Encyclopedia of

SCIENCE AND TECHNOLOGY COMMUNICATION

Encyclopedia of

SCIENCE AND TECHNOLOGY COMMUNICATION

VOLUME
1

SUSANNA HORNIG PRIEST

EDITOR

University of Nevada, Las Vegas

Los Angeles | London | New Delhi
Singapore | Washington DC

For information:

SAGE Publications, Inc.
2455 Teller Road
Thousand Oaks, California 91320
E-mail: order@sagepub.com

SAGE Publications Ltd.
1 Oliver's Yard
55 City Road
London EC1Y 1SP
United Kingdom

SAGE Publications India Pvt. Ltd.
B 1/I 1 Mohan Cooperative Industrial Area
Mathura Road, New Delhi 110 044
India

SAGE Publications Asia-Pacific Pte. Ltd.
33 Pekin Street #02-01
Far East Square
Singapore 048763

Printed in the United States of America

Library of Congress Cataloging-in-Publication Data

Encyclopedia of science and technology communication / edited by Susanna Hornig Priest.
      p. cm.
Includes bibliographical references and index.
ISBN 978-1-4129-5920-9 (cloth)
   1. Science news--United States. 2. Communication in science—United States. 3. Communication of technical information—United States. 4. Science and state—United States. I. Priest, Susanna Hornig.

Q225.2.U6E53 2010
501'.4—dc22   2010002998

This book is printed on acid-free paper.

10 11 12 13 14 10 9 8 7 6 5 4 3 2 1

Publisher:	Rolf A. Janke
Assistant to the Publisher:	Michele Thompson
Acquisitions Editor:	Jim Brace-Thompson
Developmental Editor:	Sanford Robinson
Reference Systems Manager:	Leticia M. Gutierrez
Reference Systems Coordinator:	Laura Notton
Production Editor:	Carla Freeman
Copy Editors:	Amy Freitag, Renee Willers
Typesetter:	C&M Digitals (P) Ltd.
Proofreaders:	Theresa Kay, Jenifer Kooiman
Indexer:	Joan Shapiro
Cover Designer:	Gail Buschman
Marketing Manager:	Amberlyn McKay

Contents

List of Entries

Reader's Guide

The Reader's Guide is provided to help readers find entries on related topics. It classifies entries in 18 categories: Associations and Organizations; Audiences, Opinions, and Effects; Challenges, Issues, and Controversies; Changing Awareness, Opinion, and Behavior; Critical Influences and Events; Global and International Aspects; Government Agencies (U.S.); History, Philosophy, and Sociology of Science; Important Figures; Journal Publications; Key Cases and Current Trends; Law, Policy, Ethics, and Beliefs; Major Infrastructural Initiatives; Practices, Strategies, and Tools; Professional Roles and Careers; Public Engagement Approaches; Theory and Research; Venues and Channels. Some entries appear in more than one category.

Associations and Organizations

Agricultural Communicators of Tomorrow
American Association for Public Opinion
  Research
American Association for the Advancement of
  Science (AAAS)
American Medical Association
American Medical Writers Association
Association for Communication Excellence
Center for Science in the Public Interest
Council for the Advancement of Science Writing
Environmental Defense Fund
ETC Group
Greenpeace
International Science Journalism Associations
National Association of Science Writers
Physicians for Social Responsibility
Public Communication of Science and
  Technology
Royal Society
SciDev.Net
Scientists' Institute for Public Information
Search for Extraterrestrial Intelligence
Sigma Xi
Society for Risk Analysis
Society for Technical Communication
Society of Environmental Journalists
Union of Concerned Scientists

Audiences, Opinions, and Effects

Active Audiences and Science
Attentive Public
Audiences for Science
Children's Television and Science
Communicating Science to Children
Gender Representations of Scientists
Health Literacy
Interpretive Communities
Knowledge Gap Hypothesis
Popular Science and Formal Education
Public Understanding of Research
Public Understanding of Science
Role Models in Science
Science Indicators, History of the NSB Project on
Science Literacy
Scientist–Journalist Relations
Surveys
Technological Literacy
Trust and Attitudes

Challenges, Issues, and Controversies

Abortion
Alien Abduction
Alternative Medicine
Asteroid Impacts
Bioterrorism

Science, Technology, and Society Studies
Scientific Consensus
Scientific Ethos
Scientific Journal, History of
Scientific Method
Scientific Societies
Technological Determinism
Tenure System
Two Cultures
Understanding Expertise
Visible Scientist

Important Figures

Asimov, Isaac
Attenborough, David
Carson, Rachel
Carver, George Washington
Clarke, Arthur C.
Crick, Francis
Darwin, Charles
Dawkins, Richard
Dewey, John
Einstein, Albert
Feynman, Richard
Franklin, Benjamin
Galilei, Galileo
Gould, Stephen Jay
Hawking, Stephen
Kuhn, Thomas
Latour, Bruno
McClintock, Barbara
Mead, Margaret
Mendel, Gregor
Merton, Robert K.
Muir, John
Nelkin, Dorothy
Nye, Bill
Oppenheimer, J. Robert
Popper, Karl
Sagan, Carl
Snow, C. P.
Teller, Edward
Venter, J. Craig
Watson, James D.

Journal Publications

Issues in Science and Technology
Nature

Public Understanding of Science (Journal)
Science
Science and Engineering Ethics
Science Communication
Science, Technology, & Human Values

Key Cases and Current Trends

Agricultural Biotechnology
Alternative Energy, Overview
Architecture, Sustainable
Astrobiology
Astronomy, Public Communication of
Avian Flu
Biofuels
Bioinformatics
Bovine Somatotropin (BST or BGH)
Fuel Cell Technology
Gene
Gene Therapy
Holography
Low-Level Radiation
Nanotechnology
Nutrigenomics
Nutrition and Media
Obesity Epidemic
Pandemics, Origins of
Recombinant DNA
Reproductive Medicine
Satellites, Science of
Severe Acute Respiratory Syndrome
Solar Energy
String Theory
Sustainability
Synthetic Biology and Genomics
Toxicogenomics
Wind Power

Law, Policy, Ethics, and Beliefs

Big Science
Bioethicists as Sources
Censorship in Science
Clean Air Act
Clean Water Act
Community "Right to Know"
Conflicts of Interest in Science
Embargo System
Endangered Species Act
Environmental Impact Statements

Environmental Justice
Ethical, Legal, and Social Issues (ELSI)
Eugenics
Food Libel Laws
Gene Patenting
Institutional Review Board
Nanotechnology, Regulation of
Planetary Protection
Precautionary Principle
Religion, Science, and Media
Research Ethics, Overview
Risk Analysis
Risks and Benefits
Science Communication and Indigenous North
    America
Social Justice
Technology Assessment
Toxic Substances Regulation

Major Infrastructural Initiatives

Hubble Space Telescope
Human Genome Project
Manhattan Project
Particle Accelerators
Space Program, Overview
Space Shuttle
Superconducting Super Collider

Practices, Strategies, and Tools

Effective Graphics
Interviewing Scientists
Metaphors in Science Communication
Narrative in Science Communication
Physician–Patient Communication
Risk Communication, Overview
Scientists as Sources
Strategic Communication for Science and
    Technology
Translational Research
Visual Images in Science Communication

Professional Roles and Careers

Agricultural Journalism
Beat Reporting
Career Paths, Medical Writing/Medical
    Journalism

Career Paths, Science/Environmental Journalism
Crisis Communication
Disaster Coverage
Environmental Journalism
Freelancing
Government Public Information
Medical Journalism
Public Relations and Science
Scientist–Journalist Relations
Social and Behavioral Science Reporting
Technical Communication
Weather Reporting

Public Engagement Approaches

Citizen Science
Citizens Jury
Consensus Conference
Deliberative Democracy
Deliberative Polling
Public Engagement
Science Café
Town Hall Meetings
Upstream Engagement

Theory and Research

Agenda Setting and Science
Conversation and Science Communication
Cultivation Theory and Science
Deficit Model
Diffusion of Innovations
Digital Rhetoric and Science
Discourse Analysis and Science
Evaluation of Science Communication
Framing and Priming in Science Communication
Information Seeking and Processing
Information Society
Information Subsidies
Opinion Leaders and Opinion Leadership
Optimistic Bias
Planned Behavior, Theory of
Psychometric Paradigm
Rhetoric of Medicine
Rhetoric of Science
Social Amplification of Risk Framework
Social Epistemology
Spiral of Silence and Science

About the Editor

Susanna Hornig Priest is a professor of journalism and media studies at the University of Nevada, Las Vegas. She has taught mass communication theory and research methods at the undergraduate and graduate levels since 1989. She holds a doctoral degree in communications from the University of Washington; a master's degree in sociology from the University of Nevada, Las Vegas; and a bachelor's degree in anthropology from the University of California, Berkeley. Her own research is centered on the role of science in American society and culture, its expression in the mass media, public engagement in science and science policy, and public opinion formation. She is also interested in the social roles of new media technologies.

Priest has served as a member of the Research and Publications committees of the Association for Education in Journalism and Mass Communication and as chair and research chair of the association's Science Communication Interest Group. She is a fellow of the American Association for the Advancement of Science, past associate editor of the journal *Public Understanding of Science,* and current editor of the journal *Science Communication.* She regularly serves as an advisor to a wide range of academic projects, government agencies, and private organizations on communication, public engagement, and public opinion issues and reviews research submissions for a variety of academic organizations and scholarly journals. Her current research is supported by grants from the National Science Foundation and other sources.

Her publications include more than 30 refereed research articles and nearly 20 book chapters, plus two books.

Contributors

Eric A. Abbott
Iowa State University

Len Ackland
University of Colorado at Boulder

Robert W. Adler
University of Utah

William Allen
University of Missouri

Joachim Allgaier
University of Vienna, Austria

Nick Allum
University of Essex, United Kingdom

David Amber
Freelance Science Writer

José Azevedo
Porto University, Portugal

Ayelet Baram-Tsabari
The Technion, Israel

Luca Tancredi Barone
Freelance Science Journalist

Deborah R. Bassett
University of Washington

Alice Bell
Imperial College, London

Stephen A. Banning
Bradley University

John C. Besley
University of South Carolina

Linda Billings
George Washington University

Susana Biro
Universidad Nacional Autónoma de México

Rick Borchelt
U.S. Department of Agriculture

Jason Borenstein
Georgia Institute of Technology

Frederic E. Bouder
King's College London

Bonnie Bressers
Kansas State University

S. Camille Broadway
University of Texas at Arlington

Dominique Brossard
University of Wisconsin–Madison

Joe Browder
Environmental Issues Consultant, Washington, D.C.

Massimiano Bucchi
University of Trento, Italy

Estrella Burgos
National Autonomous University of Mexico, Mexico City

Karen Burnham
University of Houston

William E. Burrows
New York University

Radford Byerly Jr.
University of Colorado

Archie Carr III
Wildlife Conservation Society

Christian F. Casper
North Carolina State University

Leah Ceccarelli
University of Washington

Bobby Cerini
Australian National University

David Chittenden
Science Museum of Minnesota

Rochelle Christian
Australian National University

Michel Claessens
European Commission

Karina Clement
Commonwealth Scientific and Industrial Research Organisation (CSIRO), Australia

Cynthia-Lou Coleman
Portland State University

Peter Collins
The Royal Society

Colleen Connolly–Ahern
Pennsylvania State University

Julia B. Corbett
University of Utah

James Cornell
International Science Writers Association

Susan E. Cozzens
Georgia Institute of Technology

Lisa Craypo
Samuels and Associates

Ned Crosby
*Promoting Healthy
  Democracy, Minneapolis*

Urs Dahinden
*University of Applied Sciences
  HTW Chur, Switzerland*

Tinsley Davis
*National Association of Science
  Writers*

James W. Dearing
Kaiser Permanente Colorado

M. Robin DiMatteo
*University of California,
  Riverside*

Alistair S. Duff
*Napier University, United
  Kingdom*

Sonya Forte Duhé
University of South Carolina

Sharon Dunwoody
*University of Wisconsin–
  Madison*

John Durant
MIT Museum

Edna F. Einsiedel
University of Calgary

Gerald L. Epstein
*OTA, the Office of Technology
  Assessment Alumni Network*

Larry E. Erickson
Kansas State University

William Evans
University of Alabama

Declan Fahy
*Dublin City University,
  Republic of Ireland*

Steven L. Fales
Iowa State University

Andrea Feldpausch
Texas A&M University

Martina Franzen
University of Bielefeld, Germany

Lynn J. Frewer
*University of Wageningen, the
  Netherlands*

Sharon M. Friedman
Lehigh University

Lynne Timpani Friedmann
Friedmann Communications

Steve Fuller
*University of Warwick, United
  Kingdom*

Miguel García-Sancho
*Spanish National Research
  Council (CSIC)*

Michele S. Garfinkel
J. Craig Venter Institute

Barbara Gastel
Texas A&M University

Ellen J. Gerl
Ohio University

Joye C. Gordon
Kansas State University

Hannah Grankvist
Linköping University, Sweden

Clair Grant-Salmon
SciDev.Net

Ted Greenhalgh
*University of Nevada,
  Las Vegas*

Robert J. Griffin
Marquette University

Joshua Grimm
Texas Tech University

Jacob Groshek
Iowa State University

Alan G. Gross
University of Minnesota

Karl Grossman
*SUNY College at Old
  Westbury*

James A. Guikema
Kansas State University

William Kinglsey Hallman
*Rutgers, The State University
  of New Jersey*

Megan K. Halpern
Cornell University

Joseph E. Harmon
Argonne National Laboratory

Gavin D. J. Harper
Cardiff University

Lisa M. Butler Harrington
Kansas State University

Claire Harris
*Commonwealth Scientific and
  Industrial Research
  Organisation (CSIRO),
  Australia*

Kelly B. Haskard
*Texas State University, San
  Marcos*

J. Scott Hauger
Techné

Robert L. Heath
University of Houston

David Henry
*University of Nevada, Las
  Vegas*

Susana Herrera Lima
ITESO, Guadalajara, Mexico

Heidi Lee Hoerman
University of South Carolina

Richard Holliman
*The Open University, United
  Kingdom*

Julie Homchick
University of Washington

Yue Hu
George Mason University

Jerry L. Hudgins
*University of
  Nebraska–Lincoln*

Lee Humphreys
Cornell University

H. Scott Hurd
Iowa State University

Deborah L. Illman
University of Washington

Jann Ingmire
JAMA *&* Archives *Journals*

Gerald Jaax
Kansas State University

Lela Jacobsohn
The Children's Hospital of Philadelphia

Branden Johnson
New Jersey Department of Environmental Protection

Richard Johnson-Sheehan
Purdue University

Karyn Ogata Jones
Clemson University

Marina Joubert
Southern Science

LeeAnn Kahlor
University of Texas

Aries Keck
Loki Studios

William Keith
University of Wisconsin–Milwaukee

Lisa Keränen
University of Colorado at Boulder

Vincent Kiernan
Georgetown University

William J. Kinsella
North Carolina State University

Jan Knight
Columnist, SEJournal

Henry Ko
Monash University, Australia

Van Kornegay
University of South Carolina

Bill Kovarik
Radford University

Marjorie Kruvand
Loyola University Chicago

Kate Ksobiech
University of Nevada, Las Vegas

Jennifer Kuzma
University of Minnesota

Sally Lawrence
Samuels and Associates

Joan Leach
University of Queensland, Australia

Suman M. Lee
Iowa State University

Bruce V. Lewenstein
Cornell University

Ragnar E. Löfstedt
King's College London

Robert A. Logan
University of Missouri (Emeritus)

Nancy Longnecker
University of Western Australia

Jose A. Magpantay
University of the Philippines

Edward W. Maibach
George Mason University

Lesa Hatley Major
Indiana University Bloomington

Alejandro Manrique
Freelance Science Writer

Jessica Marshall
University of Minnesota

Lucia Martinelli
Istituto Agrario di san Michele all'Adige, Italy

Luisa Massarani
Museum of Life, Rio de Janeiro, Brazil

Katherine A. McComas
Cornell University

Alan H. McGowan
The New School, New York

Merryn McKinnon
The Australian National University

Mike McRae
Commonwealth Science and Industrial Research Organisation, Australia

Jennifer Medlock
University of Calgary, Canada

Michael D. Mehta
Thompson Rivers University, Canada

Felicity Mellor
Imperial College London

Matteo Merzagora
TRACES *(Théories et Réflexions sur l'Apprendre, la Communication et l'Education Scientifiques), Paris*

Howard W. Mielke
Tulane University

Ellen Mika
OTA, *the Office of Technology Assessment Alumni Network*

Carolyn R. Miller
North Carolina State University

Jon D. Miller
Michigan State University

Steve Miller
University College London

Tiago Moreira
Durham University

Patricia Moy
University of Washington

Henk A.J. Mulder
*University of Groningen, the
Netherlands*

Lawrence Mullen
*University of Nevada,
Las Vegas*

Jessica Nash
Youngstown State University

Chandra Mohan Nautiyal
*Birbal Sahni Institute of
Palaeobotany, Lucknow,
India*

Kathryn A. Neeley
University of Virginia

Kurt Neuwirth
University of Cincinnati

Jeff Niederdeppe
Cornell University

Kristian Hvidtfelt Nielsen
Aarhus University, Denmark

Matthew C. Nisbet
American University

Mary Nucci
Rutgers University

Garrett J. O'Keefe
Colorado State University

Cristina Olivotto
European Space Agency

William P. Palmer
*Curtin University of
Technology*

Shobita Parthasarathy
University of Michigan

Manoj Patairiya
*National Council for Science &
Technology Communication*

Amy R. Pearce
Arkansas State University

Greg Pearson
*National Academy of
Engineering*

Joseph N. Pelton
Arthur C. Clarke Foundation

Núria Pérez-Pérez
*University of Pompeu Fabra,
Barcelona*

Hans Peter Peters
*Forschungszentrum Jülich,
Germany*

Tarla Rai Peterson
Texas A&M University

Nick Pidgeon
Cardiff University

Jérôme Pierrel
Université de Bordeaux, France

Diego Pineda
*Immunizations for Public
Health*

Andrew Pleasant
*Rutgers University and Canyon
Ranch Institute, Tucson*

Gail Porter
*National Institute of Standards
and Technology*

Maria Powell
*University of Wisconsin–
Madison*

Susanna Hornig Priest
*University of Nevada, Las
Vegas*

Margaret S. Race
SETI Institute

William Ramsey
*University of Nevada, Las
Vegas*

Carol Reeves
Butler University

Chubo Ren
Washington State University

William D. Rifkin
*University of New South
Wales, Australia*

Anthony J. Roberto
Arizona State University

Simone Rödder
University of Bielefeld, Germany

Michael Rodemeyer
University of Virginia

Lulu Rodriguez
Iowa State University

Tee Rogers-Hayden
University of East Anglia

Aldemaro Romero
Arkansas State University

Connie Roser-Renouf
George Mason University

Melanie Fridl Ross
University of Florida

Steven S. Ross
Corporate Editor, Broadband
Properties Magazine

Katherine E. Rowan
George Mason University

Cristine Russell
*Council for the Advancement
of Science Writing*

Jacinta Sagona
*Royal Melbourne Hospital,
Australia*

Sergei A. Samoilenko
Kansas State University

Sarah Samuels
Samuels and Associates

Peter M. Sandman
*Risk Communication
Consultant*

Dietram A. Scheufele
University of Wisconsin

Steven Selden
University of Maryland

P. Simran Sethi
University of Kansas

James Shanahan
Boston University

Jae-Hwa Shin
*University of Southern
Mississippi*

Michael Siegrist
ETH Zurich, Switzerland

Helena Silverstein
Lafayette College

Janas Sinclair
*University of North Carolina
    at Chapel Hill*

Cobi Smith
Australian National University

Kim Smith
*North Carolina A&T State
    University*

Brian G. Southwell
University of Minnesota

Richard A. Stein
Princeton University

Jocelyn Steinke
Western Michigan University

S. Holly Stocking
Indiana University

Daniel Stout
University of Nevada, Las Vegas

Kristen Alley Swain
University of Mississippi

Dafna Tachover
*Law Offices of Dafna
    Tachover, Princeton
    Junction, New Jersey*

Karen Taylor
*University of Alaska
    Fairbanks*

Ricky Telg
University of Florida

Toby A. Ten Eyck
Michigan State University

Paul B. Thompson
Michigan State University

Stephen Thornton
University of Limerick, Ireland

Denise Tillery
*University of Nevada,
    Las Vegas*

Natalie Tindall
University of Oklahoma

Simon Torok
*Commonwealth Scientific and
    Industrial Research
    Organisation (CSIRO),
    Australia*

Chris Toumey
University of South Carolina

Mark Tucker
Purdue University

Tari Turner
Monash University, Australia

Rae Tyson
*Former USA TODAY
    Environment Editor*

Sheldon B. Ungar
*University of Toronto
    Scarborough*

JoAnn Myer Valenti
*Tampa, Florida, (Emerita
    Professor)*

Shari R. Veil
University of Oklahoma

Vivianne H. M. Visschers
ETH Zurich, Switzerland

Alana M. Vivolo
*The Children's Hospital of
    Philadelphia*

Caroline S. Wagner
*SRI International and George
    Washington University*

Paul Walker
Murray State University

Sherrie Flynt Wallington
Harvard University

Bud Ward
*Editor, The Yale Forum on
    Climate Change & the Media*

Eric Thomas Weber
University of Mississippi

Thomas M. Welch
*Iowa Department of
    Transportation*

Catherine Westfall
Michigan State University

Bryan B. Whaley
University of San Francisco

Summer L. Williams
Westfield State College

Amelia A. Williamson
Freelance Science Writer

Kris Wilson
Emory University

Kim Witte
Michigan State University

Qingjiang Yao
University of Iowa

Chance York
Kansas State University

Tanya Zanish-Belcher
Iowa State University

Xiaoquan Zhao
George Mason University

Introduction

Science Communication as an Interdisciplinary Field

In the academic world, the term *science communication* refers both to a set of professions (such as science journalism and public information work) and to an interdisciplinary scholarly research specialization. Much of this research is aimed at improving our understanding of the best ways to communicate complex information, especially to people who are not scientists. Science communication specialists are concerned with giving people useful information about health, environment, and technology—as well as science itself. In order to do this, we also need to improve our understanding of how people think, form opinions, and process information. We need to identify the best ways to provide the information people actually want and need to know. And we need to understand some very complex issues, involving both the actual science behind both public opinion and the news and the ethical, environmental, and other policy issues it may raise.

Most people who are science communication scholars use the tools and techniques of social and behavioral science or the humanities to analyze messages and arguments and to assess their influence. Like other communication scholars, they are also concerned with the relationship between access to information and better decision making in a democratic society. They may analyze the ethical and policy issues associated with information access and information distribution, such as the relationship between information and power. While studies designed to make messages more effective are often described as "instrumental," meaning directed toward a narrow practical purpose in order to make things function more smoothly, science communication research can also be "critical," meaning directed more generally toward the analysis of conflicts and problems in

society, such as an unfair distribution of power or influence. Issues in science communication often involve areas beyond the science itself, such as research ethics or environmental justice.

In order to ask and answer research questions in these areas, science communication scholars are generally trained in a social science discipline such as communication studies, media studies, sociology, or political science, or in a closely allied humanities field, such as philosophy or rhetoric. Practicing science communicators may be trained in one of these fields or in the professional side of journalism or public relations; they may also be scientists who have decided it is important to devote part or all of their careers to communication activities. As a result, the field is broadly interdisciplinary, which makes it all the more interesting.

Media Theory and Research About Science Communication

Like other communication scholars, science communication scholars generally rely on media theory to understand the influence of media messages or other media content. They take concepts such as agenda setting and cultivation, often derived from studies in political communication or from media effects work, and then apply them to science communication problems and cases. They use typical social and behavioral science research methods such as surveys, experiments, focus groups, interviews, and observations to improve our knowledge in this area. They may also analyze the rhetoric of messages or study their ethical and political implications. Case study research may focus on important historical events, such as the near nuclear disaster at Three Mile Island, for the lessons they may provide. Another group of science communication scholars looks at the history of science communication and science journalism, including the efforts by well-known scientists to draw public attention to their findings.

Sometimes work originating in social sciences other than communication is directly relevant to the field, such as sociological studies of the nature of social movements. For example, theory and research derived from the study of social movements, such as resource mobilization theory or actor network theory, helps us to understand how the environmental movement came into being, as well as how more recent and more specific movements concerned with chemicals, food additives, or technologies thought to be harmful arise. Theory and research derived from the study of political and advertising campaigns helps us to understand how to design campaigns in public health, such as the promotion of vaccination or smoking cessation or the avoidance of exposure to HIV/AIDS or food-borne illnesses. This literature is also used in the design of campaigns (both pro and con) surrounding the adoption of controversial science or technology, such as stem cell research or nuclear power generation.

One specialized area of theory and research that is largely unique to science communication is the area of risk communication. People often have trouble understanding information expressed in probabilities, yet they are generally very aware that almost all new technologies have risks as well as benefits. Weighing the risks against the benefits of a new technology is at least as much a matter of applying social values as it is a matter of numerical calculation, but it is still important to know how to help people start with solid scientific information where it is available. Knowing the social psychology of how people react to information about risk expressed in probabilities can facilitate the achievement of this goal.

Professional Practice in Science Communication

Alongside these important issues in scholarship are equally important issues having to do with questions that are of primary interest to professional practitioners in science communication, rather than scholars. These involve both strategic and ethical decisions, sometimes closely connected to the concerns and insights of scholars

and sometimes not. For example, how should reporters cover the issue of climate change? Should the views of scientists who do not believe that climate change has been caused by human activity be included alongside the views of those who do, in order to give a "balanced" story, or does this mislead the public into thinking that both of these positions are equally accepted within the scientific community? Should the opinions of maverick scientists promoting unpopular theories be publicized—after all, it may sometimes turn out they are right—or should only widely accepted science that has already been published by peer-reviewed journals be reported as news? Scholars study these issues, but it is members of the professional community who must decide what to do.

A few scientific journals will not allow scientific results to be discussed in public and reported before the review process is complete and the journal issue has been published. This helps avoid the problem of untested results receiving wide publicity, especially important if it may persuade someone to change their diet, medical treatment, or behavior in some way that could turn out to damage their health (or at least their pocketbook). But it also slows down the process through which new findings will reach the public and diminishes the transparency of science. Insights into these sorts of professional and policy dilemmas may come from science communication scholarship, but in the end these policy decisions cannot usually be resolved by research.

Some critics have argued that science and environmental journalists should let scientists review their stories prior to publication, or even that these journalists should be licensed to practice their trade, but to others these proposals seem inconsistent with freedom of the press. On the other hand, there is increasing pressure on weather reporters to have at least some training in the science of meteorology. Should science journalists, in general, have scientific training? Or is this a conflict of interest because it might make them less likely to lean toward one side in situations where science can become controversial? It is quite natural for those with scientific education to feel positive about most scientific advances; does this make them better journalists because they are sympathetic, or less adequate ones because they are less able to be critical?

Those practicing science communication are not just science journalists, however. Physicians, nurses, and other medical professionals who wish to communicate better with their patients on an interpersonal basis are also science communicators. So are public information specialists working for government, public relations specialists working for universities or science-oriented corporations, and environmental advocates working for nonprofit nongovernmental organizations. As traditional newsgathering organizations around the globe undergo economic restructuring, our societies continue to have economies and ways of life that are highly dependent on science and technology, the range of science communication professions is likely to increase in ways presently not fully imagined. A global call for increased public engagement in science and science policy has also expanded our thinking about the best ways to practice science communication.

Making good use of scientists as sources and scientific information as a resource in professional work takes special skills. A bewildering maze of government agencies, as well as universities and research institutions, are in the business of providing this information—and like other types of sources, these organizations often have agendas of their own they are trying to promote. Around the world, the state of science development varies tremendously, and different policy approaches to governing science, technology, and associated risks are in place. These development and policy differences can be important things to understand in analyzing international trends and issues involving science. The science itself can also be daunting, alongside its ethical and legal implications and the social and policy issues it forces us to confront.

What This Encyclopedia Offers

This encyclopedia tries to provide as much information as possible on this entire range of interrelated issues in one place. While much of this information may have been published elsewhere, it is scattered across many different parts of the library, from science, engineering, and medicine to the social and behavior sciences and humanities to the professional fields of journalism and public relations. It is the goal of this encyclopedia to make as much information as possible available in a single source, with clear pointers suggesting where to begin the search for more.

Users of this volume will include undergraduate and graduate students in journalism (including those in specialized courses in science journalism and environmental journalism, but also those in general journalism courses) who have been assigned a story or other project on a science-related topic; communication, mass communication, and media studies students at any level who are writing a term paper or designing a research project and are interested in finding out more about this interdisciplinary field; and working journalists, public information officers, and public relations specialists who may or may not be science specialists—or who may be just starting out in the field—and are looking for quick information and guidance available in a single place.

Entries range from those illustrating the application of media theory and research to problems in science, technology, environment, and health; to case studies of controversial issues in science and technology and biographies of well-known scientist-communicators; to studies of how science journalism is actually done and the problems it faces; and to guidance on using scientific sources, plus helpful descriptions of the missions and structure of prominent science-related agencies and organizations (especially those in the United States, although entries are also included that discuss the state of science and science communication in Africa, Australia, Canada, East Asia, Europe, India, Latin America, and Mexico). By putting this unique collection of science communication material together in a single place, it is my hope that the field will be advanced and that newcomers to it will start to find their way around it with somewhat less difficulty.

Interdisciplinary fields are inherently challenging, but also inherently interesting. Problems of communication across disciplinary boundaries are substantial, but also quite fascinating, in part because they tend to cause us to question our assumptions about the natural order of things. I hope that users of this collection will rise to the challenges—and learn to relish the complexities and nuances of those challenges.

Susanna Hornig Priest
University of Nevada, Las Vegas

ABORTION

Stripped of moral, religious, and legal considerations, abortion is simply the termination of a pregnancy. But there is nothing simple about abortion or at least, debates over abortion, and the contest over whether and when abortion should be legally permissible has been at the center of the so-called culture war. The abortion debate has shaped party politics, electoral campaigns, legislative agendas, and judicial appointments. It has led to political rallies, protests, blockades, bombings, and the killing of abortion providers. The lasting conflict and the reach of the controversy into debates over stem cell research, sex education, fertility treatments, population control, and more ensure that abortion will remain newsworthy.

From some moral, religious, and cultural vantage points, abortion is murder. Others view abortion as a fundamental right that, whether grounded in privacy, liberty, equality, or autonomy, must remain unfettered to ensure full emancipation. For many, the morality of abortion depends on when during pregnancy it is performed or what an individual's reasons are for undergoing the procedure. Perspectives about abortion are not merely contrasting; they are frequently impassioned and irreconcilable. Seeking compromise among those who stand on opposite sides of the abortion spectrum can appear futile, and encouraging tolerance of diverse viewpoints may, in the context of this debate, seem unprincipled.

Still, a vast number of women do terminate their pregnancies, abortion is legally permissible in many countries, and the worldwide trend is toward liberalizing restrictions on the procedure. This trend notwithstanding, regulation of abortion has become more restrictive in the United States over the past 20 years.

While the contest over abortion continues to be waged on many fronts and in numerous venues, the U.S. Supreme Court has been pivotal in defining the terms and contours of the debate. After providing a general overview of the incidence of abortion, this entry will outline how the Supreme Court has interpreted the U.S. Constitution as both granting a right to choose abortion and permitting considerable government latitude in regulating this right.

Incidence of Abortion

It has been estimated that over 40 million abortions are performed worldwide each year. While the number appears to be on the decline, about one pregnancy out of every five is terminated by abortion. In 2003, according to the Guttmacher Institute, the global abortion rate—that is, the number of women of childbearing age who have an abortion—stood at 29 out of every 1,000.

Government regulation of abortion varies considerably. However, more restrictive rules do not necessarily correspond with a lower rate of abortion, and abortion rates are sometimes lower where the procedure is legal and readily available. Western Europe, for example, where abortion is legally permitted except in rare circumstances, boasts the lowest rate of abortion at 12 for every 1,000 women. In Africa, by contrast, legal restrictions are far more common, but the abortion rate is estimated at 29 per 1,000 women. While restrictions do not always coincide with a lower incidence of abortion, they often overlap with increased health risks. For example, the Guttmacher Institute reports that abortion is generally safe where permissive abortion laws exist and often unsafe where the procedure is subject to heavy restriction.

In the United States, the abortion rate has been on the decline, dropping from 29 per 1,000 women in 1981 to 19 in 2005. Still, it is estimated that, excluding miscarriages, 22% of all pregnancies in the United States are terminated, leading annually to the performance of about 1.2 million abortions.

Abortion and the U.S. Supreme Court

Prior to 1973, decisions about whether to regulate abortion in the United States were in the hands of the states. In the 1960s and into the early 1970s, legislation criminalizing abortion except in rare instances was the rule in most states, though liberalization of these restrictions increased between 1967 and 1972. But it was not until the U.S. Supreme Court entered the fray that abortion was legalized nationally.

Roe v. Wade

In 1973, the Supreme Court curtailed state authority to regulate abortion, handing down the much praised and often derided decision in *Roe v. Wade*. By a 7-to-2 margin and in a decision authored by Justice Harry Blackmun, the Court overturned a Texas statute that banned all abortions except those performed to save a woman's life. The Court reached this decision by declaring that women have a fundamental right to abortion rooted in the Constitution's implicit protection of privacy and the Fourteenth Amendment's explicit protection of liberty. The decision had the effect of invalidating restrictive abortion provisions throughout the country.

The Court applied a stringent and protective level of judicial scrutiny to the statute at issue in *Roe*. It did not, however, confer an absolute right to choose abortion. The state's interest in regulating abortion, the Court explained, increases as pregnancy advances and specifically permits government action at two points: the second and third

trimesters. According to the Court, the onset of the second trimester marks the moment when the state has a compelling and justifiable interest to regulate on behalf of a woman's health. By contrast, decisions about abortion during the first 3 months of pregnancy must be left to the woman and her physician. The onset of the third trimester marks the point of viability, when the fetus is capable of living outside the womb and when the state's interest in the unborn becomes compelling enough to warrant regulation on its behalf. But the state may not, even at this stage, prohibit abortions necessary to protect a woman's life or health. In short, *Roe* established that abortion regulations must be justified by a compelling government interest. Applying this standard to the first 6 months of pregnancy, states may not proscribe abortion and may only regulate in months 4 through 6 to preserve maternal health. Moreover, in months 7 through 9, states may regulate and even ban abortion to promote fetal life, except where maternal health or life is at stake.

Roe catapulted the nascent pro-life movement and triggered a spate of legislative initiatives testing the scope of the Court's ruling. Responding swiftly to the Court's declaration that women have a fundamental constitutional right to choose abortion, many states crafted bills aimed at limiting access to the procedure. These included provisions that restricted public funding of abortion, required hospitalization for abortion, prohibited advertising for abortion services, outlawed specific abortion procedures, mandated parental involvement for minors seeking abortion, and mandated spousal notification for married women seeking abortion. In addition, states imposed such things as informed consent requirements, waiting periods, and viability testing.

This legislative campaign ushered in an era of contentious litigation. During the decade following *Roe,* the Supreme Court overturned most efforts to control reproductive rights, though it upheld restrictions on using public funds for abortion. However, in the mid-1980s and into the 1990s, the composition of the Court shifted and so did legal precedent.

Planned Parenthood of Southeastern Pennsylvania v. Casey

In 1992, the Supreme Court handed down its decision in *Planned Parenthood of Southeastern*

Pennsylvania v. Casey, reviewing a Pennsylvania bill that mandated informed consent, a 24-hour waiting period, parental consent for minors, and spousal notification for married women. The Court affirmed the constitutionality of all but the spousal notification component of the law, reversed earlier rejections of informed consent and waiting periods, and scaled back the protections afforded in *Roe.* Notably, while sustaining *Roe's* holding that the state may not outlaw abortion prior to fetal viability, *Casey* discarded the trimester framework and declared that the state may regulate to protect potential life from the moment of conception. States may, consistent with the Constitution, declare a preference for childbirth over abortion and craft laws designed to persuade women to choose childbirth instead of abortion. Furthermore, *Casey* lowered the standard of judicial scrutiny that the Court applied in *Roe* and that typically applies to government dictates concerning fundamental rights. *Casey* held that states only need a rational, rather than a compelling, interest to justify abortion restrictions and that such restrictions would pass constitutional muster unless they impose an "undue burden" on women, or put otherwise, unless they place a "substantial obstacle" in a woman's path to terminating her pregnancy.

While *Casey* rolled back the constitutional safeguards advanced in previous rulings, it may be best known for what it did not do, namely, overturn *Roe.* The Court rebuffed calls to reverse *Roe* and instead reasserted what it described as *Roe's* central holding that the Fourteenth Amendment of the Constitution protects a woman's right to choose to terminate her pregnancy prior to viability without undue interference from the state.

Neither the game-changer that pro-life forces hoped for nor the unmitigated defeat that pro-choice forces envisioned, *Casey* nevertheless altered the terrain of the abortion contest. *Casey* invited states to devise measures aimed at discouraging, though not preventing, abortion and signaled greater deference to the state's interest in regulating on behalf of the unborn.

Gonzales v. Carhart

Maybe the most notable, controversial, and recently successful example of efforts to act on this interest is legislation proscribing so-called partial-birth abortion. Though variable in their details, these bills ban a method of terminating pregnancy that, according to supporters of the procedure, decreases the possibility of medical complications and, according to opponents, is not only horrific but also the equivalent of infanticide. The federal version of the ban, enacted in 2003, prohibits physicians from vaginally delivering a live fetus to the point where either the entire head or any part of the fetal trunk past the navel is outside the woman's body for the purpose of performing an act that the physician knows will kill the partially delivered fetus. While an exception permits use of the procedure to save the woman's life, the federal ban does not incorporate a more general health exception.

The Supreme Court upheld the federal partial-birth abortion ban in the 2007 ruling in *Gonzales v. Carhart,* reversing course from *Stenberg v. Carhart,* its 2000 decision rejecting a similar Nebraska law. The Court declared that the ban has the legitimate purpose of advancing the government's interest in expressing respect for the dignity of human life, even though the law permits use of another abortion procedure to terminate the life in question. The Court also ruled that the lack of a health exception does not on its face have the effect of imposing a substantial obstacle. The Court defended this holding by noting that the prohibition would be unconstitutional if it subjected women to significant health risks. However, the Court held, the availability of safe alternatives, medical uncertainty about the related health risks, and Congress's finding that the ban imposed no health risk provide sufficient basis to conclude that women are not unduly burdened by the law.

While the legal implications of the Court's logic in *Gonzales* remain to be seen, the symbolic and political victory for the pro-life movement was clear. For the first time, the Supreme Court upheld the prohibition of a particular abortion procedure and endorsed an abortion regulation lacking an explicit health exception. In addition, the decision marked the successful culmination of the pro-life movement's mobilization of graphic and disturbing descriptions of a particular method of abortion. As described by the Supreme Court in its 2007 ruling, the procedure involves the delivery of an unborn child, leaving only the head inside the womb, and then puncturing the skull of the unborn with scissors or other sharp instrument and sucking out the baby's brains, crushing the fetus's skull with forceps, or decapitating the fetus before crushing and removing the skull. These graphic accounts, repeated by legislators, activists, pundits, and finally, the Supreme Court itself, gave the pro-life movement the rhetorical upper hand that translated into legislative and judicial victory.

The appeal to images continues, with the pro-life movement now promoting legislation that would mandate the use of ultrasounds in provision of abortion services. Oklahoma, for example, enacted a bill that requires physicians to perform an ultrasound before an abortion, display the images so that they are within the view of the woman, and explain the images as they appear. Legislators tout such measures as a means for ensuring that a woman's consent to abortion is fully informed, but pro-life proponents freely admit that ultrasound legislation is designed to capitalize on the power of images and persuade women to continue their pregnancies.

Future Prospects

Ultrasound provisions are already being challenged in the lower courts and may well find their way onto the Supreme Court's docket in the coming years. If not these measures, then others will likely make their way to the high court for further adjudication. For example, the pro-life movement is pushing for measures that would define legal personhood, with all its attendant rights, as beginning at the moment of fertilization. Should such provisions pass, they would, like others before them, become the subject of legal challenge.

In addition to ruling on direct government regulation of abortion, the courts have confronted other types of cases generated by the abortion debate. Sit-ins, sidewalk counseling, blockades, and other forms of protest at abortion clinics have led to legal battles pitting the First Amendment right to freedom of speech against the right to obtain medical services. Free speech cases have also emerged from government efforts to restrict recipients of federal funds from providing information and advice about abortion. And still other cases involving First Amendment rights have been generated by policies establishing "Choose Life" specialty license plates that can be purchased from the state.

Ongoing efforts to control abortion contribute to perennial speculation about whether the Supreme Court will reverse its original holding in *Roe*. The prospects of such reversal continue to galvanize both pro-life and pro-choice proponents, with one side calling for the election of Republicans who will support the appointment of conservative justices and the other advocating the election of Democrats who will apply a pro-*Roe* litmus test in the judicial selection process.

The Court's support for *Roe* remains slim, uncertain, and subject to a changing of the guard. With the death of former Chief Justice William Rehnquist and the retirement of Justice Sandra Day O'Connor, a detractor of *Roe* and a coauthor of *Casey* were replaced by Chief Justice John Roberts and Justice Samuel Alito, whose positions on reproductive choice remain unclear. Joining O'Connor in retirement is another *Casey* coauthor, Justice David Souter. Furthermore, Justice John Paul Stevens is approaching the age of 90, and several other justices are in their 70s, some having battled notable health problems.

There are, of course, other issues—some divisive—that influence the selection of justices and that contribute to speculation about how the Court might shift in the future. But where prospective justices stand on the constitutional right to abortion is at the forefront, and nothing about the ongoing culture war and continued efforts to regulate reproductive decisions suggests that the Court's central role in the abortion debate will diminish.

Helena Silverstein

See also Reproductive Medicine; Science and Politics; Stem Cell Research

Further Readings

Balkin, J. M. (Ed.). (2005). What Roe v. Wade *should have said: The nation's top legal experts rewrite America's most controversial decision.* New York: New York University Press.

Ginsburg, F. D. (1998). *Contested lives: The abortion debate in an American community.* Berkeley: University of California Press.

Gonzales v. Carhart, 550 U.S. 124 (2007).

Hull, N. E. H., Hoffer, W. J., & Hoffer, P. C. (Eds.). (2004). *The abortion rights controversy in America: A legal reader.* Chapel Hill: University of North Carolina Press.

McDonagh, E. L. (1996). *Breaking the abortion deadlock: From choice to consent.* New York: Oxford University Press.

Planned Parenthood of Southeastern Pa. v. Casey, 505 U.S. 833 (1992).

Roe v. Wade, 410 U.S. 113 (1973).

Rose, M. (2006). *Safe, legal, and unavailable? Abortion politics in the United States.* Washington, DC: Congressional Quarterly Press.

Saletan, W. (2003). *Bearing right: How conservatives won the abortion war.* Berkeley: University of California Press.

Stenberg v. Carhart, 530 U.S. 914 (2000).

Tribe, L. H. (1992). *Abortion: The clash of absolutes.* New York: W. W. Norton.

Active Audiences and Science

Active audience is a term referring to a group of people who are knowledgeable about a certain public issue, highly involved with it, and furthermore, willing to act upon it. An audience is usually considered as an unorganized aggregate of people or a loose form of mass public in a society, not necessarily associated with a particular issue. However, when it comes to active audiences, the concept is similar to the concept of active publics, whereby a group of people are well aware of an issue of interest, personally involved with it, and active participants in solving the problem.

As the definition of active audiences indicates, several factors stand out to differentiate active audiences from passive ones. First, cognitive factors such as level of awareness or knowledge about an issue are important. The degree to which people see a certain problem as an important social issue affects their attitudes toward the issue in determining whether they are active or passive. For example, people who recognize the danger and threat of bioterrorism as a vital issue and gain more knowledge about it are more likely to become active audiences than those with less knowledge about the issue.

Second, personal involvement with the issue matters. Even when people recognize an issue as socially important, the extent to which they consider the issue as "their own" problem or the extent to which they believe the issue directly affects their lives determines their degree of liveliness as an audience. For example, people may not become active audiences when they realize the potential threat of bioterrorism as an important social issue because they do not believe it is "their" issue. They may not be concerned about it because they believe the government is responsible for solving the problem. The more personally connected to the issue people are, the more active they become.

Third, people do not perceive an issue only through what is termed the *cognitive route*. The level of emotional attachment to an issue can play an important role in differentiating active audiences from passive ones. Active audiences may form when people feel angry about, disappointed, or helpless about a certain issue or the way the issue is handled. A high intensity of public sentiment and emotion toward an issue creates active audiences. For example, many South Koreans reacted angrily at the Korean government's decision to reopen the Korean market to U.S. beef in the spring of 2008. U.S. beef products had been banned in Korea for several years due to the fear of mad cow disease. People saw the government's decision to reopen the market as a hasty and irresponsible move, sacrificing public health to the interests of foreign trade. Many scientific and technical arguments and heated debates among journalists, government officials, activist groups, and citizens surrounded this issue (such as whether the U.S. and Korean government inspection systems for mad cow disease are trustworthy, whether beef products from cows less than 3 years old are safer than older ones, and the actual risk probability of mad cow disease). However, knowledge and personal involvement alone are not enough to explain the hundreds of thousands of people who participated in street protests against the government day and night for several months. People were captivated by a strong fear for the safety of their health and an even stronger anger toward their government.

Active audience is not a fixed concept, but rather a dynamic concept, based on situational and environmental change. Passive audiences can quickly become active audiences when conditions are met. One triggering event or incident may rapidly change levels of knowledge, personal involvement, and emotion among people and quickly transform them into active audiences. This transformation can also happen gradually over time.

Some scholars pay particular attention to the transformation of inactive audiences and their potential to become active audiences.

The revolutionary change and development in communication technology and the way people communicate with each other are believed to significantly affect the formation of active audiences and their behaviors. New communication environments characterized by the use of the Internet, blogging, social network media, and mobile communications change the way information flows in society. This environment provides unprecedented opportunities for people to generate, disseminate, and communicate ideas and opinions with others beyond the limitations of time and space. People now have the ability to start organizing themselves in cyberspace around a certain issue or problem and to become more active in solving the problem. For example, individuals have posted video clips of their experiences with faulty products (such as burning laptops or broken toys) to YouTube or similar sites, resulting in rapid diffusion of their experiences throughout the online community. Naturally, emerging active audiences in cyberspace armed with empirical evidence are powerful social entities. Companies and other organizations risk damage to their reputations and businesses if they neglect to communicate effectively with these audiences.

What, then, is effective communication with respect to active audiences? Many scholars and practitioners in public campaigns and public relations generally agree on a two-way communication strategy. Two-way communication starts with careful and genuine listening to active audiences. Even though the voices of active audiences are not always clear and uniform, it is highly recommended that a sincere effort be made to understand the core thoughts and feelings of active audiences surrounding an issue. Organizations can communicate effectively and solve conflicts with active audiences by continuously adapting and adjusting organizational interests to active audiences' interests and finding a common ground that both parties can live with. Finding a win-win zone is often the key to effective communication.

Suman M. Lee

See also Attentive Public; Audiences for Science; Online Media and the Sciences; Public Engagement; Public Relations and Science

Further Readings

Grunig, J. E. (1989). Publics, audiences and market segments: Models of receivers of campaign messages. In C. T. Salmon (Ed.), *Information campaigns: Managing the process of social change* (pp. 197–226). Newbury Park, CA: Sage.

Grunig, J. E. (1997). A situational theory of publics: Conceptual history, recent challenges and new research. In D. Moss, T. MacManus, & D. Vercic (Eds.), *Public relations research: An international perspective* (pp. 3–48). London: International Thomson Business Press.

Hallahan, K. (2000). Inactive publics: The forgotten publics in public relations. *Public Relations Review, 26,* 499–515.

Lee, S., & Rodriguez, L. (2008). The four publics of anti-bioterrorism information campaigns: A test of the situational theory. *Public Relations Review, 34,* 60–62.

Price, V. (1992). *Communication concepts 4: Public opinion.* Newbury Park, CA: Sage.

ACTOR-NETWORK THEORY

From its inception at the beginning of the 1980s, actor-network theory (ANT) has enjoyed considerable success in the social sciences; it is drawn upon in sociology, geography, organizational studies, political science, and cultural studies. One of the key dimensions of this is the fact that ANT is not—properly speaking—a theory; that is, it does not constitute a set of interlinked, conditional propositions that make predictions about states of the world. Rather, ANT is a malleable set of conceptual tools and methodological strategies that enable researchers to investigate and organize empirical materials and helps us understand the dynamics of actions involving key actors in issues of science and science policy. As such, it provides context for understanding patterns of communication in these areas. ANT's interest in the interaction between science, technology, and society should make it an attractive resource for science communication students and scholars.

A factor that has contributed to ANT's success was social scientists' perceived need to understand new forms of socioeconomic organization that emerged in the 1980s through 1990s, in which networks and flows—of money, information, knowledge, and so on—trespassed the territorial boundaries and forms of regulation of the nation-state. In this new economy, social scientists and policymakers recognized that research and innovation were of key importance. The problem was how to understand the role of knowledge in society: Was it the case that science and technology were "pushing" or propelling socioeconomic change, or was it that socioeconomic forces were "pulling" or demanding new ideas and inventions? To this, ANT provided a useful and interesting answer: the idea that social relationships and structures are in a constant and dynamic interaction with scientific knowledge and technological devices. It is this idea of a coproduction of science-technology and society—encapsulated in the notion of the sociotechnical—that makes ANT different from other approaches to understanding science in society. To be able to understand the significance of these ideas, it is necessary to review the intellectual context in which ANT took shape.

Emergence of ANT

ANT emerged within a rich context of intellectual change in the social sciences. The middle of the 1970s had seen the appearance of a "new" sociology of science that claimed not only to study the institutional norms that govern scientists' conduct, but also to understand the relationship between scientific knowledge and the social contexts in which it was produced. This generated a variety of studies where the knowledge claims made in fields as different as neurology or statistics were seen as shaped by the social networks that scientists maintained with other scientists and/or powerful social groups. This meant that new discoveries and inventions were driven by the social and economic interests of these groups and not just by experimentation and the application of reason, particularly where there was uncertainty and controversy about the issues at stake.

In the early 1980s, two French social scientists—Bruno Latour and Michel Callon—challenged the view that scientists should be seen as passive recipients of the interests and strategies of others and thus the idea that science was simply a social construction. They proposed instead that in devising their projects, experiments, or papers, scientists actively engaged with powerful social groups, influencing their ideals of social and economic organization and change. For Latour and Callon, this was an interactive, dynamic process, wherein experimentation and material reality played a crucial role.

To describe this process, they used the concept of *translation*. Drawing on the work of the French philosopher of science and mathematics Michel Serres, Latour and Callon proposed that scientific and technological change was a process of translation. First, it entails the transformation of a social or economic problem into a scientific problem (for example, to reduce car pollution, we need to create alternative engine designs); this requires a significant amount of simplification (translation) of a complex problem into credible and feasible laboratory experiments. If this transformation is accepted by interested social groups and fellow scientists, it is possible for researchers to work through the problem within a confined set of instruments and concepts.

Finally, if a result is achieved, the objects and ideas created in the laboratory are tried out in the so-called real world. A new social and technological reality comes into being: New relationships or networks between people and between people and things (such as cars) are created in the same process. But note that all the steps in the process of translation are predicated by a conditional clause (an "if" statement), and ANT researchers are interested in describing and understanding both success and failure in establishing these networks. Like the successes of networks, failures cannot be explained only by looking at social or material forces alone. Thus, ANT researchers prefer to think of social and material entities as being involved in networks equally as actors so as to avoid making assumptions about where the driving forces of the process lie. An actor-network is accordingly a set of relationships between human and nonhuman entities drawn together by a particular activity of concern (ranging from particle physics to car design to neurosurgery to primary education).

ANT and Public Understanding of Science

ANT questions assumptions about the role of various actors in knowledge-making processes. In the field of public understanding of science (PUS), since the 1980s, researchers have drawn on the sociology of science to critique what they saw as the main assumption of science policymakers: that knowledge had to be disseminated to a public that was ignorant of the facts of science. This deficit model of science in society is underpinned by a view of laypersons as people whose knowledge falls short of accredited scientific knowledge. This view clearly ignores the highly relevant knowledge people have of their own social and material contexts: where and how they live together in everyday life. Furthermore, scholars argued that instead of being a neat boundary between science and society, these categories are in fact outcomes of negotiated, social processes, and that in assuming the existence of a public, policymakers ignore the rich and diverse ways through which various lay groups contest science and provide serious, alternative forms of knowledge to understand problems of public concern.

To understand such phenomena, ANT, as conceived in the 1980s, was ill prepared because it tended to emphasize and favor the perspective of scientists and engineers that were at the center of the network. In addressing this problem, ANT-influenced scholars have focused on the ways in which different forms of knowledge are produced and interact in fields such as medicine, economics, or biology. Also suggested is the idea that the concept of network is too restrictive to understand these complex, diverse processes. The existence of a network denotes fixed points and relationships, whereas what was needed to capture these processes were notions that encapsulated fluidity, where partial changes to the sociotechnical relationships did not entail the collapse of the whole.

Thus, an important area of research involves understanding how grassroots groups work together in the creation of new research areas. In this, it is crucial that knowledge making is not constrained by claims to authority, legitimacy, or professional boundaries: Fluidity is important not only for knowledge making, but also for enabling lay groups to participate in collective decision making. The process of actively blurring the boundaries between science and society suggests a more complex perspective on societal and political significance. Not only is a diversification of the forms of knowledge brought to bear in the public space of most contemporary societies taking place, but also these societies are seeing a proliferation of

the group identities and institutional forms created to produce those forms of knowledge. This means that it is insufficient to think of publics as "lay" or as "expert" because claims to expertise are multiple (for example, the "expert patient"), and this has consequences for the way in which we think about science communication.

Instead of viewing science communication as a matter of diffusing information or influencing the way the public thinks about issues (the public relations model), there is a need to acknowledge this social and political complexity; since the 1980s, this has involved recognizing the way in which knowledge is embedded in social practices. To best understand this, it is perhaps useful to use the example of research and innovation in the area of Alzheimer's disease. In this biomedical field, there has been an increased research interest and public investment in the characterization of preclinical risk profiles leading to dementia. It is argued that early diagnosis of dementia and particularly of Alzheimer's disease will facilitate the prevention of the diseases and lower the prevalence of the condition in the general population. However, in a study of the different ways lay and expert constituencies work to define and negotiate the boundaries between normal and abnormal cognitive aging, it has been found that caregivers, patients, and advocates found new research on risk conditions for Alzheimer's disease largely irrelevant to their lives and would have preferred human and financial resources being invested in the exploration of forms of care.

This perspective was different from that of younger citizens who mostly valued knowledge about these risk conditions for how it enabled them to plan for the future. As this research made clear, scientific expertise had not been sufficient to frame the whole problem and define its context; there were diverse views on what Latour might call "the matter of concern" in relation to dementia (that is, what was to be studied and how), although such views were not publicly explored in the determination of research priorities and problems. It is from this perspective that one can understand increased calls, from both scholars and policymakers, for systems of public discussion that support dialogical exchanges between heterogeneous groups and constituencies to find, frame, and work through research problems.

Dialogic Communication

In this, the study and practical application of forms of dialogic communication are of particular relevance. Although still an emerging research area, dialogic approaches to communication, often drawing on the work of Russian philosopher and semiotician Mikhail Bakhtin, highlight the interactive, coproduced character of communication. As such, dialogue is a quality of communication that can be enhanced or hindered through institutional and technical means. This has enormous parallels with the ANT approach to the formation or demise of sociotechnical networks: It is necessary to understand which institutional and technical means support dialogue and collective exploration of common concerns.

Dialogic ideals are important, but dialogic devices can also work as technologies of legitimization with respect to the perspective of scientists, researchers, or powerful groups. For this reason, it is necessary to construct "dialogic fora," where the rules of communication are tailored to the issue at hand. Issues where uncertainty is high and that are ill defined might be occasions that facilitate the emergence of genuine collaborative relations between groups, whereas in issues that are strongly framed by science and that enjoy sustained institutional support, other rules might have to be set up to balance exchanges. These are issues that should become central in a research and policy agenda that supports the relationship between dialogical forms of communication and interactive knowledge production.

Tiago Moreira

See also Deficit Model; Latour, Bruno; Merton, Robert K.; Public Understanding of Science

Further Readings

Callon, M., Lascoumes, P., & Barthe, Y. (2009). *Acting in an uncertain world: An essay on technical democracy.* Cambridge: MIT Press.

Latour, B. (1987). *Science in action.* Cambridge, MA: Harvard University Press.

Latour, B. (2005). *Reassembling the social: An introduction to actor-network-theory.* Oxford, UK: Oxford University Press.

Law, J., & Mol, A. (Eds.). (2002). *Complexities: Social studies of knowledge practices.* Durham, NC: Duke University Press.

AFRICA, SCIENCE IN

Africa, home to 840 million people, is lagging behind in reaching the world's Millennium Development Goals to halve world poverty by 2015. The continent battles with chronic poverty and hunger, rampant disease, civil conflict, and political unrest in many parts. Environmental degradation, failing agriculture, lack of access to clean water, population growth, rapid urbanization, and loss of biodiversity add to the daunting list of challenges. The continent is not doing well on the education or science fronts either. Advances in science and technology are held back by poor education and research infrastructure, escalating brain drain, and a widening digital divide. Africa contributes only 1.4% of the world's scientific publications, with South Africa and Egypt accounting for more than half of the continent's share. While improved science communication cannot solve Africa's problems by itself, it clearly has a contribution to make.

Africa will never be strong and prosperous with such a weak education system and poorly developed science and technology base. Policy leaders acknowledge that they will only be able to improve quality of life on the continent with the help of scientific knowledge and skills. This will require bold leadership and a massive investment in building continent-wide science and innovation capacity. Without it, Africa will remain largely excluded from the global-knowledge-based economy.

Under the auspices of the African Union, the New Partnership for Africa's Development (NEPAD) has been designed to address the many challenges facing the African continent. It steers an action plan for African science as part of its strategic framework for Africa's renewal, and seeks to use science and technology to accomplish socioeconomic goals.

African Science Academies

A network of academies of science play an important role in increasing the profile of science and technology on the continent and in providing policy advice to national governments. The U.S. National Academies of Science support this network through the African Science Academy

Development Initiative, supported by a grant from the Bill & Melinda Gates Foundation. The African Academy of Sciences (AAS), with its head offices in Nairobi, Kenya, aims to drive scientific and technological change in Africa through initiatives to promote networking, capacity building, and scientific excellence and relevance. The Academy of Science for the Developing World has a Regional Office for sub-Saharan Africa hosted at the AAS to support research achievers and the communication of research results and outcomes to policymakers. There are also national chapters in Madagascar, Senegal, Zimbabwe, Kenya, and Ghana. Finally, most national science academies in Africa belong to the Network of African Science Academies.

Pan-African Science Agencies, Networks and Research Centers

The African Ministerial Council on Science and Technology operates under the auspices of NEPAD as a high-level platform for developing policies and setting priorities on science, technology, and innovation for African development, while the International Council for Science regional office for Africa, based in Pretoria, South Africa, promotes scientific collaboration, capacity building, and the mobility of African scientists and invests in securing and using Africa's indigenous knowledge. The organization is also working toward developing closer links between science and policy, wider dissemination of scientific information of value to Africa, more equitable access to scientific information, and the participation of all scientists—regardless of race, citizenship, language, political stance, or gender—in international scientific endeavor.

The United Nations Educational, Scientific and Cultural Organisation (UNESCO) has a Regional Bureau for Science in Africa based in Nairobi, Kenya. The African Network of Scientific and Technological Institutions (ANSTI) was set up by UNESCO to train young scientists and broaden the experience of senior scientists. ANSTI also publishes the *African Journal of Science and Technology*. The International Development Research Centre serves and funds research in Africa through regional offices in Dakar, Senegal and Nairobi, Kenya, with an emphasis on research that will inform and influence policy decisions. And the Consultative Group on International

Agricultural Research has a number of research centers in Africa including the Africa Rice Center in Benin, the International Institute of Tropical Agriculture in Nigeria, the International Livestock Research Institute in Kenya, and the World Agroforestry Center in Kenya. The council for the Development of Social Science Research in Africa, with its head office in Dakar, Senegal, focuses on research in the social sciences. The Council for Scientific and Industry Research in South Africa and the Medical Research Council, a leader in community health and HIV/AIDS research that is also in South Africa, are other examples of active research efforts on the continent.

Higher Education in Africa

The Association of African Universities, with headquarters in Accra, Ghana, strives to raise the quality of higher education in Africa and to promote the role of universities in science and technology development on the continent. It has close to 200 members from 45 African countries. Yet the lion's share of research-focused universities in Africa is in South Africa. The National Research Foundation in South Africa funds and coordinates research in the country and administers a network of centers of excellence, specialist research chairs, and national research facilities.

Science Journalism, Science Communication, and Research News Services

Sustainable development of Africa's science and technology potential will require the support of its policymakers and citizens. Therefore, more organizations in Africa are now following the global trend toward an investment in making science and technology more accessible to the general public via the mass media, as well as other initiatives to encourage public interest, engagement, and participation in science. For example, the South African Agency for Science and Technology Advancement coordinates a wide range of science communication initiatives in the country, including national science week, science Olympiads, and science platform months.

Growing evidence documents the ongoing development of science communication activities and organizations in Africa. Every year, close to 60,000 people attend the annual SciFest Africa in South Africa's Eastern Cape Province. SciFest Africa has spawned several smaller festivals elsewhere in Southern Africa. Science centers in Southern Africa collaborate via the Southern African Association of Science and Technology Centres. There are several networks of science journalists, including the Uganda Science Journalists Association and the Network of Climate Journalists of the Greater Horn of Africa. The World Federation of Science Journalists invests in the development of science journalism capacity on the continent through online courses and mentorship schemes. News services devoted to science and technology news from Africa and to making research-based policy advice more accessible to governments and institutional policymakers include the Africa Science News Service, Research-Africa.Net, SciDev.Net, and Science in Africa.

Marina Joubert

See also Europe, Research System in; National Development, Science and Technology in

Further Readings

The African Academy of Sciences: www.aasciences.org

The African Network of Scientific and Technological Institutions: www.ansti.org

The New Partnership for Africa's Development: www .nepad.org

South African Agency for Science and Technology Advancement: www.saasta.ac.za

United Nations Education, Scientific and Cultural Organization, Science in Africa: www.unesco.org/ science/science_africa.pdf

AGENDA SETTING AND SCIENCE

In 1963, Bernard Cohen observed that the news media may not tell people what to think, but they do tell them what to think about. This observation was the germ of the idea of agenda setting. Agenda setting proposes that the media agenda is related to the public agenda at any given time and, moreover, that the relationship is causal: The news media cause people to rank issues more importantly on their own agenda of issues that are important to them. Maxwell McCombs and Donald Shaw first tested this theory with voters in Chapel Hill, North Carolina. They found that news media agendas (measured using content analysis of major news outlets) were highly correlated with the public agenda (using surveys of undecided voters in the 1968 election). Since then, dozens of studies have confirmed, amplified, and extended the theory, which is still one of the major theories of media effects.

Agenda setting came as part of a response to the then dominant view that the mass media had limited effects in terms of shaping public opinion. Agenda setting, along with theories such as cultivation and spiral of silence, found ways to demonstrate various types of media effects without claiming that the media had the very powerful effects claimed in some of the first observations that were made about media in the early part of the 20th century. As such, these newer theories offer middle-ground explanations of media effects.

Agenda setting was first tested with simple correlations between news agendas and public agendas. Later tests sought to show causality, and a variety of ways of testing agenda setting have emerged. Some look at agendas in the aggregate and compare those to aggregated public agendas. Others look at agenda setting at the microlevel, testing whether individuals' agendas are correlated to news agendas. Others look at issue salience over time, comparing the ups and downs of issue coverage to series data about public opinion to establish possible causal relationships. Finally, some studies use experimental methods, especially to determine whether exposure to particular news stories influences individual response to issue questions. Often these studies are pursuing questions of *framing* or *priming*, which some theorists connect with agenda-setting theory.

The vast majority of agenda-setting studies have been conducted on political issues; many fewer deal with science or technology. However, one observation from agenda setting is highly relevant to science and the environment. Agenda setting proposes that unobtrusive issues (those that are not readily apparent to us from personal experience) will be more susceptible to agenda-setting effects, because we are more reliant on the media to determine whether those issues are important.

Because science, technology, and the environment are often unobtrusive issues, media coverage of these issues may be especially important to draw public attention to them. Some examples show this importance of this effect. Researchers have shown that public attention to environmental issues is related to news coverage of those issues, consistent with an agenda-setting effect. Moreover, media attention to those issues is often seen to be cyclical. In 1972, Anthony Downs proposed an explanation for this, arguing that environmental issues would at first seem dramatically dangerous and thus receive attention. However, he argued that the public would eventually realize the cost of solving environmental problems, and would then turn their attention elsewhere. While some scholars have disputed the details of his theory, cyclical patterns of attention have been demonstrated by several researchers, spanning the period from the 1960s to today.

Even the environment, which is obviously an important issue, rarely rises to the top spot on the public agenda. Issues such as the economy, war, crime, and immigration tend to overshadow scientific and technical issues. Therefore, the public is highly reliant on media to alert them to important scientific debates. Issues such as plant biotechnology (for example, genetically modified organisms, or GMOs, including food crops), stem cell technology in medicine, and the debate over climate change have all been shown to receive cyclical coverage; public attention to those issues also rises during these cycles.

Thus, agenda-setting theory, along with framing research, has begun to explore more complex dynamics of how such issues rise to attention and how they are then dealt with within the policy sphere. Some science problems, such as the issue of acid rain, are solved within the policy sphere, and then attention goes away. Other issues, such as the case of GMOs in the United States, never create enough opposition to warrant policy attention, and then media attention again disappears. Yet other issues, however, may go through multiple cycles, as attention rises and falls as specific focusing events occur to redraw attention to the issue. In the case of climate change, there have been at least two major cycles of media attention: one in the late 1980s and early 1990s and one in recent years. As no easy solution presents itself to this possibly intractable problem, it is likely that other cycles of news attention will emerge when and as the events of the day present themselves as worthy of public attention.

A final note about agenda setting for science: There is little evidence that attention to science is motivated solely by real-world events. While new scientific studies and environmental conditions can present themselves as opportunities for news attention, just as often pseudo-events and political debates draw attention to science. What agenda setting tells us is that the public is unlikely, on its own, to pay attention to science and technology issues. Going beyond agenda setting, more recent studies are focusing on the issue of framing, particularly in determining how various stakeholders in any given scientific debate manage to convey their interpretation of the issue to the public and to the policy community.

James Shanahan

See also Agricultural Biotechnology; Climate Change, Communicating; Cultivation Theory and Science; Framing and Priming in Science Communication; Spiral of Silence and Science

Further Readings

Downs, A. (1972). Up and down with ecology: The "issue-attention" cycle. *Public Interest, 28,* 38–51.

McCombs, M., & Reynolds, A. (2002). News influence on our pictures of the world. In J. Bryant & D. Zillman (Eds.), *Media effects: Advances in theory and research* (pp. 1–18). Mahwah, NJ: Lawrence Erlbaum.

McCombs, M., & Shaw, D. (1972). The agenda-setting function of the mass media. *Public Opinion Quarterly, 36,* 176–187.

Nisbet, M., & Huge, M. (2006). Attention cycles and frames in the plant biotechnology debate: Managing power and participation through the press/policy connection. *Press/Politics, 11*(2), 3–40.

Agricultural Biotechnology

Agricultural biotechnology is the application of modern biotechnology techniques, particularly recombinant DNA (rDNA) gene splicing, for developing new varieties of food crops and animals with useful genetic traits. In the mid-1990s, the introduction of the first genetically modified (GM) food crops launched a major global controversy that continues today. In the United States, many farmers grow GM crops, and an estimated 75% of the processed food products contain ingredients from GM crops. In Europe, however, there is strong public opposition to GM foods and crops based on concerns about safety, environmental impacts, the lack of benefits, and moral and ethical issues. In addition, the European Union (EU) has adopted much stricter regulations on genetically modified organisms (GMOs), and relatively few have been approved.

Numerous studies have sought to explain the apparent divergence of U.S. and European public opinion about GM foods and crops. Studies have examined the effects of the European media's more extensive coverage of the biotechnology controversy, including greater attention to biotechnology opponents. While the difference in media coverage and focus may account for some of the difference between the European and U.S. responses, studies show that other factors are also likely to be relevant and that public opinion on both sides of the Atlantic is more complex and nuanced than broadly believed by policymakers.

The Technology

Genes are sequences of DNA that contain the inheritable instructions that enable all organisms to function. Through a series of steps, genes control the expression of thousands of proteins that, among other things, account for the characteristics, or traits, of a particular organism. Such genetic traits can be valuable for agriculture; small naturally occurring genetic variations can make the difference between a plant that tastes sweet and one that is bitter. For centuries, humans have been selecting and crossbreeding plants and animals to develop foods that are more nutritious or easier to grow. As a result, almost all of today's food crops and animals are genetically different from their ancient predecessors.

In 1973, Dr. Herbert Boyer and Dr. Stanley Cohen learned how to "cut" a gene sequence from one organism, and recombine it, or "paste" it, into another organism, where the gene would retain its original function. Since plants, animals, and humans share common genes, this new gene-splicing technique, called *recombinant DNA* or *rDNA transformation,* made it possible to move genes (and their useful traits) between completely unrelated organisms. The technology opened up a new world of possibilities for animal and plant breeders to develop new varieties. Organisms no longer needed to be sexually compatible; a useful gene found in a bacterium could be spliced into a corn plant. Further, the ability to add just a single new gene gave breeders much more precision and predictability than traditional trial-and-error breeding, allowing the faster development of useful novel varieties. While all plants and animals have been genetically changed by conventional breeding, the phrase *genetic modification* or *genetic engineering* has the popular meaning of referring to the use of rDNA technology to modify a plant or animal.

Introduction of GM Food

The adoption of agricultural biotechnology began in earnest in 1996 with Monsanto's commercial introduction of soybeans that had been genetically modified to be tolerant to Monsanto's Roundup herbicide. This new trait enabled farmers to control weeds more easily by spraying an entire field with Roundup without killing the soybeans. Using similar biotechnology tools, crops such as corn, cotton, and potatoes were modified to include genes from a bacterium that made the plants resistant to insect pests. Virus protection has also been engineered into a number of less commercially significant food crops, such as papaya. The largest agricultural biotechnology companies are Monsanto, DuPont, and Syngenta.

By 2008, only 13 years after GM crops were first introduced, U.S. Department of Agriculture estimates that 80% of the corn, 92% of the soybeans, and 86% of the cotton planted in the United States are biotechnology varieties. From this standpoint, agricultural biotechnology may well be the most rapidly adopted agricultural technology in U.S. history.

Public Opinion in the United States and in Europe

The widespread use of GM foods and the apparent absence of active opposition in the United States are often contrasted with European rejection of GMOs. While there are differences in the public opinion toward biotechnology in the United States and in Europe, consumer attitudes on both sides of the Atlantic are more nuanced and complex than often portrayed.

Studies have shown that most Americans remain uninformed about GM foods and are unaware of the extent to which GM food is already in their diets. Some studies also suggest a low salience for GM food issues in the United States. Surveys by the International Food Information Council showed that very few respondents identified GM food as a concern in response to an unprompted question about food safety concerns. Other studies have shown that GM food issues rank low in overall food safety concerns.

On the other hand, numerous public opinion studies have consistently found that significant minorities of Americans express opposition to or concern about food biotechnology on the basis of its safety, environmental impacts, and moral and ethical aspects. In some cases, these results are not very different from European poll results. Studies have examined the apparent discrepancy between these results and the relative lack of active public opposition to biotechnology in the United States. Some studies have suggested that opposition to GM food in the United States may exist, but that it receives less media attention. Susanna H. Priest suggests that the relative absence of public opposition in the United States may be due to a "spiral of silence" that discourages the open expression of dissent from the perceived mainstream view, which is partly framed and reinforced by media coverage of the issue.

Studies also show that opinions of Americans, like Europeans, are influenced by the purpose for which biotechnology is being used. Thus, there is greater support for the use of biotechnology to produce drugs or improve nutrition than to make crops easier to grow. This research suggests that consumers may apply a utilitarian risk–benefit analysis in forming their opinions. Other studies have considered additional factors believed to influence public attitudes toward biotechnology, including level of education and knowledge, trust and group identification, cultural attitudes toward technology in general, and trust in government, scientists, and experts.

As the Eurobarometer and other studies show, the majority of Europeans also express concerns about the safety of GM food and environmental risks, and they also question the benefits, which are seen as accruing to U.S. farmers and U.S. multinational companies. Significantly, Europeans are much less likely than Americans to trust government, scientists, and experts and far more likely to trust consumer and environment activist groups on this issue. Public opposition is much more apparent in Europe than in the United States. Even in the few cases where European policymakers have approved GM foods, supermarkets and restaurants will not offer them due to negative public opinion and fear of activist opposition.

Several studies have examined the role of the media in influencing the divergence of opinions and opposition in the United States and in Europe. While elite media coverage of biotechnology issues in Europe has been framed in ways similar to those in the United States, European media have given more attention to dissenting opinions, potentially helping to legitimize the greater expression of dissent in Europe. In comparison, the U.S. media have tended to reflect more mainstream official, industrial, and scientific viewpoints. An additional factor influencing both public opinion and media coverage was the widely publicized admission by the British government in 1996 that, despite earlier assurances to the contrary, eating meat from cattle infected with mad cow disease could in fact cause serious human illness. Media saturation coverage of the mad cow crisis contributed to widespread public fears in Europe about the safety of the food supply and distrust of government assurances, even as the first GM crops were being introduced in Europe.

Policy Divergence

These divergent perspectives about biotechnology are also manifested in public policy, where the United States and the European Commission have adopted dramatically different policy approaches. U.S. regulatory policy is grounded in the principle that biotechnology presents no unique risks and that any risk of a product should therefore be evaluated based on the nature of the product, not on the process by which it was made. Thus, all new food products should be regulated the same way, whether made from a GM crop or from a conventional one. In the United States, GM products are regulated under the same laws as apply to other products, such as food, pesticides, and pharmaceuticals. Since GM food is usually considered to be "substantially equivalent" to conventional food, no labeling of GM food is required.

In contrast, Europe has adopted a regulatory approach based on process. All GM crops and foods go through a safety review and approval process under a law that applies exclusively to products of biotechnology. The European Union (EU) also requires most foods derived from GM crops to be labeled, and products must be able to be traced to their source from the "farm to the fork." The EU regulatory approach reflects a broader policy called the "precautionary principle," which argues that restrictions are appropriate where there is scientific uncertainty and a risk of significant and irreversible harm to the environment or public health. Though a number of GM crops and foods have passed European safety reviews, few have received final approval in the EU's political decision-making process. In 2006, the World Trade Organization sided with the United States in maintaining that Europe's failure to approve any GM crops between 1999 and 2003 violated trade agreements.

Global Adoption

Adoption of agricultural biotechnology in the rest of the world has been a mixed picture. Governments and farmers have been uncertain about how to weigh potential benefits against European opposition, consumer concerns, potential environment risks, and market uncertainties. These concerns were vividly illustrated in 2002 when several sub-Saharan African nations suffering famine initially rejected U.S. food aid that contained GM varieties of corn. Worldwide, however, adoption of GM crops has continued to increase. In 2007, according to the International Service for the Acquisition of Agri-Biotech Applications, 114.3 million hectares of GM crops were planted globally, up from 67.7 million hectares in 2003, although the vast majority (86%) continues to be grown in just four countries: the United States (50%), Argentina (17%), Brazil (15%), and Canada (7%). Another 9% comes from GM cotton planted in China and India, with the remaining 5% scattered over 17 countries. In addition to the 23 nations currently growing GM crops, another 29 have given regulatory approval for importing at least one GM crop.

GM Food Perspectives

While proponents of biotechnology view it as a straightforward extension of plant and animal breeding techniques, opponents tend to view it as a radical departure. Proponents emphasize that rDNA breeding is safer and more precise than conventional breeding since it involves the movement of only selected genetic materials with known functions, compared to the random exchange of genetic material in traditional breeding. They also argue that the risks of biotechnology are no different than risks associated with many other accepted forms of breeding, including mutagenesis. However, critics respond that current rDNA techniques cannot control the location in the genome where the introduced genetic material will be inserted, and this could lead to unpredictable effects. They also argue that combining genetic material from widely separated species is new and creates uncertain risks.

Food Safety Issues

These contrasting perspectives have led to the question whether foods derived from GM crops or animals are safe to eat. U.S. regulators and most scientists (as reflected in reports from the National Academy of Science) take the position that while biotechnology could theoretically change a food's toxicity or nutritional value, the risks of doing so are comparable to the same risks that can occur in conventional breeding as well. The U.S. Food and Drug Administration (FDA) considers most foods derived from GM crops to be "substantially equivalent" to conventional food and therefore just as safe. Another question is whether a new gene could make the food allergenic to some consumers. This issue arose in the case of StarLink corn, a GM variety that the Environmental Protection Agency refused to approve out of concern that the new introduced protein could be a food allergen. Some critics have also raised the concern that the antibiotic resistance genes that are in some GM foods as a by-product of the gene-splicing process could increase antibiotic resistance in humans, but the FDA's position is that the risk is very low.

Biotechnology proponents point to the absence of any reported adverse human health effects during the 12 years that GM foods have been on the U.S. market as evidence of safety. Critics respond that there is no ongoing governmental monitoring or research program to find such effects. Critics also point to the lack of long-term testing on humans and to some animal feeding studies that they believe show possible adverse effects. Proponents dispute the significance of these studies.

Proponents also argue that GM food can be safer and more nutritious than conventional food. For example, Bt corn is less susceptible to mycotoxin contamination. Biotechnology is also being used to develop strains of rice with beta-carotene to alleviate vitamin A deficiency in populations that subsist almost entirely on a diet of white rice.

Environmental Issues

GM crops also raise a number of environmental issues. One set of environmental concerns deals with the potential for GM plants and animals to spread the novel genes to other plants and animals. Critics refer to this as "biological pollution" and argue that once it has occurred, it will be difficult to clean up. Commercial GM gene sequences have been found in native land races of maize in remote sections of Mexico. There are also concerns that GM herbicide resistance traits will eventually be passed into weedy relatives of canola.

Gene flow is a natural phenomenon. The question is not whether it will happen, but whether such gene transfers are likely to persist and whether it makes any environmental difference if they do. Ecologists state that novel traits are likely to die out unless they somehow provide the plant or animal with a fitness advantage over its competitors. In reports for the National Academy of Science, scientists have expressed more concern about the gene flow from GM animals than GM plants. For example, fertile GM fish that escape into the ocean and mate with wild fish could, under some scenarios, cause the demise of the wild species altogether. In such cases, the question is whether physical and biological containment systems would be adequate to mitigate that risk.

Like conventional chemical pesticides, plants modified to be pest resistant raise additional environmental issues. One concern is potential harm to beneficial insects and other "non-target" insects. A 1999 report that GM corn could kill Monarch butterflies launched an international storm of reaction. Later research showed that in real-world conditions, Monarch larvae are unlikely to be exposed to lethal levels of pest-resistant corn pollen. Another concern is that pests will evolve resistance to the pesticide in these crops if they are constantly exposed to it, making the plants (and the pesticide) ineffective. As of 2008, pest resistance to GM crops has not developed as a major problem in the United States, though it has been reported in China.

Biotechnology proponents point to a number of environmental benefits from GM crops. Technologies that allow farmers to achieve higher yields per acre mean that more food can be grown on less land. More efficient farming, particularly in the developing world, could reduce the pressure to convert marginal lands (such as tropical rainforests) for farming. GM crops allow farmers to reduce the use of some chemical pesticides on some crops, and herbicide-resistant crops make it easier for farmers to use no-till agriculture methods, which help preserve soil integrity and reduce soil erosion. Advocates also point to potential environmental benefits of future GM crops, such as drought-resistant crops that will reduce the need for water.

On a much broader scale, however, some critics dismiss biotechnology as a part of an unsustainable industrialized agriculture system that depends on monocultures, cheap oil and chemicals, and short-term technology fixes.

Moral and Ethical Issues

In 1998, Prince Charles voiced concerns about the morality and ethics of biotechnology when he argued that GM foods were taking humans into what he felt was an area that belonged only to God. Public opinion polls both in the United States and in Europe confirm that many people feel that scientists are "playing God" with the fundamental building blocks of life. Polls also show that the public is significantly more uncomfortable with the genetic modification of animals than with plants, in part due to ethical and moral concerns.

Economic Issues

The economic benefits of biotechnology are also debated, particularly the question of how the economic benefits are distributed. The evidence that biotech crops are more profitable for U.S.

farmers is mixed. While farmers save money by not buying pesticides or having to till, those savings are at least partly offset by the higher price (and possible lower yield) of GM seeds. However, the rapid adoption of biotech seed varieties certainly indicates that most American farmers find value in biotech varieties.

Further, some farmers also object to Monsanto's policy that forbids farmers from saving seed from their crops and replanting them in the next season. Monsanto argues that such restrictions are needed to protect its patented GM seeds from illegal reproduction. Critics contend that it is unfair to patent seeds and prohibit their reproduction through legal licenses and biological means (such as a gene that would render the seeds sterile), particularly for developing-country small farmers.

There are also economic issues associated with managing the drift of GM seeds and pollen in the environment. Farmers who find unwanted GM crops growing on their land may be liable for patent infringement. Organic growers do not want to have pollen or seeds of GM crops mixed up with their organic crops. Growers do not want experimental or unapproved varieties of GM crops mixed in with their food crops, since it could make their entire crop unmarketable. These and related issues are the subject of various lawsuits in the United States and Canada that may address the unresolved questions of liability for unintended gene flow.

Conclusion

The global controversy over agricultural biotechnology is driven by public opinions that reflect different perspectives on risk, benefits, and trust— social values that have been shaped by culture and history as well as by media and communication efforts. Finding a near-term resolution to these controversies is likely to prove difficult.

Michael Rodemeyer

See also Department of Agriculture, U.S.; Food Safety; Precautionary Principle

Further Readings

Brossard, D., Shanahan, J., & Nesbitt, T. C. (Eds.). (2007). *The public, the media and agricultural biotechnology*. Oxfordshire, UK: CAB International.

Federoff, N., & Brown, N. M. (2004). *Mendel in the kitchen*. Washington, DC: Joseph Henry Press.

Gaskell, G., Allansdottir, A., Allum, N., Corchero, C., Fischler, C., Hampel, J., et al. (2006). Europeans and biotechnology in 2005: Patterns and trends. *Eurobarometer, 64*(3). Retrieved August 13, 2008, from http://ec.europa.eu/research/press/2006/pdf/pr1906_eb_64_3_final_report-may2006_en.pdf

Jasanoff, S. (2005). *Designs on nature*. Princeton, NJ: Princeton University Press.

Priest, S. H. (2001). *A grain of truth: The media, the public and biotechnology*. Lanham, MD: Rowman & Littlefield.

Priest, S. H. (2006). Public discourse and scientific controversy: A spiral-of-silence analysis of biotechnology opinion in the United States. *Science Communication, 28*(2), 195–215.

Priest, S. H., Bonfadelli, H., & Rusanen, M. (2003). The "trust gap" hypothesis: Predicting support for biotechnology across national cultures as a function of trust in actors. *Risk Analysis, 23*(4), 751–766.

AGRICULTURAL COMMUNICATORS OF TOMORROW

National Agricultural Communicators of Tomorrow (National ACT) is a collegiate student organization that strives to stimulate interest in the profession of agricultural communications on the local, national, and international levels; promote the interchange of ideas among students and faculty members at colleges and universities offering academic programs in agricultural communications; and provide opportunities for personal and professional growth between students and agricultural communication professionals. Membership is composed of undergraduate and graduate students actively interested in agricultural communications. More than 15 chapters from universities across the United States and Canada affiliate with National ACT.

National ACT meets each year with agricultural communication professionals at the Agricultural Media Summit. National ACT also sponsors several annual events, including a mid-spring professional development workshop, a critique and contest where students receive feedback from professionals on their communication materials, and scholarships. A student officer team and faculty adviser manage National ACT. Universities desiring to start a National ACT chapter can visit the National ACT Web site.

National ACT traces its beginning to 1968, when agricultural communications students from the University of Illinois conceived the idea of a national student group and sent surveys to universities that offered curricula in agricultural journalism or agricultural communications. Responses from 22 universities indicated that more than 250 students were enrolled in such programs at 15 universities. Respondents indicated that a national organization for students in agricultural communications would be valuable. As a result of the encouraging responses, students and faculty advisers from the University of Illinois, Iowa State University, and the University of Missouri met in Burlington, Iowa, in early 1969 to discuss the feasibility of such a group and to formalize plans for a national meeting. This initial group envisioned a national organization that would provide students with professional development opportunities, leadership experiences, networking opportunities, and a conduit for agricultural communication and journalism students across the country to interact. After two meetings, the planners had drafted a constitution and asked the American Association of Agricultural Communicators in Education (AAACE, now known as ACE) to serve as the parent organization. Members of ACE endorsed the arrangement at their 1969 meeting. In July 1970, 23 students from seven universities met with ACE to form the American Association of Agricultural Communicators of Tomorrow, now known as National ACT. The universities represented included Colorado State University, Delaware Valley College, University of Georgia, University of Illinois, Iowa State University, University of Missouri, and The Ohio State University.

Although National ACT has seen many changes over the years, a few concepts have served as an important part of the organization. The first is ACT's ability to relate to the whole career field in agricultural communications. The programs that ACT sponsors at the national, regional, and chapter levels try to reflect the interests of all students studying agricultural communications or agricultural journalism. A good example of academic and professional diversity can be seen in the categories represented in National ACT's annual contest. A second concept is maintaining affiliation with the varied professional agricultural communications organizations. Throughout the years, ACT has worked with these organizations in many capacities, including holding the national meeting with different organizations and providing mentoring programs, scholarships, and internships. The value of these affiliations is not always seen immediately or while ACT members are attending college. Rather it is seen after they graduate when they use contacts made to find jobs and improve their network of agricultural communications. A final concept is providing students with opportunities to develop knowledge needed for a career in agricultural communications. This concept is accomplished in many ways. When students compete in critique contests, for example, they receive an evaluation of their skills and learn about ways to improve them. In addition, workshops provide students with opportunities to learn more about what is expected of them when they enter the agricultural communications field.

Ricky Telg

See also Agricultural Journalism; Association for Communication Excellence

Further Readings

Ettredge, T. M., & Bellah, K. A. (2008). A curriculum for university agricultural communication programs: A synthesis of research. *Proceedings of the 105th annual meeting of the Southern Association of Agricultural Scientists, Agricultural Communication Section.* Dallas, TX. Retrieved April 27, 2009, from http://agnewsarchive.tamu.edu/saas/2008/Ettredge.pdf

Morgan, A. C. (2009). Competencies needed by agricultural communication undergraduates: An industry perspective. *Proceedings of the 106th annual meeting of the Southern Association of Agricultural Scientists, Agricultural Communication Section.* Atlanta, GA. Retrieved April 27, 2009, from http://agnews.tamu.edu/saas/2009/morgan.pdf

National Agricultural Communicators of Tomorrow: http://gonact.org

Reisner. A. (1990). An overview of agricultural communications programs. *Journal of Applied Communications, 74*(2), 8–17.

Rhoades, E., Ricketts, J., Irani, T., Lundy, L., & Telg, R. (2005). Critical thinking dispositions of agricultural communication students. *Journal of Applied Communications, 89*(1), 25–34.

Telg, R. W., & Irani, T. (2005). Integrating critical thinking into agricultural communication curricula. *Journal of Applied Communications, 89*(3), 13–22.

Toomey, A. C., & Telg, R. (2009). Critiquing the contest: Assessing the benefits of a collegiate academic competition. *Proceedings of the 106th annual meeting of the Southern Association of Agricultural Scientists, Agricultural Communication Section.* Atlanta, GA. Retrieved April 27, 2009, from http://agnews.tamu.edu/saas/2009/toomey.pdf

AGRICULTURAL JOURNALISM

Agricultural journalism, a specialized field of communications, focuses on reporting news and information about the food system from "farm to fork" or "gate to plate," as some practitioners phrase it. Agricultural journalists face unusual challenges in covering this specialized subject, which encompasses the scientific, technological, economic, political, environmental, health, and social impacts of an enterprise spanning the interests of farmers, multinational agribusinesses, and consumers.

In many ways, agricultural journalism is just good journalism—getting accurate information for a story, checking and assessing facts, putting opposing views into a balanced perspective, and writing the story clearly and concisely while maintaining independence and objectivity. However, agricultural journalists have additional specialized knowledge and related sources in fields including science, technology, markets, health risks, and public policy for the food system.

These journalists must be ready to cover plant molecular biology, the chemistry of ethanol and other biofuel production, environmental effects of agricultural pesticides, the rise of concentrated animal feeding operations and other aspects of so-called industrial agriculture, and the application to farming of such new technologies as the Global Positioning System (GPS) and computer databases. This at a time when public concerns about food safety, the cost of food, the impacts of climate change, and feeding an increasingly populated world are more prominent than ever.

Roots of Agricultural Journalism

The story of agricultural journalism is reflected in the major changes in North American agriculture over the past two centuries. Agricultural journalism has its roots in the needs of North Americans for reliable information about farming in the New World. The first U.S. periodical on agriculture, *The Agricultural Museum,* appeared in 1810. Its editor, the Reverend David Wiley, wrote that such a publication was needed because "common farmers are slow in changing" their approach to agriculture (p. 2). Wiley saw the provision of information, as well as examples of these farmers' "more enlightened neighbors," as ways to change their prejudices. He promised to provide his readers with current information on farming practices because, in his view, "the magazines, museums and other periodical works" available at the time were "of little service to the agriculturalist" (p. 2).

The Agricultural Museum lasted only 2 years, but other periodicals soon followed. For the most part, these covered a wide range of agricultural interests, including crops, livestock, and horticulture. These publications included the agricultural journals *American Farmer,* begun in 1819, and *Plough Boys* and *New England Farmer,* begun in the 1830s. John Stuart Skinner, publisher of *American Farmer* and the Baltimore, Maryland, postmaster, is considered the "father" of U.S. agricultural journalism.

Thereafter, the number of new farm magazines rose rapidly. Many succeeded, but some disappeared quickly. By 1840, 30 farm publications existed, with total circulation surpassing 100,000. Notable among the monthly magazines of the mid-1800s was the *American Agriculturalist,* which featured scientific knowledge and practical aspects of farming in its articles. New printing technology, expanded transportation networks, and free postal service to rural areas made farm publications more affordable and obtainable. Demand for this information grew as farming spread through the Midwest and into the West.

In the second half of the 19th century, daily newspapers added farm writers. Agricultural experiment stations at land grant colleges published information bulletins on a wide range of subjects of interest to farmers. Between 1880 and 1920, the number of farm magazines grew from 157 to 400, with total circulation in 1920 of 17 million. As opportunity grew for professional agricultural journalists, so too did university programs to train them. The first college course in agricultural journalism was taught in 1905 at what today is known as Iowa State University. These trends continued even as the North American population was becoming more urban and less rural.

Agricultural Journalism in the 20th Century

Throughout most of the 20th century, farmers—and agricultural journalists—needed to keep up with the increasing pace of scientific understanding and technological development in farming, including new machinery, hybrid seeds, soil fertility, agrichemicals, genetically modified organisms, computerization, and so-called precision agriculture. Agricultural journalists adopted new communication technologies. In the 1920s, radio first brought timely weather, crop, and market reports to rural areas, as well as farming advice and information about government programs. The U.S. Department of Agriculture and local stations began transmitting farm news to rural areas via television in the 1940s and 1950s. Aided by the growth of advertising, magazines kept pace, with 390 publications by 1955 and circulation at that time over 20 million. Some agribusinesses began to produce their own farm magazines and compete with independent publishing companies. Seven agricultural publications arrived in the mailbox of the average farm in 1970.

Then the hard times came. The farm crisis of the 1980s, during which large numbers of subscribers lost their farms and magazine advertising declined, forced many publications out of business. The number of farms dropped, and their size grew, yet the need for specialized information about agriculture rose. Farm publishing followed these trends. Among the best general-interest farm magazines remaining were *Farm Journal, Progressive Farmer,* and *Successful Farming.* Specialized agricultural interests were addressed by many publications, such as *Pork* and *Dairy Herd Management.*

Farm news coverage by newspapers and broadcast stations in the United States and in Canada has declined markedly since 1970, according to a survey by Canadian journalist Thomas Pawlick. This led to a trend toward what Pawlick called "the invisible farm," a disappearance of agriculture from public consciousness. The trend was fueled in part by concentration of ownership in news media companies whose cost-cutting measures eliminated many farm writers. Also, by 1990 only 2% of the U.S. population lived on farms. Pawlick argues that the nonfarm public got agriculture-related news from only the food sections of metropolitan daily newspapers, which increasingly offered consumer-oriented stories focused on the sources of food.

In the late 20th century, fewer than 20 U.S. universities had agricultural journalism programs oriented toward training journalists for the farm press and mainstream news media. In the 1990s and 2000s, many switched to agricultural communications programs more oriented toward preparing students for careers in public relations and advertising in agribusiness, agricultural extension, academia, government agencies, and special interest groups.

Like practitioners of some other journalism specialties (such as business, environmental, and science reporters), agricultural journalists have sometimes been viewed as unquestioning advocates for agriculture and its industrial, political, and technological elites, rather than as independent, open-minded observers who challenge the authority of powerful agricultural institutions. This agricultural boosterism is reflected in what some critics believe is a reluctance on the part of the farm press to pursue controversial stories and to question agricultural interests on such issues as the environment, water pollution, and food safety.

For example, in the 1980s, George DeVault, an organic farmer who was editor and publisher of *The New Farm* magazine, criticized the American Agricultural Editors Association (AAEA), one of the leading professional membership organizations for agricultural journalists, as a "tightly knit fraternity" made up to a large extent of "good old boys and girls" engaged in public relations for farm suppliers, with farm writers relegated to publishing press releases about those suppliers' products. Others have argued that as the audience declines for many farm media companies and as advertising dollars dwindle because of economic problems, farm editors have become more willing to bow to the wishes of advertisers in story selection and placement, further compromising the credibility of the media organization.

On the other hand, many agricultural journalists maintain that their integrity as independent gatekeepers of information about the food system is intact. The AAEA, like other farm media organizations, sees itself as free of agribusiness influence, and its code of ethics holds that members should avoid conflicts of interest and be honest, accurate, thorough, and fair in their work. Agricultural journalists argue that because of their interest, background, and contacts in agriculture, they are best suited to explain its scientific, technological, business, social, and public health complexities.

Although many agricultural publications have moved at least part of their information product onto the Internet, the future of agricultural journalism is likely to be rooted in the same forces that shaped its beginning: a pressing need for reliable information that is explained clearly, understandably, and accurately. Yet, just as farming has radically changed over the past two centuries, those who report and write about it are attempting to adapt to agriculture's 21st-century realities. These realities include a lack of public understanding about agriculture, an increasing rural–urban conflict, rising corporate power, loss of family farms, concern over the environmental impacts of farming, questions about food quality and safety, genetic engineering, nutrition, international markets, infectious diseases, and access to food worldwide. In short, agriculture today is recognized as just one part of an interconnected global food system.

As agricultural journalism scholars Jim Evans and Owen Roberts write, the "farm story" has evolved into a food, science, trade, or other related story increasingly aimed at consumers in urban, as well as some rural, areas. No longer does almost everyone farm. But everyone eats. Agricultural journalists, especially those who have long focused on agricultural production stories, are grappling with this transition to the diverse meaning of the global food system they must cover. They will also need to adjust to the new audiences for information about how this system works, how it is changing, and what that change means to the average person, on or off the farm.

William Allen

See also Agricultural Communicators of Tomorrow; Career Paths, Science/Environmental Journalism; Climate Change, Communicating; Environmental Journalism; Food Safety

Further Readings

Boone, K., Meisenbach, T., & Tucker, M. (2000). *Agricultural communications: Changes and challenges.* Ames: Iowa State University Press.

Evans, J., & Roberts, O. (n.d.). *Great laments in rural-urban relations—and why these issues are so difficult to cover.* Available at the International Federation of Agricultural Journalists Web site: www.ifaj.org/fileadmin/user_upload/Professional_Development/2008_urban_rural_relations2.pdf

Pawlick, T. F. (2001). *The invisible farm: The worldwide decline of farm news and agricultural journalism training.* Chicago: Burnham.

Wiley, D. (1810). Introduction. *Agricultural Museum, 1*(2), 1–3. Available at http://books.google.com

ALCOHOL, RISK COMMUNICATION FOR

Risk communication aimed at curbing excessive alcohol consumption represents a major area of communications research, largely because of the negative consequences alcohol abuse holds for both individuals and society. According to the Centers for Disease Control and Prevention, excessive alcohol use constitutes a major public health crisis. In fact, heavy drinking (drinking more than two drinks per day on average for men or more than one drink per day on average for women) and binge drinking (drinking five or more drinks during a single occasion for men or four or more drinks during a single occasion for women) represent the third greatest lifestyle-related cause of death in the United States. Moreover, excessive alcohol use is also related to a host of societal ills, including motor vehicle accidents, criminal activity, and injuries among users. Clearly, government and other societal institutions have a vested interest in minimizing the effects of excessive alcohol consumption.

The negative outcomes associated with drinking excessive amounts of alcohol have resulted in numerous attempts to prevent or moderate alcohol use through the use of mass-media-based social marketing campaigns. However it is important to note that the success of media-based campaigns depends on the credibility of some media, especially television, that have been shown both to model unhealthy behaviors and to downplay the negative effects of health-threatening behaviors, including excessive drinking. Research indicates mixed results for social marketing campaigns. This, in turn, has led to another stream of research based on interpersonal communications models, some focused on experiential learning.

The Protection Motivation Model

Landmark research on protection motivation theory (PMT) by Ronald W. Rogers provides the theoretical basis for many social marketing campaigns, including those aimed at curbing excessive alcohol use. PMT outlines the conditions under which individuals are motivated to modify behaviors to protect their own health. According to this model, people are most likely to modify unhealthy behaviors when (a) the perceived severity of the health threat is high, (b) they believe they are vulnerable to the negative outcomes of health behaviors, (c) changing behaviors is likely to be very effective at mitigating the perceived health threat, (d) the cost of changing health behaviors is low, and (e) they believe strongly that they are capable of changing their current behaviors.

Anti–alcohol abuse social marketing campaigns based on the protection motivation model generally rely on fear appeals, underscoring the negative consequences of excessive alcohol use and binge drinking. Campaigns of this kind have been run in countries around the world, including in the United Kingdom, Australia, Canada, and the United States. While these campaigns have been successful at communicating the threats associated with drinking, researchers indicate that they have been less successful at helping individuals realize that they are capable of avoiding dangerous drinking behaviors, largely because the campaigns provide little advice on avoiding situations that lead to dangerous drinking behaviors.

The communications literature indicates mixed results on the effect of fear appeals. In a recent meta-analysis of health communications

message tactics, researchers found significant differences between the health intentions of men and women who received messages focused on the personal consequences of health behaviors: Men responded most positively to unemotional messages, while women responded best to emotional messages. Similarly, vivid messages about personal consequences appear to increase health intentions for white audiences, while dramatically decreasing them for nonwhite audiences. These findings indicate that anti-alcohol communications may be more effective when targeted to specific groups.

Social Norms Campaigns

College students are at high risk for dangerous alcohol behaviors. According to some researchers, this is because college students generally believe that excessive drinking during college is normal, that their own excessive drinking is a means of increasing their social standing among their peers, and that hangovers and other negative consequences associated with dangerous drinking are a rite of passage. In a landmark nationwide study of more than 17,000 college students, H. Wesley Perkins and Henry Wechsler found perceptions of alcohol consumption norms at their colleges to be the greatest predictor of personal alcohol abuse by students: The more that students perceived alcohol to play a significant role in the culture of their particular university, the greater the likelihood that they had encountered personal problems with alcohol during the academic year.

As a means to counteract these ideas, nearly half of colleges and universities have responded with media campaigns designed to discourage heavy drinking and binge drinking based on social norms; many of these campaigns have been supported by federal funding that was meant to change the attitudes of college students about drinking. These campaigns seek to assure students that drinking on their campuses is not as prevalent as they believe. For example, the University of California, Berkley instituted the "Don't Tell Me How to Party" campaign, featuring a diverse range of actual students who shared information about their ability to be moderate and still have a good time. The assumption of these campaigns is that once students who overestimate the amount of drinking done by their fellow students understand the true norms, their drinking is likely to fall in line with those norms, thus reducing the incidence of heavy drinking and binge drinking on campuses.

According to published research, the results of the social norms campaigns have been mixed. For example, in their evaluation of one social norms campaign conducted on a large university campus, Lindsey D. Polenc, Ann Marie Major, and L. Erwin Atwood found that while more than 90% of students were familiar with their campus's campaign, which was featured prominently in advertising on campus and throughout the surrounding community, fewer than one third of students surveyed actually believed the main message of the campaign, that most students drink between zero and four drinks when they party. Their research indicated that heavy drinkers—the most important target of social norms campaigns—were least likely to be influenced by the campaigns, taking cues from their friends' actions, rather than from campuses as a whole.

Other studies support these findings. For example, research looking at a wide range of health-related social norms issues, such as exercising, cigarette smoking, and alcohol use, found that in the case of alcohol, the most significant predictor of binge drinking was personal alcohol attitude; that is, students who said they liked to drink to get drunk were more likely to engage in binge drinking, while those who believed that drinking to get drunk was harmful were less likely to engage in binge drinking. Normative judgments about the amount of alcohol consumed by the "average" student at a university were not a significant predictor of binge-drinking behavior in that study.

In the widest study of its kind, the Harvard School of Public Health College Alcohol Study (CAS), which began in 1992 and ended in 2006, indicated no significant decreases in drinking behaviors at schools that had instituted social norms campaigns, compared with those that had not instituted social norms campaigns. These results of the CAS have been widely debated, however, because CAS did not include any measures for the quality of the campaigns instituted and because administrators' self-reports of the existence of social norms campaigns were used to

determine the social norms and nonsocial norms pools used in the analysis.

Socially Situated Experiential Learning Model

The importance of personal experience and individual attitudes about drinking appears to be a significant factor in whether or not students engage in risky alcohol-related behaviors: Students, parents, and even faculty share information about mythic campus drinking episodes, thus reinforcing the idea that excessive drinking is a norm during the college years. The fact that so much of the information about expected drinking behaviors is transferred from one person to another has led some researchers to explore the inclusion of interpersonal communications into alcohol awareness campaigns. Linda C. Lederman and Linda Stewart's work on socially situated experiential learning (SSEL) models has been used to create campaigns that include both mediated messages and interpersonal interactions, using students' peers as the delivery agents.

The key to the effectiveness of SSEL in health campaigns is participation. Experiential learning means that students must take part in activities that reinforce the anti–dangerous drinking messages. For example, Duke University attempted to curb excessive drinking with a series of alcohol-free parties in 2000. However, the university was forced to abandon the strategy when it became clear that the targets of the campaign—heavy drinkers and binge drinkers—were avoiding the events.

One way to encourage student participation in health campaigns is through curriculum infusion. In this approach, students work to spread anti–dangerous drinking messages as part of their coursework. For example, the "RU Sure" campaign, which was undertaken at Rutgers University, gave students in advanced communication courses an opportunity to help the university implement its social norms campaign by taking their messages directly to first-year students through a series of interactive events held in residence halls, designing posters, and researching campaign effects. Many students reported that the experience of working on the campaign as role models for younger students had positively affected their own drinking behaviors, making them more aware of peer pressure and less likely to engage in dangerous behaviors themselves. The general student population was shown to be aware of the campaign and to understood the messages of the campaign, but it was unclear whether or not the campaign had contributed to less dangerous drinking on campus.

Special Groups

While college students have received the majority of attention in anti–dangerous drinking campaigns, other campaigns have been designed to reach specific targets seen as particularly at risk for dangerous drinking behaviors. One group that has received particular attention is underage drinkers, adolescents who use alcohol although it is illegal to do so. The U.S. Department of Health calls alcohol the "drug of choice" for adolescents because of its wide availability. Three quarters of U.S. 12th graders in one survey reported that they had tried alcohol; 29% of them said they had engaged in binge drinking within a 2-week period.

Considering the severe consequences of underage drinking—including the possibility of damage to the endocrine system, which regulates normal development of bones, organs, and muscles—the National Institute on Alcohol Abuse and Alcoholism has made curbing underage drinking a priority. The U.S. government indicates that school- and family-based intervention programs, in which communication and experiential learning are key components, are important intervention methods for reducing underage drinking. Often, these interpersonal approaches are partnered with environmental interventions (for example, raising the prices of alcohol through taxation, increased law enforcement activity, zero tolerance policies) and media campaigns to create an increased consciousness of the dangers of underage drinking for minors, as well as for members of the community who might knowingly or unknowingly give minors access to alcohol. The government's Underage Drinking Prevention campaign includes resources for parents, schools, and communities, as well as an Ad Council public service announcement campaign created by advertising agencies Deutsch Inc. and Global Hue called "Start Talking Before They Start Drinking." This media campaign consists of television and radio commercials, as well as magazine and television advertisements, and encourages parents to talk to their children about the dangers

of alcohol abuse before they are teenagers and less likely to listen.

While all dangerous drinking behaviors have the ability to impact the lives of people other than those drinking, pregnant women's drinking behaviors may have a direct effect on the fetuses they are carrying because fetuses exposed to alcohol through their mothers' drinking are at risk for developing fetal alcohol spectrum disorders (FASD), which the Substance Abuse and Mental Health Services Administration, a division of the U.S. Department of Health and Human Services, describes as "an umbrella term" that covers a broad range of possible physical, mental, behavioral, and/or learning disabilities that might result. The only way to prevent FASD is to abstain from alcohol use during pregnancy, and the U.S. Centers for Disease Control recommends that all pregnant women—and even those planning to become pregnant—completely avoid alcohol, as there is no known amount of alcohol that has been proven safe to drink during pregnancy. However, research indicates that one of the problems with the message of complete abstinence from government sources is a countervailing message pregnant women receive, both through the media and directly from their doctors, that there are "safe limits" of alcohol use during pregnancy.

One type of campaign that has been used to counteract the mixed messages that women receive about alcohol—including the positive messages about alcohol contained in alcohol advertising—is community-based narrowcasting campaigns. Narrowcasting campaigns use media channels to reach microtargets, specific at-risk populations. Researchers at the University of California, Los Angeles conducted two community-driven campaigns—comprised of print advertisements in civic establishments, in retail outlets, and in clinics—in two different disadvantaged communities of Southern California, targeting women 18 to 35 years old. They found that women who visited clinics were most likely to remember seeing the anti-FASD message, indicating that women's involvement with reproductive issues may increase their attention to messages about FASD. This is a significant finding since it indicates that the use of expensive mass media, such as radio or television, may not be necessary to reach priority populations with anti-FASD messages.

From an interpersonal perspective, dialogic research has been used to gather insight into which voices are important to women as they make decisions about drinking while pregnant. A University of Iowa–based study found that anti-drinking media messages aimed at pregnant women, or women who are thinking of becoming pregnant, should underscore both individualism (that choosing not to drink while pregnant is a positive choice) and responsible motherhood (that good mothering includes making choices that take into account the health and welfare of a fetus). The study also found that relational closeness made speaking to another person about her drinking during pregnancy more likely. This indicates that it might be possible to employ close family members to deliver interpersonal anti-FASD messages to at-risk individuals.

Conclusion

Clearly, communications is an important weapon in the fight against dangerous alcohol consumption. Mediated campaigns have proved successful in their ability to alert many populations about the potential dangers of heavy drinking and binge drinking. But while the protection motivation model indicates that understanding a threat and believing that the remedy is both affordable and executable should lead to change in negative health behaviors, research has found mixed results for the ability of fear appeals to change the dangerous drinking behaviors of at-risk populations, partly because college students see their drinking as a normal and temporary part of life. They are willing to put up with the negative consequences of excessive drinking behaviors because they believe those behaviors help them attain their social goals of fitting in and being popular. Research in this area is ongoing and is currently focused on combining media campaigns with interpersonal communications strategies to affect behavior change in addition to awareness.

In fact, a major trend in alcohol risk communication is that of multiple messaging. This trend is evident in the highly tailored campaigns that have been created for special at-risk groups, including underage drinkers and pregnant women, who are at risk for causing FASD in their fetuses through their intake of alcohol. The combination of reminders of the dangers of alcohol use in different media, and through different interpersonal channels, including school- and community-based initiatives, as well as peer counseling, seem most likely to result in not only awareness, but also behavior change, which is the desired outcome of all alcohol risk communication.

Colleen Connolly-Ahern

See also Anti-Drug Campaigns; Anti-Smoking Campaigns; Communication Campaigns in Health and Environment; Health Communication, Overview

Further Readings

Baxter, L. A., Hirokawa, R., Lowe, J. B., Nathan, P., & Pearce, L. (2004). Dialogic voices in talk about drinking and pregnancy. *Journal of Applied Communication Research, 32*(3), 224–248.

Cameron, K. A., & Campo, S. (2006). Stepping back from social norms campaigns: Comparing normative influences to other predictors of health behaviors. *Health Communication, 20*(3), 277–288.

Cismaru, M., Lavack, A. M., & Markewich, E. (2008). Alcohol consumption among young consumers: A review and recommendations. *Young Consumers, 9*(4), 282–296.

Connolly-Ahern, C., & Broadway, S. C. (2008). "To booze or not to booze?" Newspaper coverage of fetal alcohol spectrum disorders. *Science Communication, 29*(3), 362–385.

Glik, D., Prelip, M., Myerson, A., & Eilers, K. (2004). Fetal alcohol syndrome prevention using community-based narrowcasting campaigns. *Health Promotion Practice, 9*(1), 93–103.

Keller, P. A., & Lehmann, D. R. (2008). Designing effective health communications: A meta-analysis. *Journal of Public Policy & Marketing, 27*(2), 117–130.

Lederman, L. C., Stewart, L. P., & Russ, T. L. (2007). Addressing college drinking through curriculum infusion: A study of the use of experience-based learning in the communication classroom. *Communication Education, 56*(4), 476–494.

Perkins, H. W., & Wechsler, H. (1996). Variation in perceived college drinking norms and its impact on alcohol abuse: A nationwide study. *Journal of Drug Issues, 26*(4), 961–974.

Polonec, L. D., Major, A. M., & Atwood, L. E. (2006). Evaluating the believability and effectiveness of the social norms message "Most students drink 0 to 4 drinks when they party." *Health Communication, 20*(1), 23–34.

Rogers, R. W. (1975). A protection motivation theory of fear appeals and attitude change. *Journal of Psychology, 91*(1), 93–114.

Wechsler, H., & Nelson, T. F. (2008). What we have learned from the Harvard School of Public Health College Alcohol Study: Focusing attention on college student alcohol consumption and the environmental conditions that promote it. *Journal of Studies on Alcohol and Drugs, 69*(4), 481–490.

ALIEN ABDUCTION

Alien abduction is a familiar theme in popular culture. As described by those who claim to have experienced it, alien abduction (in this entry, abduction, for short) is the physical seizure, or kidnapping, of a human being by an extraterrestrial intelligent being. Since the advent of space exploration in the mid-20th century, the subject of abduction has waxed and waned in popularity as the focus of newspaper reports and magazine features, true confessions and science fiction, television documentaries and big-budget Hollywood movies, and millions of World Wide Web sites.

John E. Mack (1929–2004), the most authoritative scientist to study this subject (see "Research and Information"), called abduction a "phenomenon." Using this nomenclature, Mack established abduction as a subject suitable for scientific study, and nothing more. By the time he concluded his program of research, he had not solved the mystery of abduction. To date, no one has been able to explain this phenomenon in a way that satisfies experiencers, believers, and skeptics alike. No one has proved that alien abduction is real. And no one has proved that it is not real.

Alleged abductees (henceforth, abductees) and their advocates argue that extraterrestrial intelligent beings do exist and have, indeed, visited Earth and have taken human beings from the planet. It is widely accepted in the space science community that life may exist somewhere beyond Earth. No one, however, has found any evidence as of yet that extraterrestrial life exists. And even scientists who accept the possibility of extraterrestrial life may not necessarily accept the idea of extraterrestrial intelligent life or the possibility of travel by such beings over distances measured in light-years.

Assuming that science is the best authority to defer to on the question of the reality of abduction, it is the case that science has not obtained any evidence, or otherwise validated any claims, of extraterrestrial life, extraterrestrial intelligent life, extraterrestrial vehicles or other technologies, or terrestrial visitations by extraterrestrial intelligent beings. The possibility of the existence of any and all of these things remains an open question for scientists and others to explore.

The Narrative

Stories of alien abduction are virtually all first-person accounts (there is at least one reported claim of an eyewitness to an abduction). Some abductees report single abduction events. Others report multiple abductions over many years. Abduction stories typically involve alien spacecraft, often referred to as unidentified flying objects (UFOs) known as unidentified aerial phenomena.

Abduction accounts tend to follow a common outline, and they tend to feature occurrences that contemporary science would deem impossible (or, at best, extremely unlikely) in the known physical world. The abductee is physically seized and moved from a building (typically a home) or a vehicle or from the outdoors and transported by some sort of beam of energy or transferred from a terrestrial to an extraterrestrial environment, most typically a spaceship. The location of the spaceship does not seem to be especially relevant.

Humanoid beings assumed to be of extraterrestrial origin are said to commit these abductions. Humanoid characteristics of these beings include intelligence (that is, the capability to produce technology) and bipedalism. Most abductees describe these beings as looking like the prototypical E.T. figure seen everywhere in popular culture: hairless and bipedal, with two eyes, two arms, and two legs. Some are reported to be friendly; others are reported to be unfriendly.

Abductees often report seeing bright lights, floating as if in the absence of gravity, traveling through solid objects, and being undressed and restrained or paralyzed. A prominent feature of many abduction accounts is a physical inspection akin to a medical examination, often reported as invasive or painful. Some abductees report that the alien beings install implants in their bodies, and some report that they have scars from their encounters. Others report that the aliens impregnate them and sometimes remove the hybrid fetuses. Other aspects of abduction stories include telepathic communication, altered consciousness, spiritual awareness, and revelations about the state of the environment on Earth.

Perhaps the best-known abduction claim is the story of husband and wife Barney and Betty Hill's abduction from their car on the road from Montreal, Quebec, to Portsmouth, New Hampshire, in 1961. Their story has been recounted in a book and a made-for-TV movie and repeated in many other media treatments of abduction.

Theories

Psychologists, psychiatrists, debunkers, and journalists have offered many possible explanations for the abduction phenomenon. Theories include sleep apnea, sleep paralysis, nightmares, waking dreams, hallucinations, near-death experiences, out-of-body experiences, hysteria, spurious or false memories, repressed and recovered memories, sadomasochistic fantasies, a psychiatric syndrome, a desire to escape the self, personality pathology (for example, fantasy proneness), and shared cultural delusion. Abductees and others argue that none of these theories adequately explains the phenomenon.

The idea of repressed and recovered memory, a product of Freudian psychoanalytic theory, offers a possible explanation for the way some people might cope with trauma, such as abduction. In the 1990s, the idea of repressed and recovered memory was so hotly contested that members of the psychology community organized to establish that what Freudians called repressed and recovered memory was, rather, false memory. This group established the False Memory Syndrome Foundation with the goal of displacing the idea of repressed and recovered memory with the idea of false memory. Psychologist Elizabeth Loftus is one well-known advocate of the false-memory theory, and she (among others) frequently served as an expert source in media reports about abduction throughout the 1990s. Loftus was affiliated with the False Memory Syndrome Foundation.

Other theories offered to explain abduction include a belief in government conspiracies. The idea of abduction is often connected with the idea of a government cover-up of extraterrestrial visits to or presence on Earth, typified in the story of the so-called Roswell incident, an alleged crash of an alien spacecraft in New Mexico in 1947. Another possible explanation offered for abduction stories is the human need for mythic narratives to demystify certain aspects of reality.

Research and Information

In the 1990s, Mack, a tenured professor of psychiatry at Harvard Medical School and an established authority on emotional trauma, initiated a 10-year alien abduction research program. Called the Program for Extraordinary Experience Research (PEER), Mack's research initiative generated controversy, criticism, and publicity. Mack took claims of abduction seriously, arguing that claimants had experienced some sort of trauma and warranted attention. Mack's PEER concluded without being able to produce an explanation for the abduction phenomenon. PEER's archives are now maintained by the John E. Mack Institute. Other well-known examiners of the abduction phenomenon include artist Budd Hopkins and Temple University historian David M. Jacobs.

A controversial aspect of Mack's work with abductees was the use of hypnosis, a contested research method, in helping abductees recall their experiences. As an MD and as an academic, Mack was appropriately credentialed to study abduction. Hopkins, a self-proclaimed abduction researcher, also used hypnosis to help abductees recall their experiences.

In 1992, a scholarly conference on abduction was convened at the Massachusetts Institute of Technology, cochaired by Mack and MIT physics professor David Pritchard. Speakers included Hopkins and Jacobs. Conference proceedings were published under the title *Alien Discussions,* and author C. D. B. Bryan wrote a popular book about the conference.

Other scholars, researchers, and observers, some with sufficient credentials to establish them as experts and others operating as self-proclaimed authorities, have explored the abduction phenomenon. The Library of Congress has catalogued an extensive body of literature on abduction, including case studies, conference reports, psychological analyses, and social studies.

The bulk of literature on abduction is popular rather than scholarly, however. A substantial body of fringe media addresses the topic of abduction, including mass-published and self-published books and videos, along with magazines such as *Fate* ("published continuously since 1948," it claims), *Flying Saucer Review* ("the international journal established in 1955 . . . and read by Prince Philip since the 1950s," it claims), *Fortean Times,* and *Mysteries.* Abduction is also a popular topic at UFO and other fringe science conferences, such as UFOs and Bible Prophecy, The Culture of Contact, and annual Mutual UFO Network (MUFON) symposia. These conferences draw both believers and skeptics, among speakers and attendees.

The World Wide Web offers access to an immense volume of information on abduction, much if not most of which would be difficult to verify, from organizations ranging from Alien Abduction Crisis Centers of America and All Other Terran Territories to Malevolent Alien Abduction Research, MUFON, and *Truthseekers Review.* Many abduction sites, including alienresistance.org (the term *alien resistance* is trademarked), alien-hub.com, and aliencentral.com, do not provide information on the sources of their content.

Advocates of the conventional scientific world-view tend to argue that claims of abduction do not stand up to logic and reason. Self-proclaimed skeptics such as the Committee for Skeptical Inquiry (CSI) have examined and dismissed claims of alien abduction. CSI describes itself as an organization dedicated to "critical investigation of paranormal and fringe-science claims from a responsible, scientific point of view." (Formerly, CSI was known as the Committee for Scientific Investigation of Claims of the Paranormal.) CSI continues to publish the magazine *Skeptical Inquirer,* which periodically has taken up the subject of abduction. The J. Allen Hynek Center for UFO Studies (CUFOS) offers information on abduction, including an article published in the CUFOS journal *International UFO Reporter* titled "Abductions and Researcher Bias: How to Lose Your Way."

Conclusion

While scholarly interest in the subject is minimal, abduction has become a sort of popular culture franchise, generating the marketing and sales of a wide variety of products, some intended for practical use and others for entertainment. Consumers can buy abduction-protection handbooks; abduction insurance; alien abduction lamps; abduction games and bumper stickers; devices to stop abductions, block UFOs, and prevent extraterrestrial contact; home alien abduction kits; and Location Earth dog tags to ensure that abductees make it back home. Amazon.com even hosts an alien-abduction customer community.

Cable television and the Hollywood film industry offer a broad array of content about abduction, ranging from documentaries, series, and miniseries on the Fox, Sci-Fi (now Syfy), Discovery, and History channels to movies such as *The X-Files.*

For students, researchers, and practitioners in journalism and mass communication, there is no ultimate, authoritative source on the subject of abduction. Anyone interested in exploring the abduction phenomenon must judge independently the veracity and reliability of information collected in the course of studying the subject.

Linda Billings

See also Astrobiology; Search for Extraterrestrial Intelligence (SETI); Skepticism

Further Readings

Billings, L. (2005). *Sex! Aliens! Harvard? Rhetorical boundary-work in the media (a case study of the role of journalists in the social construction of scientific authority).* Doctoral dissertation, Indiana University. (Available from ProQuest Dissertations and Theses database)

Bryan, C. D. B. (1995). *Close encounters of the fourth kind: Alien abduction, UFOs, and the conference at M.I.T.* New York: Knopf.

CSI: The Committee for Skeptical Inquiry: www.csicop.org

Fate magazine: http://fatemag.com/wordpress/about/welcome-to-fate

Flying Saucer Review: www.fsr.org.uk

Jacobs, D. M. (Ed.). (2000). *UFOs and abduction: Challenging the borders of knowledge.* Lawrence: University of Kansas Press.

Loftus, E., & Ketcham, K. (1994). *The myth of repressed memory: False memories and allegations of sexual abuse.* New York: St. Martin's.

Mack, J. E. (1994). *Abduction: Human encounters with aliens.* New York: Scribner.

ALTERNATIVE ENERGY, OVERVIEW

Alternative energy is derived from sources that are renewable, do not use up natural resources or harm the environment, or can replace fossil fuels such as coal, natural gas, and oil. Alternative energy is generated for electricity and heating from sources such as moving water, the sun, wind, geothermal energy from the earth's heat, biomass from vegetative or waste material, and biogas from anaerobic digestion. Given the looming energy crisis facing much of the world, alternative energy is destined to become an even more important area for science communicators.

Renewable energy sources can restore themselves over short periods of time and do not diminish. Green power, a subset of renewable energy, is clean technology that provides the highest environmental benefit. Green energy sources produce electricity with less impact on the environment than conventional power technologies and produce no anthropogenic greenhouse gas emissions. Brown energy sources, the nonrenewable or polluting energy sources, generally consume water; require mining, drilling, or extraction; or emit greenhouse gases and air pollution during combustion. Categorization of nuclear energy is debatable because it emits no greenhouse gases yet requires mining, extraction, and long-term radioactive waste storage.

Concerns about skyrocketing oil prices, world energy security, and impacts of greenhouse gases have driven growth in multiple renewable energy industries. By mid-2007, investments in more than 140 publicly traded renewable energy companies exceeded $100 billion. Key business initiatives include green tags, which represent proof that 1 megawatt-hour of electricity was generated from an eligible renewable energy resource, and the Leadership in Energy and Environmental Design (LEED) green building rating system.

The commercialization of renewable energy over the last century has involved three generations of technologies. First-generation technologies, already economically competitive, include biomass, hydroelectricity, and geothermal heat and power. Second-generation technologies, market ready and currently deployed, include solar heating, photovoltaics (PVs), and new forms of bioenergy. Third-generation technologies, which require continued research and development efforts to make significant contributions, include advanced biomass gasification, biorefinery technologies, solar thermal power stations, hot dry rock geothermal power, and ocean energy.

Net energy analysis, which indicates the efficiency of an energy technology, compares the amount of energy a technology delivers to society to the total energy required to find, extract, process, deliver, and otherwise upgrade that energy to a useful form. One net energy measure, energy return on investment, is the ratio of energy delivered to energy costs. Another measure, life cycle cost analysis, compares the electricity generated to the amount of energy needed in the manufacture, transport, construction, operation, and other stages of a technology's life cycle.

Solar

Every hour, the sun delivers as much energy to the earth as all humans use in a year. The energy from 20 days of sunshine is equal to all energy available in the world's reserves of coal, oil, and natural gas. Solar energy can be harnessed from passive solar heating, rooftop solar cells that convert sunlight to electricity, and large solar plants that use the sun's heat to generate steam.

PV cells use thin polysilicon film to convert sunlight into electricity. The power produced by a solar array, a set of PV cells, will depend on weather conditions, the sun's position, and the capacity of the array. During suboptimal conditions, solar energy can be stored using molten salts, which are low-cost and can efficiently deliver heat. Thin film nanotechnology panels, which cost half as much as traditional PV cells, are expected to be widely available by 2010. The average price for a PV module was $100 per watt in 1975; it is expected to drop to $2 per watt by 2010.

PV production has increased nearly 50% each year since 2002. Although solar power is the world's fastest growing energy technology, it produced less than 0.05% of U.S. electricity and only 0.66% of the world's electricity in 2007. The top five PV-producing countries are Japan, China, Germany, Taiwan, and the United States. Although Germany is the top market for installed solar energy, the amount of useable solar resources in the United States far exceeds what Germany has because Germany's skies are cloudy two thirds of the time.

Solar vehicles are prototype electric vehicles powered by solar energy obtained from solar panels on the surface of the vehicle. Most solar cars have been built for races. However, small PV panels are available on the market that can be installed on a car roof to generate about 50 miles a day of renewable electricity. Battery electric vehicles could be fitted with solar cells to extend their range and allow recharging while parked in the sun.

Other experimental uses of solar power include solar towers, solar ponds, thermogenerators, solar chemical processes, photoelectrochemical cells, and solar tracking devices. A solar tower is a large greenhouse in which air is heated by sunlight, and a turbine converts the expanding air into electricity. A solar pond is a saltwater pool that collects and stores solar energy. Solar thermogenerators, which convert a temperature difference between dissimilar materials into an electric current, have been used to power deep space missions.

Thermochemical and photochemical solar processes use solar energy to drive chemical changes to produce a storable and transportable fuel. For example, hydrogen fuel can be produced using heating solar concentrators to drive steam reformation of natural gas and by using concentrated sunlight to decompose zinc oxide, which then reacts with water to produce hydrogen. A photoelectrochemical cell, consisting of a semiconductor immersed in an electrolyte, uses sunlight to drive chemical reactions such as electrolysis.

Tracking PV systems use imbalances caused by the movement of a low-boiling-point fluid to respond to the sun's movement. Tracking PV systems produce 25% more electricity than fixed-tilt PV systems. One such device is the light mill, a glass bulb containing a set of vanes mounted on a spindle. Each vane has a dark side and a white side. The dark side becomes warm when absorbing light, while the white side reflects light and stays cool. The motion of gases from the hot to the cool side of each vane causes the vanes to rotate.

Passive solar methods convert sunlight into low-grade energy without the use of PVs, other active mechanical systems, or other energy sources. These technologies convert sunlight into usable heat, promote air movement for ventilation, or store heat. Passive solar technologies include direct and indirect solar gain for space heating, water heating, thermal mass, and phase-change materials for controlling indoor air temperatures, cookers, furnaces, chimneys for enhancing natural ventilation, earth sheltering, and solariums. Shading systems that respond to the movement of the sun are used in buildings to maximize natural lighting during winter and to reduce glare and cooling loads.

Wind

Wind power is the production of wind energy using wind turbines. Most wind power generates electricity, although windmills are also used to grind grain or pump water. Individual turbines can provide electricity to isolated areas, while large-scale wind farms connect to electrical grids. Although wind power has relatively low production costs, windiness varies. Much of the energy comes in short bursts when wind speeds are higher. Wind energy has less consistent output than fuel-fired power plants, and utilities using wind power require backup generation. Danger to fish, bats, and birds is a common complaint against wind turbine installation, but the number killed by turbines is negligible compared to the numbers that die because of other human activities. By 2008, worldwide wind power produced 1% of global electricity consumption and increased fivefold between 2000 and 2007. Wind energy could possibly supply 20% of all U.S. energy consumption.

Geothermal

Geothermal power is energy generated by heat stored beneath the earth's surface or from absorbed heat in the atmosphere and oceans. It is used commercially in more than 70 countries. The most easily accessible sources of geothermal power are natural hot springs near the earth's surface. These areas are located mainly in the United States, Central America, Indonesia, East Africa, and the Philippines. In most locations, hot dry rock geothermal, a newer technology, utilizes the high temperatures found in rocks several miles below ground.

High-pressure water, pumped down a borehole, travels through fractures in the hot rock and is forced out of a second borehole. The superheated water is converted into electricity using a steam turbine or power plant system. The cooled water is then injected back into the ground to heat up again. Geothermal power plants are unaffected by weather conditions and operate continuously, but they have been known to trigger minor earthquakes. In 2007, geothermal power supplied less than 1% of the world's energy. However, the potentially extractable geothermal resources of the entire earth, using systems such as hot dry rock mining, could provide all of the world's energy needs for several millennia. The amount of heat within 33,000 feet of the earth's surface contains 50,000 times more energy than all the oil and natural gas resources in the world.

Another geothermal technology is the geothermal heat pump, a heating and air conditioning system a few feet below the surface that captures available heat in the winter and puts heat back into the ground during the summer. Also known as geoexchange systems or ground-source heat pumps, they can be used in nearly any region. Although the cost of installing a residential geothermal heat pump can be twice that of a conventional heating system, it can reduce the heating and cooling costs by 35% to 70%.

Biofuels

Biofuels are produced from biomass, the organic material that stores sunlight in the form of chemical energy. Producing biofuels provides a disposal mechanism for municipal, agricultural, and industrial organic wastes. Biofuels are produced from manure, other biodegradable wastes, and living or recently dead biological material. Common plant materials include corn, soybeans, wood waste, switch grass, crop residues, straw, hemp, willow, sugarcane, and palm. Although biofuels emit as much carbon dioxide into the atmosphere as fossil fuels, they are considered carbon neutral because biomass absorbs carbon dioxide from the atmosphere while it is growing. Although the biomass energy industry in the United States only produces about 0.5% of the U.S. electricity supply, this level of power generation annually avoids 11 million tons of carbon dioxide (CO_2) emissions from fossil fuel combustion.

Biomass processing methods include anaerobic digestion of decaying biomass to produce methane, fermentation and distillation to produce ethyl alcohol, heating organic wastes in the absence of air to produce combustible gas, hydrogasification of biomass to produce methane and ethane, hydrogenation conversion of biomass to produce oil using carbon monoxide and steam under high pressures and temperatures, destructive distillation of high-cellulose organic wastes to produce methyl alcohol, and acid hydrolysis of wood wastes to produce and distill sugars.

An energy crop is a low-cost, low-maintenance harvest used to make biofuels. Ethanol fuel is relatively easy to process from common food crops such as sugarcane and corn. Flexible-fuel cars, trucks, and minivans are designed to run on fuel blends containing up to 85% ethanol. Consumers who drive flexible fuel vehicles can choose fuels based on price and availability. Algae can produce 30 times more energy per acre than terrestrial crops. If algae fuel replaced all the petroleum fuel in the United States, it would require 15,000 square miles, less than one seventh the area of corn harvested in the United States in 2000.

Cellulosic ethanol, produced from wood, grasses, or the nonedible parts of plants, is chemically identical to ethanol from other sources. A preferred alternative to corn ethanol, cellulosic ethanol is produced from raw materials that are abundant and diverse. It reduces greenhouse gas emissions by 85% compared with reformulated gasoline, while corn ethanol often does not reduce CO_2 emissions at all if it uses natural gas to provide energy for the process. Cellulosic ethanol requires more processing to make the sugars available to the microorganisms used in fermentation.

Biodiesel, produced by mixing oils with sodium hydroxide and methanol or ethanol, can be produced from oils derived from rapeseed and soybeans, mustard, flax, sunflower, and hemp, as well as waste vegetable oil, animal fats, and algae grown in sewage. It can be used in any diesel engine when mixed with mineral diesel. The U.S. market for biodiesel more than tripled from 2004 to 2005 and then quadrupled by the end of 2006 to more than 1 billion gallons.

Electric Vehicles

Hybrid electric vehicles, which became widely available in the late 1990s, combine a conventional propulsion system with an onboard rechargeable energy storage system to achieve better fuel efficiency. They typically use a small, multispeed internal combustion engine with electric motors and prolong the battery charge through regenerative braking. Many shut down at idle and restart when needed. Hybrid electric vehicle types include electric–internal combustion, pneumatic, fuel cell, hydraulic, and human/environmental power hybrids. Pneumatic hybrids use an onboard air compressor to drive the pistons, which can be quickly refilled at service stations equipped with heat exchangers or in several hours at home by plugging the car into an electric outlet. Examples of human/ environmental powered hybrids are motorized bicycles, solar electric cars, and tribrid vehicles powered by onboard PVs, grid-charged batteries, and pedals.

A fuel cell uses hydrogen fuels with oxygen from air to produce electricity and heat, without producing CO_2. Fuel reacts with an oxidant in the presence of an electrolyte. A fuel cell works by catalysis, separating electrons and protons of the fuel and forcing the electrons to travel though a circuit to convert them to electricity. Fuel cells are compact and lightweight, have no major moving parts, and are extremely reliable. They can operate continuously, as long as necessary flows are maintained. A hydrogen fuel cell uses hydrogen as fuel and oxygen as an oxidant. Electrochemical extraction of energy from hydrogen is inefficient because it requires adding large amounts of energy to water or hydrocarbon fuels. Hydrogen is only as clean as the energy source used to produce it. Although hydrogen fuel cells emit only water and heat as waste, pollution is generated during the production of the hydrogen because production typically requires the combustion of petroleum or natural gas. Fuel cell vehicles could account for a third of the market share by 2050 if hydrogen and fuel cell costs could be greatly reduced and effective incentives implemented.

A plug-in hybrid electric vehicle, also known as a grid-connected hybrid or gas-optional hybrid, has an internal combustion engine and batteries that can be recharged by plugging into a home outlet or other electric power source. Kits and services can convert existing hybrid electric vehicles into plug-ins. Most are passenger cars, but there are also plug-in passenger vans, utility trucks, buses, motorcycles, and military vehicles. The cost for electricity to power plug-in hybrids for all-electric operation is less than a fourth of the cost of gasoline. Plug-in hybrids use no fossil fuel if their batteries are charged from renewable energy sources. The flow of electricity can be reversed to allow them to provide emergency backup power in the home and to provide power that can be sold back to the grid.

All-electric vehicles are powered by chemical energy stored in rechargeable battery packs, electric motors, and motor controllers instead of internal combustion engines. Batteries can be charged from the electric grid, but the vehicle generates no pollution if its batteries are charged from renewable energy sources.

Water Power

Many hydroelectric plants have operated more than a century. Hydropower is clean, inexpensive, and can be used at long distances from the water source. However, large-scale systems release significant CO_2 during the construction and flooding of the reservoir and can disrupt ecosystems. Forms of water energy include hydroelectric dams; river watermills; waterwheels that power machinery; damless hydro plans in rivers, streams, and oceans; vortex power derived from artificial vortices; and power extracted from ocean waves and tides.

The ocean energy industry, still in its infancy, harnesses the energy of waves using buoys, underwater turbines, and other devices to generate electricity and desalinate and pump water. Waves are constant, predictable, and have high energy density. Another form of ocean energy is blue energy, retrieved from the difference in salt concentration between seawater and river water. Ocean energy can reach 100,000 watts per square meter, compared to 1,000 watts per square meter for solar energy. Future wave energy facilities could cover large areas, raising concerns about the health of fisheries and the ecosystem.

Adoption Factors

Lack of government support, information dissemination, community participation, and consumer awareness prevent the adoption of alternative energy. The perceived aesthetics of some energy systems can adversely affect the market value of real estate. Higher costs of renewable energy technologies compared with conventional technologies, inadequate workforce training for production, market control of the national grids by centralized power plants, and difficulty introducing commercially viable innovations and numerous small energy sources into the grids also prevent adoption of renewables.

Government policy typically favors existing conventional energy over renewables and near term over long term. Fossil fuel subsidies, lack of net-metering policy and utility interconnection, inadequate financing options for renewable energy projects, prohibitive permitting codes, and lack of incentives for consumer adoption of renewables all hinder development of renewable energy. Lowering income taxes, raising taxes on environmentally destructive activities, and creating subsidies for energy innovations could create a more responsive market for renewables.

Kristen Alley Swain

See also Biofuels; Environmental Defense Fund; Fuel Cell Technology; Solar Energy; Wind Power

Further Readings

Brown, L. R. (2006). *Plan B 2.0: Rescuing a planet under stress and a civilization in trouble*. New York: W. W. Norton. Available at www.earth-policy.org/Books/PB2/Contents.htm

International Energy Agency. (2008). *Worldwide trends in energy use and efficiency*. Paris: Organisation for Economic Co-operation and Development. Available at www.iea.org/Textbase/Papers/2008/indicators_2008.pdf

Krupp, F., & Horn, M. (2008). *Earth: The sequel: The race to reinvent energy and stop global warming*. New York: W. W. Norton.

Renewable Energy Policy Network for the 21st Century. (2009, May). *Renewables 2007 global status report*. Paris: Author. Available at www.ren21.net/globalstatusreport

United Nations Environment Programme. (2006, January). *Changing climates: The role of renewable energy in a carbon-constrained world*. Paper prepared for Renewable Energy Policy Network for the 21st Century. Available at www.risoe.dk/rispubl/art/2006_120_report.pdf

Worldwatch Institute. (2006). *American energy: The renewable path to energy security*. Washington, DC: Author. Available at www.worldwatch.org/files/pdf/AmericanEnergy.pdf

ALTERNATIVE MEDICINE

Understanding the history, issues, and trends related to alternative medicine has increasing importance for science communicators, as a growing number of adults and children in the United States are regular users of alternative medicine and seek information about these therapies. In this entry, alternative medicine is discussed, particularly its history and present use in the United States. Key differences between conventional medicine and alternative medicine are summarized, areas of ongoing controversy are described, and gaps in communication research are identified. Although alternative medicine has global use and implications, this entry will largely focus on alternative medicine in the United States.

A Brief History

Strictly speaking, alternative medicine refers to treatments that are used instead of conventional medicine. *Complementary and alternative medicine* and *traditional, complementary, and alternative medicine* are terms that are frequently used when discussing alternative medicine. Complementary medicine refers to therapies that are used in conjunction with mainstream treatment, while traditional medicine refers to medical practices that predate Western medicine and are still used in traditional societies in many parts of the world. *Integrative medicine* and *holistic medicine* are also terms used to refer to alternative medicine. Both terms imply a fusion of alternative and mainstream approaches that address a patient's total wellness.

Conventional medicine is also referred to as allopathic medicine, mainstream medicine, Western medicine, biomedical approaches to medicine, and science-based medicine. Globally, alternative medicine refers to medical practices that fall outside the domain of mainstream Western medical practices as are used in industrialized nations such as in the

United States, Canada, the United Kingdom, Australia, and Europe. Many of these practices have their origins in developing nations, such as in China or India, or among the indigenous peoples of industrialized nations, and are thus considered traditional medicine rather than alternative medicine. Acknowledging the importance of all of the above differentiations, the term *alternative medicine* will be used throughout this entry (for consistency) to refer to alternative, complementary, integrative, and traditional medicine as the combined medical counterpart to conventional Western medicine.

Alternative medicine as it is largely practiced in the United States today originated in the combative struggles between various natural therapies and schools of thought and conventional medicine taking place from the early 1800s to the early 1900s. These early therapies had emerged as a reaction against ineffective and painful medical practices of the early 1800s. Various alternative medicine approaches, such as homeopathy, water therapy, and hypnotism, gained popularity in the late 1880s and early 1900s, reflecting the political trends of the times, including democratization of medical knowledge and identification with the Romantic period in art and literature, in which nature was highly valued. Despite the popularity of alternative therapies, practitioners and the various schools of thought were not well organized, and by the early 1900s, had largely fallen out of favor, losing public attention to the scientific discoveries of that period.

Alternative medicine reemerged in the late 1960s and 1970s as interest in alternatives to conventional medicine arose as part of the larger counterculture distrust of authority and disillusionment with the mainstream that infused the United States during the Vietnam War era, as well as the growing costs of conventional health care that would characterize the 1980s. Although alternative medicine grew in popularity throughout the 1980s, alternative medicine went largely unacknowledged by the conventional medical establishment until the early 1990s when, after two centuries, the field came into its own with federal and scholarly recognition.

In 1991, the U.S. Congress passed legislation that allocated $2 million to establish the Office of Alternative Medicine within the National Institutes of Health. In 1993, results of the first wide-scale survey on alternative medicine use in the United States were published, which showed that 34% of U.S. adults used alternative medicine, a much higher figure than was previously assumed. In 1996, the state of Washington passed the first legislation in the United States that required every health insurance plan in the state to cover services provided by licensed alternative medicine practitioners. The expansion of the Office of Alternative Medicine to the National Center for Complementary and Alternative Medicine in 1998, and the increase in budget to $50 million, reflected a broader societal trend of placing higher value on alternative medicine and of viewing alternative therapies as complementing mainstream medicine rather than replacing it. This trend has continued with the growing use of the term *integrative medicine* to refer to alternative medicine. For example, in 1996, Andrew Weil, a medical doctor, established the program in Integrative Medicine in the Department of Medicine at the University of Arizona, creating the first integrative medicine residency program in the nation. Other universities, including Columbia University, followed suit. It appears likely that the model of integrated medicine will continue into the 21st century.

Differences Between Alternative Medicine and Mainstream Medicine

Some of the key differences between alternative and mainstream medicine include the training of practitioners, the empirical basis, and the choice of medical model. Mainstream medicine is practiced by medical doctors and nurses who have been trained in medical schools or colleges and who have received either a doctorate in medicine (MD), a degree in nursing such as a registered nurse (RN), or another degree such as a PhD in psychiatry. Alternative medicine practitioners do not require specific licensing, and until the early 21st century, there were few schools that provided accredited training for practitioners. Mainstream medicine is based on an empirical tradition of Western scientific principles. Alternative medicine is based on many different traditions, including esoteric and spiritual traditions such as Hinduism and the yin and yang philosophy of Chinese medicine. These approaches are not considered to be scientific in the Western tradition because they have not been empirically tested and proven.

Mainstream medicine has traditionally relied on a biomedical model of patient care that emphasizes physical treatment of the patient, an authoritarian communication style, and lack of preventive care. In contrast, alternative medicine practitioners employ a biopsychosocial model of patient care that emphasizes consideration of all aspects of a patient's life in addressing his or her health, a patient-centered communication approach, and preventive care. Since the latter part of the 20th century, many mainstream medical practitioners have adopted a biopsychosocial approach to health care as consumer preference for this approach has grown, displacing the earlier patriarchal model of health care.

From the outset, the relationship between alternative medicine practitioners and traditionally trained medical doctors has been contentious. However, as a growing body of scientific research supports the effectiveness of popular alternative therapies for specific health conditions (for example, acupuncture has been shown to be successful in treating pain associated with migraines and cancer), more medical doctors and health care professionals are referring their patients to selected alternative therapies. An analysis of survey data between 1982 and 1995 suggested that many medical doctors in the United States refer their patients to popular alternative therapies including acupuncture, chiropractic treatment, and massage. The findings suggested that medical doctors are less likely, however, to refer their patients to alternative therapies for which there is not scientifically based evidence of effectiveness or that take the place of conventional medicine, such as homeopathy or herbal medicine.

Among health care professionals, there is some evidence to suggest that medical doctors in the United States and in Canada have more negative attitudes toward alternative medicine than do other health care professionals, such as nurses or pharmacists. Overall, however, conventional medicine health care professionals report that they want more information and education about alternative medicine. Studies on the perceptions of alternative medicine practitioners suggest that they appear to view their field as supporting conventional medicine, not replacing it. Although the relationship between the two sides has improved dramatically from the animosity that characterized

much of the previous two centuries, there is still a need for interaction and collaboration between conventional medicine and alternative medicine providers, particularly in ensuring that patients who are being treated by both types of caregivers receive safe and effective treatment.

Type and Frequency of Usage Among U.S. Population

The most popular forms of alternative medicine in the United States are acupuncture, traditional Chinese medicine, naturopathy, nutritional supplements, chiropractic treatment, massage, meditation, and yoga. The National Center for Complementary and Alternative Medicine groups alternative medicine into the following broad five categories: whole medical systems (such as naturopathy), mind–body medicine (such as meditation), biologically based practices (such as the use of herbs and supplements), manipulative and body-based practices (such as chiropractic treatment), and energy medicine (such as therapeutic touch).

A 2007 National Health Interview Survey found that approximately 38% of adults in the United States used one or more alternative therapies, compared to 36% in 2002. The survey found that reported usage was highest among women, those with higher levels of education, and those with higher incomes. All age groups reported using alternative therapies, with the highest reported use in the 40 to 69 combined age ranges. Significant usage was indicated in American Indian/Alaska Native, white, Asian, African American, and Hispanic populations, with the highest use in American Indian/Alaska Native and white populations in which 50.3% and 43.1%, respectively, of these populations reported using alternative therapies.

The 10 most frequently used alternative therapies in the United States, in order of use, are nonvitamin, nonmineral natural products (such as herbal supplements), deep breathing, meditation, chiropractic and osteopathic treatment, massage, yoga, diet-based therapies, progressive relaxation, guided imagery, and homeopathic treatment. The three most common supplements used are fish oil/omega-3, glucosamine, and echinacea. Americans use alternative therapies most commonly to treat back, neck, and joint pain. The 2007 survey included the first survey of children's use of alternative medicine in the United States and found that approximately 12% of children under the age of 18 in the United States use alternative medicine, most commonly vitamins and supplements for back and neck pain and head or chest colds. White children are most likely to use alternative medicine, as well as children with multiple health conditions, children whose parents have higher education, children whose parents use alternative medicine, and children whose parents are unable to afford conventional care.

While most Americans use alternative medicine in conjunction with conventional medicine, the majority do not talk to their conventional practitioner about their use. In widely cited survey findings from 1990 and 1997, David M. Eisenberg and his colleagues found that less than 40% of patients who use alternative medicine in the United States disclose their use to their conventional medicine physicians. Reasons for not doing so include that people fear receiving a negative response from their physicians or that their physicians did not ask them. This trend, unchanged in a decade of research, poses risk for potential adverse interactions between prescription medication and herbs and supplements. Overall, visits to alternative medicine practitioners increased by 47.3% from 1990 to 1997. The increase was related to more people using alternative therapies rather than the same number of people making more visits.

Considering that annual out-of-pocket expenses for alternative treatments in the United States are estimated to exceed $27 billion, a figure comparable with expenditures on all other conventional treatments combined, identifying what motivates people to use alternative medicine poses interesting research questions. Historical studies of alternative medicine suggest that as early as the 1800s, patients were drawn to alternative medicine because they enjoyed the personalized and lengthy attention given by the alternative medicine practitioners and because they were dissatisfied with the level of care for their specific condition provided by conventional medicine. These reasons appear to hold true in current times.

Social scientists have suggested that people use alternative medicine either because they are dissatisfied with mainstream medicine, they want more control over their health treatment, or they find alternative medicine more in line with their personal beliefs about health. One study found that those who reported using alternative therapies were more likely to identify with environmentalism, feminism, spirituality, and self-growth psychology. Research in the United Kingdom has suggested that U.K. residents are motivated to use alternative medicine because of the positive patient–provider relationship, relaxation, empowerment, and self-awareness. Many ethnic communities in the United States and other nations prefer traditional medicine to conventional medicine. Reasons include an emphasis on family, community, and spirituality that is often absent in Western medicine. The heightened use of alternative medicine in the last two decades indicates a changing public view of health and health care that emphasizes a holistic, patient-centered approach.

Controversies

Ongoing controversies related to alternative medicine include charges that alternative therapies (particularly herbs and supplements) are untested and unsafe, that alternative medicine may be harmless but that alternative therapies are not beneficial to health and that consumers are being duped, and disagreement over whether the government should regulate alternative medicine.

When Eisenberg and his associates found in 1990 that less than 40% of alternative medicine users discussed their usage with their conventional doctors, he urged doctors to be more proactive in discussing alternative medicine with their patients, particularly since herbal supplement use may pose a safety risk for potential adverse interactions with prescription medications. However, survey data from 1997 indicated that people still were not disclosing their alternative medicine use to their doctors. Given that herbal supplements are the most commonly used alternative medicine in the United States and that at least 17 dietary supplements have been found to adversely affect kidney function, many critics charge that unregulated alternative medicine products present a health and safety risk to consumers. In 1999, the U.S. Food and Drug Administration banned the sale of colloidal silver as medicine after some users experienced permanent skin and organ discoloration; however, colloidal silver is still sold as a nutritional supplement in health food stores around the nation.

Other critics charge that alternative medicine is simply medical quackery that has become big business. Between 1990 and 1997, there was a 45.2% increase in estimated expenditures for alternative medicine in the United States, and nutritional supplements alone are a $23 billion industry. Stephen Barrett, a former psychiatrist and founder of the Web site Quackwatch, credits the placebo effect for the seeming effectiveness of alternative medicine and calls for controlled clinical trials to scientifically determine which alternative therapies are effective.

There is considerable disagreement over whether the government should regulate alternative medicine. In 1994, Congress passed the Dietary Supplement Health Education Act, which prohibits the Food and Drug Administration from regulating herbs and dietary supplements unless they contain a known hazard to human health. Some critics argue that federal regulation of herbs and dietary supplements is needed to ensure product quality and consumer safety. Some critics of alternative medicine suggest that regulation will imply legitimacy of questionable medical treatments. Some proponents of alternative medicine oppose federal regulation, suggesting that regulation may make products more expensive and less easily available and will interfere with consumer freedom to make health care choices.

Current Issues in Communication About Alternative Medicine

Scholarly studies of media representations of, news coverage of, and communication about alternative medicine are virtually absent. Health communication scholars have called for analyses of media representations of alternative medicine, provider-to-consumer information, and identification of provider and user understandings of health and health care. Very little research has been conducted on alternative medicine in the area of science communication. This could be a result of the long-held bias in scientific thought against alternative medicine as pseudoscience or a result of researchers' fears that their work would be misused in support of questionable therapies.

A number of communication-related issues affect the field of alternative medicine. These include lack of communication between alternative medicine practitioners and conventional practitioners and lack of communication to the patient on the health and safety of alternative medicine. There is little research on why or how patients decide to use alternative medicine, how they access information about alternative medicine, their adherence to treatment, and public perception of information about alternative medicine. Very little research concerns the interaction between alternative and conventional medicine practitioners. More collaboration between the two fields is needed to improve research, education, and practice.

The widespread access to the Internet in the early 1990s and subsequent availability of health information online helped create patients who are more active in their own treatment than in previous generations. Research indicates that the majority of online health-related information is authored by laypeople rather than by medical professionals and that approximately a third of such information recommends alternative approaches that have not been scientifically verified and may be harmful. Other research suggests that the amount of online information about alternative medicine overwhelms the user with the resultant effect of reinforcing the user's acceptance of mainstream medical advice.

Recent research on public attitudes about science and medicine indicates that people gather information from a variety of sources including the Internet, the mass media, and friends and family members. Public understanding of health and health care is influenced by a variety of factors including an individual's cultural and religious beliefs. Theories that the mass media have strong effects on the public have largely been discarded for theories that people seek information to accommodate beliefs they already hold. More research is needed on how people from diverse backgrounds understand health and health care and how health organizations can effectively meet their needs.

Conclusion

Alternative medicine continues to grow in popularity and use. As health organizations discover ways to incorporate alternative approaches into conventional medicine to better serve diverse populations, alternative medicine will likely become integrative medicine. Rather than dismissing alternative medicine wholesale, medical doctors will need to become knowledgeable about alternative therapies to learn how to communicate effectively with their patients, many of whom are using alternative therapies. Research is needed on the various ways in which people understand and make sense of their health and health care for health care professionals to communicate effectively with different populations, particularly in cross-cultural settings.

Alternative medicine has global health care and economic implications, including export opportunities for developing nations that grow the herbs that are used in traditional medical formulas, providing health care for poor and rural communities that do not have Western medical treatment facilities or practitioners, and reducing medical expenses by providing preventative and self-treatment for minor health conditions.

Additional scientific research on the effectiveness and safety of alternative therapies is needed. Disagreements over the need for U.S. federal regulation of medicinal herbs and supplements and for additional accreditation and licensure opportunities of alternative medicine practitioners will likely continue. Reliable information for the public in the form of news coverage and online information is needed. Health care professionals are increasingly called upon to educate themselves and their patients about alternative medicine, especially herbs and dietary supplements.

Deborah R. Bassett

See also Health Communication, Overview; Health Communication and the Internet; Physician–Patient Communication; Pseudoscience; Science Communication and Indigenous North America

Further Readings

Astin, J. (1998). Why patients use alternative medicine: Results of a national study. *Journal of the American Medical Association, 270*(19), 1548–1553.

Barnes, P., Bloom, B., & Nahin, R. (2008). Complementary and alternative medicine use among adults and children: United States, 2007. *National Health Statistics Reports, 12*, 1–24.

Bodeker, G., & Burford, G. (2007). *Traditional, complementary and alternative medicine: Policy and public health perspectives.* London: Imperial College Press.

Commission for Scientific Medicine and Mental Health: www.csmmh.org

Committee on the Use of Complementary and Alternative Medicine by the American Public & Board on Health Promotion and Disease Prevention. (2005). *Complementary and alternative medicine in the United States.* Washington, DC: National Academies Press.

Du Pré, A. (2000). *Communicating about health: Current issues and perspectives.* Mountain View, CA: Mayfield.

Eisenberg, D. M., Davis, R. B., Ettner, S. L., Appel, S., Wilkey, S., Van Rompay, M., et al. (1998). Trends in alternative medicine use in the United States, 1990–1997. *Journal of the American Medical Association, 280*, 1569–1575.

National Institutes of Health National Center for Complementary and Alternative Medicine: http://nccam.nih.gov

Quackwatch, Inc.: www.quackwatch.org

Weil Lifestyle, LLC: www.drweil.com

Whorton, J. C. (2002). *Nature cures: The history of alternative medicine in America.* New York: Oxford University Press.

AMERICAN ASSOCIATION FOR PUBLIC OPINION RESEARCH

Public sentiment about various issues—whether they be social, political, or scientific—stands at the heart of any democratic system. Citizens express their opinions and convey their interests to decision makers, who ideally should consider such views when implementing policy. The news media, charged with informing citizens about the world around them, highlight events, issues, and concerns and often report public opinion about these concerns. For science-related issues as for many others, opinion polls are a news staple.

In their daily interactions, some citizens seek information and advice from others, while others attempt to persuade their friends and family to adopt particular views or vote for a specific candidate. Indeed, assessing public opinion on a particular issue and identifying the forces that shape such sentiment are critical in understanding society. Despite theoretical and methodological differences in studies of public opinion, individuals interested in this field often turn to the American Association for Public Opinion Research (AAPOR).

Founded in 1947, AAPOR is a nonprofit professional association of individuals interested in the study and measurement of public opinion. Its membership is roughly evenly distributed across academia (in disciplines that include communication, health sciences, political science, psychology, and political science); the commercial sector (for example, market research companies, polling organizations, the news media); and government and nonprofit organizations.

Alongside its sister organization, the World Association for Public Opinion Research, and through its activities and those of its seven regional chapters, AAPOR is dedicated to several key missions, including the advancement of theory and methodology related to public opinion research and the upholding of professional standards.

Advancement of Public Opinion Theory and Methods

AAPOR's efforts toward the advancement of public opinion research manifest themselves in various forms. Its official journal, *Public Opinion Quarterly,* reaches an interdisciplinary audience with theoretical and methodological studies of public opinion, analyses of public opinion trends, and book reviews of relevant monographs.

AAPOR also promotes public opinion research through its annual conference. At its conference, researchers from around the globe present the latest research on a variety of topics, including elections and voting (such as the influence of race, gender, and partisanship on vote choice, or the accuracy of exit polling); methodological issues (involving measurement issues, sampling, questionnaire design, interviewer effects, Web surveys, and the problem of nonresponse); and public opinion on specific political and social issues such as health care, the environment, gay marriage, stem cell research, or immigration. Sessions at the AAPOR conference also deal with the latest technologies used to collect public opinion data and the impact of technological shifts (such as the increasing number of cell-phone-only telephone users) on the validity of the data collected.

Professional Standards

AAPOR is committed to maintaining high standards of scientific competence and integrity in all phases of research ranging from data collection to the reporting of such data. The organization has been responsible for creating a number of standard definitions related to public opinion research. For example, response rates, or the proportion of eligible sample units (generally, individual respondents) cooperating in a survey, have declined significantly in recent years. This decline is noteworthy because it has led consumers of public opinion data to question the quality of the survey conducted. According to such a perspective, how much faith can one have in survey data collected when over half the individuals contacted to participate in the survey refused to do so?

Despite the general prevalence of this assumption, this line of thinking has begun to lose currency among survey experts as research illustrates few differences between studies with higher response rates and those with lower rates. To address misunderstandings and inconsistencies involving the calculation of response rates and related statistics, AAPOR has published a document outlining the computation of such figures across various modes of survey administration (such as face-to-face, telephone, mail, Internet). The organization also has made available an online response rate calculator for these computations.

AAPOR's standards extend to the reporting of data. According to its standards for minimal disclosure, public opinion researchers are expected to report particular details regarding how the research was conducted. These pieces of information include, among other things, the sponsorship of the survey, who collected the data, when the data were collected, the sample size, exact question wording, and mode of data collection. The disclosure of such information allows others to better evaluate poll findings.

Educating and Interacting With the Broader Public

Issues that concern AAPOR have an impact not only on researchers interested in public opinion, but also on the broader public. For instance, AAPOR's concern with professional standards includes a concern with how public opinion data are reported by journalists, particularly significant given how many news stories include survey data. Partnering with the journalism-oriented Poynter

Institute, AAPOR has created an online journalism polling course that trains interested parties to critically and accurately report public opinion data. For the broader audience interested in how to critically consume public opinion data, AAPOR highlights on its Web site a number of questions that should be asked when evaluating a given study.

Given the increasing frequency with which polls (including Internet surveys, election polls, exit polls, and so on) are conducted, as well as great variance in poll results and their interpretation, AAPOR regularly spearheads initiatives to assess the accuracy of election and exit polls. Ad hoc committees have undertaken studies of how poll results on the same issue can end up differing vastly and how interviewer demographics can affect exit poll results. In addition, because polls are so commonplace, concern has increased over whether the public is able to differentiate between valid scientific polls and illegitimate polls. AAPOR has made efforts to educate lay audiences about some of the latter, a category that includes "push polls" or surveys that appear to be political polls, but really are telephone calls designed to persuade voters to cast their ballot in a particular manner. AAPOR also has contacted the media in cases where findings of poorly or unscientifically conducted polls have been reported as legitimate.

Given the widespread use of polls, and given the critical role public opinion plays in democratic systems, AAPOR's efforts to improve the conduct and understanding of public opinion research can help shed much needed light on issues central to society.

Patricia Moy

See also Deliberative Polling; Science Indicators, History of the NSB Project on; Surveys

Further Readings

American Association for Public Opinion Research: www.aapor.org

Gawiser, S. R., & Witt, G. E. (n.d.). *20 questions a journalist should ask about poll results* (3rd ed.). Retrieved July 12, 2009, from http://ncpp.org/?q=node/4

Keeter, S., Miller, S., Kohut, A., Groves, R. M., & Presser, S. (2000). Consequences of reducing nonresponse in a national telephone survey. *Public Opinion Quarterly, 64*(2), 125–148.

AMERICAN ASSOCIATION FOR THE ADVANCEMENT OF SCIENCE (AAAS)

The American Association for the Advancement of Science (AAAS) is a nonprofit organization dedicated to advancing science around the world through education, advocacy, and leadership. Founded in 1848, it is the world's largest general scientific society, made up of nearly 120,000 individual and institutional members as well as some 262 affiliated societies and academies of science that represent 10 million individuals. The association's headquarters are located in Washington, D.C.

In addition to membership activities and public outreach, each week AAAS publishes the peer-reviewed journal *Science*, which is considered one of the world's most prestigious scientific journals. AAAS also publishes numerous scientific newsletters, books, and reports and is in the vanguard of programs intended to raise the level of understanding for science worldwide.

EurekAlert!

As part of its outreach efforts, AAAS operates the global news service EurekAlert!—an online portal through which universities, medical centers, journals, government agencies, corporations, and other organizations engaged in research can deliver news on science, medicine, and technology to the media and the public. Launched in 1996, EurekAlert! serves approximately 5,500 reporters working in 60 countries and about 5,000 public information officers (PIOs), typically people who perform the tasks of a media relations or public relations officer.

EurekAlert! provides news in English, Spanish, French, German, Japanese, and Chinese. In addition to posting traditional news releases, PIOs can also upload digital images, audio files, and video files to an online multimedia gallery to augment printed news materials.

The public can freely access the searchable database of EurekAlert! for breaking news stories and in-depth information resources on scientific, technological, and medical topics.

To help research institutions with science-news story placements, EurekAlert! offers communication seminars that afford PIOs and public relations managers the opportunity to glean insights from reporters representing a wide range of media organizations—including print, online, and broadcast outlets—on what they seek in science-news stories.

Annual Meeting

Each year, at the AAAS Annual Meeting, science and technology professionals—from across disciplines and around the world—gather to discuss new research, emerging trends, and the interaction of science and technology with society. The AAAS Annual Meeting is one of the most widely recognized interdisciplinary scientific events of its kind, encompassing the breadth of the sciences, education, engineering, and technology.

Over the course of 5 days, upward of 10,000 scientific experts, entrepreneurs, educators, and policymakers attend the meeting. Hundreds of symposia are presented in addition to plenary and topical lectures. A variety of special events designed to engage schoolchildren and the public are also presented. Audio and video recordings of topical lectures, symposia, and public town halls from past meetings are available as an educational resource.

The AAAS Annual Meeting draws upward of 1,000 newsroom registrants. These include reporters (print, broadcast, Web), freelance writers, editors, producers, PIOs, science journalism professors, and students.

Dozens of daily briefings are provided to newsroom registrants about breaking research news presented at the annual meeting. Newsroom registrants have access to copies of speaker presentations and background materials via an on-site "papers room." Embargoed news releases pertaining to research presented at the meeting are available on-site and also in advance via EurekAlert! Much of this material is prepared by PIOs in support of their researchers' presentations at the AAAS Annual Meeting.

Science writers and science communicators new to the profession, as well as journalism students in training, can take advantage of mentoring opportunities at the meeting offered under the auspices of AAAS and the National Association of Science Writers.

Science Magazine

The editorial focus of this international weekly science journal is on publishing important original scientific research and research reviews. Unlike other scientific journals that focus on a specific field, *Science* covers the full range of scientific disciplines with a special emphasis on biology and the life sciences because of the expansion of biotechnology and genetics in recent decades.

Science's print subscriber base, institutional subscriptions, and online access reach an estimated readership of 1 million people. *Science* accepts papers from authors around the world. Competition to publish in *Science* is intense, with less than 10% of submitted articles accepted for publication. All research articles are subject to peer review before they appear in the journal.

Science also publishes science-related news, opinions on science policy, and other matters of interest to scientists and others who are concerned with the wide implications of science and technology.

The AAAS Office of Public Programs works closely with PIOs to coordinate news announcements and media efforts for research forthcoming in *Science*. For example, PIOs are alerted in advance when a paper from their institution is scheduled for publication and can post news releases and link related visuals through the AAAS Web site and have mention of these materials in a weekly *Science* press package sent to reporters.

Other AAAS News Sources

- *ScienceNOW*—A news portal that includes daily news stories from the *Science* magazine news staff.
- *Science Update Radio*—A daily, 60-second broadcast feature covers discoveries in science, technology, and medicine, presented in an entertaining and informative format. Listeners can submit science questions, either to a toll-free phone line or online, for on-air answers.
- *Science for Kids*—A portal with news releases and artwork of interest to younger readers.
- *Science Sources*—A continuously updated, searchable, international database of the contact information for public information officers at more than 1,500 universities, medical centers, laboratories, and other research organizations.

This resource assists journalists and other science communicators in finding the experts and information they need to prepare timely, accurate stories.

- *RSS Feeds*—Provide free content from Web sites such as aaas.org, EurekAlert! and *Science* online, consisting of article headlines, summaries, and links to full-text articles on the Web.

Science Multimedia Center

Access to a variety of special features with a multimedia focus provides access to science not only in words, but also in images, sound, and motion.

- *Science Podcasts*—These are weekly online audiocasts built around stories in *Science* and its related sites.
- *ScienceShots*—An image gallery of interesting, novel, or amusing scientific images and links to a variety of content and features elsewhere on the *Science* sites.
- *Images and Slide Shows*—These presentations showcase striking images or interesting photo essays associated with content on the *Science* sites.
- *Video and Seminars*—Includes video presentations tied into *Science* special issues and supplemental video from *Science* research papers.
- *Science Online Seminars*—Authors of selected breakthrough research papers discuss their work.
- *Interactives*—Enhanced Web versions of posters, illustrations, and other material.

Social Media

AAAS uses social media to augment member outreach. Within the AAAS group on Facebook are fan pages for many of the organization's individual programs, such as the journal *Science, Science Careers, EurekAlert!* and *Science*NOW. These fan pages are freely accessible to both members and others who share an interest in science.

On the professional network LinkedIn, AAAS has created a virtual Rolodex for AAAS members around the globe, and provides a forum for discussion and job postings. A separate group connects current and former AAAS Science & Technology Policy Fellows. Twitter provides breaking news from *Science* and *Science*NOW, and live reports from events hosted by *Science* Careers. Both AAAS and the journal *Science* have channels on YouTube for the posting of selected association and research-related videos.

Communications Awards

The AAAS Science Journalism Awards recognize outstanding reporting for a general audience and honor journalists for their coverage of the sciences, engineering, and mathematics. Since its inception in 1945, the awards have honored more than 300 individuals for their achievements in science journalism in the categories of large and small newspapers, magazines, television, radio, online, and children's science news.

The winning journalists help to foster the public's understanding and appreciation of science, and their work serves as foremost examples for other writers to emulate. Independent screening and judging committees select the winning journalists and their entries based on scientific accuracy, initiative, originality, clarity of interpretation, and value in fostering a better understanding of science by the public. Committees composed of reporters, editors, and scientists screen and judge the entries. An online archive of transcripts of winning entries is available as a resource.

The AAAS Award for Public Understanding of Science and Technology recognizes working scientists and engineers who make outstanding contributions to the popularization of science.

Communicating Science: Tools for Scientists and Engineers

There is increased recognition by research organizations and by funding agencies that more scientists should be directly involved in education and public outreach. Scientists and engineers who foster information sharing and respect between science and the public are essential for the public communication of and engagement with science. However, traditional scientific training typically does not prepare scientists and engineers to be effective communicators outside of academia.

In response to this need in science communications, the AAAS Center for Public Engagement with Science and Technology has partnered with the National Science Foundation to provide resources for scientists and engineers, both online and through regional workshops to help researchers communicate more broadly with the public.

Communicating Science Broadly: Tools for Scientists and Engineers online resources include Webinars with how-to tips for media interviews and strategies for identifying public outreach opportunities.

In regional workshops small, interactive groups of participants learn to distill their data into short, meaningful messages; prepare for media interviews; reach new audiences through social networking sites such as Facebook; and rehearse the use of props and gestures for their talks. The workshops are supported by online resources that offer a variety of tools, background materials, and even more Webinars that can help scientists become better storytellers.

AAAS Science & Technology Policy Fellowships

Fellowships are awarded to highly qualified individuals interested in learning about the science-policy interface while applying their scientific and technical knowledge and analytical skills to the federal policy realm.

The fellowships increase the involvement and visibility of scientists and engineers in the public-policy realm and support the AAAS objectives to improve public policy making through the infusion of science and to increase public understanding of science and technology.

Selected Issues

AAAS has had long-standing success in bringing science to the public through work with schools, science journalists, and science museums and centers; through radio, television, and Internet broadcasting; and through numerous publications translating science into more understandable terms.

The AAAS Center for Public Engagement with Science and Technology provides a venue for multidirectional dialogue on many of the topics that have recently captured national and international attention, such as the following:

- Stem cell research and cloning
- Evolution and science education
- Science, technology, and national security

- Bioterrorism
- Energy policy
- Sustainable development
- The environment
- Climate change
- Genetic medicine
- Emerging infectious diseases
- Genetically modified foods
- Space exploration
- Nanotechnology

The center supports a series of ongoing activities intended to boost public awareness and understanding of the nature of science and the work of scientists while at the same time increase public input into scientific research and policy agendas by creating a vehicle for dialogue among policymakers, the general public, and the scientific community. These activities have included such efforts as these:

- Town hall meetings on issues such as oceans, evolution, and climate change
- "Family Science Days," planned in collaboration with local universities, science centers, and others, during the AAAS Annual Meeting
- "Meet the Scientist" events at AAAS headquarters
- A "glocal" strategy to promote local public engagement regarding global science-related issues by working with local opinion leaders, policymakers, school board members, clergy, and the news media
- The Science Insights and News Service to increase the volume of scientific leadership through news opportunities such as newspaper op-ed placements and an AAAS Science Talk Experts & Speakers service

Sections of the AAAS

The AAAS has 24 sections, with each being responsible for a particular concern of the association. Reporters, PIOs, and science communications professionals tend to affiliate with Section Y—the Section of General Interest in Science and Engineering. A primary goal of sections is to prepare and submit symposia topics for future AAAS Annual Meetings. In this regard, Section Y is often the main source of symposium topics on aspects of science communications.

The sections also nominate, from within their section membership, candidates for the honorific title of AAAS Fellow. These are well-respected scientists and individuals within AAAS who are recognized for meritorious efforts to advance science or its applications. Among Section Y members who have been elected as Fellows are many of the nation's top science news reporters and science communications professionals.

Service as a section committee member and as a section officer affords science writers and PIOs a leadership track for increased responsibility within AAAS as well as increased visibility within the greater science communications community. Both are considered valuable in career development.

Affiliates

AAAS affiliates include 262 societies and academies of science, serving more than 10 million members. Among those affiliates with a focus on science communications and educational outreach are state and regional science academies, the Council of Science Editors, and the National Association of Science Writer.

The AAAS has established affiliation with these and other organizations as a means of advancing the common purpose "to further the work of scientists, to facilitate cooperation among them, to foster scientific freedom and responsibility, to improve the effectiveness of science in the promotion of human welfare, and to increase public understanding and appreciation of the importance and promise of the methods of science in human progress."

Lynne Timpani Friedmann

See also Embargo System; Science; Scientific Societies

Further Readings

American Association for the Advancement of Science: www.aaas.org

AMERICAN MEDICAL ASSOCIATION

The American Medical Association (AMA) is an important source of information about public health and the latest medical research. It is one of the most trusted and credible sources for health care professionals seeking the latest clinical medical information and for journalists writing stories for the public about medical and health issues.

The AMA was founded in 1847 by Dr. Nathan Davis. It has been an instrumental organization in advocating higher standards for medical education and for creating a better health care delivery system in the United States. Although the AMA is the country's largest organization of physicians, it also helps physicians help patients, as noted in the AMA's mission statement: "To promote the art and science of medicine and the betterment of public health." The AMA accomplishes this through several avenues. The AMA's leadership and its House of Delegates set policy on important issues facing medicine, including those in public health. The AMA's Council on Science and Public Health provides information and recommendations on medical, scientific, and public health issues. The AMA also continues to work on improving the U.S. health care system by helping to remove the barriers to access to health care and by working to eliminate racial and ethnic health care disparities.

An important way the AMA provides medical and health information to the public is through its various publications. *The Journal of the American Medical Association* (*JAMA*) is one of the premier peer-reviewed general medical journals in the world. *JAMA* started in 1883 with Dr. Davis as the first editor. *JAMA* is published 48 times a year and is the most widely circulated medical journal in the world. About 6,000 manuscripts are submitted to *JAMA* each year from researchers around the world who want to have their studies published in the journal. Approximately 8% of the manuscripts actually get published in *JAMA*. Manuscripts that are accepted go through a strenuous peer-review process in which experts carefully review the papers before publication, statisticians review the data, and manuscript editors work with the authors to make sure the studies conform to the *JAMA* format and standards for integrity.

JAMA is editorially independent from the AMA, meaning that the AMA has no influence over the content in the medical journal. The *JAMA* editor in chief has the final word on what is published in the journal. *JAMA* has several critical objectives in addition to its goal of publishing the best medical science through original, important articles. *JAMA* also strives to educate physicians, other health care professionals, and the public.

There are nine specialty medical journals published by the AMA called, collectively, the *Archives*. The journals are *Archives of Pediatrics & Adolescent Medicine, Archives of General Psychiatry, Archives of Neurology, Archives of Dermatology, Archives of Surgery, Archives of Ophthalmology, Archives of Internal Medicine, Archives of Facial Plastic Surgery,* and *Archives of Otolaryngology—Head & Neck Surgery.* These journals are published once a month except for *Archives of Internal Medicine,* which is bimonthly, and *Archives of Facial Plastic Surgery,* which is published every other month. Similar to *JAMA,* the *Archives* journals are editorially independent from the AMA. The *JAMA* and *Archives* family of 10- peer-reviewed journals makes a strong presence in the medical research world.

The studies published in *JAMA* and *Archives* journals are often reported in the consumer media on various Web sites, in newspapers, and on radio and television. The public's interest in receiving the latest medical news is apparent by the number of stories seen in various media outlets every day. The journals have a strict policy regarding the release of information to the public. The journals provide early access to the medical studies for journalists who agree to honor an embargo set by the *JAMA* and *Archives* editors, meaning that no stories should be posted, printed, or broadcast until the agreed upon time.

The purpose of this agreement is to allow reporters time to read the medical studies and to interview the authors before writing their stories. The editors like the arrangement because it is an orderly release of the information that they argue leads to an accuracy in reporting that results in improved patient care and public health. There are exceptions to the rules, of course, especially when there is a paper of such extreme public health concern that it needs to be released immediately. The biggest challenge is to make the information understandable to a lay audience with varying degrees of knowledge of medicine and science. *JAMA* and *Archives* journals have their own communications experts who specialize in translating this complex language into more accessible language for the media and, therefore, the public.

Some of the most prominent medical books in the world originate at the AMA. The *AMA Manual of Style* is in its 10th edition. This is a premier reference book that sets the standard for medical publishing guidelines, including a glossary of terms, legal and ethical concerns in publishing, and copyright issues. *Users' Guides to the Medical Literature* is another important reference book that helps readers correctly interpret medical studies and helps physicians bring that information to the clinical side for treating patients. The AMA also publishes many other clinical books to assist physicians and publishes practical books to cover the business side of medicine.

The AMA has a long history of helping doctors help patients through education, publishing the latest medical research and advocating for improvements in public health. The dissemination of this information through the news media and now directly to consumers through Web sites is an important outreach for the AMA. The AMA and *JAMA* and *Archives* reach out to physicians through various publications and forums, such as the House of Delegates, the policy-making body of the AMA. But they also want to reach patients— the consumers of health care—to make sure they are as informed as possible and have access to the health care they need.

Jann Ingmire

See also American Medical Writers Association; Embargo System; Health Communication, Overview; Health Communication and the Internet; Medical Journalism

Further Readings

American Medical Association: www.ama-assn.org
Fontanarosa, P. B. (2008). Update on *JAMA*'s policy on release of information to the public. *Journal of the American Medical Association, 300*(13), 1585–1587.

AMERICAN MEDICAL WRITERS ASSOCIATION

Long before Johannes Gutenberg invented the printing press, the seeds of what we now know as medical writing were planted. Consider the Greek physician Hippocrates, who in addition to his fame as the "father of medicine" also is recognized for a sizable collection of books that are considered the oldest surviving complete medical texts. Flash forward through the centuries, to the birth of a full-fledged communications profession. Today, thousands of modern medical journals line library shelves, health books for consumers routinely soar to the top of the best-seller list, pharmaceutical regulatory documents could fill many warehouses, and articles of every type populate myriad Web sites, newspapers, and magazines. And this is not to mention the existence of a bevy of writers researching and producing all of this copy and of editors polishing what they have written.

In 1940, a group of physicians recognized the need for an organization dedicated to teaching aspiring medical writers and editors about the craft. They formed the American Medical Writers Association (AMWA), now the world's leading resource for medical communicators, to promote excellence in medical communication and to provide educational resources in support of that goal. A nonprofit association, AMWA brings together more than 5,600 communicators and educators working in all areas of health and medicine throughout the world. The organization offers an extensive education program, provides a forum for networking and interactive meetings, promotes a code of ethics, maintains an informative Web site, and publishes the quarterly *AMWA Journal*.

AMWA's membership is eclectic and includes administrators, advertisers, college and university professors, other educators, freelance writers and editors, journal editors, multimedia producers, pharmaceutical writers, public relations specialists, publishers, reporters, researchers, scriptwriters, statisticians, students, writers and editors working in academic institutions, translators, and others.

Paths to Medical Communication

AMWA members pursue many different career paths within medical communication. Many have worked as professionals in scientific research or health care before transitioning into the more technical areas of medical communication. These individuals typically have a science, medical, or related degree (often an advanced degree). In fact, about 54% of the organization's members have a science or health care degree. Other members, about 20%, hold degrees in journalism, communication,

English, or liberal arts; many of them worked in nontechnical communication positions in public relations, advertising, marketing, corporate communication, publishing, or teaching before pursuing medical communication.

A 2007 survey showed that just 4% of AMWA members hold an academic degree in medical or technical writing. As educational institutions expand programs offering degrees and certificates in medical communication, however, an increasing number of graduates will begin their careers as medical communicators. AMWA membership includes free access to periodic salary surveys that collect data from more than 1,700 medical communicators nationwide, which is also available for sale to nonmembers.

AMWA Resources

AMWA provides resources to better prepare writers and editors for a career in medical communication and to pair employers with skilled communicators. These include continuing education opportunities, access to members-only features such as online job listings, Listserv access, and a searchable database of freelance members (available to others by subscription), and chances to network with experienced medical communicators.

AMWA offers both novice and experienced medical communicators more than 100 workshops designed to enhance their skills in many facets of medical communication. These workshops are available during AMWA's 3-day annual conference each fall and in other settings such as at local or corporate-site conferences. Many are part of AMWA's certificate program. Three certificates are available: core, science fundamentals, and advanced. Enrollment in the program is required to receive credit for completed workshops; participants may choose from a wide variety of general and specialty workshops.

Core workshops help participants improve editing, writing, communication, and bibliographic skills; learn how to develop and manage a freelance business; learn the skills necessary for writing for the pharmaceutical industry, public relations, advertising, marketing, or Web or multimedia; discover the latest methods for educating writers and editors; and brush up on statistics. Advanced workshops provide experienced medical communicators with in-depth consideration of issues in writing, editing, management, bibliographic research, education, and other topics of interest. Science workshops provide the opportunity for deeper understanding of basic concepts in science and medicine. Some core certificate workshops are offered as self-study opportunities.

The science fundamentals program was developed for medical communicators whose university education did not emphasize science and for those who want to expand their knowledge beyond their original field of scientific study. The track features introductory workshops in basic sciences, anatomy and physiology, diseases, diagnostic methods, and treatments. These workshops provide information and tools for writing about the sciences, including terminology, basic concepts and systems, commonly used methods, and key references and resources.

The advanced certificate is designed for those who have earned AMWA core certificates or who have a minimum of 5 years of relevant experience. Earning an advanced certificate requires the completion of at least eight advanced workshops. Some advanced workshops have core workshop prerequisites.

Melanie Fridl Ross

See also Medical Journalism

Further Readings

American Medical Writers Association: www.amwa.org

ANTI-DRUG CAMPAIGNS

This entry describes large-scale public anti-drug education, prevention, and communication campaigns undertaken in the United States in the last 30 years. Particular examples of campaigns are used and their purpose, approach, and effectiveness highlighted (such as the "Just Say No," Drug Abuse Resistance Education, or DARE; National Youth Anti-Drug Media Campaign, or NYAMC; and Project ALERT campaigns). While the description of campaigns from the 1980s onward may offer some insight into the recent evolution of U.S. anti-drug activities, this entry is not intended as a complete historical record of these efforts. The

focus here is on public health education and communication campaigns, as opposed to other initiatives such as those addressing supply and demand issues; thus, other policy actions and legal initiatives (such as increased punishment for users) are generally not included. This concentrated scope allows sufficient detail for the reader to gain a solid understanding of the mass media and school-based anti-drug initiatives launched and implemented in the United States in recent decades.

Important Role of Science Communication

In the recent years, we have seen an increase in the use of mass media to deliver health messages, including anti-smoking, anti-drug, and provaccination campaigns. In addition, news outlets have become more involved in disseminating information about health to the general public. The successful use of mass media has increased exposure to health-related messages among audiences who have not been reached in the past. The introduction of social networking tools (such as Facebook and Twitter) has offered an additional, and innovative, tool for dissemination of health messages, especially among youth.

As in other areas of national public health, recent national and local efforts to address youth illicit drug use have increasingly employed public media campaigns targeted at prevention. The popular use of mass media campaigns by government and nonprofit entities extends beyond the area of youth illicit drug use; recent examples include the U.S. Centers for Disease Control and Prevention's youth physical activity campaign, VERB, and the American Legacy Foundation's "Truth" anti-tobacco media campaign, Truth. National agencies' decisions to invest in these often costly mass media campaigns indicate a level of confidence in the effectiveness of the public health communication campaign approach. The implicit assumption is that these financial costs will be outweighed by the savings and other gains generated from reducing the health problem in question.

The Problem of Illicit Drug Use Among Youth in the United States

Illicit drug use among youth 12 to 18 years old has represented a significant public health problem in recent decades. After a relatively dramatic decline in the 1980s, Monitoring the Future studies have shown that teen and preteen drug use rose dramatically between 1991 and 1997. Over the past decade, Monitoring the Future studies report the prevalence of the use of some illicit drugs (such as marijuana, amphetamines, and crystal meth) among youth has declined, although the use of other drugs seems to have reached a plateau (including LSD, cocaine, and sedatives). Furthermore, in some cases, drug use has increased slightly (such as for inhalants and MDMA, also known as ecstasy). Today, Monitoring the Future studies show nearly 15% of youth in eighth grade have used an illicit drug, and by high school graduation, nearly half of youth will have tried an illicit drug.

The costs associated with illicit drug use are substantial. In 2004, the U.S. Office of National Drug Control Policy (ONDCP) estimated that the annual cost to society of illicit drug use is $181 billion. In addition, illicit drug use takes a significant toll on the physical and psychological health of youth and on the individuals, family, and community who surround them. The Substance Abuse and Mental Health Services Administration and other organizational authorities agree that early illicit drug use has the potential to lead to lifelong dependency and can influence other unhealthy, risky behaviors such as delinquency, physical violence (and associated injuries), and premature sexual activity, including unplanned pregnancy and exposure to sexually transmitted diseases.

Among all illicit drugs used by youth, marijuana is the most commonly used and the most readily obtainable. In a 2008 Monitoring the Future study, marijuana use in the previous 12 months was reported by 32% of 12th-grade youth, 25% of 10th graders, and 10% of 8th graders; nearly 85% of sampled 12th graders reported that marijuana was easily accessible. In recent years, the ONDCP reports abuse of prescription drugs and over-the-counter medication as one of the fastest growing forms of drug abuse in the United States, particularly among adolescents. In 2007, approximately 5% to 10% of 12th graders used these medications for the purpose of getting high, with 6% to 7% using over-the-counter cough and/or cold medication, 10% using Vicodin, and 5% using OxyContin.

Modern Anti-Drug Campaigns

The "Just Say No" Campaign

Under President Ronald Reagan's administration and the U.S. War on Drugs, First Lady Nancy Reagan championed the "Just Say No" public anti-drug campaign in the 1980s. The campaign was a multicomponent intervention and served as an umbrella for many initiatives, including classroom-based curriculum delivery and national mass media messages.

Research conducted by University of Houston Social Psychology Professor Dr. Richard I. Evans and his research group in the 1970s focused on substance abuse prevention and advanced a social inoculation model. This model contributed to the development of the "Just Say No" campaign; the approach was to inoculate young people with the social skills and self-efficacy (that is, confidence in their skills and abilities) to overcome peer pressure. The campaign attempted to teach resistance skills by offering a variety of ways to literally say "no" to drug use offers by friends or other peers, with the aim that these skills would enable youth to avoid drug use.

The "Just Say No" campaign included public service advertising, classroom courses, entertainment education, and mass media coverage. Beyond the public funding that supported the campaign materials and classroom curriculum, Nancy Reagan's status as First Lady garnered her significant media attention, allowing her to appear on television talk shows and entertainment programs, receive news coverage, and author articles. In addition, an entertainment education goal was accomplished when "Just Say No" campaign messages were integrated into the storylines of popular television programming at the time, such as in *Diff'rent Strokes* and in *Punky Brewster*. Through this variety of communication channels, by 1993, the campaign had reportedly reached more than 25 million U.S. youth.

Because the "Just Say No" campaign fell under the rubric and within the timeline of the national War on Drugs, most evaluation commentary has focused more broadly on the entire effort of the War on Drugs, rather than on the campaign itself. Several researchers have suggested the War on Drugs had no effect on illegal drug use, with some arguing that illegal drug use was already in decline several years before Reagan took office and declared a war on drugs, and the trend then simply continued downward. Rather, it is more widely acknowledged that the main impact of the War on Drugs was the increased incarceration rates of drug users and suppliers; between 1980 and 2001, the U.S. Department of Justice reported that the number of drug users and suppliers in state and federal prisons increased dramatically.

Scientific evaluations of the "Just Say No" campaign (including exposure to "Just Say No" posters, T-shirts, and other materials; media coverage of Nancy Reagan's speeches and appearances; and so on) are scarce. However, many other drug use prevention initiatives (in addition to those aimed at alcohol and tobacco) emerged during the time of and in conjunction with the philosophy of "Just Say No," and these have therefore been associated with the "Just Say No" moniker. Many different interventions that adopted a psychological inoculation approach during this period were referred to as "Just Say No" initiatives. Some researchers assert there is evidence of success for these interventions, especially when the social inoculation and/or peer pressure resistance approach is combined with social skills training. While these evaluation studies do suggest positive effects, the evaluated interventions were not exclusively related to "Just Say No" and were focused on prevention of the use of tobacco rather than of the use of illicit drugs.

Other evaluations focused on school-based illicit drug use prevention programs, and the results were more ambiguous. In addition, there has been critical commentary from researchers and others that the "Just Say No" ideology was ineffective in keeping youth away from illicit drug use, and also that while unsuccessful in its stated purpose, the "Just Say No" campaign successfully served a more political purpose of reassuring parents that schools were at least trying to do something about substance abuse problems among students.

The DARE Program

One of the most broadly implemented anti-drug school programs and another initiative frequently associated with "Just Say No" was the DARE program. Launched in the early 1980s, DARE became one of the most widely used drug education curriculums of the 20th century. By 1986, the U.S. Congress had passed the Drug-Free Schools and Communities Act, which mandated that schools adopt a drug abuse prevention program; this facilitated broader dissemination of DARE, a well-funded and long-standing program in the United States even more than a decade after its start. Legislation helped to ensure the continued funding of risk behavior prevention programs such as DARE with the Improving America's Schools Act of 1994. The program continues nationally, as of 2008, 25 years after its founding.

Although the messages delivered by the DARE program are generally similar to other classroom-based drug education curriculums, DARE is distinct in that trained law enforcement officers teach each session. In its original conception, local law enforcement instructors delivered an in-class curriculum in schools, predominantly in a lecture style. In recent versions of DARE, the program is designed to be more interactive for students by using technology, discussion groups, and role-playing, with officers intended to be more like coaches than authority figures. The content focus remains on the risks and harmful effects of drug use, as well as on peer pressure resistance and strategies for drug offer refusals; it attempts to persuade youth to resist drug use. At times, the program has asked students to sign a pledge that they will not use drugs.

In terms of reach, DARE programs exist for kindergarten through 12th grade, and approximately 75% of U.S. school districts implement some form of the DARE program. As of 1990, DARE programs were reported to reach over 3,000 communities across the United States and an estimated 20 million students. At various times during the DARE campaign, multiple sources suggest that DARE reaches close to 10 million students annually.

Administration of the DARE program in the United States was estimated to cost over $1 billion per year. Funding for DARE comes from a number of different federal agencies and from private sources including foundations, corporations, and individuals. In addition, training of the law enforcement officers on a state level and local implementation of the DARE programs frequently are supported by funds from other governmental sources such as state legislature appropriations, state agencies, counties, cities, school districts, and police agencies, as well as private sources such as individuals and fund-raising efforts in the local community.

Yet DARE school-based programs have shown little efficacy. Several researchers have found that the DARE curriculum had little or no effect on overall illicit drug use. Additional evidence suggests that DARE may only delay drug use, meaning adolescents who participate in the program will engage in the same rates of illicit drug use as those adolescents who have not participated in DARE, but these students will do so at older ages. Finally, multiple studies, from the early 1990s up to 2007, point to a boomerang effect of DARE exposure in which those who completed the DARE program were more likely to engage in illicit drug use than those who had not participated in DARE.

Because of the evidence indicating limited, if any, significant anti-drug effects of DARE, in 2001, Surgeon General Dr. David Satcher placed DARE in the "does not work" category of drug abuse prevention programs. In 2003, The U.S. General Accountability Office reported that the program was counterproductive among certain subpopulations and was prone to a potential boomerang effect in which those who graduate from DARE later have higher rates of drug use than others who did not participate.

Partnership for a Drug-Free America

The founding of the nonprofit organization Partnership for a Drug-Free America (PDFA) in 1986 was an early facilitator of a more widespread use of print and broadcast public service announcements (PSAs). Initiated as a project of the American Association of Advertising Agencies, the organization was driven by the goal of reducing the demand for drugs among young people by influencing their attitudes, beliefs, and other cognitions in an anti-drug direction via the use of advertising and mass media outlets. An underlying belief was that if advertising can persuade consumers to purchase products, then it may also be able to influence their health behavior choices, including whether to try drugs.

In 1987, PDFA became well-known for its anti-narcotics campaign with the advertisement

centerpiece, "This Is Your Brain on Drugs." The ad equated a person's brain to an egg, and frying an egg to what the brain looked like when using drugs. In 1989, this ad, in addition to other PDFA PSAs, received praise from President George H. W. Bush as "hard-hitting and carefully targeted." PDFA was also recognized for another ad campaign well known for the exclamation, "I learned it by watching you!" In this PSA, a father finds a box containing drugs and paraphernalia in his son's bedroom and confronts his son, vehemently demanding to know how he was introduced to drug use. The son responds with the above exclamation indicating that he learned the behavior from his father. The ad claims that "parents who use drugs have children who use drugs," highlighting the role of parents in youth decision making about drug use.

Such media campaigns paved the way for later campaigns such as the NYAMC, on which PDFA also collaborated.

NYAMC

In 1998, the ONDCP initiated the NYAMC, a large-scale health communication campaign that is still ongoing as of December 2008. The campaign's primary purpose was threefold: to prevent drug use initiation, to empower youth to reject illegal drugs, and to persuade occasional drug users to stop. The target audience for these objectives was youth 9 to 18 years old. The predominant focus of the NYAMC has been on preventing initiation of drug use, especially marijuana use.

From 1998 to 2004, the U.S. Congress dedicated nearly $1 billion toward funding this campaign, which included paid media advertising and community outreach activities in the form of partnerships with civic and faith service organizations. The NYAMC utilized a multimedia approach to reach parents and youth, including heavy use of television in addition to radio, online, and print advertising; campaign Web sites; parenting skills brochures; and school-based materials.

Separate campaign components were designed for parents and youth. The parent campaign attempted to show parents that they play an important role for their children as a strong influence against drugs. As part of this effort, the campaign for parents was centered around the brand signature "Parents: The Anti-Drug" and made use of this phrase as well as others (such as "Communication: The Anti-Drug") to promote productive parent behaviors and engage parents in using practical skills to teach youth about drugs.

The youth campaign focused on the brand signature "My Anti-Drug" to provide youth a sense of ownership and support their need for individuality. In the beginning of the campaign, youth were asked to share what motivates them to choose not to use drugs, or their "anti-drug," either online or by mail; this approach was supported by the phrases "What's Your Anti-Drug?" and asking youth to use their own "anti-drug" to create phrases such as "Soccer: My Anti-Drug," thus emphasizing positive alternatives to drug use.

Other later ads focused on negative consequences of drug use and resistance skills, especially starting in 2002, as the campaign narrowed focus to marijuana use. In particular, the campaign portrayed marijuana use as a risky behavior by showing immediate dangers of use in a portion of the NYAMC referred to as the Marijuana Initiative. In recent years, the campaign shifted to an "Above the Influence" approach aimed at preparing teens to stand up to peer pressure, teaching about negative consequences, and conveying the advantages of choosing to live above the influence of drugs.

After several years of the fully launched campaign, the results, as reported in the official Congress-mandated evaluation, were disappointing. Although the campaign was able to access many media channels and obtain extensive media coverage, the evaluation of the campaign found no positive effects on youth cognitions, intentions, or behavior with respect to marijuana use. The data from the National Survey of Parents used to evaluate the campaign showed no consistent anti-drug impact. Moreover, the results of the evaluation, as described in 2008 by Robert Hornik, Lela S. Jacobsohn, Robert Orwin, Andrea Piesse, and Graham Kalton, suggested unintended boomerang effects on the youth audience: Over time, those who had greater exposure to campaign messages were more likely to demonstrate prodrug outcomes, including more favorable norms and intentions regarding marijuana use, as well as actual marijuana use, than those with less exposure.

Subsequent research supports an explanation for the boomerang effect detected involving normative

implications of the campaign's mass media ads. The high levels of exposure of these anti-drug messages may have significantly increased the visibility of and attention given to marijuana use by youth. This kind of high visibility may have suggested that the behavior of marijuana use is a substantial problem affecting a large portion of the targeted population, or that "everyone is doing it." In other words, the aggregate or cumulative product of the campaign ads was a metamessage suggesting high marijuana use prevalence among youth peers. These perceptions of prevalent use in turn led to other promarijuana outcomes. The implications of the finding were a reinforced focus on pretesting to rule out boomerang effects, with a special emphasis on trying to get a sense of the aggregate effect by testing collections of ads together and multiple exposures rather than simply single ad pretesting.

Potential Models of Success

Not all anti-drug campaigns show no or unwanted effects on adolescent illicit drug use. Some in-school programs and community-based media efforts have been reported to lower risk factors associated with future illicit drug use and to decrease the prevalence of use among youth.

Project ALERT attempts to equip youth with effective strategies to resist the pressures of drug use, including alcohol, marijuana, tobacco, and inhalants. The primary goals are to prevent initiation of drug use, to prevent those who have already tried drugs from becoming regular users, and to affect the risk factors associated with drug use. The in-school skills-based curriculum consists of 11 lessons designed to be taught once a week with three follow-up sessions in the subsequent year. The program aims to teach seventh- and eighth-grade students how to identify internal and external pressures, to increase refusal skills and self-efficacy to resist prodrug social influences, and to build nonuse beliefs and cognitions.

Delivery of the Project ALERT program in the classroom involves small-group activities; role-playing exercises, including rehearsal of taught skills; instructional videos; and facilitated classroom discussions, using teachers and in some cases teens as instructors. Project ALERT was distributed widely starting in 1995, and since then, the program has been implemented in approximately

3,500 U.S. school districts with over 40,000 teachers trained as intervention instructors. Based on multiple randomized control group studies, in 2003, Phyllis L. Ellickson, Daniel F. McCaffrey, Bonnie Ghosh-Dastidar, and Douglas L. Longshore at the RAND Corporation found that Project ALERT was effective in preventing marijuana, alcohol, and cigarette use, with the largest effects on marijuana use. Students who participated in Project ALERT were 38% less likely than other students to initiate marijuana use.

Other school-based approaches, such as Project SMART and Project STAR, have also demonstrated positive results on preventing drug use in select studies, and school- and community-based media campaigns such as "Be Under Your Own Influence" have shown promise with strong findings of effectiveness in marijuana use prevention, particularly when conducted in conjunction with in-school prevention curricula.

Importance of Strong Campaign Evaluations

Even with these examples acknowledged, it is important to bear in mind that media campaigns can have unintended, unfavorable effects. As suggested by the review of modern anti-drug campaigns above, public service and health communication campaigns do have the potential to boomerang and leave the target audience worse off than if nothing had been done at all. Several observational research studies have concluded that public health campaigns and interventions, including anti-drug programs, can produce unfavorable effects, particularly for subgroups of the campaign audience.

This caution underscores the importance of thorough and rigorous evaluation of anti-drug campaigns; this includes formative evaluation in the form of pretesting as well as summative or outcome evaluation to assess the effects of the implementation of a campaign. Such evaluations should be framed in the context of the theories used to design the campaign content and the behavior change model used to predict its path of effects, and most often these are overlapping.

Most importantly, strong evaluations allow for ongoing iterative improvement of campaigns. Therefore, concern over boomerang effects is by no means the only or even the primary impetus to evaluate. Rather, the opportunity to demonstrate positive effects confidently and to increase the size of these effects should serve as more than sufficient motivation to continue to develop strategies and to evaluate efforts to reduce and prevent drug use. Careful evaluation of anti-drug campaigns is the key means by which lessons can be learned from past endeavors and inform future initiatives.

Lela Jacobsohn and Alana M. Vivolo

See also Anti-Smoking Campaigns; Communication Campaigns in Health and Environment; Vaccines, Fear of

Further Readings

Bukoski, W. J., & Evans, R. I. (Eds.). *Cost-benefit/cost-effectiveness research on drug abuse prevention: Implications for programming and policy* (NIH Publication No. 98-4021, pp. 59–82). Washington, DC: U.S. Government Printing Office.

Drug-Free Schools and Communities Act of 1986, Pub. L. No. 99–570, Subtitle B of Title IV (1986).

Ellickson, P. L., McCaffrey, D. F., Ghosh-Dastidar, B., & Longshore, D. L. (2003). New inroads in preventing adolescent drug use: Results from a large-scale trial of Project ALERT in middle schools. *American Journal of Public Health, 93,* 1830–1836.

Ennett, S. T., Tobler, N. S., Ringwalt, C. L., & Flewelling, R. L. (1994). How effective is Drug Abuse Resistance Education? A meta-analysis of Project DARE outcome evaluations. *American Journal of Public Health, 84,* 1394–1401.

Fishbein, M., Hall-Jamieson, K., Zimmer, E., von Haeften, I., & Nabi, R. (2002). Avoiding the boomerang: Testing the relative effectiveness of anti-drug public service announcements before a national campaign. *American Journal of Public Health, 92,* 238–245.

Hornik, R. C., Jacobsohn, L. S., Orwin, R., Piesse, A., & Kalton, G. (2008). Effects of the National Youth Anti-Drug Media Campaign on youths. *American Journal of Public Health, 98,* 2229–2236.

Improving America's Schools Act of 1994, Pub. L. No. 103-382 (1994).

Jacobsohn, L. S., & Hornik, R. C. (2008). High brand recognition in the context of an unsuccessful communication campaign: The National Youth Anti-Drug Media Campaign. In W. D. Evans & G. Hastings (Eds.), *Public health branding applying marketing for social change* (pp. 147–160). New York: Oxford University Press.

Jensen, E. L., Gerber, J., & Mosher, C. (2004). Social consequences of the War on Drugs: The legacy of failed policy. *Criminal Justice Policy Review, 15,* 100–121.

Johnston, L. D., O'Malley, P. M., Bachman, J. G., & Schulenberg, J. E. (2008). *Monitoring the Future national results on adolescent drug use: Overview of key findings, 2007.* (NIH Publication No. 08-6418). Bethesda, MD: National Institute on Drug Abuse.

Lynam, D. R., Milich, R., Zimmerman, R., Novak, S. P., Logan, T.K., Martin, C., et al. (1999). Project DARE: No effects at 10-year follow-up. *Journal of Consulting and Clinical Psychology, 67,* 590–593.

Slater, M. D., Kelly, K. J., Edwards, R. W., Thurman, P. J., Plested, B. A., Keefe, T. J., et al. (2006). Combining in-school and community-based media efforts: Reducing marijuana and alcohol uptake among younger adolescents. *Health Education Research, 21,* 157–167.

Substance Abuse and Mental Health Services Administration, Office of Applied Studies. (1999). *The relationship between mental health and substance abuse among adolescents.* Rockville, MD: Author. (OAS Analytic Series No. 9, DHHS Publication No. (SMA) 99-3286)

U. S. General Accounting Office. (2003, January 5). *Youth illicit drug use prevention: DARE long-term evaluations and federal efforts to identify effective programs.* Retrieved December 5, 2008, from www .gao.gov/new.items/d03172r.pdf

U.S. Office of National Drug Control Policy. (2004). *The economic costs of drug abuse in the United States: 1992–2002.* Washington, DC: Executive Office of the President (Publication No. 207303)

ANTI-SMOKING CAMPAIGNS

Anti-smoking campaigns refers to purposeful efforts, usually involving some form of mass media, to reduce cigarette smoking in a population. These efforts include paid media campaigns to reduce cigarette smoking, anti-smoking campaigns that operate through donated media time, and coordinated attempts to generate awareness about negative aspects of smoking. There is a long history of anti-smoking campaigns in the United States and abroad, a history shaped by changes in scientific knowledge about cigarette smoking and its effects. Careful study of the lessons learned from these campaigns can inform broader thinking

about science and technology communication. This entry begins with a brief history of cigarette smoking in the United States, followed by an overview of anti-smoking campaigns that have occurred since 1960. Next, it reviews the evidence about anti-smoking campaign effectiveness, paying attention to specific types of messages that have been used effectively in these campaigns. The entry concludes with a discussion of contemporary issues in anti-smoking campaigns, including differences in smoking rates between population groups and concerns about continued funding.

Trends in Cigarette Smoking in the United States

The prevalence of cigarette smoking in the United States varied dramatically over the past century. Cigarette smoking gained popularity in the late 19th century following the mass manufacturing and marketing of machine-rolled cigarettes. Although several organizations voiced concerns about the health effects of smoking, cigarette consumption increased dramatically between 1900 and the early 1960s. A sharp acceleration in cigarette smoking rates occurred during the 1940s, aided by cigarette companies' successful efforts to link smoking with patriotism and U.S. military efforts in World War II. By the mid-20th century, cigarette smoking was seen as a socially acceptable and normative behavior.

The late 1950s and early 1960s brought increased concerns about the health effects of smoking, culminating in the 1964 publication of the first Surgeon General's Report on the health effects of smoking. U.S. smoking rates have declined since the late 1960s, with accelerated reductions following the 1986 Surgeon General's Report on the health effects of secondhand smoke and the 1998 Master Settlement Agreement punishing cigarette companies for denying the harmful effects of their product. Today, approximately 20% of U.S. adults smoke.

Anti-Smoking Campaigns Since 1960

The first nationally coordinated anti-smoking media campaign in the United States occurred between 1967 and early 1971. Anti-smoking activists successfully lobbied the Federal Communications Commission to apply the Fairness Doctrine to cigarette advertising, which required that broadcasters donate one free anti-smoking ad for every three cigarette commercials. This legal move resulted in widespread public broadcasting of anti-smoking ads, most of which focused on the health effects of cigarette smoking. Scholars estimate that over $200 million worth of donated time was used for anti-smoking campaign messages. The campaign stopped in 1971, when cigarette companies agreed to halt all broadcast advertising for their products.

The next two decades witnessed the development and evaluation of several controlled community intervention trials related to cigarette smoking. These trials assessed the impact of anti-smoking media campaigns alongside broader community efforts (school-based tobacco education, community education, and other events) in small sets of matched communities. Notable examples include the North Karelia Project in Finland, the Stanford Three-City and Five-City Projects in California, the Minnesota Heart Health Program, the Quit for Life Programs in Australia, and the Community Intervention Trial for Smoking Cessation (COMMIT) in the United States. These trials often combined anti-smoking messages with broader efforts (for example, messages to improve diet) to reduce cardiovascular disease risk.

Starting in the mid-1980s, several states launched anti-smoking campaigns to reduce smoking. Minnesota implemented the first statewide smoking prevention campaign in 1985, followed by large-scale efforts in California (1990), Massachusetts (1994), Arizona (1995), Oregon (1997), and Florida (1997). Likewise, Australia developed a national anti-smoking media campaign in 1997. Many of these campaigns expanded their message beyond a sole focus on the health effects of smoking to issues such as nicotine's addictiveness, the harms of secondhand smoke, and deceptive behavior by cigarette companies in marketing their product.

Anti-smoking campaigns received a large boost from two events in the late 1990s: (1) the U.S. Food and Drug Administration's (FDA) 1997 decision to limit regulations on direct-to-consumer advertising for pharmaceutical products and (2) the 1998 Master Settlement Agreement (MSA) between 46 state attorneys general and the five largest tobacco companies. The FDA's decision made it legal for

pharmaceutical companies to market smoking cessation medications directly to consumers through broadcast advertising. The MSA provided states with a large sum of money to spend on anti-smoking campaigns and created the American Legacy Foundation, a new organization that launched a coordinated national campaign (Truth) in 2000 to reduce youth smoking. The Truth campaign spent over $100 million a year, with messages focused on cigarette company efforts to market their deadly product to teens. Two cigarette companies, Philip Morris and Lorillard, also launched national anti-smoking campaigns in the late 1990s, although many scholars have questioned their motives and effectiveness.

The infusion of these anti-smoking campaign resources has created substantial levels of exposure to anti-smoking messages in the United States. According to Melanie Wakefield and colleagues in 2005, the average U.S. household was exposed to 12 pharmaceutical ads, six anti-smoking ads sponsored by public health groups, and three and a half anti-smoking ads sponsored by cigarette companies in 2003. Levels of exposure were higher in states that funded their own anti-smoking campaigns.

Anti-Smoking Campaign Effectiveness: What Works?

Anti-smoking campaigns have been studied extensively. Research in this area is subject to a variety of methodological limitations that prevent definitive assessments of which types of campaigns maximize effectiveness in reducing smoking rates. Nevertheless, what we know to date strongly supports the assertion that anti-smoking campaigns are effective strategies to prevent youth from starting to smoke and to persuade adults to quit.

The first evidence of anti-smoking campaign success came from analyses of the Fairness Doctrine campaign in the late 1960s. A series of studies concluded that the coordinated national campaign reduced smoking in the U.S. population between 1967 and 1971.

Evidence from the controlled community intervention trials in the 1970s and 1980s painted a blurrier picture. On the one hand, several of these trials (North Karelia, Stanford Three-City Project, Minnesota Heart Health Program) found lower rates of smoking in communities that received anti-smoking interventions than in communities that did not. On the other hand, several of these trials (Stanford Five-City Project, COMMIT) failed to find meaningful differences between intervention and control communities. These findings led to a degree of skepticism about the role of anti-smoking campaigns in reducing population smoking rates. Nevertheless, Robert Hornik recently argued that the trials failed to find differences because the control communities were exposed to a substantial volume of anti-smoking messages from outside sources such as the national news media. Both intervention and control groups in these trials witnessed declines in smoking rates over the study period, supporting the conclusion that anti-smoking campaigns do indeed contribute to reductions in smoking.

Recent evaluations of state and national anti-smoking campaigns provide further evidence that these efforts reduce youth smoking initiation and increase adult smoking cessation. Well-designed evaluations in Australia, California, Florida, and Massachusetts concluded that campaigns reduced smoking in these locations. Data also suggest that the Truth campaign contributed to reductions in U.S. youth smoking rates in the early 2000s. Other studies found that pharmaceutical advertisements for smoking cessation medications increase quit attempts and successful quits. Combining insights from controlled trials, state and national campaign evaluations, and studies of pharmaceutical ad effects, nearly all systematic reviews of the evidence have concluded that anti-smoking campaigns are effective in reducing youth and adult smoking rates. Most also agree that media campaigns are most effective when accompanied by anti-smoking interventions in schools or communities.

The evidence is less clear about which types of anti-smoking messages are most effective in reducing youth and adult smoking. Message themes used in existing campaigns can be roughly characterized by five categories: long-term consequences of cigarette smoking (disease and death), short-term effects of smoking (for example, odor, shortness of breath), harms of secondhand smoke, cigarette company behavior, or resources to help smokers quit. Efforts to assess the comparative effectiveness of each approach are limited by the fact that few campaigns exclusively utilize a single message theme. Assessments of effectiveness also depend on the campaign's target audiences. Messages sharing resources to help smokers quit, for example, seem unlikely to appeal to a teen who is thinking about trying cigarettes, but they may be appropriate for an adult smoker who is thinking about quitting.

Despite these caveats, emotional messages about the long-term consequences of smoking appear particularly effective in convincing youth to avoid smoking and in prompting quitting among smokers. Likewise, campaigns that combine messages about the consequences of smoking with information about cigarette company efforts to market their deadly product seem to work at reducing youth smoking. There remains much to learn about specific characteristics of anti-smoking messages that maximize success among diverse audiences.

Contemporary Issues for Anti-Smoking Campaigns

Anti-smoking campaigns face a variety of challenges for the future. One major concern is the large difference in smoking rates by education. The prevalence of smoking among U.S. adults has declined steadily over the past 40 years, but disparities in smoking rates by education increased over this time period. Anti-smoking campaigns are often less effective in promoting smoking cessation among less educated smokers compared to smokers with more education. Less educated smokers face substantial barriers to sustained cessation, including lower access to treatment, more permissive workplace cultures and policies, lower social support for quitting, and more sources of stress in their social environment. Future campaigns will need to consider these barriers when developing messages to promote cessation among this group.

There also remains a great deal of uncertainty about the availability of resources for future anti-smoking campaigns. While the MSA was intended to provide states with resources to conduct anti-smoking campaigns, many states used these funds for other purposes. Several states that once funded large campaigns, including Florida and Massachusetts, saw their campaign budgets reduced or eliminated by state legislatures. National campaigns have also seen dramatic budget cuts. The Truth campaign's annual budget declined from over $100 million in 2000 to approximately

$20 million by 2008. It remains unclear whether anti-smoking campaigns will continue to be funded, particularly during times of economic uncertainty.

Jeff Niederdeppe

See also Anti-Drug Campaigns; Cancer Prevention and Risk Communication; Communication Campaigns in Health and Environment; Drug Advertising; Surgeon General, U.S.

Further Readings

Avery, R., Kenkel, D., Lillard, D. R., & Mathios, A. (2007). Private profits and public health: Does advertising of smoking cessation products encourage smokers to quit? *Journal of Political Economy, 115,* 447–481.

Brandt, A. M. (2007). *The cigarette century: The rise, fall, and deadly persistence of the product that defined America.* New York: Basic Books.

Hopkins, D. P., Briss, P. A., Ricard, C. J., Husten, C. G., Carande-Kulis, V. G., Fielding, J. E., et al. (2001). Reviews of evidence regarding interventions to reduce tobacco use and exposure to environmental tobacco smoke. *American Journal of Preventive Medicine,* 20(Suppl. 2), 16–66.

Hornik, R. C. (2002). *Public health communication: Evidence for behavior change.* Mahwah, NJ: Lawrence Erlbaum.

Office of the Attorney General. (n.d.). *1998 Master Settlement Agreement.* Available at http://ag.ca.gov/ tobacco/msa.php

Niederdeppe, J., Kuang, X., Crock, B. N., & Skelton, A. (2008). Media strategies to promote smoking cessation among socioeconomically disadvantaged populations: What do we know, what do we need to learn, and what should we do now? *Social Science and Medicine, 67,* 1343–1355.

U.S. Department of Health and Human Services. (2008). *The role of the media in promoting and reducing tobacco use.* NCI Tobacco Control Monograph Series Vol. 19. Washington, DC: U.S. Department of Health and Human Services, National Institutes of Health, National Cancer Institute.

Wakefield, M., Szczypka, G., Terry-McElrath, Y., Emery, S., Flay, B., Chaloupka, F., et al. (2005). Mixed messages on tobacco: Comparative exposure to public health, tobacco company- and pharmaceutical company-sponsored tobacco-related television campaigns in the United States, 1999–2003. *Addiction, 100,* 1875–1883.

ARCHITECTURE, SUSTAINABLE

While architecture is often seen culturally as a design-based activity that results in the production of a visually and aesthetically pleasing built environment, the design of sustainable buildings requires an approach that is informed by a knowledge of emergent technologies available to achieve this, as well as a sound grasp of the applied field of "building science." Practitioners apply these principles in the design of buildings, and architectural technologists inform their work with a functional understanding of the technologies that can be used to reduce a building's energy and materials input demand. Grounding science and technology communication in this way helps to make it relevant, demonstrating to an audience that what may appear to be abstract concepts can be put to use in everyday contexts.

A range of examples of how science can be communicated through the medium of sustainable architecture is available, including the idea of passive solar design, the concept of embodied carbon, the use of products that rely on natural energy flows, the implications of various forms of plastic, alternative building materials, insulation, and the exploration of alternative energy technologies.

The idea of passive solar design is informed through a knowledge of the geometry of the earth–sun relationship and through an understanding of the angle of incident solar radiation striking any point on the earth's surface—and also how this changes both daily and seasonally. Some designs for sustainable buildings will rely on thermal mass systems to store heat energy to even out temperature variations over the course of a day—or even, in some applications, seasonally. Exploration of such buildings can be used as a platform for communicating key thermodynamic concepts and for communicating ideas about how different materials possess specific heat capacities. In addition, a new class of building materials referred to as "phase change materials" can be used to store thermal energy; exploring the properties of these materials can be used as a catalyst to discuss states of matter and how materials change state as heat is applied.

The concept of embodied carbon is crucial to understanding how society can adapt the design of buildings so that builders use different materials in construction that have required less energy in their manufacture and result in a product with a decreased carbon intensity. Underpinning these relatively new terms, which have only entered the vocabulary in the latter part of the 20th century, is a sound knowledge of energy transformation processes and efficiency. If the efficiency of energy transformation processes at each step can be accounted for, and the carbon emissions for burning a given unit of fuel is known, then it is possible to calculate how much carbon is emitted in the production of a given quantity of a certain material.

In addition, it is possible to contrast materials that harness natural energy flows with others. For example, an exploration of timber and natural products can be used as a main theme from which can branch such diverse subjects as photosynthesis, plant cell biology, and cellulose fibers; this exploration can also be used to discuss what gives these products structural strength with respect to manmade products that are used in buildings. By way of contrast, the increased use of plastics as facade and finish materials can be used to explore a rich vein of issues associated with petrochemistry, following the development of plastics use in buildings from its humble origins through realization of plastics' ultimate unsustainability to more modern solutions to the problem, such as bioplastics, which afford the utility of modern plastics plus the benefit that they are derived from natural products.

Cement and concrete products are among those widely used in traditional building; however, an exploration of the carbon emissions from the cement manufacturing industry can be achieved while teaching the molecular science that accompanies an understanding of the process of calcination. In the search for reduced carbon alternatives to cement, it is possible to explore traditional building techniques, which can be used to explore lime, previously used as a mortar to bind bricks and stone, and in light of the awareness of the impact of cement, students can explore the lime cycle and the chemistry that dictates the different phases that lime goes through in the cycle. This can be accompanied by a dramatic demonstration of the process of slaking, whereby hydration of calcium hydroxide results in a highly exothermic reaction.

Insulation, while it may appear to be a mundane subject, is actually a diverse subject that can be used to communicate the science of heat transfer—through conduction, convection, and radiation—and the mechanisms that different insulators use to try and reduce heat transfer between building elements. From one end of the diverse range of insulation products comes natural insulation such as sheep's wool, which when discussing presents the opportunity to explore how the follicles of animals in the *Caprinae* family produce wool—and how the scaling and crimp of that wool help to retain air, providing an insulating effect. Bales of straw can be used as a structural material that provides an insulating effect, as well as form. An exploration of this might involve asking the audience to question the properties of the material and the science that underpins this material's performance. A conversation that explores more modern insulation can be used as a forum to discuss the materials science and chemistry used to make these materials—and, in contrast, one can look at the Mylar films used to make "space blankets" and to insulate satellite components from the sun's radiation. By way of discussion of the different methods of heat transfer, a communicator might explore why these materials have different applications—why do we use wool at home and a space blanket in space? How does the science of heat transmission inform the applications of these materials?

Finally, what about the question of what makes us comfortable in buildings? The best way to communicate thermal comfort is by its absence—if the audience is made thermally uncomfortable, then a discussion of the effects could follow. To understand thermal comfort, the underpinning science of human physiology and metabolic rate must first be understood, coupled with an understanding of heat transfer between the body and its environment.

Furthermore, sustainable buildings increasingly employ integrated renewable energy technologies, which in themselves provide a rich opportunity for science communication. A practitioner will look at building technologies as black box components that can be assembled in given configurations to provide a certain performance—but the scientist will question how the device works.

Solar photovoltaic technologies can be used in science communication to understand some of the principles of photonics and how the photovoltaic effect applies to semiconductor p-n junctions, allowing silicon wafers to generate electricity. A second class of electricity-generating solar cell, the

Gratzel cell, or photochemical solar cell, is also likely to find increasing application in building-integrated form. A simple Gratzel cell can be constructed using glass slides coated with tin oxide, anthocyanin dye (from red berries), and some iodine. Understanding the photochemistry of such a device can be used as a platform for teaching an array of molecular science concepts—such as reduction and oxidization and the process of how chemical reactions can be used to shuttle electrons.

Solar water heating technologies fall roughly into two classes of system: flat plate collectors and evacuated tube collectors; both technologies can be used to communicate. Indeed, many modern solar thermal collectors use selective surfaces—these can be used as a vehicle for teaching materials science. Building-integrated wind turbines are a collection of novel technologies that are used to harness wind power on a smaller scale than conventional utility-scale wind turbines. While large-scale wind power is an economically proven technology, there is fierce debate about the efficacy of wind power on smaller scales, especially when installed in sites with a suboptimal wind resource. Investigation of how wind speed and rotor size correlate directly to power output can be used to communicate concepts of energy transformation, aerodynamics, and power laws. Exploration of the Betz theorem can be used to communicate why there is a limit to the amount of energy a turbine can extract from the wind.

Heat pumps are devices that can be used to pump heat from an external source into a building to provide heating. The advantage is that the energy input, usually electricity, to pump the heat is much smaller than the total amount of heat energy moved—resulting in improved heat output for a given unit of energy, over conventional solutions—using resistive heating elements. Exploration of heat pumps can be used to communicate the second law of thermodynamics, that heat cannot of itself pass from a cooler body to a hotter body. It is the heat pump technology that allows the work to be done to accomplish this. Furthermore, by getting an audience to look at heat-pump thermal cycles—for example, the vapor-compression refrigeration cycle—a science communicator can explore with the audience the thermodynamic laws of systems that can be treated as closed loops.

Gavin D. J. Harper

See also Alternative Energy, Overview; Solar Energy; Sustainability

Further Readings

Alread, J., & Leslie, T. (2007). *Design-tech: Building science for architects*. Burlington, MA: Architectural Press.

Brown, T. S. (2006). *The science of building*. Charleston, SC: BookSurge.

McMullen, R. (2007). *Environmental science in building*. New York: Macmillan.

ASILOMAR

The famous meeting often known as Asilomar, officially the International Congress on Recombinant DNA Molecules, took place at the Asilomar Conference Center, California, in 1975. Over 100 leading scientists, mostly biologists, together with a handful of lawyers and physicians (along with members of the press), came together to propose guidelines for self-regulation of recombinant DNA technology (also known as genetic modification or GM). The legacy of this meeting is substantial not only because it was a historic time in which scientists voluntarily addressed the hazards of their work, in this case biohazards, but also because they arguably avoided the imposition of stricter regulations through doing so.

Similarly, while Asilomar is heralded as stimulating debate on GM hazards, it is also referred to as containing debate within specialized circles, restricting public discourse. For those interested in science and technology (S&T) communication, Asilomar is an event that can still be used as a lens through which to analyze relationships between S&T and society. Reference to Asilomar helps one pose questions of whether a contested issue remains within public debate or if it has actually been removed from the public sphere through debate and whether the issue has been defined in purely scientific terms, and if so, what the effects of this might be. After introducing Asilomar, a case study of GM in New Zealand will be provided to illustrate how Asilomar is more than just a historic event, but is a useful reference point with continuing application.

From Concerns to Recommendations

Asilomar, rather than an event sparked by new developments in biology, can be seen as initiated because of the unknowns that accompanied those developments. In the early 1970s, researchers discovered how to cut and splice together the DNA of disparate species, and there were growing concerns about whether such experiments might create dangerous new organisms. One of the key figures in the Asilomar story was the chair of the conference, Paul Berg, a professor of biochemistry at Stanford University Medical Center, who had been working with recombinant DNA technology. In an experiment in 1972, he cut into fragments (or cleaved) the SV40 (monkey virus); then he cleaved another virus (bacteriophage lambda). He then spliced the DNA of the two viruses together. His plan was to place the new genetic material into a laboratory strain of the *E. coli* bacterium. However, he did not continue with the experiment due to fears, prompted by his colleagues, that the product of his work might escape into the environment, infecting the workers in the laboratory.

Such concern about potential biohazards associated with recombinant DNA technology prompted a group of scientists to write to the National Academy of Sciences (NAS) requesting an ad hoc committee be formed to investigate the risks involved. A committee was established by the NAS, and it recommended convening an international conference of practitioners to explore the matter, as well as a temporary moratorium on all recombinant DNA experiments.

Asilomar can thus be seen as developing from concerns among scientists themselves. The Asilomar conference produced and published principles for dealing with the risks and recommendations for containment. These principles proposed that containment issues should always be taken into consideration in designing experiments using recombinant DNA and that containment effectiveness should reflect the estimated risk involved as well as possible.

The recommendations were for various levels of biological and physical barriers to contain the newly created organisms. These recommendations were based on the perceived risks of the experiment and varied from minimal, low, and moderate to high risk. While the minimal risk level of containment recommendations included such things as not eating and drinking in the lab, the high risk containment recommendations included utilizing facilities designed to contain highly infectious microbiological agents. These facilities are equipped with isolation systems, with air-locks, and with systems to remove contaminants in exhaust air, liquid, and solid wastes.

Furthermore, Asilomar attendees proposed a voluntary moratorium on experiments that they thought may not be able to be contained by their recommended precautions. These included both the cloning of recombinant DNA either derived from highly pathogenic organisms or which contained toxic genes and large-scale experiments using GM that could make products that were potentially harmful (whether to humans, animals, or plants).

Why Was Asilomar Important?

Three key aspects can be seen as central to Asilomar's legacy through the way scientists defined the risks. First, their voluntary approach can be seen as leading to self-regulation, which was implemented across many countries. However, this in itself has been seen, arguably, as a way of avoiding stricter regulation, for as the policy processes of the nations were set into motion, the emergence of voluntary guidelines may have diverted attention from the need to regulate the experiments. Second, Asilomar had been touted as building public trust in the belief that science was in reasonably responsible hands through the cautionary approach taken by the scientists. However, Asilomar marked a shifting of the burden of proof from scientists having to prove safety to critics (various publics) to having to prove it dangerous. This is the opposite of the precautionary principle. Thus, the Asilomar process could be used by scientists to marginalize critics of GM by saying that there was a consensus on the safety of certain experiments established through the Asilomar recommendations.

Finally, and most important, from an S&T communication perspective, confining the risks only to scientific biohazards can be seen as scientizing the debate—that is, narrowly defining the issue while ignoring broader socioeconomic, moral, and spiritual issues. This contains debate within specialized circles, effectively removing the issue from public discourse.

At the time of the Asilomar conference in 1975, recombinant DNA technology was not a public issue—little was known of it beyond scientific circles. This way of defining the relationship between science and broader publics was a core aspect of Asilomar and its legacy. Maxine Singer, one of the organizers of Asilomar, suggested that Asilomar was important because it allowed them to take a scientific approach to the issues. What this meant was that GM could thus come onto the public stage as a narrow set of scientific concerns. In particular, the discussion could be restricted to questions of what research should be carried out and under what precautions. The possibility of a public debate on recombinant DNA technology was seen as having the potential to interrupt research. Thus, Asilomar can be seen as acting as a subterfuge, detracting attention from sociocultural issues.

It is this dimension, the use of the Asilomar legacy of scientizing debate and thus removing it from public discourse, that will be considered in the following case study of GM in New Zealand.

A Case Study of Asilomar's Legacy in New Zealand

New Zealand remained publicly quiet on GM for a protracted period, with biotechnology not gaining dominance in public discourse until the 1990s when it became a popular topic. At this time, there were many attempts by various sectors to influence the public on GM. People in New Zealand came together to create nongovernmental organizations (NGOs) specifically to organize resistance against GM. For example, GE-Free (genetic engineering free) New Zealand, a large umbrella group for most of these environmental groups, emerged from the Nelson Environment Centre to concentrate solely on GM issues. However, it was not just opposition to GM that was being actively cultivated; government and industry were keenly trying to create support for GM. The New Zealand Life Science Network, a pro-GM umbrella group, was formed by scientists and industry to foster support for GM. Furthermore, Crown Research Institutes (previously government research facilities now operating as commercial entities undertaking GM

experiments and dependent on private funding) consequently hired the public relations company Communication Trumps to help create a favorable public environment for GM.

With active groups attempting to mobilize various publics to support and to reject GM, and some vocal publics renouncing GM, genetic engineering became an important issue in the 1999 national elections. The postelection establishment of the Royal Commission on Genetic Modification (RCGM) could be seen as a victory for environmentalists, for New Zealand's environmental political party, the Greens, had made their desire for a commission into GM one of their main campaign issues. The elections had ushered in a change in New Zealand's coalition government that was not able to form a majority and as a result, gave the balance of power to the Greens.

The new Labour/Alliance government established this commission, which begin on May 8, 2000. Commissions of inquiry are rare formal settings for public conflict. Furthermore, as a Royal Commission, it was the highest level governmental inquiry possible in New Zealand. Royal Commissions involve a team of independent professionals, including a judge, who undertake a comprehensive investigation into an issue and provide nonlegally binding recommendations to government. With the establishment of a Royal Commission, public concerns were therefore seen as being taken seriously.

However, a tendency toward scientization and reliance on expertise was strong throughout the inquiry. This was highlighted in the handling of the public submissions on GM. Approximately 10,000 out of the 11,000 public submissions were either strongly against, or tending to be against, GM (9,998 or 92% of the 10,861 submissions), but these were dismissed by the commissioners when they stated that the terms of reference did not direct them to conduct the inquiry as if it were a referendum.

Emphasis in the inquiry was thus on the experts' submissions by those referred to as interested persons (IPs). This interaction with IPs is traditionally seen as one of the most important aspects of a commission, and this was one issue around which many of the concerns about the RCGM revolved. Being awarded IP status was crucial for groups since it was the only way they could present oral evidence to the commission and defend their evidence under cross-examination. Furthermore, this status entitled them to cross-examine others.

IPs were specifically defined as those whose interest in the proceedings was separate from the interests of the public more generally. This definition can be seen as attempting to separate the "experts" from the "publics." By doing so, a potential barrier to participation by public interest groups was created, as expertise was presumably easier to establish for groups in the GM industry than for environmental or other groups representing public opposition to GM.

A further barrier was that all IPs were required to present their arguments within a template consisting of 16 stand-alone questions. In setting this condition of separate answers that could not be cross-referenced, the commission constrained those submitting, denying the need to contextualize some arguments about GM within the framework of a particular worldview. For those operating from a reductionist scientific perspective, in which issues can be seen in isolation to each other, this was not an obstacle, and bioproponents expressed that they had not experienced it as a problem. In contrast, environmentalists expressed frustration in not being able to present a holistic answer addressing interrelated aspects of their concerns about GM. This meant they could not adequately contextualize their answers within their own worldviews by explaining the values that underlay their positions. In effect, this meant that reductionist scientific answers (in this case, answers supporting GM) were advantaged, while the holistic responses (in this case, answers opposing GM) were disadvantaged by the process. Thus, the commission, which was widely perceived a priori as a conduit to support the wishes of the public majority, instead facilitated disempowering this majority.

Asilomar (and the parallel New Zealand case) can thus be seen as analyzing recombinant DNA issues from purely scientific terms in isolation of broader considerations and sparking the beginnings of GM regulation across the globe. However, the legacy of Asilomar is not so much regulation itself, as it is the way it reflects a particular relationship between S&T and other publics in which truly public debate is marginalized. Asilomar, for S&T communicators, therefore, can represent a historic reference point for framing questions to oneself about the S&T issues at hand by asking: Is the case playing out in Asilomar's legacy?

Tee Rogers-Hayden

See also Agricultural Biotechnology; Consensus Conference; Deficit Model; Public Engagement; Risk Analysis

Further Readings

Berg, P., Baltimore, D., Brenner, S., Roblin, O. R., III, & Singer, M. F. (1975). Summary statement of the Asilomar Conference on recombinant DNA molecules. *Proceedings of the National Academy Science, 72*(6), 1981–1984.

Gottweis, H. (1998). *Governing molecules: The discursive politics of genetic engineering in Europe and the United States.* Cambridge: MIT Press.

Hindmarsh, R., & Gottweis, H. (Eds.). Recombinant regulation: The Asilomar legacy 30 years on. *Science as Culture* [Special issue], *14*(4), 299–412.

Rogers-Hayden, T. (2005). Asilomar's legacy in Aotearoa New Zealand. *Science as Culture* [Special issue], *14*(4), 393–410.

Rogers-Hayden, T., & Hindmarsh, R. (2002). Modernity contextualises New Zealand's Royal Commission on Genetic Modification: A discourse analysis. *Journal of New Zealand Studies, 1*(1), 41–62.

Royal Commission on Genetic Modification. (2001). *Report of the Royal Commission on Genetic Modification.* Wellington, New Zealand: Author.

ASIMOV, ISAAC (1920–1992)

Isaac Asimov is considered one of the most prolific science writers of all time and one of the most prolific authors, regardless of genre, of the 20th century. In all, he is credited with nearly 500 books, including hundreds of works of nonfiction, and had a profound influence on the development of science fiction and the popularization of science.

Asimov was born on January 2, 1920, in Petrovichi, Union of Soviet Socialist Republics. His family emigrated to the United States in 1923 and settled in Brooklyn, New York. He became a naturalized citizen in 1928. His family owned candy stores, which also sold science fiction magazines;

Asimov started out from a young age as a science fiction fan.

He was a smart child, learning to read before attending school and skipping grades so that he was only 15 when he entered Seth Low Junior College, and he later graduated from Columbia University in 1939 at the age of 19.

His first published story was in his high school literary magazine. He had a fan letter published in the magazine *Astounding Stories,* whose editor, John W. Campbell, would become a guiding force in Asimov's early career. When Asimov finished his first science fiction story, "Cosmic Corkscrew," in 1938, Campbell rejected it but encouraged him to continue writing. *Amazing Stories* published "Marooned Off Vesta"—Asimov's first professionally published story—in 1939 and "Nightfall," one of his most famous stories, in 1941.

Asimov's relationship with *Astounding Stories* (which would later become *Astounding Science Fiction*) and with Campbell would see the production of some of his most important stories, those from the *Robot* and *Foundation* series. In the 1950s, Asimov branched out from *Astounding Science Fiction* to publish in *Galaxy Science Fiction* and *Fantasy & Science Fiction,* and he also began publishing novels with Gnome Press (later he would publish with Doubleday).

His novels and short story collections include *Pebble in the Sky* (1950); *I, Robot* (1950); *The Stars, Like Dust* (1951); *Foundation* (1951); *Foundation and Empire* (1952); *The Currents of Space* (1952); *Second Foundation* (1953); *The Caves of Steel* (1954); *The Martian Way and Other Stories* (1955); *The End of Eternity* (1955); and *The Naked Sun* (1957). Asimov also wrote mystery novels and a series of books for children (the *Lucky Starr* novels, published under the pseudonym Paul French) such as *David Starr, Space Ranger* (1952); *Lucky Starr and the Pirates of the Asteroids* (1953); and *Lucky Starr and the Oceans of Venus* (1954). The many collections and anthologies of his work included *Robot Visions* and the posthumous *Magic: The Final Fantasy Collection.* Later, several novels and stories were made into films, including *I, Robot* and *The Bicentennial Man.*

The *Foundation* series, a major assemblage of Asimov's work produced in the 1940s and 1950s, was published in magazines as stories and then collected into a trilogy of novels—*Foundation,* *Foundation and Empire,* and *Second Foundation.* The series, which traces the history of an imagined future society, was inspired by Edward Gibbon's *Decline and Fall of the Roman Empire.* The series received the Hugo Award as the best all-time science fiction series from the World Science Fiction Convention in 1966. Asimov continued the series in the 1980s with *Foundation's Edge.* His last novel, *Forward the Foundation,* was published posthumously in 1993.

There was a long break between Asimov's science fiction of the 1940s and 1950s and science fiction written decades later. Meanwhile, Asimov had a university career at Boston University's School of Medicine, beginning in 1949, and he stayed affiliated with the university throughout his lifetime. Asimov also started working on nonfiction books in the 1950s. His first was *Biochemistry and Human Metabolism,* which he cowrote with colleagues from Boston University's School of Medicine. He became a major popularizer of science in addition to his career in science fiction. He turned out to be a profoundly able explainer of science for laypeople, writing about a diverse spectrum of areas, including physics, mathematics, astronomy, and earth science.

He also wrote on subjects outside of science, such as the Bible and Shakespeare. He was well known for his public speaking ability and storytelling, and he wrote several autobiographies, including *Memory Yet Green* (1979) and *I. Asimov: A Memoir* (1994), as well as *It's Been a Good Life* (2002), a posthumous collection of autobiographical writings.

Asimov's many awards include several additional Hugo Awards for his short stories and novels, as well as a special Hugo Award for distinguished contributions to the field (1963). Other Asimov awards include the Science Fiction Writers of America Grand Master Award (1986). He was inducted into the Science Fiction and Fantasy Hall of Fame in 1997. *Fantasy & Science Fiction* dedicated a special issue to him in October 1966, and his name was attached to a magazine begun in 1976, *Isaac Asimov's Science Fiction Magazine.* The American Humanist Society named him 1984's Humanist of the Year; he later became president of the society.

With a reach that extended throughout the publishing and film worlds, Asimov's life, from 1920 to

1992, paralleled the rise of 20th-century Big Science and was interwoven with the rise of science fiction.

David Amber

See also Science Fiction

Further Readings

Asimov, I. (1979). *In memory yet green: The autobiography of Isaac Asimov 1920–1954*. New York: Doubleday.

Asimov, I. (1980). *In joy still felt: The autobiography of Isaac Asimov 1954–1978*. New York: Doubleday.

Asimov, I. (1994) *I. Asimov: A memoir*. New York: Doubleday.

Asimov, I., & Asimov, J. J. (2002). *It's been a good life*. Amherst, NY: Prometheus.

Asimov, I., & Asimov, S. (1996). *Yours, Asimov: A life in letters*. New York: Doubleday.

Isaac Asimov Home Page: www.asimovonline.com

ASSOCIATION FOR COMMUNICATION EXCELLENCE

The Association for Communication Excellence in Agriculture, Natural Resources, and Life and Human Sciences (ACE) is the primary professional organization for academicians and communication practitioners whose major focus is agricultural and applied communications at colleges, universities, and government agencies. The international organization was first established in 1913 as the American Association of Agricultural College Editors (AAACE). Other U.S. agricultural communication milestones of this era included the offering of the first university agricultural journalism course in 1905, the beginning of Cooperative Extension in 1914, and the first radio news broadcast in 1916.

AAACE changed its name to the Agricultural Communicators in Education in 1978 and to its current name in 2003. The organizational name changes reflect the evolving professional roles of ACE members from largely publications and print-media-based communications in the early 20th century to today's wide range of expertise in publishing, marketing, management, and information technologies. The new nomenclature also reflects expansion of land grant university communications beyond primarily agricultural subject matter to environmental and consumer science areas.

ACE fulfills its mission by raising the visibility of this specialized communication field and by providing professional development opportunities for its members. Professional development needs of ACE's 550 members are served through 14 special interest groups that span such areas as electronic media, graphic design, distance education, writing, research, management, diversity, and international affairs. Professional development is also offered through ACE's popular Critique and Awards Program, which recognizes excellence in members' communications work. ACE also recognizes nonmembers' significant contributions to the field of agriculture, natural resources, or life and human sciences with its prestigious Reuben Brigham Award, established in 1947. The award is named for one of the venerable early leaders of the profession who also served as the organization's 11th president in the mid-1920s.

The organization's flagship activity is its international conference, which has been held annually for the past 95 years except for 1 year during the Great Depression and 3 years during World War II. ACE conferences offer dozens of professional development sessions, demonstrations of new technology, well-known speakers and presenters, networking opportunities, and panel discussions focused on critical industry issues. Technology interests of ACE members are further served through joint meetings held every 2 years with the National Extension Technology Conference. Also offered are regional meetings and special workshops and educational programs such as the Media Relations Made Easy national workshops and ACE's newly developed Leadership Institute. Throughout the year, ACE disseminates information to its members and to the profession through its Web site and electronic lists focused on various communication subjects. Finally, ACE publishes a periodic newsletter, which has been distributed under various titles since 1919, and special publications such as *The Communicator's Handbook*, now in its fourth edition.

Agricultural communication and agricultural journalism faculty who teach, conduct research, and administer academic programs participate in ACE special interest groups in which they share curriculum materials, present research, and discuss topical issues in the field. Although they constitute a minority of the ACE membership, academicians make distinct contributions to the profession through specialized research and evaluation programs that help guide communication practitioners' activities. They also make contributions to a growing scholarly literature of agricultural and applied communication. ACE supports college and university programs in agricultural communication by collaboration with and mentoring of student members of the Agricultural Communicators of Tomorrow national student organization, established in 1970.

The focus on scholarship in agricultural communication was galvanized in the early 1950s with AAACE's launching of the National Project in Agricultural Communications. This Kellogg Foundation–funded project involved agricultural communication academicians and practitioners in the development of research-based educational materials for its members, the offering of consulting services to improve land grant university communications, and the sponsorship of various communication studies. AAACE members fulfilled key roles as writers and presenters on such topics as oral communication, written communication, and training methods. Although the project formally ended in 1960, it is remembered for its significant impact on the profession and is considered a milestone event in ACE history.

Today, research and professional development information is disseminated to ACE members through its annual conferences, special workshops, and through ACE's quarterly refereed publication, the *Journal of Applied Communications*. As its name suggests, content of the *Journal of Applied Communications* includes a unique focus on practical and utilitarian topics, such as various types of audience and readership analyses, case studies of new and emerging communications technologies, and development of academic agricultural communication curricula. The journal is considered one of the primary outlets for scholarship in agricultural communication and agricultural journalism.

ACE historical documents and archives can be accessed from Special Collections, National Agricultural Library, Beltsville, Maryland.

Mark Tucker

See *also* Agricultural Communicators of Tomorrow; Agricultural Journalism; Land Grant System, U.S.

Further Readings

American Association of Agricultural College Editors. (1967). *AAACE: Origin and development, 1913–1967*. Champaign: University of Illinois.

Association for Communication Excellence in Agriculture, Natural Resources, and Life and Human Sciences. (2002, July). *The records of Agricultural Communicators in Education (ACE)*. Retrieved June 29, 2008, from www.aceweb.org/publications/ace_archives_registry.pdf

Association for Communication Excellence in Agriculture, Natural Resources, and Life and Human Sciences: www.aceweb.org

Carnahan, W. E. (1993). *The presidents of ACE*. Columbus: The Ohio State University.

ASTEROID IMPACTS

Asteroids are small stony bodies that orbit the sun along with the planets. The orbits of some asteroids bring them near Earth. During the 1980s, scientists from a range of disciplines debated whether an asteroid colliding with Earth might have caused the extinction of the dinosaurs. In the 1990s, a small group of astronomers and defense scientists argued that the possibility of a future asteroid impact with Earth was a threat to civilization and required immediate action. Both the impact extinction hypothesis and the asteroid impact threat attracted widespread media coverage and public interest. In both cases, the notion of global annihilation drew on nuclear imagery and the networks of cold war science. These two episodes illustrate the role of popular media in the development of multidisciplinary research and in the promotion of new research topics, as well as the tensions this can cause. They also serve as examples of the sometimes close relationship, both discursively and institutionally, between natural science and defense science.

The Extinction Hypothesis

In 1980, geologist Walter Alvarez, with his father, the Nobel-Prize-winning physicist Luis Alvarez, and nuclear chemists Frank Asaro and Helen Michel, proposed that a layer of iridium-enriched clay found in a gorge in northern Italy was evidence of an impact by a 10-km-wide asteroid. They predicted that a similar layer would be found at other sites around the world, a prediction later confirmed. They also presented geochemical evidence that showed that the layer was located at the boundary between the Cretaceous and Tertiary periods (the K-T boundary) and thus was contemporary with the extinction of the dinosaurs. Their paper, published in the journal *Science,* reached a multidisciplinary audience of scientists. Physicists, geologists, astronomers, paleontologists, and evolutionary biologists joined in debate about the validity of the impact hypothesis. Broadly, while physical scientists were quick to accept the hypothesis on the basis of the geological evidence and astronomical knowledge about asteroids, life scientists rejected the hypothesis as unable to explain the full complexities of the fossil record.

The ensuing controversy, with its newsworthy combination of dinosaurs, global catastrophe, and celebrity scientists—for example, television astronomer Carl Sagan and paleontologist and popular science writer Stephen Jay Gould offered their views—was readily converted into newspaper and magazine articles and television documentaries. *Time* magazine, for example, published a brief account of the Alvarez team's findings a year before their paper appeared in *Science,* and the magazine returned to the story a further five times in the following years. It helped that dinosaurs already had a significant presence in public culture. Although earlier researchers had proposed impacts as an extinction mechanism and others had recorded the concentration of particular metals in the K-T boundary clay, the identification of a specific impact event at the time of the dinosaur extinction ensured that the Alvarez hypothesis reached a wide audience.

Both media reports and commentaries in scientific journals helped draw the geochemical findings to the attention of scientists in disciplines other than geology and geochemistry. A survey in the mid-1980s found that 30% of British and German paleontologists reported having first heard of the impact extinction hypothesis in scientific commentaries rather than in research papers, and a further 10% reported first hearing of it in the mass media.

The debate sometimes became heated. Alvarez referred to paleontologists as "stamp collectors"; Gould called physical scientists "arrogant"; paleontologist Robert Bakker said the idea of an asteroid impact had become "more a religion" than something with a scientific basis. Despite its role in enabling multidisciplinary approaches, the scientists frequently accused the media of corrupting the debate and fueling hostilities. Disciplinary communication practices were also criticized. When some astrophysicists entered the debate with claims that extraterrestrial mechanisms could account for a supposed periodicity in extinction events, the editor of *Nature,* John Maddox, complained that they were circumventing the normal channels of scientific publication by circulating preprints to select groups of colleagues—something that was standard practice in physics and astronomy, but not in other disciplines.

The Threat of New Impacts

The discovery, published in 1991, of a suitably large contemporaneous crater in the Yucatan Peninsula in Mexico lent further support to the view that an impact had played some role in the K-T extinction, although the precise nature of that role remained open to debate. By this time, a group of astronomers and planetary scientists had begun to use the evidence of past impacts to draw attention to the possibility of future impacts. Accumulating evidence over the previous few decades indicated that impacts were an ongoing feature of solar system dynamics rather than a completed phase of solar system history. Improved detection methods meant astronomers were identifying increasing numbers of near-Earth asteroids, and planetary probes had revealed the extent of impacts on other planets. The possibility of future impacts had been discussed in 1980 by Alvarez and others in the process of formulating a new vision for the National Aeronautics and Space Administration (NASA). The following year, NASA sponsored a conference at Snowmass, Colorado, on the consequences of asteroid impacts for human society, aligning the discussion of asteroids with the traditional popular view of comets as harbingers of human catastrophe.

However, the impact threat received little further scientific attention until 1989, when a NASA press release about the close approach of an asteroid then known as 1989FC attracted widespread media coverage. At about the same time, planetary scientist Clark Chapman and astronomer David Morrison published a popular book called *Cosmic Catastrophes* that included a chapter on the asteroid impact threat. The heightened public profile created political interest, resulting in two congressionally mandated NASA workshops, one on the detection of near-Earth asteroids and the other on means of deflecting a potential impact.

The Detection Workshop recommended that a new network of telescopes, named the Spaceguard Survey, should be set up to monitor all near-Earth objects with a diameter greater than 1 km. A decade later, the survey had catalogued half of all such objects and found none to be on a collision course with Earth. The Interception Workshop was held at Los Alamos National Laboratory. The majority of participants were weapons scientists, some of them closely associated with the Strategic Defense Initiative (SDI), the space-based missile defense system known to its critics as Star Wars. The weapons scientists argued that the greatest threat came from asteroids smaller than 1 km, a move that allowed for potential compatibilities between asteroid deflection systems and missile defense systems.

Impact science was already informed by the products of warfare. The study of asteroid impact craters had developed through comparison with the results of nuclear tests and nonnuclear battlefield craters. Now the scientists discussed the possible use of nuclear weapons to deflect incoming asteroids and the construction of a space-based defense shield to protect Earth. Many of the astronomers and planetary scientists were uneasy about the proposals of the weapons scientists. However, they also regularly invoked the language of war to describe the impact threat—for instance, referring to asteroids as "killers," "the enemy," "missiles," and "stealth weapons"—and they continued to meet with the weapons scientists over many years to discuss the merits of various mitigation technologies. The two U.S. contributions to the Spaceguard Survey both utilized military facilities.

Media's Role in Promotion

Both civilian scientists and defense scientists drew on science fiction stories to articulate their vision of a threatened Earth. For instance, the Spaceguard Survey took its name from a similar survey described by science fiction author Arthur C. Clarke in his 1973 novel *Rendezvous With Rama*. Clarke further elaborated his idea of an asteroid detection system in a short story published in *Time* magazine in 1992 and in a novel, *Hammer of God*, published the next year. Another science fiction novel cited by the impact scientists was *Lucifer's Hammer*, a 1977 postcomet-strike survivalist tale with strong racist undertones by Larry Niven and SDI advocate Jerry Pournelle. The impact threat was also presented in film. Inspired by a widely reported 1967 student exercise at Massachusetts Institute of Technology about a predicted close approach by the asteroid Icarus, the 1979 B-movie *Meteor* told of attempts to deflect an asteroid on a collision course with Earth. A similar scenario was presented in two 1998 Hollywood movies: *Deep Impact* and *Armageddon*. Both the 1998 films employed scientific consultants and served to further raise the public profile of the impact threat.

The visibility of the impact threat was further aided by the images of the impact of Comet Shoemaker-Levy with Jupiter in 1994, an event that again received widespread media coverage. Over the years, scientists had actively promoted the impact threat. Several, such as Chapman and Morrison, wrote popular books on the subject. Others contributed to newspaper articles or agreed to be interviewed for television documentaries. They construed asteroids as risky objects demanding some sort of action by framing impacts in terms of actuarial risk assessments, deriving annual death rates for once-in-500,000-years events and comparing these to the death rates from more familiar hazards such as food poisoning. They established a promotional organization called the Spaceguard Foundation, encouraged political bodies such as the United Nations to consider the impact threat, and successfully called for government funding of detection surveys. However, despite these promotional efforts, the scientists were often dismayed by the media's treatment of the issue.

As astronomical surveys started processing large numbers of objects, they occasionally identified asteroids that had not yet been observed sufficiently to rule out the possibility of impact with Earth on particular dates. The prospect of a specific asteroid impacting on a specific date in the near future made for regular stories in the news media on a roughly annual basis. Although journalists typically used conditional verbs, scare quotes, and humor to signal the improbability of impact, the scientists felt that the news articles failed to convey the uncertainties and small probabilities attached to potential impacts. They also complained of a "giggle factor" and thought that scientists' credibility was damaged by follow-up stories about revised calculations ruling out an impact. The reporting of asteroid 1997 XF11 in March 1998 raised particular concerns and led to discussions about how to manage the release of new observational data. On the one hand, astronomers needed to alert other astronomers so that further observations could be made; on the other hand, some felt that only fully checked and certain data should be released to the public. With an active constituency of amateur astronomers also monitoring asteroids, the division between public and science was not straightforward, and some scientists worried that withholding information would lead to charges of cover-ups.

In one attempt to control media coverage, planetary scientist Richard Binzel introduced a color-coded numerical scale, which he named the Torino Scale, to summarize for public audiences the danger posed by individual asteroids. However, journalists made little use of what was a predictive scale based on subjective categories. A more conceptually robust scale, the Palermo Scale, was adopted for use in computerized asteroid surveys in Italy and in the United States, but astronomers felt that its mathematical derivation made this scale inappropriate for public use. However, when in 2002 asteroid NT7 became the first asteroid to receive a positive Palermo rating for an impact within the next 100 years, indicating a risk of impact greater than the background risk, the media picked up the story, once again producing light-hearted pieces with playful headlines such as the British *Daily Star*'s "Armageddon Outta Here!" The coverage prompted another round of discussions among the impact scientists about how best to control the media. Having successfully placed asteroid impacts on the media agenda, thereby raising the political profile of the issue and securing funding for their surveys, scientists were reluctant to accept the news values of journalists that made stories about the "end of the world" irresistible.

Felicity Mellor

See also Astronomy, Public Communication of; Gould, Stephen Jay; National Aeronautics and Space Administration, U.S.; Sagan, Carl; Science Fiction

Further Readings

Clemens, E. S. (1986). Of asteroids and dinosaurs: The role of the press in the shaping of scientific debate. *Social Studies of Science, 16*, 421–456.

Davis, D. (2001). "A hundred million hydrogen bombs": Total war in the fossil record. *Configurations, 9*, 461–508.

Glenn, W. (Ed.). (1994). *The mass extinction debates: How science works in a crisis*. Stanford, CA: Stanford University Press.

Mellor, F. (2007). Colliding worlds: Asteroid research and the legitimization of war in space. *Social Studies of Science, 37*, 499–531.

ASTROBIOLOGY

The subject of astrobiology is of great interest to a wide variety of public audiences, and this interest is likely to grow as astrobiology investigations are launched on a growing number of space exploration missions. Astrobiology is the study of the origin, evolution, distribution, and future of life in the universe. It is a multidisciplinary field of research, drawing on knowledge and expertise in astronomy, biology (particularly microbiology and evolutionary biology), chemistry, earth and planetary sciences, physics, and many hybrid or subdisciplines. Astrobiology also involves, to a lesser extent, studies in the humanities (primarily philosophy and theology) and social sciences. The idea that life on other planets might actually exist (or have existed in the past) obviously captures public attention.

Astrobiology encompasses the search for evidence of prebiotic chemistry (chemical steps leading to the origin of life), signs of past or present life on Mars and other bodies in our solar system, habitable environments in our solar system, and habitable planets outside our solar system. It also encompasses laboratory and field research focused on understanding the origins and early evolution of life on Earth and on Earth itself, as well as studies of the potential for life to adapt to challenges on Earth (for example, climate change) and in space (for example, cosmic radiation and reduced gravity). Today, astrobiology investigations on planetary exploration missions are focusing first on determining whether other planetary environments are now or have ever been habitable.

The search for evidence of existing or past extraterrestrial life should be distinguished from the search for evidence of extraterrestrial prebiotic chemistry or habitability, and the search for evidence of extraterrestrial life should be distinguished from the search for evidence of extraterrestrial intelligent life. The search for evidence of extraterrestrial intelligent life is a very different enterprise than the search for evidence of extraterrestrial life. Search for extraterrestrial intelligence projects look for evidence of extraterrestrial technology—for example, radio signals that are not of natural or other known origins—as markers of intelligent life.

The study of the origins and evolution of life on Earth, the origin and evolution of Earth itself and its sister planets, the origins and evolution of life in the universe, and the origins and evolution of the universe itself are intricately intertwined. In their research on these topics, astrobiologists have learned that life as we know it—that is, carbon-based cellular life—can survive in virtually all terrestrial environmental extremes, from areas subject to nuclear radiation to permafrost and the Earth's deep subsurface. At the same time that studies of the origin, evolution, and distribution of life on Earth are revealing that life is highly resilient, these same lines of research are helping to reveal how life and its environment are deeply interdependent, improving understanding of life on Earth and prospects for life elsewhere, contributing to the understanding of global climate history and evolution.

The U.S. National Aeronautics and Space Administration (NASA) funds an astrobiology research program that is focused on three basic questions: How does life begin and evolve? Is there life beyond Earth, and if so, how can we detect it? What is the future of life on Earth and in the universe? Astrobiology research around the world tends to focus on these three questions as well. Australia, Canada, France, Germany, Russia, Spain, and the United Kingdom are among a growing number of nations that are funding astrobiology research. International collaborations in astrobiology are common.

The term astrobiology was officially established in the lexicon of space science in 1995 when NASA established its astrobiology program. The science encompassed by the field of astrobiology is not new, however. Scientific study of the origin, evolution, and distribution of life in the universe was well under way before NASA was established in 1958. For example, the theory of cosmic evolution underlying the study of the origin, evolution, and distribution of life in the universe predates the 20th century, the theory of chemical evolution leading to the origin of life dates back to the 1920s, and laboratory synthesis of amino acids under simulated early-Earth conditions first took place in 1953.

In 1959, scientists coined the term exobiology to describe the study of the origin, evolution, and distribution of life in the universe. NASA funded its first exobiology project in 1959 and established an exobiology research program in 1960. NASA's Viking missions to Mars, launched in 1976, included three biology experiments designed to look for evidence of life. The scientific consensus is, and long has been, that those experiments did not yield any evidence of biological activity on Mars. Nonetheless, a few scientists continue to argue over the interpretation of those results.

In 1995, NASA broadened the boundaries of exobiology to establish astrobiology as a program encompassing studies of chemical evolution in interstellar space, the formation and evolution of planets, and the natural history of Earth in addition to exobiology and evolutionary biology. Since 1995, the field of astrobiology has grown rapidly, the pace of discovery has been brisk, and the possibility of extraterrestrial life is now a serious scientific question. In 1996, NASA-sponsored scientists announced that they had found what they believed to be fossil evidence of ancient microbial life in a Martian meteorite (ALH 84001). Here again, however, the scientific consensus is that while fossil evidence of past microbial life on Mars may very well exist, analysis of ALH 84001 has not yielded any evidence of Martian life.

Recent research findings that are relevant to astrobiology include evidence of past and perhaps even present liquid water on Mars, an ice-covered liquid water ocean on Europa, the discovery of hundreds of extrasolar planets, plumes of water-ice particles erupting from Saturn's moon Enceladus, the possibility of liquid water beneath the surface of Titan, and identification of new forms of microbial life in an ever widening range of extreme Earth environments.

Detecting evidence of extraterrestrial life is a daunting task. Instruments must be extremely sensitive, and spacecraft must be sterile to avoid contamination of results. In situ analysis of planetary materials is far more limited than terrestrial laboratory analysis, and as yet, no samples of planetary materials have been collected and returned to Earth. Astrobiologists are identifying biomarkers—for instance, the presence of certain gases at certain levels in a planetary atmosphere—that would be signals for the possible presence of extraterrestrial life as we know it. Earth life is carbon based, requires water as a solvent, and needs energy (solar, geothermal, or chemical). At the same time, they are also attempting to define biomarkers for extraterrestrial life as we do not know it—noncarbon based, using solvents other than water, and perhaps involving different energy sources and chemical reactions.

Linda Billings

See also Astronomy, Public Communication of; National Aeronautics and Space Administration, U.S.; Planetary Protection; Search for Extraterrestrial Intelligence (SETI)

Further Readings

Committee on the Limits of Organic Life in Planetary Systems, Committee on the Origins and Evolution of Life, National Research Council. (2007). *The limits of organic life in planetary systems.* Washington, DC: National Academies Press. Available at www.nap.edu/catalog.php?record_id=11919

Dick, S. J., & Strick, J. E. (2004). *The living universe: NASA and the development of astrobiology.* New Brunswick, NJ: Rutgers University Press.

Grinspoon, D. (2003). *Lonely planets: The natural philosophy of alien life.* New York: HarperCollins.

NASA Headquarters Library, Astrobiology bibliography: www.hq.nasa.gov/office/hqlibrary/pathfinders/astro.htm

ASTRONOMY, PUBLIC COMMUNICATION OF

The public communication of astronomy shares many features with that of other scientific disciplines:

It has been done both by scientists and others; over time, the audiences have grown, thanks to material and social factors, and now include women, children, and most social classes; and all the media available have always been used. However, it is different in at least two important ways. The subject of stars, planets, and comets has been a part of popular culture from the very start. Space and time have always sparked our imagination and inspired our fears and admiration. And unlike, say, neutrinos or mitochondria, stars and galaxies are a part of nature that can still be studied by nonprofessionals. So today amateurs can participate in the production of new knowledge about the universe.

Planets and stars have always been a part of culture, even before astronomy itself existed. Apart from their obvious use for the calculation of calendars, they have been included in everything from cosmogonies to folk tales. Probably because they are the largest things we see in the sky and their movements are regular, the sun and the moon were worshipped by ancient cultures such as the Egyptian and the Aztec. And the positions of all the heavenly bodies were (and still are) considered to have an effect on our lives. Comets, on the other hand, are both more spectacular and more unpredictable and have generally been considered omens of ill fate.

As we have learned more about the universe, the subject of the cosmos has not disappeared, only adapted to each local context. Since the end of the 19th century great sagas are told in science fiction, where heroes and villains of all sizes and shapes fight among galaxies and black holes using the wildest technology imaginable. Today, our fears of the unknown remain and have been displaced from comets to unidentified flying objects. Both knowledge and questions about the cosmos have also inspired works in all the forms of high culture such as painting and music. In poetry, we find great examples, such as Alfred, Lord Tennyson—who had many scientist friends—wondering about formation of planets, or John Updike—who read a lot about science on his own—joking about the "attitudes" of neutrinos.

We could say that public communication of astronomy appeared with the first astronomer, for they have always been in contact with the general public. But nonastronomers have also been successful in this endeavor. One of the first, and still one of the best, examples of this case is *Conversations on the Plurality of Worlds,* a delightful book written toward the end of the 17th century by the French poet Bernard de Fontenelle. This agile dialogue between a lady and a gentleman of the court is divided into six nights in which the sun, the moon, the planets, and their order and movements are discussed. Through this book, the lay reader of the time became aware of Nicolaus Copernicus's heliocentric theory and especially of the Cartesian way of understanding the world. The piece probably became a best seller because it found the right balance between form and content: Fontenelle packaged pretty heavy science into the very friendly form of courtly culture. A good example of a similarly best-selling author of our day who is not a professional scientist is Timothy Ferris, whose 2002 book, *Seeing in the Dark,* documents the important role of amateur astronomers.

Perhaps the best-known astronomer and science communicator of all time is the American Carl Sagan, but he is definitely not alone. Through history, all professional astronomers have communicated their results to those around them. At the beginning of the 17th century, Galileo Galilei talked and wrote about his discoveries with the telescope and their implications for our worldview. He even traveled to other Italian cities in order to demonstrate the use of the instrument so others could confirm his results. Since then, many others have done the same, such as Camille Flammarion, who was especially interested in the possibility of life on other planets, or Arthur Eddington, who explained the very complicated subject of relativity for a general audience. When royal societies and observatories began to appear in Europe, they all spent some of their time and effort on what we now call public relations. In his time, Isaac Newton had little contact with others, but he always made sure his work and that of the Royal Society were well known in England and abroad. Observatories such as those of Paris, Rome, or Greenwich all permitted visitors and produced simple texts for broad audiences. Today, these same efforts can be seen coming from the National Aeronautics and Space Administration and the European Space Agency, as well as from each of the observatories and many individual researchers throughout the world.

The knowledge about the universe produced by astronomers has always attracted large audiences. Through time, these have been limited only by social or material factors such as spare time, the ability to read, or the subjects that were considered culturally appropriate. As noted, as early as the 17th century, women were invited to read about and discuss the cosmos. By the 18th century, science was considered a proper subject for children as well. Their small and very illustrated books had the main purpose of teaching them to read and giving them moral instruction, but they also included astronomy and other parts of nature. Such is the case of another best seller, *The Newtonian System of Philosophy Adapted to the Capacities of Young Gentlemen and Ladies.* This English book, which was supposedly written by Tom Telescope, was called a "philosophy of tops and balls" by the critics of the time. It is also a dialogue about nature, but in this case, one taking place between children.

The means for communicating astronomy in each period have always included everything that was available at the time. To the public lectures and books that were customary since at least the 17th century, other products were added as new means were invented or perfected. The appearance of mass media such as radio and television had the effect of spreading astronomy in society even further. Today, we can find the subject in articles in magazines and shows on radio and television. In all of these cases, we listen, read, or watch the message coming from popularizers. Internet is different, better in a sense because it allows us a certain degree of interaction with the source and with other readers. But it is also still possible to engage in a completely different activity: observing through the eyepiece of a telescope. Since these were invented in the 17th century, anyone who could afford one could have a telescope.

In fact, for the longest time, there was no clear distinction between professional and amateur astronomers. Anyone who had a good telescope and made careful and relevant observations could be considered an astronomer. But the introduction of physics and chemistry and the construction of large and expensive telescopes in the 19th century marked the beginning of the professionalization of astronomy. This process can be understood by looking at the life and works of Agnes M. Clerke, who was excluded from professional astronomy despite her abilities and knowledge. From the beginning of the 20th century, only a very few persons who have been awarded a specialized degree and have access to very sophisticated instruments can be considered professional astronomers; all the rest are called amateurs.

Today, there are a great variety of amateurs, however. Some enjoy making their own telescopes, many just buy them and prefer the observations, and all participate in groups to share their experiences. There are numerous groups of amateur astronomers throughout the world, from really large ones such as the British Astronomical Association, to groups of just a dozen people in smaller towns or villages. Amateurs do not keep to themselves, but also interact with professional astronomers to discuss the newest results or to participate in observations that can help in the production of new knowledge. There is plenty of work for all tastes, ranging from the lonely search for new comets to the carefully coordinated observation of variable stars.

Susana Biro

See also European Space Agency; Galileo Galilei; National Aeronautics and Space Administration, U.S.; Sagan, Carl; Search for Extraterrestrial Intelligence (SETI)

Further Readings

Chapman, A. (1998). *The Victorian amateur astronomer: Independent astronomical research in Britain 1820–1920.* West Sussex, UK: Praxis.

Ferris, T. (2002). *Seeing in the dark.* New York: Simon & Schuster.

Fontenelle, B. (2008). *Conversations on the plurality of worlds.* London: Tiger of the Stripe.

Lightman, B. (1997). Constructing Victorian heavens: Agnes Clerke and the "new astronomy." In B. Gates & A. Shtier (Eds.), *Natural eloquence: Women reinscribe science* (pp. 61–75). Madison: University of Wisconsin Press.

Riordan, M., & Turney, J. (2000). *A quark for mister mark: 101 poems about science.* London: Faber & Faber.

Secord, J. (1985). Newton in the nursery: Tom telescope and the philosophy of tops and balls, 1761–1838. *History of Science, 23,* 127–151.

ATTENBOROUGH, DAVID (1926–)

One of the best-known natural history filmmakers, David Attenborough has inspired people around the world about the planet they live on and the plants and animals they share it with. With a broadcast career spanning over 50 years, Attenborough has traveled throughout the world making the once inaccessible aspects of nature and science accessible to the general public. He is one of the best-known science personalities and science communicators of the 20th century.

Attenborough was born on May 8, 1926, in London, England. He was the middle child of the family. His siblings included elder brother Richard, younger brother John, and two sisters—Jewish refugees from Europe whom his parents adopted during World War II.

From an early age, Attenborough exhibited curiosity about the world around him, spending much of his childhood collecting rocks, fossils, and other natural artifacts. One of his sisters gave him a piece of amber that held the remains of early animals—this would be the focus of one of his television documentaries many years later. Collecting became a lifelong passion; Attenborough still enjoys collecting fossils and books.

Attenborough decided early on in his life that if he were to continue to higher education, he would study zoology, botany, and geology, which he did when he was awarded a scholarship to Cambridge in 1945. In 1947, he was called up for National Service, which he completed with the Royal Navy, stationed in North Wales and the Firth of Forth.

Attenborough's career as a communicator began at the publishing house Hodder & Stoughton, where he worked editing children's science textbooks. He then moved to the BBC, where he worked as a producer in the 1950s, one of a team of only six for the channel. He produced a variety of nonfiction programs ranging from interviews and sermons to political programs, cooking shows, and the ballet. From here, Attenborough moved onto natural history programs before eventually becoming the controller of BBC2 in 1965.

BBC2 had a policy of presenting programs that no other channel did. In this role, Attenborough helped introduce many new programs and sports to television viewers, such as snooker, 1-day cricket matches between county sides, and linked television programs such as *The Six Wives of Henry VIII*, which was written specifically for the channel. In the 1960s, documentaries—particularly 50-minute documentaries—were scarce on television, and documentary series did not exist on television at all until Attenborough and BBC2 introduced them.

Attenborough's first television appearance was completely coincidental. In 1954, a scheduled presenter for the live program *Zoo Quest* canceled at the last minute due to sudden illness. Because it was a live show, cancellation or use of other material were not viable options. So Attenborough was brought down from the control room and presented the program himself. In 1957, Attenborough formed the Travel and Exploration Unit for the BBC, which allowed him to produce and present *Zoo Quest* and other documentaries and series such as *Travelers' Tales* and *Adventure*.

Attenborough left producing shows for a few years when he took an administrative role as the director of programs for the BBC from 1969 to 1972. In 1973, he abandoned administration and returned to developing documentaries. He has produced many landmark series for the BBC, including the well-known *Life* series, which began with *Life on Earth* (1979), *The Living Planet* (1984), and *The Trials of Life* (1990).

These initial series were broad in content, largely focusing on the ecology, taxonomy, and different stages of life. Attenborough then turned his attention to more specialized series, including documentaries on life in Antarctica (*Life in the Freezer*, 1993), *The Private Life of Plants* (1995), and reptiles (*Life in Cold Blood*, 2008). In total, there are 79 programs in the *Life* series.

Attenborough has often used his programs to promote greater environmental awareness, including the impact humans have had on the natural environment and the ways in which these impacts can be halted or reversed. He is also an advocate for the teaching of evolution and natural selection in schools and strongly opposes creationism and intelligent design.

The regard in which Attenborough is held within the scientific and academic communities has been shown by the honors bestowed upon him. These include the naming, or renaming, of species such as the Mesozoic reptile *Attenborosaurus conybeari;* a New Guinea species of echidna, David's longbeaked echidna (*Zaglossus attenboroughi);* and the oldest known fossil of a fish giving live birth, *Materpiscis attenboroughi,* in honor of Attenborough's role in highlighting the scientific importance of various sites, species, and environments. Attenborough has

been awarded honorary degrees from the Universities of Leicester, Aberdeen, and Exeter and Kingston University of London.

Such has been his contribution to the public through his documentaries that in 1985 he was knighted. He has won numerous awards for his contributions to the public understanding of the natural environment including the Descartes Prize for Outstanding Science Communication Actions (2004), the Nierenberg Prize for science in the public interest (2005), and the Institute Medal from the Institute of Ecology and Environmental Management, United Kingdom (2006) in recognition of his outstanding contribution to the public perception and understanding of ecology.

Attenborough retired from making documentaries following the release of *Life in Cold Blood* in 2008. However, he continues to be a public spokesman for matters of scientific importance such as curbing population growth to environmentally sustainable levels and health awareness campaigns (blood pressure and hypertension). He has continued to promote environmental awareness and sustainability, emphasizing that the actions of individuals all contribute to making a difference. Attenborough's voice will remain synonymous with wildlife documentaries, and his work will continue to intrigue and inspire people about the world around them.

Merryn McKinnon

See also Environmental Journalism; Television Science

Further Readings

Attenborough, D. (Writer). (1990). *Trials of life: A national history of behaviour* [Documentary series]. Collins, UK: BBC.

Attenborough, D. (2002). *Life on Air: Memoirs of a broadcaster*. London: Random House.

British Broadcasting Corporation. (n.d.). *Sir David Attenborough*. [Science & Nature: TV and Radio Follow-Up]. Retrieved May 30, 2009, from www .bbc.co.uk/nature/programmes/who/david_ attenborough.shtml

ATTENTIVE PUBLIC

The term *attentive public* refers to a group of individuals within a society who have a high level of interest in a subject or issue and who believe that they are reasonably well informed about that subject. The term is a part of a broader conceptualization of issue specialization first advanced by Gabriel Almond in 1950 in regard to public awareness and involvement in foreign policy issues. Donald Devine applied the concept to politics generally, defining an attentive public for politics; although this application of the attentive public has not been carried forward in the literature, there is still substantial attention paid to individuals who do not vote and abstain from the political process. Further, the concept is very useful to science communicators because it defines one important audience and may be helpful in thinking about the level of communication appropriate to this audience.

Jon Miller and Kenneth Prewitt applied the concept to science and technology policy and were able to identify an attentive public that reported a high level of interest in scientific and technological issues and who claimed to be "very well informed." In addition to its application to science and technology policy and to politics generally, this concept has also been applied to energy policy, local school policies, and cross-national studies of science policy. Early measurements of the attentive public found that about 10% of adults in the United States qualified as members of the attentive public for science and technology.

In subsequent work, the attentiveness paradigm has been extended to include an *attentive public,* an *interested public,* and a *residual public* for any specialized issue or cluster of issues. In this conceptualization, members of the attentive public are both very interested in an issue and believe that they are very well informed about that issue. Members of an interested public report a high level of interest in an issue or subject, but do not think that they are very well informed about it. Members of the residual public for any specific issue or cluster report lower levels of interest in the subject and usually report corresponding lower levels of knowledge or understanding.

Attentiveness and Issue Specialization

To understand the rationale for and function of the idea of an attentive public, it is important to understand the present structure of the U.S. political system and the extraordinary changes that have occurred over the last 60 years. In the six decades since the end of World War II, most citizens have faced a growing number of competing demands for their time. Although the workweek has been stable for most industrial occupations for several decades, the effective workweek for many professional and technical occupations has been increasing. The number of two-job families has grown steadily for several decades. Most evenings, the typical resident of the United States can choose from 50 to 150 cable television channels, several thousand rental videos, multiple live musical or dramatic performances, athletic events, community college or university classes, and millions of Web sites. As many prominent scholars have argued, the competition for the individual's time has been growing over the last several decades, and that pressure continues to increase.

In this marketplace for the individual's time, politics and public policy issues are but one competitor among many. Each individual citizen must decide how much time, energy, and resources to devote to becoming and remaining informed about politics and to overt acts of participation. The evidence suggests that politics has been losing a portion of its market share of time for many adults. This decision to follow or not to follow political affairs is referred to as *political specialization.* While there are many measures of adult political specialization, one simple indicator is the proportion of adults who take the time to vote in national and local elections.

Among those citizens who decide to devote some of their time and energy to public policy issues, there is a second level of specialization involving the selection of issues to follow. The range of issues at the national level alone is far too broad for any individual to maintain currency, and when state and local issues are included, the full range of potential public policy issues is too vast for any individual to master. At the same time, the information threshold for many political issues has increased, requiring more specialized information to be knowledgeable about almost any given public policy issue. Inevitably, all citizens who follow political affairs must focus their attention on a significantly smaller set of issues, and research suggests that few citizens follow more than two or three major issue areas. This focusing on a limited range of issues is referred to as *issue specialization.*

It is important to note, however, that this is not the same process as *single issue* politics that revolve totally around one strongly felt position, but rather a rational and gradual narrowing, not necessarily overt, of the number of topics on which an individual can hope to remain adequately informed.

Those citizens who choose to follow a particular issue or cluster of issues and who feel that they are reasonably well informed about the areas are referred to as the attentive public for that issue. Thus, those citizens who follow foreign policy issues would be referred to as the attentive public for foreign policy, and those citizens who follow agricultural policy issues would be referred to as the attentive public for agricultural policy. An individual may be a member of more than one attentive public, but for the reasons outlined above, few individuals are able to follow a large number of issues.

Consequences of Issue Attentiveness

Individuals who are attentive to an issue are significantly more likely to follow that issue in various news media, to talk to their friends and family about that issue, to use candidate and party positions on that issue in making political choice decisions, and to contact public officials urging a particular course of action. Recognizing this specialization of interest, many candidates at the national and state levels seek to organize support within these communities of interest and to pledge to support policy positions desired by particular groups. In some cases, there may be a high level of policy agreement within an attentive public, but sometimes there are deep divisions. The continuing division of the attentive public for science and technology over issues such as nuclear power is a timely example.

It is also important to note that the growing specialization of information resources supports and advances the growth of attentive publics. The growth of cable television channels, access to the Internet, and the exponential growth of specialized Web sites not only compete with other activities for time, but also provide far more information on almost any topic at lower costs (in both money and time) than at any time in human history. It is now possible for millions of adults with a high level of interest in almost any issue or subject matter to find information and colleagues in cyberspace. The full

implications of this change will not be completely understood for several years, but all of the factors that stimulated the growth of issue specialization in the first place are still in place and growing in importance.

Implications for Science and Technology Communicators

The emergence of issue specialization poses new opportunities and new challenges for science and technology communicators. The attentive and interested publics are a ready market for science information. The growth and success of the "Science" section of the *New York Times* is directly attributable to the growth of the attentive public in the United States. The "Science" section provides sophisticated science information to a targeted audience of several million who have the resources to find and pay for it and the ability to read and understand it. The published reports (in print and online) from the National Academies of Sciences, Engineering, and Medicine are experiencing substantial sales growth as these resources become available to millions of attentive citizens through the Internet.

At the same time, there is a growing and important demand for scientifically accurate and conceptually simpler explanations of medical issues and conditions. Millions of adults are being told by their health professionals that they have a condition that is at least partially related to their genetic inheritance. Popular television commercials for statins have been able to convey to millions of adults that undesirably high levels of cholesterol may be related to what one eats and to one or more of one's relatives. Only a minority of U.S. adults understand the concepts of genetic structure and inheritance at a level sufficient to make sense of a good deal of new medical information, and the growth in popularity and use of online resources such as PubMed, WebMD, and similar Web sites testify to the growth of public interest in and demand for comprehensible information in this area.

It is clear that one level of communication is no longer sufficient (if it ever was). The most specialized and sophisticated audiences—the attentive public for science and technology and the attentive publics for other science issues and topics—demand more advanced material, and other audiences demand simpler material. Science communication is a growing area, but a fractured market and the emergence of multiple attentive publics is one part of that process.

Jon D. Miller

See also Health Communication and the Internet; National Academies, U.S.; Online Media and the Sciences; Science Indicators, History of the NSB Project on

Further Readings

Almond, G. A. (1950). *The American people and foreign policy.* New York: Harcourt Brace.

Devine, D. J. (1970). *The attentive public.* Chicago: Rand McNally.

Miller, J. D. (1983). *The American people and science policy.* Elmsford, NY: Pergamon.

Miller, J. D. (2004). Public understanding of, and attitudes toward, scientific research: What we know and what we need to know. *Public Understanding of Science, 13,* 273–294.

Miller, J. D., & Kimmel, L. G. (2001). *Biomedical communications: Purposes, audiences, and strategies.* New York: Academic Press.

Miller, J. D., Pardo, R., & Niwa, F. (1997). *Public perceptions of science and technology: A comparative study of the European Union, the United States, Japan, and Canada.* Chicago: Chicago Academy of Sciences.

Miller, J. D., Suchner, R., & Voelker, A. (1980). *Citizenship in an age of science.* Elmsford, NY: Pergamon.

Popkin, S. L. (1994). *The reasoning voter.* Chicago: University of Chicago Press.

Prior, M. (2007). *Post-broadcast democracy.* New York: Cambridge University Press.

Putnam, R. D. (2000). *Bowling alone.* New York: Simon & Schuster.

Rosenau, J. A. (1974). *Citizenship between elections.* New York: Free Press.

AUDIENCES FOR SCIENCE

Science journalists have been accused of putting both science and "objectivity" on a pedestal. Typically, they write for people who are already interested in science, persuaded of its value, and committed to its support. This describes a type of journalist who may fail to appropriately address concerns and controversies and who can sometimes be tempted to function, rather than as society's watchdog, as a sort of public relations agent for promoting science via one-sided messages.

It is thus especially ironic that persuasion research has shown us the most persuasive messages are generally two-sided, acknowledging criticisms as well as supporting arguments.

Support for science is likely to be strongest where people believe that their ethical, environmental, health, safety, economic, and other societal and values-based concerns are being addressed rather than ignored. While members of the attentive or interested public for science described by scholars are likely to be predisposed toward embracing new developments, they are a minority. Science journalism that ignores criticisms, fails to address concerns, and assumes that audiences are in favor of most science is likely to be ineffective in recruiting support—or generating interest—from other segments of the public.

Yet much of science journalism seems to assume a monolithically proscience audience—what we might refer to as the "fans" of science—and ignores the more typical reader who might be very well educated, but who does not always take the value of particular developments in science on faith. In fact, the audiences for science are quite diverse—and different from what science journalists often appear to imagine.

Science news that is written only for the "fans" of science or "converts" to a scientific worldview misses an important opportunity. The idea that a marketplace of ideas promotes healthy democratic debate is well established in liberal democratic theory. Those of us who would like to see broader public awareness and acceptance of a scientific point of view should embrace encouragement of the broadest possible debate and not be tempted to fall back on propagandistic approaches. Public debate, public engagement, and the consideration of criticisms and concerns should be encouraged. This is in the interests of science, as well as in the interests of democracy.

As with most rules, this one may have some exceptions. Sometimes society runs out of time for debate. Experts tell us we must address climate change now, for example. Similarly, looming pandemics, food safety crises, hurricane evacuations, and other societal emergencies call for a swift collective action rather than extended discussion. Yet, in the long run, cultivating public support for science could depend on our being better able to capitalize on opportunities for public deliberation.

The Variety of Audiences for Science

A single, monolithic public for science hardly exists. Rather, there is a broad range of publics or audiences—some enthusiastic and some skeptical—with different levels and types of interests in science. While the attentive public for science consists only of the small percentage of people who follow scientific developments closely, ranging from scientific workers to investors to those for whom science is simply a strong personal interest, science can reach many other publics who are also concerned with its trajectory, especially as it is seen as touching their lives.

In our high-tech economy and science-dependent society, many people recognize that their health and quality of life depend on advances in science, medicine, environment, and technology. In order to generate interest and support from the broadest possible range of audience members, science communicators need to connect developments in science to these broader everyday concerns. Targeting only the most enthusiastic and engaged segment of society will fall very short of reaching the potential audiences for science.

Everyone who relies on technology to get to work, play, or the grocery store; everyone whose health depends on good medical care; everyone whose quality of life is affected by the success with which we manage to protect our environment; everyone whose job is affected by advances in technology—in short, everyone—is a potential audience member for information about science.

In other words, almost everyone cares about some aspects of science under some circumstances. Sometimes, however, people need to be shown the connections.

The audiences for science include factory workers, nurses and physician's assistants, patients, cooks, groundskeepers, gardeners, programmers, soldiers and sailors, farmers, students, foresters, transportation planners, teachers, consumers,

people who like parks, people who manage parks, automobile owners, bicycle riders, pilots, environmentalists, natural resource managers, both users and designers of electronic gadgets, and all people who need health care, transportation, housing, jobs, and food—in short, everyone, not just geeks and nerds and people with PhDs.

People are especially likely to care about science and technology (S&T) not only when these seem helpful, but also when these appear harmful: when they appear to threaten the integrity of their environment, challenge their ethical principles or their way of life, or endanger the safety of themselves and their families. One reason why knowledge or awareness and attitudes do not correlate very well in many cases is that people may become extremely well informed as a result of reservations or opposition, not only because they are fans.

Science communicators need to think broadly about these audiences and not always concern themselves only with packaging information for the small proportion of the population that is most closely attentive to new scientific developments.

Even though quite a number of S&T broadcasts and publications (especially magazines) are directed toward those with a special interest in science, newspapers (whether in print or online) generally are not. Their present tendency to dedicate less space to science may be regrettable in some ways, but if it forces S&T back into the forefront (the front page and its electronic equivalent, for example), where it will be represented as an ordinary part of life and the economy, this could be a small blessing in disguise. Specialized coverage has its own audience, but this is only one among many.

Elite and Other Specialized Audiences

Even though pretty much everyone is a member of one or more potential S&T audiences, there are also very important specialized audiences—largely composed of society's elite—with particular interests in science. Chief among these are scientists themselves.

Major science journals such as *Science* and *Nature* include not just research reports presented in academic journal style, but also news, policy pieces, reflections, letters, and other commentary, as well as research summaries written for educated but nonspecialist audiences—for example, the sociologist who wants to read about string theory or the chemist who wants to read about new developments in archeology.

In other words, these hybridized journals are news magazines about science as much as they are scientific journals. They represent one end of a continuum, with purely popular reports of science of the type appearing in newspapers and general-purpose magazines at the other. *Scientific American* and *Discovery* are somewhere in between; they represent material written for an educated and interested, but not necessarily science, specialist audience. Television coverage of science—such as the well-known *NOVA* broadcasts—serves a similar audience.

The political and policy-making elite is another diverse group with a special relevance to science, whether or not they take a personal interest in it. Few members of the U.S. House or Senate have scientific training; although some of their staffers might, this is likely to be rare as well. People who lead and manage the various government agencies that are concerned with science, including those that provide research grants to scientists, may be trained in science, but may not practice it.

Some agencies and organizations recognize this as a problem and have developed various means to address it. For example, the National Science Foundation uses *rotators*—working scientists, engineers, and social scientists who take a year or two off to work for the agency, but who do not intend make a career of it—in many critical positions in its grant-making divisions. The American Association for the Advancement of Science has a Science and Technology Policy Fellowships program specifically designed to place individuals who have been trained—and often who have worked extensively—in scientific fields in positions working side-by-side with policymakers or agency managers.

However, in general, those who serve in legislative bodies that consider S&T regulation are not necessarily trained in science, and those who lead and manage government S&T-related agencies may be trained in science, but may not currently practice it.

From a strategic communication or public relations perspective, these decision-making elites are crucial audiences for science, but they are unlikely to read either research journals or specialized science magazines—nor are they likely to be found

Web surfing science blogs—on a regular basis, if only due to shortages of time. They likely do read major newspapers and news magazines, however. For these audiences, coverage of policy issues is at least as important as coverage of developments in the science itself.

Recent reductions in the numbers of sophisticated senior science journalists in major news organizations in the United States may therefore be a particular loss with respect to reaching these elite audiences. Only a very few publications—such as *Issues in Science and Technology*—actually specialize in S&T policy issues; this simply may not be enough to fill the gap.

Different Audiences, Different Views on Science

Neither scientific information nor the opinions of scientific experts necessarily are enough to shape the perspectives on S&T of these various audiences, from ordinary people to high-level decision makers. For example, public opinion research in both the United States and in Europe has shown that people are divided as to whether scientific or ethical considerations are more important to making decisions about science, and they are also divided as to whether they believe that the opinions of experts or those of ordinary people are more important.

While not everyone is a fan of science, the culture of the United States is nevertheless generally very proscience and protechnology, despite the existence of great religious and political diversity, which in turn means that significant subgroups may be skeptical about S&T or oppose some elements of it. Yet even in this proscience culture, only about a quarter to a third of the population believes that science is generally benign, that scientific facts are more important than ethics, and that science policy decisions are best left to scientific experts. This suggests that there are some audiences (or publics) who should be open to discussion about the ethics of policy, an area to which very little news coverage is generally devoted.

With scientific facts accounting for only a small proportion of scientific attitudes, what else matters to public opinion formation? Analysis of recent controversies over biotechnology, such as genetically modified foods, cloning, and stem cell research, suggest that different patterns of trust in leaders or spokespeople—whether scientific, environmentalist, political, or religious—have much to do with what different nonscientist audiences think about these issues. While some might see this as confirming an assumption that audiences and publics are irrational—or at the least nonrational—in their opinions, this perspective is limited.

There is nothing inherently irrational about listening to experts or other opinion leaders. Someone who is not a physicist and wants to know about physics is well advised to consult someone who does. Someone who is not sure about the ethics or policy of certain S&T developments may be well advised to consult someone who has ethics or policy expertise. So far, so good. Our reservations about this tendency for audience opinions to be persuaded by powerful others arise because we fear that people may listen to the wrong experts, whether on the topic of science or science policy. And since all values are not shared, especially obvious in pluralistic societies such as that of the United States, who is to say which experts are the "correct" ones?

In addition, through a process known as social amplification, risks that resonate with people's concerns (such as those associated with various forms of biotechnology) often receive extensive public attention and elaboration, while other risks (such as those associated with various forms of nanotechnology) are attenuated and receive virtually little public attention.

No easy fix exists for this situation; it may be that the best we can do in this respect is to promote the kind of dialogue that exposes everyone to alternative points of view, as idealistic as that sounds. Shrinking news holes will not help this situation, nor will the emergence of the Internet as a primary news source unless people learn to look beyond the electronic pundits most likely to reinforce their own perspectives.

Yet some hope might be found in the values that are broadly shared: health, peace, political stability, safety, economic security, justice, and (arguably) environmental integrity. Science in the service of these values will find attentive audiences everywhere.

The Future of Science Audiences

The audiences for science news are diverse, but how well are they being served by the existing news system—especially during periods such as the first decade of the 21st century, during which severe economic stresses took their toll on specialized reporting? While some specialized audiences are served by particular publications and broadcast materials that stress science, from those for the merely interested to those for the most highly scientifically literate, not everyone will take time out to educate themselves on most S&T issues. General-purpose news organizations, from newspapers and newsmagazines (in both traditional and new media forms) to broadcasters, will be hard-pressed to fill the void.

Recently, a group of research universities have taken things into their own hands, banding together to form their own direct-to-news-consumer research Web site called Futurity. But it seems unreasonable to expect this or other similar promotional efforts to serve the watchdog role of the journalist with respect to S&T—let alone provide information relevant and accessible to the full range of audiences, from ordinary citizens to policy specialists, or of topics, from the science itself to its social and ethical implications, that it might be of interest and value to society to consider.

Fortunately, efforts to develop new forms of science communication—from science museums and science centers that address a broad range of S&T issues more proactively, to the use of new formats such as science cafés and citizen juries for connecting ivory tower science to citizen debate—abound. We also learn about science in all kinds of unexpected places, from fiction to advertising, even posters and T-shirts.

But caveat emptor applies ever more strongly to today's audiences for S&T information because neither fiction nor advertising nor the promotional arms of research universities are in the business of telling the whole story, and while Web sites cover the full spectrum of perspectives, their quality is unpredictable and their agendas may be invisible. The new frontier of science communication will need to stress the cultivation of critical thinking skills for the consumers of information about science—which is all of us.

Susanna Hornig Priest

See also Active Audiences and Science; Deliberative Democracy; Science Indicators, History of the NSB Project on; Science Literacy

Further Readings

Gaskell, G., Einsiedel, E., Hallman, W., Priest, S., Jackson, J., & Olsthoorn, J. (2005). Social values and the governance of science. *Science, 310,* 1908–1909.

Miller, J. D., Pardo, R., & Niwa, F. (1997). *Public perceptions of science and technology: A comparative study of the European Union, the United States, Japan, and Canada.* Chicago: Chicago Academy of Sciences.

Priest, S. (2008). North American audiences for news of emerging technologies: Canadian and U.S. responses to bio- and nanotechnologies. *Journal of Risk Research, 11*(7), 877–889.

Sturgis, P. J., & Allum, N. (2004). Science in society: Re-evaluating the deficit model of public attitudes. *Public Understanding of Science, 13*(1), 55–75.

AUSTRALIA, SCIENCE IN

Australia is large in area (7,682,300 sq km, roughly similar in size to the continental United States) and small in population (21.5 million in November 2008, according to the Australian Bureau of Statistics). With a vibrant scientific community, Australia has 0.3% of the world's population and produces 2% of the world's research.[1] This entry provides basic information on the major agencies and institutions most involved in Australian science, as well as Australian organizations benefiting science communicators.

Government

The Federal Minister for Innovation, Industry, Science and Research has responsibility for a portfolio that includes the Commonwealth Scientific and Industrial Research Organisation (CSIRO), Australian Research Council (ARC), Australian Institute of Marine Science, Australian Nuclear Science and Technology Organisation, Questacon, and the Department of Innovation, Industry, Science and Research (DIISR). DIISR includes a number of divisions including Science and Research and has oversight of the Cooperative Research Centre program, Questacon, and National Science Week. DIISR houses the Office of the Chief Scientist, who is responsible for providing advice to government on a wide range of scientific and technological issues. National Science Week has run since 1997 and includes public events across the country that showcase science, scientific research, and related issues.

Universities

Thirty-seven of Australia's universities are public, and only two are private. Thirty-eight of Australia's universities are represented by Universities Australia, which provides information about Australian universities, development of education and research policy, and advice on government policy.

A greater percentage of Australia's researchers are employed in higher education institutions than in most other Organisation for Economic Co-operation and Development countries. In the United States, less than 20% of the country's researchers are employed by universities and government organizations compared to almost 80% in Australia, according to a 2004 report by the Australian Vice Chancellor Committee. Similarly, most of Australia's research infrastructure is in universities and other public institutions. Thus, Australian universities are important sources of information about current scientific research.

The Group of Eight is a coalition of Australia's most research-intensive universities. These universities have a broad disciplinary base and strong professional education. They range widely in size (13,400 students at The Australian National University compared to 58,000 at Monash University in 2008) and age (University of Melbourne was founded in 1853 while Monash was founded in 1958). All have strong international enrollments and collaborations. Indeed, international education is the top third or fourth export earner for Australia.

CSIRO

The CSIRO is the national science organization. It was formed in 1926 to conduct research to support agriculture, mining, and manufacturing. CSIRO scientists have many internationally significant accomplishments including invention of atomic absorption spectroscopy in 1956 and development of plastic (polymer) banknotes in the 1980s.

CSIRO is well recognized, respected, and supported within Australia, with over 6,500 staff researching in 16 divisions and nine flagships. Divisions cover a broad range of disciplines from entomology to materials science and energy technology.

Multidisciplinary flagships have been established to conduct research focused on specific issues of national significance. Industry partnerships and collaboration characterize the flagship program that was initiated in 2003, and in 2009, the program includes flagships for climate adaptation, preventative health, water, and niche manufacturing.

State Agencies

Each state and territory also has various agencies that conduct and support research and activities related to their brief. State departments of education have primary responsibility for primary and secondary schooling. Examples of other state agencies with responsibilities in some area of science include the Departments of Primary Industries, Environment and Conservation, Water, Mines, Energy, and Innovation and Industry.

Research Funding

Support for scientific research in Australia is provided by a number of different agencies and organizations, as described below.

ARC

The ARC is a statutory authority of the Australian Government. It manages the National Competitive Grants Program that provides a significant share of Australia's funding for research and research training across the sciences, social sciences, and humanities. The ARC advises the government on its research investment.

National Health and Medical Research Council (NHMRC)

The NHMRC is Australia's main funding agency for health and medical research. In addition to providing research funding, it provides guidelines for ethical behavior in health care and medical research and develops advice on health for government, health professionals, and the broader community.

Cooperative Research Centres (CRCs)

The CRC program was established in 1991 by Australia's federal government. Since that time, 168 CRCs have been established in six sectors: manufacturing technology, information and communication technology, mining and energy, agriculture and rural-based manufacturing, environment, and medical science and technology.

Key characteristics of CRCs are research partnerships between research organizations and industry. All CRCs include at least one university partner, and most include CSIRO. Commercialization, technology transfer, and education are important objectives of these research organizations.

Rural Research and Development (R&D) Corporations

Fifteen rural R&D corporations cover the spectrum of agricultural industries. The R&D corporations use grower levies and government funds to provide grants to researchers via a competitive application and review process. Through efforts in research and development, the Rural R&D Corporations reported in 2006 that the productivity of Australian agriculture has doubled over the past 25 years.

Science Centers and Museums

The major interactive science centers and museums in Australia include Questacon in Canberra, the Powerhouse Museum in Sydney, Scitech in Perth, and Scienceworks in Melbourne.

Visitors are welcome, and educational and communication resources are produced by museums in each capital city and many regional centers plus a wide range of other facilities such as the Australian Antarctic Division in Tasmania and Australia Telescope in Parkes, New South Wales.

Indigenous Science

Australia's original aboriginal peoples are thought to have migrated from Asia 50,000 to 60,000 years ago. From the end of the 20th century, there has been growing acknowledgment that indigenous knowledge is valuable. Indigenous science can offer knowledge of the Australian environment that has been accumulated over thousands of years. Fire management is one area in which indigenous science and Western science are collaborating.

Learned Academies, Associations, and Federations

The Learned Academies include the Australian Academy of Science, Australian Academy of Technological Sciences and Engineering, Australian Academy of the Humanities, and Academy of Social Sciences in Australia. The academies and organizations listed below provide points of contact for their communities and advice to the Australian government relating to their expertise.

Federation of Australian Science and Technology Societies (FASTS)

FASTS was formed in 1985 in response to cuts to science funding in the 1984 federal budget. It represents 60 scientific associations and societies by promoting consensus views on policy issues to government, industry, and the community. FASTS provides evidence to parliamentary committees and organizes forums about specific issues, as well as an annual Science Meets Parliament at which approximately 200 scientists meet face-to-face with members of parliament. FASTS also provides advice via ex officio membership for the president on the Prime Minister's Science, Innovation and Engineering Council.

Australian Science Teachers Association (ASTA)

ASTA is a federation of the eight state and territory science teachers associations. It promotes the profession of science teaching and provides teaching resources and professional development opportunities for its membership of about 4,000. ASTA publishes a journal, *Teaching Science,* and organizes an annual conference, CONASTA.

Australian Science Media Centre (AusSMC)

AusSMC is a national, independent, not-for-profit organization. Incorporated in 2005, it aims to provide evidence-based science to the public via the mainstream media through an independent service to news reporters providing reliable information and access to experts when major science stories break.

Australian Science Communicators (ASC)

ASC is an umbrella group that includes scientists, journalists, educators, and communicators. It provides meetings for science and technology communication professionals and fosters the professional communication of science and technology through promoting high standards in the crafts of journalism and other forms of science communication.

Nancy Longnecker

Note

1. Information provided by A. D. Robson, Chair, Group of Eight, personal communication, 2008.

See also Europe, Research System in; National Development, Science and Technology in

Further Readings

Council of Rural Research & Development Corporations' Chairs: www.ruralrdc.com.au
Australian Bureau of Statistics: www.abs.gov.au
Australian Government. (n.d.). *Our country.* Retrieved November 5, 2008, from www.australia.gov.au/about-australia/our-country
Australian Vice Chancellor Committee. (2004). *Beyond backing Australia's ability: The AVCC response.* Retrieved November 5, 2008, from www.universitiesaustralia.edu.au/documents/publications/AVCC-Response-to-BAA2.pdf
Commonwealth Scientific and Industrial Research Organisation. (2008). *The history of CSIRO: A summary of CSIRO's history and its achievements.* Retrieved November 5, 2008, from www.csiro.au/org/CSIROHistoryOverview.html
Michie, M. (2002). Why indigenous science should be included in the school science curriculum. *Australian Science Teachers Journal, 48*(2), 36–40.
Tropical Savannas CRC. (n.d.). *Fire agreement to strengthen communities.* Retrieved November 5, 2008, from www.savanna.cdu.edu.au/view/250363/fire-agreement-to-strengthen-communities.html
Universities Australia: www.universitiesaustralia.edu.au

AVIAN FLU

Avian influenza (AI), or "bird flu," is a contagious respiratory disease of animals caused by influenza viruses that typically infect birds. While AI viruses are characteristically species-specific, they can acquire the ability to infect humans. One AI virus, classified as the highly pathogenic H5N1, has affected more than 80 species of wild birds, led to the death or destruction of millions of domestic birds, and caused illness in hundreds of humans, killing more than half. Most humans have become ill with the H5N1 virus through close contact with infected birds. However, public health officials are concerned that the virus could develop into a form that could easily spread from human to human, creating an outbreak of illness that could rapidly spread around the world (a pandemic). In response, widespread efforts by national and international health organizations have been instituted to prepare for and to mitigate the potential impacts of a pandemic influenza outbreak, including attempts to use communication to alert and educate the public. Because of the potential threat to humans, news media often pay close attention to AI developments. To better understand the threat of AI, this entry explores the basic science of influenza, the impact of AI on wild and domestic birds and on humans, its potential to cause a pandemic, and what is being done in response.

Influenza Basics

The term *influenza* is thought to be derived from the Italian word for "influence." Influenza viruses belong to the Orthomyxoviridae family of RNA viruses, which are classified into three groups, known as Types A, B, and C. Type A viruses cause infections in birds, humans, and some other mammals. Type B viruses typically infect only humans, while type C viruses, which are rare, infect both humans and pigs.

Influenza A viruses are further classified into subtypes based on structural proteins projecting from their surfaces like spikes. One type of spike contains the glycoprotein hemagglutinin (H), an enzyme that helps the virus attach to and penetrate host cells. The other type of spike contains the enzyme neuraminidase (N), which helps the virus enter the host cell and to exit after replication. There are 16 different types of H and 9 different types of N known, creating 144 possible combinations. Subtypes of viruses are identified by their particular combination of H and N proteins.

According to the U.S. Centers for Disease Control and Prevention (CDC), human infections have been caused mainly by influenza A viruses containing the H1, H2, and H3 and N1 and N2 proteins, although only some subtypes (that is, H1N1, H1N2, and H3N2) are currently in general circulation among people.

Animals (including humans) can acquire protective immunities against influenza viruses by developing antibodies against these H and N proteins. Such antibodies are also the basis of influenza vaccines. However, mutations in viruses can cause chemical alterations in these proteins, yielding new strains of a virus that existing antibodies do not recognize. As a result, relatively minor variations (antigenic drift) in a virus can leave people vulnerable to getting the flu more than once. Consequently, influenza A and B viruses cause seasonal flu epidemics every year. Because viruses are constantly changing, there is no universally effective vaccine for influenza. Therefore, yearly seasonal flu vaccinations must be updated to match changes in the currently circulating flu viruses.

Abrupt, major mutations (antigenic shift) happen only occasionally, but may produce new strains to which no one has immunity, creating the potential for a pandemic. According to the World Health Organization (WHO), three such pandemics occurred during the 20th century. In 1918 to 1919, an H1N1 virus referred to as "Spanish flu" caused an estimated one third of the world's population to become sick, killing 40 to 50 million people worldwide, many within days of infection. Subsequent pandemics were both milder and kept in check by vaccines developed to fight the viruses. In 1957, an H2N2 virus called "Asian flu" killed an estimated 2 million people, and in 1968 to 1969, an H3N2 virus, the "Hong Kong flu," killed an estimated 1 million.

AI in Birds

All known subtypes of Type A viruses infect birds and are therefore referred to as AI viruses. AI virus strains are further classified as being either low pathogenic (LPAI) or highly pathogenic (HPAI) based on their ability to infect and kill domestic poultry, such as chickens and turkeys.

Viruses with the same combination of H and N proteins (such as H7N7 or H5N1) can have both

LPAI and HPAI variants. However, most AI viruses are LPAI strains with symptoms that are typically mild or not present at all. Consequently, they may easily go undetected, especially among wild birds, which typically do not exhibit symptoms when infected. In fact, according to WHO, all 16 H and 9 N subtypes of influenza viruses are known to infect wild waterfowl, such as ducks, geese, and swans. Routine tests of wild birds are nearly always positive for some AI viruses, though most are harmless. Yet because AI is continually present in wild bird populations, waterfowl serve as a natural reservoir of these viruses.

While LPAI viruses don't often cause harm in wild birds, the U.S. Department of Agriculture (USDA) notes that in domestic poultry, these viruses can cause symptoms that may include lack of energy and appetite, purple discolorations, swelling, nasal discharges, coughing and sneezing, diarrhea, lack of coordination, soft-shelled or mis-shapen eggs, and drops in egg production. Though these symptoms are typically mild, they can cause discomfort for the birds and economic losses for their owners.

In contrast, outbreaks of HPAI viruses in poultry are typically much more dramatic. They spread very quickly, causing disease in multiple organs and tissues, resulting in massive internal bleeding. As a result, deaths of entire flocks of birds frequently occur, often within 48 hours. Indeed, die-offs of thousands of birds have been associated with outbreaks of the highly pathogenic H5N1 virus.

Only viruses of the H5 and H7 subtypes are known to be highly pathogenic. However, LPAI forms of H5 and H7 viruses also exist. Indeed, according to WHO, H5 and H7 viruses are typically introduced to poultry flocks as LPAI. However, if permitted to circulate in poultry populations, the viruses can mutate into HPAI forms within a few months. As a result, the discovery of any H5 or H7 virus in poultry is always treated seriously.

Once introduced, AI can be spread from bird to bird through direct contact. It can also spread through contact with feces, blood, saliva, or nasal secretions from infected birds, contaminated surfaces (such as dirt or cages), or other materials (such as water or feed). In addition, AI viruses can be easily transmitted from farm to farm through the movement of live birds (wild or domestic), by

contaminated equipment, vehicles, egg flats, crates, and cages, and by people whose clothing or shoes have come in contact with the virus. WHO notes that HPAI viruses can survive indefinitely if frozen and for long periods in the environment, especially when temperatures are low. For example, the highly pathogenic H5N1 virus has been shown to survive in bird feces for at least 35 days at 4°C (39°F) and for 6 days at 37°C (99° F). Moreover, according to the USDA, 1 gram of contaminated feces can contain enough virus to infect 1 million birds. Therefore, to prevent the introduction of AI into their flocks, commercial poultry producers typically employ strict biosecurity procedures. These include restricting access of people and vehicles to their farms, protecting flocks from contact with wild birds, and disinfecting clothing, shoes, surfaces, and equipment.

To reduce the spread of disease, when H5 or H7 types of viruses are found in domestic poultry, potentially infected flocks are killed, and their carcasses are subjected to special treatment and disposal procedures. When practical, vaccination of surrounding flocks may sometimes be used to further reduce the threat of disease transmission. However, these methods are most effective when applied to large commercial farms, where birds are housed indoors.

Controlling the virus has proven more difficult in rural areas of developing countries where poultry is typically raised in small backyard flocks. As a result, outbreaks of highly pathogenic H5N1 AI, first documented in Southeast Asia in 1997, have become the largest and most severe on record. Countries throughout Asia, Africa, and Europe have been affected by the H5N1 virus, resulting in the death or destruction of millions of birds. In addition, to contain the spread of the disease, trade restrictions have been placed on countries with reported cases of HPAI, forbidding the export of uncooked poultry products. The resulting economic losses have been severe, especially in countries where poultry are important sources of both protein and income. Nevertheless, the highly pathogenic H5N1 virus remains a threat, causing new outbreaks and spreading to new areas, likely through a combination of the movements of migratory birds and through legal and illegal trade in wild and domestic birds used as food, pets, and breeding stock and in cockfighting.

AI in Humans

Influenza A viruses are known to infect many species of animals, including birds, pigs, whales, horses, seals, cats, ferrets, and other mammals, including humans. While most AI viruses are normally species-specific, they can acquire the ability to infect humans either through mutation or genetic reassortment. This is often facilitated by intermediate animals, such as pigs, that are susceptible both to AI viruses that normally infect birds and those that normally infect humans. If both human and bird viruses are present in a pig at the same time, they could mix genetic information, producing a new virus with the ability to infect humans, but with H and N proteins from the bird virus not recognized by existing human antibodies.

The CDC reports that some LPAI viruses are known to infect humans, resulting in symptoms ranging from very mild (for example, conjunctivitis) to those of influenza-like illnesses (for example, fever, cough, sore throat, muscle aches). Some HPAI viruses also infect humans with resulting illnesses ranging from mild to severe and fatal, causing respiratory illness (for example, pneumonia, acute respiratory distress, or viral pneumonia), sometimes accompanied by nausea, diarrhea, vomiting, and neurologic changes. Of particular concern is the highly pathogenic H5N1 virus. Since 2003, hundreds of people have been made ill by the virus in Asia and in Africa, with more than half dying.

The WHO presently considers direct contact with infected poultry, and surfaces and objects contaminated by their feces, as the main route of human infection with highly pathogenic H5N1. Most human cases have occurred in rural areas in Asia and in Africa where families keep small backyard poultry flocks. These birds are often permitted to roam freely, share outdoor areas where children play, and enter homes. Because infected birds shed large quantities of virus in their feces, these circumstances provide ample opportunities for exposure.

Unfortunately, because backyard poultry flocks are an important source of income and food for many households in such areas, for economic reasons, families are likely to sell or consume birds when signs of illness appear. Although cooking poultry and eggs to 74°C (165°F) has been shown to effectively inactivate the H5N1 virus, exposure can occur during the process of slaughtering, plucking, butchering, and preparing poultry for cooking.

Pandemic Influenza

While the large number of deaths from the highly pathogenic H5N1 virus has been tragic, public health officials are particularly concerned that when humans become infected, the genetic material of the virus could mix with that of seasonal flu viruses, making direct human to human transmission possible. This has spurred efforts by national and international health organizations and by private industry to prepare for and mitigate the impacts of a potential pandemic influenza outbreak. These include close monitoring of AI outbreaks, development of diagnostic tests and vaccines based on existing strains of H5N1, and the stockpiling of antiviral drugs and other medications that may be useful in treating those infected and in preventing the spread of the disease. Because the number of ill and dead resulting from a pandemic would likely overwhelm available resources and create severe social disruptions, public health campaigns are also focused on helping individuals, schools, and businesses prepare for pandemic influenza.

William Kingsley Hallman

See also Centers for Disease Control and Prevention, U.S.; Communication Campaigns in Health and Environment; Department of Agriculture, U.S.; Health Communication, Overview; Pandemics, Origins of

Further Readings

U.S. Department of Agriculture: www.usda.gov/birdflu

U.S. Department of Health and Human Services: www .pandemicflu.gov

U.S. Department of Health and Human Services, Centers for Disease Control and Prevention: www.cdc.gov/flu/ avian

U.S. Geological Survey, National Wildlife Health Center: www.nwhc.usgs.gov/disease_information/avian_ influenza

World Health Organization: www.who.int/en

B

BEAT REPORTING

Media organizations develop systems to provide information of interest to their audiences and to cover a broad range of emerging and ongoing issues within their communities. Beat reporting is part of a newsroom's system for managing and prioritizing news coverage. Beats are subject-matter divisions for potential news reporting. Typical news beats may include police, courts, government, education, business, sports, health, science, travel, entertainment, and lifestyle. Much like "beat cops"—police officers who patrol a certain geographic area—beat reporters may be assigned a particular geographic area. The government beat, for example, is often subdivided into city, county, state, and national government beats.

Beats also may be subdivided by level. For example, the education beat may be divided between K–12 and higher education. Similarly, the court beat may be divided into state and federal court beats. Larger beats also may be subdivided into areas of specific topical interest. The sports beat often is divided according to level—high school, college, and professional—and along topical lines, with reporters focusing on specific sports such as football, basketball, baseball, or hockey. Generally speaking, the larger the news organization, the more beats it covers and the more specific those beats are. At smaller organizations, one reporter may cover the entertainment beat, while a larger organization may have separate film, theater, television, art, and music reporters.

Often considered specialized beats, requiring additional background and specific area expertise, the health, science, and technology beats often do not exist in the very smallest news organization—such as those with five or fewer reporters. At somewhat larger institutions, one reporter may cover all three beats. At the largest organizations, however, several reporters will be assigned to these beats, and the beats may be subdivided along topical lines. For example, in some cases, the science beat may be divided into life, environmental, and physical science beats. In 2002, the *New York Times,* which has one of the few remaining stand-alone science sections, had more than 20 staff writers and regular contributors assigned to the section.

Expectations

Media organizations typically designate journalists as general assignment or beat reporters. General assignment reporters do not have a specific subject area or geographic area on which to concentrate, but write and produce news stories on an as-needed basis, acting on tips, responding to breaking news events, and providing support to beat reporters. Beat reporters are expected to develop subject-matter expertise, cultivate authoritative sources, and generate story ideas within their specialty area. Beat reporters are responsible for primary coverage of breaking news within their area of expertise, as well as for developing long-term, investigative, feature, and trend stories—often referred to as "enterprise" stories—from their beats.

Journalists' development of subject-matter expertise and a network of relevant sources are the primary advantages of beat reporting. With experience and expertise, science, technology, and health reporters have the background to (a) understand the specialized jargon, basic concepts, and underlying assumptions of the sources they cover and (b) anticipate breakthroughs and identify developing trends. Large networks of expert sources provide beat reporters with a more readily available pool of people qualified to comment on developments within the beat and in time, with more and better ideas for likely stories. Generally speaking, dividing news coverage into beats should produce stories with more depth and breadth in those subject-matter areas.

Challenges

Although beat reporting should produce better journalism, it also creates challenges and obstacles to good news coverage. Working on a beat influences how a reporter conceptualizes and approaches a story. For example, a national government reporter might focus a health care reform story on the political ramifications of the reform effort or on the number of votes that a particular proposal may receive. A business reporter may look at how health care reform will affect corporate profits, small-business owners, or the insurance industry. A health reporter might focus that same story on the fallout for health care consumers or look at how reform efforts will affect health care providers. News organizations thrive when they can foster a diversity of viewpoints and approaches to community issues. One of the challenges, however, is that long-term beat reporters may come to see issues only through the lens of their beat, which may limit their approaches to stories or exclude perspectives not consistent with the beat.

A pool of credible expert sources willing to talk to journalists is one of the advantages of beat reporting. However, a beat reporter must be wary of an overreliance on certain sources because it could limit the range of viewpoints and potential story ideas. Beat reporters deal frequently with the same sources, and successful reporters often develop positive relationships with their sources. The challenge for reporters is to keep the source relationships friendly without pandering to the sources and without avoiding stories or approaches because they could alienate important sources. Reporters who cover one beat long-term also sometimes run into the problem that they begin to write for the experts whom they cover rather than for their audiences, choosing topics more of interest to experts or using jargon that is familiar to the reporter and the sources, but not to the audience. This is definitely a potential problem in science journalism.

Although science beat writers are more knowledgeable and skilled than general assignment and other beat reporters in handling science topics, they still struggle because of the broad span of potential topics. Unless they work for a large organization with multiple science reporters, science journalists must be able to switch among physical, environmental, and life sciences, often covering astronomy one day and zoology the next. Except at the largest news organizations with the highest specialization among beats, it may take many years for reporters to develop the requisite expertise to credibly cover the breadth of potential topics.

Because science, health, and technology beats are considered specialized, the reporters assigned to these beats tend to be more experienced reporters who have spent several years writing on other beats. Having veteran reporters improves the quality of stories on a specialized beat. However, when newspapers go through reorganization and staffing cuts, veteran reporters often are the targets of corporate buyout and early retirement offers. For example, five experienced science reporters were among those at the *Boston Globe* who took early retirement offers during an early cost-cutting effort. The *Boston Globe* has since dropped its science section.

Beats are a way for the media to efficiently cover stories over multiple subject areas. They also reflect news organizations' preferences and priorities—in terms of staffing, financial support, and commitment to coverage. The division of labor in the newsroom signals the level of a news organization's commitment to science, technology, and health coverage. An organization that hires one science reporter and one health reporter but multiple government, education, and police and courts reporters is indicating the direction of its coverage and the perceived importance of these various beats.

S. Camille Broadway

See also Career Paths, Science/Environmental Journalism; Newspaper Science Pages

Further Readings

Cornell, J. (2009, July). *The rise and fall . . . and possible rise again . . . of science journalism.* Paper presented at the meeting of the First International School of Scientific Journalism and Communication (Communicating Energy) held at the Ettore Majorana Foundation and Center for Scientific Culture, Erice, Italy.

Lacy, S., & Matustik, D. (1984). Dependence on organization and beat sources for story ideas: A case study of four newspapers. *Newspaper Research Journal, 5*(2), 9–16.

McCluskey, M. (2008). Reporter beat and content differences in environmental sources. *Journalism and Mass Communication Quarterly, 85*(1), 83–98.

Shoemaker, P., & Reese, S. (1996). *Mediating the message: Theories of influence on mass media content* (2nd ed.). White Plains, NY: Longman.

BIG SCIENCE

The term *Big Science* came into vogue in the 1960s thanks to two important books by physicists, *Reflections on Big Science,* by Alvin Weinberg, and *Little Science, Big Science . . . and Beyond,* by Dereck de Solla Price. Both authors focused on the rapidly increasing size and expense of scientific projects, identified this increase in scale as a distinctive feature of science in the post–World War II era, and worried about the consequences of the "disease" of Big Science. In his oft quoted book, Weinberg identified the "triple diseases" of Big Science: "journalitis, moneyitis and administratitis." Journalitis stemmed from the need for public support for large, expensive projects, which led to the requirement that scientific results be published in the popular press as well as in scientific journals, thus blurring the line between journalism and science. Moneyitis was the rush to invest money at the expense of thought, while administratitis was the overabundance of science administrators characteristic of large-scale projects.

Despite the implication that presenting science in forms intended for nonscientist audiences led to "disease," Weinberg was quick to publicize his critique in the nonscientific press. The discussion of Big Science tended to be shaped all the way around by professional self-interest. Weinberg, an administrator at the national laboratory at Oak Ridge in the 1960s, told the public that funding for Big Science ought to be confined to national laboratories to prevent the spreading of its contagion. Big Science bashing was still popular decades later. For example, those who coveted money allocated for the Human Genome Project in the 1990s referred to it as Big Science when speaking to the press or in the halls of Congress in the hope that invoking the pathological connotations of the term would derail its funding.

Other scientists found a way to turn the term Big Science inside out. For example, starting in the late 1960s, those promoting the construction of new, larger particle accelerators used the expense and size of their enterprise to advocate for even larger funding allocations. Such promoters traded on the U.S. predilection for the grand, arguing that the rapidly increasing federal expenditures for such equipment signaled the superior value of this type of research. The next step was to argue that this superior science, which was intrinsically expensive, required more funding to continue to grow and prosper and thus meet its grand destiny. The argument that large projects were grand and superior—and therefore, provided increased national prestige—was also used to leverage federal funding. Local newspapers often added the angle that such projects offered jobs to the communities where they would be built.

Scholars studying the organization and history of science have also proceeded down the trail blazed by Weinberg and Price. Some mapped the effects of growth in various fields such as high-energy physics research, space science, laser research, and large-scale biological science. Others challenged the notion that Big Science was a modern phenomenon, detailing the extent to which teams used complicated devices and procedures, for example, in astronomical laboratories, long before World War II. Still others came up with ways to categorize Big Science based on how work is conducted and controlled. They noted, for example, the differences between a locally administered particle accelerator or a large telescope and a far-flung collection of individually administered research projects such as the Human Genome Project. These alternate ways of thinking of Big Science also led to studies that deemphasized individual cases and instead focused on how science grows larger.

Along the way, some scholars began to question whether it was helpful for nonscientists to use the label *Big Science* at all. They noted that this was a loaded term because it had long been used by researchers to help win over the public and federal funding officials. These wary scholars worried that those interested in investigating large-scale projects—rather than arguing for or against funding for such projects—were picking up a rhetorical tool ill suited for their work. For one thing, uncritical acceptance of the Big Science concept might mean accepting the values of those promoting large-scale projects. There was some evidence for this concern: Scholars who studied Big Science tended to lavish almost all their time and attention on the grandest projects, particularly those in high-energy physics and astronomy. The critics identified another problem: To their ears, the very term Big Science implied that the most important feature of large-scale research was its growth and scale. Therefore, in their opinion, scholars of Big Science were limiting the parameters of their subject matter, as well as their critical perspective. To avoid what they referred to as a preoccupation with bigness, these scholars suggested focusing on the systems and networks that form and facilitate the development of large-scale projects. They also encouraged greater study of large-scale projects in a wide variety of scientific fields (for example, in the biological sciences), as well as the investigation of different scales of large-scale science (for example, the large, but not necessarily the largest, particle accelerators).

Whatever the merits of such arguments, scholars have continued to be fascinated by the continued development of large-scale research. Recently, for example, some have argued that Big Science has evolved into something they call "megascience." This new form of Big Science began developing at the end of the 1970s when the price tags for equipment, groups, bureaucracy, and time scales grew larger even as resources for large projects (scientists as well as federal funding) became limited. As a result, researchers were forced to downsize where they could. In the era of megascience, resources were so scarce that researchers could be a part of only a limited number of measurements or experiments, facilities could support only a limited number of projects, and nations could support only a limited number of facilities. In that sense, megascience was actually smaller than Big Science.

Weinberg, however, would still be appalled at Big Science in the 21st century. Clearly, moneyitis, administratitis, and journalitis are alive and well. Large-scale research requires large infusions of money and great attention to raising it, and the large, complicated apparatus of such projects—plus the pressure for accountability to the public and federal government that goes with this expense—has led to an ever-larger number of science administrators. And of course the size, expense, and need for public accountability means that large-scale science is of significant interest to both journalists and the public, while those advocating such projects need journalism more than ever before.

Catherine Westfall

See also Human Genome Project; Particle Accelerators

Further Readings

de Solla Price, D. (1963). *Little science, Big Science . . . and beyond.* New York: Oxford University Press.

Capshew, J. H., & Rader, K. (1992). Big Science: Price to present. *Osiris, 7,* 3–25.

Galison, P., & Hevly, B. (Eds.). (1992). *Big Science: The growth of large-scale research.* Stanford, CA: Stanford University Press.

Weinberg, A. (1967). *Reflections on Big Science.* Cambridge: MIT Press.

Westfall, C. (2003). Rethinking Big Science: Modest, mezzo, grand science and the development of the Bevalac, 1971–1993. *Isis, 94,* 30–56.

BIOETHICISTS AS SOURCES

Bioethicists are increasingly used by reporters as expert sources in media stories about science and technology. Prompted by controversial topics such as genetically modified food, human cloning, and nanotechnology, reporting on bioethical issues has grown while a new type of expert, the bio-ethicist, has gained credibility and prominence through the media. Journalists and bioethicists have developed a mutually beneficial relationship, although many news consumers are unsure about who bioethicists are and what they do.

Bioethicists specialize in studying the ethical aspects of the life sciences, health care, and technology. The field of bioethics emerged in the late 1960s at the intersection of science, medicine, and ethics. Over time, bioethicists have become an accepted source of moral guidance, a role once reserved for clergy members and philosophers. Bioethicists advise patients and health care professionals on making difficult medical decisions, such as end-of-life care. They also play a part in science and technology policy making and counsel research institutions, hospitals, government agencies, and the courts on ethical issues surrounding scientific, medical, and technological developments.

Before the 1990s, reporters covering science and technology primarily used scientists, physicians, and industry and government officials as expert sources. Since then, reporters have expanded their traditional list of expert sources by using bioethicists to help them make sense of the complex bioethical issues that often accompany developments in science and technology. Still, bioethicists had a relatively low profile in the news media until 1997, when Dolly the sheep became the first mammal to be cloned. Cloning is the production of a new, genetically identical animal from a single parent animal. Reporters covering Dolly sought out bioethicists to explain and comment on cloning and its ethical consequences, including the possibility that humans could be cloned. Worldwide media coverage on Dolly helped make bioethicists recognized public figures. In 2004 to 2005, bioethicists were again in demand as expert sources when the lengthy death of Terri Schiavo, a Florida woman with irreparable brain damage, spurred intense debate about right-to-life and right-to-die issues and captured the media spotlight.

Expert sources differ from other types of news sources reporters use during the news-gathering process to provide information for stories. Reporters use expert sources in the hope of enhancing the credibility and authoritativeness of their work; the experts, in turn, help shape the news by providing comment and context for stories. But it can be difficult for reporters to choose expert sources, including deciding which sources have real expertise and which simply have information. And although public opinion research indicates that people believe in experts less and less, studies have shown that reporters rely more and more on expert sources of all kinds. In general, however, there has been little research on who expert sources are and how they are used, as well as on how reporters determine their expertise.

Bioethicists are used most often as expert sources in media stories on science, medicine, and technology, with strong ethical implications. They have provided information and opinion on a wide range of topics, including the deaths of patients stranded at a New Orleans hospital after Hurricane Katrina, debate over whether consumers should be told about food exposed to radiation to kill microorganisms, developments in stem cell research, and the use of high-tech surgery to prolong the lives of pets.

The use of bioethicists as expert news sources involves several special issues. One of these is the diverse backgrounds and perspectives of bioethicists. Bioethicists may be philosophers, scientists, physicians, theologians, or lawyers by training; Catholic, Protestant, Buddhist, Muslim, or Jewish by religion; and conservative, liberal, feminist, or libertarian in terms of worldview, to name just a few of the many possible categories. Each type of bioethicist offers a unique perspective and approach to solving moral dilemmas. Yet despite these fundamental differences, reporters tend to use bioethicists interchangeably. In most media stories in which bioethicists are used as expert sources, a single bioethicist is quoted, meaning that the views of one bioethicist represent those of the entire profession. That is significant because while two scientists used as expert sources may provide nearly identical explanations of what stem cells are, it is far less likely that two bioethicists will offer similar opinions on the ethics of stem cell research.

Another issue is that the same bioethicists tend to be quoted in media stories time and again. Although there are an estimated 2,000 bioethicists in the United States, only a relative few have become frequent news sources. These bioethicists tend to be articulate and accessible. They understand the ways in which reporters work and can be counted on to provide catchy quotes while meeting reporters' deadlines. While reporters doing all types of stories often habitually rely on those expert sources who are responsive and have something interesting to say, using the same few bioethicists over and over in media stories may limit the boundaries of discussion on a bioethical issue.

As expert sources, bioethicists are much more likely to be used to provide opinion rather than fact. And while bioethicists may play a variety of roles in stories, they most frequently serve as critics or skeptics. As a result, reporters regularly use bioethicists to counterbalance the often optimistic views of scientists, researchers, and government officials about science and technology. Bioethicists, thus, help highlight the controversy basic to these issues, making media stories more newsworthy.

As science and technology advance in the 21st century, reporters are likely to continue to turn to bioethicists to help interpret and comment on the bioethical issues that go along with these developments. And by using bioethicists frequently as expert sources, journalists increase the influence and credibility of bioethicists, thus helping to ensure their repeated use.

Marjorie Kruvand

See also Ethical, Legal, and Social Issues (ELSI); Interviewing Scientists; Scientists as Sources; Understanding Expertise; Visible Scientist

Further Readings

Boyce, T. (2006). Journalism and expertise. *Journalism Studies, 7*(6), 889–906.

Goodman, K. W. (1999). Philosophy as news: Bioethics, journalism and public policy. *Journal of Medicine and Philosophy, 24*(2), 181–200.

Pence, G. E. (1999). The bioethicist and the media. *The Princeton Journal of Bioethics, 2*(1), 47–52.

Rosenfeld, A. (1999). The journalist's role in bioethics. *Journal of Medicine and Philosophy, 24*(2), 108–129.

BIOFUELS

The identification and development of new sources of energy is a major challenge for our future and will continue to appear in news reports on a regular basis. This entry provides some basic background on a particular type of alternative energy source that is beginning to receive more attention: biofuels. These are sources of energy (solid, liquid, or gas) derived from biomass, which is defined as any organic matter that is produced and available on a recurring basis. Biofuels, therefore, are considered to be renewable sources of energy. The energy is supplied by the sun through photosynthesis, which captures solar energy and combines it with atmospheric carbon dioxide to convert it to chemical energy in various plant compounds. After the plant material is harvested, converted to a usable fuel, and burned for its energy, carbon dioxide is released to the atmosphere to begin the cycle anew.

Biofuels are distinguished from fossil fuels, which are derived from plant matter that grew and was deposited millions of years ago. Coal and petroleum are sources of fossil fuel. When fossil fuels are burned, large amounts of carbon that had been immobilized for eons are released into the atmosphere, increasing levels of carbon dioxide beyond the capacity of living plants and other earth systems to absorb it. In 150 years of increasing fossil fuel use since the beginning of the Industrial Revolution, atmospheric carbon dioxide levels have increased from 150 parts per million to 330, causing the atmosphere to retain heat (the greenhouse effect) and resulting in global climate change.

Interest in biofuels is based not only on a need to reduce emissions of carbon dioxide but also on the growing awareness that the world is running out of oil. Liquid transportation fuels are vital to industrial economies; with escalating petroleum costs (a fourfold increase from 2004 to 2008) as well as the reality that global demand for oil is beginning to exceed supply, many countries are turning to biofuels for transportation. Currently, the chief biofuels are ethanol, made from plant carbohydrates, and biodiesel, made primarily from plant oils. In 2006, world total ethanol production was 10 billion gallons, and world biodiesel production was about 1.6 billion gallons. Approximately 90% of global biofuel production was concentrated in the United States, Brazil, and Europe. European nations have tended to favor biodiesel made from rapeseed, while the United States and Brazil have focused more on ethanol from corn and sugarcane.

First-generation biofuels refer to ethanol made from sugarcane or corn starch and biodiesel made from soybean oil, canola oil, or palm oil. Waste animal fats can also be made into biodiesel. For ethanol, the starch from corn kernels is broken down to sugars, which are then fermented by yeast to produce ethanol. With sugarcane, sugar is simply squeezed out of the sugarcane and fermented. This general process has been used for hundreds of years to produce a variety of alcoholic beverages and is a mature technology. Biodiesel is made by mixing the plant oil with methanol to produce a methyl ester (biodiesel) and a coproduct, glycerin, that has a number of uses, including its use in cosmetics. First-generation biofuels have caused controversy because of concerns that diverting crops and cropland from food to fuel will have negative consequences for the food system. For this reason, the U.S. Department of Energy and the U.S. Department of Agriculture agree that first-generation biofuels will only be able to meet about 15% of U.S. liquid transportation fuel demand, which was approximately 150 billion gallons per year in 2007. To reduce the U.S. reliance on petroleum, the U.S. Congress passed the 2007 Renewable Fuel Standard, a mandate for 36 billion gallons of biofuels to be produced annually by the year 2022.

Achieving this goal will require the production of second-generation biofuels, which are produced from a variety of different conversion technologies and use nonfood biomass as the feedstock. Biochemical conversion uses plant fiber from grasses, crop residues, or wood to produce ethanol. Plant fiber is composed mainly of cellulose, a polymer (chain) of six carbon sugars, and hemicellulose, a polymer of five carbon sugars. Enzymes break down the cellulose and hemicellulose to constituent sugars, and microorganisms ferment the sugars to ethanol. This process is more difficult than the conversion of sugar or starch to ethanol because plant fiber contains large amounts of lignin, a substance that glues the fibers together and gives plants rigidity. Lignin, therefore, must be removed before the enzymes can do their work. This has been a costly and time-consuming process, but recent technological advances have improved the process to the point that a number of new commercial cellulosic ethanol plants are under construction, with some predicted to be in operation by the year 2010. An alternative technology for producing biofuels is thermochemical conversion, which uses high temperatures and restricted air to convert biomass either into a gas or a bio-oil. The gas can be burned directly or converted biochemically to a variety of fuels, including ethanol, ammonia, hydrogen, and diesel. Bio-oil, comparable to petroleum in composition, can also be converted into different fuels using processes similar to petroleum refining.

A major challenge for second-generation biofuels is producing the biomass in a way that does not compete with food production or degrade the environment. Massive amounts of material will need to be grown, harvested, transported, and stored. The current agricultural infrastructure was not designed to do this and will need to be redesigned. It is unlikely that biomass will be able to be transported long distances economically. Thus, the industry probably will be dispersed geographically, with different biomass feedstocks prevailing in different regions of the country. In some regions, crop residues will be part of the mix. In others, dedicated energy crops will be used, including grasses and trees. Using perennial plants wherever possible will be important for conserving soil and water. Municipal solid wastes, totaling 245 million tons in the United States in 2005, are another potential feedstock, particularly for thermochemical conversion.

In reality, however, biofuels can be only part of the energy future. The world simply cannot produce enough biofuel to replace petroleum-based fuels. Wind and solar electricity generation, as well as other new technologies, will be needed, in combination with increasing efficiency and energy conservation, to meet the increasing energy demands of the nation and world, as the era of inexpensive fossil fuels comes to an end.

Steven L. Fales

See also Alternative Energy, Overview; Climate Change, Communicating; Department of Agriculture, U.S.; Department of Energy, U.S.

Further Readings

Brown, R. C. (2003). *Biorenewable resources: Engineering new products from agriculture.* Ames: Iowa State University Press.

Mastny, L. (Ed.). (2007). *Biofuels for transport: Global potential and implications for sustainable energy and agriculture*. Sterling, VA: Worldwatch Institute.

Perlack, R. D., Wright, L. L., Turhollow, A. F., Graham, R. L., Stokes, B. J., & Erbach, D. C. (2005). *Biomass as feedstock for a bioenergy and bioproducts industry: The technical feasibility of a billion-ton annual supply*. Oak Ridge, TN: U.S. Department of Energy. Available at http://feedstockreview.ornl.gov/pdf/billion_ton_vision.pdf

BIOINFORMATICS

Developments in bioinformatics are driving many of the advances in genetics and genomics that are broadcast in today's news. For instance, on June 26, 2000, British Prime Minister Tony Blair and U.S. President Bill Clinton held a joint press conference, linked via satellite, to announce the completion of the "draft" of the human genome. The *New York Times* published a startling headline: "Genetic Code of Human Life Is Cracked by Scientists." The sequencing of the 3 billion base pairs constituting the human genome was the culmination of over a decade of work.

The Term *Bioinformatics*

Paulien Hogeweg and Ben Hesper coined the term bioinformatics in 1978 to refer to the study of informatics processes in biotic systems. Bioinformatics is the application of information technology to the field of molecular biology and more generally asking biological questions with a computer. There was a time when biology happened mostly in dissection labs and test tubes and under microscopes. Due to the development of genomic technologies, biology has been transformed from a science in which the human effort was mainly oriented toward data gathering to a science that generates a huge volume of data. Many scientists today refer to the next wave in bioinformatics as systems biology, a new approach to tackling new and complex biological questions.

Use of Sophisticated Analytic Tools

Bioinformatics is about searching biological databases, comparing sequences, and looking at protein structures. Systems biology involves the integration of genomics, proteomics, and bioinformatics information to create a whole-system view of a biological entity.

The origins of bioinformatics derive from the existence of biological databases. The first bioinformatics or biological databases were constructed a few years after the first protein sequences of amino acids became available, resulting from work on insulin in 1956. After the formation of the databases, tools became available to search sequence databases. Since these early efforts, significant advances have been made in automating the collection of sequence information. Rapid innovation in biochemistry and instrumentation has brought us to the point where the entire genomic sequence of several organisms are known. Projects to elucidate more than 100 prokaryotic and eukaryotic genomes are currently under way. The Internet is the virtual laboratory in which genomic research is now conducted.

In the early 1990s, scientists at the European Organization for Nuclear Energy (CERN) invented the World Wide Web (WWW) technology on the Internet (the now ubiquitous computer network developed earlier in the United States). The Web was the platform that solved many problems of maintenance, update, access, and integration of databases in molecular biology. In a way, without the WWW technology, the Human Genome Project would not have been possible.

The information archive within each organism is its genetic material (DNA and RNA). The human genome is only one of the many complete genome sequences known. The ENCODE Project (ENCyclopedia Of DNA Elements) has the ultimate goal of developing methods for comprehensive identification of functional regions of the human genome, including coding and regulatory regions.

Roderic Guigó, one of the main characters in the race for the genome project culmination, said that life begins when the nucleotides are arranged in the sequence of the genome. It is the particular order of nucleotides in this sequence, rather than its physical and chemical properties, that dictate the biological characteristics of living beings.

The human genome sequence is now complete, and it is joined with 18 archaea, 155 bacteria, and over 30 eukarya (the cow genome has been sequenced recently, according to an April 24, 2009, report in *Science*), as well as many other organelle and viral sequences that are now known.

Key databases containing this information include the archive of nucleic acid sequences known as the International Nucleotide Sequence Database Collection, maintained by Genbank, based at the U.S. National Center for Biotechnology Information, in Bethesda, Maryland; the EMBL Nucleotide Sequence Database, or EMBLBank, based at the European Bioinformatics Institute, in Hinxton, U.K.; and the Center for Information Biology and DNA Databank of Japan, located at the National Institute of Genetics in Mishima, Japan.

The archive of amino acid sequences of proteins is maintained by The United Protein Database, a merger of the databases SWISS-PROT, The Protein Identification Resource, and Translated EMBL. Three systems use Web technology to facilitate access to genomic information via distributed databases: ENSEMBL in Europe and NCBI and Genome Browser, both in the United States.

The implementation of genetic information occurs through the synthesis of RNA and proteins. However, not all DNA is expressed in proteins or structural RNA. Most genes contain internal untranslated regions called introns. Some regions of the DNA sequence are devoted to control mechanisms, and for a substantial number of regions, we do not yet understand the function. Proteins, in contrast, show a great variety of three-dimensional configurations with diverse structural and functional roles. Originally, bioinformatics concentrated on the study of the genome, but today it also extends to the study of the proteome, involving the patterns of gene expression and the complex networks of regulatory interactions associated with protein functions.

Alignment: Toward Structure and Function

Aligned sequences of nucleotide or amino acid residues are typically represented as rows within a matrix. In the precomputer era, sequences of DNA, RNA nucleotides, or protein amino acids were assembled, analyzed, and compared manually. Later, these problems were solved using algorithms instead. An algorithm is a complete and precise specification of a method for solving a problem. As soon as computers became available, the computational biologist started to enter these manual algorithms into the machines.

In general, this new discipline called bioinformatics could be summarized in the term *alignment*. In bioinformatics, a sequence alignment is a way of arranging the sequences of DNA, RNA nucleotides, or protein amino acids to identify regions of similarity that may be a consequence of functional, structural, or evolutionary relationships among the sequences. Sequence—structure—function: This is now a central concept of both molecular biology and bioinformatics.

Protein sequence alignment has become an essential task in modern molecular biology research. A number of alignment techniques have been documented in the literature, and their corresponding tools are made available as both freeware and commercial software. The two most commonly used programs are the Basic Local Alignment Search Tool (BLAST) and FASTA. BLAST finds regions of local similarity between sequences. The program compares nucleotide or protein sequences to sequence databases and calculates the statistical significance of matches. BLAST can be used to infer functional and evolutionary relationships between sequences and to help identify members of gene families. BLAST was developed to provide a faster alternative to the earlier FASTA without sacrificing much accuracy.

These programs are an ideal starting point to determine whether a related sequence, or a family of sequences, already exists in a database. The results from these programs will provide evidence of function, utility, and completeness of the gene product. Within the last decade, the sensitivity of sequence searching techniques has been improved by profile-based or motif-based analysis, which uses information derived from multiple sequence alignments to construct and search for sequence patterns.

An Applied Science

Computers were essential to today's developments in genomics, both for determination of the sequence and for development of applications to biology and medicine. Computer programs are used to make inferences from the data archives (containing information about genomes and proteins, mainly) of modern molecular biology, to make connections among them, and to derive useful and interesting predictions. Biological systems information retrieval is possible thanks to bioinformatics. The range of possible applications of bioinformatics is enormous: molecular biology, clinical medicine, pharmacology, biotechnology, forensic science, anthropology, and many other disciplines.

Núria Pérez-Pérez

See also Gene; Human Genome Project; Internet, History of

Further Readings

Claverie, J.-M., & Notredame, C. (2003). *Bioinformatics for dummies*. Hoboken, IN: Wiley.

Guigó Serra, R. (2007). Bioinformàtica [bioinformatics]. *Les biotecnologies: Treballs de la Societat Catalana de Biologia* [The biotechnologies: Works of the Catalan Society of Biology], *58,* 11–24.

Lesk, A. M. (2008). *Introduction to bioinformatics*. Oxford, UK: Oxford University Press.

BIOTERRORISM

In the fall of 2001, a bioterrorism attack using letters laced with anthrax spores killed five U.S. citizens. Termed "Amerithrax" by the FBI, the attacks stunned the nation and elevated domestic bioterrorism into the public consciousness. Bioterrorism and biowarfare are closely related activities that use biological organisms as weapons. Both exploit microbes or toxins for their deadly or disruptive effect; both are destined to remain important topics of both policy analysis and science communication. However, bioterrorism and biowarfare generally differ in a number of important characteristics. These differences might include motivation for use, resources necessary to execute an attack, likely perpetrators, potential targets, delivery strategies, and potential effect.

Biowarfare is a state-sponsored activity and is defined as the intentional use of microorganisms or toxins derived from living organisms to produce death or disease in humans, animals, and/or plants. Biowarfare agents are usually intended for military purposes and have potential for both operational (on the immediate battlefield) and strategic (beyond the theater of conflict) use. In contrast, bioterrorism is the random use of disease-producing microorganisms or toxins, generally for nonmilitary purposes. Examples include demoralizing or intimidating a population or country, exacting revenge, and affecting national or international policy. Bioterrorism is far less likely to be state sponsored.

Under certain circumstances, bioweapons are capable of producing significant numbers of casualties and causing widespread panic or severe economic damage. Plausible threats or even hoaxes can have a profound and destructive effect. It is this potential that earns biological agents, along with nuclear and chemical weapons, a place in the classic triad of weapons mass of destruction. Both bioterrorism and biowarfare are universally prohibited by either domestic criminal laws or by international treaties or agreements.

History of Biowarfare

The potential for use of biological organisms as weapons has been a concern for many decades. Indeed, there are numerous historical accounts of incidents when deliberate activities with polluted or contaminated materials were deemed responsible for significant sickness and disease in humans. Anecdotal examples include Scythian archers (440 BCE) dipping arrowheads in the blood of corpses to increase lethality of the projectiles, Mongols catapulting deceased plague victims over walls of besieged cities in the Crimea (14th century), and the purposeful distribution of smallpox-contaminated blankets among indigenous tribes in the United States.

The 20th century saw global military and ideological conflicts that spurred many of the world's industrialized nations' attempts to develop biological weapons. During World War II, several Imperial Japanese Army units covertly engaged in offensive biowarfare programs, including terminal experiments on prisoners of war and use of bioweapons against unsuspecting civilian populations in Manchuria and China. During the cold war, the United States and others conducted clandestine offensive biowarfare research and development programs on human, plant, and animal pathogens. In 1969, the United States unilaterally terminated its offensive biowarfare programs.

Alarmed by the proliferation of bioweapons programs, the international community sought to establish restraints. The 1972 Biological and Toxin Weapons Convention (BWC) was the first multilateral disarmament treaty banning the production and use of an entire category of weapons and theoretically halted offensive biowarfare programs in signatory states. However, there was no effective verification regime to monitor treaty compliance. Mounting evidence of Soviet noncompliance with the BWC resulted in the 1992 Trilateral Agreement on biological weapons between the United States, the United Kingdom, and Russia—the successor state to the Union of Soviet Socialist Republics. Neither the Trilateral Agreement nor the BWC could solve the dilemma of accurately assessing dual-use biological programs and facilities—those useful for both peaceful or defensive purposes and those with offensive military aims.

Even after the cold war, the prospect of covert, state-sponsored offensive biowarfare programs remains an international compliance and public health dilemma. Bioterrorism is the legacy of cold war state-sponsored biowarfare programs. Controlling proliferation, or the illegal spread of specialized bioweapons technologies or pathogens from state-sponsored BWC programs, poses one of the great biodefense challenges. Although spectacular advances in molecular biology provide critical tools to counter bioterrorism, commercially available biotechnology equipment has increased the possibility that bioweaponeers could either enhance the effectiveness of existing pathogens or could engineer novel or designer microbes for nefarious purposes.

Overview

Microorganisms are ubiquitous, present by the trillions in virtually all known environments, and are essential to life as we know it. There are a relative handful of microbes that can be injurious or have pathogenic effects for humans, plants, and/or animals. There are many factors that influence whether a particular organism is pathogenic and still others that can make it a potential weapon of mass destruction. The following provides a brief review of some of the important factors in biowarfare and bioterrorism.

Weaponization

Most potential biowarfare or bioterrorism threats require weaponization to be effective. Weaponization is usually a complex series of processes, preparations, treatments, and delivery systems designed to optimize the harmful effect of the organism. In most cases, weaponization involves creating an aerosol or airborne delivery capability while maintaining or enhancing the pathogenicity of the agent. An airborne attack can be launched from a distance, can greatly increase the number of victims, can be difficult to detect and counter, and can decrease the likelihood the perpetrator would be caught. Classic agents such as anthrax, plague, botulinum toxin, and tularemia would require some degree of weaponization to cause mass casualties. However, some pathogens have intrinsic characteristics that can obviate the need for sophisticated weaponization technology to be an effective weapon.

Highly contagious viruses such as smallpox and foot-and-mouth disease (FMD) are examples. Because of the level of sophistication and infrastructure required, state sponsorship has historically been thought necessary for successful biological weaponization efforts. Yet the general availability of advanced biotechnology methods and equipment has significantly altered this perception. The 2001 Amerithrax attacks that killed 5 and sickened 17 others show the complex challenges faced in assessing weaponization capabilities. According to published reports, the characteristics and quality of anthrax spores used in the seven known Amerithrax letters varied from sample to sample. Early letters reportedly contained spores with crude preparations that showed little or no advanced technology, while other samples displayed sophisticated properties that suggested a highly trained, competent, or even state-sponsored origin. Definitive conclusions about weaponization, if known, are not yet available in open sources.

Availability

A bioweaponeer must first acquire an organism to use it as a weapon. Most agents thought to be useful as bioweapons have natural reservoirs in plants, insects, animals, or man, providing variable availability to potential perpetrators. Examples would include agents such as anthrax, plague, botulinum, tularemia, FMD, and equine encephalititis. Smallpox, one of the most feared bioweapons, has only one natural host: humans. Global vaccination programs resulted in eradication of smallpox as a naturally occurring disease, making it theoretically impossible to obtain the virus from natural sources. Infectious disease and biodefense research programs in government, industry, and academia use pathogenic organisms in their work. To reduce the risk of theft, or the potential for dual-use activities that might serve as a source of bioweapons, laboratory safety, control, security, and oversight measures have been greatly increased in recent decades. Advancing biotechnology makes genetic modification and enhancement of known pathogens, or even the creation of new classes of novel bioweapons, possible. And finally, proliferation of dangerous organisms or bioweapons from covert or defunct offensive bioweapons programs is a lingering concern.

Asymmetry, Deterrence, and Retaliation

One of the benefits of having top-tier military combat power is that adversaries recognize an overt attack against the United States would likely result in a swift and severe retaliatory response. As such, a strong military generally serves as an effective and potent deterrent against attack. However, if a perpetrator cannot be precisely isolated, has blended into innocent populations, or has been identified as associated with a nation-state, the power of deterrence and retaliation is largely neutralized. Either a lone wolf or someone part of a small group that purchased, stole, or produced a bioweapon would likely not be intimidated by the threat of retaliation. This is called asymmetry since the national response cannot be proportional to the insult.

Agroterrorism

Agroterrorism is the malicious use of plant or animal pathogens to cause significant disease or disruption in the agricultural or food sector, and it poses a significant threat. Cold war biowarfare

programs invested significant resources to develop, weaponize, and test agents that would primarily affect plant and animal targets; the intent was to develop weapons to damage agricultural infrastructure and national economies. The ability to produce safe, plentiful, and inexpensive food contributes greatly to national prosperity. Consequently, a successful attack on agricultural infrastructure could have dire national economic consequences, with a ripple effect extending far beyond the direct cost of goods lost. FMD in particular poses a great threat to agriculture.

Unique characteristics of the FMD virus make it an ideal candidate for use as an economic bioterrorist weapon. It is endemic in much of the world, making it easily obtainable in nature. It is incredibly contagious by aerosol from one animal to the other, obviating the need for weaponization technology, and it affects multiple animal hosts. Intensive production practices for cattle and swine make them particularly vulnerable to FMD. Since effective vaccines are not currently available, the introduction of FMD into susceptible animals would immediately halt meat exports to FMD-free countries. The projected impact of an outbreak would be in the tens to hundreds of billions of dollars. Although it is not a human disease hazard, the economic, psychological, and symbolic effects of a bioterrorist attack with FMD would likely be a national disaster.

Countermeasures

Perhaps our most critical vulnerability to bioterrorism involves the lack of effective countermeasures for bioweapons, such as vaccines, antibiotics, antivirals, and protective equipment. Each potential biological agent or class of biological agents has different characteristics that make defensive measures or strategies vary from agent to agent. For the dozens of potential bioweapons identified, we have effective countermeasures for only a relative handful.

The Power of Bioterrorism: A Case Study

From late September 2001 through November 2001, at least seven letters containing brownish to whitish powdered anthrax were sent through the U.S. mail system. Five persons subsequently died from pulmonary anthrax infection, and 17 more became ill from the spores. The attacks had unprecedented and far-reaching effects. They terrorized a nation already unnerved by the 9/11 attacks, paralyzed the U.S. Postal Service, resulted in antibiotic therapy for thousands of people, and created a crisis in public confidence in the government. Law enforcement and intelligence agencies invested extraordinary resources to identify and apprehend the perpetrator, with no apparent success. Massive biodefense initiatives were launched, including emergency response programs and extensive biocontainment facility construction projects. Vaccine, treatment, and other medical countermeasures research and development programs were strengthened. Ambitious detector development programs, such as BioShield, were launched to provide critical warning for populated areas in the event of an aerosol bioweapons attack. Comprehensive new biosafety and security regulations were implemented, changing the landscape of biomedical research.

This response for five fatalities might seem disproportionate to the actual event. However, the recognized potential for bioweapons to inflict mass casualties dictated the extraordinary response. With a more efficient delivery and a wider dispersal of spores, the Amerithrax attack could have been a tragedy of considerable dimensions. Most believe that this event, eventually resulting in actions costing tens of billions of dollars, was likely the work of a single person or small group with a comparatively modest financial investment in the thousands or tens of thousands of dollars. Until apprehended, it is impossible to know the motives of the Amerithrax attacker, but this seminal event dramatically embodies the asymmetric power of bioterrorism.

Gerald Paul Jaax

See also Centers for Disease Control and Prevention, U.S.; Cold War Rhetoric

Further Readings

Alibek, K., & Handelman, S. (1999). *Biohazard: The chilling true story of the largest covert biological weapons program in the world—told from inside by the man who ran it.* New York: Random House.

Centers for Disease and Control and Prevention, Emergency Preparedness and Response: www .bt.cdc.gov/bioterrorism

Miller, J., Engelberg, S., & Broad, W. (2001). *Germs: Biological weapons and America's secret war.* New York: Simon & Schuster.

U.S. Army Medical Department, Borden Institute. (2007). Medical aspects of biological warfare. In *The textbooks of military medicine.* Washington, DC: Department of Defense, Office of the Army Surgeon General, U.S. Army Medical Department, Borden Institute. Available at www.bordeninstitute.army.mil

BOVINE SOMATOTROPIN (BST OR BGH)

Bovine somatotropin (BST), also known as bovine growth hormone (BGH), is a hormonal product that is part of the natural process of lactation in cows. Since the 1930s, the injection of natural BGH has been used sporadically in dairy cattle to increase lactation rates to meet consumer demands for milk and other dairy products. In the 1980s, it was found that BGH could be produced synthetically, making it more readily available. This BST is referred to as rBST, or recombinant BST—reference to the recombinant DNA or genetic engineering technology used to produce it. Similarly, rBGH is used to refer to recombinant BGH. (The two terms are interchangeable.) This was one of the first uses of molecular genetic engineering, although an artificial rennet used in the making of cheese was developed at about the same time.

By the late 1990s, over 1,800 research papers on rBST had been written, reflecting intense scientific interest in genetic engineering rather than any sudden interest in dairy farming. But at the same time, controversies arose about the idea of changing the way milk is produced, and these received substantial news coverage, as did other controversial aspects of agricultural biotechnology of which this was one of the first. The use of rBST has represented a special challenge for risk communicators because of the broad range of views that exist about it. While some dairy farmers saw rBST use as a way to increase milk output (and profits), others were concerned that this practice would help larger farms win out over smaller family ones. The use of rBST also touched off a number of controversies over food safety and animal welfare. This entry reviews the main controversies over animal welfare, food safety, and industrial food production associated with artificial hormone use in dairy cows.

Animal Welfare Issues

As animal welfare experts have pointed out, animals used in food production are often under a good deal of stress. These animals are frequently moved from place to place—one place for birth or hatching, another for early growth, another for later growth, and another for slaughter—and can be held in cramped or crowded living areas, often fed a diet meant to bulk them up as quickly as possible. The industrial production system is designed to help bring profits to the people who raise the animals. The animals are not pets, but are an investment for farmers, ranchers, meat processors, and others in the food industry. The idea is that the bigger and faster one can make an animal grow, the more profit one will make from that animal.

As with steroid use in humans, however, faster growth can lead to a number of problems. Putting a lot of weight onto young animals can cause problems in their joints and vital organs and can create other health issues. With the use of artificial BGH, dairy cattle are being asked to produce more milk than is normal. While some animals can handle the extra load, others develop a disease known as mastitis, which involves inflammation of the udder. Afflicted animals must then be given drugs to cure them, leading to more handling by humans and to more stress. Some studies have even shown that animals given rBST tend to live shorter lives.

Animal rights activists have argued that the use of BGH should be banned for the sake of animal welfare. Mastitis is an uncomfortable disease that is caused by overproduction, so the animal is suffering in two ways—her health is impacted, and she has to spend more time producing milk and standing at a milking machine. If the substance is not banned, they argue, the milk produced from cows given BST should at least be labeled so that consumers can have a choice about purchasing BST-free (or more accurately rBST-free) milk. This is seen as a way to let consumers voice their concerns for the animals, and surveys show that people do

like to have their food labeled with respect to all kinds of issues. Industrial interests have argued against labeling, saying that it is too easy to provide false information on a label. While labeling is still an issue for many food-related topics, technically, all milk contains traces of the naturally occurring hormone BST, and it is not clear that the levels are any different for milk produced using artificial BST than for milk that is not. Eventually, the controversy died down in the United States, which some observers have attributed to U.S. news coverage having become more positive by the mid-1990s.

Food Safety

Two issues discussed above may have raised red flags for readers with regards to food safety: the use of a synthetic hormone (rBST) in dairy production and the use of drugs to treat dairy cattle with mastitis. Since natural BGH is already present in milk supplies, many scientists and farmers argue that the additional BGH is not problematic for humans consuming milk produced through its use—whether natural or synthetic. Studies of cross-species somatotropin exposure have found that while same-species exposure does have an impact—for example, human somatotropin has been used on children whose growth has been stunted—there is no evidence of cross-species interactions (such as human exposure to BST). Therefore, even if rBST use resulted in milk with higher levels of growth hormone, it would be unlikely to have any influence on humans who consume it. Regulatory agencies in over 30 countries have deemed rBST use to be safe. In addition, cattle with mastitis are typically taken out of production until their disease clears up, so drug residues in the milk from treating them with antibiotics should not be an issue.

However, others feel that milk should contain only what is found in it naturally. Increased levels of BGH in cattle, even if it is a substance that is normally found in milk (and even though studies show that using rBST does not increase the amount of BGH in milk), are not natural. Given that there is little evidence calling the safety of additional BGH in dairy cattle into question, some people are calling for a halt to BGH treatments until more medical tests are done to check the safety of BGH in humans (and whether or not rBST is really the same as naturally occurring BGH). Some groups have even claimed that milk from rBST-treated cattle can cause cancer. In addition, traces of some drugs can still be found in animals long after treatments for something such as mastitis have stopped. Many drugs that have been deemed safe for animals have not been approved for humans. Little is known about what would happen if residues of these drugs made their way into the food supply. Some have argued that exposure to animal antibiotics can weaken the human immune system and make the antibiotics ineffective as harmful organisms evolve resistance toward them.

One of the problems with concerns over food safety and dairy products is that the latter are a major component of the U.S. Department of Agriculture's (USDA) food pyramid. According to the USDA, most people should have two to three servings of dairy products each day. While eliminating dairy products may keep consumers away from both rBST and the naturally occurring saturated fats found in many dairy products, this is also a threat to healthy bones and teeth. Giving up dairy products can be as much of a health issue as continuing to consume them.

Industrial Food Production

The use of BGH also costs money, as with any drug, whether animal or human. Farmers who have a small profit margin may find that they are unable to afford new drugs, and some fear they could start losing even more of their market share to larger farmers who can afford the latest medical care and technology. Larger dairy farms are able to use the profits from rBST-boosted milk production to buy more animals, giving them even more milk production so they can continue to lower their costs. Smaller farmers find it increasingly hard to compete, so they must sell out or find a niche market for their milk and milk products. In states where small dairy farms are an integral part of the agricultural identity—such as Wisconsin and Vermont, where there has been a great deal of vocal opposition to rBST—this can have an economic impact beyond the potential direct impact on small dairy farms. Tourism, for example, could suffer as well.

While many of us may appreciate lower milk prices (which, historically, have also been heavily

affected by government subsidies in the United States and elsewhere), there are a number of concerns with an increasingly concentrated food supply. First, as mentioned above, the more animals one puts into a confined space, the greater the risk of stress among the animals. More stress can lead to more health issues, which means that more drugs are needed to treat the animals. As more drugs are involved with animals in food production, the greater the chances that some of these drugs will find their way into the food supply. Avoiding this cycle can actually benefit the smaller farmer, who is able to keep the stress level of animals lower than in large dairy operations. In the end, some argue that the price of using rBST may be the same as not using it. Larger farms can produce more milk, but they spend more money on treating their animals and on public relations if something does go wrong.

Another concern with a concentrated food supply is that if a problem does occur in production, it can spread very rapidly. Milk that is sold in the United States to consumers and dairy product manufacturers (such as cheese makers) must be pasteurized, which means that it has been heated to a certain temperature (161°F for 15–20 seconds) to kill bacteria that might spread diseases such as tuberculosis and listeria. Science has not found a microorganism that has evolved a resistance to these kinds of high temperatures, so milk should be safe from most diseases if treated properly (though pasteurization does nothing to the BGH in the milk). Some cattle from these herds, however, are culled. If any of the culled animals are infected with some disease, it can make its way into the food supply and be disseminated widely in a relatively short time. If something were to ever go wrong with the milk supply at a large production facility (say, the pasteurization process failed), the same thing could happen—people could consume a large amount of bad milk before the problem was found and fixed.

A number of recent food concerns—such as those involving peanut butter, spinach, and tomatoes—highlight this problem. While only one or two food manufacturing plants or areas may be infected, the way food is widely disseminated from these central locations can spread the problem across a region (or farther, to an entire country or even across national borders) within a matter of days or weeks.

Milk is unique in that it has a shorter shelf life than some foods, but this also means that we tend to consume it shortly after purchasing it. If there is a problem, such as the one detected in 2003 with milk that had been mixed with eggnog, the consumer may experience problems (in this case, limited to people who were allergic to eggs) before they hear about the recall.

While many argue that the use of rBST is safe because it is very similar to natural products found in milk, others are still not so sure. Anyone who is curious or concerned about this practice has plenty of opportunities to find out more about it—from the full spectrum of these views.

Toby A. Ten Eyck

See also Agricultural Biotechnology; Department of Agriculture, U.S.; Food Safety; Recombinant DNA

Further Readings

Gregory, N. G., & Grandin, T. (2007). *Animal welfare and meat production.* Wallingford, UK: CABI.

Leiss, W., & Powell, D. (1997). *Mad cows and mother's milk.* Montreal, QC, Canada: McGill-Queen's University Press.

Nottingham, S. (2003). *Eat your genes* (Rev. ed.). New York: Zed.

BREAST CANCER COMMUNICATION

Communication about breast cancer is prevalent and occurs across all domains and contexts of human communication. Several aspects of the screening, diagnosis, and treatment of breast cancer have resulted in controversy, and recent technological and scientific innovations and discoveries are leading to changes in the way scholars, activists, and others talk about breast cancer. Communication is an important tool in increasing breast cancer awareness and the adoption of appropriate prevention strategies.

Mass media efforts to communicate the causes, diagnosis, treatment, and survival of breast cancer began fairly recently in U.S. history, perhaps most notably with reports of the experiences of First Ladies Betty Ford and Nancy Reagan. Today, media coverage about breast cancer is widespread and varied, addressing issues ranging from diagnosis and treatment, to fund-raising and research, to genetic factors linked to the disease. Public discourse about breast cancer has been greatly affected by the efforts of grassroots, private, and governmental organizations created to provide education, raise awareness and funding for research, and improve access to tools for the screening, diagnosis, and treatment of the disease.

Breast cancer became a highly politicized health topic in the late 20th century, as a coalition of national voluntary organizations and others collaborated to increase federal funding for breast cancer screening programs, influence policymakers to devote more funds to breast cancer research, and protect the rights of breast cancer survivors. These organizations, including Susan G. Komen for the Cure, have continued focused efforts to influence policy at local, state, and federal levels; provide education about breast cancer to a broad array of publics; and fund breast cancer research and outreach activities. Organizations such as the American Cancer Society also perform services designed to help breast cancer survivors and their families cope with illness and recovery.

A number of organizations have also established partnerships with for-profit corporations to conduct fund-raising and awareness efforts, a practice that has caused some to criticize the ethics of employing a cause such as breast cancer in the marketing of products and services. Despite its critics, the practice has gained a foothold in U.S. culture, and the iconic pink ribbon, first worn on a lapel or collar to designate support of breast cancer awareness, is now a recognizable symbol that can be found everywhere—from yogurt labels and cereal boxes to cable television network logos. The results of the efforts of those involved in the breast cancer movement, culminating in Breast Cancer Awareness Month currently recognized each October, is an example of a highly successful social marketing campaign.

Recent scientific discoveries of genetic mutations associated with an increased risk for developing breast cancer have also affected media coverage about breast cancer and have clear implications for interpersonal, organizational, and professional communication about breast cancer. The discovery of these BRCA genes has led to the involvement of medical professionals such as geneticists and genetic counselors in communication about breast cancer and has resulted in public debates about the ethics of how this kind of information should be used and who should have access to it. Public and political discourse about the risks of organizations such as employers or insurers having access to such information has led lawmakers and others to propose steps to prevent genetic discrimination, whether for breast cancer or for any other genetic condition or predisposition.

Women who discover they have a genetic predisposition to developing breast cancer may choose to manage their behaviors in a variety of ways. For example, they may choose to do nothing; they may increase their personal screening behaviors; they may discuss their personal risk with family members, friends, genetic counselors or other medical professionals; or they may even undergo prophylactic mastectomy (preventive removal of one or both breasts). Clearly, the knowledge of such a predisposition can create significant stress and anxiety for a woman and her family members, and specific communication behaviors are often employed in an attempt to manage anxiety and uncertainty. The role of professionals such as genetic counselors in managing health is an area that merits further study by communication researchers as we continue to learn more about the role of genetics in the development of breast cancer.

The science of the early detection of breast cancer is also not without controversy; scholars, activists, and medical professionals have criticized current screening methods and have called for the need for advancements in this area. Mammography has been specifically criticized as an inadequate or outdated technology, despite its widespread use as a primary method of screening and diagnosis among women over age 40. General recommendations on the practice of breast self-examination for the early detection of breast cancer, once advising this to be done monthly for all women over age 18, have been reduced due to findings that the practice did not appear to result in increased cancer diagnoses, based on a recent, well-publicized study of Chinese women. Another well-publicized recent controversy involves the discovery of an increased risk of breast cancer linked to hormone replacement therapy, a treatment widely prescribed to counteract negative effects of menopause.

The occurrence of breast cancer can have a significant impact on family communication and relationships, particularly when a genetic predisposition to developing breast cancer is found within a family. Family members may feel conflicted about their roles and expectations in attempting to provide support to the breast cancer survivor, and the person with breast cancer is likely to be concerned about the effects of the diagnosis on family members. Families have also been shown to be conflicted about responding to, or seeking, knowledge of a genetic predisposition to breast cancer. Breast cancer survivors and their family members often seek support from others in attempting to cope with the diagnosis. Cultural and religious beliefs related to cancer, personhood, and illness are likely to affect communication about breast cancer and the extent to which one seeks diagnosis, treatment, and support. Others who may provide supportive communication to breast cancer survivors and their families include medical professionals, friends, members of voluntary organizations and churches, and representatives of government organizations. Such formal and informal communication activities may involve interpersonal or mediated forms, or both.

The Internet is a technological innovation that will have significant effects on breast cancer communication, now and in the future, as more individuals gain access to the technology and become comfortable with its use. The Internet is emerging as a significant communication resource for breast cancer survivors and other involved parties, not only in providing information and support, but also as a forum for information sharing and advocacy. Computer-based and computer-assisted breast cancer education programs and tailored screening interventions also represent new methods to employ technology in breast cancer communication efforts.

Karyn Ogata Jones

See also Cancer Prevention and Risk Communication; Computer-Tailored Messages; Health Communication, Overview

Further Readings

Andrykowski, M. A., Munn, R. K., & Studts, J. L. (1996). Interest of learning of personal genetic risk for cancer: A general population survey. *Preventive Medicine, 25*(5), 527–536.

Champion, V., Ray, D., Heilman, D., & Springston, J. K. (2000). A tailored intervention for mammography among low-income African-American women. *Journal of Psychosocial Oncology, 18*(4), 1–14.

Green, J., Richards, M., Murton, F., Statham, H., & Hallowell, N. (1997). Family communication and genetic counseling: The case of hereditary breast cancer. *Journal of Genetic Counseling, 6*(1), 45–61.

Jones, K. O., Denham, B. E., & Springston, J. K. (2006). Effects of mass and interpersonal communication on breast cancer screening: Advancing agenda setting theory in health contexts. *Journal of Applied Communication Research, 34*(1), 94–113.

Jones, K. O., Denham, B. E., & Springston, J. K. (2007). Differing effects of mass and interpersonal communication on breast cancer risk estimates: An exploratory study of college students and their mothers. *Health Communication, 21*(2), 165–176.

Jones, K. O., & Pelton, R. (2009). Attribute agenda setting and breast cancer in newspapers. *Journal of Health & Mass Communication, 1*(1), 77–89.

Thomas, D. B., Gao, D. L., Ray, R. M., Wang, W. W., Allison, C .J., Chen, L., et al. (2002). Randomized trial of breast self-examination in Shanghai: Final results. *Journal of the National Cancer Institute, 94*(19), 1445–1457.

C

CANADA, SCIENCE COMMUNICATION IN

While traditional, elite-focused forms of consultation and advice gathering dominate the science and technology (S&T) policy landscape in Canada, new trends have emerged. The predominant model of communication with citizens has been a one-way flow of information from policy and scientific elites to the mass public. More recently, though, there has been a broad shift toward experimentation with more participatory forms of public engagement that encourage a two-way model of communication, one that provides a forum for dialogue and mutual learning among citizens, experts, and policymakers.

These more participatory engagement activities have remained for the most part experimental. Significant barriers remain in the Canadian context to integrating more inclusive, two-way communication opportunities as regular practice in the Canadian system. The objective of this entry is to identify and describe these barriers. It will first review Canada's parliamentary structure, including the role of the prime minister and cabinet, and the influence this structure has on S&T communication opportunities. It will then describe the standard template of public consultation used by federal government departments, one that emphasizes one-way, government-initiated communication, and explain why this makes it difficult to accommodate more dialogic and nontechnical

forms of communication. Then, Canadian experiments with more participatory forms of engagement will be highlighted, followed by a conclusion examining ways to overcome barriers to including two-way communication practices more regularly alongside the traditional one-way forms.

Government Context for S&T Communication in Canada

Canada adheres to a Westminster model of parliament similar to that in the United Kingdom. The two-house legislature is composed of the House of Commons, an elected body of 308 members of Parliament (MPs) representing constituencies from across the country, and the Senate, 105 senators who are appointed by the prime minister. Generally, the governing party wins the majority of the seats in the House of Commons, a system that gives the governing party (and especially the prime minister) substantial power to implement policies and regulation (as compared to the presidential system within the United States, where there is a clearer separation between the legislative and executive branches).

Theoretically, MPs play a key role in communication between their constituents and the government. A government of Canada poll conducted in the year 2000 showed that two thirds of Canadians regard individual communication with their MPs as a valued channel of involvement in policy issues. However, while they are well placed to hear views from their citizens (through town hall meetings,

meetings at their constituency office, and so on), conveying those views to the party caucus and to the prime minister is difficult, especially if those views contradict the party's position on key issues. Individualism among Canadian MPs is not encouraged.

Another avenue to communicate about S&T issues within Canada's parliamentary system is offered by parliamentary committees. These are permanent committees that hold public hearings on bills currently being considered for legislation, where presentations from witnesses—who can be scientific experts, stakeholders, other public servants, or unaffiliated citizens—are heard. In practice, however, parliamentary committees have provided a limited venue for S&T communication, especially with respect to nonexperts. They generally depend on formal hearing procedures with technical witnesses who address specific points within proposed bills rather than political witnesses who can debate the underlying values and principles that direct the bill. Communication is further hampered by the adversarial and partisan style of interaction on these committees. Their activities are not well covered in the media, which cuts off another opportunity for broader public discussion and debate.

A less often used yet characteristic mode of communicating between the government and external groups and individuals in Canada is through the use of public inquiries and Royal Commissions. Commissions and inquiries are created by the federal cabinet, generally for one of two purposes: (1) to gather advice on a complex and/or contentious policy problem (such as the Royal Commission on New Reproductive Technologies) or (2) as a fact-finding investigation into a specific incident (such as the Krever Inquiry into Canada's blood system). Commissions and inquiries are conducted independently of the government and have the power to subpoena witnesses, hire staff, conduct research, and requisition documents. They are seen as important sites for policy learning and are instrumental in generating broader public debate. (The Berger Inquiry into building an extensive gas pipeline through the Mackenzie Valley is an example of doing both.) Cynics suggest, however, that governments strike commissions for the purpose of avoiding controversial policy issues rather than addressing them, and the government is not bound to implement the recommendations. Commissions

are conducted as isolated events, and thus, they are not part of institutionalizing in-depth consultation with citizens and stakeholders in a regular, ongoing manner.

On the regulatory front, public consultation is a requirement for all departments and agencies. Through the Cabinet Directive on Streamlining Regulation, these regulatory bodies must identify interested and affected parties and provide them with the ability to participate in "open, meaningful, and balanced consultations" throughout the regulatory process. A required part of meeting this directive is publishing draft regulations in the Government of Canada's official publication, the *Canada Gazette*. This gives interested groups and individuals an opportunity to review and comment on a proposed regulation, albeit at the final stages of the regulation-making process.

Traditional Government Approach to Public Involvement

In the last 10 to 15 years, the federal government has become more active in engaging with citizens and nonexpert stakeholders in S&T policy development. Most of this work is conducted by the public service, a nonpartisan body of professionals who remain in place through successive governments. Public consultations are generally organized in an ad hoc manner by and for a specific department (such as Health, Industry, or Agriculture). A common consultation format consists of the following elements: preparation and circulation of a background document, a series of stakeholder meetings or focus groups in at least one major center per province (reflecting the importance in Canada of balanced regional representation), prepared questions and answers, a 1-800 number and Web site to permit submission of comments, and provision of a workbook to allow citizens to respond to specific questions. These activities often occur quite late in the policy process when there is pressure to make a decision, providing no opportunity to go back to citizens for further input. Furthermore, public consultation activities are small in number and in influence compared to the expert committees that dominate S&T consultation.

Many departments within the government, and especially the prime minister's office, are increasingly using public opinion polling as a prime mode of getting feedback from citizens. Frequently, the total number of participants in a consultation is of prime concern because government ministers like to say that a large number of people participated, no matter how superficial that participation may have been. In this environment, institutionalizing more open and two-way communication and dialogue has been described as a hugely ambitious goal. Another barrier in involving publics in S&T policy processes is Canada's science-based decision-making framework. The framework is based on a "sound science" approach in which decisions are based on technical and "objective" risk assessments, making it difficult to accommodate more "subjective" or value-oriented inputs into the policy process. Without designated entry points for this kind of input into policy making, there is little opportunity for publics to play a significant role.

Participatory Experiments

Despite this situation, other approaches have emerged. This section highlights recent experiments with more inclusive forms of public consultation by the Canadian federal government.

Parliamentary Committees

In an attempt to hear more directly from individual citizens, parliamentary committees have started to experiment with online consultations as part of the committee process. For example, in 2005, the Standing Committee on Social Affairs, Science & Technology created a Web site in conjunction with its work on Mental Health, Mental Illness and Addictions in Canada. The Web site used a consultation workbook presenting an overview of issues in conjunction with an online questionnaire asking about views on the current mental health system and for judgments of different scenarios for change in the system. More than 1,200 contributions were received from service providers, users of the system, their family members, and concerned citizens. Unfortunately, the parliamentary context of the consultation impacted the outcomes of the consultation and highlights the challenges in undertaking more in-depth, longer-term consultation initiatives. Just as the input period came to a close, an election was called and the committee was dissolved (pending reconstitution under the new government).

Commissions and Inquires

The Romanow Commission on the Future of Health Care in Canada (2001–2002), created as a fact-finding commission, is considered to be the most comprehensive consultative exercise ever undertaken in Canada. It incorporated many standard federal consultation methods such as ensuring provincial and territorial representation, holding expert roundtables, and providing open public hearings for stakeholders and citizens. Supplementing this consultation were televised forums (with call-in sessions with citizens), policy dialogue sessions held on university campuses, and an online consultation workbook (which was completed by more than 20,000 people). The most innovative part of the initiative was a set of 12 public dialogues with 40 randomly selected participants each, held in major centers throughout Canada.

These in-depth dialogue events examined participants' current views on health care and were able to probe deeper into underlying value questions and consider how trade-offs could be made with those with opposing views. What was significant about this process in relation to health care is that previous consultation efforts had concluded that Canadians were not capable of making trade-offs on how their health care is delivered, a view echoed by elite groups within Canada. These discussions provided a methodology that allowed underlying values to be considered and trade-offs negotiated. The outcomes of were remarkably consistent across the 12 groups involved and were ultimately confirmed by a follow-up telephone poll with a representative sample of 1,600 Canadians. The discussions also had influence on the final report of the commission. First, the report incorporated demands for transparency and accountability that had emerged from the dialogue (and that had been unexpected by members of the commission), and second, it recommended conducting regular follow-ups (which did not occur).

Policy Creation

In 2001, Health Canada experimented with a deliberative consultation based on a citizens jury model of public involvement. The topic was xenotransplantation, a controversial process that involves the transplantation of animal organs into humans. The department had released a draft *Proposed*

Canadian Standard for Xenotransplantation in 1999 and had been advised to hold public consultations. Citizens juries and other deliberative models of consultation, such as consensus conferences, are geared toward complex issues such as xenotransplantation because they have an element of learning and promote the integration of technical and social aspects in deciding which policy path to follow. In a citizens jury, participants are randomly selected (and often roughly match the broader demographics of the region or country in which they are being held). The participants receive background information on the issue, they hear from and question experts from a wide variety of backgrounds (in the xenotransplantation case, those representing law, infectious disease, ethics, animal welfare, and transplant recipients), and then discuss the issue among themselves before coming to a judgment on it. Six citizen forums with 107 participants were held across Canada, along with telephone and Web site surveys with citizens and a mail-in survey sent to stakeholder groups. The Public Advisory Group (PAG) overseeing the consultation felt that the most informative data came from the citizen forums and clearly demonstrated that "ordinary" citizens could grapple with complex policy issues. However, there has been no further public consultation since the release of the PAG report in 2002, and Canada has not finalized a standard on xenotransplantation, so it is difficult to assess how the consultation effort was integrated into the policy-making context.

Controversy around biotechnology was a catalyst for the federal government in supporting further public involvement and dialogue. The Canadian Biotechnology Strategy, released in 1998, represented a drastic shift from earlier versions of the strategy that made no mention of public involvement by making citizen engagement one of three key pillars of the strategy. The strategy also created the Canadian Biotechnology Advisory Committee (CBAC), which had a dual mandate of providing policy advice and creating opportunities for all Canadians to join a "national conversation" on biotechnology policy. CBAC was innovative because it provided an organizational structure that provided ongoing funding for the committee to conduct public involvement activities (as opposed to the more ad hoc nature of most involvement initiatives), and just as important, it was directly linked to high-level policymakers (the ministers of the seven departments involved in biotechnology policy) through a coordinating committee, providing opportunity for citizen views to reach a high level in the government. Another unique feature of CBAC was the appointment of two laypeople to the committee, which otherwise consisted of experts (in the fields of ethics, economics, biology, and so on).

CBAC was criticized, however, for narrowly defining some of its issues for consultation, for example, on the issue of genetically modified (GM) food, which led to more than 50 nongovernmental organizations refusing to participate in any further stakeholder consultations with the group. In response to these criticisms and in conjunction with stakeholder groups, CBAC created a dialogue tool (focused on GM foods, but broadly applicable to S&T issues) that aims to facilitate discussion among diverse stakeholders on the social, ethical, environmental, and health implications of a given technology. The tool structures dialogue so that participants can discuss the risks and benefits in detail and express various levels of acceptability. The tool represents a step toward more two-way communication and dialogue, but it was not implemented by CBAC before the organization was shut down in 2007.

Conclusion

Public communication on S&T issues in Canada has for the most part been done on an ad hoc basis. Policy elites and decision makers remain skeptical about the value and benefits of engaging citizens in ongoing dialogue on policy issues and generally revert to traditional one-way communication methods with the Canadian publics, either top-down communications about S&T issues or strictly defined public consultation opportunities. Furthermore, the dominant science-based, decision-making framework provides a very narrow opening for accommodating public views that are beyond the technical considerations of policy issues.

Above all else, integrating two-way communication techniques into S&T governance in Canada will require a dramatic shift in policy culture. Although there has been some experimentation with more deliberative forms of engagement at the federal level, the current policy environment inhibits broadscale change. General skepticism across the government and public service remains an issue, but more important, there is a lack of leadership and political will at the highest levels. The structure of the Canadian political system concentrates a lot of power in the prime minister's office, and this has only intensified within the recent Conservative-led government. More and more decisions are being made at this level, with little input from the general public and stakeholders, let alone backbench MPs in the governing party.

Jennifer Medlock

See also Citizens Jury; Consensus Conference; Deliberative Democracy; Public Engagement; Town Hall Meetings

Further Readings

Gamble, D. (1978). The Berger Inquiry: An impact assessment process. *Science, 199,* 946–952.

Maxwell, J., Rosell, S., & Forest, P.-G. (2003). Giving citizens a voice in healthcare policy. *British Medical Journal, 326,* 1031–1033.

Phillips, S. (with Orsini, N.). (2002, April). *Mapping the links: Citizen involvement in policy processes.* Discussion paper prepared for Canadian Policy Research Networks, Ottawa, ON, Canada. Available at www .cprn.org/doc.cfm?doc=169&1=en

Turnbull, L., & Aucoin, P. (2006, March). *Fostering Canadians' role in public policy: A strategy for institutionalizing public involvement in policy* (Research Report Pl07). Ottawa, ON, Canada: Canadian Policy Research Networks. Available at www.cprn.org/doc.cfm?doc=1404&1=en

CANCER PREVENTION AND RISK COMMUNICATION

Health-related risk involves the probability of a negative health event, such as being diagnosed with cancer. The importance of risk depends not only upon this probability, but also upon the severity of the disease in question and its potential negative consequences of morbidity and mortality. Risk communication involves the open exchange between physicians and their patients regarding health-related information about risks toward the goal of more informed decisions about prevention and treatment. Although physicians and patients may be the primary communicators about patients' risks of developing cancer and possible preventive actions (such as cancer screening), risk information is also communicated by the media, in public health campaigns, and by researchers in published findings in scientific journals. It is important for the general public to be able to interpret how risk information is presented in advertising and marketing arenas in addition to how it is presented at the doctor's office.

In the context of cancer prevention, risk communication involves several elements: a focus on behavioral, environmental, and/or genetic risks; discussion of risks and benefits of various cancer screening procedures; and possibly genetic counseling for those with a family history of cancer. This kind of risk communication is a form of science and technology communication. Health-related risk and cancer information is communicated about by many individuals from physicians to scientists to journalists to patients, and clarity of the information is crucial to ensuring that informed decision making takes place. Furthermore, because cancer is both a leading cause of death and preventable with change in several behavioral risk factors (such as smoking), communication about cancer risk to the general public is of considerable importance. This entry discusses types of cancer prevention activities for which effective risk communication is essential, theories about the perception of health risks, communication between doctors and patients (particularly the exchange of information, discussion of risks and benefits of cancer screening, and shared decision making), and factors affecting the efficacy of health communication about risk.

Prevention, Behavior, and Risk Communication

The types of cancer for which screening has been demonstrated to be most effective include breast cancer, cervical cancer, and colorectal cancer. Yearly mammograms are effective in early detection of breast cancer for women of appropriate age; there is disagreement about when screening should begin, but many suggest that mammograms should be done every 1 to 2 years for women over age 40 and that they are generally not needed for women under the age of 40 unless there is significant risk or symptoms.

Some research findings have suggested that mammograms are most effective for women over age 50. Papanicolaou (Pap) smears for women 21 years or older or who are younger and sexually active are effective in early detection of cervical cancer. Cervical cancer screening rates are generally high because of the efforts of public education campaigns, the routine nature of the test in many women's annual gynecological exams, and the level of knowledge of female patients and their health care providers about cervical cancer. Colorectal cancer can be detected early, and death rates can be reduced through fecal occult blood tests and sigmoidoscopy and other screening tests before age 50, as well as colonoscopy after age 50. Screening rates for colorectal cancer remain low despite evidence of the benefits because of the complexity of the various screening options and the requirements on the part of the patient being screened (such as cleansing of the colon and possible sedation).

Risk communication regarding screening focuses on urging people to receive regular, age-appropriate screenings. If there is some uncertainty about the benefits of regular screening (for example, for prostate-specific antigen testing for prostate cancer), risk communication might best be focused on giving patients information to make informed decisions in light of the risks and benefits. Cancer prevention may also involve health behaviors such as eating a low-fat diet, avoidance of tobacco, low to moderate alcohol consumption, and regular exercise and may involve counseling at-risk patients to change relevant health behaviors. More recently, cancer prevention also can include genetic counseling, which involves providing information about potential increased risk to patients who may have a genetic predisposition for certain types of cancer, particularly breast and colorectal. Such communication focuses on informing younger patients about mammography or preventive surgery in the case of breast cancer to help them make informed choices in consideration of the risks and benefits and determine which risks may be tolerable and which should be reduced through preventive actions.

Patient Perceptions of Risk

A crucial element in the process of risk communication is the patient's perception of risk. Perception involves the individual's opinion about the severity of the particular type of cancer and his or her level of control over the risk. People attach very different levels of significance to an outcome, possibly due to their personal knowledge of and experience with the disease. For example, people vary in how serious they believe colorectal cancer can be. In their communications with patients, health care professionals must attend to the perceptions that the patient brings to the encounter. There is evidence that females, for example, overestimate their lifetime risk of breast cancer; a physician could keep in mind this bias when communicating with the patient about breast cancer risk. People may underestimate risk of colon cancer, for example, because of lack of knowledge about the disease and about the risk factors; accurate understanding of risk is needed to recognize the benefits of screening.

A number of well-tested theories have attempted to explain how patients make decisions about engaging in preventive health behaviors based partially on their consideration of individual risk. One of the earliest proposed theories is the health belief model, which states that several elements are necessary for patients to engage in preventive health actions. First, patients must perceive that the disease to be prevented is severe, that they are susceptible or at risk, and that the benefits of the preventive action outweigh the costs. Second, patients must have self-efficacy or confidence in their ability to act to reduce their risks. A crucial element in risk communication involves a patient's perceptions of his or her susceptibility to disease. If, for example, a patient believes she has high risk for cervical cancer, she is more likely to have annual cervical cancer screenings than if she believes that her risk is low. Interventions to increase cancer screening and other preventive behaviors using these theories have focused on individualizing risk communication and on providing information that applies directly to patients' individual concerns and needs.

Communication About Risk

Several common strategies may guide communication about risk for all types of communicators including scientists, health care professionals, and members of the media. These involve the following steps: determining the purpose of communicating about risk, identifying which persons should receive the information, considering the perceptions of those persons, ascertaining the best channels for the communication, describing the risk in understandable terms with appropriate context, and providing suggestions for behaviors and actions that the person can take or ways that he or she can gain additional information.

Communication between health care provider and patient is a central route for the transmission of risk communication related to cancer prevention and will be the focus of the remainder of this entry. A crucial element of this exchange is transmission of information in a way that makes sense to the patient and is thorough, with sufficient time devoted to the exchange to ensure that the patient is fully informed. If a patient does not understand the information he or she is given about risks and benefits of cancer screening, the patient is unlikely to follow through with the health care provider's recommendations. Thus, it is crucial to present risk information in a way that maximizes the patient's understanding and confirms with the patient that he or she understands what has been discussed. It is wise to avoid medical jargon or terms that may be unfamiliar to a typical patient, and it may be beneficial to ask the patient to repeat back the information that he or she just learned. It is also necessary to give the patient adequate time to ask any questions that he or she may have.

The presentation of risk communication can involve qualitative or quantitative information. Quantitative information is presented in probabilities or numbers and can involve *relative risks*, *absolute risks*, or *odds ratios*. Relative risks are the percentage of an outcome in a group exposed to the risk versus a group of individuals not exposed to the risk. Absolute risks are lifetime percentage risks. Odds ratios involve the odds of a potential outcome in people who face the possibility of some risk versus people who do not face the possibility of the risk. Use of these terms can be confusing for patients, so clarity is crucial for enhancing the patient's understanding. Quantitative information on risk should be presented in a balanced format; for instance, absolute and relative risk could be presented together, and it should be clear through word use that relative risk involves comparisons and absolute risk involves lifetime risk.

According to the work of Gerd Gigerenzer, patients need to have transparent representations of risks with percentages translated for them into frequencies taking into account conditional probabilities and their associated frequencies. Other work suggests that presenting risks in percentages is an option that may be clearer for patients, although percentages less than 1% may be difficult for some patients to interpret. The language that accompanies the numbers is critical. Terms such as *rare* or *probably* may mean different things to different people. Use of accepted language or terminology for different levels of risk such as the level of risk of 1 in less than 100 (for example, high) or from 1 in 100 to 1 in 1,000 (for example, moderate) may be helpful.

Quantitative information alone can be difficult to understand. Qualitative information about risk may involve discussion of the causes of cancer, as well as the risk factors and consequences. Such information may be put in context, such as by showing a film with individuals discussing their experiences with certain types of cancer prevention strategies or treatments. Other methods of contextualizing risk may involve comparing risks of dying of certain types of cancer to dying of other diseases such as coronary heart disease or the risk of dying in a car accident.

Risk information in qualitative or quantitative formats can be presented in a number of ways, including visual, numeric, and written. Graphical presentation may be helpful for patients (for example, using a histogram, line graph, or pie chart). Some evidence indicates that combined formats (such as visual and numerical and written) for presenting risk information may be the most effective, as well as the most preferred by patients. Benefit information can also be presented in a chart or graph to examine, for example, deaths prevented by certain preventive behaviors (such as yearly screening for colon cancer). It is, of course, important to present possible side effects or negative outcomes and to give patients a balanced perspective.

Framing of information is another aspect of risk communication. Messages about cancer prevention behaviors can be framed as either a gain (such as survival) or as a loss (such as mortality). A *gain-framed* message focuses on attaining positive outcomes, or avoiding negative ones, by engaging in a health behavior, whereas a *loss-framed* message focuses on a negative outcome from failing to engage in a health-related behavior. In the case of skin cancer prevention, for example, a gain-framed message might be, "Wear sunscreen to promote the health of your skin," and a loss-framed message might be, "If you don't wear sunscreen, you increase your susceptibility to skin cancer."

Framing risk in terms of both losses and gains may be the most balanced approach to the presentation of risk information. Similarly, tailoring information about cancer risk involves specifying the message to apply to a specific person's concerns or needs for promoting behavior change (for example, a particular woman's concerns about mammography). In cancer prevention, tailoring may also apply to lifestyle risk factors of an individual person (including smoking, lack of exercise, or low consumption of fruits and vegetables). Although many people are fearful of cancer, fear-based messages generally are not persuasive in changing smokers' behavior. For example, smoking cessation messages might show a person who is unable to speak normally due to the effects of the cancer, but unless these messages are moderately fear arousing combined with specific information a patient can use to change his or her behavior, these messages are unlikely to be effective in influencing the majority of patients to change their behavior.

Shared Decision Making

Typical communication between physician and patient has changed over the past several decades, from a relationship in which physicians were more dominant and the primary decision makers to one in which physician and patient collaborate and share in making medical decisions. This change requires patients to be informed and willing to take on the role of partners in their care and physicians to share decision-making power and work together with patients. Patients who are informed and active in their care tend to be more committed to treatment decisions and more adherent to recommendations. It is critical in a process of shared decision making to realize the individual needs of each particular patient. Some patients, for example, may prefer quantitative information about risk, whereas others may prefer qualitative information. It is important for the health care provider to determine the patient's preferences through a process of communicating and questioning.

Various tools may aid the process of shared decision making. Decision aids may be helpful for patients in making choices among different health-related options, by guiding them through the steps involved in gathering needed information to make a decision. Decision aids including videos, interactive computer programs, Web sites, and booklets can assist in the process of presenting and discussing risk information. One such strategy involves patient and physician discussing together the procedure in question, the reason for considering it, the expectation of the outcome, the probability, alternatives, risks, expenses, and the final step of making the decision of whether to undergo the procedure or not. There also exist decision models for breast cancer that help women to make decisions about breast cancer screening based on knowledge about their personal risk of developing and dying of cancer in conjunction with the benefits and costs of screening.

Other factors can affect risk communication and cancer prevention activities, including access to medical care, patient cultural beliefs, and low health literacy or numeracy. If patients have limited access to medical resources because of poverty or other circumstances, they are unlikely to engage in appropriate cancer screenings or receive necessary health behavior counseling. Cultural beliefs may affect rates of screening in particular ethnic groups; for instance, rates of mammograms and Pap smears are lower in Hispanic women than in other ethnic groups. Many patients struggle with poor understanding of health information and particularly with understanding numbers related to health information. For many, the lack of clear understanding of the risks and benefits of cancer prevention activities may be a barrier to taking preventive action. It is important for health care providers to be aware of patient barriers; large-scale risk communication campaigns should be targeted to patients in the highest risk groups.

Kelly B. Haskard and M. Robin DiMatteo

See also Breast Cancer Communication; Communication Campaigns in Health and Environment; Health Communication, Overview; Physician–Patient Communication; Risk Communication, Overview

Further Readings

Arkin, E. B. (1999). Cancer risk communication: What we know. *Journal of the National Cancer Institute Monographs, 25,* 182–185.

Croyle, R. T., & Lerman, C. (1999). Risk communication in genetic testing for cancer susceptibility. *Journal of the National Cancer Institute Monographs, 25,* 59–66.

Edwards, A., Elwyn, G., & Mulley, A. (2002). Explaining risks: Turning numerical data into meaningful pictures. *British Medical Journal, 324*(7341), 827–830.

Fischhoff, B., Bostrom, A., & Quadrel, M. J. (1993). Risk perception and communication. *Annual Review of Public Health, 14,* 183–203.

Ghosh, K., Crawford, B. J., Pruthi, S., Williams, C. I., Neal, L., Sandhu, N. P., et al. (2008). Frequency format diagram and probability chart for breast cancer risk communication: A prospective, randomized trial. *BioMedCentral Women's Health, 8,* 18.

Julian-Reynier, C., Welkenhuysen, M., Hagoel, L., Decruyenaere, M., & Hopwood, P. (2003). Risk communication strategies: State of the art and effectiveness in the context of cancer genetic services. *European Journal of Human Genetics, 11*(10), 725–736.

Lipkus, I. M., Skinner, C. S., Dement, J., Pompeii, L., Moser, B., Samsa, G. P., et al. (2005). Increasing colorectal cancer screening among individuals in the carpentry trade: Test of risk communication interventions. *Preventive Medicine, 40*(5), 489–501.

Nekhlyudov, L., & Partridge, A. (2003). Breast cancer risk communication: Challenges and future research directions: Workshop report (United States). *Cancer Causes and Control, 14*(3), 235–239.

Schwartz, L. M., Woloshin, S., & Welch, H. G. (1999). Risk communication in clinical practice: Putting cancer in context. *Journal of the National Cancer Institute Monographs, 25,* 124–133.

Vernon, S. W. (1999). Risk perception and risk communication for cancer screening behaviors: A review. *Journal of the National Cancer Institute Monographs, 25,* 101–119.

Career Paths, Medical Writing/Medical Journalism

Medical writing, including medical journalism, has become an increasingly recognized area of specialization for communication professionals. Various career opportunities exist in this realm, educational pathways for medical writers have become increasingly defined, and various professional organizations now serve medical writers. This entry identifies such career niches, educational pathways, and professional organizations. The entry focuses mainly on medical writing in the United States, but much of the content also applies to medical writing elsewhere.

Career Niches

Medical journalists for popular media are the most visible medical writers. Newspapers with sizeable circulations commonly employ medical reporters. Syndicates such as the Associated Press have medical reporters whose work appears in many newspapers and elsewhere. Medical reporters cover medical research advances, new health care technologies, health policy issues, and occurrences in the health care industry. They also write feature articles on health topics. Some do investigative reporting on wrongdoing in the medical field.

Other popular media also employ medical writers. News magazines and some other magazines have medical writers on their staffs, and many magazines publish articles by freelance medical writers. National television networks and some local television stations have medical reporters. National Public Radio has medical reporters. Medical Internet sites also employ medical writers. Some medical writers write books for the public.

Many medical writers work in public information or public relations, for example, at hospitals, medical schools, and health-related associations such as the American Heart Society and the American Cancer Society. Among items commonly prepared by these medical writers are news releases, articles for newsletters and other publications, brochures, and materials for Web sites. This type of writing is also done by medical writers working at government agencies, such as the National Institutes of Health and the Centers for Disease Control and Prevention. Some public relations agencies have medical writers. Many medical writers enter careers in public information or public relations after working as reporters for newspapers; movement in the other direction appears much less common.

Medical writers also work in the pharmaceutical, biotechnology, and medical device industries.

For example, before approving a new drug, the Food and Drug Administration requires extensive research to help show that it is safe and effective; medical writers participate in preparing the reports on this research. Medical writers for industry also write such items as patient information materials, informational materials for health professionals, news releases, and items for posting on the World Wide Web.

A related career niche is medical editing. Some medical editors are employed by popular media, public information or public relations offices, or health-related companies. Some work for publishers of medical journals, medical textbooks, and other items for health professionals. Also, some help medical researchers refine their writing before submission for publication. With English having become the international language of science, many authors who are not native speakers of English especially want such editorial help. Some medical communicators specialize in medical editing from the start; others are promoted from writer to editor.

Medical writers and editors can have staff positions or work on a freelance basis. Some do both.

Educational Pathways

Until recently, little formal education in medical writing was available. Thus, medical writers typically have come from related backgrounds and learned medical writing on the job. Many have majored in journalism or English or had at least bachelor's degrees in biology or biomedical science; some have attended medical school or obtained other health professional degrees. Medical writing has tended to attract people who like both writing and biomedical science.

In recent decades, opportunities for formal education in medical writing have increased. For example, master's degree programs now exist in medical journalism and pharmaceutically oriented medical writing. In addition, courses in medical writing are available through more general undergraduate and graduate programs, especially those in science journalism.

Whatever degrees they pursue, prospective medical writers can benefit from courses in both communication and science. They can also benefit from internships in medical writing. Sites providing such internships include magazines and other popular media, pharmaceutical and other companies, and public information offices of medical schools, government agencies, associations, and hospitals. Internships in medical writing can provide valuable experience and aid in obtaining employment.

Professional associations also provide instruction in medical writing, for example, at their conferences. This instruction can aid those entering medical writing without academic training. It also is an important source of continuing education. Because communication fields and medical fields keep evolving, medical writers must continue to learn.

Professional Associations

Various professional associations serve medical writers. The Association of Health Care Journalists is targeted mainly to health care reporters for the popular media. The American Medical Writers Association serves mainly writers and editors working in the pharmaceutical industry, for institutions or associations, for medical journals, or as freelancers. Organizations specifically for those in pharmaceutical communication include the Drug Information Association. Organizations in related fields—such as the National Association of Science Writers, Council of Science Editors, and Public Relations Society of America—include many members who are medical writers or editors and offer much that is about or relevant to medical writing. Associations in medical writing and related realms publish periodicals in their fields, post resources on the World Wide Web, hold conferences, and otherwise facilitate education of and communication among medical writers. These associations can be good ways to learn about opportunities for education and employment in medical writing.

Barbara Gastel

See also American Medical Writers Association; Beat Reporting; Health Communication, Overview; Medical Journalism; National Association of Science Writers

Further Readings

Gastel, B. (2005). *Health writer's handbook* (2nd ed.). Ames: Iowa State University Press.

Gray, T., & Hamilton, C. W. (2008). Findings from the 2007 AMWA salary survey. *American Medical Writers Association Journal*, 23(1), 4–8.

Iverson, C., Christiansen, S., Flanagin, A., Fontanarosa, P. B., Glass, R. M., Gregoline, B., et al. (2007). *AMA manual of style: A guide for authors and editors* (10th ed.). New York: Oxford University Press.

Kanel, S., & Gastel, B. (2008). Careers in science editing: An overview to use or share. *Science Editor*, 31(1), 18–22.

Career Paths, Science/ Environmental Journalism

Using two different Web-based mapping services does not always identify the same route. But all of them, ultimately, will get the user to the same destination. The same is true of finding the "correct" career path for science or environmental journalism. Indeed, the prescribed route may depend solely on who is asked.

If one were to ask an academic, he or she is more than likely to recommend a traditional approach: journalism school. If one were to ask a scientist, the recommendation may be altogether different. If one were to ask three working journalists, the questioner will probably get three different answers. What is really the correct answer? There probably is not one. Indeed, any number of choices will probably get someone to his or her destination. One just may take a little longer than another. But some choices may significantly increase the odds of actually landing a job.

Journalism school will provide a strong academic background—not to mention an array of near-real journalism experiences. As students complete assignments—and perhaps write for school newspapers—they become very comfortable with the rigors of daily journalism. But they may not pick up the necessary science or environment background to pursue a journalism career in that field.

Others would advocate a science degree, with journalism skills as an afterthought. This approach has been used widely by the radio and television networks—as well as by some Web-based science, health, and environment sites. No doubt many have noticed the number of medical doctors who report on health issues for those outlets. In other words, having a science background is viewed as more desirable than having a journalism degree. The assumption is that it may be quicker to teach a medical doctor how to be a journalist than it will be to train a journalism graduate to understand complex issues and write about them in a way that is understandable to a lay audience.

Along the way, a science background also helps in interviewing scientists, who are more likely to talk freely with someone who obviously knows their field. However, there is no single formula for success as a science journalist. So what is the best path? Assuming that a combined science and journalism background might be the best alternative, one should consider the following advice.

Someone about to enter college should find a school with strong science and journalism programs. A student who is already in college should strongly consider supplementing his or her education with journalism or science courses. The ideal is immersion in both fields: Students should learn the science and practice how to write about it. Finding a science specialty might be even better. A good grounding in statistics can be immensely valuable.

What else will help? Without a doubt, students should join a science-based journalism group. Most have discount memberships for students. And they provide excellent opportunities to learn the craft—and to network with scientists and other journalists. One should think job opportunities. Two organizations, for example, are the Society of Environmental Journalists (www.sej.org) and the National Association of Science Writers (www .nasw.org). Membership benefits are enormous, both for working journalists and for students. Both organizations offer informative newsletters, chock full of articles about issues of importance. Both also have resource-rich conferences that have proved beneficial to students and working journalists for decades.

In addition, both of these groups sponsor an array of workshops and other career-enriching opportunities. Plus, both organizations are conduits for other opportunities that are offered by academic institutions, government agencies, or other science organizations. These sessions offer invaluable background on a plethora of relevant science and environmental issues.

What else can be done to prepare for a journalism career covering science and/or the environment?

One should read and watch—and that means Web-based sites, science publications, and the mainstream press. Along with the myriad science-based programs available on cable television, all these media have mastered the art of communicating complex subjects to a lay audience. There is a lot to learn from successful professionals. One should find faculty members who are scientists with writing experience and find journalism professors with an understanding of science writing. Then pick their brains.

Internships should be considered as well. Science internships can help with understanding of complex issues. Journalism internships can help teach how to communicate those same issues. And both could, potentially, lead to a first job out of college—or prepare someone for a career change if he or she has already graduated and is working in another area.

Ultimately, there is no precise formula for success. Talking to a dozen journalists will likely produce a dozen different opinions about the proper way to break into the field. But in the end, it would not be surprising if those opinions could be distilled into one key point: Those interested should concentrate on both science and journalism to increase the odds of a rewarding career.

Rae Tyson

See also Career Paths, Medical Writing/Medical Journalism; Environmental Journalism; National Association of Science Writers; Society of Environmental Journalists

Further Readings

National Association of Science Writers: www.nasw.org
Society of Environmental Journalists: www.sej.org

Carson, Rachel (1907–1964)

Rachel Carson was a U.S. marine biologist and author who is best known for writing *Silent Spring,* a book that documented what the improper usage of pesticides such as DDT did to the environment. Published in 1962, *Silent Spring* was first serialized in the *New Yorker,* allowing its message to penetrate the public conscience and gain notoriety among its detractors. The book is credited with bringing about the environmental and "green" movements. Carson's other books were *Under the Sea-Wind* (1948), *The Sea Around Us* (1951), *The Edge of the Sea* (1955), and *The Sense of Wonder* (1965).

Early Life and Career

Born in Pennsylvania, Carson was fascinated by nature and the ocean since childhood. At an early age, she developed a strong respect and adoration for nature. She received a Bachelor of Arts degree from the Pennsylvania College for Women in 1929. After her senior year of college, Carson received a fellowship with the Woods Hole Marine Biological Laboratory. In 1932, Carson graduated from The Johns Hopkins University with a master's degree in zoology.

A mentor at the U.S. Bureau of Fisheries helped her secure a part-time position as a writer. As Carson climbed the government ranks to become an editor and writer for professional journals and consumer publications, she also freelanced, contributing articles and book reviews to the *Baltimore Sun, Collier's, Reader's Digest,* and the *Atlantic.*

Her 1937 *Atlantic* article, "Undersea," jump-started her interest in professional writing. The first book she wrote, *Under the Sea-Wind* in 1941, was a critical success, and the second book, *The Sea Around Us,* was a best seller. Following the success of *The Sea Around Us,* Carson retired from the federal government and wrote her third book, *The Edge of the Sea,* an exploration of different seashores and sea animals.

Origins of *Silent Spring*

The idea behind the *Silent Spring* project had percolated within Rachel Carson for years. In the mid-1940s, she learned about the dangers of DDT. What prompted Carson to write about these chemicals was a 1957 to 1958 lawsuit to block the aerial spraying on DDT on private property.

According to her contracts with Houghton Mifflin and the *New Yorker,* Carson was to serve as the editor for a book regarding the impact toxins had on the environment and have her chapter appear in the magazine. As the research ensued, she realized that the book should come from a single author and that she should write that book. That book was *Silent Spring*. Originally titled *Man Against the Earth*, *Silent Spring* focused on the toxic side effects of commonly used chemical pesticides and the irresponsible, dangerous use of these insecticides, herbicides, and fungicides.

In 1962, *Silent Spring* was published as a series of *New Yorker* articles and as a Houghton Mifflin book. Before the article was first serialized and before the book was published, a counter campaign, launched by the chemical industry, targeted Carson's credibility and that of *Silent Spring*. Chemical companies sent informational pieces to legislators, editors, publishers, and influential citizens. Houghton Mifflin and the *New Yorker* were pressured not to publish Carson's work, and the opposition attempted to control and massage the media coverage of the issue.

The book drew Americans into an engaging public debate about pesticide dangers. Some saw *Silent Spring* as a call to reconsider the misuse of pesticides and examine society's connection with nature. Others perceived *Silent Spring* as faulty, biased science pushed upon the U.S. public and as the end to modern society, and they believed Carson called for the ban of all pesticides. (She did not.) Carson herself wrote that she did not intend for chemical insecticides never to be used. Rather, she sought to keep from making "poisonous and biologically potent chemicals" available indiscriminately to those ignorant of their risks. According to Priscilla Murphy, the remarkable aspect of the debate was that the hot topic under debate was generated by one person, a sole writer whose only forum was "the simple dyad" of author and reader. The book was named a Book-of-the-Month-Club selection, and the Consumer Union put out a special edition for its members. Carson appeared in a special news program, *CBS Reports*, which aired with limited advertiser support and under "cease and desist" warnings from one chemical company.

As she spent 4½ years researching and writing *Silent Spring*, Carson suffered personal setbacks and health problems. Her beloved mother died, and she was diagnosed with breast cancer in 1960. The cancer rapidly metastasized. Two years after the publication of *Silent Spring*, Carson died on April 14, 1964.

Natalie Tindall

See also Environmental Journalism; Narrative in Science Communication

Further Readings

Carson, R. (2002). *Silent spring* (40th anniversary ed.). Boston: Houghton Mifflin.

Lear, L. (1997). *Rachel Carson: Witness for nature*. New York: Henry Holt.

Lyttle, M. H. (2007). *The gentle subversive: Rachel Carson,* Silent Spring, *and the rise of the environmental movement*. New York: Oxford University Press.

Marco, G. J., Hollingworth, R. M., & Durham, W. (Eds.). (1987). Silent Spring *revisited*. Washington, DC: American Chemical Society.

Murphy, P. C. (2005). *What a book can do: The publication and reception of* Silent Spring. Boston: University of Massachusetts Press.

Waddell, C. (Ed.). (2000). *And no birds sing: Rhetorical analyses of Rachel Carson's* Silent Spring. Carbondale: Southern Illinois University Press.

CARVER, GEORGE WASHINGTON (CA. 1864–1943)

George Washington Carver, agricultural scientist, educator, humanitarian, and the son of slaves, is believed to have been born around 1864. Mary Carver, George's mother, was a slave belonging to Moses and Susan Carver in Diamond Grove, Missouri, although it is unclear who his father was. Mary Carver and the infant George were kidnapped by slave raiders, and although the baby was eventually returned to the Carvers, his mother never was. Raised by Moses and Susan Carver, young George learned all about the plants and his local community. From the very beginning, he was dedicated to learning, for he believed it was God's will, and as a teenager, he left his home for nearby Neosho, Missouri. There he resided with Andrew and Mariah Watkins while he attended school. Eventually, Carver would become well-known as a science educator and science communicator and for his agricultural research.

To further his quest for learning, he traveled to Kansas, hoping to expand his educational opportunities. He graduated from high school but was denied enrollment at Highland College after he arrived and they realized he was African American. He supported himself by homesteading and taking in laundry. He was welcomed to Simpson College (Indianola, Iowa) in 1890, where his talent for art and botany were apparent. His art teacher, Etta Budd, was concerned about Carver's ability to support himself. She encouraged Carver to pursue a career in botany and horticulture through her father, Joseph Budd, Horticulture Department Chair at Iowa Agricultural College (IAC, now Iowa State University) in Ames, Iowa. Carver entered the college in 1892 and specialized in botany and mycology, the study of fungi. During his time at IAC, he participated in the Welch Eclectic Literary Society, was elected quartermaster in the student military company, and was active in the YMCA. While there were early moments of racial difficulty, Carver eventually won over the student body, which subsequently nicknamed him "Doctor." In 1894, Carver attended the Columbian World Exposition in Chicago with other IAC students, where he displayed his paintings. He graduated as the college's first African American student and authored the class poem for his senior class.

IAC hired Carver as an assistant botanist on the faculty, and he also served as an extension specialist for the college, which was a land grant institution. He received his master's degree in 1896 and shortly thereafter accepted an appointment with Tuskegee Institute (now Tuskegee University), based on a personal invitation from its president, Booker T. Washington. His Iowa connections continued to serve him well throughout his career. During his time at IAC, he developed connections with three future U.S. Secretaries of Agriculture, James "Tama Jim" Wilson, Henry A. Wallace, and Henry C. Wallace.

Carver was named the director and instructor in scientific agriculture and dairy science at Tuskegee and found his position very challenging. He organized the department, taught classes, and focused on research and extension work throughout the state. He was also named the director of Tuskegee's Experiment Station and made particular efforts at expanding technology and potential new crops for the African American agricultural community. He sponsored farmer's institutes, created a demonstration school on wheels (called the Jesup wagon) to travel to local communities, and

George Washington Carver graduation photograph, 1894, Iowa Agricultural College. Reproduced by permission.

Source: Special Collections Department, Iowa State University Library.

published numerous extension bulletins on agriculture and food preparation. His 1925 bulletin, "How to Grow the Peanut and 105 Ways of Preparing It for Consumption," offered farmers a nutritional and soil-enriching alternative to a cotton-based system. During Carver's time at Tuskegee, cotton was at great risk from the boll weevil. His research also focused on food and industrial uses not only for the peanut, but also for the sweet potato, cotton, clay, corn, soybeans, and pecans. Carver is known as the "father of chemurgy" for his work in converting organic material to industrial uses. He received patents for a cosmetic based on peanuts and two other inventions, and the Carver Penol Company was formed to market a combination of creosote and peanut juices used in massage, but his goal was always to share his research and findings with the public. Throughout his career, Carver was also an excellent plant collector, and he contributed numerous specimens to botanical collections.

Carver's true gift, however, was in his teaching and his ability to make science come alive for his audience. This talent served him well in the classroom and in the presentations he made to white audiences and communities. As the 20th century continued, he was called upon frequently to speak, and in 1921, he appeared before the U.S. House of Representatives Ways and Means Committee on behalf of peanut growers. He may have been perceived as nonthreatening and above the racial fray, although he had directly experienced racism. He was also regarded as an eccentric genius researcher, whose poor dress contrasted with the flower he wore daily in his buttonhole. He spoke all over the country to farming and industrial groups and developed friendships with Thomas Edison, Henry Ford, Mahatma Gandhi, and other prominent individuals. He was deeply religious, although distinctly nonsectarian, and he always saw his research and teaching as part of God's plan.

Carver received many honors in his lifetime, including being named a Fellow of the Royal Society (1916), receiving the Spingarn Medal (1923), and receiving the Roosevelt Medal for Outstanding Contribution to Southern Agriculture (1942). The George Washington Carver Museum at Tuskegee was dedicated in 1941. Carver died on January 5, 1943, but his honors continued. His birthplace in Diamond, Missouri, was named a national monument in 1943. Commemorative postage stamps (1947 and 1998) and a 50-cent coin (1951) were also commissioned in his honor. He was elected to the Hall of Fame for Great Americans (1977) and inducted into the National Inventors Hall of Fame (1990). He received honorary degrees from Simpson College, University of Rochester, Selma University, and Iowa State University.

Tanya Zanish-Belcher

See also Land Grant System, U.S.

Further Readings

Kitchens, J. W., & Kitchens, L. B. (Eds.). (1975). *George Washington Carver papers at Tuskegee Institute archives* [Microfilm]. Tuskegee, AL: Carver Research Foundation, Tuskegee Institute.

Kremer, G. R. (Ed.). (1987). *George Washington Carver in his own words.* Columbia: University of Missouri.

McMurry, L. O. (1981). *George Washington Carver: Scientist and symbol.* New York: Oxford University Press.

Legacy of George Washington Carver (Iowa State University): Web site available at www.lib.iastate.edu/spcl/gwc/home.html

CENSORSHIP IN SCIENCE

The term *censorship* often suggests prohibitions on obscene or indecent material, not scientific statements. In the past few years, many Americans have heard about censorship in relation to various celebrities accused of saying or doing something considered indecent or obscene, often in cases involving on-air personalities. However, censorship can mean many things other than attempts to prevent this kind of inappropriate material from reaching audiences. For example, the term censorship is also used to describe press restrictions in effect under conditions of war or other national emergencies. And one of the most famous censorship cases from history was about science: the case of Galileo Galilei, who was told by religious leaders in the early 1600s that it was heresy for him to assert that the sun, not the Earth, was the center of the universe. At the time Galilei was alive, the Church was the authority on issues related to the natural world.

In modern times, various mechanisms have been put in place to try to make sure that the science people are exposed to is "good" science in the sense that published scientific findings are based on approved scientific methods. One key mechanism is the peer-review system, which means that scientific papers are evaluated by others, often anonymously, who ask whether the research has been carried out according to accepted standards. Some scientists who have been rejected in this way may claim they are being censored, but many scientists would agree that the system is not about censorship, but about providing checks and balances that will continue to keep scientific research legitimate.

Other cases are not so clear-cut. There are some fields—such as the study of the paranormal (ghosts, UFOs, or mysterious disappearances)—that are not considered as legitimate as the familiar sciences such as physics, biology, or psychology. Whether reactions to this kind of study from the scientific community should be thought of as censorship is an open question. There are, however, other cases in which the effort to censor someone doing scientific research is much clearer. And censorship is not limited to extremist views or to the events of previous centuries. Many examples of censoring science can be founded in recent times.

Climate Change

According to the June 19, 2003, *New York Times*, the Bush administration changed a report from the Environmental Protection Agency (EPA), deleting many of the statements on the effects of climate change. An opinion piece in the *Boston Globe* a few days later, on June 23, 2003, stated that George W. Bush claimed he was looking for what he considered sound science on the subject. EPA administrator Christine Todd Whitman left her post shortly thereafter.

Whitman was not the only individual who was caught up in this controversy over global warming. National Aeronautics and Space Administration (NASA) scientist James Hansen concluded that historical trajectories of Earth's climate pointed to an increase in global temperatures that was beyond anything that could be predicted by natural processes. After he reported these findings in the late 1980s, numerous bills were introduced into Congress that were meant to decrease (or at least contain) carbon emissions produced in the United States (such as those in car vehicle exhaust or emissions from coal refineries). By the time Bush became president in 2001, none of the bills had yet become law, and Bush announced that his campaign promises to limit carbon emissions were unrealistic. A few years later, Bush's political appointees were accused of preventing reporters from interviewing Hansen and other NASA scientists whose views disagreed with those of the White House.

Editing a report does not always mean it has been censored, nor is it censorship to disagree with someone else's opinion. Censorship occurs when messages are removed from circulation or their publication is prevented, when they are changed in meaning with the intent of suppressing particular findings, or when someone is prevented from speaking. In other words, if Hansen says that climate change is real and someone else says he or she disagrees, that is not censorship. If Hansen is told to keep quiet or his opportunity to speak or report his findings is taken away, then it is censorship.

Endangered Species

There are numerous reports on the negative impacts that activities supported by business and political interests may have on the flora and fauna of our planet. When scientists study these impacts, their reports are often changed or silenced by those who stand to lose if an endangered plant or animal stands in their way. In various places across the United States, business interests have fought with zoologists, ecologists, and biologists over the impact of their operations (such as mining or logging) in a certain area. This includes asking for court-issued gag orders on scientists and their findings when their reports show that a new business operation could have a negative impact on a plant or animal. The business group may then hire their own scientists to do a study, and it is typical that these scientists will come to a different conclusion—that doing business in an area will have no negative impact on the local ecological system.

Efforts at censoring biological reports have been alleged in cases such as the spotted owl (harmed by logging), sea turtles (harmed by shrimp harvesting), and dolphins (harmed by tuna fishing). In each case, critics have charged that efforts were made to suppress scientific reports showing a detrimental outcome to these animals under current or planned business practices. While reports did finally come to light showing the conflicts between humans and animals, individuals and groups were accused of trying to keep them from being seen or heard by the public.

Human Origins

In a 1998 book titled *Forbidden Archeology*, Michael A. Cremo and Richard L. Thompson argue that mainstream scientists are reluctant to accept the idea that humanlike creatures have been on Earth for far longer than has been believed. These authors believe that *Homo sapiens* would have needed a very long time to evolve—that we are really the product of millions of years of change. The authors contend that archaeologists and paleontologists keep finding bits and pieces of older and older humanoids, proof that the human line stretches back much further in time than is currently accepted. They argue that million-year-old bone fragments that appear to share similar DNA to humans have been found but that the people trying to publish these findings have been told their science is unfounded and does not fit with current scientific thoughts on the developmental of the human race.

Other scientists say that this work is ridiculous at best, arguing that very little of the evidence presented in *Forbidden Archeology* is available for testing. For example, no evidence is available from the Hueyatlaco archaeological site in Mexico, the site of a study during the 1960s—some say because the Mexican government took all the artifacts and hid them away and therefore no more tests can be run on them. The original research team has argued that they used standard scientific dating methods and found that the artifacts were approximately 250,000 to 300,000 years old, yet current scientific thought states that humans did not come to the Americas until about 10,000 to 25,000 years ago. Was the evidence for an earlier arrival really censored by those with a vested interest in saying that humans did not come to the New World until much later?

Within the scientific community, many individuals have built entire careers and reputations on particular theories, and to give credence to new theories could mean that their cherished ideas have been wrong. While Cremo and Thompson may be wrong themselves, they claim that the evidence that would support their theory has been suppressed.

Censorship and Bioterrorism

In April 2002, Abigail Salyers, the president of the American Society for Microbiology, wrote an editorial that appeared in *Science* (one of the top scientific journals in the world) concerning government censorship after the 2001 bioterrorism attacks in the United States in 2001 involving anthrax. According to Salyers, government officials became concerned that terrorists might be able to use scientific research on viruses and other diseases to wage biological warfare in the United States and abroad. Given these fears, there was a push from some officials for some kind of government oversight of scientific articles and other communications. Salyers, however, argued that by censoring scientific publications, the public would be led to a false sense of security, and scientists who needed to know certain information in case of an emergency would not have access to it.

Protecting the public is a very real concern for many scientists and government officials, especially during crises such as the terrorist attacks of September 11, 2001. According to Salyers, public opinion in the early years of the 21st century has started to turn against scientists, as people begin questioning a seeming lack of accountability on the part of the scientific community. Scientists often say that their work is purely scientific and that if something bad happens because of it, it is likely to be the fault of others putting their ideas to wrongful ends, not the scientific work itself. This denial of responsibility could make censorship more likely.

Full disclosure of how someone has gone about doing his or her research, including information on funding sources, may be our best protection against bogus science, not censorship. In each of the cases presented in this entry, dissenting and conflicting views can be found; total censorship, meaning that only one side of a story is known, did not develop. With the advent and spread of new communication technologies—from telephones to the Internet—total censorship is rare. Yet powerful interests can still distort scientific results. One of the more notorious cases from recent history is the tobacco industry, in which scientists continued to say that smoking was neither addictive nor a health threat long after their research was finding these problems. Not releasing findings, a form of self-censorship, may reflect fears of retribution—or simply the loss of a paycheck. The future is likely to bring us more such cases.

Toby A. Ten Eyck

See also Conflicts of Interest in Science; Galilei, Galileo; Peer Review; Research Ethics, Overview; Scientific Ethos

Further Readings

Atkins, R., & Mintcheva, S. (Eds.). (2006). *Censoring culture*. New York: New Press.

Collins, H., & Pinch, T. (1998). *The golem*. New York: Cambridge University Press.

Gedicks, A. (1993). *The new resource wars.* Boston: South End Press.

Vaughn, J. (2006). *Environmental politics: Domestic and global dimensions.* Belmont, CA: Wadsworth.

Center for Science in the Public Interest

The Center for Science in the Public Interest (CSPI) describes itself as a consumer advocacy organization with "twin missions": (1) to conduct innovative research and advocate for health and nutrition programs and (2) to provide people with useful consumer information about their health and well-being. CSPI was founded in 1971. In both its founding and its work over the years, the center has been an extension of the consumer advocacy approach pioneered by activist Ralph Nader.

CSPI's founders were Michael F. Jacobson, who has a doctorate in microbiology and has been the organization's executive director since 1978; Albert Fritch, a chemist; and James Sullivan, a meteorologist. All had worked together briefly at Nader's Center for the Study of Responsive Law, also based in Washington, D.C., which had been established 3 years earlier to conduct research and engage in educational projects designed to encourage major U.S. institutions to focus on the needs of the citizen-consumer.

CSPI, with more than 900,000 members and a staff of 60, continues to emphasize issues of health—especially those involving food safety and nutrition—and a variety of other consumer-oriented issues. As explained on the Web site, the organization has adopted three main goals:

- To make useful, objective information available to the public and policymakers in areas such as food, alcohol, health, and the environment, and to conduct related research
- To advocate for the interests of citizens before regulatory, judicial, and legislative bodies with respect to these and other issues
- To make sure that science and technology are used for the public good and to encourage scientists to engage in activities supportive of the public interest

CSPI's newsletter, *Nutrition Action Healthletter,* is not only its principal channel of providing information to the public but also (via subscription fees) a major source of funds for the nonprofit group. Foundation grants typically make up between 5% to 10% of CSPI's $17 million annual revenue (figure for 2006). This has included grants from organizations such as Heinz Endowments, Rockefeller Family Fund, The Rockefeller Foundation, Beldon Fund, C.S. Fund, and the Robert Wood Johnson Foundation. The center stresses that it accepts no corporate contributions or government grants, and *Nutrition Action Healthletter* accepts no advertising.

CSPI led efforts that won passage of the Nutrition Labeling and Education Act of 1990, which requires nutrition information on most food labels. An early CSPI campaign was against the use of sulfite preservatives, believed to be the cause of numerous deaths due to anaphylactic reactions; the campaign resulted in the Food and Drug Administration's banning sulfites from fresh fruits and vegetables. The center gained worldwide attention for its studies on the nutritional value of restaurant meals. Through litigation and media attention, CSPI has worked to stop deceptive food labels and advertising in many instances. It has been in the forefront in the recent successful campaign to stop the use of trans fats by restaurants and food processors. *The Boston Globe* once described CSPI as the "most respected nutrition advocacy group" in the United States.

One of CSPI's foci is encouraging healthier diets for children. It has worked with citizens groups and legislators around the country to get foods of poor nutritional quality out of schools. Its Integrity in Science project has developed a database of nearly 5,000 scientists, physicians, and nutritionists who are believed to have financial ties to food, energy, chemical, and other companies. That project has spurred regulatory agencies to drop scientists with conflicts of interest from advisory committees and is credited with spurring major newspapers, including the *Washington Post* and the *New York Times,* to advise readers when the scientists they quote have consulted for or received grants from industry.

In an autobiographical note introducing the 35-year history of CSPI and posted on its Web site, executive director Jacobson recalls that when he left the Massachusetts Institute of Technology in 1969, after having just received his PhD in microbiology, he had plenty of career opportunities in "academia, government, and, of course, industry." But in 1970, Jacobson went to Washington, D.C., a few days after the 1970 Earth Day celebration; he decided to use his "scientific training to help solve" a few of the "health or environmental problems" in the United States. Jacobson reports that he began by working in Ralph Nader's office, writing a book about food additives; here, he met the two other scientists who later helped him create CSPI, a "vehicle" to turn "our concerns into action."

The organization also has its critics. In a statement given at a Food and Drug Administration public meeting on obesity in 2003 and also posted online, David Martosko, director of research for the Center for Consumer Freedom, called CSPI a "radical nutrition activist group" that had "never met a tasty food" that it could not complain about. CSPI, for its part, lists the Center for Consumer Freedom on its Integrity in Science site as a nonprofit organization receiving corporate funding, the recipient of $900,000 in donations from the Philip Morris Corporation and numerous smaller grants from the food and restaurant industry.

Jacobson's latest book (on which the staff of the center is listed as a coauthor) is *Six Arguments for a Greener Diet: How a Plant-Based Diet Could Save Your Health and the Environment.*

Karl Grossman

See also Communication Campaigns in Health and Environment; Food and Drug Administration, U.S.; Health Communication, Overview

Further Readings

Center for Science in the Public Interest: www .cspinet.org

Jacobson, M. J., & Staff of the Center for Science in the Public Interest. (2006). *Six arguments for a greener diet: How a plant-based diet could save your health and the environment.* Washington, DC: Center for Science in the Public Interest.

Nutrition Labeling and Education Act of 1990, Pub. L. No. 101-535.

CENTERS FOR DISEASE CONTROL AND PREVENTION, U.S.

The U.S. Centers for Disease Control and Prevention (CDC) is an agency within the Department of Health and Human Services (HHS). It is dedicated to promoting health and quality of life by preventing and controlling disease, injury, and disability and to preparing for new health threats in the United States. The CDC is an important provider of critical information related to its mission; this information often forms the backbone of breaking news about emerging health-related conditions. In addition, the CDC's National Center for Health Marketing provides resources and information specifically related to health communication efforts. Communication is central to the accomplishment of the CDC's public health mission.

The Communicable Disease Center, the predecessor of the CDC, was established on July 1, 1946, in Atlanta, Georgia. It was then a branch of the U.S. Public Health Service, a part of the Department of Health, Education and Welfare, which later became HHS. In the very beginning, the CDC focused on controlling malaria, largely through the use of the pesticide DDT. However, the founder of this small agency, Joseph W. Moustin, envisioned a more crucial role that the CDC could play in public health. Moustin pushed the CDC to expand its mission to include concern with any communicable diseases except for tuberculosis and venereal disease, which at that time had separate units in Washington, D.C. Moustin's dreams were realized as the CDC quickly became the center of epidemiology work for the United States.

One of the keys to the CDC's success has been disease surveillance. In 1949, Alexander Langmuir launched the first-ever disease surveillance program to monitor the progression of disease. This program confirmed the eradication of malaria, which became one of the first milestones of the CDC's achievements in public health. The surveillance program later successfully traced poliomyelitis cases in children to defective vaccine. It also traced the cause of a massive influenza epidemic in 1957. These achievements showed the CDC's indispensability in protecting citizens' health. It was not long before the CDC finally acquired the responsibility of monitoring and responding to venereal disease and tuberculosis. By the 1970s and 1980s, the CDC was successfully tracking and monitoring a broad range of new disease outbreaks including Legionnaires' disease (1976), toxic shock syndrome (1980), and acquired immunodeficiency syndrome (AIDS, first documented by CDC in 1981).

The CDC continued to expand its focus with the establishment of new programs and the acquisition of existing programs. With the addition in the 1950s and 1960s of a variety of new programs, the CDC became a much more diversified agency that had broadened its scope beyond monitoring communicable disease. Therefore, in 1970, its name was changed to the Centers for Disease Control, and the acronym CDC was retained. As part of its growth, the CDC joined with international public health programs in worldwide disease control efforts. One of the most noticeable contributions was the global eradication of smallpox, which was officially accomplished by 1977. The CDC is now one of only two repositories in the world that has the smallpox virus, which is contained in its high-security Biosafety Level 4 laboratories.

According to the Preventive Health Amendments of 1992, the U.S. Congress changed CDC's name again to the Centers for Disease Control and Prevention to acknowledge its contribution in the prevention of "disease, injury and disability"; however, the well-known acronym CDC was kept. By the 21st century, the CDC's efforts extended well beyond the traditional meaning of public health. To respond to the September 11, 2001, terrorist attacks and subsequent anthrax attacks, the CDC took on the responsibility of guarding the United States against bioterrorism.

Currently, the CDC is widely acknowledged as a leading public health agency with an annual budget of $8.8 billion (FY 2008). Apart from its headquarters in DeKalb County, Georgia, the CDC has branches in 10 other locations throughout the United States and in Puerto Rico. In 2005, the CDC completed its first major organizational restructuring in more than 25 years. Under the new structure, there are about 15,000 employees grouped under the CDC Office of the Director, coordinating centers, and national centers. The coordinating centers are a newly added leadership and organizational level between the office of the director and the various national centers. The coordinating center structure is intended to better integrate the work of the national centers through enhanced collaboration and innovation across organizational boundaries. These coordinating centers include the Coordinating Office for Global Health, the Coordinating Office for Terrorism Preparedness and Emergency Response, the National Institute for Occupational Safety and Health, the Coordinating Center for Environmental Health and Injury Prevention, the Coordinating Center for Health Information and Service, the Coordinating Center for Health Promotion, and the Coordinating Center for Infectious Diseases. Four coordinating centers oversee the activities at specified national centers, while the other three deal with agency-wide issues.

Since its establishment more than 60 years ago, the CDC has been committed to protecting health and promoting quality of life through the prevention and control of disease, injury, and disability. Rather than simply treating illness or disease care, the CDC's mission is focused on health protection and health maintenance. It has continued to conduct surveillance on a wide range of health threats—from infectious diseases to bioterrorism to environmental hazards. The CDC experts are poised to go whenever called to the sites of disease outbreaks, ferret out the cause, and provide technical assistance. The CDC has also funded state and local health departments, organizations, and academic institutions engaged in a broad spectrum of public health programs and research. The CDC has such an extensive impact that every American inevitably benefits from the organization's ideas, guidance, or recommendations regarding health-related issues.

Chubo Ren

See also Communication Campaigns in Health and Environment; Health Communication, Overview; Health Communication and the Internet; Public Health Service, U.S.

Further Readings

Centers for Disease Control, U.S. (1996). Historical perspectives: History of CDC. *Morbidity and Mortality Weekly Report, 45*(25), 526–530.

Centers for Disease Control, U.S.: www.cdc.gov

Government Accountability Office, U.S. (2008, February). *Centers for Disease Control and Prevention: Changes in obligations and activities before and after fiscal year 2005 budget reorganization* (GAO-08-328R). Washington, DC: Author.

Sencer, D. J. (2006). CDC's 60th anniversary: Director's perspective. *Morbidity and Mortality Weekly Report, 55*(27), 745–749.

CHERNOBYL

On April 26, 1986, around 1:23 in the morning, unit 4 of the Chernobyl nuclear power plant near Pripyat, Ukraine, exploded, sending millions of radioactive particles into the atmosphere. More than 350,000 people had to be evacuated or resettled from the most contaminated areas of Belarus, Ukraine, and Russia. The nuclear cloud traveled over much of Europe, falling as radioactive rain. Decades after the accident 4.5 million people continue to live in irradiated areas. This entry provides an overview of the multiple causes of devastation in addition to the consequences that continue to be felt by generations of Chernobyl survivors. Communication failures were an important component, and the fate of the disaster's survivors continues to appear in contemporary news reports.

Causes of the Disaster

Human, technological, and systemic failures, alongside communication failures, came together to cause the Chernobyl catastrophe. The consequences of these multiple failures are still being felt today.

Human Failure

Operators were conducting an experiment on the RBMK-1000 graphite-moderated uranium reactor to determine how much energy would continue to be expended by the turbine rotor if the reactor should fail. The experiment was started in the afternoon of April 25, 1986, as scheduled. However, at the request of a load dispatcher in Kiev, the removal of the unit from the grid was delayed. Since that day operators had already begun reducing output as needed for the experiment, unit 4 was kept operating with the core cooling system switched off, clearly breaching safety rules.

The operators conducting the test in the early morning of April 26 also violated multiple nuclear safety rules. The operators shut off the automatic controls, blocked the protection systems, and reduced the operational reactivity reserve below the permissible level, rendering the emergency power reduction system useless. To quickly increase power, the graphite control rods were removed by hand, causing the reactor to become more sensitive to fluctuations. When the cooling water overheated and turned to steam, the control rods could not be lowered fast enough. Because the heat was so intense, the tips of the graphite rods that were inserted caused a reaction that only increased the temperature further. The resulting explosions blasted the thousand-ton "safety" cover off the top of the reactor and shot burning graphite and radionuclides high into the air.

Very few operators in the entire plant were actually trained in nuclear technology. Most operators were electrical engineers with experience in coal and gasification plants. While an explosion at such a thermal power station will no doubt cause destruction, the devastation will not continue to be found in cancer-causing radioactive particles for literally hundreds of years after the explosion, as is the case with nuclear power plants. Peter Gould, in his analysis of the democratic consequences of Chernobyl, explained that little shared knowledge exists between electrical engineers and atomic engineers. Grigori Medvedev, a nuclear physicist who once worked at Chernobyl, documented that operators were hired and promoted based not on their knowledge and ability to work with nuclear technology but on their standing in the Communist Party and on past experience with the station director at thermal plants. The safety programs should not have been ignored during the test, but the operators had little knowledge as to the devastation such lax protocols could inflict. Six operators, including the chief engineer and station director, were eventually prosecuted for "violations of discipline."

Technology Failure

Graphite-moderated reactors are inherently more dangerous than the more common water-moderated reactors. In water-moderated plants, reactivity decreases as temperature increases. In graphite-moderated plants, reactivity increases as temperature increases, making the reactor unstable when energy is reduced. The design of the control rods was specifically noted as a contributing factor in the disaster. The "controlling" aspect of the rods is located above graphite tips. While fully inserted rods do slow down a reaction, the graphite tips actually speed up a reaction. This design flaw was unknown to the operators when they attempted to quickly insert the rods into the already overheated reactor. Charles Perrow is among the scholars who refer to the complexities specific to nuclear power management. Specific to Chernobyl, the safety systems put in place as redundancies actually contributed to the accident.

System Failure

Operators also had little knowledge of the possibility of failure. All incidents were filtered through Moscow, Russia. Reports of known "failures" at nuclear power stations were withheld not only from the public, but also from personnel at other nuclear power stations. The Three Mile Island accident had occurred 6 years earlier in the United States, and yet Chernobyl operators were working under the assumption that accidents do not happen at Soviet nuclear power stations. Despite the *perestroika* (restructuring) and *glasnost* (transparency) of Mikhail Gorbachev's rule, the preexisting bureaucracy smothered any negative news in the industry. In his book, *No Breathing Room,* Medvedev detailed his struggle with government censors as he fought to publish articles warning of nuclear catastrophes in the years prior to Chernobyl. With no acknowledgement of failure there was no opportunity for operators to learn from the accidents that had occurred at other nuclear facilities. The system created hubris that manifested itself in the disregard for training requirements and safety protocols. The secrecy continued even after the explosion, costing further lives and obliterating trust in government.

Communication Failure

Following the explosion, the operators wrongfully assumed the reactor was still intact and even ignored reports that it was not, all the while suffering the effects of radiation. Hundreds of unknowing firefighters were sent up to the burning roof, returning with a "nuclear tan." Over the course of the next 10 days, helicopters dumped sand, clay, and minerals on the fire, and military personnel collected the strewn radioactive graphite from around the decimated reactor by hand. An estimated 600,000 *liquidators*, the term used to describe those involved in the cleanup operations, were exposed to high levels of radiation until the reactor was finally entombed in its now deteriorating concrete sarcophagus. According to official reports, just 31 people died as a direct cause of the incident. However, shortly after the explosion, Moscow officials directed physicians not to cite radiation as the cause of death.

The assumption that the reactor was still intact also delayed the evacuation of the region until 2:00 p.m. on April 27, 1986, exposing hundreds of thousands of people to radiation. The people of Pripyat and the villages within a 6-mile zone around the reactor were evacuated first. The people were told to dress lightly and take as little as possible, for they would only be gone for a few days. The town of Pripyat today remains a ghost town filled with personal belongings, as the radioactivity level is still too high to allow citizens to return. Even worse, because the radiation dispersed unevenly, some evacuees were moved to even more contaminated areas and had to be moved again. Through the end of May 1986, the city of Chernobyl and surrounding villages in an 18-mile radius were evacuated as well.

Even during the evacuation of Pripyat, no public warnings were issued notifying the world of the nuclear cloud making its way across Europe. The radiation was detected in Sweden before a statement was made on April 28 stating that there had been an accident but that everything was under control. May Day celebrations were held outdoors even as radioactive rain fell on some parades. Optimistic news reports denounced the "lies" generated by Western media. As radiation levels in milk and foodstuffs began to increase, contradictory warnings were issued, creating more distrust of central authorities. The official message from the Soviet Union was that the accident was contained, but that children should stay indoors and no one should drink milk or eat food from his or her gardens.

The Soviet Union was not the only government providing conflicting messages. Radiation numbers were averaged to downplay the danger in countries across eastern and western Europe. Peter

Gould analyzed the responses of the countries affected by the nuclear fallout. He found that, with the exception of Germany, the countries with the highest dependency on atomic power also had the greatest tendency to manipulate or suppress the facts surrounding radiation levels. In some countries, people were instructed to stay indoors, and milk and foodstuffs were imported until radiation levels declined. In other countries, no warnings were issued or only reassuring messages were provided. Because media overlapped across countries, no one knew whom to trust. The exaggeration of U.S. media and officials as to the number of people killed and the effect of the radiation only intensified the confusion.

The direct causes of the accident including the human, technological, and systemic failures created a grave situation. However, lives could have been saved and consequences could have been limited with appropriate communication following the explosion. The next section focuses on the multiple consequences of the disaster still being felt today.

Consequences of the Disaster

The disparities caused by the fallout from Chernobyl continue to be disputed. Lack of health reporting before Chernobyl makes it difficult to make comparisons before and after the event. In addition, the breakup of the Soviet Union and the resulting economic downturn in the former Soviet states only increased the risk for health disparities. While organizations continue to argue over the impact of the disaster, most agree that one of the greatest risks is to the mental health of those living with the uncertainty of how Chernobyl will continue to impact their lives.

Health Consequences

The United Nations Scientific Committee of the Effects of Atomic Radiation (UNSCEAR) has reported an increase in thyroid cancer linked to Chernobyl. Specifically, about 4,000 cases had been identified by 2002 in children and adolescents exposed to iodine radioisotopes following the explosion, and many more are likely to be identified. According to reports of the Chernobyl Forum, a regular meeting of the International Atomic Energy Agency, the World Health Organization,

and other international organizations, no link has been found to solid cancers (such as lung cancer) or even leukemia, which was assumed would occur based on the increase found following the atomic bombs on Hiroshima and Nagasaki, Japan. UNSCEAR also reports no link has been found between Chernobyl and an increase of birth defects, despite the number of children shown on Chernobyl charity Web sites. However, because of the fear of birth defects, there was an increase in abortions following Chernobyl. Other organizations have reported contradictory cancer numbers to UNSCEAR's findings. For example, *The Other Report on Chernobyl* predicts 30,000 to 60,000 excess cancer deaths caused by Chernobyl.

Social and Economic Consequences

Evacuees lost their jobs, their homes, and the social circles to which they had been accustomed. Contaminated land became useless for agricultural production. The economic breakdown following the breakup of the Soviet Union exacerbated the consequences of Chernobyl, leading to an increase in unemployment, a decrease in birth rates, and overall lower standards of living. Despite the restrictions on picking mushrooms, berries, and other local foodstuffs, those with no other food source have had to eat what was available, increasing their exposure to radiation. Poverty caused by resettlement and land use restrictions has caused more people to claim Chernobyl-related benefits, thereby labeling themselves *Chernobyl victims*.

Psychological Consequences

The stigma associated with being contaminated by Chernobyl has led to higher levels of stress and worse perceived health. In fact, the secondary effects linked to stress and poor living conditions are believed by some to have caused more deaths than the radiation. Fatalism is common in the most contaminated regions, and suicides have been reported, particularly in the population of liquidators. An increase in smoking, drinking, drug use, and promiscuous sex has also been found, specifically in young adults who were children at the time of Chernobyl. The belief that victims of the disaster are already tainted has lowered the perception that they are at risk for other ailments. The continued uncertainty as to the long-term effects of low-dose radiation continues to diminish trust in government agencies. Continued research, while needed to determine the consequences of Chernobyl, furthers feelings of helplessness in Chernobyl survivors.

Shari R. Veil

See also Crisis Communication; Nuclear Power; Three Mile Island

Further Readings

Abbott, P., Wallace, C., & Beck, M. (2006). Chernobyl: Living with risk and uncertainty. *Health, Risk & Society, 8*(2), 105–121.

Burlakova, E. B., & Naidich, V. I. (2006). *20 years after the Chernobyl accident: Past, present, and future.* New York: Nova Science.

Gould, P. (1990). *Fire in the rain: The democratic consequences of Chernobyl.* Baltimore: Johns Hopkins University Press.

Marples, D. R. (1996). *Belarus: From Soviet rule to nuclear catastrophe.* New York: St. Martin's.

Marples, D. R. (1996). The Chernobyl disaster: Its effect on Belarus and Ukraine. In J. K. Mitchell (Ed.), *The long road to recovery: Community responses to industrial disaster* (chap. 7). New York: United Nations University Press.

Medvedev, G. (1991). *The truth about Chernobyl.* New York: Basic Books.

Medvedev, G. (1993). *No breathing room.* New York: Basic Books.

Mould, R. F. (2000). *Chernobyl record: The definitive history of the Chernobyl catastrophe.* Bristol, UK: Institute of Physics.

Perrow, C. (1999). *Normal accidents: Living with high-risk catastrophes.* Princeton, NJ: Princeton University Press.

United Nations Scientific Committee of the Effects of Atomic Radiation. (2000). *Sources, effects and risks of ionizing radiation.* UNSCEAR Report to the General Assembly, with Scientific Annexes, United Nations, New York.

CHILDREN'S TELEVISION AND SCIENCE

Television holds great potential as a teaching and learning medium. Particularly for young children, this dynamic, colorful, and often musical broadcast medium is naturally appealing; children voluntarily watch it and can learn much from age-appropriate and relevant content. Well before formal educational settings, children are exposed to televised offerings, and this has a significant impact; what they view influences their behavior, values, and learning.

According to the *Sourcebook for Teaching Science,* U.S. children average about 1,500 hours per year watching television, yet only about 900 hours per year in school. Studies have shown that Americans rank among the lowest of students in industrialized nations in science, and many abandon science courses in the upper grades. Considering that Americans are comparatively low performing in science yet spend much time watching television, the potential for increasing interest in science and expanding scientific knowledge through this medium is great. This entry maps previous efforts to bring science to children's television in the United States and examines the possible impact of science education programming on the enjoyment and learning of science and on stimulating interest in science.

Motives for watching television vary with the type of program and the type of child. Among other reasons, children watch television for entertainment, to increase or decrease social contact, to pass the time, to avoid doing other things, and to obtain information about the world. Unlike the carefully managed content of media produced for school programs, most children's television programs aired on commercial channels initially went largely unregulated and do not necessarily have proven educational value. Increased time in front of the television has been linked with decreased educational performance and negative health issues.

To address this issue, Congress passed the Children's Television Act (1990), which mandated that television aimed at younger audiences must meet their educational and informational needs, and programming improved substantially. Although many early family and adult science programs influenced children's science programming, the more noteworthy ones are mentioned in the following section.

History of Science Programming for Children

Commercial network television began its rise in the postwar United States, and even in early experimentation with content, programmers included informational and scientific segments in television schedules. It was from this broader realm of educational television that children's science television originated. Yet for any show's success, mass audiences needed to be entertained as well as enlightened, yet many of the early programs aimed merely at disseminating science content to viewers. Over a few short years, the number of networks grew, media presentation skills improved, and viewers' attention became divided among numerous options, some with more exciting approaches and visual techniques. The introduction of dynamic productions particularly enamored younger viewers, preferences that were soon noted and captured in children's programs. By 1951, networks featured 27 hours of children's programs per week. Children's educational programs peaked in 1953, dropped sharply before 1960, increased slightly that decade, persistently fell until the 1990s, then steadily increased throughout the 1990s and 2000s.

Premiering in 1951, *Watch Mr. Wizard* was one of commercial television's early attempts to make science enjoyable and understandable for children. Host Don Herbert presented laboratory demonstrations in a simple, informal manner. The show featured children helpers, had a target audience of 12-year-olds, and ran continually on the National Broadcasting Company network until 1965. *Watch Mr. Wizard* won three Thomas Alva Edison National Mass Media Awards and the prestigious Peabody Award, and at its peak, it presided over nearly 50,000 Mr. Wizard fan clubs. Teachers used the show's themes in their classrooms, and Mr. Wizard products such as science kits and books were highly sought after by children. Decades later, the program gave rise to the updated and faster paced *Mr. Wizard's World* (Nickelodeon, 1983–1991).

Beginning in 1954, *Disneyland,* created by Walt Disney Studios, brought the marvels of science and nature to families through a progressive and attention-grabbing combination of animation and cinematography. Initially aired on the American Broadcasting Company (ABC) network, this highly successful series created compelling natural history narratives using nature as characters and plot. Throughout its 12-year run, 20% of *Disneyland*'s offerings were related to science, nature, space, and technology.

In the 1960s, government support for a non-profit public broadcasting system originated with the Public Broadcasting Act (1967). The aim was to provide information and education to viewers of all ages. Shortly thereafter, the newly established Public Broadcasting Service (PBS) network began to forge its identity around science programs. Preeminent during this time was the Children's Television Workshop (CTW), which revolutionized children's programming by offering educational shows for preschoolers on PBS such as *Sesame Street* (1969 to present), during which prescience segments were introduced. Although less successful due to decreased funding and low public awareness, CTW produced its first health-related series, *Feeling Good,* in 1974. Featuring celebrity guests and humorous characters, the show promoted informed health choices and educated minority and lower socioeconomic status families on healthy eating and exercise.

But *3–2–1 Contact* (1980–1988) became the first U.S. children's television program specifically designed to promote scientific thinking and the awareness of science as a career, particularly for women and minority children. At its height, the show reached 7 million viewers and was syndicated in 26 countries. Its use of young hosts and the popular Bloodhound Gang, in which three teen science sleuths solved particular mysteries using science concepts and problem-solving skills, set the standard for subsequent educational children's shows and remains an effective format for young audiences. Overlapping with this show was the national Science Journalism Award–winning *Newton's Apple* (1982–1988).

Then in the 1990s, perhaps in direct response to the CTW or simply due to increased competitive pressure and the expansion of channel capacity due to the proliferation of cable networks, an unprecedented growth occurred in science programming for children. U.S. youth audiences were introduced to *Bill Nye the Science Guy* (PBS, 1993–1994), *Beakman's World* (the Learning Channel, 1992), *The Voyage of the Mimi* (PBS, 1984–1990), and *The Magic School Bus* (PBS, 1994–1997), among many others.

The massive expansion of cable and satellite television throughout the 1980s and 1990s greatly broadened children's options and exposure to information. In 1996, the popular cable channel Discovery Kids originated; it was a spin-off from the regular Discovery Channel, which focused on science, history, and space technology. In the following decade, a plethora of children's programs with explicit or implicit science themes bombarded the screens, including *Curious George* (PBS), *Go, Diego, Go* (NickJr), and *Assignment Discovery* and *Animal Planet* (The Learning Channel).

Many of the original and even the more modern children's science programs run in syndication today worldwide and on one or more U.S. broadcast or cable television channels. Televised programs frequently have Internet Web sites devoted to interactive content and streaming video of past episodes.

Enjoyment of Science Programming

With vast opportunities to view noneducational programs, questions arise about whether children will voluntarily watch science programming and if so, will they enjoy it. The answer to both questions is yes. As with any programming designed for children, several factors influence enjoyment of science programs. Children are discerning critics; hence, the presentation style and format, including the length of the program, energy or pace, use of music, animation, humor, sound effects, graphics, special effects, and level of science content should be age appropriate for maximum attention and enjoyment. Also, program producers assume children have short attentions spans and prefer recognizable characters and stories to which they can relate. For these reasons, science programs typically run 30 minutes or less, use child actors, and cover topics pertaining to nature. Further, studies show child viewers are more likely to voluntarily watch and enjoy programs that use a feature story embedded with science compared to programs that are overtly labeled as science content.

Studies also suggest that exposure to different types of television material may influence children's beliefs and attitudes toward science and scientists. For example, children who frequently watch science fiction programs show a high liking for science. On the other hand, regular watching of noneducational cartoons is associated with low evaluations of scientists.

Teaching Science

Educational television for children can teach some subject matter more effectively than others.

For instance, mathematics and science topics have been more successfully taught via television than topics from history, literature, or the humanities. The general conclusion is that scientific concepts can be taught and durably retained by child viewers, but there are certain important considerations.

Consider *Sesame Street.* It is the most studied children's program, and research supports the assertion that preschoolers can learn skills from it that influence educational success. Regular viewers of educational programs at age 5, including *Sesame Street,* later show superior high school grades in subjects including math and science. Despite these data, examination of the effectiveness of pre-science segments introduced on the early episodes of *Sesame Street* suggested that the presentation of scientific content was appropriate but that the format design was at that time ineffective at teaching the concepts. This was attributed to lack of structure in presenting the information, and improvements have since been made.

More recent studies also support the notion that the structure of the program is important for comprehension of science extracted from television. For instance, older child viewers learn more when science content is embedded and presented in a relevant context. Science concepts entwined within the context of a story format are more effective at teaching science than concepts presented on their own or out of context. Repetition of key science concepts combined with graphic representation and several different examples are also deemed effective strategies. Postviewing teacher- or parent-led discussions about the scientific material are encouraged for comprehension, synthesis, and retention of the information.

Although a powerful argument exists for television's use as a teaching tool, it is not necessarily a substitute for hands-on interactive science experiences in the classroom, in the laboratory, or at home. Studies do not promote television consumption as preferable to high-quality manipulative play or discovery learning.

Role Models

Results from several studies contend that young males hold more positive attitudes toward science, engage in more science activities, and are more interested in pursuing science careers than young females. Such gender-specific behaviors, attitudes, and characteristics are linked to images from popular television series. Character portrayals on children's programs show twice as many male characters and twice as many male scientists as female characters and scientists.

Girls are more likely to think of scientists as being male, tend to develop a masculine image of science, and possess negative attitudes toward science, scientists, and scientific activities. This type of socialization has been a concern because television so frequently presents only basic or stereotypical images of gender roles. From *Johnny Quest* (ABC, 1964–1965) to *Jimmie Neutron* (Nickelodeon, 2002–2006), systematic observation of children's programs suggests most characters are sex stereotyped, with women generally underrepresented and less focal to the program. Females are frequently portrayed as laboratory assistants or science journalists and less frequently as science specialists. Considering that children wish to be like popular same-sex personalities, television images of female scientists who are portrayed as competent, knowledgeable, and attractive may serve as important role models and sources of information about science to young girls who may have few such real-life models. Consistent with this view, research supports the idea that girls may be positively affected by viewing programs with female characters engaged in and enjoying science. However, there is potential for a backlash effect as boys viewing females in science roles may express heightened beliefs that the field is not appropriate for women.

A related concern is the lack of science programs featuring key characters from underrepresented minorities. There is growing awareness that minorities have been consistently absent from leading science roles on television aimed at both adults and children. Only within the last decade have programmers sought to redress this balance. Some of the newer children's science shows more commonly depict racial and ethnic diversity in both hosts and guests and reflect growing sensitivity toward alternate backgrounds and interests. For example, *DragonflyTV* (PBS, 2002–present) adds modern graphics and popular music to real-life problems that are solved using applied science concepts, most often by female and minority hosts.

Conclusion

Sixty-plus years of children's television research shows that science programming can be successfully aimed at children, to increase either their learning, enjoyment, or appreciation of science and to change their attitudes toward it. This medium has great potential for influencing the pursuit of science in school and science careers later in life. Children's television programs can teach scientific content, but many factors influence their effectiveness. A growing body of research suggests character role models in science programming for children do influence young viewers' reactions to science.

Amy R. Pearce

See also Communicating Science to Children; Nye, Bill; Television Science

Further Readings

Children's Television Act of 1990, 47 U.S.C. §§ 303a, 303b, 394 (1990).

Hofferth, S. L., & Sandberg, J. F. (2001). How American children spend their time. *Journal of Marriage and the Family, 63*(2), 295–308.

Huston, A. C., & Wright, J. C. (1998). Television and informational and educational needs of children. *Annals of the American Academy of Political and Social Science, 557,* 9–23.

LaFollette, M. C. (2002). A survey of science content in U.S. television broadcasting, 1940s through 1950s. *Science Communication, 24*(1), 34–71.

Mares, M. L., Cantor, J., & Steinbach, J. B. (1999). Using television to foster children's interest in science. *Science Communication, 20*(3), 283–297.

Museum of Broadcast Communications. (n.d.). *Children and television.* Retrieved July 28, 2008, from www.museum.tv/archives/etv/C/htmlC/childrenand/childrenand.htm

Public Broadcasting Act, 47 U.S.C. § 396 (1967).

Steinke, J., & Long, M. (1996). A lab of her own? Portrayal of female characters on children's educational science programs. *Science Communication, 18*(2), 91–115.

Citizen Science

This entry describes developments in the field of public understanding of science that led to Alan

Irwin's conception of citizen science. Irwin's concept turns the public understanding of science idea on its head and explores science–society issues from the point of view of the citizens and what they consider to be relevant. This idea inspired and influenced a range of formal and informal science and technology communication initiatives and projects, which will be described in the second part.

In the 1980s, there was dissatisfaction among members of the scientific community with how members of the public perceived science. A number of mainly quantitative surveys also determined that the public was not scientifically literate enough to make informed decisions involving science. Another tendency during that time was a growing lack of trust in scientific and technological expertise as a consequence of scientific crises such as the radiation accident of the Chernobyl nuclear power plant in the former Soviet Union or the scientific uncertainties involved in the outbreak of mad cow disease (bovine spongiform encephalopathy) in Europe. Many citizens realized that they are highly dependent on scientific and technological experts to assess, calculate, measure, and predict the potential risks and benefits of the implementation of new technologies or particular scientific, technological, medical, or environmental policies.

Members of the population grew increasingly suspicious toward scientific experts since so many of the new risks, hazards, and dangers that affect citizens' lives have had their origins in scientific and technological practices. Various efforts have been made to enlighten the public about science and increase and foster a better public understanding of science. As a consequence, a range of promotional strategies and initiatives were established to better disseminate scientific knowledge and to educate the public about science. The assumption behind these initiatives was that a public that was more educated about science would take up more science and would better appreciate the value of science. In this view, there is a divide between educated scientific experts and an ill-educated public that is "ignorant" about science and needs to be educated by the experts. This asymmetric and simplified model of science–society relations that described the public as being deficient in scientific knowledge soon came under attack and was labeled the *deficit model* of science communication by a range of critics.

Science studies scholars and sociologists that empirically investigated science–society relationships found that in practice things were more difficult and complex. For instance, it was found that some citizens deliberately choose not to take up scientific knowledge for various reasons. All efforts to educate them about science were doomed to fail because they did not see it as their job to deal with scientific questions. From this point of view, it is the task of the expert to deal with scientific and technical issues. Other studies found that the scientific knowledge of the experts was too abstract to be applied to specific and local contexts. In this case, scientific experts did not manage to adapt their expert knowledge to relevant contexts of application because they failed to incorporate the local knowledge of the citizens. In fact, in some cases, the local and situated knowledge of the citizens clashed with the technical knowledge of the experts, and the experts lost their credibility among the citizens because they could not provide solutions that made sense to the locals. Not only did scientists not consider the viewpoints and concerns of citizens as being relevant to their problems, but also nonexpert citizens had problems making sense of the advice they got from the scientific and technical experts.

The overall conclusion from this kind of research is that it is not the members of the public who are ignorant about science; rather, it is the way the members of the public and their knowledge concerning science was constructed by the scientific community as ignorant with respect to what the members of the public actually think and know about science. The end result is a broadening and blurring of the concept of expertise and a better understanding of the value and relevance of the situated expertise of citizens.

Irwin's Conception of Citizen Science

Consequently, Irwin, a British sociologist, developed the concept of citizen science to look at the relationship between science and society not only from the view of the scientific community but also from the point of view of the citizens who are affected by the developments of science and technology. Irwin suggests that the citizens affected by particular scientific and technological developments should not be seen only as a purely passive audience. Science is not a monolithic block: There are a huge variety of scientific disciplines that work on different topics and use different methodologies. However, neither is the public monolithic. Members of the public differ in personal experiences and knowledge, educational achievements, cultural backgrounds, personal beliefs, income, and so on. The deficit model of science communication failed to problematize the heterogeneity of the public, which is in fact better understood as various publics for science (with a varied range of situated expertise). Further work on the divide between expert and lay knowledge explored the uptake of lay knowledge by the scientific community.

One conclusion from this work is that situated lay knowledge usefully contributes to and can become an integral part of scientific knowledge. However, this is still an asymmetric process because scientific experts must still certify the local and situated knowledge of the citizens so that it can enter the scientific realm. In this regard, it should also be noted that authors such as Charles Leadbeater and Paul Miller have observed that many enthusiasts with no specialist training became so advanced in their hobbies—for instance, in astronomy, open source software development, or music production and distribution—that they are actually pursuing these activities according to professional standards. These so-called professional amateurs usefully contribute to expert fields, often without having any form of specialist training.

Irwin also investigates practical ways that the different situated and local experiences of citizens could be incorporated into the working processes and practices of scientific and technological experts to the benefit of both the citizens and the experts. He argues that the relevance of the outcomes of scientific research for the everyday lives of citizens must be taken into account, especially if these outcomes will affect their lives. Furthermore, the idea of taking citizens' concerns seriously and their points of view as relevant points of departure for scientific research is also a way of decreasing the tension and distance between lay citizens and scientific experts.

Science Shops as an Ideal Type of Citizen Science

Irwin offers a case study about science shops as an ideal type of the interaction between citizens and scientific experts. There are many different types and sorts of science shops, but the basic idea behind this initiative is that citizens go to the science shop with a problem that occurred in their local environment. The task of the science shop is then to translate the problem of the citizens into a scientific problem and to find the relevant experts in the scientific community that can contribute to the solution of the problems of the citizens. In other words, the science shop asks what science can do for citizens.

Such forms of science–society interactions can teach us a lot about society and about science itself. Irwin found, for instance, that many of the problems defined by citizens were of a transdisciplinary nature and did not match the compartmentalization of scientific disciplines. Therefore, it was often rather difficult to find experts with the relevant expertise for solving problems from everyday life contexts. Furthermore, the study showed that the scientific enterprise hardly rewarded the participation of scientific experts in science shop initiatives. For instance, in most cases, it was not possible to publish results stemming from citizen requests for research in peer-reviewed journals, but considerable resources were still needed to solve these often complex and difficult problems.

Citizens Participating in Scientific Research

The term citizen science is now also used to describe a range of initiatives concerned with public engagement in science and informal science education activities. In these projects, which are based at universities and other scientific institutions, volunteers with no specialist scientific training participate in real scientific research. Compared to the idea of science shops, the interaction is directed by the scientific experts who generally tell the nonspecialists how they can contribute to the research projects. In many cases, the volunteers contribute to the data collection, for instance, by observing birds for the Cornell Laboratory of Ornithology, measuring local rainfall, or providing computational services through their home PCs. Professional scientists will collect the data, analyze it , and then publish the results in scientific journals. The idea behind these projects is that the participation in actual scientific research projects will have strong learning effects and transcend the limitations of one-way communication coming solely from science and technology experts by making citizens an actual part of the research.

However, little research on the impact of participating in such citizen–science projects has been carried out, and there are still difficulties with the assessment. Also, as in many projects promoting public engagement with science, it has to be assumed that the self-selection process of the participants ensures that many of the volunteers already have an interest in science that is above the average interest of the general population.

Science Education for Scientific Citizenship

The concept of citizen science has also influenced formal science education programs in many countries. The idea of science education for scientific citizenship aims at preparing younger citizens for an everyday life in societies that are enriched with science and technology. Many political issues and debates involve decisions that are interrelated with scientific and technical theories, knowledge, and explanations. The political concept of citizenship implies not only citizen rights but also citizen duties, such as the responsibility to participate in decisions that affect society as a whole.

The scientific citizenship approach in science education is therefore a crucial prerequisite and preparation for citizens to participate effectively in societies that are saturated with science and technology. It is also argued that to become informed and form a personal opinion it is necessary for citizens to develop an idea of how society shapes science and how science shapes society. Furthermore, it is argued that citizens require some understanding of the processes of science so that they can get an understanding of how, for instance, the reliability and validity of scientific claims can be assessed and make informed judgments and decisions involving science and technology that affect their lives. This argument suggests that when citizens know how to deal with scientific information and knowledge, they will be more capable of participating and deciding about issues that concern their lives and involve scientific content.

Scientists alone cannot provide consensual solutions to socioscientific problems; in many cases, scientific expertise is met by an opposing counterexpertise. Here the argument is that the scientific citizenship approach requires a general education, developing transferable skills so that citizens can critically assess new information about science and participate in decisions about scientific issues. Various programs teaching science for citizenship also include lessons on how science and technology are communicated in the media, since the media will be a major information source about science for most of the citizens of tomorrow. Some science education experts also argue for a science education that helps the citizens of tomorrow apply scientific knowledge to their own personal contexts whenever they need it. As a consequence, the content of the science curriculum must be useful and relevant to the lives of the learners, and not only for the minority that chooses to pursue a career as a scientific or technological expert. School science, in this sense, has to respond to the new social contexts of science, technology, and knowledge production, helping young people to engage reflexively with science-related issues.

Joachim Allgaier

See also Chernobyl; Deficit Model; Mad Cow Disease (BSE); Public Understanding of Science; Science Shops

Further Readings

Irwin, A. (1995). *Citizen science: A study of people, expertise and sustainable development*. London: Routledge.

Leadbeater, C., & Miller, P. (2004). *The pro-am revolution: How enthusiasts are changing our economy and society*. London: Demos.

Phillips, T., Lewenstein, B., & Bonney, R. (2006). A case study of citizen science. In C. Donghong, J. Metcalfe, & B. Schiele (Eds.), *At the human scale: International practices in science communication* (pp. 317–334). Beijing, China: Science Press.

Ratcliffe, M., & Grace, M. (2003). *Science education for citizenship: Teaching socio-scientific issues*. Maidenhead, UK: Open University Press.

CITIZENS JURY

The history of the citizens jury process was begun independently by Peter Dienel, in Wuppertal,

Germany, in January 1971, and Ned Crosby, in Minneapolis, Minnesota, in March 1971. Although Dienel called it a *Planungszelle,* and Crosby called it a citizen committee, both were manifestations of approximately the same concept, namely, to what extent can a democratic process similar to a court-room jury empower citizens, as jurors, to engage in reasonable and informed discussion on public policy issues?

Dienel created his method based upon work he did at a conference center where he observed many groups having dialogues with each other and upon his views on democracy stemming from his doctoral work in sociology. He decided to work with groups of 20 to 25 randomly selected people for an event lasting 4 or 5 days. He brought in witnesses with different views to speak with the groups. Often they were broken into small groups to enhance the ability to speak with each other more easily. One of Dienel's innovations was to hold two Planungszellen at the same time on the same topic in neighboring rooms, with witnesses going back and forth between the two.

Crosby's approach stemmed from his doctoral thesis on social ethics and decision making. He randomly selected a group of people to have them discuss public policy in a reasonable way in a situation where they could show concern for each other (borrowing this from the reason-in-ethics moral philosophers). He was also aware of the many small group studies in social psychology showing the irrationality of people under certain group dynamics. He proposed to structure juries to minimize such dynamics. By the time Dienel and Crosby learned of each other's work in 1985, the two processes were surprisingly similar.

According to a chapter by Crosby and Doug Nethercut (2005), these are the seven elements that make up a citizens jury process:

1. Randomly selected participants that represent a microcosm of the community

2. As large a group as possible (not greater than 24) conducive to deliberation

3. Witnesses rather than staff present high-quality information and answer jurors' questions

4. Promotion of high-quality deliberation through careful facilitation

5. Minimal staff bias

6. Strive for a fair agenda and hearing process

7. Provide sufficient time for the process (typically 5 days)

In the 1990s, the Citizens Jury model became more widely adopted around the world. In 1994, the Citizens Jury process spread to Britain with the launch of a booklet from the Institute for Public Policy Research (IPPR) of London. In an effort to maintain uniformity in procedures, the Jefferson Center placed a trademark on Citizens Jury process by that time to prevent its commercial use. (The center was prepared to let anyone use the method at no charge, so long as they followed a set process.) The IPPR, however, did not uphold the trademark, which meant that anyone could conduct a Citizens Jury in Britain according to whatever process they wanted. This ultimately led the process to be much more widely used in the United Kingdom, where best estimates are that over 300 events have been run under that name. Citizens juries are also now being run with some regularity in Australia, and the process is beginning to spread around the world.

Today, many methods may be referred to as a citizens jury. Some have questioned whether these facsimiles, which vary in their resemblance to the original process, are as useful as they could be. To date, however, there have been no large-scale evaluations of citizens juries to offer comparative evidence of their success. Even so, many would argue that citizens juries remain an important tool of deliberative democracy. Still, the future of citizens juries is unclear. John Gastil and Peter Levine, in *The Deliberative Democracy Handbook,* note the fairly rapid rise in interest in deliberative methods in general, but they say that it is impossible to know if this is the start of something lasting or the height of a movement that will fade.

Looking ahead to the use of citizens juries in science and technical communication, one possible direction is to experiment with combining different methods of deliberation with citizens juries. These could include methods that deliberate for longer periods, such as citizens assemblies, or incorporate sophisticated fact-checking methods, such as consensus development conferences. This would enable the deliberating citizens to get help understanding scientific and technical disputes, while allowing the scientists and the technologists to refer value questions to the citizens.

Ned Crosby

See also Consensus Conference; Deliberative Democracy; Deliberative Polling; Public Engagement

Further Readings

Abelson, J., Forest, P. G., Eyles, J., Smith, P., Martin, E., & Gauvin, F. P. (2003). Deliberations about deliberative methods: Issues in the design and evaluation of public participation processes. *Social Science and Medicine, 57,* 239–251.

Crosby, N., & Nethercut, D. (2005). Citizens juries: Creating a trustworthy voice of the people. In J. Gastil & P. Levine (Eds.), *The deliberative democracy handbook: Strategies for effective civic engagement in the 21st century* (pp. 111–119). San Francisco: Jossey-Bass.

Gastil, J., & Levine, P. (Eds.). (2005). *The deliberative democracy handbook: Strategies for effective civic engagement in the 21st century.* San Francisco: Jossey-Bass.

CLARKE, ARTHUR C. (1917–2008)

Arthur Charles Clarke has been described in many ways: as a "true Renaissance person," a scientist and inventor, a cosmic dreamer, and the father of satellite communications. During his 90-year lifetime and 70-year career, he wrote nearly 100 books, both fiction and nonfiction. Always, his prime mission was to explore the mysteries of the world and the cosmos. In his scientific and engineering writings, he opened many new doors, most notably in the fields of radar and satellite communications. He not only inspired generations through his writing but also first envisioned the geosynchronous satellite system on which today's global electronic communication system is based.

Clarke is most celebrated for his science fiction, which won every top honor in the field. In fact, *Rendezvous With Rama* alone won the Hugo, the Nebula, the Jupiter, and the Campbell Memorial

Arthur C. Clarke

Source: Photo by Karl H. Anders, MD.

awards. He later earned the Edgar Award, named in honor of Edgar Allan Poe.

Clarke's fiction classics include *Childhood's End, Fountains of Paradise,* and *3001: The Final Space Odyssey.* (Both of these books anticipate the creation of a so-called space elevator—a futuristic device that might one day lift cargo and humans to "Clarke orbit." This is one of his many predictions that has yet to be realized.)

His books and almost countless short stories have now been translated into many languages. Yet it was the screenplay that he cowrote with Stanley Kubrick for the movie *2001: A Space Odyssey*—based on Clarke's short story "The Sentinel"—that best explains how he became a household name around the globe. The American Film Institute ranks *2001: A Space Odyssey* as one of the top 10 movies of all time. Ironically, only after the film was released did Clarke actually go back and finish writing the book that made him so famous.

Clarke's compelling science fiction would have brought him fame, but this was only one of his talents. His scientific writings, inventions, and predictions led to his recognition as a "true Renaissance man." His writings spanned science, energy, the oceans, the environment, mathematics, computers, and communications as well as world peace, futurism, and politics—always with a hint of his wry British humor. His famous "Arthur C. Clarke's Three Laws" from his 1962 *Profiles of the Future* captures the spirit of this much beloved guru:

1. When a distinguished but elderly scientist states that something is possible, he is almost certainly right. When he states that something is impossible, he is very probably wrong.

2. The only way of discovering the limits of the possible is to venture a little way past them into the impossible.

3. Any sufficiently advanced technology is indistinguishable from magic.

It was Clarke's technical writings that most won him respect and admiration in the scientific world. Many astronauts, including John Glenn, have indicated that Clarke first inspired them. In the spring of 1945, Clarke circulated a paper outlining a radical new idea. It explained how three rocket-launched communications satellites positioned in geosynchronous orbit could provide a global network using earth stations that did not have to track across the sky. Later that year, Clarke published his full landmark paper "Extra-Terrestrial Relays" in *Wireless World*. It explained in detail the orbital mechanics of the geosynchronous orbit. Clarke showed that a satellite traveling in circular orbit some 22,230 miles (35,870 kilometers) above the earth's surface would appear stationary in this sky. This is because this "magic" orbit at this precise altitude would have precisely the right velocity to travel around the globe once a day, and this velocity would generate sufficient centrifugal force to exactly overcome the gravitational pull at this height. Only one unique solution to this particular set of conditions applies—no other orbit can meet these special conditions.

In 1945, Clarke's article in *Wireless World* was not even the cover article, and he garnered a mere 15 pounds for his efforts. Yet Clarke's article ultimately led to a multibillion-dollar industry, now with over 300 geosynchronous satellites ringing the globe. Communication satellites in this unique orbit currently provide over 10,000 satellite television channels daily, millions of telephone and mobile communications channels, and multiple Internet connections and data channels worldwide. To honor Clarke, the International Astronomical Union has designated this special ring around Earth the "Clarke Orbit."

However, the geosynchronous communications satellite was not the only Clarke contribution to humanity. At the start of World War II, he entered the British armed forces and first worked as an accountant. When his greater mathematical talents were recognized, he was promoted to technical officer. In this capacity, he worked on what was then called radio direction finding, or radar. He made major contributions to the development of ground controlled approach radar that is the basis for today's autopilot landing for aircraft. This he did while only in his mid-20s in the service of the British Radar Establishment working under the supervision of Nobel laureate Luis W. Alvarez. (Alvarez would later be one of the physicists who worked on the Manhattan Project to develop the atomic bomb.) Reportedly, it was Clarke who suggested that the truck equipped with the radar for the ground controlled approach equipment be pulled back farther from the landing strip in the first test. If he had not made this suggestion, both he and Alvarez would almost surely have been killed, and history would have been rewritten.

Clarke, like Isaac Newton, had no famous forebears and was the son of a farmer from Somerset, England. He was born in the seashore town of Minehead, England, and later moved to Taunton, England, where he attended school. As a youth, he showed special talents in math and science at the Huish Grammar School. He was experimenting with rockets and optical communications by the time he was a teenager, and he had a lifelong interest in telescopes and astronomy. When he went for the British Civil Service entrance examinations at the tender age of 19, he scored exceptionally well. Once in government service in London in 1936, he became known as a mathematical whiz and acquired the sobriquet: "Fastest slide rule in Whitehall." Since he was barely 20, he was also among the youngest.

After the end of the war, Clarke knew he must acquire greater education. He thus entered Kings College, London and zoomed through his courses to receive his degree in only 2 years—an almost impossible feat for any normal student. By 1948, he had his degree in hand. By this time, at the age of 31, he had published several technical articles and was starting to launch his science fiction writing career. In a few short years, by the early 1950s, he would vault to the front ranks of the profession.

Many believe that Clarke spent his life as a confirmed bachelor, but in fact, on June 15, 1953, just as his career was in its ascendancy, he acquired a wife after a 3-week whirlwind courtship in New York City. Marilyn Mayfield Clarke, a "strikingly beautiful" social director for large vacation resorts, was an unexpected choice in many ways. She was American, a strict Presbyterian, jaw-droppingly gorgeous, social in nature, and definitely not a scientist or an intellectual. A very English, agnostic, intellectual scientist who was not all that handsome and very focused on his writing was probably not the best possible match.

When the couple moved to a rural setting in England, with Clarke constantly consumed with writing his books and articles, the marriage quickly developed stresses and strains. By Christmas of 1953, just 6 months after the wedding, a dispute over religion resulted in a clear rift. In January 1954, just as Clarke's writing career had succeeded, he and Marilyn agreed to separate. This seemed to lead quite naturally to a new chapter in Clarke's life.

Clarke became quite interested in the new scuba technology and traveled to Australia to explore the Great Barrier Reef. He had from his youth trained himself to hold his breath underwater for 3 to nearly 4 minutes. For someone who could not expect to go into space, the oceans offered an earthbound weightlessness and adventures in a whole new alien world. This led to his preoccupation with exploring the seas and writing several books about his experiences in the 1950s. After exploring the Great Barrier Reef, he next went to Colombo and the southwest coastline of Sri Lanka, which also offered magical oceans to explore. Thus, he ultimately decided to take up residence in Colombo, Sri Lanka, where he lived out his life. There he not only wrote, but also eventually owned and operated Underwater Safaris Ltd., a scuba diving company for tourists and explorers, which he operated with a Sri Lankan partner.

Over his 90-year life, Clarke achieved amazing things. He provided us with key inventive technical insight in the areas of satellite communications, radar, and ocean thermal energy conversion, among many other areas. He wrote some of the most memorable science fiction stories of all time.

He worked on several movies—most notably *2001: A Space Odyssey*. He was a gifted athlete and diver as well as one of the world's best table tennis players. (Not surprisingly, he invented a robotic partner so that he could practice returning 60-mph serves.) Clarke twice served as chairman of the British Interplanetary Society and garnered countless other awards including a knighthood from Queen Elizabeth and the British Empire. He was both an innovative mind and a noble human being with more than ample amounts of wit and wisdom. The Arthur C. Clarke Foundation continues to give awards in his name for the most innovative people in the world of the arts and science.

Joseph N. Pelton

See also Satellites, Science of; Science Fiction

Further Readings

McAleer, N. (1992). *Arthur C. Clarke: The authorized biography*. Chicago: Contemporary Books.

CLEAN AIR ACT

The Clean Air Act (1963), a landmark federal environmental law, is aimed at reducing air pollution in the United States. Widely regarded as a dramatic success in improving air quality and reducing health problems in the late 20th century, the act has changed the way Americans live and conduct business by regulating emissions that create smog, acid rain, toxic air pollution, and other airborne hazards produced by such sources as factories, power plants, and motor vehicles. The overall benefits of the law have included trillions of dollars and countless lives saved. Even so, millions of U.S. residents still breathe polluted air. Air pollution, its effects, and our progress in combating it are constantly in the news, especially in urban areas; this entry provides a brief introduction to the primary legal foundation of these efforts.

What is known today as the Clean Air Act is actually a body of federal legislation dating back to 1955. The act motivated scientific research on the nature and health effects of air pollution and led to steady improvement of control programs at the local, state, and federal levels. The act regulates six main types of pollutants: particulate matter, ground-level ozone, carbon monoxide, sulfur oxides, nitrogen oxides, and lead. Today, the U.S. Environmental Protection Agency (EPA) considers particulate matter and ground-level ozone the most extensive threats to human health.

The Clean Air Act is made up of Public Law 159 and several amendments added in subsequent years that strengthened federal environmental enforcement as the nation's leaders recognized that post–World War II urbanization, the spread of the suburbs, industrial development, and increased vehicle use were causing a rise in the amount and complexity of air pollution. They feared the harm this would do to people, crops, livestock, and property.

The first federal air-pollution law was the Air Pollution Control Act of 1955, which authorized research on air pollution. The Clean Air Act of 1963 expanded research on monitoring pollution problems and helped state and local agencies develop or improve control programs. The Clean Air Act Amendments of 1966 added grants to maintain control programs, and the Air Quality Act of 1967 expanded the federal role in overseeing state air-quality standards and control.

Cultural changes and increased awareness of environmental concerns in the 1960s led to public demand for even more federal effort to combat air pollution. In his State of the Union address in January 1970, President Richard Nixon made dozens of proposals concerning the environment, including one that led to the formation of the EPA and several others that advocated strengthening the federal role in air-pollution control through the Clean Air Act. By the end of the year, Congress had passed, and Nixon had signed into law the Clean Air Act Amendments of 1970, which established the structure for managing the nation's air quality that still exists today.

The newly created EPA, an executive agency, took over administration of the act from the Public Health Service, which previously had overseen U.S. air-pollution law. Under the act, EPA officials set about developing comprehensive federal air-quality standards and implementing their expanded enforcement authority. EPA provided guidance on the standards to the states, which were responsible for developing and implementing state-level plans for meeting them. Another key provision of the act

was to require significant reductions in emissions from motor vehicles.

Among EPA's first successes under the act was eliminating lead from gasoline. Toxic to humans when inhaled, lead was known to damage the brain and other organs, especially in children, leading to learning disabilities, lowered IQ, and other health problems. EPA began a phase-out of lead in gasoline in the mid-1970s. Over the next two decades, lead levels in the air and in children's blood dropped precipitously.

Another major pollution problem addressed by the act was air pollution from motor vehicles, petroleum refineries, and chemical manufacturing facilities. To put the vehicle problem in perspective, total vehicle miles traveled between 1970 and 2005 in the United States rose 178%. Vehicles today account for 75% of the carbon monoxide released, more than half the nitrogen oxide, and about half the smog-causing volatile organic compounds. EPA has required auto manufacturers to build cleaner engines, and petroleum refineries cleaner fuels. In addition, regions with significant pollution problems were required to create vehicle inspection and maintenance programs for cars, trucks, and buses. Today, new car emissions are more than 90% cleaner than in 1970.

The federal legal authority for air-pollution control was extended by the Clean Air Act Amendments of 1977 and 1990. Among other issues, these amendments addressed new scientific understanding, gaps in pollution protection, acid rain, and visibility in more than 100 national parks, including Yosemite, the Grand Canyon, and the Great Smokies parks. The act now requires publicly available air-pollution monitoring reports for industrial facilities and other stationary sources of pollution. It also established the Air Quality Index, perhaps best known for the code orange and code red designations used by weather forecasters to indicate locally unhealthy air, especially ozone pollution.

One of the controversies that surround the act is how to assess the health risks posed by pollutants and establish standards that include a margin of safety when the science is uncertain. Some critics of the act argue that no scientific basis exists for establishing a safe level of some pollutants, such as ground-level ozone. However, EPA officials have maintained that a reasonable and safe standard exists somewhere on the continuum between known serious health effects and no known health effects. Just where is a matter of judgment? As scientists have provided a clearer picture of the risks of specific pollutants over the years, EPA has adjusted its standards based on the new evidence.

Despite the act's requirement that air-pollution standards be set based only on protecting public health and not on cost and attainability, the process of setting and revising the standards has been replete with expert disagreement, political conflict, and lawsuits. Industry and environmental groups have repeatedly sued the EPA, but the EPA's decisions on health risks and pollution standards generally have been upheld by federal courts, including the U.S. Supreme Court. Some critics have accused the EPA of acting too slowly in response to air pollution issues and placing unnecessary administrative burdens on industry and on state and local governments.

In addition to curtailing airborne lead pollution, the act has enabled government to make significant progress toward improving other air-pollution problems around the country. For example, sulfur oxides and nitrogen oxides, two of the primary pollutants targeted by the act, had been significantly reduced by 1990. However, many areas, especially large cities, still struggle with air pollution. Carbon monoxide, particulate matter, and ozone levels in these areas still violate national standards and cause major health problems.

It is important to note that the significant improvements in air quality under the act have occurred amid steady growth in U.S. population, energy consumption, vehicle use, and economic activity. An EPA report to Congress in 1997 estimated the accumulated benefits of the act from 1970 to 1990 at between $6 trillion and $50 trillion. The report estimated the cost of complying with the act at about a half-trillion dollars ($520 billion). Some experts argue that such accomplishments mean the act is no longer needed. Yet many others maintain that it is decades away from achieving many of its major aims and that the risks of air pollution remain high, especially as the effects of climate change play out in the decades ahead.

William Allen

See also Clean Water Act; Endangered Species Act; Environmental Protection Agency, U.S.; Toxic Substances Regulation

Further Readings

Bachmann, J. (2007). Will the circle be unbroken: A history of the U.S. National Ambient Air Quality Standards. *Journal of the Air & Waste Management Association, 57,* 652–697.

Clean Air Act, 42 U.S.C. § 7401–7626 (1963).

Findley, R. W., & Farber, D. A. (2004). *Environmental law in a nutshell.* St. Paul, MN: West.

U.S. Environmental Protection Agency. (2007, April). *The plain English guide to the Clean Air Act* (Publication No. EPA-456/K-07-001). Available at www.epa.gov/air/caa/peg

CLEAN WATER ACT

The Clean Water Act (CWA), sometimes referred to as the Federal Water Pollution Control Act, is the major federal statute in the United States governing pollution of surface waters (rivers, lakes, coastal waters, and wetlands, as opposed to groundwater). The act's broad impact on U.S. water pollution control practices means that it is important for communicators and others interested in federal water policy to understand it. Congress adopted the statute essentially in its current form in 1972, thus revolutionizing water pollution control law and policy in the United States in two major ways. First, the CWA reversed the traditional view that it was acceptable to discharge pollutants into waterways unless and until harm was proven. Instead, discharges are now presumptively prohibited unless in compliance with a government-issued permit that imposes treatment requirements and other conditions to protect human health and the environment. The burden is now on the discharger to show compliance with applicable discharge limits and other requirements, rather than on the public or some affected downstream user to prove harm.

Second, the law expands the concept of pollution beyond the notion of noxious chemical wastes or sewage. The statutory definition of pollution includes almost any man-made alteration of the integrity of the nation's waters, which can include changes in water body characteristics such as hydrology, stream bank conditions, sediment quality or condition, or biodiversity. The ambitious main goal of the law is not merely to prevent discharges of waste materials but to maintain the "chemical, physical, and biological integrity" of U.S. waters, as well as to restore them.

Significant progress has been made in reducing some forms of water pollution since Congress adopted the 1972 law. Most of the United States is now served by modern sewer systems and sewage treatment plants, and acute outbreaks of water-borne infectious disease such as cholera and typhoid have largely been eradicated in this country as a result. Direct releases of industrial chemicals into waterways have been curtailed, reducing risks to human health and environmental quality. However, neither of these problems has been solved completely, and other, more diffuse but still damaging forms of water pollution have received far less attention. Thus, although the law can be called a qualified success, much more work remains before the complete goals of the CWA will be achieved.

History

Until the middle of the 20th century, legal solutions to water pollution in the United States were addressed mainly by common law, the system by which legal principles are established by judges through adjudication of individual cases. Although individual case decisions are limited to the facts of that case, a body of law evolves gradually through the accumulation of precedent in those decisions. Addressing a nationwide problem such as water pollution through such a dispersed system of decisions, however, was difficult. Major sources of pollution were often localized, but the harm was spread over such a large population that few individual plaintiffs had sufficient incentive or resources to file lawsuits to abate the pollution. Where governments brought such cases, it was often difficult to meet the stringent requirement to show harm to obtain relief, in part because of the lack of scientific methods necessary to prove linkages between individual pollution sources and harm. For example, in the famous common law public nuisance case of *Missouri v. Illinois* (1906), Supreme Court Justice Oliver Wendell Holmes found that Missouri failed to prove a connection between sewage discharges from Chicago diverted downstream to the Mississippi River by reversing the flow of the Chicago River and an increased incidence of typhoid in St. Louis.

In 1899, Congress amended the Rivers and Harbors Act, a federal law designed to provide federal aid and regulation of navigation on waterways, to require permits from the U.S. Army Corps of Engineers for activities that might impede navigation. In a provision of this law that later became known as the Refuse Act, permits were required for, and designed to regulate, the discharge of garbage or other materials that might interfere with that navigational goal. That requirement was used entirely for its original intended purpose of protecting navigation until the early 1960s, when the federal government began to use this provision to address the growing problem of industrial water pollution. In a series of decisions, the U.S. Supreme Court ruled that the law was drawn with sufficient breadth to encompass chemical pollution and physical impediments to navigation. Still, this solitary provision was a blunt and infrequently used tool for addressing a problem of nationwide scope.

The first federal statute designed specifically to tackle water pollution as its main goal was the Federal Water Pollution Control Act of 1948. Reluctant to tread too heavily on the traditional domain of state land use and water policy, however, in this initial law and for the ensuing two decades, the federal role in water pollution control was limited largely to providing federal funds to build municipal sewage treatment plants. In 1965, Congress amended the law to require states to adopt water quality standards for interstate waters and to establish a somewhat cumbersome procedure to resolve interstate pollution disputes.

Faced with growing public pressure to address a growing water pollution crisis, Congress concluded in reports leading up to the 1972 amendments that national water pollution control law and policy were "inadequate in almost every respect." Congress rewrote the law almost entirely as a result, and passed it overwhelmingly over a veto by Nixon (issued due to the president's concern over the bill's price tag for federal sewage treatment plant subsidies, not because he disagreed with the need for a stronger national water pollution control law). Although Congress adopted additional amendments in later years (most notably in 1977 and 1987), the basic approaches adopted in the 1972 version of the law remain intact in all major respects.

Major Provisions and Requirements

In the CWA, Congress adopted a multipronged approach to water pollution control. Rather than supplanting state and local efforts, the law embraces a partnership of the federal, state, and local governments to address various aspects of the problem. The law contains minimum principles and requirements that apply nationwide, supported by the federal government's authority over navigable waters under the commerce clause of the U.S. Constitution. Those minimum federal requirements also preempt noncomplying state and local laws under the supremacy clause of the Constitution. However, Congress left considerable latitude to state and local governments to implement the CWA according to local conditions and priorities, so long as those minimum requirements are met.

The 1972 CWA transformed U.S. water pollution control law by flatly prohibiting discharges of pollutants without permits that assure application of minimum treatment requirements (end-of-pipe obligations of individual dischargers) and compliance with ambient water quality standards (standards that establish goals for whole bodies of water in the face of pollution from multiple sources). Those requirements can be enforced through a range of administrative, civil, and criminal sanctions, including citizen suits allowing any affected person to sue those who violate the requirements of the law.

More precisely, the CWA prohibits any person from discharging any pollutant into any navigable water from any point source, defined as any "discrete or confined conveyance" such as a pipe or a ditch. Dischargers covered by the CWA must obtain a permit from either the U.S. Environmental Protection Agency (EPA) or from a state water quality agency with an EPA-approved program. Those permits impose effluent limitations that reflect the stricter of two kinds of controls. First, all dischargers must meet "technology-based limits" at least as stringent as those that can be met using what EPA has determined reflects the best technology to treat that kind of waste from that category of facility. The best technology findings vary with the type of discharger, kinds of pollutants, and other factors but aspire to a statutory goal of zero discharge, the complete elimination of pollutant discharges into the navigable waters. A secondary goal of this system is national uniformity and fairness. By requiring similarly situated dischargers around the country to meet similar or identical pollution control requirements, Congress prevented states from competing for jobs by lowering these requirements.

Second, dischargers must meet stricter "water quality-based" limits where necessary to assure attainment of instream water quality standards. Those standards consist of designated uses for all waters (such as swimming or other contact recreation, drinking water, or protection of various kinds of fish and aquatic life), and water quality criteria sufficient to protect those uses. Water quality standards are established by individual states but require EPA review and approval, and EPA must adopt federal standards where the state standards are not sufficient. Water quality standards complement the system of minimum technology-based controls for individual point sources by ensuring that aggregate pollution from all sources within a watershed does not impair real-world uses such as fishing, swimming, and providing public drinking water. For water bodies that remain polluted despite existing controls, the law requires states to calculate the total amount of pollution a water body can receive without violating the standards, to allocate those amounts among sources within the watershed, and to develop and enforce strategies to reduce pollution to the degree needed to meet the standards.

A separate provision reminiscent of the Refuse Act described above authorizes the U.S. Army Corps of Engineers, applying regulatory standards adopted by EPA, to issue permits for the discharge of dredged or fill material into waters of the United States. This provision is used primarily to protect wetlands, which are often destroyed or damaged by discharges of fill material to convert them to fast land for development, at the expense of important aquatic ecosystem functions and wildlife habitat. Implementation of this program is controversial because it applies to a large number of individual landowners rather than a comparatively small number of industrial facilities and because landowners sometimes argue that denial of a permit or conditions in a permit constitutes an unconstitutional "taking" of their property in violation of the Fifth and Fourteenth Amendments to the U.S. Constitution.

Other provisions address pollution from more diffuse sources such as farms and logging sites—so-called nonpoint sources—that generate contaminated runoff and other impairments of water bodies. Most notably, the CWA requires states to adopt comprehensive nonpoint source water pollution control plans designed to ensure that this large category of diffuse sources does not cause violations of water quality standards despite the extensive efforts to regulate point sources described above. However, unlike the point source control programs, EPA has no authority to require various sources of pollution to adopt minimum controls, and EPA similarly lacks authority to implement nonpoint source control programs when state efforts are deemed insufficient.

Key Remaining Issues and Problems

Several key and related problems continue to plague U.S. water pollution control efforts despite decades of significant progress under the CWA programs described above. First, despite major reductions in point source discharges of pollutants, a large percentage of rivers, lakes, and coastal waters continue to violate water quality standards all over the country. Moreover, states routinely continue to report real-world indicators of use impairment, such as fishing advisories, beach and shellfish bed closures, and similar evidence of ongoing pollution.

One main reason for that ongoing pollution has been the law's relatively ineffective approach to nonpoint source pollution, which is still the largest remaining source of most waterway impairment in the country. Similarly, EPA and the states have paid far more attention to reducing discharges of chemical pollutants than to physical, hydrological, and other changes to water bodies that continue to cause considerable harm. For example, a stream may be harmed just as much by excessive water withdrawals for irrigation as by direct pollution, and fish may be harmed as much by dredging and channelizing a stream's banks as by discharges of wastes.

In recent years, implementation of the CWA has also suffered from uncertainty over the scope of waterways covered by the statute. In a series of cases, the U.S. Supreme Court has curtailed the kinds of water bodies included in the statutory definition of "waters of the United States." Usually in heavily split decisions (with dissenting opinions filed by some of the Justices), the Court has ruled that Congress only intended to include wetlands and tributary streams with a "significant nexus" to navigable waters, regardless of the role of those water bodies in overall watershed health. Most experts, however, believe that the health of wetlands and smaller tributaries are critical to the integrity of larger, downstream waters.

Conclusion

The Clean Water Act has been an extremely successful environmental statute and has resulted in significant reductions in discharges of chemical pollutants and biological wastes into the nation's waters. However, many water bodies around the country remain degraded due to polluted runoff, aquatic habitat loss and impairment, and other factors that have not yet been addressed under the law. As a result, the act's ambitious statutory goal has not yet been fully realized.

Robert W. Adler

See also Carson, Rachel; Clean Air Act; Environmental Impact Statements; Environmental Protection Agency, U.S.

Further Readings

Adler, R. W., Landman, J. C., & Cameron, D. M. (1993). *The Clean Water Act 20 years later.* Washington, DC: Island Press.

Arnold, C. A. (Ed.). (2005). *Wet growth: Should water law control land use?* Washington, DC: Environmental Law Institute.

Clean Water Act, 33 U.S.C. §1251 et seq. (1972).

Craig, R. (2004). *The Clean Water Act and the Constitution.* Washington, DC: Environmental Law Institute.

Missouri v. Illinois, 200 U.S. 496 (1906).

Novotny, V., & Brown, P. (Eds.). (2007). *Cities of the future: Towards integrated sustainable water and landscape management.* London: IWA.

Rivers and Harbors Act, 33 U.S.C. § 403 (1899).

CLIMATE CHANGE, COMMUNICATING

Climate change is an urgent problem. Climatologists describe climate change as the biggest challenge humans have ever faced and warn that we must respond immediately to the threat if we are to avert its worst consequences. Effective communication is necessary to generate such a response, but there are significant barriers to overcome, given both the complexity of the science and the volatile current message environment, with its high levels of partisanship, purposeful disinformation, and public misunderstanding. These obstacles can and must be successfully addressed if communicators are to educate and engage the public in the policy solutions and the personal behavior changes that will help to avert the threat.

The Intergovernmental Panel on Climate Change (IPCC) has warned that without dramatic reductions in our carbon emissions, human civilization faces a future of greatly increased flooding, droughts, crop failures, extreme weather events, mass extinctions, and the displacement of millions of people. (The IPCC is an international body of scientists convened in 1988 by the United Nations and the World Meteorological Organization to review and summarize the relevant literature on climate change.) Climate change is inevitable—and indeed, is already occurring—but the worst effects can still be mitigated with appropriate public policies and widespread adoption of personal and commercial actions that reduce greenhouse gas emissions.

Informing the public about the urgency of the issue and educating them about the policy options and personal and commercial means for responding is a challenging task for communicators given the following barriers:

- Public understanding of the causes and consequences of climate change is not high, nor is awareness of the methods that can mitigate its effects.
- Action has been hampered by political partisanship and industry disinformation campaigns.
- Principles of fairness in news coverage have given a far greater voice to the handful of skeptics than is merited by either their numbers or their evidence, and publication of their views has fostered a widespread perception in the public of scientific controversy where none actually exists.
- The issue remains a low policy priority for most Americans and is likely to remain so until the perception of controversy is overcome and

people clearly understand both the dangers we face and the actions we must take to avert the dangers.

Global bodies, most prominently the IPCC, have been calling for immediate and dramatic cuts in carbon emissions. Although the United States delayed action for much of the last decade, both the Obama administration and Congress have begun taking major steps to reduce U.S. emissions through legislation, regulation, and stimulus spending.

The public response to these initiatives has been generally positive, given that recognition of the danger is growing. In the fall of 2008, a majority of Americans believed that every level of government should be doing more to address climate change. Over two thirds believed that climate change is occurring, and about a third saw it as a threat to them and their families—even while they believed climate scientists are still divided. Half expressed the belief that humans could reduce global warming but that it is unclear at this point whether we will do what is needed. Of those who believed both positive and negative outcomes will follow from national action to reduce global warming, over 90% believed that the nation should take action, in spite of their concerns.

Many Americans, however, still perceived the problem as primarily distant—occurring to people in distant places far in the future or as affecting plants and animals, but not humans. About one in five were still unsure what to believe, and some remained doubtful regarding the reality of climate change, its human sources, or the need for change.

This entry reviews the ways that climate change has been covered in the U.S. media, focusing on the factors that have slowed progress toward solutions. It then turns to specifics of communicating climate change, detailing what needs to be taught and how.

Media Coverage of Climate Change

On a sweltering June day in 1988, National Aeronautics and Space Administration scientist James Hansen told a Senate committee that the greenhouse effect was changing the climate and that droughts and heat waves would increase, thereby drawing the public's attention to the issue for the first time. As he and other scientists began sounding the alarm, journalists were faced with reporting on a new and extremely complex scientific issue of great public significance that required significant expertise. Studies have shown that these reporters lacked understanding of the basic science underlying climate change. To compensate, they relied on "balanced" reporting styles, seeking out opposing voices on the issue, and in the early 1990s, they turned increasingly to politicians and interest groups, rather than to scientists, for information. Unable to assess for themselves the validity of the claims of climatologists, they relied on the principles of fairness, providing the public with both sides of the issue and leaving the public to decide for itself whether the claims of danger were valid or not.

Balanced reporting is a time-honored approach to news coverage, and it adds conflict and drama to news stories. But in this context, it has created a false impression of controversy in the public mind. The opposing voices the media turned to were a small number of skeptical scientists, most of whom were funded by the coal and oil industries. These skeptics operate largely on the margins of the science community, promoting their views in the media but not in the peer-reviewed scientific literature. They have been repeatedly shown to exaggerate and misrepresent research, but lay audiences are unlikely to detect their distortions.

Federal policymakers have used these few dissenting voices to keep public discussion and legislative action focused on the preliminary step of determining whether climate change exists, thereby inhibiting public policy discussion from moving forward to the question of how the United States should respond. Balanced reporting has thus pitted a handful of skeptics against the thousands of scientists who support the consensus view, giving a minuscule minority a strong media presence. In addition, there is well-documented evidence of the Bush administration suppressing scientific information, weakening reports on the dangers, and exaggerating the level of uncertainty in the science.

Partisanship was minimal when climate change first appeared in the news; it grew during the late 1990s when the nation was debating the Kyoto Protocol, a 1997 agreement to reduce greenhouse gas emissions ratified by 182 nations (but not by the United States). Because the public has difficulty assessing the scientific evidence directly, most people have relied on their own trusted sources of information to assess the validity of the danger. When conservative voices began arguing against the existence of dangers from climate change, Republicans began to become polarized from Democrats on the issue, and today climate change has become one of the defining issues distinguishing the two parties.

Further, presentation of the skeptics' views in news coverage has fostered the misimpression among Americans of scientific controversy over the reality of climate change and its causes, thereby stalling support for mitigation policies and the passage of federal legislation. Communications from scientists and the public's lack of understanding of scientific methods may have also contributed to this public perception of scientific controversy and doubt. Scientists' strong tendency—based on their training—is to emphasize the limits and uncertainties in their research, and the public infers from their statements that scientists are divided and unsure. Indeed, in recent polls, more Americans are certain that climate change is occurring than are certain that scientists agree on its reality and causes. Many people feel that so long as the scientists are unsure of the danger, legislation or personal action is premature—a position promoted by some partisans as a delay tactic to postpone federal legislation on the issue. Creating change—both in public policy and in personal and commercial practices—is difficult, while maintaining the status quo is relatively easier. So long as the perception of controversy exists, inertia is likely to impede change.

The evidence presented by the IPCC clearly refutes any assertion of controversy and uncertainty, as does a review of the nearly 1,000 articles published in refereed scientific journals between 1993 and 2003 on climate change. Not one of those articles disagrees with the consensus opinion that climate change is being caused by human activities. Further, a study comparing the magnitude of the projected effects of climate change, and the use of language such as *catastrophic, urgent, worse than previously thought,* and *irreversible* to describe those effects, finds that the projected impacts justify the strong terminology and are not alarmist, as the skeptics would have it.

Though news coverage has created a partisan divide, there are signs that the divide is weakening: The presidential candidates of both parties in 2008 favored legislation to combat climate change, the skeptics are now receiving less media attention, and increasing numbers of conservative politicians and Evangelical Christians have spoken publicly in favor of aggressive action. As the administration and Congress develop broad new policies to reduce emissions, the circumstances are ripe for communication that moves beyond the question of whether climate change has human causes and advances us toward an informed discussion of the solutions.

The Challenges Facing Climate Change Communication

Given the current environment, communicators can ask themselves, what, specifically, do we need to tell the public? Scientific literacy in general is low in the United States, and for this particular issue, the public is confused on several dimensions, most notably the difference between destruction of the ozone layer and climate change. While most all Americans are aware of climate change, for many this means simply that they have heard of the issue but do not understand either the causes or the consequences, both of which have important implications, as discussed below.

Before considering what needs to be communicated, it is essential to recall that people have their own reasons for using any informational content. To successfully convey information to audiences, one must understand their motivations and satisfy their perceived information needs, while still supplying them with valid information that is germane to helping them make good decisions. Audience motivations differ from the motivations of communicators: People typically acquire scientific information for its social uses in conversation, to satisfy social norms that people should be informed on public issues, or because the information is personally useful for some reason. Because climate change involves particularly complex information, the entry costs are very high—that is, it requires a lot of effort to become expert on the issue, and this inhibits people from actively seeking and carefully attending to information on the topic.

While communicators may be inclined to teach the underlying science of climate change, inform the public on the policy options, and encourage intelligent, informed discussion and debate, it is also important to remember that these goals are not necessarily foremost in the minds of audience members. Nor is persuasion—changing people's minds about the issue—a very likely outcome.

What the media can do quite effectively is to communicate the significance of an issue: When a topic receives a great deal of coverage, audience members infer that it is important. And audiences are particularly likely to assess the significance of climate change by the amount of coverage it receives for a number of reasons:

- It involves complex science, of which the average individual has little understanding.
- It has long-term and gradual effects, which cannot be easily observed by any single individual.
- Its effects are global in scale and therefore distant from most Americans.
- It cannot be easily connected to any single dramatic event, such as Hurricane Katrina—we can legitimately say that climate change increases the frequency of events such as Katrina, but not that it caused any particular event.

Unfortunately, the same characteristics that make the media more powerful in communicating the importance of climate change to the public simultaneously make it less likely that the mass media will cover the issue on a steady, continuing basis: News media tend to focus on dramatic, discrete, and local events. Dramatic or unusual weather triggers coverage, as do political events relating to the issue, but slow cumulative changes in temperature and rainfall do not make for exciting reading and hence receive little attention. Thus, while the issue is not one that the media are naturally inclined to promote, people are unlikely to recognize its importance unless they do.

Communicating the Causes of Climate Change

If people do not understand the causes of climate change, they will have difficulty assessing proposed options to mitigate its impact. Moreover, studies have shown that when people have a clear understanding of the causes, they express stronger intentions to take appropriate action. Hence, an informed public requires some understanding of the greenhouse effect and the role of greenhouse gas emissions in creating it.

Unfortunately, the greenhouse effect competes in the public mind with ozone depletion: Many Americans believe that climate change is occurring because the hole in the ozone is letting in too much heat, thereby conflating climate change, a more recently publicized environmental issue, with the ozone hole, which has been recognized and publicized for a longer time. Given their confusion about the cause, many Americans incorrectly believe that eliminating the use of aerosol spray cans will reduce climate change. The use of chlorofluorocarbons in aerosols has long been banned because they contributed to creating the ozone hole, and eliminating aerosols has no impact on climate change.

Conveying a useful model of climate change thus remains a major challenge, made more difficult by the low scientific literacy of Americans. Approximately two thirds of the public is not scientifically literate, and three quarters are unable to read and understand news with basic science constructs, such as DNA, molecules, or radiation. Given these limitations, communicators have been seeking a first-rung theory or a bridging metaphor—a clear, simple, and concrete image that would convey to the public the greenhouse effect and its impacts.

Another contrast with ozone depletion is useful. The hole in the ozone layer received much less media coverage than climate change has received, but the public was more aware of the issue. Potent bridging metaphors existed for ozone depletion that helped the audience grasp it immediately: *Star Wars*, the Strategic Defense Initiative, video games, and children's television all depicted external threats that were held at bay by shields that had to be maintained. Even more broadly, the metaphor of a hole in the ceiling was widely used and is easily grasped by anyone.

Climate change, by contrast, has no clear metaphor that enables the audience to easily and immediately grasp the threat. The term *climate change* seems innocuous, and given the widespread confusion of climate with weather, it may be interpreted as nothing more dangerous than the changing of the seasons. *Global warming* and *greenhouses* both have positive connotations, as may the depiction of global warming as a blanket around Earth. Increasingly common pictures depicting the globe in flames do not convey anything about the causes of the change, nor the solutions, and are frightening—a

questionable combination as will be discussed below. Communicators need to intensify the search for a metaphor that is easily understood, connotes both the causes and potential consequences of climate change, implies what type of response is needed, and reassures people that responses will be efficacious. This sounds like an extremely tall order, but a consideration of the hole-in-the-ceiling metaphor for ozone depletion reveals that it does, in fact, entail all of this.

Communicating the Consequences of Climate Change: Talking About the Risk

Many Americans are still unaware of the dangerous consequences of climate change and view the prospect of warmer winters, longer summers, and longer growing seasons as positive. And many of those who are aware of the dangers view these consequences as occurring in the distant future to people in distant lands. As a result, climate change is not viewed by the majority of Americans as a high policy priority—as compared with, say, the economy, the war in Iraq, education, or health. This is true of both Republicans and Democrats. Those who do recognize the dangers, however, have greater willingness to make personal changes and support aggressive policy actions. Studies show that people who recognize climate change as a serious national problem tend to hold five beliefs:

- Climate change is real.
- They are certain that it is real (as opposed to thinking that climate change is probably real).
- It will be bad for people.
- Humans are causing it.
- Humans can solve the problem.

While the majority of Americans now agree that climate change is real and that humans have caused it, there is relatively less understanding that the consequences may be very bad for people and that we have the capacity to mitigate these consequences.

A temptation for communicators, then, is to attempt to frighten people into an awareness of the graveness of the situation with warnings of impending doom. There is an intuitive appeal to using fear-inspiring messages to motivate action, and a large body of experimental research supports the efficacy of fear in motivating a broad range of self-protective actions.

Numerous authors warn against the use of fear with climate change, however, because it may lead people into denial, in which they reject, distort, or avoid the messages. Or fear may leave people with feelings of hopelessness and despair: For example, people might think, why bother conserving energy if we are all going to die anyway? Communicators may justly ask if they should use frightening content, and if so, how they should use it to avoid having their messages backfire?

The answer to this question lies in the central importance of providing people with hope and useful options for addressing the threat. Any message that warns of the dangers of climate change should also clearly provide solutions—solutions that are both effective and feasible. Fear alone may backfire, but fear with accompanying solutions can foster hope and resolve in the audience.

Values and Framing in Climate Change Communication

In light of the urgency of their message, communicators can easily forget that the most prevalent effect of media use is reinforcement of prior beliefs—not persuasion and behavior change. People selectively use media content consistent with their existing values and beliefs, and these beliefs are then strengthened by the content. Selective exposure and reinforcement effects are especially likely with climate change communication, given the partisanship of the issue.

Studies have shown that Democrats generally have strong egalitarian values, which lead them to take environmental threats seriously because these threats harm other people and species, denying them access to a livable environment. Republicans, in contrast, generally have strong hierarchical and individualistic values, which incline them to favor traditional values and practices and to oppose governmental limitations on individual freedoms. Environmental regulations, therefore, are seen as the greater threat by Republicans, while environmental damage is seen as the greater threat by Democrats.

When messages are framed to be consistent with the audience members' values, individuals are more likely to attend and be influenced by the content. Because conservatives are less likely to respond to the high-risk messages discussed above, some communicators are attempting to influence them with messages that appeal to their values—emphasizing the business and economic opportunities of green technologies, the national security advantages of energy independence, and our responsibility for sound stewardship and protecting our children's future.

Another frame currently under development focuses on the public health consequences of climate change—the harm that will occur to people here in the United States—in terms, for example, of increased asthma, heat stroke, and vector-borne diseases. By replacing polar bears with vulnerable populations at home, communicators may increase the salience of the issue among those who currently perceive the threat as distant while simultaneously moving from the contested political issue arena to the broadly accepted domain of public health.

The Special Challenge of Communicating About Personal Behavior Change

Little research to date has measured the extent to which people are changing their behavior in ways that help to mitigate climate change. People do report to pollsters that they are changing their behaviors, but many confess to confusion over the types of change needed. The multitude of new how-to books, newsletters, blogs, and public service announcements sometimes contradict each other with advice on what to change, and advertisers hoping to benefit from the growing green consumer market further confuse the message. Federal standards for labeling products, such as the Energy Star program, can help consumers sort through the conflicting claims.

Moreover, many of the most important behaviors—transportation, diet, home energy use, and product consumption (that is, overconsumption)—are highly entrenched and difficult to change. As Americans become more informed on the causes and consequences of climate change, they are likely to become more motivated to change their personal behaviors, but even the best communication can only go so far in helping people change deeply entrenched behaviors. Many people will require superior options to those that are currently available to them (for example, an ultra-fuel-efficient vehicle large enough to carry all members of their family) before they are able to effect significant changes in their lifestyle.

Conclusion

To effectively inform the public about climate change, communicators must continue to reinforce and clarify the seriousness and at the same time provide people with hope and acceptable options for solving the problem. Bringing the human consequences of climate change to life with vivid, concrete examples and anecdotes that are consistent with the best available scientific evidence is likely to increase audience receptivity to personal, commercial, and public policy responses to address the problem.

The public is confronted daily with many messages on myriad topics, most of which receive only superficial attention and are immediately forgotten. To combat this tendency, communication about climate change should present clear messages, consistently, over a long period. Some teachers say that repetition is the mother of all skills; it is certainly an important part of the formula for effective public communication.

Given the strong partisanship and complexity of the information, choosing information sources wisely is also an extremely important element of effective communication on this issue. Sources may be two-edged swords, however: prominent Democratic voices, such as Al Gore, may alienate as many Republicans as they persuade Democrats. Messages such as the "We Can Solve It" campaign's pairing in a single public service announcement of prominent liberals and conservatives (for example, Nancy Pelosi and Newt Gingrich)—both of whom express their commitment to solving climate change while acknowledging that they disagree on almost everything else—are likely to be an effective method of taking advantage of the importance of sources, while simultaneously avoiding their dangers. Another option is to seek sources not aligned with either party, such as public health officials.

Studies of public health campaigns have long demonstrated that personal behavior changes and significant public policy changes rarely involve a simple one-step process. Rather, change is typically gradual and entails a number of small steps. Many observers have pointed out that as a nation we are addicted to lifestyles that are not sustainable, and while the need for change is urgent, communicators would do well to recognize that people are at many different stages in the change process. Some are already highly motivated to adopt a green lifestyle; others are unconvinced that climate change is occurring or that any type of change is needed.

Given this wide distribution of beliefs and practices, communicators will increase their impact if they target their messages according to the common beliefs and behaviors of their audiences. Studies show that messages that increase people's perceptions of their risk are the place to start with groups that do not yet recognize the problem. For those who already recognize the risk, however, messages explaining what to change and how to do it and messages that support the individual's belief that these changes will effectively avert the worst consequences of climate change may prove more effective.

Connie Roser-Renouf
and Edward W. Maibach

See also Agenda Setting and Science; Environmental Journalism; Public Engagement; Uncertainty in Science Communication; Weather Reporting

Further Readings

Kolbert, E. (2006). *Field notes from a catastrophe: Man, nature, and climate change.* New York: Bloomsbury.

Maibach, E., Roser-Renouf, C., & Leiserowitz , A. (2009). *Global warming's six Americas 2009: An audience segmentation analysis.* Available at http://climatechange.gmu.edu

Mann, M. E., & Kump, L. R. (2008). *Dire predictions: Understanding global warming: The illustrated guide to the findings of the IPCC.* New York: Kindersley.

Moser, S. C., & Dilling, L. (Eds.). (2007). *Creating a climate for change: Communicating climate change and facilitating social change.* New York: Cambridge University Press.

CLONING

Cloning is an umbrella term for processes of duplicating genetic material, whether animal or human. Scientists refer to a *clone* as a group of two or more cells or organisms with identical genetic information that have been derived from a single cell or organism. Clones result naturally from asexual reproduction in bacteria, plants, and animals, and they are also produced deliberately by a variety of technical strategies.

In media reports and public debates on cloning, the concept usually refers to artificial rather than natural clones, and the term is used mainly to refer to the individual that has been derived by a cloning procedure (rather than the parent). The stereotypical popular clone is a same-age, look-alike copy of a single parent.

Debates on cloning provide an opportunity to observe the social aspects of a novel technical option. Research into how cloning is constituted in these debates has demonstrated that in the years following the announcement of the first cloned mammal, the famous sheep Dolly, the prospect of human cloning has shifted from science fiction to scientific practice; at the same time, it has become particularly controversial. Media scholars and social scientists are concerned with the discursive frames and strategies that shape the debates and with how the discussion of a particular technique is linked to more general expectations about the role of science in a democratic society. This entry discusses the technoscientific developments and the media and public debate on both animal and human cloning.

The Science and Technology of Cloning

The term *cloning* was first introduced at the beginning of the 20th century. Its root is the ancient Greek term κλων, meaning "twig" and referring to the process whereby a new plant can be created from a twig. A basic characteristic of cloning is that sexual reproduction is bypassed. The production of cloned DNA fragments, cells, or embryos is an important technique in the toolbox of molecular biotechnology. Cloning requires knowledge of embryology, genetics, and reproductive technology. It complements two other key technologies, genetic engineering (the transfer of genetic material from one organism to another) and genomics (the mapping, sequencing, and functional analysis of the entire genetic makeup of an organism).

Scientists today apply a variety of cloning strategies. Every biology student clones genes by transferring and amplifying DNA fragments in unicellular organisms such as bacteria. This strategy generates multiple copies of a DNA fragment and can be used

to introduce a gene into the genetic makeup of a different species.

Cloning a cell or an embryo, achieved by splitting embryos, is more demanding. Basic research in animal embryology dates back as far as the late 19th century, when the German embryologist Hans Driech produced multiple individuals from split sea urchin embryos. In the early 20th century, Hans Spemann successfully manipulated salamander eggs to remove the cell nucleus, the part that contains most of the genetic material in a cell. The eggs were then renucleated with the nucleus from an early embryo. Spemann was replacing the egg cell nucleus with another embryonic one but was already thinking ahead to using the nucleus of a more specialized cell. Such experiments were realized in the 1950s when U.S. embryologists Robert Briggs and Thomas King transferred the nuclei of frog cells in different phases of tadpole development into frog eggs.

A second technological innovation that has contributed to the successful cloning of mammals is in vitro fertilization (IVF). Assisted reproductive technologies have been employed since the first child was born as a result of successful IVF of a human egg in 1978. It has been argued that the development and wide-scale implementation of IVF has not only been crucial in the development of the technological capacities for cloning but also—by legitimizing IVF as a normal and unproblematic option—has facilitated the emergence of a cultural imaginary for cloning, as well as of a legislative framework for dealing with cloning applications.

The technique of nuclear transplantation developed by embryologists and the skills acquired in manipulating mammal eggs through the refinement of reproductive technology eventually led to micromanipulation techniques involving transfer of the nucleus of a donor cell into an oocyte from which the cell nucleus and associated genetic material have been removed. The manipulated oocyte containing the DNA from the donor cell is subsequently treated with chemicals or electric current to stimulate cell division. The variant of nuclear transplantation that is most used today is somatic cell nuclear transfer (SCNT), in which the donor cell nucleus can be derived from any somatic cell—that is, from any body cell other than a sperm or egg cell.

SCNT produces genomic clones: Only the hereditary information in the transferred nucleus is identical to that of the donor parent but not the entire genetic makeup because DNA is also present outside the nucleus of animal cells. Dolly the sheep, the first mammal to develop from a cell derived from an adult tissue, was created using SCNT. Dolly is hence not identical to, but a genome clone of, the Finn Dorset sheep whose mammary gland provided the cell nucleus that was injected into an egg taken from a blackface ewe.

Before Dolly, scientists thought that the processes through which embryonic cells differentiate into specialized body cells could not be reversed. Following 276 failed attempts, Dolly's birth demonstrated that during the development of the mammary cell there was no irreversible modification: A cell that has already specialized for a particular role in an organism could be reprogrammed once the nucleus was transferred into an egg.

Recent developments, such as the creation of five human embryos using DNA from adult skin cells by Californian researchers in 2008, aim to provide a source of viable human *embryonic stem cells*. Embryonic stem cells are cells that have the capacity to divide and self-renew and to develop into different types of body cells. They are therefore thought to be promising tools for research and therapy. Stem cells obtained from cloned embryos have the advantage that a patient's body will not reject them after transplantation, provided that the patient is the donor of the somatic cell.

Another line of research is the reprogramming of adult somatic cells into embryonic stem cell–like cells, so-called induced pluripotent stem cells. In 2009 this was achieved in mice by inserting a single gene into the genome of an adult cell. Reprogramming adult cells avoids both the need for human oocytes and the use of true embryonic stem cells and therefore, circumvents the ethical issues linked to human egg donation and the use of embryos for research purposes.

Scientists looking for alternative sources for human oocytes are also working on the creation of human-animal admixed embryos (often also called hybrid embryos), a technique that has been legalized in the United Kingdom with the Human Fertilisation and Embryology Act of 2008.

Cloning Animals

The development of micromanipulation techniques led to the birth of Molly and Megan, two lambs cloned from the nuclei of embryonic stem cells, in 1996 at the Roslin Institute in Edinburgh, Scotland, and to the successful transfer of the nucleus of an adult somatic cell, creating Dolly. Born on July 5, 1996, she hit the headlines when the scientists who had created her published a paper describing their work in the scientific journal *Nature*.

The article by Ian Wilmut and his colleagues was scheduled for publication on February 27, 1997, but a science journalist with the U.K. newspaper *The Observer* broke the news embargo on February 23, drawing on information that he had obtained from a TV production. Within hours, Dolly gained worldwide prominence that was retained throughout the 6 years of her short sheep life. She died of a respiratory infection in 2003; her body is on display in the Edinburgh-based National Museum of Scotland.

Dolly was not the first mammal ever cloned, but the fact that secured her worldwide scientific and media attention was that the nucleus of the embryo from which she developed was that of a fully differentiated somatic cell of an adult sheep, a cell of an animal that has already reached maturity and whose characteristics are therefore known. Since then, mice, cows, rabbits, cats, pigs, goats, and dogs have been cloned from adult cells: Polly (another Edinburgh sheep), Snuppy (the South Korean dog), Uschi (the German cow), Copy-Cat (the U.S. cat clone), and Injaz (the camel from Dubai) populate labs and barns. But with about one or two viable offspring for every 100 attempts, the safety and efficiency of animal cloning is still very low, and abortions, stillbirths, malformations, and developmental abnormalities are very common.

The major incentive to clone animals is the genetic improvement of livestock both for medical and commercial purposes. By transferring a human gene into an animal, scientists have created transgenic sheep, goat, and cattle that produce human proteins or antibodies in their milk or blood. Transgenic animals may also serve as models for diseases such as diabetes and for xenotransplantation: In the future, genetically modified pigs could provide organs such as hearts, livers, and kidneys to human patients.

Animal cloning is also used to create more productive and hence more commercially valuable animals. An example is the cloning of high-quality breeding bulls to enhance the amount of donor sperm available from a particular parent animal. By creating a genetic twin, private companies also offer replacements for pet cats and dogs that have died.

Cloning Humans

Cloning occurs naturally in humans in the form of monozygotic, or identical, twins. Monozygotic twins are derived from a single fertilized egg and hence share their basic genetic makeup. But they are of course not identical as the English term seems to imply. The idea of human cloning in the sense of creating or copying a person has surfaced in myth, religious discourse, and popular culture for a long time. In a context of the general techno-scientific optimism in the 1960s and 1970s, human cloning as a potentially beneficial option was put forward by scientists such as Nobel laureates Joshua Lederberg and James D. Watson.

At the end of the 20th century, the birth of Dolly shifted the possibility of cloning humans from science fiction to science practice. A distinction was introduced with regard to what happens after the application of nuclear replacement technology to human cells. The creation of a cloned human embryo for use (and eventual destruction) in research is now distinguished from the reproduction of a human being.

Therapeutic cloning refers to SCNT to clone a human embryo from which stem cells can be derived for therapies or cure, applications of the technique that do not involve the creation of genetically identical individuals through implanting the embryos into a womb. Therapeutic cloning is also referred to more critically as research cloning to indicate that the therapeutic prospects lie far in the future. *Reproductive cloning,* by contrast, is the use of SCNT to clone a human embryo that is subsequently implanted into a woman's womb for gestation.

The main argument in favor of reproductive cloning is the expansion of reproduction opportunities. Cloning advocates have challenged the distinction between therapeutic and reproductive cloning by arguing that reproductive cloning is a technical extension of IVF and as a form of infertility treatment, is therefore a therapy.

Following the birth of Dolly, numerous announcements of intentions to clone humans have been made. In December 1997, the U.S. physicist Richard Seed announced that he was ready to clone people for the purpose of producing children for infertile couples. In March 2001, Panos Zavos, professor emeritus of reproductive physiology-andrology at the University of Kentucky, and Severino Antinori, an Italian fertility expert famous for helping post-menopausal women to conceive, staged a media event to announce their plans to clone humans.

Just after Christmas of 2002, the Raëlians (a religious sect that believes human life was created by extraterrestrials) announced the birth of a cloned baby named Eve at a Hollywood, California, press conference featuring their scientific director, Brigitte Boisselier. In 2004, it was again Zavos who announced the implantation of an embryo that was suggested to have been cloned from the tissue of a deceased child.

In response to Zavos's 2004 announcement, 14 U.K. scientists wrote an open letter in which they called upon journalists to cease reporting dubious claims about human reproductive cloning. But unlike Boisselier or Seed, Zavos had some scientific credentials and therefore was to be taken seriously. There was no simple way for science journalists to know whether someone had been successful in an attempt to clone a human being, and in every case there has been broad global news reporting on these "maverick" announcements.

In 2004 and 2005, the South Korean researcher Woo Suk Hwang and colleagues published groundbreaking work on the creation of human embryonic stem cells and the establishment of stem cell lines from somatic cells—the first claims of human cloning that had been peer-reviewed for a high-profile scientific journal. Both results turned out to be fabricated, however, and the two *Science* papers were retracted. Furthermore, an investigation committee from Seoul National University found that Hwang had pressured junior members of his lab to donate eggs for the cloning experiments.

Cloning in Media and Public Debates

Debate on Dolly

The cloning of animals and humans has been featured in films and popular books for more than 100 years, but Dolly's birth has become the point of reference for most of today's news reports about cloning. Reporting on Dolly has from the beginning not been restrained to a discussion of animal cloning. Many scholars have argued that the intensified debate in the aftermath of her birth indicates that the creation of a cloned sheep made it clear human cloning would soon be an option as well. It was this idea rather than the reality of animal cloning that caused such intense emotional debate.

The newsworthiness of cloning has been attributed to its links to deeply rooted myth and popular images: the mix of attraction and fear with regard to the prospect of human cloning, the role of stakeholders such as scientists and politicians, the promotional strategies of scientific institutions, and the human interest in an animal personality with a name and an image. The resonance of the issue has been explained by the history of the "playing God" theme in stories of the artificial creation of human beings and in images in everything from the biblical creation myth to popular novels and films, particularly science fiction. These well-established cultural representations of cloning served as a framework for the debate.

Cloning in Print Media and Films

As with genomics in general, media coverage of cloning is influenced by staged media events and announcements by maverick scientists. Yet debates on cloning are typical media discourses on biomedicine in that they are largely dominated by well-established actors such as scientists and government leaders. Arguments and positions are put forward by a variety of speakers in their attempts to frame the debate. Science communication scholars have traced the demarcation of a number of boundaries, most importantly the boundaries between animal and human, between maverick scientists and the scientific establishment, between a rational view of the embryo as a collection of cells versus a view of the embryo as potential human being, and between reproductive and therapeutic cloning.

In a comparison of the elite British press coverage from 1997 to 2004 with popular films that were released between 1978 and 2003, Eric Jensen has found two sharply divergent discourses: While the press discourse was one of unqualified hope and hyped claims of future cures, the film narratives constructed cloning as inherently dangerous, often wielded by hubristic scientists in the tradition of Frankenstein, with human reproductive cloning ultimately used for destructive purposes. He concludes that the debate induced, legitimized, and reproduced perceptions of an uncritical acceptance of therapeutic cloning as hope and cure while attaching fears to reproductive cloning.

This separation of options in order to legitimize a good, ethically unproblematic option by separating it from another that is perceived to be unethical is a recurring strategy of boundary work in the debate over technical innovations and has also been demonstrated for the case of gene therapy.

Brigitte Nerlich and David Clarke have demonstrated that news reporting on cloning reinforces stereotypical images of science and scientists through the use of metaphors. To refer to clones as products or copies invites further inferences, such as clones used as a means to an end and cloned children as consumer options. References to standard works of literature and popular films such as Mary Shelley's *Frankenstein,* Aldous Huxley's *Brave New World,* and the films *The Boys From Brazil* and *Multiplicity* abound, as do historical references to eugenics and genocide and arguments about the opening of Pandora's box.

The doom scenarios in popular films frame public policy debates in that reproductive cloning is seen as a threat that must be banned. Dorothy Nelkin and Susan Lindee have argued that from the 1960s on, human cloning has been associated with genetic engineering and the artificial creation of life, pervasive themes in horror films and science fiction fantasies. Genetic determinism prevails: One's personality and behavior are reduced to one's genes. Films such as *Gattaca* show the transition from a society that is oriented toward religious or other values to a society in which individuals are reduced to their genetic makeup. Only recently have there been a few explicit attempts to produce alternative imaginings, such as the German-Canadian drama *Blueprint,* a 2003 film that presents cloning as a plausible reproductive choice.

In the majority of films and news reports, however, different kinds of arguments are put forward against human reproductive cloning—arguments related to technological feasibility; to the psychological well-being of the clone, especially risk of loss of individuality; and to the impact on society as a whole, such as fears of eugenics, the disintegration of family structures, and dystopias of enhanced humans created for a purpose. The ethical debates center on the moral status of the embryo: Should early human embryos be treated as if they were persons or not?

Cloning advocates have argued that of these objections, only religious or other moral motives will remain. Those who claim that cloning will not become a real option are said to underestimate the power of the marketplace and the power of individual desire as driving forces behind the use of cloning technologies.

A study by Joan Haran and colleagues concludes that the largely negative figuration of religious and other collective activism in the U.K. elite press means that these groups are effectively expelled from the legitimate public; rather, they are positioned as operating against the imagined public interest. In U.S. discourse, however, religious groups are seen as much more relevant in discussions about the governance of biomedicine.

Media and social scientists interpret debates in the light of their own normative positions on the role of science in society. Some adopt a critical stance toward the scientific community's attempts to defend their authority by scrutinizing the extent to which interested scientists set the terms of debate. Efforts of the scientific establishment and institutions such as the Science Media Centre in the United Kingdom to counter the claims of maverick scientists help ensure that the public's perceived antipathy to human reproductive cloning does not interfere with therapeutic applications and economic benefit.

Other scholars have attributed the demarcation of therapeutic and reproductive cloning to the media themselves, motivated by an interest in policy regulation favorable to therapeutic applications. Yet others emphasize the need for better-informed political and ethical discourses that overcome what they see as prejudices regarding the links between cloning and eugenics, blasphemy, and the loss of human individuality, arguing that the picture of human cloning should be shaped by scientific facts rather than images from literature and films.

Matt Nisbet and Bruce Lewenstein's longitudinal analysis of newspaper coverage of biotechnology in the U.S. media has shown that—while the character of the coverage in general is overwhelmingly positive, emphasizing scientific progress and economic prospects—the cloning debate in the late 1990s is a departure from this trend. They describe the debate as a crisis with sharp increases in the coverage of ethical issues and controversy. In other work, Susanna Priest has shown that the controversy was not about scientific facts, their interpretation, or their implications for policy, but over the ethics of making particular use of the technique. The debate about Dolly changed media framing of biotechnology to a debate that explicitly incorporated ethical considerations and that was largely confined to that dimension, with the implication that it served to maintain the existing distribution of power rather than upset it.

Researchers have concluded that both the optimistic print media discourse and the dystopian scenarios in popular films indicate an impoverished public debate on the issue and undermine the ideal of an informed, reasoned debate that would address the full range of questions about society's desired ends with regard to biomedical advances. While cloning debates were linked to wider debates about the governance of science and its role in shaping society, they expose the deficit of effective and independent science critics.

Public Perception

Studies of public perception have shown a broad disapproval of human cloning. U.S. and British citizens polled after Dolly felt that human cloning should be outlawed, as did the majority of journalists, ethicists, and policymakers. Furthermore, research revealed a deep-felt ambivalence involving beliefs in the power of science on the one hand, and mistrust toward both science and systems of regulation on the other. Widespread attention was given to threats to identity, individuality, and human dignity and to the moral unacceptability of human cloning, but with little or no analysis of what it means to be human or what exactly is morally objectionable.

Human reproductive cloning is rejected as a beneficial activity, but is perceived as a trend that is beyond societal control. In their reaction to public ambivalence and mistrust, scientists and politicians were found to focus on the media as both the cause of the decline in trust in science and also as part of the potential solution to this crisis.

Conclusion

A sharp dichotomy exists in thinking about cloning with regard to animals and humans. While animal cloning for medical and commercial purposes is gaining increasing legitimacy, human cloning remains much more controversial. A distinction between human cloning for therapeutic or reproductive purposes has been introduced that detaches therapeutic cloning from the horrors and fears of human copying and associates it instead with the promise of cures characteristic of genomics discourses in general.

While therapeutic cloning takes center stage in the vision of the future of regenerative medicine, reproductive cloning remains linked to the dystopian views of science fiction scenarios. The focus has shifted from fully cloned human beings to the micromanipulation of cloning processes, images of the removal of a nucleus from a cell replacing images of multiple clones.

Simone Rödder

See also Gene; Maverick Science and Journalism; Science Fiction; Stem Cell Controversy; Watson, James D.

Further Readings

Alcibar, M. (2008). Human cloning and the Raelians: Media coverage and the rhetoric of science. *Science Communication, 30,* 236–265.

Haran, J., Kitzinger, J., McNeil, M., & O'Riordan, K. (2008). *Human cloning in the media: From science fiction to science practice.* London: Routledge.

Horst, M. (2005). Cloning sensations: Mass mediated articulation of social responses to controversial biotechnology. *Public Understanding of Science, 14,* 185–200.

Hwang, W. S., Ryu, Y. J., Park, J. H., Park, E. S., Lee, E. G., Koo, J. M., et al. (2004). Evidence of a pluripotent human embryonic stem cell line derived from a cloned blastocyst (retracted). *Science, 303,* 1669–1674.

Hwang, W. S., Roh, S., II, Lee, B. C., Kang, S. K., Kwon, D. K., Kim, S., et al. (2005). Patient-specific embryonic stem cells derived from human SCNT blastocysts (retracted). *Science, 308,* 1777–1783.

Jensen, E. (2008). The Dao of human cloning: Utopian/dystopian hype in the British press and popular films. *Public Understanding of Science, 17,* 123–143.

Klotzko, A. J. (Ed). (2001). *The cloning sourcebook.* New York: Oxford University Press.

Maio, G. (2006). Cloning in the media and popular culture. *EMBO Reports, 7,* 241–245.

Nelkin, D., & Lindee, M. S. (1995). *The DNA mystique: The gene as a cultural icon.* New York: W. H. Freeman.

Neresini, F. (2000). And man descended from the sheep: The public debate on cloning in the Italian press. *Public Understanding of Science, 9,* 359–382.

Nerlich, B., & Clarke, D. D. (2003). Anatomy of a media event: How arguments clashed in the 2001 human cloning debate. *New Genetics and Society, 22,* 43–59.

Nisbet, M. C., & Lewenstein, B. V. (2002). Biotechnology and the American media: The policy process and the elite press, 1970 to 1999. *Science Communication, 23,* 359–391.

Priest, S. H. (2001). Cloning: A study in news production. *Public Understanding of Science, 10,* 59–69.

Silver, L. M. (2001). Thinking twice, or thrice, about cloning. In A. J. Klotzko (Ed.), *The cloning sourcebook* (pp. 61–69). New York: Oxford University Press.

Stanford Encyclopedia on Philosophy. "Cloning": http://plato.stanford.edu/entries/cloning

Wilmut, I., Schnieke, A. E., McWhir, J., Kind, A. J., & Campbell, K. H. S. (1997). Viable offspring derived from fetal and adult mammalian cells. *Nature, 385,* 810–813.

Wilmut, I., Tudge, C., & Campbell, K. H. (2001). *The second creation: Dolly and the age of biological control.* Cambridge, MA: Harvard University Press.

COLD WAR RHETORIC

When World War II "ended in a thunderclap," observed Joseph H. Rush of the Association of Oak Ridge Scientists in 1947, the war had made science "politically interesting" and had interested scientists in politics. These interests manifested themselves in the rhetoric of the cold war that defined much of the public discourse for the next four decades. The cold war's inception is marked variously with such events as the August 6, 1945, explosion of the atomic bomb on Hiroshima, Japan; Japan's surrender shortly thereafter; articulation of the Truman Doctrine in the president's March 1947 address to the U.S. Congress; assistance for Greece and Turkey; and publication the same year of George F. Kennan's anonymous memo in *Foreign Affairs* advocating that the U.S.

adopt a policy of containment vis-à-vis the Soviet Union. That multiple moments, or some combination of them, might be said to account for the origins of the cold war testifies to rhetoric's significance in U.S. foreign policy. For although no one can dispute the materiality of nuclear weapons, an act of surrender, the provision of assistance to allies, and so on, imparting meaning to such events is a function of rhetoric.

Rhetoric originated as a practical art of persuasion following the overthrow of tyranny at Syracuse, Sicily, in the sixth century BCE. Citizens found themselves in a complicated situation. Free to make their own decisions, they were uncertain about how to proceed. In ensuing decades, rhetoric emerged and matured as an essential means for deliberating public policy and making laws in legislative bodies, settling disputes over the appropriateness of the laws in courtrooms, and both celebrating and censuring events, leaders, and community values on ceremonial occasions. Speakers in these arenas sought to influence audiences through some combination of their own expertise on subjects (*ethos*), their skill in assessing and appealing to audience emotions (*pathos*), and the construction of compelling messages grounded in sound logic and strong evidence (*logos*). From these roots evolved the foundation of a rhetorical tradition in which speakers (and, later, writers) prepared messages delivered through appropriate channels to influence audiences in response to situational or contextual dynamics.

Two-and-a-half millennia later, rhetoric continues to include the performance and analysis of persuasive discourse, but its meanings and uses have also broadened markedly. Thus, since scholarship of cold war rhetoric began in the last quarter of the 20th century, research has included attention to advocates' modes of argument, language choices, appeals to ideology, use of narrative and myth, and skill in public presentation, among other concerns. But beyond such traditional assessments of public policy deliberations, scholars have also examined the rhetorical dimensions of film, popular culture, covert as well as overt acts, pamphlets, and social movements; rhetoric's role in the construction of social reality; and many other topics. Despite increasing diversity in explorations of cold war rhetoric, however, one theme relevant to an encyclopedia of science and technology recurs:

Science became increasingly central to political speech, and scientists became increasingly prominent players in political life. Attention to the emergence of the scientists' movement in the 1940s and to presidents who made use of science in their political rhetoric illustrates these points.

Scientists as Cold War Rhetors

If there is disagreement that U.S. use of the atomic bomb marked the inception of the cold war, there is less dispute that the bomb sparked scientists' collective interest in politics, driving the scientists' movement of the 1940s and 1950s. Although the great majority of those involved in atomic science research—90% by most estimates—united in the immediate postwar period to promote internationalism and civilian control of nuclear power, the scientists' movement was not a single, unified collective action. New issues surfacing in the early years of the cold war, including questions concerning the role of science in military planning, loyalty programs, civil defense, and concerns over the genetic consequences of atomic—and hydrogen—bomb tests, diffused initial solidarity.

Two distinct factions of the movement, the Idealists and the Realists, ultimately took center stage to compete for the attention and support of their peers and the U.S. public. Immediately after the war, the Idealists held favor. In two key legislative battles of 1946, they garnered support through a carefully planned and well-executed campaign. Idealists contributed both to the defeat of the 1946 May-Johnson bill, which favored a strong military role in postwar control of the atom, and to the enactment of the McMahon bill, which ensured civilian control of nuclear power. Details of the first wave of the Idealist movement illuminate scientists' newfound interest in politics. Three dimensions of the campaign reflected their skill in moving from the laboratory to the political arena: their perception of the significance of educating the public about the atom, their role in the educational process, and the message strategies they employed. Although Realist advocates disagreed with the Idealist perspective, they adapted these same techniques to their own rhetorical purposes as the cold war progressed.

The educational process began with organization at the local level. This was logical, since the Manhattan Project that developed the atom bomb encompassed diverse laboratories across the country. Groups such as the Atomic Scientists of Chicago, the Association of Los Alamos Scientists, the Association of Oak Ridge Engineers and Scientists, and the Association of Cambridge Scientists emerged as the importance of scientists' new political role became clear. In time, recognizing that their potential strength lay in unity, the local groups cast their net more widely, first as the Federation of Atomic Scientists and eventually as the Federation of American Scientists. Once organized, they created speakers bureaus, sponsored lecture series, and targeted the general public with articles by and about scientists in such popular periodicals as *Reader's Digest*, the *Saturday Review of Literature, U.S. News and World Report*, and the *New York Times Magazine*. More learned periodicals emerged for the education of one another, as well as of potential opinion leaders. The *Bulletin of the Atomic Scientists* appeared in December 1945 and quickly became the most noteworthy of these, evolving into the "journal of conscience" among atomic scientists. Once the educational objective was in place and the infrastructure was solidifying, attention turned to the organizational members' role in the education process.

Ultimately, they assumed the mantle of scientist–citizen, which proved a critically important role in shaping the social organization of the postwar world. A crucial first step to the development of an ethos in political affairs was for scientists to overcome a schism between themselves and the U.S. public. That division stemmed in part from the scientists' lack of public presence, use of complex language in the conduct of their work, and reclusive image. To overcome this division, Idealist strategists sought first to establish scientists' credibility as public figures and then to pursue identification between the public and the scientist–citizen. Expertise and moral responsibility constituted the dimensions of credibility through which they pursued construction of their ethos with the public and with political leaders. And their successful advocacy on the May-Johnson and McMahon bills could be traced in large part to their skill in promoting identification between their own values and aspirations and those of the decision makers they sought to persuade.

Scientists who addressed committees, met with members of Congress in small groups, and delivered public addresses exhibited three influential traits. They showed respect for Congress, demonstrated that they did not want control or power for themselves, and put the common good first. In short, they affirmed the values of other dimensions of society and argued persuasively for the common bonds between culture's scientific and nonscientific spheres. Once the public and decision makers viewed the scientist–citizen as an ally whose values they shared, the challenge became to create and advance a message guided by those values and supportive of the one-world perspective.

In *Cold War Rhetoric*, Robert L. Scott notes the centrality of language in postwar politics, contending that even the term *cold war* is itself a rhetorical construct. Moreover, once the World War II allies found themselves in opposition to one another, language defined their new roles. U.S. leaders, for instance, continued to refer to countries opposed to the Soviets as "allies," while those in accord with the Soviet Union were Russian "satellites." In similar fashion, Idealist strategists understood that how they defined issues and described their objectives was intimately linked to the prospective success of their claims. Thus, in the immediate aftermath of the war, they made peace the center of their message, and defined progress and science as essential instruments of peace. Los Alamos physicists J. Robert Oppenheimer and Robert Wilson, for instance, argued that the options were "cooperation or annihilation." And cooperation, they and their colleagues maintained, included harnessing the resources of scientific and technological progress to advance peace.

The force of progress as a persuasive term in 1940s and 1950s United States cannot be overstated. After living through nearly two decades of sacrifice, first during the Great Depression and then during the war, the public was eager for the material benefits that postwar science and technology promised. Thus, virtually all of one appliance manufacturer's print and electronic media advertising carried the slogan, "At General Electric, progress is our most important product." Scientists, too, understood the appeal of progress and defined it as a fundamental value of their work. Scientific discoveries underlay researchers' commitment to peace, Oppenheimer wrote in the *Saturday Review of Literature*, because in a world in which science and technology are used for war, "not only the preferences and tastes of scientists are in jeopardy, but [so is] the substance of their faith: The general recognition of the value, the unqualified value, of knowledge, of scientific power, and progress." And peace and progress, from the Idealist perspective, depended on international cooperation in scientific inquiry, even with the U.S.'s postwar adversaries.

As the cold war intensified, however, Idealist appeals for one-world control of nuclear research struck many as problematic, particularly when one third of scientific research related to war. Moreover, revelations of scientists trading in espionage, as well as denials by others that any of their research had ever been disclosed to foreign powers, yielded an image of Idealists as grossly naïve at best, and potentially dangerous at worst.

Nonetheless, the scientist–citizen did not disappear from the political conversation. Rather, the Idealists were succeeded by Realists, whose convictions about science's role in the cold war differed markedly from those of their predecessors. Despite their substantive divergence from Idealist thinking, though, their rhetoric revealed remarkable parallels in persuasive strategies and tactics. Like that of the Idealists, Realist rhetoric addressed issues of credibility, peace, and language, albeit differently. They constructed appeals designed to reconstruct scientists' credibility in the wake of espionage scandals.

Thus, the Realists' task was not so much to create a scientific ethos in public affairs, but to assure the public that they, too, understood that the cold war demanded vigilance to counter communist malevolence. This was not to suggest a disposition toward war, however, for Realists (like the Idealists) expressed a commitment to peace. They disagreed with the "cooperation or annihilation" formula, however, arguing that peace could best be ensured through military strength. And Realists did not reject the importance of science and technology in pursuit of progress, but rather, they urged a view that depicted victory in an arms race as the most important consequence of scientific and technological inquiry. At the same time that scientists surfaced as influential players in postwar political culture, the products of their laboratory work became increasingly prominent in mainstream political discourse. Perhaps nowhere is this more evident than in presidential rhetoric.

Science in Presidential Rhetoric

Presidential speech is central to any overview of cold war rhetoric. For beginning with Harry Truman and continuing through George H. W. Bush, east–west tensions pervaded every president's foreign policy discourse and decisions. And scientific discovery was integral to the deliberations from which those decisions emanated. Atomic power and space exploration, independently and in combination, are two of the foremost achievements that reflect science's centrality in cold war rhetoric. Just as the rhetoric of the scientists' movement entailed diversity of objective and argument, even if there were parallels between factions' discursive habits, so too there is no single cold war presidential rhetoric. Rather, extant scholarship on Presidents Truman, Dwight Eisenhower, John Kennedy, and Ronald Reagan alone reveals their use of a wide range of subjects and a breadth of evaluative means.

Truman's significance derives in part, of course, from timing, by his occupation of the White House when events came together to end the war on both the European and Pacific fronts. But it is also the case that he understood the significance of U.S. leadership in war and in peace, and he recognized the relationship between the power of speech and the making of policy. His announcement of the atomic bomb, explanation of the Truman Doctrine, delineation of science's role in postwar diplomacy, and explication of technology's importance in transforming domestic culture are but four illustrations. Nuclear issues also influenced Eisenhower's rhetoric, but the arrival of the space age complicated the links between science and politics further than Truman could have imagined. Despite a modest reputation as a speaker, Eisenhower was a master propagandist. He demonstrated a capacity for conceptualizing both what needed to be said and how to say it in his "Atoms for Peace" speech in 1953, at once an explanation of the atom's potential in peacetime and a warning to the Soviet Union not to underestimate the United States. His major address on science and security in 1957 was designed to assuage U.S. fears in the wake of the Soviet launch of *Sputnik* in 1957, and he warned in his 1961 farewell address of the "military-industrial complex" made possible in large part by rapid advances in 20th-century science and technology.

Kennedy was tested early in his tenure by the 1962 Cuban Missile Crisis, demonstrated a propensity for skillful cold war diplomacy in guiding negotiations of the 1963 Nuclear Test Ban Treaty, and proved prescient by announcing that the United States would land a man on the moon by the end of the 1960s. Hailed as a potentially unlimited resource for scientific research, the space program's uses in cold war persuasion were equally limitless. Reagan illustrated one such use when he merged research on space with nuclear arms policy in articulating the Strategic Defense Initiative (SDI). He intimated the goal of SDI in a 1983 televised speech to the nation when he asked, "What if free people could live secure in the knowledge that their security did not rest upon the threat of instant U.S. retaliation to deter a Soviet attack, that we could intercept and destroy strategic ballistic missiles before they reached our own soil, or that of our allies?" His vision offered an alternative to the formula that dictated a choice between either "cooperation" or "annihilation," suggesting that "peace through strength" entailed a capacity to defend against other nations' atomic weapons.

Perhaps predictably, Reagan's critics derided SDI as "science fiction," while his supporters characterized the policy as a sign of genius. Whether either depiction ultimately proves wholly accurate, Reagan's conception of SDI culminated a progression of science's role in presidential speech, dating from Truman's presidency. Close reading of the chief executives' discourse reveals that while there are indeed significant differences in the presidents' views on science, technology, foreign affairs, and domestic policy, there are also recurring themes that comprise a sort of topoi, or topical system, of cold war presidential rhetoric. Not all cold war presidents are alike in speech and policy, of course. But just as Idealist and Realist scientists attended to parallel discursive challenges in advancing divergent arguments, so too do diverse presidents return to common themes. As Truman was the first to engage the challenge posed by the nuclear era, his rhetoric provides a fitting lens through which to view the emergence and evolution of the themes' place in presidential rhetoric.

On August 6, 1945, en route to the United States from the Potsdam Conference, Secretary of State Henry Stimson handed Truman a message indicating that the day before the United States had dropped the atomic bomb. Truman issued a statement that at once announced the devastating attack on Hiroshima and foreshadowed both his own administration's approach to public discourse on nuclear power and the rhetorical tack that would often define subsequent presidential commentary on technological innovation. Truman's initial goal was to work for international control of atomic power, provided an agreement with the Soviet Union that included verifiable compliance could be reached. Increasing suspicion and concern that the Soviets were proceeding with less than complete candor, however, soon led to a carefully crafted campaign to frame nuclear energy as an integral facet of U.S. cold war foreign policy. The overriding aim was a commitment to peace, but the realities of the Soviet threat mandated a call for peace through strength. Because such a rhetoric stimulated "nuclear fear" in the U.S. public, however, Truman engaged in a concurrent effort to define the harnessing of atomic power not as a feat to be remembered in terms of the destructive force unleashed on Japan, but as a natural force with unlimited potential to benefit humanity.

Substantial evidence suggests that Truman was sincere in his public commitment to international control of the atom, to his promise to share scientific knowledge with other nations, and to his pledge to disarm once a satisfactory arms control agreement could be reached. Yet the realities of the postwar world soon demanded an alternative approach to the use of nuclear energy in political decision making. Consequently, Truman advanced a foreign policy tied directly to atomic superiority, a policy that served as a precursor to Eisenhower's "atoms for peace" and Reagan's "peace through strength" strategies.

Four defining traits issued from Truman's rhetoric on behalf of that policy. First, he made clear the centrality of peace in his administration's thinking about U.S. policy in the atomic age. Thus, for example, when he spoke at Philadelphia's Girard College he said that it "is our endeavor and the effort of the government of the United States to have that age accomplished for the welfare and the peace of the world, and not for its destruction. That is what we work for, is peace in the world." When his critics quickly noted that the lives lost at Hiroshima and Nagasaki did little to reflect that goal, Truman countered that he and his advisers had contemplated the lives lost at two sites against those saved—both Japanese and American—by ending the war quickly. It was, he averred, the most difficult decision he had ever made. But he also concluded that the world had seen destructive technologies invented in war become engines for progress in peacetime, and he was convinced that pattern would repeat itself.

The only obstacle to putting U.S. success with atomic power to collective use, he argued in advancing his second theme, was Soviet intransigence. In 1946, a commission of leaders from the United States, Britain, Canada, France, China, and the Soviet Union met to discuss international control of nuclear power. The U.S. proposed—once an effective system of international control was in place—to stop making the bomb, to dispose of existing bombs, and to provide an international agency with all details of the country's knowledge of atomic science and weapons production. Only the Soviet Union hesitated, demanding a selective veto over other nations' calls for information. Such demands not only proved an obstacle to international agreements, but also anticipated increased hostility, tension, and secrecy in foreign relations. By 1949, the Soviet Union obtained its own nuclear weapon, and the arms race was fully engaged.

In response to Soviet resistance to cooperative ventures, a third feature of cold war presidential rhetoric surfaced. Truman cast the United States in the role of benevolent caretaker, a first among equals, charged with shepherding Western nations to the forefront in scientific research. He vowed to lead the allies to victory in the "battle of the laboratories," just as they had won the battles of air, land, and sea. And though he was motivated by the common good to follow technological achievement on its own terms, he was even more committed to using science to promote and preserve freedom. As Truman observed in an address on foreign policy at the George Washington Masonic Memorial in 1950, U.S. principles "have uplifted the hearts and hopes of generations of men. At the same time, through the progress of science, the nations of the world have been drawn together into a common destiny. Our security and progress are today more closely related than ever before to the advance of freedom and self government in other lands."

While thus putting the Soviet Union on notice that the United States would marshal technology as necessary in international affairs, the promise of peace made in his Hiroshima announcement required that Truman also articulate the atom's domestic value. He did so throughout the balance of his presidency in at least four ways: by linking nuclear power to research in natural science, particularly solar energy; by depicting atomic power as an extension of extant domestic technology, drawing parallels (for example) to water power that ensures agricultural productivity; by aligning the prospect of benefits from a nuclear age with the promise of the nation's future; and by animating science, as when he spoke of technology in terms of human traits. As Truman observed in 1948 while addressing the American Association for the Advancement of Science, "We need more than anything else the honest and uncompromising common sense of science. . . . The [scientific] method is characterized by open-mindedness, honesty, perseverance, and above all, by an unflinching passion for knowledge and truth."

In imparting animate traits to inanimate technology, Truman not only foreshadowed the presidential rhetoric of Eisenhower, Kennedy, and Reagan, but he also anticipated significant change in the nature of what is studied as rhetoric. By the 1950s, atomic age themes had surfaced in such popular culture venues as the Walt Disney Studios' *Our Friend the Atom*, science fiction literature, and film. There is, then, much more to cold war rhetoric than this orientation to the scientists' movement and presidential discourse can begin to address. But even as rhetoric changes in function and scope, a fair starting point for its understanding is to ascertain how sources conceptualize and transmit messages through appropriate media to influence audiences in response to situational or contextual variables.

David Henry

See also Manhattan Project; Nuclear Weapons; Oppenheimer, J. Robert; Rhetoric of Science; Space Program, Overview

Further Readings

Bostdorff, D. M. (2008). *Proclaiming the Truman doctrine: The cold war call to arms.* College Station: Texas A&M University Press.

Brockriede, W., & Scott, R. L. (1970). *Moments in the rhetoric of the cold war.* New York: Random House.

Gaddis, J. L. (2005). *The cold war: A new history.* New York: Penguin.

Langston, T. S. (2007). *The cold war presidency: A documentary history.* Washington, DC: CQ Press.

Mann, J. (2009). *The rebellion of Ronald Reagan: A history of the end of the cold war.* New York: Viking.

Medhurst, M. J. (Ed.). (1994). *Eisenhower's war of words: Rhetoric and leadership.* East Lansing: Michigan State University Press.

Medhurst, M. J., & Brands, H. W. (Eds.). (2000). *Critical reflections on the cold war: Linking rhetoric and history.* College Station: Texas A&M University Press.

Medhurst, M. J., Ivie, R. L., Wander, P., & Scott, R. L. (1997). *Cold war rhetoric: Strategy, metaphor, and ideology.* East Lansing: Michigan State University Press.

Osgood, K. (2006). *Total cold war: Eisenhower's secret propaganda battle at home and abroad.* Lawrence: University of Kansas Press.

Parry-Giles, S. J. (2002). *The rhetorical presidency, propaganda, and the cold war, 1945–1955.* Westport, CT: Praeger.

Public Papers of the Presidents. The American Presidency Project, University of California, Santa Barbara: www.presidency.ucsb.edu

Wittner, L. S. (2009). *Confronting the bomb: A short history of the world nuclear disarmament movement.* Stanford, CA: Stanford University Press.

COLONIZING OTHER WORLDS

The idea of colonizing other worlds has been persistent throughout the history of the space age in official and public discourse about space exploration and in the realm of science fiction. Common rationales offered for the human colonization of outer space are to fulfill human destiny or execute a biological imperative, to spread Earth life throughout the universe, to expand economic development into space, and to protect the human species against global catastrophe.

Primary proponents of space colonization include space advocacy groups and aerospace industries. Challenges to colonizing other worlds include the high cost of space transportation and space-based operations, limited understanding of the effects of varying gravity on human and other life, and the need to consider how new human societies should operate in nonterrestrial environments. U.S. government space policy avoids the use of the term *colonization* because of its negative connotations. Nonetheless, colonization continues to be a popular term among space advocates, along with the term *settlement*.

In the 21st century, advocates continue to promote space flight as the fulfillment of a biological necessity and as a means of extending U.S. free enterprise, with its private property claims, resource exploitation, and commercial development, into the solar system and beyond. The mass media tend to replicate these views with little analysis of their ideological underpinnings or their technical and economic soundness.

History

U.S. and European space exploration advocates of the 1920s, 1930s, and 1940s promoted the idea of conquering, exploiting, and colonizing outer space. Among the best known of these advocates are the Russian-Soviet space flight theorist Konstantin Tsiolkovsky, the U.S. rocket builder Robert Goddard, and Germany's Werhner von Braun. Tsiolkovsky was influenced by the late 19th century Russian mystic philosopher Nikolai Fyodorov, who believed that humanity was intended to leave Earth and spread out into space.

Other early advocates of space colonization included science fiction author Olaf Stapledon, who asserted that humankind should colonize other planets to exploit their resources for Earth's benefit, and rocket designer Krafft Ehricke, who claimed that it was humankind's destiny to expand throughout the universe. In the 1950s, books such as journalist Willy Ley's 1959 *The Conquest of Space*, with illustrations by space artist Chesley Bonestell, and a series of articles in *Collier's* magazine (also illustrated by Bonestell) titled "Man Will Conquer Space Soon!" helped to popularize the idea of colonizing other worlds. The Walt Disney Company played a role in this popularization as well.

In the 1960s, U.S. and Soviet human space flight programs and the race to land on the moon kept public attention focused on the idea of human expansion into space. In the 1970s, the idea of colonizing space got a major boost from physicist Gerard K. O'Neill (1927–1992), then at Princeton University. O'Neill presented his ideas for building human colonies in outer space to futurists, aerospace professionals, public audiences, and even the U.S. Congress. O'Neill conceived of massive human colonies suspended in space at so-called libration points between the Earth and the moon, lunar mining outposts designed to produce construction materials for human communities in space, and space-based generation of solar power to fuel these communities. At a time when concerns about rapid population growth, limited Earth resources, waning fossil energy supplies, and environmental degradation were prominent in public discourse, O'Neill's conception of human colonies in space seemed appealing in some quarters.

Since then, the U.S. government has developed several plans for human expansion into the solar system, including the 1986 report of the National Commission on Space, President George H. W. Bush's 1989 Space Exploration Initiative (which turned out to be an unfunded mandate), and President George W. Bush's 2004 "Vision for Space Exploration." During the 2008 presidential election season, Democratic members of Congress criticized Bush's "vision" as another inadequately funded mandate.

At the same time, the space community and the mass media—films, television, popular magazines and books, and most recently computer games—have continued to play a key role in sustaining and popularizing the idea of colonizing space. Just a few examples of the vast array of media products that feature colonies in space are *Serenity* (film); *Battlestar Galactica* (TV program); Kim Stanley Robinson's *Red Mars*, *Blue Mars*, and *Green Mars* series (books); and *Halo* (video game). To catalogue the wide array of media products addressing the subject of space colonies is beyond the scope of this entry. The enduring popularity of the idea of colonizing other worlds among public audiences may be an indication of public support for expanding human presence into the solar system. Or it may simply be an indication that most people find it interesting and entertaining to think about what life would be like elsewhere.

Rationales

Preservation and perpetuation of human civilization is a popular rationale for colonizing outer space. Astronomer and public scientist Carl Sagan

(1934–1996), for example, was an advocate of the idea that humankind must establish settlements in extraterrestrial environments to ensure against the possible destruction of Earth and its inhabitants by a catastrophic comet or asteroid impact. (Sagan once said he preferred the term *space cities* to *space colonies* to avoid negative connotations attached to the word *colonization*.) Others have argued for human colonies in space to accommodate Earth's rapidly growing population. This argument makes sense only if one accepts that human population growth should be unfettered.

Planetary engineering is a term developed by advocates of space colonization to describe the idea of using technology to alter the physical environment of a planet. *Terraforming* is a term developed to describe a particular form of planetary engineering—that is, the engineering of the physical environment of a planet to make it like Earth to enable habitation by humans.

The concepts of planetary engineering and terraforming are used primarily as tools for thinking about the evolution of planetary environments. Engineering or terraforming a planet would require technologies that are not available today, along with immense investments that no one is willing or able to make today. In addition, planetary engineering or terraforming could pose risks to indigenous extraterrestrial life forms, should they turn out to exist. The ethics of engineering other planets are a major consideration.

The idea that colonizing space is a matter of genetic predisposition or human destiny is a belief rather than a fact (see section on ideology below). This belief is widespread, nonetheless. Historians have documented exploration and colonization (on Earth and in space) as a cultural rather than a biological phenomenon—that is, exploration and colonization are products of particular times and places—particular social, economic, and political milieus. Modern (17th–20th century) exploration was conducted to expand commerce, stake political claims, and display military power. It may or may not be the case that the conquest-and-exploitation approach toward expanding human presence into space is a suitable or viable approach in the 21st century.

Advocates of the idea of extending terrestrial economic development into the solar system generally are promoting the idea of expanding Western-style capitalism into space. Legal, ethical, and other issues relating to the expansion of capitalism into the solar system—such as questions of claims on extraterrestrial resources, private property rights in space, and legal and regulatory regimes for space-based businesses—remain largely unexplored outside a small community of space law experts. (See section "Law and Policy" below.)

Ideology

Space colonization is often framed as a practicality, but it is as much an ideological position as a practical matter. The ideas of frontier pioneering, continual progress, manifest destiny, free enterprise, and rugged individualism have been especially prominent in U.S. cultural narrative. This story of what it means to be American constructs a rationale for U.S. exceptionalism. It provides a U.S. belief system, an ideology. This ideology constructs Americans as independent, pioneering, resourceful, inventive, and exceptional. It establishes that liberal democracy and free market capitalism constitute the only viable form of political economy.

The belief that colonizing space is a matter of human destiny rests on the assumption that humankind has both a genetic predisposition to explore and the power and the right to control nature. This belief is at the core of the idea that outer space is a frontier to be conquered and exploited for human benefit. Embedded in this conception of the space frontier are the assumptions that humankind has, and presumably should have, dominion over nature (which encompasses the universe) and that capitalism is a model of political economy that should be replicated throughout the universe.

U.S. space advocacy movements and initiatives have deployed the values and beliefs sustained by this national narrative in advocating for the colonization of other worlds. So-called grassroots space advocacy groups, such as the Mars Society, National Space Society, Space Studies Institute, and Space Frontier Foundation were chartered to promote the idea of expanding human society into the solar system.

The L5 Society, a precursor to the National Space Society, was founded in 1975 to promote space colonization, as it was then being advocated by Princeton University physics professor Gerard K. O'Neill (see "History" above). "The Colonization of Space," O'Neill's first paper on the subject, was published in the September 1974 issue of *Physics Today*. O'Neill adopted the term *the high frontier* to describe outer space as an environment to settle and exploit. In the Reagan administration, the term was co-opted by military space advocates to describe their vision of near-Earth space as a territory to be weaponized.

O'Neill founded the Space Studies Institute in 1977 to promote his space colonization agenda. Through the 1980s and 1990s, the institute conducted studies and conferences on topics such as energy and materials from space, engineering with lunar and asteroidal materials, and pathways to the so-called high frontier. In 1988, other advocates of manifest destiny in space created the Space Frontier Foundation to promote the colonization agenda. The Mars Society, founded in 1998, also advocates colonization.

Government Rhetoric

U.S. government rhetoric about space exploration typically avoids the term *colonization* because of its negative connotations, preferring the term *settlement* or *outpost*. Nonetheless, over the past 50 years, the frontier metaphor, the ideology of progress, and the belief in U.S. exceptionalism have been prevalent in government rhetoric about expanding human presence into space, as well as the rhetoric of advocacy groups.

The National Commission on Space, appointed by President Ronald Reagan to develop long-term goals for space exploration, titled its final report "Pioneering the Space Frontier." Reagan's Commission asserted that humankind is destined to settle other worlds and expand free enterprise into space. The George H. W. Bush administration cited an imperative to expand into the space frontier in its official rhetoric about the civilian space program, Clinton administration space policy perpetuated the idea of inevitable human expansion into space, and the George W. Bush administration pursued an agenda of incorporating space resources into Earth's economic sphere through Bush's "Vision for Space Exploration."

Law and Policy

The fundamental legal framework for human activities in space is the 1967 United Nations

Treaty on Principles Governing the Activities of States in the Exploration and Use of Outer Space, Including the Moon and Other Bodies, commonly known as the Outer Space Treaty. According to this treaty, for the good and in "the interests of all countries," we should explore and utilize outer space, which should be the "province of all mankind." The treaty states that space exploration and development will be conducted "in accordance with international law," with "free access" to all "celestial bodies" for all. The treaty prohibits "national appropriation by claim of sovereignty" of any part of space "by means of use or occupation, or by any other means." Signatories to the treaty are obligated to take responsibility for "national activities" of either governmental or nongovernmental entities.

The Outer Space Treaty does not specifically address human outposts or settlements or colonies in space, but rather provides a framework for their operation. A regulatory regime will likely be necessary to govern human settlements in space. Experts in space law and policy have been debating for some time over whether and how the treaty affects commercial operations in space, extraterrestrial resource claims, and long-term human presence in space. The International Institute of Space Law (an arm of the International Astronautical Federation) and the U.N. Committee on the Peaceful Uses of Outer space (COPUOS) are leading repositories of expertise on space law. (COPUOS has two standing subcommittees: a Scientific and Technical Subcommittee and a Legal Subcommittee.) Several universities around the world house programs or experts in space law and policy.

Large-scale, long-term human settlements in space are further into the future than their advocates may indicate. The persistence of long-standing barriers to this development, such as the high cost of space transportation and the need for an in-depth global dialogue on legal, regulatory, and ethical considerations relating to this development, will ensure that colonizing other worlds takes place slowly, if at all.

Linda Billings

See also Astrobiology; Space Program, Overview

Further Readings

Billings, L. (2007). Ideology, advocacy, and space flight: Evolution of a cultural narrative. In S. J. Dick & R. D. Launius (Eds.), *Societal impacts of space flight* (pp. 483–500, NASA SP-2007-4801). Washington, DC: National Aeronautics and Space Administration. Available at http://history.nasa.gov/sp4801-part2.pdf

Clarke, A. C. (Ed.). (1967). *The coming of the space age.* New York: Meredith Press.

Ley, W. (1959). *The conquest of space.* New York: Viking Press.

O'Neill, G. K. (1977). *The high frontier: Human colonies in space.* New York: Morrow.

Pyne, S. J. (2003). *Seeking newer worlds: The future of exploration.* Sarton Lecture, American Association for the Advancement of Science, Denver, CO. Available at www.public.asu.edu/~spyne/FUTURE.pdf

Sagan, C. (1994). *Pale blue dot: A vision of the human future in space* (1st ed.). New York: Random House.

United Nations treaty on principles governing the activities of states in the exploration and use of outer space, including the moon and other bodies, commonly known as the outer space. (1967). Available at www.oosa.unvienna.org/oosa/SpaceLaw/outerspt.html

COMMUNICATING SCIENCE TO CHILDREN

Children are at the center of some of the most controversial topics in science communication. Science, health, and technology news stories often carry images of children—on topics ranging from vaccinations to climate change, nutrition, genetics, or digital media—and yet the audience for such reporting tends to be decidedly grown up. News media aside, however, a significant quantity of science communication is aimed at children, in school if nowhere else. The science communicated in school is noticeably less contentious than that found in science news, science so established that it is sometimes several decades (even centuries) out of date.

This entry's title might be too didactic for some tastes—communicating to children—but in many respects it is realistic. When it comes to science communication's more youthful audiences, the deficit model approach (that is, assuming the audience is ignorant and in need of scientific instruction) is widely acceptable; so much of children's lives are plotted around learning. Arguably, the possessive apostrophe in the phrase "children's science communication" could be misplaced: Children may be the audience of such media products, but they do not necessarily have ownership of them. Even examples of child-to-child science communication tend to be initiated, mediated, controlled, and even censored by adults, largely led by adult ideas of children and adult ideas of which scientific issues will affect young people (now or in their future).

Sites for Communicating Science to Children

Science communication for children happens in a range of different spaces, in various forms of (multi) media. Although young people are often associated with electronic communication, science for children is just as likely to take place outdoors; there is a powerful tradition of connecting science, nature study, health education, and the outdoors movement. Arguably most science communication for children takes place in some form of school environment. Even outside the classroom, informal learning and "edutainment" products are branded with the logos of educational policy programs or at least reflect the topics and concerns of school curricula.

School science is especially noteworthy as an area of science communication that comes under the close inspection of a range of nonscientists: parents, nonspecialist teachers, businesspeople, politicians, community leaders, and others. As Dorothy Nelkin wrote in her study of arguments over creationism, education is often seen as an ideological instrument, a tool both for social reform and, sometimes in conflict with this, for the preservation of cultural values. This can make school science a contentious subject, and an area where more than just science gets covered. There is a long tradition of using science to teach children what is seen as the magnificence of God's creation. Arguably, even explicitly nonreligious science education reverberates with such messages today, if only through appeals to the sublime. There is also a history of teaching ideas of society through examples drawn from scientific views on, for example, ants or stardust—making scientific study a parable for moral or political lessons.

It is noticeable that some science communication spaces are especially full of children, whereas others tend to ignore young audiences. Science museums have long been associated with young people, especially when it comes to interactive exhibits. Indeed, some museums worry this damages their brand when it comes to chasing the young professional market (though others equally cash in on adult nostalgia for memories of childhood science experiences). Young people's media often exist quite separately from those aimed at adults, a no-go area for the old just as much as adult media can exclude under-18s. This might be due to concerns over child safety, with explicit barriers for unaccompanied adults. It may also be because grownups do not want to be bothered with what they see as childishness or because media producers think a no-adults-allowed aesthetic will appeal to young audiences.

It is worth emphasizing that museums are also sites full of cross-generational science communication. Family learning projects are often based on the realization that if one wants to talk to adults, one may well have to deal with the children that accompany them (and vice versa). Similar points can be made about science toys: Chemistry sets and so on may not seek to educate adults via their children, but they have often been sold as projects for parents and children to share. In contrast, television programs, Web sites, and books for children over 7 are more likely to talk directly and singularly to the child. This varies immensely by genre and age group, however: A science of skateboarding Web site aimed at teenagers assumes completely different generational identities and relationships from a Baby Einstein DVD.

Imagining the Child and Science

The relationship between science and children is not a simple business, with a range of agendas, histories, norms, and concerns at work. Arguably, this complexity is at least in part due to the diversity of ways science and the child can be defined. Each different pairing of definitions of science with those of childhood produce different ways of thinking about the whys, hows, whats, meanings, and morality of science communication for young people.

We might imagine children as inherently naïve, in need of a scientist's mature and expert knowledge, but we should not assume children are always placed at the bottom of the comparison. Romantic images of the child as positively innocent and in some way at one with nature may be juxtaposed with ideas of science as destructive, corrupting, and unnatural. Equally, we might choose to think of science as inherently childlike in some way—curious and playful—or that children could, or should, be thought of as little scientists for similar reasons.

One important characteristic of children is that they change, making them an interestingly variable audience for science communication. Children grow up, and in doing so, may one day become professional scientists. Thus, science communication will address children as current outsiders and, simultaneously, as potential insiders. Some educationalists apply a semi-Kuhnian idea of scientific progress, hoping future generations will challenge scientific orthodoxy in ways that will lead to better science (while also teaching the central tenants of the current paradigm right alongside prompts to revolt). This liminal identity of science communication's child audiences is also at the heart of many recent controversies in school science: Do we prepare students for future lives as scientists or as citizens? Some argue a curriculum can do both; others worry that by preparing children for one role, we somehow damage their ability to productively do the other.

Children's Agency and Science

It is perhaps temping to describe science communication for children as a form of intergenerational hegemony. However, there are questions of children's dependence on adults and intergenerational continuity that make children's marginality a rather different issue from, for example, marginalization by gender, race, or class. Still, there are inequalities of power to be reflected upon and different cultural identities to be aware of. Science policy questions may often be about regulating children's lives (either as children now or as adults later) but are largely considered a matter for their parents' generation.

Child health policy perhaps presents the biggest challenge to the idea of child passivity with respects to science. Child patients can develop lay expertise of their condition, just as adults can. There are also child–patient knowledge communities, pro-anorexia Web sites being the most contentious of these, but there are more conventionally supportive ones too. On the other side of the issue, parents' feelings and knowledge matter immensely in child health, and it is worth remembering that young patients may need or want to rely on the support and guidance of older people.

The topic of the environment also brings out particularly contentious questions of child agency, as it is assumed future-oriented environmental policy is most likely to affect younger generations. However, it is worth repeating David Buckingham's warning that the prevalence of ecology in children's news programs could be seen as a way of labeling it a kid's topic, putting off action rather than addressing the future needs of children today.

When it comes to education policy, there have been several challenges to the norm of assuming a deficit model. Discovery learning—popular in the mid- to late 20th century and still prevalent in areas of the science center movement—makes for an interesting case study. Loosely, this is rooted in the idea that it is wrong to indoctrinate children with the beliefs of the previous generation; rather, children should be allowed the freedom to discover nature for themselves. However, as many commentators have pointed out, this only works in as much as one believes that scientific research comes straight from simple lab-bench interaction with the natural world. Several classroom ethnographers noted that in practice, discovery learning tended to be highly teacher led, with any student results that challenged scientific orthodoxy accommodated as experimental error.

Another challenge comes from the science, technology, and society (STS) education movement. (STS is an acronym also used to identify the more academic field of Science and Technology Studies, with which there are connections, but in this entry, the acronym will refer to science, technology, and society.) This typically maintains the educationalist's position that knowledge of science is useful and that children should be educated in it but that knowing about science is more useful than scientific knowledge itself, and indeed, this knowing might be used by students to empower themselves against the might of the scientific establishment. However, it is noticeable that any engagement with science policy is largely conceived of in terms of students' future lives (that is, their adult lives) rather than something that involves them as children. Further, the various controversies surrounding STS education tend to focus on whether university scientists, educationalists, teachers, businesspeople, or politicians should have the greatest role in forming science curricula; the child's point of view is mentioned only in terms of maintaining children's interest.

Conclusion

In some respects, the children of science communication are to be seen but not heard. Children are at the center of much science news, and yet they are rarely involved in discussions over science policy. Still, children are the audience for a significant quantity of science communication, generally produced by adults and principally based on teaching established ideas. The deficit model approach might be criticized for treating nonscientists as if they were children, but when the audiences actually are children, it is largely unquestioned. The apparent characteristics of the child—greater mischief, curiosity, ignorance, or innocence—can be seen as a challenge or worry to be curtailed and trained. These attributes may also be seen as indicative of an exciting possibility, especially for those with an eye on future scientists developing new and so-far-unthought-of ideas and products. There is also the argument that in the spirit of at least some form of democracy, young people should be allowed greater power to speak to, and about, science.

Perhaps science communication for children is a form of intergenerational hegemony after all. Equally, perhaps children's lack of agency with respect to science is justified, or at least indicative of cultural norms much larger than the specifics of science communication. There are no easy answers to any of this, and theories of children's science communication can come down to quite complex philosophical questions (or, more pragmatically, specific knowledge of the people involved). Whatever one's personal view, the generational politics of children's engagement with science is something to be aware of.

Alice Bell

See also Children's Television and Science; Kuhn, Thomas; Nye, Bill; Popular Science and Formal Education; Science Centers and Science Museums

Further Readings

Bell, A. (2008). The childish nature of science: Exploring the child/science relationship in popular non-fiction. In A. Bell, S. Davies, & F. Mello (Eds.), *Science and its publics* (pp. 79–98). Newcastle, UK: Cambridge Scholars.

Buckingham, D. (2000). *The making of citizens: Young people, news and politics.* New York: Routledge.

Driver, R. (1983). *The pupil as scientist?* Buckingham, UK: Open University Press.

Mickenberg, J. (2006). Tools of science. In J. Mickenber, *Learning from the left: Children's literature, the cold war and radical politics in the United States* (chap. 6). Oxford: Oxford University Press.

Nelkin, D. (1982). *The creation controversy: Science or scripture in the schools.* New York: W. W. Norton.

Toon, E. (2004). Teaching children about health. In J. Golden, R. Meckel, & M. Prescott (Eds.), *Children and youth in sickness and in health* (pp. 85–106). Westport, CT: Greenwood.

Turner, S. (2008). School science and its controversies; or, whatever happened to scientific literacy? *Public Understanding of Science, 17*(1), 55–72.

COMMUNICATION CAMPAIGNS IN HEALTH AND ENVIRONMENT

Communication campaigns have functioned as vehicles of public information and persuasion throughout history. Issues driving them have included religion, politics, and culture—and more recently, the marketing of commercial goods and services, value-driven causes, and economic and social development. Such campaigns have often provided publics with scientific and technical content, either implicitly as the bases for campaign appeals or explicitly as the foci of the programs. By far the most conspicuous uses of such science and technology-based campaigns have centered on health and environmental issues, the emphasis in this entry.

According to Ronald Rice and Charles Atkin, in this context, a useful broad definition of public communication campaigns is that they are directed to a large and "relatively well-defined" audience in an attempt to "inform, persuade, or motivate" changes in behavior; they are typically designed to produce "noncommercial benefits" and are directed to both individuals and society more generally via "organized communication activities" that involve the mass media and are "often complemented by interpersonal support." Recent technological advances suggest adding that individual and social media play an increasingly important role and that community-level involvement and participation have become more critical.

Characteristics of Successful Campaigns

Several decades of empirical research and theorizing on the uses and effects of public communication campaigns have led to four overarching strategies and tactics gleaned from observing more successful programs:

1. Campaigns should be planned and designed by drawing from social science–based theory appropriate to the given topic, context, audience, and goals. Theory-based design not only provides rationales and evidence for what has previously succeeded (or not), but also provides a rigorous framework for strategic planning and establishing realistic outcomes. Possibilities include drawing from such classic psychological models as social learning and reasoned action, the sociological approach of diffusion of innovations, communication-based constructs such as framing and message analysis, or multifaceted risk analysis and communication models, as well as more general paradigms such as social marketing. The choice of a suitable theory for the program at hand can be daunting, but it is critical.

2. Formative evaluation research carried out prior to the campaign has shown significant value in effective program planning and design. Such research includes examining audiences' existing knowledge, attitudes, motives, and behaviors with respect to the campaign topic, as well as examining their communication patterns and preferences. More broadly, formative research should include attention to the situational or community setting in which the program will take place, including the

institutional resources, availability and accessibility of public response mechanisms, and the willingness of organizational or community leaders to facilitate or impede the program goals. Pilot testing of campaign themes and messages with target publics through expert interviews, focus groups, and/or surveys can be invaluable.

3. Individual and community participation in campaign planning, design, and execution can lead to greater effectiveness on several levels. Such involvement can aid in more clearly understanding the audience's view of a problem, which may differ markedly from that of program leaders. If an audience is being asked to take steps to resolve a problem, views are gained as to the kinds of steps that may be potentially viable, versus those that are likely to be rejected. And, of course, one size will not fit all. Public participation allows a finer delineation of the variations in an audience (or segments), leading away from attempts to focus on one grand, general audience descriptor. Finally, participation can build greater involvement with the issue, with less of a sense of top-down hierarchical communication efforts, particularly characteristic of those of governmental agencies that have sometimes been found less than effective.

4. The campaign should be implemented with clear, appropriate, and ultimately measureable goals, given the audience makeup and setting; the goals should be spelled out conceptually and operationally, in such a way that they are subject to eventual assessment. Strategies and tactics for accomplishing the goals should be clearly formulated, with a well-orchestrated dissemination plan utilizing professional quality messages and materials. While this may seem obvious, many public sector campaigns lack measureable goals or attention to obtaining adequate resources for quality campaign deployment. Such shortcomings can subvert programs that have the best of intentions. Final summative evaluation rounds out the requirements for appropriate campaign implementation.

Public Health Campaigns Versus Environmental Campaigns

Public health communication programs have for decades been far ahead of environmental and natural resources programs on all of the above dimensions. Health programs benefit from a longer tradition and a far more extensive support system, greater personal public interest and thus financial support for addressing health issues, and greater coherence among a multitude of health organizations at all levels. Insofar as program funding is concerned, the U.S. health promotion and research by the National Institutes of Health (NIH) alone far outweigh funded environmental efforts, which are apt to be tied more to resources from nonprofit advocacy organizations. That distinction may lead to something of a credibility gap as well.

Nonetheless, environmental and health campaigns today share many of the same strategies and tactics, theoretical models, assessment techniques, and the like; environmental campaign paradigms have lagged behind mainly in scale and sophistication. Both types of programs are generally motivated to serve the public good. Both require volitional inputs from individual citizens. The campaigns attempt to build awareness of problems and potential solutions, inform, build or change opinions or attitudes, motivate, and ultimately impact behaviors. Health campaigns naturally lean toward behaviors with more personal and therefore more salient outcomes. Heart disease prevention, cancer screenings, vaccinations, beneficial nutritional habits, and reduced substance abuse affect everyday physical, psychological, and social patterns, notably including mind–body functioning and sense of self.

As individuals and as a society, we are quite naturally likely to place a significantly higher premium on personal health than on any other aspect of our lives. Personal and familial survival—and in some cases, population survival—is often at stake, and that is emotionally felt. On the other hand, many if not most health campaigns are aimed at public health issues with implications for populations, not just for individuals. Personal actions are promoted as a stepping-stone for serving the greater public good.

Environmental campaigns, however, for the most part are implicitly and explicitly aimed at a greater public and ecological good, with individual actions assumed to be aimed likewise. Taken to the extreme, survival of the physical environment is critical to individual survival, but almost inevitably, this possibility is more removed from everyday life. Climate change may well be mankind's downfall someday, but someday can easily be seen as a distant if not invisible event. It is not in the here and now; it is more remote physiologically and psychologically, more arguable, and less certain.

Similarly, advocacy for energy conservation, recycling, water and air protection, and protection of other natural resources, habitats, and nonhuman species receive strongly positive opinion responses in most public polls, but they are less likely to enter into the daily activities of most of the public. Granted, many individuals ignore their health or most aspects of it with their everyday lifestyles, but protecting aspects of the external environment still remains more difficult to promote. Indeed, in instances in which environmental risks can be shown to directly endanger human health, such as radon exposure or drinking water pollution, the success of remedial campaigns can be expected to be considerably higher.

Environmental information programs are further limited by the nature of environmental issues and potential solutions. The concept of interconnectedness is inherent to ecological systems, and efforts at greater sustainability involve consideration of the complex interactions among biological, physical, and social science approaches to the world, often in combination with humanistic, cultural, political, and economic forces. Conflicting evidence within individual fields concerning a specific research question is endemic to science, but in environmental arenas, the conflicts often rise to the level of which scientific approaches, such as biological versus physical, are more appropriate, and of course, the evidence can become more muddled when multidisciplinary efforts are used. Examples abound in efforts to better understand climate change; air, land, and water quality; and the role that human development has in this equation. Such conflicts arise in simply outlining the problems, let alone delineating potential solutions.

Further, the consequences of environmental actions, positive or negative, are usually not immediately observable, taking away an important motivating factor in behavior change campaigns. And recommended actions that favor environmental remediation typically involve risks including relatively large economic ones—with at least some uncertainty over the payoff or eventual success. In many, if not most, instances, environmental successes are dependent not on individual or small-group behavioral change, but on change by a critical mass of individuals or communities, leading many campaigns into systems-level program efforts that not only must impact individuals but also organizations and often institutional and political bodies. None of the above should imply that human health problems and solutions are inherently simple, but they do tend to be relatively more easily visualized and understood, at least in the public view.

Important Strategic Models: Diffusion and Social Marketing

Two broad research-based strategic models applied to both health and environmental campaigns over the years have met with some success: diffusion of innovations and social marketing. Their different approaches can inform us as to which of several widely varying strategies should underlie campaign implementation, whether in the health or environmental realm, and when and where they may be more applicable, or at the least more useful as starting points for planning. The diffusion approach has roots in social change programs going back to the 1940s, with the introduction of new agricultural practices to farm producer populations, and focuses research on two components. The first is more social systems based, and it examines the stages of diffusion of a new practice or product over time in a given population, from groups typically defined as innovators, early adopters, early majority, late majority and laggards, or nonadopters. The time lag in successful diffusion efforts typically accelerates after innovators and early adopters, usually about 20% to 25% of the population, adopt the product or practice. Patterns of influence among these groups vary with population and innovation characteristics.

The second component is more individually based, and it examines the characteristics of the adoption process itself, ranging from awareness of the innovation, to persuasion, to the decision stage, to implementation and decision confirmation of the adopted innovation. Attributes of the innovation affecting the process include its relative advantage regarding existing alternatives, compatibility with individual or cultural values, complexity of use, ability to use the innovation during a trial period, and ability of others to observe the results of its adoption. Campaigns using this view of behavior have been successful in introducing agricultural practices that are more environmentally compatible, as well as other sustainable practices and products, new medical techniques within the health community, and a host of more commercial product innovations.

Social marketing is a more recent paradigm, developed in the 1970s on the assumption that certain kinds of individual and social changes could be promoted through campaigns based on traditional commercial marketing techniques. For example, the marketing-based five Ps—product, price, placement, promotion, and positioning—have been adapted to a range of health-related products and practices that compete against others that may have less desirable outcomes. The paradigm, although it has limits to its applicability, has increased the emphasis placed upon preliminary marketing research or needs assessment in campaigns and on the attention paid to the cost of behavior change relative to other options. Previously used most often in health programs, recent efforts to apply social marketing to environmental situations have met with mixed success, particularly when combined into a community-based marketing plan.

Social marketing has been viewed as a more exchange-based model, involving something given for something gained. Diffusion appears more relational; social dynamics among groups and individuals are more pertinent. Each approach has amplified our perspective on social influence processes in the campaign environment, and especially with respect to health, environmental, and other science or evidence-based programs. A range of social-psychological and related social science theories can be subsumed under each in particular circumstances.

Ethical Considerations for Campaigns

Regardless of the approach and theory applied, and despite intentions that are typically good, health and environmental campaigns are open to ethical concerns. These have traditionally centered around the intention of campaigns to influence personal behavior through persuasion techniques that can be equally effective against the public good as on its behalf. When does positively inspired social influence become propaganda for the purposes of the state or of other social institutions? Can many campaigns be seen as aimed at both of these ends? Who decides which issues receive the imprimatur of governmental or civic foundation funding and support? How is that decision reached? Similarly, the ethics of promoting a health or conservation practice based upon mixed or even flawed evidence must be considered. Given the relatively simple messages of many media campaigns, are audiences being asked to respond more on emotion than on good reasoning? These are only a sampling of some of the many ethical themes that are likely to confront communication campaign efforts in the near future.

Evaluating Campaigns and Their Impact

The application of social science research and evaluation to health-related campaigns spans perhaps 50 years at most, at least with any degree of internal or external validity. Even so, the number of programs that undergo virtually no evaluation, or only the most spurious, anecdotal efforts, remains substantial, especially at local and even statewide levels. The parallel situation for environmental programs is even less encouraging. Expense is of course a major factor. A fully assessed health or environmental program, beginning with the appropriate formative research process and finally summative evaluation using adequate sample numbers and measurement designs and tools, normally takes a significant amount out of the budget for the campaign itself.

Of course, the legitimacy of the expense of evaluation has to be stacked against the wisdom of running extensive public campaigns with little clue as to their effectiveness. Further, one can argue that the knowledge gained by performing robust assessments of particular types of exemplary campaigns can be carried over to future ones; what is learned in one series of programs can be transferable to others. One example is the lessons learned from the appropriate use of fear levels in health campaigns over the years and that this does not appear to work under certain conditions (such as high-fear messages in an existing high-fear climate) but that they may work in others (such as high-fear messages used to build awareness in a low-fear climate, with immediate activities to help quell the fear). Similarly, building in community involvement and

participation in both public health and environmental campaigns over the past two decades can been seen as at least in part an outgrowth of formative research efforts, which in many cases began to create local interest in problems and programs prior to actual campaign activity.

The role of the federal government and in particular NIH in instigating and funding the assessment of major health campaigns has been enormous. Most federally sponsored campaigns require capable evaluation, and in most cases, the agencies involved financially support this research. This has led to thousands of such studies over the years, some bare-bones undertakings that might be based on anecdotes, many empirically driven post-program numerical assessments, some carefully designed full-scale before-and-after field experiments, and a smaller number of well-validated, theory-based, hypothesis-testing effects studies. A host of the latter two types regularly make their way into the scientific journals focused on the emergent field of health communication or in broader publications concerned with communication research and/or public health issues.

The body of evidence, often contradictory, can appear overwhelming at times. Complex meta-analyses of the research have provided some clarification. The analyses generally conclude that health communication campaigns have affected health-related behaviors of segments of the public, clearly among statistically significant numbers of targeted populations. The actual percentages of such populations that are impacted are often in the range of 10%, with high variability. This raises a policy question of whether affecting, for example, 10% of a population is enough or is cost-effective, which is more appropriately addressed politically and economically than through the evaluation research itself.

Research indicates that behavioral change is more apt to result from health programs as a consequence of interpersonal influence and more recently has often been shown with increased community-level and other organizational involvement and networking. Traditional mass media sources appear to have their impact more in promoting awareness, knowledge, attitudinal dispositions, and perhaps motivation to act. A host of intervening factors also come into play, including population demographics and lifestyle habits, access to health information sources and health support facilities, and individual perceptions, values, personal networks, and other dispositions that at times seem only remotely related to health practices.

As for the impact of more personal and social media technologies, the research is just getting under way with new paradigms and techniques for simply observing and measuring these phenomena. Conventional wisdom points to these new media as building more off of the effectiveness of interpersonal and networking communication modes than that of "older" electronic media and print, with speed and interactivity the keystones. Hypothetically, these media could provide greater access to population subgroups—including now underserved ones—previously below the radar of many previous campaigns. This could allow closer tailoring of messages and interventions to individual dispositions, potentially with increased impact.

The focus above has been on health campaign assessment and impact because that is where the lion's share of such work has been done. On the environmental front, most likely more success has been tied to community-level organizing and participation, including public advocacy efforts aimed at political and other policy-making bodies. These impacts do not lend themselves as easily to social science measurement tools, but anecdotal evidence of meaningful results cannot be negated. One must consider as examples the rise of climate change on the public agenda, which has been documented by analyses of both media coverage and public opinion. The swelling of concern and documented behavior change with respect to energy conservation provides further evidence, as do the countless community-level recycling and other conservation efforts. The green revolution in commercial products and consumer practices may in part be an artifact of recent economic stresses and savvy commercial marketing, but their origins also include formal and informal environmental communication efforts on numerous fronts.

Garrett J. O'Keefe

See also Diffusion of Innovations; Evaluation of Science Communication; Health Literacy; Planned Behavior, Theory of; Social Marketing

Further Readings

Cox, R. (2006). *Environmental communication and the public sphere*. Thousand Oaks, CA: Sage.

Hornik, R. C. (Ed.). (2002). *Public health communication: Evidence for behavior change*. Mahwah, NJ: Lawrence Erlbaum.

Israel, B. A., Eng, E., Schulz, A. J., & Parker, E. A. (2005). *Methods in community-based participatory research for health*. San Francisco: Jossey-Bass.

McKenzie, J. F., Neiger, B. L., & Smeltzer, J. L. (2009). Planning, implementing and evaluating health promotion programs (5th ed.). San Francisco: Pearson.

McKenzie-Mohr, D., & Smith, W. (1999). *Fostering sustainable behavior: An introduction to community-based social marketing*. Gabriola Island, BC, Canada: New Society.

O'Keefe, G. J., & Shepard, R. L. (2002). Overcoming the challenges of environmental public information and action programs. In J. Dillard & M. Pfau (Eds.), *The handbook of persuasion: Theory and practice* (pp. 661–690). Thousand Oaks, CA: Sage.

Rice, R. E., & Atkin, C. K. (2001). *Public communication campaigns* (3rd ed.). Thousand Oaks, CA: Sage.

Rice, R. E., & Atkin, C. K. (2009). Public communication campaigns: Theoretical principles and practical applications. In J. Bryant & M. B. Oliver (Eds.), *Mass media effects* (3rd ed., pp. 427–452). Mahwah, NJ: Lawrence Erlbaum.

Santos, S. (2007). Risk communication. In M. G. Robson & W. A. Toscano (Eds.), *Risk assessment for environmental health* (pp. 463–488). San Francisco: Jossey-Bass.

Schiavo, R. (2007). *Health communication: From theory to practice*. San Francisco: Jossey-Bass.

Sexton, K., Marcus, A. A., Easter, K. W., & Burkhardt, T. D. (1999). *Better environmental decisions: Strategies for governments, businesses and communities*. Washington, DC: Island Press.

COMMUNITY "RIGHT TO KNOW"

In 1986, the U.S. Congress passed the Emergency Planning and Community Right-to-Know Act (EPCRA). Though it was debated and passed as a stand-alone law, it ended up packaged as part of another 1986 law, the Superfund Amendments and Reauthorization Act (SARA). The act is known either as EPCRA or as SARA Title III. This vitally important act mandates public communication of information regarding the release of toxic chemicals into the environment, creates an important resource for both the public and journalists regarding these releases, and demonstrates the power of making environmental information available.

The new law was billed as a response to two emergencies, the catastrophic 1984 chemical release at a Union Carbide plant in Bhopal, India, and a distressingly similar but not catastrophic 1985 release at Union Carbide's facility in Institute, West Virginia. As befits its focus on chemical emergencies, EPCRA set up a network of State Emergency Response Commissions and Local Emergency Planning Committees, and it obligated every individual facility deemed capable of launching a chemical emergency to develop its own emergency response plan.

But the best-known part of EPCRA had very little to do with emergency planning. Section 313 required the U.S. Environmental Protection Agency (EPA) to establish a Toxics Release Inventory (TRI), a nationwide list of routine chemical releases to air, land, and water from every covered factory, power plant, and so forth. Facilities have to file their TRI reports annually. A couple of years later, EPA releases the data to the public—not only the totals, but also the raw numbers for every facility in the country. Interested citizens can get chapter and verse on releases from any facility or geographical area of any chemical that is covered.

Section 313 is the community right-to-know part of EPCRA. Importantly, Section 313 does nothing—absolutely nothing—to regulate chemical emissions. It is not about controlling what gets emitted; it is exclusively about communicating what gets emitted. Nonetheless, its effects have been little short of revolutionary. And because those effects are publicity driven and market driven, they are in many respects immune to the ebb and flow of regulatory fervor in Washington, D.C. Even during the environmentally lax presidency of George W. Bush, the annual TRI obligation continued to exert strong pressure on companies to reduce their reportable emissions.

In the two decades since EPCRA became law, U.S. environmental activists have gotten used to the annual flood of TRI data. They tend to focus more on the (genuine) flaws of Section 313 than on its extraordinary mandate of transparency. But it has arguably been one of the most effective environmental laws ever.

There is a lesson here for other areas of environmental regulation: When companies are doing things the public disapproves of, it may not be necessary to make them stop directly. It may be sufficient to make them tell and to let the public make them stop. Of course, addressing a problem such as global warming requires a lot more than just expanding TRI to cover greenhouse gases. But that would surely be a useful, easy, and early step.

Corporate Obligation to Know

TRI forces facility managers to at least know what they are emitting. It is not just a community right-to-know law. It is a corporate obligation-to-know law. It may surprise some readers to learn that the management of most facilities have traditionally had very little idea of how much of what they were emitting. This is true not just of mom-and-pop operations, but even of huge complexes owned by multinational corporations.

In some cases, clearly, they did not know because they did not want to know—often because their attorneys told them they would be better off not knowing. The way toxics liability law has evolved in the United States, a company that knowingly emits potentially dangerous chemicals is far more vulnerable to tort litigation than a company that unknowingly emits the same chemicals. "We had no idea" is a better defense than "We knew about it but didn't think it was worth fixing."

Prior to TRI, companies were usually under no obligation to characterize their emissions. But if they did so voluntarily, they might have an obligation to inform their stakeholders. Then they would face a classic Catch-22: Either tell the stakeholders and invite litigation, or keep the information secret and reap the whirlwind if it gets out anyhow. It was far better not to know—at least better for the company, though obviously not for its neighbors or its employees. It was arguably malfeasant for a company to acquire this dangerously volatile information until EPCRA Section 313 made it obligatory to do so. While a doctor is in better legal shape if he or she considered a possible diagnosis but wrongly concluded that it did not apply, a factory's management is in better legal shape if it has never stopped to wonder exactly what is coming out of its stacks. However, since 1986, Section 313 makes the company stop to wonder what it is emitting whether it wants to or not, thus eliminating the defense of ignorance.

Even without the perverse effects of litigation defense, a facility's management might not have known much about their emissions before EPCRA Section 313. Consider, for example, a wire manufacturer that operated a copper smelter in Georgia for decades without wondering whether the smelter's emissions might include dioxins. Only when dioxins were added to the TRI list did the company discover not just that it had reportable dioxin emissions, but that its copper smelter was in fact the largest single-point dioxin source in the state among facilities covered by TRI, and one of the largest in the country. Once the company knew about its dioxin emissions, it obviously had to do something about them. After costing out various emissions reduction technologies, it quickly decided to close the smelter.

Pressure, Competition, Litigation, and Husbandry

Why did the wire manufacturer feel obligated to do something about its dioxin emissions, even though it violated no federal or state law? More generally, why has the TRI requirement led to significant emissions reductions, even though it does not mandate any reductions at all? For at least five reasons:

- *External pressure.* TRI numbers are published. Local activists look at them when deciding what to campaign about. Local journalists look at them when deciding what to report about. Local residents look at them when deciding what to worry about. Workers look at them when deciding how safe their workplace is, and investors look at them when deciding which stocks are likely to suffer from environmental controversy. All this attention readily converts into pressure on individual facilities as questions about emissions and emission trends come up routinely.
- *Internal pressure.* Even when these sorts of questions have not come up yet, companies

know they might come up at any time. The result is significant internal pressure from corporate management seeking to achieve lower overall TRI numbers. Vague corporate goals such as sustainability and social license to operate need credible, trackable metrics. Every U.S. company that publishes an annual environmental report or corporate social responsibility report includes a section on TRI emissions. And every company wants its TRI trend line to point downward.

- *Competition.* A lot of the pressure is competitive. It takes a real expert to know how many pounds of a given chemical add up to a serious problem. The answer depends on the chemical—some TRI chemicals are measured in tons, others in fractions of an ounce. The answer also depends on where the emissions are going; the same amount shipped to a landfill may be a lot less harmful than if it is going out the stacks. What everyone can relate to is the comparative information. Which company is the biggest emitter in the area? Which is one of the top ten in the country? Companies that struggle successfully to get lower on the list thereby expose other companies to unwanted scrutiny in their stead and thus motivate those other companies to get lower too.
- *Litigation.* Like activists, journalists, neighbors, workers, and shareholders, plaintiff attorneys also study the TRI list, looking for good class action prospects. Getting lower on the list reduces the probability of becoming a litigation target. And for companies that are already litigation targets, getting lower on the list gives them a more positive story to tell to prospective plaintiffs, and (if things go badly for the company) to juries.
- *Husbandry.* TRI emissions are wasted chemicals. Once TRI was implemented, a lot of companies were shocked to learn how many tons of useful chemicals they were wasting. Especially in the early years, facilities often found that their TRI emissions reductions more than paid for themselves when the recovered chemicals were reused as raw materials for their own manufacturing or converted into raw materials for some other facility.

And so the TRI numbers have gone down—and pretty impressively. Consider the grossest of all measures: total emissions of all chemicals from all facilities in all industries (for comparability, using just the chemicals and industries that have been covered since the outset). In 1988, the total was 3.01 million pounds. In 2006 (the latest year available as this is written in mid-2008), the total was 1.24 million pounds, 59% lower. (Meanwhile, the U.S. population increased by 22%.) Total TRI emissions went down every year except 1997 and 2004. Progress in the first 6 years of the Bush administration, from 2000 to 2006, was a 22% drop from 1.60 million pounds to 1.24 million pounds.

Anyone who wants to do their own trend analysis can access the EPA data online; specify the geographical location, the industry, and the chemical or chemicals; and look at the results for every year from 1988 to 2006.

Three More Benefits

Section 313 of EPCRA has had three other highly desirable impacts that deserve to be mentioned.

1. *Use as a tool of policy making.* TRI has been a potent tool of policy making—for lawmakers, for regulators, for companies, even for local emergency planning committees. If one analyzes the TRI data by geographical area, one learns where the hot spots are—which neighborhoods are enduring the most pollution, and thus which are most vulnerable to particular diseases linked to particular emissions. If one analyzes the data by industry, one learns which industrial processes are the biggest sources of particular pollutants, so one can zero in on altering or replacing those processes. If one analyzes by company, one learns who the corporate leaders and bad actors are. If one analyzes by chemical, one learns which pollutants are on the way out and which are getting worse, and thus, which ones most deserve research attention to assess their impacts and regulatory attention to get them under better control. And all the relevant information is public. Policymakers, companies, activists, and citizens are working from the same online data set.

2. *Generation of a raft of imitators.* TRI opened the door to a raft of federal and state right-to-know laws. Among the federal progeny of Section 313 are the following:

- The Hazard Communication Standard (administered by the Occupational Safety and Health Administration), requiring employers to warn their employees about workplace chemical hazards and to make available detailed Material Safety Data Sheets on each chemical.
- The Beach Bill (a 2000 amendment to the Clean Water Act), requiring states to notify the public when beaches become unsafe for swimming or other recreational activities.
- The Safe Drinking Water Act (originally passed in 1974 and amended in 1986 and 1996), requiring public water suppliers to tell their customers when they exceed specified contaminant levels and making them mail every customer an annual report on the level of contaminants in the system and the health concerns associated with each contaminant.
- Securities and Exchange Commission regulations, requiring publicly traded companies to disclose their environmental liabilities and pending enforcement actions above certain thresholds.
- Clean Air Act Risk Management Plan, requiring facilities that use extremely hazardous chemicals over threshold amounts to model their worst-case accidents and then brief their neighbors on what might happen, how bad it might get, and what they are doing to address it.

Many state and local governments have also followed up with their own right-to-know laws. The best known of the state right-to-know provisions is California's Proposition 65, adopted as a voter initiative in 1986 (the same year as EPCRA). It requires businesses to provide warnings prior to exposing individuals to listed carcinogens or reproductive toxins. Prop 65 is responsible for the warning signs in grocery stores, restaurants, and other public facilities throughout California. It is also responsible for changes in the composition of thousands of consumer products, at the hands of manufacturers seeking to avoid a Prop 65 labeling obligation.

3. *Establishment of a validated principle.* TRI has validated the concept of right to know as an engine of environmental improvement. In 1986, it was not obvious that making companies publish

their emissions data would exert such powerful downward pressure on emissions. No one doubts that now.

Moreover, it was not obvious in 1986 that "outsiders" actually ought to have a right to know what was ending up in their air and water. That seems obvious today, even to most corporate managers. But in 1986, many environmental professionals believed that ordinary folks would not know what to do with emissions data, that access to technical information should be restricted to people with the technical expertise to evaluate it, and that companies had a right to negotiate emissions standards with regulators without having to reveal confidential information to an interfering public.

It took good risk communication to persuade lawmakers otherwise. In 1981, 4 years before Congress passed EPCRA, the country's first municipal right-to-know ordinance was proposed in Philadelphia, Pennsylvania. When a skeptical city council scheduled hearings, one proponent testified with a large metal gas canister behind her. The canister was filled with compressed air, but its label suggested it contained an unknown chemical. As she gave her reasons why Philadelphia needed right to know, she casually turned the valve on the canister—and kept talking as a sinister "ssssss" of escaping gas filled the air. When several council members asked what the gas was, she assured them it was safe—that they had no need to know, since the experts were confident there was no risk. The council made her stop emitting compressed air—and the ordinance passed.

Right-to-Know Risk Communication

Section 313 obligated every covered facility to talk with its neighbors and other stakeholders about its emissions, but not technically—all that was technically required was to tell EPA about its emissions. But companies knew that EPA would make their TRI data public. Smart companies quickly realized that they would be wise to do so themselves, and do it first.

Even in the days before the Web, when making information public was lot less convenient than it is today, Section 313 launched thousands of environmental dialogues between industrial facilities and their neighbors. The need to communicate

became even more pressing after the Environmental Defense Fund (EDF) started putting all the TRI data online in 1998. EDF created the original Scorecard site that initially became the dominant Web site for localized industrial emissions information. Later, EPA did the same thing, and EPA's surprisingly user-friendly TRI Explorer is now the go-to Web site for TRI information. (Since 2005, the Scorecard has been managed separately from EDF, and unfortunately, it is no longer up-to-date.)

Because it forced local industrial facilities to talk to their neighbors, Section 313 was a huge shot in the arm for the then brand-new field of risk communication. The first national conference with risk communication in its title was titled simply National Conference on Risk Communication. It was sponsored jointly by the Conservation Foundation, the National Science Foundation, and EPA, and it took place in 1986, the year EPCRA was passed. In the decade that followed, how to explain the TRI numbers became a risk communication staple. Many of today's leading risk communication practitioners and consultants got their start helping companies talk about their TRI emissions, and not just about the pounds.

TRI risk communication has invariably focused on why particular numbers went up or down, on how much risk is associated with particular emissions, and on how well the company has fulfilled its previous promises and what it is prepared to promise for the future. And when companies are foolish enough to wait for EPA to release the data—and for an activist or a journalist to find it—then TRI risk communication focuses largely on why the company kept the information secret.

When companies talk to their stakeholders about their TRI emissions, they typically have at least four goals:

- To put the numbers in a context, the company considers appropriate before some critic puts them in a context the company likes a lot less. Risk communication teaches that this should not mean telling people there is nothing to worry about; it should mean explaining which emissions the company considers most worrisome and which it thinks are less so (even if the poundage is substantial).

- To focus attention on the company's TRI improvements. If a company is savvy about risk communication, it outsources much of the credit for those improvements to the stakeholders who most actively applied pressure to achieve them. The improvements are more credible when the company shares the credit.
- To explain the company's TRI deficiencies—emissions that went up or failed to go down enough. A company that understands risk communication will make these explanations apologetic rather than defensive and accompany them with actionable improvement goals. Smart companies also establish accountability mechanisms so that people can watch as the company struggles to achieve the goals.
- To acknowledge and validate people's concern about the emissions. This is the goal that departs most from the TRI numbers themselves. How much anger and fear people feel about a company's emissions is more a function of the way the relationship is handled than of the actual data. Good risk communication does not just mean explaining the data; it means validating people's concerns, apologizing for the company's past transgressions, and sharing control and credit.

Environmentalists sometimes worry that a company's "good" risk communication might replace actual emissions reduction. And companies sometimes hope that will be the case. But trying to improve relationships with stakeholders without improving actual performance as well is profoundly unlikely to work. People quickly understand that the so-called improvement is a strategic distraction—mere public relations—and that generates more anger and fear.

But improving performance without improving relationships with stakeholders does not work either. People stay upset and therefore tend not to notice that the numbers went down. Companies have to do both. This is one of the core lessons of risk communication. The chief arena in which it was learned was EPCRA Section 313 right to know.

TRI Drawbacks

The most serious drawback of Section 313 is also the most obvious: It doesn't address the risk associated with various pollutants, only their quantity. "Pounds of pollution" is an extremely gross measure of environmental or health impacts. What people really want the right to know is how endangered they are, not how much stuff has been emitted to the air, water, or ground. Even a technical ignoramus realizes that the risk is going to depend on what's being emitted and where it's being emitted, not just on how much of it is being emitted.

EDF's Scorecard offered a fairly rudimentary measure of risk. EPA now says it is trying to do something more sophisticated. It is merging TRI data, data from its National-Scale Air Toxics Assessment (NATA), and geographic information systems data (on Google Earth) into something called TRI-NATA Explorer, which is eventually supposed to enable people to map their risk, at least their inhalation risk. Meanwhile, the annual TRI reports provoke dialogue about risk, but they inform that dialogue only with information about pounds.

Other drawbacks that are frequently mentioned:

- Right to know translates into action only if politically active stakeholders mobilize around the information (or if companies anticipate that they are likely to do so). Not surprisingly, then, TRI's impact on emissions has occurred mostly in politically active communities.
- Some of the incentives in TRI are wrong. A company can reduce its numbers by switching from a chemical that is covered to one that is not, or from a chemical that is emitted by the ton to one that is emitted in much smaller quantities—changes that do not necessarily reduce risk and may actually increase it. Similarly, a company that outsources a high-emitting process or hires an off-site waste processor can reduce its own numbers without reducing total emissions.
- TRI data are self-reports, with no meaningful way to police their accuracy. In many cases, they are not actually data at all; "reasonable estimates" are permitted instead where actual data would be burdensome to collect.
- TRI covers only 600+ chemicals—which is far from all the chemicals emitted. Recurrent battles focus on what chemicals should be added to (or deleted from) the list.
- Since 2005, EPA has been trying to weaken (one critic says "dismantle") the TRI program with

changes such as switching from annual to biennial reporting and increasing as much as tenfold the thresholds for having to report about particular chemicals. These efforts have been partially successful and are continuing as of mid-2008.

- There is also a movement afoot to make federal right-to-know law preempt more draconian state laws, such as California's Proposition 65.

These drawbacks notwithstanding, TRI has proved its worth. More than any other U.S. law, it has established that transparency can lead to environmental improvement, and thus that requiring transparency—right to know—is an efficient tool of environmental regulation.

Peter M. Sandman

See also Environmental Defense Fund; Environmental Journalism; Environmental Protection Agency, U.S.; Risk Communication, Overview; Toxic Substances Regulation

Further Readings

Emergency Planning and Community Right-to-Know Act, 40 C.F.R. § 350–372 (1986).

Florini, A., & Stiglitz, J. E. (2007). *The right to know: Transparency for an open world.* New York: Columbia University Press.

The Right-to-Know Network: www.rtknet.org

Safe Drinking Water Act, 42 U.C.S. § 300f et seq. (1974).

Superfund Amendments and Reauthorization Act, 42 U.S.C. § 9601 et seq. (1986).

U.S. Environmental Protection Agency. (n.d.). *Toxics Release Inventory program.* Retrieved August 15, 2008, from www.epa.gov/tri

U.S. Environmental Protection Agency. (n.d.). *TRI Explorer.* Retrieved August 15, 2008, from www.epa.gov/triexplorer

COMPUTER-TAILORED MESSAGES

Imagine that a person wants to convince someone to stop smoking or start exercising, select one political candidate or position over another, or purchase a certain product from a particular business. Previous theory and research suggest one good way to increase one's chance of successfully persuading another would be to increase the personal relevance of one's message. For example, if one wants to convince someone to start exercising, one might begin by asking him or her what he or she sees as the biggest benefits (such as weight loss, better health, improved appearance or strength, or decreased stress) and barriers (such as cost, time, being self-conscious about one's appearance, a belief that exercise is boring, or having tried in the past and failed) to exercising. Then, rather than addressing every reason someone may or may not want to exercise to every person one tries to influence, one could customize his or her message to focus on just the motivations that are important to each individual.

Until recently, it was difficult and costly to develop and disseminate customized messages, especially on a large scale. However, recent advances in computer and other communication technologies have made it both possible and practical to create individualized communication via computer-tailored messages. *Tailored messages* are intended to reach one specific person based on characteristics that are unique to that person. Tailored messages are typically created by asking individuals to answer a series of questions (for example, about their beliefs or behavior) and then using a computer algorithm (a series of instructions or decision rules) to generate messages that are highly customized for each individual. To illustrate, an individual might be asked a series of questions about his or her perceived susceptibility to kidney disease and then receive a computer-tailored message designed to increase only those perceptions that are currently low. The final message can take on a variety of forms (such as letters, pamphlets, or Web pages) and can be delivered through a variety of channels (in the mail, over the Internet, or via telephone—including cell phones, in person, using personal handheld assistants, and so on).

To provide a point of reference, tailored messages are often compared to generic and targeted messages, both of which are still very common but allow for no or very little customization. *Generic messages* are designed to reach a large number of individuals in the general population but are not customized to any particular subgroup or individual within that population. An example of a generic message would be a kidney disease prevention pamphlet or Web page designed for the general public. At least some of the information in a generic message will likely be relevant to everyone who reads it, but readers will have to search through a lot of potentially irrelevant information to find the facts that are applicable to them.

Targeted messages, on the other hand, are developed for a specific subgroup of the general population whose members are similar on one or more demographic (for example, ethnicity), psychographic (for example, levels of perceived threat or efficacy), or behavioral (for example, stage of change) variables. An example of a targeted message would be a kidney disease prevention pamphlet or Web page designed specifically for Hispanics who are over the age of 40, since this subgroup is at greater risk for kidney disease than members of the general population. Targeted messages are an improvement over generic messages because they take important characteristics of a subgroup into account and use some customization to increase the relevance of the message to individuals within that subgroup. However, targeted messages use a single version of a message to communicate with all members of a subgroup and therefore do not address important factors that likely vary from person to person, a weakness that is exactly what computer-tailored messages are designed to do.

Do Computer-Tailored Messages Work?

Results across dozens of studies and several recent meta-analyses provide compelling evidence that computer-tailored messages can be an effective way to change knowledge, beliefs, and behaviors. Tailored messages dealing with numerous topics and target audiences, guided by a variety of different theoretical perspectives, have been shown to be more likely to change people's behavior than if individuals receive no message or only generic or targeted messages. Computer-tailored messages work best when they involve more than one contact and are tailored based on both behavior and one or more theoretical constructs. A considerable amount of evidence suggests that computer-tailored messages work and that, in some instances, they can work as well as human-delivered interventions provided in one-on-one, small group, or classroom settings by health care providers, professional counselors, peers, or other facilitators.

Application Across Communication Contexts

Although the use of computer-tailored messages is fairly common and well studied in the area of health communication, people working in other communication contexts including marketing and politics also use tailored messages on a regular basis. (In these contexts, the use of computer-tailored messages is sometimes referred to by other names such as narrowcasting.) For example, retailers such as Amazon.com use rudimentary tailoring when they make recommendations based on an individual's search or purchase histories, as do services such as TiVo when they make suggestions based on the television shows an individual watched or recorded. Google AdWords and Yahoo! Sponsored Search both use similar processes to produce customized ads based on the terms people enter into their search engines.

An even clearer example of tailoring is when Amazon.com asks customers to actively take part in the tailoring process by using its Recommendations Wizard, which includes a series of questions and rating systems designed to help Amazon.com make more effective individualized recommendations. Similarly, TiVo has a feature that viewers can use to rate the programs they like and dislike, ratings TiVo then uses to generate better-customized suggestions in the future.

In politics, those canvassing for various candidates or causes can ask potential voters a few simple questions and then play a short customized video clip. Further, candidates may try to find out which issues potential voters find most important and then call, e-mail, direct mail, or visit each of these individuals with their message on just these topics. In short, politicians can use computer-tailored messages to adapt and disseminate their messages to individuals in a variety of ways. The examples discussed in this section represent just a few of the many possible contexts and uses for computer-tailored messages.

Conclusion

Computer-tailored messages represent a relatively new and cost-effective way to reach a large number of individuals with customized content in a variety of communication contexts. Further, the on-demand nature of computer-tailored messages delivered over the Internet has the added potential to reach anyone, anywhere, and at any time if they have the necessary equipment. Finally, computer-tailored messages share some of the benefits of both mass media and interpersonal communication in that they can reach a large number of individuals with messages that are both interactive and easily adapted. This strategy is one that health and other risk communicators are likely to find increasingly useful and effective.

Anthony J. Roberto

See also Communication Campaigns in Health and Environment; Fear Appeals; Risk Communication, Overview

Further Readings

Goodman, B., & Rushkoff, D. (Writers & Directors). (2003). The persuaders [Television series episode]. In R. Dretzin, B. Goodman, & M. Soenens (Producers), *Frontline*. Boston, MA: WGBH Educational Foundation.

Kreuter, M., Farrell, D., Olevitch, L., & Brennan, L. (2000). *Tailoring health messages: Customizing communication with computer technology*. Mahwah, NJ: Lawrence Erlbaum.

Noar, S. M., Benac, C., & Harris, M. (2007). Does tailoring matter? Meta-analytic review of tailored print health behavior change interventions. *Psychological Bulletin, 133*, 673–693.

Noar, S. M., Black, H. G., & Pierce, L. B. (2009). Efficacy of computer technology-based HIV prevention interventions: A meta-analysis. *AIDS, 23*, 107–115.

Noar, S. M., Harrington, N. G., & Aldrich, R. S. (2009). The role of message tailoring in the development of persuasive health communication messages. In C. S. Beck (Ed.), *Communication yearbook 33* (pp. 73–134). New York: Lawrence Erlbaum.

Sohl, S. J., & Moyer, A. (2007). Tailored interventions to promote mammography screening: A meta-analytic review. *Preventive Medicine, 45*, 252–261.

CONFLICTS OF INTEREST IN SCIENCE

In 1942, sociologist Robert Merton included "disinterested" as one of the four behavioral norms of scientists, meaning that scientists were not to have emotional or financial ties to their research. Although critics have called Merton's norms overly idealistic, the last several decades have witnessed growing concerns in the scientific community regarding scientists' objectivity in the face of increased pressures to seek sponsored funding for their research. With some exceptions, the news media offer little coverage of such issues. This entry provides a definition of conflicts of interest and then discusses issues related to the management of conflicts of interest. It then offers examples of conflicts of interest in science and an overview of research examining public views about conflicts of interest in science.

Defining Conflicts of Interest

Few issues can cast as much suspicion over the truth of scientific results as the accusation of real or potential conflicts of interest among scientists. Broadly construed, conflicts of interest occur when individuals, groups, or organizations have an interest in a decision or outcome and the opportunity to influence the process to get the decision or outcome they prefer. In his 2001 coedited book on conflicts of interest, Michael Davis provides a more precise definition, stating that conflicts of interest occur when an individual is asked to exercise his or her judgment on behalf of an individual or organization, and the individual making the judgment has a special interest that could result in a judgment that would be different if that interest did not exist. Scientists with a conflict of interest might be referred to as having a *vested interest* or a *stake* in the outcome, suggesting that the scientists might be influenced to act in favor of that interest.

Science offers many scenarios that could give rise to conflicts of interest. For example, if a scientist receives funding from a specific organization and is then asked to evaluate the efficacy of a product that organization makes, the scientist would have a financial conflict of interest. Specifically, the financial interest may influence the scientist to evaluate the product differently than if no financial tie existed. Another example is when a physician accepts gifts from pharmaceutical corporations. Although accepting gifts is not necessarily unethical, it could give rise to the physician favoring one pharmaceutical's product over another, equally effective drug. Another example would arise if a scientist were asked to review grant proposals, one of which was submitted by his or her collaborator or former student. The prior relationship between the scientist and his or her collaborator or former student could lead the scientist to give more favorable reviews of this submission than if the relationship did not exist.

It is important to point out the difference between *bias* and conflict of interest. Being biased implies that an individual is not neutral in his or her judgment, meaning that he or she is predisposed toward one view or another. Having a conflict of interest does not mean that an individual is biased, but rather that the conditions are ripe for bias to occur. In the examples given above, the state of conflict has not necessarily resulted in a biased decision, but it has created a greater potential for biased decisions to occur.

In his discussion of conflicts of interest, Davis described three scenarios in which conflicts of interest can lead to biased decisions. In the first scenario, an individual has a conflict of interest but is unaware of it and, consequently, does nothing to reduce its real or potential influence on his or her judgment. Although this individual has not deliberately sought to deceive, the conflict of interest may still result in the individual acting (unknowingly) in a biased manner. In the second scenario, the individual is aware of the conflict but hides it. By most standards, the deliberate nondisclosure of a conflict of interest would be viewed as unethical behavior, not to mention that the behavior again results in no action to reduce the potential for resulting bias. In the third scenario, the individual is aware of the conflict of interest and discloses it but yet still exercises his or her judgment. Although disclosure is preferable to nondisclosure, the conflict means that there is still a greater potential for bias to occur. Furthermore, it could harm the integrity of the decision-making process if people do not agree with the decision to allow the conflicted individual to participate.

Managing conflicts of interest among scientists has become more important. Along these lines, for certain types of conflicts of interest, guidelines help scientists determine whether they should remove themselves from a potentially compromising situation. For example, science is moving toward greater transparency of funding arrangements and

disclosure of conflicts of interest, with growing requirements in the peer-reviewed literature for authors to disclose any financial conflict. Even such transparency may not reduce bias, however. Some observers have questioned whether scientists can receive funding from industry and remain unbiased. For example, research concerning the food and beverage industry has found that authors with financial ties to industry—and whose ties were fully disclosed in the article—were still more likely to publish supporting views of that industry's product than other researchers who had no such ties.

Types of Conflicts of Interest

Although financial conflicts of interest are the most visible, most regulated, and most often disclosed, many types of conflicts of interest exist. Other types include professional, personal, and ideological conflicts of interest. As in the example provided earlier, professional ties may result in one scientist giving a more (or less) favorable review to a journal article submitted by colleagues (or competitors) in his or her field. To reduce the potential for bias, scientific peer review is usually blind so that reviewers cannot identify the author of the article they are asked to evaluate. Most journals today request authors to remove any information that could be used to identify who they are. Of course, the peer-review process is not always perfect, as reviewers are sometimes able to discern the identity of the author by examining the references, acknowledgements, or embedded document properties information (if it is an electronic copy).

Personal conflicts of interest can occur when a family member has a stake in the outcome of a scientist's research. This interest may lead to a scientist losing objectivity under pressure to produce favorable results. Along these lines, in medical science, physicians are discouraged from treating family members as patients due to the potential loss of objectivity. Ideological conflicts of interest, which can arise due to religious or political views, may compel a scientist to discount an area of research or discredit scientific findings that compete with his or her worldview or political agenda. Religious views, for example, may lead some scientists to oppose research on stem cells derived from human embryos or may motivate others to discount research findings related to evolution.

By far, however, financial conflicts of interest are the most prominent in science and seem likely to become even more frequent due to pressures on scientists to seek external funding for their research. Increasingly, such external sources are industrial partners, which have a financial stake in seeing a return on their investments. Although the U.S. government still funds the greatest share of scientific research and development in the United States, the National Science Board has reported that recent years have seen a decrease in government funding and a growth in industry funding. The prospect of increased industry funding in areas traditionally sponsored by U.S. government agencies has given rise to new ethical questions. John Ziman, in a 2002 article, has discussed how the two traditions of science—academic and industrial—have become more entangled in recent decades, giving rise to increased ethical dilemmas in science. These can include pressures for scientists to pursue research that has greater commercial potential than more basic or academic science. As academic scientists are encouraged and rewarded for entrepreneurship in seeking grants and patents for their work, so too have universities required greater oversight for possible misconduct. Annual conflict of interest disclosures have become the norm in an effort to identify potential abuses of the system.

Certainly, not all industries have a malicious intent to influence the results of the science they fund. At times, however, relationships between scientists and industrial partners can give rise to the appearance of conflicts of interest, even if no real conflict exists. For example, according to a 2003 news report, a U.S. Food and Drug Administration advisory committee came under fire when it became public that the committee, which recommended the return of silicon breast implants to the consumer market, included a large number of plastic surgeons. Indeed, even the suggestion of a conflict of interest can at times breed suspicion or skepticism about scientists' findings. On the other hand, sometimes the scientist seeks to behave in an ethical manner but is thwarted by the funding agency. In one notorious example, authors of an article examining the effectiveness of a new AIDS drug were restricted from publishing their findings by the funding organization, which did not want to release the data. The *Journal of the American Medical Association*

decided to publish the incomplete data in spite of the sponsor's concerns.

Other egregious examples of conflicts of interest in science arise when an industry seeks to legitimize its research by establishing research centers or front groups. Often, these efforts are couched in terms that appear to legitimize the science as objective. Few would recognize, for example, that the Advancement of Sound Science Coalition was once the name of a front group for Philip Morris, manufacturer of cigarettes and other consumer products. The terms *sound science* and *junk science* were coined by interest groups seeking to politicize scientific evidence and at times delay agency action.

In an effort to obscure the source of funding, some industries have established their own research groups. U.S. tobacco companies have provided some of the most visible examples of attempts to "launder" scientific data. The Center for Indoor Air Research, for example, was formed by three tobacco companies in the late 1980s to conduct research on the effects of tobacco smoke on indoor air quality. Although this center had a stated mission of promoting unbiased science, some observers suggested that it used special grants to support tobacco companies' interests and divert attention from the harms of tobacco smoke.

Public Views and Media Coverage

Few studies have actually examined what the public believes about conflicts of interest in science or how these beliefs might influence the public's trust in scientific results. One question is the extent to which the public knows about conflicts of interest in science. Some research has examined the extent to which people were willing to tolerate real or potential conflicts of interest among U.S. Food and Drug Administration advisory committee members. This research found that people were more willing to accept real or potential conflicts of interest when they believed that there were fair procedures in place to ensure that conflicts were appropriately managed.

U.S. interest groups such as the Union of Concerned Scientists and the Center for Science in the Public Interest have sought to raise awareness of and attention to risks to scientific integrity brought about due to conflicts of interest. The Union of Concerned Scientists, for example, pays particular attention to how the federal government uses science and treats federal scientists. A recent complaint reported in the *New York Times* in 2007 centered on one federal agency's efforts to suppress another federal agency's research related to global climate change. The Center for Science in the Public Interest reports on financial ties between scientists and corporate interests and, at the time of this writing, keeps a searchable public database on its Web site for users to look up scientists and see who has funded their research.

In terms of general exposure to science, we know that most people get their information about science from television, followed closely by the Internet. Despite some notable exceptions of investigative reporting that have uncovered conflicts of interest in science, the media may not devote much attention to conflicts of interest in science in general coverage. One study by Daniel Cook and others examined over 1,000 stories about science published in newspapers in 2004 and 2005 and found that the stories often did not report scientists' conflicts of interest even if these were disclosed in the original scientific journals. One question is whether the lack of disclosure of scientists' financial ties may lead to a lack of public awareness about conflicts of interest in science. To date, no one has examined the extent to which television or Internet news stories on scientific discoveries or reports disclose conflicts of interest among scientists.

With regard to how journalists should report on conflicts of interest in science, some may question whether it is the journalist's responsibility to disclose conflicts of interest of scientists in general news stories or whether this disclosure is better left to the editorial pages. On the other hand, few would argue against having journalists evenhandedly report the potential biases of sources. Regardless of how this is resolved, the popular press a has long way to catch up to the level of disclosure in scientific journals.

Katherine A. McComas

See also Center for Science in the Public Interest; Merton, Robert K.; Peer Review; Research Ethics, Overview; Union of Concerned Scientists

Further Readings

Brown, D. (2000, November 1). Scientists report bid to block publications of an AIDS study: Results not favorable to biotech firm's antiviral product. *The Washington Post*, A10.

Cook, D. M., Boyd, E. A., Grossmann, C., & Bero, L. A. (2007). Reporting science and conflicts of interest in the lay press. *PLoS ONE, 2*(12), e1266.

Davis, M. (2001). Introduction. In M. Davis & A. Stark (Eds.), *Conflict of interest in the professions* (pp. 3–19). New York: Oxford University Press.

Dean, C. (2007, January 31). Scientists criticize White House stance on climate change findings. *The New York Times*, A17.

Hilts, P. (2000, November 1). Company tried to block report that its HIV vaccine failed. *The New York Times*, A26.

International Committee of Medical Journal Editors. (1993). Conflict of interest. *Lancet, 341*, 742–743.

Lesser, L. I., Ebbeling, C. B., Goozner, M., Wypij, D., & Ludwig, D. S. (2007). Relationship between funding source and conclusion among nutrition-related scientific articles. *PLoS Medicine, 4*(1), 41–46.

Levine, J., Gussow, J. D., Hastings, D., & Eccher, A. (2003). Authors' financial relationships with the food and beverage industry and their published positions on the fat substitute olestra. *American Journal of Public Health, 93*(4), 664–669.

McComas, K., Tuite, L. S., Waks, L., & Sherman, L. A. (2007). Predicting satisfaction and outcome acceptance with advisory committee meetings: The role of procedural justice. *Journal of Applied Social Psychology, 37*(5), 905–927.

Merton, R. K. (1973). *The sociology of science: Theoretical and empirical investigations* (N. W. Storer, Ed.). Chicago: University of Chicago Press.

National Science Board. (2008). *Science and engineering indicators 2008*. Arlington, VA: National Science Foundation.

Rowland, C. (2003, November 5). Chief of FDA panel says implants vote "misguided": Safety of silicone is called unproven. *The Boston Globe*, A1.

Ziman, J. (2002). The continuing need for disinterested research. *Science and Engineering Ethics, 8*(3), 397–399.

CONSENSUS CONFERENCE

The consensus conference is a type of forum specifically designed for citizen (or citizen and expert) discussion and communication about issues in science, technology, and health that confront society. The original consensus conference model was based on an approach to medical research assessment originating in the health care sector in the United States during the 1960s. It was (and is) used to bring experts together to arrive at a consensus about the state of the research evidence on a given medical or research question. This process was adapted in Denmark by the Danish Board of Technology in the 1980s, introducing the use of a citizens' panel to the process of technology assessment. This version brings together a lay citizen panel and an expert panel to provide an opportunity for lay citizens to deliberate on a technology based on learning about the topic, hearing from and questioning a range of experts, deliberating, and then coming up with recommendations and key issues that need to be addressed.

There are two premises underlying the concept of the citizens' consensus conference. First is the idea that citizens are entitled to a say on issues that affect their lives. In the past, science and technology were frequently treated as an exception to this value and were left to the domain of technical experts. Consensus conferences are among a range of models of public deliberation that have been designed to bring science and technology back into the public domain. These deliberative models of technology assessment include a wide variety of approaches: citizen juries, deliberative polls, scenario workshops, and other forms of public engagement that incorporate both discussions and learning via engagement with information resources and with specialists. The deliberative poll combines the features of a public opinion poll (with a randomly selected group of around a thousand citizen participants) and processes of deliberation. A scenario workshop involves citizens (or some mix of citizens, stakeholder representatives, and policy decision makers) in considering different visions or scenarios of possible futures or discussing solution options to particular problems. New ideas and recommendations for future actions or policies are discussed. Citizen juries are based on selection of citizens in much the same way a legal jury is chosen and invited to hear evidence on a community or policy issue and to deliver a judgment.

The second premise of consensus conferences is the idea that laypeople are able to grasp and deal with complicated technical matters and can bring valuable insights that may not otherwise be considered by experts.

The consensus conference procedure typically involves four sets of actors: an advisory committee, a lay panel, an expert panel, and a project management team. The panel of laypeople is composed of citizens of divergent backgrounds. The expert panel is defined broadly to incorporate not just scientific experts, but experts from areas that have relevance for a given technology topic, such as legal scholars or practitioners, regulators, ethicists, occupational experts (for example, farmers), experts from different interest or advocacy organizations, or people with experiential expertise (for example, transplant patients). Conflicting expert views are sometimes juxtaposed.

Lay panelists are typically selected by sending out invitations to 1,000 or 2,000 randomly selected adult citizens. Among those who respond to the invitation, 15 to 20 are selected, with as much of a mix as possible in terms of age, gender, education, profession, and geographic location.

The citizens receive a thorough briefing on the subject, typically through a background document or set of related readings, so they are well prepared to pose questions to the experts. Additional information is gained through meetings with experts in the course of two subsequent weekends. During the first weekend, the citizens get to know each other and start to formulate questions around which the conference will revolve. They also participate in choosing the types of experts they want to hear from. These experts are then invited during the second and third weekends, during which time the experts present information on a range of topics, which may include economic, scientific, legal, social, and ethical aspects of the issue.

The third weekend typically involves a meeting open to the public, the media, and policymakers. On the first day, the selected experts do short presentations. On the second day, the morning is spent on the lay panel asking individual experts for elaboration and clarification of their presentations. Members of the audience also have an opportunity to ask questions. A break is then scheduled on the afternoon of the second day when the lay panelists continue their deliberation and prepare their final report. The panel sometimes works in smaller groups to hone parts of the final report. A writer who is not part of the panel is in the room to assist in the process as the panel works on the final document. As the final report is drafted, the panelists continue to provide each other feedback, to debate on key points, and to arrive at a consensus on the ideas and recommendations in the report. Some panels have been known to work through until the late hours of the night. The consensus conference process, as its name suggests, encourages participating lay panelists to arrive at a consensus on the issues identified and their recommendations.

On the third and last day of the conference, the lay panel presents the final document to the experts and the audience, including the media. The experts are given the opportunity to clear up misunderstandings and correct factual errors. However, they have no influence on the views expressed by the panel. This citizens' report is typically delivered to members of Parliament or other relevant policymakers.

Throughout the process, the roles of the expert and lay panels are clearly delineated, and the process is transparent and well documented. It is rarely the case that minority statements are included in the report. This is based on the fact that consensus among the lay panelists is achieved through open deliberation, that the process emphasizes the identification of key questions or issues that need to be addressed, and that it is recognized that decision makers may be more likely to respond to the issues raised when they are not marked by divisions among many different perspectives.

The advisory or steering committee is typically a three to four member group, chosen for their expertise to represent the breadth of the topic areas. These advisers to the project team play a key role in initially identifying key topic areas that might be covered in discussions about the issue. They are also key to setting up the framework of the introductory material to be used to familiarize lay panelists with the topic. The project management team also helps to compile essential documents on the given topic. In some instances, a journalist or science writer might be hired to summarize the information into a background document that is 15 to 20 pages long and that is understandable to lay citizens. This document is intended to present the subject in general terms and describe the status of the technology, including key developments, areas of uncertainty, or conflicts among experts. The steering committee then approves the document.

Some topics are more suitable for the deployment of consensus conferences than others. These include, for example, technology issues that are topical (those receiving attention in public arenas such as the media), are controversial (perhaps the subject of debate in the public realm or representing new and controversial technologies being considered for adoption), can benefit from the illumination of the different perspectives on the issue, rely on contributions from a range of experts to help clarify the different dimensions of an issue, and require clarification of public views and positions. An example of this type of issue is genetically modified foods, an issue that became the focus of consensus conferences in many different countries including Australia, Canada, Denmark, South Korea, the United Kingdom, and the United States.

Consensus conferences have been viewed as a way of opening up the black box of expertise by making explicit the conflicts among experts and their commitments, as well as by displaying the sometimes fluid nature of both lay and expert knowledge. It is a process that brings to light the range of values that citizens emphasize as they consider whether or how a given technology ought to be embedded in society.

Edna F. Einsiedel

See also Citizens Jury; Deliberative Democracy; Deliberative Polling; Science Café; Technology Assessment

Further Readings

Joss, S., & Durant, J. (Eds.). (1995). *Public participation in science: The role of consensus conferences in Europe.* London: Science Museum.

Medlock, J. E., Downey, R., & Einsiedel, E. F. (2007). Governing controversial technologies: Consensus conferences as communication tool. In D. Brossard, J. Shanahan, & T. C. Nesbitt (Eds.), *The public, the media, and agricultural biotechnology* (chap. 13). Oxford, UK: CABI International.

CONVERSATION AND SCIENCE COMMUNICATION

Although many people in the 21st century live in an environment saturated with mass mediated information, talk between people continues to be a regular part of most people's lives, and one topic of conversation is contemporary science. Such talk can be a source of information that both complements and contradicts information broadcasted by mass media organizations. As such, it is not surprising that scholars increasingly consider conversation occurring in social networks to be an important object of inquiry for science communication research. In addition to considering the ways in which talk between people can facilitate or hamper science education, many scholars view deliberation and discussion among people formally working outside of scientific institutions as critical to science-related governance and policy making. Some science and technology scholars even argue that assessing the presence of, and quality of, dialogue among publics (as well as between scientists and publics) is crucial from an ethical perspective.

Everyday Conversation Versus Formal Science Education

Scholars do not yet have a full account of how specialized scientific knowledge can be translated most effectively into public understanding, nor are the central dynamics in the interplay between public sentiment and official support for scientific investigation well understood. Simply acknowledging that conversation between laypeople can play a role in shaping public understanding of science raises an important point of controversy for some scholars. Some see formal science education as the most plausible, and perhaps ideal, route for knowledge translation and thus tend to emphasize the role that formal education plays. Others, however, see communication occurring outside of classrooms as vital, if not central, in understanding public sentiment, understanding, and behavior.

One account of how publics come to understand science is the so-called popularization perspective. From that perspective, scientists supposedly develop knowledge and communicators, then spread that knowledge in simplified form. More recently, however, others have challenged the popularization account as an oversimplified description of how scientific knowledge functions— or ought to function—in a society. As an alternative, some have emphasized the central role of audiences in engaging in, and often generating, the

discourse necessary to develop scientific findings relevant to society and to resolve emergent concerns. Rather than popularization, this rival approach suggests that the process instead is best described as secularization, a more balanced process of communication between scientists and various publics. From this perspective, the hierarchy of popularization is replaced by a more even exchange.

Science communication scholars working in the social representations tradition often side with the secularization account and in some ways even go beyond that perspective to describe everyday social life as an ultimate constraint on the communication of scientific knowledge. From this perspective, formal science knowledge is important to individuals outside of the scientific professions only insofar as such knowledge facilitates the basic social interplay that is a part of everyday life. People use science knowledge in their engagement with others. As a result, social representation scholars interested in science communication claim that public understanding of scientific knowledge and public prioritization of such knowledge are ultimately shaped both by the resonance of such knowledge with existing public discourse and with the connections people see between scientific observation and the basic tasks of survival and social interaction. This perspective suggests why laypeople do not talk about all scientific topics with equal frequency. Some topics might be more compelling in their resonance with day-to-day life than others. Moreover, scholars working in this tradition acknowledge that inaccurate representation of scientific fact sometimes can be functional for individuals.

Defining Conversation

What exactly counts as conversation? Interpersonal communication scholars largely would agree that interaction between two people occurs when one person's pattern of behavior is somehow influenced by another person's such that their behavior differs from what we would have expected prior to the point of contact between the pair. Moreover, most usually agree that interpersonal communication requires that the two (or more) communication partners are mutually co-oriented; in other words, both need to be aware of their participation in the interaction. When a verbal exchange of that sort occurs, we can count that as conversation. As to what counts specifically as conversation about science, scholars generally agree there is benefit in casting a wide net and assuming that any conversation that can influence or reinforce beliefs related to contemporary scientific investigation is relevant. Two people discussing genetically modified fruit in the grocery market may or may not explicitly claim to be "talking about science," but they are likely engaged in a behavior that matters for science communication scholars.

As such, conversation not only constitutes a simple mechanism for scientific information repetition and exposure to science-related knowledge among participants, but also comprises a relatively complex dyadic or group variable vulnerable to an array of factors that relate to human needs and desires and environmental constraints. Conversation is not a simple function of exposure to science education materials nor does it always coincide in its effects with the goals of formally planned science communication efforts.

Where does conversation occur? The archetypal conversation between colleagues at a water cooler during a work break is not the only sort of exchange relevant to science communication scholars. Although early research on interpersonal communication focused on face-to-face interaction, many now agree that talk between people can occur in a variety of settings. For example, communication scholars now look at a variety of electronic applications for exchange, online and elsewhere, such as bulletin boards, e-mail, chat rooms, and text messaging. Current research suggests that online discussion can be consequential. Though participants do sometimes report some differences in their perceptions of conversations occurring online and those occurring face-to-face, evidence suggests that at the very least all sorts of interpersonal exchange can affect beliefs and reinforce or complicate science education efforts.

Many important challenges remain in studying conversation as it relates to science communication. For example, development of conversation measures beyond simple frequency indicators has been vexing for mass communication scholars. While interpersonal communication scholars have ways of assessing dyadic exchanges, finding ways to incorporate such measures into large-scale survey research and campaign evaluations has been difficult.

Predicting Conversation About Science

Under what circumstances might we expect people to talk about science? On some level, we know that general predictors of conversational engagement seem also to hold with specific regard to science and technology. Scholars have found that individual differences and personality tendencies predict likelihood of talking about science. Those who are high in sensation-seeking tendency in general, for example, have been found to be more likely to report having recently had conversations about science, even after controlling for other predictors of science-related conversation, such as educational attainment and employment with a science-related organization.

At least one factor that appears to be particularly relevant to talk about science specifically is one's own confidence in engaging in such conversation. Such confidence seems to be linked to perceptions regarding one's own ability to understand concepts related to science, technology, engineering, and mathematics. Personal knowledge and confidence in that knowledge appears to play a significant role in determining whether a person engages people around her or him in dialogue linked to science and technology.

Exposure to some types of educational media content might boost one's sense of topical understanding and conversational competency. All else being equal, we can expect that talk about that topic will be more likely to ensue among those exposed to such programming. Evaluation of the Discoveries and Breakthroughs Inside Science project funded by the U.S. National Science Foundation and run by the American Institute of Physics highlights exactly such a pattern. Experimental data from that evaluation demonstrated that science news exposure can indirectly affect conversation about science by bolstering perceived understanding of science.

Effects of Conversation on Science Communication Outcomes

Exactly how might conversation be linked to science communication efforts formally organized by institutions and groups? Scholars working at the intersection of interpersonal and mass communication offer some help, as they have identified three primary ways in which talk and media campaigns can affect one another. Those categories of relationships include conversation as a planned or unintended media campaign outcome, conversation as a mediator of media campaign effects, and conversation as a moderator of campaign effects.

Many science communication efforts intend to prompt public discussion of science, and so in those instances, conversation might be seen as an outcome of organized science communication efforts. At the same time, there are many instances in which conversations between people act to enlarge the circle of people exposed to the original set of science education materials by indirectly presenting messages and ideas to people who otherwise did not have a chance to engage the original materials. Two people talking about global warming might actually provide a venue for indirect exposure to an organized science education campaign, as one person in the conversation might either use information gleaned from earlier exposure to materials or explicitly mention messages promoted through such materials. In that instance, we might view interpersonal communication as a mediator of science communication project effects. On a third plane, we also know that conversations between people can affect the possibilities for success of science communication efforts. Religious community discussion of controversial scientific investigation can dampen response to mass media messages noting a new scientific discovery, just as talk occurring in social networks can amplify memory for breast cancer screening guidelines originally mentioned in the news.

All three categories of roles for interpersonal conversation suggest an array of possibilities that not only account for some past findings in the science and technology communication literature but that also could pose hypotheses for future investigation.

Future science communication project evaluations likely will need to address the existence of social networks among audiences and the conversations that occur in those networks with regard to particular science and technology topics.

Brian G. Southwell

See also Evaluation of Science Communication; Popular Science and Formal Education

Further Readings

Hilgartner, S. (1990). The dominant view of popularization: Conceptual problems, political uses. *Social Studies of Science, 20,* 519–539.

Hwang, Y., & Southwell, B. G. (2007). Can a personality trait predict talk about science? Sensation seeking as a science communication targeting variable. *Science Communication, 29*(2), 198–216.

Southwell, B. G., & Torres, A. (2006). Connecting interpersonal and mass communication: Science news exposure, perceived ability to understand science, and conversation. *Communication Monographs, 73*(3), 334–350.

Southwell, B. G., & Yzer, M. C. (2007). The roles of interpersonal communication in mass media campaigns. In C. Beck (Ed.), *Communication yearbook 31* (pp. 420–462). New York: Lawrence Erlbaum.

Wagner, W. (2007). Vernacular science knowledge: Its role in everyday life communication. *Public Understanding of Science, 16*(1), 7–22.

COUNCIL FOR THE ADVANCEMENT OF SCIENCE WRITING

Created at the dawn of the space age, the Council for the Advancement of Science Writing (CASW) has sought for 50 years to enhance the quality of science journalism for the general public. Led by distinguished journalists and scientists, this nonprofit U.S. educational organization develops and supports a wide range of programs and resources designed to increase public understanding of science. It seeks to provide reporters, editors, and writers from all media a better understanding of important science and technology developments and to promote best practices in communicating those findings and their significance to a wide audience.

Its initiatives include an annual 4-day program for journalists and other science writers on cutting-edge science, travel fellowships for journalists, stipends for graduate science journalism education, efforts to improve local science coverage, an annual medical science-reporting prize, and programs on science journalism for the scientific community. In doing so, CASW works closely with other journalism organizations.

For its efforts to raise "the quality of science news" that reached the public, the council in 2003 received the prestigious Public Service Award from the National Science Board, which oversees the U.S. National Science Foundation.

CASW History

The explosion of science and technology in the 1950s created new challenges for journalists faced with explaining how polio vaccines work, what the structure of DNA is, and why satellites do not fall from the sky. While major publications had long had specialty science writers, the Soviet launch of the first *Sputnik* satellite in late 1957 triggered tremendous public demand for coverage of the space race, and the ranks of journalists assigned to this beat suddenly expanded. A small group of leading U.S. science writers recognized the need for better training of journalists covering not only space exploration but also other new developments in science and technology to improve the quality of their news and feature stories.

To realize that ambition, the CASW was incorporated as a nonprofit educational organization in 1959 and held its first meeting in early 1960. Its founders were active in the National Association of Science Writers (NASW), a professional membership group started in 1934. However, the council's independent, nonprofit status allowed it to raise the resources needed to support enhanced programs to educate science writers and thereby improve public understanding of science. Foundations, scientific institutions and societies, government agencies, corporations, and individuals have provided financial support over the years. But CASW's programs stay close to its journalistic roots and remain under the sole discretion of its strong professional staff and governing council. The council is comprised of about 15 prominent journalists, educators, and public information officers, with leading scientists serving in an advisory role.

New Horizons in Science Briefing

The centerpiece for carrying out CASW's educational mission is New Horizons in Science, an annual program for journalists that draws upon the world's leading scientific minds to present the most promising developments across diverse disciplines, including physical and environmental sciences, biomedical research, and technology. The program's organizers seek to identify potential advances before they hit the headlines, along with scientists able to clearly explain their work and its potential societal impact.

Since its start in 1963, New Horizons has established itself as a preeminent meeting for beginning and seasoned science journalists and other communicators. The breadth and depth of the ambitious program allows them to learn about findings in emerging science and to become familiar with fields they have not previously covered. And it provides access to leading scientists. Many of the program's presenters have later gone on to win the Nobel Prize and other prestigious awards in science and to become academic and government leaders, including presidential science advisers.

New Horizons is independently organized by CASW to find the best and brightest in science from a variety of educational, government, or private institutions. Hosted by a different prominent university or research center each year, the meeting provides seminars, informal get-togethers, and added opportunities for participants to tour laboratories or take field trips to see scientific research firsthand. In recent years, host institutions have included the University of Texas at Austin, Stanford University, the Pacific Northwest National Laboratory, Johns Hopkins University, and Carnegie Mellon University.

Since its founding, CASW has maintained a close relationship with the NASW. In 2005, the two organizations joined forces to provide one-stop shopping for science writers: NASW's professional development and skills workshops are followed by CASW's New Horizons briefing. The 2010 meeting at Yale University marks two important anniversaries, NASW's 75th and CASW's 50th.

Outreach to Journalists and Scientists

CASW has long put high priority on improving science journalism and communications by supporting educational and professional development of current and future science writers. Travel fellowships to attend the New Horizons meeting and NASW workshops are awarded to professional journalists with limited resources, including staff at smaller media outlets and freelance writers. To support next-generation science writers, CASW's Taylor/Blakeslee fellowships grant stipends for graduate science writing education, with student recipients numbering about 100 thus far.

CASW also welcomes opportunities to link veteran science writers with editors and reporters at smaller media outlets to encourage local science coverage. It has sent journalists to newsrooms and offered regional workshops for nonspecialist print and electronic reporters on topics such as the environment, health care, and child psychology. It hopes to expand its training efforts to improve the accuracy of online Web sites that increasingly provide science content for the general public.

CASW's own Web site provides access to science writing resources, including "A Guide to Careers in Science Writing." The organization has provided financial support for publications to improve science coverage, including the NASW *Field Guide for Science Writers* (2nd edition, 2005) and its quarterly journal, *ScienceWriters*. It helped underwrite *News and Numbers: A Guide to Reporting Statistical Claims and Controversies in Health and Other Fields* by the late science writer Victor Cohn and his colleague Lewis Cope.

Cohn was a CASW founder and longtime *Washington Post* health and medical writer. In his memory, the council in 2000 established the annual Victor Cohn Prize for Excellence in Medical Science Reporting to recognize career contributions for a body of work over the last 5 years. Honorees have included leading journalists from the *New York Times, Newsday,* the *Washington Post,* the *Wall Street Journal,* the *New Yorker,* the Associated Press, National Public Radio, public television, and freelance newspaper and magazine writing.

From its inception, CASW has involved the scientific community in its efforts to improve science information for the public. Prominent scientists have long participated in the organization's work, including recent advisers Nobel Prize–winning physicist Leon M. Lederman and Stanford University biologist Donald Kennedy. Recognizing the need to encourage researchers to explain their work and its potential societal impact, CASW organizes panels and seminars on science writing and communication for scientific meetings and institutions. These informal programs provide an opportunity to have leading science writers talk about how and why scientists should speak with the news media, with a special emphasis on younger researchers who may be less familiar with—and more reluctant to work with—the press. In recent years, CASW has sponsored seminars at universities such as Yale, Duke, Johns Hopkins, and Harvard, as well as at gatherings of organizations such as the American Association for the Advancement of Science, the scientific research society Sigma Xi, and the Cambridge Science Festival.

Global Outreach

The need for clear, accurate, and insightful science journalism has never been greater, as citizens worldwide are confronted with challenging public issues with a strong science component, including climate change, energy needs, nuclear proliferation, stem cell research, genetically modified food, and the teaching of evolution. While the United States is suffering severe cutbacks in staff science writing jobs and coverage in mainstream print and electronic media, science journalism is expanding internationally, particularly in developing countries. The rapid growth of the Internet is providing new opportunities—and challenges—for improving the quality of science news in the global marketplace.

CASW is committed to improving science writing around the world. In 1979, it joined with NASW to lead an official delegation of science writers to China, as the doors were reopened to Western journalists. It organized foundation-sponsored trips for U.S. science journalists to Africa in 1991 and to Central and South America in 1995. In 2007, it provided financial support for a U.S. visit by leaders of the newly formed Arab Science Writers Association who were partnering with the NASW. In 2009, CASW was elected as the first associate member of the World Federation of Science Journalists, which consists of 40 membership associations from Africa, the Americas, Asia-Pacific, Europe, and the Middle East. The federation plays a leading role in advancing international science journalism and networking science writers from developed and developing countries. U.S. science journalists will work with their Arab counterparts in organizing the next world conference in Cairo in 2011, with CASW among the sponsors.

Cristine Russell

See also Career Paths, Medical Writing/Medical Journalism; Career Paths, Science/Environmental Journalism; National Association of Science Writers; National Science Foundation, U.S.; Space Program, Overview

Further Readings

Bishop, J. E. (2005). CASW history: *The 5 W's of CASW*. Available at http://casw.org/casw/history

Cohn, V., & Cope, L. (2001). *News and numbers: A guide to reporting statistical claims and controversies in health and other fields* (2nd ed.). Ames, IA: Wiley-Blackwell.

Council for the Advancement of Science Writing; http://casw.org

National Association of Science Writers: http://nasw.org

CREATIONISM

Creationism is the belief that the universe was created by a divine entity, identified as God in Judeo-Christian theology. Creationist understandings of the formation of the earth fall along a diverse spectrum, but most creationists believe that the universe was created from nothing, that evolution cannot explain the development of life, that humans and apes have different ancestors, and that the Noachian flood covered the earth as documented in the Bible. Under some circumstances, conflicts have arisen between advocates of science communication and science education and strict creationists. These conflicts generally receive significant media attention.

Creationists can be placed into one of two categories: young-earth and old-earth creationists. Young-earth creationists follow a strict, literal interpretation of the story of human creation as it appears in the Bible; they believe that the entire universe was created in six 24-hour days. The exact age of the earth assumed varies to some extent, with some estimating that the earth was created between 10,000 and 20,000 years ago, while others agree with an estimate by Irish Archbishop James Ussher, who deduced that the creation occurred sometime in the evening on Saturday, October 22, 4004 BCE. Young-earth creationists (also called strict creationists) believe that God created the world (and humankind) basically in present form. They reject the idea that humans (or other creatures) evolved from lower life forms.

Old-earth creationists follow the creationist beliefs that God created everything, but they believe that this occurred much earlier than dates provided by young-earth creationists. Some old-earth creationists believe in gap theory, which suggests that time continued to pass in the gap between the first and second verses of Genesis. Others follow the day-age theory, which states that the story of the earth and universe being created in 6 days is true, but that each day could have been longer than 24 hours (even millions of years). Still others believe that that God created certain species of animals and that limited evolution (microevolution) occurred to account for the wide range of species on the planet (for example, they may believe that God created the cat, which evolved into the tiger, lion, leopard, and so on). These old-earth approaches are supported with certain types of scientific affirmation, such as radiometric dating, but scientists do not generally accept the beliefs of the old-earth creationists.

While these individuals tend to be religious and with low levels of formal education, a recent survey showed 25% of college graduates believe in some form of creationism. As for public opinion, surveys consistently reveal that about 40% to 50% of the U.S. population accepts the Biblical account of creationism, while similar numbers of people accept the evolutionary account that humans evolved over time. The accuracy of these polls has been questioned, as surveys do not distinguish between old-earth and young-earth creationists, and it is often unclear how familiar respondents are with the terms and concepts being used. Furthermore, these beliefs also do not necessarily translate into beliefs that school curriculum should be changed; while fewer than half of Americans believe in evolution, according to this poll data, a majority nevertheless feel that evolution should still be taught in schools.

In the middle of the 19th century, science was being practiced on a limited basis in colleges and universities in the United States. Churches operated many of these institutions, and about a third of the faculty members were clergymen. However, between 1850 and 1900, a fundamental shift in academics occurred as graduate education was further developed. College professors began to engage in more research activity, and loyalties shifted from the individual university to the larger field. Therefore, Darwinism was soon embraced, and because scholars began publishing more, these professors (rather than secondary school teachers) began authoring more textbooks. As a result, by the 20th century, evolution had been thoroughly incorporated into biology textbooks and teaching materials, and references to creationism disappeared from those pages.

Through the early 1900s, the idea of teaching evolution met little resistance. There was no serious animosity toward evolution in the general public, and even religious leaders did not speak out against evolution being taught in schools. However, by the 1920s, the fundamentalist movement had hit full stride as growing unrest from increased urbanization and demographic changes resonated with some segments of the population.

These fundamentalists generally believed in a literal interpretation of the Bible and felt it was necessary to rescue the United States from the perceived evils of atheism and modernism. The 20th century had witnessed unprecedented growth in secondary school enrollments, which led to the fastest growth in high school enrollment in the history of the United States. Little was known about evolution among the general public, and many parents saw these teachings as going against their religious beliefs. The fundamentalists seized upon this and launched an antievolution movement as a way to help cure the perceived ills in U.S. society. Laws against teaching evolution were soon passed in the state legislatures of Kentucky and Oklahoma, but it would be the antievolution law passed in Tennessee that would garner the most national attention.

Scopes Trial

In 1925, the Tennessee legislature passed the Butler Law, which made it illegal for teachers at public schools to teach anything that contradicts the Biblical teaching that God created humans. When the American Civil Liberties Union (ACLU) heard that Tennessee had passed this law, the organization placed an advertisement for a Tennessee teacher who was willing to violate this statute. Leaders in Dayton, Tennessee, read the announcement and saw it as an opportunity to put their town on the map by hosting a courtroom battle between evolution and creationism. After conferring with John Scopes, a science teacher, a warrant was sworn out for his arrest for violating the Butler Law. The ACLU had its test case.

The prosecution asked former secretary of state and presidential candidate William Jennings Bryan, who was called "The Great Commoner" and who had recently launched the antievolution movement, to represent the state, and he agreed to do so without compensation. Famed attorney Clarence Darrow volunteered to argue for the defense, and these two men became the main figures in the trial. The event drew much media attention, with live radio updates from the courtroom and over 2,300 daily newspapers tracking the trial. Those following the case were treated to an array of passionate speeches, with Darrow arguing for the freedom of speech and Bryan arguing for the right to uphold values and tradition.

Because the judge insisted that the trial was about whether or not Scopes broke the law and not about the validity of evolution, no expert witnesses were allowed to testify. In a famous maneuver to get around this, Darrow called Bryan to the stand to testify as an expert on the Bible. In the cross-examination, Darrow's questioning showed that even Bryan did not accept a completely literal interpretation of the Bible. The trial ended as expected, with Scopes found guilty of breaking the law—he was fined $100. Darrow and the ACLU filed an appeal, but Bryan would not see the case past Dayton—he died in his sleep 5 days after the trial was over.

Upon appeal, the Tennessee Supreme Court reversed the conviction of Scopes on a technicality because the $100 fine had been levied by the judge and not by the jury. As a result, Scopes was freed, and yet, the law was upheld, preventing the ACLU from appealing the verdict to the Supreme Court. Not only was the case prevented from having its constitutionality tested (which had been the ACLU's plan from the beginning), but the verdict also produced a chilling effect in regard to the teaching of evolution. The word *evolution* and references to Darwinism disappeared from textbooks, sometimes being replaced by religious quotations.

By 1942, most high school teachers in the United States did not teach their students about evolution. Antievolution groups forced biology professors who did not teach creationism to resign in states such as Georgia and South Carolina. Mississippi passed a law against teaching that humans had evolved, and in 1928, Arkansas voters passed an antievolution statute with 63% of the vote. In a number of states, antievolution propositions were only barely defeated; in Missouri, one legislator even suggested the penalty for violating an antievolution law should be spending a month imprisoned in the St. Louis Zoo.

However, while the creationists officially achieved a victory with the guilty verdict at the Scopes trial, many felt the Scopes trial hurt the cause more than helped it. Creationists were ridiculed in the press, especially following Bryan's testimony in the courtroom. Media outlets touted the trial as an embarrassment to the antievolution movement. In the years following his death, Bryan's supporters did manage to pass laws against teaching evolution in other states to promote creationism, but the antievolution movement quickly lost steam. The charismatic Bryan was the face of the movement, and when he passed away, the ability to reach states beyond those in the South was greatly diminished. By 1928, fundamentalists were more concerned with the fact that Al Smith, a Catholic, was running for president; after the Great Depression hit a year later, teaching creationism in schools was no longer a pressing matter.

Creationism on Trial

Funding for sciences slowly grew following the decline of the antievolutionist movement, gaining momentum during World War II. However, when the Russians launched the *Sputnik* satellite in 1957, a nationwide panic ensued in the United States as the state of science education was sharply critiqued. Edward Larson's account of creationism in the court system explains that, in 1927, the combined expenditures for scientific research by the state and federal governments was .02% of the gross national product (GNP); by 1960, federal expenditures had reached 1.5% of GNP. This steadily increasing funding of science grew rapidly, and this emphasis extended into science education.

Textbooks began including evolution again, and states began repealing antievolution laws (including the Tennessee law for which Scopes was arrested). While the early antievolutionist movement had focused on preventing the teaching of human evolution, by the 1960s the goal was to enforce the teaching of cosmic creationism. However, evolutionists had momentum on their side and began to fight back through the courts.

Creationists sought to stem the tide of disappearing antievolution laws, but in 1965, another lawsuit was filed, this time challenging the 1928 Arkansas law that made it a crime to teach evolution in public schools. A devout Christian and Arkansas native, Susan Epperson was an ideal plaintiff because there could be no accusations of tampering by the ACLU or other outside organizations. The state repealed the antievolution law, although this was challenged by the Arkansas Attorney General's Office, and the decision was reversed by the Arkansas Supreme Court, which, in a peculiar move, overturned the decision with an unsigned opinion that was only two sentences long. In 1968, the Supreme Court agreed to hear *Epperson v. Arkansas* and ruled that, by preventing evolution from being taught, the state was attempting to establish a religious position in the public schools that favored those who followed a literal interpretation of the Bible.

This decision united and mobilized creationists, who launched a number of campaigns to have references to evolution stricken from textbooks or, at the very least, disclaimers included in those texts calling into question the validity of evolution. In 1970, creationists launched their first lawsuit in *Wright v. Houston Independent School District*, where a parent argued that her daughter's teachers were violating her right to religious freedom by teaching only evolution. However, the court ruled that creationism would not receive equal time in the classroom. In 1972, the plaintiff in *Willoughby v. Stever* argued that, by teaching evolution, the government was trying to establish secularism as the official religion in the United States. This was also rejected.

Creation Science

With multiple lawsuits failing and the established precedent of *Epperson,* creationists regrouped and developed creation science as a way to get their teachings included in public schools. According to creation science, the Bible should be viewed as a scientific text, and therefore, scientific observations must conform to that content. If observations do not match those in the Bible, then the observations are either incorrect or have been skewed by Satan. Thus, rather than arguing that evolution is an immoral idea that has no place in the public schools, creationists could argue that creation science was a scientifically feasible alternative to Darwinism. Strict readings of the Bible, modeled after Henry Morris's *The Genesis Flood,* produced a body of scholarship that supported the ideas of young-earth creationists while emphasizing the importance of equal time for both evolution and creation science. This would be tested in a pivotal court case that once again featured Arkansas.

The *McLean v. Arkansas Board of Education* case of 1982 was billed as another "monkey trial," but it would be different from *Scopes.* Judge William Overton was known for relying heavily on precedent and therefore allowed a string of expert witnesses to testify for both sides. Furthermore, because he was appointed (by President Jimmy Carter), Overton did not have to worry about reelection and was therefore unconcerned with public opinion. While other judges had shied away from defining the line between creationism and science, Overton tackled it head-on, explicitly stating in his decision that creation science was "religion masquerading as science," and because it "fails as science," creation science should not be taught in public schools.

Intelligent Design

The idea of intelligent design first emerged in the wake of Overton's decision to remove creation science from school curricula. The movement was founded when Berkeley law professor Phillip E. Johnson wrote a critique of evolution titled *Darwin on Trial* in 1991. Five years later, the concept was laid out in greater detail in Michael J. Behe's *Darwin's Black Box: The Biological Challenge to Evolution.* In his work, Behe suggests that, like a mousetrap (which will not work without certain components), humans have certain processes (genetic cascades, pseudogenes, the Krebs cycles, and so on) that are "irreducibly complex," meaning that they could not have evolved and therefore must have been created by a designer. No definition of the designer is given, though the designer is presumed to be omnipotent. Scientists almost universally reject intelligent design and argue that it is

a Trojan horse strategy for creationism to again be taught in public schools.

A number of state school boards have debated whether to include intelligent design in the curriculum, including Ohio and Kansas. In 2005, parents in Dover, Pennsylvania, sued the school district for requiring intelligent design to be taught as an alternative to evolution. In the *Kitzmiller v. Dover* case, Judge John Jones, who was appointed by President George W. Bush, ruled that the law requiring a statement about the uncertainties of evolution to be read to the class was unconstitutional. In his finding, Jones stated that intelligent design was essentially religion in disguise, just as Overton had declared in the creation science trail 23 years earlier. While some school boards across the country are still advocating equal time for intelligent design and evolution in public schools, creationism, creation science, and intelligent design remain on the fringes of educational legitimacy.

Joshua Grimm

See also Intelligent Design in Public Discourse; Religion, Science, and Media

Further Readings

Eve, R. A., & Harrold, F. B. (1991). *The creationist movement in modern America.* Boston: Twayne.

Larson, E. J. (2003). *Trial and error: The American controversy over creation and evolution.* New York: Oxford University Press.

Moore, R. (2000). *Evolution in the courtroom: A reference guide.* Santa Barbara, CA: ABC-CLIO.

Nelkin, D. (1982). *The creation controversy: Science or scripture in the schools?* New York: W. W. Norton.

Scott, E. C. (1997). Antievolution and creationism in the United States. *Annual Review of Anthropology, 26,* 263–289.

Young, C. C., & Largent, M. A. (2007). *Evolution and creationism: A documentary and reference guide.* Westport, CT: Greenwood.

CRICK, FRANCIS (1916–2004)

Francis Harry Compton Crick was not only codiscoverer of the DNA double helix, but also maintained a long career as a science communicator. Born near Northampton, England, the son of a shoe manufacturer, Crick began a PhD in physics before World War II at University College, London. During the war, he worked for the Royal Navy on the design and the detection of mines. Like many physicists after the war, he decided to move to biology and applied for funding in 1947. He began cell biophysics in Cambridge, England, and in 1949, he opted for protein crystallography, rejoining Max Perutz's unit for the study of the structure of biological systems at the Cavendish Laboratory, directed by Lawrence Bragg. There, he worked toward a PhD on protein structure but, with James D. Watson, discovered the structure of the double helix of DNA before graduating in July 1953.

In Cambridge, Crick also participated in the creation of the first Laboratory of Molecular Biology (LMB) in Europe. Later the same year, he received the Nobel Prize of Medicine together with James D. Watson and Maurice H. F. Wilkins for their work on DNA. In the LMB, Crick worked on the genetic code and then chromosome structure. In 1977, he left the field of molecular biology to pursue research in neuroscience. In this field, he focused on consciousness and worked at the Salk Institute in San Diego, California.

As a molecular biologist, Crick was the discipline's best-known theoretician. He did perform experiments, but as Matt Ridley has aptly noted in his biography, Crick's greatest skill was conjecturing. Throughout his career, he wrote numerous papers reporting hypotheses and models. The double helix paper was one of them. His prominent ability was to synthesize a great number of facts in a theoretical model. He was also good at explaining new theory in a clear and captivating way. In the 1960s, the then nascent field of molecular biology was indeed characterized by new jargon about the cell.

While biochemists saw the cell as a factory that produces proteins, molecular biologists saw the cell as an information machine that deals with information flux, from DNA to proteins. Both metaphors were powerful, but the latter was fashionable in the postwar era when computers started to disseminate. From the molecular biology point of view, DNA stores genetic information into the sequence of its four bases (A, C, G, and T). The DNA sequence is translated into a protein sequence written in a 20-letter alphabet. The genetic code and a complex biochemical apparatus are needed to realize this translation. Crick made a contribution at every step of this scheme, which was uncovered between 1950 and 1965. He provided the main theoretical framework of information transfers in molecular biology, the so-called central dogma.

After uncovering the double helix structure, which suggests how genetic information is stored and copied, he attempted to theoretically decipher the genetic code, but failed. He nevertheless made invaluable contributions both theoretically (involving the adaptor and the wobble hypothesis) and at the bench (showing with Sydney Brenner that the code is made of triplets of bases). The adaptor hypothesis stated that proteins are not directly molded on DNA but that an adaptor molecule exists between the two. This molecule was discovered soon after and was called transfer RNA. The wobble hypothesis explained how different triplets of bases have the same meaning in the protein's alphabet.

At the end of the 1960s, Crick felt that molecular biology was globally understood and, like other molecular biologists, he turned to embryology and finally to neuroscience. After having solved what many saw as the riddle of life (that is, DNA), he tried to solve the riddle of consciousness. One common thread of his whole career is indeed his fight against vitalism, the idea that life cannot be explained by standard physical and chemical laws. He explained his views in his first book, titled *Of Molecules and Men.* Alas, in neuroscience, he was less successful than in molecular biology. In the former field, he used his reputation as a Nobel Prize winner to attract scientists into the study of consciousness. His main collaborator in this last area was the younger neuroscientist Christof Koch.

The double helix ultimately achieved an iconic status in popular culture. The photograph taken by Anthony Barrington Brown in 1953 of Crick and Watson staring at their model of the double helix is often reproduced. In the famous book *The Double Helix,* Watson described the discovery as a race for the Nobel Prize, involving colorful characters. Its noted first sentence reports that Watson never saw Crick in a modest mood. The book became the paradigmatic story of a science competition. At first, Crick tried to prevent Watson from publishing because he considered the book to be a fragment of Watson's autobiography, written for laymen. As a result, the story is told from one side, and the science behind the helix is simplified. Later, Crick revised his judgment, acknowledging that Watson's book did include a large amount of science.

Crick did not write his own account of the discovery of the double helix, but he did write a preface for Robert Olby's *Path to the Double Helix* in which he praised Olby for stressing the scientific aspects of the discovery. The British Broadcasting Corporation made a docudrama (that is, half documentary, half drama) called *Life Story* about the discovery and broadcast it in 1987. While Crick judged in his autobiography that this docudrama was a success and that the story told was good, he was more concerned with science itself than with related stories of science. Indeed, he felt that the DNA structure was not made by Watson and Crick, but that Watson and Crick were made by the DNA structure. In popularization articles he wrote for *Scientific American* about the genetic code or the brain, as well as in every book he wrote, science's results, not scientists, were the main characters.

While *Of Molecules and Men* stemmed from lectures, his second book, *Life Itself,* is an extended version of a hypothesis he published together with Leslie Orgel about the origin of life. The thesis is that because he cannot explain why the genetic code is universal, then life may have originated from outer space. His third book, *What Mad Pursuit*, is something of a scientific autobiography, while his last book, *The Astonishing Hypothesis,* is a materialist assault on consciousness.

Despite being a first-class scientist and scientific popularizer, Crick was not vocal in the public controversy about recombinant DNA in the 1970s. He did not participate at the Asilomar Conference on recombinant DNA in February 1975, nor did he take on responsibility in the Human Genome Project like Watson. Rather, it seems that he was more interested in speculating about a new hypothesis than in science policy. Crick's public figure as a scientist is strengthened by the fact that his papers were acquired by the Wellcome Trust and the Heritage Lottery Fund in 2001 to be made available online to the public. In the meantime, Crick concentrated on neuroscience until the very last week of his life. His last paper about the brain, titled "What Is the Function of the Claustrum?" was written a few days before he died of cancer.

Crick married Doreen Dodd in 1940. Together, they had a son, Michael Francis Compton Crick. They divorced in 1947, and 2 years later, Crick married Odile Speed. This second marriage brought him two daughters, Gabrielle and Jacqueline.

Apart from his Nobel Prize, Crick was a Fellow of the Royal Society (elected 1959) and belonged to the Order of Merit.

Jérôme Pierrel

See also Human Genome Project; Watson, James D.

Further Readings

Crick, F. H. C. (1966). *Of molecules and men.* Seattle: University of Washington Press.

Crick, F. H. C. (1981). *Life itself: Its origin and nature.* New York: Simon & Schuster.

Crick, F. H. C. (1988). *What mad pursuit: A personal view of scientific discovery.* New York: Basic Books.

Crick, F. H. C. (1994). *The astonishing hypothesis: The scientific search for the soul.* New York: Scribner.

Olby, R. (1974). *The path to the double helix: The discovery of DNA.* Seattle: University of Washington Press.

Olby, R. (2009). *Francis Crick: Hunter of life's secrets.* Cold Spring Harbor, NY: Cold Spring Harbor Laboratory Press.

Ridley, M. (2006). *Francis Crick: Discoverer of the genetic code.* New York: Atlas Books/HarperCollins.

Watson, J. D. (1968). *The double helix: A personal account of the discovery of the structure of DNA.* New York: Atheneum.

CRISIS COMMUNICATION

From natural disasters such as Hurricane Katrina to human-made tragedies such as 9/11, these sudden events are all considered crises. A crisis can be just about anything that will disrupt an organization, industry, or company. A crisis can also disrupt an organization's reputation, products, and services. Broadly defined, a crisis is an unstable, disruptive situation. Frequent types of crises may include everything from fires to fatalities to mergers and murders to layoffs and lawsuits. Whether frequent or rare, a crisis is a major occurrence. Most crises involve some element of science or technology, whether this means following the path of a storm or identifying how a technology has gone wrong.

Crisis communication is what is communicated before a situation occurs, when a situation erupts, and after the situation is stabilized. During crises of any magnitude, effective communication is key. Furthermore, it is important to understand who should communicate when a crisis occurs and what should be said. This entry provides basic guidance for crisis communication situations.

Have a Plan

What type of crisis might impact a particular organization? While one can only hope that a crisis will never occur, it is important to be prepared. That is exactly where a crisis communication plan comes into play. No matter how large or small the organization, it should always have a crisis communication plan in place. The plan should include everything from key internal and external people to contact, to emergency and evacuation plans, to details regarding off-site operations if the situation warrants. While the plan should be thorough, it also needs to be tested to ensure its success.

Select a Spokesperson

In addition to having a crisis plan ready to activate at any moment, an organization must also determine who should serve as the organization's spokesperson. Depending upon the crisis, there are times when the spokesperson is someone whose regular job duties include public relations or public communication. However, depending upon the magnitude of the crisis, some public relations specialists argue that a top official or someone with appropriate authority or visibility should act as the key contact or spokesperson. If there are issues the spokesperson cannot answer, the organization may choose a team of spokespersons. Whether it is one individual or a team, the spokesperson must be selected very carefully and their role understood. Who speaks can be just as important as what he or she says. Nonetheless, it is critical that the spoken and written positions be consistent.

Rules to Follow

The organization must also be aware that once a crisis occurs, the media will be there. In fact, the media's presence should be thought of as an opportunity to get the organization's message out to the public. Appropriate crisis communication training should not happen when a crisis occurs, but rather beforehand. Key personnel in any organization should be prepared to handle the spokesperson's role, if necessary, when dealing with the media.

When crises do occur, the media want information instantly and around the clock. Oftentimes, the media will become aware of an incident before internal publics do. One should not be surprised if the media show up to a crisis before key company personnel.

How a company handles the media once a crisis occurs is even more important. The crisis communication plan should include an area where the media would be located. Where will spokespeople address the media if the organization's property is not accessible? Has the organization prepared for an off-site location media headquarters? Once the media do arrive, how should their questions be handled? The organization should provide brief remarks or even a news conference to update the media regarding the situation. When strategically communicating with the media during a crisis, here are the rules to follow:

Rule 1: Prepare, prepare, and prepare. While there may not be much time to prepare when a crisis does occur, the simplest way to prepare for a news interview is to address the issue using the five W's—who, what, when, where, why, and sometimes how. These are facts that a journalist must include in his or her story. Most likely, these five W's will be addressed in the news briefing that is delivered before any questions are even asked.

Rule 2: Know the subject. When asked to respond to a crisis situation, an effective spokesperson must know everything possible about the subject. Since the spokesperson has agreed to the interview, most likely in advance, or has chosen to have a news briefing, he or she should be well prepared and know the subject matter.

Rule 3: Be correct. If reporters should ask a question that the organization's spokesperson does not have an answer for or is unsure about, the spokesperson should tell them they will find the answer and get back with them. A spokesperson must be correct. A reporter would prefer to have the right answer later than the wrong answer right away. Chances are, with the availability of the Internet, the reporter will have already done his or her homework and will actually have some of the answers to the questions. Although the reporter may already know the answer, he or she stills need the spokesperson to state that answer on camera. Reporters may also be verifying that the answers people are giving them are accurate.

Rule 4: Be quotable. Every single word told to a reporter has the potential to be on the evening television newscast—local or national—in the morning newspaper, or even in the headlines on the Internet. Every single word said to a reporter is critical, so spokespeople must follow the next rule: They must be quotable. The best quotes or sound bites have passion. They are not filled with numbers and statistics. Great quotes are generally less than 15 seconds.

There is a reason for that, too. The average television newscast is about 30 minutes. Once commercial breaks, weather, and sports are subtracted, the actual time for news may be anywhere from 6 to 8 minutes. If an entire news story or news package is approximately 1 minute, and the reporter has to give both sides of the story, an organizational spokesperson will be lucky to get a total of 15 seconds. To be quotable means to keep responses short, tight, and to the point.

Rule 5: Select three key points. When preparing to talk to the media, spokespeople should select at least three key points to use in the interview. Those points should be the quote seen in the newspaper or the sound bite heard on the evening news.

So what should the message be? No matter what the crisis, there are some basic rules that will help develop key points. Much about message development is just basic common sense. For example, human life is almost always the most important point to talk about first. Most crises involve at least potential impact on human lives, and it is critical that whether a spokesperson is representing an individual, a company, or an organization, he or she is sensitive to the impact on human life. Take, for example, an explosion that occurs at a chemical refinery where employees are missing. Even though the refinery may have to stop production, the most important point should be

about the search for the missing employees. To talk about the economic impact when employees are missing would not be appropriate. Other key points might be whether the explosion is contained. A third point might be how people can get help if debris from the explosion has damaged their homes.

Reporters may ask questions that take the conversation away from the issues the spokesperson wants discussed in the interview. If a reporter does try to take the event in an unwanted direction, it is important for the spokesperson to bridge back to the three key points. To do this, spokespeople use phrases such as "What is most important . . ." or "That's a good question, but what I want you to understand is . . ." Then the spokesperson must be sure to bridge back to his or her key points.

Bridging does not mean evading the reporter's question. Even though the bridge can be an effective technique for inserting a key message, the spokesperson or other source still needs to answer the reporter's question. It does mean that he or she is strategically communicating the message. Spokespeople need to be clear as to what the answers to the questions are. No matter how many different ways a reporter asks the same question, the response should remain the same.

When communicating key points, the spokesperson needs to look the part. That not only means the appropriate attire but also showing the appropriate emotion. Being sincere and human will help make that person believable.

Rule 6: Do not ramble. When speaking to any reporter, print or electronic, it is very important for the spokesperson not to ramble. That means the spokesperson should keep the response short, tight, and to the point. As pointed out earlier, keep the response to seconds—not minutes. If a spokesperson does ramble, the media most likely will not call again for an interview. Spokespeople must remember that there just is not enough time in a newscast. Print reporters may tape record the interview. Both print and electronic reporters generally are working on tight deadlines and do not want to go through massive amounts of video or audio tape or written notes to get the perfect sound bite or quote.

If a spokesperson does ramble, he or she is most likely disobeying an earlier rule—to be quotable. It is imperative that when someone is being interviewed that the person sticks to the key points; otherwise, the person will miss that great opportunity to tell his or her side of the story.

Rule 7: Never say "no comment." The response of "no comment" to many folks screams guilty. If one were to think about it, if a defendant is walking out of the courtroom and the reporter shoves a microphone in his or her face, when the defendant shouts no comment, many assume he or she may be hiding something. If the person has not done anything wrong, then why will he or she not talk to the media?

Saying no comment may also mean missing an opportunity to get a key message across. Every attempt should be made to determine if other responses could be used0 rather than saying no comment. This is a good time to remember to use the bridging technique to lead back to the three key points.

Rule 8: Do not deal with "what-if" situations. Oftentimes, we will hear a reporter ask, "Well, what if?" Bottom line—spokespeople should not try to deal with what if situations. Answering a what if question will only bring trouble. For example, why would anyone want to answer the following question: What if the sun does not come up tomorrow? Spokespeople should not speculate. Instead, they should use bridging techniques and move the interview back to the key points.

Rule 9: Do not go off the record. The best bet when dealing with the media as sources is to realize that the journalist's job is to get information. Therefore, anything someone says or otherwise puts in front of a reporter is on the record, meaning that everything said can be quoted and attributed. In fact, leading journalism professionals often urge reporters to keep sources on the record.

Off the record information, some argue, should never be used by a reporter or used only rarely and only with approval of a news supervisor. Ethical codes from such journalism professional organizations as the Radio-Television News Directors Association for electronic journalists and the Society of Professional Journalists address this issue of dealing with sources. Furthermore, no one should confuse off the record with background information used by reporters to understand the context of a story.

Today, many reporters will use the Internet as a tool for background information. In addition, however, reporters may also ask experts for information to help the reporter understand the issues at hand. Generally, reporters are not asking to quote this kind of source. But the source and the reporter must clearly agree whether the information is to be used only for background purposes.

Furthermore, just because a camera is not rolling does not mean that the person being interviewed is off the record. One should remember that a reporter's job is to tell stories; therefore, everything someone tells a reporter is generally considered on the record.

Rule 10: Be visual. The final rule to follow when dealing with the media is to be visual, especially when dealing with TV news reporters. After all, television is a visual medium. Even the print medium lends itself to photographs and graphics. Being visual might also help explain what is often difficult to explain to a lay audience. This is especially true for scientific stories. If trying to state the size of something, use analogies that everyone can visualize. For example, one could say that the amount of chemical emitted would just fit inside a soda can or water bottle. If the amount is much larger, appropriate analogies may be that the liquid would fit in an average size swimming pool or inside a football stadium.

By following these 10 rules when responding to the media, the source has a much better chance of strategically getting his or her message out. This is the organization's opportunity to tell its side of the story.

During crisis situations, communications is truly key, and such communications must occur prior to any event, during the event, and certainly after the event. In all crisis situations, from natural to manmade disasters, those speaking out must fight fear with facts. During crises, communications may be the best tool an organization has to survive.

Sonya Forte Duhé

See also Disaster Coverage; *Exxon Valdez*; Hurricane Katrina; Public Relations and Science; Three Mile Island

Further Readings

Anthonissen, P. (2008). *Crisis communication: Practical PR strategies for reputation management and company survival.* London: Kogan Page.

Coombs, W. T. (2007). *Ongoing crisis communication: Planning, managing, and responding.* Thousand Oaks, CA: Sage.

Fearn-Banks, K. (2007). *Crisis communications: A casebook approach.* Mahwah, NJ: Lawrence Erlbaum.

Levick, R., & Smith, L. (2007). *Stop the presses: The crisis and PR desk litigation reference* (2nd ed.). Washington, DC: Watershed Press.

Ulmer, R. R., Sellnow, T. L., & Seeger, M. W. (2006). *Effective crisis communication: Moving from crisis to opportunity.* Thousand Oaks, CA: Sage.

CULTIVATION THEORY AND SCIENCE

Cultivation theory emerged in the late 1960s as an alternative to the predominant theoretical approaches of the time that emphasized relatively short-term and direct effects of the mass media. The theory was first articulated by George Gerbner of the Annenberg School, University of Pennsylvania. Cultivation itself was seen as part of a larger three-part framework called "cultural indicators." Gerbner's perspective focused on the more long-term, subtle, and indirect impacts of media messages.

In Gerbner's view, every society has methods of storytelling—ways of passing along ideas about one's culture, including underlying ideas about science, scientists, and the environment. These ideas are not communicated in a single program or even a short-term series. Rather, they are often buried in the stories that everyone is exposed to, and they form the basis for rather uniform images of how members of a society see themselves and their culture. For example, repeated portrayals of scientists as respected heroes might be expected to convey an underlying belief that scientists help society. On the other hand, repeated portrayals of mad scientists who have evil intent or whose accidents cause societal harm might convey underlying doubts and concerns about scientists and science. Over time, by psychological mechanisms that are still being debated, audiences absorb the underlying messages in a rather passive way.

Cultural Indicators

Gerbner's cultural indicators approach asserted that television, which emerged as a mass medium in the 1950s and was almost ubiquitous in households by 1970, has taken over as society's storyteller. This occurred because television was uniformly present in households and was watched more than any other medium. The average U.S. resident watches about 3 hours of television per day. In the 1960s, a lack of diversity of channels meant that everyone was being offered about the same mix of programs. Even in the current media environment with more than 200 channels offered to many, the actual programs and program types viewed are about the same.

These are three aspects of the cultural indicators framework:

1. *Institutional process.* This investigates the systematic pressures and constraints that affect how media messages are selected, produced, and distributed. Gerbner was concerned that media messages are being created by commercial companies with a marketing and profit motive and that the result has been stories that promote products and present images designed to draw, hold, and sell to audiences.

2. *Message system analysis.* This quantifies and tracks the most stable, pervasive, and recurrent images in media content. In this context, content analysis methods of selected weeks of television offerings are analyzed in terms of the underlying themes or stories they tell.

3. *Cultivation analysis.* Surveys are usually used to measure the extent to which television viewing contributes to audience members' conceptions about the real world. To the extent that viewers regard what they see on television as portraying reality (television reality) rather than actual reality, a case can be made that television is having long-term impacts on the stories people learn. These television perceptions, in turn, cause people to change behaviors.

The primary application of the theory has been focused on television and violence, due in large measure to societal concerns in the late 1960s and 1970s about the impacts television might be having, especially on children. Gerbner and colleagues received substantial research funding from the National Institute of Mental Health, the National Science Foundation, and other funders that enabled them to develop and test cultivation theory in this specific area. Later, the theory was applied to a number of other areas, including gender, age, the environment, health, and science.

The television and violence studies documented a consistent pattern of violence in television programs that far exceeded its true presence in society. Nancy Signorielli's 1990 continuation of the cultural indicators approach examining a 17-year period found that between 63% and 80% of programs in prime time and on weekends contained at least some violence. The numbers of murders, beatings, and other violence were carefully counted whether they occurred in cartoon shows or news programs because the underlying premise of the cultural indicators approach is that it is the overall and underlying messages about violence, rather than its context, that is important. Since very few people did not see programs of this type, it was concluded that the effects would be rather uniform despite the fact that people view a variety of different specific programs.

To measure possible impacts of this viewing on audiences, two indexes were constructed, one to measure "alienation and gloom," and one for a "mean world index." The first used items such as "In spite of what some people say, the lot (situation/condition) of the average man is getting worse, not better" (agree/disagree). The second used items such as "Would you say that most of the time people try to be helpful, or that they are mostly just looking out for themselves?" Results showed that those who were heavy viewers of television (often defined as viewing 4 hours or more a night) tended to score higher on the two indexes.

Cultivation and Science

In 1987, Gerbner began to address how issues relating to science might be cultivated by television. In terms of television content, he found that although scientists were portrayed in a positive way 83% of the time, doctors were portrayed positively 95% of the time, and police were portrayed positively 97.5% of the time. Thus, by comparison, scientists were portrayed less positively. During programs, 5% of scientists killed someone, and 10% got killed, giving scientists the highest violence rate of any occupational group. Given these results, Gerbner reasoned that the effect of viewing television would be a negative view of scientists and science.

In a national survey, which included an index of favorability or unfavorability to science, he found that heavy viewers of television were less favorable about science. This was true among subgroups too, broken down by age, newspaper readership, and viewing of Public Broadcasting System (PBS) science documentaries. Gerbner concluded that mainstreaming was occurring, which is the idea that those who view heavily will be most likely to distrust scientists across subgroups (that is, they will be most likely to give the "television answer"). Thus, even though those who view PBS science documentaries overall were much more positive about science than other groups, PBS viewers who were heavy viewers were relatively less positive.

James Shanahan and Katherine McComas applied the cultivation theory approach to television portrayals of the environment. They found very little coverage of the environment overall. Instead, what they found was a strong bias toward urban and indoor settings for television programs. They reasoned that this would cause heavy viewers to be less concerned about the environment. In subsequent surveys, they found mixed results. Heavy viewers of television were less likely to be willing to sacrifice for the environment, but there were no differences between heavy and light viewers for specific pollution issues.

Susanna Priest examined mass media content and public responses to issues concerning biotechnology. She concluded that while mass media may have a long-term, subtle, and indirect impact, audiences bring with them schemas or agendas of their own that they impose on mass media coverage. These more basic ideas about science may come from long-term portrayals by the mass media and interact with and guide interpretations of mass media content when issues such as biotechnology arise.

Assessing Overall Impacts

In a 1997 meta-analysis of the contributions of cultivation theory over the past two decades, Michael Morgan and James Shanahan conclude that across topics ranging from violence to science, there is an underlying cultivation correlation of .09 (representing a relationship, but a relatively weak one) between the long-term portrayals of topics on television and the worldviews of audiences. Heavier viewers, who are almost always less educated, experience a greater impact. What this means is that over time, there is a rather small but consistent impact from extensive television viewing that affects societal ideas about science, violence, and other topics. Gerbner argues that although television is by no means the most powerful influence on people, it is the most common, the most pervasive, and the most widely shared.

Eric A. Abbott

See also Television Science

Further Readings

Gerbner, G. (1987). Science on television: How it affects public conceptions. *Issues in Science and Technology, 3*, 109–115.

Gerbner, G., & Gross, L. (1976). Living with television: The violence profile. *Journal of Communication, 26*(2), 173–199.

Morgan, M., & Shanahan, J. (1997). Two decades of cultivation research: An appraisal and meta-analysis. In B. R. Burleson (Ed.), *Communication yearbook 20* (pp. 1–46). New York: Routledge.

Priest, S. H. (1995). Information equity, public understanding of science, and the biotechnology debate. *Journal of Communication, 45*(1), 39–54.

Shanahan, J., & McComas, K. (1999). *Nature stories: Depictions of the environment and their effects.* Cresskill, NJ: Hampton Press.

Signorielli, N. (1990). Television's mean and dangerous world: A continuation of the cultural indicators perspective. In N. Signorielli & M. Morgan (Eds.), *Cultivation analysis: New directions in media effects research* (pp. 85–106). Newbury Park: Sage.

DARWIN, CHARLES (1809–1882)

Charles Robert Darwin, Fellow of the Royal Society, was an English naturalist who realized—and presented compelling evidence—that all species of life have derived over time from common ancestors through the process he called natural selection. The debate on Darwin's theory of evolution is a unique case for observing some particular ways in which science is perceived and experienced in society. His works were best sellers in his English Victorian society, and his theory has been popularized by several generations of authors, including those who are alive and writing today. The fact that biological variation occurs became accepted by the scientific community and much of the general public in his lifetime, while his theory of natural selection came to be widely seen as the primary explanation of the process of evolution in the 1930s and now forms the basis of modern evolutionary theory. In modified form, Darwin's scientific discovery is the unifying theory of the life sciences, providing a logical explanation for the diversity of life.

The Voyage of the *Beagle*

At 22 years old, Darwin was a young university graduate, planning a career as a clergyman. A 26-year-old naval officer, Robert FitzRoy, had been given command of HMS *Beagle* for a second surveying voyage to South American waters. He was determined to take along a naturalist capable of studying the little-known areas that the ship would visit. Darwin was recommended by John Stevens Henslow, his professor of botany, from whom he had learned a great deal about scientific method. So, in 1831, Darwin received an astounding invitation: to join the HMS *Beagle* as a naturalist for a trip around the world. The *Beagle* voyage would provide Darwin with a lifetime of experience to ponder and with the seeds of the theory he would work on for the rest of his life.

From Plymouth, England, the *Beagle*'s first stop was the Cape Verde Islands. Then the ship proceeded to Brazil, where she was stationed at Bahia. Over the next 2 years, the *Beagle* went to Rio de Janeiro, Montevideo, Bahia Blanca, Patagonia, and the Falkland Islands. Then, via Valparaiso and Lima, the *Beagle* arrived at the Galapagos Islands. Crossing the Pacific and coming back through Asia, visiting Australia, the island of Mauritius, Cape Town, and then Brazil again, the *Beagle* finally arrived home. After a 5-year journey (December 1831–October 1836), Darwin, in his later *Autobiography,* called this trip the most important event of his life.

At the end of the travel, in May 1838, FitzRoy edited the *Narrative of the Surveying Voyages of His Majesty's Ships* Adventure *and* Beagle as the official narrative of the first and second voyages in four volumes. Darwin's *Journal and Remarks, 1832–1835,* forms the third volume, which adapted his shipboard diary into a book. This volume contains, in the form of a journal, a history of the voyage and a sketch of observations in natural history and geology. In its preface, Darwin demonstrates his special interest in general readers, noting that he has condensed some parts and expanded others to better adapt the book to general readers. Darwin's interest in science became a lifelong devotion. He avidly read the scientific travel accounts of Alexander von Humboldt and also read his works related to the Canary Islands. Another influence on Darwin was the work of the astronomer John Herschel. His *Preliminary Discourse* (1831) became the authority on correct methods of scientific investigation. *Principles of Geology* by Charles Lyell (1830) opened Darwin's eyes to a view of Earth as characterized by a long history of gradual change.

Maturation of the Theory of Variation by Natural Selection

In the years after *Beagle*'s return, Darwin was interested in how species might be related to one another. Species Darwin encountered included those living on isolated islands such as the Galapagos Islands. From making delighted, detailed observations of individual species and pondering the connections among them, Darwin achieved the simple conclusion that all species are in fact related. Fossils also raised many questions about the origin of species; they clearly showed that in the past ages, the world had been inhabited by different species from those existing today. New species had appeared at many different times in Earth's history. Fossils also revealed how new species tended to appear where similar species had previously lived.

Darwin also began to think about marriage and settled on his cousin Emma Wedgwood, and they were married in January 1839. Darwin's health soon began to deteriorate, and Emma would care for him throughout his life.

The relationships between old and new species, as shown in fossils, would become one of the main lines of evidence leading to Darwin's theory of variation by natural selection and the statement that all organisms have descended with modification from a common ancestor. Darwin kept his idea a secret because he was afraid of what his colleagues would think. He was writing up his theory in 1858 when a young naturalist named Alfred Russel Wallace sent him an essay that described the same idea, prompting immediate joint publication of both of their theories in the *Journal of the Linnean Society* on July 1, 1858.

Darwin's great work *On the Origin of Species by Means of Natural Selection,* published in 1859, was a popular success. The first printing sold out the day of publication. It is written in such uncomplicated English that readers could easily recognize what it meant. By 1859, the fact of evolution was widely accepted, although the mechanism was still in doubt. There were hundreds of book reviews and countless works written in opposition or in support, and a second edition of 3,000 copies was printed in January 1860.

The Descent of Man, and Selection in Relation to Sex was first published in 1871. A second and largely corrected edition of it appeared in 1874. Darwin was convinced that species were mutable productions, and he could not avoid the belief that man must come under the same law. In his *Autobiography,* Darwin specifies how the *Descent of Man, and Selection in Relation to Sex* followed from the logic of *On the Origin of Species by Means of Natural Selection.*

The Modern Evolutionary Synthesis

The world today is recognizably the same as when Darwin considered it, and his fundamental questions remain. The modern evolutionary synthesis is a union of ideas from several biological subspecialties, particularly genetics and population biology, that led to a theory of evolution that recognized the importance of mutation and variation within a population. Natural selection then became a process that altered the frequency of genes in a population, and this defined evolution.

Modern evolutionary synthesis is also referred to as the new synthesis, the modern synthesis, and the evolutionary synthesis. The modern theory of the mechanism of evolution differs from the original Darwinism in three aspects. First, it recognizes more mechanisms of evolution in addition to natural selection, for instance, genetic drift, mutation, and migration. Second, it recognizes that characteristics are inherited via discrete entities called genes. And third, it postulates that speciation could be due to the gradual accumulation of small genetic changes. This point is today an object of some controversy among evolutionists. The modern synthesis is a theory about how evolution works at the level of genes, phenotypes, and populations, whereas Darwinism was concerned mainly with organisms, speciation, and individuals.

This description would be incomprehensible to Darwin because he and his contemporaries were unaware of genes. The modern evolutionary synthesis showed that Mendelian genetics is consistent with natural selection and gradual evolution. The Czech monk Gregor Mendel (1822–1884) is often called the father of genetics for his study of the inheritance of certain traits in pea plants. Mendel showed that the inheritance of these traits follows particular laws, which were later named after him. He proved that the genetic factors behaved as if they were indivisible particles and that they did not blend or dilute themselves in the course of interbreeding. Mendel's paper was neglected and was not rediscovered again until 1900. Ultimately, the modern synthesis solved many difficulties and much confusion among biologists that had existed in the early years of the 20th century.

The Contemporary Creationism Controversy

In those days, Darwin recognized that his main lines of evolutionary thinking could not be observed directly but could only be deduced from indirect evidence. In his *Autobiography,* he noted that he had gradually come to see the Old Testament as presenting a "false history." Creationism means the taking of the Bible, particularly the early chapters of Genesis, as literally true guides to the history of the universe and to the history of life, including our history as humans. Creationists are strongly opposed to the idea of a world created by evolution, particularly to the world as described by Darwin in his *On the Origin of Species by Means of Natural Selection.* Darwin knew that unless a theory had been induced from observable facts, it was nothing more than a hypothesis. But today, following the modern synthesis, evolution is abundantly corroborated.

Núria Pérez-Pérez

See also Creationism; Intelligent Design in Public Discourse; Mendel, Gregor

Further Readings

Bowler, P. J. (2003). *Evolution: The history of an idea* (3rd ed.). Berkeley: University of California Press.

Complete Work of Charles Darwin Online: http://darwin-online.org.uk

Darwin, C. (2002). *Autobiographies* (M. Neve & S. Messenger, Eds.). New York: Penguin.

Darwin, C. (1979). *The illustrated origin of species.* London: Faber & Faber.

Darwin Correspondence Project: http://www.darwinproject.ac.uk

Eldredge, N. (2005). *Charles Darwin, discovering the tree of life.* New York: W. W. Norton.

DAWKINS, RICHARD (1941–)

Clinton Richard Dawkins is a British science writer and zoologist, who was appointed the first Professor of the Public Understanding of Science at Oxford University. He was elected a Fellow of the Royal Society in 2001 and of the Royal Society of Literature in 1997. His published works have been popularizations of Darwinism, original contributions to evolutionary theory, defenses of scientific rationalism, and critiques of religion. All but one of his books have been aimed at nonspecialist readers.

Dawkins was born in Nairobi, Kenya, on March 26, 1941, where his father moved during World War II to join the Allied forces. Dawkins studied zoology as an undergraduate at Oxford University, where he also took his doctorate, specializing in ethology, the science of animal behavior, and working under Nobel Prize–winning ethologist Niko Tinbergen. Afterwards, Dawkins held academic positions at the University of California, Berkeley, and the University of Oxford, where he was appointed reader in zoology in 1990.

The Selfish Gene

His career as a public scientist began in 1976 with the publication of his first book, *The Selfish Gene.* It remains his seminal work and a classic of popular science writing. It argued that Darwinian natural selection operated at the level of the gene, and organisms have existed chiefly as vehicles for replicating genes. It contended that even seemingly altruistic behavior among animals, such as birds risking their lives to warn the flock of a predator, can be driven by selfish genes to ensure their survival.

The book has been translated into 13 foreign languages and has sold more than 150,000 copies in English alone. It was expanded into a second edition in 1989 and republished as a 30th anniversary edition in 2006, along with a companion volume of essays titled *Richard Dawkins: How a Scientist Changed the Way We Think* (2007). Critics have uniformly praised his engaging prose, which uses clever analogies and striking metaphors to communicate scientific ideas.

Dawkins made no sharp distinction between popularization and original scientific work. Even though it was primarily aimed at nonspecialist audiences, he viewed *The Selfish Gene* as a creative contribution to scientific knowledge. It was pioneering in modern popular science writing for its presentation of ideas and arguments that had not been agreed on or accepted within the scientific community. It drew on the work of neo-Darwinian scientists, including William Hamilton, Robert L. Trivers, G. C. Williams, and John Maynard Smith, whose work merged classical Darwinian evolution with population genetics.

Dawkins had been drawn to the philosophical dimensions of zoology since his undergraduate studies. *The Selfish Gene*'s central ideas contributed to philosophical and moral debates that had been occurring in the late 1970s, following the publication of entomologist E. O. Wilson's controversial *Sociobiology* (1975). Critics objected to Dawkins's anthropomorphizing of genes and tended to take literally his vivid metaphors explaining genetic survival strategies. Critics, including British neurobiologist Steven Rose, argued that Dawkins's views were a form of genetic determinism, written from a neoliberal political perspective, criticisms Dawkins has continually denied. He is politically center left and has said he always voted labor or liberal in U.K. elections. In *The Selfish Gene*, Dawkins noted that he did not advocate morality based on evolution and argued that humans were not compelled to follow their genes' selfish drives.

The Darwin Wars

The Selfish Gene also fitted into large scientific and cultural debates over the political and philosophical interpretations of Darwinism, debates that have collectively been called "the Darwin wars." There have been several protagonists in this contested terrain, but the dominant personalities have been Dawkins and Harvard paleontologist Stephen J. Gould. Their academic rivalry, frequently expressed in popular science books, has focused on differing specialist interpretations of the dynamics of evolution. However, Dawkins and Gould have been united in their strident opposition to creationism because opposing it could give their views creditability, although Dawkins has refused to directly debate creationists.

Dawkins's next book, *The Extended Phenotype* (1982), was his only title to be consciously aimed at the specialist in biology. It extended his original concept of the selfish gene to the idea that a gene can reach far outside its own molecular walls, sometimes into other organisms, to increase its chances of evolutionary survival. He viewed the book as his main piece of original research.

His third book, *The Blind Watchmaker* (1986), was awarded the *Los Angeles Times* Literary Prize and the Royal Society of Literature Award. It is an extended explanation of how evolution has created what he called the beautiful biological complexity of the natural world, themes he has explored in his books *River Out of Eden: A Darwinian View of Life* (1995), *Climbing Mount Improbable* (1996), *The Ancestor's Tale* (2004), and *The Greatest Show on Earth: The Evidence for Evolution* (2009). *A Devil's Chaplain* (2003) is a collection of previously published essays on science and society themes.

The Blind Watchmaker was a refutation of both creationism and intelligent design. It demonstrated how the structure of the human eye and the sonar of bats, instead of being designed by a higher intelligence, were formed by the natural and gradual evolution over time through the replication of genes over generations. An original feature of his work was his self-created computer program of images, biomorphs, that evolved in complex patterns similar to biological life forms.

Professor of Public Understanding of Science

In 1995 Dawkins was appointed as the inaugural Charles Simonyi Professor of Public Understanding of Science at Oxford. The first of its kind in the United Kingdom, the chair was created with an endowment from former Microsoft executive

Charles Simonyi to bolster science's cultural standing. The post was to be held by an eminent scientist who would contribute to the lay public's understanding of some scientific field.

The first book Dawkins published in this role was *Unweaving the Rainbow: Science, Delusion and the Appetite for Wonder* (1997), which defended science as a cultural force, as well as debunked various forms of pseudoscience and challenged pseudoscientific thinking, especially some forms of cultural relativism and postmodernist critiques of science. He also argued that science writing was best when it adopted an unadorned prose writing style.

In *The Selfish Gene*, Dawkins also applied Darwinism to cultural evolution, using the concept of the meme. Memes are replicating units of cultural transmission, analogous to genes as biological units of reproduction. Natural selection could thus be used to explain how ideas spread through history and society. Songs, theories, beliefs, and values were all examples of memes, but the most prominent example in Dawkins's writing was religion.

Using the analogy of a computer virus, Dawkins argued that religion was a virus of the mind, which was open to infection from parasitic and self-replicating ideas. Scientific ideas were memes, too, but they succeeded in replicating because they were proven to be true, while faith has failed as an idea because it does not meet the standards of evidential proof achieved through the application of the scientific method.

Dawkins's cultural criticism has focused increasingly on critiques of religion. His view was given its sharpest expression in *The God Delusion* (2008), which challenged a range of theological arguments advanced in favor of a creator. The book has sold more than 1.5 million copies and has prompted book-length counterarguments, including writer John Cornwell's *Darwin's Angel: An Angelic Riposte to* The God Delusion (2007) and Oxford theologian Alister McGrath's *The Dawkins Delusion? Atheist Fundamentalism and the Denial of the Divine* (2007), coauthored with Joanna Collicutt McGrath.

Dawkins has become allied with wider cultural movements of atheism, skepticism, and humanism. He founded the Richard Dawkins Foundation for Reason & Science to promote rational scientific

thinking and oppose what he characterized as an attack on science from organized ignorance.

An articulate and capable media performer, he has written widely for British publications, been featured as a commentator in various media, and has presented several broadcasts, including episodes of BBC's flagship science program *Horizon* and the documentaries *The Genius of Charles Darwin, The Enemies of Reason,* and *Root of All Evil?* broadcast on the U.K. Channel 4. He edited the 2003 edition of *The Best American Science and Nature Writing* and *The Oxford Book of Modern Science Writing* (2008), as well as wrote forewords to several books.

Dawkins holds honorary doctorates in literature and science. Among the several awards he has received are the Royal Society's Michael Faraday Award for advancing the public understanding of science and the Shakespeare Prize for contribution to British culture. He has one daughter and lives in Oxford with his third wife, actress Lalla Ward.

Declan Fahy

See also Creationism; Darwin, Charles; Gould, Stephen Jay; Intelligent Design in Public Discourse; Religion, Science, and Media

Further Readings

Cornwell, J. (2007). *Darwin's angel: An angelic riposte to* The God Delusion. London: Profile Books.

Dawkins, R. (1982). *The extended phenotype*. New York: W. H. Freeman.

Dawkins, R. (1986). *The blind watchmaker*. New York: Longman.

Dawkins, R. (1989). *The selfish gene* (2nd ed.). Oxford, UK: Oxford University Press.

Dawkins, R. (1995). *River out of Eden: A Darwinian view of life*. New York: Basic Books.

Dawkins, R. (1996). *Climbing mount improbable*. New York: W. W. Norton.

Dawkins, R. (1997). *Unweaving the rainbow: Science, delusion and the appetite for wonder*. New York: W. W. Norton.

Dawkins, R. (2003). *A devil's chaplain: Selected essays*. Boston: Houghton Mifflin.

Dawkins, R. (2004). *The ancestor's tale*. Boston: Houghton Mifflin.

Dawkins, R. (2007). *The God delusion*. London: Black Swan.

Grafen, A., & Ridley, M. (2006). *Richard Dawkins: How a scientist changed the way we think*. Oxford, UK: Oxford University Press.

Kohn, M. (2005). *A reason for everything: Natural selection and the English imagination*. London: Faber & Faber.

McGrath, A., & McGrath, J. C. (2007). *The Dawkins delusion? Atheist fundamentalism and the denial of the divine*. Downers Grove, IL: InterVarsity Press.

DEDUCTIVE LOGIC

Deductive logic is a category of reasoning that is fundamental to the sciences and technology and, therefore, especially important for science communicators and others concerned with understanding science. In fact, deductive logic is important anywhere computers are used. Deductive logic forms the basis of all computer code and is often taught in computer science curricula, not just in philosophy departments.

Logic itself is commonly understood as the relationships and principles of reasoning. The phrase "the process of reasoning" generally refers to the way in which one or several sentences give reason to believe some conclusion, which is itself another statement. For instance, when Jack is taller than Tom and when Tom is taller than Allen, someone can know from these two premises that Jack must be taller than Allen. This example is an instance of deductive logic.

Deductive logic is generally contrasted with inductive logic. Inductive logic is the kind of reasoning that is founded upon premises that support a conclusion with a degree of likelihood or probability, not with necessity. For example, when Jill sees clouds outside, she reasons that it will rain. She does not know this with certainty, but this is not her fault. Until a sign appears that implies there will necessarily be rain, something that is not yet the case, Jill cannot know for sure what the weather will do. By contrast, consider that when there is fire, there must be oxygen present. This is true because fire itself is a process that requires oxygen. So wherever there is fire, there is at least some oxygen.

Arguments that involve necessity, such as the kind involving fire and oxygen, are different in kind from inductive arguments. It is important not to assume that in all deductive arguments the conclusion necessarily does follow from the premises, however. That is because the argument can simply be a bad one, called invalid. Take the following as an example: Jack is a bachelor; therefore, Jack is married. This is an example of a deductive argument, but it is one in which the necessary characteristics of bachelorhood are mistakenly related to being married. In fact, to be a bachelor implies that one is not married. This argument would be called deductive, but invalid. The valid version looks like this: Jack is a bachelor; therefore, Jack is not married.

There are several different kinds of deductive argumentation. The simplest kind is an *argument from definition*. The example of bachelorhood is one of these. How terms are defined bears important consequences, however, since the definitions used imply consequences than can be better or worse for particular purposes. Controversies can arise over the proper way to define terms. Some controversial examples have included terms such as *planet, marriage,* or *enemy combatant.*

Another kind of deduction is called *natural deduction*. Natural deduction generally refers to the forms that arguments take. There are certain shapes that our arguments frequently form. When someone substitutes other terms and categories into well-designed deductive arguments, some forms never lead to false conclusions. Those are the arguments that are called valid. For example, one argument form, called modus ponens, is especially common and important to the study of logic. In modus ponens, the arguer says that if some condition P is true, then condition Q is also true. He or she then claims that P is true. Therefore, according to these reasons, it must be that Q is also true. This form of argument has been shown time and time again to be irrefutable. There could be mistakes made in filling in the details, but the form itself cannot lead someone from true premises to a false conclusion. When an argument has proper form but has premises that are not true, the argument is called valid but unsound. In fact, all deductive arguments that are either invalid or that have one or more false premises are considered unsound. Therefore, a sound argument, technically speaking, is a valid, deductive argument in which the premises are true.

A further sort of deductive argument is called *propositional logic* and is associated with Venn diagrams and categories. Certain categories of things bear necessary consequences. For instance, all human beings are mortal. Based on this categorical statement, it is also true that no human beings are immortal. If someone knows that some fruits are apples, they also know that it is false that no fruits are apples. While statements like these can sound obviously true in these examples, the examples are chosen because of how simply they demonstrate these principles. In technical matters, it is very important to check one's reasoning to avoid mistakes.

In deductive arguments, the purpose is not looking for conclusions that are likely to be true. The test for the quality of a deductive argument is whether the conclusion must be true. If the argument's conclusion could be false with true premises, then the argument is deemed invalid. The test of the quality of a deductive argument is called the counterexample method. Instead of testing to see whether a conclusion could be true with some premises, the real test for a deductive argument is whether or not there could be even one example in which the same form could be used with different terms to yield a true set of premises and a false conclusion.

This is important because if the answer is yes, someone cannot say with certainty that true premises in such an argument necessarily support the conclusion. As the standard for deductive arguments is truth-preserving necessity, to find a counterexample to someone's argument is to show that his or her reasoning is flawed.

Eric Thomas Weber

See also Inductive Logic; Scientific Method

Further Readings

Copi, I. M. (1986). *Introduction to logic.* New York: Macmillan.

Hurley, P. J. (2003). *A concise introduction to logic* (8th ed.). Belmont, CA: Wadsworth.

Toulmin, S. (1994). *The uses of argument.* New York: Oxford University Press.

DEFICIT MODEL

Every so often, at least in the Western world, there seems to be a bit of a panic: politicians, media professionals, and ordinary citizens do not know enough science to value, appreciate, and rationally discuss it and the issues it poses. It happened in Britain in the late 1820s, and the upshot was the foundation of the British Association for the Advancement of Science. U.S. scientists and politicians were shocked in the 1950s to discover that the Russians had successfully launched the first artificial satellite, *Sputnik*; surveys showed that the average American knew very little science. The result was an intense drive for scientific literacy in the education system. Crises in funding for scientific research in the mid-1980s coupled with concerns that the "Asian tiger" economies, led by Japan, were outstripping Europe gave rise to the latest phase of actions to promote the public understanding of science across the European Union. And despite the change in rhetoric to include *dialogue* and *debate,* behind much of what passes for engaging the public is still aimed at redressing some perceived deficiency among ordinary citizens. Where science is concerned, there is a public deficit, and it is the job of the scientific community to address it—that, in a nutshell, is what the deficit model entails.

In 1985, the Royal Society—Britain's premier scientific society—produced the report "The Public Understanding of Science" that urged the media to carry more science and told scientists that they had a duty, no less, to communicate with the public about the work that they did, changing the ethos of several decades during which researchers who did make their work accessible to their fellow citizens had been shunned as self-serving attention seekers, who were not very good scientists anyway. Instead, thousands of scientists, from the humble PhD student to the superannuated Fellow of the Royal Society, were encouraged—and sometimes funded—to give public lectures, take part in science fairs, and be friendly to the media—all aimed at increasing the public understanding of science and scientific literacy. Analyzing the motives for this activity in 1987, Oxford scholars Geoffrey Thomas and John Durant found that these ranged from macroeconomics and national prestige, to enabling citizens to be involved in informed democratic debate and to lead fulfilled lives, to enhancing moral behavior.

Thomas and Durant later surveyed levels of scientific literacy—defined by knowing a dozen or so key facts of science, understanding the scientific method, and appreciating the social importance of science—and found that most people were ignorant of science by the definition used. Previous surveys in the United States showed similar results; later, surveys across Europe confirmed the (gloomy) picture, and the European Union took steps to rectify the situation. Moreover, unlike previous concerns about the citizen–science relationship, the latest phase has been globalized. Surveys carried out in Japan, India, China, Korea, Brazil, and South Africa—to name but a few non-European and non-U.S. countries—have all shown similar deficits in the scientificity of the public.

Survey Results and the Deficits They Show

Behind all of these surveys is the notion that the results provide some sort of performance indicators and that—as with indicators of economic activity, for example—action can be taken to improve the performance. And behind that assumption is the sometimes explicit, but usually implicit, notion that to know more science is to like it better. So what evidence does this model of a somewhat deficient public rest upon?

The surveys carried out regularly in the United States and in the European Union, and from time to time by other countries, tend to show similar results. Somewhere between 50% and 60% of lay citizens can correctly answer any particular true-false question of a set of 12 facts correctly (the so-called knowledge quiz), which might suggest a scientific literacy rate of about 50% to 60%. But that percentage halves when people answering the questionnaire are also asked to explain what it means to study something scientifically. And it halves again when people who think astrology (rather than, or as well as, astronomy) is scientific are discounted, leading the more pessimistic to report scientific literacy rates below 20%. So the conclusion is drawn that citizens should know more about science—a deficit to be filled.

The same surveys often ask not only what citizens know but also what their interests are and how well-informed they feel themselves to be. The results are clear: People who say that they are very or fairly interested in sports, for example, report that they are very or fairly well-informed. But people who claim that they are very or fairly interested

in matters scientific (including medical) feel that they are much less well-informed than they would like. So there is evidence that people realize they are deficient in science and that they would like to know more—they desire the deficit to be filled. Incidentally, people report to be approximately twice as interested in science as they are in sports—though one would not realize this from a glance at commercially successful newspapers. Finally, on an individual level, there is a correlation between knowing more science and being more positive toward it, although the relationship is more complex than the more simplistic versions of the deficit model of science communication imply.

Critiques of the Deficit Model

Much of the science literacy and public understanding of science campaigns of the last two decades have thus been based on the three premises: Citizens need to know more science, they want to know more science, and if they knew more science, they would like it better. A clear strategic program can (and did) unfold. So what were the results?

For a start, the performance-indicator approach to the results of surveys hit (at least) one brick wall: Despite the plans and funded activities aimed at raising scientific literacy as defined by the leading surveyors, the scientific literacy indicators stayed stubbornly static year after year; if there were positive changes in the aggregate numbers of citizens answering the knowledge quiz correctly, there were negative changes in levels of interest (see, for example, the results of the Eurobarometers from 1992–2005)—not what the simple deficit model implied, but perhaps a case of "familiarity breeds contempt."

One of the most succinct critiques of the deficit model was given by Alan Gross. He summed it up by saying that it simultaneously assumed public deficiency plus scientific sufficiency. In his view, the model implies a passive public that requires science to adapt itself, in order to be communicated, to the limited capacity and experience of the public. Deficit model science communication was top-down, one-way, and patronizing. It failed to take account of the lay expertise that resided with citizens individually or in their social groups. Nor was it a communication process aimed at empowering citizens or negotiating new knowledge.

Moreover, analyses of the science–society dynamic have pointed out that historically there had been at least three identifiable deficits implicit in the overall deficit model: a deficit of knowledge associated with the initial U.S. push for scientific literacy post-*Sputnik*; a deficit of public attitude, embodied in the post-1985 public understanding of the science movement; and—just as the deficit model is being declared dead—a deficit, or crisis, of trust coupled with a deficit of expert understanding of the public, a mismatch between the hopes and desires of citizens and what science seems to be delivering.

How Dead Is the Deficit Model?

Critiques of the deficit model may give the impression that such an approach to science communication is decidedly old-fashioned and has been largely abandoned. As a genuine approach to dealing with relations between science and citizens, it is clearly—on its own—inadequate. That said, there is a gap or a deficit between what trained scientific researchers know and what the lay public knows. Or at least there should be, if scientists are earning their salaries, funded directly by taxpayers or indirectly by consumers. Clearly communicating the facts derived from laborious and costly research programs—where they have a bearing on the public as a whole, as groups, or as individuals—has to be worthwhile and important. Science has much to say about global warming, health, and even personal beliefs about the origin of life or of the universe. So, in that sense, the deficit model lives on.

But there is another, more insidious way in which the good old-fashioned deficit model is still alive and kicking. Today's rhetoric around science communication is all about science and society (or science in society), with notions of two-way communication, dialogue, debate, engagement, and so on predominating. So how does all of this work out in practice?

One key area of contested science in Europe is the issue of genetically modified (GM) food and whether or not it has a place in the countryside, the supermarket shelves, or the stomachs of citizens. In 2003, the government of the United Kingdom decided to hold a public dialogue and to invest more than 1 million dollars in ascertaining what the British felt about the issue. Focus groups, public meetings, and opinion polls all came back

with the same response: No! But that was not what the government, or the scientific community, really wanted to hear. And although GM foods are not widely available in the United Kingdom or in the rest of Europe, there is a strong feeling that the public came up with the wrong answer and that it needs to be better persuaded so that European biotech companies can sell to their home markets.

All of this raises the question, Is the move to engagement, dialogue, and debate simply a recognition that two-way communication is a requirement if citizens are to be persuaded that governments and scientists are right? If so, then the new deficit to be overcome is a lack of listening by the public. Or maybe not: Maybe citizens have heard and have not liked what they heard; maybe the real deficit is a lack of listening on behalf of scientists and politicians. After all, if genuine dialogue is to take place, both sides have to listen as well as to speak.

Steve Miller

See also Attentive Public; Audiences for Science; Public Understanding of Science; Science Literacy

Further Readings

Gross, A. G. (1994). The roles of rhetoric in the public understanding of science. *Public Understanding of Science, 3*(1), 3–23.

Thomas, G., & Durant, J. (1987). Why should we promote the public understanding of science? In M. Shortland (Ed.), *Scientific literacy papers* (pp. 1–14). Oxford, UK: Oxford University Department for External Studies.

DELIBERATIVE DEMOCRACY

Deliberative democracy is a political theory that requires legitimate decision making to be based on deliberation among citizens. The theory is often contrasted with the purely aggregative voting methods used in many democratic societies, as well as the self-interested bargaining typified in economics. Deliberative democracy is compatible with science and technology communication theory in that both broad theories promote participation, engagement, and accessible knowledge for all people, not just for the powerful or elite.

In contrast to methods of public engagement with science and technology such as cafés scientifique (or science cafés), deliberative procedures are generally more focused on outcomes and decisions rather than on purely discussions. While enhanced knowledge and participation are benefits in both types of activity, deliberative processes typically involve a definitive conclusion of some sort. Consensus conferences typically seek this type of conclusion, as do citizen juries and deliberative polls.

Controversial issues such as stem cell research, nuclear technology, and genetic modification have been the subject of deliberative democracy initiatives in attempts to ensure that political decisions reflect people's interests and preferences and thereby justify and legitimize policy.

Deliberative democracy is associated with fairer decision making because it is assumed that when contributing to a public discussion, people consider the common good, not just their own interests. Whereas when voting privately, people may be inclined to make decisions for their own benefit, without considering impacts on others, discussing views publicly encourages people to reflect on the rationality of their perspective and on how others will perceive it. Considering an issue from different perspectives could lead to a change in attitude, which could be more aligned with the public good. Through deliberation, it is expected that citizens and their representatives will arrive at decisions that all can find acceptable, even though individuals' reasons for accepting a decision might be different.

In addition, public discussion and deliberation allows people to gather more information, which can lead to fairer opinions coupled with greater education. This knowledge transfer, although perhaps less significant for political theorists, has significant appeal for science and technology communicators. Because deliberation allows time and resources for listening to different perspectives and because it encourages consideration of rational arguments, it often promotes public understanding of science and technology, given the likelihood that aspects of science and technology are often present in contentious policy issues.

How deliberative democracy should happen is the subject of deliberation itself. Some authors argue that rationality should not be a rigid condition of deliberative participation. Indeed, some argue that rhetorical or emotional arguments can have a valid place in deliberation and should not be excluded from decision-making processes, as long as such persuasive techniques do not involve coercion or undermine processes of collective decision making. Some take issue with the perceived superiority of expert opinions and claimed objectivity of science. Particularly when used to justify and inform political decisions, value judgments behind science should also be considered.

Deliberative theorists are divided on whether the public has inherently different interests and desires; deliberation involves conflict unless there is harmony in people's values and desires, which will lead to consensus. Either way, respect for others' contributions is an important condition of effective deliberation. Since deliberation does not guarantee that consensus around a decision will be reached, the process can include better representation of different views and better engagement with a range of people; if an ultimate decision is not compatible with some perspectives, however, the benefits of engagement can be lost if people feel their opinions are not reflected in the outcome. For this reason, it is essential that deliberation procedures and eventual decision making are transparent so that people can see how their contribution and perspective fit into the broader picture.

Transparency also guards against manipulation. Persuasive groups or individuals with more power or better communication skills can sway deliberative processes. It is not guaranteed that after discussion, the perspective that best reflects public good will dominate. Political equality is a concern for deliberative theorists; although it is unrealistic to expect everyone to participate in deliberative processes, it is important that every person capable of rational communication has the right to participate and that deliberative methods are focused on accessibility for different types of people.

The term *deliberative democracy* first appeared in 1980, in a book chapter by Joseph M. Bessette called "Deliberative Democracy: The Majority Principle in Republican Government." The idea originated as part of a discussion on constitutional democracy. Many deliberative democracy theorists are focused on the idea's application in political settings; however, in science and technology communication, deliberative processes are used by organizations with other focuses as well.

Deliberative democracy is increasingly a part of decision making in health sciences, where organizational policies are sometimes made in consultation with patients and caregivers.

Cobi Smith

See also Citizens Jury; Consensus Conference; Deliberative Polling; Science Café; Upstream Engagement

Further Readings

Elster, J. (Ed.). (1998). *Deliberative democracy.* Cambridge, UK: Cambridge University Press.
Fishkin, J., & Laslett, L. (2003). *Debating deliberative democracy.* Malden, MA: Blackwell.
Guttman, A., & Thompson, D. (2004). *Why deliberative democracy?* Princeton, NJ: Princeton University Press.

DELIBERATIVE POLLING

James S. Fishkin has pioneered (and trademarked) deliberative polling as a way of combining the generalizability of a random sample opinion survey with the citizen–expert and citizen–citizen dialogue characteristic of high-quality public engagement. Deliberative polls also usually include a media component aimed at bringing the experience of deliberation to a wider audience.

The goal of deliberative polling is to find out what a random sample of citizens would think if they had the time and resources necessary to carefully consider an issue. In contrast, most public opinion surveys include many subjects with little knowledge or engagement on a topic, resulting in unstable answers and superficial opinions. Consistent with the political theory of deliberative democracy, deliberative polls include an opportunity for participants to hear from carefully selected experts on multiple sides of an issue followed by an opportunity to discuss the issue with fellow participants in cooperation with a trained moderator.

While most deliberative polls do not focus on science issues, several have looked at energy topics or have dealt with policy issues such as health care and housing that require the consideration of social science research findings.

The main challenge facing deliberative polling is the cost associated with assembling a large enough random sample (at least several hundred, sometimes more) of a population in a single place. Most forms of citizen deliberation use only a small number of participants (often fewer than 20). Whereas other engagement formats aimed at fostering citizen deliberation may request that participants work together to produce a joint report or consensus statement, deliberative polls rely on pre- and postparticipation questionnaires with participants to assess the impact of participation. Finally, like most forms of public engagement, deliberative polls are meant only to provide guidance to decision makers, but participants who spend a weekend focused on a single issue may come to expect that their views should hold more weight. While the process of deliberative polling has resulted in opinion change on some issues (but not necessarily all), it consistently leads to increased knowledge and issue understanding.

Fishkin has also argued that, given the results of deliberative polling, governments should consider implementing a national day of citizen discussion—that is, a deliberation day—prior to major elections. Such a day would be aimed at enhancing citizens' consideration of electoral candidates.

John C. Besley

See also Citizens Jury; Consensus Conference; Deliberative Democracy; Public Engagement

Further Readings

Ackerman, B. A., & Fishkin, J. S. (2004). *Deliberation day.* New Haven, CN: Yale University Press.
Fishkin, J. S. (1997). *The voice of the people: Public opinion and democracy* (2nd ed.). New Haven, CT: Yale University Press.
McCombs, M. E., & Reynolds, A. (1999). *The poll with a human face: The National Issues Convention experiment in political communication.* Mahwah, NJ: Lawrence Erlbaum.

DEPARTMENT OF AGRICULTURE, U.S.

The U.S. Department of Agriculture (USDA) was established in 1862 and has a stated mission to provide leadership on food, agriculture, natural resources, and related issues. The secretary of agriculture, who is appointed by the president of the United States and serves as a cabinet member, administers the policies and programs of the department. This entry provides a brief overview of the mission areas, offices, and agencies that make up USDA, which is a key source for up-to-the-minute information about all issues involving food and agriculture in the United States.

Farm and Foreign Agricultural Services strive to strengthen the agricultural economy through the delivery of the commodity, credit, conservation, disaster, and emergency assistance programs.

Farm Service Agency is administered directly by state and county offices. County committee members are elected by local producers to resolve local issues. The committee members certify farmers for farm programs and support loans and pay out subsidies and disaster assistance.

Foreign Agricultural Service (FAS) is primarily responsible for USDA's international activities, including improving foreign market access and the competitive position of U.S. products, building new markets, and providing food aid and technical assistance to foreign countries. FAS coordinates agricultural trade negotiations with the U.S. Trade Representative Office.

Risk Management Agency (RMA) is comprised of three divisions: Insurance Services, Product Management, and Risk Compliance. The agency's mission is to promote, support, and regulate risk management to strengthen agriculture's economic stability. RMA manages and operates the Federal Crop Insurance Corporation by approving premium rates, administering subsidies, supporting products, and reinsuring the private sector insurance companies.

Food, Nutrition and Consumer Services works to end hunger and improve health in the United States through federal domestic nutrition assistance, dietary guidance, nutrition policy coordination, and nutrition education.

Center for Nutrition Policy and Promotion develops and promotes dietary guidelines, defines and coordinates nutrition education policy, and translates nutrition research for consumers, policymakers, professionals, and the media.

Food and Nutrition Service provides children and low-income people with access to food and nutrition education through the administration of nutrition assistance programs, such as the Food Stamp Program; the National School Lunch Program; Women, Infants and Children; and the Emergency Food Assistance Program, among others.

Food Safety oversees the commercial supply of meat, poultry, and egg products to ensure proper safety, labeling, and packaging. The mission area works with the Food and Drug Administration, the Centers for Disease Control and Prevention, and the Environmental Protection Agency to coordinate a national food safety strategic plan.

Food Safety and Inspection Service sets food safety standards, maintains inspection oversight, monitors recalls of meat and poultry products, and enforces regulatory standards.

Marketing and Regulatory Programs facilitate the marketing of U.S. agricultural products and set national and international standards for the health and care of plants and animals.

Agricultural Marketing Service (AMS) standardizes, grades, and coordinates the marketing of food, fiber, and specialty crops including cotton, dairy, fruit and vegetable, livestock and seed, poultry, and tobacco. AMS oversees marketing agreements, administers research and promotion, and purchases commodities for federal food programs.

Animal and Plant Health Inspection Service (APHIS) has a stated mission to protect and promote U.S. agricultural health through the regulation of genetically engineered organisms, the administration of the Animal Welfare Act of 1966, and the support of wildlife damage management activities. APHIS strives to detect pests and diseases to quickly eradicate outbreaks and minimize threats to the agricultural industry.

Grain Inspection, Packers, and Stockyards Administration includes the Federal Grain Inspection Service and the Packers and Stockyards Program. The Federal Grain Inspection Service facilitates the marketing of grain products by establishing quality standards, regulating handling practices, and managing federal, state, and private inspection and weighing services. The Packers and Stockyards Program monitors, reviews, and investigates livestock, meat, and poultry competition to guard against deceptive and fraudulent trade practices.

Natural Resources and Environment is a mission area, while under the USDA, funded by the Department of the Interior appropriations to promote good land management while preventing damage to natural resources and the environment.

Forest Service (FS) manages public lands in national forests and grasslands. FS's mission is to sustain the health, diversity, and productivity of the nation's forests and grasslands.

Natural Resources Conservation Service (NRCS), formerly the Soil Conservation Service, provides technical and financial assistance to encourage the conservation of soil, water, and other natural resources. NRCS also assesses natural resource conditions and trends in the United States through the National Resources Inventory.

Research, Education and Economics (REE) seeks to create a safe, sustainable, and competitive food and fiber system through integrated research, analysis, and education. The agencies that make up REE create and disseminate biological, physical, and social science knowledge related to agricultural research, economic analysis, statistics, extension, and higher education. REE also maintains the National Agricultural Library, which houses one of the world's largest agricultural information collections.

Agricultural Research Service (ARS) is USDA's chief scientific research agency. Research in the ARS is categorized into three key areas: (1) animal production, product value, and safety; (2) national resources and sustainable agricultural systems; and (3) crop production, product value, and safety.

Cooperative State Research, Education, and Extension Service (CSREES) funds and supports research, education, and extension programs through the land grant university system and other partner organizations. CSREES also administers the 4-H youth development program.

Economic Research Service (ERS) conducts research to inform economic and policy issues involving food, farming, natural resources, and rural development. The four research divisions of ERS include Food Economics, Information Services, Market and Trade Economics, and Resource and Rural Economics.

National Agricultural Statistics Service (NASS) conducts hundreds of surveys every year and makes reports available regarding many aspects of U.S. agriculture. NASS also conducts the Census of Agriculture every 5 years in every county in the United States as a source of consistent and comparable data.

Rural Development (RD) seeks to help rural areas grow by offering financial and technical resources. RD provides funding to support public facilities and services such as water and sewer systems, housing, health clinics, emergency services, and electric and telephone service in rural areas. RD also administers community empowerment programs to improve the self-sufficiency of rural communities.

Shari R. Veil

See also Agricultural Biotechnology; Agricultural Journalism; Food and Drug Administration, U.S.; Government Public Information

Further Readings

Animal Welfare Act of August 24, 1966, Pub. L. No. 89-544 (1966).

U.S. Department of Agriculture: www.usda.gov/wps/portal/usdahome

DEPARTMENT OF ENERGY, U.S.

The U.S. Department of Energy (DOE), administered by the U.S. secretary of energy, is responsible for energy policy and nuclear safety. Its responsibilities include the nation's nuclear weapons program, nuclear reactor production for the U.S. Navy, energy conservation, energy-related research, radioactive waste disposal, and domestic energy production. DOE initiatives focus on energy security, nuclear security, scientific discovery, and environmental responsibility. Many federal agencies that handled energy policy between World War II and the energy crisis of the 1970s were placed under the auspices of DOE in 1977. With energy-related issues involving everything from nuclear power to energy production alternatives and from global warming to vehicle fuel efficiency gaining attention in the news, journalists and other science communicators will need to understand DOE's current role.

The Advanced Energy Initiative of 2006 mandated a 22% increase in funding for clean energy technology research at DOE, including greater investment in zero-emission coal-fired plants, solar and wind technologies, and nuclear energy, as well as more funding for ethanol production research and development of mass market electric and hydrogen fueled cars. The initiative seeks to develop technologies that would allow a plug-in hybrid electric vehicle to have a 40-mile range operating solely on battery charge, make cellulosic ethanol cost competitive with corn-based ethanol by 2012, and mass produce hydrogen fuel cell vehicles by 2020. It commits new funding for clean coal research; addresses spent nuclear fuel and proliferation risks; promotes the development of clean, reliable, and affordable nuclear energy; seeks to make solar photovoltaic technologies cost competitive by 2015; and expands access to wind energy.

The Energy Independence and Security Act of 2007 mandates a 20% reduction in U.S. gasoline usage by 2017. The act requires production of 35 billion gallons of renewable fuels by 2017 to displace 15% of the projected annual gasoline use and reforms the Corporate Average Fuel Economy standards for cars.

Key Agencies

The Energy Information Administration is a statistical agency within DOE that provides official data, forecasts, and analysis to inform policy making, ensure efficient markets, and support public understanding of energy and its interaction with the economy and environment. By law, its data are prepared independently of policy considerations, and the agency does not formulate or advocate policy conclusions. It issues a wide range of weekly, monthly, and annual reports on energy production, stocks, demand, imports, exports, and prices and prepares analyses and reports on special topics.

The DOE National Nuclear Security Administration is responsible for managing the U.S. nuclear weapons stockpile, nuclear nonproliferation, naval reactor programs, and radiological emergencies. The Office of Secure Transportation is responsible for secure transportation of nuclear weapons and materials and conducts other missions supporting national security.

The Federal Energy Regulatory Commission manages the Strategic Petroleum Reserve and the interstate transmission of natural gas, oil, and electricity. It also regulates natural gas, hydropower projects, and other energy industries that are in the economic, environmental, or safety interests of the United States. It oversees these industries in an effort to achieve reliable, affordable energy in a fair, competitive market. The commission seeks to promote the development of a strong energy infrastructure and competitive markets and to prevent market manipulation. The DOE Office of Cyber Security maintains the Computer Incident Advisory Capability service, which has provided computer security bulletins since 1989. It also provides advice about how to obtain protection from viruses, hoaxes, and other malicious entities on the Internet.

National Laboratories

DOE sponsors more basic and applied scientific research than any other federal agency, and it employs more than 30,000 scientists and engineers. Most DOE research is funded through the following 21 laboratories and technology centers within its national laboratories system.

The Ames Laboratory synthesizes, analyzes, and engineers rare earth metals and their compounds and conducts research about energy generation and storage. The Argonne National Laboratory, the first national laboratory in the United States, is one of DOE's largest multidisciplinary research centers. It supports more than 200 research projects across the sciences, ranging from studies of the atomic nucleus to global climate change.

The Brookhaven National Laboratory conducts research in the physical, biomedical, and environmental sciences, as well as in energy technologies and national security. The Fermi National Accelerator Laboratory studies the fundamental nature of matter and energy through basic high-energy physics research. The Idaho National Laboratory conducts applied engineering research in environment, energy, science, and national defense areas.

The Lawrence Berkeley National Laboratory conducts research in biology, nanoscience, new energy systems, and integrated computing. The Lawrence Livermore National Laboratory is responsible for the design and engineering of the nuclear stockpile, while the Los Alamos National Laboratory contributes to nuclear deterrence capability. The National Energy Technology Laboratory ensures that U.S. fossil energy resources can meet increasing demand for affordable energy without compromising quality of life for future generations.

The National Renewable Energy Laboratory develops renewable energy and energy efficiency technologies and practices that address the nation's energy and environmental goals. The New Brunswick Laboratory houses the Nuclear Materials Measurements and Reference Materials Laboratory and the National Certifying Authority for measurement calibration standards. The Oak Ridge Institute for Science and Education studies health risks from occupational hazards, assesses environmental cleanup, responds to radiation medical emergencies, and supports national security and emergency preparedness.

The Oak Ridge National Laboratory conducts research to increase the availability of clean, abundant energy; restore and protect the environment; and contribute to national security. The Pacific Northwest National Laboratory seeks to increase U.S. energy capacity and reduce dependence on imported oil, prevent and counter terrorism, and reduce environmental effects of human activities. The Princeton Plasma Physics Laboratory conducts plasma and fusion science, with a leading international role in developing the theoretical, experimental, and technology innovations needed to make fusion practical and affordable. The Radiological and Environmental Sciences Laboratory conducts measurement quality assurance programs and provides technical support and quality assurance metrology.

The Sandia National Laboratories develop technologies that ensure safety of the nuclear weapons stockpile; enhance energy infrastructures; reduce proliferation of weapons of mass destruction, the threat of nuclear accidents, and the potential for damage to the environment; and address new threats to national security. The Savannah River Ecology Laboratory independently evaluates ecological effects of DOE's Savannah River National Laboratory nuclear materials operations through ecological research, education, and outreach. The Stanford Linear Accelerator Center designs, constructs, and operates electron accelerators and related experimental facilities for use in high-energy physics and synchrotron radiation research. The Thomas Jefferson National Accelerator Facility uses continuous beams of high-energy electrons to discover the underlying quark and gluon structure of nucleons and nuclei.

Finally, DOE and its contractors are also responsible for the design, testing, and production of nuclear weapons. Nuclear components of weapon systems are designed and manufactured by Los Alamos National Laboratory, while Lawrence Livermore National Laboratory also designs these components, Sandia National Laboratory does the engineering, the Nevada Test Site tests the systems, and the Pantex ordnance plant in Texas conducts the final assembling and dismantling of weapons and warheads.

Kristen Alley Swain

See also Alternative Energy, Overview; Fuel Cell Technology; Nuclear Power

Further Readings

Council on Environmental Quality, Executive Office of the President of the United States. (2006). *Advanced Energy Initiative*. Available at http://georgewbush-whitehouse.archives.gov/ceq/advanced-energy.html

Energy Independence and Security Act of 2007, Pub. L. 110-140 (2007).

U.S. Department of Energy: www.doe.gov

Dewey, John
(1859–1952)

John Dewey, among the 20th century's most famous and influential philosophers, was born in Burlington, Vermont, on October 20, 1859. He studied at the University of Vermont, graduating in 1879, and then after teaching high school in Pennsylvania until 1881 and in Vermont until 1882, he attended Johns Hopkins University, where he earned his PhD in 1884. In 1886, he married Alice Chipman, who died in 1927. In 1946, he married Roberta Lowitz Grant, who survived him when he died on June 1, 1952. Dewey's long life spanned the U.S. Civil War and both World Wars, not to mention countless other conflicts, industrial developments, and societal changes. His influence as a scholar has been substantial in a number of fields, including philosophy, psychology, the social sciences, and education. His work has helped focus attention on the crucial role of the dissemination of knowledge in democratic societies.

Few philosophers have had as great an impact on their societies as John Dewey. Dewey is most famous for his work in the area of education. Prior to his famous work, *Democracy and Education,* published in 1916, education in the United States followed the European system that was founded on what some scholars have dubbed the "banking theory" of knowledge—that is, in the old way of doing things, as an authority the teacher would deposit his or her wisdom in the empty minds of students. Creative thinking was discouraged, and challenges to authority were treated as heretical. Dewey, however, saw that people were not prepared and empowered for addressing the problems of their own environments, a problem which meant that education was generally abstract, disconnected from students' interests, and often appeared pointless. Dewey understood that in a democratic society, students needed to be guided through a process of learning to address public problems around them. Sometimes history will help us to solve problems, sometimes to create art, but the overall point of studying subject matter was to become reoriented, according to Dewey. Education should address the overall project of developing more intelligent citizens, he thought, who are more able to pursue their own goals as well as to live together harmoniously.

The great influence that Dewey's practical and democratic philosophy has had on disciplines such as education, sociology, psychology, and philosophy is rarely seen in the context of his whole body of work. Dewey came to hold the views he did about education because of how he thought about knowledge and inquiry in the first place. In the traditional approach to the subject of knowledge, an idea was understood as a picture or a mirror of the thing in the world that it represents. With that metaphor supporting all the human sciences, people sought to make more and more accurate pictures. They aimed to achieve certainty about the world using an approach to the sciences that ignored the scientists' purposes and desires. While Dewey understood and valued the avoidance of unjust or misleading bias and lack of objectivity, he recognized the unavoidable nature of inquiry as always undertaken from a given perspective—that is, following the modern insights of philosopher Immanuel Kant, Dewey noted that what we perceive in the world must be conditioned by the kind of observer who perceives it.

In response to these developments, Dewey preferred thinking of knowledge and ideas as a map, metaphorically speaking. A map is drawn for a purpose, though that does not by itself mean that the map lacks objectivity or is biased. Nevertheless, a map must leave out some things while focusing on others. In addition, a map is a kind of tool that in some ways represents things in the world, but a map can never be mistaken for a possibly perfect picture of all there is to the reality of what one is mapping. Also, a map should be judged on whether it is useful and good. It is a true map if it in fact can help one get from point A to point B or if it can help one achieve some other objective for which it is drawn.

With the map metaphor in place, Dewey conceived of inquiry and therefore science as a process of making clear what our objectives are, since some objectives are not properly formed and need to be rethought. Then observations, experiments, and hypotheses can be developed for learning more about the problems we hope to address. Sometimes we find out that our idea of the problem we wanted to study was unclear, inaccurate, not really a problem, or in some other way in need of revision. That is normal, thought Dewey, and is a crucial part of the process of inquiry. In his influential book, *Logic: The Theory of Inquiry,* Dewey presented his outlook on how to rethink the process of inquiry in a way that revised the traditional picture of the theory of knowledge and science. If we do not recognize the purposes we have in inquiry, we can so easily be misled or work on problems that are not worth our efforts. Dewey's theory of inquiry and science, therefore, saw human purposes as matters to be developed, refined, and discussed publicly. Public feedback and debate, he argued, are some of the most powerful forces for refining human intelligence.

With his sense of the power of criticism and public scrutiny, Dewey developed a robust democratic theory. He argued that the demands of public responsibility require educated inquirers and open channels for debate. He saw a need for schools to be available to all citizens, when they had been previously available only to the wealthy. As such, Dewey was an active advocate for public education. Some have called Dewey the patron saint of education.

In the 20th and 21st centuries, philosophy of technology has emerged as a substantial field of study. Industrialization and mechanization have had powerful consequences for enabling human beings to be more comfortable and to live longer. They have also brought with them some devastating costs and possibilities for humankind, however. Given that Dewey was a great advocate for the advancement of human intelligence through education and the sciences, critics of technological progress believe that Dewey was a part of the problem. Followers of Martin Heidegger's philosophy of technology, for instance, thought that people like Dewey did not recognize the worries that arise due to technology. In fact, Dewey has been shown to have been profoundly aware of the costs of technological development and to have had the seeds of a philosophy of technology of his own.

Larry Hickman, director of the Center for Dewey Studies at Southern Illinois University, has written extensively on the subject of a Deweyan philosophy of technology. He explains that to address problems of technology and science, science and technology must be used even more. The solution to environmental degradation has been scientifically driven. Recycling and fuel-efficient light bulbs and automobiles are developed with the help of technological sciences. In sum, Dewey's philosophy of technology, as Hickman has expressed it, holds technological development to be the application of intelligence to address problems. So we must not turn our backs on science and technology when our technological developments come at a cost. Our science and technology need to be enhanced, in fact, such that costs can be balanced or minimized. In this sense, Dewey was a defender of science and likely would be today.

Students of journalism and communication will find a guiding theorist in Dewey. In the fifth chapter of his famous book, *Experience and Nature,* Dewey explained why communication is the greatest of all tools that humanity possesses. Just as ideas are maps and therefore tools for developing, refining, and achieving goals, so too is communication a tool. Dewey describes communication as "wonderful," the building block upon which all public inquiry is founded. Teams of scientists, politicians, educators, and journalists would all be impossible without the ability to make one's own ideas, amazingly, travel from one person's private realm of thoughts to another's. In this way, we see how Dewey's views about knowledge and inquiry led him to see great potential in tools such as language. Language, science, and technology are tools human beings can use collectively to maximize their happiness and future prospects and to address new problems as they arise. With language, education, science, and technology, people can and do pursue greater and greater human ends.

Eric Thomas Weber

See also Deliberative Democracy; Scientific Method

Further Readings

Dewey, J. (1944). *Democracy and education.* New York: The Free Press.

Dewey, J. (1988a). *The later works, 1925–1953: John Dewey: Vol. 1. 1925: Experience and nature* (J. A. Boydston, Ed.). Carbondale: Southern Illinois University Press.

Dewey, J. (1988b). *The later works, 1925–1953: John Dewey: Vol. 2. 1926: The public and its problems* (J. A. Boydston, Ed.). Carbondale: Southern Illinois University Press.

Dewey, J. (2008). *The later works, 1925–1953: John Dewey: Vol. 12. 1938: Logic: The theory of inquiry*

(J. A. Boydston, Ed.). Carbondale: Southern Illinois University Press.

Dewey, J., Hickman, L. A., & Alexander, T. M. (1998). *The essential Dewey* (Vols. 1–2). Bloomington: Indiana University Press.

Hickman, L. (1992). *John Dewey's pragmatic technology.* Indianapolis: Indiana University Press.

Hickman, L. (Ed.). (1998). *Reading Dewey: Interpretations for a postmodern generation.* Indianapolis: Indiana University Press.

Hickman, L. (2001). *Philosophical tools for technological culture: Putting pragmatism to work.* Indianapolis: Indiana University Press.

Rorty, R. (1979). *Philosophy and the mirror of nature.* Princeton, NJ: Princeton University Press.

DIFFUSION OF INNOVATIONS

Diffusion is a multifaceted perspective about social change in which innovations are communicated over time among the members of a social system. Key to understanding this research and practice paradigm is acknowledgment of its emphasis on diffusion as (a) an inherently processual activity that occurs over time (see Figure 1), (b) the relations among people and their organizations as channels through which influence is exchanged in a network of social relations as individuals decide how to respond to an innovation they have previously learned about (see Figure 2), (c) perceptions by potential adopters of innovation characteristics that partly determine whether they will adopt the innovation or not, and (d) the enabling and constraining force of the sociomedia-environmental context in accounting for diffusion.

Scholars dating at least to the German social philosopher Georg Simmel and the French sociologist Gabriel Tarde theorized about imitative behavior at the level of small groups and within communities and the relation between these microlevel processes to macrolevel social change. In the 100 years since, researchers have tended to conceptualize diffusion either at the macrosociological level of sector, system, national, or state change; the social psychological or communicative level of local relationships and how those linkages affect adoption patterns as in a classic study by Elihu Katz and Paul Lazarsfeld; or the psychological level

of how individuals perceive innovations in the form of a codified set of pros and cons. Beginning in the 1960s, diffusion concepts have been operationalized and used to purposively spread prosocial innovations through development communication in Colombia, Pakistan, Brazil, Nigeria, India, Finland, Korea, Tanzania, Bolivia, and Vietnam.

Since 2000, diffusion studies have traced and explained the spread of kindergartens across cultures throughout the world, the spread of schools-of-choice policies among the 50 states in the United States, the diffusion of tobacco control policies back and forth between Canadian and U.S. political jurisdictions, the adoption of participatory approaches in community health system planning, the spread of e-commerce, and the online spread of social norms among adolescents. Studies such as these form the basis of the generalized codification of key concepts and the general pattern of diffusion over time from a literature of more than 5,500 publications as best synthesized by the communication scholar Everett M. Rogers in his successive editions of *Diffusion of Innovations.* Diffusion concepts have also contributed importantly to theoretical and conceptual development of social learning theory, technology transfer, dissemination strategy, social network theory, entertainment education, and now the science and practice of translational studies.

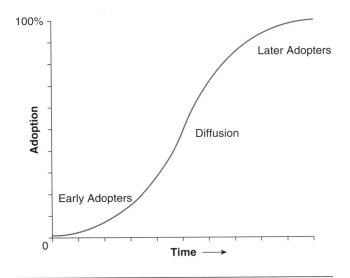

Figure 1   Diffusion is a nonlinear process of social influence over time.

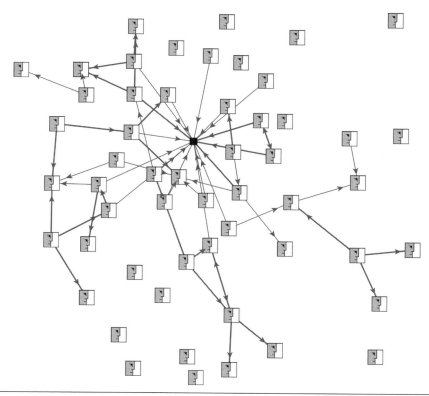

Figure 2   A Sociogram of Who Seeks Advice From Whom for a Certain Innovation

Notes: Arrows show advice-seeking directionality. The solid black node is the informal opinion leader. Innovations seeded by opinion leaders diffuse more rapidly and completely.

An Example of How Diffusion Works

Imagine a chemistry professor who wants to demonstrate her willingness for professional development because her 3-year progress review is only 1 year away. She volunteers to attend a half-day workshop about problem-based learning in the sciences organized by her university's center for teaching excellence. The workshop is interesting to her, yet she decides nothing. Three weeks later, she has a chance conversation in the mailroom with a more senior assistant professor whom she likes. Though she has never seen the other professor teach, she admires her colleague's teaching ability based on students' casual comments about what a good teacher she is and the fact that the friend has won a university teaching award. In the mailroom, the award-winning teacher talks as she recycles a flyer about constructivism as a basis for better teaching. The chemistry teacher, alert, listens. She mentions the problem-based learning workshop.

The award-winning teacher reveals that she organizes many of her classes around problem-based learning. Back in her office, the chemistry teacher decides to try problem-based learning with her chemistry students.

The preceding scenario demonstrates a typical diffusion decision process for an individual: Knowledge is gained through the largely one-way communication of information (in the workshop); persuasion occurs through the two-way communication of social influence in the form of informal, extant local opinion leadership (during the conversation); and a positive adoption decision is made to try a new practice. And note what did not happen: Information alone, in whatever form, is insufficient to move the individual toward a positive decision or even serious contemplation of innovation costs and benefits when the innovation in question is consequential to the potential adopter. Talking was key. And it was not just anyone who was able to prime the chemistry teacher's memory in a productive way. It was someone she knew and already believed to be expert and trustworthy. If someone other than this role model advocates or serves as a social model for the use of problem-based learning, the chemistry teacher likely would not have made the decision she did. Opinion leaders constitute a small proportion of system members (often about 5%), so random approaches to recruitment, volunteerism or self-selection, marketing or advertising, or defaulting to positional authority such as a company president or college dean will usually be ineffective in jumpstarting diffusion.

Main Elements of Diffusion

An *innovation* is anything that potential adopters perceive to be new, inclusive of new ideas and beliefs, explicit and tacit knowledge, processes and protocols, policies, and even value belief systems, according to Rogers. Frequently, studies of the diffusion process focus on scientific or technological innovations and how these are communicated. In the diffusion paradigm, the first 2.5% of adopters are called innovators; the next 13.5% are early adopters (a category that includes the subset of local, informal opinion leaders); this is followed by the early majority (34%), late majority (34%), and laggards (16%). Diffusion conceptualizes individuals as progressing through stages of change as they first confront, make sense of, and then routinize that which was new to them.

Newness is key in the diffusion processes since the perception of newness creates uncertainty in the mind of potential adopters about what they should do or how they should respond to the opportunity presented to them about the innovation. Uncertainty, in turn, leads to a feeling of discomfort or cognitive dissonance, which propels the individual to seek out first descriptive information about the innovation (typically through efficient mediated communication channels such as the Internet) and then evaluative information about how well the innovation performs (most often through nonmediated and mediated interpersonal discussion and observation of others' behaviors). It is at this point that perceptions of the attributes of innovations become important. Simplicity, low cost, and effectiveness, as well as how observable the innovation's results are and how readily tried an innovation is, are all attributes positively related to individual-level adoption and systemwide diffusion.

Thus, in diffusion processes, communication of information through mass and specialty media often precedes the communication of personal influence through informal communication networks, especially local networks. Because people tend to communicate with others whom they recognize as similar to themselves, real and perceived heterophily—differences among people—slows diffusion. Innovations can spread rapidly within one clique or network of like individuals and then take years to achieve acceptance in other networks where members differ in terms of demographics, ethnicity, behavior, and situation.

Linking Macro- With Microphenomena

Many diffusionists take a macrostructural perspective on diffusion, especially those in population planning, demography, economics, international relations, anthropology, and linguistics. Such scholars conceptualize waves of innovations washing over societies and serving as the means by which social change occurs, as in agenda building or agenda setting. Their units of adoption are countries or cultures. A macro-orientation to diffusion is highly enticing to scholars because of its deductive and parsimonious potential based in a simple mathematical law of nature that describes a logistic (S-shaped or exponential) growth curve (see Figure 1). Marketing scientists, epidemiologists, demographers, and political scientists create and test mathematical models of diffusion based on the predictive potential and eloquence of this orientation.

Other scholars, including many in communication studies, conceptualize diffusion at a microlevel of analysis by focusing on the predictors of positive adoption decisions by individuals or organizations, on interpersonal relations and how they mediate the effects of information exposure about innovations, or on local social networks and how network position is related to adoption decisions.

The diffusion paradigm is noteworthy, especially in the work of Rogers, for deliberately offering explanations based on empirical studies of how macrochange processes are linked to microindividual and group level processes. The explanations offered show both how microlevel units of adoption (usually people) are influenced by system norms, as well as how system change is dependent on individual action. Diffusion is one of the very few social theories that persuasively link macro- with microlevel phenomena.

Mass Media, Specialty Media, and New Media

Mass communication channels are the most efficient means for spreading awareness of innovations that have popular or broad appeal. When the innovation in question is only an idea, as in knowing something new, awareness equates with adoption. Often, however, agencies or organizations have objectives that require more of adopters. To adopt, they must engage in a new practice, buy a new service, or commit to learn a new routine. In these cases, mass communication functions to raise awareness and, for some, produce information-seeking behavior. For innovations with specialized appeal, such as new medical procedures or disease prevention interventions, specialty media in the form of targeted magazines, industry newsletters, and conference presentations function to spread awareness.

The promise of new media, especially the Internet and portable telecommunications, is high, and not only for speeding up the awareness of innovations. New media, especially formats such as tailored interactive Web pages that allow for various portrayals of innovations, can be designed to encourage choice and a sense of ownership among potential and actual adopters, to show social modeling of the innovation, and to increase efficacy. Customized Web sites can, for example, increase the likelihood that modifications made during the implementation of adopted innovations will not be counterproductive. Insisting on innovation fidelity by discouraging or prohibiting adaptation is negatively related to adoption. Portable digital assistants and cell phones can be used to reinforce decisions in diffusion-based health campaigns.

Innovation Quality and Diffusion

Many people assume that high quality, especially when paired with low cost, will result in rapid diffusion. This expectation is often not met. Many innovations that have a tangible basis spread because of other factors, such as bandwagon effects in which managers or administrators are afraid of lagging competitive rivals or because the decision to adopt is decoupled from responsibility for implementation. In both cases, diffusion can be extensive, but implementation and use can be quite limited.

The diffusion literature includes many examples of advantageous innovations that do not achieve widespread use, even after many years and when campaigns are conducted to publicize them. This is so even for highly effective "best practice" innovations that have demonstrated, empirical advantages compared to alternative ways of achieving the same ends, and it is so even when studying diffusion within the same organization, where the rate of adoption might be expected to be more rapid than the adoption across separate organizations. Concerning innovation diffusion, what is best and what is used are frequently different.

Cases from the diffusion literature do not stop at highlighting effective innovations that do not diffuse; we also have cases of innovations with very important implications for adopters that spread prior to the communication of any information about their effectiveness, such as in the rapid imitation of strike behavior by 18th-century coal miners as studied by Carol Conell and Samuel Cohn. Fads and fashions occur regularly; having an innovation received by potential adopters as fashionable can be highly desirable. Yet other studies have documented the diffusion of ineffective innovations.

In sum, while effectiveness is typically positively related to positive adoption decisions, the correlation can be weak, with other factors more highly correlated with adoption. Social influence is one of those factors.

Diffusion as a Social Process

Opinion leaders influence the decisions that others make about innovations that are communicated to them. Opinion leaders are the reason why diffusion can be such a very efficient process to jumpstart: An innovation source or sponsor need only communicate an innovation to a special small subset of all possible adopters for the innovation to spread through a social system. Their existing influence and the extent to which followers monitor the attitudes and behaviors of opinion leaders can do the rest as long as opinion leader attitudes are favorable toward the new practice and followers positively identify the opinion leader with the innovation. The social influence of opinion leaders, either by talking or by example setting, is what drives the diffusion curve up, giving it its characteristic S shape. Opinion leaders are also responsible for innovations not diffusing, by ignoring an innovation (passive rejection) or by speaking out against it (active rejection). Studies of higher-order aggregates demonstrate opinion leader effects through interorganizational networks and among counties and nations.

Different individuals take different amounts of time to adopt innovations. For some, only one or two people in their personal networks or reference groups are required to adopt before they adopt; for others, nearly all others in their personal networks or reference groups must adopt before they finally convert. These differences are thresholds that vary person to person for any particular innovation.

Beginning with the empirical results of Bryce Ryan and Neal Gross published in 1943, diffusion has been understood to be a social process. While knowledge is often gained through the largely one-way communication of information, especially with the increased information search capabilities of new communication technologies, persuasion occurs through the two-way communication of social influence, most commonly in the form of local informal opinion leaders who are already in place and who already influence the decisions of others. Information alone, whether in one-on-one counseling or in a training workshop, Web site, brochure, and so on, is insufficient to move the individual toward a positive decision or even serious contemplation of innovation costs and benefits when the innovation in question is perceived to be consequential by the potential adopter.

Opinion leaders are perceived as expert and trustworthy, influential, credible, popular, near-peer friends, and accessible. The trait opinion leadership tends to be stable across time and operates consistently across social systems such as hospitals, schools, towns, and even distributed networks. However, in intervention work, opinion leaders are especially effective when they are not asked to do too much. Asking opinion leaders to advocate, persuade, promote, or educate in ways they normally would not with their colleagues is asking them to risk their status within the system in question by formalizing what is an informal role.

Intervening to Diffuse an Innovation by Using Opinion Leadership

Many intervention studies have demonstrated the viability of identifying informal opinion leaders and then recruiting them to help in a diffusion-based campaign. Consider the international problem of ineffective obstetrical practices.

In thousands of hospitals, evidence-based birthing practices are underused, while ineffective and harmful practices continue. Previous efforts at improving birth attendant performance in Mexico and Thailand by providing access to the latest information about evidence-based practices resulted in no change in what birth attendants do. Fernando Althabe and colleagues decided to test whether identifying informal opinion leaders via the formative administration of a sociometric questionnaire to identify opinion leaders who are best connected in social systems (see Figure 2) and then intervening with them in hospitals might help. Published in *The New England Journal of Medicine* in 2008, the study randomly assigned 19 hospitals in Argentina and Uruguay to receive a multifaceted behavioral intervention involving opinion leaders, workshops, training, one-on-one academic detailing, reminders, and feedback.

Desirable practices increased, and undesirable practices decreased at the intervention hospitals as compared with control hospitals. At intervention hospitals where opinion leaders had been sociometrically identified by questionnaire and then contacted and recruited to help, the rate of use of prophylactic oxytocin during the third stage of labor increased from 2.1% to 83.6%! Opinion leading birth attendants were key to the 18-month intervention's success, and they were eager to help by talking with their work colleagues in positive terms about evidence-based birthing practices. Importantly, practice changes were sustained for 12 months after the end of the intervention.

James W. Dearing

See also Conversation and Science Communication; Opinion Leaders and Opinion Leadership; Translational Research

Further Readings

Althabe, F., Buekens, P., Bergel, E., Belizan, J. M., Campbell, M. K., Moss, N., et al. (2008). A behavioral intervention to improve obstetrical care. *New England Journal of Medicine, 358*(18), 1929–1940.

Conell, C., & Cohn, S. (1995). Learning from other people's actions: Environmental variation and diffusion in French coal mining strikes, 1890–1935. *American Journal of Sociology, 101*(2), 366–403.

Dearing, J. W., Maibach, E., & Buller, D. (2006). A convergent diffusion and social marketing approach for disseminating proven approaches to physical activity promotion. *American Journal of Preventive Medicine, 31*(Suppl. 4), S11–S23.

Katz, E., & Lazarsfeld, P. F. (1955). *Personal influence: The part played by people in the flow of mass communications.* New York: Free Press.

Manning, K. C., Bearden, W. O., & Madden, T. J. (1995). Consumer innovativeness and the adoption process. *Journal of Consumer Psychology, 4*(4), 329–345.

Rogers, E. M. (2003). *Diffusion of innovations* (5th ed.). New York: Free Press.

Ryan, B., & Gross, N. C. (1943). The diffusion of hybrid seed corn in two Iowa communities. *Rural Sociology, 8,* 15–24.

Weimann, G. (1994). *The influentials: People who influence people.* Albany: State University of New York Press.

DIGITAL DIVIDE

Digital divide generally refers to the relative advantage individuals or groups of people gain over others as the result of their access to and use of communicative technologies, such as the Internet. This gap—or divide—is considered digital largely because many technological advances over the last half of the 20th century have been based on digital, as opposed to analog, technology. While some scholars have limited use of the term *digital divide* specifically to Internet diffusion and access, there are many who conceptualize being digital as including a wide variety of other information and communication technologies (ICTs) such as cellular phones, satellite television receivers, and personal computers. As these technologies were initially developed, there was little concern that they might contribute to the stratification of societies principally because they were cost prohibitive. More recently, however, it has become apparent that digital communication devices can be economically mass produced and distributed to a vast number of individuals—along with relevant knowledge and skill sets.

It has been well established, most notably by Everett Rogers, that innovations are typically diffused in an S-shaped curve where the number of adopters continues to grow so long as a relative advantage is perceived. Crucially, though, digital media technologies were not uniformly available or accepted in all sectors of national and international populations at equivalent rates due to economic, technological, political, and cultural factors. As a result of disparate adoption rates, a cleavage developed and then widened between digital haves and have-nots. It is important to note that the effects of the digital divide reach far beyond the actual diffusion of the innovations themselves. Most scholars now agree that technologies, digital or otherwise, are value-free and should be viewed as deterministic. This is to say that no technology is inherently good or bad or democratic or capitalistic. Rather, these and any other moral characteristics exist in the individuals and the crucial uses they make of communication technologies. In the case of the digital divide, the unequal diffusion of digital communication technologies often reinforces socioeconomic, political, and cultural chasms precisely because of the different uses that individuals make of these technologies.

Equally important are the ways in which the digital divide operates on a number of different social levels. First, there is an easily observable individual level digital divide. Here, individuals who have access and are able to harness the advantages of digital technologies contribute to their own socioeconomic advancement above other individuals with less access to digital technologies or who have merely lower levels of technology literacy. Second, intrastate digital divides are increasingly apparent among populations within different countries such that entire regions are technologically behind the diffusion curve of the rest of the population. This situation typically increases the economic and cultural distance of such regions (such as more rural areas) from other areas of the nation. Third, interstate digital divides have emerged across different countries that have high and low levels of digital technology diffusion. This particular development positions less developed countries as even less able to compete equally in the globalized marketplace because of the very same limitations in resources and infrastructure that had already hindered their development.

In other words, instead of promoting a more equitable social arena with more opportunity for socioeconomic, political, and cultural unification, the unequal distribution of digital communication technologies can actually contribute to the maintenance and even the exacerbation of social hierarchies. Moreover, the effects of the digital divide can be felt across social levels, and it is evolving and ongoing—that is, even in the instance that an individual, region, or nation can catch up to a certain level of digital technology deployment, the rapidity with which new innovations are reached nevertheless renders them technological laggards who are unable to fully engage with their more advanced counterparts. Such a situation has been particularly evident during the transition to broadband Internet and Web 2.0 applications where only a relatively small portion of the online population can actually make full use of the Internet's most participatory and perhaps most efficacious functions.

Nearly all scholars and policymakers agree that the digital divide needs to be narrowed on all social levels. Closing those gaps, however, remains a challenging task. In many cases, ICTs are most likely to benefit individuals, groups, and nations who have the resources to adopt them relatively early in their diffusion curve—so long as the particular technology, service, or device is also deemed by other individuals and groups to offer similar relative advantages. Investment in unproven technologies, though, is often fraught with risks and realistically may be undertaken only by those individuals or groups with a certain level of resources and expertise in existing technologies. In some cases, communication technologies have been reported to enable *leapfrogging*—a phenomenon that suggests that stages of technological, financial, and human investment can be bypassed during the development process. One such example is the relatively widespread implementation of cellular phones in countries where little to no landline phone infrastructure existed, but few other examples have been empirically observed. This apparent lack of examples has led scholars to consider leapfrogging a largely theoretical idea, with few practical applications.

Research has also demonstrated that simply providing access to digital media technologies is unlikely to entirely resolve any existing digital divides. This is because not all users are able to complete the same functions or use the technology to the same capacity as other, more experienced users. Thus, there is evidence of a second-level digital divide even among populations that already have access to and use digital communicative technologies. Precisely because the digital divide operates both across as well as within social and technological levels, ICTs still, paradoxically, threaten to fragment and disempower those individuals, groups, and nations that exist as being digital have-nots from those with the technological, financial, and personal resources to tap the remarkable potential of modern digital media technologies.

Jacob Groshek

See also Diffusion of Innovations; Knowledge Gap Hypothesis; Technological Determinism; Technological Literacy

Further Readings

Norris, P. (2001). *Digital divide: Civic engagement, information poverty, and the Internet worldwide.* New York: Cambridge University Press.

Rogers, E. (2003). *Diffusion of innovations* (5th ed.). New York: The Free Press.

Sunstein, C. R. (2007). *Republic.com 2.0.* Princeton, NJ: Princeton University Press.

van Dijk, J. A. G. M. (2006). *The network society: Social aspects of new media.* Thousand Oaks, CA: Sage.

DIGITAL RHETORIC AND SCIENCE

Rhetoric has been defined historically as the use of symbols, including language, in the act of persuasion. It can be argued that all communication is rhetorical in that it seeks to change belief or influence action. Some people think that science is not rhetorical, or in other words, that scientists simply uncover facts and present these facts plainly without needing to persuade. However, many scientists and researchers in the fields of communication studies, English, and rhetoric argue that when scientists present the results of their research, they are not just reporting facts, but are instead making arguments about how findings should be interpreted, establishing their own credibility, and attempting to create confidence in and enthusiasm for their work. Lawrence Prelli argues that scientific discourse aims to persuade others to attach particular meanings to particular phenomena and that, like all rhetoric, scientific rhetoric is greatly influenced by the intended audience and the geographic and cultural environment in which it takes place. Thus, scientific rhetoric in England in the 17th century was different from that in the United States in the 19th century; likewise, an argument made by a geologist is different from one made by an astrophysicist or a molecular geneticist. Similarly, we might expect that scientific rhetoric is affected by the medium of communication: oral discussion at a scientific conference, publication in a print journal, and various forms of electronic digital media, especially on the Internet and the World Wide Web.

If rhetoric is the art of persuasion, then digital rhetoric is the art of persuasion in digital media such as Web sites, Weblogs (or blogs), wikis, and e-mail. Scientists who work at some distance from each other have traditionally communicated at professional conferences, by mail, and by writing articles in scientific journals. Scientists still communicate in these ways, but much of their communication is now taking place online. Many scientists, especially those employed at universities, keep professional Web sites with information about their research. Scientists also use e-mail to communicate with each other one-on-one, and they use e-mail Listservs to communicate with groups of scientists with interests similar to theirs. Some of this activity may result from the rise in what is called "Big Science"—beginning with the Manhattan Project—in which many researchers from all over the country or the world work together on large projects, especially in fields such as high-energy particle physics, which requires the use of enormous, highly specialized facilities such as the Large Hadron Collider (LHC) on the border between France and Switzerland. Many of the scientists who work on projects that use the LHC work on site, but others work far away. Digital media allow scientists working far from each other to communicate quickly.

Regardless of whether a small group of scientists work together in a laboratory at a single institution or hundreds of scientists collaborate across the globe, the results of a research program must be periodically reported. When scientists have research results to report, they often publish research articles in online journals. Some of these journals let readers comment on these articles online, giving scientists a new way to discuss the latest research findings. Also, most major funding agencies now require grant proposals to be submitted through electronic systems, such as grants.gov and the National Science Foundation's FastLane system. Many scientists also write about science in blogs for other scientists, for the general public, or for both, and they contribute to wikis, which are Web sites that can be edited or modified by readers.

Important features of scientific rhetoric that may be affected by digital media include audience, authorship, and genre. We discuss these issues in digital scientific rhetoric below.

Audience and the Scientific Community

At its most basic level, communication occurs between two parties: a sender and a receiver. More broadly, communication takes place within a community. The audience in science might be a colleague down the hall, a collaborator across the globe, or the many scientists working in a particular field of research. The group of other scientists that a particular scientist interacts with professionally has been called an *invisible college*, a term that captures both the very important professional connections that exist between colleagues and the much less formal nature of the relationship between researchers who work at different institutions compared to members of the same department or agency. By enabling more communication to take place online in public spaces, digital media may be making these invisible colleges more visible and more concrete than they used to be.

Audience is an important topic in rhetoric because the intended audience for a communication is a major factor in the structure, form, and rhetorical purpose of that communication. For example, Ann Blakeslee examined how a group of physicists carefully tailored an article they were writing for a journal that is read mostly by chemists. They realized that they could not write the article the same way for chemists as they would if they were writing for other physicists, so they connected their research to issues that they felt would be of particular interest in the field of chemistry. Digital media enlarge the potential audience for a publication, so other groups such as the public have much greater access than they used to. A consequence of this may be that the exclusivity of the scientific community is weakened. This seems to be especially true in blogs about science, which are often read by scientists and laypeople.

Another important aspect of digital media that sets it apart from traditional print media is that it is interactive, making the audience's role potentially different from that in print media—that is, as Barbara Warnick points out, electronic media allow users to interact with other users, with the documents they are using, and even with the system itself. James P. Zappen argues that the interactivity afforded by electronic media emphasizes dialogue more than persuasion because they facilitate cooperative building up of knowledge. Thus, students and citizens may be able to contribute to scientific knowledge in new ways, influencing funding decisions or contributing data through field observations of birds or other natural phenomena.

Authorship

Digital media have called many of our assumptions and practices about authorship into question. Not only have they provided new technologies for collaborative authorship (such as Google Docs and proprietary systems such as Lotus Notes that are used within large companies and agencies), but they have also made it more difficult for us to keep thinking of the author as someone who originates and controls a text. Because digital texts are so easy to replicate, parts of a text may be copied and included in another text, or a text may be changed and still attributed to the original author. In addition, digital works that include links or are available in a linked environment may be encountered far from their original contexts, or a reader may link in and link out following his or her own train of thought rather than the author's.

Traditional rhetoric teaches that the character of the author is possibly the most important factor in persuasion because we need to judge credibility before believing something. In science, these judgments are often made on the basis of the author's affiliation and expertise, the methods used, and the quality of the reasoning. In the digital environment, because of the loss of authorial control, these judgments may be more difficult for the audience to make. Barbara Warnick has suggested that under these conditions, we judge credibility in ways that go beyond specific authors to include the digital environment in which a text is located; for example, features such as ease of navigation, expertise, and convenience may not have the same importance for the credibility of a medical Web site such as Medline as they do for a media Web site such as CNN.

Digital media also make it possible for scientific authors to modify data displays, such as electron micrographs or any other data produced by scientific instruments, by enhancing color or contrast or by changing the scale or scope of a graph. Thus, to preserve the credibility of data, many scientific journals have developed strict guidelines on what kinds of changes are allowable.

Genres and Media

Scientists use a variety of media and *genres,* or types of communication. A medium is a technology or vehicle for communication, such as e-mail or blogs. A genre may be thought of as a collection of texts that have something in common, such as a similar form or a common location in a particular medium. Recently, scholars have considered a text's social action to be the most important characteristic in determining its genre. In other words, an e-mail message calling a meeting of a research team and an e-mail message asking a coworker for a piece of information might look very similar, but they may actually be intended to accomplish different things, so they might be considered to be of different genres.

The set of genres used in a particular community can tell us a lot about that community, including its values and social structure. Even comparing the genres used by scientists in different fields can be instructive. For example, high-energy physicists often make extensive use of online *preprints,* which are drafts of articles that are published at the arXiv e-print repository (www.arxiv.org) hosted by Cornell University. These e-prints are a primary way that scientists in these fields learn about the latest research. Usually the research reported initially in e-prints is published in traditional journals later on. Journal articles in these fields are not used to communicate cutting-edge research but instead are used, in effect, to "stamp" the work as being professionally valid so that the scientists receive credit for the work. In contrast, biochemists typically do not communicate new research via preprints but rather through traditional journals, which also double as professional "currency," much in the same way that journal articles in physics do. The differences in the genre sets in these fields may reflect that the high-energy physics community is smaller and more closely connected than the biochemistry community is because they are more willing to communicate important research findings with less formal vetting.

New media have made possible other new genres. Some of these include electronic annotations and comments about research articles in online journals, online laboratory notebooks reporting new data in nearly real time, and blogs in which scientists and laypeople discuss the latest issues in science.

Conclusion

As more and more communication in science takes place in digital form, the rhetorical nature of this communication in these spaces is drawing increased attention from researchers. Important areas of future research in this area include how online credibility is determined by readers when the message source cannot be readily ascertained and how this might vary between scientific fields, how similar ideas and expressions are used across multiple texts (a phenomenon sometimes called *intertextuality*), the predicted demise of the journal and the evolution of the research article, and public communication of science in blogs and other online media.

Christian F. Casper and Carolyn R. Miller

See also Audiences for Science; Big Science; Invisible College; Scientific Journal, History of

Further Readings

Bazerman, C. (1988). *Shaping written knowledge: The genre and activity of the experimental article in science.* Madison: University of Wisconsin Press.

Blakeslee, A. M. (2001). *Interacting with audiences: Social influences on the production of scientific writing.* Mahwah, NJ: Lawrence Erlbaum.

Crane, D. (1972). *Invisible colleges: Diffusion of knowledge in scientific communities.* Chicago: University of Chicago Press.

Crawford, S. Y., Hurd, J. M., & Weller, A. C. (1996). *From print to electronic: The transformation of scientific communication.* Medford, NJ: Information Today.

Prelli, L. J. (1989). *A rhetoric of science: Inventing scientific discourse.* Columbia: University of South Carolina Press.

Swales, J. M. (2004). *Research genres: Explorations and applications.* Cambridge, UK: Cambridge University Press.

Warnick, B. (2007). *Rhetoric online: Persuasion and politics on the World Wide Web.* New York: Peter Lang.

Zappen, J. P. (2005). Digital rhetoric: Toward an integrated theory. *Technical Communication Quarterly, 14,* 319–325.

Ziman, J. (1968). *Public knowledge: The social dimension of science.* Cambridge, UK: Cambridge University Press.

DISASTER COVERAGE

Science and technology play a role in every part of life. When disasters occur—be they those that are sudden, catastrophic, and widespread or those that occur slowly and in a constrained location—people will seek out experts to provide answers, insight, or advice. Science and technology communicators may be called on to help facilitate this process.

Science and technology have an important role to play in understanding why disasters happen and how to recover from them and rebuild. When earthquakes and tsunamis occur, scientists such as seismologists and geologists may be asked to explain tectonic plates and how their movements cause such devastating effects. People may ask meteorologists how hurricanes form and ask climatologists if they are increasing in frequency because of climate change. If there is an explosion at a factory or a chemical process goes wrong, then engineers, chemists, or physicists may be asked to explain why.

Disasters create high stress, anxiety, fear, thoughts about death, and grief, particularly for people directly affected by the loss of loved ones or property. Key questions are usually, Why did this happen? and How do we try to ensure it does not happen again?

This entry examines possible roles and responsibilities for science and technology experts in disaster situations and the key considerations for experts participating in public discussion. The case study summarizes the media coverage of the Commonwealth Scientific and Industrial Research Organisation (CSIRO, Australia's largest research agency) after devastating bushfires in Victoria, Australia, in 2009. Further discussion suggests areas for organizations to focus on to contribute to the dissemination of accurate science and to develop their capacity to respond to inquiries about disasters.

Science Communication in Relationship to Disaster

It is important for anyone planning to communicate the science of a disaster to examine the perspective of communication. In some cases, individual scientists or organizations will need to formulate a communication plan because they have directly contributed to the disaster. This is a very different situation from providing explanations from the perspective of an expert assisting society to understand the disaster.

A significant amount of published literature and online information describes best practices for organizations responsible for managing or communicating risk, offering advice to prepare for a disaster, or even those directly causing a disaster (for example, in the case of an explosion at a chemical plant). Science and technology representatives may have a role in what leads up to disasters and may also be called on to answer questions about them, potentially affecting the reputation of the quoted person or their agency, or even leading to legal or criminal action.

News Cycle

When a disaster first occurs, there may be no remaining information technology infrastructure in the local area to connect with the wider world. Communicators and reporters who are present at the location will have an especially important role to play. The media becomes a vital link between the disaster-affected region and the rest of the world.

Immediately following a disaster, there may be a huge amount of media attention as communities try to find out what is happening, governments try to deal with the situation and warn people, and media try to disseminate stories to the rest of the country and internationally. Experts will be sought to explain what has happened and to provide specialist angles. Communication staff may have to field hundreds of calls from journalists around the world.

With the instantaneous access provided by online and other media, coverage of the disaster will quickly flow around the world: Close to 1.7 billion people were using the Internet in 2001 at the time of the Gujarat earthquake in India. In their paper about the use of the online environment for media reporting and the formation of online communities, researchers Kris Kodrich and Melinda Laituri found that the Internet raised the awareness of the Gujarat earthquake and helped create a global community transcending national boundaries and enabling multiple lines of communication.

Initially, the media profile of scientists with relevant expertise is elevated following a disaster. While it is important to convey accurate information regarding the cause of the disaster and its impacts, it is also important that scientists do not appear opportunistic in such an emotionally charged time. The public may misinterpret scientific comment as exploitation of the situation for personal or institutional promotion. Experts and communicators should assist the media to understand the issues, without inappropriately promoting their organization. It is also wise to put forward only those spokespeople who have a strong reputation, have had media training and experience, and are experts in the particular field.

Another consideration is to be cautious of the tone of the messages being delivered, as poorly framed pessimism could cause additional alarm unnecessarily. Experts providing public comment in such a situation must consider the devastating effects on those touched by the event and ensure that their comments are not only scientifically accurate, but also considerate of people's loss. In the sensitive time soon after a disaster, objective explanations for the occurrence of the disaster can help calm those wondering if it will happen again soon and can also assist with the healing process for those affected.

One common complaint from communities affected by disasters is that there is much initial attention, but then interest wanes, and the rebuilding of lives and livelihoods takes years.

As the acute phase of the disaster reduces, people will start to reflect on more in-depth explanations or longer-term implications of the disaster, and this again provides a situation where people may turn to science and technology for answers. The media will probably still be reporting on the disaster, but they will be seeking new angles for their stories. There may be focus on who is to blame and weighing into this debate can potentially cause inaccurate and emotionally charged attention from both the media and society. In the long term, experts may be asked to provide advice on the cleanup and rebuilding effort as well. They may also be asked to provide opinions to the media, to government, or even to legal inquiries regarding the disaster, its impacts, and the likelihood of a similar event reoccurring. Communicators may be required during all these stages to play facilitating or coordinating roles between experts and the wider community.

Case Study: Bushfires in Australia, February 2009

On February 7, 2009, catastrophic bushfires occurred in Victoria, in southeast Australia. Communities suffered widespread loss of life and property. Australia's CSIRO has significant expertise and experience in bushfire research, including fire behavior, fire-resistant materials, and the impact of climate change on fire risk. This scientific expertise has many audiences, including fire-aware or at-risk communities and individuals; state and national fire, forest, land, water, and environmental agencies; farmers and land resource users; scientists (Australian and international); the general public; and policymakers and politicians.

This wide-ranging group of audiences was considered in the preparation of the bushfire communication strategy, which was put into practice in February 2009. The bushfires generated hundreds

of media inquiries for CSIRO and other science institutions from local and international journalists. The greatest peak in media coverage for CSIRO occurred in the first 10 days after the fires, with most of this concentrated in the first 2 days.

CSIRO scientists were initially sought to provide insight into the following issues:

- Why the bushfires were so catastrophic
- Why the fires behaved the way they did
- What people should do if caught in a bushfire
- Whether the fires were related to climate change

In the week after the bushfires, further analysis of the events occurred, and many people raised questions over the adequacy of warning systems and the validity of protection systems, such as bunkers. Areas the media subsequently covered in more detail included the following issues:

- Questions of who was to blame for the devastation
- Fire behavior, progress, and movement
- Fire and fuel load management and controlled burning
- Bunkers and other ways to protect from fire
- Appropriate responses to the fire (relating to fire authorities' "stay or go" policy: either prepare, stay, and defend, or leave early)
- Climate change
- A future Royal Commission
- Questions of whether funding had been sufficient and correctly targeted for fire research

The coverage of CSIRO-related bushfire communication recorded online around the world occurred in Australia-Oceania (66%), North America (19%), Europe (8%), Asia Pacific (2%), Asia (2%), Middle East (2%), and Africa (1%).

Analysis of visitors to the CSIRO organization's Web site revealed that in the first 2 weeks after the bushfires, there was approximately a 10-fold increase in the page views on the bushfire introduction and bushfire research overview pages. The additional online traffic from people searching for fire information resulted in approximately an extra 10,000 page views per week (on top of the average 220,000 per week). From CSIRO's perspective, the majority of the media inquiries resulted in accurate dissemination of the science.

Organizational Strategy

To ensure that accurate science and suitable experts were available to add constructively to the public discussion of the bushfires, CSIRO immediately launched a crisis communication strategy. This strategy aimed to do the following:

- Prepare and support scientific experts for explaining their science at such a distressing time
- Effectively manage the high volume of media and public inquiries
- Provide the media with experienced CSIRO spokespeople with relevant research expertise
- Monitor potential issues and related media coverage

The strategy operated under three primary guidelines: first, to facilitate media accessibility to expert comment from CSIRO; second, to focus on the science (specifically the spokesperson's field of expertise); and third, to avoid speculation on the causes of the fires so as not to preempt the official investigation and Royal Commission. The strategy included steps that enabled CSIRO to do the following:

- Rapidly assemble experts and communication staff with relevant knowledge and engage with them frequently, such as via daily telephone conferences
- Develop and circulate a contact list for efficient internal use and to identify secondary spokespeople to reduce the load where possible
- Connect quickly with organizational contacts (including management, legal contacts, and media liaison) and external stakeholders such as collaborating science agencies and government departments with responsibilities related to the disaster
- Establish a dedicated 24-hour central contact point for media, government, and general public inquiries
- Assist spokespeople to develop key messages, ensure that these key messages were discussed among those who are commenting in the media, and seek wider input to the key messages from relevant parts of the organization
- Establish a designated section of the organization's Web site to include summary information, spokespeople's resumes, and common questions and answers (these worked particularly well at reducing the load on scientists for basic information)
- Provide active support, including on-the-ground media liaison, to spokespeople through advice and assistance in managing relationships with key stakeholders
- Provide experts visiting disaster areas with advice on appropriate attire and equipment when doing so—it is especially important for experts to be easily identified in their official capacity, as affected communities might grow resentful of sightseers
- Monitor daily media reporting of issues
- Avoid spokesperson fatigue through careful management of inquiries and streamlining organizational demands on key scientists
- Proactive scoping of media coverage to identify which areas media inquiries might cover

In summary, the following points should be considered to ensure the provision of relevant science information during a disaster:

Have procedures in place to deal with any disaster. It is important to have current, clear, well-documented, and well-supported procedures in place prior to a disaster. This allows an organization to respond rapidly if disasters occur. Do as much brainstorming as possible about areas of science or technology that could be called upon when things go wrong and when questions arise regarding who may be affected and what the potential ramifications could be. The process will take time, but will undoubtedly help emergency response and increase confidence regarding putting in place processes that will result in the best outcomes for the scientists, the organization, the media, and the general public.

Engage with as many people as possible. At the time of a disaster, organizational representatives will no doubt have to call on others for support and guidance. If a strategy has previously been discussed with management, legal consultants, media advisors, and relevant government departments, it will be easier and faster to implement the strategy. Ensure everyone understands and is supportive of the process and ready to assist when called on for support.

Have suitable scientific and media contacts. It is important to scope possible areas of expertise that can be called upon during a future disaster and identify relevant contacts, both in partner or collaborative organizations and in the media. It must be ensured that scientific spokespeople have had media training and are equipped to cope with the situation. At the time of a disaster and associated heightened interest, a media conference can be a far more effective and efficient vehicle for disseminating information than numerous individual interviews.

Develop and discuss key messages. In the time available, it is important to develop clear key messages that are easily understood. These should be discussed among the identified key spokespeople. They should also be canvassed with others from relevant parts of the organization to acknowledge diversity in expert opinion. In multidisciplinary areas, many experts may have a valid view on what has occurred, so points of difference and common ground should be identified. Once developed, the key messages can then be provided to all involved in the communication effort. Clear messages, delivered by relevant scientists with training and experience in dealing with the media, provide the best chance of media and public uptake of accurate science. Such coordination and preparation also reduces the likelihood of confusion about the take-home message and ensures the integrity of scientists and the organization is maintained.

Make sure resources and expertise are adequate. Professional communication expertise is vital in organizations. There should be adequate resources, including media liaison officers, Web writers and designers, science writers, and administrative and operational support for those in the field.

Conclusion

Science and technology have an important role to play in helping the community understand the where, why, how, when, and what of natural and human disasters. When disasters occur, there can be much pain, suffering, fear, and loss. Science and technology experts need to be on hand to explain the science behind disasters, and they have a responsibility to provide accurate information that is respectful and mindful of those most directly affected. In many cases, organizational communicators have a significant role to play in enabling access to accurate scientific information as well as credible experts.

Although using windows of opportunity is a legitimate method of raising science awareness, in the case of disasters, society will judge harshly an expert who is seen to be opportunistic or disrespectful of the situation. Reputations and credibility will be at stake. Undertaken properly, communication by science experts can help communities come to terms with disasters and be better prepared for future events; handled poorly, the communication could lead to further and inexcusable suffering, alongside professional damage to the spokespeople and their agencies.

Claire Harris, Simon Torok, and Karina Clement

See also Chernobyl; Crisis Communication; Risk Communication, Overview; Three Mile Island

Further Readings

Baruch, F. (2005, January). We need the right words to weather the storm. *The Washington Post.* Retrieved July 15, 2009, from www.washingtonpost.com/wp-dyn/content/article/2005/09/30/AR2005093002078.html

Chui, G. (2006). Earth sciences. In D. Blum, M. Knudson, & R. M. Henig (Eds.), *A field guide for science writers* (2nd ed., pp. 236–242). Oxford, UK: Oxford University Press.

Gunawardene, N. (2009, July 12). *Reporting disasters: How to keep a cool head when all hell breaks loose.* Blog posted to *Moving images, moving people.* Retrieved August 21, 2009, from http://movingimages.wordpress.com/2009/07/12/reporting-disasters-how-to-keep-a-cool-head-when-all-hell-breaks-loose

Gunawardene, N., & Noronha, F. (Ed.). (2007). *Communicating disasters: An Asia Pacific resource book.* Bangkok, Thailand: UNDP Regional Centre in Bangkok and TVE Asia Pacific. Available at www.tveap.org

Kodrich, K., & Laituri, M. (2005). The formation of a disaster community in cyberspace: The role of online news media after the 2001 Gujarat earthquake. *Convergence: The International Journal of Research Into New Media Technologies, 11*(3), 40–56. doi: 10.1177/135485650501100304

Leiss, W., & Powell, D. (2004). *Mad cows and mother's milk: The perils of poor risk communication* (2nd ed.). Montreal, QC, Canada: McGill-Queen's University Press.

DISCOURSE ANALYSIS AND SCIENCE

Discourse analysis is the study of the features of discourse, both written and spoken, in their social context. For written discourse, these features include word choice, grammatical structures, organizational strategies of texts, or groups of related texts. Applied to science communication, discourse analysis focuses on laboratory notebooks, published research articles, technical reports, textbooks, and public communications, all within their particular social contexts. Researchers also study drafts, revision notes, and other unfinished texts that offer insight into a writer's choices and communication strategies. With its focus on how language shapes and is shaped by social structures and institutions, discourse analysis provides insight into the choices that science communicators make when they write and how those choices are informed by social and institutional forces. Discourse analysis helps researchers and practitioners identify how conventions of scientific discourse are formed and how social forces shape and maintain them.

To illustrate how discourse analysis contributes to our understanding of science and technology communication, this entry will discuss the definition of discourse analysis in more detail, present specific examples of research questions from this approach, explain some of the most important work in discourse analysis, and outline controversies regarding linguistic and rhetorical studies of science.

Background and Examples

Discourse analysis has its origins in the field of sociolinguistics and maintains an emphasis on the ways that language interacts with social institutions, values, and communities. In concrete terms, social institutions can include the academic system of tenure and publishing, values include prestige or reputation of individuals or institutions, and communities might range from an entire discipline (for example, all biologists) to a small subset of the discipline (a small team of biologists working on a project to evaluate a wetland area threatened by development). Discourse analysis research methods have been applied to scientific communication as part of an overall trend of examining the ways that scientific knowledge is constructed and transmitted through language. Scholars who use this method begin from the assumption that the language we use acts on our perceptions and social conventions in powerful ways.

A variety of approaches can be used to analyze relationships between language and social institutions. A researcher might work closely with a scientist, reading drafts of grant proposals, viewing comments from peers and reviewers, and interviewing the scientist to discover the rationale behind revisions from one draft to the next. The researcher would also analyze the social context: Is the scientist tenured, or does tenure depend on receiving this grant? How are reviewer comments influenced by ongoing controversies in the discipline, and how does the scientist respond to those comments? What resources does the scientist have access to as he or she works to get the grant funded? Similarly, a researcher using discourse analysis to study press releases introducing new technologies might observe a writer interviewing a technical expert, follow the process the writer uses to draft and revise the press release, and interview the writer to learn why this topic is considered significant and how the text will be distributed.

Perhaps the most controversial assumption of discourse analysis as a research method is the notion that the specialized language of science makes scientific research possible. To demonstrate the mutual relationship between language and scientific language, linguist Michael Halliday studied the way that early scientific writers such as Isaac Newton often transformed verbs (such as *refract*) into nominalizations (*refraction*). This linguistic analysis shows how scientific language enabled scientific researchers to see the world in terms of abstract processes, such as the behavior of light, that can be generalized into sets of natural laws. In that way, Halliday suggested, scientific language coevolved with and enabled modern scientific thought.

Relativistic Views of Science and Language

The assumption that language both constructs and is constructed by scientific knowledge is shared by sociologists of science such as Bruno Latour and Steve Woolgar, as well as linguistics scholars such as Greg Myers. Some critics associate these scholars with a relativistic view of science: Latour and Woolgar's claim, for example, that scientific facts are socially constructed has been interpreted to mean that scientific knowledge can be reduced to a set of agreements among a group of experts, without any reference to an objective reality. However, the notion that social institutions, values, and communities influence and are influenced by the language of science is not necessarily a relativist position. It is possible to analyze the relationship between the language of science and its surrounding social context without neglecting the special relationship between science and accurate representations of nature. Discourse analysis does not necessarily disregard the facts of nature as either irrelevant or entirely socially constructed; instead, it considers the ways those facts are represented to be a result of human relationships, institutions, values, and communities.

Denise Tillery

See also Latour, Bruno; Rhetoric of Science

Further Readings

Gee, J. P. (1999). *Introduction to discourse analysis: Theory and method.* New York: Routledge.

Halliday, M. A. K. (1993). *Writing science: Literacy and discursive power.* Pittsburgh, PA: University of Pittsburgh Press.

Latour, B., & Woolgar, S. (1986). *Laboratory life: The social construction of scientific facts.* Princeton, NJ: Princeton University Press.

Myers, G. (1990). *Writing biology: Texts in the social construction of science.* Madison: University of Wisconsin Press.

DRUG ADVERTISING

When people switch on U.S. television today, they will find—in addition to dramas, comedies, and news—a sea of consumer advertisements enticing them to eat burgers, buy cars, and talk to their doctors about drugs. Prescription drug pitches, known as *direct-to-consumer* (DTC) advertising, emerged on TV, on radio, and in magazines after 1997 and have altered the landscape of how consumers learn about medicine. Before that time, most patients heard about drugs from their doctors or from friends and family members. Today, U.S. consumers find out about prescription drugs from TV and the Internet, often before having a conversation with a doctor, nurse, or pharmacist.

Assessing the Controversy

The advertising of drugs has been controversial in many quarters, with opponents arguing that marketing campaigns create unnecessary desire for high-cost new drugs when low-cost and generic drugs will suffice. Opponents decry such ads as helping create a drug culture in North America, where the solution to a problem is always swallowing a pill. Proponents of DTC advertising, on the other hand, argue that ads help consumers identify symptoms that could signal an underlying disease and prompt visits to physicians where illnesses can be better managed. Ads inform consumers and thus educate patients about illnesses and treatments, and some mental health advocates have argued that the ads reduce the stigma surrounding conditions such as depression.

The controversy over advertising has played out on pharmaceutical company Web sites, in medical publications, in the U.S. legislature, and on consumer advocacy blogs, with scant attention in popular media. For example, in a study of news and editorial coverage of the DTC issue from 1997 until 2004, researchers found about 216 stories in eight major daily U.S. newspapers—fewer than five articles per newspaper each year. Opponents of drug marketing argue that consumers have been subjected to the onslaught of advertising without being invited to participate in the discourse surrounding the issue. In other words, advertisements began appearing in 1997 with little input from the individuals most affected by the ads: patients.

While consumers are pivotal in the drug marketing culture, physicians claim they are being bypassed in the decision-making process. As a result of DTC advertising, some doctors say patients demand drugs. Since the advent of drug ads, researchers report that patients are much more likely to ask their doctors for a specific brand name drug they have seen on TV. Although some drugs may not be suitable for some patients, many physicians feel pressured to bow to such requests and fear that patients will find avenues to obtain drugs regardless of whether they are warranted. Rather than lose a patient, some physicians say they feel compelled to prescribe unnecessary medicines.

The Shifting Balance of Power

Drug advertising resulted in a sea change in the medical field when pharmaceutical companies began to target patients directly, changing how consumers think about health information and altering their relationships with physicians. One perspective is that patients' approaches to their health care have become more consumer focused or market driven. In other words, competition for patient dollars and attention has intensified as power has shifted from a physician-centered medical system to one that pivots on the needs and choices of the patient. Medical sociologists refer to this as the countervailing powers theory in which patients, physicians, hospitals, insurers, and state and federal agencies vie for power and authority in a complex health network. Much like John Kenneth Galbraith's theory of checks and balances in the economic system, countervailing powers theory in the medical field posits that authority will shift as one group in the system gains a greater financial footing over the others.

The infusion of DCT advertising has shifted power from physicians to consumers and from federal regulatory agencies to pharmaceutical companies. In the United States, in the decade since the U.S. Food and Drug Administration relaxed regulations about prescription drug advertising, the impact on drug spending has been unprecedented. During the first year of deregulation, spending on ads totaled about 1 billion U.S. dollars. Ten years later, in 2007, $5.4 billion was spent on ads. To put this in perspective, the same amount would completely eliminate hunger and starvation among children in Africa, according to the head of the World Food Programme.

Financial and Social Costs

The impact of advertising has also affected the consumer's pocketbook. For every $4 a patient spends on a prescription drug, $1 goes to advertising. Today, spending is at an all-time high, with what some critics describe as skyrocketing prices. Americans spent a record $140.6 billion on prescription drugs in 2001, an increase of more than 15% from the previous year, and in 2005, the price tag jumped to a record $252 billion spent on prescription drugs—a dollar figure equal to the gross national product of Denmark. According to the Kaiser Family Foundation, drug expenses constitute "the fastest growing segment" of spending in the health care arena.

Evidence that drug prices have more than doubled since the advent of DTC advertising is incontrovertible, but whether such ads truly educate consumers is less clear, in part because researchers have paid more attention to whether the ads result in greater sales, rather than trying to determine if DTC advertising results in increased knowledge. Critics, therefore, charge that ads create a desire for drugs rather than educate consumers about the application and efficacy of drugs.

Surveys have shown that when patients talk to doctors about advertised medicines, they are likely to get a prescription for them, and researchers report that such requests have increased over time. Since 1997, about 1 in 3 patients has talked to her or his doctor about drugs seen on TV, and the most recent national survey conducted by Prevention Magazine reported that nearly one in two patients now talks to doctors about an advertised drug. Researchers interpret the findings as an indication that ads work. Indeed, the surveys also reported that as many as 75% of consumers who asked for a drug from their doctor received it. Opponents of DTC advertising charge that doctors are responding to patient requests for drugs that may be costly and inappropriate and thus drive prices even higher.

The Vioxx Case

In one noteworthy case, advertising was blamed for patient demand for the drug Vioxx, with some members of the U.S. legislature accusing drug companies of enticing consumers to buy harmful medicine. The heavily advertised Vioxx, a name brand pain reliever, was withdrawn in 2004 after studies demonstrated a linkage between the drug and serious cardiovascular events (heart attack and stroke). Marketing of Vioxx was intense, with spending in 1 year about $160 million—more than that spent on advertising the soft drink Pepsi ($125 million). Leaders in the U.S. Senate called for curbs on DTC advertising and requested that the Government Accountability Office study the issue and consider federal restrictions on advertising.

Merck, the pharmaceutical company that made Vioxx, agreed to pay $4.85 billion to settle 27,000 lawsuits brought against Vioxx. Senators also took the Food and Drug Administration to task, accusing the agency of lackluster attention to drug safety. In 2007, California Congressman Henry Waxman introduced a bill that would ban DTC advertising for a 36-month period and authorize the FDA to prescreen ads. Waxman publicly took to task the pharmaceutical industry for claiming that ads educate consumers and that the promotional materials distort scientific evidence about drugs. Ads tout the benefits of prescription drugs while downplaying the risks, and advertising fails to educate consumers, he said.

Advertising Today

Despite the high-profile controversy surrounding Vioxx, DTC advertising continues to play a prominent role in the mediated consumer landscape: The most popular drugs are those that are the most heavily advertised. According to IMS Health, an organization that tracks drug marketing, antidepressants led prescription sales in 2007. The other top-selling drug categories include lipid regulators (treatments for cholesterol), codeine and combination pain medications, ace inhibitors (treatments for hypertension and congestive heart failure), and beta blockers (for cardiac arrhythmia and hypertension).

Forbes magazine noted that the top-selling brand name drugs include Lipitor, a cholesterol pill from Pfizer; the asthma inhaler Advair (GlaxoSmithKline); the blood thinner Plavix (Bristol-Myers Squibb and Sanofi-Aventis); Nexium, the heartburn pill (AstraZenaca); and Zocor, a statin that lowers cholesterol (Merck). In each case, the top-selling drug has been heavily advertised. For example, drug companies spent $181 million advertising Lipitor in 2007, followed by $175 million for Plavix, according to *Consumer Reports*. GlaxoSmithKline spent $121 million marketing Advair, while AstraZeneca invested $97 million for Nexium, and in 2003, Merck spent $91 million to advertise Zocor.

Critics charge that marketing dollars would be better spent on providing health care to the poor or on developing new drugs and that pharmaceutical companies have earmarked twice as much of their budget for marketing compared with developing new medicines. The impact of DTC advertising on prescription sales in the United States has influenced how other countries think about marketing. In 2008, Canada and the European Union considered legislation that would allow the practice. However, authors of an editorial in the *British Medical Journal* advised against DTC ads, arguing that no country has ever been successful in ensuring that ads provide accurate and balanced information about drug risks and benefits to consumers. The authors note that patients are poorly served when governments allow such ads. Clearly, the controversy over advertising prescription drugs continues to unfold globally.

Cynthia-Lou Coleman

See also Food and Drug Administration, U.S.; Physician–Patient Communication; Science in Advertising

Further Readings

Angell, M. (2004). *The truth about the drug companies: How they deceive us and what to do about it.* New York: Random House.

Avorn, J. (2005). *Powerful medicines: The benefits, risks, and costs of prescription drugs.* New York: Random House.

Breggin, P. R., & Breggin, G. R. (1994). *Talking back to Prozac: What doctors won't tell you about today's most controversial drug.* New York: St. Martin's.

Cardy, P., Cayton, H., & Edwards, B. (1999). *Keeping patients in the dark: Should prescription medicines be advertised direct to consumers?* Philadelphia: Coronet Books.

Kramer, P. (1997). *Listening to Prozac: A psychiatrist explores antidepressant drugs and the remaking of the self.* New York: Penguin.

Nesi, T. (2008). *Poison pills: The untold story of the Vioxx drug scandal.* New York: St. Martin's.

Peterson, M. (2008). *Our daily meds: How the pharmaceutical companies transformed themselves into slick marketing machines and hooked the nation on prescription drugs.* New York: Farrar, Straus & Giroux.

E

East Asia, Science Communication In

Although located in the same area, societies in East Asia have very different political and economic systems, which also make their patterns of science communication divergent. What follows is an introduction to science communication in a few of the major societies in East Asia.

Mainland China

Since the May 4th movement in 1919, which introduced the concepts of science and democracy to the Chinese people, science has gradually taken the upper hand in China's public discourse, particularly after the establishment of the People's Republic of China (PRC) in 1949. In the 1970s and 1980s, a popular saying in China was that one could succeed anywhere with learned scientific knowledge. Guosheng Wu, director of Center of Science Communication at Peking University (CSCPU), called such worship of science "scientism." The Communist Party has been a fervent adherent to such scientism and has devoted much effort the popularization of science and technology (or PST), which could be seen as the main initial form of science communication in the PRC.

Xiaomin Zhu, a scholar at China's PST Institute, divided China's PST effort into five historic periods. The first is the institutionalization period (1949–1958). At its beginning, the government of the PRC wrote in the temporary constitution that the nation needed to dedicate itself to PST, and the PST Association was established to implement this policy. By the end of 1958, the PST Association had built branches in 27 provinces, more than 2,000 cities and counties, and about 4.6 million local communities, with an estimated 102.7 million members and volunteers. The second period, the period of expansion (1958–1966), began when the PST Association and the Association of Scientists were merged into the new China Association for Science and Technology (CAST). CAST organized Chinese scientists to promote successful scientific practices in industrial and agricultural production, and it encouraged workers and farmers to do their own studies. The PST movement discontinued its activities in the third period, the Cultural Revolution era (1966–1976), when most of the science and technology (S&T) organizations in China were dismantled or shut down.

The fourth period is the recovery period (1976–1990). In 1978, the National Science Conference was held, which was broadly seen as the "spring of science." At the conference, Deng Xiaoping, then the top Chinese leader, said that S&T were the "first productive force" and set S&T development as the top priority of China's development. In this decade, CAST opened 13,000 township agricultural technical schools, training 80 million peasants. It also created more than 600 science wagons equipped with devices to play movies and radios and provide exhibitions in rural areas with poor transportation conditions. In 1986, a new national newspaper, *Science & Technology Daily*, was launched, sponsored by the Ministry of Science and Technology

(MST), the Committee of Science and Science in National Defense, China Academy of Science, and CAST. The newspaper is now published 7 days a week and hires about 180 journalists, operating 31 domestic and 13 international bureaus.

A delegation from the American Association for the Advancement of Science (AAAS) witnessed China's PST development in 1980. Its report to the AAAS described how China used film, radio, and television in science communication. Science film, with subjects in health, natural history, new technology, and so on, played a significant role, particularly in rural areas. In 1979, Shanghai showed 200 science films, reaching 160,000 people; in a rural commune close to Shanghai, 100,000 people viewed 100 science films. Radio reached almost every Chinese person through receivers and loudspeakers, and radio stations at all levels had a decent amount of science programs. There were only four television channels and 3 million television sets at that time, but a few hours of educational programming during the day were still warranted, primarily blackboard lectures on electronics, computer science, and foreign languages. In prime time, there was about 1 hour of science programming each week.

Zhu's fifth period, reflective exploration, was from 1990 to 1998. Since 1992, CAST and MST have been conducting national surveys of science literacy every 2 years (except 1998). The government and the public were concerned with the low national science literacy and the proportion of people performing superstitious activities, such as fortune telling, shown in the early surveys. The first National Symposium on PST Theories held in 1991 formed a consensus that PST needed to take the responsibility of eliminating superstition. In 1994, the fourth International Conference on Public Understanding of Science was held in Beijing. Chinese PST scholars began to reexamine the traditional concept of PST based on the international science communication literature.

The pattern of science communication in China changed after Zhu's fifth period. In 2002, the National People's Congress passed the PST Law, stating that the mass media will give "full play to their own advantages" to make PST successful. In 2006, the State Council announced a 15-year plan, the *Outline of the National Scheme for Scientific Literacy*. More mass media were dedicated to science communication. In 2002, about 250 PST

journals and newspapers were published, with a total circulation of 53 million copies. In 2001, the 10th channel of China Central Television was created as the S&T channel, carrying relevant programs more than 20 hours a day. Many provincial and local television stations also created their own S&T channels. A 2007 poll showed that 90% of Chinese people obtained their science information mainly from television, 60% from newspapers, followed by personal communication (35%), radio (21%), science magazines (13%), and books (12%).

Some major Chinese newspapers, however, such as the *People's Daily* and *China Daily*, were still found to have decreased the amount of their science news. Science journalist Hapeng Jia believes that the stereotype that science news is boring has contributed in part to those decreases.

Internet and Short Message Service (SMS) communication also became widely used in science communication, particularly in what political communication scholar Zhou He called, in his dual discourse universe theory, the "private discourse universe," as opposed to the official public discourse universe represented in the state-run media system. In 2003, when news about the breakout of severe acute respiratory syndrome (SARS) was censored, more than 300 million SMS messages were sent out informing people about the disease. In May 2007, a SMS message that reached a million Xiamen residents revealed that the city government was building a 1.58 billion dollar chemical plant close to the downtown. A protest by about 2,000 people, organized via the Internet, finally forced the government to relocate the chemical plant. In January and May 2008, people in Shanghai and Chengdu also organized, via the Internet and SMS, to protest the building plans for a magnetic levitation train and two chemistry plants. Such public participation pushed scholars to redefine PST. Wu argues that we should replace PST with science communication, a concept suggesting a more two-way information flow. Huajie Liu, another researcher at CSCPU, believes that China is in the middle of a transition from PST, a classic top-down model that set scientists as experts providing moral models, to public understanding of science, a deficit model. Some places in China are now shifting from the deficit model to the reflective model, a dialogue and democratic model that examines science from the perspective of the citizens. Driving forces of the three models are government, the science community, and the public.

Hong Kong

In Hong Kong, government is a major promoter of science communication. Education Television, created in 1971, is a government station exclusively devoted to scientific and educational programming. Its programming is also broadcast on the channels of two major commercial televisions stations in Hong Kong. Further, the government buys time and space from the mass media to advertise its science and health campaigns. Another major venue for science communication is the Science Museum, opened in 1991. The four-storied building has a regular exhibition area (6,500 square meters) and a special exhibition area (745 square meters), usually housing over 500 exhibits. It is also equipped with computer classrooms, science movie theaters, and interactive games. The museum often organizes activities together with schools.

Hong Kong scientists also engage themselves in science communication. For instance, Nancy Ip, winner of the 2004 UNESCO Award for Outstanding Women Scientists, believes that scientists need to reach out to the public and help people understand science's social contributions and impacts. She participates in science program production in mass media and science exhibitions that provide opportunities to talk with students and citizens. Scientists' organizations, such as the Hong Kong Astronomical Society, also help to promote science.

Hong Kong public reaction to science content in the media has also been studied. For example, Kamen Lee surveyed 3,035 Hong Kong female teenagers and found that they are more easily activated by the passionate concerns rather than the rational arguments or judgments in the environmental ads. Lee also found that, in a society with the tradition of collectivism like Hong Kong, individuals expected others to share responsibility with them and were less likely to behave by themselves. Science and health campaigns, in addition to pure information, also need to increase individuals' perceived responsibility to act.

Taiwan

Scholars usually regard 1987 as a significant year in Taiwan's communication studies, when martial law and its historical restrictions on the press were lifted. Before 1983, science news was only a subgenre of education and culture news. But from 1983 to 1988 (when the ban had been totally lifted), the mass media institutionalized their science news teams. Ying-chun Hsieh, the most prominent science communication scholar in Taiwan, acknowledged that before 1988, the mass media covered science news regularly. Her study, however, showed that the stories often emphasized nonscientific themes. When Samuel C.C. Ting won the Nobel Prize for Physics in 1976 and Yuan Tseh Lee won the Nobel Prize of Chemistry in 1986, both being men from Taiwan, the media coverage focused on their personal background and touched on their scientific studies only briefly. After the press ban was lifted, as both Hsieh and Shangping Han (a science journalist in Taiwan) noted, many new media outlets were created, and the existing ones expanded the amount of their overall coverage, but the volume of science news did not increase while that of superstitious stories, such as geomancy, was boosted.

Han proposed several reasons for the scarcity of science news in Taiwanese newspapers in this period: (a) Newspaper managers did not value science news very much, possibly because they did not take it as their responsibility to educate the citizens; (b) science news was mainly obtained from press conferences held by governmental officials or public relations professionals, which limited the sources and biased the stories; (c) scientists were reluctant to talk with journalists, which might be seen as reputation hunting or might even get them in trouble; and (d) the media favored only certain types of science stories, such as those about governmental policies, high-tech stories (for example, those about computer, nuclear, and medical sciences), and scientists who studied abroad. Another factor Han found to undermine science journalism is that only novices were assigned to cover science. Sociologist Yiyuan Li argued that three social factors also hindered science communication in Taiwan: (1) authority, in that all collective societies, scientists, journalists, and the public in Taiwan tended to follow their political leaders, bosses, and teachers and tended to accept scientists as authorities, in opposition to the spirit of scientific inquiry; (2) pragmatism, in that the mass media only focused on practical technology, but ignored basic scientific values; and (3) after modernization destroyed the domination of Confucianism, superstition became prevalent. Hsieh also noted that Taiwan's education system, which assigned students to science or liberal arts majors in high school, decreased public science literacy and cultivated what C. P. Snow called the "two culture" pattern.

Governmental officials are no longer major sources of science news since Taiwan has transformed into a democratic society in the 21st century. A 2003 content analysis of the island's three major newspapers, *United Daily*, *China Times*, and *Liberty Times*, found that 63% of the science stories talked about marketing of and shopping for technical products, and these used salespeople, doctors, managers, and shoppers as sources. Around a third (29%) talked about the products and techniques themselves; these cited engineers, technicians, or the technical organizations. Only 9% of the stories were about scientific theories and research, using scientists as sources. Most of those pure science stories, moreover, were translated from foreign media. To increase coverage of pure science in the mass media, in 2007, the National Science Council launched a Taiwan Science Popularization and Communication Promoting Plan, which as of 2009 had subsidized 15 films, 9 news programs and columns, and 5 feature programs and columns on television and in newspapers on science. The government also sponsored a series of lectures and exhibitions devoted to scientific matters.

In 2002, consensus conference was introduced to Taiwan, which has been used to address more than 20 controversial S&T issues. At those conferences, typically around 20 citizen participants read a balanced and comprehensive package provided by the experts and then discussed among themselves and with experts their recommendations for policies. The processes were broadcast on television. A study involving two consensus conferences on surrogate motherhood and mandated prenatal testing and screening, held in 2004, found that the conferences could increase science literacy of both the participants and the audiences and could change their attitude. Citizens could also identify bias and expert stereotypes through participation in these conferences.

Japan

Japan's science literacy is quite high among East Asian countries. A 1991 survey showed 3% of Japanese people were science literate; while not a large percentage, this is higher than for most Asian countries. Japanese people also have a positive attitude toward S&T. According to a 2005 poll, 51% of Japanese people believed that nanotechnology was "to some extent" useful for the society, and 37% believed that it was "very much" useful. But the government still has a sense of urgency because the Third Trends in International Mathematics and Science Study in 1999 surveyed middle school students in 38 countries and reported that Japanese students did not like mathematics and science, although they performed well in the knowledge tests. In 1996, Japan passed the Basic Law of Science and Technology, one goal of which is that all Japanese, including young people, should be given opportunities to increase their understanding of and interest in S&T. Since 1996, Japan has issued three Science and Technology Basic Plans (FY1996–FY2000, FY2001–FY2005, and FY2006–FY2010) to benefit society and to encourage the public to support S&T.

The major tool to disseminate scientific knowledge is still the mass media. About 70% of Japanese people reported in a poll that they gained medical and scientific information mainly from television. A survey by the Society for Techno-Innovation of Agriculture, Forestry and Fisheries showed that about 60% of Japanese know the genetic modification (GM) technique from newspapers and television. Japan's media have a long history of science coverage. Most of the newspapers and television stations established S&T teams in the 1950s and the 1960s, covering nuclear energy, space, and computer science emerging at that time. Newspapers are also credited as more accurate and reliable than television. But a content analysis on *Asahi Shimbun* and *Yomiuri Shimbun*, two major newspapers having circulations of 8 and 10 million, respectively, still found that their coverage of GM food shifted focus to respond to public interests. Science magazines' history can be traced back to the end of World War I. Although the Japanese economic bubble in the 1980s ended the prosperity of Japanese science magazines, some influential ones such as *Newton* and *Trigger* still have a large readership in the country.

Partly because governmental agencies such as the Science Council of Japan have called on scientists to be public communicators and have regularly organized forums for scientists to talk with journalists, Japanese scientists have good contact with journalists. A cross-national survey found that 71% of Japanese scientists received media coverage at least once in the recent 3 years. Compared to the United States, United Kingdom, France, and Germany, however, fewer Japanese scientists were pleased (47%), and many more felt mixed (32%) or mostly dissatisfied (5%) about their experience with the media. Although Japanese scientists acknowledged that journalists listened to them carefully, they felt that their research was not explained very well partly because journalists like to ask biased or unfair questions. In the 2001 International Conference of S&T Journalists held in Tokyo, Japanese scientists also criticized journalists for preferring negativity and misleading the public by overemphasizing the risks of some scientific studies, for chasing the insignificant studies that may be easy to report but ignoring those significant and complicated projects, for sloppy writing and using too much jargon in their stories, and for following politicians' leads when choosing story subjects. Journalists complained that there were no appropriate science courses for them to take in college.

Scientists are also blamed for less-than-perfect science communication. Since 1997, to merge into the international academy, Japanese scientists have gradually adopted English as their primary working language, which increasingly isolates scientists from Japanese policymakers, journalists, and the public. Ambiguous terminology is another barrier. A study that interviewed 64 Japanese life science researchers found that they used the common term *mouse model* with four different dimensions of meaning. While the researcher might mean to indicate that the results based on the mouse cannot be applied to humans, the media coverage might actually emphasize the possible application.

Now, Japanese scientists are trying hard to reach out to the public. A group called Zero to One, organized by S&T graduate students from universities in Tokyo, fosters interdisciplinary discussions among young scientists and offers science classes in schools. Since 2005, many science cafés have been opened, where public members can chat with noted scientists, watch science movies, or use the affiliated science libraries. Those outreach efforts are critical when the public has lost its confidence in scientists after disasters such as AIDS

caused by blood transfer and the JCO Company's nuclear "leak." The consensus conference appeared in Japan in 1998. It is an ideal forum for citizens to request scientists to respond to their needs and has been used to address issues such as GM food, the Internet and society, and nanotechnology.

South Korea

In 1999, to hold onto its advancing position in information science, the South Korean government issued its "Vision 2025: Korea's Long-Term Plan for Science and Technology Development" report, which included the recommendation that the country encourage "public awareness of S&T policy." The Korean Science Foundation (KSF), as stated in its mission, is committed to "advancing public understanding and knowledge" regarding science and technology, and it has made efforts in the following media: television, print media, and the Internet.

Television

Science TV, an exclusive science television channel, was launched in 2007 under a contract among the MST, KFS, and the YTN media group. It runs for 24 hours per day. The foundation also sponsors production and distribution of science television programs and films through other television channels. The state-run Korea Educational Broadcasting System offers one terrestrial television channel, one radio channel, and three satellite television channels, all exclusively dedicated to adult education and student extracurricular education, including science education. Most of the programs are also available online.

Print Media

Since 2004, the KSF has been financing its staff, journalists, and freelancers to write science stories for 11 selected newspapers. Since 2006, KSF has also encouraged those newspapers to cover science development in the United States, Europe, and Japan. In 2007, the KSF began to sponsor *The Youth Science & Economic Newspaper*. Research has found that major Korean newspapers provide little scientific information in their science stories. A study showed that concerning Woo Suk Hwang's scandal about his cloning research, *Chosun Ilbo*—the oldest, largest, and most elite newspaper—at first covered the "achievement" as a source of national pride and then tried to defend Hwang when the fraud was revealed. Another study examined how *Chosun Ilbo* and *Hankyoreh*, a liberal counterpart of the former, covered Korean public health professionals' protest against a governmental policy in 1999 and 2000. Both newspapers tended to use governmental officials and physicians as primary sources and used verbatim quotes from them, providing little interpretation or background information regarding the science involved.

Internet

South Korea's Internet penetration rate was 76% by the end of 2008, the highest in Asia. KSF hence created a science Web site (www.scienceall .com) to reach young students, housewives, and opinion leaders. The Web site provides cartoons, video clips, and three-dimensional animated games of scientific experiments; an open database about scientists and their expertise; and an open database of background information for science journalists to fact-check their stories. By the end of 2006, the Web site had approximately 2.26 million registered users. KSF also established an online newspaper, *Science Times*, in 2003, which is updated from Monday through Friday. By November 2007, around 220,000 adults and 700,000 students subscribed to the newsletter of the online newspaper.

A Sogang University Researcher, Hak-Soo Kim, has argued that South Korea needs to shift from the deficit model, which represented the scientists' viewpoints, to a new model of public engagement in science communication. Kim analyzed data from two national surveys and found that 27% of Korean people tend to associate science with certain products (computers, electronic devices, transportation, and so on), 17% with research activities (experiments, microscopes, laboratories, and so on), and 13% with evaluative attributes (such as good, useful, difficult, complex, and so on). The public chooses what it cares about, not simply following what the scientists want them to know. Based on his model, Kim proposed three suggestions for improving South Korea's science communication: (1) The topic should be what the public is willing to engage with, (2) communication should

try to relate the issue in question to science's problem-solving or resolving ability, and (3) it is essential to establish a science community in which people have high collective engagement in science.

Qingjiang Yao

See also Cloning; Consensus Conference; International Science Journalism Associations; Public Understanding of Science; Snow, C. P.

Further Readings

Chen, D.-S., & Deng, C.-Y. (2007). Interaction between citizens and experts in public deliberation: A case study of consensus conference in Taiwan. *East Asian Science, Technology and Society: An International Journal, 1,* 77–97.

Cheng, D., & Zhou, H. (2007). Science communication on demand. In M. Claessens (Ed.), *Communicating European research, 2005* (pp. 31–35). Dordrecht, the Netherlands: Springer Netherlands.

Ishizu, S., Sekiya, M., Ishibashi, K.-I., Negami, Y., & Ata, M. (2008). Toward the responsible innovation with nanotechnology in Japan: Our scope. *Journal of Nanoparticle Research, 10,* 229–254.

Kim, H.-S. (2007). A new model for communicative effectiveness of science. *Science Communication, 28*(3), 287–313.

Korea Science Foundation. (2007). *Scientific C=content.* Retrieved October 11, 2009, from www.ksf.or.kr/en/sub02/sub2_02.jsp?gubun=2

Lee, K. (2008). Making environmental communications meaningful to female adolescents: A study in Hong Kong. *Science Communication, 30*(2), 147–176.

Logan, R. A., Park, J., & Shin, J.-H. (2004). Elite sources, context, and news topics: How two Korean newspapers covered a public health crisis. *Science Communication, 25*(4), 364–398.

Peters, H. P., Brossard, D., Cheveigné, S. D., Dunwoody, S., Kallfass, M., Miller, S., et al. (2008). Interactions with the mass media. *Science, 321,* 204–205.

Pitrelli, N. (2005). The new "Chinese dream" regards science communication. *Journal of Science Communication, 4*(2), 1–5.

EFFECTIVE GRAPHICS

Information graphics, information design, and visualization through the use of computer graphics represent the intersection of science communication and mass media fields, such as journalism and graphic design. Scientists, graphic artists, journalists, and even the audiences they seek to reach now have a wide range of tools available to translate quantitative data and complex processes into visual displays.

This entry briefly explores the history and context of the visual display of numeric data, looks at the forms of visuals that are most frequently used to communicate these concepts, and discusses the principles and processes behind their effective use.

History

Pictorial symbols preceded the written word as a form of universal communication, and despite the march of time and the development of complex alphabets, they continue to be an effective means of transmitting information, often working in concert with the written word.

The first books made it easier to store and retrieve information, but they also created an opportunity for the emergence of new forms of visual communications. Diagrams began appearing in manuscripts as early as the 9th century that illustrated philosophical belief systems and family trees. Drawings were also used to illustrate the first medical and botanical books.

The development of new scientific tools during the 16th and 17th centuries brought new, more accurate ways of visualizing information. The mariner's compass, the aneroid barometer, and the bubble level are examples of innovations that resulted in significant improvements in the accuracy of plotting topographic measurements and nautical charts.

Some graphic innovations were simply the result of finding novel ways to represent quantitative data. Statistical graphics, such as the familiar pie, bar, and line charts that are commonplace in today's popular media and scientific journals, first appeared in a book published in 1786 by a little-known Scottish writer and engineer named William Playfair. His *Commercial and Political Atlas* contained 44 charts that analyzed the changing fortunes of England's balance of trade.

In the 1920s, artists at the Vienna Museum of Social and Economic Studies established a style of creating information graphics to show comparisons in numbers and averages that relied on the use of stylized symbols. This system was designed to be readable to anyone regardless of language or culture, and artists dubbed the technique "ISOTYPE," which stands for the International System of Typographic Picture Education.

With the advent of the Internet, many publications began producing online and print versions, and this presented challenges as well as opportunities for visual representation of information. Often, graphics produced for print had legibility problems when they were translated online because of their small type, and line art did not reproduce as well on the screen. As a result, publishers had to decide whether to create two versions of every graphic or opt not to reproduce a graphic that appeared in print in the online version.

Despite these new challenges, the new medium did allow for more experimentation with new forms of informational representation. Online informational graphics can incorporate animation and interactivity with users. One such site, Many Eyes, also lets users upload their own data sets and analyze them using up to 19 different visualization models.

Proper Use of Informational Graphics

A variety of forms of visual representation exist that are best suited to illustrate just about any type of quantitative data. The type of graphic that is most appropriate depends on the data available and what the creator of the graphic wants that data to show. There are several strategies to consider when picking a graphic format:

- Showing parts of the whole
- Looking for relationships between data points
- Comparing one set of values with another
- Tracking up or down trends over time
- Analyzing text for themes or associations
- Applying data patterns over a spatial area, such as a county or state boundary
- Displaying natural phenomenon in the physical environment
- Showing a chronology of events
- Showing a process or cause and effect relationship

Following are some of the most common forms of visual representation of data, along with general guidelines for the treatment of the data and design of the visual.

Tables

Tables are arrangements of text or numbers usually organized in ranks, intervals, or alphabetical order and displayed with some type of organizational grid of columns and rows.

These are guidelines to follow when organizing data sets for tables:

- Numbers should be arranged in meaningful patterns: ascending or descending order, chronological order, or class intervals.
- When arranging in class intervals, intervals should be made equal and there should be no overlapping intervals.

An example of a class interval would be to arrange the average household income of a particular population into four intervals where each interval spans an amount that equals $15,000.

$1 to $14,999.00

$15,000 to $29,999

$30,000 to $44,999

$45,000 to $59,000

Pie Charts

Pie charts are used to show relationships between one part and the whole, for example, data that are arrayed in percentages. Pie charts need not be limited to a circular arrangement divided up in pie slices. Any visual that can be divided into proportional and accurate segments (for example, a rectangular dollar bill) can serve to compare parts to the whole.

Circular pie charts work best when they are limited to 8 to 10 slices. More than 10 divisions are usually hard to label, and the patterns are less discernible and, thus, less meaningful. Whenever the number of divisions becomes too cumbersome, the data should either be combined or collapsed into fewer categories, or another graphic format, such as a table, should be used.

Bar and Column Charts

Bar and column charts compare the frequencies of different categories with each other. The only difference between the two is that in a column chart the categories, such as countries of the world, are arranged on the horizontal x-axis and the values, such as poverty rates, are arranged on the vertical y-axis. On a bar chart, the categories occupy the vertical y-axis, and the values occupy the horizontal x-axis.

Why pick one over the other? The major reason is whether the room allocated for the chart in a presentation is vertical or horizontal. Column charts tend to occupy more space vertically, whereas bar charts frequently occupy more horizontal space. Also, if the labels of categories are very long, it is frequently easier to stack them vertically on the y-axis of a bar chart than on the horizontal x-axis of a column chart.

A key guideline to follow with bar and column charts is to make sure that the numbers on the value scale do not exaggerate, minimize, or otherwise distort the comparisons of bars or columns. For example, in a column chart where all the data points in the data set range from 75 to 95, a y-axis value scale that ranges from zero to 100 would show far fewer differences between categories than one that ranges from 50 to 100.

Scatterplots

Scatterplots show relationships between numeric variables with a series of dots or points charted on an x- and y-axis, and they are an effective way to create a visualization of all points in the data set involving two variables (Figure 1).

Each dot or point in a scatterplot represents one piece of data, and usually, all the points in the data set are represented in the plot, creating a complete census. In addition, the size of the dot can also track a third variable, with bigger dots representing higher values and smaller dots representing less (Figure 2).

Tag or Word Clouds

Tag or word clouds are a relatively new form of visualization that provide a means to visually analyze the textual content of documents and Web sites by showing the weighted importance of words with font size and color. Tag or word clouds of two similar documents can be used as a visual tool of comparison. For example, a word cloud that

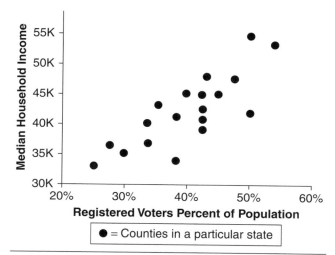

Figure 1   Illustration of a Scatterplot Showing Household Income and Percent of Population Registered to Vote for Each County Within a State

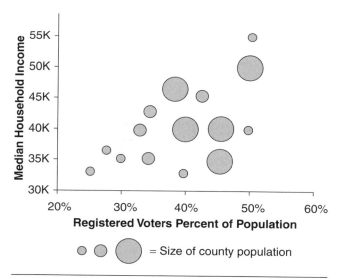

Figure 2   Illustration of a More Complex Scatterplot in Which the Size of the Dot Representing Each County Reflects That County's Population Size

compared the most often used words in Barack Obama's inaugural address with those of George Bush's could illustrate the textual differences in the emphasis of the two speeches. Figure 3 provides a word cloud visualization of a text taken from a grant proposal about communication issues.

Fever or Line Charts

Fever or line charts show trends in data over some time interval, such as years, hours, or seasons, where the y-axis represents some categorical value, such as income, and the x-axis represents some time-based value, such as age, months, or years. Most all data sets can potentially have some time element associated with them and therefore could be plotted on a line chart.

Maps

Maps can be divided into three different categories: maps that locate something; maps that display data over an administrative area, such as infectious disease rates by state; and maps that display data that represent natural phenomenon, such as average rainfall or elevation.

Data maps that display data over an administrative area usually rely on some type of color or shaded legend to display ranges. When creating a legend that measures one variable in a map, such as poverty rate, the designer should use only one color with dark shades representing larger values and lighter shades representing lower values. When displaying more than one variable in a map, such as top cash crop by state, it is best to use a unique color to represent each variable. Also, when constructing a legend, the intervals of data displayed should be equal to each other and there should be no overlapping intervals.

A legend that could be applied to a state map of poverty rates, for example, might have four intervals that each represent 10 percentage points, with shading that gets progressively darker as the rates increase: 90% to 99% might be black, 80% to 89% dark gray, 70% to 79% light gray, and 60% to 69% white.

Diagrams

Diagrams can show processes, cause and effect relationships, or sequences of events or can be used for simple schematic identification. These types of graphics have the potential to be the most illuminating and to more fully engage a reader. However, they also require a great deal of research and writing time to produce. Unlike many of the other formats mentioned above, diagrams cannot typically be generated automatically by computer

Figure 3   Illustration of a Word Cloud, a New Variety of Graphic That Reflects the Relative Importance of Words in a Given Text (in this case, a grant proposal about communication)

software. They usually require the illustration skills of an accomplished artist as well as someone who can write in a clear, succinct fashion to boil down a complicated process to a few key points.

Conclusion

Since Paleolithic artists first painted primitive, but nuanced, images on the cave walls of Lascaux, visual illustrations have been used as stylistic adornments, as tools to communicate complicated ideas, as means to represent spatial information, and as ways to explain complex processes and to tease out patterns and trends that might otherwise be hidden in quantitative data.

Data visualization is an interdisciplinary field that is part art and part science. It is where the hard facts of data meet with creative expression to create visual formats that aid in human understanding and comprehension. With the democratization of powerful new tools for displaying visual information, scientists, journalists, educators, and laypeople now have more opportunities to share and collaborate in creating new forms of visualization

that cast new and insightful lights on the world around us.

When they are properly conceived, designed, and executed, informational graphics are visual amplifiers to data, and they validate the cliché that a picture is worth a thousand words.

Van Kornegay

See also Visual Images in Science Communication

Further Readings

Holmes, N. (1990). *Designer's guide to creating charts and diagrams*. New York: Watson-Guptill.

Meggs, P. B., & Purvis, A. W. (1998). *The history of graphic design* (4th ed.). Hoboken, NJ: Wiley.

Meyer, E. K. (1997). *Designing infographics*. Indianapolis, IN: Hayden Books.

Salkind, N. J. (2004). *Statistics for people who hate statistics* (2nd ed.). Thousand Oaks, CA: Sage.

Tufte, E. (2001). *The visual display of quantitative information* (2nd ed.). Cheshire, CT: Graphics Press.

Einstein, Albert (1879–1955)

Albert Einstein is one of the most influential and recognized scientists in history. He is best known for his theories of special and general relativity and his postulation of mass–energy equivalence as expressed by the famous equation $E = mc^2$. In 1905, often called his miracle year, Einstein published five papers, one of which (on his quantum theory of light) won him a Nobel Prize in 1921. Einstein has become the iconic scientific genius of the 20th century, and his picture continues to be featured seemingly everywhere, even a half century after his death.

After measurements taken during a total solar eclipse in 1919 proved Einstein's theory of general relativity was correct, his popularity soared, and he instantly became an international celebrity. *Time* magazine named Einstein Person of the Century in its final issue of 1999. Einstein's theories radically changed the way we view the universe, laid the groundwork for modern physics, and led to some of the most significant scientific and technological advances in human history.

The Early Years

Albert Einstein was born into a Jewish family in Ulm, Germany, on March 14, 1879. Einstein's interest in science was first sparked at the age of 5 when his father showed him a compass and explained that magnetism caused the needle to always point north. He was fascinated by the fact that there are forces in nature that cannot be seen, and the experience left a lasting impression on him.

In 1885, Einstein began his education at the age of 6 at a neighborhood Catholic primary school in Munich, Germany. He moved on to secondary school in 1888 and became interested in physics, math, and philosophy the following year. By the time he was 11, Einstein could prove the Pythagorean theorem by himself, and by age 12, he had taught himself calculus.

In 1894, Einstein's family moved to Italy but left him behind in Munich to finish his schooling. Einstein was unhappy, however, and left school after his teacher told him he would not amount to anything because of his irreverence. The following year, Einstein tried to enroll in the Swiss Federal Polytechnical Institute 2 years early, but he failed the nonscience parts of the entrance exam. In 1896, he retook the exam and began school that fall. Four years later, Einstein graduated, and in 1902, he began working as a clerk in the Swiss Patent Office in Bern, Switzerland.

Year of Miracles

In 1905, at the age of 25, Einstein had a sudden burst of progress and published five scientific papers, including three of his most important, in his spare time while working at the patent office. In that 1 year, Einstein proposed his revolutionary quantum theory of light, helped prove the existence of atoms, was able to explain Brownian motion, radically changed the way we think of space and time, and came up with science's most famous equation: $E = mc^2$.

Einstein submitted his first paper of the year—the one that would earn him a Nobel Prize in 1921—to *Annalen der Physik* (Annuals of Physics) in March, and it was published 3 months later. In the paper, "On a Heuristic Point of View Concerning the Production and Transformation of Light," Einstein put forth his revolutionary particle theory of light. For two centuries, scientists had thought of light as a continuous wave. Einstein, however, postulated that light is actually made up of many point-like particles—light quanta—later termed photons. By thinking of light as particles, Einstein laid the foundation for quantum theory and was able to explain the photoelectric effect—something that had puzzled scientists for almost 20 years.

On April 30, Einstein completed his thesis, titled "A New Determination of Molecular Dimension," in which he studied the properties of molecules in fluid. At the time, there was still no definitive proof for the existence of molecules or atoms, and Einstein sought to determine the size of molecules and thus move one step closer to proving their existence. Einstein submitted his thesis to the University of Zurich in July and was officially awarded his PhD in January 1906.

Eleven days after completing his dissertation, Einstein submitted another paper to *Annalen der Physik*, titled "On the Motion of Small Particles Suspended in Liquids at Rest Required by the Molecular-Kinetic Theory of Heat." In this paper,

Einstein not only was able to prove that atoms and molecules actually exist, but also to explain a phenomenon known as Brownian motion. For more than 80 years, scientists had been trying to figure out why small particles, such as pollen, suspended in liquid appear to jiggle around. Einstein was able to show that it was the result of the millions of random collisions that occur between the molecules in the liquid. The paper was published in July and became Einstein's most cited work.

In June, Einstein submitted his famous paper on special relativity to *Annalen der Physik* titled "On the Electrodynamics of Moving Bodies," and it was published in September. Einstein's relativity theory—an idea he had been working on since 1899—states that all uniform motion is relative and that there is no absolute and well-defined state of rest. This means the laws of physics are the same in all reference frames—whether one is at rest or moving at a constant velocity. His theory also stated that the speed of light is constant and that time must slow down as one moves faster. Einstein's theory is called special relativity because it only applies to observers moving at a constant velocity relative to one another. It would take Einstein another decade to broaden his theory to a general theory of relativity that incorporated accelerated motion.

Three months after submitting his special relativity paper, Einstein sent off a short follow-up paper on relativity called, "Does the Inertia of a Body Depend on Its Energy Content?" In this three-page paper published in *Annalen der Physik* in November, Einstein presents his conclusion that mass and energy are simply different manifestations of the same thing and that they are interchangeable. This idea is the basis for Einstein's famous equation $E = mc^2$, although he did not actually write down the equation until 1907. It also led to the creation of the atom bomb 40 years later.

It is hard to believe that even after his miracle year, Einstein was still not very well-known within the scientific community, much less around the world. It was not until after Einstein's theory of general relativity was shown to be correct that he gained celebrity status.

General Relativity and Rise to Fame

After more than 10 years of work, Einstein was finally able to extend his theory of relativity to include acceleration, and thus gravity, and his paper titled "The Foundations of the General Theory of Relativity" was published in *Annalen der Physik* in 1916. Einstein's new theory unified his theory of special relativity and Isaac Newton's universal theory of gravitation and described gravity as a property of the geometry of space-time. According to Einstein's theory, mass curves space-time like a bowling ball placed in the center of a rubber sheet. Thus, gravity is simply the result of matter traveling across curved space-time. Not only did Einstein's new theory simplify Newton's theory of gravitation, it was also able to explain a long-standing problem in the calculation of Mercury's orbit.

Einstein's theory of general relativity also made new predictions for how light bends in a gravitational field. Einstein predicted that the trajectory of light from a distant star would curve as it traveled through the strong gravitational field around our sun. To test this prediction, scientists could measure the position of a distant star in normal conditions and then compare it to measurements taken when the alignment was just right for the light to pass close to our sun. If the star's position appeared to shift, Einstein was correct. The experiment, however, required a total solar eclipse to photograph the star.

The next total solar eclipse occurred on May 29, 1919, in two locations—off the west coast of Africa near the equator and in Brazil—and a team of scientists went to each location to test Einstein's prediction. Three months later, once the photographs had been developed and analyzed, measurements confirmed that the gravitational field did, in fact, bend the light and that Einstein was correct. When the news was announced publicly in November, Einstein instantly became an international star and was bombarded by the media and fans from around the world.

In 1917, Einstein added a cosmological constant to his theory of general relativity. At the time, scientists strongly believed the universe was static. To make his theory work for a static universe, Einstein introduced a cosmological constant—a force that opposes the pull of gravity and keeps the universe from collapsing—into his equations. Twelve years later, U.S. astronomer Edwin Hubble discovered the universe is not static and is expanding as a result of the big bang, so Einstein took the cosmological constant out of his equations and called it his biggest blunder.

In 1998, however, scientists found that the universe is not only expanding, but that the expansion is accelerating. This means there must be a force overcoming the pull of gravity to make the universe's expansion accelerate. Scientists call this force dark energy, and so after 80 years, Einstein's so-called biggest blunder may not really be a blunder after all.

The Atom Bomb and Later Years

In 1939, Einstein learned of research using uranium and nuclear fission to produce an explosive chain reaction. He quickly realized this could lead to massively destructive bombs, and in August 1939, Einstein wrote a letter to President Franklin D. Roosevelt warning him that German scientists may already be working on such research. As a result, Roosevelt assembled a board to investigate the possibilities of uranium, but progress was slow. In March 1940, Einstein heard Berlin researchers were making progress in producing chain reactions with the potential of creating huge explosions and again wrote Roosevelt, urging him to speed up research in the United States. In response, Roosevelt called a series of meetings that led to the launch of the Manhattan Project in December 1941.

Roosevelt had invited Einstein to attend the meetings, but he declined, not wanting to get more involved. Even if he had wanted to become more involved, many considered Einstein a potential security risk, despite his officially becoming a U.S. citizen in June 1940, and he was largely kept in the dark regarding work on the bomb.

In 1944, Einstein began to have second thoughts about what the creation of an atom bomb would mean and encouraged policymakers to rethink their actions. By March 1945, it was clear that Germany did not have a bomb and that the country's defeat was only weeks away. Einstein wrote another letter to Roosevelt, voicing his concerns about dropping a bomb when it might not be necessary to secure victory. However, Roosevelt did not receive the letter before he died, and on August 6, 1945, the United States dropped the first atom bomb on Hiroshima, Japan. Three days later, a second bomb was dropped on Nagasaki, Japan.

When the U.S. government released its report on the development of the bomb, much to Einstein's dismay, it named his 1939 letter to Roosevelt as playing a major role in the launch of the Manhattan Project. Einstein said that if he had known Germany would not be successful in building a bomb, he would have never written to Roosevelt.

On April 11, 1955, just days before his death, Einstein signed a joint manifesto with British philosopher Bertrand Russell and several other prominent scientists urging all nations to renounce nuclear weapons. Six days later, on April 17, Einstein died from internal bleeding caused by the rupture of a previously diagnosed aortic aneurysm. Einstein's unprecedented contributions to science paved the way for modern physics, fundamentally changed the way we understand the universe, and led to some of the most significant advances in history, making him one of the most famous scientists of all time.

Amelia A. Williamson

See also Manhattan Project; Nuclear Weapons; Visible Scientist

Further Readings

Brian, D. (1996). *Einstein: A life.* New York: Wiley.

Calaprice, A., & Lipscombe, T. (2005). *Albert Einstein: A biography.* Westport, CT: Greenwood Press.

Isaacson, W. (2007). *Einstein: His life and universe.* New York: Simon & Schuster.

White, M., & Gribbin, J. (1994). *Einstein: A life in science.* New York: Dutton.

EMBARGO SYSTEM

An embargo is an information subsidy in the form of an agreement between a news source and a journalist under which the source gives the journalist access to information before it is given to the public, and in return, the journalist agrees not to disseminate news about the information until a designated day and time.

Embargoes are used throughout journalism. However, they are particularly prevalent in journalism about science and technology—most commonly, in news about research published in major journals—because of the combination of the perceived difficulty in reporting on these topics and the control that the scientific establishment can exert over access to information.

For example, the journal *Science* is published on Fridays. However, selected journalists are allowed to read advance copies of papers in a given issue of the journal up to a week ahead of the publication date. During this embargo period, a journalist may interview sources and prepare an article or broadcast report, but the news itself cannot be disseminated until 2 p.m. on the day before the journal issue's publication date.

A participating journalist knows that he or she will not be "scooped" on the story by competitors because all have agreed to abide by the same release time. If the embargoed news leaks out prematurely, the embargo is considered to be vacated, and journalists who had agreed to the embargo are free to disseminate the news immediately. If the leak is traced to a journalist who received information under embargo, the journal can discipline the journalist by withholding future access.

Among technology journalists, embargoes are known as nondisclosure agreements, or NDAs, after the term for the legal contract used to formalize the arrangement. NDAs are commonly to control the timing of news regarding new computer hardware and software.

Proponents of embargoes argue that they promote journalism that is accurate and thorough by giving journalists sufficient time to digest technical material and interview a range of experts. In addition, according to Eliot Marshall's 1998 discussion of embargoes, embargoes on medical journals are timed so that physicians will have received their journals by the time news is disseminated, so physicians will be able to read the journal articles in question and answer patient inquiries in an informed manner. Empirical support for these claims is equivocal at best.

Critics of embargoes, as reported by Vincent Kiernan in 2004, argue that this system plays on journalists' penchant for pack behavior to highlight research from a few journals while discouraging journalists from pursuing independent investigative research into science and technology institutions.

A common error is confusing an embargo with the Ingelfinger rule. Many journals follow versions of the Ingelfinger rule, named for Franz Ingelfinger, who enunciated it in 1969, according to the article "Definitions of 'Sole Contribution,'" while editor of *The New England Journal of Medicine*. The Ingelfinger rule seeks to restrict the actions of scientists by declaring that the journal will not publish studies that have been previously disseminated to the public, but the rule does not regulate what journalists can do with information that they do obtain.

Origins of the embargo system are murky. In the United States, pioneers were Morris Fishbein, the politically powerful editor of *The Journal of the American Medical Association* from 1924 to 1950, and Howard W. Blakeslee, a Chicago-based reporter for The Associated Press and a preeminent early science journalist. According to Fishbein's 1969 autobiography, Fishbein gave Blakeslee access to page proofs of the journal each week, steering Blakeslee toward those items that Fishbein deemed most newsworthy.

Initially, much of the impetus for embargoes came from journalists rather than from the scientific establishment. As science and medical journalism developed into a distinct professional specialty in the 1930s and 1940s, early science and medical journalists sought to establish their bona fides with scientists who were suspicious of the journalists' skills and motivations. In 2006, Kiernan reported in his book *Embargoed Science* that journalists argued that embargoed access would help journalists produce news reports about science and medicine that were accurate and dignified.

Securing cooperation from scientists was difficult at first, but particularly in the post–World War II scientific boom, scientists and their organizations began to perceive that the benefits of news coverage outweighed its risks. Consequently, according to Kiernan's *Embargoed Science*, they began to embrace embargoes on journals and conference papers.

In the 1960s, as television journalism emerged as a serious competitor to daily newspapers, science journalists began to argue among themselves and with the scientific establishment over whether the terms of scientific embargoes benefited certain media over others. For example, an evening embargo time would enable a television station to report a scientific finding as breaking news in its evening broadcast; however, the news might seem stale in the next day's morning newspaper and would be far too old for inclusion in the next day's evening newspaper, according to Kiernan's *Embargoed Science.*

In subsequent decades, particularly in conjunction with the research-fueled growth of the biotechnology and pharmaceutical industries that started in the 1980s, nonjournalists such as investors have sought to ferret out embargoed information as a tip-off to news that could affect stock prices and government regulatory action, as reported by Marshall in 1998.

The development of the Internet has reshaped the embargo system. Embargoed materials previously were disseminated by fax and overnight mail; now, major journal publishers maintain password-protected Web sites from which approved journalists can download embargoed information. The most prominent is Eurekalert! operated by the American Association for the Advancement of Science, which disseminates embargoed information for both the association's own *Science* and for other publishers' journals. This use of Web technology has broadened the number of journalists using embargoed materials and extended their reach around the world.

However, this broadening effect also has undercut some of the social controls that enable the embargo system to persist. Few of the journalists participating in the embargoes now know each other personally, which weakens social strictures on violating the embargo. Moreover, the fashion in which the Internet makes news reports instantly available throws much more publicity on embargo violations whenever they are committed. In general, the growth in social networking technology and the free, decentralized flow of information that it enables seem destined to make the embargo system "leakier" in coming decades.

Vincent Kiernan

See also American Association for the Advancement of Science (AAAS); Interviewing Scientists; *Nature; Science*

Further Readings

Definition of "sole contribution." (1969). *New England Journal of Medicine, 281,* 676–677.

Fishbein, M. (1969). *Morris Fishbein, MD: An autobiography.* Garden City, NY: Doubleday.

Kiernan, V. (2004). Embargoes and science news. *Journalism and Mass Communication Quarterly, 80,* 903–920.

Kiernan, V. (2006). *Embargoed science.* Champaign: University of Illinois Press.

Marshall, E. (1998). Embargoes: Good, bad or "necessary evil"? *Science, 282,* 860–867.

ENDANGERED SPECIES ACT

To save a species from extinction, only a limited number of mechanisms are available through which to take appropriate action. A concerned person might write articles and books about the endangered plant or animal species; he or she might make speeches and lead demonstrations to move public opinion. A wealthy citizen might attempt to purchase the critical habitat of the species in question, thus guarding its place to live for all time. These types of initiatives can often be effective, and they frequently appear as part of a successful campaign to save an endangered species. But with the introduction of the Endangered Species Act (ESA) of 1973 into this rather meager mix of options for the conservationist, a powerful new tool became available: the lawsuit.

If law is a framework of rules and regulations that help guide the affairs of human beings, then endangered species law is a mechanism to, in effect, give wild plants and animals standing—a voice—within that framework. The advent of endangered species law was stimulated, and is still supported, by the direst of consequences: extinction. An endangered species is in danger of being eliminated from the biosphere. And for biological organisms, extinction is, of course, an irreversible condition. Extinction is forever.

In nature, extinction may occur over very prolonged, evolutionary time periods—a million years or more—or as the result of some sudden catastrophic event. As a new species of plant or animal adapts to the environment, changing genetically ever so gradually with each generation, it may outcompete and displace (drive to extinction) its predecessor. Fossils recovered from beneath the earth give a record of this ancient process of extinction and renewal. On a more abrupt time frame, extraordinary weather on a planetary scale, volcanic eruptions, earthquakes, and tsunamis can result in extinction of plants and animals. The notably sudden disappearance of the dinosaurs from the earth some 65 million years ago is now generally attributed to the earth being struck by a large asteroid. It is reasoned that the dust, water vapor, and other debris that would have followed this horrific collision would have been enough to darken the atmosphere of the entire planet, bringing on an endless winter in which the giant reptiles could not survive.

In modern times, species most often become at risk of extinction because of the acts of mankind. Specific causes of this risk fall into three general categories: overexploitation, such as excessive fishing, hunting, or harvesting; habitat destruction, including pollution of the environment; and exotic species introductions, leading to competitive exclusion of local biota by plants or animals from other continents. Often a specific entity, be it an industry, an agricultural scheme, a governmental agency, or even an individual, can be identified as being responsible for putting the species in danger. With endangered species laws in place, that entity can be challenged by another party, an environmental group, for example, and brought before a judge to have the risk to the species formally addressed. With the power of law, the threatening party must appear. Before the court, he or she is free to argue his or her side of the story: There is no guarantee how the court action will turn out. Either party might win the case. Indeed, today, if the laws are adhered to thoughtfully and if regulatory agencies are performing responsibly, legal interventions to save species—lawsuits—are not necessarily called for. Under the law, the plight of the endangered species must be weighed against the requirements of the human enterprise, and adjustments must be made in the plans to ensure survival of imperiled wildlife.

That has not always been the case. For generations in the United States, projects purportedly beneficial to broad economic development, or to narrow personal gain, including direct exploitation of wildlife such as great whales and the American bison, were considered logical and even noble elements to the U.S. character and to the American Dream. If such activities resulted in the direct destruction of populations of plants or animals or to the grievous degradation of unique habitat and ecosystems, such was the price of doing business. To the proponents of the projects, to politicians,

and even to society in general, it was felt that surely the significance of the economic gain of the enterprise outweighed the disappearance of certain plants and animals from the landscape.

The change in U.S. public attitudes, and in the legislative landscape pertinent to endangered species, can be confidently traced to a single paramount event in 1973: the passage of the ESA legislation signed by President Richard Nixon.

Wildlife Law Before the ESA

To be sure, the ESA is not the first historical example of U.S. wildlife law. In fact, some key concepts in wildlife management date back to medieval times in Europe. For example, defining fish and game (but not plants) as the property of the king (or more generally, the state) is both an ancient and a very helpful notion when presented with the need to manage, protect, or restore populations of wild animals. In the United States, the authority of the government to assume stewardship over wildlife has rarely been challenged. The methods of implementing that stewardship, on the other hand, have regularly stirred controversy.

Landmark wildlife law began to appear in the early part of the 20th century. Laws pertaining to game—identifying game species, declaring closed seasons to allow reproduction, and creating "bag limits"—were vital advances for the status of many mammal and bird species in the country. Curtailing the slaughter of herons and egrets came about during this period (1910). The birds were shot in the thousands during breeding season so that the elaborate plumage of the courting birds could be harvested to decorate women's hats.

In concert with the new wildlife laws, Congress also authorized the establishment of a federal wildlife agency, the U.S. Fish and Wildlife Service (FWS), and called for the designation of a National Wildlife Refuge System. These developments matured to offer crucial functions in wildlife management and conservation in the United States, as well as provide for increasingly popular, and sustainable, outdoor recreation opportunities for the public.

Development of the Endangered Species Concept

These early advances in wildlife law would ensure useful, if often only partial, frameworks to respond to the more contemporary notion of the endangered species. The National Wildlife Refuges, for example, either by coincidence or—more recently—by design, secured critical habitats necessary for the survival of numerous species of plants and animals in this country. But the idea of the endangered species would present the public and the lawmakers with both a managerial and an intellectual challenge.

From out of New England to help bridge the intellectual gap came one of greatest U.S. natural history writers: Rachel Carson. With her book *Silent Spring,* published in 1962, Carson alarmed the nation and launched the modern environmental movement. The "silence" in *Silent Spring* was the author's suggestion that if society did not move forcefully to protect the environment, there would come a dawn with no birds calling, such was her concern for the sinister effects of pollutants, especially pesticides, in the biosphere as she wrote the book. In the years that followed, conservation organizations flourished, new federal and state agencies were created, notably the Environmental Protection Agency, and a plethora of environmental laws were pushed through, including the ESA.

The lesson taught by *Silent Spring,* and one reiterated repeatedly as endangered species law has been applied, has both an ethical and a very practical facet to it. On the one hand is the notion that a species has the right to survive on this earth, that it is somehow immoral for human beings to cause the extinction of the unique products of the evolutionary process. Often accompanying this proposition is the suggestion that the presence of species of plants and animals in our lives enriches our very humanity and that to struggle to protect nature for aesthetic reasons is an entirely reasonable endeavor, one that should even stand up in a court of law.

On the other hand is the suggestion that an endangered species is often an indicator of danger to us as fellow occupants of the earth's biosphere and that to relieve the stresses and threats to that organism is to make the world safer for our own existence. At the time of the release of *Silent Spring,* no species illustrated this principle better than the bald eagle, the symbol of the United States. In the early 1960s, there were fewer than 500 breeding pairs of these magnificent birds remaining in the entire span of the lower 48 states (although eagles in Alaska maintained a robust population). There

were several explanations for their decline from their original continental abundance, but what appeared to have them on the brink of extinction was an insecticide known as DDT.

The bald eagle was given special protection by the federal government as early as 1940 by way of the Bald Eagle Protection Act and was subsequently listed as an endangered species under the ESA. Following the urgings of *Silent Spring,* Congress also banned the further use of DDT as an insecticide in 1972, and the public watched anxiously as the fate of this most recognizable of all birds in the country, in a sense the very embodiment of the United States, hung in the balance. In June 2007, with great ceremony in front of the Jefferson Memorial in the nation's capitol, the bald eagle was removed from the federal list of endangered and threatened species. The moment highlighted a dramatic success story for species recovery under the auspices of the ESA.

There are now as many as 10,000 breeding pairs of eagles in the lower 48 states—and the public can enjoy the satisfaction and pride of witnessing the noble emblem of our country soaring among the clouds.

The ESA in Practice

Over the past 40 years or so, through the discipline of endangered species law, society has learned how to save species, and almost as a collateral benefit, how to make the environment healthier for all living things. Under the ESA, the road to recovery begins with listing. A plant or animal species may be declared (that is, listed) as endangered or threatened depending upon its status in the wild, with the endangered declaration being the more critical. Determinations of the viability of wildlife populations normally require research, monitoring, and data from the field. Accordingly, the listing process is, or at least should be, science based, making the ESA a particularly interesting domain for biologists and setting the stage for ferocious philosophical debate, often pitting scientific fact against economic expectations.

The ESA is implemented by FWS and the National Marine Fisheries Service of the National Oceanic and Atmospheric Administration (NOAA), the latter taking responsibility for marine (saltwater) endangered species issues. The initiative to list threatened and endangered species can be undertaken by either agency. But an individual or organization can also step in to urge the governmental agencies to begin the listing process. This intervention can be by means of a simple petition or, once again, through court action.

Once the species is listed, certain other crucial activities can begin. Among these is enforcement. Individuals or corporate entities that continue to do damage to the species or its habitat can be brought to task. Arrests can be made, fines levied, and licenses to develop or harvest revoked. Violators of the provisions of the ESA may even go to prison.

The listing of an endangered species is normally followed by a recovery plan, a strategy (as the term suggests) to restore the species to a viable condition whereby it no longer needs to be listed. Recovery may call for working directly with individual and groups of organisms, for example, by launching captive propagation programs, a method that was crucial to the recovery of the black-footed ferret in Wyoming and in other western states. Or recovery may entail working with habitat, both by identifying and securing critical habitat, and by refurbishing ecosystems, such as unique forests, river banks, or seashores, to allow the species to carry out essential phases of its life history, such as feeding, breeding, or finding shelter, and to flourish once again.

One other challenging device employed by FWS and NOAA fisheries under the provisions of the ESA is the Habitat Conservation Plan (HCP). This is a proactive means of avoiding catastrophes for endangered species. Learning that his or her property includes critical habitat for an endangered species, the developer or miner or timber company may use the HCP to demonstrate to federal authorities and the public at large just how the project will go forward without jeopardizing the species of concern. Very often, the principle of mitigation will be employed in such projects, a concept which seeks to balance losses in such things as critical habitat in one location with gains, perhaps a gift of land, in another. In any case, the HCP seeks to permit cautious, thoughtful development to proceed without undue negative consequences for nature.

The ESA can be complemented by state and local provisions to protect species. In addition, local interest, sensitivity, and insight can sometimes be ensured in enforcing ESA provisions and advancing recovery plans by passing the implementation authority down from the federal agency to state wildlife management agencies.

Habitat destruction is generally considered the most common, and often the most irreversible, explanation for a species of plant or animal to have become endangered. But in the past and continuing into the present day, direct exploitation—harvesting for commercial or subsistence use—has raised the specter of doom for countless types of organisms. (The most alarming and seemingly untouchable example of destructive direct exploitation today may be industrial taking of innumerable species of fish and invertebrates in every ocean on the planet.) The ESA can respond to some of these harvest challenges, but the legal mechanism with the most comprehensive scope to attend to commercial use of wildlife is the Convention on International Trade in Endangered Species of Fauna and Flora, or CITES. The CITES treaty was ratified by the United States in 1973, the same year that saw passage of the ESA. Indeed, over time, the two legal mechanisms have complemented one another repeatedly. CITES exists out of the now global recognition that international trade in, for example, elephant ivory, sea turtle scales (tortoise shell), rare cactus plants, parrots for pets, and black coral can precipitate extinction. CITES, as a plurinational treaty organization, is particularly interesting and in a sense, superior to the ESA because it allows advocates, including scientists, in one country to influence policy—and wildlife harvest—in another. Thus, if frighteningly rare hyacinthine macaws are found to have been smuggled from Brazil into Holland, the European community might threaten an embargo on Brazilian coffee until the illegal trade is curtailed.

As examples of endangered species law, the ESA rallied the United States and became a beacon and a model for worldwide concern and attention for imperiled plants and animals. CITES became a shared global mechanism to directly address some of the most pressing threats.

Archie Carr III

See also Carson, Rachel; Environmental Protection Agency, U.S.

Further Readings

Bald Eagle Protection Act of 1940, 16 U.S.C. § 668–668d (1940).

Burgess, B. B. (2001). *Fate of the wild: The Endangered Species Act and the future of biodiversity*. Athens: University of Georgia Press.

Carson, R. L. (2002). *Silent spring* (40th anniversary ed.). Boston: Houghton Mifflin.

Convention on International Trade in Endangered Species of Wild Fauna and Flora: www.cites.org

Endangered Species Act of 1973, 7 U.S.C. § 136, 16 U.S.C. § 1531 et seq. (1973).

Endangered Species Program, U.S. Fish and Wildlife Service: www.fws.gov/endangered

Primack, R. (2006). *Essentials of conservation biology* (4th ed.). Sunderland, MA: Sinauer Associates.

ENVIRONMENTAL DEFENSE FUND

The Environmental Defense Fund (EDF), more than any other of the new environmental groups formed in the United States in the 1960s, illustrates the sweeping changes that have taken place in the public interest world, from the last 20th-century time of great U.S. social and political unrest, to the current wave of activism in the first decade of the 21st century. In the period that spawned the U.S. environmental movement, from the late 1960s through the mid-1970s, remnants of state-sanctioned racism, divisions over the Vietnam War, and criminal activity in the White House created broad public engagement in debates about U.S. values and the federal government's responsibilities. With eyes opened by struggles over race, war, and corruption, the Americans were ready to pay attention to other issues.

No social cause benefited more from that attention than the changing and increasingly effective environmental movement. The EDF's roots are in Rachel Carson's 1962 book, *Silent Spring*. Carson's warning that misuse of DDT and other persistent pesticides was wiping out bird populations had intrigued President John F. Kennedy and alarmed environmental groups such as the National Audubon Society and National Wildlife Federation.

Industry's futile attempts to discredit Carson only stimulated more environmental activism. The EDF grew from the urgency of a small team of lawyers and scientists who were unwilling to accept the impending loss of eagles and other birds of prey and who were impatient with the mainstream environmental community's slow response to U.S. wildlife's unnecessary death from pesticides.

In 1967, in the closing hours of National Audubon's annual convention, Victor Yannacone, a young lawyer from New York, ignored protocol and in questions from the floor demanded to know why Audubon was not litigating to prevent the extinction of raptors. After getting polite but uncommitted replies, Yannacone noted that he and his friends were organized to do the job. Yannacone, scientist Charles Wurster, and others had already been going to court to stop the dangerous misapplication of pesticides.

This was the beginning of the EDF. Yannacone quickly moved on to other legal adventures, but Rod Cameron replaced him, and with Chief Counsel Lee Rodgers, the organization survived and grew. EDF's legal success against inappropriate use of pesticides helped the bald eagle, the osprey, and other endangered birds to recover.

EDF's groundbreaking legal work against DDT and toxic substances, its litigation against a river-destroying Corps of Engineers project in Florida (the Cross-Florida Barge Canal), and other cases helped establish the legal principle that U.S. citizens have standing to ask that courts require the enforcement of environmental laws. With the Natural Resources Defense Council, the Center for Law and Social Policy, the Sierra Club Legal Defense Fund (now Earth Justice), and Ralph Nader's young attorneys, EDF built environmental law into a formidable tool in defense of nature and public health.

Two other creative EDF leaders have helped shape EDF and influence the trajectory of U.S. national environmental activism. Before becoming EDF's president in the early 1970s, Arlie Schardt had covered civil rights for *Time Magazine* and then worked for the American Civil Liberties Union. EDF was then under attack by antienvironmental politicians who repeated false claims that one of EDF's founding scientists was a racist. Arlie Schardt's commitment to social equity was beyond question. Schardt promptly erased the organization's debts and strengthened its legal and science abilities. Then he moved EDF beyond litigation into the forefront of work on national environmental policy. He created EDF's first legislative and communications offices.

Schardt also used EDF's influence to expand collaboration at the highest level among old-line national conservation organizations and the new activist environmental groups. When more traditional organizations tried to ignore politically hard-hitting groups such as the Environmental Policy Center or Friends of the Earth or to exclude their women project leaders from White House and federal agency meetings with national environmental leadership, EDF insisted that the other activist groups be at the table.

EDF had been transformed into an organization that used gifted lawyers and scientists inside and outside the courtroom, with political strategists and communications specialists lobbying Congress and the White House, dealing directly with economic interests, and helping to shape U.S. national and global environmental agendas. EDF's next transition, with a new focus on economics and the business marketplace, came from the leadership of Fred Krupp, who became president of the EDF in 1984.

Krupp's realization that understanding economics and working directly with business leaders could bring good environmental results was not new. Alliances of mutual interest between environmentalists, major corporations, labor unions, and other economic interests had taken place for decades and are still pursued by most national environmental groups. But Krupp's strategy made the pursuit of business-negotiated resolution of environmental conflicts the core of EDF's mission. His insights into ways of engaging industry defined EDF and eventually became conventional wisdom in the debate about global climate change—the foundation of most industry, government, and public-interest proposals for reducing greenhouse gas emissions. EDF's attempt to act as industry's collaborator and consultant has led not only to some successes and some potentially important opportunities, but also to some dissonance, both within EDF and with other environmental organizations.

In four decades of leadership, EDF has helped establish environmental law in the United States, rescued U.S. iconic wildlife from extinction, saved generations of children by banning lead in gasoline, and used brilliant legal, scientific, and analytical skills in defense of nature and humanity in the United States and around the world. Now, facing global-scale problems such as climate change and the preservation of biodiversity, it is too early to tell if having big environmental groups join with big financial and industrial companies to design market-based solutions will actually restore a healthy atmosphere, preserve what is left of the best of nature, and provide economic and social opportunity for people on earth.

It is challenging and potentially rewarding for environmentalists to join with industry in thinking about positive solutions, though environmental leaders' history of trying to pick winners in the energy business has not always been successful. In fact, some technologies and alternative fuels promoted by industry, and blessed by environmental groups as climate solutions, actually create more greenhouse gases and destroy more natural habitats than the fuels the alternatives would replace.

Business leaders take economic risks to be rewarded for picking winning strategies. It is up to the public interest community to see that nature and society do not suffer the environmental costs of those choices. But industry's willingness and ability to succeed in business while actually reducing greenhouse gas emissions depends on analysis that openly reveals the environmental benefits and costs of all proposed solutions and on rules that uniformly require the enforcement of strong environmental standards to every enterprise.

Whether market-based solutions will protect the earth from the most severe impacts of climate change remains to be seen. Most likely, organizations such as EDF will also need to keep using their other tools, the same tools that industry itself uses to influence policy: lobbying, litigation, and public pressure.

Joe Browder

See also Carson, Rachel; Union of Concerned Scientists

Further Readings

Environmental Defense Fund: www.edf.org

ENVIRONMENTAL IMPACT STATEMENTS

The environmental impact statement (EIS) is a device that allows study, contemplation, and commentary by a broad spectrum of interested parties before commencing with a project or activity that might threaten the environment or cultural assets. A relatively new legal mechanism, EIS requirements recognize that such engineering works as road building, dam construction, and port channelization can have far-reaching and often unexpected ecological and cultural impacts, and before the bulldozers and draglines go to work, these impacts must be identified and responded to. Communication is a key component; the EIS process involves the use of communication by whatever means are available and appropriate to reach and involve interested parties.

Origins

Following a very gradual awakening of public interest and concern for the environment, an enlightenment encouraged by such U.S. figures as John Muir, Henry David Thoreau, and Aldo Leopold, the EIS became a significant instrument in the U.S. environmental movement in 1970. Most observers agree that the breakthrough was precipitated by yet another U.S. writer, Rachel Carson, and her book *Silent Spring,* published in 1962. The EIS was devised as a legally binding way to pause the developmental process and to enrich it with insights from the biological and social sciences and numerous other disciplines, combined with broad public input.

An EIS might be required by any level of government. A municipality, for example, might call for an EIS before proceeding with a new parking garage. A county might demand an EIS before issuing permits for a new coal-fired electric plant. The state might develop an EIS prior to introducing new timber harvest rules for forests on state lands. At the national level in the United States, the EIS is the centerpiece of the federal National Environmental Policy Act of 1969 (NEPA). Signed into law by Richard Nixon on January 1, 1970, it helped mark the beginning in this country of a new era of environmental awareness and responsibility.

Considered by scholars to be a remarkably straightforward, efficiently worded piece of environmental legislation, the introductory paragraphs of NEPA begin to articulate environmental policy for the nation and are eloquent in stating the purpose and urgency of the groundbreaking law that declares the encouragement of "productive and enjoyable harmony between man and his environment" to be the official national policy of the United States (see the NEPA Web site for full text of the statute and other useful information). These sentiments indicated that the U.S. government and, more importantly, the public were learning a fundamental lesson from ecology that says, metaphorically, that everything is related to everything else. The environmental impact statement was to become the required exercise to identify and address these many things.

The Florida Barge Canal Statement

The first EIS ever drafted in the United States was prepared not as a result of a federal mandate, but as an innovation by a private conservation group, the Florida Defenders of the Environment (FDE). The novel document was titled *Environmental Impact of the Cross-Florida Barge Canal: With Special Emphasis on the Oklawaha Regional Ecosystem* and was published in 1970, the same year that NEPA was signed into law.

A canal cutting across the mid-section of the Florida peninsula had been under consideration by Congress since 1930 as a means to facilitate barge traffic from the Gulf of Mexico to the East Coast of the United States. By 1936, a section of canal had been dug from the Gulf of Mexico inland for a few miles, but the project was abandoned. Formal authorization to resume construction came out of Congress during World War II, but funding shortages and other limitations prevented any significant work. After some false starts, the project began again in earnest in 1964, under the direction of the U.S. Army Corps of Engineers.

Startled by the magnitude of the project and then learning that the canal construction would destroy an extraordinary river in central Florida, the Oklawaha, conservation-minded citizens led by biologist and activist Marjorie Carr were galvanized into action, and the FDE came into being. The group consisted of biologists, economists, lawyers, and other highly trained individuals, many holding faculty positions in universities around the state. As a scholarly group, it soon occurred to FDE that the sensible way to challenge the redoubtable canal project was to examine its costs and benefits methodically and scientifically, to remove guesswork and speculation from evaluation of the project, to verify or disprove the alleged economic rewards of completing the project, to predict and highlight dangers to wildlife and aquatic systems, to give a higher profile to the esthetic values of the threatened river than the canal proponents were willing to acknowledge, and to do this in a single document created by authors with irrefutable qualifications in the form of an EIS.

The strategy worked for FDE. After consideration of the EIS, governmental authorities in Tallahassee, the state capital, and in Washington, D.C., turned against the barge canal project, and in due course, it was deauthorized by Nixon.

The cross-Florida barge canal project was found to be deeply flawed on numerous economic and environmental counts. One of these was particularly surprising and troubling. Among the contributors to the EIS were specialists in Florida's unique geology and underground hydrology. These scientists brought to light the possibility that the proposed canal would be cut into the limestone bedrock of the peninsula at various points along its course. Limestone is a notably porous matrix, and the hydrologists suggested that canal waters would likely pass freely into deep underground water systems, or aquifers, thereby contaminating them. In this way, canal construction would threaten the drinking water supplies of the nearby city of Ocala and possibly even the enormous metropolis of Orlando to the south. It was the type of unexpected finding that made the EIS process, initiated in this case by FDE and perpetuated for the entire country by NEPA, so sensible and so crucial to wise environmental management.

The Environmental Protection Agency: Implementing NEPA

The agency primarily responsible for implementing NEPA and reviewing environmental impact statements at the federal level is the Environmental Protection Agency (EPA). The duties of EPA are formidable. The number and variety of projects around the country requiring an EIS review each year is staggering. To understand the scope of the EIS mandate and to highlight the wide variety of potential environmental impacts that might arise as this country continues to evolve, it is instructive

to study a list of activities under review in 2008 by the EPA:

- Renewal of a license to operate a nuclear power plant in the state of New York
- A subsistence hunting quota for bowhead whales by Native Americans in Alaska
- A plan to restore snapper and grouper fisheries in the South Atlantic Region
- Construction of a light-rail in Texas
- A highway extension at the Florida–Alabama state line
- Construction and operation of a pressurized natural gas pipeline in Wyoming
- Development of the flight systems and earth-based ground infrastructure for the Moon, Mars, and Beyond program
- A land transfer proposal in the Santa Fe National Forest of New Mexico
- Development of a wind energy project in Rhode Island and Massachusetts
- An electric power line project in California
- An elk management plan in Rocky Mountain National Park, Colorado
- Construction of a new facility for the Smithsonian Institute in downtown Washington, D.C.

Each of these projects will be evaluated in a systematic way. Reviewers will look for potential impacts of three sorts: direct impacts, such as the destruction of a bald eagle nesting tree; indirect impacts, such as pollution of a deep aquifer jeopardizing human populations far removed from the actual project site; and cumulative impacts, the sum total of all perturbations, any one of which might be tolerable but which, taken together, can pose a significant threat. By law, for each project a "no-action alternative" will also be considered, wherein reviewers judge what the consequences of not doing the project at all might be. Where risks are perceived, "other reasonable courses of action" are considered, whereby the project's goals might be achieved and the environment protected simply by changing the location of the activity or the manner in which it is developed. And, of course, mitigation measures are considered, compensatory actions that might make up for unavoidable impacts to the human environment by the proposed project.

After more than 35 years, NEPA and the EIS process have helped moderate the footprint of U.S. society on the landscape by requiring careful study of each increment of development, each new road, each new bridge, and each new factory. The EIS can add rationality to the developmental process and can steadily guide society toward a relationship of improved productive harmony with nature.

Archie Carr III

See also Carson, Rachel; Endangered Species Act; Environmental Protection Agency, U.S.

Further Readings

Clark, R., & Canter, L. (Eds.). (1997). *Environmental policy and NEPA: Past, present and future.* Boca Raton, FL: St. Lucie Press.

Florida Defenders of the Environment. (1970). *Environmental impact of the cross-Florida barge canal: With special emphasis on the Oklawaha regional ecosystem.* Gainesville, FL: Author.

National Environmental Policy Act: www.nepa.gov

ENVIRONMENTAL JOURNALISM

Environmental journalism refers to news coverage of events, issues, and conditions related to the health of environments and ecosystems. Environments include land, air, and water and may be natural (a lake or forest, for example) or built (such as a reservoir or city park). *Ecosystems* refer to interrelated populations of animals, plants, and other species within a given habitat, including human communities, and they also may be natural (for example, a wildlife habitat, such as a spawning ground) or built (such as a fish farm).

Many venues for environmental information exist, but environmental journalism refers only to materials published by news outlets that adhere to, and grapple with, the professional practices of journalism, including aiming for objectivity and balance. News refers to information prepared by journalists for general audiences and disseminated in newspapers, magazines, radio and television newscasts, and on the Internet. This includes specialized and niche publications, such as online environmental news services and regional environmental periodicals that follow the journalistic tradition. It generally does not include advocacy materials, such as public relations brochures or magazines published by environmental groups.

News stories from the environment beat often focus on human actions that have contributed or might contribute to the deterioration of environments and ecosystems, including their impacts on human health. Environmental news also can be purely explanatory, such as describing how air pollution travels from one part of the world to another or relaying details of research into the medicinal properties of endangered plants. Environmental journalists also strive to provide news that people can use, such as tips on how to "go green."

This basic description belies the rather complex nature of environmental journalism. As news professionals Craig L. LaMay and Everette E. Dennis noted, the environment story can contain many tensions, including a wide range of conflicting public and political views about environmental protection. Further, the environment beat is known as one that transcends boundaries—that is, the environment story often is also a political, government, or economic story, and it can even involve crime, sports, or a combination of two or more of the above—and others as well. Stories about the environment usually contain scientific elements because of the need to explain why environmental problems occur, what their real or potential impacts are, and how they might best be solved. However, a common thread among environmental news stories is a stated or implied focus on the effects of human action on the biosphere and its human and nonhuman inhabitants.

Origins

Environmental problems, including their discovery and efforts to solve them, are part of U.S. history. As such, so are journalistic reports of these problems. Media historian William Kovarik traced U.S. environmental news coverage to as far back as 1739, when Andrew Bradford of *The American Weekly Mercury* and Benjamin Franklin of *The Pennsylvania Gazette* sparred in print over the dumping of tannery and slaughterhouse wastes into Philadelphia's Dock Creek, which Franklin opposed because of the wastes' foul odor and potential to harm human health, while Bradford viewed Franklin as attacking the freedom to conduct business. In a collection of case studies, Kovarik and his colleague Mark Neuzil documented a variety of approaches to mass media environmental coverage from the mid-19th to early 20th centuries, including magazines' contributions to the creation of regulations to stop the overhunting of wildlife and *New York World* editor Walter Lippmann's efforts in the 1920s to help the "Radium girls," five women who suffered and eventually died of radium poisoning contracted in the factory where they worked. Other researchers have traced news attention to acid rain to 1910 and discovered cautionary news reports about the dangers of DDT dating to 1944, 18 years before the 1962 publication of *Silent Spring,* Rachel Carson's landmark book on DDT and other pesticides. Research also has confirmed that the Progressive Era crusade to conserve the nation's forests received copious news attention during the first decade of the 20th century, largely attributable to the public relations efforts of Gifford Pinchot, the nation's first chief forester.

Many scholars, however, assess this early coverage as sporadic, too heavily focused on natural resource conservation, and too lightly focused on pollution to be collectively considered anything more than a precursor to environmental journalism. They also fault it for ignoring early evidence of health risks associated with commonly used chemicals, including radium, whose dangers were known among members of the scientific and industrial communities by the time the Radium girls began handling it on a routine basis. Further, they have documented that early environmental coverage was severely compromised by journalists' ready reliance on the public relations efforts of corporations who used forests, other natural resources, and chemicals to make their products. Perhaps most importantly, researchers have found that early coverage failed to explicitly link human action and environmental harm, a conclusion that also is often drawn about contemporary environmental news.

Scholars thus usually trace the birth of U.S. environmental journalism to the 1960s, when the modern environment movement began to take shape, and often pinpoint it to 1969, when the *New York Times* assigned reporter Gladwin Hill to cover the environment full time and other news outlets followed suit. After environmentalism crystallized on April 22, 1970, the first Earth Day, scholars found that U.S. environmental news coverage at last was taking steps to focus on what scientists and environmental communication scholars have recognized as one of the most important ideas of the 20th century, namely, that all earthly life is interconnected.

The Environment Beat

Environmental journalism is usually considered a subcategory of science news, which early on was linked to concerted efforts on the part of the new scientific community to promote mass media coverage of its research, considered by some a public service and by others a form of advocacy. *National Geographic Magazine,* for example, was founded in 1888 by a group that included geographers, meteorologists, cartographers, biologists, and engineers who aimed to disseminate research findings among the U.S. population in order to increase their knowledge of the world where we all live. But science as a news beat did not fully develop until after both World Wars, when public and news media interest in scientific issues was catalyzed by the devastation caused by weapons such as tear gas and the atomic bomb.

At first only a handful of reporters had covered science news. Organizations such as the National Association of Science Writers formed and began efforts to foster relationships between journalists and scientists to help ensure that important findings reached the public in accurate forms. Then after World War II, space exploration, and the cold war, competition for prowess in this area attracted more journalists to science. While only about 60 science writers were working before World War II, by 1960 nearly one fourth of 1,500 U.S. daily and Sunday newspapers had assigned a full- or part-time reporter to cover science, medicine, and technology. Also, by the 1960s, science journalists were reporting on research related to human–ecosystem interaction. General science news then and now focuses on discoveries in fields of study ranging from astronomy to zoology and how these discoveries become applied to everyday life. At least a basic knowledge of science is considered an important tool for both science reporters and environmental journalists, who share the common challenge of mastering scientific concepts to translate sometimes complex information in ways that are not only accurate but also enticing to their audiences. Further, science reporters and environmental journalists differ from those who cover beats with more easily visualized turfs, such as city hall and public schools. Yet according to researchers David Rubin and David Sachs, environmental journalism is distinct from science coverage because the environment beat always involves reporting on the direct and indirect human health effects of pollution as well as effects related to the disappearance of indigenous species and other types of degradation.

Contributing to environmental journalism's distinctiveness was the societal paradigm shift that began to form during the 1960s and fully emerged during the 1970s. Events such as the Union Oil spill off the coast of Santa Barbara, California, and the Cuyahoga River fire, caused by routine industrial dumping of thousands of tons of chemical wastes into the river's waters, helped bring public concerns about human abuse of the natural world to the forefront. Government agencies, citizen activists, industry spokespeople, scientists, and academics competed for their version of environmental events and issues to be heard. In the process, a new vocabulary and new ideas began to form. "Environment," once a common referent to a person's general social surroundings, began to signify recognition of humanity's place as but one species among many that faced extinction if human behavior did not change.

For their part, journalists began to realize that environmental coverage was a sorely needed but new type of territory, one requiring that they find new ways to help their audiences weed through competing interpretations, including scientific explanations, of environmental problems and the risks they posed. However, the newly emerging environment beat did not make an easy transition into newsrooms, where beats were organized around governmental and other societal institutions.

Criticism

By some accounts, this transition is still taking place. Environmental journalists must vie for attention to their work within their own news organizations, a situation that often requires that they (a) conform to the traditional criteria of newsworthiness, such as conflict; (b) adhere to a standard focus on immediacy, or current events; and (c) use established approaches to newswriting, including summarizing the news in about 30 words or less in the first paragraph of a news article or the first seconds of a newscast.

Communication scholars have found that when journalists adhere to traditional news practices, they present environmental topics as isolated crises of high drama rather than as occurrences that are part of a continuous chain of events linked to socially sanctioned behaviors, such as overconsumption and oil dependency. Studies also suggest that, like many reporters, environmental journalists rely heavily on government and industry leaders to source their stories, a reliance that contributes to a status quo presentation of environmental problems that ignores other views and perhaps deflects responsibility away from the institutions that these leaders represent.

Researchers also have found that the news media as a whole send contradictory messages, promoting both conservation and consumption and downplaying environmental problems in their circulation areas while focusing on less severe conditions farther away. Communication scholar Allan Mazur has concluded that the news media have an inexplicably short attention span when it comes to the environment, even when evidence of problems is abundantly clear.

Such findings are important because research also indicates that most people, including policymakers, learn about environmental issues via the news media. This may be because the environment is unobtrusive—a majority of Americans have not experienced environmental problems firsthand, and many of these problems are not immediately visible, such as air pollution and rainforest destruction. Thus, it is commonly agreed, when news reports focus on environmental issues, they attract attention and perhaps shape attitudes and prompt action. Likewise, when journalists neglect environmental issues, the polity and the public ignore them, with potentially devastating repercussions. Some environmental risks may never be covered by the press or covered only at a point of crisis, long after the possibility of averting them has passed. Overall, news researchers find, the news media presentation of environmental problems can result in citizen apathy.

Environmental Journalists

Environmental journalists themselves have organized efforts to tackle the challenges inherent to their beat. One such effort dates to 1970, when newspaper journalists formed the California Academy of Environmental News Writers. Twenty years later, a national group, the Society of Environmental Journalists (SEJ), formed and has continued to grow, counting more than 1,000 members among its current ranks. One of this group's stated aims is not only to stimulate more coverage of environmental issues but also to improved approaches to it. To that end, it has supported efforts to provide journalists with special training, as have a variety of other organizations.

An examination of SEJ's history suggests that the environment beat has long since passed the stage where its topics could be neatly categorized as being either about conservation or about pollution. Environmental journalists cover topics ranging from acid rain to zoos and report on toxic risks to all forms of life and associated with products ranging from children's toys to dismantled ships. They also trace the effects of livestock farm waste-disposal systems and sewage sludge and take stock of the environmental costs associated with war. Longtime reporters have judged contemporary environmental journalism as much more complex than in the past, perhaps especially so with the emergence of bioterrorism, a topic they also cover.

In an effort to clarify the state of U.S. environmental journalism, David Sachsman, James Simon, and JoAnn M. Valenti conducted a national census to survey environmental journalists working at daily newspapers and in television news at the turn of the century. They found that newspapers were more likely than television stations to have a reporter covering the environment on a regular basis. However, most of these journalists spent no more than about half of their time covering the environment because they also performed other duties, such as covering breaking news occurring on any beat. The journalists reported that they most often used state environmental quality offices, local environmental groups, and individual citizen activists to source their stories, and their stories most often took a government angle, although they also often used a human-interest frame. Most reporters interviewed rejected the idea that environmental journalists should be advocates for environmental protection, preferring instead to adhere to objective reporting. Most also opposed a public journalism approach, wherein journalists would work with community leaders to solve environmental problems.

Accolades and the Future

Despite challenges and criticisms, environmental journalism has come a long way in a relatively short period of time. A sign of this has been the awarding of the Pulitzer Prize to news organizations for their environment coverage. In 1967, the *Milwaukee Journal* and the *Louisville Courier-Journal* each won a Pulitzer Prize for, respectively, campaigns for tougher water pollution regulation in Wisconsin and for tighter control of strip mining in Kentucky, each deemed to be "a notable advance" with respect to national resource conservation efforts. More recently, the *Los Angeles Times* won a Pulitzer in 2007 for its series on the state of the oceans, while the *New York Times* won a 2008 Pulitzer for its investigation of toxic ingredients in products imported from China, leading to crackdowns by U.S. and Chinese officials.

Yet the environment, like all news beats, sometimes succumbs to economic downturns. When news organizations struggle, the environment beat may be among the first to go, either in total or by being combined with another. To many, this vulnerability is worrisome, given the complex and global environmental challenges of the present day. At the same time, however, the environment has become firmly established as an important news beat. And reporters, better trained and with more collective experience behind them than in the early years of their beat, will continue to report the environmental story.

Jan Knight

See also Beat Reporting; Carson, Rachel; National Association of Science Writers; Newspaper Science Pages; Society of Environmental Journalists

Further Readings

Allan, S., Adam, B., & Carter, C. (Eds.). (2000). *Environmental risks and the media.* London: Routledge.

LaMay, C. L., & Dennis, E. E. (Eds.). (1991). *Media and the environment.* Washington, DC: Island Press.

Neuzil, M., & Kovarik, W. (1996). *Mass media and environmental conflict: America's green crusades.* Thousand Oaks, CA: Sage.

Nieman Foundation. (2002). Environment reporting: Exploring the beat [Special section]. *Nieman Reports, 56*(4), 30–89.

Rubin, D. M., & Sachs, D. P. (1973). *Mass media and the environment: Water resources, land use and atomic energy in California.* New York: Praeger.

Sachsman, D. B., Simon, J., & Valenti, J. M. (2006). Regional issues, national norms: A four-region analysis of U.S. environment reporters. *Science Communication, 28*(1), 93–121.

ENVIRONMENTAL JUSTICE

The environmental movement in the United States has traditionally focused on resource conservation and species preservation, while international efforts have been more expansive and incorporated the concept of environmental justice. Environmental justice efforts can generally be defined as advancing equal and fair access to the environments in which people live, work, worship, and play, supporting equal protection under the law and just enforcement of all environmental regulations. Environmental justice involves rectifying the disproportionate burdens select communities have suffered as a result of the placement of environmental hazards. The United States has seen an increasing inclusion of environmental justice within the framework of the environmental movement since the late 1960s. News accounts of environmental issues are sometimes inspired by environmental justice considerations, and environmental reporters need to be aware of this issue.

Environmental justice seeks to highlight and rectify the inequitable distribution of natural resources and the disproportionate placement of environmental toxins through grassroots activism and legal action. This entry chronicles the environmental justice movement, tracing its history and achievements and providing examples of the fight for equal and fair participation in our environment.

Framework

The civil rights movement established a framework for addressing disparities caused by the perceived weakness or inferiority of select groups of people and their lack of access to power structures. Predicated on the acknowledgment of environmental racism, environmental justice defines environmental rights as civil rights. Environmental racism is the social injustice represented by the disproportionately large number of health and environmental risks cast upon communities of color. Historically, communities of color have been unable to accrue sufficient financial, political, and legal resources to organize and oppose the sitting of toxic facilities. Polluting industries are also attracted to low-income neighborhoods and neighborhoods of color because land values, labor, and other costs of doing business are lower. Globally, this can be seen in actions such as the export of electronic waste from developed nations to developing ones. Companies may perceive these communities to be the paths of least resistance.

Legal History

In the United States, the civil rights movement laid the groundwork for environmental justice through the use of litigation and mass movements as instruments of change. The Civil Rights Act of 1964 provided a legal remedy to discriminatory actions with respect to African Americans and women by encouraging desegregation and prohibiting discrimination in public facilities, government, and employment.

Lawsuits set the framework for congressional action, created remedies for impacted communities, and galvanized a national movement. Ralph Abascal's 1969 lawsuit filed on behalf of six nursing migrant farmers in California eventually led to congressional hearings and the banning of the toxic synthetic pesticide dichlorodiphenyltrichloroethane (DDT) in 1972. In the early 1970s, U.S. Public Health Services determined lead poisoning disproportionately impacted African American and Hispanic communities, and the President's Council on Environmental Quality acknowledged that racial discrimination adversely impacted poor urban communities and degraded the quality of their environment. The 1979 lawsuit *Bean v. Southwestern Waste Management Corporation* was the first U.S. suit to charge that the decision to issue a permit for a solid waste facility constituted racial discrimination, violating the equal protection clause of the Fourteenth Amendment.

These struggles were brought to national attention in 1982 when residents of Warren County, North Carolina, protested plans to situate a toxic waste landfill in their community. The landfill was to store soil contaminated by 30,000 gallons of oil containing polychlorinated biphenyls (PCBs) that had been illegally sprayed along roadsides in 14 North Carolina counties. PCBs are persistent organic pollutants that do not easily degrade and accumulate in the tissue of animals and humans at higher rates than can be absorbed and eliminated.

At the time, Warren County, chosen from 90 proposed sites, had the highest percentage of African American residents in the state. The county was 64% African American, and out of North Carolina's 100 counties, ranked 97th in per capita income. Shocco Township, the site of the landfill, was 75% African American. Local residents joined forces with national civil rights organizers, African American church leaders, elected officials, environmental activists, and labor leaders. Over 400 protestors were arrested in the 2 weeks after the site opened. While the demonstrators were unsuccessful in blocking the landfill, they brought attention to the disparate treatment of low-income communities of color and galvanized local citizens around environmental issues. Decades later, the state of North Carolina was required to spend over $25 million to detoxify the Warren County PCB landfill, a process that was completed in 2003.

The Warren County protests prompted the Congressional Black Caucus to request that the U.S. General Accounting Office investigate the racial composition of communities hosting hazardous waste landfills. The resulting 1983 G.A.O. study, "Siting of Hazardous Waste Landfills and Their Correlation With Racial and Economic Status of Surrounding Communities," stated that in the southeastern United States, three of the four communities with hazardous waste landfills contained a majority of African American residents. In all four of these communities, at least 26% of the population had incomes below the federal poverty level.

The Warren County struggle was also the catalyst for the landmark 1987 "Toxic Waste and Race" report compiled by the United Church of Christ (UCC) Commission for Racial Justice. In this report, Rev. Benjamin Chavis Jr. originated the term *environmental racism*, defined as racial discrimination in the official sanctioning of the life-threatening presence of poisons and pollutants in minority communities through strategic sitting, government policy, unequal enforcement of laws and regulations, and the exclusion of minority stakeholders from mainstream environmental groups, decision-making boards, commissions, and regulatory bodies. The UCC study highlighted the direct correlation between the location of hazardous waste sites and minority populations. UCC determined that areas with the highest concentration of people of color also had the largest number of commercial hazardous waste facilities and that three out of five African Americans and Hispanics lived in neighborhoods containing uncontrolled toxic waste sites. The report also discovered that African American children comprised 50% of all children afflicted by lead poisoning and that pesticide poisoning had the largest impact on Hispanic farm workers and their families.

Grassroots organizing against lead and asbestos poisoning was prominent in the Midwest. Hazel Johnson founded People for Community Recovery (PCR) on the South Side of Chicago. Known as the "Mother of Environmental Justice," Johnson spearheaded a campaign to remove asbestos in local homes and schools and to educated community members about the record concentrations of lead poisoning hazards in the community's public housing development. These efforts resulted in a series of lead reforms and outreach programs by the Chicago Housing Authority.

The 1990s marked a period of further substantiation of environmental racism and greater pursuits toward environmental justice. The U.S. Congress passed seminal environmental protections through the 1990 Clean Air Act that provided further grounds for lawsuits regarding environmental harm. However, by ignoring the existing concern regarding discrepancies in how toxins and pollutants were accumulating and impacting populations of color, the Environmental Protection

Agency (EPA) was open to scrutiny. In response to a charge from the Congressional Black Caucus that the needs of people of color were left unaddressed, EPA created an Environmental Equity Workgroup that, 2 years later, determined the allegations were true and that racial minority and low-income populations experienced greater exposure to air pollutants, hazardous waste facilities, and pesticides. The report, "Environmental Equity: Reducing Risks for All Communities," included recommendations to give greater priority to environmental equity, reduce risk for vulnerable groups, and increase efforts to involve communities of color and low-income communities in environmental policy making. On the recommendation of the report, EPA established the Environmental Equity Office, now the Office of Environmental Justice, in 1992 to support its environmental equity outreach and policy efforts.

In February 1994, President Bill Clinton signed Executive Order 12898, "Federal Actions to Address Environmental Justice in Minority Populations and Low-Income Populations," directing federal agencies to address the disproportionate and unfavorable public health and environmental impacts of their programs on minority and low-income populations. The order also encouraged increased access to public information and stakeholder participation in issues regarding human health and the environment.

More recently, the UCC released an update of its original report "Toxic Wastes and Race at Twenty: 1987–2007." The study reaffirmed that race and place matter. Significant racial and socioeconomic disparities persist in the placement of hazardous waste facilities and polluting industries. Legal remediation is inconsistent, and communities of color and low-income communities continue to face unequal protection under the law. In response, environmental sociologist Robert Bullard (known as the "Father of Environmental Justice") presented the Senate Subcommittee on Superfund and Environmental Health hearing titled "Oversight of E.P.A.'s Environmental Justice Programs" with a letter signed by over 100 environmental justice, civil rights, health advocacy, and faith-based groups. The letter endorsed the 2007 UCC report findings and recommendations to codify Environmental Justice Executive Order 12898, reinstate the Superfund tax, require industries to provide safety data on harmful chemicals introduced to market, promote cleaner production and waste management technologies, and reestablish a private right of action to prove discrimination under Title VI of the Civil Rights Act of 1964.

Cultural History

The environmental justice movement is made up of people who do not typically identify themselves as environmentalists. These citizens, grassroots organizers, and advocates have a vested stake in the environment but may not participate in organizations exclusively dedicated to nature conservation. While environmental groups have dedicated themselves to highlighting the plights of species extinction and climate change, the environmental justice movement strives to put a human face on these issues and address the preservation of communities through the inclusion of local stakeholders.

In 1989, the nonprofit Gulf Coast Tenants Organization and residents of the 100-mile corridor between Baton Rouge and New Orleans, Louisiana, led a "toxic march" through the region. "Cancer Alley," as it is sometimes known, contains 128 petrochemical companies and is infamous for the highest rates of cancer, birth defects, and miscarriages in the United States. Most victims of these health problems are African Americans who live and work along the Mississippi River.

The community-led initiatives and grassroots activism that define the environmental justice movement continue to reshape the traditional environmental movement. In January 1990, nine activists of color wrote a letter to the "Big 10" national environmental organizations, including Greenpeace, World Wildlife Fund, National Wildlife Federation, Natural Resources Defense Council, The Nature Conservancy, and Sierra Club. The activists challenged the nonprofit groups to increase the racial and ethnic diversity of their staffs and boards of directors and to engage in dialogue with activists of color on the environmental crisis impacting their communities.

In 1991, the First National People of Color Environmental Justice Summit was held in Washington, D.C., and attended by over 650 grassroots and national leaders from all 50 states. Summit delegates outlined 17 "Principles of Environmental Justice," meant as guidelines for organizing and relating to government and non-governmental organizations. The principles were later translated into Spanish and Portuguese and distributed at the 1992 Earth Summit in Rio de Janeiro. Over 1,200 delegates representing grassroots, academic, church, and labor organizations from around the world gathered at the Second National People of Color Environmental Justice Summit in 2002, an almost 200% increase in participation, and more than half of the 86 sessions were led by women.

Environmental justice gained an institutionalized presence with the founding of the Deep South Center for Environmental Justice at Xavier University in Louisiana in 1992. Built on the idea that knowledge of daily community life must be integrated with scientific research to create effective environmental policy, the center promotes collaboration between scientific researchers, policymakers, and communities, and it focuses on developing minority leadership in the areas of environmental, social, and economic justice along the Mississippi River Corridor.

Recent Events

Recent environmental events demonstrate that the struggle for environmental justice is ongoing and amassing greater interest. Hurricane Katrina in New Orleans, Louisiana, in 2005 highlighted socioeconomic disparity in environmental planning and emergency response to environmental disasters. The United Nations Climate Change Conference in 2007 sought to develop a roadmap to tackle climate change, but it failed to set binding targets for reducing greenhouse gas emissions and used market mechanisms as the primary means of change. Because agrarian-based developing nations are most vulnerable to climate disruptions, these official decisions spawned sideline discussions among activists working to increase civilian participation and define just climate parameters and policies. The growing "green jobs" movement expands environmental justice and uses employment as an instrument of social change, working to revitalize low-income communities and communities of color through the transformation of blue-collar jobs and the creation of localized jobs in renewable energy, recycling, and other environmental industries.

Conclusion

Environmental justice requires us to rethink our relationship with our own and neighboring communities and to expand our understanding of the environment; it is as much about saving people as it is about preserving wildlife. Neither nature nor toxins adhere to boundaries or make distinctions between low-income and high-income areas or between predominantly white areas and communities of color. Mistreatment of our environment will ultimately impact everyone and result in costs to our health, communities, economies, and natural resources. The struggle for clean air, clean soil, and clean water benefits everyone.

The low-income communities and communities of color that have been excluded from environmental discussions must be given the tools and opportunity to participate. Because environmental issues are global ones, they cannot be addressed without a comprehensive collaboration between many communities, each with their own needs and approach. Acknowledging and understanding political and social divisions of race, class, and gender are fundamental to shifting global patterns of environmental inequality in the direction of justice for all.

P. Simran Sethi

See also NIMBY ("Not In My Backyard"); Superfund

Further Readings

Bean v. Southwestern Waste Management Corporation, 482 F. Supp. 673 (1979).

Bullard, R. (1990). *Dumping in Dixie: Race, class, and environmental quality.* Boulder, CO: Westview Press.

Bullard, R. (Ed.). (1993). *Confronting environmental racism: Voices from the grassroots.* Boston: South End Press.

Clean Air Act Amendments of 1990, 42 U.S.C. § 7401 et seq. (1990).

Chavis, B. F., Jr. (1987). *Toxic wastes and race.* Boston: South End Press.

Civil Rights Act of 1964, Pub. L. No. 88-352, 78 Stat. 241 (1964).

Lee, C. (1993). Beyond toxic wastes and race. In R. Bullard (Ed.), *Confronting environmental racism: Voices from the grassroots* (pp. 41–52). Boston: South End Press.

United Church of Christ Commission for Racial Justice. (1987). *Toxic wastes and race in the United States: A national report on the racial and socio-economic characteristics of communities with hazardous waste sites.* New York: Author.

United States Environmental Protection Agency. (1992). *Environmental equity: Reducing risk for all communities* (Vols. 1–2). Washington, DC: Environmental Equity Workgroup, Office of Policy, Planning, and Evaluation, USEPA.

United States General Accounting Office. (1995). *Hazardous and nonhazardous waste: Demographics of people living near waste facilities.* Washington, DC: Author.

ENVIRONMENTAL PROTECTION AGENCY, U.S.

Established in 1970, the U.S. Environmental Protection Agency (EPA) describes itself as the U.S. environmental steward. With a mission to protect human health and the environment, the agency engages in six major areas of activity: (1) to develop regulations to implement environmental laws passed by Congress; (2) to enforce environmental laws, regulation, and standards; (3) to provide grants to states, nonprofit organizations, and educational institutions; (4) to study environmental issues; (5) to support pollution prevention and energy conservation measures; and (6) to promote environmental education so that Americans realize the benefits of clean land, air, and water.

In the 1960s, environment issues were surfacing as a political and social concern. With the publication of Rachel Carson's *Silent Spring* in 1962 and the first Earth Day celebration in 1969, the stage was set for official federal action concerning the environment. President Richard Nixon established the Environmental Quality Council 4 months after his inauguration. The National Environmental Policy Act (NEPA) was signed into law January 1, 1970, establishing national environmental policy and outlining goals for the protection, maintenance, and enhancement of the environment. Fueled by the effort of Roy Ash, founder of Litton Industries, the EPA, an autonomous regulatory body designed to oversee enforcement of environmental policy, cleared regulatory

hurdles and was established December 2, 1970. Today, the EPA employs more than 17,000 individuals and has an annual budget in excess of 7 billion dollars.

The EPA manages its mission under five strategic goals addressing land, air, water, human exposure and health, and ecological conditions and compliance. Structured over 14 headquarter offices and 10 regions, agency divisions are responsible for the execution of the agency's programs. A key priority is that EPA decisions be based on sound scientific data, analysis, and interpretation. As such, Congress established the EPA Science Advisory Board (SAB) in 1978 with the charge of advising EPA on matters of relevant science. Largely composed of independent scientists and experts, the SAB acts as a federal advisory committee and must announce its meetings in the *Federal Register* and provide opportunities for public comment.

EPA efforts to facilitate effective communication between the agency and the public include distribution of information, solicitation of public involvement in decision making, and enforcing laws requiring information disclosure on the part of entities that may pose potential threats to environment and health. As a distributor of information, the EPA has made available a large family of publications on various topics and maintains an extensive Web site for lay audiences. Information is made available in English, Spanish, Chinese, Vietnamese, and Korean. Special efforts to target publics include the EPA's Environmental Kids Club designed for 5- to 12-year-olds. The EPA also maintains a teaching center with educational resources to promote environmental education in both formal and informal settings. Annually, the agency also produces a performance and accountability report for citizens. The EPA's Office for Public Affairs is the primary center responsible for public outreach and communications. The Office for Public Affairs maintains divisions for public outreach, media relations, and Web communications.

As well as basing environmental decisions on sound science, the EPA solicits involvement from the public, acknowledging that doing so enhances the quality of decision making and the deliberative process. After 2 years in development, the agency produced an official Public Involvement Policy in 2003. The policy encourages EPA officials to promote early and meaningful public involvement; to identify, communicate, and listen to affected populations; to involve the public in the development of alternatives and conflict resolution; and to foster partnerships that facilitate public involvement.

This policy outlines seven specific steps to facilitate effective public involvement and asserts that "the Agency should approach all decision making with a bias in favor of significant and meaningful public involvement" (U.S. Environmental Protection Agency, 2003, p. 4). The National Service Center for Environmental Publications followed the Public Involvement Policy with a 20-page framework for implementing it. Specific communicative techniques include workshops, community meetings, mailing lists, and use of the *Federal Register* and media outlets to publicize opportunities for public involvement. The EPA's Web site also provides opportunities for public input. Moreover, several EPA regulations include procedural outlines for public involvement, ranging from broad mandates such as the Freedom of Information Act to the very specific Rules of Practice Governing Hearings, Under the Federal Insecticide, Fungicide, and Rodenticide Act.

The EPA, as well as other federal agencies and commissions, is charged with enforcing the many laws mandating disclosure of information by those potentially causing environmental harm. The EPA makes both hard data and compliance data available through its Enforcement and History Online Web presence, which offers extensive capabilities to information seekers including facility searches, regional searches, analysis of trends, and reports and resources. Other services and Web-based outlets hosted by the EPA provide mandated environmental disclosure data concerning specific areas such as the Envirofact Data Warehouse (for water data) and AirData.

A notable contribution to communication practices made by the EPA is its recent attention to the area of risk communication. In 1995, the EPA created the National Risk Management Research Laboratory (NRMRL) in a reorganization of several offices. While communications is not within the stated mission of this laboratory, risk management professionals acknowledge that risk management includes risk assessment and communication of hazards. Risk communication is the process of communicating about potential physical hazards with the goals of helping publics understand risk management, to form perceptions of hazards based

on scientific perspectives, and to participate in decisions regarding how to manage risks. In 2007, the NRMRL's publication of *Risk Communication in Action: The Risk Communication Workbook* marked a significant move by the EPA to acknowledge concepts of risk communication based on values, persuasion, perceptions, and presentation of data.

With less than a half of a century of existence, the EPA has emerged as a significant federal arm serving as a protector of the environment and human health. Through concentrated scientific and enforcement efforts, the agency strives toward mitigation and prevention of environmental damage. As a communicator, the agency seeks to make environmental data public, to inform citizens about environmental issues, and to involve publics in the decision making of the agency.

Joye C. Gordon

See also Environmental Impact Statements; Environmental Journalism; Government Public Information; Public Engagement; Risk Communication, Overview

Further Readings

National Environmental Policy Act, 42 U.S.C. § 4321 et seq. (1970).

U.S. Environmental Protection Agency. (2003). *Public involvement policy of the U.S. Environmental Protection Agency*. Available at www.epa.gov/publicinvolvement/pdf/policy2003.pdf

U.S. Environmental Protection Agency. (2008). *Performance and accountability report: Environmental and financial progress*. Available at www.epa.gov/ocfo/par/2008par/par08report.pdf

U.S. Environmental Protection Agency. (2008). *Risk communication in action: The risk communication workbook*. Available at www.epa.gov/nrmrl/pubs/625r05003/625r05003.pdf

U.S. Environmental Protection Agency: www.epa.gov

ETC GROUP

In recent years, civil society organizations[1] such as the ETC Group (or Action Group on Erosion,

Technology and Concentration) have played an increasingly important role in shaping debates on science and technology issues and in stimulating global policy dialogues on the appropriate development of transformative technologies and their socioeconomic implications. With a small complement of staff, this Canadian-based advocacy group has successfully lobbied governments and consulted with international bodies on a global scale. It has focused its attention on topics such as plant genetic resources, biotechnology, intellectual property rights, biopiracy, nanotechnology, geoengineering, synthetic biology, and human genomics. The ETC Group is a registered civil society organization in Canada and in The Netherlands, while Friends of the ETC Group is a private, nonprofit organization in the United States.

In the early 1970s, Pat Mooney, Hope Shand, and Cary Fowler founded a precursor organization to the ETC Group known as RAFI (Rural Advancement Foundation International) that was based in Winnipeg, Canada. RAFI was one of the first civil society organizations to pioneer advocacy-based research on the rights of farmers in the developing world, and it played a significant role in lobbying for the *International Treaty on Plant Genetic Resources for Food and Agriculture* that came into effect on June 29, 2004. In 2000, RAFI transformed itself into the ETC Group, which has dedicated its advocacy work to support the development and deployment of technologies that could benefit marginalized peoples on global and regional levels but does not undertake grassroots, community, or national work. As such, the ETC Group is strongly oriented toward conservation and the sustainable development of cultural and ecological diversity. To achieve these goals, the ETC Group conducts and freely distributes policy-relevant research, leads educational programming initiatives, and has consultative status on a variety of bodies such as the United Nations Economic and Social Council, United Nations Biodiversity Convention, Food and Agriculture Organization, United Nations Conference on Trade and Development, and with the Consultative Group on International Agricultural Research.

To understand how this organization evolved over time, it may be useful to characterize their work in the following way. In phase one (between the early 1970s and 2001), this civil society organization focused it energies on agricultural issues and developed a niche for itself in the fields of agricultural biodiversity, food security, and the impacts of emerging biotechnologies on the rural poor. In a second phase (2001–2008), the ETC Group shifted its emphasis to questions of technological convergence and focused on nanotechnology, synthetic biology, geoengineering, and human genomics.

In the first phase of its development, the ETC Group managed to colonize areas that were relatively underexamined by civil society organizations. For example, in 1981, this organization explored how the development of herbicide-tolerant plant varieties could pose threats to food security. The ETC Group coordinated civil society organizations from around the world to explore these issues by showing how pesticide companies were purchasing seed companies on a global scale and how they were simultaneously developing genetically modified plants that were tailor-made to work with proprietary brands of pesticides. In 1998, the ETC Group discovered that several large biotechnology companies were developing patented sterile seed technology that could also have implications for food security and have negative impacts on small-scale farmers in the developing world who have practiced seed saving techniques for generations. Through the work of this organization, this so-called terminator technology was stalled in its bid to reach the commercialization stage. The ETC Group also played a key role in drawing attention to intellectual property rights issues and is credited with coining the term *biopiracy*, which refers to the unfair capture of indigenous knowledge (usually genetic and genomic resources from local plants) by multinational corporations for the purposes of commercial exploitation.

In 2001, the ETC Group shifted into a second phase of its development with the release of an influential report on technological convergence and nanotechnology. This work was subsequently followed up on with separate reports on nanotechnology in food and agriculture, medical applications of nanotechnology, and ultimately a competition sponsored in 2007 by this organization to develop an international symbol for products containing potentially hazardous nano-materials. The ETC Group also moved into the synthetic biology and human genomics debates in

2006 and 2008, respectively, with reports on the implications of synthetically manufacturing DNA molecules and the advent of direct-to-consumer DNA testing kits. In 2007, the ETC Group released a report on geoengineering and reviewed critically a variety of proposed ocean fertilization projects for sequestering carbon dioxide for carbon crediting purposes under the Kyoto Protocol to the *International Convention on Climate Change*.

The ETC Group is a prime example of a civil society organization whose focus on facilitating policy dialogue helps bridge the gaps that exist currently between developed and less developed countries. With an emphasis on fairness, equity, cultural sensitivity, and sustainability, the ETC Group has played a key role globally in raising awareness of issues that normally get poor coverage by the mass media or receive little scholarly attention in academia. The ETC Group translates complex scientific information and cutting-edge technological advancements into socially relevant chunks that represent a unique brand of science communication that spans multiple disciplines, various stakeholders, and has global reach.

Michael D. Mehta

Note

1. More commonly used in Canada than in the United States, the term *civil society organizations* refers to the broad range of formal and informal nongovernmental organizations and groups that participate in civic affairs such as policy development.

See also Agricultural Biotechnology; Nanotechnology, Regulation of; Resource Mobilization; Synthetic Biology and Genomics

Further Readings

ETC Group: www.etc.org

ETHICAL, LEGAL, AND SOCIAL ISSUES (ELSI)

The acronym ELSI (pronounced *Elsie*) entered common use as the result of a unique research

initiative conducted by the U.S. National Institutes of Health (NIH) for the Human Genome Initiative (HGI), a global effort to sequence the human genome. It is now used to refer very broadly to research on the ethical, legal, and social issues that accompany scientific and technical change. ELSI research has two direct ties to communication. First, topics studied by ELSI research are often of critical importance in science communication and news coverage of science and technology. Second, ELSI programming at science funders such as NIH and the National Science Foundation (NSF) is the institutional home for a great deal of communications research.

It was widely recognized that the NIH Human Genome Project (HGP) would be attended by a number of issues that lay beyond the purview of traditional NIH sponsored research in basic and medical science. Among them would be the possibility that genetic screening would be used to exclude people from insurance or employment and to make decisions about terminating a pregnancy. In addition, the HGI itself was already seen to be having broad cultural significance in the form of speculation about *genetic determinism*—a term that referred broadly to views that traits of character, personality, and racial or ethnic identity had a basis in human genetics. HGP's first director, James Watson, proclaimed that where people once understood their fates to be determined by the stars, now they know that "fate is in our genes."

Thus, when the U.S. Congress authorized a new funding stream for the HGP in 1989, they required NIH to develop a plan for dealing with these issues in a systematic fashion. The ELSI program was the result. The original ELSI program supported research and policy forums intended to track closely with the basic science work being conducted under the auspices of the HGP. Eric Jungst was the first director of ELSI programming at NIH. Researchers in a wide range of science studies disciplines began to craft proposals that could be tied to questions in human genetics. As genetics and genomics became more central to questions in medicine, the goals of the ELSI initiative were broadened to be inclusive of many social and ethical questions associated with biomedical research. Watson originally announced that 5% of HGP funding would be dedicated to ELSI work. Although this figure was quickly halved, it still represented a more than doubling of the funding available to U.S. researchers in science studies, and especially to those who emphasized ethics. Thus, the ELSI program is significant in part simply because of the way that it created a new era of legitimacy and opportunity for social scientists, philosophers, and other scholars conducting research on the broader social implications of science and technology.

Expanding ELSI Concepts and Activities

When the HGP was completed, NIH and the U.S. Department of Energy continued to issue requests for proposals in the ethical, legal, and social issues raised by the basic science research that the agencies support. ELSI has become a term used to refer broadly to scholarship on the broader implications of science and technological innovation, without regard to whether this research is funded through agencies that utilize the ELSI acronym to describe their program. ELSI type work began to be funded both by national science agencies in Europe and by the European Union in the wake of controversy over agricultural biotechnology and problems encountered in the discovery and management of risks from prion diseases such as bovine spongiform encephalopathy, popularly referred to as "mad cow" disease. One of the largest ELSI initiatives has been sponsored by Genome Canada under the acronym GE³LS, which stands for Genomics, Ethics, Environmental, Economic and Legal Studies. Genome Canada projects are distinctive both for their size (GE³LS projects have exceeded 5 million in Canadian dollars) and for the emphasis that has been placed upon integrating science studies work more closely with ongoing genomics research and technology development.

As the concept of ELSI has been broadened, it becomes apparent that studies of this sort did not begin with the NIH ELSI program in 1989. The U.S. NSF had been funding such research (albeit at a significantly lower total dollar commitment) through a series of programs since the 1970s. Rachelle Hollander was the primary architect of an NSF program titled Ethics and Values in Science and Technology (EVIST). The EVIST program was merged into a more comprehensive initiative in the 1990s, but NSF continues to operate a program in Societal Dimensions of Engineering, Science and Technology (SDEST). NSF has also dedicated a

significant resource commitment to research on Social and Ethical Issues in Nanotechnology (SEIN) under the National Nanotechnology Initiative (NNI). NIH and the Department of Energy funding on nanotechnology has utilized the original ELSI acronym, while the U.S. Department of Agriculture launched its first competition for proposals on social and ethical implications of nanotechnology in 2007.

Nanoscience and nanotechnology has proved to be an important focus for ELSI-type research. The U.S. Congress created the NNI by passing the U.S. 21st Century Nanotechnology Research and Development Act in 2003. Although the act does not provide for new funding streams, it directs federal agencies to develop a coordinated plan to foster research on nanotechnology. It also specifies that research in the physical and biological sciences must be accompanied by research that anticipates and evaluates the broader social and ethical implications expected to follow from this domain of science. Testimony before Congress articulated two primary rationales for this unprecedented specification. One was the prior success of ELSI research sponsored through the HGP. The other was the public furor associated with agricultural applications of recombinant DNA techniques in the creation of genetically modified organisms. NSF has funded several groups undertaking normative or policy relevant studies in conjunction with the NNI, including a large multi-institution project called the Center for Nanotechnology in Society based at Arizona State University, University of California at Santa Barbara, the University of South Carolina, University of California at Los Angeles, and Harvard.

The welter of acronyms associated with these programs reflects the bureaucratic requirements at these distinct funding agencies. Agencies specializing in the funding of specific domains in the biological and physical sciences have developed programs to support social science and humanities research that bears upon their particular area of science. In fact, there are often overlaps both in research methods and even in individuals conducting these diverse studies on the implications of science and technological development. Thus, while from the perspective of funding agencies there are programs in ELSI, GE³LS, SDEST, and SEIN, there is in actuality a loosely unified research community of social scientists and humanities scholars who migrate back and forth among all these programs for support of their research. Some studies are identifiably based in a specific social science or humanities discipline, while others are markedly multidisciplinary and interdisciplinary in their approach.

Themes in ELSI Research

Given the range and variety of sciences or technological innovations studied by ELSI researchers, it is virtually impossible to characterize ELSI research either in terms of central themes or unique research methods. However, one characteristic that distinguishes most ELSI studies from other social science studies of science and technology is a clear normative orientation. Not all ELSI research has a focus on ethics as such, but most studies do isolate and analyze issues. ELSI studies often identify aspects and implications of science and technology that could be construed as problematic or as calling for some sort of response either from the research community or from policymakers. Other times they emphasize social controversy concerning the nature of the science itself, its regulation and sponsorship or unintended consequences in the realm of environment and social organization. Some ELSI studies have prescribed appropriate policy or behavioral responses to the problems and ills they have diagnosed. Thus, HGP ELSI studies that noted how genetic profiles could affect insurability or employment prospects often called for legislation to ban such uses of genetic information.

Other than normativeness, it would be difficult to single out any other characteristic that would describe more than a fraction of ELSI research that has been conducted over the 40-year history of such research. ELSI research has been conducted by philosophers, sociologists, political scientists, historians, economists, anthropologists, geographers, legal scholars, linguists, and theologians, as well as by scientists trained in the physical and biological sciences. It has deployed classical forms of content and conceptual analysis as well as surveys, archival research, ethnographic interviews, focus groups, and participant observation. It has been undertaken by single investigators and by collaborative teams of researchers from multiple disciplines. Although genetic sciences are disproportionately represented among the topics for ELSI research, virtually every conceivable type of science could be the object of an ELSI study. A few general themes in ELSI work bear special mention.

First, studies on the use of human subjects have had significant effects on the research process in biomedical and social science. In 1979, a National Commission for the Protection of Human Subjects of Biomedical and Behavioral Research issued a study that has come to be known as the Belmont Report. The study focused on high profile abuses of human subjects such as the Tuskegee syphilis study in which the disease was allowed to run its course in a population of African American subjects so that researchers could track its progress. This observation continued long after it was recognized that penicillin could provide a safe and effective cure. Subjects believed they were receiving treatment for the disease and were never offered an opportunity to receive more effective drug therapies. The Belmont Report highlighted these and other abuses and established the need for informed consent and for institutional committees to review protocols in which human subjects were utilized. ELSI style work has continued to refine and develop appropriate guidelines for the research process, especially as research has involved potentially sensitive collection and use of genetic information on individuals and on vulnerable populations.

Second, ELSI-type studies have revealed a number of ways in which science and technology can become entangled with unequal power arrangements. In particular, such studies have focused on the changing nature of personal privacy in technologically advanced societies. Innovations ranging from remote sensing with satellite data to radio frequency identification can allow social actors with money and privilege to obtain potentially valuable information about the activities of others. ELSI-type studies have resulted in both legislation and privately enacted policies that would strictly limit the use of surveillance technologies in situations where individuals could expect privacy. It has also led to the creation of advocacy groups specifically focused on privacy, as well as to actions undertaken by labor organizations on behalf of their members. Privacy impacts from genetic and electronic technologies continue to be both controversial and a frequent object of study by ELSI researchers.

Third, ELSI research has played a role in the rise of new policy and governance mechanisms intended to increase the effectiveness of public participation in decision making. Here, ELSI studies converged with social movements focused on environmental protection and empowerment of women and minorities, but influential studies on managers of technologically based public works programs brought the need for broader participation to the attention of the science community. Cognizance of the way that minorities have been disproportionately exposed to industrial pollutants brought about calls for environmental justice. Langdon Winner's idea of the "technological constitution of society" illustrated how choices over putatively technical domains such as the telephone system or the electric power grid can have long-lasting effects on social interdependencies and the quality of life. Studies on risk perception surfaced a variety of public concerns not previously associated with the regulation of technologically based risks. Collectively, these concerns have merged under the goal of democratizing science, and new ELSI research has been undertaken to test the effectiveness of various modes for accomplishing this goal.

Communications research has been particularly relevant to this last category of ELSI studies. In 1996, the National Research Council issued a report titled *Understanding Risk* that underlined the importance of a well-designed communication process both to provide public input into programs of scientific risk assessment, and also to avoid serious misunderstandings and reactions of public outrage associated with unsophisticated attempts to translate studies on the probability that new technologies would cause hazardous outcomes to a public made increasingly aware of technological risks. ELSI research was in part the basis for *Understanding Risk,* and communication focused research has become increasingly central to ELSI research in its wake.

Paul B. Thompson

See also Human Genome Project; Research Ethics, Overview; Watson, James D.

Further Readings

Clayton, E. W. (2003). Ethical, legal and social issues in genomic medicine. *New England Journal of Medicine, 349,* 562–569.

Meslin, E. M., Thomson, E. J., & Boyer, J. T. (1997). Bioethics inside the beltway: The ethical, legal, and social implications research program at the National Human Genome Research Institute. *Kennedy Institute of Ethics Journal, 7,* 291–298.

Mnyusiwalla, A., Daar, A. S., & Singer, P. A. (2003). "Mind the gap": Science and ethics in nanotechnology. *Nanotechnology,* **14,** R9–R13.

U.S. 21st Century Nanotechnology Research and Development Act, Pub. L. No. 108-153 (2003).

Wynne, B. (2001). Creating public alienation: Expert cultures of risk and ethics on GMOs. *Science as Culture, 10,* 445—481.

Eugenics

During the late 19th and early 20th centuries, a belief in biological determinism became the basis for the movement known as *eugenics.* For many, eugenics was seen as a secular religion, providing the modern world with a new, biologically based Ten Commandments. Eugenicists planned to create this better world by controlling and improving the inheritance of society's next generation. Despite this rhetoric of social improvement, 20th-century eugenics was associated with racism and ethnic bias, maintenance of the social status quo, support for the powerful over the powerless, and putting the interests of the native born over those of the newcomer. Before it was rejected as poor science and unacceptable social policy, eugenics was used against the interests of large numbers of Americans and against democracy. More contemporary advances in genetics and genomics are at the heart of a number of public policy issues currently being debated as to how this knowledge should be used; this entry provides valuable historical context for some of today's ongoing debates about genetic manipulation.

The history of humankind's desire to construct an explanation for varying levels of human performance and to improve the next generation of human beings can be traced to sources including Plato's (348–347 BCE) classic text, *The Republic.* In that volume, Socrates explains that human differences are best understood as a reflection of human essences. An individual's behavior is a direct expression of the stuff of which that person is made. And as those essences scale upward in quality from iron and brass to silver to gold, so too do the moral and civic qualities of the citizens who possess them, in this view. To reframe the argument in terms unknown to Plato or Socrates, we are what our genes make us; we are determined by our biology. And some have argued on this basis that human improvement depends primarily on manipulating and improving humanity's biological inheritance.

In the early 20th-century United States, native-born Anglo-Saxon intellectuals had become anxious about their status in the face of rapid social change. Since the end of the Civil War, increases in immigration, urbanization, crime, and social dislocation had transformed U.S. society. Rapid changes were also taking place in the life sciences, and eugenicists drew upon the work of August Weismann and Gregor Mendel to solve these vexing problems. With strong support from eugenicists, laws were passed that required the restriction of immigration from southern and eastern Europe, the segregation of those judged unfit; the rejection of interracial marriage; and forced state-sponsored sterilization. Regarding this last legislation, over 60,000 U.S. citizens were sterilized against their will. At the more popular level, school textbooks lauded the promise of eugenics, motion pictures warned of eugenic decline, and Fitter Families Contests offered medals to those of presumed eugenic excellence.

While not inconsistent with the state of scientific knowledge early in the 20th century, eugenics had lost its scientific support by the end of that century's second decade. Its lack of scientific legitimacy, disregard for human rights, and close association with the European Holocaust sealed its fate. By the end of World War II, early 20th-century eugenics was moribund. However, a combination of 21st-century parents' desire for perfection in their offspring combined with advances in molecular genetics and fertility treatments may make a 21st-century neoeugenics a possibility. It may be feasible to achieve the eugenicists' dream of changing and improving the human germ plasm, to undertake the as yet untested process of genetically modifying in vitro human zygotes. This does not necessarily suggest a return to the racist and antidemocratic eugenics of the past. If, unlike the eugenics of the past, there is to be a politically acceptable and morally responsible eugenics in the future, it will have to maintain currency with advances in life science,

sustain a vision of a just society consistent with democratic values, and satisfactorily resolve the ethics of human manipulation.

British and U.S. Roots

Eugenics began in Britain with Francis Galton (1822–1911), who coined the term, meaning "well-born," in 1883. Galton observed that the leaders of British society were far more likely to be related to each other than chance alone might allow and concluded that it was the ruling classes' superior biological inheritance that determined their social positions. Finding nature far more important than nurture, Galton recommended competitions for potential marriage partners, thereby assuring that only "best" would marry "best" and, more importantly, that superior progeny would be produced.

In the United States, eugenics was a product of the Progressive Era, combining insights from the developing field of biology, a concern for human improvement, and a desire to control human inheritance. Its supporters, coming from across the political spectrum, urged the application of science to human betterment and focused on four major policy initiatives: the restriction of immigrants from southern and eastern Europe, the segregation of those judged socially unfit, the forced sterilization of the supposedly feebleminded, and laws restricting interracial marriage.

As Daniel Kevles notes, this mainline form of eugenics was strongly associated with nativist and racist attitudes, and it achieved substantial success. For example, in 1924, in the face of increased immigration from eastern and southern Europe, Congress passed an immigration reform law requiring quotas based on the 1890 census, a time when the U.S. population comprised greater numbers from northern and western Europe. A decade later, these quotas would deny those trapped before the juggernaut of World War II access to U.S. shores. Also, in 1924, with the Supreme Court's *Buck v. Bell* case, supporters of eugenics succeeded in legalizing state-enforced sterilization. In the *Buck* case, a poor white girl was charged with having a "feebleminded" mother, to being feebleminded herself, and with giving birth to a feebleminded child. In concluding for the majority and for sterilization, Chief Justice Oliver Wendell Holmes Jr. announced, "Three generations of imbeciles is enough." However, as Paul Lombardo has reported, the concern for the purity of the nation's gene pool overpowered the facts in this landmark case. Carrie Buck's daughter was not feebleminded; she was an award-winning elementary school student. Three generations had not appeared before the Court.

By the 1930s, a more moderate, nonracial, nonnativist reform eugenics had replaced its mainline counterpart. Using the IQ tests developed by eugenicists in World War I, it focused on meritorious individuals rather than on racial or family groups. Unlike mainline eugenics, reform eugenics provided a role for environment in human development. It supported human improvement through the marriage of society's most talented individuals in combination with environmental reform, and high school science textbooks of the era supported this biologically driven, merit-based eugenics. While reform eugenicists focused on public schools to classify citizens based on their assumed innate capacities, they could not avoid the class-based nature of the tests or the segregated nature of U.S. society in determining social advance. Whether negative or positive, mainline or reform, eugenics legitimated the social status quo, supported the powerful over the powerless, and privileged the native born over the newcomer.

U.S. Eugenics: Responding to Rapid Changes in Society and Science

U.S. eugenics' success in restricting immigration, segregating the putatively unfit, supporting state-imposed sterilization, and limiting interracial marriage was not simply as an expression of social anxiety based on racism or fear of immigrants. While these were surely factors, its success is best understood as the interaction between society and science in a time of rapid change and modernization.

Social and Economic Developments

The period during which the U.S. eugenics movement developed was one of dramatic and socially unsettling changes in technology, demographics, and science. For example, between 1870 and 1910, 900,000 patents, a rough measure of technical and scientific advance, were issued in the United States. One effect of these advances when applied to

industry was the transformation in the scale and structure of the U.S. economy. The great concentrations of wealth produced by industries such as railroads, meatpacking, and steel made famous the names of men such as Edward Harry Harriman, Cornelius Vanderbilt, and Andrew Carnegie. But it was also a time of profound economic imbalances. By the last decade on the 19th century, the top 1% of the U.S. population controlled more than 50% of the nation's wealth, while the bottom four quintiles controlled a mere 1.2%. Further, economic instability created a series of economic depressions or "panics" between 1873 and 1897.

The decades after the Civil War also witnessed massive waves of immigration to the United States. Coming first from western and then from eastern and southern Europe, immigrants settled in urban centers and suffered the dislocations of the Industrial Revolution. Between 1870 and 1900, 12 million persons immigrated to the United States. And an additional 13 million arrived between 1900 and 1914. By 1900, immigrants comprised more than half of the industrial workforce, and immigrant adults were the majority in 90% of cities with populations over 100,000. While they provided a way forward for these immigrants, these cities nevertheless suffered increases in crime, violence, disease, and economic instability.

Of the many challenges facing the United States in last decades of the 19th century and the turning of the 20th, however, perhaps none was as destructive as that of U.S. race relations. The end of Reconstruction in 1877 saw aggressive racism spread across the nation as violence against African Americans increased, and the 1896 *Plessy v. Ferguson* Supreme Court decision made segregation legal in education.

By the turn of the century, the position of U.S. native-born, Anglo-Saxon elite was challenged by economic instability, urbanization, deepening inequality, immigration, and racism. These were challenges that demanded a program of repair. And for those who would champion eugenics, rapid changes in biological science appeared to provide just the tools that were needed for such a program.

Advances in Life Science

The late 19th century, much like our own period, was a period of revolution in biology.

Among the many changes taking place was the rejection of popular environmentalist assumptions regarding human improvement. The French naturalist Jean-Baptiste Lamarck (1744–1829) had theorized that the muscles of the blacksmith developed through years at the forge would be transmitted to his children as "acquired characters." This suggested that social improvement could take place through environmental reform. But experimental biology made the testing of theories central to scientific advance. And Lamarckism was demolished by the empirical studies of the German biologist August Weismann (1834–1914).

Weismann's work distinguished between *somatic,* or body, cells that died with the organism, and sperm and egg, or *germinal,* cells that were passed from parent to offspring. Germ plasm, as he called it, was continuous from generation to generation; it was unaffected by environmental change. The blacksmith's children would not be born with powerful biceps. For 20th-century mainline eugenicists, Weismann pointed to biological determinism as the basis for human improvement. If germ plasm was unchangeable and transmitted from generation to generation, then improving humankind required the control of the behavior of germ plasm's carriers. If Anglo-Saxon germ plasm was judged superior to that of Polish immigrants or of the "feebleminded," then immigration restriction and sterilization would be scientifically justified.

In 1900, U.S. eugenicists also found support for their policies in the rediscovery of Mendel's (1823–1884) mid-19th-century breeding experiments. Mendel, a Moravian Abbott, carefully bred peas in his garden and recorded the patterns of inheritance of their different traits for generations. He discovered that if he controlled for traits such as size, color, and texture, he could predict the qualities of future generations with mathematical precision. He proposed that his plants' traits were expressions of what he called "determiners." U.S. eugenicists believed that determiners in human germ plasm were expressed in a wide variety of complex moral, intellectual, and social traits. Lobbying for a series of social polices, these eugenicists assumed that single genetic elements controlled traits such as intelligence, patriotism, shiftlessness, pauperism, boat building, and a tendency to wander; by controlling the genetic elements, they believed they could control the traits. However, as Columbia

University geneticists under the leadership of Thomas Hunt Morgan would soon discover, these simplistic Mendelian views were wrong.

The Demise of U.S. Eugenics

Beginning in the 20th century's second decade, Morgan and his students at Columbia began a series of groundbreaking studies of fruit fly genetics. Their studies revealed the remarkable complexity of the chromosomal inheritance of fruit flies and the role of environment in their expression. By implication, human intelligence and morality were far too complex to be understood or controlled in simple Mendelian terms. Mendelian, or mainline, eugenics was moribund. Yet the belief in biological determinism regularly returns, claiming a place in public policy using arguments based on bell curves and postulating genes for complex human behaviors. It is, of course, true that there are direct and unambiguous links between specific genes and medical conditions. Huntington's disease and Down syndrome can be traced directly to genetic and chromosomal errors. In these cases and in others, biology determines human health and behavior. But the consensus of the geneticists who have studied the issue is that the determination of complex human behavior by genes alone is not so easy to demonstrate.

Conclusion

While we are again living in a time of profound scientific and social transformation, the eugenics of the 20th century is not likely to return. But the possibility of making permanent changes in a zygote's DNA, changes transmissible to future generations, may become a possibility in the future through the process of inheritable genetic modification. Insofar as this would be the realization of the eugenic goal of modifying of the germ plasm of future generations, the prospect of a 21st-century neoeugenics is worth considering. Parents are already using preimplantation genetic diagnosis to achieve what Michael Sandel calls "perfection" in their offspring. And as the *Wall Street Journal* reports, surveys reveal that prospective parents express interest in using this technique to select for athletic ability, height, or intelligence.

But care must be taken not to see a potential neoeugenics as synonymous with its early 20th-century counterpart. Unlike the popular eugenics of the 20th century, so closely linked to racism, class bias, and anti-Semitism, tomorrow's neoeugenics will have to meet the strictest of criteria: It will have to maintain currency with advances in life science, it will have to sustain a vision of a just society consistent with democratic values, and it will have to satisfactorily resolve the ethics of human manipulation.

Steven Selden

See also Ethical, Legal, and Social Issues (ELSI); Gene; Gene Therapy; Human Genome Project; Mendel, Gregor

Further Readings

Buck v. Bell, 274 U.S. 200 (1927).

Cravens, H. (1978). *The triumph of evolution: American scientists and the heredity-environment controversy, 1900–1941.* Philadelphia: University of Pennsylvania Press.

Davenport, C. B. (1913). *Eugenics Record Office bulletin no. 9: State laws limiting marriage selection in light of eugenics.* Cold Spring Harbor, NY: Eugenics Record Office.

Galton, F. (1883). *Inquiries into human faculty and its development.* London: J. M. Dent.

Gautam, N. (2009, February 12). A baby please. Blond, freckles—hold the colic. *The Wall Street Journal.* Retrieved February 18, 2009, from http://online.wsj.com/article/SB123439771603075099.html

Gould, S. J. (1981). *The mismeasure of man.* New York: W. W. Norton.

Kevles, D. (1985). *In the name of eugenics: Genetics and the uses of human heredity.* New York: Knopf.

Lombardo, P. (2008). *Three generations, no imbeciles: Eugenics, the Supreme Court, and* Buck v. Bell. Baltimore: Johns Hopkins Press.

Paul, D. (1995). *Controlling human heredity: 1865 to the present.* Atlantic Highlands, NJ: Humanities Press.

Pernick, M. (1996). *The black stork: Eugenics and the death of "defective" babies in American medicine and motion pictures since 1915.* New York: Oxford University Press.

Plessy v. Ferguson, 163 U.S. 537 (1896).

Sandel, M. (2007). *The case against perfection: Ethics in the age of genetic engineering.* Cambridge, MA: Belknap Press.

Selden, S. (1999). *Inheriting shame: The story of eugenics and racism in America.* New York: Teachers College Press.

EUROPE, RESEARCH SYSTEM IN

Today, Europe (along with the United States and Japan) is one of the three major international players in science and uses its large resources of funding, scientific infrastructure, and personnel to produce substantial outputs in terms of publications, patents, and Nobel Prizes. As both science and science communication have become increasingly globalized, Europe's contemporary role has become increasingly visible outside Europe, as well as within it. In addition, the European Union (EU) has made important efforts to study the science–society interface and to improve communication between European scientists and the European public to ensure that public awareness keeps pace with rapid scientific and technological development.

Without disregarding the great achievements in mathematics and astronomy in ancient Egyptian and Asian cultures, it is legitimate to say that the foundations of science in its present form evolved to a large extent in Europe. This includes substantial advances not only in knowledge but also in the development of specific scientific methods and the evolution of the social organization of modern science. Several centuries BCE, Greek mathematicians developed the study of mathematics as a scientific discipline and developed the idea of a strict proof or a set of explicit methodological rules used to separate truth from error. In the beginning of the 17th century, Francis Bacon, the great British philosopher, laid the philosophical foundations of empirical science, or science based on systematic observation and experimentation. Important research instruments such as telescopes and microscopes were first constructed and used by European researchers such as Galileo Galilei in Italy and Antoni van Leeuwenhoek and Christiaan Huygens in the Netherlands. Isaac Newton developed his theory of classical mechanics in London. Researchers such as Louis Pasteur in Paris and Robert Koch in Berlin created the microbiological basis of modern medicine, Gregor Mendel in Austria created the basis of today's genetics, and James Clerk Maxwell, a Scot, the theory of electromagnetism. The university, still a major organizational form of science worldwide, was shaped in its current form in Europe.

However, in the beginning of the 20th century, the global center of science moved from Europe to the United States, and Europe lost its leading role. In the 1960s and 1970s, Japan also emerged as an important player—second after the United States in a comparison of individual countries, third if one treats Europe as a unit. In the decades to come, the positions of all three leaders will be challenged by the rapid modernization of China and India, which have shown a tremendous dynamism in the expansion of their research and development (R&D) systems. Meanwhile, Europe is rivaling the U.S. dominance in international science. This is due in part to the growing importance of new players such as China but also to the improved efficiency of R&D in Europe, caused by the increasing integration and internationalization of European research, as well as high growth rates for R&D expenditures in Europe.

In this entry, "Europe" refers primarily to western Europe, in particular to the European Union (EU) countries plus a few additional ones such as Switzerland and Norway that are not EU members but cooperate closely with it. Description of the R&D systems in the former Union of Soviet Socialist Republics, including Russia, and other post-Soviet countries is beyond the scope of this discussion. While statistical indicators show that Europe's R&D capacity is indeed concentrated in Western Europe (the most important countries in this respect being Germany, France, the United Kingdom, Italy, and Sweden), it should be noted that some Eastern European countries have a workforce of well-trained and experienced scientists and engineers, and—in selected scientific and technological areas, such as space technology, these are also home to major scientific and technical achievements.

While the EU funds research and develops a common research policy, in particular aiming to promote cooperation among European research groups and increased mobility of researchers within Europe, its budget for R&D is still rather limited if compared to the national budgets of the large EU member states. For example, while the European Commission (EC) distributes roughly 5.5 billion euros annually for R&D throughout Europe, the German government alone spends about 17 billion euros for R&D in Germany, and the aggregated government budgets for R&D of the 27 EU member states add up to some 81 billion euros. In other words, more than 90% of R&D expenditures in Europe are still provided by national budgets and distributed according to national R&D policies. While this entry may imply that Europe (as a whole) can be meaningfully compared with the United States and Japan in terms of scientific and technological development, this is only partly true—even taking into account that the impact of EU funding is larger than its mathematical weight.

In addition, some European coordination of research also takes place outside the EU context: Several European research organizations such as the European Laboratory for Particle Physics (also known as European Organization for Nuclear Research, CERN) and the European Space Agency (ESA) were founded and are funded by individual agreements of European countries that occurred outside the EU framework. When talking about Europe as an entity in international comparisons of R&D systems, it is important to remember that European research is still governed by a mixture of 27 individual national policies and a number of multinational endeavors, as well as the common policy and funding framework of the EU.

The 27 countries of the EU together produce slightly more internationally recognized scientific publications than the United States. However, considering not only the number of publications but also their impact (generally measured by how often these papers are referenced in other papers), the U.S. research system may be said to be more productive of high-impact science than the European system, yet with roughly the same amount of government funding. This idea is confirmed by looking at the proportion of Nobel Prizes given to researchers in the United States versus in Europe. Of the 267 Nobel laureates in physics, chemistry, and medicine in the last 40 years (1969–2008), 58% were from the United States, while only 35% were citizens of a European country.

Several reasons may account for the higher research productivity of the U.S. R&D system. First, research in the EU is still largely divided into 27 national research systems with separate budgets and policies. This leads to uncoordinated parallel research and makes it difficult to concentrate sufficient resources on larger projects or goals. Even if the total funding of scientific research in Europe is roughly comparable to the U.S. funding (201 billion euros in the EU compared to 251 billion spent by the United States in 2005), the European system may be less efficient with respect to top achievements: Many small pyramids do not reach the same height as one large one, even if the same resources are used in their construction. Second, as the United States is the top player in science, U.S. universities and other research organizations are attractive employers for researchers from elsewhere. Research organizations in the United States can choose from among the best researchers in the world (feeding what is called the "brain drain"). Finally, the larger U.S. R&D system increases the possibility for division of labor and specialization, and it probably increases competition among researchers, motivating them to be more productive, while political, cultural, and language boundaries in Europe may still shield researchers somewhat from international competition.

European Research Organizations

To define European research organizations, two criteria are applied in this entry: geographical location and political-legal organization. Based on the wider geographical criterion, all research organizations located in Europe would be termed European; based on the narrower political criterion, only those research organizations that are governed and funded by supranational European bodies, whether the EU or specific intergovernmental agreements among European states, would be included. Based on a combination of both criteria, four categories of research organizations are distinguished in the discussion below, from narrowest to broadest definition: (1) those operated and funded by the EU, (2) those based on agreements among European countries (whether or not EU member states), (3) those based on international agreements between European and non-European countries but located in Europe, and (4) those of a national character, that is, universities and other national research organizations of European countries. In terms of number, budget, and R&D potential, this last category is by far the largest one. However, particularly expensive research instruments and experiments increasingly tend to be funded and operated as joint ventures on a European level.

Organizations Operated and Funded by the EU

The Joint Research Centre (JRC) has its headquarters in Brussels (Belgium) and its main site in Ispra (Italy), with other locations in Europe; it has a staff of 2,750 and an annual budget of 350 million euros. The JRC is part of the EC and serves as an umbrella organization for seven very different research institutes at five locations in Europe. Its main mission is to support the EC with scientific knowledge relevant for policymaking and regulation, particularly in the fields of environment, climate change, health, nuclear safety, and energy.

Organizations Based on Individual Agreements Among European Countries

The ESA has its headquarters in Paris and research centers in several European countries, with a staff of 1,900 and an annual budget of 3 billion euros. ESA is the west European equivalent of the U.S. National Aeronautics and Space Administration (NASA), although much smaller, and it is a partner with NASA in the International Space Station (ISS). ESA also cooperates closely with the Russian Federal Space Agency. Major recent achievements of ESA include development of the *Ariane 5* rocket, the research laboratory Columbus for the ISS, and the space probe Rosetta, which investigates asteroids. ESA is also responsible for the selection and training of European astronauts involved in U.S. and Russian space missions, although ESA does not have its own manned spaceflight vehicle.

The CERN is located in Geneva (Switzerland), with a staff of 2,650 and an annual budget of 986 million Swiss francs. CERN is the world's largest center for high-energy physics. Research at CERN is done by accelerating subatomic particles to very high velocities before they hit a target or other particles. Analyzing the collisions helps researchers understand the physical laws of matter and the evolution of the universe. Several thousand researchers from all over the world use the facility. A team at CERN was the first to produce antimatter (in 1995). CERN is also the home of the new Large Hadron Collider (LHC), a new type of accelerator in which beams of protons are accelerated in opposing directions to almost the speed of light. The World Wide Web was invented at CERN in 1989; it was originally intended to improve communication among collaborators at different locations.

The European Southern Observatory (ESO) has its headquarters in Munich (Germany) and operates sites in Chile, with a staff of 600 and an annual budget of 120 million euros. ESO operates a number of advanced optical telescopes and other astronomical instruments at three locations of the Chilean Atacama Desert at altitudes of up to 5,000 meters above sea level. These locations were chosen to minimize the disturbing influence of the atmosphere for astronomical observations. The task of ESO is to study the southern part of the sky, which can only be done from locations south of the equator.

The European Molecular Biology Laboratory (EMBL) has its main site in Heidelberg, Germany, and has four other sites in Europe, a staff of 1,400, and an annual budget of 120 million euros. The EMBL conducts basic research in molecular biology and is involved in advanced training of researchers, in part through an international PhD program. Research areas include cell biology, developmental biology, gene expression, structural biology, and bioinformatics. The research units are supported by core facilities; through partnerships, researchers also have access to specialized facilities. Alongside the European members of EMBL, Israel is also a member state.

The Institut Laue-Langevin (ILL) is located in Grenoble (France), with a staff of 450 and an annual budget of 80 million euros. The ILL is one of the leading facilities in neutron science and technology, important for the study of the structure of materials including the relationship between microstructure of materials and macroscopic characteristics. The heart of the ILL is a high-flux nuclear research reactor, the most intense source of neutrons worldwide. The ILL provides a large-scale facility that can be used for many different research purposes and grants external users access to its facilities based on a peer-review proposal selection process (for academic science) and/or a fee structure (for industry).

The European Synchrotron Radiation Facility (ESRF) is also located in Grenoble (France). It has a staff of 600 and an annual budget of 80 million euros. Synchrotron radiation is used to study the structure of materials at the atomic and molecule level. Unlike conventional X-rays, radiation produced by synchrotrons is shaped like a laser beam, very intense and focused. The ESRF operates one of the three most powerful synchrotrons of the world. It is used by researchers from academic organizations and from industry in many fields of science, including biology, chemistry, medicine, and physics.

The Joint European Torus (JET) is located in Culham (United Kingdom) and has a staff of 800 and an annual budget of 60 million euros. Founded and operated by the *European Fusion Development Agreement*, a legal construction including the European Commission and national fusion research organizations of most EU countries and Switzerland, JET is currently the largest operating test nuclear fusion reactor. It is used for research on the use of nuclear fusion for the production of electric power based on a reactor design called "Tokamak." Constructing a nuclear fusion reactor is a technological challenge, and JET is used to study the many problems that have to be solved before a commercial fusion reactor is feasible.

International Research Organizations With Facilities Located in Europe

The ITER facility will be located in Cadarache (France). ITER is a large-scale international project (with an estimated construction cost of 10 billion euros) to build a nuclear fusion test reactor. The construction is expected to begin in 2010 and, according to plans, ITER should be operational in 2016. The project is funded by an international consortium that includes the European Community, the United States, Japan, South Korea, Russia, China, and India.

National Universities and Research Organizations in Europe

More than 90% of the European R&D capacity and many hundreds of individual organizations fall into this category; this section provides only a brief summary. A common element of the research infrastructure in Europe (as elsewhere) is the university. European universities have had a long history; the first were founded around 1200 in Italy (Bologna), the United Kingdom (Oxford, Cambridge), France (Paris), and Spain (Salamanca). Many European universities today are facing problems of underfunding and low-research productivity, and—with the exception of the top British institutions—few European universities make it to the top in international rankings. A key problem is that Europe lacks equivalence among different programs, examinations, and degrees in different countries, and the multitude of European languages is an additional barrier to the mobility of students and faculty. Attempts are currently being made to overcome these problems.

European countries differ regarding the dominance of universities in R&D. Several countries have large, prestigious research organizations and laboratories outside the university system that represent a significant part of national R&D capacity (and government spending for science). For example, in France, the Centre National de la Recherche Scientifique (National Center for Scientific Research) carries out research across the full spectrum of scientific fields. It operates its own laboratories and joint labs with universities, and it employs about 11,000 researchers. Germany has four associations with different research focuses, each named after a prominent German researcher: the Max Planck Society, the Fraunhofer Society, the Helmholtz Association, and the Leibniz Association. About 27,000 researchers are employed in the research centers and institutes belonging to these associations. Other European countries also have research facilities outside the university system; an interesting example is the Gran Sasso National Laboratory in Italy, a laboratory built in a huge cave inside a mountain to shield experiments from cosmic radiation.

A European Research Area?

In 2000, the EU agreed on the vision of a European Research Area (ERA). The idea behind ERA is to create a unified area all across Europe in which research is coordinated, funded, and governed in very much the same way as it is within a single country today and in which researchers move and interact seamlessly as they do within their home countries. Internationally, ERA is intended to establish Europe as a competitive actor and strong collaborating partner in R&D, able to take a leading role in international initiatives.

To build ERA, the overall strategy of EU research policy is to regroup and intensify efforts

at a European level and to coordinate them with national and international initiatives. Although several steps have been taken in that direction, there are still strong national and institutional barriers that impede ERA from achieving its complete realization. As further steps in the realization of ERA, the EC launched new initiatives in 2008 in areas such as the management of intellectual property, the promotion of mobility and careers of Europe's researchers, the legal framework for pan-European research infrastructures, and international cooperation.

Since 1984, EU research policy has been implemented through a series of Framework Programmes. The Seventh Framework Programme (FP7) covers the period of 2007 to 2013 and has a budget of 53 billion euros, representing a 63% increase compared to the Sixth Framework Programme. Still, EU R&D expenditures remain, in relative terms, quite low, and this represents a major weakness. The latest available data (for 2005) show that the EU devotes 1.8% of its gross domestic product (GDP) to R&D compared to 2.6% and 3.3% for the United States and Japan, respectively. Although the governments of the EU member states and the EC committed themselves in 2001 to increase research spending to 3% of GDP by 2010, this objective will not be met; only two member states exceeded the 3% target in 2005: Sweden (3.9%) and Finland (3.5%).

Over 70% of the FP7 budget will be used to foster collaborative research across Europe and other partner countries in selected priority areas. Compared to earlier Framework Programmes, FP7 innovates in several ways. For example, FP7 has allowed the creation of the first pan-European agency for funding basic research, the European Research Council. FP7 also funds new Joint Technology Initiatives, which are industry-driven, large-scale, multifinanced actions, supported by a mix of public and private funding.

As the EU Framework Programmes account for a mere 5% of the total R&D expenditures in the EU, one might think that the impact of the EU research policy is rather modest. In reality, as most EU-supported projects are cofunded (with only 50% of the budget provided by the EU), FP7 controls more than 10% of all European research funding. In addition, most member states match their own research priorities with those of the

Framework Programmes, and FP7 money is poured directly into the research work. According to internal commission reports, EU policy directly influences some 25% of the research carried out in Europe. Another major effect of the Framework Programmes consists in the strengthening of interpersonal networks among European researchers by providing strong incentives for cross-national collaborations; funding of research projects out of the EU budget usually requires the involvement of researchers from several European countries.

Framework Programmes have expanded in terms of budgets, areas, and funding opportunities. While the first Framework Programme focused on applied research and the transfer of its results to industry, FP7 also supports activities related to the advancement of the European research system such as the training and qualification of researchers and the development of research infrastructures. In particular, FP7 offers Marie Curie mobility fellowships and training grants, which are also open to non-European researchers. One of the aims of the Marie Curie initiative is to reduce the "brain drain" in Europe mentioned earlier, the loss of productive researchers being offered attractive jobs in the United States, especially for researchers from the Eastern and Central European countries. Regarding research infrastructure, FP7 foresees a European Strategy Forum on Research Infrastructures that will provide support to the planned European Spallation Source, the High Performance Computing Facilities for Europe, and several other large-scale efforts.

Part of the EU strategy is attention to and improvement of the relationship of science to its societal context. For a long time, the EC has regularly monitored public perceptions of and attitudes toward science and technology through special Eurobarometer surveys. Many European policymakers and research managers are concerned that public acceptance of technical innovations is lower in Europe than in the United States or Japan and that this more critical public attitude may be a disadvantage in international technological and economic competition. The EU thus makes large efforts to improve communication of research to the European public by means of publications, conferences bringing together researchers and journalists, and guidelines and media training for researchers. A section called "Science in Society" in FP7 funds research on the science–society relationship as well as outreach, public dialogue, and public engagement initiatives. These activities are somewhat ambiguous in their implicit and explicit goals; some understand them as means to advocate a positive public opinion of science and technology, while others see them as an attempt to increase the role of the public in the governance of science.

Conclusion

Taken as a unit, internationally, Europe is currently the second largest player in scientific research in terms of absolute expenditures and personnel—behind the United States and before Japan. With respect to R&D expenditures relative to GDP, Europe is far behind the United States and Japan, however, and its research productivity seems to be somewhat lower than that of the United States. The cultural richness and diversity of Europe regarding languages, traditions, research infrastructures, and R&D policies may be a factor contributing to creativity, but it obviously leads to reduced research efficiency as well.

While Europe is much more than a loose group of countries tied together geographically, it cannot yet be understood as a coherent actor with fully coordinated and integrated national R&D policies. Europe is probably more divided, less coordinated, and less consistent in its policies than are its competitors, the United States and Japan. Guided by the vision of a ERA, the EU is currently trying to move toward more integration of European research. It aims at increasing mobility of researchers within Europe, fostering cross-national collaborations of researchers, increasing attractiveness for R&D personnel on the international job market, and building a more powerful European research infrastructure than any individual European country could afford.

The biggest share of European resources in R&D is still nationally controlled by the individual member states, however. While the balance between the national and the EU level will probably continue to move toward a greater weight at the European level, the ambiguity in the description of the European research system as a geographical unit or as a unified actor in R&D policy will continue to exist, at least for a while.

Hans Peter Peters and Michel Claessens

See also European Space Agency; Particle Accelerators; Scientific Method

Editor's note: The vast majority of organizations and programs discussed in this entry have presences on the World Wide Web. Given the number of these involved and the ephemeral nature of Web addresses, we elected not to include all of them here. However, a quick Internet search should reveal them without difficulty in almost all cases.

Further Readings

European Commission. (2008). *Science, technology and innovation in Europe.* Luxembourg: Office for Official Publications of the European Communities. Available at www.imamidejo.si/resources/files/doc/KS-EM-08-001-EN.pdf

European Organization for Nuclear Research: http://public.web.cern.ch/public/Welcome.html

National Science Board, U.S. (2008). *Science and engineering indicators 2008.* Available at www.nsf.gov/statistics/seind08

EUROPEAN SPACE AGENCY

The European Space Agency (ESA) is the European organization devoted to the development of space programs in its 18 member states: Austria, Belgium, Czech Republic, Denmark, Finland, France, Germany, Greece, Ireland, Italy, Luxembourg, the Netherlands, Norway, Portugal, Spain, Sweden, Switzerland, and the United Kingdom. Canada also takes part in some projects under a cooperation agreement. Thanks to a cooperative approach, ESA is able to undertake space-related activities that would not be affordable by any single European country. ESA is organized in directorates dedicated to different space programs, among which are Human Spaceflight, Science, Earth Observation, and Telecommunication. Over the last few years, communication and education have played a growing role in the agency: in the Legal Affairs and External Relations directorate, there is currently a department for communication and a separate one for education.

ESA was originally funded in 1975 by 10 founding members as a result of the merging between the European Launch Development Organisation and the European Space Research Organisation. These two organizations had been created in 1964 as a result of a commission study aimed at investigating the possible avenues for European cooperation in space. The need to create a European space organization was strongly felt in the post–World War II scientific community, which saw in international collaborations the best way to reboost European science and technology after the dramatic years of the war and thus becoming competitive on the international level. ESA was created as an organization with no military purposes. It is currently established in France, Germany, Italy, the Netherlands, and Spain.

The corporate communication and education departments work closely with teams and other staff in each directorate to ensure that the media or educational materials and activities are updated with the latest news and achievements. The ESA portal is the main tool for public outreach, together with mailing lists, press releases, and events, mostly organized to celebrate space missions and major project milestones, according to dedicated mission communication plans.

ESA communication and education is often carried out in close collaboration with the other international space agencies, such as U.S. National Aeronautics and Space Administration (NASA) or Japanese Aerospace Exploration Agency. A peculiar aspect that has to be taken into account from communicators at ESA is the multiculturalism of the agency, which sometimes requires different strategies (for example, because of different school curricula in the different countries), as well as different languages.

As in most public international organizations, outreach is funded and supported for a number of reasons. First, European citizens have to be informed about the latest advances in the space field from a European perspective, as an outcome of an investment of public money. This is a right of taxpayers, but it is also a necessity for ESA to show to stakeholders, decision makers, and European citizens the achievements and benefits of a space program for Europe. This shared knowledge represents a common ground necessary to obtain general support from the citizens and funding for future missions. In cases of debated and expensive projects, such as the International Space Station, ESA communication is particularly sensitive to the need to sustain and support its strategic approach and promote benefits for European citizens.

ESA communication key messages are constantly evolving to reflect the reasons that justify a public investment in space, which naturally follow the evolution of society itself. (The key messages of a space program during the cold war or in a period of economic crisis are necessarily different.) The goal of ESA communication is therefore to inform the public about the benefits and challenges—political, economical, social—of a strong European space program. To achieve that, it is also important for ESA to create a visible corporate identity, as NASA has already successfully accomplished.

Second, ESA has a vested interest in contributing to the scientific literacy of European students to help educate the future manpower that will work on space programs, ranging from space engineers to lawyers, from scientists to managers specialized in international collaborations. Ensuring the existence of a qualified workforce in the European job market is indeed a condition sine qua non for Europe to maintain a role and take on leadership in space activities at a worldwide level. Because it is an agency based on the forefront of scientific and technological knowledge, the availability of highly qualified European professionals is a vital requirement for ESA. This interest is reflected in several educational programs for university and postgraduate students, including internships, participation in workshops, and student space experiments. The students' involvement goes beyond higher education, also addressing pupils and their teachers from primary school onward, consistent with the broad European effort to make students attracted to the study of scientific and technical disciplines from a younger age.

In a more general framework, communication and education are a fundamental mandate of ESA because it has the responsibility to contribute to a scientifically literate and aware society, with the long-term objective of contributing toward the creation of a knowledge-based society, and ESA is able to play a significant role in this effort. ESA communication and education meet the needs of citizens, students, and educators who are interested in space and who search for information about space for their pleasure, education, or work. For its part, ESA aims to reach a greater proportion of the public and to trigger further interest into space, science, and technology, leveraging the inspirational values (especially for students) and overall benefits of the space adventure.

Cristina Olivotto

See also Europe, Research System in; National Aeronautics and Space Administration, U.S.; Particle Accelerators

Further Readings

European Space Agency: www.esa.int

Russo, A., Krige, J., & Sebesta, L. (2000). *A history of the European Space Agency, 1958–1987*. Noordwijk, the Netherlands: European Space Agency.

EVALUATION OF SCIENCE COMMUNICATION

When do science communication projects work? How do we know when science communication is effective? These are seemingly simple but nonetheless vexing questions that evaluation scholars have faced for decades. Some of the challenges facing evaluation experts who study science communication are similar to those faced by those who study strategic communication campaigns. At the same time, there are some unique challenges that science communication evaluation efforts often involve, due in part to the nature of funding for such efforts and in part to philosophical differences between many science communication staff and, for example, commercial advertising professionals. These challenges cut across several dimensions, including definition of audience, outcome identification, and measurement issues. Some recent large-scale project evaluations, such as those connected with the Discoveries and Breakthroughs Inside Science project or the ScienCentral project, offer further insight into these issues.

Audience Definition

Who should science communication efforts target? Many have documented the gap in scientific literacy that lies between the general populations of many countries and scientific professionals. Some scholars argue that this gap threatens societal health and needs to be narrowed, at least in part so that sound policy on scientific research can be formulated through democratic means. That stance suggests the need for science communication efforts that address a relatively wide audience. Other researchers have argued that the audience for science communication efforts is always going to be a relatively small minority of a general population due to limits in educational background and specific interest. From that perspective, recommended projects might only be intended to speak to a relatively select group.

Defining who makes up a target audience is nonetheless vital to project evaluation. If a project is intended to address beliefs about genetically modified food among a general population, an appropriate evaluation design will focus on effects that are apparent for that whole group. Alternatively, evaluation designs that permit assessment of interactions, for example, differential project effects according to demographic segmentation or other group characteristics, might be most appropriate if a project is more narrowly focused. For example, if a project is only intended to improve attitude toward science education policy among active voters, then looking for effects among the general public might miss important outcomes.

A different type of science communication evaluation effort involves reporters or policymakers as an intended audience rather than lay people. The academic literature documents a number of such efforts in recent years, many of which stem from concern about the chasm between scientists and journalists. Although important differences between scientists and journalists exist in terms of educational background and scientific understanding, some recent evidence suggests that the chasm is not an insurmountable one. Interviews with epidemiologists and stem cell scientists, for example, have revealed widespread interaction with reporters and editors and a drop in general apprehension about peer reaction to such interaction compared with the past. Lingering concerns remain, however, both on the part of scientists who are worried about being misquoted and misrepresented and journalists who do not always get the information they need for stories from interviewed scientists. Regardless of these specific findings, it is clear that the audience

definition for science communication projects involving scientists or journalists (or both) differs in important ways from general public efforts. Identification of a sampling frame is sometimes easier for such efforts; a survey of a census of identified reporters rather than a sample is sometimes possible due to the smaller audience size, for example. At the same time, generalizability limitations sometimes arise with such investigation; a study of science journalists working for major metropolitan newspapers may or may not generalize to general assignment reporters for local TV news stations due to differences in story length and focus.

Which Outcomes to Evaluate?

A major challenge faced by science communication evaluation professionals involves the question of outcomes. Unlike many strategic communication campaigns, which often involve persuasion as a means of influencing individual behavior, what constitutes success for science communication efforts is often more difficult to discern. Consider, for example, an effort to improve science journalism as a means of affecting public understanding of science. Many science professionals would object to the notion that such projects are strategic efforts intended to affect individual behavior or even the general reputation of scientists. Learning for the sake of learning might be the most appropriate goal from such a perspective. Others have argued that public perception of scientific research and intended support for such endeavors is a perfectly legitimate indicator of communication success.

This situation poses some obstacles for evaluation design. Underlying most justifications for science communication projects, nonetheless, are theoretical models of the direct and indirect effects of science-related messages. Appropriate evaluation explicitly identifies those models of variable relationships, measures relevant variables, and seeks to empirically demonstrate hypothesized relationships. If scientific knowledge gain is deemed appropriate because of its connection to favorable attitudes toward continued funding for scientific research, for example, then first demonstrating that exposure to a science communication effort results in knowledge gain and then demonstrating an indirect link to attitude toward funding for research would be a useful approach.

If the goal of a science communication effort does not involve individual beliefs, attitudes, or behaviors, however, different possibilities exist for outcomes measurement. Imagine, for example, efforts intended to affect the priority given to, and prevalence of, particular scientific topics in mass media coverage. In such instances, scholars have conducted content analyses to determine, for example, the rank order of particular key word presence in newspaper and television news coverage. Such studies, in turn, raise the question of which key words to assess. In cases of content analysis, the outcomes assessed are variables describing content, not people.

This array of possibilities underscores the primary importance of carefully considering what the appropriate unit of analysis will be for any particular science communication evaluation. Studies of public opinion regarding climate change, for example, often will assess population-level shifts in percentages of people reporting a particular belief over time. Alternately, research on the impact of framing messages about climate change in a particular way often will require experimental approaches whereby some people are randomly assigned to see one set of messages and then compared to others randomly assigned to not see those messages. In yet a different example, evaluation of efforts to affect press coverage of nanotechnology would require not time or an individual as a unit of analysis, but rather a news article. Misunderstanding the units of analysis that most appropriately correspond theoretically to the intended impact of a campaign can lead to evaluation missteps.

Moderating Factors

There are a number of reasons why science communication efforts will not work uniformly across people, a possibility that should be addressed in evaluation research but which is sometimes overlooked. For example, scholars have looked at which factors contribute to retention of presented science content and concluded that those with more initial familiarity with science tend to remember more content. In other words, those rich in scientific knowledge tend to get richer as opposed to a situation of uniform knowledge gain across all groups.

On a different plane, brain chemistry differences appear to affect media style preferences, a pattern with implications for media-based project evaluation. Work on so-called sensation-seeking tendency, for example, highlights the idea that individual differences in one's biological composition explain why some individuals prefer more stimulation than others do. Those higher in sensation-seeking tendency may prefer more fast-paced or stimulating media content than their peers (though we also know such editing also can diminish overall comprehension). In such situations, evaluation that accounts for potential variation in content style preference by assessing known individual difference factors can be more powerful in discerning effects than research that only looks for general effects across all people.

Despite popular commentary on the impact of ideology on engagement with, and interpretation of, science information, evidence regarding the effect of political and religious perspective on science communication outcomes remains mixed. Despite the relationship of religious perspective to many beliefs about science, for example, a number of evaluation scholars have not found anticipated differences in science material comprehension or retention. While political or religious ideology may very well affect the extent to which a particular group might be persuaded by a particular presentation, then, evaluation scholars may not necessarily find differences in the relationship of project exposure to other outcomes as a function of such stances.

Science Communication and Framing

Aside from individual-level moderators, we also know that the way in which scientific information is presented, or framed, can have a demonstrable impact on audience engagement and interpretation. Researchers have found that inclusion of sufficient context, for example, is critical in determining audience belief certainty. Research on interpretation of climate change news coverage has found that readers provided the most context and background had the most reported certainty in their beliefs about global warming after reading the story, whereas study participants in a control condition and those presented a story that focused on scientific controversy reported the least certainty.

Some have argued that such framing effects directly suggest that all science communication efforts related to a particular topic are not equal. That realization, in turn, has led some to question the generalizability of studies on science communication effects. We know that mass media content related to science varies widely, both in terms of topics presented and in terms of the ways such topics are framed. Consequently, the present science communication evaluation literature does not yet provide a concrete answer to the question of whether science communication affects individual perception or other outcomes. Some of the reported variation in study results likely stems from differences in the way content has been framed, differences that themselves are not always reported in academic articles in this arena.

Determining the effect of framing poses important evaluation challenges. Some designs allow for comparison of the effect of exposure to one message frame to that reported by a control group that does not engage the message in question, but technically such a design does not allow researchers to tease apart exactly which aspect of the sometimes myriad message differences between treatment and control actually is responsible for demonstrated effects. Designs that allow for comparison of a variety of comparable message frames seem to offer some advantage in this regard.

Measurement Issues

Measurement is a challenge lurking for many project evaluations; science communication projects are no exception. The key variables for many science communication projects, for example, exposure, memory, beliefs, and attitudes, are often not well measured. Reliance on self-reported survey items is partly responsible for this pattern. Another important factor is insufficient variable definition.

Consider message retention as an example. We know that memory is not monolithic. The human brain employs a variety of related but distinct memory systems, and thus, we should consider memory to be multidimensional. Consequently, evaluators face an array of options for measurement, each of which has distinct theoretical implications that are ignored at one's own risk. For those evaluation professionals interested in tapping basic memory for presented content, for example, at least

two individual memory performance task options are relevant: a recognition task or a recall task. We know that the two types of measures are related. Nevertheless, recognition is typically considered distinct from unaided recall of information.

In the case of science communication evaluation, unaided recall would be a respondent's ability to offer detail about particular program or project content when asked an open-ended question at some point after initial exposure to that content. Recognition, in contrast, would be a more basic ability to respond to a closed-ended question about past exposure to content when presented that content once again. Whereas recall suggests a relatively high degree of current information salience and accessibility, recognition involves a somewhat lower standard of past cognitive engagement. Unaided recall questions may provide a keener sense of what is most salient to a respondent at the time of interview. Measuring recognition, though, should more exhaustively tap exposure that has simply been encoded at some point in the past. Deciding which of these two types of memory tasks to employ for an evaluation, then, should not simply be a function of convenience but instead should hinge on the model of effects and intended impact for the program in question. Projects intended to increase the salience of earthquake preparedness among a population might choose to focus on unaided recall, whereas projects focused on detailed knowledge acquisition might choose recognition tasks.

Impact of Program Modality

Does the medium used for science communication affect effectiveness? Studies suggest that project modality does not necessarily dictate success. Rather than assuming wholesale differences between media in presentation effectiveness, for example, inherent differences between television and Internet-based programs, recent research has examined specific attributes of presentation that might facilitate effectiveness. This move is consistent with technological trends in platform convergence; more and more mass communication is occurring digitally, meaning a single platform is increasingly delivering all kinds of content.

Recent evaluation efforts have found widespread memory both for project content presented over the Internet and for content presented via television news stories, for example. Teaching science through television can work. While some scholars have found potential differences in comprehension for print versus Internet-based presentations of science content, others have reported few, if any, general differences between presentation formats. Individual differences in modality experience and preference seem to moderate some of these effects.

Examples of Past Science Communication Evaluations

The U.S. National Science Foundation has funded a number of science communication evaluation projects in recent decades. The ScienCentral and Discoveries and Breakthroughs Inside Science projects have each distributed science news stories to TV news affiliates, for example. Evaluations of those projects have focused on a variety of outcomes and have attempted to document effects in noteworthy ways. Such studies have typically focused on effects that occur outside of the laboratory and look at effects occurring over time with large populations. In these ways, such work represents improvement over past evaluation research.

Researchers evaluating the ScienCentral work have looked at retention of story content as one important outcome. Consistent with discussion above, they also have looked at possible factors affecting such retention, not only finding that past experience with science predicted greater story retention, but also finding that general educational background and religious beliefs did not play major roles. While exposure, memory, and knowledge gain are centrally appropriate outcomes, evaluations also have focused on other relevant variables. For example, researchers investigating the impact of the Discoveries and Breakthroughs Inside Science project have looked at perceived ability to understand science and conversation with others about science as possible outcomes affected by exposure to the science news project in question.

What many of these examples highlight is the impact of careful evaluation design prior to project implementation on the eventual utility of results. Rather than relying on difficult-to-generalize focus group findings based on conversations with convenience samples of participants, for example, a number of these designs have employed combinations of large-scale surveys with representative samples,

random assignment to experimental condition when possible, and multilevel model approaches allowing for individual-level and community-level variables to simultaneously predict outcomes. By doing so, evaluations of science communication efforts have become increasingly scientific.

Brian G. Southwell and Jessica Marshall

See also Audiences for Science; Conversation and Science Communication; Framing and Priming in Science Communication; Science Indicators, History of the NSB Project on

Further Readings

Brossard, D., & Shanahan, J. (2006). Do they know what they read? Building a scientific literacy measurement instrument based on science media coverage. *Science Communication, 28,* 47–63.

Corbett, J. B., & Durfee, J. L. (2004). Testing public (un)certainty of science: Media representations of global warming. *Science Communication, 26,* 129–151.

Eveland, W. P., & Dunwoody, S. (2001). User control and structural isomorphism or disorientation and cognitive load? Learning from the Web versus print. *Communication Research, 28,* 48–78.

Miller, J. D., Augenbraun, E., Schulhof, J., & Kimmel, L. G. (2006). Adult science learning from local television newscasts. *Science Communication, 28,* 216–242.

Southwell, B. G., Blake, S. H., & Torres, A. (2005). Lessons on focus group methodology from a science television news project. *Technical Communication, 52,* 187–193.

Southwell, B. G., & Torres, A. (2006). Connecting interpersonal and mass communication: Science news exposure, perceived ability to understand science, and conversation. *Communication Monographs, 73,* 334–350.

Treise, D., & Weigold, M. F. (2002). Advancing science communication: A survey of science communicators. *Science Communication, 23,* 310–322.

EVIDENCE-BASED MEDICINE

What are evidence-based medicine (EBM) and evidence-based practice (EBP)? According to the international organization the Cochrane Collaboration, as well as various prominent researchers and practitioners such as David Sackett, Iain Chalmers, and Paul Glasziou, EBM is the use of current best evidence in making decisions about the care of patients or the delivery of health services.

While EBM was the first term coined for this approach to clinical practice, it quickly became clear that an evidence-based approach also applies to nursing, allied health, and other forms of clinical practice, and so the term EBP is now more widely used because it encapsulates the evidence-based approach to clinical decision making.

EBP is the integration of the best available clinical evidence from systematic reviews of relevant research with clinical expertise and patient preferences and values, and the implementation and evaluation of the use of best evidence in practice. A key element of EBP is to make sense of multiple research studies by evaluating study quality and analyzing aggregated outcomes to get an overall summary of the validity and outcomes.

The field of EBP owes much of its impetus to the Cochrane Collaboration, founded in 1993 and named after the British epidemiologist Archie Cochrane (1909–1988). The Cochrane Collaboration is an international not-for-profit organization that produces systematic reviews of evidence regarding the effectiveness of health care interventions. The reviews are used to help inform evidence-based decision making in health care settings. They are created by hundreds of contributors worldwide.

Synthesis of evidence is practiced not only at this international level, but also on national and local levels, where universities and health services may have centers doing reviews of evidence to inform and answer specific clinical questions to inform EBP. Well-known centers involved in this effort include the Centre for Reviews and Dissemination at the University of York, various McMaster University centers, and the Centre for Evidence Based Medicine at the University of Oxford.

The complete process of integrating evidence into health care decision making has five steps, which are discussed in detail in the "Further Readings" list and are also summarized below.

The Five Key Steps in EBP

1. Formulate an Answerable Clinical Question

The basic tool in EBP is the PICO question—that is, population, intervention, control, and outcome. To answer any question about improving health care outcomes, we need to know the population or patient group for which the treatments are used. The intervention, or experimental, treatment needs to be known, as well as the control or comparison treatment. Finally, we need to know what outcomes are being compared or measured.

For example, someone may want to ask about elderly patients (the population) taking Vitamin D supplements (the intervention) compared to calcium supplements (the comparator or control) to improve muscular strength and bone density (the outcomes).

This PICO approach also applies to questions about diagnosis or exposure and helps to identify the components of questions underlying clinical practice decisions. These components are then used in Step 2 to identify the best available evidence to answer these questions.

2. Find the Best Evidence

After formulating an answerable clinical question in the form of a PICO, the next step is to find the best available evidence. This requires systematically searching sources of medical and health care research—including databases such as MEDLINE, CINAHL, EMBASE, and the Cochrane Library. Databases of evidence-based guidelines can also be searched for evidence and guidance. These sources include the Scottish Intercollegiate Guidelines Network, the U.K. National Institute of Healthcare and Clinical Excellence, and the New Zealand Guidelines Group. Health professional bodies may also create their own evidence-based guidelines.

When searching for evidence, elements of the PICO question are used to determine the relevance of the population, intervention, comparison, and outcomes used in the research to answer the original question.

3. Critically Appraise the Evidence

The next step in EBP is to assess the quality of the studies by appraising the research methods. By appraising the methodological quality of a study, we can determine the risk of bias in the study, or the likelihood that the results may not reflect the truth. The poorer the quality of a study, the more opportunity for bias and the less we can trust the conclusions.

The elements used to appraise the quality of the study depend on the type of study and include the subject selection, allocation blinding, follow-up, and assessment of outcome, exposure, and intervention. Blinding, or masking as it is also known, is where the participants are unaware to which treatment they are exposed. Proper randomization (where participants are assigned to treatments by chance) and the blinding or masking of all study participants helps reduce biases that may otherwise contaminate study outcomes and give false results. The methods used to follow up and measure the results, including the methods and tools used to measure the intervention treatment, the comparator-control treatment, and the outcomes, are also important. Inappropriate methods used to assess outcomes, interventions, and comparators-controls introduce bias and errors into a study. In EBP, there is a continuum of quality of evidence from high quality to low quality. In general terms, there is a hierarchy of evidence depending on the type of study, with higher levels of evidence being less open to bias. These are briefly explained as follows:

Systematic Reviews and Meta-Analysis

Systematic reviews summarize the best available research evidence to answer a particular clinical question using rules established in advance to minimize bias. Systematic reviews are useful to digest large numbers of studies, assess the consistency of results from these studies, analyze the quality of studies, and assist in decision making. However, systematic reviews are usually very time-consuming to produce. Meta-analysis is the technique of statistically combining the results of multiple studies to determine the overall effectiveness of a treatment. For example, we may find several studies with similar PICO, each of which has results of differing magnitudes for a specific outcome (such as mortality). If we want to determine the overall effect of a drug on mortality we can perform a meta-analysis to provide the summary effect. The utility of meta-analysis is in eliminating the reliance on a single study's result and allowing all the evidence to be analyzed together.

Randomized Controlled Trials (RCT)

RCTs are trials where there is an intervention and control treatment group, with patients randomly allocated to either group by researchers. This is considered the gold standard method to test treatments. Properly conducted RCTs can eliminate many sources of bias and methodological weaknesses present in other trial methods. These are conducted prospectively, where the methods are planned before the study begins, and data are collected in real time as the study is occurring. However, RCTs may not always be ethically or logistically feasible and may be too restrictive in some cases to be useful for real-world situations.

Controlled Trials

These are trials where patients are selected and put in either an intervention group or control group. Researchers allocate people to either group, but not randomly. Controlled trials are conducted prospectively. A major problem with controlled trials is that groups may differ on certain baseline characteristics, such as age, gender, or disease severity, and these differences, rather than the intervention, may explain the study results.

Cohort Studies

In cohort studies, there are two groups of patients studied, and these are selected on the basis that one group was exposed to the treatment or exposure of interest (such as a drug or high-fat diet), whereas the other group was not exposed to any treatment. The outcomes of this treatment or exposure are examined either prospectively or retrospectively. Cohorts are a strong study design and are particularly useful for common outcomes, especially where it is not ethical or feasible to randomly allocate people to receive the exposure of interest (such as cigarette smoking). An issue with cohort studies is that either group may differ on baseline characteristics, and as with controlled trials, these differences may explain the results, rather than the results being due to the intervention.

Case Control Studies

Case control studies include two groups of patients: cases and controls. Cases are selected because they have an outcome of interest, usually a disease or condition (such as cancer, heart disease, or miscarriage). Controls are selected because they do not have the outcome of interest. Case control studies are always retrospective because the outcome must have occurred for patients to be included as cases, and researchers then look back in time to determine whether one group or the other had increased rates of a particular exposure. Case-control studies are useful for rare outcomes and common exposures, but they have a high probability of bias.

Case Studies and Case Series

Case studies and case series are the lowest grades of clinical evidence in EBP. Case studies are usually based on rare events and report on the patient's diagnosis and treatment course and the outcomes from these actions. A case series is a number of case studies grouped together. These are retrospectively examined and can lead to development of hypotheses leading to further research. Case studies and case series cannot be used to determine the effectiveness of a treatment as no comparison is made to people who do not receive the treatment.

4. Integrate the Evidence With Clinical Expertise and Patient Values for Decision Making or Change Processes

In this step, the research evidence identified and appraised in Steps 2 and 3 is combined with clinical expertise and patient preferences to make decisions about health care practice. Clinical applicability relates to the utility of evidence in the context of the clinical environment. To be useful, EBP must combine scientific rigor and the realities of clinical practice. This means there is a need to understand the clinical environment and the way it operates, and to incorporate patient and consumer experiences and preferences in decision making. Even if evidence points to the superior effectiveness of a treatment under very defined and strict conditions, if those conditions cannot be replicated in practice, then this evidence may not be very useful because those conditions are not available outside of the research environment. It is also important to recognize and integrate into the decision relevant consumer and patient experiences—the qualitative aspects of the health care journey—that can inform health care practices. Faced with the same research evidence, individual consumers may make very different decisions about the appropriateness of interventions such as radical mastectomy or circumcision. Consumer advisory committees and consumer input into health care processes are increasingly common in health care services, and this is a sign that there are complex processes that need the contextual experiences that only patients can provide to make health care more effective.

5. Evaluate Decision or Change Outcomes

This is an important step in EBP to determine if evidence has been integrated into clinical practice and has actually had a positive effect on health outcomes. Only once the change has been evaluated properly using the relevant evaluation tools can it then be determined if further action is needed to improve the integration of evidence into practice or if further questions need to be asked.

Other Evidence Used in Health Care Decision Making

Health technology assessments are slightly different than the process of comparing treatments and are mainly concerned about evaluating the effectiveness of medical devices, pharmaceuticals, and surgical procedures, whether they be diagnostic tests, implants, or other devices. For diagnostic tests, it is important to evaluate the sensitivity and specificity of tests to determine how accurate they are. Sensitivity measures the proportion of people with an illness or condition who are correctly identified as positive by a test, and specificity measures the proportion of people without an illness or condition who are correctly identified as negative by a test.

There is also a need not only to find the best evidence for treatment effectiveness, but also to find the most cost-effective treatments from a health policy and governance perspective. Health economics applies the tools and techniques of economics to the health care system. The aim of applying economic analysis to health care delivery is to minimize waste and maximize efficient and effective use of resources for the most benefit. Cost effectiveness analysis informs health care policy as to whether a treatment should be implemented or not, based on the balance of the costs of the treatment and the benefits it provides.

The Current Limitations of EBP

EBP requires good research and good methods for incorporating consumer views. While the field of

EBP is rapidly developing, some limitations remain in both these areas. There are limited rich data on patient experiences, and the methods for integrating patient experiences into EBP are still being developed. Research is not currently available to answer all questions, for example, there is a lack of studies involving certain racial minorities, women, certain age groups, ethnic groups, or in populations with many comorbidities. Other issues include biases that exist in what studies get funded and what studies get published. This skews the scientific evidence that is created, and EBP can only support decisions based on the available studies. An example of this is that usually studies that find significant or positive findings are favored for publication, as opposed to those with so-called negative findings that do not identify an effect. With these in mind, the methodologies of EBP are continually evolving to take into account existing and new limitations.

Henry Ko and Tari Turner

See also Health Communication, Overview; Health Literacy; Physician–Patient Communication; Scientific Method

Further Readings

Agency for Healthcare Research and Quality, U.S. Department of Health and Human Services: www.ahrq.gov

Centre for Clinical Effectiveness, Southern Health, Australia: www.mihsr.monash.org/cce

Centre for Evidence Based Medicine, University of Oxford, UK: www.cebm.net/index.aspx?o=1001

Centre for Reviews and Dissemination, University of York, UK: www.york.ac.uk/inst/crd

Cochrane Collaboration: www.cochrane.org

Egger, M., Smith, G. D., & Altman, D. (Eds.). (2001). *Systematic reviews in health care: Meta-analysis in context* (2nd ed.). London: BMJ.

Evidence-Based Medicine for Primary Care and Internal Medicine: http://ebm.bmj.com

Higgins J. P. T., & Green S. (Eds.). (2008). *The Cochrane handbook for systematic reviews of interventions.* Hoboken, NJ: Wiley. Available at www.cochrane-handbook.org

National Institute for Health and Clinical Excellence, UK: www.nice.org.uk

Sackett, D., Rosenberg, W. M. C., Gray, J. A. M., Haynes, R. B., & Richardson, W. S. (1996). Evidence based medicine: What it is and what it isn't. *The British Medical Journal, 312,* 71–72.

EXXON VALDEZ

An online search of *Exxon Valdez* turns up over 4 million sites. Two decades after the event, this massive oil spill remains a very hot topic. The infamous March 1989 spill of 11 million gallons of crude oil into Alaska's Prince William Sound permanently scarred not only a dramatic ecosystem but also the giant oil company, Exxon. When the *Valdez* hit a reef, spewing heavy crude into a critical fishery, covering thousands of sea birds and marine mammals with black goo, and fouling beyond repair a shoreline ecosystem and native culture, Exxon scored the worst oil spill in U.S. history. The incident quickly became a crowning example of just how serious manmade environmental disasters can be, as well as a textbook case of bad corporate public relations.

The general crisis communication rule is to tell the truth and do so quickly. It took 10 days for the company's New York–based public relations staff to release an apology and a promise "to be there for the duration" as attempts at cleanup began. To date, few have bought the apology, and the legal battle over punitive damages against the oil giant only recently concluded.

In 1994, a federal jury ordered $5 billion to be paid to thousands of people damaged by the wreck, at the time, the largest punitive damage award in the nation's history. Exxon claimed the Clean Water Act does not provide for punitive damages and appealed the ruling; the company had already paid out $3.4 billion in damages and fines. After hearing the case in February 2008, the U.S. Supreme Court ruled in June of that year, finally ending the battle and giving one of the world's most profitable corporations what appeared to the 32,677 plaintiffs to be a mere slap on the hand. The final ruling sliced a $2.5 billion punitive damage judgment from a lower court (which had already cut the original award in half) to just $507.5 million.

Justice David Souter, writing for the majority (in a 5 to 3 decision), described Exxon's conduct as "worse than negligent, but less than malicious" and ruled that a ratio between punitive and compensatory damages of no more than 1 to 1 was appropriate in maritime cases. Justices Stephen Breyer, Ruth Bader Ginsburg, and John Paul Stevens disagreed. Justice Samuel Alito, who owns Exxon stock, had recused himself from the case. The hard-hit fishing villages in Alaska, now paying $6 a gallon for gas to power their boats, decried the verdict in news reports.

Anger against the former Standard Oil Company of New Jersey, now known as the Exxon Mobil Corporation, persists in the environmental and anti-big-business communities and especially among the over 30,000 Native Alaskans who had sought recompense for ecological, financial, and legal damages caused by the oil slick. Lives and livelihoods were changed forever. The old Standard Oil Company, accused of doing business with the German Nazis in the World War II era, had been reborn as Exxon, and the company had seemed able to maintain a less high-profile reputation in later years, their ads featuring a cartoon character urging consumers to "put a tiger in your tank." During the Arab oil embargo of the 1970s, the company promised it was prepared for any accidents along the then-proposed trans-Alaska pipeline.

Apparently, this was not quite so. Research by the U.S. National Oceanic and Atmospheric Administration some 19 years after the *Valdez* spill showed oil residue still lingering just beneath the water surface. Scientists report a collapse in the adult herring population, eggs, and larvae, with survivors marked by liver lesions and depressed immune systems. Herring, a food source for other species, have never returned to pre-*Valdez* health. Yet some scientists hired by Exxon gave the sound a clean bill of health. Otters and eagles have rebounded. Nature has fought hard to recover. Yet generations of fishing families—and the fish on which they depended—have been stopped cold by residue from the crude spill. Alaska fishermen blame the loss of herring from the sound on the now-damaged waters. The industry claims killer whales have eaten all the fish.

The U.S. Oil Protection Act of 1990, passed after the *Valdez* disaster, requires more tug escorts with tankers, and citizen groups have forced improved monitoring. The *Valdez* Principles, which require corporations to take responsibility for any harm to the environment and not to compromise the ability of future generations to sustain their needs, have been adopted worldwide as an ethical protocol. Meanwhile, it was estimated that some 6,000 of the Alaskan Natives, landowners, and other victims of the *Valdez* spill had died while waiting for compensation for their losses. One commercial fisherman quoted at newsminer.com in February 2008 told a reporter, "Corporations have no conscience."

When the news of the accident first broke, officials blamed a "drunk captain" in the ultimate driving under the influence case. News reports claimed Captain Joseph Hazelwood had consumed vodka prior to the collision. No one denied Hazelwood had left the bridge when the tanker hit Bligh Reef, a violation of seafaring regulations. The *Valdez* carried 53 million gallons of crude on board. Hazelwood claimed he had strayed out of the shipping lane to avoid ice. The 1,000-foot tanker hit the reef just after midnight. Oil oozed into the sound, eventually fouling 1,200 miles of coastline. Media informed a worldwide audience with stark images of blackened seabirds, otters, and seals; beaches covered in sludge; and bloated whale carcasses. An entire ecosystem had been devastated.

The post-*Valdez* era for the company, which has now merged with Mobil Oil, continues to record astounding profits. With oil prices reaching over $100 a barrel, company profits reached $40.6 billion in 2007. But there have been hints of a subtle shift in direction. Recent reports suggest the company will give up their hold on the red, white, and blue gas stations, leaving the signage and operations at the pumps to independent owners. And even more unexpectedly, members of the Rockefeller family, descendants of the original tycoon John D. Rockefeller, pushed resolutions at a recent shareholder meeting for the company to take global warming more seriously and to look for alternative energy sources. However, that proposed shift in priorities, an effort seen as a move to avoid future *Valdez* disasters and repair the company's sullied reputation, was soundly defeated.

Exxon Shipping Company v. Baker did not bring the hoped for level of satisfaction to those involved. Headlines announcing the Supreme

Court decision proclaimed the disaster finally over. But in terms of its impact on science communication, disaster coverage, and environmental reporting, there remains no closure for the notorious *Exxon Valdez* case.

JoAnn Myer Valenti

Note: As this publication went to press, Exxon had finally agreed not to contest the $500 million in interest due to Alaskans harmed by the spill.

See also Clean Water Act; Crisis Communication; Disaster Coverage

Further Readings

Clean Water Act, 33 U.S.C. §1251 et seq. (1965).

Exxon Shipping Co. v. Baker, 490 F.3d 1066 (9th Cir. 2007).

Lebedoff, D. (1997). *Cleaning up: The story behind the biggest legal bonanza of our time*. New York: Free Press.

Smith, C. (1993). News sources and power in news coverage of the *Exxon Valdez* oil spill. *Journalism & Mass Communication Quarterly, 70*(2), 393–403.

Valenti, J. M. (2005). Exxon's whipping cream on a pile of manure. In P. Patterson & L. Wilkins (Eds.), *Media ethics: Issues and cases* (5th ed., chap. 3). Boston: McGraw-Hill.

FEAR APPEALS

Fear appeals are messages designed to scare people by describing a threat that is both personally relevant and serious. Fear appeals are one type of *motivational appeal,* which can be broadly defined as a message intended to increase an individual's drive to engage in a particular behavior. Virtually any human emotion or need can serve as the basis of a motivational appeal. Examples of emotional appeals are numerous and include appeals to pity and guilt (for example, the "Feed the Children" campaign), humor appeals (for example, Fetman, Garland, & Associates' "Life's Short. Get a Divorce" billboard), and appeals to pride and patriotism (for example, the 2008 John McCain presidential campaign's "Palin Power" or "Country First" slogans). Further, biological needs might be used to capture people's attention via sex appeals (for example, People for the Ethical Treatment of Animals' "I'd Rather Go Naked Than Wear Fur" campaign), social needs can be targeted using bandwagon appeals (for example, Microsoft's "I'm a PC" ad), and esteem needs might be targeted by ingratiation appeals (for example, Allstate Insurance's advertised "stand" that "you deserve more than your 15 minutes of fame").

Though these and other types of motivational appeals are popular in the United States, fear appeals are among the most commonly used and most thoroughly studied type of motivational appeal, and the issues they raise are directly relevant to effectively communicating health and environmental risks. Fear appeals are often marked by their use of vivid language (for example, "You can see the path of the bullet dragging bone fragments from the skull across the brain"), personalistic language (for example, "If it can happen to me, it can happen to you"), or graphic images (for example, police photos, X-rays, or other pictures of injuries and disease). A classic example of a fear appeal message is The Partnership for a Drug-Free America's "Fried Egg" drug prevention campaign that originally aired in the mid-1980s (that is, "This is your brain. This is drugs. This is your brain on drugs. Any questions?" accompanied by a frying egg image). Another, more recent example is Health Canada's smoking prevention messages on cigarette packs (for example, "Smoking causes lung cancer," "Tobacco smoke hurts babies," and "Tobacco use can make you impotent"—all accompanied by full-color, graphic images and often with strategy tips to help people quit smoking).

Given their pervasiveness and potential effectiveness in changing people's behavior to reduced exposure to risks, this entry focuses specifically on fear appeals. The next section will contain a brief introduction and overview of early fear appeal theories and research, followed by an in-depth discussion of the extended parallel process model (EPPM), which superseded these earlier theories by explaining both the successes and failures of fear appeal messages. The entry will conclude with a few important recommendations for those who wish to use fear appeal messages more effectively or study them in more depth.

Early Fear Appeal Theories

The first formal fear appeal theories appeared in the 1950s, and the EPPM is an integration and extension of several of the fear appeal theories that have been developed since that time (including the fear-as-acquired drive model, the parallel process model, and protection motivation theory). Though all of these theories introduced important elements into the fear appeal literature, each also had one or more shortcomings that the EPPM was designed to overcome. For example, the fear-as-acquired drive model posited that a moderate amount of fear arousal would be most effective at producing attitude and behavior change and that too much fear would backfire; this model proposed a curvilinear or inverted U-shaped relationship between fear and changes in attitude and behavior. However, many fear appeal studies contradicted this hypothesis and suggested a more linear relationship between these two variables (that is, asserting that as fear increases, attitude or behavior change will also increase).

While the parallel process model distinguished between situations in which individuals will focus on and attempt to develop strategies to avoid a danger or threat (that is, danger control) and situations in which they will focus on and try to control their fear (that is, fear control), it did not specify when one process would dominate over the other, nor did it specify what specific factors would elicit these different responses.

Finally, while protection motivation theory acknowledged the importance of also addressing the effectiveness and easiness of the recommended response in a fear appeal message, it focused exclusively on when fear appeals lead to message acceptance and danger control processes. While this theory does a good job of explaining when fear appeals succeed, it does not explain the specific factors leading to message rejection. The EPPM integrated the best parts of these and similar fear appeal theories and research and extended them to more effectively explain both when fear appeals will be likely to succeed and when they will be likely to fail. A more detailed discussion of the EPPM is provided next.

The EPPM

The EPPM is concerned with the effects of perceived threat and efficacy on attitude and behavior change. Perceived threat includes both an individual's *perceived susceptibility* (that is, the perceived likelihood or chance that the threat will occur) and *perceived severity* (that is, the perceived magnitude or seriousness of the threat), whereas perceived efficacy is comprised of both an individual's perceptions of *response-efficacy* (that is, the perceived safety and effectiveness of the recommended response) and *self-efficacy* (that is, the perceived ease or simplicity with which the individual can engage in the recommended response). Examples for each of these terms are provided below.

According to the EPPM, an individual's response to a fear appeal message will be very different depending on her or his levels of perceived threat and efficacy (see Figure 1). Put somewhat differently, the EPPM posits that perceived threat motivates action, and perceived efficacy determines the nature of that action (that is, whether people attempt to control the danger or control their fear). So an effective fear appeal message must not only contain a strong threat component but also include a strong efficacy component. To illustrate, one could imagine that the effects of a hypothetical bicycle safety fear appeal message are being evaluated. Recent data suggest that only one third of bicyclists wear a helmet on all or most trips, so the goal or recommended response of the message might be to get bicyclists who do not currently wear a bike helmet to start doing so to reduce the risk or threat of a head injury during an accident. Three outcomes are possible according to the EPPM depending on individuals' levels of perceived threat and efficacy, as detailed below.

No Response

When perceived threat is low, *no response* will occur—that is, if an individual does not believe that she or he is susceptible to a threat (for example, someone who thinks that bicycle head injuries are uncommon and that it is unlikely he or she will sustain a head injury even if he or she has an accident) or if she or he does not believe the threat has severe consequences (for example, someone who thinks that bicycle injuries typically lead to only minor scrapes and bruises), the person will not be

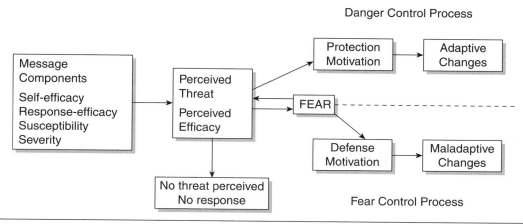

Figure I   The Extended Parallel Process Model

Source: Adapted from Witte, K. (1992). Putting the fear back into fear appeals: The extended parallel process model. *Communication Monographs, 59,* p. 338. Copyright © 1992 by Taylor & Francis, Ltd. Reprinted by permission of the publisher. The journal Web site is www.informaworld.com.

motivated to pay attention to the message and, therefore, will not respond to it. In this instance, the hypothetical message has failed to promote a perception of threat, so the message recipient is not motivated to engage in an appraisal of efficacy or to respond to the message.

Individuals who do not ride a bike would go through a similar process since the threat is not relevant to them. This highlights the importance of having a clear idea of the intended audience, in this case bicyclists, when developing and evaluating fear appeal messages. Unfortunately, researchers sometimes test fear appeal messages using a general population and find no effects. However, when researchers control for individuals for whom the message has no relevance (that is, in our example, those who rarely or never ride bikes), then effects are more likely to emerge.

Fear Control Response

When perceived threat is greater than perceived efficacy, individuals engage in *fear control,* which is a response designed to control or limit one's degree of fear rather than reduce the actual threat or danger—that is, if an individual believes that she or he is susceptible to a threat (for example, someone who thinks that thousands of serious bicycle injuries occur in the United States every year, and he or she has had a couple of close calls) and believes the

threat has severe consequences (for example, someone who thinks that a bicycle accident can result in traumatic brain injury or even death), the individual's level of perceived threat will be high. This high perception of threat motivates the individual to act, which leads her or him to engage in an appraisal of efficacy. If, during the appraisal of efficacy, the person does not believe the recommended response is effective (or low response-efficacy, such as someone who thinks that bike helmets do not provide much protection in case of an accident) or does not believe that she or he has the ability to engage in the recommended response (or low self-efficacy, such as someone who thinks that bike helmets cost too much and that he or she cannot afford one), then the person's level of perceived efficacy will be low. In this case, because being afraid is an uncomfortable state, the person will take steps to reduce the fear that do not necessarily decrease the actual danger. For example, the person might refuse to believe that the threat is real, or he or she might simply ignore any information that is provided about the health threat.

Danger Control Response

An individual will engage in *danger control* when both perceived threat and perceived efficacy are high—that is, she or he will think carefully about the recommended response and adapt her or his behavior to reduce the danger. In this instance, the hypothetical message has accomplished all of its goals by convincing the person that a personally relevant and serious threat exists by providing an effective means to reduce the threat (for example, by communicating that bike helmets are a good way to prevent head injuries) and by showing the person he or she is able to perform that action (for example, by communicating that bike helmets are worth the price and are easy to use). It is only when both perceived threat and perceived efficacy are high that a person will focus on potential solutions to the problem, which will likely lead to attitude or behavior change in the advocated direction.

Conclusion

Research on dozens of topics and many different populations indicates that developing effective fear appeal messages involves more than simply convincing a person that a personally relevant and serious threat exists. Effective fear appeal messages must also include a means of reducing the threat that is both effective and easy to perform. The EPPM also highlights the importance of considering and measuring both danger control and fear control responses when assessing the effectiveness of fear appeal messages; just because recipients of a fear appeal message do not engage in the recommended response does not mean the message did not influence them in some other, less productive manner. Finally, the importance of talking with intended audience members before developing a fear appeal message to determine what might be most threatening or efficacious to them cannot be overstated. Sometimes social, economic, or spiritual threats might be even more motivating than a physical threat, and often the only way to find this out is to get it directly from the intended audience. Regardless of what fear appeal message developers think, it is ultimately the intended audience members' perceptions of both threat and efficacy that will determine whether or not they will follow the recommendations made in the message.

Anthony J. Roberto and Kim Witte

See also Communication Campaigns in Health and Environment; Computer-Tailored Messages; Risk Communication, Overview

Further Readings

Gass, R. H., & Seiter, J. S. (2007). *Persuasion, social influence, and compliance gaining* (3rd ed.). Boston: Allyn & Bacon.

Goodall, C. E., & Roberto, A. J. (2008). *An inconvenient truth*: An application of the extended parallel process model. *Communication Teacher, 22*, 97–100.

Roberto, A. J. (2004). Putting communication theory into practice: The extended parallel process model. *Communication Teacher, 18*, 38–43.

Smith, S. W., Rosenman, K. D., Kotowski, M. R., Glazer, E., McFeters, C., Keesecker, N. M., et al. (2008). Using the EPPM to create and evaluate the effectiveness of brochures to increase the use of hearing protection in farmers and landscape workers. *Journal of Applied Communication Research, 36*, 200–218.

Witte, K. (1992). Putting the fear back into fear appeals: The extended parallel process model. *Communication Monographs, 59*, 329–349.

Witte, K. (1998). Fear as motivator, fear as inhibitor: Using the extended parallel process model to explain fear appeal successes and failures. In P. A. Andersen & L. K. Guerrero (Eds.), *The handbook of communication and emotion: Research, theory, applications, and contexts* (pp. 423–450). San Diego, CA: Academic Press.

Witte, K., & Allen, M. (2000). A meta-analysis of fear appeals: Implications for effective public health campaigns. *Health Education Behavior, 27*, 591–614.

Witte, K., Meyer, G., & Martell, D. (2001). *Effective health risk messages: A step-by-step guide*. Thousand Oaks, CA: Sage.

FEYNMAN, RICHARD (1918–1988)

Richard Phillips Feynman (1918–1988) was born in Queens, New York. At an early age, Feynman displayed exceptional mathematical abilities, which earned him acceptance into the Massachusetts Institute of Technology. After graduating with a degree in physics, he attended Princeton and received his PhD in 1942. He ultimately became widely known as a science teacher, communicator, and popularizer, as well as a scientist.

While researching his PhD, Feynman met and married his first wife, Arline Greenbaum, despite knowing she was diagnosed with tuberculosis. Although they were often separated by his work on the Manhattan Project, the marriage was apparently happy. Arline eventually succumbed to her illness in 1945. In 1952, Feynman was briefly married to Mary Louise Bell, but later married Gweneth Howarth, with whom he would spend the rest of his life. They had a son, Carl, in 1962 and adopted a daughter, Michelle, in 1968.

Feynman had many hobbies and nonscientific interests including lock picking, playing the drums, painting, and juggling. He died in 1988; wry wit intact, his last words were, "I'd hate to die twice." His reason? He found dying "boring."

Feynman the Physicist

After Feynman completed his PhD, he obtained a faculty position at the University of Wisconsin–Madison, but he was persuaded by his mentor Robert Wilson to join the Manhattan Project, the secret U.S. program to develop the atomic bomb at Los Alamos, New Mexico. He was assigned to Hans Bethe's theoretical physics division, where he oversaw the human computational group and contributed to the development of mathematical equations, most notably the Bethe-Feynman equation used to calculate the explosive yield of nuclear fission weapons. Feynman observed the Trinity atomic bomb test with enthusiasm, but after seeing the devastation caused by the Hiroshima and Nagasaki bombs, he became depressed over the possibility of the complete destruction of civilization.

Due to his contacts from working on the Manhattan Project, when the war ended, Feynman had offers to join several prestigious research universities. He chose to follow Hans Bethe to Cornell University and taught theoretical physics while working on a variety of physics problems, most notably those of spinning objects. While his research during this period was somewhat eclectic, his equations for predicting speeds across rotating objects would have a direct bearing on his Nobel Prize–winning work in quantum electrodynamics.

By 1951, the cold Ithaca, New York, winters had convinced Feynman that a move to a milder climate was in order, and he accepted a position with the California Institute of Technology in Pasadena, California. His most notable research there included additional work on the theory of quantum electrodynamics (for which he shared the Nobel Prize in Physics in 1965), a functional path integral formulation of quantum mechanics,

the superfluidity of supercooled liquid helium, and a model of the weak decay of neutrons. He also played an important part in developing the first massively parallel computer system and promoting nanotechnology research.

The final years of Feynman's life were marked by his involvement as part of the Rogers Commission investigating the *Challenger* disaster of 1986. He was dismayed to learn the National Aeronautics and Space Administration management team often misunderstood the safety data presented by contractor engineers working on the shuttle program and was shocked to find that they would take these misunderstandings as evidence of the mission's safety. Feynman found many other egregious misuses of safety information, leading him to recalculate the mission managers' often-cited shuttle safety factor of 1 in 100,000 to a much more sobering (and accurate) 1 in 100 to 200.

Feynman, the Science Popularizer

Teaching physics was one of Feynman's great pleasures in life. He felt science should be accessible to anyone and that all topics should be completely explainable at a college freshman's level. To this end, he developed a number of teaching tools including Feynman Diagrams, a map that tracks particles and aids in calculating interactions between them. Working with colleagues in the early 1960s, he also developed the Feynman Lectures on Physics, which have sold over a million copies and are still widely read today. Many of his other lectures and talks have also been transcribed or edited into books.

Feynman wrote a number of books about physics, his life, and his hobbies, many specifically designed for the general public. His books often recount amusing anecdotes from his life but focus on making the underlying science or methods (sometimes very complex) accessible to the readers. Even today, over 30 years since his death, he is still one of the most colorful and well-known advocates for science.

Feynman, the Visionary

Feynman introduced the term *nanotechnology* to the world in 1959 during a presentation at California Technical Institute titled "There's Plenty of Room at the Bottom." He described many of the opportunities that working with nanoscale structures offered and hypothesized about the ways to create the machines needed to assemble these structures. It would be another 30 years before researchers would create the first "Feynman machine" and jump-start the nanotechnology juggernaut that rumbles forward today.

Although widely considered the "spiritual grandfather" of nanotechnology, Feynman's critics have pointed out that he did not pursue the work he proposed in his presentation. However, he did promote further research by offering prizes to researchers who accomplished milestone feats in nanotechnology, and his presentation did influence some key players in developing the tools needed to manipulate individual atoms. When discussing Feynman's impact, detractors tend to downplay contributions to nanotechnology made by those who were, in turn, influenced by his 1959 presentation.

This question of Feynman's contribution to nanotechnology will continue to be debated by science historians. Feynman's legacy as one of the world's first-rate physicists and science communicators remains a strong one, however, regardless of just how much credit he is given for inventing this new field.

Ted Greenhalgh

See also Manhattan Project; Nanotechnology; Space Shuttle

Further Readings

Brown, L. M., & Rigden, J. S. (Eds.). (1993). *Most of the good stuff: Memories of Richard Feynman*. New York: Simon & Schuster.

Feynman, R. P. (1985). *Surely you're joking, Mr. Feynman: Adventures of a curious character* (R. Leighton, Ed.). New York: W. W. Norton.

Feynman, R. P. (1988). *What do you care what other people think? Further adventures of a curious character* (Ralph Leighton, Ed.). New York: W. W. Norton.

Gleick, J. (1992). *Genius: The life and science of Richard Feynman*. New York: Pantheon.

FOOD AND DRUG ADMINISTRATION, U.S.

The Food and Drug Administration (FDA) is the federal agency responsible for ensuring the safety of foods (other than meat and poultry) and of therapeutic biological products such as vaccines, cosmetics, medical devices, radiological products, human drugs, and veterinary drugs. Originally called the Bureau of Chemistry, the agency name was changed to the Food and Drug Administration in 1930. Although currently housed within the Department of Health and Human Services, historically the FDA has been housed in the Department of Agriculture, the Federal Security, the Public Health Service, and the Department of Health, Education, and Welfare, the predecessor to Health and Human Services. In 1862, Charles M. Weatherill was appointed the first chemist of the Department of Agriculture. In 1883, Harvey Wiley became the chief chemist and campaigned for a federal food and drug law. This transformation came with increased regulation, responsibilities, and duties for the agency.

Prior to 1906, the U.S. government was primarily concerned about food and drug safety within particular segments of the general population. A public scandal about contaminated or adulterated medicine given to U.S. troops rushed the passage of the 1848 Drug Importation Act. Signed by President James K. Polk on June 26, 1848, the act established customs laboratories on the borders. The introduction of the law came at the request of pharmacists and physicians who questioned the purity of the medicines they prescribed and compounded.

By the start of the 20th century, many U.S. households had shifted from an agrarian lifestyle and economy to an urban environment, affecting jobs, housing, and consumer goods. Prepared foods and drugs were readily and easily available in the marketplace. Yet the quality of those products was questionable, and state laws were varied and inconsistent in the regulation of the quality of these foods and drugs. In this era of exploding foods, blinding lash dyes, questionable patent medicines, and fermenting catsups, some measures were taken to assure consumers about the drug and food quality. Passed 4 years before the 1906 Food and Drug Act, the 1902 Biologics Control Act called for the regulation of the manufacture and sale of biologics.

The passage of the 1906 Pure Food and Drug Act (also called the Wiley Act) was prompted by internal forces such as Harvey Wiley and by organized social movements that demanded the government regulate the safety and labeling of food and drugs. To understand the effects of preservatives on the human body and to have evidence to build their case for a federal pure food and drug standards act, Wiley and his staff of chemists collected samples of adulterated food and drugs and performed food additive experiments. Also, Wiley built a broad coalition of business leaders, chemists, physicians, women's club members, and journalists who supported food and drug reform. As the Department of Agriculture chemists continued their research and as Wiley cemented support among various groups, journalists and other writers prodded the conscience of the U.S. public by tackling the food industry and upsetting the nation's collective stomach. The most famous muckraker author who wrote about food standards was Upton Sinclair, author of *The Jungle,* which vividly described the unsanitary conditions of the Chicago meatpacking yards. Other authors included Samuel Hopkins Adams of *Colliers* and Ray Stannard Baker at *McClure's Magazine,* who wrote about food safety and drug standards. The publishers of *Ladies' Home Journal,* Cyrus H. K. Curtis and Edward Bok, refused advertising from patent medicines and medicines laced with high percentages of alcohol.

The 1906 Pure Food and Drug Act called for the prevention of the manufacturing, sale, and interstate distribution of foods, drugs, medicines, and liquors that had been "adulterated or misbranded or poisonous or deleterious" and called "for regulating traffic therein." The modern FDA was formed by the 1906 passage of the Food and Drug Act. Suzanne Junod wrote that the 1906 act transformed the business and manufacturing practices, introducing sanitary procedures, and updated equipment, shaping new industries such as refrigeration and ushering in improvements in drug and food safety. She argued that business benefited from these early federal regulations, which eliminated spoilage and other waste and helped gain the confidence and goodwill of consumers.

The 1938 Food, Drug, and Cosmetics Act, which replaced the 1906 law, added the requirements that the companies conduct premarket testing of all new drugs and that the FDA approve the drugs before their marketing. After an elixir called sulfanilamide caused 107 deaths in fall of 1937,

the new law was pushed onto the congressional and presidential agenda.

Other key events in the history of the FDA include these:

1951: Congress passed the Durham-Humphrey Amendment, which required harmful drugs to be dispensed by prescription and under the care of a licensed health care provider.

1958: Per the Food Additives Amendment, additives manufacturers must seek FDA approval of new additives before the additives are included in food products.

1960: The Color Additive Amendments is enacted. Manufacturers of any dyes used in food, drugs, cosmetics, and medical devices must establish safety and seek FDA approval before marketing to the public.

1962: The Kefauver-Harris Drug Amendment instituted tighter regulatory controls over pharmaceutical drugs.

1970: The first patient package insert was used.

1995: FDA considers cigarettes "drug delivery devices." However, this regulatory action was subsequently struck down (in 2000) by the Supreme Court, in a 5 to 4 verdict.

2004: The Food Allergen Labeling and Consumer Protection Act was passed. This amendment to the Food, Drug, and Cosmetic Act requires food labels to list any ingredients that may be a major food allergen.

Today, the FDA is composed of various centers, offices, and affiliated organizations that help to fulfill the mission of the organization. These include the Center for Biologics Evaluation and Research, Center for Devices and Radiological Health, Center for Drug Evaluation and Research, Center for Food Safety and Applied Nutrition, Center for Veterinary Medicine, National Center for Toxicological Research, Office of Regulatory Affairs, Joint Institute for Food Safety and Applied Nutrition, and National Center for Food Safety and Technology.

Natalie Tindall

See also Drug Advertising; Food Safety; Health Communication, Overview

Further Readings

Food Allergen Labeling and Consumer Protection Act, Pub. L. No. 108-282 (2004).

Food and Drug Act, 21 U.S.C. § 1 et seq. (1906).

Food, Drug, and Cosmetics Act, 21 U.S. C.§ 301 (1938).

Goodwin, L. S. (1999). *The pure food, drink, and drug crusaders, 1879–1914*. Jefferson, NC: McFarland.

Junod, S. W. (2000). Food standards in the United States: The case of the peanut butter and jelly sandwich. In D. F. Smith & J. Phillips (Eds.), *Food, science, policy, and regulation in the twentieth century* (pp. 167–188). London: Routledge.

Maeder, T. (1994). *Adverse reactions*. New York: William Morrow.

Pure Food and Drug Act of 1906, 21 U.S.C. §§ 1–15 (1906).

Young, J. H. (1989). *Pure food: Securing the federal Food and Drugs Act of 1906*. Princeton, NJ: Princeton University Press.

FOOD IRRADIATION

Food is needed for survival and is a major component of developing cultural and personal identities, but food can also be harmful. Throughout history, humans have been trying to find ways to safely and effectively store and preserve food, including salting, fermentation, and canning. When new food technologies are developed, risk communicators try to promote (or challenge) these technologies in ways that are interesting and informational to both the press and the general public. One such technology that has gained a good deal of media spotlight over the past several years is food irradiation.

Food irradiation is a relatively new technology for many people in the general public. It became headline news in the 1980s and has continued to be a topic of debate through the early part of the 21st century. This technology, however, has a history that is over 100 years old, dating back to a patent issued in 1905 in the United Kingdom. By 1929, U.S. cigar makers were using X-ray technology to kill beetles that were infesting their cigar shipments. These new machines were continually breaking down, so the manufacturers turned to newly discovered and cheaper pesticides to do the job.

Things began to change when the nuclear age provided more accessible radioactive materials and better technology, fueled in large part by the cold war. Given better and more reliable nuclear technologies, interests were renewed in the practical applications of radioactive material. As early as 1947, food irradiation experiments were being conducted in the United States and in other countries. By the 1950s, institutions such as Massachusetts Institute of Technology and the University of Washington were conducting their own irradiation experiments, often with financial backing from the U.S. Atomic Energy Commission.

The process of irradiation involves exposing food to ionizing energy, which can include radioactive materials, such as cobalt 60 or cesium 137, X-rays, or high-energy electron beams. The ionizing radiation breaks down the molecular structure of the cells that are present in the food at the time of exposure, killing bacterial organisms, such as *E. coli* and salmonella, and insects, such as fruit flies. The molecular reconfiguration of many fruits and vegetables keeps them from spoiling or sprouting quickly, which for the consumer means a longer shelf life.

The first full-scale food irradiation plant was opened near Mulberry, Florida, in 1992. Within the Mulberry plant, food is loaded onto a conveyor belt and then transported to the treatment room, which contains the radioactive material (in this case, cobalt 60). The food is then bombarded with the electrons that are breaking free of the cobalt. After the food is treated (the length of the treatment depends on government designated dosages and thickness of the food and packaging), it is taken out of the room and sent to its final destination.

What can be risky about food that is bacteria-free and maintains a longer shelf life? For some opponents, there are a number of issues. First, irradiation facilities are an environmental risk due to the presence of radioactive materials (there is also a possibility of accidents while shipping radioactive materials to these facilities). Second, irradiation breaks down beneficial nutrients as it is killing harmful bacteria. It can also be used to compensate for poor handling practices by food producers and manufacturers, and it alters the flavor and texture of some foods. Finally, there is an argument over whether or not food that has been irradiated can be labeled as *fresh*, as irradiation can actually cook the food that is exposed to it, much like microwaving food, if the dosage is too high; if the dosage is too low, irradiation can be of little use.

In 1980, a joint committee made up of members from the World Health Organization, the Food and Agriculture Organization, and the Organisation of Economic Co-operation and Development agreed that a dose of 10 kilograys would not pose any toxicological threat to consumers, and this has been accepted as the high end for irradiation, though in some countries, such as the Netherlands and South Africa, higher doses (up to 75 kilograys) are used to completely sterilize meat or food for terminally ill patients. In the United States, where food irradiation is considered a food additive, the approved level for most foods is 1 kilogray or lower, though up to 30 kilograys have been approved for herbs and spices for the purpose of controlling foodborne pathogens.

The fight over food irradiation appears to be long from over in the United States. Not all scientists agree that it is a safe and effective way to treat food. Some have argued that the same process that kills bacteria could harm humans in the case of an accident, and others have argued that it provides a false sense of security, as irradiation may kill some bacteria but do nothing for viruses such as hepatitis. In addition, accidents involving radioactive material started to become highly visible in the 1970s. Still, the U.S. Food and Drug Administration has approved irradiation for a number of foods, including a 1963 ruling permitting irradiation of wheat, wheat flour, and potatoes.

The future of irradiation will be decided in a number of arenas, including the government, the press, and the market. Most U.S. government agencies have given the green light for irradiation, though political pressures could change the tide, or at least silence these proponents if this becomes a platform issue for popular political candidates. The press has given space to both supporters and opponents, and given the lack of knowledge the general public has about this process it would be easy for a vocal minority (either in favor or opposed to irradiation) to dominate the public discussion. Finally, irradiated products have been made available to the public in various grocery stores. Some have sold, while the marketability of others is still in question. For risk communicators, this points to fertile ground for studying the ways

in which various agencies and arenas play into the success or failure of a technology.

Toby A. Ten Eyck

See also Food Safety; Low-Level Radiation

Further Readings

Bruhn, C. M. (2001). United States consumer choice of irradiated food. In P. Loaharanu & P. Thomas (Eds.), *Irradiation for food safety and quality* (pp. 169–173). Lancaster, PA: Techomic Production.

Diehl, J. F. (1995). *Safety of irradiated foods* (2nd ed.). New York: Marcel Dekker.

Sapp, S., & Korsching, P. F. (2004). The social fabric and innovation diffusion: Symbolic adoption of food irradiation. *Rural Sociology, 69,* 347–369.

Ten Eyck, T. A., & Deseran, F. A. (2001). In the words of experts: The interpretive process of the food irradiation debate. *International Journal of Food Science and Technology, 36,* 821–831.

FOOD LIBEL LAWS

Every information campaign, whether it is promoting a commercial brand name or a new scientific discovery, relies on legitimacy. A story of a homeless person isolating the gene that causes obesity is not likely to be considered trustworthy due to a lack of credibility, while a NASA scientist contending that there has been a meeting between the President of the United States and the Martian political movement lacks plausibility. These two cases are extreme examples of stories that are likely to be ignored by a large portion of the population due to a lack of legitimacy. There are, however, stories where the boundaries are not so clear. Some of these include efforts to defame someone or something, including campaigns meant to threaten various aspects of the food industry. The food industry has countered these attacks by backing food libel laws.

The concepts of *libel* and *slander* have a long history, though both words have become more common in everyday usage with the rise of the mass media. Slander is typically tied to spoken words (such as radio and television broadcasts), while libel is linked to the written word (newspapers). Both words connote a mistreatment of someone or something, typically without provocation or just cause. In U.S. courts, it is typically the plaintiff that must prove that the libelous or slanderous statement was done specifically to ruin a reputation and that there is no evidence to support such statements. This is very often difficult to do, as any evidence pointing to the slightest truth can render a libel action moot.

With regard to food and libel, negative news coverage of the growth promoter Alar in apples in 1989 moved a number of states to begin drafting libel laws that would protect their food producers and manufacturers. These laws were tested in one of the most famous cases of food libel in 1996, when Oprah Winfrey announced on her television show that she was going to stop eating hamburgers. This was prompted by a guest who warned the talk show host and her audience that mad cow disease (bovine encephalitis) could find its way into the U.S. meat supply. After the comment, a number of groups in Texas, including that state's agricultural commissioner, asked for Winfrey to be sued under the food libel laws (also known as veggie libel laws and food disparagement laws). Winfrey was sued by the Texas Cattlemen's Association but won her case in 1998. By the end of that ordeal, 13 states have passed similar laws (Alabama, Arizona, Colorado, Florida, Georgia, Idaho, Louisiana, Mississippi, North Dakota, Ohio, Oklahoma, South Dakota, and Texas), though the Arkansas State Legislature struck down a food libel bill in 1999.

The United Kingdom also has food libel laws, which were used by McDonald's to sue Greenpeace in 1990. According to Eric Schlosser, who wrote *Fast Food Nation,* the U.K. libel laws are much easier on the plaintiff, as it is the person or organization accused of being libelous that must prove their statements are correct, and they cannot refer to scientific findings unless they are the scientists themselves. In the McDonald's case, which came to be known as the "McLibel case," three activists apologized for their actions, while two others decided to fight the corporation. The trial began in 1994 and ended in 1997, when the judge found that some of the information passed out by the activists did fit the definition of libel, though not all of it (which is what McDonald's had

contended). The court awarded McDonald's £60,000, which was lowered to £40,000 later, though by that time the corporation had said it would not seek to collect the money.

While libel laws are important for protection against malicious attacks on one's reputation, they can have a chilling effect on risk communication when applied to something as broad as an industry. Scientists, as well as other individuals and organizations that might feel the need to speak against some practice or potential hazard, may be threatened into silence, as even a wrongful case of libel can have negative ramifications. For example, if a food scientist was to contend that certain industry practices run the risk of spreading a virulent bacteria across the United States and was then sued by the industry under the food libel laws, his or her organization might also come under attack, leading to a withdraw of legitimacy from important consumers. This might include the industry itself, as many food scientists either work for the food industry or receive funding from it. Given the amount of financial resources controlled by the food industry, as well as how many lay consumers rely on this industry for survival, making such a statement cannot be done quickly or without institutional backing.

There are groups that are fighting against food libel laws. The Center for Science in the Public Interest has created FoodSpeak: Coalition for Free Speech, which argues that the food libel laws are anticonstitutional, as they disregard First Amendment rights regarding free speech and freedom of expression. *Mother Jones,* a magazine with over 250,000 subscribers in 2004 (as well as a Web presence), has also called the food libel laws an attack on First Amendment rights. In a February 24, 1998, article, they mentioned six food libel suits that included ice cream, beer, and large flightless birds.

Food libel laws are only one area at the intersection of libel and risk communication. Concerns with being held responsible or sued for comments may lead to self-censorship among those engaged in risk assessments, management, and communication. Agencies and institutions with a vested interest in other commodities may look to these types of laws to protect their own sales, while other groups may see this kind of regulation as a way to raise support for their own causes, whether that is commodity specific (such as Greenpeace trying to raise awareness of environmental issues) or related to freedom of speech rights. Risk assessors, managers, and communicators must take libel and slander into consideration when dealing with developing and disseminating messages that could cause harm to another individual, group, or industry.

Toby A. Ten Eyck

See also Center for Science in the Public Interest; Food Safety; Nutrition and Media

Further Readings

Arnold, A., & Sandlin, J. (1998). *Fear of food.* Bellevue, WA: Free Enterprise Press.

Atkins, R., & Mintcheva, S. (Eds.). (2006). *Censoring culture.* New York: New Press.

Kretkowski, P. D. (1998, February 24). Food fights. *Mother Jones.* Available at http://motherjones.com/politics/1998/02/food-fights

Schlosser, E. (2001). *Fast food nation.* Boston: Houghton Mifflin.

FOOD SAFETY

Communication about food safety is complex. This is, in part, because food safety covers a range of different issues, including microbial contamination of food (for example, in the domestic environment), optimization of nutrition and consumer food choices, and development of effective communication about the risks and benefits of food processing technologies such as genetic modification of food crops and (more recently) nanotechnology used in food production. In addition, food choice is important for all consumers. On the one hand, food choices are representative of that class of behaviors that are frequently repeated by consumers and can be described as habitual. Against this, consumers may also be suspicious of new foods that are outside of their experience or produced using novel technologies, a phenomenon known as food neophobia. Communication about food safety may involve communication about both risks and benefits associated with consumption of a specific food product, and the impacts of these risks and benefits may also vary across the population and be associated with different degrees of uncertainty. Finally, people need to eat to live, and so making safe food choices also becomes an issue of survival and can potentially influence an individual's quality of life.

Food-Related Risk Perception and Communication

In line with research in other risk domains, research into risk perception and communication in the area of food safety initially focused on understanding why laypersons' risk perceptions differed from "expert" risk assessments and the implications of the results of this research for the development of effective risk communication. In terms of perception, the extent to which a potential food risk is perceived to be unnatural or potentially catastrophic or to which an individual perceives exposure to be involuntary increases their risk perceptions. These psychological dimensions are reliable predictors of people's responses to potential risks associated with different foods and have been shown to systematically vary across different types of food hazards. In addition, individual differences in consumer perceptions of, and responses to, food hazards, as well as communication about the associated risks, have also been a focus of empirical investigation. For example, risk perceptions, food safety related behaviors, consumer responses to food safety incidents, and consumer use of information may be dependent on the consumer's own personality characteristics as well as other hazard-related variables.

Another concept that has been extensively studied in relation to consumer perceptions of food safety is the concept of trust in food risk communication. Research in this area also has implications for the practice of food risk management. The influence of specific food safety incidents on consumer risk perceptions and behavior (for example, in a crisis context) may also influence the effectiveness of risk communication practices. For example, people may respond negatively to a message from an information source that has mishandled a food safety incident in the past or failed to convey accurate information that takes into account both technical risk estimates and consumer concerns.

Cultural and historical variation in both consumer perceptions of food risks and trust in local and international regulatory institutions, across different geographical regions and within different social contexts, implies consumer responses to information about food safety may be prone to cross-cultural differences. Individual differences in consumer evaluations of risks (for example, the extent to which an individual perceives that he or she has control over his or her own health status through, in this case, making safe or otherwise healthy food choices) may also be influential determinants of consumer responses to communication.

Despite the potential for variation in perceptions of food-related risk, there is evidence to suggest that consumers are less concerned about natural or familiar food risks, and for this reason, people may make inappropriate and unhealthy food choices or take inappropriate risks regarding, for example, domestic food hygiene practices when these are both familiar and perceived to be under personal control.

An example is provided by the development of communication interventions to prevent the occurrence of food poisoning incidents originating in the domestic environment. Food poisoning represents an important public health issue. The introduction of food safety objectives reflects the need to promote public health through reduction in the number of cases of foodborne illnesses. From the perspective of public health, it is far more useful to set food safety objectives at the point of consumption, as this is the point where microbial load determines the probability of illness occurring. To meet food safety objectives, changes in consumer behavior (for example, regarding inappropriate storage and food preparation practices) may reduce the incidence of foodborne illness. As a consequence, the goal of improving public health can only be obtained through implementation of appropriate and effective communication interventions.

Domestic food preparation is an example of a human activity that involves frequently repeated behaviors embedded in an individual's routine activities and is associated with lifestyle choices (for example, the selection of healthy foods). An important factor that needs to be taken into account in any discussion of lifestyle risks is that of optimistic bias or unrealistic optimism. People tend to rate their own personal risks from a particular lifestyle hazard as being less than those experienced by an average member of society or in comparison to another individual with similar demographic characteristics. Optimistic biases tend to be much greater for lifestyle-related hazards (such as food poisoning contracted in the home or illness experienced as a consequence of inappropriate dietary choices) compared to those perceived to be associated with technologies applied to food production, where people perceive much less personal control over exposure. People exhibiting optimistic bias may not take precautions to reduce their risk from a hazard.

The risks of food poisoning are typically prone to optimistic biases. Although targeting information to those individuals most at risk may optimize use of available resources, this cannot be done unless there is an understanding of which consumers are most at risk. Important first steps in targeting risk communication associated with food safety are to differentiate or segment consumers who are most at risk as a consequence of both attitudinal factors and their vulnerability to the risks, identify potential barriers to communication relevant to these individuals, and utilize this information in optimizing risk communication. Understanding those social-psychological factors that determine consumer behavior is important if consumer protection is to be optimized. For example, despite that consumers appear to be knowledgeable about how to prepare food safely, other factors (for example, optimistic bias or habitual food preparation practices) may result in incidences of domestic food poisoning.

It is also recognized that some segments of the population are more at risk than others for adopting unsafe food preparation practices. For example, there is evidence to suggest that young single males are most likely to create a contaminated meal. This suggests that a stratified risk communication strategy is important if risk communication is to be targeted to those who are most vulnerable. It has been found that embedding relevant emotional cues associated with food safety (for example, disgust) in information about food safety increased both consumer awareness of food safety risks and consumers' motivation to behave in such a way as to protect their health from the risks of food poisoning. In another example, it has been found that including information about safe food preparation in a recipe increased food safety relevant behaviors. In other words, the message included in the recipe activated an existing attitude to produce a positive effect in terms of consumer health protection. One conclusion is that consumers possess more knowledge about safe food preparation than they used to, and activating this knowledge at the same time the behavior is being conducted is important. Communication about food safety might usefully exploit recipes or instructions on food packaging to activate existing knowledge about food safety held by consumers.

Risk-Benefit Communication

Food consumption often involves consumers making a trade-off between the risks and benefits associated with the consumption of a particular food product. For example, fish represents a product where consumers have to balance the health benefits of eating fish (for example, beneficial effects associated with omega-3 fatty acids) against possible safety risks (for example, adverse effects associated with contamination). If consumers are to make informed consumption choices, they will need to base these decisions on information about both risks and benefits. People receiving integrated risk-benefit messages may not interpret risk and benefit information independently. Generally, as risk perception associated with a specific issue increases, benefit perception associated with the same issue decreases, and vice versa. However, further research is required to understand the fundamental cognitive mechanisms underlying consumer decision making under circumstances where both health risks and benefits are associated with food choices. It is possible that perceived risk and benefit might be inversely correlated because people have a need to avoid conflict between different beliefs held simultaneously—that is, it is difficult for consumers to perceive high risks and high benefits associated with the same food hazard at the same time. Nonetheless, consumers are faced with decisions about both risks and benefits associated with specific food choices, and developing effective communication about both is a priority.

An example may serve to illustrate the complexities associated with risk-benefit communication. Consumer preferences regarding information about the net health impact of both risks and benefits on life expectancy and integrated risk-benefit measures (for example, quality of life and disability adjusted life years) have been examined. The perceived complexities of these integrated measures have been reported as being difficult for consumers to interpret. Communication of such integrated risk-benefit messages represents a challenge for future research.

In addition, the order in which risk or benefit information is provided may influence the relative impact of information on risk or benefit attitudes held by consumers. For example, the information provided first (either risk or benefit information) may differentially influence consumer attitudes toward a particular food. The impact of communication about both risks and benefits may also be affected by the prior attitudes held by the consumer toward a particular food or food production process. For example, people may not pay attention to information that contradicts an already strongly held attitude about a particular food. If people perceive that eating a specific food is potentially risky, they may not attend to information about the potential benefits associated with the same food, and vice versa. Similarly, if people are very negative about the application of a particular food processing technology to food production, they may only attend to risk messages about the same technology, but avoid messages about benefit.

Communicating Uncertainty

Different types of uncertainty have been found to be important to the general public, including within the area of food safety. For example, uncertainty linked to lack of knowledge, and the potential impact or extent of a particular hazard, should it occur, needs to be included in food-safety-related communications. The public also requires information about what is being done to reduce uncertainties where these exist. Indeed, consumer perceptions were that regulatory institutions were withholding uncertainty information. In line with this, various challenges associated with the communication of uncertainty have been identified. For example, individuals appear to have difficulties in interpreting low probabilities and associated events and tend not to seek out probabilistic information under conditions of uncertainty. In addition, heuristics or cognitive decision rules may exert influence on interpretation of uncertain events associated with food safety issues. For example, the availability heuristic results in people estimating greater probabilities of the occurrence of future events if they can recollect past examples of similar incidents. Developing effective communication about uncertainty is important if food safety communication is to be transparent (that is, if it acknowledges uncertainties where these exist) and create an environment where consumers can make accurate and informed decisions about food safety issues.

The Role of Trust

Consumer trust in different actors and institutions responsible for guaranteeing and controlling food safety, as well as trust in the information provided by different information sources that communicate about food safety or food-related risks, plays an important part in developing effective communication about food safety. Consumer perceptions of risk and benefit may be dependent on consumer trust in institutions with responsibility for consumer protection and in the food industry and producers with responsibility for the supply chain. Other dimensions of trust, such as perceived honesty and concern about public welfare and consumer protection on the part of risk communicators, might overrule perceived competence as a determinant of risk perceptions and attitudes toward food safety issues. Indeed, existing attitudes held by consumers toward food hazards or food production technologies might influence whom the public trusts. For example, if consumers have a strongly held attitude about a potentially hazardous activity, they are more likely to trust a source that provides a message that agrees with their existing attitude and to distrust a source that provides a message that disagrees with what they already believe.

Various approaches to improving trust can be identified. For example, consumer evaluations of the effectiveness of food risk management are primarily driven by whether consumers perceive effective and proactive consumer protection systems are being put into action. As a consequence, risk communication should also include information about proactive consumer protection strategies if trust in food risk managers and institutions is to be developed and maintained. Increased transparency about scientific uncertainties associated with combined risk-benefit communication has the potential to increase perception of honesty

associated with the information source, while at the same time to reinforce perceptions of transparency in the process of food risk analysis. Maintaining public trust in regulatory activities associated with food risk requires transparency and openness in communication practices. As a consequence, the effective communication of uncertainty and variability associated with risk (and benefit) assessment is increasingly important.

Conclusion

Developing effective risk communication about food safety issues requires understanding of consumer perceptions, needs, and behaviors. Risk communication is likely to be most effective when targeted at specific groups of consumers with similar needs and interests. Understanding how individuals differ in, for example, their food safety information needs and preferences, how different individuals process food-related risk (and benefit) information, and how these may vary according to psychological and other individual differences will help risk communicators in developing and communicating their messages.

Lynn J. Frewer

See also Agricultural Biotechnology; Food Libel Laws; Nanotechnology; Risk Communication, Overview; Uncertainty in Science Communication

Further Readings

Alhakmi, A. S., & Slovic, P. (1994). A psychological study of the inverse relationships between perceived risk and perceived benefit. *Risk Analysis, 14,* 1085–1096.

Fischer, A. R. H., & Frewer, L. J. (2008). Food safety practices in the domestic kitchen: Demographic, personality and experiential determinants. *Journal of Applied Social Psychology, 38,* 2869–2884.

Frewer, L., Lassen, J., Kettlitz, B., Scholderer, J., Beekman, V., & Berdal, K. G. (2004). Societal aspects of genetically modified foods. Entransfood [Special issue]. *Food and Chemical Toxicology, 42(7),* 1181–1193.

Miles, S., & Scaife, V. (2003). Optimistic bias and food. *Nutrition Research Reviews, 16,* 3–19.

Nauta, M. J., Fischer, A. R. H., van Asselt, E. D., de Jong, A. E. I., Frewer, L. J., & de Jonge, R. (2008). Food safety in the domestic environment: The effect of consumer risk information on human disease risks. *Risk Analysis, 28,* 179–192.

van Kleef, E., Houghton, J. R., Krystallis, T., Pfenning, U., Rowe, G., van Dijk, H., & Frewer, L. J. (2007). Consumer evaluations of food risk management quality in Europe. *Risk Analysis, 27,* 1565–1580.

Verbeke, W., Vanhonacker, F., Frewer, L. J., Sioen, I., de Henauw, S., & van Camp, J. (2008). Communicating risks and benefits from fish consumption: Impact on Belgian consumers' perception and intention to eat fish. *Risk Analysis, 28,* 951–967.

FRAMING AND PRIMING IN SCIENCE COMMUNICATION

Scientific and technological issues are increasingly becoming policy issues, with different stakeholders trying to influence the debate. It is therefore imperative for science communicators to understand the importance of processes such as framing and priming, two theories of media effects with roots in psychology, communication, and other social science disciplines. Although they are often presented as related, they refer to two different processes. They are, however, both very important to science and technology communicators since they refer to powerful media effects that can influence audiences' perceptions of scientific issues. They can also be used as strategic tools to affect audiences' attitudes toward complex issues and the type of decisions individuals might make to address risky situations potentially posed by new technologies.

Defining Framing

A communicator faced with the challenge of writing about a complex scientific issue, be it for a persuasive speech, a newspaper article, a magazine story, or a blog, will most likely end up emphasizing a specific dimension of the issue over numerous others to make the story more compelling or more relevant to the audience. To highlight the favored interpretation of an issue, communicators will use specific metaphors, visuals, symbols, and other culturally relevant devices. They may be doing so intentionally to persuade a specific audience (through speechwriting, for instance) or by necessity to efficiently present a complex issue as in the case of journalistic science writing. By doing so, communicators are framing the issue, much like artists would do when choosing a specific frame to present a painting in a particular light.

In communication theory, *frames* refer to the mode of presentation used by communicators (journalists and others) to characterize an issue in a way that resonates with their audiences. Different frames for the same issue do not simply diverge in terms of content; rather, frames differ in how they present ambiguous stimuli such as complex scientific issues. For instance, a news story about an emergent technology such as nanotechnology could present the technology as the next plastic, therefore evoking potential technological breakthroughs. The same news story could have characterized nanotechnology as the next asbestos, which would have conveyed a very different interpretation of the issue. These diverging media frames could both be used by audiences to make sense of nanotechnology, although each might produce different effects on those audiences' perceptions.

Research on framing is not limited to the communication discipline. For instance, the first formal work on framing can be attributed to sociologist Erving Goffman, who argued in the 1970s that individuals apply socially shared interpretative schemes when encountering information, which he called interpretative frameworks. These frameworks help people classify new information and make sense of a complex world, much like frames tailored to audiences in media discourse help audiences make sense of complex information.

In the late 1970s and 1980s, psychologists Daniel Kahneman (who won a Nobel Prize in Economics for this research) and Amos Tversky used experiments to show that different ways of presenting a risk-related situation (as either a loss or as a gain) but with identical informational content led to different choices regarding the best option to follow. In other words, the same message framed in terms of loss or in terms of gain was interpreted differently by subjects and led to different behavioral intentions. Their principle of *loss aversion* states that avoiding a loss seems to be a more powerful motivator than achieving a gain.

Research in sociology and political communication, and more recently in science communication, has added to the body of knowledge on framing accumulated in other disciplines. In an article published in 1999, Dietram Scheufele proposed a process model of framing that was elaborated in the context of political communication but that can be applied to other contexts such as science and technology communication. In this model, he distinguishes between frame building, the process by which media frames are produced, and frame setting, the process by which media frames impact audiences.

Media Frame Building

Different sets of variables, such as cultural norms, values, and organizational pressures and routines, can influence how a news story is framed. Journalists' own political and ideological orientations can also affect the type of frames they will use in a story. Influences external to the newsroom are also important to consider since different groups in society are likely to try to shape media discourse about a specific issue through the strategic use of frames. Press releases presenting new research in science and technology will often emphasize specific frames, just as will press releases from different interests advocating for a specific issue. And elite groups such as political and corporate actors are likely to be actively engaged in the frame building process as well, through quotes provided to the media and other communication and lobbying efforts.

Media Frame Setting

Frame setting refers to the process through which audiences are influenced by media frames. At the most basic level, and particularly for novel issues such as new technologies for which people lack any existing considerations, frames help people figure out what the issue is about and reach some kind of understanding about it. Frames can also help people make sense of information by influencing which schemas (or categories) are activated in people's brains when they process information. People will then use these cognitive schemas to reach a judgment about a specific issue, by linking their existing beliefs, values, and attitudes to the issue under consideration. It is therefore important to note that although media frames can affect

audiences' attitudes, these effects depend on predispositions, schemas, and a wide range of individual traits that will ultimately influence how people process messages. In other words, individuals will process frames through their own perceptual filters (religious beliefs, moral schemas, patterns of trust, and so on), which means that any given frame may mean different things to different people.

Frames do not always shape the way in which an individual interprets or understands an issue; framing effects only occur if the frame is resonant with an individual's existing schemas. The underlying mechanism by which framing effect occurs is represented by the applicability model of information processing and by the knowledge activation process described by David Tewksbury and Vince Price in 1997. Each individual possesses a unique set of existing knowledge constructs in his or her memory. The activation of a particular knowledge construct at any time depends on certain characteristics such as its chronic and temporary accessibility, as well as the salient attributes of the current situation.

When an individual is exposed to a news story emphasizing a certain aspect of an issue, the activation of relevant frame-related thoughts by the news frame is dependent on the extent to which the information and message featured in the news frame match the knowledge construct held by the individual. The more the knowledge construct and the news frame resonate with each other, the more likely the news frame will render the knowledge construct applicable for issue interpretation. As a result, the knowledge construct is more likely to influence subsequent decision making and judgment. In other words, individuals are not passively influenced by a news message. Rather, they actively interpret relevant information in the media message to make subsequent judgments.

Defining Priming

Priming theory has its roots in cognitive psychology and has extensively been studied in political communication. More recently, its effects have been explored in health communication and science communication. Unlike framing theory, which is based on an applicability model, priming theory is based on a memory-based (or accessibility-based) model of information processing. People make decisions and reach a judgment about a specific issue based on the considerations that are the most accessible to them at that time. If a first stimulus has made accessible certain considerations, individuals will use these considerations when asked to formulate a judgment. Priming therefore implies that two successive cognitive tasks will be performed. First, a stimulus activates a particular node in memory. If a second related stimulus occurs, the node is already activated, thus making a judgment in response to the new stimulus easier.

Priming therefore posits that media can make certain issues or certain aspects of an issue easily brought to mind and, therefore, can influence the standards audiences use when forming attitudes and judgments about specific issues. As applied to media and science, news content could suggest to audiences what issues they should use as standards to evaluate scientists or other scientific issues under consideration by making some issues particularly salient through media coverage and, therefore, accessible to individuals when rendering subsequent judgments. Survey research is another context in which priming can occur if the questions asked are not ordered carefully. For instance, if a respondent is asked to rate how much risk he or she sees in a technology, the individual is likely to keep this consideration in mind if asked right afterward to rate how much he or she supports the technology.

Framing and Priming as Strategic Communication Tools in Science Communication

Frames can be used in public relations campaigns and other strategic communication efforts. By selecting frames that resonate with an audience's preexisting knowledge, beliefs, and cultural values, communicators can make a message more persuasive. They can also influence a specific debate by setting the vocabulary and metaphors used to discuss the issue. For instance, Greenpeace has widely used the term *frankenfood* to define food biotechnology as a risky technology, while industries such as Monsanto have promoted through extensive communication efforts their view that food biotechnology will help solve world hunger.

Priming can be used in strategic communication in the context of an integrated communication campaign. For instance, one could imagine a campaign for which teasers, in the form of billboards or Twitter messages (to cite just two potential communication media), prepare an audience for subsequent messages. By making salient certain aspects of a campaign before its full deployment, priming can increase the campaign's effectiveness, particularly for issues that are completely novel to the public.

Framing in Relation to Priming

In short, the main difference between framing and priming lies in the type of psychological process in play for each of these effects. The concept of framing is based on applicability, while the concept of priming is based on accessibility. The applicability effect refers to a frame's making information or other associations applicable to an issue or topic, whereas accessibility refers to the influence of activated thoughts on subsequent evaluations.

Of course, framing and priming effects are related in that they both can occur as a consequence of news stories exposure. Although distinct in nature, they can be expected to happen concurrently. In the long run, the lasting effects of media exposure on audiences' attitudes toward science and technology will most likely be due to a plethora of effects, including framing and priming.

Dominique Brossard

See also Metaphors in Science Communication; Strategic Communication for Science and Technology

Further Readings

Brossard, D., Kim, E., Scheufele, D. A., & Lewenstein, B. V. (2009). Religiosity as a perceptual filter: Examining processes of opinion formation about nanotechnology. *Public Understanding of Science, 18*(5), 546–568.

Goffman, E. (1974). *Frame analysis: An essay on the organization of experience.* Cambridge, MA: Harvard University Press.

Kahneman, D., & Tversky, A. (1979). Prospect theory: Analysis of decision under risk. *Econometrica, 47*(2), 263–292.

Nisbet, M. C., & Scheufele, D. A. (2007). The future of public engagement. *The Scientist, 21*(10), 38–44.

Price, D., & Tewksbury, D. (1997). News values and public opinion: A theoretical account of media priming and framing. In G. A. Barett & F. J. Boster

(Eds.), *Progress in communication sciences: Advances in persuasion* (Vol. 13, pp. 173–212). Greenwich, CT: Ablex.

Scheufele, D. (1999). Framing as a theory of media effects. *Journal of Communication, 49,* 103–122.

Scheufele, D., & Tewksbury, D. (2008). Framing, agenda setting, and priming: The evolution of three media effects models. *Journal of Communication, 57,* 9–20.

Tewksbury, D., & Scheufele, D. (2009). News framing theory and research. In J. Bryant & M. B. Oliver (Eds.), *Media effects: Advances in theory and research* (3rd ed., pp. 17–33). New York: Routledge.

FRANKLIN, BENJAMIN (1706–1790)

Famous as an author, a humanist, an inventor, a musician, a philosopher, a printer, an internationally known scientist, and a statesman, Benjamin Franklin was one of the most remarkable of the Founding Fathers of the United States. He was one of the signers of the Constitution and served as one of the most influential diplomats of the new nation. Although he was often looked on as an amateur in his scientific work, he earned renown in the history of physics for his many discoveries related to electricity and lightning.

A product of the 18th century Age of Enlightenment, a period when reason was advocated as the primary source for authority in cultural life, Franklin invented the lightning rod, bifocal eyeglasses, the Franklin stove, a carriage odometer, and the glass harmonica. He communicated his extraordinary accomplishments in graceful, smart prose, and as a self-taught master of many subjects—including publishing and journalism, as well as science and engineering—he remains a popular icon of U.S. initiative and curiosity, as well as an early science communicator.

Benjamin Franklin was born on January 17, 1706, in Boston, Massachusetts. Franklin's formal schooling ended early, but he continued his education on his own by reading every book he could get his hands on. He taught himself simple algebra and geometry, English grammar, foreign languages, history, and science. He began an apprenticeship in his brother James's printing shop and moved to London to continue his training as a printer; he

then returned to Philadelphia to open his own printing shop. In June 1727, he helped to establish the Junto, a society of young men who met together on Friday evenings for friendliness and self-improvement that has been described as the first U.S. club. In 1729, he began the publication of the *Pennsylvania Gazette,* and in 1730, he married Deborah Read.

He proposed Pennsylvania's first university and the first U.S. city hospital and organized the country's first subscription library. Annually, from 1732 to 1758, he published *Poor Richard's Almanac,* where many polemics in favor of U.S. independence appeared alongside aphorisms and commonsense observations. Franklin became known as one of the first important writers in U.S. journalism. He is also remembered as one of the U.S. great thinkers. His ideas and words of wisdom helped to lay the foundation for the United States. At 42 years of age, he was wealthy enough to retire and started to carry out his experiments with electricity, thereby embarking on a new career of scientific research.

In 1750, he wrote to the British Royal Society, the oldest scientific organization in the world, expounding his electrical theory that stated that there were two kinds of electricity, positive and negative. His book *Experiments and Observations on Electricity* was published in London in 1751. Franklin proposed that electricity flowed from one place to another, a phenomenon everyone had observed, because of the "desire" for a negative material to move to a positive one in order to achieve natural balance. He claimed that electricity would therefore be attracted to a positive iron rod and away from properties that might otherwise lie in its path. So he performed his now famous kite experiment in 1752: As has been widely reported, at least, he attached an iron wire to a kite and was hit by the shock from a storm cloud. Franklin's lightning conductors would catch the imagination of Europe in the 1770s.

In 1753, he was awarded the Copley Medal of the Royal Society, the highest award in science at that time. Three years later, in April 1756, he became Fellow of the Royal Society because of his contributions to the theory of electricity. Many important British scientists regarded Franklin's scientific achievements as equivalent to those of Isaac Newton and the most important world scientists of the 18th century.

From 1757 to 1762, he served as representative of the Pennsylvania Assembly and traveled to England, where he was highly respected as a scientist. While in London, he invented the glass harmonica, based on a set of water-tuned wineglasses. Adam Smith may have consulted Franklin for his *Wealth of Nations* when he lived in London. He also discussed with Thomas Malthus many ideas on demography and the increase of the population that were used in the second edition of *Essay on the Principle of Population*.

Franklin became a hero in the United States when he fostered the efforts to have the British Parliament repeal the unpopular Stamp Act, the tax imposed by the Parliament on the colonies. The Hutchinson Letters Affair started at the end of 1772, when Franklin got an anonymous packet of letters. They were written by Thomas Hutchinson, Royal Governor of Massachusetts, to ask his superiors in England for more troops to Boston to fight the American rebels. Franklin allowed others to read the letters, which were published the following year in the *Boston Gazette*. Bostonians were angry with Hutchinson and forced him to leave for England. Once Franklin admitted his responsibility for leaking the letters, his reputation in England deteriorated, and he returned to the United States.

By the time he came back to Philadelphia in 1775, the American Revolution had already begun, and he joined the delegates who drafted the Declaration of Independence on July 4, 1776, becoming one of its signatories. He was subsequently appointed postmaster general, executive head of the U.S. Postal Service, under the Continental Congress, the convention of delegates from the 13 colonies that became the governing body of the United States during the American Revolution.

Franklin felt comfortable whether in London or Paris, where he eventually settled in as a minister plenipotentiary from the United States to negotiate peace treaties with England and other countries. He helped to unite his newly independent country and to manufacture an alliance with France that greatly contributed to the U.S. victory in 1783. Franklin was elected foreign member of the Paris Academy of Science in 1772, a high international distinction. He read many of his papers there, and he even had the chance to meet the distinguished philosopher Voltaire at a public session.

When he arrived in France, he was very popular, and people had a high esteem for him as a natural philosopher, referring to him as "Dr. Franklin." He watched the Montgolfier brothers, Joseph Michael and Jacques Ètienne, in Paris when they became the first men to fly in a balloon in August 1783.

If the world today is concerned about energy, Franklin had already envisaged a practical way to conserve it. In his essay "An Economical Project" of 1784, one of the pieces he wrote in Paris, he introduced the idea of saving candles if people would just get up earlier in summer. He suggested that the people of Paris should use sunshine instead of candles and rise when the sun rises instead of sleeping until noon. He even calculated the amounts of savings by getting up with the light and sleeping with dark between March and September, the origin of what is now called daylight savings time and applied by the United States and many other countries.

Franklin returned to the United States in 1785. He attended the Constitutional Convention as a delegate and acted as a conciliator in the debates over the Constitution at Philadelphia in 1787. At age 84, Franklin died in Philadelphia on April 17, 1790. More than 20,000 mourners attended his funeral.

Alejandro Manrique

Further Readings

Cohen, I. B. (1995). *Science and the Founding Fathers— Science in the political thought of Thomas Jefferson, Benjamin Franklin, John Adams and James Madison.* New York: W. W. Norton.

Meador, R. (1975). *Franklin—Revolutionary scientist.* Ann Arbor, MI: Ann Arbor Science.

Wright, E. (Ed.). (1970). *Benjamin Franklin, A profile.* New York: Hill & Wang.

FREELANCING

A freelancer is a self-employed individual who pursues a given profession without having a long-term commitment to a single employer. Science communication fields where freelancing is common include journalism and other forms of science writing, copywriting, editing, and public relations–media consulting. Each plays an important role in communicating science.

Freelancers typically come from the ranks of traditional journalism, university public information, and corporate communications positions where they gained work experience and editorial contacts prior to striking out on their own. Other freelancers are scientists turned writers. To make the transition and be competitive in the market, scientists often take courses on journalism basics, interviewing skills, and feature writing; attend specialized science-writing seminars and workshops; and/or complete science-journalism fellowships or certificate-degree programs.

Freelancers generally enjoy a greater variety of assignments than those in a full-time staff position and usually have more freedom to choose their work schedule. The experience can lead to a broader portfolio of work and the establishment of a network of clients. A major drawback to freelancing is the uncertainty of obtaining work, uneven cash flow, and the lack of benefits usually provided by an employer such as a pension, health insurance, paid holidays, sick leave, and bonuses.

Freelance science journalists sell their work to local newspapers, syndicates, magazines, and electronic media outlets. The pay for freelance science journalism varies from pennies per word to dollars per word. For decades, the industry average for magazine articles has been $1 per word. But consider that a 3,000-word magazine article may take a month to produce, and one such article per month translates into a $36,000 annual salary for an experienced freelancer. This is hardly a living wage; thus, freelancers must either juggle a great many assignments to make ends meet, hold a full-time job and freelance on the side, or have other means of financial support.

Freelance medical writers can earn more by writing for hospitals, pharmaceutical companies, government agencies, medical schools, or nonprofit organizations. This type of writing may include writing educational booklets for patients, clinical study protocols, regulatory documents, and brochures for investigative drugs. Freelancers may also be called upon to ghostwrite articles or research papers for physicians or create in-depth presentations based on materials provided by a client.

Freelance technical writers, as the name implies, write and edit highly specialized material for biotech, pharmaceutical, and technology companies. This type of science writing is sparse in that ideas must be communicated with a minimal number of words. Successful technical science writers tend to have very strong organizational skills and a keen eye for detail, plus a keen awareness of audience to judge what background knowledge can be assumed and what must be provided.

Freelance science marketing writers produce sales materials, news releases, annual reports, Web content, catalogs, and other collateral material for biotech and pharmaceutical companies. While these companies have marketing professionals on staff, the insight a freelance science writer brings to the marketing process can make the end result more effective.

Freelancing is first and foremost a business. While a flexible work schedule and a variety of assignments are attractive to those considering this career option, the reality is freelancers are entrepreneurs responsible for finding work, negotiating contracts, managing their time to complete assignments, and handling myriad details required of a small business, ranging from licensing, marketing, bookkeeping, and taxes to insurance and retirement accounts. Sometimes a freelancer finds it advantageous to join forces with one or more other freelancers and/or vendors to form a virtual agency to serve a particular client's needs for short- or long-term projects. This versatile agency model can help a freelancer land jobs that require targeted, specific experience and skills outside the scope of one individual. The composition of a virtual agency's talent base can expand or contract depending on client needs and the availability of other work.

A freelance business can grow to the point that it becomes desirable to hire part-time or permanent employees to help with administrative duties. Becoming an employer brings with it the obligation to obtain an employer identification number from the federal government; withhold, report, and pay payroll taxes; and provide workers' compensation insurance, among other responsibilities.

Impact of the Internet

Technology has made freelancing easier, but that does not mean it is easy to be successful. In the pre-Internet days, the magazine industry relied on freelance writers for the content of their publications rather than finance the payroll and benefits for full-time staff writers. Newspapers were also an important outlet for freelance writers, particularly in the late 1980s, when nearly 100 newspapers published a weekly science section.

Over the last few decades, all of this has changed. Internet and cable news, blogs, and podcasts have led to consolidation in the newspaper and TV news broadcast industries; the size of long-established magazines has shrunk as readers and advertisers migrate to new media outlets. This trend is changing the opportunities and challenges for freelance writers to communicate science to the public. Thanks to the Internet, however, today it is easier than ever to find ideas, research story background, and identify experts—whether by tagging every news story containing "global climate change" or simply by initiating a search on Google or Electric Library or perusing the dozens of online news-tip sources.

More and more editors are willing to accept e-mail queries of story ideas. This provides faster feedback to a writer than waiting for letters to transit via the U.S. Postal Service. Job Web sites such as monster.com, guru.com, and elance.com are sources for freelance science writers to locate writing opportunities and instantly link with potential clients. Networking with established science writers via online forums—such as those offered by the National Association of Science Writers, Society of Environmental Journalists, and American Medical Writers Association—can help create a path to success, as well as be a good way for freelancers to keep their finger on the pulse on industry trends that impact their ability to earn a living.

The Internet has opened up many freelance opportunities and expanded available markets, even while it has closed or narrowed some outlets. In addition, technology allows freelancers to work anywhere in the world so long as they have Internet access.

Conference News Reporting

There are myriad science, medical, and technology conferences held annually. Most receive little or no media coverage because news organizations have, in recent years, curtailed out-of-town assignments for staff reporters, choosing to send them to only a handful of "major" conferences such as the American Heart Association, Alzheimer's Association, and Society of Neuroscience annual meetings. This presents an opportunity for freelancers to create a lucrative business as news correspondents for less-reported meetings.

Freelancers who live in metropolitan areas with a large transportation hub and the conference infrastructure that attract such meetings find they can operate a successful business without the burden of travel and hotel expense. They research meeting schedules, often available years in advance, as well as target publications prior to contacting editors to offer their services as an on-site correspondent. Freelancers can often generate several assignments from one meeting. Because a meeting may be held in a city only once or not return for several years, these should be considered one-time assignments. Thus, researching new meetings and making cold calls to new editors is an ongoing process.

Other freelancers are road warriors who follow select meetings, sometimes around the globe, to report from them year after year. Editors value the reliability of a writer with depth of knowledge of a scientific field that they can trust to turn in thoughtful, analytical news reports. Some freelance writers earn six-figure incomes as road warriors, but to do so necessitates hundreds of days of travel per year and often the hiring of a support staff as a home base to book airline and hotel reservations, manage the writer's assignment calendar, and handle invoices, banking, taxes, and other day-to-day business operations.

Consultants

Some individuals who begin their careers in science writing and science communications by working as public information officers within universities and in corporate communications positions later start consulting practices. This form of freelance is focused on building relationships with all the publics of a client organization (that is, employees and their families, customers, vendors, journalists, alumni, donors, and government regulators). Successful consultants are effective communicators adept at problem solving, able to see multiple points of view, and have the ability to remain calm even in the most hectic situations. Consultants are often called upon to assist in crisis communication.

Consultants also support science- and technology-based companies by writing news releases, annual reports, and product introductions. They can provide temporary staffing for nonprofit organizations, universities, and research institutions and work with the leadership of scientific professional associations on long-range strategic planning. The same business issues that freelance writers grapple with (business planning, budgeting, marketing, and contract negotiation) also pertain to the field of consulting. Science communications consultants are served by many of the same science-writing organizations to which freelance writers belong. In addition, the Counselors Academy of the Public Relations Society of America is dedicated to providing principals of public relations agencies and freelance consultants with the resources to grow their firms and counseling skills.

Occasional Freelancing

It can take months—even years—for a freelance writer to develop a reputation and client base. For that reason, many freelancers start out by writing occasional articles on the side while still holding onto full-time jobs. Some find occasional freelancing to be a fulfilling and profitable arrangement and never feel the need to become full-time freelance writers. A good rule of thumb is not to give up a full-time job without having between 6 months' and 1 year's worth of savings, more if a writer is the sole support for a household. This is because it takes times to secure assignments; more time to research, conduct interviews, and write articles; and then there is the wait as an invoice goes through a client's accounting cycle for payment. This can mean several months before the first paychecks come in.

Writers Groups

Because of the solitary nature of freelancing, writers benefit by joining and becoming active in professional writing organizations. Most require some form of credentials to join, such as published writing samples and/or sponsorship by another professional writer. The better-known associations include the National Association of Science Writers (NASW). This U.S. organization for science writers has many members who are freelancers. The organization supports them with a freelance committee, online job bank, Listserv, and dedicated Web site section with information on contracts, health insurance, negotiating, self-publishing, and other resources. NASW holds an annual professional development workshop with many topics devoted to freelance issues.

Freelancers make up a large segment of the Society for Environmental Journalism's (SEJ's) membership. To build a stronger and more closely connected network of educated environmental journalists and editors, SEJ provides information on contract negotiation, copyright issues, time management, and story selling. There is a dedicated section on the SEJ Web site for freelancers (beginners and professionals) that offers free newsletters, a Listserv, a writers' directory, market listings, and more.

The American Medical Writers Association offers an extensive continuing education program available to professionals in the medical and allied scientific communication fields. Core workshops—available at national and regional meetings as well as online—provide opportunities to improve editing, writing, communication, and bibliographic skills as well as how to develop and manage a freelance business writing for the pharmaceutical industry, public relations, advertising, marketing, or Web-multimedia.

Awards and Fellowships

For marketing purposes, winning awards is a good way to enhance the reputation of a writer, particularly a freelance writer. The online news service Newswise maintains a listing of science-writing awards. Many of these competitions will accept the work of freelance writers. Newswise also maintains a list of journalism grants and fellowships, many of which are open to freelance writers. Fellowships are an opportunity to develop writing skills as well as build a network of peers and editors.

Lynne Timpani Friedmann

See also American Medical Writers Association; National Association of Science Writers; Society of Environmental Journalists

Further Readings

Blum, D., Knudson, M., & Henig, R. M. (Eds.). (2005). *A field guide for science writers: The official guide of the National Association of Science Writers* (2nd ed.). New York: Oxford University Press.

Harper, T. (Ed.). (2003). *The ASJA (American Society of Journalists and Authors) guide to freelance writing.* New York: St. Martin's.

National Association of Science Writers. (n.d.). *All about freelancing.* Available at www.nasw.org/resource/freelancing

FUEL CELL TECHNOLOGY

A fuel cell is a relatively simple device for separating electrons from their atoms via a chemical process and thereby deriving electricity from the flow of electrons. Hydrogen is the best-known source of fuel cell electricity, but other elements are also viable in certain circumstances. Fuel cells are attractive because they constitute an energy process that contributes no pollution, and especially no greenhouse gases. They generate only electricity, heat, and small amounts of water. For this reason, they will continue to be prominent in discussions of our energy future. In addition, they have very high levels of potential efficiency for converting the power source to useful energy. It is not unusual for fuel cells to have efficiency rates of 40% or more; an incandescent lightbulb, by contrast, has a rate of only 5% of its energy converted to light. The other 95% is lost.

William Grove, a Welsh physicist, built the first working fuel cell in 1839. While this technology was gradually developed over more than a century, it gained serious attention when the U.S. National Aeronautics and Space Administration used fuel cells in the *Gemini* and *Apollo* spacecraft of the 1960s. This demonstrated that sources of electricity can be used that weigh much less than conventional batteries.

A hydrogen fuel cell works by injecting pressurized hydrogen into a series of small channels on one side of the cell (the anode), which is separated from the channels on the other side (the cathode) by a platinum-coated membrane. This membrane permits the protons of the hydrogen atoms to pass through to the other side, but not the electrons.

Thus, it is known as a proton-emitting membrane, or PEM. The electrons are channeled externally to a circuit to yield electricity, and they are then recombined on the other side with the protons and some oxygen. This combination of hydrogen and oxygen creates a small quantity of water. The fuel cell also generates heat during this process. Sometimes the heat is problematic because it degrades the efficiency of the fuel cell, but in other cases, this by-product is captured and used to heat water or buildings.

Fuel cell technology has three principal kinds of applications: vehicular, stationary, and portable. Vehicular applications have received more attention than the others as governments and industries seek alternatives to transportation powered by fossil fuels that cause global warming. Several leading auto companies have produced hydrogen fuel cell prototype vehicles. These are electric cars that run on hydrogen instead of batteries. It should be noted, however, that this kind of application has problems that should not be underestimated. An automobile needs a very large stack of fuel cells to generate enough electricity to move the vehicle, and this adds a lot of weight to the vehicle. It also needs a large tank of pressurized hydrogen if the vehicle is going to have more than a local range. Finally, hydrogen fueled vehicles need an infrastructure of refueling stations. This is far from impossible, but it confronts us with a chicken-and-egg situation: People will not own hydrogen fuel cell vehicles if they cannot refuel conveniently, but refueling stations will not be attractive investments until there is a critical mass of hydrogen fuel cell vehicles. Several cities in several countries now have refueling stations, and it remains to be seen how many more will be added in the near future.

Stationary applications may not be as captivating as the idea of fuel cell vehicles, but they deserve serious attention. If a residential or commercial building has a fuel cell and a reliable source of hydrogen, then it can be independent of a local or national electrical grid. This leads to several possibilities. Hospitals and other facilities that need absolutely reliable power sources can use fuel cells as back-up power when an electrical grid fails. Thousands of homes in Japan use hydrogen fuel cells for heating, lighting, cooking, and everything else that comes from electricity. A small number of buildings in several countries use solar or wind power to separate hydrogen from water or other sources and then store the hydrogen for use when solar and wind power fail, for example, at night or when wind velocity declines. These stationary applications demonstrate that a fuel cell with a reliable source of hydrogen constitutes a dependable source of electricity. They also point to the value of distributed sources of energy: Hydrogen can be produced locally anywhere, thereby minimizing reliance on regional or national electrical grids that are vulnerable to overloads, human error, or terrorist attacks.

Portable applications are also attractive. Television cameras, two-way radios, and other devices require many conventional batteries if they are used for more than a few hours. In recent years, some portable fuel cells have come onto the market, powered by small hydrogen canisters. These devices yield electrical power for longer time periods than ordinary batteries, and they weigh less.

Challenges

While the operation of a hydrogen fuel cell is very clean ecologically, there are major challenges to acquiring the hydrogen. The principal sources are natural gas, water, and methane. For each, it takes energy to separate out the hydrogen. When the necessary energy comes from solar, wind, biomass, hydropower, or other renewable nonpolluting sources, then the entire system is very clean. But under current conditions, conventional energy sources are usually used to separate the hydrogen, and these sources consist almost entirely of coal and nuclear power. So the back end of the hydrogen fuel cell process is very attractive, but the front end can be ecologically problematic. This ought to be taken into account when weighing the benefits of hydrogen fuel cells.

Another set of issues concerns storage and transportation. Hydrogen, as the lightest element of the periodic table, requires extremely leak-proof containers to store and move. This is not impossible, but it is not trivial. When the hydrogen is separated locally, however, transportation costs are minimized.

A final question is the operating life of the fuel cell. Impurities in the hydrogen will eventually coat the platinum catalyst of the PEM membrane and thus degrade the efficiency of the fuel cell. This can be mitigated by maximizing the purity of the hydrogen, maximizing the platinum's reactive surface, and protecting the platinum catalyst.

In addition to hydrogen, there are more than a dozen other energy carriers that feed into fuel cells. Hydrogen receives the most attention because this is the most plentiful element in the world, but it is likely that a spectrum of energy carriers will serve specialized purposes, depending on variations in storage, transportation, and operating conditions such as temperature and humidity.

Even though fuel cell technology has the potential to contribute to solutions to our energy problems, it has received less attention than the renewable forms of energy, particularly solar, wind, and biomass. One outreach effort designed to address the lack of awareness was the Citizens' School on Fuel Cell & Hydrogen Technology, which the University of South Carolina in Columbia offered for 2½ years. Nevertheless, the fuel cell technology community is still a relatively small network of engineers, technicians, and entrepreneurs. At this point, it is difficult to envision in detail what the broader societal issues will be when this technology is better appreciated.

Future Directions

Still, one can imagine some possible issues. Fuel cell technology, like many other emerging technologies, will not be financially attractive until there are economies of scale: Investors will benefit when they can move from successful prototypes to affordable mass-produced devices. Perhaps this will happen without government involvement. Some governments assist solar technology with tax credits and other incentives. If assistance like this gets solar energy to desirable levels of economies of scale, then there will be a good case for doing the same for fuel cell technology. And yet one cannot take it for granted that national or local governments will assist this technology's development.

Another question has to do with the role of one energy technology in relation to other such technologies. Fuel cell technology will not be a magic bullet that solves all of our problems, and the same is true of every other newer energy technology. Instead, it is worth asking how a particular technology will become a part of a portfolio of multiple technologies that together deliver a large-scale solution. For fuel cell technology, and especially for hydrogen-driven fuel cells, two considerations are apparent. First, this technology is especially suited to distributed networks. Hydrogen is expensive and difficult to transport over long distances, but it can be separated from other elements wherever there is natural gas, water, methane, or other sources. There will be multiple local sources of hydrogen, and multiple local methods for separating this element from its sources. Meanwhile, fuel cell technology that uses other energy carriers might be more suitable for other local conditions.

Second, this will not be a stand-alone energy technology. Because it needs energy to separate the energy carriers that go into the fuel cells, the future of fuel cell technology depends on its relation to the kinds of energy that make possible the separation process. The more that fuel cell technology can take advantage of clean renewable energies, and thus distance itself from coal and nuclear energy, the more attractive it will be as a contribution to our portfolio of clean energy technologies.

Chris Toumey

See also Alternative Energy, Overview; Climate Change, Communicating; Solar Energy; Wind Power

Further Readings

Ogden, J. (2006). High hopes for hydrogen. *Scientific American, 295*(3), 94–101.

Service, R. F. (2007). Platinum in fuel cells gets a helping hand. *Science, 315,* 172.

Wald, M. L. (2004). Questions about a hydrogen economy. *Scientific American, 290*(5), 66–73.

G

GALILEI, GALILEO (1564–1642)

The life and works of Galileo Galilei have been recounted numerous times and in a variety of ways in the 400 years since he lived. He has been studied as one of the first modern scientists, as an astronomer, a physicist, and a man of the late Italian Renaissance. Here we will look at him from a more social angle, which has been less explored and is especially relevant in this encyclopedia: the role that public communication plays in the development of science. In Galileo's time, what we now know as science was not at all well defined. Neither the practices nor the people and places were clearly established. This meant that the study of nature could be done in more than one way, and Galileo created his own approach, and he used all the means of communication at hand to promote it.

At the beginning of the 17th century, Galileo was a teacher at the University of Padua, in the north of Italy. He had learned mathematics mostly on his own and obtained this teaching position by a combination of his intellectual abilities and his good connections. This was not unusual in his time. Inside the universities of that time things were very strictly defined: Teachers were to review and at most comment on the classics with their students. Mathematicians were something like technicians who used their knowledge for practical tasks such as designing fortifications or hydraulic systems. Philosophers, on the other hand, were in charge of the theoretical discussions of the essence and structure of things in nature, such as life or the universe. The social structure was such that these two kinds of professionals did not mix.

In the period in which Galileo worked at Padua, when he was not busy teaching, he studied the motion of bodies. For this purpose, he read the works of his predecessors and also thought about and did experiments. He soon found that he did not agree with all of the knowledge inherited from Greece and Rome. He could not say this in the university, of course, but he discussed it with friends, wrote letters to other mathematicians, and taught it to his private students. And because he was a mathematician, he definitely could not discuss it with the philosophers, who were practically the owners of the subject.

Universities of that time were rather constraining, both in the subjects that could be taught and in their social structure. Through his letters we can see that Galileo was constantly looking for a way out, and he had his eye on a position in the court. In 1610, he had a lucky break, for among his first telescopic observations he discovered four little stars gyrating around the planet Jupiter. He dedicated this discovery to the house of the Duke of Medici, whose founding father Cosimo was identified with the figure of Jupiter. As a result, he managed to move both physically and professionally: He went from the university in Padua to the court in Florence and became the "philosopher and mathematician of the Grand Duke."

In his new position, Galileo had more liberty, a better salary, and the protection of a very powerful court. And with the title of philosopher, he could now discuss with others of this rank. But he also acquired new responsibilities, among which was entertaining the members of the court with novelties about nature and the instruments that could be used to study these. This is why he addressed his writings to a mixed audience: other philosophers and mathematicians, of course, but also the educated class who were the members of the court.

Thus began a new period of Galileo's life, in which he was a public figure and did not represent only himself, but also his patron. In the years that followed, he wrote and published several treatises in which he discussed subjects related to what we now call physics and astronomy. Throughout these texts, he was not only showing his results but also proposing a new way of going about obtaining them. With his work he was laying the foundations for what we call modern science, which combines observation, experiment, measurement, comparison, and the feedback between theory and practice. This went against the established ways of doing things and soon made him enemies among the ranks of philosophers and theologians.

After some time, the support Galileo received from the Florentine court declined. He then looked to Rome and found endorsement from one of the first scientific societies, the Lincean Academy. With them he published several important works and met many important people. Once again, Galileo was lucky, for his friend the Cardinal Barberini was elected pope. Taking advantage of this, Galileo got permission to publish a book discussing the controversial topic of the old Ptolemaic and the new Copernican systems for explaining the universe.

The trouble and the very famous trial that resulted were only partly a result of the content of his *Dialogue Concerning the Two Chief World Systems*. As he had been doing since he moved to the court in Florence, Galileo opted for a very public discussion of his ideas. This was dangerous because he was playing by the rules of the court, and in this case he was not successful. In general, however, we can say that he did quite well in promoting his novel way of doing things by communicating to a wide audience.

Susana Biro

See also Astronomy, Public Communication of; Censorship in Science; Kuhn, Thomas

Further Readings

Allan-Olney, M. (1870). *The private life of Galileo: Compiled principally from his correspondence and that of his daughter.* Boston: Nichols & Noyes. Available at www.archive.org/details/privatelifegali00allagoog

Biagioli, M. (1993). *Galileo, courtier. The practice of science in the culture of absolutism.* Chicago: University of Chicago Press.

Drake, S. (1978). *Galileo at work: His scientific biography.* Chicago: University of Chicago Press.

Galilei, G. (1890–1909). *Le opere di Galileo Galilei* [The works of Galileo Galilei]. (A. Favaro, Ed., 20 vols.). Florence, Italy: Tip. di G. Barbèra.

Galileo Project: http://galileo.rice.edu/index.html

Secord, J. (2004). Knowledge in transit. *Isis, 95,* 654–672.

GENDER REPRESENTATIONS OF SCIENTISTS

Images of scientists in the mass media are a major source of information for popular views of scientists. People are much more likely to see scientists on television and in films or read about scientists in newspapers and magazines than they are to have direct interactions with actual working scientists. Subsequently, the ways in which scientists are portrayed in the mass media often leave lasting impressions on people's views of science and scientists. Media images of scientists, particularly those found in television programming, have been found to be one of the primary sources of information about scientists for adults as well as for children and adolescents.

Gender representations of scientists in the mass media convey and reinforce cultural beliefs and expectations about scientists that influence people's perceptions of the role of men and women in the scientific, engineering, and technical (SET) workforce. Science communication researchers have used both quantitative and qualitative research methodologies, most often content analysis, textual analysis, and thematic analysis, to examine gender representations of scientists in a variety of mass media, including television programs, films, newspapers, magazines, books, and Web sites. Research in science communication often investigates gender representations by comparing differences in the number of male and female scientists presented in media content and also by documenting specific variations in the depictions of male and female scientists.

Images of male scientists and engineers have dominated the mass media in the United States in both past and contemporary images. The number of media images of male scientists is not only greater than the number of media images of female scientists in most media content, but more screen time and more print space have been devoted to male scientists. The typical media image of a scientist is that of an adult, white male who wears a laboratory coat or scientific apparel and directs a team of subordinate research assistants. Media images of scientists that show male scientists more frequently and in positions of high status in the scientific workforce reinforce the long-standing gender stereotype of science as a male domain or a profession more appropriate for men. While the percentage of male scientists shown in media content mirrors the greater percentage of males in the actual U.S. scientific and technological workforce, researchers argue that presenting more female scientists and showing them more often in the mass media is critical for presenting a more balanced vision of the SET workforce and for altering gender-stereotyped values in society.

The greater frequency of images of male scientists over female scientists has been documented in a variety of media. Research by Marcel C. LaFollette on U.S. magazines from 1910 to 1950 found male scientists appeared much more often than female scientists as the focus of biographies and interviews. Researcher Nancy Signorielli noted in her study of men and women in occupations in the U.S. workforce in primetime network television dramas in the 1980s that male scientists outnumbered female scientists by three to one. Elfriede Fursich and E. P. Lester's analysis of the *New York Times'* "Scientist at Work" columns noted that only 2 of the 11 scientists profiled were female scientists.

Research on gender representations of scientists in children's television programming has been a focus of much of the research in this area; and, as with other types of media content, male scientists appear more frequently than female scientists. A study of children's educational television programs from the 1980s noted male scientist characters outnumbered female scientist characters by two to one; however, a later study of these and other children's educational television programs by Marilee Long and her colleagues indicated no differences in the frequency or screen time for male and female scientists. More recent research on television programs broadcast in 2006 found that male scientist characters outnumbered female scientist characters for cartoon programs such as *Dexter's Laboratory* and *The Adventures of Jimmy Neutron: Boy Genius,* drama programs such as the *CSI* programs, and some educational programs such as *MythBusters.* Across all programs male scientist characters were found to be present in more scenes than were female scientist characters.

Mixed Messages

When female scientists are shown in the mass media, the images of female scientists often present mixed messages about the contributions of women in science and reinforce traditional gender stereotypes. Some female scientists in media portrayals are shown as extraordinary women or "superwomen" who are unusually intelligent, while other female scientists are shown as lacking the expertise, skills, and abilities needed to be a scientist. In some media images, female scientists are shown as competent and diligent researchers in the laboratory, while in others they are most admired for their domestic abilities at home. Some portrayals focus on women scientists as exemplary wives and mothers whose extraordinary energy and organizational skills also allow them to succeed professionally, other portrayals more realistically focus on the challenges women scientists face in juggling work and family responsibilities, and still other portrayals either completely ignore any mention of work and family balance issues or focus on the personal sacrifices that women scientists have made by forgoing marriage and children in order to devote themselves entirely to their careers. Some media images focus on the attractiveness and the potential distraction that female scientists create for male colleagues in the workplace, while other images present women scientists as unattractive, unpopular, and socially inept loners who work all the time.

Challenging Gender Stereotypes

Gender differences also have been noted in the depictions of the professional status of scientists in the mass media. The professional status of media representations of scientist characters reflects the importance of scientists' roles within the scientific community. Historically, media representations of male scientists have shown them as primary investigators or research leaders in the scientific workplace. More recent depictions of male scientists, such as those shown on the *CSI* television programs, present male scientists in more collaborative or subordinate professional roles. Depictions of women scientists in the scientific workplace typically have been more varied than those for male scientists and have shown women in numerous roles from that of a primary researcher or research team leader to a research assistant to a student. Over time, media portrayals of female scientists' professional status appear to have improved as women scientists are now more likely to be shown as primary scientists leading a team of researchers or lead investigators rather than as research assistants or subordinates. The depictions of women scientists in an expanded array of professional roles challenge traditional gender stereotypes that formerly placed women scientists almost exclusively in secondary roles subordinate to male scientists.

Gender representations that present counter-stereotypes or offer images of women scientists that challenge traditional gender stereotypes have been noted in popular films, in a PBS documentary television program, and more recently in broadcast programming on children's television. A textual analysis of popular films from the 1990s and a case study of the film *Contact* noted improvements in the representations of women scientists. Many of the images found in films showed female scientists in high status positions in the scientific community and presented female scientists as intelligent, competent, determined, and independent. The portrayals of female scientists in some popular films, however, still emphasized the appearance and feminine attributes of women scientists, and both overt and subtle discrimination against female scientists was evident in depictions of their interactions with male colleagues. Recent research on cartoon, drama, and educational television programs that featured scientist characters found women scientist characters portrayed more equitably in regards to their professional roles in the scientific community and depictions of marital and parental status.

Effects on Public Perception of Scientists

Two theoretical perspectives in the social sciences describe the potential impact that gender representations of scientists in the mass media can have on public views of scientists. Albert Bandura's social learning theory explains that children learn about gender roles not only from an array of role models such as parents, teachers, and peers but also from media models such as characters in television programs and in films. Sandra L. Bem's gender schema theory describes how media models can then influence perceptions of gender roles. Gender schema theory explains that throughout childhood and into adolescence, children develop specific views about gender roles as defined by the culture and society in which they live. According to this theory, children have a tendency and readiness to process information they learn based on gender or sex-linked associations that are part of their gender schemas. Gender schemas represent the networks of information or knowledge stored in memory that people call on to interpret new information that they learn. Gender representations of scientists, then, are sources of information not only about scientists and science but also about gender roles.

Based on these theoretical perspectives, recent research has gone beyond a documentation and analysis of media content and has begun to explore the potential influence of gender representations of scientists on people's perceptions of scientists and attitudes toward science. Research has examined adolescents' sources of information for their views of scientists and examined adolescents' reactions to stereotyped and counter-stereotyped gender representations of women scientists. This research found that adolescents cite television as a source of information about scientists and adolescent boys who reported the media as being important in their lives had more negative views toward women in science. These findings suggest some support for the influence of gender representations of scientists on young people's perceptions and attitudes.

Gender-stereotyped representations of scientists in the mass media perpetuate the often-held view that the SET fields are a male domain and create views that contribute to the existing gender gap in the SET workforce. Examining the potential influence of both stereotyped gender representations of scientists and counter-stereotyped gender representations of scientists in the mass media may help determine ways to address the gender gap in SET and to predict children's future interest in SET professions. The link between gender representations of scientists in the mass media and the gender gap in SET fields appears to be an important factor in seeking ways to increase the number of future scientists in the SET workforce where critical shortages are beginning to become evident. Science communication research on gender representations in media content not only helps researchers to better understand the ways in which science is communicated to the public, but also helps them gain a better understanding of strategies for changing public images of scientists in order to enhance the efficacy of programs to promote greater representation of girls in SET and women in the SET workforce.

Jocelyn Steinke

See also Children's Television and Science; Television Science

Further Readings

Bandura, A. (2002). Social cognitive theory of mass communication. In J. Bryant & D. Zillmann (Eds.), *Media effects: Advances in theory and research* (2nd ed., pp. 121–153). Mahwah, NJ: Lawrence Erlbaum.

Bem, S. L. (1981). Gender schema theory: A cognitive account of sex typing. *Psychological Review, 88*(4), 354–364.

Fisch, S. M., Yotive, W., McCann Brown, S. K., Garner, M. S., & Chen, L. (1997). Science on Saturday morning: Children's perceptions of science in educational and non-educational cartoons. *Journal of Educational Media, 23*(2–3), 157–167.

Fursich, E., & Lester, E. P. (1996). Science journalism under scrutiny: A textual analysis of "Science Times." *Critical Studies in Mass Communication, 13*, 24–43.

LaFollette, M. C. (1988). Eyes on the stars: Images of women scientists in popular magazines. *Science, Technology and Human Values, 13*(3–4), 262–275.

Long, M., Boiarsky, G., & Thayer, G. (2001). Gender and racial counter-stereotypes in science education television: A content analysis. *Public Understanding of Science, 10*, 255–269.

Signorielli, N. (1993). Television and adolescents' perception about work. *Youth and Society, 24*(3), 314–341.

Steinke, J. (2005). Cultural representations of gender and science: Portrayals of female scientists and engineers in popular films. *Science Communication, 27*, 27–63.

Steinke, J., Lapinski, M., Zietsman-Thomas, A., Nwulu, P., Crocker, N., Williams, Y., et al. (2007). Middle school-aged children's attitudes toward women in science, engineering and technology and the effects of media literacy training. *Journal of Women and Minorities in Science and Engineering, 12*(4), 295–323.

Steinke, J., & Long, M. (1996). A lab of her own? Portrayals of female characters on children's educational science programs. *Science Communication, 18*(2), 91–115.

Steinke, J., Long, M., Johnson, M., & Ghosh, S. (2008, August). *Gender stereotypes of scientist characters in television programs popular among middle school-aged children.* Paper presented to the Science Communication Interest Group, Association for Education in Journalism and Mass Communication. Chicago, IL.

GENE

Biologists currently define a *gene* as a fragment of the DNA molecule containing the necessary information to direct the formation of a particular protein. However, this concept has been the subject of change and controversy during the last 100 years. The idea of a "gene" was first formulated in the early 20th century as a physical unit believed to be present in all living organisms and responsible for hereditary transmission from parent to offspring. Up to the middle of the century, the gene was identified with proteins, the molecules involved in the chemical reactions triggering growth, nutrition, and the main processes characterizing life. When in the early 1950s it was postulated that genes were instead associated with the deoxyribonucleic acid (DNA) found in the cell nucleus, this molecule gradually became the center of biomedical research.

Even today, when the sequence of chemical units composing the DNA of many species and the mechanisms underlying the formation of proteins are known, there are still scientific and social debates over the precise nature of the gene and, especially, its capacity to determine our fate. Important public policy issues have arisen as the result of contemporary advances in genetic science, and cultural fascination with the gene continues to be reflected in public discourse, including popular news accounts about many of these developments.

Origin of the Concept of Gene

The origins of the concept of the gene lay in the so-called rediscovery of Mendel's laws. In 1907, Danish botanist Wilhelm Johannsen used this term to designate a number of units present in every living organism and involved in hereditary transmission according to the rules that Gregor Mendel had formulated in 1866, following his experiments with peas. Simultaneous research during the first decade of the 20th century showed that these units were actually located in the chromosomes, a series of bodies present in every plant and animal cell. A common assumption at that time was that genes were formed by proteins, because these latter were the main functional molecules known to be involved in all processes identified with life.

The formulation of the gene concept fostered the discipline of genetics, in which researchers, using mathematics, physics, and other tools, investigated how genes transmitted heritable characters through generations and what happened if these units were altered—that is, mutated—by external factors, such as radiation. The widespread view inside and outside science during the first half of the 20th century was that of an absolute power of genes to direct inheritance. This strengthened sociopolitical movements such as eugenics, which sought to improve the hereditary fate of families and communities by selective breeding. Eugenics proposals were established before the gene was postulated—raising dichotomies such as that between "good" and "bad" blood—but this new concept gave these proposals apparent scientific respectability, especially between the 1910s and 1940s. These ideas led to both progressive campaigns designed to avoid diseases among lower classes and to "social hygiene" directed against the handicapped or certain races in both the United States and Nazi Germany.

Discovery of the Role of DNA

Since the late 1940s, there was experimental evidence that DNA, instead of proteins, was the substance forming the genes and involved in hereditary transmission. This view was reinforced with the postulation of the double helix and confirmed in a series of experiments during the mid-1950s. The discipline of molecular biology was born and with it a new approach to studying the role of genes, distinct from the study of genetics, which since then is often referred to as "classical" genetics. (Classical genetics, however, has persisted as an independent field.)

Molecular biology increasingly focused on the physical and chemical study of the mechanisms by which DNA exerted its role as the genetic material. This DNA focus was strengthened by the formulation, in the late 1950s, of the central principle according to which genetic information was always believed to be transmitted from DNA to proteins, rather than the reverse. This one-directional model of genetic action drove the experimental strategy of molecular biologists during the first decades of the development of the discipline.

The double helical structure had portrayed DNA as two coiled strands, each formed by a sequence of chemical units, or nucleotides. The genes were nucleotide fragments within each sequence, and one of the first problems for molecular biology was referred to as understanding the genetic code, that is, how a particular sequence of nucleotides in DNA specified a protein, formed by a sequence of different chemical units, the amino acids.

Human Genome Project

The genetic code began to be unraveled between 1961 and 1967, and with it the way in which genes directed the formation of proteins began to be understood. The following decade, a series of techniques directed to the study of the nucleotide sequence of DNA emerged; and since the late 1970s, the genome or DNA molecules characteristic of different organisms—first simple viruses, and then the worm *C. elegans*, yeast, and the bacterium *E. coli*—were determined. The Human Genome Project (HGP), aimed at specifying the human DNA sequence, was first discussed in the mid-1980s and launched officially in 1990.

The conclusion of the HGP and subsequent determination of the human genome sequence between 2000 and 2001 raised a new definition of the gene. Genes were no longer undefined physical entities in the chromosomes or undetermined nucleotide arrangements within the DNA molecule. They were precise sequences of information formed by a long and linear arrangement of As, Cs, Ts, and Gs—symbols for adenine, cytosine, thymine, and guanine, the nucleotides constituting the DNA molecule. These sequences could be processed by a computer and stored in a database, relying on the new discipline of bioinformatics to do so.

The possibility of obtaining human DNA sequences increased the social and scientific expectations for the power of genetic information. Political leaders, prominent biologists, and media reports portrayed a new era in which the secrets of evolution and cures for diseases would be "read" in our DNA sequences. Some social scientists warned about a new form of eugenics in which genetic information contained in databases could be used to discriminate against citizens suffering from a disease or possessing certain other traits.

Genetic information also became a source of wealth and business. The HGP was marked by a race to finish the sequence between an international public consortium and the private company Celera Genomics. Despite both institutions reaching an agreement at the end of the project, a debate about the ownership of DNA sequences emerged and is still present. If genetic information can be the object of patents, all the achievements derived from it—including treatments for diseases—could be proprietary and therefore subjected to royalty payments to the researcher who determined the sequence. During the 1980s and 1990s, a number of biotechnology companies were created to commercialize sequencing instruments, as well as diagnostic kits and drugs based on a particular DNA sequence.

The social and scientific enthusiasm with the power of genetic information has gradually faded. Shortly after the conclusion of the HGP, it became increasingly apparent that the transition between identifying DNA sequences, gathering clues to evolution, and finding cures for diseases was not that straightforward. Both social and natural scientists are currently arguing for a shift from genomics to "post-genomics" and a new concept of the gene arising as a consequence.

The fact that sequences alone do not determine how genes direct the functioning of the body points toward the importance of the interactions of DNA with other components outside the genome. New biological approaches expanding after 2000 conceive the cell as a system in which DNA is no longer the center or even the prime mover. Rather, it is an element in permanent connection with proteins and other cell components. Systems biologists also argue for the importance of the environment surrounding the cell as a factor that may make a gene act in one way or another.

Post-genomics has also been characterized by a new understanding of genetic control. During the HGP, the parts of the sequence that did not contain genes—that is, that did not determine proteins—were considered as "junk DNA" of unknown function. It was also estimated that there were around 100,000 genes in our genome. After the conclusion of the project, this figure was reduced to 20,000 to 25,000, with the rest of the human DNA sequence involved in the regulation of the expression of this smaller number of genes. The bulk of the DNA sequence, consequently, makes genes act, remain inactive, or synthesize one protein or another. Biologists no longer talk about genes in isolation, but about batteries of interconnected genes, as well as discontinuous DNA sequences—that is, exons separated by introns—which can act as genes depending on regulation.

The idea of the gene as a linear and continuous text of nucleotides is, therefore, being replaced by the network as the dominant concept in current thinking. The idea is now that there are fragmented genes that are no longer believed to act unconditionally, but in coordination with their environment. Today, the gene is still a controversial concept that remains under development. Recognition of its pervasiveness, however, is one of the most astonishing events of 20th-century biology.

Miguel García-Sancho

See also Bioinformatics; Eugenics; Human Genome Project; Mendel, Gregor; Watson, James D.

Further Readings

Beurton, P. J., Falk, R., & Rheinberger, H. J. (Eds.). (2000). *The concept of the gene in development and evolution: Historical and epistemological perspectives.* Cambridge, UK: Cambridge University Press.

Cook-Deegan, R. (1994). *The gene wars: Science, politics and the Human Genome Project.* New York: W. W. Norton.

Fox Keller, E. (2000). *The century of the gene.* Cambridge, MA: Harvard University Press.

Kevles, D., & Hood, L. (Eds.). (1992). *The code of codes: Scientific and social issues in the Human Genome Project.* Cambridge, MA: Harvard University Press.

Morange, M. (2001). *The misunderstood gene.* Cambridge, MA: Harvard University Press.

Sarkar, S. (1998). *Genetics and reductionism.* Cambridge, MA: Cambridge University Press.

Sloan, P. R. (Ed.). (2000). *Controlling our destinies: Historical, philosophical, ethical and theological perspectives on the Human Genome Project.* Notre Dame, IN: University of Notre Dame Press.

GENE PATENTING

The 1953 discovery of the DNA double helix revolutionized the biomedical world and catalyzed the advent of an entirely new group of disciplines—from genomics, the study of entire genomes, to more specialized areas including toxicogenomics, nutrigenomics, pharmacogenomics, and so on—that as a group promised profound changes in disease prevention, diagnosis, and treatment. The development of genomics was catalyzed by the initiation of the Human Genome Project, an unprecedented international collaboration launched in 1990, which proposed to map the human genome, understand the genetic basis of disease, and create a freely accessible body of data to support continuing research and progress. Some of these advances have become the subject of controversies, and one of the most recent debates, with profound medical, legal, scientific, and social implications, revolves around gene patenting. While genetics-related controversies regularly surface in the news and public discussion, the legal ownership of genetic information is a highly technical subject in its own right and will be explored in this entry.

The patent system was originally established to encourage scientific advancement. A patent is a "negative right" that protects the patent holder's property rights by excluding others from manufacturing, selling, or using the patented product, while at the same time promoting progress by allowing free access to the details of the invention. By providing inventors exclusive property rights for a limited period of time, which is usually 20 years in the United States and the European Union, this system enables them to capitalize on their invention. In return for this protection, inventors must disclose the details of their invention to competitors and to the public. Public access to the details of the invention is intended to enhance future advancement and to prevent duplication and the associated waste of resources.

While it is widely accepted that the existing patent system is in the public interest and its contribution to innovation is proven, its suitability in context of the human genome is the topic of intensive debates.

Criteria for Patentability

The basic criteria for patentability in the United States are usefulness, nonobviousness, and novelty, while the equivalent criteria in the European Union are novelty, inventive step, and industrial applicability. These two sets of requirements are very similar, and the differences are mostly in terminology. By this definition, natural chemical compounds, natural species of plants and animals, and abstract ideas cannot be patented. The patentability of human genes is rooted in a 1912 precedent in which a patent was granted for the isolation and purification of adrenaline, a hormone that did not exist in nature in that exact form and that, after purification, could be used for the medical treatment of humans. In that case, the court held that a substance, after it is purified from nature, is patentable, and under the same precedent, even though a human gene itself cannot be patented, a DNA sequence that is purified or isolated from it was deemed patentable.

It is often difficult to clearly define the criteria distinguishing naturally occurring compounds from products of invention. Linda J. Demaine and Aaron X. Fellmeth, writing in *Science*, describe how a patent for purified alumina was denied in the 1930s, based on the fact that the product was only slightly more pure than the natural form of the compound and was not deemed to be particularly inventive. However, while live organisms were considered a naturally occurring phenomenon and, as such, not patentable, this was changed in 1980 with the landmark Supreme Court decision in *Diamond v. Chakrabarty*. In this case, a patent application filed by a microbiologist,

Ananda Chakrabarty, involved a bacterium that was engineered to break down crude oil and had potential applications in treating oil spills. The patent was initially rejected based on the consideration that living things cannot be patented.

The Court of Customs and Patent Appeals overturned this initial decision, and subsequently the United States Patents and Trademarks Office appealed to the Supreme Court, which granted the patent. In its 5-to-4 decision, the Supreme Court noted that a strain of genetically engineered bacteria is patentable because it is not "naturally occurring" and argued that the bacterium was not a product of nature, but was produced by the person who engineered it and, thus, can be patented. While *Diamond v. Chakrabarty* did not involve human genes, the same principles were later applied to human genes that could be patented if they were isolated from their natural environment and subsequently manipulated.

Genomics research was still limited at the time of this decision, and it was not until the beginning of the new millennium, with the initiation of the Human Genome Project, that gene patenting became the focus of vehement debates, opening some of the most complicated legal, ethical, and public policy dilemmas in recent history.

Legal, Public Policy, and Ethical Arguments

The Human Genome Project created a surge of patent applications. As of 2005, it was estimated that patents had been granted to approximately 20% of all human genes. A widespread argument in opposition to gene patenting asserts that, considering the three requirements under the existing patent system—novelty, nonobviousness, and usefulness—genes do not necessarily meet the legal criteria for patenting. With regard to novelty, the approach that patent offices have adopted is that, even though genes exist in nature, they are not readily available, because further efforts are required for their isolation, and these manipulations are sufficient to show novelty. However, many disagree.

One prevalent opinion is that genes already exist in nature, and therefore naturally occurring genes should never have been patented. What could be patented, instead, are nonnaturally occurring DNA sequences, along with processes designed to sequence, analyze, or manipulate the genetic material. The second requirement is nonobviousness, for which the equivalent criterion in the European Union is inventiveness: The applicant must show that the invention, when compared to existing knowledge, is not obvious to the "skilled person." When examining this requirement, the patent office is asking whether the gene sequence would have been obvious to this "skilled person" before it was isolated.

This approach was heavily criticized for not imposing a genuine difficulty in demonstrating inventiveness because the mere fact that the gene sequence is not obvious does not indicate that it is innovative. Furthermore, extensive debates surround the issue of whether gene sequences can still be considered "nonobvious" at all in light of recent advances in biotechnology. Critics claim that identifying a gene sequence was technically complicated and labor intensive in the past, and could therefore have been regarded as innovative, but as a result of recent advances in sequencing technologies, the mere process of isolating a gene cannot continue to be regarded as innovative for the purpose of patenting.

For example, decades ago, DNA had to first be sheared into small fragments, then cloned, amplified, and sequenced. Recent technologies such as the next-generation sequencing eliminated the cloning requirement, and DNA can now be directly amplified by a technique known as polymerase chain reaction. An even more recent approach, known as next-next generation sequencing, or true single-molecule sequencing, eliminated the amplification step as well and allows even single DNA molecules bound to a surface to be sequenced.

Completion of the 5375-base genome of the first genome to be sequenced, that of a bacteriophage, required intensive work and represented a milestone in the field. It was recently estimated that at that time, sequencing of the more complex *Escherichia coli* (E. coli) bacterium would have required a thousand years, and that of the human genome, a million years. Currently available technologies allow between 10 and 80 million base pairs to be sequenced within an hour, with continually decreasing costs. In light of these advances, several authors have pointed out that the eligibility of DNA sequences for patenting should have decreased and that the inventiveness requirement should now be more difficult to fulfill.

To satisfy the third criterion for patenting, "utility" in the United States or "industrial applicability" in the European Union, patent applicants need to show that their invention has a useful purpose and is operative. In January 2001, the United States Patents and Trademark Office amended this requirement and announced the implementation of a three-way test, requiring utility to be specific, substantial, and credible. However, the mere concept of utility is very complex and has not been sufficiently explored. Jane Calvert emphasizes that while "novelty" and "inventiveness" are internal to the science surrounding the genes, "utility" is more related to the outside world and, as a consequence, has to be examined in a much broader social, political, and ethical framework.

The concept of utility is further complicated by genes that have several functions, some of which may be found years apart, and by genes that are implicated in more than one medical condition. In this context, Calvert warns that gene patents could enable patent holders to claim rights over future gene functions that are discovered, even though they were completely unknown at the time the patent was granted. As an example, so-called noncoding DNA, which represents over 97% of the human genome, was initially thought to lack any important roles, but later research showed that it serves important functions, such as shaping the structural organization of chromosomes, and that it can be used as a valuable tool in genetic fingerprinting, an application that was not apparent at the time it was initially described. The patenting of noncoding DNA sequences by Genetic Technologies Limited, an Australian firm, has become the subject of extensive controversy, and many researchers question the novelty and inventiveness of such patents. It was argued that a higher standard, more than just a theoretical possibility of a future function, should be set for the utility requirement in gene patents.

The Nuffield Council on Bioethics, a U.K.-based advisory group, concluded that, based on these considerations, granting a patent for a DNA sequence should become the exception, rather than the norm. Some authors argue that DNA sequences should not be patented at all. They claim that because the rationale of the patent system is to protect the investment of the owner, in view of the ease and lack of significant investment required to discover sequences with existing technology,

patenting DNA sequences is unjustifiable, especially taking into account that while the future rewards to the alleged owner could be significant, the direct and indirect costs to the public could be huge.

Perhaps the more important question is really not whether a genetic "invention" meets the legal criteria for patenting, but how the rights conferred to the inventor would impact the public. The public costs of gene patenting represent the focus of an argument that opposes gene patenting from a health care public policy standpoint. It is argued that while a patent system is in the public interest, the patenting of genes is not, and different considerations should exist with regard to genes. Genetic factors play increasingly important roles in medical decisions, such as predicting adverse effects to a therapeutic compound, adjusting doses during treatment, or selecting a medication. Private ownership of genes allows the owner to decide the price for diagnostic tests and medications that use the patented gene.

Gene patenting is therefore expected to increase health care costs, and many health care professionals are concerned that this will cause genetic testing and associated treatments to become too expensive, even prohibitive, for many patients, and could thus limit or bar access to some health care. Gene patenting also causes research in the field to be more costly and, because it excludes others from developing alternative tests and treatments unless they obtain licenses and pay royalties, development of competing tests, which in individual cases could provide superior diagnostic tools and be more affordable, is problematic. Furthermore, for many diseases that are caused by more than one mutation in the gene, gene patenting could decrease the likelihood of finding new mutation-disease associations that could confer therapeutic and diagnostic benefits to patients.

The health care costs that occur as a result of patenting practices might become even higher as a consequence of *patent stacking,* a term used to describe the situation when different aspects of the same innovation are patented in several different ways, and often by different patent holders. As royalties need to be paid to each patent owner, this can further delay progress and increase costs, which ultimately are supported by consumers.

Ethical debates related to gene patents represent one of the most controversial topics in the life sciences. A major controversy revolves around the fact that patented items are considered to be the intellectual property of the patent holder, who has certain rights over the property, yet human genes are part of our common heritage and, therefore, they should belong to the public domain. Philosopher David Resnik has pointed out that, when genes are patented, humans are being treated as property, and because it is morally wrong to treat humans as property, the act of patenting human genes is also morally wrong. Based on these considerations, gene patenting is in contrast to the most fundamental moral principle that no person should own another, or even another person's body parts or genes.

The *BRCA* Legal Battle

The patentability of genes is at the center of a lawsuit that was submitted by the American Civil Liberties Union (ACLU) and the Public Patent Foundation, a nonprofit organization. The lawsuit, *Association for Molecular Pathology, et al. v. U.S. Patent and Trademark Office, et al.,* was filed on May 12, 2009, in federal Court in New York City against 12 defendants, including the U.S. Patent and Trademark Office, Myriad Genetics, and the University of Utah Research Foundation, which hold the patents for *BRCA1* and *BRCA2,* the genes linked to certain types of hereditary breast and ovarian cancer.

The plaintiffs include cancer patients, several professional organizations, and health and research professionals, who argue that as a result of the exclusive rights granted to the patent holders in these cases and the price tag that the patent owners set, many cannot afford to take this crucial test, which allows some patients to make life-changing decisions.

The patents offer Myriad Genetics exclusive rights over the *BRCA1* and *BRCA2* genes and prevent others from further studying these genes without getting a license and paying royalties. Myriad established a monopoly for the genetic test, and currently there is no other way to test for the presence of *BRCA* mutations without infringing the Myriad patent. In the summer of 2001, Myriad sent letters to several agencies worldwide, informing them that testing for *BRCA* mutations has to be performed through the Myriad laboratory or by

using their license, a highly controversial move that was criticized by patients, practitioners, researchers, and governmental agencies alike.

The lawsuit argues that *BRCA1* and *BRCA2,* as "products of nature," should never have been patented in the first place, and it also contests genetic patenting in general, claiming that it hinders research and, by granting monopoly on a piece of information, it violates the First Amendment, which protects the free exchange of knowledge. Furthermore, the plaintiffs claim that the patent prevents the development and commercialization of improved tests and treatments that may be lifesaving. A 2001 publication by Sophie Gad and collaborators provides an example: The authors report the identification of a previously unknown rearrangement in the *BRCA1* gene in an American family with French/German ancestry. That mutation was initially missed by the patented Myriad test.

The lawsuit attempts to prevent genes from being patented in the future or, at least, to significantly limit the rights afforded to patent owners and restrict their ability to hinder progress. The *BRCA1/BRCA2* patent controversy, the most referenced case in the literature so far, is expected to impact many future decisions and guidelines with regard to other gene patents.

For all these reasons, it is argued that patents may not be the best way to compensate for the discovery of genes and gene sequences. Several authors recommended, as a possible solution, retaining the patenting of inventions involving genes or gene sequences, but making sure that the gene itself, or the gene sequence that is part of the invention, are not patented. In this way, inventors' rights to profit from their invention are ensured but, at the same time, others would be able to conduct research with the same gene without cumbersome limitations, giving them an opportunity to develop alternative tests and therapeutic approaches and ensuring continued progress in the public interest.

An alternative is to protect inventions by the use of *trade secrets,* which are another form of protecting intellectual property. However, based on several considerations, including the fact that they encourage secrecy rather than the public dissemination of the information, this alternative was predicted to cause even more harm than the current patent system. Other suggested proposals include "compulsory licensing," which would require a patent holder to license the use of the patented gene for a reasonable price, and the "experimental use exemption," which would exclude researchers conducting investigations for noncommercial purposes from infringement liability.

In 1996, an amendment known as the Ganske-Frist law was enacted in the United States to protect medical practitioners from patent-infringement lawsuits while performing medical or surgical procedures within a health care establishment, university, or clinic, but based on the consideration that it excludes biotechnology patents and gene-based diagnostic testing, several authors have proposed that it should be amended. Another proposal known as "patent pooling," in which several patent owners license patents to one another and/or to third parties, provides several benefits, such as reduced time and costs associated with obtaining individual licenses, and could facilitate advancement. It appears, therefore, that many concerns about gene patenting are not addressed by the current patent system, and yet they would not necessarily be addressed by removing human genes from the patent system altogether either.

The debate about human gene patenting is only a small facet of the controversy that is currently unfolding with regard to gene patents. Additional heated debates are questioning whether genes of plant and animal origin, stem cells, or genetically engineered microorganisms can be patented, and whether they should be. All these topics are of great public interest, and they impact virtually every discipline and every aspect of life.

For example, when scientists wanted to make golden rice, a strain engineered to produce a vitamin A precursor, available in developing countries and use it to prevent many of the disorders associated with vitamin A deficiency, they ran into approximately 70 patents that belonged to over 30 institutions. Subsequently, a humanitarian board was established, and licenses were granted free of charge in several countries, but this example illustrates the challenges of navigating through what has become known as the "patent thicket," an increasingly common situation in which the number of overlapping patents that investigators face acts as a disincentive for innovation and advancement. Gene patenting will most likely continue to represent a challenging and controversial topic in the years to come, continuing to occupy an important position at the interface between the biomedical, legal, and social sciences.

Dafna Tachover and Richard A. Stein

See also Gene; Human Genome Project; Venter, J. Craig

Further Readings

Burge, D. A. (1999). *Patent and trademark tactics and practice*. New York: Wiley.

Calvert, J. (2004). Genomic patenting and the utility requirement. *New Genetics and Society, 23*(3), 301–312.

Caulfield, T., Bubela, T., & Murdoch, C. J. (2007). Myriad and the mass media: The covering of a gene patent controversy. *Genetics in Medicine, 9*(12), 850–855.

Committee on Intellectual Property Rights in Genomic and Protein Research and Innovation, National. (2006). *Reaping the benefits of genomic and proteomic research: Intellectual property rights, innovation, and public health*. Washington, DC: National Academies Press.

Demaine, L. J., & Fellmeth, A. X. (2003). Natural substances and patentable inventions. *Science, 300*, 1375–1376.

Diamond v. Chakrabarty, 447 U.S. 303, 309 (1980).

Gad, S., Scheuner, M. T., Pages-Berhouet, S., Caux-Moncoutier, V., Bensimon, A., Aurias, A., et al. (2001). Identification of a large rearrangement of the *BRCA1* gene using colour bar code on combed DNA in an American breast/ovarian cancer family previously studied by direct sequencing. *Journal of Medical Genetics, 38*(6), 388–392.

Levenson, D. (2010). ACLU case against Myriad Genetics. *American Journal of Medical Genetics Part A, 152A*(1), viii.

Marshall, E. (2009). Biotechnology: Lawsuit challenges legal basis for patenting human genes. *Science, 324*, 1000–1001.

Nuffield Council on Bioethics. (2002). *The ethics of patenting DNA*. Available at www.nuffieldbioethics.org

Resnik, D. B. (1997). The morality of human gene patents. *Kennedy Institute of Ethics Journal, 7*(1), 43–61.

Shapiro, C. (2001). Navigating the patent thicket: Cross licenses, patent pools, and standard setting. In E. Jaffe, J. Lerner, & S. Stern (Eds.), *Innovation Policy and the Economy* (Vol. 1, pp. 119–150). Cambridge: MIT Press.

Thompson, A. K., & Chadwick, R. F. (Eds.). (1999). *Genetic information: Acquisition, access, and control.* New York: Kluwer Academic/Plenum.

Verbeure, B., Van Zummeren, E., Matthijs, G., & Van Overwalle, G. (2006). Patent pools and diagnostic testing. *Trends in Biotechnology, 24*(3), 115–120.

GENE THERAPY

Gene therapy involves the direct genetic modification of cells of the patient in order to achieve a therapeutic goal. There are two possible types of gene therapy interventions that can be performed on individuals. Such interventions can be performed on an individual's somatic cells (that is, any cell in an organism that is not a reproductive cell) or on the gamete or gamete forming cells, called germ line cells. This entry briefly reviews the ethical and social issues that have arisen in somatic gene therapy, while having a larger focus on the issues present in germ line gene therapy. Developments in gene therapy often appear in the news, but rarely do such accounts fully analyze these issues.

Somatic gene therapy has the potential to treat a wide range of disorders, including inherited conditions, cancers, and infectious diseases. In gene therapy, an exogenous genetic sequence, called a *transgene,* is introduced into human subjects with the aim of correcting phenotypic (expressed) or genotypic (inherited) abnormalities or to provide cells with new functions. To date, human gene therapy research has been focused almost exclusively on the modification of somatic cells because these genetic modifications only affect the individual patient. By contrast, direct germ line gene therapy is still in its infancy. Germ line gene therapy affects the germ line and therefore also the genome of future generations. Germ line gene therapy has been discussed as a means to treat mitochondrial diseases, that is, diseases due to DNA deviations in genes in the mitochondrial DNA, by ooplasmic transfer. Otherwise it is currently used in the creation of transgenic animals.

Somatic gene therapy currently lies in the uncertain gray area between novel research topic and therapeutic reality. The first decade of human gene therapy has so far demonstrated that there are no quick solutions to developing systems that are capable of delivering genetic material to the correct cells, in sufficient quantity to have a lasting therapeutic effect, without toxic side effects resulting from either the vector used to carry the genetic material or overexpression of the gene product. Further, the clinical efficacy and safety of somatic gene therapy remains disputed and no form of it is yet in routine use. Over years of professional discussion of somatic gene therapy, an ethical consensus has evolved that views somatic gene therapy as an extension of conventional medical interventions. The ethical issues associated with somatic gene therapy are the same as in other experimental treatment as it relates to clinical research, fundamentally. The ethical issues in this case are the risk-benefit ratio, the criteria for enrollment of patients, the informed consent process, conflicts of interest, and the fear of misuses.

However, most ethical and social critique of human gene therapy has focused on the problematic nature of germ line gene therapy, which has been deemed both controversial and technically distant. Objections to it often stem from ideas about what is *natural* and arguments against intentionally causing genetic changes in future generations. However, in recent years there has been a provocative precedent for germ line gene therapy, because there are now children who have three biological parents as a result of the medical intervention referred to as ooplasmic transfer.

Germ line gene therapy interventions are different than somatic gene therapy in the sense that they would produce changes that could be transferred to the descendants of the person receiving the intervention. In many of the official statements that endorse somatic gene therapy, this particular difference is the only one sited in their goal of proscribing or postponing research aimed at developing human germ line gene therapy. However, behind these official statements lies a longer argument. This argument revolves around four sets of concerns: eliminating the disease, scientific uncertainties, social risks, and concerns for future generations.

Eliminating Diseases

Because of the difficulties associated with somatic gene therapy, there has been some pressure to move into the direction of germ line gene therapy. The debate about the ethics of gene therapy has recently resurfaced, and the moral demarcation line between somatic gene therapy and inheritable genetic modifications has been questioned.

Several arguments have been presented in favor of germ line gene therapy. The arguments in support of intentional germ line gene therapy aim to defend interventions directly intended to affect the germ line, and they also try to diminish concern about any unintended germ line effects resulting from somatic gene therapy. Further, it is argued that that germ line gene therapy could potentially be an effective and efficient treatment for diseases that affect many different organs and their cell types. It could also be an alternative to somatic gene therapy techniques for diseases expressed in nonremovable or nondividing cells. Germ line gene therapy has been presented as positive because it has the benefit of actually treating a disease and curing a patient. It has also been claimed that germ line gene therapy may be much more efficient than somatic gene therapy, and that, in contrast to somatic gene therapy, it may reduce the incidence of certain genetic diseases in the human gene pool.

Scientific Uncertainties

There seems to be a consensus between opponents and proponents of germ line gene therapy that, in its current state, it would be unacceptable to move into human trials. The reason for this is that germ line gene therapy poses too many unpredictable, unavoidable, and serious long-term risks to the genetically altered individuals and their offspring to be justified. In order to justify this move, several important issues concerning germ line gene therapy and its techniques would need to be solved. The genes concerned must be stably integrated, expressed correctly and only in the appropriate tissues, and reliably targeted to the correct location on a chromosome.

Opponents of germ line gene therapy hold that there are no real justifications for using germ line gene therapy to eliminate conditions, except in those cases where germ line gene therapy is the only option, that is, when diseases are transmitted via the germ line. The reason is that many genetic diseases could be addressed through the less risky means of carrier screening, prenatal screening followed by abortion, or (perhaps) somatic gene

therapy in the future. The question whether current barriers should in the end dissuade society from contemplating clinical trials in the future still remains.

We have, whether unintentionally or not, already crossed the boundary between somatic gene therapy and germ line interventions in humans. This has been done through ooplasmic transfer where transplantation of mitochondria-rich cytoplasm from one egg into another was performed in an attempt to avoid genetic mitochondrial diseases. This permanently imported new mitochondrial DNA has effected inheritable genetic changes in humans.

Social Risks

A general argument in favor of germ line gene therapy is that, from a social and economic point of view, it is a more efficient method than somatic gene therapy, which must be repeated generation after generation. Arguably, germ line gene therapy also fits better with today's increasingly preferred model of disease prevention and health promotion. Further, germ line gene therapy, by its attempt to prevent disease in individuals rather than to select against individuals according to genotype, would allow the maintenance of our commitment to the value of moral equality regardless of our acknowledged biological diversity.

Thus, the ethical issues associated with germ line gene therapy have a higher level of social implications because this therapy could open the door to genetic enhancement, implying that manipulations of specific phenotypic traits could be used to produce improved individuals. Critics of germ line gene therapy have also raised the question of whether there is a risk that those who do not fit an alleged genetic norm may be seen as nonnormal and in need of therapy or correction, which is understood as problematic or at least ethically questionable.

When considering the moral aspects of different forms of gene therapy, it has been claimed that if we permit somatic gene therapy, we are taking the first step on a slippery slope that will ultimately lead to our acceptance of germ line gene therapy. If we allow diseases such as diabetes and sickle cell anemia to be prevented or cured by altering the genetic makeup of individuals, it will gradually cause a blur in the distinction between health and disease, which eventually could lead to our inability to distinguish between legitimate medical treatments and morally unacceptable eugenics, as in the creation of "improved" individuals.

Concerns for Future Generations

The ability of germ line modifications to shape the inheritance of future generations raises major ethical concerns. Germ line gene therapy might change the attitudes toward the human person, the nature of human reproduction, and the parent-child relationship. It could also exacerbate prejudice against people with disabilities. Germ line gene therapy for enhancement purposes is particularly problematic. Efforts to improve the inherited genome of people might commodify human reproduction and foster attempts to have "perfect" children by "correcting" their genomes. Some types of enhancement applications might lead to the imposition of harmful conceptions of normalcy. The dilemma is that technologies originally developed for germ line modifications with therapeutic purposes are likely to be suitable for enhancement applications as well. Thus, going forward with germ line gene therapy to treat disease or disability will make it difficult to avoid use of such interventions for enhancement purposes, even when this use is considered ethically unacceptable.

Opponents of germ line gene therapy have objected that the use of the technology implies a change in the prerequisites for the future individual concerned, which will undermine our moral community; children born after genetic interventions will be genetically programmed in accordance with their parents' wishes. This will, according to the German philosopher Jürgen Habermas, make them unable to act autonomously in the same sense as their parents did. The main argument for this notion is that the child born after germ line modification is not "author of its own life plan," and that a person whose life plan has been designed by somebody else is not able to participate in the communicative dialogue that constitutes our ethics and community. As opponents see it, future generations have a right to determine their own destinies. Further, germ line interventions violate the right of the individual and his or her descendants to have their own unique genetic identities.

Conclusion

The cultural and social uses of gene therapy have expanded far beyond scientific knowledge. How we think about life, including disease and disability, human capabilities and failings, social problems, kinship, and quality of life, are all influenced by the new genetic paradigm in medicine. Medicine has moved from just explaining illness from genetic causes into trying to change the genetic makeup of humans in order to improve health.

Hannah Grankvist

See also Conflicts of Interest in Science; Ethical, Legal, and Social Issues (ELSI); Risks and Benefits

Further Readings

Habermas, J. (2003). *The future of human nature.* Cambridge, UK: Polity Press.

Juengst, E. T., & Grankvist, H. (2007). Ethical issues in human gene transfer: A historical overview. In R. E. Ashcroft, A. Dawson, H. Draper, & J. R. McMillian (Eds.), *Principles of health care ethics* (2nd ed., pp. 789–796). Chichester, UK: John Wiley & Sons.

Walters, L., & Palmer, J. G. (1997). *The ethics of human gene therapy.* Oxford, UK: Oxford University Press.

GOULD, STEPHEN JAY (1941–2002)

Stephen Jay Gould, Harvard University paleontologist, evolutionary biologist, and educator for more than 30 years, as well as a curator at the university's Museum of Comparative Zoology, was also a monthly columnist for *Natural History* magazine and a writer admired for his brilliant literary style. His work is read by almost everyone with an interest in science, from layperson to professional. In the last years of his career, Gould also taught biology and evolution at New York University.

Gould published over 20 books in his career and rivals Richard Dawkins in his fame as a popularizer of evolution. His *Ever Since Darwin: Reflections in Natural History,* a collection of essays from his *Natural History* column, was published in 1977; a second volume of collected essays from the magazine appeared in 1980 as *The Panda's Thumb* and won a National Book Award.

Among countless other awards Gould received for his writing, his 1989 *Wonderful Life: The Burgess Shale and the Nature of History,* a book on the evolution of early life based in the study of the fossils of the Cambrian fauna, won an Aventis Prize in 1991 and was a finalist for a 1991 Pulitzer. In his book, he argues that chance was one of the decisive factors in the evolution of life on earth. In *Full House: The Spread of Excellence From Plato to Darwin* (1997), Gould again states an innovative argument, that progress is not the "goal" of evolution, using the apparent disappearance of 400 hitters in baseball as a convenient example.

Gould was also known for a strong sense of social responsibility, opposition to creationism, and long-standing concern with the relationship between science and politics. He was deeply involved in the legislative challenge mounted against the governor of Arkansas's proposal that creation "science" be taught in schools alongside evolution. In the book *The Mismeasure of Man* (1981), he presents an extended critique of the methods and motivations underlying biological determinism. He considers that the social and economic differences between human groups are independent of biological capabilities such as intelligence. In this book, Gould rejects IQ tests as based on pseudoscientific theories used to defend racist ideologies.

Gould's scientific contributions were also substantial, winning him a Charles Schuchert Award in 1975 and a Paleontological Society Medal in 2002, both awarded by the Paleontological Society. Gould and Niles Eldredge published their theory of punctuated equilibrium, a new interpretation of the fossil record, in 1972. They pointed out that, on the evidence of the fossil record, many species show little change over long periods of time and then are quite suddenly replaced by new species. The earlier view had been that such discontinuities are simply gaps in the fossil record, but Gould and Eldredge argue that the discontinuities reflect the fact that the evolutionary process involves long periods of stability punctuated by periods of rapid change. Nowadays, scientists are still arguing over how often the fossil record shows a punctuated pattern and how such a pattern might arise.

Gould immersed himself in a morphological tradition (that is, an approach to the study of the forms and structure of organisms) stressing that the most significant features of organic life are the similarities that link organism to organism. Adaptation is in many cases secondary or nonexistent. Moves of this nature did not find favor within more conventional Darwinians, especially those working experimentally on rapidly reproducing organisms where natural selection is a vital tool. Gould proposed an "expanded Darwinism" where natural selection and adaptation are undoubtedly important when one is considering organisms in their day-to-day life and microevolution. But as one looks at more long-term matters, it is apparent that other factors, including chance, increasingly come into play.

Gould died of lung cancer in 2002 at the age of 60, 2 months after publication of his nearly 1,400-page *The Structure of Evolutionary Theory* and 20 years after a successful battle with another form of cancer, abdominal mesothelioma, which is often fatal. In the second part of this last book, Gould presents a constructive critique of contemporary Darwinism and presents his own major contributions to macroevolutionary theory.

Núria Pérez-Pérez

See also Dawkins, Richard

Further Readings

Gould, S. J. (2002). *The structure of evolutionary theory.* Cambridge, MA: Belknap.

Ruse, M. (1999). *Mystery of mysteries. Is evolution a social construction?* Cambridge, MA: Harvard University Press.

GOVERNMENT PUBLIC INFORMATION

Federal, state, and local government agencies with science- and technology-related missions very frequently employ professional communications specialists to assist journalists and the public in accessing information about government programs. These specialists work to ensure that information about how the agency has spent taxpayer funds is available in plain English, that agency managers have access to advice about how to best communicate with various audiences important to the success of the agency, and that specific questions from journalists or the public are answered in an accurate and timely way.

These professional science communicators work for a variety of different types of agencies. For example, at the federal level, some organizations directly conduct scientific field or laboratory research, such as the National Aeronautics and Space Administration (NASA) or the National Institute of Standards and Technology (NIST). Some agencies provide funding to universities and others to conduct research, such as the National Science Foundation. And a large number of agencies at the federal, state, or local level, such as the U.S. Department of Agriculture, the U.S. Food and Drug Administration, and the U.S. Environmental Protection Agency, conduct programs related to health, food safety, energy, environment, law enforcement, military, and manufacturing that require science and technology communications.

According to the U.S. Office of Personnel Management, as of December 2008, a total of about 9,000 people were employed by the federal government as public affairs specialists, writer/editors, technical writers, audiovisual specialists, editorial assistants, and exhibit specialists. Only a fraction of this number specializes in science and technology communications. Many more people in the field work for state or local government offices with science- and technology-related missions.

The function of government public affairs, communications, or information offices within science and technology agencies is similar to that of counterpart offices within universities or other nonprofit organizations—to help the agency succeed in its mission by maintaining good relationships with major stakeholder groups. Stakeholder groups, sometimes referred to as publics, are collections of people with similar interests whose support or opposition can strongly affect the agency's welfare and can either help or hinder it in accomplishing its mission. Examples include the news media; federal, state, or local agency officials; members of Congress or other elected officials and their staffs; academic or corporate leaders; researchers, engineers, and other technically trained specialists; doctors, nurses, and other health care specialists; or segments of the broader public, such as educators, parents, science enthusiasts, or students.

Two-Way Communication

Strong two-way communication—in which the government agency strives to be open and transparent in its decision-making processes and actions, regularly provides information on its activities, and routinely seeks feedback from its stakeholder groups—is the hallmark of excellent government public affairs or information programs. Government agencies have both a legal and ethical obligation to provide detailed descriptions of their activities to the public and to seek input for improving their operations.

Many government science communicators specialize further in media relations. They actively maintain good relationships with journalists working for the general news media or the trade and technical press who regularly write about science and technology topics. These relationships help ensure that the government employees can target news of specific research accomplishments to journalists likely to write about these topics, as well as help journalists find agency experts on specific topics to interview.

Government science communicators also frequently train their agency's scientists and engineers to help improve their communications skills. Without such training, technical experts often unintentionally use jargon rather than lay language in describing their research and may fail to provide enough context for journalists to write accurate, clear articles about their work. Government public information specialists help agency scientists and engineers to understand the constraints most journalists must operate under, including tight deadlines, demanding editors, and limited space for explaining complex topics. Most government researchers discuss their work with the news media only rarely, and some are intimidated by the prospect of broad public exposure. Without the reassurance and training provided by their agency's media relations specialists, many government scientists and engineers would be unwilling to participate in media interviews.

Some journalists view public relations specialists in general and government media relations experts in particular as obstacles to direct contact with scientists and engineers. In most science and technology agencies, however, media specialists substantially increase the amount of information available to the public. They do this not only by encouraging agency employees to provide interviews, but also by serving as in-house journalists who interview agency technical staff about the results of their research and then translate news of those results into lay language in the form of news releases, Web sites, newsletters, magazines, blogs, videos, or as other types of communications products.

Many different types of audiences beyond journalists benefit from access to descriptions of governmental technical topics in plain English. Policymakers use these materials to better understand the scientific principals behind important policy issues such as regulation of greenhouse gases, medical research using stem cells, or protection of endangered species. Educators use lay language in government public information products to continually improve textbooks and lesson plans using information on the latest scientific and technical results. Manufacturers and service industry managers use these lay language summaries to learn how the latest research can help them improve their current products and create new ones. Even scientists and engineers benefit from lay language news of government technical achievements because it helps them learn about results beyond their own narrow fields of study. Often some of the greatest advances in science occur at the boundaries of technical disciplines, and government public communication helps encourage information sharing at these boundaries. Without the skills of the government science communicator to translate these technical accomplishments into accessible language, many research accomplishments would lay undiscovered and unused within the pages of thousands of technical journals.

Whereas previously the commercial news media were the only outlets reaching large public audiences, the World Wide Web now allows government agencies to provide detailed information about their programs in forms directly to relevant audiences. Many agencies use Web-based software tools to provide real-time e-mail or cell phone alerts about adverse weather events, health concerns, natural disasters, or other news topics, allowing citizens to connect with others with similar interests, or to encourage visitors to their Web sites to comment on agency programs or ask questions of agency experts.

Government agencies are also increasingly maintaining accounts with the most popular commercial Web sites, especially so-called social media or social networking sites, and posting agency-created content including videos, news releases, photos, blogs, feature articles, and conference announcements. These new technologies have dramatically increased the ability of agencies to broadly disseminate results of government-funded research and other science- and technology-related programs. At the same time, social networking tools have allowed the many publics affected by and interested in these programs to provide direct feedback to agencies—that is, to participate in a two-way communications flow that ultimately helps improve government programs.

Working in Government Public Information

Government public information officers at science and technology agencies train for their jobs in many different ways. Most have bachelor's or master's degrees in fields such as journalism, communications, or English. Some have degrees in science fields such as physics, chemistry, biology, environmental science, or astronomy that are related to their specific agency's mission. Still others have degrees in both a related science and in journalism/communications. Some university master's degree or certificate programs specialize in training science and engineering graduates with excellent communications skills to be science journalists. Some of these graduates ultimately are employed as government science information specialists.

While many of the skills learned by journalists are also helpful to government science communicators, there are key differences between the two professions. Journalists write articles, create radio programs, or produce videos about science and technology topics as neutral bystanders. While they may specialize in a particular field, such as the environment, health, or computer technology, each day they talk to different sources at many different institutions. Their job is to report the news as truthfully as possible and to stay as objective as possible by not becoming too close to their sources.

Government science communicators, on the other hand, write articles, create radio programs, produce videos, write speeches, post Web sites, publish employee newsletters, and provide tours to the public to help their agencies advance their missions. They are participants in government science- and technology-related programs rather than bystanders. They typically know the scientists or engineers they are interviewing well and get updates on progress of their technical work frequently. The public information specialists' efforts to translate and disseminate results of a scientist's work may result in new collaborations with university researchers or in a company licensing a patent from the agency that results in a new product being marketed. A skilled government science communicator typically knows about these impacts through continuing contact with the agency's technical staff and is considered an important contributor to the research group's success.

Continuing education opportunities for government public information officers is available through workshops provided by professional associations, such as the National Association of Science Writers, National Association of Government Communicators, and the Society for Technical Communications. Large scientific societies, such as the American Association for the Advancement of Science and the American Chemical Society, also provide regular seminars and workshops on best practices for communicating science and technology to the public.

Multimedia skills have become increasingly important for government public information specialists. The Internet is now the top source of information for everyone from school children to senior policymakers. As broadband connections become more commonplace, content typically available only in written documents is increasingly provided in both video and audio forms. A generation of journalists trained primarily in print journalism is now frequently writing video scripts, producing radio interviews, or creating slide shows with photos, text, animation, and music. This means that government public information specialists must also have these skills. To meet the public's high expectations for such content, government science and technology agencies now routinely provide high quality multimedia content on their Web sites.

Ethical and Legal Requirements

An important element of a government public information officer's training is knowledge of ethical standards and legal requirements. Government public information specialists literally work for the public. Whereas public relations experts working for private organizations may choose whether to provide information requested by journalists or the public, government information specialists are often required to do so, either ethically, legally, or both.

Federal and state laws and regulations describe what information government agencies must provide on request and how accessible the information provided should be for citizens with disabilities, limited English proficiency, or other special needs. Examples of these laws and regulations at the federal level include the Freedom of Information Act, executive orders by the president, the Federal Advisory Committee Act, Americans with Disabilities Act, records retention regulations from the National Archives and Records Administration, and the Whistleblower Protection Act.

General professional and ethical codes of conduct require that public information specialists report on agency research results in a factual way that does not exaggerate accomplishments and that properly attributes opinions and facts provided in information materials. For example, materials prepared by agency public information specialists or by contractors paid by government agencies must be clearly identified as government-sponsored information. For materials about science and technology research, communicators are ethically obligated to include any important qualifiers that put research results in perspective. This is especially important when discussing the results of medical research to avoid raising unrealistic hopes within the public that a cure for a specific condition is imminent when in fact many years of research may remain before new, effective treatment options will be available.

In recent years, concerns about the potential for manipulation of scientific information for political purposes have been widely reported. Organizations such the Union of Concerned Scientists have responded by pointing out the importance of broad, unfettered dissemination of scientific and technical information to public health and safety. In March 2009, President Barack Obama issued an executive order prohibiting political officials from suppressing or altering scientific or technological findings and conclusions. In addition, a number of federal science and technology agencies and cabinet-level departments have public communications policies designed to protect scientific integrity by explicitly allowing scientists and engineers to speak freely to the media or the public about their research results. These policies acknowledge the important role that is played by public information specialists in helping scientists and engineers successfully describe their research results to the media. At the same time, such policies explicitly allow technical experts to interpret their taxpayer-funded results and accept media interview requests without permission from agency public information offices. As a result, an additional important role for federal government science communicators is to ensure that agency scientists and engineers understand their rights and obligations for public communication of their research results.

Gail Porter

See also Department of Agriculture, U.S.; Environmental Protection Agency, U.S.; Food and Drug Administration, U.S.; National Aeronautics and Space Administration, U.S.; National Science Foundation, U.S.

Further Readings

Blum, D., Knudson, M., & Marantz Henig, R. (2006). *A field guide for science writers: The official guide of the National Association of Science Writers.* New York: Oxford University Press.

Borchelt, R. E. (2001). Communicating the future. *Science Communications, 23,* 194–211.

Dozier, D. M., Grunig, L. A., & Grunig, J. E. (1995). *Manager's guide to excellence in public relations and communications management.* Mahwah, NJ: Lawrence Erlbaum.

National Aeronautics and Space Administration. (2006). *NASA policy on the release of information to the news and information media.* Retrieved February 9, 2009, from www.nasa.gov/audience/formedia/features/communication_policy.html

Porter, G. J. (Ed.). (2002). *Communicating the future: Best practices in communicating about science and technology to the public.* Gaithersburg, MD: National Institute of Standards and Technology.

Union of Concerned Scientists. (2008). *Federal agency media policies inconsistent: Some stifle, some support scientists sharing information with the press, new study finds.* Available at www.ucsusa.org/news/press_release/federal-agency-media-policies-0152.html

U.S. Department of Commerce. (2008). *Public communications* (DAO 219-1). Retrieved April 30, 2008, from http://dms.osec.doc.gov/cgi-bin/doit.cgi?204:112:708e5734262ec0a03bf925e749484c9eb24a509a90ab8daaf91019431a09f860:297

The White House. (2009). *Memorandum for heads of executive departments and executive departments and agencies, subject: Scientific integrity.* Retrieved March 9, 2009, from www.whitehouse.gov/the_press_office/Memorandum-for-the-Heads-of-Executive-Departments-and-Agencies-3-9-09

GREENPEACE

Greenpeace, one of the largest environmental advocacy organizations, is best known for dramatic protests over marine environmental issues that capture media attention. The environmental activist group is famous for members who place themselves in harm's way. From a small antiwar group formed in 1971 in Vancouver, Canada, the organization had grown by the early 21st century to an international organization with 5 ships, 2.8 million supporters, 27 national and regional offices, and presence in 41 nations.

Among its thousands of dramatic protests, Greenpeace activists have infiltrated nuclear test sites, shielded whales from harpoons, protected fur seals from clubs, and blocked ocean-going barges from dumping radioactive waste. The strategy was inspired by a confrontational but nonviolent philosophy rooted in the Quaker concept of bearing witness and also in the nonviolent interventions of Mahatma Gandhi and Martin Luther King Jr. The organization's strict adherence to nonviolence has led to breakaways by some who want more muscular activism (for example, Paul Watson, founder of the Sea Shepherd Society).

Greenpeace tactics were also influenced by political street theater and the work of Saul Alinsky, the Provos of Amsterdam, and the Diggers of San Francisco. Greenpeace raised street theater and protest tactics to a new level using global media. The effect, according to Greenpeace cofounder Robert Hunter, was a "mind bomb"—that is, an action designed to create a dramatic new impression to replace an old cliché. The most obvious example of a "mind bomb" was to overturn the image of heroic whalers to that of heroic ecologists risking their lives to save the gentle giants of the sea. This approach caught the world's attention and dramatically changed the political terrain for commercial fishing and whaling operations after Greenpeace's first whaling protests in June 1975.

Greenpeace organizers first noticed the power of dramatic protest in 1971 when they imagined a new kind of protest amid an intense international controversy over U.S. nuclear weapons testing in the Aleutian Islands of Alaska. They chartered a fishing trawler to sail into the test area in the expectation that the U.S. government would have to call off the test. The trawler originally had the name *Greenpeace,* while the group originally called itself the "Don't Make a Wave" committee, the fear at the time being that nuclear weapons tests could create tidal waves. The trawler *Greenpeace* sailed from Vancouver on September 15, 1971, but turned back after arrests, other delays, and being held back by winter storms.

When the United States detonated the bomb two months later, Greenpeace was ignored in the United States—however, the Canadian media saw the protests as visionary and helpful. French nuclear testing was also an early prominent target of Greenpeace protests. When a small Greenpeace sailboat that sailed into the French nuclear testing area of Moruroa in the summer of 1972 was seriously damaged in a collision with a French warship, the protest led to headline coverage around the world. The Greenpeace antiwhaling campaign began in 1974 with training on zodiac inflatable boats using outboard motors. The summer campaign in 1975 was launched to confront whaling vessels on the high seas off the U.S. and Canadian Pacific Coast. When a Russian factory whaling ship fired a harpoon perilously close to one zodiac in late June, the incident touched off a media frenzy at a scientific meeting of the International Whaling Commission in London. The fight to save the whales changed that day, according to Rex Weyler, a Greenpeace historian.

Greenpeace campaigners continued attacking the extermination of the last whales and presented

Michael Bailey of Greenpeace blockades a Soviet whaling ship in the North Pacific, July 1976.

Source: Photo by Rex Weyler. ©Rex Weyler, Greenpeace, 1976. Reproduced by permission.

evidence that even flimsy rules against taking young whales were being ignored. Meanwhile, similar campaigns were mounted against radioactive waste dumping at sea and against killing seals for fur. By the early 1980s, the combination of tactics—dramatic confrontations and impassioned arguments—led to bans on sealing by the European Union and a moratorium on most whaling by the International Whaling Commission. It also led to financial success, and in 1978, Greenpeace was able to buy a 417-ton research ship, the *Sir William Hardy,* and rename it the *Rainbow,* in honor of a Cree Indian prophesy. According to the prophesy, when the earth was poisoned by humans, a group of people from all nations calling themselves Warriors of the Rainbow would band together to defend nature.

With success in Europe and the United States, Greenpeace decided to protest French nuclear testing on Mururoa Atoll in the Pacific Ocean. The *Rainbow Warrior* was taking on provisions in Auckland, New Zealand, on July 10, 1985, when explosions ripped through its hull, killing crewman Fernando Pereira and sinking the ship. Two agents with the French Direction Générale de la Sécurité Extérieure (DGSE) were arrested by late July, and by September 22, 1985, the French government conceded that its scuba diving agents planted magnetic mines and sank the vessel. The French agents were jailed briefly, but released after France threatened to block New Zealand exports to the European Union. The French apologized and paid $7 million to Greenpeace, but the nuclear tests continued and no one in the French government was held accountable.

Yet the bombing of the *Rainbow Warrior* underscored the prominence that Greenpeace had attainted in the 15 years since its founding. By the early 1990s, it was considered the "green giant" of the environmental movement with protests of every conceivable environmental issue underway in every corner of the globe. Usually the protests involved actions designed to highlight an issue in a dramatic or humorous way, such as dumping marbles in the Department of the Interior lobby in Washington, D.C., because the Secretary of the Interior had "lost his marbles." Another imaginative tactic was to have children pass out asthma inhalers at coal industry conferences. Greenpeace also fanned the flames of international outrage in 1995 when the Nigerian government executed environmental activist Ken Saro-Wiwa, who had led a nonviolent campaign against Shell Oil Company.

Despite its popularity, Greenpeace was not always considered a serious environmental group and was often excluded from coalitions working in legal or legislative arenas. The organization was also criticized by other environmental groups in the 1990s as misrepresenting some issues—for example, collecting money from sponsors for a weak program of dolphin protection. One vocal Greenpeace critic, cofounder Patrick Moore, quit the organization in 1986 and began working for forestry, nuclear power, and chemical interests. He criticized "scare tactics" within the environmental movement, saying in 2008 that Greenpeace was an organization that had lost its way due to "extremism and politically motivated agendas." Others in the environmental movement have dismissed Moore's criticism as self-interested.

Another criticism of Greenpeace has been that with so much general popular support for environmental reform, a dramatic media-targeted protest may seem like a cliché. This may have been more so in the United States and Europe, where, after a growth peak in the early 1990s, the organization went through serious restructuring. Yet Greenpeace continued growing on an international level in the early 21st century, helping regional and international activists mount protests involving a variety of issues, such as toxic waste in Africa, illegal logging in the Amazon, undercover sale of whale meat in Japan, nuclear power in Asia, and drift net fishing in the Pacific. For all the controversy and drama it generates, Greenpeace still manages to catch the imagination of the environmental community.

Bill Kovarik

See also Environmental Journalism; Nuclear Power; Nuclear Weapons

Further Readings

Brown, M., & May, J. (1991). *The Greenpeace story.* New York: Dorling Kindersley.

Heller, P. (2007). *The whale warriors: The battle at the bottom of the world to save the planet's largest mammals.* New York: Free Press.

Weyler, R. (2004). *Greenpeace: How a group of ecologists, journalists, and visionaries changed the world.* Emmaus, PA: Rodale Books.

H

HAWKING, STEPHEN (1942–)

Some have called Stephen Hawking the most brilliant physicist since Albert Einstein. Hawking has been quick to point out that he was born 300 years to the day after Galileo Galilei died and that he holds the same professorship at Cambridge University Isaac Newton once held.

If visible scientists are scientists well-known to the public, then Hawking is not just a visible scientist—he is a rock-star scientist.

Hawking was born on January 8, 1942, in Oxford, England, and spent most of his childhood in St. Albans, a town 20 miles north of London. In 1959, he received an open scholarship to University College, Oxford, where he began studies at the age of 17. In 1962, he received his first-class honors degree from Oxford and then began studying for a PhD in cosmology at Cambridge University, where he pursued his interests in black holes, singularities, and other areas of interest—sometimes thought of as the physics of the very big and the very small.

In 1965, Hawking received his PhD and began a fellowship in theoretical physics at Cambridge's Gonville and Caius College, where he often collaborated on space-time research with mathematician Roger Penrose. He became a staff member of Cambridge's Institute of Astronomy in 1968 and worked with Penrose on mathematics and thermodynamics related to black holes. Hawking was named a Fellow of the Royal Society in 1974, then spent a year as the Fairchild Distinguished Scholar

at the California Institute of Technology. In 1978, he received the top theoretical physics honor, the Albert Einstein Award of the Lewis and Rose Strauss Memorial Fund.

His work focuses on black holes, particle physics, quantum gravity, and other areas related to the origin of the universe and work toward developing a grand unification theory, or theory of everything, that would link Einstein's theory of relativity with quantum mechanics. By the 1980s, he was working on big bang issues. Was there a big bang, or were there universes that produced other universes? Is there a beginning? Is there an end? If there is a singularity at the end of a star's collapse, was it possible that there had been a singularity at the beginning of the universe? He and Penrose showed that the answer was yes.

Hawking has received many of the most prominent awards in science, including the Eddington Medal of the Royal Astronomical Society (1975), the Pius XI Gold Medal (1975), the Maxwell Medal of the Institute of Physics (1976), the Franklin Medal of the Franklin Institute (1981), the Gold Medal of the Royal Society (1985), the Paul Dirac Medal and Prize (1987), the Britannica Award (1989), and the Royal Society's Copley Medal (2006). He has also received honorary degrees from a variety of universities, including Oxford (1978); Chicago (1981); Leicester, Notre Dame, and Princeton (1982); Newcastle and Leeds (1987); and Tufts, Yale, and Cambridge (1989).

Greater fascination has surrounded Hawking's life and the interconnection of his life with the study of such "big picture" scientific questions than for perhaps any other modern scientist. In 1973, Hawking showed that particles are emitted by black holes. Then he formulated the theory that black holes could emit subatomic particles (Hawking radiation). In 2004, Hawking said he was wrong in his previous black hole theory—instead of black holes devouring everything, he said that stuff may be preserved, with mass sent back into the universe.

Hawking has amyotrophic lateral sclerosis, also known as Lou Gehrig's disease. It was first noticed during his time at Oxford and progressed during his time at Cambridge. When he was originally diagnosed, doctors predicted, incorrectly, that he would live for only another 2 1/2 years. The progression of the disease was such, however, that he would eventually require a wheelchair and full-time nursing care. A case of pneumonia in 1985 forced an operation that would also leave him without a voice. Later, a device dubbed "the equalizer" would allow him to communicate through a computer and speech synthesizer attached to his wheelchair.

Hawking cowrote *The Large Scale Structure of Space-Time* (1973) with G. F. R. Ellis. It was a highly technical, mathematical book—very different from what would follow 15 years later. In 1979, the same year he was named Lucasian Professor of Mathematics at Cambridge, he coedited with Werner Israel *General Relativity: An Einstein Centenary Survey.* He published *Three Hundred Years of Gravitation* (Cambridge University Press) in 1987.

In 1988, he published *A Brief History of Time: From the Big Bang to Black Holes,* a book that includes historical coverage, as well as coverage of how his own theories fit into the timeline of our understanding of cosmology, general relativity, and quantum physics. The ideas presented in *A Brief History of Time* may have their own importance in the scientific world, but they are not necessarily the most important elements with respect to the ultimate impact of the book—and Hawking's career as a science communicator.

A Brief History of Time became extremely important to the general public as a readable window on the world of physics. It was intended from the beginning for a lay audience and became a best seller, with ripples through magazines, movies, and television. Hawking consciously chose the layman's path for *A Brief History of Time,* choosing trade publisher Bantam over an academic publisher such as Cambridge University Press. The only equation in the book is $e = mc^2$ (following advice from the publisher, who said that equations hurt book sales).

And then came more books in the science popularization arena, including *Black Holes and Baby Universes and Other Essays* (1993), *The Nature of Space and Time* (with Roger Penrose, 1995); *The Illustrated A Brief History of Time* (1996), *The Universe in a Nutshell* (2001), *The Future of Spacetime* (with Kip S. Thorne, Igor Novikov, Timothy Ferris, and Alan Lightman, 2002), *On the Shoulders of Giants: The Great Works of Physics and Astronomy* (2002), and *The Theory of Everything: The Origin and Fate of the Universe* (2002). *A Briefer History of Time* (with Leonard Mlodinow) appeared in 2005, and later, he co-wrote a children's book with his daughter, Lucy Hawking: *George and His Secret Key to the Universe* (2007).

Hawking became a household name who appeared in cameo roles on popular television and whose *A Brief History of Time: From the Big Bang to Black Holes* continues to attract readers. Today, his contributions as a communicator and his status as a celebrity may even rival his reputation as a scientist.

David Amber

See also Visible Scientist

Further Readings

White, M., & Gribbin, J. (1992). *Stephen Hawking: A life in science.* New York: E. P. Dutton.

Boslough, J. (1985). *Stephen Hawking's universe.* New York: William Morrow.

Hawking, S. (1988). *A brief history of time: From the big bang to black holes.* New York: Bantam.

Ferguson, K. (1992). *Stephen Hawking: A quest for a theory of everything.* New York: Bantam.

HEALTH COMMUNICATION, OVERVIEW

Health is an emerging area within the field of communication. Health communication includes the practice and study of communication strategies to prevent diseases or illness, and to promote individual and public health or quality of life. The pace of health communication research and practice has increased and expanded dramatically over the last three decades. Increased awareness of the incidence and the range of health issues around the world have led to the integration of research from disciplines such as medicine, nursing, sociology, psychology, law, and business. Health communication researchers and professionals have developed a variety of tools and methods to intervene at the individual level of behavioral processes associated with health and to advance systematic improvements related to the performance of health care organizations and issues within society in general.

Crucial milestones were the formation of the Health Communication Divisions of the International Communication Association in 1975 and the National Communication Association in 1985. In 2009, the Association for Education in Journalism and Mass Communication also expanded the focus of its Science Communication Interest Group to encompass communication of science, health, technology, and risk. These organizations have given voice to a generation of researchers who had been working in the field in relative isolation. In 1989, *Health Communication,* the first journal specifically regarding health communication, was launched, followed by the *Journal of Health Communication,* first published in 1996. Before this, research on health communication issues were published in journals devoted to other social sciences and medicine and tended to focus on specific aspects of the relationship between the practice of medicine and communication processes. By the early 1990s, however, the field was invested with a theoretical and methodological rigor and was characterized by synthetic and sophisticated perspectives on the interactions between health care providers and consumers in a variety of contexts.

Current perspectives on health communication include analyses of communication processes from the vantage of senders, channels, receivers, and feedback. These processes occur at the individual, organizational, and societal levels of communication in health contexts or settings. At the individual level, health communication can help increase awareness of health problems and their solutions, providing individuals with actionable methods to prevent or treat illness. Interpersonal communication among health care administrators, physicians, nurses, patients, and their family members is critical to the delivery of health care and patient outcomes. At organizational level, health communication often relates to procedures and policies that govern health organizations and may involve resolution of group or system conflicts among health care providers. At the societal level, health communication addresses community issues such as health disparities, the development of social networks, and the role of support groups. Health communication influences the public agenda, effects policy changes to improve health care systems, and encourages the establishment of social norms that promote health.

Federal and state government agencies, often under the auspices of health boards, have taken a lead role in promoting effective communication. For example, the U.S. Health and Human Services Department publication titled *Healthy People 2010* outlined a number of key indicators for health communication strategies focusing on health improvement. The document advocates education campaigns related to physical activity, healthy weight, nutrition, sexual behavior practices, tobacco use, substance abuse, injuries, and violence. Health communication interventions also have moved beyond the individual level to address global issues such as poverty, environmental issues, and needed reform of the health care system.

The role of the media has been a crucial aspect of health communication. Health communication professionals work in concert with media outlets to further their goals. Examples of the collaborative relationship between the media and health communication professionals include developing health promotion campaigns to target specific audiences. In recent years, health communication delivery strategies have changed dramatically with the advent of online and social media. For example, telemedicine has expanded the delivery of health care and health communication to virtual environments.

Although the development of health communication theory and practice has a relatively short history, it has reached a critical point of development. Although insights from a variety of theoretical traditions in the social sciences have been adopted, health communication has tended to focus on practical applications and implementation techniques. The field has struggled, valiantly in many instances, to stay abreast of the rapidly evolving scientific and clinical advances that characterize the health care field in general. Yet health communication has enormous potential to alleviate suffering, improve mortality rates, enhance patient satisfaction and quality of life, and promote the overall physical and psychological well-being of society in general. Given the complexities and multiplicities of health communication processes, the need for effective communication strategies cannot be overemphasized.

Individual Level of Health Communication

Four major communication processes occur at the individual level in health contexts: (1) professional–patient, (2) professional–professional, (3) professional–family, and (4) patient–family relationships. For example, communication between health care professionals and patients affects or is affected by conflicting values, power differences, unshared meanings, and potential misunderstandings. Communication at the individual level is a crucial determinant of the effectiveness of health care. Communication at the intraprofessional level often involves role uncertainty, misunderstanding, differences in goals, and questions about the nature of collaboration and competition for overscarce resources. Interpersonal communication between health care professionals and patients' family members may result in misunderstandings based on miscommunication or misperception. Communication between patients and their family members is often related to issues concerning coping and decision-making processes. Communication among different interest groups such as health care providers, insurance companies, or other politically involved parties tends to center on issues of conflict of interest, resource allocation, or professional judgment.

Interpersonal conflict is an inevitable aspect of the communication process. Conflict has been defined in scholarly literature as differences that arise between parties in terms of perceived incompatibility, beliefs, roles, values, and goals. In part because they often involve matters of life and death, professional identity, and the financial stability of individuals and organizations, health communication processes tend to intensify conflicts. Thus, resolution of tensions is a key goal of health communication. Studies have documented how conflict resolution promotes better health

care processes and outcomes. Proactive communication enables resolution processes and generates positive outcomes.

Organizational Level of Health Communication

Health care organizations are the most common sites for the interaction between patients and health care providers. Norms, conventions, and institutional culture broadly influence the character and nature of the relationships among stakeholders. Although it may seem on the surface as though interactions between a doctor and a patient are uncomplicated, an entire nexus of embedded norms colors the relationship. For example, a physician with a small private practice may perceive that he or she has relative freedom in interactions with patients, and patients may report a higher level of direct communication; however, the interests of an accrediting body such as the American Medical Association, insurance companies, and the opinions of peers, media, and government regulations may nevertheless affect the doctor's communication with his or her patients.

The essential challenge of health communication at the organizational level is to coordinate and manage the flow of information about the increasingly complex practice of medical science for layperson consumers while simultaneously building interpersonal relationships with a broad array of interest groups. Health communication specialists have played a vital role in the development of team-based approaches that build collaboration among individuals with different specializations and skills. Drawing on the strengths of individual members with different backgrounds, interdisciplinary teams can address the complexities of patient care by sharing different perspectives. A crucial role of health communication is to help team members understand the perspectives of their peers and overcome some of the biases that result from working with others in highly specialized fields.

Societal Level of Health Communication

The field of health communication is also instrumental in mediating the relationships between health care providers, social service agencies, and patients or their families. Making individuals aware of their alternatives, such as support groups and other social networks, is an increasingly important function of health communication. In this way, health communication serves as a complement to structured health care systems and facilitates the overall health of society. For example, community-based social support groups can help reduce the gaps in delivering health information to underserved populations.

Health communication professionals have recognized and embraced the importance of issues of diversity in the health care arena. Cultural difference, combined with socioeconomic, ethnic, and lifestyle variance, has challenged health communication specialists to develop integrative approaches to serve their constituents. Understanding and addressing diversity issues leads not only to better health care outcomes, but also to greater efficiency. There is ample research documenting how health care systems have failed to account for communication differences among individuals with diverse backgrounds. For example, institutional culture sometimes impedes effective communication among health care providers serving diverse constituents.

The delivery of messages and the use of channels in health communication depend on factors such as age, gender, ethnic background, regional differences, and socioeconomic status. For example, older patients often appreciate communication styles informed by traditional media channels, whereas younger patients may prefer online or emerging forms of social media. Women may be more attuned to expansive discussion of health topics, whereas men may prefer succinct and direct answers. Recognition and appreciation of these differences is an aspect of health communication. As the demographic makeup of countries such as the United States shifts, a broadening of cultural differences and increasing incidence of language barriers presents increasing challenges for health communication.

Behavioral factors, such as sexual practices, drinking, smoking, diet, physical activities, and routine screening tests, also present challenges that are strongly associated with health communication as well. Negative stereotypes or biases, reinforced by cultural norms and media representations, are frequently associated with such diseases as HIV/AIDS, alcoholism, and morbid obesity. These stereotypes can affect how health care professionals approach and deliver treatment, as well as the receptiveness of the health care consumer. Health communication researchers have presented strategies to reduce expressions and incidence of stereotypes or bias in health care systems.

One daunting task addressed in *Healthy People 2010* is the elimination of health disparities, which researchers have shown are connected to health literacy. Those who have the least access to health information, health care, and other social supports and resources are often less knowledgeable about health issues and are thus more vulnerable to chronic or untreated health problems. Many studies have shown that low health literacy is found at a disproportionately high level among specific racial and ethnic groups and non-English speaking or reading populations. Tailored health messages and health campaigns that target these populations is a key means of overcoming health disparities. However, health disparities along with health literacy disparities cannot be resolved without making concomitant efforts to change health professionals' perspectives and build effective and efficient social networks to support these underserved populations. For example, training health care professionals with basic interpersonal communication skills relative to diverse populations can help overcome the language barrier and misunderstanding between health care providers and consumers.

Effective Health Communication Campaigns

Developing effective health communication campaigns requires a great deal of planning and deliberation, incorporating both theory and research-based examples. Research has shown that health campaigns and their messages have the greatest effect, particularly in the short term, when they are strategically planned. For example, strategically planned health interventions have reduced the incidence and morbidity of diseases, self-destructive behaviors such as tobacco use, and other poor health outcomes.

The *Healthy People 2010* initiative identified several attributes of effective health campaigns. First, they should be accurate. Second, the content should be made available to the target audience. Third, health campaigns should present a balanced view that takes competing perspectives into consideration. Fourth, they should be presented in a consistent manner so as not to cause confusion. Fifth, health campaigns should take into account cultural, ethnic, linguistic, and other differences to be effective. Sixth, they should be based on the most recent and reliable clinical evidence and theoretical formulations. Seventh, health campaigns should be designed to reach the largest number of people within the target population. Eighth, the message delivery should be repeated and reinforced. Ninth, the content should be delivered in a timely fashion. Tenth, the message should be readily comprehensible to the target audience.

Meeting these criteria may be achieved through testing and evaluation. At the onset, audience research, including surveys and other forms of analysis, help health campaign planners to ensure that the messages are designed and targeted to specific demographic groups. Focus groups and other forms of pilot testing also help refine the message and ensure that they are being communicated effectively. Health messages are presented using a variety of media channels, including radio, television, newspapers, and increasingly, new forms of distribution such as the Internet. Depending on the demographic and psychographic characteristics of the audiences, some media channels may be more effective than others. For example, health campaigns presented in newspapers or magazines tend to be more effective at reaching older, more educated audiences, whereas a billboard or public service announcements on television may appeal to younger, less literate audiences.

A number of models of health campaigns have been proposed. Some theoretical applications have included the theory of reasoned action (TRA), the health belief model (HBM), and the extended parallel process model (EPPM). These theories have been especially influential for scholars and health professionals working at the level of individual behavior. HBM proposes that six factors affect an individual's reception of health messages: perceived severity, perceived susceptibility, perceived benefits, perceived barriers, cues to action, and self-efficacy. The first two categories describe a recipient's assessment of likely outcomes of behavioral interventions. Benefits and barriers concern the individual's calculation of the cost of achieving the desired result. Self-efficacy and cues to action are related to the confidence and necessary stimuli required to effect behavioral change.

In contrast, TRA places emphasis on the individual's attitudes toward making a behavioral change. TRA suggests that individuals' attitudes toward a health-related behavior and their evaluations of the behavioral outcomes affect assessments of the relative value of performing it; subjective normative beliefs, motivation to comply with the norms within a social network, and intent to perform a given behavior depend partly on individuals' beliefs about what others think they should do. Individual beliefs about resources or constraints also determine personal control and participation in the behavior. Finally, EPPM focuses on the message recipient's reaction to information about health threats. If the individual does not perceive that the threat is eminent, he or she tends to ignore or avoid the message. On the other hand, if a perceived health threat is dire, individuals are motivated by fear to take recommended action.

While these theories have had enormous influence on the development of health campaigns, recent research has challenged these models. Scholars have pointed out that health campaigns designed using HBM, TRA, and EPPM have a significantly higher degree of success in reaching members of higher socioeconomic strata. A growing number of health communication scholars and professionals have called for a radical reconsideration of health communication campaigns to meet the needs of at-risk and marginalized individuals with the goal of overall behavioral changes.

In developing health campaigns and the messages, particular attention is warranted to reach at-risk populations that historically have tended to benefit at a lower rate due to the correlation between literacy, including health literacy, and the positive benefits of health communication campaigns. A power differential between health campaign designers and message recipients in lower socioeconomic groups has often been found and leads to the failure of campaigns, in part because they have been perceived by the intended recipients as efforts to dominate and control.

Impact of Technologies on Health Communication

The dissemination of health messages through public health campaigns seeks to change individual awareness, attitudes, and behaviors. Mass communication channels such as television, radio, newspapers, and billboards have been the traditional media channels used to create desired health campaign outcomes. Nonmedia channels, including community intervention programs and particularly community-based programs that support individuals through group-level interventions, have also been found effective. Many researchers have examined the relative effectiveness of mass media channels versus interpersonal communication, but an increasing number of recent studies have shown that multiple channel strategies are most effective.

One key issue in designing and implementing effective health communication is to use appropriate channels and tailor messages that target specific audiences. This approach should target the demographic, psychographic, socioeconomic backgrounds and characteristics, language systems, media habits, knowledge, and health-related attitudes of the intended audiences.

For example, Latino media channels, particularly television and radio, have been effective in targeting the U.S. Hispanic population. Health communication channels are evolving as well. While the previous generation tended to receive health messages from direct interaction with health care providers, newspapers, or television, today an increasing number of consumers receive health messages from the Internet and other new media sources. Technological advances have increased the number of media channels, thus allowing more ready access to health messages that are often tailored to specific demographic groups. However, the digital and wireless revolutions also have contributed to a health literacy gap based on socioeconomic and generational discrepancies.

Interactive media allow individuals quick and easy access to health information and services, facilitating widespread and efficient distribution of health information among patients or other health information consumers. However, while the advance of technology into health communication contexts may bridge the boundaries of geographical and cultural differences, this advance creates a digital divide insofar as there are unreachable populations. Widespread use of interactive health communication and telehealth

applications also have the potential to obfuscate with inaccurate, misleading, or in some cases conflicting information. The jumble of competing health messages on the Internet is one case in point. The quality control of information seems to be a challenge for the information consumers who may make a decision based on the messages that they receive. On the other hand, some health-related government or agency Web sites, notably the National Institutes of Health, National Library of Medicine, and Centers for Disease Control sites, provide accurate, valid, and research-based information. In addition, the collection of personal health information presents new challenges for institutions that collect and manage this information due to privacy and confidentiality issues.

Jae-Hwa Shin

See also Communication Campaigns in Health and Environment; Health Communication and the Internet; Health Literacy; Knowledge Gap Hypothesis; Physician–Patient Communication

Further Readings

Atkin, C., & Wallack, L. (1990). *Mass communication and public health*. Newbury Park, CA: Sage.

Jackson, L. D., & Duffy, B. K. (Eds.). (1997). *Health communication research: A guide to developments and directions*. Westport, CT: Praeger.

Harris, L. M. (Ed.). (1995). *Health and the new media: Technologies transforming personal and public health*. Mahwah, NJ: Lawrence Erlbaum.

National Cancer Institute. (1989). *Making health communications work* (Publication No. NIH 89–1493). Washington, DC: U.S. Department of Health and Human Services.

Northouse, L. L., & Northouse, P. G. (1998). *Health communication: Strategies for health professionals* (3rd ed.). Stamford, CT: Appleton & Lange.

Shin, J. H. (2009). Developing constructive and proactive conflict management strategies in healthcare. *Journal of Communication in Healthcare, 2*(1), 78–94.

Thompson, T. L., Dorsey, A., Miller, K. I., & Parrott, R. (2003). *Handbook of health communication*. Mahwah, NJ: Lawrence Erlbaum.

U.S. Department of Health and Human Services. (2002). *Healthy people 2010* (2nd ed.). McLean, VA: International Medical.

HEALTH COMMUNICATION AND THE INTERNET

The impact of the Internet on health communication is so comprehensive that it has spawned a new discipline, which is called consumer *health informatics,* or *e-health*. The partial integration of health education, patient education, medical informatics, and health communication (the disciplines that preceded consumer health informatics) into e-health provides abundant opportunities and important challenges.

The opportunities include enhancing the nation's health literacy and creating the potential for health communication to evolve from social and commercial marketing to the use of informatics in provider–patient communication, patient-to-patient communication, patient education, and support for personalized medicine. Some of the challenges include the impact of the Internet on health disparities and discomfort among health care providers with the salience of the health information some people find on the Internet.

The Internet's transformative impact on the practice of—and research about—health communication is tied to the U.S. public's acceptance of the Web as a primary health information source. The National Cancer Institute's Health Information National Trends Survey (HINTS) recently found for the first time that the Internet eclipsed other mass media as a primary source of consumer health information. HINTS also reported that health information on the Internet sometimes is perceived as a more credible source than legacy media, such as broadcast health news or information on television and radio as well as print news/information from newspapers, magazines, books, and brochures. The Pew Internet and American Life survey recently found that 70% of Americans (with access) now report they routinely seek medical information on the Internet, and recent surveys report rising trends in U.S. consumer Web-based health information seeking.

Electronic Communication in Patient Care

In addition to its popularity, the expansion of health information and communication on the Internet is tied to its unique attributes and functionality as a mass medium and to the evolving use and potential of information technology in patient care. In terms of its characteristics as a mass medium, the Internet fosters individual participation, enables a customization of information, and provides both instant consumer access and a search capacity to manage large stores of health information. The Internet uniquely blends all legacy media (audio, video, photography, print, display, and multimedia) to make either learning or Web surfing more compelling. Also in contrast to legacy media, the Internet gives a potential voice to the user by enabling mass communication without comparatively high start-up costs.

Health communication experts Linda Neuhauser and Gary Kreps add that in contrast to legacy media, the Internet alters the potential cost-effectiveness of direct-to-consumer mass communication, mass health education, noncommercial public health interventions, and social marketing initiatives by making it affordable for health care organizations to communicate directly with patients. Cost-effective consumer educational and health services–oriented Web sites now flourish in clinical centers, medical organizations, and provider groups throughout the United States and other nations.

The Internet also provides an unprecedented resource for interpersonal health communication, using e-mail as well as blogs and Listservs for interactive peer and affinity groups of patients with common illnesses or conditions. The Web provides a cost-effective, accessible medium to enable patients and caregivers to exchange information, experiences, and emotions, and it enhances the creation of often useful and uplifting support communities across geographical boundaries. The latter is especially advantageous to families and patients with rare diseases and conditions, or to advance health-related exchanges between persons who share similar sociocultural and religious backgrounds.

Electronic Communication Within the Health Professions

The ubiquity of the Internet and information technology also may transform e-health and health communication's utility within public health research and routine clinical practice. Before the Internet, health communication initiatives focused mostly on noncommercial public health intervention campaigns (such as encouraging women to obtain a mammogram), social marketing and health promotion (for example, discouraging illegal drug use), or commercial marketing (including direct-to-consumer pharmaceutical advertising). While these initiatives continue, medical informatics extends e-health into clinical decision making for the first time. For example, in some clinical settings, information technology is a tool for providers to retrieve patient information and current research findings and provides an advisory resource that helps physicians make difficult clinical decisions. These same tools can be adopted for patient use, so health consumers are able to retrieve their medical records—perhaps with direct links to health information on the Internet tailored to a person's medical needs and literacy level.

While access to interchangeable medical records creates important privacy considerations and challenges, the trend is toward an integration of electronic patient medical records, patient health records, and public health information. The availability of de-identified, aggregate, interchangeable patient data on the Web significantly improves the body of individual as well as public health evidence. In addition, the combination of patient care use, providing tailored health information to consumers, enhancing public health research, preventing clinical errors, and improving clinical decisions all reinforce e-health's practical utility within the health care delivery system.

The high cost of medical care and treating chronic diseases (such as diabetes and arthritis) also are forcing a shift in health policy and medical economics toward early detection, self-management, and preventive care. These developments accelerate the expansion of e-health into clinical care because they create obligations for providers and patients to manage long-term conditions by staying updated via tailored, Internet-based, health education and information services.

All these developments pale compared to the potential revolution in medical diagnoses, preventive care, and clinical intervention that may result from genetic and molecular medicine. While analyses of multiple genes to determine flaws and resulting health risks are in their formative stages, major medical research institutions, such as the U.S. National Institutes of Health, anticipate a personalized, predictive, and preventive future in medical care—all of which depend on informatics-based analytical tools and the use of e-health in patient education.

Overall, e-health and medical informatics are poised to become a cornerstone of clinical care, which transforms their utility and importance. For the first time, health communication will not be confined to efforts that educate consumers about public health challenges, healthier lifestyles, and advertising medical products. E-health migrates health communication from population to personal outcomes and potentially integrates health communication, evidence-based care, and patient care.

Do E-Health Initiatives Work?

However, all this progress heightens the burden to demonstrate that personal and public health outcomes are therapeutically affected by e-health's expanded applications. Although modest evidence suggests that well-tailored health communication interventions can help targeted populations make better clinical decisions, as well as correct patient misinformation, encourage persons to seek care, expand health information seeking, encourage communication with providers, improve patient compliance with provider instructions, and change attitudes about seeking care, there is less evidence that e-health-based patient education is medicinal. Yet two relatively new subdisciplines affiliated with health education, patient education, and health communication—information therapy and health literacy—assess whether therapeutic patient clinical outcomes result from health information interventions (via e-health and other means).

Health literacy is defined by the U.S. Institute of Medicine as the degree to which individuals have the capacity to obtain, process, and understand basic health information and services needed to make appropriate health decisions. Health literacy's underlying purpose is to elevate the functional understanding of health across all patient populations. Health literacy starts with the premise that most Americans, regardless of socioeconomic or educational status, find it difficult to understand health and medical information, physician and provider instructions, signage in medical centers, prescription labels, and similar communications. Indeed, the National Assessment of Adult Literacy, the first comprehensive, nationally standardized assessment of the nation's health literacy, conducted in 2003, found that only about 12% of Americans had a proficient, functional understanding of health information.

In addition, some initial research reported by the Office of the U.S. Surgeon General suggests important associations among adult health literacy levels and some health services' utilization (for example, adults with higher health literacy spend fewer days in a hospital than people with low health literacy), as well as some clinical outcomes (adults with high health literacy are more likely to comply with immunization and screening recommendations than those with low health literacy). Other interesting findings reported by the surgeon general suggest that health literacy levels may be a more robust predictor than demographic characteristics and environmental factors (such as age, income, educational status, and urban or rural location) of how adults use clinical and other health services. Demographic and environmental factors once were thought to be the best predictors.

While health literacy began as a separate discipline from e-health, the assessment of health literacy and interventions—as a strategy to improve individual and public health as well as advance accompanying health communication initiatives—is attracting the attention of health communicators and medical organizations. The findings that specialized health literacy efforts coupled with e-health tools may enhance health outcomes have the potential to streamline and enhance health communication initiatives and better demonstrate the clinical efficacy of e-health efforts. The findings that there may be clinical benefits derived from communication-based or informational interventions also could reinforce the health care community's investment in e-health and patient education initiatives.

E-Health and Health Disparities

Despite health literacy and other boosts to e-health's momentum, ongoing countertrends exist. Parallel to the opportunities fostered by consumer health informatics are contentious issues that include the perceived overuse of the Internet (by some highly attentive audiences) and its influence on clinical care, combined with the underuse of the Internet (by less attentive audiences) and its impact on health disparities.

For example, some critics of e-health's sociocultural impact note that reduced access to the Internet among some U.S. populations, coupled with the cost of computer hardware and software, creates a digital divide. A digital divide, in turn, helps foster a vicious cycle of health disparities in the United States. Similar to the well-established knowledge gap hypothesis in mass communications theory, in health care the information-rich are perceived to have access to plentiful health resources, including Internet access, while medically underserved audiences are significantly less likely to use computers, have access to the Internet, or use e-health services. The U.S. Department of Health and Human Services identified the vicious cycle of health disparities as a critical public health, clinical care delivery, and sociocultural challenge because a higher frequency of acute, chronic, and communicable disease or illness and morbidity or mortality rates cluster within medically underserved groups. While the topic of health disparities is too large to address here, one of the future challenges in e-health is to ensure Web health services are available to medically underserved audiences. The U.S. Department of Health and Human Services recently prioritized improving access to Internet among low income, minority, and other medically underserved audiences, partially to address at least one component of the vicious cycle that fosters health disparities in the United States.

Turning to the other side, there is discomfort with e-health from some health care providers who find some highly attentive Internet users are too much influenced by the health information and advice they receive on the Web. In contrast to rare Internet use by some medically underserved audiences, some health care providers note that undue influence and overuse of Web-based health resources can also occur. Some physicians have suggested health and medical information on the Internet is perceived by some patients to be more credible and salient than health information and advice provided by health care providers, family, and peers. Critics decry the Internet's influence in instances where health information is not evidence based, promotes commercial products and services that are not regulated (such as some vitamins and nutritional supplements), or provides access to health care services that bypass U.S. regulation (such as selling and distributing drugs and medical devices on international Web sites that have not been approved by the Food and Drug Administration).

The Future of E-Health

Certainly, the future of e-health brightens when the Internet is used as a source of evidence-based information and facilitated communication instead of as a resource for disinformation or anxiety that providers feel forced to rebut in clinical care and public health interventions. Consumer health informatics resources have the potential to be clinically disruptive or to interfere with lines of communication between health care providers and patients. More positively, however, physician and public health concerns have fostered innovative services, such as the Health on the Net Foundation's seal of approval, to establish the accuracy and evidence base of Web-based health information resources. Health on the Net and similar services seek to provide authoritative medical information. But their existence underscores that e-health's public impact needs monitoring and leadership to ensure its remedial use.

Finally, the future of e-health depends on research that integrates its subdisciplines, which include health communication, mass communication, consumer health informatics, health literacy, risk perception, information therapy, public understanding of science, health education, and health information seeking. The separate development of related e-health disciplines potentially detracts from the integration of research efforts and the development of common terminologies, operational definitions, conceptual foundations, and other keys to advance research in a more linear, stepwise manner. While there are numerous challenges to create a common discourse among e-health's many disciplinary divisions, the demonstration of e-health's benefits to individual and public health partially depends on integrative efforts and multidisciplinary leadership.

Robert A. Logan

See also Computer-Tailored Messages; Digital Divide; Health Communication, Overview; Health Literacy; Knowledge Gap Hypothesis

Further Readings

Health on the Net Foundation: www.hon.ch

Institute of Medicine of the National Academies. (2004). *Health literacy: A prescription to end confusion.* Washington, DC: The National Academies Press.

Kassirer, J. (2000). Patients, physicians and the Internet. *Health Affairs, 19*(6), 115–123.

Logan, R. A. (2008). Health campaigns research. In M. Bucci & B. Trench (Eds.), *Handbook of public communication of science and technology* (pp. 77–92). New York: Routledge.

National Assessment of Adult Literacy: http://nces.ed.gov/naal/health.asp

National Cancer Institute. (2008). *Health information trends survey.* Retrieved October 24, 2008, from http://hints.cancer.gov

Neuhauser, L., & Kreps, G. (2003). Rethinking communication in the e-health era. *Journal of Health Psychology, 8*(1), 7–22.

Office of the Surgeon General. (2006). *Proceedings of the Surgeon General's workshop on improving health literacy: Health literacy, literacy and health outcomes.* Retrieved November 5, 2008, from www .surgeongeneral.gov/topics/healthliteracy/pane11.htm

Pew Internet and American Life Project. (2008). *Reports/health: The engaged e-patient population.* Retrieved November 5, 2008, from www.pewinternet.org/PPF/r/259/report_display.asp

Smith, E. A., & Malone, R. E. (2008). Philip Morris' health information Web site appears reasonable but undermines public health. *Public Health Nursing, 25*(6), 554–564.

U.S. Department of Health and Human Services. (2000). *Healthy people 2010* (Conference ed., Vols. 1–2). Washington, DC: Government Printing Office.

HEALTH LITERACY

The concept of health literacy initially emerged and continues to gain strength as an approach to improving health status and health systems because numerous research studies clearly link low levels of education and literacy with poor health and early death around the world.

Health literacy is a key component of the complex relationship between knowledge, attitudes, behavior, and health outcomes from the individual to the societal level. For example, a health literate person is able to improve individual health decision making and reap benefits from healthier lifestyle choices. In addition, a health literate individual is more aware of the social, economic, and environmental determinants of health and is more prepared to engage in individual and collective actions that can improve the status of those determinants.

Health literacy is increasingly applicable and relevant to practice within health care and health research systems around the world. Most of the major advances in health since the beginning of the 20th century are due to the application of new knowledge and technologies such as immunizations and preventive medicine. Health literacy is the fundamental skills and abilities that allow health systems and health care professionals to promote those new advances and allow individuals to receive, understand, and use that information in their daily lives.

The evidence base on health literacy includes significant findings that people with lower health literacy often experience the following:

- Poorer adherence to medical regimes
- Poorer understanding of their own health
- Less knowledge about medical care and conditions
- Poorer understanding of medical information
- Lower understanding and use of preventive services
- Being less likely to seek health care early
- Being less likely to ask questions of a health care professional
- Poorer self-reported health
- Increased hospitalization
- Increased health care costs
- Poorer health status
- Being less likely to receive needed kidney transplants
- Earlier death

The ongoing shift in the global burden of disease away from infectious diseases and toward chronic diseases and illness further increases the importance of health literacy. That shift requires increased patient self-management as well as behavior and lifestyle changes. Thus, there is an increasing need for an active and informed public with the health literacy skills to ensure, for example, that people maintain their prevention and treatment plans, including proper self-care that promotes good health. A continuing emergence of self-care and long-term care protocols as basic treatment, combined with cutbacks in health services (furthering the need for self-care) and increasing complexity in routes to access care, compound the need and utility of a fully engaged health literate public.

Further, as nations (in particular the United States) grapple with the ongoing need for health care system reform—in part driven by the shift in the burden of disease—health literacy is beginning to play a strong role in providing a conceptual basis and direction for health care reform. For instance, at the September 2009 U.S. Institute of Medicine workshop on health literacy and prevention, the argument was advanced that a complete understanding of health literacy leads to key recommendations that urge transitioning away from the current sick care system and moving toward a true health care system that embraces prevention. The recommendations included the following:

- Ensure that all health communication be at the appropriate literacy level for the audience
- Require health literacy training for all health care workers
- Establish health literacy learning standards across the life span
- Create centers of excellence for each state to develop and share best practices appropriate to local contexts
- Incorporate health literacy into national health surveillance efforts
- Build demonstration projects specifically targeting reductions in health disparities by using health literacy
- Create and monitor standards for hospital operations (via Joint Commission) based on principles of health literacy
- Emphasize health literacy as a solution in *Healthy People 2020* goals

Adopting such recommendations would lead to reduced costs, increased efficiency, and elimination of health disparities.

Support for the level of public engagement with the health care and health research systems that health literacy creates is found in almost every major contemporary public document that addresses health, development, or the environment. That policy discussion has led some to argue that both health and health literacy should be considered human rights, an argument perhaps most clearly advanced in the form of a formal policy document by the Constitution of South Africa.

Three domains of potential action are presented when considering health and health literacy as a human right. The first level is to respect the right to health and health literacy by not interfering with anyone's ability to be healthy or to be health literate. The second level is to protect the right to health and health literacy by making sure no one interferes with an individual's ability to be healthy or to be health literate. The third level is to fulfill the right to health and health literacy by fostering environments that encourage people to lead healthy lives, prevent ill health, and constantly improve their health literacy skills and for society to be prepared and willing to step in when any factor attempts to prevent people from reaching those ends.

Defining Health Literacy: A Field in Transition

At the end of the first decade of the 21st century, multiple and partially conflicting definitions of health literacy continue to appear in the academic and policy literature. For example, the U.S. Institute of Medicine (IOM) and the document *Healthy People 2010* in the United States define health literacy as the degree to which individuals have the capacity to obtain, process, and understand basic health information and services needed to make appropriate health decisions. A U.S. Agency for Healthcare Research and Quality effort limits that definition to just "patients' ability." An American Medical Association ad hoc committee on health literacy defined health literacy as a constellation of skills, including the ability to perform basic reading and numerical tasks required to function in the health care environment.

Researchers Ilona Kickbusch and Daniela Maag, most active in regard to European and World Health Organization policy, offer a context-driven definition of health literacy as having the capacity "to make sound health decisions" in ordinary life, whether at home or work, in the community, or within the health care system, the marketplace, or the political arena. Health literacy by this definition is cast as a critical empowerment strategy to increase people's control over their health, their ability to seek out information, and their ability to take responsibility. However, the generalities in the definition defy using this as a basis for measurement. Further, the notion of a "sound" decision is as judgmental as the IOM's goal of an "appropriate" decision.

Researchers in Canada, particularly Irving Rootman, and the World Health Organization have offered a definition of health literacy as people's ability to find, understand, appraise, and communicate information to engage within the demands of different health contexts to promote health across the life course. Christina Zarcadoolas and colleagues offer a comprehensive definition in their 2006 book, *Advancing Health Literacy: A Framework for Understanding and Action*. That definition neither limits nor conflicts with others by defining health literacy as the wide range of skills and competencies that people develop to seek out, comprehend, evaluate, and use health information and concepts to make informed choices, reduce health risks, and increase quality of life.

Recently, an effort to produce consensus on a definition of health literacy that included researchers and practitioners across multiple fields in the United States and Canada defined health literacy as the skills and abilities that determine the extent that all people can find, understand, evaluate, communicate, and use health information and concepts to make informed choices, reduce health risks, navigate the health care system, reduce inequities in health, and increase quality of life in a variety of settings across the life course.

A review of the most commonly cited definitions reveals several key attributes that are in common across these definitions (see Table 1). At least by default, this finding makes it clear that there is some consensus—albeit unspoken—that health literacy is a multidimensional construct. Areas of potential consensus seem to be possible around several domains of skills and abilities such as using, understanding, finding, and evaluating.

The Two-Sided Nature of Health Literacy

Despite a very strong early move in the United States to depict health literacy as something the public is lacking, current research and practice are increasingly embracing an approach that depicts

Table 1   Attributes in Commonly Cited Definitions of Health Literacy

Attribute of Health Literacy	Number of Definitions Attribute Appears Within
Skills, capacity, ability	5
Understand	5
Use, make decisions, apply	4
Find, access, obtain	4
Evaluate, process, appraise	4
Function	2
Read	1
Numeracy	1
Communicate	1

health literacy as a two-sided social construct in that it applies equally to the public and health care professionals. (See Figure 1.)

In this view, health literacy applies to all people—whether laypeople or health care professionals—in any part of the health system, as well as to the systems themselves.

For example, an individual can be health literate by having skills needed to find, use, understand, and use information. Health care professionals can be health literate by presenting information in ways that improve understanding and ability of all people to act on the information. Systems also can be health literate by providing equal, easy, and shame-free access to and delivery of health care and health information. Ultimately, many of the same health literacy skills and abilities underpin outcomes at individual, community, and system levels.

Health care system and professionals		The public
Level of demand	Health	Ability to participate
(Sending and receiving skills)	Literacy	(Sending and receiving skills)

Figure 1   The Two-Sided Nature of Health Literacy

Growth of the Field and Awareness of Health Literacy

While roughly a decade passed between what seem to be the first, in 1974, and the second, in 1985, uses of the phrase *health literacy* in peer-reviewed academic literature, the field has more recently experienced very rapid growth in terms of the number of peer-reviewed journal articles (see Figure 2). Currently, there are over 1,300 peer-reviewed articles published that refer to health literacy in the title, keywords, or abstract. However, to put that in perspective, the ISI Web of Knowledge database alone has over 3,500 articles on the white-tailed deer (*Odocoileus virginianus*).

Another indicator of the growth of the field is the number of individuals subscribed to the U.S. National Institute for Literacy's Listserv that focus on health and literacy (see http://www.nifl.gov/mailman/listinfo/Healthliteracy). Data provided by the Listserv manager, Julie McKinney of World Education, Inc., indicates that the number of subscribers nearly doubled from slightly over 500 in 2004 to nearly 1,000 in April 2009.

Finally, a third indicator of the growth and impact of the field of health literacy is the number of times the phrase *health literacy* appears in newspaper coverage. In the United States, major newspapers (as identified by the Lexis/Nexis database) used the phrase only 20 times during 1999. During 2007 and 2008, the phrase appeared in major newspapers approximately 140 times each year. (See Figure 3).

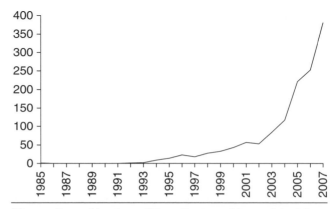

Figure 2   Number of Peer-Reviewed Journal Articles With the Phrase *Health Literacy*

Sources: Databases: PubMed, ISI Web of Science, Academic Search Premier, CINAHL, ECO, Ingenta, Science Direct.

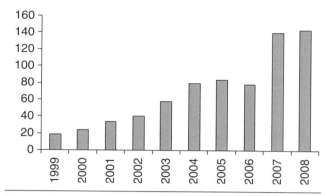

Figure 3   Appearance of the Phrase *Health Literacy* in U.S. Major Newspapers, 1999 to 2008

Source: Based on Lexis/Nexis database of major U.S. newspapers.

The Level of Health Literacy in the United States

In 2003, the National Center for Educational Statistics conducted the National Assessment of Adult Literacy (NAAL). This methodology attempted to measure English literacy and health literacy of U.S. adults over 16 years of age. The NAAL assessed both English literacy and health literacy in terms of three broad domains—prose, document, and quantitative.

Embedded within the NAAL assessment of English literacy were 28 questions (12 prose, 12 document, and 4 quantitative) that make up the NAAL health literacy scale. These questions address three health content areas: clinical (3 questions), prevention (14 questions), and navigation (11 questions). (See Figure 4.)

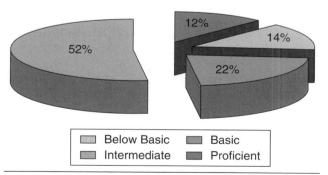

Figure 4   Health Literacy Levels in the United States as Measured by the National Assessment of Adult Literacy

Source: Based on U.S. government data.

There are two critically important findings that derive from this assessment of the health literacy of Americans. First, 88%, or nearly 9 out of 10 U.S. adults, are below the proficient level in health literacy. Thus, health literacy is clearly an issue everyone faces. Second, as health literacy improves, people say they are increasingly healthier. (See Figure 5.)

Through the early part of the 21st century, a wave of journal articles has reported findings supporting the assertion that most Americans do not have the necessary skills to comprehend most health materials. The NAAL data clearly indicate that the health literacy of "most Americans" is below the proficient level in health literacy. Therefore, "most health materials" deemed too difficult for most Americans must require a proficient level of health literacy. While this may seem extreme, the only other possible explanations are that the 300 studies are incorrect, the NAAL is incorrect, or that a limited approach to measuring health literacy does not capture the broad range of skills and abilities that people actually use to make informed decisions and change health-related behaviors.

Challenges in the Measurement of Health Literacy

Overall, it is worth noting that the NAAL health literacy component seems to assess only the ability

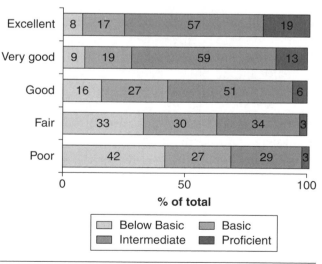

Figure 5   Self-Reported Health by Health Literacy Level as Measured by the National Assessment of Adult Literacy

Source: Based on U.S. government data.

to find information in text, plus sometimes to apply that information numerically. As far as can be ascertained from what has been published, there is no assessment of the skills needed to critically evaluate information about health or to put this information to use.

A further and important limit is that the NAAL limited assessment to individual skills and not the contexts in which health literacy skills are used in actual practice. In that sense, the NAAL measures only half the issue. This shortcoming is not limited to the NAAL, as it applies to all existing screeners of health literacy. These limitations reflect methodological, epistemological, and political challenges inherent to assessing health literacy as the attempt involves bridging diverse disciplinary perspectives and preferred methodologies. Thus, the current state of health literacy measurement is best described as incomplete.

Numerous attempts have been made to create measures of health literacy—but in a strict sense, they are best described as screeners rather than true measures. In part, this is because to date, none of the definitions of health literacy discussed above have been explicitly used as the conceptual basis for any of the many attempts to measure health literacy. As a result, there is a drastic mismatch between the skills and abilities included in the definitions and practice of health literacy and the skills and abilities assessed in existing measures of health literacy. The measures predominately focus only on an individual's ability to read health-related materials or to possess health-related knowledge.

There is also a mismatch between the measures of health literacy in existence and the content of health literacy curricula in use today. There is a growing body of curricula attempting to address health literacy issues. These target a wide variety of audiences and content areas.

A comparison of the content and targeted audiences of these curricula with the content and populations used to initially validate existing health literacy measures also reveals a large mismatch between measures of health literacy and actual practice. For instance, of the five broad audiences targeted by health literacy curricula—health care professionals, university students, medical students, participants in Adult Basic Education (ABE), English for Speakers of Other Languages (ESOL), and English as a Second Language programs, and

the general public—existing measures of health literacy were initially validated with, at best, members of two of the five (ABE and/or ESOL students and the general public). Further, existing measures of health literacy address only about one quarter of the broad and growing range of contexts and content present within health literacy curricula.

Despite a steady increase in their number, existing measures of health literacy fail to align with the growing body of theoretical and applied work. Existing measures are mainly focused on assessing what individuals cannot do in clinical contexts. What people can do, the interaction of health literacy with public health issues, the role of health literacy in prevention of poor health and chronic diseases, and the entire body of theory and conceptual frameworks of health literacy remain relatively unmeasured as a result. Building a new comprehensive measure of health literacy is the next significant and necessary task facing health literacy research and practice. Until that is accomplished, the state of health literacy measurement can only be described as incomplete at best.

Future Directions for Health Literacy Research and Practice

Clearly, one of the most pressing areas of future research needed is the development of a comprehensive measure of health literacy. That work can lead to the development of short and easy-to-use measures that reflect the emerging consensus in definitions of health literacy and health literacy curricula. Efforts to create valid and reliable national data sets as well as to evaluate the effectiveness of the growing number of health literacy interventions remain hampered by the lack of an acceptable measure of health literacy that is useful across multiple contexts and audiences.

The U.S. Office of the Surgeon General recently convened a workshop on health literacy, the World Health Organization recently convened an international meeting on health literacy, and there is a growing interest among researchers and practitioners in both clinical and public health contexts around the world. However, the field remains disjointed due to a lack of consensus on definition.

For instance, the lack of a comprehensive and widely shared definition and measure of health literacy lead many efforts to mistakenly assume that health literacy is simply the understanding of health information. That is an incorrect oversimplification. Health literacy is the skills and abilities that are required to find, understand, evaluate, communicate, and use that understanding—not simply the understanding itself. Efforts that move forward based on that misunderstanding of health literacy will inherently fail to provide people with the skills and abilities they need to live healthier lives. More unfortunate, that approach continues a top-down bias that blames people for not understanding what health care professionals may well be poorly communicating about health. While there are signs that a consensus on a comprehensive approach to health literacy is possible, there is a continuing need for an organized and global effort to create the path toward that consensus.

Conclusion

At the heart of health literacy are a few simple truths that are applicable to clinical and public health professionals around the world. These truths include knowing the audience—including the audience programs already have as well as the audience they want. Knowing the audience (or patients, or community) means that practitioners know how this audience prefers to receive information, what barriers are in place that keep people from using that information, and engaging with them to develop solutions to those barriers.

Health literacy necessarily requires that practitioners involve their audience(s) early and often. The ultimate goal is to empower people to take better care of their health, prevent disease, and create more efficient and equitable health care systems. That level of empowerment and engagement will not be the result of what some have called an "appropriate decision" as an outcome of health literacy skills. The primary goal of health literacy is more accurately described as an informed decision.

The goal of an informed, versus appropriate, decision is based on the evidence not only common to health literacy, but also common across the continuum of science and technology studies and public communication of science:

- People cannot be forced to make the "right" decisions as defined by a health care or scientific system.

- Science will always change—what is "right" today for one person or situation may not be equally true in all cases today or tomorrow.
- Evidence about health and science produced by the research system may indeed be global, but the use of that evidence is inevitably local.
- Thus, all people (public and health care professionals) need the health literacy skills to make an informed decision in the context of their lives and professions.

Health literacy has always existed. Research and practitioners, however, only began to identify the construct over the past two decades. Today, there is a surge of interest in both research and practice involving health literacy in both clinical and public health contexts. The field will continue to build evidence of the effectiveness of health literacy interventions and evidence of how to build better interventions. Health literacy interventions that work can and will be targeted toward health care professionals and the public at large—this reflects the two-sided nature of the concept. Health literacy has great potential to help people make more informed health decisions, help health care professionals have more and more effective engagement with the public, and help health care systems reduce costs, increase effectiveness, and reduce inequities in health.

Andrew Pleasant

See also Health Communication, Overview; Health Communication and the Internet; Science Indicators, History of the NSB Project on; Science Literacy; Surgeon General, U.S.

Further Readings

Kickbusch, I., & Maag, D. (2006). Health literacy: Towards active health citizenship. In M. Sprenger (Ed.), *Public health in Osterreich und Europa* (pp. 151–158). Graz, Austria: Festschrift Horst Noack.

Kutner, M., Greenberg, E., & Baer, J. A. (2005). *First look at the literacy of America's adults in the 21st century* (No. NCES 2006-470). Washington, DC: U.S. Government Printing Office.

Nielsen-Bohlman, L., Panzer, A. M., & Kindig, D. A. (Eds.). (2004). *Health literacy: A prescription to end confusion.* Washington, DC: Institute of Medicine of the National Academies.

Nutbeam, D. (2000). Health literacy as a public health goal: A challenge for contemporary health education and communication strategies into the 21st century. *Health Promotion International, 15*(3), 259–267.

Pleasant, A. (2008). A second look at the health literacy of American adults and the National Assessment of Adult Literacy. *Focus on Basics, 9*(B), 46–52.

Pleasant, A., & Kuruvilla, S. (2008). A tale of two health literacies? Public health and clinical approaches to health literacy. *Health Promotion International, 23*(2),152–159. Retrieved February 28, 2008, from http://heapro.oxfordjournals.org/cgi/content/abstract/dan001v1

Rootman, I., & Gordon-El-Bihbety, D. (2008). *A vision for a health literate Canada: Report of the expert panel on health literacy.* Ottawa, ON: Canadian Public Health Association.

World Education. (2009). *Health literacy special collection: Tools and resources for health literacy initiatives.* Available at http://healthliteracy.worlded.org

World Health Organization. (2008). *Closing the gap in a generation: Health equity through action on the social determinants of health: Final report of the commission on social determinants of health.* Geneva, Switzerland: Author.

Zarcadoolas, C., Pleasant, A., & Greer, D. (2006). *Advancing health literacy: A framework for understanding and action.* San Francisco: Jossey-Bass.

HIGHWAY SAFETY

Highway safety is a complicated science that rises to an art form as ordinary drivers perceive what engineers communicate to them in the road design, what government policies and education campaigns communicate in laws and in shaping public discourse, and what the culture of the driving public adds to their perception. This area of scientific and communication research ultimately has a profound impact on the well-being of citizens and the communities where they live and travel.

Highway safety is a worldwide concern because an estimated 1.2 million people lose their lives in road crashes each year, and as many as 50 million are injured. It is expected that close to 2 million lives will be lost each year on roadways by the year 2025. This human cost of transportation progress impacts both developing and advanced nations. The widespread loss of human lives and the impacts

of life-changing serious injuries are now considered a public health epidemic, sometimes known as "the disease of mobility." Over 40,000 roadway fatalities occur each year in the United States, and these motor vehicle crashes are the number one cause of death for persons age 34 and younger. This entry examines the factors involved in motor vehicle crashes and the solutions for reducing losses that both improve the roadway systems and attempt to change the culture of the motoring public.

Crash Losses Are Predictable and Preventable

This loss of human lives and the resulting economic impact have become unacceptable in many countries. Meanwhile, vehicle ownership and travel have been expanding worldwide. The most dramatic recent increases in traffic casualties occur in developing countries with very poor, congested roadways shared by motor vehicles and other modes including pedestrians, bicycles, scooters, and animal-pulled carts and wagons. In higher-income countries, high-speed congestion, distracted driving, vulnerable motorcyclists, and aging drivers confound efforts to reduce crashes.

Added to the profound impact on public health, roadway fatalities and injuries have a substantial impact on the global economy. The global cost is estimated to be $518 billion per year in U.S. dollars. The economic loss to low-income and middle-income countries exceeds the amount of economic development funds they receive each year. Within major U.S. metropolitan areas, the cost of traffic crashes is nearly 2.5 times the cost of congestion, at $164 billion for traffic crashes and $67.6 billion for congestion. And yet, communities and governments routinely demand more funding for relieving congestion than for improving traffic safety.

Roadway traffic crashes are not just accidents. They are predictable and therefore preventable events. However, both roadway crashes and the solutions are complex.

Addressing Crashes Worldwide

Globally, the World Health Organization declared road safety a worldwide public health epidemic for 2004 and tried to advocate a systems approach to road safety, which takes into consideration the key aspects of the system: the road user, the vehicle, and the infrastructure. Today, the World Bank will fund roadway safety programs, just as it funds responses to health epidemics, to improve the human condition.

The 2005 U.S. transportation bill was titled Safe, Accountable, Flexible, Efficient, Transportation Equity Act: A Legacy for Users (SAFETEA-LU), placing particular emphasis on decreasing fatalities and serious injuries on U.S. roadways and requiring that diverse stakeholders participate in planning and implementing effective strategies. This shift in thinking helped fuel nationwide discussion among mixed disciplines involved in health, highways, and law enforcement, and resulted in the American Automobile Association inviting experts in these diverse fields to contribute opinion papers to the publication *Improving Traffic Safety Culture in the United States: The Journey Forward.*

Australia and most Western European countries have implemented aggressive and comprehensive multidisciplinary highway safety programs, resulting in significant decreases in roadway fatalities, as well as decreases in the public's willingness to tolerate the numbers of their fellow citizens who are killed in motor vehicle crashes. These countries typically establish a safety goal of zero deaths and build public and legislative support for safety laws, which have proven to change driver behavior. Traffic fines are increased and tolerance for high-risk behaviors such as drunk driving, speeding, and red light running is reduced in both citizens and law enforcement. Australia, for example, set and met a goal for reducing roadway fatalities by one half in just a few years using this aggressive approach.

Identifying Crash Mitigation Strategies

In the United States, driver condition and behavior is a contributing factor in 95% of all crashes. It is the primary factor in 67% of crashes. Roadway design and weather conditions that drivers often blame for their crashes are a contributing factor in only 28% of crashes and are the primary factor in only 4% of crashes. Vehicle condition is a contributing factor in 8% of crashes.

With this mixture of factors combined, solutions to roadway safety cannot focus on just the driver or just the roadway design. Roadway safety programs must address the five Es of roadway safety: engineering, enforcement, education, emergency response, and everyone else (that is, driver behavior and the influence of culture).

Typically, the highest number of roadway fatalities—and also the greatest opportunities to reduce fatal crashes—are associated with unrestrained vehicle occupants (no seat belts), impaired drivers, lane departure crashes (involving single vehicles that run off the road or those that cross the centerline or median), and young drivers.

Implementing Crash Mitigation Strategies

Although the countermeasures for specific aspects of crash conditions and outcomes seem simple enough to identify, fully implementing these measures may not follow so directly because human behavior can appear to be such a mystery. In a 2008 best-selling book, *Traffic: Why We Drive the Way We Do (and What It Says About Us)*, author Tom Vanderbilt combined scientific research and common observations of the complicated and confounding nature of human driving behavior in approaching an answer to this complicated area of applied science. The book includes discussion of the powerful nature of the social climate and the culture that impact how and whether safety strategies can be identified, implemented, and communicated.

Human Factors and Traffic Policy and Enforcement Implementation

In the United States, a number of proven and widely implemented human behavior policies have reduced certain types of crashes, injuries, and fatalities, but they have not resulted in full implementation or full compliance among either governing entities or the driving public. Here are some examples:

- Despite safety belt laws, over one half of U.S. highway fatality victims were not wearing seat belts.
- Despite decades of traffic laws and drunk driving culture change, impaired drivers still contribute to over 40% of all fatal crashes.
- Motorcycle fatalities in the United States have more than doubled in recent years, exceeding

5,100 fatalities per year, yet only 20 of the 50 states require all motorcyclists to wear a safety helmet.

♦ About 60% of all fatal crashes were lane departure crashes, despite how simple it seems it should be for drivers to stay on the road.

Driver behavior is very difficult to change solely through driver education and public information campaigns because drivers tend to underestimate risk, believe their driving skills are superior, believe crashes happen to other people, and seem to want other drivers to behave so that they are not threatened.

Further, driver behavior is difficult to change because people see more reward than risk with behaviors such as speeding, running red lights, not wearing helmets, multitasking (text messaging, using cell phones), or driving in bad weather. In many countries, successful behavior-based safety programs have included key elements such as public awareness of the consequences of fatal and major injury crashes; a sound and realistic comprehensive; multidisciplinary safety plan; sound data for evidence-based decisions; political leadership; and a supportive media.

A broad change in national safety culture has resulted in a number of countries adopting legislation and polices such as the following:

- Automated speed and red-light-running enforcement cameras
- Meaningful moving violation fines
- Allowable blood alcohol content at or below 0.05
- Immediate license loss for all drunk driver offenses
- Random breath testing for alcohol
- Mandatory helmet use for motorcyclists and bicyclists
- Requiring all vehicle occupants to use occupant protection (such as seat belts)
- Restricted driving privileges for teen drivers

Such efforts can help change the way we think about driving responsibilities and consequences in much the same way that smoking in public or driving drunk has become unacceptable, resulting in changed social behavior across much of our culture.

Infrastructure and Roadway Improvement Implementation

Making major safety improvements to roadways is often very expensive, and in most cases, not cost effective. Using data to identify and implement appropriate countermeasures with limited resources is an ever-present challenge. Although today's travelers drive exponentially more miles than in the past, modern roadway crashes generally occur as rare and random events over an entire roadway system. A location with a high number of fatal and major injuries in one 3- to 5-year time period may not be likely to be considered a high-crash location in the next time period, even if no improvements are made. Methods of weighing costs and benefits can direct funds to locations where property losses accumulate from minor crashes instead of where lives are lost in severe crashes.

Selecting Systemwide Infrastructure Improvement Policies

Establishing a systemwide, low-cost improvement policy could effectively reduce the most severe and most common types of crashes without completely rebuilding roads or installing high-cost improvements at a few high crash locations. These policy decisions are best made using available data that correlate common crash causes and proven countermeasures.

For example, lane departure occurs on all roadways, and even occurs where there is no apparent geometric condition for a driver to get off track. Installing 4- to 6-foot-wide paved shoulders with rumble strips will both alert drivers before they leave the pavement and provide room for driver correction before a crash occurs. Data analysis indicates these enhancements reduce the frequency and severity of crashes. A policy adding paved shoulders and rumble strips to roadways with a certain level of traffic (such as 3,000 vehicles a day) would address the randomness of single vehicle run-off-the-road crashes and optimize the return on investment for limited available safety funds.

Implementing Systemwide Infrastructure Improvement Policies

Policy implementation strategies also allow for the opportunity to target limited safety improvement funds to prioritize worst first, using data analysis to identify higher-incident locations. Although paving roadway shoulders and installing shoulder rumble strips in a systemic manner will take a number of years, and will most likely occur as the roadways become resurfaced, major gains can be immediate and proven, with additional gains achieved over time. For example, for the first treatments, 7 to 10 years of crash data could identify rural corridors with exceptionally high single vehicle run-off-the-road fatal and major injury crash rates (for example, 4 or 5 times the state average). As safety gains are proven, accelerating the installation of additional paved shoulders and shoulder rumble strips could be warranted. A similar approach could be used to target high-crash rural curves.

Well-chosen systemic safety improvements could be integrated with an agency's pavement resurfacing program and result in safety improvements to some roadways, with valuable cumulative improvements even though a limited number of roadways might be affected. Most agencies program for resurfacing every roadway over 20 to 25 years. Low-cost safety improvements made over time as part of periodic resurfacing is both manageable and cost effective. Improved signing, partially paving the inside shoulder on curves, or flattening driveway slopes may address varied needs throughout the system.

Future Directions

Highway agency safety improvement programs are a very small portion of the total agency capital improvement program. These limited funds may best be used to target systemic and low-cost safety improvements. Equal effort must be placed on changing the safety culture to cause a shift in how we think about the responsibility and consequences of driving as we now do other health risks such as drunk driving and smoking in public, a strategy in which communication campaigns have obvious application.

All countries that have made significant improvements in roadway safety have focused more aggressive efforts on changing driver behavior, which is the primary contributing factor in fatal crashes. This requires adopting some controversial legislation and enforcement policies—in essence, creating a change in the safety culture of those countries.

The United States, for example, does not presently have an adequate safety culture. If countries across the world do not embark on a movement toward changing the safety culture, the number of traffic fatalities and serious injuries will increase and perpetuate this public health epidemic.

Thomas M. Welch

See also Communication Campaigns in Health and Environment; Optimistic Bias; Risk Communication, Overview

Further Readings

American Automobile Association Foundation for Traffic Safety. (2007). *Improving traffic safety culture in the United States: The journey forward.* Retrieved November 16, 2009, from www.aaafoundation .org/pdf/SafetyCultureReport.pdf

Rodriguez, L. (2002, February). *Communicating highway safety: What works.* Retrieved November 5, 2008, from www.ctre.iastate.edu/reports/chs.pdf

Safe, Accountable, Flexible, Efficient, Transportation Equity Act: A Legacy for Users, Pub. L. No. 109-159 (2005).

U.S. Department of Health and Human Services, Centers for Disease Control and Prevention. (n.d.). *Motor vehicle-related injuries.* Retrieved November 16, 2009, from www.cdc.gov/health/motor.htm

U.S. Department of Transportation, Federal Highway Administration: http://safety.fhwa.dot.gov/safetealu

Vanderbilt, T. (2008). *Traffic: Why we drive the way we do (and what it says about us).* New York: Knopf.

World Health Organization. (2009). *Violence and injury prevention and disability: World report on road traffic injury prevention.* Retrieved November 16, 2009, from www.who.int/violence_injury_prevention/ publications/road_traffic/world_report/en/index.html

HIV/AIDS PREVENTION AND COMMUNICATION

As the U.S. concludes its third decade of fighting to control and contain the spread of human immunodeficiency virus (HIV) and acquired immune deficiency syndrome (AIDS), governments at all levels, health agencies, nonprofit organizations, and special interest groups have come to recognize the importance of communication to their efforts. Given that the acquisition of HIV/AIDS is a multifaceted problem, requiring a multifaceted approach to effectively prevent it from spreading within high-risk populations as well as throughout communities in general, the role of communication in all forms—interpersonal, mediated, and mass—has played and will continue to play a central role in increasing knowledge, altering attitudes, and impacting risky drug- and sex-related behaviors associated with HIV/AIDS.

As researchers have learned to target audiences, develop specific messages for those audiences (or adapt them), and deliver these with sufficient frequency via mass media and other appropriate channels, intervention results have been encouraging. Clearly, one message is typically not effective for multiple target populations; as the target audience changes demographically, psychographically, and culturally, the intervention-prevention message regarding HIV/AIDS must be altered. For example, merely translating an effective intervention message from English to Spanish, without taking into account the cultural differences between those populations, does not facilitate the shared meaning essential to a successful communication effort. Nearly 30 years of research, across multiple target audiences, with a variety of educational and/or behavioral objectives related to HIV/AIDS acquisition prevention, has shown this to be so.

In the years ahead, as the average cost of treating an HIV/AIDS patient over 20 or more years continues to rise from its current estimate of more than $600,000, and disproportionately affected states such as New York, Florida, California, and Texas struggle to absorb a significant portion of these costs, effective prevention messages and other interventions will become even more critical. With millions of dollars at stake, and a significant number of lives hanging in the balance, the fight to prevent individuals from acquiring HIV and controlling the spread of the infection within various target populations will continue.

Historical Perspective

Researchers such as Merrill Singer have asserted that HIV is not an "equal opportunity" disease;

acquiring HIV is not a random event. As metropolitan areas develop, concentric circles of poverty are generated from the inside out, with the most economically depressed area typically at a given city's geographic center. Life circumstances within that center (crime, illicit drug use, unemployment, lack of adequate housing, improper nutrition, lack of health care, and so on), coupled with sociopsychographic variables (sexual practices, religious beliefs, attitudes toward family and government, level of sensation seeking, and others), combine to increase the likelihood of acquiring HIV. In short, place and the life circumstances associated with this place make HIV more likely within this population. For these reasons, Singer labeled HIV a *syndemic* (involving the co-occurrence of multiple health-related problems) rather than an epidemic and argued that prevention efforts must focus, to some degree, on altering these life circumstances if the HIV/AIDS fight is to be successful.

At first, the syndemic notion was not especially well received by the government, health agencies, media, or nonprofit organizations engaged in preventing the spread of HIV/AIDS. Millions of dollars were spent creating interventions (such as public service announcements or educational materials designed for middle school and high school curricula to make the nation's youth or the general population knowledgeable regarding HIV. While those efforts were reasonably successful in raising awareness and knowledge of HIV/AIDS and other sexually transmitted infections (STIs) for those groups, they did little to change attitudes and/or risky sexual and drug practices among the populations that were most at risk (gay men, minorities, and injection drug users, or IDUs, among others).

Well-established communication principles would argue that media messages and school curricula were appropriately and properly utilized to increase awareness and knowledge for the general population and its youth. However, for these low-risk populations, there was little need to alter existing behaviors or change more deep-seated attitudes or beliefs.

Such was not the case, however, for the high-risk populations, which live primarily in urban areas within which a disproportionate number of HIV/AIDS cases are concentrated. For those minorities, gays, and IDUs who were significantly at risk and living in a place where HIV/AIDS was far more prevalent, these generalized messages did little to limit or control the spread of HIV/AIDS. Changing risky sexual and drug-related behaviors associated with acquiring HIV/AIDS would require a far more targeted approach given that the behavioral-attitudinal objectives were much more difficult to achieve.

In recent years, while the George W. Bush administration (2000–2008) pursued the ABC approach to combating sexually transmitted diseases (that is, abstinence, be faithful to one partner, and use condoms correctly) and focused primarily on abstinence as a required component for federally funded school interventions, its critics maintained that limiting—and sometimes even excluding—contraceptive information from the sexual education curriculum led to higher rates of STIs and unintended pregnancies. Further, if one subscribes to the syndemic approach, the same critics argued that allocating the most substantial portions of the limited available dollars to reach youth living outside of the circle of poverty is inefficient and wasteful. Those who were unhappy with the ABC approach worked, instead, to create HIV/STI interventions focused on delivering culturally relevant prevention messages to target other audiences, often through venues such as youth detention centers, Boys & Girls Clubs of America, and other locations serving those who live within economically depressed areas. The sections below briefly summarize three such attempts, highlighting the manner in which well-targeted interpersonal, group, or mass media messages, interventions, or campaigns can impact the dangerous drug and sexual behaviors of at-risk populations.

Social Networks

During the early days of the HIV epidemic, when gay men were the primary target population, Jeffrey Kelly introduced the Popular Opinion Leader (POL) intervention, derived from the framework of Everett Rogers's diffusion of innovations theory. First used in Mississippi and Louisiana gay bars, the success or failure of this approach is tied to infiltrating a relatively closed system with the desired intervention message (use of condoms with all sexual partners), delivered to 15% or more of the setting's population, by someone perceived to be a charismatic individual within

that system. Researchers identified the group's potential leaders and trained them to deliver the condom use message if and when approached by someone in the bar. Initially, leaders wore a pin resembling a traffic stoplight to attract attention. If questioned, the leader would deliver the intervention message, and condoms were readily available for all patrons.

In this concentrated environment, the POL intervention was successful; condom use increased. POL has since been transferred and adapted for other at-risk populations, such as students living in college dormitories in St. Petersburg, Russia, with mixed success.

Social networks of so-called hidden populations such as IDUs are particularly difficult to locate, let alone infiltrate with an HIV risk-reduction message. One avenue for such contact is a needle exchange program (NEP) through which drug users acquire sterile needles in exchange for used needles. Some NEPs also provide tourniquets, drug cookers, condoms, and even food.

The complexity of creating suitable, appropriate messages for targeted audiences is reflected in recent research comparing responses to a series of commonly used HIV/AIDS knowledge questions and attitudes toward condom use by IDUs in the United States and in Russia. Surprisingly, not only were responses significantly different by country of origin, but also by gender within each country. Delivering brief HIV interventions when IDUs participate in an NEP program might well be an overlooked opportunity for effective communication regarding HIV/AIDS.

Interpersonal Channels

In recent years, J. L. King's book *On the Down Low* has drawn media attention to the supposedly common underground homosexual activity of African American men who are perceived as heterosexual in their communities. Given the social stigma attached to homosexuality in the African American community, especially in its churches, it is difficult, if not impossible, to reach these men with a direct HIV risk-reduction intervention. Given this situation, some researchers have turned instead to targeting women engaged in what the women perceive to be long-term, monogamous sexual relationships with "down low" men. Interventions were designed to reach these women in venues such as beauty salons and churches, encouraging correct and consistent condom use after educating the women on the down low behavior of some African American men. Drawing from what is known as the stages of change model, knowledge of one's HIV risk must occur before the women can begin to contemplate behavioral changes (such as insisting on condom use with their partners). This approach indirectly works to combat and prevent the spread of HIV/AIDS resulting from down low activity by educating sexual partners.

Given that "cruising" for brief, anonymous, gay sexual encounters is surrounded by a cultural taboo not limited to African Americans, variations of this approach might well be successful with other target populations, utilizing the same or other appropriate venues. One such population might be Hispanic men who cruise for gay or bisexual activity while excluding those behaviors from their own definition of what it means to be homosexual by being the receiver in these sexual encounters. Further, convincing Hispanic men to introduce condoms into their primary sexual relationships with a wife or girlfriend because they are engaging in risky sexual activities outside of that relationship is an added layer of complexity.

Disclosing one's HIV-positive status in any relationship is perhaps even more problematic. A book by Kathryn Greene and her colleagues explores the advantages and disadvantages of such disclosure from multiple communication dimensions. Losing one's job, being ostracized, and divorcing are potential outcomes of disclosing HIV. On the other hand, access to social services, educating others, and finding avenues to deal with the situation can positively impact the life of an HIV-positive individual after such disclosure.

Mass Media Health Campaigns

Over the last 10 years or so, various governmental agencies and private organizations have produced, disseminated and evaluated the relative success or failure of a series of health campaigns designed to combat the spread of HIV/AIDS within and among a number of specific target populations. Recent research by Seth Noar and colleagues assessing the impact of these campaigns concluded that, when sufficiently targeted and when communication theories and principles are followed, these campaigns are reasonably effective in reaching their stated goals. Three such campaigns in the United States were the "Condoms: They Go Where You Go" campaign, targeting 15- to 17-year-olds; the "HIV: Live With It. Get Tested!" campaign, aimed at youth of color from urban areas with high levels of HIV-positive individuals; and the "Use a Condom. Every Partner. Every Time" campaign, designed for high sensation-seeking young adults 18 to 26 years old. While these researchers want more emphasis on message design in future campaigns, targeted media campaigns do indeed offer promise as a means to combat HIV/AIDS. The potential for social media (such as Facebook or Twitter) as an avenue for targeted, tailored messages has yet to be explored in any depth.

Conclusion

As scientists throughout the world search for vaccines and medications to prevent the spread of HIV/AIDS and to treat those already infected, public health officials must continue to educate the population and encourage safe drug- and sex-related behaviors in this regard. The role of communication in this endeavor is clearly critical. A wide variety of theories and principles, developed and supported by communication scholars, lead to the inevitable conclusion that messages must be constructed in relation to the specific knowledge, attitudes, beliefs, and cultural perspectives of specific target populations if they are to achieve their desired goal. Clearly, one size does not fit all: Well-researched, carefully targeted messages play an important role in the fight to combat and control HIV/AIDS.

Kate Ksobiech

See also Diffusion of Innovations; Health Communication, Overview; Health Literacy; Online Media and the Sciences; Social Marketing

Further Readings

Centers for Disease Control and Prevention. (2008, August). *Estimates of new HIV infections in the United States.* Retrieved July 30, 2008, from www.cdc.gov/hiv/topics/surveillance/resources/factsheets/pdf/incidence.pdf

Greene, K., Derlega, V. J., Yep, G. A., &, Petronio, S. (2003). *Privacy and disclosure of HIV in interpersonal relationships: A sourcebook for researchers and practitioners.* Mahwah, NJ: Lawrence Erlbaum.

Kelly, J. A., St. Lawrence, J. S., Diaz, Y. E., Stevenson, L. Y., Hauth, A. C., Brasfield, T. L., et al. (1991). HIV risk behavior reduction following intervention with key opinion leaders of population: An experimental analysis. *American Journal of Public Health, 81*(2), 168–171.

King, J. L. (2004). *On the down low: A journey into the lives of "straight" black men who sleep with other men.* New York: Broadway Books.

Noar, S. M., Palmgreen, P., Chabot, M., Dobransky, N., & Zimmerman, R. S. (2009). A 10-year systematic review of HIV/AIDS mass communication campaigns: Have we made progress? *Journal of Health Communication, 14*(1), 15–42.

Prochaska, J. O., & DiClemente, C. C. (1983). Stages and processes of self-change of smoking: Toward an integrative model of change. *Journal of Consulting and Clinical Psychology, 51*, 390–395.

Singer, M. (1994). AIDS and the health crisis of the U.S. urban poor: The perspective of critical medical anthropology. *Social Science Medicine, 39*(7), 931–948.

U.S. Department of Health & Human Services, Public Health Service. (n.d.). *Making health communication programs work.* National Institutes of Health, National Cancer Institute. Retrieved August 30, 2009, from www.cancer.gov/pinkbook

HOLOGRAPHY

Holography is the science of recording three-dimensional information on a piece of two-dimensional film. It does this by recording the light that is scattered from an object in such a way that this pattern of light can be reconstructed when the hologram is viewed. The word *holography* comes from the Greek words *holos*, meaning "whole," and *gramma*, meaning "message." Holography is one of several techniques for representing images of objects in three dimensions that are attractive to science communicators working in science centers, museums, and similar institutions. In addition, teaching about holography provides an opportunity to convey important concepts in physics.

History of Holography

Dennis Gábor (1900–1979), a physicist born in Hungary, received the Nobel Prize in Physics in 1971 for his work on holography. Gábor was limited by the light sources available at the time, which consisted of mercury arc lamps that lacked the coherence necessary to produce high-quality holograms. Holography was given a significant boost by the development of the laser in the 1960s, which was the enabling technology to allow high-quality, three-dimensional holograms to be made. Significant advances in the field of holography were made by Yuri Denisyuk in the Soviet Union (who developed a technique for making reflection holograms) and by Emmett Leith and Juris Upatnieks in the United States (who worked on a technique for making transmission holograms); all created three-dimensional holograms that are similar to those we are familiar with today.

How Holography Works

In a conventional photograph, the film medium or digital sensor captures a focused image, recording for each point a value for the intensity of the light—and in color photography, its color. This results in a static, two-dimensional image. By contrast, in holography, the image that is formed on the plate is an unfocused image. The thing that differentiates this unfocused image is that it is recorded using coherent monochromatic light such as that produced from a laser. First, a *reference beam* is shone on the plate, which creates a pattern according to the phase of the light at any one point. Then a second beam, known as the *object beam,* is reflected off the object to be recorded, again onto the plate. As the light is monochromatic, interference occurs between the two light beams. This interference is recorded on a very finely grained photographic emulsion as patterns of light and dark. The plate is then processed to fix the image. To reconstruct the hologram, a light source is used to re-create the reference beam, and light is diffracted from the reference beam in a manner that reconstructs the light field originally created by the objects—thus, the user can see a representation of the original image in three dimensions.

Use in Science Communication

Holograms provide a very visual way for science communicators to advance concepts where three-dimensional representations are especially important; in addition, the technology presents an exciting vehicle for communicating a range of physics concepts. Holography also has the potential to be used in science communication to present a three-dimensional visualization of a three-dimensional object, where the original object is not available for exhibition. The Soviet Union made particularly effective use of holography in cataloguing and preserving its treasures and artifacts as three-dimensional holograms. A particularly notable exhibition of these took place in 1985, titled "Holography, Treasures of the USSR." Holograms are particularly suitable for static displays in museums and science centers where users can view holograms at their leisure; however, careful attention should be paid to illuminating the hologram so that it is presented at optimum quality to viewers. This will depend on the technique used to produce the original hologram. For lectures or larger audiences, small holograms may present a challenge to display—small copies can be passed around for inspection. Larger holograms that could be viewed by a whole audience are likely to be prohibitively expensive. Fortunately, a range of other technologies is available that can potentially be used, as described below.

Teaching holography is a good vehicle for teaching some fundamental physics regarding interference and light waves, as well as basic photochemistry. One of the things that makes holography such an accessible subject to teach is that it sits both in the arts and sciences, and so it is appealing to a wide audience.

Other Three-Dimensional Imaging Techniques

The term *holography* refers to the specific technique of encoding an unfocused three-dimensional image onto a two-dimensional plate. There are a number of other three-dimensional imaging techniques that are often misconstrued as producing holograms and that can be used to communicate three-dimensional information. Some of these might be appropriate for different applications where holography is not suitable.

Lenticular Imaging

A lenticular image is a plastic image that is overprinted with a series of cylindrical plastic lenses. The image behind the plastic lenses consists of a number of images taken from several different viewpoints along a straight line. These images are divided into fine vertical strips, and these strips are then interspersed. Often an image is printed onto a substrate that is then laminated onto a preproduced lens sheet. Viewing the image does not require any glasses or other special equipment.

Anaglyph Imaging

An anaglyph is a type of three-dimensional image where the images for the right and the left eye are encoded using different color lenses. Normally, either red-green or red-cyan color combinations are used. The anaglyph image is normally encoded onto a single color film or video that contains information for both the right and left eyes. The eye covered by the red lens does not see images projected in red light; however, cyan images are perceived as being dark. The eye covered by the cyan lens, conversely, will not see the cyan image but will perceive the red image as dark. It is also possible to encode a limited amount of pseudocolor information when generating anaglyph images using a computer.

Polarized Three-Dimensional Imaging

It is possible to make large, color, three-dimensional images by using two projectors with opposing polarizing filters fitted over the projector lens, projecting onto an aluminized screen. The audience then wears polarizing glasses that match the encoding of the polarizing lenses on the projector. This ensures that the left eye receives the left eye information from one projector, while the right eye receives the right eye information from the other. The viewer looking at the screen without glasses will perceive a blurry color image.

Volumetric Displays

A volumetric display forms a three-dimensional representation of an image contained within a volume. A variety of different techniques can be used to accomplish this. In a swept volume display, a rapidly spinning or oscillating display is rapidly updated with information pertaining to the image at that point in three-dimensional space. As the display sweeps through the space, it scans the three-dimensional image, with persistence of vision acting to splice these slices of image together and form the impression of a three-dimensional display. Another alternative method of producing a volumetric display is to have a static volume display. The static volumetric display consists of light-emitting elements that are transparent in ordinary use, but when activated, emit light or turn opaque. Whereas the terminology of *pixels* is used to indicate a point in two-dimensional computer graphic space, the term *voxel* is used as a contraction of "VOlumetric piXEL." Volumetric displays have been created that use pulsed lasers to create a ball of glowing plasma that hovers in the air—displays have also been created that will generate dots within volumes anywhere up to as large as a cubic meter.

Gavin D. J. Harper

See also Effective Graphics; Science Centers and Science Museums; Visual Images in Science Communication

Further Readings

Ackermann, G. K., & Eichler, J. (2007). *Holography: A practical approach.* Chichester, UK: John Wiley & Sons.

Saxby, S. (2003). *Practical holography* (3rd ed.). London: Taylor & Francis.

Unterseher, F., Schlesinger, B., & Hansen, J. (1996). *The holography handbook* (3rd ed.). Berkeley, CA: Ross Books.

HOUSE SCIENCE COMMITTEE, U.S.

The House Science Committee, more precisely known as the Committee on Science and Technology of the U.S. House of Representatives, was born in the reaction of the Congress and the American people to the shocking 1957 launch of *Sputnik* by the supposedly backward Soviet Union. A second factor was congressional realization that since World War II, federally funded research and development (R&D) had become continually larger and more important and that the Congress was not organized to deal comprehensively with this burgeoning activity. Since its inception, the committee has received information on scientific and technical matters, considered it, and communicated its import to a lay Congress.

The committee's original name was Science and Astronautics, recognizing the importance of both science and its jurisdiction over the National Aeronautics and Space Administration (NASA), an agency it formed and to which it gave the authority and resources to overtake the Union of Soviet Socialist Republics (USSR) in space. For years it was colloquially referred to as the Space Committee. Its internal organization has changed in response to events. In the beginning of the committee's history, three (out of six) subcommittees divided coverage of NASA, but during the 1970s energy crisis, it had two energy subcommittees and an environment subcommittee. It now has one space subcommittee, with energy and environment combined into another subcommittee, and it is referred to as the Science Committee.

The House Science Committee is one of 20 standing authorizing or legislative committees in the House (as opposed to appropriations, rules, and special purpose committees). For example, through legislation, these committees provide an agency such as NASA with legal authority to carry out a program along with general instructions on how to do it and an upper limit on spending, and sometimes with explicit programmatic limits—instructions not to do something.

Science Committee jurisdiction comprises diverse topics: energy R&D and demonstration projects and federal civilian energy laboratories; astronautical R&D; civil aviation R&D; environmental R&D; marine research; commercial application of energy technology; National Institute of Standards and Technology (NIST); NASA; National Space Council; National Science Foundation (NSF); National Weather Service; outer space, including exploration and control thereof; science scholarships; and scientific research, development, and demonstration. Arguably, the last item gives the committee the authority to set national science policy.

This is the only House committee focused on science, technology, and space. However, other committees' jurisdictions include R&D that support's their main focus. For example, Armed Services has jurisdiction over military R&D and military space. There is no equivalent Senate committee.

The committee deals with a variety of legislation in various ways. The Space Act (also known as the National Aeronautics and Space Act of 1958) creating NASA was its first authorization and is amended occasionally as needed. The committee passed an annual authorization of NASA funding for years, but multiyear authorizations now seem to be the rule. The same is true for other agencies such as NIST and NSF and for energy R&D programs. The Science Committee spars with the House Commerce Committee over energy legislation. Commerce has broad energy jurisdiction, including nuclear and alternate energy. Neither of these technologies is mature; more research is needed to improve each, and the Science Committee claims jurisdiction over this research; the two committees continue to quarrel over the jurisdictional dividing line.

On other matters, the two committees work cooperatively. In the mid-1970s, commerce was embroiled in a very contentious reauthorization of the Clean Air Act (1977) when the ozone-Freon issue arose. Research was needed to learn more about how the ubiquitously used Freon could cause destruction of the stratospheric ozone layer—which protects the earth from harmful ultraviolet light. So the Science Committee had a claim on the issue. Because Commerce was so entangled with the Clean Air Act, it turned the whole ozone-Freon issue over to Science—the research and the regulation. Subsequently, Commerce adopted verbatim the language passed by Science into its Clean Air Act. Similar cooperation eased passage of the Resource Conservation and Recovery Act (1976). At one point, the Reagan administration ordered that a remote-sensing satellite program, LANDSAT, be turned over to the private sector, or commercialized. Wanting to see a program in its jurisdiction succeed commercially, the Science Committee passed a bill to ensure a fair and open process.

The committee is generally supportive of programs in its jurisdiction—even across party lines. This is especially true of space programs, which bring dollars and jobs to members' districts and excite members and their constituents. Sometimes the committee might better support agencies by applying healthy skepticism toward agency proposals; for example, NASA's shuttle and station programs have cost much more and accomplished much less than originally promised.

Almost all committee members lack formal technical training; exceptions usually total no more than one or two (if any) out of the 40 or 50 committee members. According to one story, a new member with a PhD once asked the committee clerk to change his hearing nameplate from "Mr." to "Dr." She responded that she would be happy to but that people might think he was staff. (Traditionally, the staff has had substantial technical training.) Members often join the committee because a large NASA or other scientific facility or contractor is in their district.

However, to date the committee has not grappled successfully, comprehensively, or open-mindedly with the question of overarching national science policy. Typical efforts have merely endorsed the status quo. Many scholars see current policy as outdated, still based on the postwar Vannevar Bush report, *Science—The Endless Frontier*. The committee made a broad and sustained effort in the late 1980s that produced many hearings and reports on specific issues, but it was diffuse, uneven, slow, and not action oriented. And a new chairman killed the effort before a final report was ever written.

Radford Byerly Jr.

See also Senate Committee on Commerce, Science, and Transportation, U.S.; Space Program, Overview

Further Readings

Clean Air Act Amendments of 1977, 42 U.S.C. § 7401 et seq. (1977).

Fuqua, D. (1986). *American science and science policy issues: Chairman's report to the Committee on Science and Technology, House of Representatives, ninety-ninth Congress, second session.* Washington, DC: Government Printing Office.

Hechler, K. (1980). *Toward the endless frontier: History of the Committee on Science and Technology, 1959–79. U.S. House of Representatives.* Washington, DC: Government Printing Office.

National Aeronautics and Space Act of 1958, Pub. L. No. 85-568, 72 Stat. 426 (1958).

Resource Conservation and Recovery Act, 42 U.S.C. §6901 et seq. (1976).

HUBBLE SPACE TELESCOPE

No other name but that of astronomer Edwin Hubble would have better fit the telescope that more than any other has deeply influenced our collective imagination over the last two decades. In 1990, the Hubble Space Telescope (HST) became the first optical telescope to be put into orbit, and it has revolutionized the way we look at the cosmos. After its wobbly beginnings, the most famous space observatory in history was destined to influence a new generation of sky lovers and change the perspectives on the universe of everyone from professional astronomers to laypeople. Having captured the popular imagination, the Hubble is often featured in journalistic accounts of astronomy and space science.

Why a Space Telescope?

For thousands of years, the only instruments humans used to observe the universe were the eyes. These are a precious pair of antennae, very sensitive to a narrow band of wavelengths from around 380 nanometers (violet-blue light) to around 750 nanometers (red-orange light), the so-called optical band. It cannot be by chance that this is exactly the range of frequencies where our own sun emits most of its radiation, something about which Darwin's theory of evolution should have a lot to say.

Just 400 years ago, Galileo Galilei inaugurated a new era in which the instrument called the telescope would begin to aid these natural antennae in observing the sky. By progressively improving the design of telescopes, over the last four centuries astronomical observatories have flourished all around the world. Inside those often cold and uncomfortable buildings, astronomers would spend long nights, keeping their eye to the eyepiece, making use of increasingly wider and more challenging telescope mirrors.

This romantic vision of the astronomer was valid until around 50 years ago. By the beginning of the 20th century, scientists had already begun to realize that there were other bands in the electromagnetic spectrum, extending beyond the visible, but that most of them were precluded from astronomical investigation. Earth's atmosphere is actually a very effective filter with respect to the radiation coming from space. It prevents the harmful frequencies—such as X-rays, gamma rays, and even most ultraviolet light—from reaching Earth. These unexplored, invisible bands could provide astronomers with rich astrophysical information, as they would discover in the years to come.

In the 1930s, astronomers discovered another important category of waves that could penetrate the atmosphere, the so-called radio window. In 1930, the U.S. physicist and engineer Karl Jansky built the first radiotelescope (the initial goal of which was to give Bell Laboratories a way to identify noise sources that affected vocal telephone transmissions), and the era of radioastronomy began. This new discipline, developed largely after World War II, for several decades provided the source of some of the most amazing discoveries in astrophysics, including radiogalaxies, quasars, pulsars, and of course the idea of cosmic background radiation.

But things were to change only slowly. Eventually, the injection of resources by the U.S. National Aeronautics and Space Administration (NASA) made possible the development of new technology for the exploration of space and, most importantly, for the launching of satellites. It was then that the era of space telescopes really began.

The first of these satellites was launched in 1958, as a reaction to the launch of the first artificial satellite, *Sputnik,* by the Soviet Union, the United States' chief rival in science and technology. This was *Explorer 1,* built thanks to the fundamental contribution of the German-born physicist and engineer Wernher von Braun, an ex–SS officer and father of the infamous V2 missiles. Together with 500 other engineers and technicians involved in the Nazi missile program, at the end of the war, von Braun had handed himself over to the Americans, who offered him an attractive post in the space program.

One of the most famous early satellites sent to space was *Uhuru* (a Swahili word meaning "freedom," an homage to the hospitality of Kenya, which had offered to launch the missile on a holiday celebrating its independence). This was the first satellite launched solely to study X-ray astronomy, and it produced the first comprehensive X-ray catalogue with 339 objects.

The boom of astronomy-dedicated space satellites dates back to the 1980s and 1990s, when dozens of satellites in all wavelengths were launched. Finally, the color palette available for astronomers was enriched to include all possible frequencies, opening new windows into the cosmos.

An Eye in the Sky

It was during this era when space telescopes flourished that a project for an optical telescope orbiting Earth was first developed. The construction of the telescope was concluded in 1985, but the actual project dates back to the beginning of the 1970s. U.S. astronomer and theoretical physicist Lyman Spitzer in his paper *Astronomical Advantages of an Extra-Terrestrial Observatory* had argued as early as 1946 that putting a telescope into space would have numerous advantages. Due to an inescapable optical phenomenon, the atmosphere blurs and distorts all light coming from celestial objects. Thus, the angular resolution achievable from Earth is limited, whereas capturing light directly from space would avoid this degradation of the quality of images. This same phenomenon is the reason why the stars seem to twinkle at night.

The idea was not as bizarre as it might have looked back then. In 1969, a National Academy of Science Ad Hoc Committee on the Large Space Telescope had prepared a report titled *Scientific Uses of the Large Space Telescope* in which they studied the issue and urged the construction of such an instrument. At first, the funding necessary to make this dream come true was not available. But thanks to a downsizing of the project (which included a reduced mirror size), the lobbying of prominent scientists, and the cooperation of the newly formed European Space Agency, NASA ultimately acquired the needed financial support from the U.S. Congress for this project.

Delays in the construction of this extremely sophisticated technology meant that the assembly of the necessary spacecraft did not take place until 1985. But its launch was further delayed due to the 1986 *Challenger* shuttle disaster. Spitzer's dream was finally launched on April 24, 1990. The telescope was placed in orbit at 569 km altitude, orbiting around Earth every 97 minutes at a speed of 8 km/s. It is a type of telescope known as a Cassegrain reflector. Light hits the telescope's main mirror (2.4 m in diameter). It bounces off and then encounters a secondary mirror. The secondary mirror focuses the light through a hole in the center of the primary mirror that leads to the telescope's scientific instruments.

We Have a Problem

Once the excitement was over, astronomers' enthusiasm was dampened when, within days, it became clear that the pictures Hubble was sending back to Earth were more blurred than expected. Millions of dollars had been spent in vain, or so it seemed. NASA finally discovered a major flaw in the primary mirror. It was too flat on one edge by 1/50th of the width of a human hair. The aberration was due to a miscalibrated instrument that had been used to grind the edges of the mirror.

Engineers were able to come up with a fix just in time for the first servicing mission in December 1993. The system used was called COSTAR (Corrective Optics Space Telescope Axial Replacement), a set of optics that compensated for the aberration and would allow Hubble's instruments to function correctly. The mission was a great success.

Since then, the flood of spectacular images HST began to send back to Earth has started shaping our imagination with respect to the frontiers of our universe. These pictures have been the best allies of astronomy communicators. For nearly 20 years, Hubble's images have not only been a precious source of discoveries for scientists, but (thanks to an excellent communication strategy, in both the United States and Europe) have also reached every aspect of our lives, from T-shirts, to cups, to posters, to millions of screensavers around the world, all the way through to lay advertisements—which perhaps represents today's real indicator of a successful communication strategy.

There have been four other servicing missions (in 1997, 1999, 2002, and 2009), which have updated and improved the HST instruments and performed routine repairs. These include replacing failed gyroscopes (which are needed to point the telescope), changing solar panels, and lifting the orbit of the HST, which tends to fall slowly down toward Earth. Many of the telescope's components, in fact, were designed to be easily removed and replaced during these servicing missions.

The Legacy of Hubble and Its Future

In a review article appearing in the January 1, 2009, issue of *Nature*, Julianne Dalcanton, a University of Washington associate professor of

The Hubble Space Telescope after its final revision. Hubble drifts over Earth after its release on May 19, 2009, by the crew of the space shuttle *Atlantis*.

Source: NASA (2009).

astronomy, traced the history of this extraordinary instrument. She credits the location of the telescope for its success, and not just with respect to the resolution: Ubiquitous light pollution on Earth makes it virtually impossible to find a really dark site from which to produce equivalent images.

The scientific advancements Hubble has made possible are so great that they are hard to summarize, ranging from understanding the structure and evolution of stars, to the exploration of black holes and their links to galaxy formation, observing the evolution of galaxies over billions of years, and testing our knowledge of the expansion of the universe. Recently, Hubble even produced the first direct evidence of a planet orbiting a star outside

our solar system. But one of the biggest successes, Dalcanton points out, is the democratization of Hubble's data. All data the HST collects are available for general use after 1 year.

Thanks to the lobbying of scientists and most importantly, of laypeople interested in science, NASA decided to postpone the decommissioning of HST to 2014. By that time, if everything works smoothly, its successor should be launched, the James Webb Space Telescope (JWST, named after a former NASA administrator), which will use a completely different telescope design. Despite its impressive new characteristics, the JWST may never replace Hubble in the hearts of those who admire the space program. It will be primarily an infrared telescope, thus sensitive to a slightly different range of wavelengths than the HST, and it will possess a 6.5-m primary mirror. The JWST will reside in an orbit about 1.5 million km from Earth, and it will have a sunshield of about the size of a tennis court protecting it from the sun's radiation.

Luca Tancredi Barone

See also European Space Agency; Galilei, Galileo; National Aeronautics and Space Administration, U.S.; Space Program, Overview; Space Shuttle

Further Readings

Hubble Space Telescope: http://hubblesite.org

National Aeronautics and Space Administration. (2009). *Gallery: Spacecraft Hubble: Final release over earth.* Available at http://hubblesite.org/gallery/spacecraft/28

Dalcanton, J. (2009). 18 years of science with the Hubble Space Telescope. *Nature, 457,* 41–50.

Lindberg Christensen, L., Fosbuy, R., & Hurt, R. (2009). *Hidden universe.* Chichester, UK: John Wiley & Sons.

National Research Council (U.S.) Space Science Board Ad Hoc Committee on the Large Space Telescope. (1969). *Scientific uses of the large space telescope.* Washington, DC: The National Academy of Sciences.

Schilling, G., & Lindberg Christensen, L. (2009). *Eyes on the skies: 400 years of telescopic discovery.* Chichester, UK: John Wiley & Sons.

Spitzer, L., Jr. (1990). Report to Project Rand: Astronomical advantages of an extra-terrestrial observatory. *Astronomy Quarterly, 7,* 131–143.

Star Witness News: http://amazing-space.stsci.edu/news

HUMAN GENOME PROJECT

The heritability of diseases and traits has fascinated humanity since ancient times. Hippocrates recognized the hereditary transmission of many diseases, and Aristotle noted that children not only have some of the same diseases as their parents but also often share similar characteristics. Most recently, the Human Genome Project marked the beginning of a new era in which mutations implicated in human disease started being discovered at an increasing pace. Breast and ovarian cancer, colon cancer, systemic lupus erythematosus, macular degeneration, prostate cancer, diabetes, and psoriasis are just a few conditions for which the genetic basis has been elucidated in the years since the Human Genome Project was initiated. These advances improved our understanding of the genetic basis of several medical conditions and revolutionized the field of genetic testing. This revolution promises to bring additional advances in coming decades, as well as new controversies, and is destined to continue to produce prominent news items.

It is widely accepted that modern genetics started in the mid-19th century with the Augustinian monk and botanist Gregor Mendel. While breeding different varieties of peas to generate hybrids, Mendel observed that certain traits disappeared during the first generation and reappeared later in mathematically predictable patterns. He called these traits *recessive,* as opposed to the ones present in every generation, which became known as *dominant.* Thomas Hunt Morgan later proposed that a collection of small elements, called *genes,* localized in discrete places on the chromosomes found in the nuclei of living cells, constitute the basis of heredity. The 1953 discovery of the DNA double helix helped elucidate the molecular basis of inheritance, and less than half a century later, in October 1990, a massive international and multidisciplinary effort, known as the Human Genome Project, was initiated to gain insight into human genetic material and to better understand the genetic basis of medical conditions.

The project, considered to be one of the most monumental accomplishments in biology during the 20th century, cost approximately 2.7 billion U.S. dollars and marked the beginning of a new era, that of the *omics* sciences, which now include genomics, proteomics, transcriptomics, metabonomics, and toxicogenomics and is constantly expanding. Completion of an initial draft of the human genome was announced on June 26, 2000, and the project was officially completed on April 14, 2003, less than 13 years after it started. The National Human Genome Research Institute (NHGRI) and the Department of Energy (DOE) coordinated this massive collaborative effort, and the actual sequencing was performed at several research centers in the United States, the United Kingdom, Germany, France, China, and Japan.

How Many Genes?

Throughout the years, the number of genes in humans has consistently been the topic of debate. The human genome is comprised of approximately 3.2 billion base pairs, which were estimated, based on early predictions, to encode up to 100,000 individual genes. It came as a surprise when the Human Genome Project revealed that only about 20,000 to 25,000 genes appear to exist in humans, far fewer than anticipated. In fact, in what has become known as the C-value paradox, for many species, it appears that genome size is not correlated with complexity. The genome of the one-celled organism *Amoeba,* with an estimated 670 billion base pairs, is approximately 200 times larger than the human genome, and *Paramecium tetraurelia,* a unicellular organism, is estimated to encode approximately 25,000 genes, similar to humans. *Drosophila melanogaster,* the fruit fly, has around 13,000 genes, and *Arabidopsis thaliana,* a flowering plant, 28,000.

Scientists now believe that the complexity of an organism is not determined by the number of genes but instead is shaped by several other factors. One hypothesis is that alternative gene splicing plays an important role. While for several decades it was believed that each gene can encode only one protein, the path from genes to proteins is actually much more complex. Each gene is first used to produce a molecule known as messenger RNA, from which certain regions known as *introns* are subsequently removed while the remaining *exons* are joined by a process known as *splicing* to generate proteins. It recently became apparent that several possible combinations might exist to reconnect the exons encoded within the messenger RNA originating from a single gene, allowing several different proteins to be generated, a process known as *alternative splicing.* Alternative splicing is thought to occur in over 85% and, according to most recent estimates, up to 95% of the human genes with multiple exons, and many diseases were linked to mutations that affect alternative splicing sites. Another hypothesis proposes that the complexity of an organism is shaped by the intricacy of the interactions between

the various genes, and ample scientific evidence supports this view.

In parallel with the Human Genome Project, the genome sequences of many other organisms, ranging from microbial pathogens to mammals, became available as a result of other sequencing projects. This has facilitated comparative analyses between the genomes of various species, providing valuable insights into the evolution of species and the migration of humans across the globe.

Interindividual Variations

The Human Genome Project provided the answer to another long-standing question: that of what similarities and differences might exist at the DNA level between individuals. Sequencing the human genome revealed that any two individuals are 99.9% identical at the DNA level. However, the most interesting part appears to revolve around the remaining 0.1% of the chromosome, which sets different individuals apart from each other. Among the 3.2 billion base pairs of the human genome, approximately 3.1 million such differences, known as single nucleotide polymorphisms (SNPs), are currently reported, and as new ones are continually discovered, their real number is projected to reach 10 million.

SNPs shape disease predisposition, adverse effects to medication, and sensitivity to environmental chemicals. In October 2002, the International HapMap project was initiated, which proposed to catalog single nucleotide polymorphisms and examine their involvement in health and disease. This initiative proposed to sequence the genomes of people from four different populations: the Yoruba ethnic group in Ibadan, Nigeria; Japanese individuals from Tokyo with ancestry in different parts of the country; Utah residents of European ancestry; and Han Chinese individuals from Beijing. The HapMap project reached its first major milestone in the spring of 2005 when it reported the identification of 1.1 million SNPs, and a second generation HapMap data set released in October contained an additional 2.1 million SNPs.

While SNPs were initially thought to represent the only type of interindividual variation, an additional source of genomic variation emerged in recent years, when investigators revealed that many genes or chromosomal regions, ranging in size from

1,000 base pairs to several millions of base pairs, are present in different numbers in different individuals. As a result, one person may have one copy, while others may harbor six or seven copies or even more. Copy number variations represent a major source of genetic variability that collectively includes more nucleotides per genome than the total number of SNPs. One survey reported 1,447 copy number variations that cover approximately 12% of the human genome. Some copy number variations are described in otherwise healthy individuals, while others were linked to cancer, neuropsychiatric conditions, autoimmune diseases, HIV susceptibility, and responses to medication. For example, a study revealed that 10% of patients with major depression who did not respond to certain medications harbored duplications of a particular gene, compared to less than 1% of individuals in the general population.

The 1000 Genomes Project and the $1,000 Genome

Interindividual DNA variations can explain why certain individuals are predisposed to specific medical conditions, do not respond to medication in similar ways, or develop adverse effects during treatment. To better understand interindividual variations, a collaborative project called the 1000 Genomes Project was launched in January 2008 between the NHGRI of the U.S. National Institutes of Health (NIH–NHGRI; Bethesda, Maryland), the Wellcome Trust Sanger Institute (Hinxton, United Kingdom), and the Beijing Genomics Institute (Shenzhen, China). By taking advantage of recent developments in DNA sequencing, which enable genomes to be sequenced much faster and more accurately than ever before, this project intends to provide high-resolution maps of SNPs and copy number variations by examining the genomes of approximately 1,200 individuals originating from Nigeria, Kenya, Japan, the United States, Italy, and China. The 1000 Genomes Project, the most detailed analysis of human genomic variation to date, proposed to sequence the equivalent of approximately two human genomes every 24 hours and is estimated to cost between $30 and $50 million.

These advances could not have been possible without developments in DNA sequencing methodologies that occurred during recent years. The first genome that was sequenced in 1977 with the method developed by Frederick Sanger, for which he later received his second Nobel Prize, was that of the bacteriophage φX174, which infects bacteria such as *Escherichia coli*, has a single-stranded genome of 5,386 bases, and encodes only 11 genes. With the currently available technologies, millions of base pairs can be sequenced within hours or days. As sequencing costs are decreasing, several companies are engaged in the race toward the $1,000 human genome, which proposes to sequence an individual's genome for $1,000 and represents the next milestone toward personalized medicine in which individual genetic and genomic characteristics would be taken into consideration during medical decisions.

Ethical, Social, and Legal Implications

Over 13 million people in the United States are impacted by approximately 15,500 different genetic disorders recognized today, and up to 30% of infant deaths are associated with genetic diseases. The discovery of increasing numbers of mutations has provided new opportunities to understand more and more medical conditions and reactions to chemical compounds, and it contributed to the development of genetic testing. The plethora of genetic information that has emerged also opens significant ethical, social, and legal challenges.

Approximately 1,200 genetic tests are currently available, and they fall into several categories that often overlap. Newborn screening detects diseases such as phenylketonuria, which often can be treated if recognized in time. Diagnostic testing helps confirm genetic conditions that are suspected based on clinical manifestations and/or family history. Predictive testing detects mutations in healthy individuals who do not have clinical disease but could develop it over time—for example, BRCA1 mutations indicate an increased risk to develop breast cancer but cannot predict whether or when the disease will develop. Preimplantation genetic testing can detect mutations in embryos, forensic testing is used to attribute paternity or solve criminal investigations, and other genetic tests are informative about predispositions to develop certain adverse responses to medications or environmental toxins.

It is important to remember the limitations of genetic testing. Most mutations have a predictive value and reveal predisposition toward a disease but, with very few exceptions, cannot tell with certainty whether or when the individual will develop the condition. For example, testing for BRCA1 and BRCA2 mutations, which were linked to breast and ovarian cancers, can provide several benefits. Carriers can decide to undergo more frequent screenings, exercise their reproductive choices, change lifestyle habits, or even make decisions about prophylactic surgery. However, a positive test could falsely make people believe that they will develop the disease, despite studies showing that 10% to 15% of women harboring mutations never become ill. In addition, not all breast and ovarian cancers are genetic, and a negative genetic test could create a false sense of security leading to decreased surveillance and the possibility to miss a tumor that is otherwise detectable in early stages by regular screening.

Even though new mutations are discovered at an increasing and unprecedented rate, we still lack the ability to meaningfully interpret their significance. Specific mutations are often linked to more than one medical condition—for example, the same chromosomal deletion has been implicated in autism, schizophrenia, epilepsy, and intellectual disability. At the same time, mutations in several different genes are often linked to the same disease, and interpreting the significance of a specific mutation often represents a challenging task.

Every genetic test brings its own ethical dilemmas. Genetic testing for cystic fibrosis, a recessive disease, can identify asymptomatic carriers who do not have the disease and will not develop it in the future but may transmit the mutation to their children, who can develop the condition if they inherit a second copy of the mutation from the other parent. It is debatable whether individuals should learn about their carrier status early, during childhood or adolescence, or only once they reach adulthood, when this piece of information becomes relevant as part of their reproductive choices. Another medical condition, Huntington's disease, is dominantly transmitted—meaning that one copy of the mutated gene is sufficient to cause disease. This genetic test has diagnostic value in symptomatic people, but it can also reveal the existence of a mutation in clinically healthy individuals decades before the onset of neurological manifestations. Children with one affected parent have a 50% chance to harbor the mutation and to develop the disease throughout their lifetime. Particularly in the absence of any currently available treatment options, the benefits provided by testing for this progressive neurodegenerative condition are widely debated.

Another source of ethical debates is the recent availability of direct-to-consumer genetic tests, which companies market directly to consumers, often without counseling and without the involvement of health professionals. One study found that of 14 companies offering health-related tests online, only 6 described the availability of counseling. In addition, it was reported that the clinical validity of the association between the mutation and disease is not always clearly established. For example, a few years ago, a company was offering direct-to-consumer apoE genetic testing to predict Alzheimer's disease risk even though, at the time, professional societies recommended against performing this test due to its insufficient sensitivity and specificity for this application.

The availability of genomic information generates fervent discussions regarding its potential misuse. Several controversies surround the status of genetic information: Should genetic test results enjoy the same degree of privacy as routine medical and laboratory tests, or do they deserve enhanced security and protection measures? Even the definition of what constitutes genetic information is debated, and with good reason. While a BRCA1 mutation indicates predisposition to breast cancer, so does family history, which can unveil the existence of breast cancer in one or several of the patient's first-degree relatives. In fact, a patient's family history has for millennia represented the foundation of all medical exams, and learning about diseases affecting family members, or even about the age at which a patient's parents or siblings died, are very powerful indicators of certain genetic diseases in the family. This view supports the idea that genetic information is not so distinct from medical information. On the other hand, genetic tests can reveal predispositions in other family members, and this represents one of the arguments in favor of considering them more powerfully private than medical tests.

Unlike other biological samples, DNA can be stored for a long time and used, many years later, to repeat the genetic test or perform a new one. For example, the amplification of DNA from viral sequences that infected 1,500-year-old Andean mummies found in Chile provided details about the migration of human populations, and HIV amplification from a stored biopsy sample that belonged to a 1959 African patient confirmed that the infection existed in the human population decades before it emerged worldwide in the 1980s. Therefore, the debates surrounding privacy and confidentiality in genetic testing involve not only the actual test results, but also the DNA sample that was used to perform the test. Furthermore, obtaining informed consent for retesting old DNA samples years after an initial test, when locating the person who provided the sample might be challenging, represents an additional source of dilemmas.

An important facet of genetic testing is the concept of incidental findings. Similar to the situation encountered in clinical medicine, when an X-ray can often reveal findings in organs that are distinct from the one that the examination was conducted for, genetic tests can also unveil predispositions to conditions that are different from the one that constituted the initial reason to perform the test. For example, a mutation in a gene that can predict cardiovascular disease risk is, at the same time, informative about Alzheimer's disease risk. It is unclear what are the obligations of health care professionals who perform a genetic test and discover that their patient is predisposed to a different or to an additional disease, particularly as it is increasingly recognized that, in addition to their right to be tested and learn about their medical conditions, individuals also have a right not to know about genetic predispositions about which they did not ask.

The availability of genetic and genomic information has far-reaching social and legal implications, and while several laws were recently passed worldwide, more legislative oversight is required to prevent potential discrimination in health insurance, life insurance, and employment. In what is probably the most widely reported example, in February 2001, the U.S. Equal Employment Opportunity Commission filed a federal lawsuit against the Burlington Northern Railway Company, claiming that the company used blood samples to perform a genetic test for predisposition to develop a form of carpal tunnel syndrome without employees' knowledge or consent. The company subsequently settled and agreed to stop testing. At the same time, workplace testing, by being able to uncover early signs of disease caused by exposure to chemicals long before clinical manifestations become apparent, also represents an important tool for health care management. Recently, it was reported that the widow of a deceased employee filed a lawsuit against the employer, who failed to include her husband in a testing program that could have detected early signs of leukemia, a condition that can result from workplace benzene exposure.

Genetic testing promises to reshape the patient–physician relationship and family dynamics. While genetic information is private and personal, it sometimes reveals details about disease predispositions in other family members. This creates a conflict for medical professionals, who have to find the balance between respecting a patient's confidentiality and notifying family members at risk or, in other words, decide whether an individual's right to privacy would prevail over a family member's right to know. It is unclear whether genetic information belongs to the individual who was tested, who might harbor mutations absent in other family members, or whether the entire family has a right to know because genetic conditions, by definition, are transmitted in families and concern families as a whole. Debates surrounding this dilemma have opened discussions surrounding even the definition of family for the purposes of genetic testing. While some scholars recommend that genetic testing and counseling be provided to the family as a unit, as this would eliminate certain conflicts of interest, others have pointed out that, in many families, adult children and parents live in different geographic areas, making it impractical to visit the same genetic counselor or physician. Ethical guidelines will play a fundamental role in addressing these issues, which represent previously unexplored facets of the biomedical and social sciences.

Richard A. Stein

See also Crick, Francis; Gene; Mendel, Gregor; National Institutes of Health, U.S.; Venter, J. Craig

Further Readings

Coulthart, M. B., Posada, D., Crandall, K. A., & Dekaban, G. A. (2006). On the phylogenetic placement of human T cell leukemia virus type 1 sequences associated with an Andean mummy. *Infection, Genetics and Evolution, 6*(2), 91–96.

Freeman, J. L., Perry, G. H., Feuk, L., Redon, R., McCarroll, S. A., Altshuler, D. M., et al. (2006). Copy number variation: New insights in genome diversity. *Genome Research, 16*(8), 949–961.

Geransar, R., & Einsiedel, E. (2008). Evaluating online direct-to-consumer marketing of genetic tests: Informed choices or buyers beware? *Genetic Testing, 12*(1), 13–23.

Gollust, S. E., Wilfond, B. S., & Hull, S. C. (2003). Direct-to-consumer sales of genetic services on the Internet. *Genetic Medicine, 5*(4), 332–337.

Greely, H. T. (1998). Legal, ethical, and social issues in human genome research. *Annual Reviews of Anthropology, 27*, 473–502.

Hayden, E. C. (2008). International genome project launched. *Nature, 451*(7177), 378–379.

International HapMap Consortium. (2003). The International HapMap Project. *Nature, 426*, 789–796.

Kawanishi, C., Lundgren, S., Agren, H., & Bertilsson, L. (2004). Increased incidence of *CYP2D6* gene duplication in patients with persistent mood disorders: Ultrarapid metabolism of antidepressants as a cause of nonresponse. A pilot study. *European Journal of Clinical Pharmacology, 59*(11), 803–807.

Kim, E., Goren, A., & Ast, G. (2008). Alternative splicing: Current perspectives. *Bioessays, 30*(1), 38–47.

Lander, E. S., Linton, L. M., Birren, B., Nusbaum, C., Zody, M. C., Bladwin, J., et al. (2001). Initial sequencing and analysis of the human genome. *Nature, 409*(6822), 860–921.

Levine, M., & Tjian, R. (2003). Transcription regulation and animal diversity. *Nature, 424*(6945), 147–151.

Meyers, B. C., Scalabrin, S., & Morgante, M. (2004). Mapping and sequencing complex genomes: Let's get physical! *Nature Reviews Genetics, 5*(8), 578–588.

Pan, Q., Shai, O., Lee, L. J., Frey, B. J., & Blencowe, B. J. (2008). Deep surveying of alternative splicing complexity in the human transcriptome by high-throughput sequencing. *Nature Genetics, 40*, 1413–1415.

Redon, R., Ishikawa, S., Fitch, K. R., Feuk, L., Perry, G. H., Andrews, D., et al. (2006). Global variation in copy number in the human genome. *Nature, 444*(7118), 444–454.

Venter, J. C., Adams, M. D., & Myers, E. W. (2001). The sequence of the human genome. *Science, 291*(5507), 1304–1351.

Wade, C. H., & Wilfond, B. S. (2006). Ethical and clinical practice considerations for genetic counselors related to direct-to-consumer marketing of genetic tests. *American Journal of Medical Genetics Part C: Seminars in Medical Genetics, 142C*(4), 284–292, discussion 293.

Weinstein, M., Widenor, M., & Hecker, S. (2005). Health and employment practices: Ethical, legal, and social implications of advances in toxicogenomics. *American Association of Occupational Health Nurses Journal, 53*(12), 529–533.

Worobey, M., Gemmel, M., Teuwen, D. E., Haselkorn, T., Kunstman, K., Bunce, M., et al. (2008) Direct evidence of extensive diversity of HIV-1 in Kinshasa by 1960. *Nature, 455*(7213), 661–664.

HURRICANE KATRINA

In late August 2005, much of the United States tracked the progress of Hurricane Katrina, as reported by the National Hurricane Center (NHC), National Weather Service (NWS) forecast offices, and news media. The hurricane strengthened considerably as it moved over the warm waters of the Gulf of Mexico and caused devastating effects on the Gulf Coast, especially in Louisiana and Mississippi. Warnings and evacuation orders were issued well ahead of the storm, but many lives were lost, and there was tens of billions of dollars in property damage. Reporting on the storm and its aftereffects was a national focus for weeks, and reporting regarding recovery efforts and the effects of displacement on coastal residents continues years after the incident. Understanding the physical conditions of the storm, as well as its effects, is important for communications efforts.

Storm History

Since the 1980s, hurricane tracking and forecasting have improved significantly, as has the ability to communicate to more people through a variety of media. Tracking the development and movement of Hurricane Katrina and the early messages of its likely landfall locations epitomize our current capabilities with respect to storm warnings.

The storm began as a tropical depression on August 22, over the southeastern Bahamas, and intensified to become a tropical storm (see Table 1) on August 24, at which time it was named Katrina. The storm reached hurricane status the afternoon of Thursday, August 25, as it approached landfall on the southeastern coast of Florida. Hurricane Katrina made its first U.S. landfall in the Miami area at 6:30 P.M. on August 25, with maximum sustained winds of about 81 miles per hour (mph). Very heavy rainfall occurred as the storm moved across southern Florida, bringing over 12 inches of precipitation in some locales. Six people died in Florida from the direct effects (wind and water) of Hurricane Katrina. Katrina weakened back to tropical storm status before entering the Gulf of Mexico early on August 26.

The storm rapidly regained hurricane status after reaching the Gulf of Mexico. At that time, gulf waters were exceptionally warm, providing Katrina with the energy to intensify. By Friday evening, August 26, Katrina was a Category 2 storm.

Once in the Gulf of Mexico, Hurricane Katrina intensified rapidly, becoming a Category 3 hurricane with 115 mph winds by the morning of August 27. In addition to increasingly strong winds, the storm nearly doubled in size on August 27, with tropical storm force winds as far as 160 miles from the center. The hurricane turned toward the northwest and strengthened to a Category 5 storm on August 28, with winds at 167 mph; it reached a 173 mph peak intensity later that day, about 195 miles southeast of the Mississippi River delta. Katrina became very large, with hurricane force winds extending about 100 miles from the storm center and tropical storm force winds to about 230 miles.

Hurricane Katrina's path turned northward early on Monday, August 29. The storm weakened considerably due to internal storm changes and made landfall in Louisiana's Plaquemines Parish, as a strong Category 3 storm with estimated maximum sustained winds of about 126 mph. Hurricane strength often is judged by atmospheric pressure in the center of the storm, as well as by wind speeds; low pressures are associated with stronger storms. Central pressure of Hurricane Katrina at the time

Table 1   Tropical Storm and Saffir-Simpson Hurricane Scale Divisions, With Maximum Sustained (1-Minute Average) Wind Speeds in Miles Per Hour (Knots)

	Wind Speeds
Tropical Storm	39–73 mph (34–63 kt)
Hurricane Categories	
1	74–95 mph (64–82 kt)
2	96–110 mph (83–95 kt)
3	111–130 mph (96–113 kt)
4	131–155 mph (114–135 kt)
5	156 mph (136 kt) and higher

Source: Data from the National Weather Service.

of Louisiana landfall was 920 millibars, a very low pressure, and the third lowest on record for hurricane landfalls in the United States. The storm center crossed over the delta area and made its final landfall near the boundary between Louisiana and Mississippi with an estimated top sustained wind speed of about 121 miles per hour. Although Katrina had weakened to just below Category 4 status, making landfall as a strong Category 3 storm, the size of the hurricane remained very large, with hurricane and tropical storm force winds extending out to about 200 miles or more from the storm center.

Grand Isle, Louisiana, received the strongest sustained wind measured at the surface, at 87 mph, as well as the strongest official gust measurement of 114 mph, but the anemometer (wind speed measuring device) ceased operating about 2 hours before the eye of the hurricane was at its closest. Another location measured a sustained wind of 82 mph before a storm surge struck it. Unofficial reports of wind gusts in Mississippi to 135 mph in Poplarville, 124 mph in Pascagoula, and 122 mph at Long Beach were received. Due to the very large storm size, sustained hurricane force winds were recorded eastward to Dauphin Island, Alabama.

Hurricane Katrina was a Category 3 storm when its center was about 23 miles east of downtown New Orleans (its closest), but such strong winds did not reach the city. According to NHC researchers, it is likely that most of New Orleans experienced Category 1 or Category 2 strength surface winds; tall buildings may have experienced winds one category stronger since winds are stronger aloft.

Katrina continued on a north-northeastward path and weakened to less than hurricane strength. As a result of the hurricane, southeastern Louisiana and southwestern Mississippi received 8 to 10 inches of rain in a broad area, with 10 to 12 inches falling over a small area of eastern Louisiana. The weakening storm produced rainfall of 4 to 8 inches in central Mississippi and in portions of the Tennessee Valley as it traveled northward, along with 42 reported tornadoes August 29 to 30, a number of which were recorded well east of the storm center track.

Major Storm Effects

The night of Friday, August 26, with good information from NWS forecasts and clear expectations of landfall in the area of New Orleans, Louisiana, to Gulfport, Mississippi, the governor of Louisiana declared a state of emergency. By Saturday, the governor of Mississippi declared a state of emergency. Evacuation orders—voluntary and mandatory—were issued for parts of Louisiana, Mississippi, and Alabama.

Hurricane winds push water ahead of them. Because they have a counterclockwise rotation, as a storm approaches shore the maximum piling up of water in a storm surge occurs in the front right portion of the storm. Given Hurricane Katrina's landfall on the far west side of Mississippi, the Mississippi coast received the highest storm surge, with heights of about 24 to 28 feet impacting Waveland, Bay St. Louis, Pass Christian, and Long Beach. Storm surge flows extended from 6 to as many as 12 miles inland in parts of Mississippi. Eastern Mississippi and Alabama coastal areas also received very significant storm surge, although it was reduced to under 15 feet for Alabama. Much smaller storm surge amounts were experienced along the northwestern Florida coast.

West of the path of the hurricane center also received a significant damaging storm surge, with waters piling up ahead of the approaching storm center. Lake Pontchartrain, a saltwater lake to the north of New Orleans separated from the Gulf of Mexico by a relatively narrow stretch of very low land, received storm surge as water was pushed

into it. Its northeastern shore received storm surge of 12 to 16 feet; a surge of 10 to 14 feet was received on the southern edge of Pontchartrain, in western New Orleans. Eastern New Orleans, as well as areas to the south, had a storm surge of 15 to 19 feet. Much of New Orleans lies below sea level, protected by levees and an engineering system to pump water out of the city. The storm surge overtopped some of these levees, and other levees collapsed in places as water eroded the levee bases. Early on Monday, August 29, about 80% of New Orleans was flooded, with portions under as much as 20 feet of water. It took about 6 weeks for all the floodwaters to be removed from the city.

The potential for major hurricane storm surge impacts along the Gulf Coast is increased by the gentle offshore slope, the low-lying setting of New Orleans, and protections not designed to withstand a strong storm and high surge. Damage potential exists throughout the region, where there has been loss of coastal wetlands that help to absorb and buffer against storms, as well as buildup of residential and commercial areas. Public recognition of the importance of coastal wetlands and barrier islands has increased since Hurricane Katrina. Unfortunately, the storm caused further loss of these buffers.

Well before Hurricane Katrina, there was good recognition that a major hurricane could cause flooding and have disastrous effects in New Orleans, at least on the part of scientists and emergency personnel. The *Times-Picayune* newspaper had featured a series of articles about the potential effects of a strong hurricane in June 2002 and *National Geographic* had a story about the potential within the year prior to the storms. Unfortunately, many thousands of people remained in New Orleans and other affected areas in spite of evacuation orders; the urging of meteorologists, government officials, and media representatives; and prior reporting on the potential for a hurricane-related disaster. Many residents had experienced the impacts of past hurricanes, including Category 5 Hurricane Camille, which struck the Mississippi coast in 1968. Such experiences motivated some residents to evacuate, but many others felt adequately prepared; the Camille Effect has been used to describe the decision of many Gulf residents to weather Katrina in place, believing that nothing could be worse than Camille. Although

Hurricane Camille was a stronger storm at landfall, it was much smaller than Katrina, had a somewhat lesser maximum storm surge, and had more localized effects.

Some of those who chose to stay in place ahead of the storm thought that the danger was insufficient to merit evacuation; others believed they lacked the resources to leave. Many of those who stayed had to be helped out of the area, following storm surge and flooding problems brought by the storm. In addition, those who had evacuated to locations within the affected area later had to be moved further. Serious concerns arose based on what was seen as inadequate government response to the disaster. (Locally based military rescue operations were generally seen positively, however.)

Hurricane Katrina was one of the worst natural and social disasters in the history of the United States. Over 1,800 people died as a result of the storm, over 800,000 people were displaced (either short-term or long-term), and the storm produced an estimated economic loss of about $81 billion, including insured losses, uninsured property, and public infrastructure.

Communications and Katrina

Forecasting by the NHC, a branch of NWS, regarding the trajectory of Hurricane Katrina and the need for residents and governments in its path to take the storm very seriously has generally been judged to have been very good. Southern Florida NWS public forecast statements related to what was to become Hurricane Katrina were issued beginning on Tuesday, August 23. Although lead times for Florida watches and warnings were less than desired, the storm was still relatively weak when it made landfall there. Broad areas of watches and warnings were issued for the Gulf Coast well ahead of landfall, with very accurate storm surge predictions about a day in advance. Statements and interviews from NHC were widely carried by the media; media outlets such as the Weather Channel, the Internet, national television networks, and local news sources gave the storm significant coverage as it approached land.

News media continued to cover the storm's aftermath over what has turned out to be the months, and years, of recovery efforts. Hurricane Katrina produced long-lasting needs for recovery

of victims' bodies, help for those trapped in affected areas, and help for evacuees, as well as the mechanics of reconstruction. Many journalists have been involved in covering Katrina-related stories, a number of whom were reporting from the field (particularly, from New Orleans) during the early days of emergency operations. It has been noted that those covering disasters often experience psychological effects, including symptoms of posttraumatic stress.

Research indicates that television sources of information about Hurricane Katrina were widely used and trusted and apparently had some effect on evacuation decisions. Specific local television stations or personalities were trusted sources of important information to residents as the storm approached. Unfortunately, many of those who did not evacuate lacked trust in local and state governments where much of the evacuation information originated.

A major critique of the role of news media in the aftermath of Hurricane Katrina, especially reporting of the New Orleans disaster, was a tendency to show people of color and women in positions needing help, whereas white males were depicted as rescuers. Reporting of looting tended to portray minority members as the criminals. An additional important concern was the uncritical dissemination of rumors (horror stories) from New Orleans during the early days following evacuation to the Convention Center and the Superdome.

In spite of the concerns related to Hurricane Katrina reporting, the role of the news media and reporters has been valued. National television and other media brought information to other parts of the country; local New Orleans reporters became especially important to both the region and the nation.

Lisa M. Butler Harrington

See also Crisis Communication; Environmental Journalism; Environmental Justice; Risk Communication, Overview; Weather Reporting

Further Readings

Kates, R. W., Colten, C. E., Laska, S., & Leatherman, S. P. (2006). Reconstruction of New Orleans after

Hurricane Katrina: A research perspective. *Proceedings of the National Academy of Sciences, 103*(40), 14653–14660.

National Hazards Center. (2006). *Learning from catastrophe: Quick response research in the wake of Hurricane Katrina* (Special publication No. 40). Boulder: Institute of Behavioral Science, University of Colorado at Boulder.

Thevenot, B. (2005). Apocalypse in New Orleans. *American Journalism Review, 27*(5), 24–31.

Times-Picayune. (2002). *Special report: Washing away.* Five-part series, June 23–27. Available at www .nola.com/hurricane/content.ssf?/washingaway/index .html

Travis, J. (2005). Scientists' fears come true as hurricane floods New Orleans. *Science, 309,* 1656–1659.

I

INDIA, SCIENCE AND SCIENCE COMMUNICATION IN

India is a large, populous, and ancient country with great geographical diversity. Inhabited by 1.2 billion people over 3,287,263 square kilometers, India has a long history in culture and in science and technology (S&T), dating back to at least 2,750 years BCE. Under British influence via the East India Company from 1600 to 1773 and thereafter the British Empire, India attained independence in 1947 and became a republic in 1950. Although the motive is debatable, the period under the British also saw the introduction of the English language, which opened a new window that certainly made a substantial difference to Indian science. With considerable emphasis on keeping society informed in relevant matters of S&T and promoting scientific thinking, science communication is gaining importance.

Scientists command respect in Indian society. Three of the 40 recipients of the highest Indian civilian order, Bharat Ratna (or Gem of India), belong to the scientific and engineering community: M. Visweswaraya (1861–1962), Chandrasekhar Venkat Raman (1888–1970), who is also a Nobel laureate; and A. P. J. Abdul Kalam (1931–), who subsequently became president of India (2002–2007). Eight Indian scientists or engineers have been foreign associates of the U.S. National Academy of Sciences, and over 40 Indian scientists have been members of the U.K. Royal Society.

Science in Ancient India

A rich heritage in science is visible in the widespread archaeological evidence of the early Indus Valley civilization, evidence that has been found in about 1,500 different places. This evidence includes remains of systematically laid out towns, structures, and beautiful bronze and other sculptures belonging to the period from around 2750 BCE to 1900 BCE. The Indus Valley civilization was followed by Vedic culture (appearing around 1500 BCE). The remains of this period include a port that can be seen in Lothal (Gujarat). Agriculture was advanced, as evidenced by vestiges of henna, shikakai, grapes, and aanwala (emblic). Education flourished in centers such as Nalanda University (in present day Bihar) and other sites in the 5th century BCE. Charak (circa the 2nd century CE) and Sushrut (circa 4th century CE) made marks in Ayurveda (or science of life). Around 300 different surgical procedures and over 100 instruments were known; the surgical textbook known as Sushrut Samhita describes rhinoplasty, for example, in detail.

The Arabic numerals were actually invented in India, although they traveled to the West via the Arab world. In the 5th century CE, Aryabhata I estimated the diameters of the earth and moon, described the earth's axial rotation, and calculated the value of the ratio of circumference of a circle to its diameter (Pi) to the fourth decimal place. The concept of the decimal system had been developed by this time. Around the 7th or 8th century CE, Brahmagupta worked out solutions to indeterminate second-order equations. Such progress continued into the 13th century, including work in chemistry by Nagarjuna (10th century) and others. The 1,500-year-old, 23-foot 8-inch, rust-free iron pillar at Mehrauli (Delhi) is testimony to the skill in metallurgy. Materials written during Emperor Akbar's time (the end of the 16th century) contained astronomical data, and Akbar's son Jehangir (1569–1627 CE) systematically recorded the behavior of birds, reptiles, and animals and recorded how an iron meteorite was used to fabricate a sword. These years also saw many architectural wonders being erected but saw few serious efforts in science. Around the same time, in 1600 CE, the East India Company entered India as merchants and gradually gained political power.

Science Under British Rule

The British government sent a viceroy in 1773; with battles constantly being fought, S&T was not a priority. However, military considerations did prompt the development of rockets in Tipu Sultan's kingdom Mysore and their use in the Srirangapatana battle in 1792. Out of personal interest, one king, Sawai Jai Singh II, built five solar observatories between 1718 and 1734, two of which still exist today. The East India Company set up the Survey of India in 1767, primarily to facilitate collection of revenue and other administrative goals rather than for research. The Asiatic Society of Bengal emerged in 1784. The first engineering institution was the College of Engineering created in 1847 (now known as the Indian Institute of Technology-Roorkee), followed by others.

The first Indian train moved between Bombay and Thane in 1853, although by and large India remained untouched by industrial and scientific development at this time. Three universities were established in 1857 at Bombay, Calcutta, and Madras (now Mumbai, Kolkata, and Chennai, respectively). The same year saw the first freedom struggle (known as the Sepoy mutiny). Establishment of the Geological Survey of India (GSI, 1861) and the Botanical Survey of India (1890) followed. The tram was introduced in Kolkata in 1873, was discontinued, and then reemerged in 1900 in its electrified version, run by pole-mounted power lines. However, the progress of research in India remained outside the government's control. This led to the founding of the Indian Association for the Cultivation of

Science in Kolkata in 1876, which fostered many talents. P. C. Ray (1861–1944) may be credited with beginning chemistry research and related industry in India, and J. C. Bose (1858–1937) invented wireless transmission before Marconi.

The 20th century saw a kind of renaissance. With the creation of a Board of Scientific Advice in 1902 and a University Act in 1904, science courses were introduced. Mathematician Srinivasa Ramanujan (1887–1920) contributed remarkable theorems and proofs. He was identified by G. H. Hardy of Cambridge University (U.K.) as a genius and became a Fellow of the Royal Society in 1918. The Indian Institute of Science (1909), a dream of industrialist J. N. Tata, materialized through a donation of land by the king of Mysore. Government founded the Indian Research Fund Association in 1911. Satya Prakash, a chemist at Allahabad University, and his colleagues founded the Vigyan Parishad in 1913, publishing research journals in Hindi. The Indian Science Congress Association was founded in 1914. J. C. Bose, whose work was termed "the dawn of the revival," established the Bose Institute in Calcutta in 1917. Raman earned a Nobel Prize in 1930 for work on the scattering of light (involving the Raman effect), termed an International Historic Chemical Landmark in 1998 by the American Chemical Society. S. N. Bose (for whom the elementary particle the boson is named) and Meghnad Saha carried out theoretical work on Bose–Einstein condensates and thermal ionization equations, respectively.

The Indian Council of Agricultural Research (ICAR) was founded in 1929. The 1930s were a period of nationalism. Through the Indian National Congress, a National Planning Committee on Science was formed in 1938, with Nehru as its chairman. In 1940, a Board of Industrial and Scientific and Industrial Research was constituted, followed by the Council of Scientific and Industrial Research (CSIR) in 1942. All through the period, philanthropist-industrialists such as J. N. Tata, Kasturbhai Lalbhai, and G. D. Birla supported the promotion of science.

Science in Independent India

Nehru, the first Indian prime minister and a Cambridge University science graduate, retained the portfolio of S&T, a practice followed for many years. The portfolios of atomic energy and space are still under the prime ministers. Nehru's enthusiasm led to the first Indian S&T policy in 1958, the latest revision having been in 2008. The basic problems of food, power, water, health, and so on naturally dominated the government's concerns. But basic sciences also continued to flourish in universities and Indian Institutes of Technology, as well as in research institutions such as the Indian Institute of Science, Bangaluru.

CSIR, now a statutory body with the prime minister as its chairman, continued to grow. In 1985, a separate department for scientific and industrial research was created under the S&T ministry. The CSIR has 37 research institutions under its umbrella and deals with research on topics as diverse as basic physics, medicines and contraceptives, hand pumps, and light aircrafts. With the union minister of agriculture as president, ICAR coordinates research and education in agriculture through 94 research institutions and 45 universities, including responsibility for dairy, poultry, and fisheries. From a stage of heavy dependence on imports up to the 1960s, India has progressed to a food-grain surplus status.

An engineer and physicist trained at Cambridge and Cavendish, Homi J. Bhabha played the pivotal role in establishment of the Department of Atomic Energy (DAE) in 1954. DAE deals with various aspects of nuclear energy and radiation and their application to energy, agriculture, and industry and with research through its five research centers, three industrial organizations, five public undertakings, and three service organizations. These institutions deal with everything from basic science to related technologies and even nuclear medicine (Tata Memorial Centre). India is a party to ITER, a seven-member collaboration for building a tokomak reactor to realize the use of nuclear fusion for energy and is also a partner in the Large Hadron Collider experiment at Geneva (European Organization for Nuclear Research, also known as CERN).

Nuclear energy production in India is still small; coal provides 55% of energy needs. Coal is under a separate ministry that concerns the exploration and development of coal and lignite reserves, research on carbonization of coal, production of synthetic oil, and other coal-related issues. The Ministry of Petroleum and Natural Gas deals with the exploration and management of coal. Its public

sector unit, the Oil and Natural Gas Corporation, explores and drills for oil and is now joined by several private companies. But it also supports research in related fields. Compressed natural gas (87 million cubic meters a day) has been introduced, leading to great relief from pollution. The Indian Institute of Petroleum, Dehradun (part of CSIR) also works on petroleum-related issues.

All minerals other than natural gas, petroleum, atomic minerals, and coal are dealt with by the Ministry of Mines, which also includes the GSI, the Indian Bureau of Mines, and public sector undertakings such as the Mineral Exploration Corporation and Hindustan Copper Limited. The GSI has been engaged in building a geological database since 1861. It carries out geological mapping, mineral prospecting, and other geological studies in areas such as glaciology, environment, natural hazards, and seismology. It is now also engaged in Antarctic research.

The vision of Vikram A. Sarabhai, also a graduate of Cambridge, led to the establishment of the Department of Space. India now has launching capabilities for polar as well as geosynchronous satellites. These satellites continue to play important roles in communication, weather forecasting, disaster warning, and resource mapping. With *EDUSAT* in orbit since 2004, distance education has been advanced. The Physical Research Laboratory, Ahmedabad has participated in lunar sample research. In a hallmark achievement, India sent *Chandrayaan* (literally meaning moon ship) in 2008 to orbit the moon and to drop a moon probe carrying payloads from the United States and several European countries.

India has also developed airplanes, tanks, missiles—the latest being the Agni series of missiles with a range of up to 3,500 kilometers—and nuclear submarines. This research is mainly through a network of over 50 organizations under the umbrella of the Defense Research and Development Organisation, formed in 1958.

The Department of Science and Technology (DST) was established in 1971. The S&T departments (or councils) in all the states and union territories resulted from the DST initiative. DST has 18 institutions organized as autonomous aided institutions (AI), whose fields of research range from plant fossils to physics and astrophysics, heart valves, and more. In addition to AIs, there is a Survey of India, Dehradun with 18 directorates. The Jawaharlal Nehru Centre for Advanced Scientific Research at Bangaluru houses some of the best-known scientific minds. DST also supports science academies, conferences, and publications.

The long Indian coastline of 7,516 kilometers, its natural resources, the role of ocean data in climate prediction, and other factors necessitated the creation of the Department of Ocean Development in 1981, but following the devastating Sumatra tsunami of 2004, the relevant ministry was reconstituted as the Ministry of Earth Sciences with nine institutions under it. The India Meteorological Department is one important constituent. Beginning in 1981, India built three bases in Antarctica and, in 2008, established Himadri in the Arctic.

The Department of Information Technology under the Ministry of Communication and Information Technology is involved in promoting e-governance. The National Informatics Centre, with headquarters at New Delhi, has units in all the state headquarters and has penetrated to every district in India's 28 states and seven union territories.

India was the first country to have a national bioinformatics network. The Ministry of Biotechnology regulates the progress in this field. It monitors and looks after issues such as biosafety and the application of the technology on behalf of the underprivileged and women, especially from the medical angle. Under the Ministry of Water Resources, several organizations are engaged in research and water-related coordination. This ministry conducts research through the Central Water Commission and about 50 divisions. Another subordinate organization, the Central Ground Water Board, is engaged in standardization of water-related methodologies.

The Ministry for Environment and Forests has a mandate for conservation of natural resources and is a node for the U.N. Environment Program; it funds research in the area of environment and forests. Among the nongovernmental institutions is the Tata Energy Research Institute, New Delhi, whose director general has been chairman of the Intergovernmental Panel for Climate Change, the 2007 Nobel recipient. Alternative fuels including hydrogen are being experimented with in several institutions, including those of DAE. The Botanical Survey of India, the Forest Survey of India, Dehradun, and the Zoological Survey of India, Kolkata document

the floral and faunal diversity and also study coral reefs, wetlands, and mangroves. There are 99 national parks, 513 wildlife sanctuaries, 41 conservation reserves, and four community reserves in addition to 39 zoos. The G. B. Pant Institute of Himalayan Environment and Development, Kosi-Katarmal, Almora (Uttarakhand), is engaged in research on the Himalayan region environment. Some of the states have their own research centers, such as the Gujarat Ecological Education and Research Foundation at Gandhi Nagar (Gujarat).

Health and family welfare concerns have been grave in India, partly due to the tropical conditions. In 1949, the Indian Research Fund Association was redesigned and shaped into the Indian Council for Medical Research at New Delhi. The council is the apex body with the Union Minister of Health and Family Welfare as its president. It promotes medical research through 21 research institutions and five regional centers, and it awards grants and fellowships. Medical research is also carried out in many universities, institutes, and colleges. Diseases such as tuberculosis, kala-azar, malaria, filarial infestation, chikunguya, and HIV/AIDS have been tackled and controlled through research and awareness campaigns.

With a long coastline, mountain chains, and vast expanses of sunlit land, India has tremendous potential for exploiting water, wave, wind, geothermal, and solar energy. Hydroelectric plants are common. The Ministry of New and Renewable Energy has several autonomous organizations under it working on various aspects of renewable energy, bioenergy (including biofuels), and synthetic fuels. Some private firms have also stepped into the area of wind energy generation.

The Ministry of Railways promotes research through its Research Design and Standardisation Organisation at Lucknow, formed by amalgamating the Central Standards Office (established 1930) and the Railway Testing and Research Centre (established 1952).

India has many academic societies, some for specialized subdisciplines. The most prominent societies are the Indian National Science Academy (INSA, New Delhi; formerly the National Institute of Sciences of India), Indian Academy of Sciences (Bangaluru), and National Academy of Sciences (Allahabad). INSA is also responsible for scientist exchange programs with foreign academies. The Indian Science

Congress Association (ISCA) holds the biggest annual meeting of scientists.

International cooperation has also certainly grown in independent India. Although India's share in research publications remains a little over 2%, there are certain areas where India is in the forefront. The science budget has doubled since 2008. Many awards encourage excellence, including the annual S. S. Bhatnagar Awards by the CSIR. To encourage young scientists, the INSA and CSIR annually bestow awards on young scientists. Many medals, endowments, and other awards have been instituted by INSA, as well as ISCA. Additional awards have been instituted by research institutions, private trusts, and other organizations. Some of the most prominent scientists find themselves nominated to the upper house of Parliament (Rajya Sabha). In an exceptional case, Meghnad Saha, best known for the Saha equation for thermal ionization, won parliamentary election as an independent candidate in 1952.

Science Communication in India

The Indian constitution considers it a fundamental duty under Article 51A (h) to develop the scientific temper, humanism, and a spirit of inquiry and reform. In accord with this, communicating science has been on the agenda of all the broadcasting agencies of the government since independence. Narender K. Sehgal, a physicist, Kalinga awardee, and leading Indian science communicator, has argued in his concept paper for the United Nations Educational, Scientific and Cultural Organization that everyone must have some minimum knowledge of S&T, although the essential knowledge may not be the same for all.

Historical Science Communication Practices

Many books were written in ancient India on science and mathematics, mostly in Sanskrit, including some riddles. However, not much record is available for any popular writings, possibly because of constraints of reproduction as books were written manually on dried leaves and because of destruction by invaders. Syed Ahmed, founder of Aligarh Muslim University, made serious efforts to disseminate science through Indian languages as early as 1866. J. C. Bose made public experimental

presentations. In the early 20th century, Ruchi Ram Sahni, a professor of chemistry in Punjab with research experience under Ernest Rutherford, went around on a bicycle giving popular lectures on science. Nobel laureate Raman was a great speaker on the subject of science. As early as 1924, Rahul Sanskrityayan, a great litterateur, published the first science fiction novel in Hindi, Baaiisavee Sadee (*Twenty-Second Century*). A purely literary Hindi magazine *Saraswati* (named after the Hindu goddess of learning) published many popular articles on science by well-known authors during the first half of the 20th century. The Oscar winner cinema personality Satyajit Ray wrote science fiction for children. With the advent of technology, science communication also leap-frogged. India has had four winners of the international Kalinga Award. To commemorate Raman's Nobel Prize–winning discovery, February 28 is celebrated as Science Day.

Publications, exhibitions, direct interactions, and radio and TV programs are now among the most common science communication activities in India. Government has initiated a number of programs through its ministries, but over the years, nongovernmental agencies have also assumed a major role in this area, either with or without governmental support.

Science Communication by Governmental Agencies

The National Institute of Science Communication and Information Resources (NISCAIR), under CSIR, collects and manages scientific information and has brought out more than 60 popular science books in English, 28 in Hindi, and several encyclopedias. The National Council for Science and Technology Communication (NCSTC) is an apex body for science communication as a part of DST. It supports the *Indian Journal of Science Communication*. But more importantly, it catalyzes and supports many science popularization activities, such as the National Children's Science Congress, science activity workshops, the Teachers' Science Congress, science-based films, and workshops for science communication training.

The National Council of Science Museums (NCSM), under the Ministry of Culture, is the largest network of these museums and centers under one umbrella anywhere. In its nearly 40-year existence, it has set up 27 science centers and/or museums visited by several million people every year. Exhibitions are also organized during the annual session of the Indian Science Congress, with most of the leading ministries and organizations showcasing their achievements. The DAE makes special efforts to spread information about nuclear energy and its applications through exhibitions and lectures.

Science Publication for the Common Person

Vigyan by Vigyan Parishad, Allahabad, is the oldest Indian popular science magazine, started in 1915. The bimonthly magazines *Awishkar* and *Invention Intelligence* by the National Research Development Corporation, New Delhi; *Down to Earth* by the Centre for Science and Environment, New Delhi; *Eureka* by KSSP; *Everyman's Science* by the Indian Science Congress Association; *Vaigyanik* (meaning scientist or scientific) by BARC; and *Vigyan Pragati, Science Reporter*, and *Science ki Duniya* by NISCAIR are some notable magazines. Vigyan Prasar (1989) has been publishing *Dream 2047* since 1997 and *VIPNET Newsletter* since 2002. Magazines in regional languages also exist, though with limited circulation. A Hindi quarterly *Vigyan Katha* (meaning science fiction) has been appearing since 2002. Science fiction and fantasy have become popular even in net forums, and there have been several discussions at the national level on the subject. The ICAR publishes a popular magazine, *Indian Farming;* a semi-technical magazine, *Indian Farmer;* and two periodicals in Hindi, one for horticulturists, vegetable growers, nurserymen, and similar audiences and a second one for farmers. Newsletters, usually limited to in-house circulation, are common in scientific institutions. A number of blogs, also in Hindi, on science have appeared.

Vigyan Prasar has also brought out original books on science for laypeople, as well as reprints and translations, mainly in Hindi and English. The publications division of the Ministry of Information and Broadcasting also has an impressive catalog of science books in several languages.

The science scene in newspapers is not as bright, the space devoted to S&T being close to 2% and shrinking. Some of the prominent newspapers such as the *Hindu,* the *Hindustan Times,* and the *Telegraph* carry weekly science supplements. However, the space devoted to science has been gradually shrinking. The *Pioneer* carries informative articles on science, usually in its Sunday magazine. Interestingly, the regional language newspapers devote more space to S&T than the English language ones. With support from NCSTC (DST), a fortnightly tabloid *Vaigyanik Drishtikonn* (meaning scientific attitude) exclusively devoted to S&T has been in circulation for about 9 years.

Radio started in the 1920s. The radio programs on farm and home average 60 to 100 minutes per day, and those on environment 5 to 7 minutes. Regional Training Institutes train staff in science popularization. The national radio channel broadcasts a science program (*Vigyan Bharati*) every Wednesday night and so do regional channels, even in the local dialects. Several science-based serials have been broadcast to fair acclaim.

Television, beginning in 1959, has spread its reach and prominently featured events like the widely watched total solar eclipse (1995) and Venus transit (2005). The popularity of foreign programs such as Carl Sagan's *Cosmos, Discovery,* and *National Geographic* (dubbed in Hindi) has been undisputed. News items on miracles are common, but the media also tries to provide balance by bringing in scientists with alternative, rational explanations for these phenomena.

Science Communication by Nongovernmental Agencies

Nongovernmental organizations are also playing a very important role in science communication in India. The All India People's Science Network (over 40 organizations), Kerala Sasthra Sahitya Parishad with over 40,000 individual members, and the 70-organization-strong NCSTC-Network have done pioneering work in science popularization. The NCSTC-Network has a strong presence in every district of India. The Bharat Jan Gyan Vigyan Society (1987) and Bharat Jan Vigyan Society (1992) have also left an imprint.

The science fiction scenario is also looking up. The status in Assamese, Bangala, Hindi, Kannada, Malayalam, Marathi, Punjabi, and Tamil languages has been reviewed in the *Proceedings for the Eighth National Conference on Science Fiction*

Writers. However, it seems it may be a long time before a genuine Indian science fiction (or even science fantasy) movie appears. Use of puppetry, street plays, and poems in science communication represent unique media, also in vogue.

Science Communication Targeted at the Young

For the past few years, there has been an emphasis on theme-based activities such as the Year of Scientific Awareness–2004, the Year of Physics–2005, the Year of Planet Earth–2008, and the Year of Astronomy–2009. Government institutions such as Vigyan Prasar, professional societies such as the Geological Society of India, and nongovernmental organizations such as the NCSTC-Network actively participate in publishing books and organizing programs especially for the young.

The National Children's Science Congress, coordinated by the NCSTC-Network, involves hundreds of thousands of children (10–17 years old) every year in working out science projects on a given theme such as "Know Your Environment." The DBT targets children through DNA Clubs in 23 states involving 300,000 students, and the Department of Environment and Forests through 84,000 Eco Clubs. They also conduct awareness programs through about 10,000 organizations. Vigyan Prasar has established nearly 10,000 VIPNET-Clubs. The Science for School Children session during the Indian Science Congress invites selected students to present their projects and listen to and interact with well-known experts for the Science for School Children.

The interaction of young students with Nobel Prize laureates is a recent program initiated by DST. Following the overwhelming response to traveling Vigyan Rail (meaning science train) in 2004, which carried a display of Indian science prepared by NCSM in its coaches, the idea was picked up by NCSTC, which resulted in a trip by another train during 2007 with exhibits provided by the Max Planck Society, Germany. It traveled 15,000 kilometers, touching 57 stations with 2.2 million visitors over 217 days.

Recognition for Science Communication

A number of prizes and awards are given by governmental as well as nongovernmental agencies for science popularization and science writing such as NCSTC's National Awards, the Indian National Science Academy's Indira Gandhi Award, and a variety of other prizes, including some by state governments, magazines, newspapers, and private and other nongovernmental organizations. In addition, various ministries provide prizes to encourage popular and technical writing on S&T, especially in the national language.

Conclusion

Science in ancient India made an impact the world over, but the momentum was not maintained for various reasons. The late 19th and early 20th centuries again witnessed some outstanding work in India. Postindependence, there has been a tremendous growth in the number of research organizations. The application of S&T in areas such as agriculture, communication, health, and nuclear energy has also made visible changes in common people's lives. The science communication picture is definitely looking up and could play an important role in translating some of the research into welfare.

Chandra Mohan Nautiyal

See also Bioinformatics; Nuclear Power; Particle Accelerators; Satellites, Science of; Science Centers and Science Museums

Further Readings

Bhargava, P. M., & Chakrabarty, C. (2003). *The saga of Indian science since independence: In a nutshell.* Bangalore, India: University Press.

Indian National Science Academy. (2001). *Pursuit and promotion of science: The Indian experience.* New Delhi, India: Author.

Misra, S. G. (Ed.). (2001). *Hindi mein Vigyan Lekhan ke 100 varsh* [100 years of science writing in Hindi] (Vols. 1–2). Uttar Pradesh, India: Vigyan Prasar.

Mukhopadhyay, P. K. (1998). Sir J. C. Bose's diode detector received Marconi's first transatlantic wireless signal of December 1901 (The "Italian Navy Coherer" scandal revisited). *Proceedings of the IEEE, 86*(1), 259–285.

Nautiyal C. M. (2008). A look at S&T awareness: Enhancements in India. *Journal of Science Communication, 7*(2), A 01, 1–10. Available at http://jcom.sissa.it/archive/07/02/Jcom0702%282008%29A01

Proceedings of the 8th National Conference for Science Fiction Writers at Aurangabad, Maharashtra, India. (2006, November). Available at www .vigyanprasar.gov.in/dream/dec2006/Eng%20 December.pdf

Rajagopal, N. R., Qureshi, M. A., & Singh, B. (1991). *The CSIR saga.* New Delhi, India: Publication and Information Division.

Scholberg, H. (1998). *The biographical dictionary of greater India.* New Delhi: Promila.

INDUCTIVE LOGIC

All scientific investigation relies on logical reasoning, and it can be important for science communicators to understand the type of logic underlying a particular scientific finding. Inductive logic is one common type of logic used in science. To define inductive logic, it is first necessary to have a firm grasp of what logic is generally, and then it will be possible to specify what kind of logic is inductive.

Logic is generally identified as the principles and relationships of reasoning. Logic concerns argumentation, but not in the everyday sense of people who are angry at one another. Rather, an argument in the logical sense is a set of two or more statements in which at least one (called a premise) is said to be a reason to believe another is true (a conclusion).

Principally, inductive logic can then be distinguished from deductive logic as follows. *Deductive arguments* are characterized by a necessary relationship between their premises and conclusions. By contrast, *inductive arguments* offer support for thinking that their conclusions are likely to be true. Thus, the relationship between the premises and conclusion in an inductive argument is characterized by probability.

There are many kinds of inductive arguments. Statistical arguments are often good examples of inductive reasoning, when the conclusion drawn is only probable. A batter who has a high rate of hitting home runs is more likely to hit another than his teammates who have hit few, for example. Arguments based on observation of signs, often predictions, are also common inductive arguments. Weather forecasts are good examples. Other forms of inductive premises are claims by authorities, whose evidence is stronger or weaker depending upon their history or the quality of their arguments and capabilities.

History and tradition can be good predictors, but only when relevant. For instance, the fact that the sun has come up every day throughout history is reason to think it will rise again tomorrow. Evidence of having seen the sun rise in the past is called *empirical.* It is evidence gained from people's senses and their memory of what these showed. In this way, traditional (past) practices are empirical predictors of future behavior, unless some other evidence or reason can help to predict a variation from traditional practices.

Finally, analogies are frequently used in inductive arguments. Consider that in biology, for example, animals that share characteristics are likely to have a more similar DNA than animals with more differences. Analogies here are relevant in testing, where mice are selected for medical drug studies because of the similarity of their immune system to humans'. Effectively, studies that are successful in mice in combating disease argue by analogy that the same or a similar treatment could be developed to help treat human beings.

Inductive logic is a crucial tool in the study of science and technology. Scientists do not only attempt to make predictions, of course. Inductive reasoning is also crucial in learning how things happened or how they have worked. When someone thinks about a space ship that does not function properly or explodes, for instance, that person often searches creatively for hypotheses that might explain the dysfunction. Once someone has a theory, he or she can create methods for testing that theory.

Some analyses of theories can involve deductive reasoning, playing out the implications of the relevant definitions, physical laws, and necessary categories of our thinking. They can also have to do with probabilities of certain consequences arising as a result of the conditions in question. In the theoretical sciences, scholars frequently start from principles and the problems we have in reconciling them with other principles or with empirical facts. Theoretical sciences can focus a great deal on deductive proofs, although to test them often includes finding ways to seek inductive evidence for the theories. In the empirical sciences, the work is very often profoundly focused on inductive reasoning.

A crucial purpose for inductive reasoning is to consider what might be the cause of a problem. For instance, when a patient visits the doctor's office, the physician asks many questions to see whether any relevant evidence turns up that could point to the cause for an illness. In diagnosing a patient, deductive reasoning can frequently be necessary, such as in deciding whether certain categories of illness make sense to consider given the symptoms at hand. At the same time, the decisions to be made about what are the most important and relevant symptoms can be crucial elements of diagnosis and are frequently based upon inductive reasoning, particularly because symptoms are signs of underlying causes.

Whether some element of a patient's history is simply an irrelevant fact versus a pertinent symptom of an underlying condition is something for which sometimes only probabilistic reasons can be given. Causal reasoning and studies are done with regard to medicines, technologies, automobile safety tests, and any area in which is it important to be able to predict or determine a causal relationship.

A final word on a philosophical controversy is worth mentioning regarding the relationship between deductive and inductive reasoning. While scholars often like deduction because it involves what some call truth preservation—necessarily true conclusions when the premises are true—scholars who call themselves empiricists have argued that the rules of deduction are known because of empirical, inductive evidence. Empiricists label this idea the problem of induction. It is a problem for those who think that deduction creates more certainty than induction.

Scholars who disagree with this point of view take several approaches. One example is to say that it is not inconsistent to learn about the physical laws of the universe or about the processes of chemical composition through experience in empirical study and inductive reasoning. While either approach may result in learning new things about the universe, certainly the kinds of reasoning involved in deductive logic differ from those in inductive logic.

Eric Thomas Weber

See also Deductive Logic; Scientific Method

Further Readings

Copi, I. M. (1986) *Introduction to logic.* New York: Macmillan.

Hurley, P. J. (2003). *A concise introduction to logic* (8th ed.). Belmont, CA: Wadsworth.

Toulmin, S. (1994). *The uses of argument.* New York: Oxford University Press.

INFORMATION SEEKING AND PROCESSING

In the context of science communication, the study of information seeking and processing is focused on what brings people to science information and, subsequently, what they do with that information once they encounter it. This area of research is of value to myriad practitioners, including scientists interested in building the public's (and policymakers') understanding of their work, educators, science museum curators, and scholars who want to maximize the potential for communication interventions to reach the public and improve the state of citizens' science knowledge. Both seeking and processing are often explored in terms of motivational factors and effort expended.

Information Seeking

People can seek information by expending very little or quite a lot of effort. Thus, information seeking is often conceptualized in terms of its intensity. Intensity can be thought of as varying along two dimensions: (1) effort involved in seeking each information source and (2) overall number of sources sought. Seeking can involve interpersonal as well as mediated sources—and often involves a combination of both. In terms of effort, information seeking is often dichotomized as active or passive. Active seeking describes a more goal-driven behavior, while passive seeking describes a more ritual-based behavior. In the case of mass mediated seeking, active seeking is characterized as stimulated beyond routine media use and is driven by such motivating factors as problem solving or the desire for autonomy. Active seeking may involve, for example, seeking out information about climate change on the Internet using search engines. Passive seeking, in contrast, is characterized as more routine and habitual and not driven by a specific goal beyond the general desire to scan one's environment. An example of passive seeking would be habitual scanning of the morning newspaper or a Web page one regularly visits. While passive seeking may seem a contradiction of terms, it is simply meant to capture information seeking that is one step up from no seeking at all. This dichotomy is similar to that offered by the uses and gratifications literature, which invokes the terms *instrumental* and *ritualized* media use.

Passive seeking can serve as a gateway to more active seeking. Motivating factors that tend to determine moving from passive to more active seeking include one's perceived need for information, the relative or perceived accessibility of information channels that can assist in meeting that need, and changing situational demands (multitasking, deadlines, etc.). In terms of perceived need, perceived personal relevance plays a notable role such that as relevance increases (for example, one experiences illness), so does the effort expended in seeking and the number of sources sought. Multichannel information seeking can involve accessing not only the major news media and the Internet but also family, friends, and experts. Sometimes, seeking may not be easily dichotomized and may vary.

Any attempts to better understand information seeking behaviors must be careful not to oversimplify the behaviors; researchers must account for the numerous potential sources of variation. That means that researchers must consider the goals that drive information seeking as well as the situation in which the seeking takes place.

In addition, it is likely that understanding the complexity of information seeking also means understanding its relationship to information processing and knowledge gain. Information seeking, it can be argued, is, in most cases, a necessary prerequisite for information processing—that is, before one can process information, he or she needs to be exposed to it. Although there are occasions in which individuals are confronted with unsolicited information (for example, billboards, unsolicited phone calls, chance encounters with a news broadcast, etc.), by and large, to encounter information, one must at least switch on the TV, pick up the newspaper, dial a phone number, link to the

Internet, and so on. So the question is, how does information seeking relate to information processing? In all likelihood, if one needs information and one or more channels are perceived to be accessible and useful, the intensity with which the resulting information will be processed will be congruent with the intensity of the perceived need, accessibility, and usefulness—that is, the intensity of the seeking will be positively related to the extent to which a person will become engaged in processing the information that he or she encounters. The more actively an individual seeks information, the more actively he or she will process it. If fewer channels are available, this level of activity would, most likely, need to increase further still. Ultimately, however, it is information processing, not seeking, which leads to influence; therefore, we must now turn our attention to information processing.

Information Processing

To understand the concept of information processing, it is first useful to review the concept's history in both the social psychology and psychology disciplines. This history has contributed to both disciplines' development of similar dual processing models of information processing, which depict two processing styles that are, essentially, automatic and conscious, respectively.

Around the time of World War II, English psychologists, called on by the military to improve pilots' abilities to learn the complex control panels of military aircraft, began to move away from behaviorism and turn their attention to information processing. Communication technology was key to this movement because at about this time, communication researchers interested in information transmission were studying the transfer of signals between telephone operators. That research was useful to psychologists interested in human information processing because it was believed that, like the nation's burgeoning telephone network, human beings could similarly be viewed as receivers and transmitters of information.

It was not long before this technology-based focus on information transfer gave way to a computer metaphor for human information processing. From there grew models of short-term and long-term memory, processing capacity, information retrieval, and information storage. However, in time, some psychologists recognized that there were shortcomings with the technology-based or computer-simulation models of information processing. As psychologists gained a better understanding of how the brain functions, it became more obvious that the standard computer metaphor could not address the question of how organisms acquired information. For example, organisms can voluntarily (and sometimes arbitrarily) devote time and resources to processing tasks. Sometimes this allocation of resources is likely to occur automatically, while at other times the organism must consciously deploy mental resources to accomplish the given task. As a result, beginning in the 1970s, the study of human consciousness became an important element in the research that developed around resource allocation and attention.

Researchers also applied this conscious-versus-automatic model to processing activities beyond attention. As with conscious attention, conscious processing is intentional and open to awareness. It requires conscious attention. Automatic processing, on the other hand, is unintentional, without awareness, and consumes little or no consciousness resources. Habitual exposure to a stimulus (or, simply, practice) is a likely contributor to automatic processing. However, it is conscious processing that is more likely to lead to active learning, which is a deliberate mental process.

As this focus in psychology on attention and processing continued to develop, a shift was taking place in mass communication research as well. Media researchers interested in audience effects were moving from a direct effects model of media influence toward a much more limited model of influence. While the circumstances following World War I seemed to confirm the direct effects model (for example, the rapid rise of Nazism in Germany, the apparent effectiveness of propaganda both at home and abroad, and the much publicized listener reaction to the 1938 radio broadcast of H. G. Wells's *War of the Worlds*), social scientists later labeled the evidence as anecdotal. More scientific study revealed that the persuasive power of the media is contingent on a large number of mediating forces, including perceptions about the sources of messages.

As the latter half of the 20th century approached, it became clear that models of information processing in a mass communication context needed to account for (at least) two modes of processing: conscious and automatic. It was also clear that media effects (for example, persuasion), regardless of whether they result from conscious or automatic processing, are moderated by a fairly large number of variables. Both of these considerations were key to the development of at least two information processing theories, the elaboration likelihood model (ELM) and the heuristic-systematic model (HSM).

The ELM is a theory about the cognitive processes responsible when an individual yields to persuasive communication. It was introduced by Richard Petty and John Cacioppo around 1981. The model shows two distinct routes to persuasion—the central route and the peripheral route. The central route involves effortful cognitive activity and is likely to lead to careful appraisal of message content, while the peripheral route involves the use of simple cues and is likely to lead to a cursory evaluation of message content. Such cues may include the perceived source of the information, design elements of the message, and so on. Because it is more effortful and relies on processing more than cues, central processing is said to lead to more lasting attitude change and is more likely to lead to behavior change than peripheral processing. When processing more effortfully, individuals are believed to make a more concerted effort to integrate the information with what they already know. Still, peripheral approaches to processing can be effective for both the sender and the receiver, particularly in the short term and when individuals have situational or processing constraints.

Like the ELM, the HSM makes a distinction regarding the dual processes that lead to persuasion. According to Shelly Chaiken, the model's creator, these two processes are designated heuristic and systematic. Systematic processing is comprehensive, analytic, and effortful. It can, however, vary in its extensiveness and still remain effective. Heuristic processing, on the other hand, is more focused on simple rules or shortcuts that can help the processor come to a judgment more quickly and efficiently. Heuristic processing tends to employs only marginal levels of effort and cognitive capacity. Heuristic processing avoids detailed processing of content; rather, it focuses on the more peripheral characteristics of a message. In addition to source identity, these characteristics include source expertise (experts are more believable), source likeability (likeable sources are more credible), message format (well-designed messages are more credible), and message length (longer messages are more credible).

In the case of both models, the perceived need to formulate a judgment can result from outside pressures (for example, the perception that an other will ask questions about the information) or internal pressures (for example, the need to assess the validity of a given message before committing time and energy to processing the message or accepting its contents). Both models also assert that less effortful processing is more likely to occur with low issue involvement, when an individual does not perceive more in-depth processing to be of much consequence, or when an individual wishes to avoid contrary information. The distinction between more and less effortful processing is similar to the conscious-automatic dual processing distinction developed earlier in psychology. Like conscious processing, systematic and central processing both are understood to be controlled and intentional. Heuristic and peripheral processing, however, are not as easily aligned with automatic processing. The theoretical rationales for both the ELM and HSM allow for peripheral-heuristic processing to be deliberate and conscious.

The HSM and the ELM share many similarities in how they conceptualize information processing. One notable difference, however, is that heuristic processing is more narrowly and more explicitly defined than peripheral processing. While peripheral processing can involve simple decision cues, heuristic processing is defined as reliance on the use of decision rules that draw from stored schemas, stereotypes, and so on. Another notable difference between the two models is that the HSM can accommodate the co-occurrence of both modes of processing without a tradeoff—that is, one can simultaneously process information heuristically and systematically with efficiency and success. The ELM does not explicitly address co-occurrence and favors central processing as the most desirable mode of processing. The HSM also addresses theoretical and methodological issues related to the co-occurrence phenomenon. Finally, another notable difference is the ability of the HSM to accommodate multiple motives for processing in addition to the desire for accuracy, which is the motive

highlighted in the ELM. The HSM also allows for processing motivated by the need to defend one's position, as well as processing motivated by the need to form an initial impression. This latter point recommends the HSM as seemingly more applicable not only to information intended to affect attitude change but also to information for which the sole intention is to introduce new concepts.

Bridging Seeking and Processing

In the last decade, there have been an increasing number of studies that seek to explore information seeking and processing in a science and/or risk communication context. One such research program was begun by Robert Griffin, Sharon Dunwoody, and Kurt Neuwirth in 1999. Those researchers integrated the above information seeking and processing concepts into a model they dub the risk information seeking and processing (RISP) model. The purpose of the model was to pull together important factors from different literatures and link them together in ways applicable to risk communication situations in general. That model posits theoretical linkages among seven factors intended to predict risk information seeking and processing:

1. Perceived hazard characteristics such as perceived likelihood of coming to harm

2. Affective response to risk such as worry

3. Perceived social pressures to be informed about risk (informational subjective norms)

4. Perceived amount of information needed about the risk (information sufficiency)

5. Beliefs about the usefulness and legitimacy of various media channels

6. Perceived information gathering capacity

7. Individual characteristics

Support for the RISP model has been robust, as it has explained variance in information seeking and processing regarding consumption of contaminated fish and drinking water, the health of the Great Lakes, and information seeking related to global warming. Those studies indicate that all of the above factors are notable predictors of information seeking and processing—and can together account for upwards of 50% of the variance in both of those concepts.

LeeAnn Kahlor

See also Risk Communication, Overview

Further Readings

Eagly, A. H., & Chaiken, S. (1993). *The psychology of attitudes.* New York: Harcourt Brace.

Gantz, W., Fitzmaurice, M., & Fink, E. (1991). Assessing the active component in information seeking. *Journalism Quarterly, 68,* 630–637.

Griffin, R., Dunwoody, S., & Neuwirth, K. (1999). Proposed model of the relationship of risk information seeking and processing to the development of preventive behaviors. *Environmental Research, 80,* 230–245.

Griffin, R., Neuwirth, K., Giese, J., & Dunwoody, S. (2002). Linking the heuristic-systematic model and depth of processing. *Communication Research, 29,* 705–732.

Kahlor, L., Dunwoody, S., Griffin, R., & Neuwirth, K. (2006). Seeking and processing information about impersonal risk. *Science Communication, 28*(2), 163–194.

McGuire, W. (1974). Psychological motives and communication gratification. In J. Blumler & E. Katz (Eds.), *The uses of mass communication: Current perspectives on gratifications research* (pp. 167–198). Beverly Hills, CA: Sage.

Rubin, A. M. (1984). Ritualized and instrumental television viewing. *Journal of Communication, 48,* 67–77.

INFORMATION SOCIETY

Although highly topical and extensively researched across several disciplines, the topic information society presents certain challenges. Not only does the term support various families of meaning, but also the very existence of an information society is a subject of scholarly controversy. Even among those who believe in the concept—perhaps a majority now—its origins, nature, and policy implications are hotly contested. Disclaimers aside, however, this entry attempts to locate the main empirical and normative currents in the global information society debate. The idea matters to those attempting to grasp the role of scientific information in society because information society theory postulates that information itself has become the foundation of the economy of a handful of highly developed contemporary societies.

Origins and Accounts of the Information Society

It might be thought that a safe way to define an information society is to say that it is an information-based or information-centered society. However, this is to imply that every community, past and present, qualifies. Knowledge of the whereabouts of potable water and other natural resources was, and still is, central to the cultures and economies of indigenous and aboriginal societies. It is better, therefore, to say that an information society is one where information is of unprecedented abundance, where there has been an information explosion, since that captures an aspect of what seems to be unique about contemporary experience in advanced nations.

Such has been the path taken by researchers in Japan, a country that can lay claim to being the leading information society. Not only did the Japanese coin the term—*Joho Shakai* (that is, information society) was first used in 1964 in the media periodical *Hoso Asahi* [Rising Sun Broadcasting]—but they have spared no effort in attempting to measure the information explosion and thus in supplying concrete evidence that informationization—or *Johoka*—was definitely occurring. Using words as their unit—a picture, incidentally, was calculated to be worth 80 words (not a 1,000, as the proverb has it)—their annual information flow census counted the total volume of data flowing across all media. The early returns confirmed that Japan was undergoing an intensive process of informationization, particularly in the area of electronic media. Censuses also revealed the flowering of point-to-point telecommunications, as distinct from traditional mass media. Indeed, as far back as the 1970s Japanese officials were predicting that personalized communications would be the nucleus of the information society—what is today, following Manuel Castells, sometimes referred to as the "network society."

As regards Western thinkers, the outstanding exponent has been Daniel Bell, whose *Coming of Post-Industrial Society* (1973) is usually credited as the foundational text of the information society thesis. Bell's position defies neat summary, but it is clear that the book's main message is that the economy of the United States has undergone a major shift from industrial manufacturing to postindustrial services and information. Data pointing in that direction had already been examined by precursors, notably the economist Fritz Machlup, whose *Production and Distribution of Knowledge in the United States* (1962) argued that knowledge—very broadly defined—had become the largest industry in the United States. Marc Porat and others did additional journeyman work in establishing the concept of the information economy, demonstrating, at least to their own satisfaction, that information workers would outnumber noninformation workers from approximately the year 1980. However, it was Bell who composed a sophisticated, and, for many, persuasive sociological story around this theme. Blue-collar, he explained, has given way to white-collar, and life for the majority has thus become a game between persons. This metamorphosis is seen as being as significant as the industrial revolution, which supplanted the agrarian form of life (game against nature) with factories and mass production (game against fabricated nature). And at the heart of the socioeconomic transformation is theoretical knowledge, which has superseded the trial-and-error inventing of the past. We are, Bell concluded, in the preliminary stages of a new, more scientific era.

What has not been specifically mentioned so far in these accounts is the computer, yet, as the information machine par excellence, the computer has played the starring role in the information society thesis. Admittedly, several of the economic and social trends that gave rise to the information society predated ENIAC (Electronic Numerical Integrator and Automatic Calculator), the world's first proper computer. However, it was the computer, as an enabling, all-purpose instrument, that accelerated and brought to fruition, as well as symbolized, those trends. The gigantic mainframes of the early postwar period, automation and robotics in the 1960s, information technology in the 1970s and 1980s, and of course now the Internet and cyberspace are all phases in the evolution of computing that comprise cumulative evidence of the information society proposition. Recent commentators have presented the convergence between computers, telecommunications, and broadcasting as axial to the future of informationization, forcing huge upheavals in business and society. Nevertheless, the information society should not be conflated with information technology applications because it is rooted in those broader socioeconomic factors described by Bell and others.

Critiques of the Information Society Thesis

The information society thesis, particularly in its more optimistic forms, has met considerable resistance inside the academy. To begin with, critics disallow the operational definitions of informationization. At precisely what point does an industrial society turn into an information society? If the measures are information employment or computer diffusion, are we talking about bare majorities? Why not totalities? And what if the criteria are ratcheted up, to include (for example) distribution of household robots or the proportion of workers in full-time telecommuting? Where does that leave even the land of the rising SONY? Such quibbles reflect an unresolved methodological debate over the extent to which postindustrialism is still just prediction—a "venture in social forecasting," to use the sobering subtitle of Bell's *Coming*.

Another frequent line of assault is that the thesis is guilty of technological determinism, the untenable premise that information technology somehow acts as an unstoppable force, dictating the direction of societal development. This assumption, more or less ubiquitous in popular discourse about new media and technology, seriously underestimates the influence of the human context in which all innovation is situated. Computers, for example, which are largely of military origin, have materialized in their current manifestations because of the particular requirements of various social systems. It is society that shapes technology, not vice versa.

Many have also cast doubt on the validity of a thesis in which the quality of information appears to have been nullified. Most information systems do not discriminate between true and false information, or even between the meaningful and the meaningless. While this does not matter to the signaling engineer, it may trouble the planner and the social theorist greatly. In the original formulations, even striptease dancers were reclassified as information workers, a droll reminder (so critics allege) of the need to challenge the supposition that information society sits comfortably above industrial society in a trajectory of social progress.

Finally, in rejecting claims of a paradigm shift, left-wing thinkers argue that there is one base that has not suffered undue disruption: the power of elites. While some new sources of advantage have emerged, there is little sign of a fundamental upset in the structures of power that developed under industrialism. The means of production, coercion, and communication, now also including cyberspace, are still largely in the hands of the same dynasties. The knowledge class, a theme of 1960s idealism, especially on U.S. campuses, has not coalesced in a politically significant manner. The information revolution is thus only the revolution of a fixed wheel. And that should not be surprising, say such realists, because information is not and will not ever be an independent force in society, but rather, it is a function of stratified economic, cultural, and political power relations. The question then becomes, whose information society?

Whatever the merits of these criticisms, descriptors such as postindustrial society, information society, and network society are now firmly established in the lexicons of academia, government, and industry. Moreover, proponents and opponents of the information society thesis are at least agreed that some of the changes that are afoot require a considered response from policymakers. The final section introduces the major policy implications.

Salient Issues on the Information Society Agenda

The overarching issue, anticipated above, is that of access to information. If information has replaced land and capital as the source of wealth (maximal information society thesis), or even if information has merely increased in importance for citizen participation in society (minimal information society thesis), then access to information has therefore become a critical matter. Some do indeed wish to speak of the information age as an age of access,

but it is certain that the distribution of access is far from equal. The persistence of information gaps and digital divides has accordingly been discussed in political circles everywhere, particularly as Internet connectivity expanded. Early initiatives typically involved a straight injection of information technology—free terminals, neighborhood cyberkiosks and the like—into information-deprived communities. Such technologically deterministic efforts are gradually giving way to more sophisticated approaches centering on information literacy, education, and employment. Nevertheless, severe inequities endure, especially between elites and the mass in developing countries.

Access, though, is only half the problem. Ownership of information, in the traditional sense of legal property rights, has appeared as another divisive item on the policy agenda. While the splendid mantra of the pioneers of personal computing, "information wants to be free," survives as a popular ideal, it is rapidly losing ground to a commodity-minded approach ultimately anchored in conservative political philosophy. Journalists and college librarians, for example, do constant battle to retain fair use clauses in copyright statutes because the trend is toward stricter, longer entitlements for corporations and their clients. The domain of intellectual property rights has been dramatically enlarged, fastening upon such unlikely objects as the venerable Christian fish symbol and even fragments of the human genetic code. But should information be treated as a private commodity or a public resource? The answer must depend entirely upon the type of information in question; yet, overall, current developments indicate that, without policy interventions, wholesale commodification will win the day.

Privacy, too, is commonly believed to be under threat, and some see its defense as the paramount ethical and legal issue facing information societies. Surveillance, in a sense, is the antithesis of the information society thesis: If information is generally exploding, then personal information cannot easily be contained. The widespread passage of freedom of information laws (an aspect of informationization that has little to do with new technology) has often been accompanied by legislation to protect personal privacy. However, even where data protection is relatively robust, there is a growing perception that individual privacy is prone to both official and commercial intrusion. The secret intelligence services, meanwhile, extend their reach, and the "panopticon"—a world where the citizen is constantly being watched, or, at least, cannot ever be sure that she or he is not being watched—becomes an irreversible reality, constitutive of a new, depreciated normality.

Another momentous issue is sovereignty. At what political level—local, national, or international—should citizens act? It could be argued that there is only one information society in existence, a borderless sociotechnical formation. So if globalization is indeed the logic of the future, then perhaps we should be seeking a world government, and yet that concept remains deeply repugnant. The impotence of the recent World Summit on the Information Society, piously devoted to information and telecommunications policy, confirmed that the world cannot speak with one voice on questions of social justice. Meanwhile, potent regional institutions develop. The European Commission, in particular, has foregrounded information society rhetoric in its pursuit of a United States of Europe, an ambition sufficiently alarming to have provoked a public backlash across the continent.

Of course, many of these problems are interrelated in myriad ways, and there are other impending issues of equal, or greater, complexity. What is to be done about the social control of artificial intelligence, robots, and cyborgs? Should statist social engineering be rehabilitated as an antidote to the ongoing social engineering by advertisers and other market actors? How can policymakers facilitate the transition from information society to knowledge society—surely the real goal? And how should postindustrial liberal democracy provide for religion and spirituality, whose revival Bell has predicted?

Conclusion

It is probably safe to report that a multifaceted, global process of informationization is under way. It seems clear, therefore, that the information society, sensibly construed, will partly define the sociotechnical context in which communication, specialist as well as everyday, operates. The resulting premium on information management—in the form, let it be hoped, of intelligent selection, interpretation, and evaluation, rather than of propaganda or

manipulation—should ensure the survival of journalism and cognate professions. The perplexed will always need a guide, even in the midst of an information explosion.

Alistair S. Duff

See also Digital Divide; Knowledge Gap Hypothesis; Technological Determinism; Technological Literacy

Further Readings

Bell, D. (1999). *The coming of post-industrial society: A venture in social forecasting.* New York: Basic Books. (Original work published 1973)

Castells, M. (2000). *The rise of the network society* (2nd ed.). Oxford, UK: Blackwell.

Duff, A. S. (2000). *Information society studies.* London: Routledge.

Machlup, F. (1962). *The production and distribution of knowledge in the United States.* Princeton, NJ: Princeton University Press.

Mattelart, A. (2003). *The information society: An introduction.* London: Sage.

Schiller, D. (2007). *How to think about information.* Urbana: University of Illinois Press.

Webster, F. (2006). *Theories of the information society* (3rd ed.). London: Routledge.

INFORMATION SUBSIDIES

The term *information subsidies* refers to the process of providing news stories, reports, facts, or other forms of information or intellectual capital to reporters or gatekeepers, with the intention of affecting the perceptions or actions of readers, viewers, or recipients of the information. This information is subsidized by the producer, typically making it less costly to the user than it would be were the user to gather it on his or her own. In turn, the subsidizing agency generally expects to gain a higher degree of influence or power over information consumers as well as advantage over competing information sources than would ensue were they not to provide the subsidy. Information subsidies are particularly important for science and technology news.

The value of subsidized information depends on two factors: how it may reduce the uncertainty in future decision making and how useful, credible, or reliable the source is judged to be. Information subsidies are valuable commodities because they reduce the amount of time and expense that reporters would otherwise spend gathering information. Information subsidies also provide opportunities for corporations, governments, or other entities to present their positions and thereby are involved directly in the news-making process. The process of wielding influence through the provision of information subsidies has been described as agenda building.

In 1982, Oscar Gandy defined an information subsidy as an effort to influence others by providing information in a controlled manner at a lower cost than were users to collect it themselves. Researchers have suggested that anywhere from 15% to 80% of news content is derived from information subsides. Nevertheless, debate continues as to the degree to which information subsidies influence reporters and gatekeepers and to how they affect media content.

Agenda Setting

Agenda-setting theory suggests that the media agenda sets the public agenda, and the public agenda sets the policy agenda. The relationships among media agenda, public agenda, and policy agenda are circular or interactive rather than linear or directional relationships. Agenda-setting theory has been linked closely to research on media effects. Researchers have also correlated it with the development of public opinion and policy formation.

Researchers Maxwell McCombs and Donald Shaw, who pioneered research into the agenda-setting process, argued that the amount of coverage given to an issue is directly related to the public's interest and perception of its importance. They demonstrated a direct correlation between the value that the media placed on an issue and voters' interest. Based on their analysis of news coverage of the 1968 presidential campaign in Chapel Hill, North Carolina, these researchers identified this phenomenon as the media's agenda-setting function. Other researchers went a step farther, arguing that the media are responsible for creating a reality that is so powerful and pervasive that the public is unable to ignore its influence even when this is presented in a subtle manner. The perceived role and influence of information subsidies on media effects are

reflective of these relationships. The argument is that social actors who provide the media with information subsidies have great influence on the process of agenda setting. This reinforces the idea that the media play a direct role in shaping public perception and policy and contends that information sources influence media content, and thus (in turn) both public perceptions and policy.

Beyond Agenda Setting

Gandy's landmark 1982 book *Beyond Agenda Setting* defined the term *information subsidy* as a reduction of the cost of information to consumers and disseminators in an effort by sources to increase consumption. Information and knowledge, according to Gandy, has tangible economic and political value. He characterized the exchange of information in terms of surplus and shortage. Advertisers, in his formulation, create a surplus of information, while information about health, for example, may be in shortage. Particularly in capitalist societies, he concludes, those with economic power use information subsidies to maintain their hegemony.

Discussions of information subsidies have suggested a relationship between news media content and news sources, while analysis of the agenda-setting process focuses on the relationship between mass media content and audience reception. Agenda building describes the overall process of creating mass media agendas, but information subsidies influence the process at the source. Gladys and Kurt Lang conceived of information subsidies as the relationship between journalists and their sources engaged in a collective process of agenda building. They argued, for example, that both the press and official sources played a crucial role in the early phase of the Richard Nixon Watergate scandal but that their power to affect public opinion waned as the events unfolded. Other scholars have demonstrated specific aspects of the interplay between the public, news organizations, and news sources to set agendas and have refined the relationship between agenda-setting theory and information subsidies. Judith Turk, for example, has shown how information sources can affect public assessment of the importance of an issue through controlled release of information subsidies.

Information, according to Gandy, is a valuable commodity that is sold or traded according to market principles. He contended that sources often seek to reduce the price of information selectively to increase its attractiveness. Information providers are sensitive to the demand for information—trying to provide too much tends to drive down the price or value, while trying to offer too little may compromise organizational goals. Finding a balance between the demand for information and the cost of production and dissemination depends, to a large degree, on understanding the interests of the target audience. Sources or gatekeepers have a vested interest in matching the prevailing outlook and ideology of information consumers. Thus, the cost of producing and disseminating news items that support the status quo tends to be lower.

For all of its elegance, Gandy's formulation today appears somewhat simplistic. Information is not merely a commodity to be bought and sold in the marketplace. Reporters often exercise ethical responsibility to their readers to present the most accurate and unbiased opinion. For this reason, journalists tend to be skeptical of sources with vested interests in advancing organizational perspectives. They often are cautious as well about using information subsidies from public relations sources. Journalists also tend to balance the information gleaned from various sources when faced with conflicting information or controversy.

Whereas sociologist Herbert Gans argued that sources play a larger role in shaping news, Gandy stressed the mutual dependency of news sources or news subsidizers, on the one hand, and journalists or news providers, on the other. In informing Gandy's contention that reporters benefit from the source–reporter relationship through saving of time and effort for gathering information, Gans compared the relationship to a dance, arguing that, more often than not, sources do the leading. Other research by Jae-Hwa Shin and Glen Cameron has characterized the degree of cooperation or conflict among sources and reporters in the news disseminating, new gathering, and news-making process as a "love and hate" relationship. This research suggests that conflicts between sources and reporters in the agenda-building process may be constructive.

Source Power

Not all sources attempt to exert influence by subsidizing journalists with information equally. Governments and other large organizations, for example, tend to be accepted readily because media cannot easily acquire the information they can provide due to limited or restricted access. Reporters, by necessity, give some sources greater or lesser weight than others. Government officials generally are considered to reflect the source's agenda more accurately than general sources. Scholar Daniel Berkowitz noted that larger organizations tend to serve as news sources to a disproportionate degree because they possess greater credibility and source power.

Source credibility often determines whether reporters use news subsidies. Gans listed credibility among the four factors that affect whether or not news outlets use information supplied by sources, the other factors being reliability, incentives, and geographic location. The source power and credibility of an entity providing a subsidy is thus based on perceptions of disinterest, newsworthiness, and timeliness. Source power and credibility can be analyzed from the vantage point of audience agendas. There is a distinction between the organizations that offer subsidies as a means of projecting power and those who earn credibility through projecting the public's interest. Gans later argued that the public tends to have greater trust in sources that appear disinterested. Journalists, he contended, tend to consider academic and government sources as reliable because there is a built-in public perception that they are unbiased parties, especially in comparison to businesses and advocacy groups. The credibility of an information subsidy is also connected to a journalist's perception of newsworthiness. Research indicates that the perceived availability and usefulness of information comes into play in the news-making process. A source's ability to generate usable news stories provides a more powerful incentive than merely providing information. Turk emphasized the significance of perceived newsworthiness of information subsidies. Berkowitz also found that local relevance and visual elements are keys to the usefulness and influence of information subsidies. The perceived credibility of a subsidy is also connected to timeliness. A combination of these factors informs Gandy's economic concept of information subsidies.

As demonstrated by Gans, journalists tend to use information subsidies from sources with whom they regularly interact. Inevitably, the symbiotic relationships that develop between journalists and sources may have either a direct or subtle influence on news content. The relationship between journalists and news sources has often been described as adversarial, as well as symbiotic. Although journalists try to avoid being influenced by information subsidies and maintain their objectivity and credibility, news sources seek to gain influence on the news agenda. Given time constrains and economic concerns, journalists and gatekeepers often find it expedient and efficient to rely on news subsidies.

Market-Driven Journalism

The practice of journalism is increasingly driven by market pressures. To meet deadlines and rapidly select pertinent information, journalists and other media gatekeepers rely on news subsides. Patricia Curtin found that 78% of surveyed journalists reported using news subsidies, particularly from nonprofit organizations and government sources, with other research estimating that 50% of news stories result directly from press releases and other information subsidies generated by public relations professionals. Some researchers suggest a lesser proportion, perhaps 15%, of news content originated from information subsidies. Regardless of the degree, information subsidies have been shown to have a significant influence on news content.

It is clear that information subsides play a useful and significant role in agenda building. Berkowitz has argued that the costs of news gathering and expediency make it necessary and essential for news providers to rely on a steady stream of information subsidies from news sources. However, some have cautioned that time pressures and source power tend to make reporters and gatekeepers dependent on a small pool of sources at the peril of ignoring competing perspectives.

As John McManus discussed in his 1994 book, *Market Driven Journalism,* various pressures on media outlets may have led to an overreliance on news subsides. The growth of 24-hour cable news networks in the last decade, concentration of media outlets under fewer corporate umbrellas, and the commercialization of news all place increasing demands on gatekeepers to accept news subsides at face value. These pressures, McManus argues, have compromised journalistic ethics. In particular, he is concerned about the loss of objectivity.

On the other hand, Shin and Cameron suggested that the "wrangle in the marketplace of ideas" and the involvement of various social actors in democratic societies promote competition among ideas that foster constructive agenda-building processes. They emphasize the value of advocacy by information sources from a perspective of social interests while noting the diminishing objectivity of journalists. With the advent of new media, news sources are challenging traditional notions of gatekeeping by seeking to reach audiences directly. Seen from this perspective, the prevalence of information subsidies and the power wielded by sources has been never greater.

Jae-Hwa Shin

See also Agenda Setting and Science; Public Relations and Science; Strategic Communication for Science and Technology

Further Readings

Berkowitz, D. (1987). Television news sources and news channels: A study in agenda building. *Journalism Quarterly, 64,* 509–513.

Curtin, P. A. (1999). Re-evaluating public relations information subsidies: Market-driven journalism and agenda-building theory and practice. *Journal of Public Relations Research, 11*(1), 53–90.

Gandy, O. H. (1982). *Beyond agenda setting: Information subsidies and public policy.* Norwood, NJ: Ablex.

Gans, H. J. (1979). *Deciding what's news: A study of CBS Evening News, NBC Nightly News, Newsweek, and* Time. New York: Vintage.

Lang, G. E., & Lang, K. (1983). *The battle for public opinion: The president, the press, and the polls during Watergate.* New York: Columbia University Press.

McCombs, M. E., & Shaw, D. L. (1972). The agenda-setting function of the mass media. *Public Opinion Quarterly, 36,* 176–187.

McManus, J. H. (1994). *Market-driven journalism: Let the citizen beware?* Thousand Oaks, CA: Sage.

Shin, J. H., & Cameron, G. T. (2003). The potential of online media relations to address false consensus between source and reporter: A coorientational analysis of PR professionals and journalists in Korea. *Journalism & Mass Communication Quarterly, 80*(3), 583–602.

Turk, J. (1985). Information subsidies and influence. *Public Relations Review, 7,* 10–25.

INSTITUTIONAL REVIEW BOARD

Department of Health and Human Services (DHHS) regulations require that institutions conducting research activities on humans and receiving federal funds must appoint a specialized review and oversight committee called the institutional review board (IRB). The IRB is mandated by the federal law 45 CFR 46—Protection of Human Subjects. The IRB system is a direct result of the need to provide structure, review, oversight, and public accountability for federally funded research activities involving humans as subjects. The overarching responsibility for IRBs is to protect the rights and welfare of persons recruited as human subjects in research conducted in the affiliated institution. While fortunately somewhat rare, questions about human subjects protections can become prominent news items, and science communicators should be familiar with the basic requirements; university-based science communication researchers, like all other researchers who use human subjects in their research for any purpose, are also bound by these rules.

Throughout history, inquisitive minds have searched for ways to improve the human condition. In the 4th century BCE, Hippocrates is credited with the dictum: "First, do no harm." Despite this early cautionary treatment principle, there are numerous historical accounts of egregious abuses of human beings used as research subjects. Revelations of inhumane experimentation by Nazi researchers during World War II resulted in the creation of the Nuremberg Code. Developed to assist the prosecuting Military Tribunal, it featured 10 ethical principles for the conduct of research involving humans.

In the United States, the infamous Tuskegee study observed untreated syphilis infection in disadvantaged minority populations who were denied treatment that was available to the general public. This study is an example of serious violations of moral and ethical principles in government-sponsored research. To increase accountability, in 1974 the government convened the National Commission for the Protection of Human Subjects of Biomedical and Behavioral Research. In 1979, the commission produced the Belmont Report, a unifying review of research and medical ethics involving humans as subjects. Although federal laws provide the regulations for IRBs, the Belmont Report provides the ethical and moral base for human subjects research and still serves as the essential reference for IRB policies.

The Belmont Report delineates three "basic ethical principles" that remain the basis for all human subjects research: respect for persons, beneficence, and justice. The principle of respect for persons involves the ethical conviction that all individuals must be free to make an independent assessment and judgment of their ability and willingness to participate as a research subject in a defined activity. Not all persons are capable of or empowered to make self-determination, and some cases may require special considerations or protections. Examples include the young, mentally disabled, incarcerated, or those susceptible to coercion. Informed consent—the process of ensuring that participants understand the research and willingly volunteer—is the key application of respect for persons.

The second principle is beneficence. This principle obligates researchers not only to try to protect research participants from harm, but also to seek to secure their well-being. The IRB must attempt to ensure that subjects receive maximum possible benefits and minimum possible harms. Regulating research that poses a degree of risk but has no immediate prospect for benefit to the actual participant involves consideration of beneficence in IRB evaluations. The performance of a comprehensive risk-benefit assessment is critical to the application of the principle of beneficence.

The third ethical principle is justice. The key premise is that a group or class that will ultimately benefit from research should not unnecessarily differ from those that bear the burden or risks of that research. Historical examples of problems would include the experimental use of disadvantaged ward patients who could not afford the medical benefits developed, unwilling prisoners in Nazi concentration camps, and the participants in the Tuskegee syphilis study. Consequently, research must be scrutinized to ensure that subjects are selected for legitimate reasons, not solely because they are conveniently available, have no viable alternatives, or have other exploitable vulnerabilities.

The Belmont Report also addresses the sometimes blurry boundaries between research (contributing to generalizable knowledge), and practice (improving the well-being of an individual patient or other participant). The report set the stage for current federal human subjects legislation and rule making. In 1991, 16 federal departments and agencies adopted a uniform set of regulations unifying federal oversight of human subjects research. The Food and Drug Administration, which has its own set of IRB requirements as they apply to clinical trials of new drugs, also adopted certain of these provisions. These uniform regulations were called the Federal Policy for the Protection of Human Subjects, or the common rule.

Using 45 CFR 46, the National Institutes of Health Office for Human Research Protections regulates all aspects of federally funded human subjects research, including in-depth requirements for IRBs. Membership must include at least five members, with varying backgrounds and qualifications that promote adequate review of institutional research activities. IRB members must be able to consider issues such as race, gender, community attitudes, cultural backgrounds, and special or vulnerable populations and be equipped to adequately represent these interests. Assessment of risk is a fundamental review consideration since risk largely determines the review mechanism, intensity, frequency, follow-up, and reporting requirements for IRB-approved research.

The need for IRB oversight may be most apparent in biomedical research projects where experimental procedures or materials pose an evident degree of risk. However, IRBs are also responsible for oversight of all human subjects research activities, including social science or behavioral research that might cause other harms such as embarrassment, psychological trauma, emotional distress, invasion of privacy, loss of social status, exposing of illegal behavior, or loss of employment, for example. Even where there is no special reason to expect any of these or any other harm to participants, researchers using human subjects still must apply for IRB oversight.

Since the original rules were designed primarily to regulate biomedical research, application of the standards to nonmedical research activities can be especially challenging for IRBs. The IRB system is an unfunded federal mandate that commonly stretches organizational resources. The ultimate challenge for IRBs is to minimize the effect of cumbersome regulatory bureaucracy, while fulfilling legal and ethical requirements to protect the interests and welfare of persons who agree to participate in research as subjects.

Gerald Jaax

See also National Institutes of Health, U.S.; Research Ethics, Overview

Further Readings

U. S. Department of Health and Human Services, Office for Human Research Protections: www.hhs .gov/ohrp

INTELLIGENT DESIGN IN PUBLIC DISCOURSE

Depending on one's perspective, intelligent design (ID) can be viewed as either the intrusion of a religiously driven pseudoscience on the successful scientific project of evolutionary theory or as an alternative theory of origins that promotes pluralistic thought and education. The public debates have been played out in an astonishing number of venues, including movies, speaking events, textbooks, books, bumper stickers, court cases, museum exhibits, and media coverage of all of these. In this entry, we will try to outline the argumentative and discursive strategies used by both sides in the debate. The main positions and theories on each side of the debate are often captured in the terminology used, such as the idea of *the watchmaker* (an argument that the design of life is so complex it surely required a designer, parallel to a watchmaker), the concept of *descent with modification* (Charles Darwin's term for biological evolution), and the term *irreducible complexity* (the ID concept that biological systems are too complex to have evolved as Darwin proposed), among others. This entry uses the terms *IDer* and *evolutionist* to label the supporters of each side, recognizing that this includes a variety of positions under each label.

Generally speaking, the main communication strategy used by IDers has been to pull the larger public into the debate and show how ID (as they believe) can contest on an equal footing with the arguments of the scientific community. Ultimately, IDers want to be seen as partaking in an internal scientific debate on the public stage, even if their position has public implications (they think all science does). This strategy represents a fairly radical departure from the clash of science and religion that has occurred from the days of Galileo Galilei to the so-called Scopes trial; IDers generally do not seek the exclusion of science, but seek to make their own inclusion equal. Evolutionists, for the most part, have tried to portray the ID community as outsiders to science because they are religiously motivated and/or do not advance any positive, testable scientific claims. However, unlike IDers, evolutionists have only reluctantly engaged in public debate, primarily because they do not see this debate as a legitimate scientific controversy. In addition, they argue that the admission of ID into science per se ends up disadvantaging mainstream biology, especially in the classroom.

Lines of Argument

The general lines of argument used by each side of the debate can help observers understand how each side makes arguments favorable to their own case and how they attack the opposition. These are useful in trying to track the terms of the debate as it has played out in the public sphere; they do not necessarily represent the best instincts of either side, but the ones that get the most "play."

Abusive Characterization

Each side caricatures the other so that all ID defenders become 6-day creationists, and all scientists are characterized as materialist, atheist Darwinians. These characterizations are typically used for mocking the opposition and often incorporate "straw person" fallacies. Standing in for the evolutionists, Richard Dawkins notoriously characterizes ID and other forms of creation science as a type of insanity. Contrarily, supporters of ID mock evolutionists as well. Ben Stein's film *Expelled* presents several dubious representations of evolutionists and the philosophical implications of evolutionary theory. Both sides attempt to create caricatures of their opposition to appear more reasonable and sound themselves.

Slippery Slope: The Dangers

Science: Proponents of ID argue that scholars and the public need to be skeptical of the intellectual and political power of scientific knowledge and language. Supporters of ID often cite historical catastrophic instances where science was motivated by ideological and political commitments, such as Nazi science. They argue that the supposed objectivity of scientific knowledge and language often masks larger ideological, political, and paradigmatic motivations. Because of this, the public should be skeptical of status quo science and investigate possible biases. With evolutionary theory in particular, IDers would like the public to recognize the secularism, philosophical materialism, and atheism they believe are implicit in the theory.

Religion: Supporters of biological evolution maintain that ID theory is religiously based in both motivation and conclusion. Ultimately, including one's religion in scientific research might lead to predetermined conclusions, thus nullifying a theory's scientific credibility. In addition, the inclusion of ID in the public school classroom was ruled a violation of the Establishment Clause of the First Amendment in *Kitzmiller v. Dover* (2005). Defenders of ID maintain that on the contrary, the theory has no religious motivation and offers a substantial scientific theory that is supported by empirical studies.

Appeal to Fairness

Relying on arguments for democratic pluralism, proponents of ID argue that the classroom and the public sphere should have room for multiple theories, particularly both evolutionary theory and ID. In this view, ID proponents are not to be seen as attempting to oust evolutionary theory from the public school classroom; rather, they are allowing both theories to speak for themselves. Critics of ID argue that including multiple theories in a classroom just for the sake of pluralism is antithetical to effective science education; we should not teach every topic and theory so that science education is fair; rather, we should teach the best current science that is well supported by research.

Another way to state this line of argument is that everything is debatable, as if scientists are unfairly trying to "shut down debate" by pointing out the accumulated mass of evidence supporting evolution; the phrase "teach the controversy" is an academic variant of the same argument. To an extent, this amounts to disagreeing about whether this is a religious or scientific debate: Are evolutionists advancing religious claims or IDers scientific ones? IDers will often try to gain entry to scientific debate through plausible examples; scientists contend that fairness should not get extended to just anyone, but only when an alternative position becomes plausible. IDers return again and again to the example of the bacterial flagellum, which they believe is characterized by "irreducible complexity." They contend that since they have evidence for their theory, they have stronger grounds for arguing for fairness dictating their own inclusion.

Wolf in Sheep's Clothing

Supporters of ID are often criticized by evolutionists for disguising creationism by the use of the term *design*. In analyzing the ID textbook *Of Pandas and People,* the National Center for Science Education (NCSE) discovered that the textbook was an exact replica of an earlier creationist textbook, *Biology and Origins,* save one difference: The word *creation* and its derivatives had been replaced by the word *design*. NCSE and other supporters of evolution have therefore accused IDers of merely adopting new vocabulary and term to distance themselves from scientific creationism. IDers argue that this shift in language is reflective of the substantive scientific research that supports their theory of ID. Supporters of evolution commonly cite the famous "Wedge Document" of the Seattle-based Discovery Institute (which promotes ID) as evidence for IDers attempting to "wedge" creationism into the public sphere through the use of ID.

Argument From Ignorance

Traditionally, this form of argument amounts to "true because not proven false" or "false because not proven true." Evolutionists maintain that IDers offer no positive claims in support of their theory and only try to show that Darwinian evolutionary theory might be flawed. Even if this is the case, evolutionists maintain that it would not, conversely, make ID true. Evolutionists also argue that ID must be wrong because it makes no positive assertion about the natural world that could be subject to scientific scrutiny and testing. IDers, however,

argue that they do advance positive, testable claims, most commonly the "irreducible complexity" argument. They also point out that evolution is "just a theory" and is therefore open to criticism.

Argument Frames

These are the background argument contexts for the argument topoi (rhetorical themes) used in this controversy. We will call these arguments "frames" because they amount to metastructures that provide a means for interpreting the arguments circulating in the media. Each of these provides a way of interpreting the significance of the lines of argument cited previously. For example, arguments from ignorance ("You haven't disproved me") take on a different meaning if they are meant to imply presumption ("my side doesn't need to prove") or underdog status ("Proving is an unfair burden on us").

Battle Over Presumption

Traditionally, certain situations of argument distribute the responsibilities of arguers in a differential way: Who has the burden of proof, and who needs to merely refute? The old Roman principle *Qui dicit probat* (meaning, whoever asserts must prove) implies that simply staking a claim brings the burden of proof. But in many situations, there is a preexisting body of belief, fact, argument, or policy (the status quo); the challenger has the burden of proof, while the status quo has presumption (it is considered true until sufficient reasons are brought against it). The status quo does not need, logically, to argue for itself but just has to poke holes and show the challenger has not met the burden of proof. In the legal setting, presumption both gives advantage to the weaker party (the accused) and avoids the possibility of a tie—in the case of equal evidence, the presumption wins.

In the case of ID, a huge number of argument resources are opened or closed by the assignment of presumption. If evolutionists have presumption, they do not have to defend their view, just attack IDers or creationists. If both sides have the burden of proof, and their proofs are incommensurate ("We see God's actions in the very places you don't"), then there is the possibility of stalemate, in which observers of the debate could reasonably conclude for either side. Scientists are quick to claim presumption for themselves, although they are not always adroit at making clear how their claim is justifiable.

This frame is applied in several kinds of topoi. For example, "it's just a theory" appears to be less a claim about what scientific theories are than the assertion that there is no presumption in this setting. "Teach the controversy" likewise positions ID and biology as competing on an equal footing. For the science community, their frequent appeals to "150 years of scientific research" or "all that is known about processes of adaptation" function as a claim to presumption, which sets in motion their reluctance to defend biology per se, and rather attack ID claims only. Again, claims about IDers' "ignorance" of biology make the most sense when seen through the framework of presumption and burden of proof; if standard biology is true, one would have to be ignorant to challenge it, and the burden falls on the ignorant.

Underdogs: For Whom Should We Root?

Lacking a clear sense of presumption in the situation, arguments made by each side seem to ask that they be given support based on their social–political disadvantage in the situation. Is this a case where the entrenched and callous establishment of Big Science musters its forces to silence a few brave people of faith? Or is it a case where scientists bravely defend rationality against the wacky legions of religious zealots who are not content to control every other aspect of public life in the United States? Obviously, these stereotypes are broadly drawn, but for "low information" consumers of this debate, this may serve an important role indicating which side deserves sympathy—which one is "my" side or "my" team.

Democracy Versus Authority

Another way of deciding who is sympathetic is through the frame of democracy and authority. The frame is applied in a slightly different way, depending on which side uses it. For scientists, science still retains its Enlightenment legacy as the democracy of knowledge: Within the purview of scientific method, all claims and claimants are equal. But religious claims seem to cheat this system and have to be regarded as authoritarian interruptions in the democracy of knowledge; they change the game by trying to enter into it, and so should rightly be ignored. For the IDers, scientific debates are no different from political debates; the only token necessary for admittance is citizenship—so let us just debate. Scientists are then behaving like authoritarians, holding themselves above others, and refusing to engage those with whom they do not agree. Much of the appeal of the fairness or teach the controversy topos comes from this frame; we live in a democracy, so everything ought to be debatable.

Regress/Slippery Slope to the Unthinkable

This frame works in tandem with the science versus religion frame and allows each side to condemn the other for the nightmarish result of siding with that other side. For scientists, the history of religion is fraught not only with discord and disagreement that cannot be solved rationally, but also with violence, from crusades and religious wars to the Inquisition. The condensation symbol for what is wrong with religion is the persecution of Galileo by the Catholic Church for maintaining truths about celestial bodies. On the other side, science is portrayed as without value or scruple, an approach to the world indifferent to the horrors that science might produce. The nightmare of science gone amok is personified not only by Frankenstein's monster, but also, and more horrifyingly, by Nazi eugenics and experiments on human beings. This frame justifies arguments that would otherwise seem very off point, ranging from "the Inquisition is obviously not far behind" to "removing God from the world leads directly to the Nazis."

Both sides in this debate use each of these lines of argument and frames to their own advantage in public discourse. The larger question of whether this is how we ought to conduct such debates remains unanswered. However, at present public communication and debate on these issues most commonly rely on these elements, so understanding them can help observers understand some of what lies beneath the surface.

William Keith and Julie Homchick

See also Big Science; Darwin, Charles; Dawkins, Richard; Galilei, Galileo; Scientific Method

Further Readings

Behe, M. J. (1996). *Darwin's black box: The biochemical challenge to evolution.* New York: Free Press.

Campbell, J. A., & Meyer, S. C. (Eds.). (2003). *Darwinism, design and public education.* East Lansing: Michigan State University Press.

Dembski, W. A. (2007). *Intelligent design: The bridge between science and theology.* Downers Grove, IL: Intervarsity Press.

Dennett, D. C. (1995). *Darwin's dangerous idea: Evolution and the meaning of life.* New York: Simon & Schuster.

Kitzmiller v. Dover Area School Distict, 400 F. Supp. 2d 707 (M.D. Pa. 2005).

Forrest, B., & Gross, P. R. (2007). *Creationism's trojan horse: The wedge of intelligent design.* Oxford, UK: Oxford University Press.

Fuller, S. (2007). *Science v. religion? Intelligent design and the problem of evolution.* Cambridge, UK: Polity Press.

Fuller, S. (2008). *Dissent over descent: Evolution's 500-year war on intelligent design.* London: Icon.

Isaak, M. (2007). *The counter-creationism handbook.* Berkeley: University of California Press.

Johnson, P. E. (1993). *Darwin on trial.* Downers Grove, IL: Intervarsity Press.

Intelligent design argument. (1998). [Special issue] *Rhetoric and Public Affairs, 1*(4).

Kitcher, P. (2007). *Living with Darwin: Evolution, design, and the future of faith.* Oxford, UK: Oxford University Press.

Larson, E. J. (1997). *Summer for the gods: The Scopes trial and America's continuing debate over science and religion.* Cambridge, MA: Harvard University Press.

Larson, E. J. (2008). *The creation-evolution debate: Historical perspectives.* Athens: University of Georgia Press.

Miller, K. R. (2008). *Only a theory: Evolution and the battle for America's soul.* New York: Viking.

Numbers, R. L. (2006). *The creationists: From scientific creationism to intelligent design.* Cambridge, MA: Harvard University Press.

Pennock, R. T. (Ed.). (2001). *Intelligent design creationism and its critics: Philosophical, theological, and scientific perspectives.* Cambridge: MIT Press.

Petto, A. J., & Godfrey, L. R. (Eds.). (2007). *Scientists confront intelligent design and creationism.* New York: W. W. Norton.

Scott, E. (2004). *Evolution vs. creationism: An introduction.* Berkeley: University of California Press.

INTERNATIONAL SCIENCE JOURNALISM ASSOCIATIONS

It has been suggested that the bug-like tendency of science journalists to swarm, or as Philippe Marcotte and Florian Sauvageau describe it, their "propensity for grouping and mingling," stems from their sense of isolation—from other types of reporters and even more so from their sources. Neither fish nor fowl, science writers tend to be a breed apart, often the only one of their kind in a newsroom—or, in the developing world, sometimes in an entire country.

Surprisingly, then, the creation of mutual support systems for science writers is a relatively recent phenomenon. Although the first national group— the German Association of Science and Technical Journalists—was founded in 1929, followed by the formation of the U.S. National Association of Science Writers (NASW) in 1934, the majority of the 55 national and regional associations counted in a 2007 survey published by the World Federation of Science Journalists (WFSJ) were formed since the mid-1970s, with many in the developing world created only in the last decade.

Internationalization of Science Journalism

The rapid and luxurious bloom of science journalism worldwide in the late 20th century mirrored in part the transformation of science research into an international endeavor. As the world became increasingly interconnected, it was clear that issues such as climate change, water shortages, sustainable development, and pandemics knew no borders. Because global problems demanded global solutions, many science journalists hoped to establish effective global networks for sharing vital information, ideally though a world union or federation of the many new national groups.

The first step toward internationalism was creation of the Ibero-American Association of Science Journalism (AIPC) in 1969 by the Spanish writer Manuel Calvo Hernando. The AIPC linked a score of national associations in Latin America (some of them extremely small) with a base group in Spain. In addition to promoting exchanges of journalists and conducting training programs, the AIPC sponsored a series of bihemispheric "congresses" that would set the model for future international conferences. Indeed, at the 1977 congress in Madrid, the Venezuelan delegation proposed creation of a World Union of Science Journalists. Although an international organizing committee was formed and some potential funders, including the United Nations Educational, Scientific and Cultural Organization (UNESCO), were contacted, this first formal expression of the "world union" concept went little further due to political, economic, and linguistic limitations.

Actually, the idea of a world union had come up even earlier—and was dismissed—during the creation of the first truly global such association, albeit one made up of individual journalists, the International Science Writers Association (ISWA). In 1966, a group of senior science writers and editors (among them Gordon Rattray Taylor of the British Broadcasting Corporation [BBC], John Maddox of *Nature,* and Dennis Flanagan of *Scientific American*) met in London to discuss the benefits of forming a loose network. The next year, using the occasion of the World's Fair in Montreal, Canada (EXPO 67), this core group, joined by several other prominent writers (including Robert Cowen of the *Christian Science Monitor,* Howard Lewis of the U.S. National Academy of Sciences, and Fred Poland of the *Montreal Star*), met to write and approve a draft constitution, to elect officers, and to debate, and finally dismiss, a motion to create a federation of associations in favor of what ISWA would become (and remains today): an "organization of individual membership." Maddox became the first president.

For the next 30 years, ISWA would provide science journalists around the world, particularly those living and working in countries without national associations, connections with the wider world of science communication. Initially serving a largely Anglo-American-Canadian group of journalists who lived or worked abroad (including the notable expatriate Arthur C. Clarke of Sri Lanka), ISWA actively sought out young journalists from emerging nations in the 1980s. Today, the organization has some 200 members in 25 countries, and through its Web site, ISWA offers them information about jobs, training, and educational opportunities, as well as assists in planning, organizing, and conducting workshops on science communication.

A World Union?

While ISWA has remained an organization of individuals, the concept of an organization made up of associations still resonated with many writers. In 1971, Giancarlo Massini of Italy's *Corriere della Sera* persuaded a group of like-minded European science journalists to form what was to become a truly multinational organization, although a purely regional one. Out of their meetings was created the European Union of Science Journalists' Associations (EUSJA).

The original union included just seven associations, but following the collapse of the Berlin Wall in 1989, there was an upsurge of interest from Eastern European countries, all of whom now play an active role in EUSJA's activities, which include exchange visits between member countries and training for young journalists. Member countries (as of March 2009) are Albania, Austria, Croatia, Denmark, Estonia, Finland, France, Greece, Germany, Hungary, Ireland, Italy, Netherlands, Poland, Romania, Russia, Slovenia, Spain, Sweden, Switzerland, and the United Kingdom. EUSJA has its headquarters in Strasbourg, France, at Euroscience—where it has its own secretariat.

Those forerunners of a world union—EUSJA, ISWA, and AIPC—would all play significant roles in organizing the first world conference of science journalists, and eventually, if somewhat painfully, the formation of an actual world federation. But despite these contributions, that first conference was essentially the result of one man's vision and persistence.

Arthur Bourne, a British science writer, world traveler, and occasional consultant to the United Nations, had tried for nearly two decades to organize a truly international conference of journalists from all parts of the world—and particularly from the emerging nations of Africa and Asia. Finally, in late 1990, Bourne, by then president of EUSJA, persuaded UNESCO to sponsor the first world conference in Tokyo, Japan. With generous assistance from Japanese business and philanthropic groups, some 50 journalists from 35 countries were invited to meet with approximately 100 of their Japanese colleagues in November 1992.

Despite the great success of the Tokyo meeting, its declaration of the need for a world association, and the continued efforts by Bourne and others to organize a follow-up, a second world conference would not be realized for another 7 years. Held in Budapest, Hungary, in July 1999, this conference reflected the changes in science journalism brought about by new technologies, as well as the changes in European society brought about the collapse of the old Soviet bloc.

The organizer and host of the Budapest meeting, Istvan Palugyai, science editor for the newspaper *Nepszabadsag,* had been a leading proponent of the federation concept at the Tokyo meeting. As such, he led the effort to write "The Declaration of Budapest," a set of eight recommendations for UNESCO aimed at improving the state (and status) of science journalism worldwide. A key recommendation was the formation of a world federation bringing national and regional associations under an umbrella organization that, among other things, could convene international conferences on a regular basis.

The next milestone was 2001, when Japanese science writer and teacher Kenji Makino organized an international mini-meeting on science and technology reporting at Tokyo's then-new innovation museum. The meeting closed with still another call for a world federation, but the accompanying draft constitution caused some controversy because the signatories to the document did not necessarily officially represent their national associations.

The third world conference would be convened within a year at the Universidade do Vale do Paraiba in Sao Jose dos Campos, Brazil. Any lingering doubts about the usefulness of an umbrella group of associations and concern over its awkward introduction in Tokyo seemed to have disappeared by this time. The result was a formal announcement of WFSJ, complete with a set of officers and a draft constitution that would be approved at the next conference, held in Montreal in 2004.

By April 2007 and the fifth world conference in Melbourne, Australia, the WFSJ was a well-established entity, with some two dozen member organizations, a sustaining budget, and active outreach and mentoring projects for reporters in the developing world. The sixth conference was held in London in the summer of 2009, by which time the WFSJ represented 40 associations of science and technology journalists around the world. Its flagship project is *SjCOOP,* which encourages partnerships between well-established science writing associations and newly formed ones in the developing world. One highly successful partnership has been that between the Arab Association of Science Journalists, representing writers from the Middle East and North Africa, and the NASW in the United States.

One other world union of science journalists also deserves mention. The International Federation of Environmental Journalists (IFEJ) was formed in Dresden, Germany, in 1993, and Darryl D'Monte, chairman of the Forum of Environmental Journalists of India, was elected its first president. The federation includes as members both associations and individual environmental journalists representing some 88 countries.

The IFEJ is a founding member of the Com+ initiative (Communicators for Sustainable Development), together with the World Bank, Global Environment Facility, InterPress Service, Conservation International, BBC, DevTV, Television Trust for the Environment, *National Geographic,* and a number of other partners. With InterPress Service, IFEJ runs an occasional feature service on sustainable development issues, among many other initiatives.

James Cornell

See also Clarke, Arthur C.; Council for the Advancement of Science Writing; National Association of Science Writers

Further Readings

Cornell, J. (1999). Report: Second world conference of science journalists meets in Budapest. *Science Communication, 21*(2), 200–202.

Cornell, J. (2002). Report: Tokyo conference sets stage for third world conference—and a New World Federation of Science Journalists. *Science Communication, 23*(4), 463–466.

Drillsma, B. (Ed.). (2006). *The barriers are down: EUSJA advances across Europe.* Strasbourg, France: European Union of Science Journalists' Associations.

International Federation of Environmental Journalists: www.ifej.org

International Science Writers Association: www .internationalsciencewriters.org

Marcotte, P., & Sauvageau, F. (2006, Winter). *Les journalistes scientifiques: Des éducateurs?* [Science journalists: Educators?]. *Les Cahiers du journalisme,*

15, École supérieure de journalisme de Lille and Université Laval.

White, J. (2007). *2007 science journalist associations guide*. Gatineau, QC, Canada: World Federation of Science Journalists.

World Federation of Science Journalists: www.wfsj.org

INTERNET, HISTORY OF

The Internet is an extremely flexible and rapidly evolving communication infrastructure. Most researchers are struggling with the challenge of understanding the significance of the Internet for our present and future life. The aim of this contribution is different: The main focus is on the history and evolution of the Internet up until now. Like many other complex technologies, the Internet is not a single innovation and was not invented in one day by a single individual. This entry presents a few of the key events and key developments in this history.

This entry begins with an explicit definition of the Internet that highlights that the Internet is much older than common wisdom usually assumes. In the following sections, three main phases in Internet history are distinguished (military, academic, and commercial). The last section sketches the current situation and possible futures of the Internet.

Definition of the Internet

In everyday conversation, most people use the term *Internet* as a synonym for the World Wide Web (WWW). However, this colloquial definition is wrong from a technical perspective: The WWW is indeed a part of the Internet, but it is only one service among many others (see Table 1).

Given that background, what is a more precise definition of the Internet? Perhaps the simplest and shortest definition would be this: The Internet is a global net of computer networks. Some authors add the technical specification that the Internet includes all communication based on the TCP/IP protocol (see below for further details).

Two points should be highlighted in this definition. First, the Internet is a global communication infrastructure that provides public access to all users. The Internet differs, in other words, from Local Area Networks (called LANs) that provide access only to a limited number of users (such as students and faculty members at the same university, employees of the same company, and so on). Second, the Internet is a metanetwork that allows for the integration of a variety of computer networks that differ with regard to hardware and software (including operating systems).

Under this broader definition, the history of the Internet does not start with the invention of the WWW (say in 1989), but much sooner: The oldest Internet service is the File Transfer Protocol (or FTP), which was invented and first used in 1970.

It is not easy to distinguish specific phases in Internet history, which is due to the fact that many development processes were taking place in parallel and had neither a clear beginning nor a specific culminating point or end. Nevertheless, the determination of phases is helpful to highlight key trends and structure the long list of facts and figures in a systematic way. For the sake of simplicity,

Table 1   Selected Internet Services and Years of Invention

Internet Service	Year of Invention	Technical Protocol	Content Type	Communication Structure
File Transfer Protocol	1970	FTP	Data, Text	Group Media (m-m)
E-Mail	1971	POP3, SMTP	Mainly Text	Private (1-1), Group (m-m), and Mass Media (1-m)
Chat	1988	Internet Relay Chat Protocol (IRCP)	Text	Group Media (m-m)
World Wide Web (WWW)	1989	Hypertext Transfer Protocol (HTTP)	Multimedia	Mass Media (1-m)

Source: Author, using data from Leiner et al. (2003).

then, three main phases can be distinguished in the Internet's history: a military, an academic, and a commercial phase that are separated by key events.

Military Phase: The ARPA-NET (1969–1985)

In the beginning of the Internet, military aims and resources were of key importance. In retrospect, the triggering event lies back in the cold war. In 1957, the Soviet Union successfully developed and launched the first artificial satellite (named *Sputnik*). This led to the so-called *Sputnik* crisis, involving the sudden awareness of the United States that the Soviets were technologically more advanced and able to launch intercontinental missiles. As a reaction to that crisis, military spending for research and development was increased to cope with this technological challenge. In 1958, several new institutional bodies were created, including not only the National Aeronautics and Space Administration but also the less well-known Defense Advanced Research Projects Agency within the U.S. Department of Defense. This agency was a longtime sponsor of the main predecessor of the modern Internet, called the ARPA-Net (Advanced Research Projects Agency-Net).

The ARPA-Net went into operation in 1969 and initially linked four nodes (meaning computers) at the following institutions: the University of California, Los Angeles; Stanford Research Institute's Augmentation Research Center; the University of California, Santa Barbara; and the University of Utah.

Using scarce resources in an economical way was a key driving force in the development of the ARPA-Net. In contrast to current times, computers in the 1960s and 1970s were extremely large (filling entire halls) and expensive. Linking computers was one approach to sharing this expensive infrastructure in an efficient way. Another approach to the economical use of the network itself was the use of packet-switching technology. Packet switching is a network communication method that divides information units into packets that are transmitted separately over the network, following paths dictated by the availability of connections, and then put back together at their final destination. In addition to the economic advantage, packet switching is also better able to guarantee a safe and robust exchange of information that can be continued even in the case of nodes on the network failing. This security aspect was also of key interest for the military sponsors of the ARPA-Net. Packet switching is still in use in the present Internet.

Several other key events marked this first phase of the Internet. In 1972, e-mail was invented by Ray Tomlinson, working for BBN Corporation. In 1973, an open protocol was created that allows access of any computer to the Internet, named TCP/IP and developed by Internet pioneers Vint Cerf and Bob Kahn. In 1983, the ARPA-Net stopped using the old protocol (called NCP) and switched to the new, open protocol, TCP/IP. Finally, the military phase ended in 1985 with the split of the ARPA-NET in two sections, MILNET for the military and ARPA-NET for civilian use.

The Academic Phase (1985–1991)

The second phase of the Internet's history can be labeled the academic phase. Academic institutions (such as universities) have had a strong influence on the Internet evolution from the very beginning of the military phase, but their impact was strongest in the years from 1985 to 1991.

The key invention in this phase was the WWW, developed by Tim Berners-Lee, Sam Walker, and Robert Caillau, working as researchers at CERN (European Organization for Nuclear Research). The WWW was initially created in 1989 and was then publicly announced and made generally available in 1991. The main innovative technological features of the WWW are hypertext documents that are interlinked to each other and can be navigated by using hyperlinks. Hypertext documents are read by means of a Web browser (such as Mozilla Firefox, Internet Explorer, and so on).

The main motive of Berners-Lee and his team was to facilitate the communication and exchange of scientific data among researchers with different nationalities and academic backgrounds who were working at CERN. Therefore, the software developed for programming hypertexts (the so-called hypertext markup language, or HTML, and its protocol, the hypertext transfer protocol, or HTTP) was conceptualized from the very beginning as open source software. Though the term *open source* was not yet in use at this time, the creators of the Internet shared the intention of today's open source movement to make the source code of their software available to the general public with relaxed or nonexistent copyright restrictions. A main innovation of the WWW was the integration of different media types (pictures, sound, video, text, and animation) in one environment.

Commercialization and Popularization Phase (1991–Present)

The third and still ongoing phase of Internet history can be called the commercialization and popularization phase. It started in 1991 with the decision of the U.S. government to allow commercial enterprises to be present on the Internet and to develop new forms of business there (often referred to as e-commerce). Since that decision, the Internet has spread much more rapidly within the general population than any other medium before it. It took only 5 years to gain 50 million Internet users in the United States, for example, which is much faster than radio (38 years) or television (13 years), according to Internet historian William Slater. This high-speed diffusion of the Internet can be attributed to several factors.

The first factor has been that hardware costs have diminished constantly and dramatically over the last few decades. According to the idea embodied in what is known as Moore's law, the power of the newest computer chip doubles every 18 months and the prices halve in the same period. This "law" does not really have the status of a scientifically grounded theory, but is rather a generalized trend based on empirical observations.

A second factor for the accelerated diffusion of the Internet has been the availability of user-friendly Internet software. The development of a new type of visual browser software allowed even those without extensive technical training to navigate easily through the Internet. Mosaic was the first visual browser and was developed by Marc Andreessen and Eric Bina at the National Center for Supercomputing Applications (NCSA) and released in 1993. Mosaic was further developed by the same team outside the NCSA and renamed into Netscape Navigator. Netscape was one of many Internet companies to experience a commercial boom due to inflated expectations. This commercial Internet hype peaked in the year 2000, which was followed by a "crash," or a rapid decay of the values of these technology stocks.

A third factor promoting the rapid diffusion of the WWW was its multimedia content. In contrast to older, text-focused services on the Internet (see Table 1), the WWW opens new and attractive options for developing and distributing entertainment content (such as music, videos, and games). These multimedia options were a key feature in making this complex technology not only accessible beyond the small elites of technicians and scientists, but also attractive for a broader audience.

Present and Future Trends

As a result of all of these favorable factors, we can see today a high and continuing diffusion of the Internet on a global level. In 2009, some 25% of the world population had access to the Internet. However, there are strong differences in Internet access (and also Internet use) between and within world regions that are discussed and investigated under the heading digital divide. Many industrialized countries already show signs of market saturation. In 2009, the Internet penetration (share of the population with Internet access) was 75% in North America, followed by Oceania-Australia with 60% and Europe with 50%. The other world regions have lower average penetration rates (Latin America, 30%; Middle East, 24%; Asia, 19%; and Africa, 7%), but some nations within these regions are on the same level as North America (such as South Korea at 77% or Japan at 74%), according to a 2009 report by the Web site Internet World Stats.

What about the future of the Internet? This short sketch of Internet history has shown that many technological developments were not the result of long-term planning and were not foreseeable at the time they started. It was neither the intention of the U.S. military nor of any of the academic institutions involved to create a new commercial infrastructure for the distribution of multimedia content. Based on that background, any statements about the further development of the Internet should be made and read with considerable caution. Nevertheless, the following three trends seem to be relevant for the next decade or so:

1. *Continuing diffusion:* The expansion of the Internet will continue in all world regions and reach levels similar to those of many industrialized countries today.

2. *Mobile access:* More users will access the Internet by wireless technologies (mobile phones, laptops with WLAN, and so on). This trend is of special relevance for those areas (such as Africa) that are in the process of building up a telecommunication infrastructure based on wireless technologies (without first having a completely developed wired infrastructure).

3. *Convergence with other media:* More and more, the content of traditional mass media such as newspapers, radio, and television will be distributed via the Internet. As a result, many familiar technological distinctions (such as that between a TV set and a computer) as well as market segmentation (such as that between TV and radio companies) will be softened or will disappear entirely.

While the details of the Internet's future cannot be predicted with certainty, it is clear that these three—continued diffusion, more wireless access, and ongoing media convergence—are practical inevitabilities.

Urs Dahinden

See also Cold War Rhetoric; Digital Divide; Media Convergence; National Aeronautics and Space Administration, U.S.; Online Media and the Sciences

Further Readings

Alesso, H. P., & Smith, C. F. (2008). *Connections: Patterns of discovery.* Hoboken, NJ: Wiley-Interscience.

Internet Society. (n.d.). *Histories of the Internet.* Retrieved September 7, 2009, from www.isoc.org

Leiner, B. M., Cerf, V. G., Clark, D. D., Kahn, R. E., Kleinrock, L., Lynch, D. C., et al. (2003). *A brief history of the Internet.* Retrieved September 7, 2009, from www.isoc.org/internet/history/brief.shtml

Miniwatts Marketing Group. (2009). *Internet world stats: Usage and population statistics.* Retrieved September 7, 2009, from www.internetworldstats.com/stats.htm

Slater, W. F. (2002). *Internet history and growth.* Retrieved September 7, 2009, from www.isoc.org/internet/history/2002_0918_Internet_History_and_Growth.ppt

INTERPRETIVE COMMUNITIES

An idealized treatment of science envisions it as a sphere of activity in which there is no need for interpretation. The specialized terminology and systematic methodology of science creates an environment in which interlocutors understand each other so perfectly that they can dispense with the messy business of untangling each other's utterances. The precision of scientific communication allows the direct transfer of meaning from one mind to another, or so the story goes. The concept of the interpretive community can help to explain how communication within science can be so effective, designed to convey meaning between experts with so little ambiguity and confusion, and why that image of scientific communication does not always match the reality of how scientific texts are encountered.

Literary critic Stanley Fish introduced the idea of the interpretive community to show how a particular meaning for a text is rooted in the shared interests and goals of a particular group of readers. A piece of literature might not have a single, objectively true meaning that is understood by all readers at all times, but a community of readers who share a set of interpretive strategies, and who look at a text from the same frame of reference and with an agreed upon procedure for determining its meaning, can unite in a shared understanding of it. Scientists who share a disciplinary vocabulary and an agreed upon set of goals and research practices constitute one such interpretive community, allowing them to suffer no loss of communicative content and endure no contentious debate over the meaning of their shared texts. Communication in science is thus ideally untainted by the murky depths of hermeneutic encounter.

But even if it were true that scientists within a discipline always make up a community of speakers who understand each other perfectly, there are situations when scientists from one discipline must communicate with scientists from another, with those who are still training to enter the discipline, or with nonscientists. It is in these cases that the concept of multiple interpretive communities becomes especially useful to the activity of describing, analyzing, and evaluating the communication of scientists.

Communicating Across
Disciplines and Other Gaps

Scientists must sometimes communicate with colleagues who occupy different specialty fields, scientists who do not share their particular disciplinary interests or goals and who operate with somewhat different expert vocabularies. Scientists from these distinct disciplines might be said to exist in different interpretive communities, and thus, they are more likely to approach an interdisciplinary scientific text with divergent beliefs about the proper meaning of that text. For example, a single passage in Erwin Schrödinger's little book *What Is Life?* was interpreted by antireductionist physicists as evidence that the author believed new complementary laws of physics would soon be discovered in biological matter, while a number of reductionist biologists interpreted that same passage as evidence that the author was confirming the presence of the already discovered quantum-mechanical laws of physics in living things.

These two readings of the text, although contradictory, both fit perfectly well with what was said in the text, as viewed by the interpretive community that developed it in each case. Which reading was most accurate is difficult to determine, and possibly irrelevant, since both interpretations helped Schrödinger achieve his stated intent of getting physicists and biologists to collaborate with each other in studying the physical aspect of the living cell.

Another situation in which scientists are likely to develop contradictory interpretations is when a discipline experiences what Thomas Kuhn described as a revolutionary shift from one paradigm to another. Insofar as the old guard and the subscribers to the new paradigm can be said to occupy incommensurable positions, they are unable to make complete contact with each other's viewpoints. Each sees the world through the lens supplied by its own interpretive community, and any canonical texts for that discipline are read and reread to support the worldview of each respective reading community.

Disciplinary communities and paradigms are two ways of categorizing readers as grouped into reception clusters that authorize divergent interpretations of a text. Another variable that can be used to identify multiple interpretive communities is

geography. For example, Charles Darwin's *Origin of Species* was interpreted differently in the 19th century by scientists in the American South who understood its meaning within the horizon of postbellum racial politics and by scientists in Russia who interpreted it in light of their dissatisfaction with Malthusian social theory. Scholarship on the geography of reading traces differences in reception that mark the presence of divergent interpretive communities bounded by spatial and geopolitical factors.

Interpretations of scientific texts can also differ across temporal boundaries, with a 19th-century interpretation of Darwin's *Origin of Species* developing differently from a 20th-century interpretation of that same text, not due to the disruption of a radical paradigm shift, but because a number of changes accumulated in the culture of its more modern readers. Both synchronic and diachronic studies of reception demonstrate that clusters of interpretation vary for important scientific texts. Whether contained by disciplinary, geographical, or historical boundaries, the existence of these different interpretive communities demonstrates that scientific texts are not always as exegetically shallow as they are sometimes made out to be; their meaning shifts and changes across fields, over space, and through time.

Interpretive Communities
and Science Pedagogy

When Fish used the concept of interpretive communities, it was in the context of authorizing a single, defensible, if temporary, reading of a literary text within the classroom environment, where requirements for evaluation demanded that meaning not be wholly idiosyncratic, but where he also knew that a single objective meaning for a literary artifact was out of reach. By legitimating readings according to the social systems of intelligibility, the practices and assumptions that inform the particular cultural or institutional communities to which he and his students belonged, a potentially anarchic deconstructive process could be given reasonable constraints.

Mapped to the study of scientific communication, this concept of the interpretive community can help to explain how students are trained to read like scientists, developing a shared set of interpretive practices that discipline them to the vocabulary, performative traditions, and genres shared by experts in their respective fields. In short, they are educated to become members of a particular interpretive community in science, just as Fish's students were trained to read a text like a literary critic. For example, a study of how graduate students and faculty members in evolutionary science read a scientific article demonstrates that those who are not yet wholly socialized into the reading practices of this interpretive community are less critical of what they read, approaching the article for comprehension rather than to test its arguments or question its findings. Also, students are more likely to read the article in a linear fashion rather than jumping between sections or skimming sections as the more disciplined faculty readers did. Presumably, over the span of their graduate education, they learn to read more like expert evolutionists do so that by the time they are ready to join the faculty, they are socialized into the reading practices that make that scientific community function so well; they become literate in a particular scientific discipline's interpretive culture.

The Public Communication of Science

Extradisciplinary actors can also constitute interpretive communities for science. One such community that has been identified is the profession of journalists, a group that usually serves as a conduit between scientists and the public. Driven by their own institutional, occupational, and social values, journalists apply a consistent set of reading frames to their reporting of scientific developments. As a result, the stories they tell often employ the same themes and quote the same types of actors, even if the science being discussed in different reports diverges greatly. When a science story becomes a key public event, it is also the case that certain favored interpretations are shared across news outlets, and a single narrative is developed that reflects the interests and assumptions of science journalists as much as, if not more than, the interests of the specific scientists whose work is being reported.

Another node along which interpretive communities might diverge in the public communication of science is political ideology. For example, the community of climate change skeptics tends to be politically conservative, while the community of

climate change adherents tends to be politically liberal. Both communities can look at the same scientific data reported in the same text and with great certainty come to opposite conclusions about the meaning of that data. Although science is mythologized as an institution that operates free of political commitments, when significant public policy implications arise, neither scientists nor members of the general public are able to avoid the coloring lens supplied by the ideological worldviews that they share with others of like mind.

Conclusion

The concept of interpretive communities in science tempers the idealized image of science as immune from the multiple meanings that attend poetry and scripture, as a perfect vector of communication that transparently conveys the intended message of scientific authors. But in exploding this myth, it does not open up the scientific text to infinite meanings. Instead, it anchors the meaning of a scientific text in the shared interpretive strategies of a particular community. It should not be forgotten that when that community is a highly disciplined one, the work that can be done by scientific communication is considerable. It is mostly when communication escapes that disciplinary community, encountering scientists from other disciplines, paradigms, locations, and times, or encountering nonscientists, that different interpretive communities make divergent claims on the meaning of a scientific text.

Leah Ceccarelli

See also Audiences for Science; Climate Change, Communicating; Kuhn, Thomas

Further Readings

Ceccarelli, L. (2001). *Shaping science with rhetoric: The cases of Dobzhansky, Schrödinger, and Wilson.* Chicago: University of Chicago Press.

Charney, D. (1993). A study in rhetorical reading: How evolutionists read "The spandrels of San Marco." In J. Selzer (Ed.), *Understanding scientific prose* (pp. 203–231). Madison: University of Wisconsin Press.

Fish, S. (1980). *Is there a text in this class? The authority of interpretive communities.* Cambridge, MA: Harvard University Press.

Kuhn, T. S. (1970). *The structure of scientific revolutions* (2nd ed.). Chicago: University of Chicago Press.

Leiserowitz, A. (2007). Communicating the risks of global warming: American risk perceptions, affective images, and interpretive communities. In S. C. Moser & L. Dilling (Eds.), *Creating a climate for change: Communicating climate change and facilitating social change* (pp. 44–63). New York: Cambridge University Press.

Livingstone, D. N. (2005). Science, text, and space: Thoughts on the geography of reading. *Transactions of the Institute of British Geographers, 30,* 391–401.

Ten Eyck, T. A., & Williment, M. (2004). The more things change . . . : Milk pasteurization, food irradiation, and biotechnology in the *New York Times. Social Science Journal, 41,* 29–41.

Zelizer, B. (1993). Journalists as interpretive communities. *Critical Studies in Mass Communication, 10,* 219–237.

INTERVIEWING SCIENTISTS

Many journalists feel daunted at the prospect of interviewing a scientist. They worry that the scientist will talk over their heads. They may have heard dark tales of scientists who refuse to be interviewed, or reluctantly agree, only to talk in jargon and roar their disapproval when a mangled media account appears. Some wonder if they can get an interview at all. But in truth, interviewing scientists has never been easier. As more and more federal agencies require public outreach efforts on the part of the scientists they fund, growing numbers of scientists understand the need for participating in media interviews. In addition, as colleges and universities seek to promote their science faculty and expand job opportunities for their students, many more scientists receive training in how to relate to journalists; as a result, more now understand the needs of journalists for clear, jargon-free explanations and bullet points and their needs for turning things around quickly on deadline. Scientific societies, too, offer a growing number of articles and workshops on how to prepare for media interviews to ensure that their scientist members are getting across what they want to, clearly and easily.

This means that much of the groundwork that journalists used to have to lay for a good interview has already been done for them. That does not mean it requires little effort to conduct a successful interview with a scientist. There remains a lot of work to do. But most of the time, it is not the daunting prospect it used to be. The most important advice for conducting a successful interview is the old Scout motto: Be prepared.

Getting Background

First, a journalist does advance reading, both of the science involved and of other journalists' accounts of the scientist and of his or her work.

One place to start is to go to the scientist's Web site, for often it summarizes the work a scientist is doing and who is funding the research, as well as providing a curriculum vitae (the extended resume used by academics) and other background information. A journalist can download from there or from the Internet any article he or she wishes to discuss. If journalist does not have time to read the work that is prompting the interview, he or she skims what he or she can, paying particular attention to titles, abstracts, conclusions, and any graphs and charts that condense the main points of the work. From the introduction and discussion sections of individual articles, the journalist gleans what he or she can of the scientific and social significance of the research. Journalists read the conclusions for significant caveats and calls for future studies. They consider any possible influences from funding sources and check the body of the text and the reference list for names of other scientists in field who might be able to comment on the findings. Finally, if a journalist gets stuck on unfamiliar terms or concepts, he or she looks them up in science dictionaries or encyclopedias.

Using LexisNexis or other online databases, a journalist can find any stories that other journalists may have written on the scientist and/or the specific research. Journalists skim for the names of additional scientists in the field, preferably experts without direct ties to their interview subject, again seeking those who could comment on the quality of the research or its scientific and social significance. Journalists also note how other journalists have handled difficult terms and concepts.

Setting Up the Interview

Most scientists shuttle between their offices and their labs or the field and may respond better to e-mail than to phone calls. So journalists e-mail their requests for interviews. That way, journalists will not get caught in what science writer Glennda Chui calls "phone-tag hell."

Journalists explain the what, where, and when. In the e-mail, journalists briefly explain the purpose of the interview—to discuss the findings and their significance, for example. Journalists note the kind of piece they are working on—a discovery story, profile, or trend or issue piece—and for whom. Journalists explain the amount of time they will need—usually no more than 20 or 30 minutes in the case of most discovery stories—and say where they would like to conduct the interview—preferably on the scientist's professional turf, so they can gather observational details as needed. They also mention their deadline and times when they are available to talk.

Once the scientist says yes to the request, journalists ask for the single best description of the research. Journalists specify that they want something relatively brief and reader friendly, if it is available. The journalist may already have it, but it does not hurt to ask, and if the journalist does have what is recommended, he or she can say so in a reply, thus impressing the scientist with his or her preparedness.

Journalists must be persistent. They cannot be afraid to e-mail the scientist again if he or she does not respond to their first e-mail request. If that does not work, they try the telephone, or if the scientist is an academic, even "shoe leather," showing up at his or her office during office hours. Journalists do not want to be pests, of course, but a little initiative can go a long way.

Prethinking Questions and Comments

To be sure a journalist makes the best use of his or her time in the interview, the journalist prethinks his or her questions and comments. As a general rule, preparing leading questions and questions that elicit yes-no answers should be avoided. Instead, open-ended questions should be prepared. Such questions ask for information or opinions without leading scientists in a predetermined direction.

Before launching into the interview, some science writers like to comment on an aspect of the research; this is a way of showing that they have taken the time to become familiar with the scientist's work. Journalists can identify some aspect of the research that they find particularly interesting or that is otherwise worthy of comment for their warm-up questions.

Some science writers like to begin their interviews by asking, "What inspired your research?" Claudia Dreifus, who conducts question-and-answer pieces with scientists for the *New York Times*, often begins with this kind of question. It gets at things not typically included in formal research accounts and can also serve as a good warm-up.

The favored first questions of broadcast journalists are these: "Tell me in your own words what you found, and why you think these findings are significant to science or society." The very general nature of these questions can lead some scientists to imagine the journalist has not prepared for the interview, but if the journalist has planned a warm-up comment that belies that judgment, these questions can be useful ones, setting the journalist up for conversational quotes about the significance of the scientist's work in his or her own eyes.

Questions about the research context should be asked. As any experienced science writer will state, one scientific study is but a piece in the scientific puzzle. So it is going to be important, once the journalist is clear on the findings, to ask how these results fit with those of prior research. Do they support and extend prior findings? And if they contradict prior findings, what accounts for that? Sometimes results that fly in the face of existing research findings do so because the new research uses more rigorous research methods. Sometimes, though, it can be for other reasons. Be on the lookout for biasing influences of funding sources, as research has found a tendency for research findings to lean in the direction of those who fund the science, especially when the science is funded by corporate sponsors.

Science stories only rarely contain much about research methods. Despite this, experienced science writers are likely to prepare a number of questions about methods. They do this if only to get clear for themselves the quality of the research, having learned the hard way that even studies that have passed peer review sometimes have serious flaws. Questions related to method tend to revolve around populations studied, sampling procedures, sample size, measures used, and the ability of a particular research design to control for extraneous variables that could muddy (or confound) the findings.

If the journalist does not have the background to prepare questions about research methodology, at least he or she can ask what was the most important thing this particular study was unable to answer about the subject. What remains uncertain? When journalists ask about the unknowns and uncertainties in the science, the chances are high that the scientist will talk about the major limitations of the research, and from such discussions, journalists cannot only decide what caveats belong in their stories but also begin to increase their knowledge of research methods. Basic texts on research design can also be helpful to increase one's knowledge of research methodology.

Risk–benefit questions should be asked. When research concerns a new medical treatment or drug, experienced science writers tend to prepare additional questions that can temper extravagant claims. Among these questions are the following: Is there any evidence of harms, and if so, to whom? Are some more likely to benefit than others? How does the new treatment or drug compare to existing alternatives? How soon is the treatment likely to become available? And what will it cost?

If journalists are working on a feature story, they are also going to want go after the little human interest stories that help to support what they think they may want to say or show about their subject (the focus). To get at these anecdotes, journalists should ask questions about whether the person they are interviewing recalls when he or she first got the idea for this study, realized he or she had found something no one had seen before, or first realized the significance of the findings, and journalists can follow up with additional questions that flesh out the incident—the time of day, thoughts and emotions, the responses of others, and so on. They can be on the lookout when they arrive for the interview for visual details (books on the shelves or cartoons on the door) that could support the feature angle they are considering. Journalists should imagine ahead of time what some of these things might be.

With whatever kind of story is being written, anticipating concepts will require additional explanation. One should be prepared to ask the scientist to make comparisons to things in ordinary life. For example, journalists may ask the following: "Could you compare this process to anything our audience is more likely to know and understand?"

Finally, journalists prepare to ask their interviewee for the names of others scientists who can comment on the quality and significance of the research, both for science and for society. Journalists cannot be afraid to ask for the names of potential critics as well as champions. Surprisingly, most scientists are willing to provide the names of those who are likely to have reservations about their work, as well as the names of those who are sure to support it enthusiastically.

Interviewing Like a Pro

When journalists show up for the interview, they thank the scientist for taking time out of a busy schedule to talk to them about the subject (be specific) for the publication or broadcast outlet involved (name them). They offer any warm-up comments and preview the kinds of questions they are going to ask and convey a sense of the level at which the scientist is going to need to pitch the answers. So, for example, if they are producing a story for a general interest audience, they might say something like this:

> I'd like to ask you about x, y, and z. It may help as you answer these questions to know that our audience consists of people at all kinds of education levels. We don't like to think of our audience as dumb, just uninformed. Some scientists I've talked to find it helpful to think of me as a member of that audience—a smart person, but someone with a high school education or even less. Alternatively, think of me as a particular person in your family who is not stupid, but doesn't know what you know and will need a lot of help to understand the research. If you talk to me as if I was that person, it may make it easier for both of us to get the kinds of explanations and easy-to-understand comments that will work in the story.

It is good to prepare, but even better to listen. As the interview unfolds, journalists do not stick rigidly to their prepared questions. Try not to read them, for example. They allow for the inevitable give-and-take that will facilitate conversation and help them to understand the science, and they record what they learn in ways that facilitate listening and conversation.

Journalists should welcome occasional tangents. They should feel free to deviate from their prepared questions, especially if the scientist gets especially enthusiastic about something. Some of the best material can come from such tangents. Journalists can always gently bring the interview back to point, by looking at their watch and saying something like, "Wow, this is going by quickly! I want to be sure we cover everything, so let me ask you . . ."

Journalists should not pretend to know more than they do. The Chinese have a saying, it is better to ask and appear ignorant than to remain ignorant. For a journalist, there is no better advice, so they should not be afraid to show their ignorance or to interrupt and ask the scientists to simplify, maybe even to create a drawing if it will help them to understand something. If the journalist does not understand it, it is going to be impossible to explain it to someone else.

Notes should be taken unobtrusively. If a journalist can, he or she should take notes while maintaining eye contact. They should use their own system or shorthand, perhaps putting parentheses around indirect quotes, so they can distinguish these from direct quotes later. Journalists might also want to write question marks in the margins and fold back an edge of that question-marked page to come back to at the end of the interview.

A backup recorder should be used. Science writers differ on the advisability of using recorders in an interview. But most like them, as they provide a backup to note taking and allow for better listening. If they do use one, they should tell their scientist they are using it to ensure accuracy. When he or she says something the journalist knows he or she is going to use, jot down the minute or number of the record. Doing that saves one from having to listen to the entire tape to get the quotes and other information the journalist is going to want to use.

Finally, at the end of the interview, journalists should review their notes for questions they had but did not get a chance to ask. A good concluding question can be "Is there anything I overlooked?" When the journalist has finished the interview, he or she thanks the scientist for the help and asks if it would be okay to call if he or she has additional questions while writing the piece; journalists should get a phone number and times that are convenient.

Postinterview Follow-Ups

It is important to fact-check the story. Many media shops that will not allow a journalist to check back with a source on a political story will allow it with science stories. So if this is allowed, it should be done, stressing to the scientists that what they have to say about the factual accuracy of the account is more important than how the piece has been put together to enhance the public's interest and understanding.

Many science writers who ask scientists to check their facts hesitate to send the entire story for fact-checking. They read just the factual passages of the story or script to the scientist, usually over the phone, as this saves time and also provides an opportunity to talk about any changes the scientists might recommend.

Studies of science news accuracy suggest that scientists often see as errors matters that have been omitted for the sake of simplicity. If it becomes necessary, journalists may need to stress that some concepts have had to be simplified so as to gain and maintain audience interest.

Journalists should always send the article (or a link) to the scientist with a thank you. Good manners never hurt anyone.

S. Holly Stocking

See also Bioethicists as Sources; Scientist–Journalist Relations; Scientists as Sources; Visible Scientist

Further Readings

Cohn, V., & Cope, L. (2001). *News & numbers: A guide to reporting statistical claims and controversies in health and other fields* (2nd ed.). Ames: Iowa State University Press.

Dreifus, C. (2001). *Scientific conversations: Interviews on science from the* New York Times. New York: Henry Holt.

Schwitzer, G. (2008). *Health news review.org: Grades for health news reporting.* Available at www.health newsreview.org

INVASIVE SPECIES

As global travel and trade increase and the global climate changes, the dispersal of species from their natural range into new areas is bound to increase, increasing the likelihood that species will become invasive, often with unexpected consequences. Effective communication with diverse stakeholders is essential for reaching a shared understanding of the perceived costs and benefits of invasive species to the environment, the economy, and society and to inform decisions that prioritize actions and resources to manage the risks posed. This entry considers the traits that make species invasive, the risks invasive species pose, methods for their assessment and management, and the important role of communication throughout the risk management cycle. Stakeholders must work together to address invasive species issues, and understanding risk perception and effective risk communication will be increasingly important components of the management of invasive species.

Invasive alien species are defined by the International Union for the Conservation of Nature (IUCN) as all organisms, animals, or plants that have a negative effect on "the local ecosystem and species" because humans have introduced them to an area that is outside of "their natural range," and they then establish themselves and become broadly distributed in these areas. It is usually because of their impacts that invasive species are of concern—and sometimes generate controversy. This entry follows the IUCN's ecological emphasis, although impacts on the economy or society may also be of concern.

Historically, species have often shifted their ranges naturally in response to changed environmental conditions. However, documented species invasions have overwhelmingly originated from purposeful or accidental introductions by humans. Growth in international trade and travel is increasing the opportunities for species to invade new areas, both through their accidental transportation and because people deliberately transport exotic species that they value for their use as food, fiber, or medicine; for their beauty; as exotica or as pets; for sport; and for their usefulness in the biological control of other organisms. In Australia, a review led by Malcolm Nairn found that more than 70% of the 290 plant species naturalized during 1971 to 1995 were introduced through human activities. However, not all species that are introduced become pests. One rule of thumb suggests that 10% of species imported are introduced to ecosystems in the receiving area, of which 10% become established, of which 10% become pests.

Characteristics of Successful Invasions

Models describing the life histories (that is, the patterns of development, reproduction, and mortality) of particular species have been used to identify traits that may favor invasiveness. Invasive species are often categorized as having high potential rates of population growth enabled by such characteristics as short life cycles and preferential allocation of resources to reproduction. Other associated traits can include small propagule size (that is, small size of seed, egg, or other part capable of giving rise to a new individual) and effective dispersal, often over long distances. A species may also become invasive in a new area through being free of the natural enemies that were present in its native range.

Models of the structure and dynamics of ecological communities have been used to identify environments that may be more favorable to invaders. Many of these model the process of succession by which one ecological community gives rise to another. In general, disturbance of communities is considered to facilitate invasion by new species, and late-successional or species-rich communities are thought to better resist invasions.

International Policy and Regulation

Internationally, many approaches are used to predict which species are likely to be invasive, what their impacts are likely to be, and how best to manage them. For members of the World Trade Organization, assessment and management of invasive species risks must accord with the Agreement on the Application of Sanitary and Phytosanitary Measures (SPS agreement), and reliance on other standards is also encouraged. Other international bodies and agreements are also concerned with the management of risks posed by invasive species, such as the Global Invasive Species Program and the International Maritime Organization's International Convention for the Control and Management of Ships' Ballast Water and Sediments.

Predicting Invasion Risk

Managing invasive species is easier if invasion risk can be predicted. Most predictive approaches assess the risks posed by individual species, although more recently, approaches based on the attributes of ecological communities have begun to be developed.

Most predictive approaches identify the pathways (such as shipping containers or transport by air passengers) by which species may arrive; assess the likelihood of the species entering, becoming established, and spreading in a new area; and assess the consequences that would result. Uncertainty often pervades these predictions and needs to be considered in making decisions. Where the risks posed are considered unacceptable, the risk may be managed by preventing or controlling the entry and the establishment or spread of species and by limiting their impact. Defining an acceptable level of risk is important and is ultimately a social decision, involving tradeoffs between preventing undesirable impacts and interference with desirable activities. Consultation with stakeholders is important at all stages of the risk assessment; an interactive exchange provides ownership of the solution proposed and can enhance the acceptance of decisions.

The probability of success at different stages of invasion is influenced by diverse factors. Entry of a species into a new area requires long-distance transport from areas the species currently inhabits. Transport may be favored by an association with humans, wide existing distribution, and a capacity to survive conditions during transport. The species' survival in the new area may depend on locating suitable habitats or hosts. Founding populations also have to overcome initial low population densities and low genetic variation. Traits that enhance the competitive ability of the invader compared with other species in the ecological community in question, such as toxicity to natural enemies, may favor establishment. Spread may follow a long lag phase during which populations evolve and adapt to local conditions, or in which repeated introductions increase genetic variability. Small propagule size or the presence of dispersal pathways such as roads or disturbed areas may favor spread, while natural barriers may limit it.

In a review, Kenneth Whitney and Christopher Gabler found that the majority of schemes to predict invasions by a species draw on the life history attributes associated with past invasions, the known distribution of the species, how well the environment in a new area matches that of the species'

current distribution, and the species' potential impacts in the new area. Maps of species' current distributions have been drawn using a range of methods, according to another review led by Benjamin Phillips, ranging from drawing a simple smoothed line to fitting a convex polygon to distribution records. Future distributions have been predicted using two main classes of methods. Correlative statistical approaches use data on a species' spatial distribution and environmental variables such as climatic conditions in its current and possible new range to predict potential distribution in a new area. Alternatively, mechanistic approaches model the relationship between species' physiological adaptations and fitness in different environments.

Rates of spread of species may be predicted using statistical models of current and historic rates of spread as a function of environmental conditions or mechanistic models of population dynamics.

Ecological Impacts of Invasion

Invasive species may affect native species and ecosystems directly or indirectly. Direct effects may occur where the invasive species is an herbivore, browser, predator, or parasite that feeds on native species. Direct effects may also result where the invasive species hybridizes with native species. Indirect effects may arise through a range of mechanisms. For example, the invasive species may act as a vector for the introduction of other species including novel pathogens detrimental to native species, compete with native species for resources, or alter the effects of natural enemies that also affect native species.

A review led by Marc Kenis on the ecological effects of invasive alien insects considered the example of the gypsy moth, *Lymantria dispar,* which is a major pest of broad-leaved forests in eastern North America. Larvae feed on oak (*Quercus spp.*) leaves and repeated defoliation increases tree deaths. Oak defoliation by gypsy moths depresses the growth rates and survival of native northern tiger swallowtail butterflies, *Papilio canadensis,* which feed on oak leaves. Gypsy moth outbreaks have also been associated with increases in the rates of attack of other native moths and butterflies by generalist parasitoids. Defoliation and deaths of oaks lead to changes in the structure and species composition of forests with further impacts on ecosystem processes.

Quantifying the impacts of invasive species and measures used to manage them are often mandated by national and international legislation and guidelines (such as the SPS agreement). Many of the resulting costs and benefits fall outside of markets and are difficult to estimate in monetary terms. This has sometimes meant that impacts on native ecosystems or cultural activities have received less attention than impacts on agriculture or human health. Efforts are being made to remedy this through the development of frameworks that account for the services provided by ecosystems and enable peoples' preferences to be taken into account.

The Importance of Evolution

Some doubt the effectiveness of current schemes to predict invasive species, which are dynamic, evolving entities. A review by Whitney and Gabler has shown the importance of evolutionary change, both for the invasiveness of species and the resistance of receiving communities. Invading populations are likely to experience evolutionary change because of hybridization of different source populations and native and other introduced taxa, small initial population size, and novel selection pressures coupled with typically rapid population growth.

For example, cane toads, *Chaunus [Bufo] marinus,* were introduced to Australia in 1935 in a misguided attempt to control agricultural pests. Ben Phillips and Rick Shine have shown that increased rates of spread of cane toads have accompanied the evolution of longer legs in toads at the invasion front, which may gain a fitness benefit by arriving at a site first and forming the founding population. Furthermore, they demonstrated coevolution with Australian red-bellied black snakes, *Pseudchis porphyriacus,* which have increased resistance to the novel toxins possessed by the toads.

Risk Management

Unacceptable risks posed by an invasive species are managed in a variety of ways. Early implementation of measures to prevent entry of a potentially invasive species may be more desirable and cost-effective than later implementation of measures to control or eradicate an established species, and measures are often put in place at national borders, or at preborders. Acceptable levels of risk may be achieved using measures that ensure freedom of vehicles, consignments, passengers, or commodities from potentially invasive species to agreed tolerance limits. These may include inspection, production of certified commodities, disinfestation treatments, and quarantines.

Measures to control or eradicate invasive species that have established or spread include poisoning, shooting, cutting, burning, trapping, and biological control. Measures may also include the regulation of movement of organisms and their vectors out of affected areas, monitoring, and public awareness campaigns.

Governments often face the difficult task of deciding how best to allocate limited resources along the biosecurity continuum. Such decisions require the efficient allocation of resources to the species that pose the greatest risks and the balancing of the differing interests of affected stakeholder groups.

Management strategies should take into account not only the level of risk, but also the degree of uncertainty in estimates of the likelihood and consequences of species invasion. Adaptive management strategies that enable variations in the measures applied as new information comes to hand may be particularly important where uncertainty is high.

Surveillance and Monitoring

Surveillance and monitoring programs form an important part of the management of these risks. Surveillance involves continuing investigation of a given population to detect the occurrence of a species. Monitoring involves ongoing programs aimed at detecting changes in a species' abundance. Early detection of the presence of a potentially invasive species can enable early intervention and reduce costs. Monitoring also provides opportunities to learn about the system of concern and evaluate the effectiveness of management actions. Sampling schemes, data collection, recording, and analysis may be explicitly targeted to address areas of uncertainty in the original risk assessment and provide evidence for future policy development.

Monitoring may underpin contingency planning, with detection of invasive species at predefined levels triggering emergency actions. Such planning can be of great benefit in enabling rapid responses to incursions and limiting the likelihood that a species will become established.

Traditionally, taxonomic expertise has played an important role in the identification of species considered to pose unacceptable risks. Recently, methods based on DNA have begun to be used. While an invasive species chip capable of rapid screening for hundreds of species is still fanciful, a review by John Darling and Michael Blum shows that DNA-based tools are already contributing to the management of the risks posed by invasive species. For example, the invasive northern Pacific seastar, *Asterias amurensis,* spread to Tasmania in the 1980s and subsequently established in Port Phillip Bay on mainland Australia. Ballast water is a vector for transportation of this species' larvae and could contribute to expansions of its range. Bruce Deagle and colleagues developed a polymerase chain reaction–based method to detect DNA of the invasive *Asterias* species in ballast water.

Public awareness may also form an important component of monitoring and surveillance schemes. The potential for informed members of the public to contribute to early detection and management of invasive species is gaining increased attention.

Risk Perception and Communication

Actions to manage invasive species are shaped by scientific and other knowledge. However, societal preferences, and people's perceptions of and attitudes toward the risks posed by invasive species, are also highly influential and are attracting new research interest. For, example Juliet Stromberg and colleagues have recently argued for a reframing of perceptions of invasive species, and for scientists to discard negatively biased viewpoints and language. They considered the case of *Tamarix,* imported and widely planted in the United States in the early 20th century as a windbreak and to stabilize soil. Concerns that *Tamarix* water use was high came to dominate during the mid-20th century, and *Tamarix* was tagged the country's second worst weed. Today, evidence of the ecosystem services provided by *Tamarix* in modified riparian communities suggests that eradication management efforts are sometimes misguided.

The future success of governments in preventing and managing species invasions will depend on the public's understanding of invasive species, their sense of shared responsibility, and their willingness to support policies for the management of invasive species. Communication requires intelligent, sympathetic thought about how to respond to any public concerns. Public awareness campaigns can encourage engagement and desirable behaviors, including involvement in actions to mitigate the spread and impacts of invasive species. Participatory approaches to policy development are also essential to constructive engagement with stakeholders. They improve the transparency and accountability of decision making, enable testing of assumptions, and provide a more complete exploration of the risks of concern and options to manage them.

Decision Making

The environmental, social, and economic costs and benefits of invasive species are experienced differently by stakeholders than from different sectors of society. These differing values can be integrated with scientific understandings of risks by using formal decision analysis, as has been shown by Lynn Maguire, who considered the example of feral pigs (*Sus scrofa*) brought to Hawaii by Polynesians and later by Europeans. The pigs damage native ecosystems and are vectors for bird diseases. Hawaiians of European and Polynesian descent are concerned about these negative impacts, but the pigs also serve important contemporary roles in the cultural activities of Polynesian Hawaiians.

Differing perceptions and values make effective communication essential to the assessment and management of the risks posed by invasive species and emphasize the value of deliberative approaches to decision making, which facilitate participation of stakeholders and the consideration of their knowledge and values, as well as those of experts.

The Future of Invasive Species

Jessica Hellman and collaborators have considered the problem of invasive species in relation to climate change, which could change patterns of trade and transport, the commodities that humans choose to deliberately import, and the survival of species accidentally transported. Climate change may also change the frequency of successful dispersal by other means such as storms. Patterns of colonization of invasive species and the spread of established populations may also be affected where climate change alters the favorability of the climate to the invasive species relative to that of resident native species. Climate change may be more favorable to invasive species than native ones because invasive species are more likely to possess traits considered adaptive in changing environments—such as broad environmental tolerances, short juvenile periods, and long-distance dispersal mechanisms—while native species are more likely to be adapted to particular local conditions. The impacts of invasive species may also be altered by climate change, with increased range sizes and abundance speculated to increase impacts on ecosystems and economic costs.

Climate change may require a rethinking of strategies to manage invasive species. In situations where changed climates are more favorable to invasive species, the effectiveness of current mechanical and chemical methods of control may be reduced. The long-term success of current biocontrol programs may also be altered; biocontrol agents are usually selected for specificity to the target invasive species, and changes in climate may change the concurrence of conditions that favor the survival of both the biocontrol agent and its target. In this uncertain future, management of invasive species will require integrated applied research, long-term thinking, adaptive management, and a renewed emphasis on monitoring and communication.

Rochelle Christian

See also Climate Change, Communicating; Risk Communication, Overview; Uncertainty in Science Communication

Further Readings

Darling, J. A., & Blum, M. J. (2007). DNA-based methods for monitoring invasive species: A review and prospectus. *Biological Invasions, 9,* 751–765.

Deagle, B. E., Bax, N., & Patil, J. G. (2003). Development and evaluation of a PCR-based test for detection of *Asterias* (Echinodermata: Asteroidea) larvae in Australian plankton samples from ballast water. *Marine and Freshwater Research, 54,* 709–719.

Hellman, J. J., Byers, J. E., Bierwagen, B. G., & Dukes, J. S. (2008). Five potential consequences of climate change for invasive species. *Conservation Biology, 22*(3), 534–543.

International Union for the Conservation of Nature. (2009). *Invasive species.* Retrieved August 9, 2009, from www.iucn.org/about/union/secretariat/offices/iucnmed/iucn_med_programme/species/invasive_species

Kenis, M., Auger-Rozenberg, M. A., Roques, A., Timms, L., Pere, C., Cock, M., et al. (2009). Ecological effects of invasive alien insects. *Biological Invasions, 11*(1), 21–45.

Maguire, L. A. (2004). What can decision analysis do for invasive species management? *Risk Analysis, 24*(4), 859–868.

Nairn, M., Inglis, A., Tanner, C., & Allen, P. (1996). *Australian quarantine: A shared responsibility.* Canberra, Australia: Department of Primary Industries and Energy.

Phillips, B. L., Chipperfield, J. D., & Kearney, M. R. (2008). The toad ahead: Challenges of modelling the range and spread of an invasive species. *Wildlife Research, 35*(3), 222–234.

Phillips, B. L., & Shine, R. (2006). An invasive species induces rapid adaptive change in a native predator: Cane toads and black snakes in Australia. *Proceedings of the Royal Society B-Biological Sciences, 273,* 1545–1550.

Stromberg, J. C., Chew, M. K., Nagler, P. L., & Glenn, E. P. (2009). Changing perceptions of change: The role of scientists in tamarix and river management. *Restoration Ecology, 17*(2), 177–186.

Whitney, K. D., & Gabler, C. A. (2008). Rapid evolution in introduced species, "invasive traits" and recipient communities: Challenges for predicting invasive potential. *Diversity and Distributions, 14*(4), 569–580.

World Trade Organization. (1995). *Agreement on the application of sanitary and phytosanitary measures.* Retrieved August 14, 2009, from www.wto.org/english/docs_e/legal_e/15-sps.pdf

INVISIBLE COLLEGE

Science is a social activity that grows through free and open communications among its practitioners. The links among scientists—ones that that extend beyond particular institutions, nations, and disciplines—have been known as the *invisible college* at least since 1645. The term describes the underlying structure of science, which operates as a communications system with formal and informal functions.

The first use of the term invisible college is often attributed to the Irish scientist Robert Boyle (sometimes called the "father of chemistry"). He used the term in a letter to his tutor to describe the interactions of a small group of like-minded natural philosophers, also known as the "virtuosi." He pointed out that a group of natural philosophers had begun a series of communications about the natural world (mostly conducted through letters) in a way that constituted an invisible college.

Boyle was writing from his estate in Ireland where he spent a great deal of time conducting research. He shared many of his findings with other amateur investigators. These early communications had begun through letters and in meetings held in London during an era of intellectual and social ferment. In the mid-17th century, new discoveries had upended much of the academic world. The improved telescopes of Galileo Galilei and other early astronomers had yielded more precise measurements of the movement of heavenly bodies. These movements were shown to follow predictable patterns that could be uncovered through scientific observation and study. These discoveries challenged the Aristotelian tenets that the heavens were not only divine and immutable, but beyond human understanding.

As the Aristotelian worldview began to give way to the measures and predictions of early astronomers and chemists, interest in the empirical exploration of nature spread across Europe. Scientific societies and academies were established almost simultaneously in five European cities. These societies were intended to facilitate the communication of ideas, the formulation of experiments, and the sharing of results, increasingly through the printed word. Between 1630 and 1830, at least 300 scientific journals were launched. Scholar Derek de Solla Price found that the growth rate of scientific literature was exponential, with the number of scientific journals growing by a factor of 10 about every 50 years since.

Boyle's invisible college of the mid-17th century included such notables as biologist Robert Hooke; mathematician William Viscount Brouncker; the Reverend John Wilkins, a future head of colleges at

both Oxford and Cambridge; and Christopher Wren, the accomplished astronomer and architect of St. Paul's Cathedral. This invisible college emerged at a time of great political strife in England. The civil wars, which began in 1642 and raged for much of the following decade, split Britain into two camps: the parliamentarians, who sought to defend Parliament's traditional role in matters such as taxation, and the royalists, who favored a stronger monarchy. But the early experimentalists (who as individuals held divergent political views) set aside these differences to pursue their shared interest in studying the "sensible realm" through experimentation. Eventually their discussions gave rise to the Royal Society of London, now the oldest scientific society in continuous existence.

An Intellectual Revolution

During a time of political revolution and civil war, the future members of the Royal Society were revolutionaries of a different kind. They asked basic questions about nature that challenged the religious and academic orthodoxy of the time. Following private introductions, they initially met informally and corresponded occasionally. In the late 1650s, a group within the invisible college began to meet more regularly at Gresham College in London. In 1660, after an inspiring lecture by the polymath Wren, the gathered group decided to form the College for the Promoting of Physico-Mathematical Experimental Learning. They took the motto *Nullius in verba* (meaning, on the word of no one) to show that they were prepared to test and seek verification of facts rather than accept received wisdom. The commitment to the external validity of knowledge and the openness of the society marked it as unique in intellectual history and set the conditions for an intellectual revolution that is still ongoing.

Today, in an era when questioning received wisdom is a cultural norm, it is difficult to fully grasp the audacity of these members of the invisible college of experimentalists in publicly declaring their allegiance to science. But their gamble paid off. In early 1660, after a republican interregnum lasting 11 years, the British monarchy was restored. The new king, Charles II, took an interest in the group's work, largely because of his friendship with staunch royalist Viscount Brouncker. In

1662, the king granted the society a royal charter, which created the Royal Society of London.

The members of the Royal Society reinvigorated a scientific world outlook that had lain dormant for centuries. As methods for seeking objective meaning about the natural world began to diffuse widely in the 17th century, these men challenged one another to question traditional thought and to seek answers through reproducible, documented experimentation. Men (no evidence exists that women were included) who alone might have been an obscure cleric here or a university mathematician there pushed each other to stretch the limits of knowledge however they could. As Thomas Sprat described in his 1772 edition of *History of the Royal Society,* these men "had no Rules nor Method fix'd," but were more intent on communicating among themselves information regarding the discoveries they had made.

The result was the birth of a new intellectual age, a scientific revolution capped by the immediate recognition of the significance of the work embodied in Isaac Newton's *Philosophiæ Naturalis Principia Mathematica* (*Mathematical Principles of Natural Philosophy*), published in 1687 under the imprimatur of Samuel Pepys, then president of the Royal Society of London. With the publication of *Philosophiæ Naturalis Principia Mathematica,* the heavenly bodies, viewed by Aristotle as divine, were brought into the range of human inquiry and shown to obey discernable laws of mathematics. More broadly, a later historian would note that the new learning, long blocked by the Aristotelians, had by this time found its way into some of the universities. The number of those concerned with natural philosophy was increasing rapidly.

The discoveries of this era remain of epic significance in the history of science. Less widely recognized, however, are the significance of the society's commitment to openness, its emphasis on recording and disseminating scientific findings, and its contributions to scientific communication. These social innovations were just as groundbreaking as the scientific method they supported. In contrast to the secretive alchemists of the Middle Ages, the Royal Society operated in the open. Its members corresponded avidly with experimentalists in any part of the world where sympathetic fellows could be found (although they seem to have been unaware of science in China, which was well established at the time). In particular, the first secretary of the Royal Society, Henry Oldenburg (a native of Bremen, Germany, living in London) took on the responsibility of, in his words, "entertaining a commerce" around the world with the "most philosophical and curious persons" to be found.

On the European continent, Oldenburg's correspondents included Christiaan Huygens, a Dutchman who published his own work on dynamics; René Descartes, a Frenchman living in Holland who suggested in his writings that unverified assumptions lay beneath the received wisdom of the scholastics (medieval philosophers who drew their inspiration from Aristotle); and Gottfried von Leibniz, a German who, working independently, invented calculus at around the same time as Isaac Newton. Correspondence was also established with members of similar societies in Italy and France. As Sprat noted of the Royal Society's members, a correspondence existed throughout all countries so much so that there was "scare a Shipthat came up the Thames that does not bring some news of "their Experiments, as well as of Merchandize."

The Universality of the College

As this emphasis on the far-flung exchange of ideas suggests, early modern science was universal in several senses. The virtuosi were mainly educated gentlemen who found patrons for their work or were wealthy enough to fund their own inquiries, correspondence, and participation in scientific meetings. As a result, their research was not limited by the need for government support. Most of the era's pamphlets and letters, along with the rare book, were written in Latin, making the results of experimentation accessible to educated individuals in a wide range of countries. And most thinkers saw their work in very broad terms as part of a common effort to understand nature, rather than an inquiry in a particular field. Early modern science, then, was subject to very few institutional, political, or disciplinary claims. These conditions persisted in some measure into the 18th century, but as science advanced, the social and political context inevitably began to change.

The earliest invisible college grew in England, but it was not a purely British phenomenon. Many continentalists were in England at the time, driven there by war or social necessity. One of the most influential members was Jan Amos Komensky, who is better known by the Latinized name Comenius. (He is often credited with having invented modern science-based education in Europe.) In the 1630s, when he was working as a minister and educator in Moravia (now part of the Czech Republic), his writings came to the attention of a man named Samuel Hartlib. Hartlib was to the 17th century what a Web portal might be today. Born in Elbing in West Prussia (now part of Poland) and educated in Germany, he immigrated to London in the 1630s to escape the Thirty Years War. His gift for languages led him to take on the role of an intelligencer—an agent for the dissemination in London of news, books, and manuscripts from throughout Europe. As an intelligencer, he met many members of the intellectual class.

Hartlib was so impressed with Comenius's writings on universal education that in 1637, he personally arranged to have the work published by Oxford University. He also convinced some members of Parliament to invite Comenius to make an official visit to London. After many letters back and forth, Comenius agreed to Parliament's request and booked a trip to London to discuss his views on education and science with governmental members and learned men.

In September 1641, the ship carrying Comenius arrived from Hanover at the London docks. As fate would have it, these same docks had very recently launched three ships for Scotland. Regrettably for Comenius and Hartlib, the ships that had vacated the docks were carrying an elite cargo: King Charles I and his family were fleeing London ahead of a revolutionary uprising by Parliament, one that led to the great remonstrance of 1641. The crisis left little time to talk about educational policy with a Moravian clergyman.

The tides and weather dictated that Comenius would reluctantly stay in London for the winter of 1641–1642. (During this time, he wrote one of his most noted essays, titled "The Way of Light.") While awaiting the return of the government—or better weather, whichever came first—Comenius had ample time to write an important treatise on education, as well as to meet with a small group of intellectuals in London organized by Hartlib. Among these contacts was a prior acquaintance of Comenius, a German expatriate and coreligionist named Theodore Haak. Haak was quite pleased to host a small gathering at his home to introduce the renowned Comenius to London intellectuals. The meeting included such leading virtuosi as John Evelyn, Wren, Boyle, and Viscount Brouncker. Some historians suggest that it was at this meeting that the idea of an invisible college of experimentalists was first broached, and that it was Comenius himself who suggested the term to the British experimentalists. (This bit of history—the role of Comenius in suggesting the formation of an invisible college and the role of the German nationals in organizing the first meetings of the Royal Society members—is not often cited in the official British-authored histories of the Royal Society.)

The New Invisible College

Recent research emerging from physics, biology, and sociology has revealed ways to analyze and model the emergence of invisible colleges. The work of Mark Granovetter, "The Strength of Weak Ties," pointed the way to studying behavior that is closely embedded in networks of interpersonal relationships. When joined to other research demonstrating that scientists tend to work together in relatively dense networks or groups of invisible colleges, new approaches to understanding the role of these networks have emerged. These studies also find that invisible colleges are often centered on a small number of prominent academics who play an important role as hubs in a social network and as gatekeepers to the field itself. Although in the early phase of this research many studies took inspiration from Kuhn and concentrated on studying the social structure of rapidly changing scientific fields, it soon became clear that such dense groups are not reserved to emerging fields, but are in fact prevalent throughout science. The interesting question for contemporary research is therefore not so much whether such dense groups of interacting scholars do in fact exist, but rather how these groups link up with one another into something that (perhaps) may be characterized as a distinct scientific field. As pointed out by Diane Crane, scholars are normally connected to several different networks at the same time through links of various strengths.

Thus, the invisible college continues to operate in the 21st century and is understood now as the essential structure by which knowledge is created.

Science operates at the international level as a network—a global extension of the invisible college. In contrast to the operations of science at the national level, where agencies manage and policy directs investment, no global ministry of science connects people internationally. Yet most scientists collaborate with colleagues abroad. The more elite the scientist, the more likely it is that he or she will be an active member of the global invisible college. These connections self-organize through the interests of scientists themselves and thus take on an emergent character similar to other networks that mark social connections in the information society.

Indeed, self-organizing networks that span the globe are the most notable feature of science at the start of the 21st century. These networks constitute an invisible college of researchers who are not tied to an institution or a discipline: scientists who collaborate not because they are told to, but because they want to; not because they work in the same laboratory or even in the same field, but because they have complementary insight, data, or skills. These networks will drive the direction of 21st-century science, subsuming and transforming the roles played by national policies and ministries in the 20th century. Scientific nationalism—where science was funded and claimed as a national asset—was a defining feature of 20th-century science; the invisible college at the international level is defining science in the 21st century.

Caroline S. Wagner

See also Galilei, Galileo; Kuhn, Thomas; Royal Society; Scientific Journal, History of; Scientific Societies

Further Readings

Andrade, E. N. da C. (1960). *A brief history of the Royal Society, 1660–1960*. London: Royal Society.

Butterfield, B. (1957). *Origins of modern science: 1300–1700*. London: Free Press.

Chubin, D. E. (1983). *Sociology of sciences: An annotated bibliography on invisible colleges, 1972–1981*. New York: Garland.

Crane, D. (1972). *Invisible colleges: Diffusion of knowledge in scientific communities*. Chicago: University of Chicago Press.

Granovetter, M. (1973). The strength of weak ties. *American Journal of Sociology, 78*(6), 1360–1380.

Piaget, J. (1968). *John Amos Comenius on education*. New York: Teacher's College Press.

Price, D. J. de S. (1963). *Little science, big science*. New York: Columbia University Press.

Stimson, D. (1948). *Scientists and amateurs: A history of the Royal Society*. New York: Greenwood Press.

Wagner, C. S. (2008). *The new invisible college: Science for development*. Washington, DC: Brookings Press.

ISSUES IN SCIENCE AND TECHNOLOGY

Issues in Science and Technology is a journal devoted to stimulating awareness and discussion of public policy related to science, engineering, and medicine. The journal was founded in 1984 and is published quarterly in print and on the Web by the National Academy of Sciences, the National Academy of Engineering, the Institute of Medicine, and the University of Texas at Dallas.

The scope of this publication is quite broad, treating subjects that range from nanotechnology and biotechnology to national defense, social science, climate, and education, among others. The journal publishes articles that "analyze current topics in science, technology, and health policy and recommend actions by government, industry, academia, and individuals to solve pressing problems," according to its Web site (http://www.issues.org). Its scope encompasses "policy for science (how we nurture the health of the research enterprise) and science for policy (how we use knowledge more effectively to achieve social goals), with emphasis on the latter" (http://www.issues.org). With a print circulation in 2008 of about 8,000, newsstand sales, and an online archive of issues back to 1996, the journal provides a forum targeting researchers, government officials, business leaders, and others concerned with public policy. A recent readership survey showed that respondents worked mostly in universities, medical organizations, and federal agencies.

Each volume contains a mix of feature articles (4,000 to 5,000 words), "Perspectives" (2,000 to 2,500 words), brief news articles ("From the Hill"), an editor's comment, letters to the editor, book reviews, and a special section called "Archives," which presents a visual subject such as artwork, a photograph, or other display relating broadly to the scope of the journal.

Feature articles are longer, more in-depth pieces that make specific policy recommendations on an issue, whereas the perspectives articles are shorter, perhaps on newer issues, with fewer if any policy recommendations.

Special collections of some of the journal's past articles are available online under the following categories: climate, competitiveness, education, energy, environment, foreign policy, national security, public health, real numbers, transportation, and universities.

The establishment of the journal in 1984 was led by Frank Press, who served as the U.S. president's science adviser and director of the U.S. Office of Science and Technology Policy under President Carter from 1977 to 1980. He was president of the National Academy of Sciences and chairman of the National Research Council from 1981 to 1993.

Deborah L. Illman

See also National Academies, U.S.

Further Readings

Issues in Science and Technology: www.issues.org

KNOWLEDGE GAP HYPOTHESIS

The 1970s marked the formalization of the *knowledge gap hypothesis,* developed by Philip J. Tichenor, George A. Donohue, and Clarice N. Olien, known as the Minnesota team, which proposed that the segments of a population that have higher socioeconomic status (SES) tend to acquire information flowing from the media at a faster rate than do segments with lower status and that the gap in knowledge between these segments tends to increase rather than decrease over time. The knowledge gap hypothesis does not suggest that the lower-SES population segments remain completely uninformed, but that the growth of knowledge is relatively greater among the higher-SES population segments. These gaps in knowledge between high-SES and low-SES populations can lead to what scholars such as Kasisomayajula Viswanath and John Finnegan have referred to as the information "haves" and "have-nots."

Historical Underpinnings

Gaps in knowledge are nothing new and have always been found among groups, thus laying the foundation for the knowledge gap hypothesis. Earlier evidence of the underpinnings of the knowledge gap hypothesis was first found by Herbert H. Hyman and Paul B. Sheatsley in 1947. In their public information campaign research, they observed that information and knowledge rarely spread equally to all societal groups. Similar observations noting that those with more education had better information and knowledge acquisition outcomes than those with little education were reported by others. Earlier intellectual contributions to the knowledge gap hypothesis can also be found in research emerging from the literature on rural sociology, diffusion of innovations, public opinion, and information campaigns. Theorizing about the social structural influences of media and the contributory aspects of the knowledge gap hypothesis can be seen in the mass media effects literature as well. However, it was Tichenor, Donohue, and Olien's celebrated 1970 study, "Mass Media Flow and Differential Growth in Knowledge," that first examined whether or not factors such as education level or socioeconomic status actually make a difference in knowledge acquisition.

The knowledge gap literature presents conflicting evidence, however, with some studies suggesting that media-generated information increases knowledge gaps, whereas other studies find no evidence of widening knowledge gaps. Along with these conflicting findings, many researchers have taken exception to the implication that SES may affect the ability to learn. As a result, the knowledge gap hypothesis was revised by the Minnesota team and later refined by others to address these concerns. The knowledge gap hypothesis continues to generate a lot of interest worldwide.

Assumptions

A central point of the knowledge gap hypothesis concerns the acquisition and control of knowledge, which scholars suggest is the basis of social power and social action. As articulated by Sir Francis Bacon, "knowledge is power." Tichenor, Donohue, and Olien have identified several predictors of why knowledge gaps should appear and widen with increasing levels of media flow into communities. Also important to note is that in the initial conceptualization of the knowledge gap hypothesis, education was used as the indicator of SES. People with more formal education were assumed to have better communication skills (higher reading and comprehension skills). Further, people who are already better informed were believed better able to store information more easily, draw from this store or background knowledge, and be aware of a topic when it is first presented. People with more education were generally seen as having a more relevant social context (that is, more reference groups and more interpersonal contacts with whom to discuss issues). More education also generally determines a person's selective exposure, acceptance, and retention of information, which some have suggested is a prerequisite for acquiring knowledge. Finally, in general, the flow of mass media information is geared toward the interests and tastes of those with more education or a higher SES status.

Knowledge Gap Hypothesis Applications

In addition to Tichenor, Donohue, and Olien's ground-breaking research, other noteworthy contributions came from works by Herbert H. Hyman and Paul B. Sheatsley (1947), James S. Ettema and F. Geraldine Kline (1977), Brenda Dervin (1980), Cecilie Gaziano (1983), Kasisomayajula Viswanath and John Finnegan (1996), and Kasisomayajula Viswanath, Shoba Ramandahn, and Emily Kontos (2007). These scholars' work, along with that of others, has presented a critical foundation for the formalization, refinement, and expansion of the knowledge gap hypothesis.

Although Tichenor, Donohue, and Olien's original knowledge gap hypothesis was applied primarily to public affairs and science news, in the United States and worldwide, knowledge gap theory has also been used to examine knowledge of politics, education, space research, environment, international issues, mass media issues, and health.

Currently, there is a great deal of focus on health issues in the United States. Several knowledge gap applications have examined health-related issues, such as diet and cardiovascular disease, health information campaigns, smoking behavior, childbirth, and infant development. For example, in one 2008 study by Minsun Shim using the National Cancer Institute's 2003 Health Information National Trends Survey (or HINTS), a survey that routinely collects nationally representative data about the American public's use of cancer-related information, the researcher applied the knowledge gap hypothesis to examine Internet use for cancer information. This study examined disparities in online information seeking by education and ethnicity, as well as subsequent gaps in cancer knowledge. Data supported the hypothesis that higher-education groups and white Americans were more likely to use the Internet for cancer information than were their counterparts, and that online information seeking enlarged to some degree the cancer knowledge gaps between education groups.

Future Work

Future knowledge gap applications should continue to focus on the astonishing advances in new media technology, including the convergence of traditional media (print, television, radio) with new media (computers, Internet, cell phones, iPods, CD-ROMs, video, audio). A groundswell of new information and information-delivery opportunities is emerging, thereby extending the information landscape beyond time and space and extending the reach of information and communication efforts. However, challenges remain. The digital divide—the perceived gap between those who have access to the latest information technologies and those who do not—continues to be an important concern. Research still reveals that more-educated and higher-income groups have greater access to both traditional media and new media information resources compared to lower-SES groups, demonstrating the persistence of the digital divide and contributing to ongoing knowledge gaps among various groups.

Scholars have also called for more examinations that seek to tease out knowledge measurement issues by utilizing cross-sectional, panel, and time-trend studies to better examine change. There is also a paucity of research that seeks to elucidate the factors that reduce knowledge gaps and erase communication inequalities. Some recent and promising work in the domain of health communication builds on the knowledge gap hypothesis, combining the social epidemiological approach with the structural approach in mass communication and offering some clarity regarding how communication inequalities may contribute to inequalities in health.

The Structural Influence Model of Health Communication (SIM), as proposed by Viswanath, Ramanadhan, and Kontos in 2007, further explores communication inequality, defined as the differences among social groups in their ability to generate, disseminate, and use information at the macrolevel and to access, process, and act on information at the individual level. This emerging framework posits a connection between social determinants of health outcomes and a broad range of mass and interpersonal communication factors. In our fast-paced and ever-changing social and information landscape, the knowledge gap hypothesis and its refinements represent a tenable lens with which to examine these social, informational, and technological changes and challenges.

Sherrie Flynt Wallington

See also Communication Campaigns in Health and Environment; Digital Divide; Health Communication and the Internet; Health Literacy; Information Seeking and Processing

Further Readings

Coleman, J. S., Campbell, E. Q., Hobson, C. J., McPartland, J., Mood, A. M., Weinfeld, F. D., et al. (1966). *Equality of educational opportunity* (No. OE-38001). Washington, DC: U.S. Department of Health, Education, and Welfare, Office of Education, National Center for Education Statistics.

Dervin, B. (1980). Communication gaps and inequities: Moving toward a reconceptualization. In B. Dervin & M. J. Voight (Eds.), *Progress in communication science* (p. 2). Norwood, NJ: Ablex.

DiMaggio, P., Hargittai, E., Neuman, R., & Robinson, J. (2001). Social implications of the Internet. *Annual Review of Sociology, 27,* 307–336.

Donohue, G. A., Tichenor, P. J., & Olien, C. N. (1975). Mass media and the knowledge gap: A hypothesis reconsidered. *Communication Research, 2,* 3–23.

Ettema, J. S., & Kline, F. G. (1977). Deficits, differences, and ceilings: Contingent conditions for understanding the knowledge gap. *Communication Research, 4*(2), 179–202.

Eveland, W., & Scheufele, D. (2000). Connecting news media use with gaps in knowledge and participation. *Political Communication, 17*(3), 215–237.

Gaziano, C. (1983). Knowledge gap: An analytical review of media effects. *Communication Research, 10,* 447–486.

Gaziano, C. (1997). Forecast 2000: Widening knowledge gaps. *Journalism and Mass Communication Quarterly, 74*(2), 237–264.

Hyman, H. H., & Sheatsley, P. B. (1947). Some reasons why information campaigns fail. *Public Opinion Quarterly, 11,* 412–423.

Kwak, N. (1999). Revisiting the knowledge gap hypothesis: Education, motivation, and media use. *Communication Research, 26*(4), 385–413.

Shim, M. (2008). Connecting Internet use with gaps in cancer knowledge. *Health Communication, 23*(5), 448–461.

Star, S. A., & Hughes, H. M. (1950). Report on an educational campaign: The Cincinnati Plan for the United Nations. *American Journal of Sociology, 55*(4), 389–400.

Tichenor, P., Donohue, G., & Olien, C. (1970). Mass media flow and differential growth in knowledge. *Public Opinion Quarterly, 34,* 159–170.

Viswanath, K., & Finnegan, J. R. (1996). The knowledge gap hypothesis: Twenty-five years later. In B. Burleson (Ed.), *Communication yearbook* (Vol. 19, pp. 187–227). Thousand Oaks, CA: Sage.

Viswanath, K., Ramanadhan, S., & Kontos, E. Z. (2007). Mass media and population health: A macrosocial view. In S. E. Galea (Ed.), *Macrosocial determinants of population health* (pp. 275–294). New York: Springer.

Kuhn, Thomas (1922–1996)

Thomas Kuhn popularized the term *paradigm* in science and, in doing so, changed the way many scientists and others view the process of scientific inquiry. His theories and descriptions had a profound influence on science education, sociology, and the way in which the history of science was applied to the philosophy of science. Many of these influences were controversial; however,

Kuhn is largely regarded as a central figure in the development of contemporary understanding of the nature of the scientific process.

Born in Cincinnati, Ohio, on July 18, 1922, Thomas Samuel Kuhn studied physics at Harvard University, receiving his doctorate degree in 1949. He worked as an assistant professor in the history and philosophy of science department at Harvard. In 1956, he moved to the philosophy department of the University of California, Berkeley. In 1964, he took the position of M. Taylor Pyne Professor of Philosophy and History of Science at Princeton. Kuhn later took a professorship at Massachusetts Institute of Technology (MIT) and, in 1983, was named Laurence S. Rockefeller Professor of Philosophy there.

While working toward his doctorate degree in 1947, Kuhn was asked to teach some simple science concepts to undergraduate humanities students as part of the general education in science curriculum. This provided what Kuhn described in an interview in *Scientific American* in 1991 as a "Eureka" moment. While searching for an example to provide to these students, Kuhn read some of Aristotle's work on basic principles of physics, which he did not initially comprehend because it was so different from Newton's work, with which Kuhn was more familiar. On some reflection, however, Kuhn realized that Aristotle's ideas were merely different from Newton's, and neither was more correct than the other—they were simply examining the same idea through a different framework.

This was a pivotal realization, moving Kuhn away from physics into the philosophy and history of science. It was during his time as a graduate student that Kuhn wrote his best-known work, *The Structure of Scientific Revolutions*. Initially published as a monograph in the *International Encyclopedia of Unified Science,* it was published as a book in 1962. Since then it has been translated into over a dozen languages and is still used as a fundamental text for students of the history and philosophy of science.

Through his publication of *The Structure of Scientific Revolutions,* Kuhn popularized the term *paradigm,* which was typically associated with areas of linguistics. Kuhn proposed that paradigms guide research and scientific efforts. He describes science as a structure consisting of three parts: pre-paradigm science, "normal" science, and revolutionary science. Pre-paradigm science, or prescience, describes the search for information on a phenomenon for which there is no shared common background or theory. Through work conducted on pre-paradigm science, normal science is created.

Normal science is where scientists are working to build on existing knowledge—that is, the central paradigm. Kuhn described scientists working within normal science as "puzzle solvers." Paradigms provide the problems for scientists to solve. Any results that do not fit with the existing paradigm accumulate until the existing paradigm is seen as unable to explain a problem. This creates what Kuhn termed a *crisis,* whereon a new paradigm is formed. The new paradigm incorporates all the previous knowledge, as well as the formerly conflicting results, thereby resolving the crisis. This final stage is called revolutionary science.

Kuhn's structure of science supports his belief that science does not progress in a linear fashion with each piece of knowledge leading to another, then another, until all the information is known. Instead, it goes through periods of radical change, with central ideas and theories often challenged or even discarded. This period of more radical change is also known as a "paradigm shift."

How we view science within a particular paradigm, which can be shaped by our sociocultural beliefs, also affects how we can evaluate science constructed within a different paradigm. Kuhn called this the "thesis of incommensurability." He developed this idea at the same time as Paul Feyerabend, an Austrian philosopher of science. The thesis states that science examined through one paradigm is "incommensurable" with the science developed under a different paradigm—they do not share any common measure or language.

Kuhn's ideas generated a lot of interest in the scientific, philosophical, and later the more general community; however, the reception of his ideas was not always favorable. Kuhn's intimation that scientists may not always adhere to rules to make decisions was in stark contrast to the belief that rules, such as the scientific method, and rational choice were the fundamentals of science. Some considered that for Kuhn to suggest otherwise was implying that science was irrational. Kuhn met further resistance to his belief that the history of science was important to the philosophy of science. These opinions were unusual for the time (the early 1960s) and generated much debate. Much of Kuhn's career was dedicated to further articulation and development of his ideas in *The Structure of Scientific Revolutions* and the thesis of incommensurability—and the latter underwent its own transformations.

Kuhn held honorary degrees from institutions such as Columbia University and the universities of Notre Dame, Chicago, Padua, and Athens. He was named a Guggenheim Fellow in 1954 and, in 1982, was awarded the George Sarton Medal in the History of Science. He died on June 17, 1996, of cancer of the throat and bronchial tubes, at the age of 73 in his home in Cambridge, Massachusetts.

Merryn McKinnon

See also Scientific Consensus; Scientific Method

Further Readings

Horgan, J. (1991, May). Profile: Reluctant revolutionary. *Scientific American, 40,* 49.

Kuhn, T. S. (1996). *The structure of scientific revolutions* (3rd ed.). Chicago: University of Chicago Press.

Kuhn, T. S. (2000). *The road since structure: Philosophical essays, 1970–1993.* Chicago: University of Chicago Press.

L

Land Grant System, U.S.

The U.S. system of land grant state colleges and universities has been supportive of science and technology communication for nearly 150 years. Initially focused on agricultural and mechanical arts education for working-class citizens, the schools were so named because they were first funded by grants of federal lands to the states. Land grant schools have been noted as the first academic institutions to (a) communicate science to the general public, (b) translate scientific discoveries into applied practices and technologies, and (c) communicate technical expertise to professionals in the field, among other communication-related innovations. Land grants initiated academic programs in scientific and technical communication, inaugurated social-science-based research programs on the uses and effects of such communication, and continue to pioneer in mass and interpersonal media transmission of science and technical innovations for use by appropriate segments of the public.

The land grant emphasis on public communication received a major boost in the early 1900s with the formalization of cooperative extension programs, so named because their purpose was literally to extend the knowledge base of the universities beyond the campus into communities—most notably, at the time, including farms and ranches. Agriculture was at the heart of land grant universities from their inception in the 1860s and remains a major player in most extension programs today.

Closely behind was education in the mechanical arts, ranging from engineering to landscape architecture and eventually home economics, which encompassed a wide range of household, childrearing, and community development skills. Natural resources education grew along with along with focuses on forestry, mining, and fishing.

So-called classical education, involving the arts and humanities, played a secondary role in the developing schools, that of broadening the intellectual and cultural scope of the students, most of whom came from modest upbringings and who were often the first in their families exposed to higher education (and in many cases to secondary school). At most institutions, basic science programs (such as physics) existed mainly to serve the applied sciences (such as mechanical engineering).

Origins

Founded under the Morrill Act of 1862, land grant colleges and universities responded primarily to a need for expanded agricultural and technical education opportunities as the nation grew. Tuition and expenses were kept uniformly low, below those of the recently established state universities that catered more to upper-middle-class students and provided heavier emphases on arts, humanities, and basic sciences, often including professional schools such as law and medicine. Private schools had their own clientele of largely upperclass students.

After the federal government granted public lands to each state to help finance the institutions,

439

further federal appropriations continued, but states were responsible for building construction, maintenance, and certain other operating expenses. States varied in how they sited and organized the fledgling schools. Some chose to build entirely new campuses dedicated to the innovative programs, and site selection was often highly competitive among communities wanting them. An early example was what is now known as the Iowa State University of Science and Technology in Ames, established over 100 miles from the already existing University of Iowa. Others merged into already existing state universities, such as what happened at the University of Wisconsin. These situations often created campus rifts between the typically less privileged newcomers and those more established, with social class tensions and arguments over technical versus classical curricula.

A second round of land grant institutions was created in 1890 in the racially segregated states of the South expressly for African American students to attend. Today these historically black colleges exist alongside their integrated state land grant counterparts and are sometimes known as "1890 land grants." In 1994, 29 Native American tribal colleges, largely in the West, received land grant designations as well.

With respect to science and technology communication, two other years stand out in the history of land grants. In 1887, the federal Hatch Act created the agricultural experiment station program, which brought federal and matching state monies to fund innovative agricultural research at the schools. The research was tied to state agricultural issues and proved to be a highly productive vehicle for increased crop productivity, better livestock health, improved farm practices, and related advances. The experiment stations provided a physical research base at the schools that demonstrated commitment to intellectual activity and the promise of discovery, expanding the previous teaching base of the schools. It also led to a need to disseminate the results of the research through station bulletins and other publications, often widely read by other researchers, agricultural policymakers, and a growing, more educated cohort of agricultural producers.

The Smith-Lever Act of 1914 formalized the service and outreach commitment of the land grants with the creation of the Cooperative Extension Service. Up to that time, many land grants and governmental agencies had created variations on outreach programs largely emphasizing rural demonstration efforts on and off campuses. Cooperative Extension unified those into working relationships among partner institutions, including the U.S. Department of Agriculture (USDA), individual states, and county agencies.

Communication and Extension

A successful communication–education structure then began to form that would last into the 21st century. Land grant institutional research in agriculture, home economics, human development, community development, natural resources, engineering, and related areas was informed at least to some extent by real-world problems. Building on findings from basic research, more applied research solutions were brought into the field for testing by academic specialists. Solutions deemed more successful were shared with extension agents trained as educators in their own areas of expertise. Usually county-based, these agents would then work with appropriate clientele to educate and train them as to the most effective evidence-based techniques for improving products and services, whether new seed corn varieties, plowing methods, childrearing practices, food safety in the home, land development practices, or water quality protection.

The county agents interacted heavily with both the research specialists and with their own constituencies. The agents were informed of the latest research findings emanating from the experiment stations and could also seek out the specialists for advice on particular problems in their own counties or on individual farmsteads. At the same time, agents disseminated relevant information to publics within their counties, while being readily available to respond to individual problems and questions. During most of the 20th century, mass media played a central role in helping specialists and agents spread the word. Experiment station personnel relied on a system of research bulletins to communicate findings to other researchers and agents, while agents reached their publics through newspapers, radio, television, and regional and specialized magazines and other publications. Weekly news columns and daily radio spots were a staple of this system, particularly in agriculture, and were closely attended to by agricultural producers.

Equally if not more important in the communication process were interpersonal and group interactions. The media's role was regarded as being more informational and useful for awareness building, while actual influence and behavioral change required a strong social component. Extension agents reached out in particular to those in a community regarded as more influential in given areas of expertise—sometimes referred to as change agents—to help reach and impact others with respect to improved practices and techniques. Social change models, such as the diffusion and adoption of innovations, were popular and seemingly effective, particularly in rural communities. The diffusion model called for relatively slow spread of new practices within a population across such groups as innovators and then early and late adopters, each with their own particular social, economic, and psychological capacities for change. The land grant schools gave rise to research on many of the social influence and communication theories and practices that later made their way into more general marketing and consumer research parlance. Key to extension-based education was constant translation of research concepts and practices into the language of the end users, the agricultural producers, homemakers, and other community members who would actually have to apply the products to their own needs and circumstances. Hands-on training, whether individually or in groups, was a mainstay of this system as well.

New Challenges

Extension communication techniques joined the electronic revolution of the late 1900s with varying degrees of effort and success. The amount of effort depended in part on the then-declining resources being accorded to extension programs more generally. Some land grant schools already highly proficient in computer technology were more easily able to transfer resources to their extension units, while others struggled. In many cases, personnel and staffing expertise were major considerations. Experiments with communication technology—ranging from use of telephone "audiotex" information retrieval systems for clientele to interactive cablevision to videoconferencing across

state meeting sites—abounded at some land grant schools but languished at others in the 1980s and early 1990s. Distance education by mail and eventually through the Internet became a staple at most of the schools. However, adequate evaluation of the impact of such attempts suffered, given the further costs required.

Even training programs to allow county agents to learn to effectively use desktop computers for e-mail, Web site use, and desktop publishing appeared hit-and-miss into the 1990s. However, by the turn of the century, the ubiquity of the Internet, decline in its costs, and ease of its use had impacted the vast majority of extension operations. Moreover, their constituents were demanding it, even in rural locales where broadband usage was hindered. Well into the first decade of the 21st century, effective extension Web sites, accessible databases, and e-mail and chat contact were mainstays of extension communication and education. Moreover, cost efficiencies began to be realized that began to compensate for reduced extension staff and budgets overall. Instrumental in many of the more successful communication transitions was the Association for Communication Excellence in Agriculture, Natural Resources, and Life and Human Sciences (ACE), initially an organization of agricultural college editors that has grown as a force incorporating educators, researchers, and specialized professional communicators, as well as information technologists.

The reduced financial support for extension (now formally under the auspices of the USDA Cooperative State Research, Education and Extension Service, or CSREES) was in part a consequence of the reduced role of agriculture, especially smaller-scale agriculture, in the U.S. economy. Another significant influence on lessening support of extension was the rise in the late 1900s of private infrastructures of agricultural information that paralleled the greater industrialization of the agricultural economy. Even small- to medium-sized farm operators were apt to seek and receive advice about their practices from area supply cooperatives and other dealers, who readily had information and advice on hand from manufacturers' representatives and other experts in farm practices. The information—whether print, electronic, or Internet-based—could be as validated and well presented as that from extension and was often more readily accessible. Larger producers relied more heavily on specialized consultants who visited their operations, offered targeted advice on specific practices, and sometimes ran sophisticated tests and experiments to try to attain optimal production results.

While some questioned the motives behind dealer-based or consultant advice, the validity and accuracy of this information was often quite high. One reason was that the research bases for the information were often the same land grant schools that provided extension information. While some have criticized what they saw as a split between more "public" sources of information through extension and related agencies and private, typically for-profit, corporate enterprises, others claimed that what was occurring was more of an interdependence between the public and private sectors, with each somewhat dependent on the other to provide the broadest base of evidence-based information as possible.

By the beginning of the 21st century, the more traditional aspects of land grant universities struggled somewhat to adjust their roles to move further beyond agriculture and engineering, most often moving into fields such as environment, energy, sustainability, public health, human and community development, and global competitiveness. These changes, of course, reflected greater emphasis on contemporary issues. Strategic planning for visions of 21st century land grants abounded in efforts to maintain appropriate applied research and outreach missions across a wider range of academic disciplines as the major land grant universities came to resemble—and more often competed with—other state universities.

Garrett J. O'Keefe

See also Agricultural Journalism; Association for Communication Excellence; Department of Agriculture, U.S.; Diffusion of Innovations

Further Readings

Anderson, G. (Ed.). (1976). *Land grant universities and their continuing challenge.* East Lansing: Michigan State University Press.

Jenkins, J. W. (1991). *A centennial history: A history of the College of Agricultural and Life Sciences at the University of Wisconsin-Madison.* Madison: University of Wisconsin Press.

Kerr, N. A. (1987). *The legacy: A centennial history of the state agricultural experiment stations, 1887–1987.* Columbia: University of Missouri Press.

National Association of State Universities and Land Grant Colleges. (2009). *2009 strategic opportunities for cooperative extension.* New York: Author.

Nevins, A. (1962). *The state universities and democracy.* Urbana: University of Illinois Press.

Seevers, B., Graham, D., Gamon, J., & Conklin, N. (1997). *Education through cooperative extension.* New York: Delmar.

Wolf, S. A. (Ed.). (1998). *Privatization of information and agricultural industrialization.* New York: CRC Press.

LATIN AMERICA, SCIENCE COMMUNICATION IN

Due to the cultural, economic, social, and historical diversity of the several countries in Latin America, science communication should not be seen as homogeneous in the region. The history of science communication in Latin America (as in many other regions) is far from being fully mapped out, but it is known that countries such as Brazil have a long tradition in the field. The newspaper *O Patriota,* for example, was already covering science issues in the beginning of the 19th century (1813), as soon as the prohibition of printing was banned in Brazil, a trend followed by other newspapers in the same century. Continuing this long tradition of Brazilians communicating science, public conferences held in the latter part of the 19th century and the first Brazilian radio, created in 1923 by scientists for communicating science issues, should be noted. An important early tool for communicating science in Latin America was the natural history museums, created in the 19th century in countries such as Argentina, Brazil, Chile, and Uruguay—to mention some of them. However, during this period, science communication had a limited impact on society for the most part, reaching mainly the elites.

After World War II, newspapers and magazines started publishing sections and articles on science and technology, as result of an effort of both individuals enthusiastic about science journalism and a more organized movement engaging several countries. A first seminar on science journalism was delivered in Chile in 1962, supported by CIESPAL, the International Center of High Studies in Communication for Latin America. In 1965, the Argentinean Association of Science Journalism was created, headed by the physicist and science journalist Jacobo Brailovsky. In 1969, the Iberoamerican Association for Science Journalism was founded, then directed by the Spanish science journalist Manuel Calvo Hernando. Another enthusiast of science journalism and cofounder of the Iberoamerican Association for Science Journalism, Arístides Bastidas, pushed the area in Venezuela, where in 1968 he created a Sunday science section in the main newspaper, *El Nacional,* and, in 1971, the Circle on Science Journalism.

As part of the same movement—which included among their main objectives creating a good atmosphere for science journalism and for training journalists for covering science stories—Colombia (in 1976), Chile (in 1976), and Brazil (in 1977) created their own national associations. Among the group who created the Brazilian Association was José Reis, who is considered to have had a key role in science journalism in Brazil. Due to his importance, the Brazilian government created the José Reis Prize for Science Communication in 1978. This more organized movement toward science journalism later reached other countries, including Peru, Ecuador, and Costa Rica—all of them in the same year, 2005—and Bolivia (in 2007), some of them with the profile of a network instead. A network for science journalists was also created in Argentina, in 2007, by the younger generation, joining together at the present moment 110 journalists who, among other activities, keep up an electronic discussion.

In 1990, the "Red Pop" network, a network on science popularization for Latin America and the Caribbean, was created. This network is not limited to science journalism. Red Pop has as its main objective to strengthen the interchange of ideas and to promote cooperation. Its meetings, carried out every 2 years in different countries, have been important forums for discussion since the network's founding, mainly for science centers.

In the 1990s, an important emphasis was given to hands-on science museums, with Mexico and Brazil being the countries that most heavily invested in creating these organizations. In Brazil, at least 100 hands-on science museums were founded, with different sizes and budgets, although still concentrated in the big cities. Chile, Colombia, and Uruguay should also be highlighted for their innovative experiences in engaging the public in science through hands-on museums. National associations for science museums were also created, once more in Brazil and Mexico, for example.

An important step taken by some countries was the consolidation of a national policy for supporting science communication. Two countries have started this process: Chile and Panama. Chile created Explora in 1995 as a "National Program for Non-Formal Education in Science and Technology," linked to the National Commission for Scientific and Technological Research and aiming to create a scientific culture in the community, in particular for children and teenagers. The annual budget is U.S.$5 million; the program includes several activities, such as a Science Week, printed material, meetings, fairs, and so on. The Panama program, called Destellos, was created in 1997 and linked to the National Secretary of Science and Technology.

In 2004, the Brazilian government created a national unit for science popularization (as it is called) linked to the Ministry of Science and Technology, with the following objectives: to support nonformal science education activities; to support hands-on science museums (including mobile initiatives such as science trucks, boats, and buses); to improve the quality of science coverage; to create the Science and Technology National Week; to push the creation of science festivals; and to support the training for science communicators. The budget for 2004 was about U.S.$7.5 million and has grown to about U.S.$15 million per year in 2008 and 2009.

Following the Latin American perspective of seeing science and technology as a tool for supporting development, the Colombian government created, in 2005, the National Policy of Social Engagement on Science, Technology, and Innovation (in Spanish, Política Nacional de Apropiación Social de la Ciencia, la Tecnología y la Innovación). It has five main action lines: to communicate Colombian science, technology, and innovation; to provide training for science communicators; to push citizen participation in science and technology; to support consolidating a scientific culture taking into consideration the interests and needs of society; and to evaluate science engagement activities. The budget per year is about U.S.$2.6 million.

With a budget of U.S.$200,000, the Uruguayan Program for Popularization of the Scientific Culture (as it is called) was created in 2007, linked to the Unit for Innovation, Science, and Technology for Development, which is in turn linked to the Ministry of Education and Culture.

Mexico does not have a national program for science communication, although the field is recognized. In Mexico, a program that deserves to be highlighted as a key initiative in science communication in Latin America is the Directorate General for Science Communication (in Spanish, Dirección General de Divulgación de la Ciencia), which is linked to the National Autonomous University of Mexico. Created in 1997, it was one of the first in the region having a whole infrastructure for science communication. It includes two science museums, a magazine for teenagers, training for science communicators, and production of books and multimedia.

Another activity carried out by several Latin American countries is the science week, which has been engaging both individuals and institutions at the national level (although the actual impact of the activity varies according to the country). The first country in the region that started organizing a science week was probably Chile, which created it in 1995 and is having its 15th version in 2009. Following this, countries such as Bolivia, Colombia, Mexico, Argentina, and Uruguay have been organizing their own science weeks. Brazil is the country with the most impressive figures: The first science week in 2004 joined 1,842 activities throughout Brazil; in 2008, 11,000 activities were organized in 450 cities and small towns.

At the present moment, Latin America is the stage for a wide diversity of activities in science communication through different tools: museums, science centers, TV, radio, magazines, newspapers, books, drama, and so on. A number of meetings have been organized in the regions, reflecting a need for more spaces for sharing experiences and for training. With respect to training, a trend toward professionalization of the field can be observed, including some long-term courses being

created in countries such as Argentina, Brazil, Colombia, Ecuador, and Mexico. Although indeed this text is far from being a complete map of science communication in Latin America, it is hoped that it succeeds in providing a general overview of activity in the region.

Luisa Massarani

Author's Note: Thanks to Diana Cazaux, Valeria Román (Argentina), Cristina Pabón, Laura Guachalla (Bolivia), Ildeu de Castro Moreira (Brazil), Eduardo Rey, José Santiago Arellano (Chile), Lisbeth Fog, Ximena Serrano, Marcela Lozano (Colombia), Margoth Mena Young (Costa Rica), Ernesto Márquez (Mexico), Zoraida Portillo (Peru), Gustavo Riestra (Uruguay), and Acianela Montes de Oca (Venezuela), who helped with compiling this information.

See also International Science Journalism Associations; Mexico, Science Communication in

LATOUR, BRUNO (1947–)

Trained as philosopher and anthropologist, Bruno Latour has become one of the most influential theorists in the field of science and technology studies (STS). He is probably best known as one of the primary developers of actor-network theory (ANT). Since the publication of his first book in STS, *Laboratory Life* (in 1979, coauthored with Steve Woolgar), Latour has sought to combine an interest in the construction of scientific facts and technological artifacts with a concern for the wider implications of science and technology in society. Latour's oeuvre is unique not only in the range of topics covered from science and technology to politics, religion, and law; it is also unique in its blending of a wide variety of disciplinary influences, including STS, anthropology, philosophy, political science, sociology, primatology, entomology, and more.

The Power of Inscription Devices

Laboratory Life is based on fieldwork done by Latour in a laboratory of the Salk Institute for Biological Studies, La Jolla, California. In the book,

Latour and Woolgar introduced the notion of inscription devices to designate laboratory apparatus or any configuration of apparatuses that enable the transformation of material substances into figures, diagrams, or recorded traces, which can be used by scientists to produce knowledge. The scientific production of knowledge is the action of putting something into a form. Scientists use all kinds of devices, including instruments, computers, and written documents, to put their objects of inquiry into scientific form, the most prominent of which is the peer-reviewed scientific article or letter. From the first, perhaps barely comprehensible, recorded traces produced in the laboratory to the final article, and then, perhaps, later to the inclusion into the accepted body of scientific knowledge, the scientific inscriptions undergo a huge change in epistemic modality, that is, the degree of possibility or necessity of some piece of knowledge. Whereas scientists typically express with due uncertainty their interpretations of the first inscriptions produced in the lab, much later inscriptions in the chain of scientific reference are phrased using a much higher commitment to the truth of the statement.

Laboratory Life also was a reflective exploration into the very idea of doing laboratory studies. Latour and Woolgar concluded that, really, the only difference between scientists and anthropologists of science is that they (scientists) have a laboratory. In other words, scientific inscription devices along with techniques for reducing the modalities of inscriptions are much more powerful tools of persuasion than the ones available for anthropologists and others wishing to study scientists at work. If one wishes to question scientific information, one has to disentangle and reinterpret all the inscriptions and all the inscription devices that constitute the information given.

Although Latour and Woolgar did not take their conclusion this far, the powerful inscription devices of science also introduce an asymmetry between scientists and laypeople. In public debates, scientists have at their disposal inscription devices that make scientific objects speak while the general public often has very few and highly unreliable inscriptions to refer to. Many contemporary issues, such as climate change, the depletion of the ozone layer, genetic modification, and technological risk, to a large extent are made possible by the inscription devices of science and technology.

In a talk given at the Darmstadt Colloquium in 2001, Latour used the term *socioscientific experiments* to designate such issues where the inscriptions of science seem to spill over from the inscription devices used by scientists to become entangled in socioeconomic and political debates. He argued that now, where the laboratory has extended its network of inscription devices to the whole planet, more than ever we need to balance scientific inscriptions with other types of evidence and experience. We have to come to an understanding of scientific information as a resource for democratic processes, not as statements that need refutation or combat in public debate.

How "Matters of Concern" Matter for Science and Technology Communication

Latour has used particular insights of STS and ANT to rethink social theory and political philosophy. In *We Have Never Been Modern* (1993), he argued that two dichotomies constitute the foundation of modern societies. First, the division between the natural and the social world prescribes different sets of laws for nature and culture. Modern societies' emphasis on humanism rests on this particular separation of natural and political powers. Second, there is a hidden dichotomy between the work of purification, which detaches humans from nature and thus enables the first division, and the work of translation, resulting in the construction of hybrid networks spanning the dichotomy between nature and culture. In Latour's interpretation of the process of modernization, the work of translation was necessary for the establishment of two separate orders of knowledge and power, but then later forgotten or hidden away.

The heirs of enlightenment, modern societies have delegated all knowledge about nature to the sciences, along with the notion of objective matters of facts. The modern constitution rests on the belief that science injects into society undisputable facts about natural objects and processes. However, as STS scholars have shown, science itself is an uncertain, partially objective, ongoing social process. Moreover, many scientific objects of inquiry are fully entangled with human decision making in society. This means that the work of translation—that is, the collective merging of scientific and political representations—becomes central to questions concerning science and technology in open democratic societies.

According to Latour, the very idea of matters of fact was an unfortunate by-product of the modern constitution. The term is used to make a distinction between what can be disputed and what cannot. Communicating matters of fact to the public is a simple and one-way process. Since there can be no dispute over matters of fact, the process consists in the conveying of scientific certainty to a wider audience.

Latour has proposed another concept to replace matters of fact, namely, matters of concern. This concept opens up for a more dialogic understanding of science and technology communication in public. Matters of concern are public issues that arise in part as a result of scientific and technological uncertainties. With regard to matters of concern, science and technology can provide no straightforward solutions. Rather, science and technology are part of the problems inherent to matters of concern, which have to be solved using many different resources pooled together from many different spheres of life: science, technology, politics, law, economics, and so on.

Controversies are constitutive elements of matters of concern—controversies in terms of how to identify relevant problems and problem solutions, controversies with respect to what are the appropriate facts and methods, and controversies about whom to involve in the process of moving ahead. Such controversies often will bring out new actors and new configurations of actors. They even pertain to questions about proper expertise and proper means of representation.

Science and technology communication is central to matters of concern. Whereas the concept of matters of fact primarily engages conditions of the production of reliable scientific knowledge, matters of concern emphasize knowledge in circulation. Processes of movement, translation, transmission, and, not least, transformation of knowledge take center stage. In those processes, scientists and engineers have to negotiate with other actors about proper understandings and implications of scientific and technological objects. This may involve conflict and change as much as mutual understanding and reconciliation. It is, perhaps, the only way to bring science and technology into democracy.

Kristian Hvidtfelt Nielsen

See also Actor-Network Theory; Science, Technology, and Society Studies; Uncertainty in Science Communication

Further Readings

Latour, B. (1993). *We have never been modern.* Cambridge, MA: Harvard University Press.

Latour, B. (2001, March). *What rules of method for the new socio-scientific experiments?* Retrieved June 4, 2009, from www.bruno-latour.fr/poparticles/poparticle/p095.html

Latour, B. (2004). *Politics of nature: How to bring the sciences into democracy.* Cambridge, MA: Harvard University Press.

Latour, B., & Woolgar, S. (1979). *Laboratory life: The social construction of facts.* London: Sage.

LOGICAL POSITIVISM

In the years prior to World War I, a mathematician, a sociologist, and a physicist would come together regularly to meet in various cafés around Vienna, Austria, to discuss philosophy in a genial, friendly atmosphere. At the core of the majority of their discussions was the nature of belief—a field of philosophy called *epistemology.* How do we know "truth" from "fiction"? This issue is at the heart of attempts to define truth, whether from a scientific or a communication point of view.

The war put a temporary hold on their association as the group disbanded and went their separate ways. It wasn't until 1922 that the mathematician Hans Hahn returned to Vienna and encouraged a newly appointed professor in the philosophy of inductive sciences to join him in rekindling the old discussions. This gentleman, a German by the name of Moritz Schlick, had published on a range of topics, from the novel special theory of relativity to the nature of truth and logic. It was with this association that the Vienna Circle was formed.

With Schlick as chairman, this gathering formally established itself in 1928 as the Ernst Mach Society, honoring the Austrian physicist and philosopher who had famously described the descriptions of natural laws as summaries of experimental data. The members of this society, including the original members Hahn, Otto Neurath, and Phillip

Frank, included mathematicians, philosophers, and physicists such as Kurt Gödel, Gustav Bergmann, Rudolf Carnap, Richard Edler von Mises, and Hahn's sister (and Otto Neurath's wife) Olga. Mach's influence was clearly reflected in a common philosophy shared by most members of the society—one that valued empiricism and logic in evaluating the strength of ideas.

In 1929, a pamphlet titled "The Scientific Conception of the World—The Vienna Circle" was printed, listing the members of the circle in an appendix at the back. This pamphlet became better known as the "Vienna Circle Manifesto," and within it was an attempt to define the characteristics of the scientific method.

The Vienna Circle Manifesto

There were two defining features of the philosophy of the Vienna Circle. One was that natural laws could only be described according to our observations. This empirical approach, called *positivism,* was fundamentally expounded by Mach, who competed with the atomists of his day by stating that unobserved conjecture had no place in science. This was not to say that proposals that were not based on direct observations were wrong or impossible, but rather that the formulation of laws should be an economical exercise based on a parsimonious expression of the facts.

Positivism has a long and varied history dating back to ancient rhetoric on the respective roles observation and reason play in describing reality. The term itself was coined in the middle of the 19th century by the French sociologist Auguste Comte, whose study of the angst experienced by his fellow countrymen after the revolution eventually led to modern secular humanism. He described three phases of a society—the theological (appeal to a greater authority, whether divine or historical), the metaphysical (appeal to human rights or the rights of an individual), and the positive (appeal to the objective, or scientific).

An outcome of this perspective, however, is that there are only two kinds of ideas—those that can be reduced to events that can be experienced, and those that cannot. The latter were termed as metaphysical in nature and were determined to be virtually meaningless concepts and therefore scientifically useless.

Language and Logical Positivism

Arguably, the goal of the Vienna Circle's discussions was to unify science under a single system of thought or practice. This process would be defined by the reduction of all statements to either observable qualities, which are therefore subject to scientific analysis and discussion, or to unobservable, metaphysical qualities, which should therefore be rejected.

Yet a persistent problem with science is the ambiguous nature of language, which routinely leads to logical fallacies and errors in reasoning, not to mention confusing descriptive qualities with the subject itself. An example of this is the term *love,* which is typically imbued with physical qualities in spite of its being a description of an emotional state. This problem can also lead to the mistaken belief that reason alone can create useful knowledge in the absence of observations, a notion referred to as *synthetic knowledge.*

Oddly, while mathematics is typically based purely in reason and can be argued to be a form of synthetic knowledge, which therefore should be rejected by logical positivism, philosophically it is analytical in nature. As such, mathematical conclusions are the only form of a priori reasoning considered by the Vienna Circle to be scientifically productive.

It is in part the use of language to describe nature that separates metaphysics from logical positivism. Rudolph Carnap's essay, "The Elimination of Metaphysics Through Logical Analysis of Language," delves into the relevance of language and how it impacts scientific inquiry. In it, he explains the metaphysical application of many words as being "meaningless," given they have no empirical equivalence. Even today, this is an accusation leveled at certain fields of science—the so-called Sokal Affair (named after physicist Andrew Sokal's well-known hoax in the mid-1990s, intended to demonstrate that certain fields, such as postmodern cultural studies, are at best less critical than other sciences and at worst are pseudoscientific) echoes the perceived significance of language in scientific inquiry.

Where Did the Logical Positivists Go?

Whereas World War I saw the first Vienna Circle dissolve only temporarily, World War II was its end. Most of the members fled to the United States when the National Socialists came to power in Germany, although Schlick was murdered by one of his students in 1936.

Logical positivism had its critics, although its advocates largely defended it as being a philosophy rather than an axiomatic, scientific system, and therefore claimed that any tautologies or logical inconsistencies that arose needed no proof.

Perhaps the most famous critic of logical positivism was Austrian-born philosopher Karl Popper. He felt that the tenets behind verification were too strict, risking the exclusion of ideas that could possibly have merit. In its place, he proposed falsification—the evaluation of an idea's worth by its ability to be disproved. For instance, if there was no way to observe a potential phenomenon (even in theory) that would demonstrate an idea as false, the idea was without scientific merit.

A clear example that supported his concerns was provided by the atomic theories that Ernst Mach opposed. In many ways, atomics were unobservable, and the language used to describe them could well be thought of as being metaphysical, even though, as technology improved, the atomic theory gained ground. Logical positivism would have meant dismissing it on such grounds, while falsification would only have done so once observations were made that contradicted the hypothesis.

Ironically, Einstein stated that Mach could be considered the "precursor" of Einstein's general theory of relativity—in spite of Ernst Mach's own rejection of the theory given its nonempirical, metaphysical quality.

A former student of Carnap's, Hilary Putnam, believed it was impossible to distinguish observations from theories. Given that all observations are technically subjective in nature, and it is only on collaboration that we agree or disagree on observed qualities, it is impossible not to use theoretical terms to describe observations. As such, defining metaphysical concepts is less "black and white" than logical positivism might call for.

Today, logical positivism is regarded as having played a vital role in our understanding of language and its role in science, as well as grounding the progress of analytic philosophy throughout the latter half of the 20th century and into modern times.

Mike McRae

See also Popper, Karl; Scientific Method; Two Cultures

Further Readings

Holton, G. (1993). *Science and anti-science.* Cambridge, MA: Harvard University Press.

Zalta, E. N. (Ed.). (2009). *Stanford encyclopedia of philosophy.* Available at http://plato.stanford.edu

LOVE CANAL

During the summer of 1976, a group of angry homeowners descended on the weekly city council meeting in Niagara Falls, New York. Their gripes were not about rising taxes, trash collection, or street maintenance. Instead, they were armed with a litany of unusual complaints, including tales of sick children, dying pets, and shriveled lawns and gardens. And nasty industrial odors had permeated the basements of their homes. Ultimately, the homeowners' complaints provided the first glimpse of an environmental nightmare that awakened the nation to the risks of improper industrial waste disposal. Subsequent media coverage of these events helped raise the environmental consciousness of the nation and shape the emerging field of environmental journalism.

In the aftermath, the neighborhood known as *Love Canal* emerged as one of the nation's worst environmental disasters, one that set off a litany of finger-pointing, corporate denials, and bureaucratic missteps. Ultimately, even Washington reacted when, in 1980, Congress created the Superfund waste cleanup program. Appropriately, President Jimmy Carter signed the landmark legislation at a ceremony that took place in downtown Niagara Falls, New York. Summarizing the whole nightmarish ordeal, the New York State Health Department, in a 1978 report to Governor Hugh Carey, minced no words. "Love Canal," it said, was "a public health time bomb."

The history of Love Canal can be traced to the 19th century, when entrepreneur William T. Love attracted enough investors to begin construction of a canal that would connect the upper and lower Niagara River. Using the elevation drop over the same escarpment that created the famous Niagara Falls, Love envisioned a waterway that would be ideal for the generation of hydroelectric power. He imagined that industries would flock to the region to take advantage of an abundance of electricity. But when Louis Tesla discovered a way to transmit power over long distances by the use of alternating current, industries no longer needed to be in close proximity to a source of electricity. Love's dream ended. And the short section of canal near the upper Niagara River became a swimming hole for local children.

Meanwhile, the lifeblood of the city—its chemical industry—continued to grow, providing jobs and vital tax revenue to the region. By the early 1920s, one of the largest companies—Hooker Chemical—was producing at such a pace at its riverside plant that it was running out of places to dispose of the waste by-products from its production of pesticides, herbicides, and other toxic organic compounds. The abandoned Love Canal was an attractive alternative. It was close to the factory and the area was, at that time, sparsely populated.

Hooker filled the 2,000-foot-long, 60-foot-wide canal cavity with some of the most toxic by-products ever produced. Neighbors recall seeing truck after truck loaded with barrels of toxic chemicals. Workers emptied thousands of tons of the toxic brew directly into the water, taking the drums back the factory to be used again. And local children continued to swim in the mess, unaware of the dangers until chased away by chemical burns and unexplained skin irritations.

In 1953, after filling the cavity to the brim, Hooker sold the Love Canal property to the Niagara Falls Board of Education for $1. The board wanted the land for a playground behind an elementary school that was built to serve block after block of new homes that housed the workers from the city's burgeoning chemical industry. The transaction, according to a 1980 series in the *Niagara Falls Gazette,* contained no warning at all about the contents of the landed gift. Company vice president Bjarne Klaussen wrote in 1952 that he felt the board had done a fine job meeting expanded demand, and he expressed his firm's interest in cooperating with the board's efforts. The 99th Street Elementary School was constructed and the abandoned canal became a playground for students and an open area for the working-class families that flocked to the new neighborhood.

The first hint of trouble came after a particularly harsh winter in 1975 to 1976. Melting snow and spring rains filled the chemical graveyard, and toxic pollutants started to seep to the surface. Groundwater flow carried the toxic brew into the basements of adjoining homes. Parents started worrying about children, who became ill after playing outdoors. Family pets were dying and backyard gardens were filled with dead vegetable plants. By the time those families stormed the city council meeting in 1976, anxiety was high—although no one in that community had any idea what the implications were. In fact, the first official response from the Niagara County Health Department was to recommend distribution of electric fans to dissipate the foul industrial odors.

Eventually, the New York State Health Department began documenting illnesses, miscarriages, and birth defects—all linked to the toxic waste in close proximity to those modest homes. In 1978, New York announced a government-funded evacuation of the neighborhood. Some 235 families left the community at government expense. In the analysis that followed, New York scientists identified more than 200 different toxic compounds, including highly toxic dioxin and benzene, along with 10 other carcinogens—all waste by-products of pesticide production. But the Love Canal disaster was far from over. Led by housewife-turned-activist Lois Gibbs, families outside the immediate evacuation area pressed for relief, concerned by the ongoing threat to their children—and diminished property values because of proximity to the notorious chemical dump.

In 1980, President Carter declared Love Canal a federal emergency, making way for the relocation of more than 700 additional families. Meanwhile, cleanup work began as homes were demolished and steps were taken to encapsulate the buried toxic wastes. And Hooker Chemical, now a division of Occidental Chemical, faced a myriad of state and federal lawsuits as government agencies sought to recover cleanup expenses and damages.

Today, the immediate Love Canal area is a barren wasteland, surrounded by an imposing chain-link fence. A treatment plant collects toxic groundwater from an underground drain system that surrounds the perimeter of the toxic graveyard.

Some homes around the periphery have been resettled. But, to this day, Love Canal remains a symbol of the environmental and health hazards associated with improper chemical waste disposal. And though thousands of other dump sites have been identified nationwide, Love Canal remains the symbol of improper industrial waste disposal. The U.S. Environmental Protection Agency's John Deegan told the *Washington Post* in 1980 that he did not believe the nation would ever be able to fully recover from Love Canal.

Rae Tyson

See also Community "Right to Know"; Environmental Journalism; Environmental Justice; Superfund

Further Readings

Beck, E. C. (1979, January). The Love Canal tragedy. *EPA Journal.* Washington, DC: U.S. Environmental Protection Agency. Retrieved December 31, 2008, from www.epa.gov/history/topics/lovecanal/01.htm

Gibbs, L. M. (1982). *Love Canal: My story.* New York: Grove Press.

Gibbs, L. M. (1998). *Learning from Love Canal: A 20th anniversary retrospective.* Retrieved December 31, 2008, from http://arts.envirolink.org/arts_and_activism/LoisGibbs.html

New York State Department of Health. (1978, September). *Love Canal: Public health time bomb* (Special report to the Governor and Legislature). Retrieved December 31, 2008, from www.health.state.ny.us/environmental/investigations/love_canal/lctimbmb.htm

University at Buffalo, The State University of New York. (n.d.). *The Love Canal collections.* University Archives. Available at http://ublib.buffalo.edu/libraries/specialcollections/lovecanal/index.html

U.S. Department of Justice. (1995, December 21). *Occidental to pay $129 million in Love Canal settlement* (Press release No. 638). Retrieved December 31, 2008, from www.usdoj.gov/opa/pr/Pre_96/December95/638.txt.html

LOW-LEVEL RADIATION

Low-level radiation is a mixed blessing. It can be used medically in radiation therapy to save the lives of cancer patients, but it also has the possibility of causing cancer when people are exposed to it over long periods of time. In addition, its use in many fields creates a radioactive waste disposal problem. Low-level radioactive wastes cannot be thrown in the trash; depending on the type of waste, they probably will have to be securely stored or buried for hundreds of years. Because radiation is always a public concern and is always newsworthy, science communicators need to know about the issue.

Few people worry much about low-level radiation. Most public attention has focused on high-level radiation exposure that might come from the explosion of a nuclear or a "dirty" bomb or from a nuclear plant accident, such as the one in 1979 at Three Mile Island in Pennsylvania or the far more serious accident in 1986 at the Chernobyl nuclear plant in the then–Soviet Union. Yet many sources of low-level radiation might pose health risks, including a naturally occurring radioactive gas or continuing exposure to sources of human-made radioactive emissions.

What It Is and Where It Occurs

Naturally occurring forms of radiation are part of "background radiation," which people are continually exposed to in varying degrees. Naturally occurring forms account for an average of 82% of the exposures in the U.S. population, according to the National Council on Radiation Protection and Measurements (NCRP). These exposures come from a variety of sources, such as cosmic radiation from outer space and internal emissions from radioactive materials ingested in food and water and from the body itself. Exposures also occur from radioactive minerals in soils and rocks. By far, the largest background exposure (52%) comes from radon, a colorless, odorless radioactive gas that originates from uranium in the soil, which can seep into people's houses in air and water. In high enough concentrations, radioactive particles from radon can damage cells that line the lungs and lead to lung cancer. Radon is the second leading cause of lung cancer in the United States and is associated with 15,000 to 22,000 lung cancer deaths each year, according to the National Cancer Institute.

Human-made low-level radiation accounts for about 18% of the total background exposure, according to the NRCP, with medical X-rays and nuclear medicine making up the majority of this human-made exposure in the United States. Other exposures can come from building materials, such as the granite in Grand Central Station in New York and consumer products such as computer screens, smoke detectors, and tobacco. Low levels of radiation also are emitted from nuclear plants and nuclear weapons facilities and from widespread fallout from aboveground testing of nuclear weapons that occurred in the United States from 1951 to 1962. However, for most people, these sources account for only a small portion of human-made background exposure, according to the NCRP.

Unless they live near or work at a nuclear power or nuclear weapons plant or have radon in their homes, the majority of people are most frequently exposed to low levels of radiation through medical and dental X-rays and diagnostic tests.

Health Effects Debate

The risk of harmful health effects from exposures to low-level radiation has been the subject of scientific uncertainty and disagreement for many years. Scientists have long known that exposure to very high levels of ionizing radiation, as this type of radiation is called, causes serious illness and death within a few days, and that lower doses of radiation can cause health effects such as cancer that may take many years to develop. Ionizing radiation, which includes X-rays and gamma rays, can cause damage in living cells by making atoms in molecules release electrons and become ions. This process can cause cell death in high doses in a short time and errors in the reproductive process called mutations in lower doses over longer periods. The mutations can eventually lead to cancer.

While these effects are clear for high-level radiation doses, many scientists have questioned whether there is a risk of health effects from chronic or continuing exposure to very low doses of radiation. The scientific debate has focused on how much exposure to low-level radiation could cause health effects.

Scientists have developed two main risk models about this question: one says that any exposure—any dose—no matter how small might prove harmful to individuals over time. This first model is called the linear-no-threshold model. The other risk model, often referred to as the threshold model, proposes that there is a level or threshold below which a minimal radiation dose will not cause damage. This risk model (there are actually several different models in this group) says that small amounts of damage done by low-level radiation over time can be naturally repaired and there is little risk of harm. This is a simple explanation of a very complex scientific argument over the threshold concept, which also applies to chemical exposures.

Over the years, many studies have been done and reports written about potential health effects from low doses of radiation. In 1999, the U.S. Department of Energy funded a long-term set of scientific studies on cellular and molecular responses to low doses of X-ray and gamma radiation. One goal of this study was to try to definitively answer the threshold question, but results of these studies have been mixed with respect to threshold effects. Since 1972, the Biological Effects of Ionizing Radiation (BEIR) committee of the National Academies, one of the most prestigious scientific organizations in the United States, has periodically reviewed accumulating scientific data about low-level radiation effects on exposed populations.

In the seventh of its series of reports on the health risks, which was issued in 2005, the BEIR VII committee agreed that a major review of the available scientific information supported the linear-no-threshold risk model, stating that even "the smallest dose" might increase risk to humans. While the biological mechanism is not completely understood, the report noted that the ionizing radiation energy can result in complex changes in the structure of molecules, including DNA, within the cells of the body, making it difficult for the body's repair mechanisms to mend them correctly. This could result in the development of cancers, particularly in "solid" organs such as the breast or prostate, over time. The BEIR VII report emphasized that the cancer risk was small, estimating that 1 cancer in 100 could result from a single low-level radiation exposure, compared to 42 in 100 from other causes. According to the report, the risk of children inheriting health effects from their parents' exposure to low-level radiation was very small compared to other inherited genetic disorders.

Despite this newest report, some scientists still believe in a threshold, at least for some types of cancers, and research is continuing. Both interpretations of the threshold concept have implications for government regulations to protect citizens, with stricter exposure regulations required for the linear-no-dose model. Because of this scientific debate and other important social, political, and economic factors, many countries have adopted different allowable exposure standards for low-level radiation, including those for both nuclear plant workers and citizens. For example, France and Japan, which depend primarily on nuclear power as their energy source, allow more radiation exposure than does the United States.

The Low-Level Radioactive Waste Problem

Health issues are not the only concerns with low-level radiation. There also is a major problem in disposing of the large volumes of radioactive wastes created in the United States. While they present much less of a radiation hazard than either nuclear fuel or high-level radioactive waste, if they are improperly controlled, these low-level wastes can cause both chronic and acute health risks, according to a Committee on Improving the Regulation and Management of Low-Activity Radioactive Wastes (LAW) of the U.S. National Academies.

Coming from many sectors of the U.S. economy, including national defense, private industry, and medical and research operations, different types of low-level radioactive wastes require long-term storage or burial until their radioactive elements decay to safe levels.

Commercial low-level waste comes from nuclear power plants and other industrial, medical, and research operations. According to the LAW committee, typical examples include protective shoe coverings and clothing, mops, rags, equipment and tools, laboratory apparatus, process equipment, reactor water treatment residues, and some hardware. These wastes are produced in every state in the country.

Slightly radioactive debris, rubble, and contaminated soils can result from decommissioned nuclear power plant sites and from site cleanup at nuclear weapons facilities. Uranium and thorium mining and milling have produced large radioactive waste piles as well as process residues and contaminated soils and equipment. Low-level radioactive waste products also are found in residues from commercial ore mining, phosphate and fertilizer production, oil and gas production, coal burning, and wastewater treatment.

Federal and state regulations on how to handle and store this low-level waste are complex, inconsistent, and confusing, according to the LAW committee. Current regulations are based primarily on the type of industry that produced the wastes rather than on the degree of risk the wastes pose for treatment, storage, and disposal. In addition to government agencies, others with a stake in deciding how to store low-level radioactive wastes include the organizations that generate the waste and have to pay for its disposal, operators of nuclear waste storage facilities and their workers, and citizens living near the waste facilities and along waste transportation routes.

Where to store all of this waste is a major problem. The U.S. Congress passed the Low-Level Radioactive Waste Policy Act in 1980 and amended it in 1985, making states responsible for disposing of most commercial low-level radioactive waste. The law required creation of a system of interstate compacts to develop and manage disposal facilities. Most states agreed to form compacts composed of three to eight states that would locate a waste site within one of the states in the group. All low-level wastes from the compact would go to this site until it was filled, and then another state in the compact would open a site. Ten compacts were formed but no new sites were developed. Economics, politics, and significant public resistance to siting waste storage facilities in peoples' "backyards" undermined this program.

Only three commercial sites exist in the United States that take various types of low-level radioactive waste, requiring long transportation routes. Barnwell, a site in South Carolina, for years conveniently took waste from generators in many states. However, because of shrinking capacity, it closed its doors on July 1, 2008, to waste from all states except those within its compact—South Carolina, New Jersey, and Connecticut. The two other low-level commercial waste disposal facilities are in Clive, Utah, which accepts the least hazardous type of low-level waste from all states, and near Richland, Washington, which accepts all classes of low-level waste from Washington, Oregon, Idaho, Montana, Wyoming, Utah, Alaska, Hawaii, Nevada,

Colorado, and New Mexico. With the closure of Barnwell, waste generators in 36 states now have no disposal options for more hazardous low-level wastes, such as those from nuclear power plants. The Nuclear Regulatory Commission, which regulates nuclear production and waste in the United States, has recommended that these generators store their low-level radioactive waste on-site for an extended period. For nuclear plants, this would add more wastes to be stored to the high-level radioactive wastes they already have on-site because technical and political issues have held up the construction of Yucca Mountain in Nevada, the designated U.S. disposal site for high-level waste.

Although not facing the major technical problems of high-level radioactive waste storage, low-level radioactive waste storage also has problems beyond limited capacity. Many of them involve public distrust of the ability of government agencies and commercial organizations to protect public health. Members of the public are concerned about risks of groundwater contamination and possible health risks from long-term exposures for site workers and people living near these sites, whether the wastes are stored at a commercial site or at a nuclear power plant. They also have fears about trucking low-level wastes over long distances to storage facilities that relate not only to potential accidents but also to national security issues. Both trucking and a large number of storage sites spread across the nation could provide possible targets for terrorists looking for material to build "dirty bombs."

In the past, public resistance to placing low-level radioactive waste sites in many states proved fierce and defeated almost all efforts to accept them, despite extensive monetary and other incentives. Because of the persistent and widespread public concern about low-level radioactive waste, a major recommendation from the LAW committee was that government agencies improve their efforts to understand levels of public knowledge about low-level wastes and to take citizens' opinions into account and directly involve them when making decisions about low-level radioactive waste management and disposal.

Sharon M. Friedman

See also Chernobyl; Department of Energy, U.S; Nuclear Waste; Nuclear Weapons; Three Mile Island

Further Readings

Committee on Improving Practices for Regulating and Managing Low-Activity Radioactive Waste. (2006, March). *Report in brief, improving the regulation and management of low-activity radioactive wastes.* Washington, DC: National Academies Press. Available at http://dels.nas.edu/dels/rpt_briefs/Low_level_Waste_final.pdf

Committee to Assess the Health Risks From Exposure to Low Levels of Ionizing Radiation. (2005). *Report in Brief, BEIR VII: Health risks from exposure to low levels of ionizing radiation.* Washington, DC: National Academies Press. Available at http://dels.nas.edu/dels/rpt_briefs/beir_vii_final.pdf

National Safety Council. (2005, July). *Understanding radiation in our world.* Available at www.nsc.org/safety_home/BringSafetyHome/Documents/Understanding Radiation.pdf

U.S. Environmental Protection Agency. (2009). *RadTown USA.* Available at www.epa.gov/radtown/

M

Mad Cow Disease (BSE)

Bovine spongiform encephalopathy (BSE), popularly referred to as *mad cow disease*, has caused such global controversy that one might expect it to be clearly proven as a very contagious and deadly human disease, but this expectation is far from true. Worldwide, fewer than 200 human cases have been blamed on infection with the BSE agent. Infection is thought to cause a human disease called variant Creutzfeldt-Jakob disease (vCJD). The human vCJD illness is somewhat different from the previously recognized classic Creutzfeldt-Jakob disease (CJD). Those affected with vCJD are younger, with a median age of 28 years (versus 68 years for CJD); the duration of illness is about twice as long at 13 to 14 months (versus 4–5 months for CJD); and patients exhibit more prominent psychiatric symptoms compared to dementia.

In all species, the disease causes some types of nervous system signs. In cattle, BSE usually occurs in cows over 4 years of age, causing difficulty walking, apprehension or the appearance of anxiety, loss of body weight, and hypersensitivity. All affected animals will die with or without treatment. The age at which the animal was affected and the clinical signs are useful tools in surveillance targeting high-risk animals.

A number of different mammals, including humans, have been identified with diseases similar to BSE, collectively termed transmissible spongiform encephalopathy (TSE). Affected natural hosts include mink, cats (domestic and captive large cats), nyala and greater kudu (African antelopes), and North American cervids such as elk, mule deer, white-tailed deer, and red deer. In the United States and Europe, sheep with the TSE or scrapie have been recognized since the 1730s.

A Brief History

In 1986 and 1987, the BSE story began to unfold in the United Kingdom with the identification of a new and unique neurological syndrome in cattle. However, it was later discovered that the story had actually begun 10 to 20 years prior to that, with the implementation of feeding cattle a ration that included meat-and-bone meal (MBM) from cattle and sheep. This was a common practice due to the high protein content in MBM and the scarcity of high-protein crops such as soybean meal.

Once a nationwide reporting system was developed in the United Kingdom, many more cases were reported. The number of new BSE cases in cattle reported per week peaked at 800 in January 1993. Other countries began to report cases in 1989, with cases reported in the Falkland Islands and Ireland, then in Portugal and Switzerland in 1990. As of 2009, a few cases are still reported, but the epidemic seems to be nearing its end. The top 5 countries by reported cases are the United Kingdom (183,841), Portugal (875), Switzerland (453), Spain (412), and Germany (312). In North America, Canada has reported 15 cases, and the United States has reported only 3 domestic-born cases.

The first U.S. case of BSE was confirmed on December 25, 2003, and became known as "the cow that stole Christmas" for those in the U.S. Department of Agriculture (USDA) who were tasked with responding to the situation and communicating to the public regarding risk concerns. The second U.S. case, in June 2005, occurred in a 12-year-old, native-born cow from Texas. In March 2006, the third U.S. case was confirmed in a 10-year-old cow from Alabama. Genetic tests suggested that this last case was spontaneous, not resulting from the feeding of contaminated MBM. This was reassuring because the U.S. feed ban had been in effect since 1997.

In response to the first U.S. case, the USDA began an intensive program of testing high-risk cattle. From June 1, 2004, to September 20, 2006, tests were run on 787,711 cattle, with only 2 animals, noted previously, being discovered. The testing procedure is very expensive, involving removal of the brain, shipment to the National Veterinary Services Laboratory in Ames, Iowa, and microscopic examination of sections of the brain, looking for the typical spongiform lesions. In 2006, the United States switched to a surveillance system, testing about 40,000 high-risk cattle per year. This level of testing is still very sensitive, designed for the discovery of BSE if the prevalence is more than one case per million cattle.

Infectious Process

The disease is thought to develop when an infectious protein particle, called a prion, contacts a normal, noninfectious prion. As new proteins are produced as a normal part of cell function, the infectious prion interacts with the normal prion, causing it to be folded incorrectly. Many organic molecules change function as they are folded differently. The buildup of incorrectly folded prion proteins in the brain causes the accumulation of plaques, which look like clear holes when the brain is examined under a microscope. This appearance is the reason for the lesion name, *spongiform,* as these lesions look like holes in a sponge.

An infectious disease is generally expected to occur when disease in other infected animals spreads to the susceptible ones. It is unclear if this process holds true for BSE, as spontaneous forms of TSE, such as Kuru, have been identified in humans. However, a likely source in the United Kingdom is sheep, as they are predominant and contribute heavily to the supply of MBM. Sheep can have a TSE disease called scrapie, which is similar to BSE. Passage of scrapie through cattle may have adapted it to its new host. However, there has never been any evidence that scrapie directly infects humans.

U.S. Actions to Prevent Animal and Human Exposure

The risk to cattle and humans in the United States had been greatly reduced because of early action by cattle producers, the USDA, and the U.S. Food and Drug Administration (FDA). All ruminants and ruminant products from countries with BSE were prohibited from entering the United States beginning in 1989.

In 1996, cattle producers implemented a voluntary ban on the feeding of any product derived from ruminants, and, in 1997, the FDA made the ban a regulation and began enforcement at feed mills. In 2004, the USDA Food Safety Inspection Service began to require the removal of specific risk material (SRM) from all cattle over 30 months of age. The FDA extended the feed ban to include the feeding of any materials from mammals to ruminants. A 2008 rule prohibited the use of entire carcasses that have not been inspected and passed for human consumption, unless the cattle are under 30 months of age or have had the brains and spinal cords removed. Another BSE firewall implemented by USDA includes a ban on nonambulatory animals, because the inability to walk can be a symptom of BSE. USDA prohibits any animals that are unable to walk from entering the human food supply.

In the United States, only three cases of vCJD have been identified since 1996, when vCJD was first recognized. All three patients had spent considerable parts of their lives outside of the United States. In comparison, 27 people in the United States died of lightning strikes in 2008. Therefore, any possibility of illness due to U.S. meat consumption can be considered highly remote.

There is also still some question as to whether vCJD is really due to consumption of meat from BSE-infected animals. Unlike for other infectious diseases, it has not been possible to directly demonstrate that consumption of infected meat by a specific ill patient produced vCJD. The evidence is circumstantial but currently termed "strong" by the

U.S. Centers for Disease Control and Prevention. The most convincing experimental trial showed that three monkeys injected with brain tissue from BSE-infected cows developed symptoms similar to human cases. Note that for the investigators in this study to cause illness, it was necessary to inject (not feed) brain tissue (not meat) directly into the central nervous system of the monkeys. However, other epidemiological evidence supports the link of increased cases of vCJD in countries with BSE. The number and timing of cases coincides with the BSE epidemic in cattle. Also, countries with no reported cases of BSE have not reported any human vCJD cases.

Detailed studies of infected cattle 30 months of age and older have clearly demonstrated that only certain parts of the animals have infectious properties, including the brain, skull, eyes, trigeminal ganglia, spinal cord, and vertebral column. In addition to these tissues, other SRMs include the tonsils and distal ileum of all cattle. Currently, these SRMs are not allowed in the food supply. This practice has greatly minimized any real or even potential risk that may have existed.

H. Scott Hurd

See also Centers for Disease Control and Prevention, U.S.; Department of Agriculture, U.S.; Food and Drug Administration, U.S.; Food Safety; Risk Communication, Overview

Further Readings

Kehrli, M. E., Jr., O'Rourke, K. I., Hamir, A. N., Richt, J. A., Nicholson, E. M., Silva, C. J., et al. (2007). *Pathobiology and diagnosis of animal transmissible spongiform encephalopathies: Current knowledge, research gaps, and opportunities* (Government white paper). Beltsville, MD: Interagency Working Group on Prion Science, Subcommittee on Pathobiology and Diagnostics.

U.S. Department of Agriculture, Animal and Plant Health Inspection Service. (n.d.). *Bovine spongiform encephalopathy (BSE)*. Available at www.aphis .usda.gov/newsroom/hot_issues/bse/surveillance/bse_ disease_surv.shtml

U.S. Department of Health and Human Services, Centers for Disease Control and Prevention. (2009). *BSE (Bovine spongiform encephalopathy, or mad cow disease)*. Available at www.cdc.gov/ncidod/ dvrd/bse/

U.S. Food and Drug Administration, Center for Veterinary Medicine. (2008). *November 2008 update on feed enforcement activities to limit the spread of BSE* (Government white paper). Rockville, MD: Author.

World Organisation for Animal Health. (2007). *Geographical distribution of countries that reported BSE confirmed cases since 1989*. Available at www .oie.int/eng/info/en_esbcarte.htm

MANHATTAN PROJECT

The Manhattan Project was the code name given to the American wartime program to build an atomic bomb at the time the project was brought under army control in 1942. Three years later, the United States dropped two atomic bombs on the Japanese cities of Hiroshima and Nagasaki, with devastating effects. The development and deployment of these weapons permanently altered the dynamics of world politics and shaped the cultural anxieties of the Cold War era. Costing $2 billion and employing hundreds of thousands of workers over the course of the war, the Manhattan Project helped establish Big Science as a dominant form of research and positioned physics as a central component of the military-industrial complex. After briefly outlining the origins and development of the project, this entry focuses on the ways in which both scientists and the military attempted to control communication about the work of the project.

Wartime Organization of Atomic Research

Government involvement with nuclear research began in October 1939, when the financier Alexander Sachs persuaded President Franklin D. Roosevelt that the Germans might be planning an atomic bomb. Sachs delivered a letter to the president that had been signed by Albert Einstein and drafted by the Hungarian physicist Leo Szilard. Szilard and colleagues at Columbia University had recently demonstrated that when a uranium atom was split by bombardment with neutrons, it produced more neutrons. If enough uranium was present, this could, in principle, lead to a self-sustaining chain reaction, releasing large quantities of energy relative to the amount of uranium. The findings confirmed Szilard's longstanding fears that fission of uranium could be used to make an exceptionally powerful bomb. In the letter to Roosevelt, he pointed out that Germany had halted all sales of uranium. Roosevelt agreed to the formation of an Advisory Committee on Uranium, later known as Section-1 or S-1. The committee would oversee Allied research into the feasibility and possible manufacture of atomic weapons.

By the time the United States entered the war at the end of 1941, S-1 had oversight of 16 separate research projects with a total budget of $300,000. The findings indicated that both U^{235}, an isotope of uranium, and the newly discovered element plutonium could be used as the basis of a bomb. By June 1942, laboratory methods of producing these two substances were ready to be scaled up to provide the quantities required for manufacture of a bomb. The project was now brought fully under military control as a new district within the Army Corps of Engineers, designated the Manhattan Engineer District after the Manhattan headquarters of its first director.

In September 1942, Brigadier General Leslie Groves was appointed to lead the Manhattan District. Groves's previous assignment had been managing the construction of the Pentagon. Working with a number of industrial contractors, he now set about building extensive nuclear research and production facilities at three isolated locations: Oak Ridge, Tennessee; Hanford, Washington; and Los Alamos, New Mexico. In addition to research laboratories and some of the world's largest industrial plants, all three sites included new towns to house workers and their families. By the end of the war, Oak Ridge was home to some 75,000 people.

Beginning in 1943, many of the Manhattan Project scientists were located at Los Alamos under the directorship of the charismatic physicist Robert Oppenheimer. With essentially unlimited funding, the scientists were able to pursue multiple solutions to the technical problems they encountered. They therefore designed and produced two types of weapons—a U^{235} bomb known as "Little Boy" and a plutonium bomb known as "Fat Man." The latter was tested on July 16, 1945, at the Trinity test site in Alamogordo while 30 scientists looked on. The explosion was equivalent to 18,600 tons of TNT, almost 4 times more powerful than

predicted. When later asked what he had thought as he watched the exploding fireball, Oppenheimer famously quoted the Bhagavad Gita: "Now I am become Death, the Destroyer of Worlds."

At the same time as the Trinity test was taking place, a Little Boy bomb was loaded onto a ship bound for Japan. On August 6, the untested bomb was detonated above Hiroshima. Three days later, a Fat Man bomb was detonated above Nagasaki. In the United States, when news of Japanese surrender arrived a few days later, the atomic bomb was heralded as bringing a quick and decisive end to the war. By the end of 1945, an estimated 210,000 people had died from the two blasts and from the radiation released by the bombs. People continued to die from the effects of radiation for years afterward.

In December 1946, the Manhattan Engineer District was terminated and its facilities and activities were reassigned to the newly created Atomic Energy Commission. Today, five of the Manhattan sites are designated as historical landmarks and have become destinations for nuclear tourists.

Discussion of the different communication cultures associated with the Manhattan Project can be organized around four overlapping periods: an early period of self-censorship by nuclear scientists prior to the establishment of the Manhattan District in 1942; a period of official secrecy and compartmentalization policed by the military from 1942 onward; a period of media management toward the end of the war in preparation for the time when the project became public knowledge; and a period from 1944 onward in which scientists attempted to regain control over nuclear policy.

Self-Censorship

In the years preceding the outbreak of war in Europe, developments in nuclear physics had been rapidly disseminated within the scientific community and widely reported in the press. Newspapers were quick to speculate that uranium fission might be harnessed as a source of power, and that it might even cause a world-destroying explosion. Some reporters, however, conveyed the doubts of many scientists that fission would have any significance outside the laboratory. The Science Service news agency, for instance, reassured readers that fears of the world being blown up stemmed not from the new science but from the fantasies of writers such as H. G. Wells.

Leo Szilard had indeed been inspired by H. G. Wells's novel *The World Set Free* when he had first sketched out the principles of a chain reaction 5 years before. From January 1939, Szilard became concerned that Hitler might coerce his scientists into building an atomic bomb. He urged his colleagues to adopt a system of voluntary censorship to prevent new insights from reaching Germany. Some objected that open exchange of information was a central principle of science, but many U.S. physicists agreed to a system whereby they would submit papers to journals to establish priority but would request that publication be deferred. Journal editors also agreed to such a system, but the proposal foundered when the French physicist Frédéric Joliot-Curie reported experimental results suggesting that a chain reaction was possible in the journal *Nature* in the spring of 1939.

The Advisory Committee on Uranium was disinclined to enforce censorship of scientific publications. However, from the start of 1940, some key results were voluntarily withheld from publication, and the National Research Council put a more formal system in place in June 1940. Papers on nuclear fission were now to be submitted to a special committee. Those judged sensitive would be distributed among a limited number of researchers only; and when finally published, they would carry their original submission date to confirm the authors' priority claims.

Compartmentalization

When Groves took control of the Manhattan District in 1942, he attempted to impose a strict policy of compartmentalization, in which classified information would be circulated on a need-to-know basis only. Army and navy procedures of classification and compartmentalization had already been adopted by the Advisory Committee on Uranium as a means of persuading the military that civilian scientists and engineers could be entrusted with secrets. However, Groves was credited with extending the procedures into a unique security system that would later become the basis of peacetime security programs. When it took over from the Manhattan District, the Atomic Energy Commission—brought into being by the only U.S. statute to restrict the dissemination of information—continued with the same security regime.

Under Groves's security policy, access to the Manhattan District sites was strictly controlled. All inhabitants had their correspondence censored, and language was further controlled through an extensive vocabulary of code words. Scientists were forbidden from talking with their counterparts at other sites without permission from senior managers, though in practice they frequently broke the rules. In the production plants, where compartmentalization was most fully implemented, measures such as the modification of meters to give dummy readings ensured that workers remained unaware of what they were producing. The policy of compartmentalization meant that, in theory, only about a dozen people knew of all aspects of the project. Even some high administration officials did not know of the project's existence.

Groves also introduced counterespionage measures, not only to prevent information being passed to the Germans but also to the Soviet allies. Phones were tapped, microphones installed in offices, and workers recruited to spy on colleagues. The army's counterintelligence branch kept Oppenheimer under particularly close observation, suspicious of his earlier links with the Communist Party. In June 1943, a counterintelligence report recommended that his directorship of Los Alamos not be confirmed. Groves, feeling that Oppenheimer's presence was indispensable, exercised his authority and ordered that Oppenheimer be granted security clearance. Groves was less trusting of Leo Szilard and insisted that he continue to be investigated, even after months of surveillance had turned up nothing suspicious. By contrast, theoretical physicist Klaus Fuchs was able to pass information to the Soviets without being suspected by the Manhattan District's security apparatus.

Groves claimed that secrecy was necessary not only for security reasons but also to prevent scientists from being distracted by interesting scientific questions that were not directly relevant to the task at hand. However, the scientists fought against compartmentalization, invoking the free exchange of ideas as the communicative ideal in science as they had when debating self-censorship. They argued that preventing scientists from talking freely to each other would delay, or even prevent, progress in their work. The scientists succeeded in undermining Groves's policy, both through individual infractions and through more formal means, most notably when Oppenheimer introduced a weekly research seminar open to all Manhattan scientists. After the end of the war, Oppenheimer claimed that even physicists not working on the project had known about it but had kept quiet for reasons of national security. However, while the scientists resisted the specific form of Groves's security arrangements, most accepted that some level of secrecy was necessary.

Media Relations

If Groves expected communication within the district to be restricted, he expected complete silence in the media. From 1943, the Manhattan District operated its own censorship office, monitoring over 400 newspapers and magazines and numerous radio stations. In June 1943, the first of a series of memos was sent to editors and broadcasters forbidding all reporting of atomic research. The memo itself could not mention the Manhattan Project or atomic bombs, so instead it imposed a blanket ban on all mention of key words such as uranium, atomic energy, or radioactive materials.

There were violations, however, due in part to ambiguities in the wording of the ban, and by 1944, Groves had recorded 104 published references to the project and related subjects since 1939, including 77 since the censorship note had been circulated. The existence of military establishments at Hanford and Oak Ridge was now common knowledge. As a result, the district changed its approach to the media at these two sites, appointing experienced newspaper employees to act as public relations officers. Editors were kept happy with a flow of innocuous information and misleading disinformation while the purpose of the sites remained secret. By contrast, Los Alamos remained largely hidden from the media, even after Jack Raper, a columnist at the *Cleveland Press,* correctly identified its purpose in 1944.

In the spring of 1945, with completion of the bombs nearing, Groves prepared for the project to become public by granting *New York Times* science reporter William L. Laurence extensive access to the Manhattan District, including Los Alamos. Before the war, Laurence had reported enthusiastically on developments in nuclear physics. He now began writing press releases for the War Department with no apparent ethical concerns about conflicts between this role and his obligations as a journalist.

The Trinity test required particularly careful media planning because, despite the remote location, there was a strong possibility that the explosion would be visible some distance away. In the event, light from the explosion was observed over 100 miles away. Laurence, who attended the test, prepared four press releases beforehand to cover all eventualities. The severest recorded a catastrophic explosion killing many senior scientists. The mildest, which was the one actually used, claimed that an ammunition magazine had exploded. Newspapers were prevented from covering the story in any detail, and at least one reporter was visited by FBI agents to persuade her not to pursue the story any further.

The bombing of Hiroshima made the existence of the atomic bomb public knowledge. As early as July 1945, the Manhattan District had prepared an official history of the project, written by physicist Henry Smyth and published after the bombings. The War Department also managed information about the project through a series of press releases that had been drafted by Laurence 2 months before the Trinity test. Laurence had also been in one of the planes that flew over Nagasaki as the Fat Man bomb was dropped. He reported watching "awe-struck" as the bomb was "fashioned into a living thing" a sculptor might proudly have created. Laurence's accounts, drawing on religious imagery about the dawn of a new era, would greatly influence nuclear imagery in the immediate postwar years.

The War Department sought to control all the news coming from Hiroshima and Nagasaki. Reporters were allowed into the cities only if accompanied by military escorts, but Australian reporter Wilfred Burchett visited Hiroshima unaccompanied. His front-page story "Atomic Plague" in London's *Daily Express* was the first report of radiation sickness in the bombed cities. Laurence, who went on to win a Pulitzer Prize for his reporting, responded in the *New York Times* by denying that radiation was killing people and repeating the official line that such stories were Japanese propaganda—despite another *Times* reporter, the similarly named William Lawrence, having written an eyewitness report of radiation sickness just days before. *Chicago Daily News* reporter George Weller, like Burchett, stole into Nagasaki unaccompanied in September 1945. His four reports on radiation sickness were censored in their entirety. They did not appear in print until 2002.

Scientists' Activism

From the summer of 1944, some of the Manhattan scientists—particularly those based at the district's metallurgical laboratory in Chicago where Szilard was now based—became concerned about how the atomic bomb might be used. They attempted to influence both the decision to bomb Japan and later nuclear policy by organizing a number of committees and petitions. Their concerns mounted as news leaked out about the recommendations of the newly formed Interim Committee. The committee of key politicians, administrators, and four nuclear scientists, including Oppenheimer, was tasked with drawing up plans for the future of atomic policy. On June 1, 1945, the Interim Committee concluded its first meetings with the recommendation that the bomb should be dropped on a mixed military/civilian target in Japan as soon as possible and without warning.

In response, a report by a committee of Chicago scientists chaired by Nobel Laureate James Franck set out the case for the international control of nuclear weapons and called for the bomb not to be used on civilian populations. The report argued that a public demonstration of the bomb should instead be made over the desert as a warning to the Japanese. The Franck Report was submitted to War Secretary Henry Stimson on June 11, but he forwarded it to the scientific panel of the Interim Committee, who—unaware that the Japanese were already preparing to surrender—concluded that they could see "no acceptable alternative" to military use of the bomb. Szilard tried circulating a petition to President Truman around the various laboratories protesting against the use of the bomb, again to no avail. The July 17 version carried the signatures of 68 scientists, but Groves prevented it being forwarded to the president.

The decision to use atomic bombs against Japan was debated intensely over the following years. Many Manhattan scientists joined their Chicago colleagues in the newly formed Federation of Atomic Scientists (FAS) to fight for atomic energy

research to be taken out of army control. They regularly spoke at public meetings and wrote for magazines, such as the FAS's own *Bulletin of the Atomic Scientists,* on the dangers of a nuclear arms race. Oppenheimer, now a high-profile public figure, wrote of "the evil of having too much power." He proposed that scientists should form an international agency to police all aspects of nuclear facilities. Szilard, in addition to his ongoing political efforts, turned to fiction to try to bring home the dangers of nuclear weapons.

Despite the scientists' activism, classified nuclear weapons research and development continued at Los Alamos and elsewhere. Today the Manhattan Project is often invoked in calls for directed research and development programs—for instance, for a "Manhattan Project for global warming" or a "Manhattan Project for AIDS"—a shorthand that empties history of its terrible consequences and erases the agonies and dilemmas of the scientists who worked on the project.

Felicity Mellor

See also Big Science; Cold War Rhetoric; Nuclear Weapons; Oppenheimer, J. Robert; Teller, Edward

Further Readings

Hales, P. B. (1997). *Atomic spaces: Living on the Manhattan Project.* Urbana, IL: University of Chicago Press.

Hewlett, R. G., & Anderson, O. E. (1962). *A history of the United States Atomic Energy Commission, Vol. 1: The new world 1939/1946.* University Park: Pennsylvania University Press.

Hughes, J. (2003). *The Manhattan Project.* London: Icon Books.

Keever, B. A. D. (2008). Top secret: Censoring the first rough drafts of atomic-bomb history. *Media History, 14*(2), 185–204.

Rhodes, R. (1986). *The making of the atomic bomb.* London: Simon & Schuster.

MAVERICK SCIENCE AND JOURNALISM

How do journalists communicate the nature of controversy among scientists to their readers, viewers, and listeners? Is the journalistic function primarily one of translation, in which journalists attempt to mirror a scientific controversy but in simpler terms for a general audience? This is a common argument of journalists, that they are "just reporting the facts." Or is the journalistic function more of transformation, in which journalists pay less attention to accurately representing the balance of scientific opinion and more attention to criteria that may heighten the newsworthiness of a scientific controversy? The latter journalistic function of transforming a scientific controversy into a story that is more newsworthy for a general audience is interesting because when science plays a large role in the story, such accounts may be especially prone to either overstating or trivializing risks.

By writing stories that are broadcast and printed, journalists communicate information about a variety of issues to viewers, listeners, and readers. Issues that have a basis in science and technology frequently make for interesting stories because important consequences of science and innovation are often unanticipated, indirect, and undesirable. Such stories often also concern *innovations,* the new ideas, processes, or technologies that in many ways define human progress.

Communication of Risk

Risk communication informs individuals about the existence, nature, severity, or acceptability of hazards. For any scientific or technological issue, exposure to mass media messages about risk, together with personal experience and interpersonal communication, may lead to individual perceptions of personal and public risk (and also to behavioral outcomes) as the result of a range of informational and influence cues. The mass media are central to this process because of their omnipresence and the high degree to which the media may influence audience members through cognitive and framing effects. An example of the media's role in risk communication is coverage of the possibility that autism in children may occur as a result of vaccination. In a content analysis of 279 newspaper articles from the British and American press, researcher Christopher Clarke found large differences between the two countries in the frames used by journalists to help readers interpret the stories. While many of the articles included an attempt by the journalists to balance viewpoints about whether or not vaccination could cause autism, many other articles include no such balancing. In this case, while the scientific studies formed a common literature across the two countries, newspaper readers could come away with very different understandings of vaccine safety depending on the country in which they lived.

Several factors complicate mass communication about issues that involve risk. The mass media sometimes distort the relevance to individuals of various risks. For their part, scientists sometimes seek publication prior to establishing the reliability of their findings. Results, when interpreted in light of other scientific findings, are often contradictory. There may be a bias by audience members against information that is based on science or technology. According to research done by Allan Mazur, increases in mass media coverage of scientific controversies are positively correlated with higher proportions of the public who think negatively about the issues. Also, the public does a poor job in distinguishing among the severity of risks, and there are a multiplying number of smaller risks that are publicized due to more sensitive detection techniques.

For journalists, issues that imbed risk and uncertainty enable the writing of stories with higher informational value. They are intuitively more interesting to most people. Topics that may seem mundane for journalistic purposes—coffee, cholesterol, biotechnology, hydroelectric dams, radon—are made more interesting by heightening risk or uncertainty. The largest circulation newspapers, magazines, and talk television programs achieve popularity largely through the sensationalism of stories that concern personal or public risk. Indeed, disputes among scientists and technical experts and the nature of probability sometimes encourage journalists to "play" with stories and write tongue-in-cheek reports. Media organizations can also directly advocate a minority scientific view, which has been viewed by the scientific establishment as irresponsible journalism.

Scientific Paradigms and Their Communication

Scientific knowledge accumulates not just through testing hypotheses and discovering objective facts, but also through social influence. Information becomes acknowledged as a scientific fact when a critical mass of scientists becomes persuaded that a certain way of understanding a phenomenon of study is most likely to be the one validated through empirical testing. Paradigms (broad theoretical assumptions) are social constructions, held together by belief and, similarly, abandoned and toppled by disbelief. A threat to a paradigm—a contrary argument—is resisted strenuously by paradigm proponents, who gain stature, credibility, and coherence from the maintenance of their paradigmatic views.

So science is based both on empirical evidence and on the persuasiveness of theories in lieu of evidence. The history of scientific fields and disciplines may be viewed as marked by occasional intellectual attacks by scientists who hold what were, at that time, minority views in contradiction to the beliefs of a majority of scientists working in related fields. The latter scientists will strive to repress minority-view scientists through both intellectual and personal counterattacks (for example, on credibility).

Journalists are trained to rely on scientific authority figures to interpret and relate appropriate degrees of risk concerning a scientific topic to the public. Journalists are also trained to distrust authorities. What happens when the journalist is presented with radically different opinions from sources? The conventional journalistic resolution is to play the quotes against each other, to let the experts "battle it out" for the right to speak for science. Scientists, the popular stereotype of disinterestedness aside, can be passionate and forceful advocates of their own beliefs, while criticizing the work of competing scientists. William Check has termed this balancing tendency of journalists a "political model of reporting" in which the journalist attempts to present each side of the issue democratically and equally. Without the means to determine the scientific truth for themselves, reporters present both sides and invite the audience member to make the choice.

Journalistic Norms and Rules

Journalists often seek to portray the most extreme conflicting authoritative positions, as a U.S. National Research Council report on risk communication issues concludes. In countries such as the United States, journalists are taught to contrast authoritative experts because of the journalistic norm of *objectivity*, which requires that journalists both gather information impartially and write a story based on that information in a way that accurately reflects the meanings of news sources. In newsrooms, the norm of objectivity is pursued through the application of journalistic rules, such as the equal-space rule, the equal-access rule, and the get-the-other-side-of-the-story rule. Journalists, in trying to accurately represent a scientific controversy through the application of these rules, balance the views of competing authority figures in trying to present an "objective" account of the story. As a result, stories involving risk may often leave audience members in a state of considerable uncertainty regarding whether, and to what extent, they should be worried about a certain risk or adopt precautions against it.

What does the journalist who is trying to be objective do? She uses conflicting authoritative positions or, when a conflicting technical source cannot be found quickly, she defaults to "man on the street" sources to provide human *balance* to her story. In writing a story about the potential for tornados, for example, she balances the warnings of an atmospheric scientist and a meteorologist with a woman who laughs off the threat and a man who says he doesn't have time for such things. The result? In the reader's interpretation, scientific risk is effectively counterbalanced with the knowledge that people just like you are using their own experience to reach a judgment that the threat at hand is unlikely. The scientists come off as uncertain; the lay people, wise. When an easy, convenient, and cost-neutral option exists that decreases their risk exposure, they are likely to take it, as in grocery store produce aisle decisions to select cucumbers instead of tomatoes that may carry salmonella. But in the absence of such alternatives, most of us take the conservative behavioral route of staying with the way things are.

The Case of Maverick Science

Balanced coverage of science- or technology-based issues is not always desirable. The political model of reporting, in which journalists rely on competing authority figures to communicate the risks associated with an issue, may be especially ill-suited for communicating to general audiences scientific theories that have not received widespread support among scientists. *Maverick science* is unorthodox scientific theory that is accepted as credible by only one or a few scientists; a *maverick* is an outspoken proponent of unorthodox scientific theory. They are typically disbelieved by hundreds, and at times thousands, of scientists with relevant expertise. A theory that has few scientific believers is disregarded by the scientific community as unlikely to be supported by empirical evidence. Disbelief does not falsify the theory or make its validation impossible, yet disbelief is an indication to journalists that the theory in question is considered by most scientists to be extremely unlikely to be supported. For journalists who value the professional norm of objectivity, it is necessary to balance the view of the maverick with the perspective of the vast majority. Journalistic "balancing" in a story concerning maverick science can itself be a form of bias; journalists may unintentionally give credibility—sometimes undue credibility—to the views of the maverick.

Occasionally, nonexperts quoted in news stories about maverick theories (such as a househusband who voices concern about microwave radiation) may embrace the maverick's ideas as their own, making the theory seem more credible and believable to nonscientist audience members. The routine inclusion by journalists of brief quoted disclaimers about the maverick's theory or credibility from authority figures who represent the relevant scientific establishment may merely act to interrupt such stories, not actually to refute the maverick within the context of the story.

Mass media audience members may also be predisposed to feel sympathetic for, or even proud of, the maverick scientist. The balanced and conflictual stories that result often resemble "David and Goliath" struggles, with a seemingly bright go-it-alone scientist bucking an intransigent, conservative scientific establishment, whose representatives subjectively attack the personal credibility and creativity of the maverick. Due to the strong value placed on individuality in the United States, American mass media audience members are predisposed to "root for the underdog" and suspend their disbelief. The quality of making unusual associations among ideas and of doing the unexpected—of being a maverick—is a cherished American entrepreneurial trait.

Maverick theories may ultimately prove to be correct or may at least convince a significant group of scientists that the theory is superior to the dominant theory, representing the beginning of what Thomas Kuhn termed a *paradigm shift* or *scientific revolution* (1962). But the possibility of a revolutionary theory is always slight. For every case of an Alfred Wegener (the German meteorologist who was ridiculed throughout the 1920s until his death in 1930 for his 1915 theory of continental drift, now commonly accepted), scores of maverick theories do not pan out.

Framing articles according to majority scientific beliefs is a good strategy for journalists and is all the more important because there is a wide discrepancy between scientific assessments of risk and public assessments of the same risk. Experts typically determine risk narrowly, based on the degree of hazard present. Some members of the public may determine risk by their personal degree of fear or outrage, as well as in response to economic, social, and political factors. Unlike scientists, members of the general public often combine beliefs in science and in superstition, experiencing little apparent contradiction. Thus, for members of the public to believe in a maverick and a highly improbable theory is a relatively simple decision, as long as the maverick is perceived to be credible. And credibility is precisely what media coverage ascribes to the maverick and his or her idea.

Playfulness, Journalism, and Risk

Another transformative function that journalists sometimes perform is tongue-in-cheek reporting about mavericks and their maverick theories. Not all news stories are intended to be serious. The personal characteristics and iconoclastic tendencies of mavericks can be quite appealing to journalists and editors. Almost by definition, the maverick is newsworthy. In the writing of such accounts, journalists assume that audience members will recognize the implicit message of many of these stories, that the maverick in question has some very unusual ideas that, despite not being credible, are still newsworthy. The maverick personality, the maverick's willingness to go it alone against great odds, the disbelief of the relevant scientific establishment—all of these conditions suggest newsworthiness to the journalist who is writing an article to entertain more than to inform. As news budgets have been cut and news divisions have blurred with entertainment divisions in media organizations, more and more attention to maverick scientists can be expected.

The journalist's presumption of audience members who have the critical ability to distinguish what is likely from what is not—to, in effect, accurately judge risk—might be questioned. One survey of journalists who wrote stories about mavericks and their ideas showed that the journalists themselves were skeptical of the mavericks and did not believe their theories. But they still wrote stories that, through the application of standard journalistic norms and rules, came out as balanced accounts of the maverick theories. In this way, journalistic balance can become bias in its misrepresentation of the state of the science.

James W. Dearing

See also Rhetoric of Science; Risk Communication, Overview; Scientific Consensus; Scientific Method

Further Readings

Check, W. A. (1987). Beyond the political model of reporting: Nonspecific symptoms in media communication about AIDS. *Review of Infectious Diseases, 9*(5), 987–1000.

Clarke, C. E. (2008). A question of balance: The autism-vaccine controversy in the British and American elite press. *Science Communication, 30*(1), 77–107.

Covello, V. T., Winterfeldt, D., & Slovic, P. (1987). Communicating scientific information about health and environmental risks: Problems and opportunities from a social and behavioral perspective. In J. C. Davies, V. T. Covello, & F. W. Allen (Eds.), *Risk communication* (pp. 108–134). Washington, DC: The Conservation Foundation.

Dearing, J. W. (1995). Newspaper coverage of maverick science: Creating controversy through balancing. *Public Understanding of Science, 4,* 341–361.

Dunwoody, S., & Neuwirth, K. (1991). Coming to terms with the impact of communication on scientific and technological risk judgments. In L. Wilkins & P. Patterson (Eds.), *Risky business: Communicating issues of science, risk, and public policy* (pp. 11–30). New York: Greenwood Press.

Kuhn, T. (1962). *The structure of scientific revolutions.* Chicago: University of Chicago Press.

Mazur, A. (1981). Media coverage and public opinion on scientific controversies. *Journal of Communication, 31,* 106–115.

Merton, R. K. (1968). *Social theory and social structure.* New York: Free Press.

National Research Council. (1989). *Improving risk communication.* Washington, DC: National Academy Press.

Plough, A., & Krimsky, S. (1987). The emergence of risk communication studies: Social and political context. *Science, Technology, & Human Values, 12*(3–4), 4–10.

McClintock, Barbara (1902–1992)

Barbara McClintock was a cytogeneticist best known for her discovery of *transposons* (a term derived from "transposition") in maize genes. In 1983, she was the first woman to be awarded an unshared Nobel Prize in Physiology or Medicine. Her work in the field of genetics continues to be of great significance in the study of genetics, cytology, and molecular biology. Her life was a case study of persistence in the face of little recognition from her peers or the public over many years, as well as gender discrimination, and provides an important lesson for science communicators to the effect that the most important discoveries are not always the most quickly recognized—nor the most visible—even in relatively recent times.

Early Life and University

Barbara McClintock was born in Hartford, Connecticut, to parents Thomas McClintock, a doctor, and Sara McClintock, a pianist, poet, and painter. Her parents allowed her to follow her own interests rather than imposing a strict regime on her, even allowing her time off from school if she felt like doing something else. This would form much of her adult character, as she followed pursuits she loved solely for the joy of it.

McClintock wanted to go to college, but despite her rather liberal upbringing for a girl at the time, her mother was against it at first. Sara had already persuaded Barbara's older sisters, Marjorie and Mignon, not to go to college, despite Marjorie being offered scholarship money to attend Vassar. Eventually, after Barbara had worked for 6 months while also educating herself in the evenings, her mother relented and allowed her to go to Cornell University.

McClintock flourished at Cornell, and she continued her graduate studies there, gaining her doctorate in botany and genetics in 1927. In the years that followed, up until she left Cornell in 1932, she was a research assistant and botany instructor.

However, she was not simply granted her place in graduate school without any problems. She was originally told she could not enroll to study genetics because she was a woman. But women were allowed to study in the botany department, so she enrolled in cytology (the study of cells) and added in courses from the plant breeding department to combine both areas of interest. In 1931, McClintock and fellow student Harriet Creighton published a paper together called "A Correlation of Cytological and Genetical Crossing-over in *Zea Mays*." This paper can be found in *The Dynamic Genome* (1992), edited by Nina Fedoroff and David Botstein.

By using a new staining technique developed by John Belling, McClintock was able to characterize the maize chromosomes by their lengths, patterns, and shapes. She continued her experiments and publications, consolidating the links she had discovered between cytology and genetics. By her mid-40s, however, McClintock's ideas were seen as so new or radical by some scientists that they were largely ignored, and her dense and complicated writing style did not make her papers easy to follow.

In 1939, she was elected vice president of the Genetics Society of America; she became a member of the National Academy of Sciences in 1944; and in 1945 she served as president of the Genetics Society.

Discovery of Transposition

McClintock moved to Cold Spring Harbor, New York, in 1941 to plant her corn there and continue her experiments, funded by a position in the Department of Genetics of the Carnegie Institution of Washington. Her research was largely unaffected by wartime projects, and her work continued as usual. In fact, other wartime problems, such as gas shortages and food rationing, were said to have left little to do at Cold Spring Harbor during that period other than work.

The results from her crop at Cold Spring Harbor lead to her discovery of the concept of transposition. Previously, it was thought that chromosomal elements were fixed in place, like beads on a string, but McClintock realized that they could in fact move into new positions. Noticing some strange patterns and blotches of color in the kernels and leaves of her plants that others had not considered, she discovered a system of control and regulation among genes. She repeated her experiments over 6 years to be sure of her results and then wrote a short paper about transposable genetic elements, published in *Proceedings of the National Academy of Sciences* and titled "The Origin of Behaviour of Mutable Loci in Maize." She attempted to present the paper at the Cold Spring Harbor Symposium in the summer but was met with silence and misunderstanding. She tried to explain again in 1956, but by this time her work was even more, not less, difficult for others to follow.

In 1960, researchers Jacques Monod and Francois Jacob created a model of a molecular mechanism for gene regulation. They proposed that protein synthesis is regulated by an operator gene and a regulator gene, not by the structural gene itself as had been previously thought. McClintock was pleased by the similarities between this new work and her own—because now, surely, the scientific world would be able to understand McClintock's work with maize. But despite publishing another paper on the subject, she still could not make people fully appreciate or understand transposition.

The Cold Spring Harbor seminar in 1960 was McClintock's last attempt to be heard by her colleagues. She felt isolated, and younger molecular biologists were becoming more successful with their ideas. Nonetheless, she continued with her work, feeling sure she was right. She won the Kimber Genetics award in 1967 and the National Medal of Science in 1970.

Recognition and Nobel Prize

By 1976, transposable elements in bacteria (known as transposons or "jumping genes") were well documented, but no conclusions had yet been drawn that paralleled McClintock's work on transposable elements in maize. Then, at the 1976

Cold Spring Harbor meeting on DNA insertion elements, plasmids, and episomes, other researchers finally made reference to the parallels between bacteria and maize. Scientists in the later 1970s and early 1980s finally recognized how important "jumping genes" were.

In 1981, then in her 70s, McClintock won eight awards, including some with monetary prizes. Then, on October 10, 1983, she discovered she had won the Nobel Prize in Physiology or Medicine for the discoveries she had made three decades earlier.

Despite her age, she continued to work on her maize research until her death on September 2, 1992, at the age of 90. McClintock's work continues to be relevant to studies going on today, and scientists are still learning from her discovery of transposons. She is also considered a source of inspiration to female scientists for her achievements in the face of sexism.

Jessica Nash

See also Gene; Gene Patenting; Gene Therapy

Further Readings

Ferdoroff, N., & Botstein, D. (1992). *The dynamic genome: Barbara McClintock's ideas in the century of genetics.* Cold Spring Harbor, NY: Cold Spring Harbor Laboratory Press.

Fox Keller, E. (1983). *A feeling for the organism: The life and work of Barbara McClintock.* New York: W. H. Freeman.

Fox Keller, E. (2000). *The century of the gene.* Cambridge, MA: Harvard University Press.

Heiligman, D. (1994). *Barbara McClintock: Alone in her field.* New York: W. H. Freeman.

McClintock, B. (1983). *Barbara McClintock— Autobiography.* Retrieved May 10, 2009, from http://nobelprize.org/nobel_prizes/medicine/laureates/1983/mcclintock-autobio.html

Watson, J. D. (2000). *A passion for DNA.* Oxford, UK: Oxford University Press.

MEAD, MARGARET (1901–1978)

Margaret Mead was one of the most prominent cultural anthropologists of the 20th century and a celebrated popularizer of science. A controversial public intellectual, she applied theories of primitive societies to contemporary culture, influencing progressive social movements including feminism and environmentalism.

Science studies scholar Rae Goodell called Mead the people's anthropologist and profiled her in *The Visible Scientists* (1975) as one of a coterie of American researchers, including Carl Sagan and Linus Pauling, who popularized and explained scientific issues for mass audiences during the mid-20th century.

Born on December 16, 1901, in Philadelphia, Pennsylvania, Mead was the eldest daughter in an academic family where her father was an economics professor and her mother had trained as a sociologist. She went to DePauw University for a year before transferring to Barnard College, where she earned a master's degree in 1923.

Mead was awarded a doctorate from Columbia University in 1929 for a study on cultural stability in Polynesia. She trained under Franz Boas, a key figure in the establishment of anthropology as a science. As head of the anthropology department at Columbia, he had the greatest impact on Mead's work, but she also worked with influential anthropologist Ruth Benedict.

Coming of Age in Samoa

Mead's research focused on ethnographic studies of Pacific island cultures; her work examined topics including child rearing, adolescence, sexuality, gender roles, and conflict between generations. Comparing these issues with modern U.S. society gave her work a public resonance. She felt that anthropology was particularly suitable for popularization and widespread media coverage because it focused on people.

Her first book, *Coming of Age in Samoa* (1928), presented the findings of a field trip between 1925 and 1926, where she worked with the people on the island of Tau in American Samoa. It became a best seller, translated into several languages and reprinted in dozens of editions. It vaulted her and her scientific specialism into public consciousness. Its analysis of young Samoan girls found that adolescence was a time of smooth transition, without the emotional or psychological difficulties common among American teenagers. Samoan girls were also more sexually liberated.

The book's clear and readable style contributed to its widespread popularity (Mead intended it to be written for teachers). It was also an original contribution to anthropology, as she interpretated her data from a viewpoint of cultural determinism, where individual personalities and values were formed largely by culture, rather than biology, which was the then-prevailing view within anthropology. Mead also revised the original introduction and conclusion of her manuscript, adding two chapters that discussed the implications of her findings for child rearing in the United States.

Mead pioneered the field of cultural anthropology, which is concerned with the history and development of human culture. Her ideas of cultural determinism spread to other disciplines, including literature, history, psychology, and sociology.

She regularly published technical works from the same research she used for her popular books: Alongside *Coming of Age in Samoa*, she wrote an academic account of Samoan culture, *The Social Organization of Manua* (1930). More than 20 of her 44 books were aimed at general readers, and she was awarded UNESCO's Kalinga Prize in 1970 for the popularization of science.

Her second book aimed at a popular readership, *Growing Up in New Guinea* (1930), fixed her popular prose style, which critics have compared to literary narratives, rather than traditional academic accounts. The book was based on her studies of the Manus, in what was then the Admiralty Islands and is now part of Papua New Guinea.

Mead was the first anthropologist to study child rearing and women from a cross-cultural perspective. Overall, she conducted more than 20 major expeditions, pioneering innovative methods of gathering anthropological data and using photographs to document her visits. In Bali, she took more than 30,000 photographs of the people there. She developed a working knowledge of the language of many of the cultures she studied. She also did a first-hand analysis of the indigenous cultures of North America.

Contested Research

Mead's fieldwork has been criticized by other anthropologists who argued that her studies were too subjective; that she selected subjects to support her hypotheses; that her writing style was glib, impressionistic, and subjective; that she focused on sex to increase her readership; and that comparisons between primitive and modern societies extended her anthropological expertise beyond its limits.

Her most trenchant critic was Australian anthropologist Derek Freeman, who challenged her Samoan research in *Margaret Mead and Samoa: The Making and Unmaking of an Anthropological Myth* (1983) and *The Fateful Hoaxing of Margaret Mead* (1998). He argued that young informants had deliberately misled Mead and that she failed to adequately address the biological boundaries of human behavior. Mead and Freeman corresponded until her death, but the controversy has not reached a consensus within anthropology.

Her standing in the scientific community was reflected in her academic appointments and honors. She became adjunct professor at Columbia University in 1954 and was chair of the department of social sciences and professor of anthropology at Fordham University between 1968 and 1970. She was the second woman and the first anthropologist since Franz Boas to become president of the American Association for the Advancement of Science. In addition, she lectured at Columbia University, Vassar College, and New York University. Twice she refused offers of a full tenured professorship at Columbia.

American Museum of Natural History

Mead had a lifelong association with the American Museum of Natural History in New York, where she worked in a series of rooms at the top of the building and used an English-made tall forked walking stick, which became her trademark (she had broken her ankle several times). She was appointed assistant curator there in 1926, associate curator in 1964, and emeritus curator in 1969. The museum gave her a position from which she could popularize anthropology. The museum opened its Margaret Mead Hall of Pacific Peoples in 1984, displaying some 1,500 artifacts.

In addition to her research, teaching, and curatorial work, Mead participated in public debates surrounding social issues. She continually expanded her range of expertise to pressing social concerns, including female sexuality, race relations, population control, violence, drugs, sex, alcoholism, the church, civil liberties, environmental degradation, and nuclear proliferation. She regarded the examination of current concerns a legitimate field of study for an anthropologist.

Her book *Sex and Temperament in Three Primitive Societies* (1935) became an influential text for the women's liberation movement. It reported a 2-year field trip she undertook in the Sepik region of Papua New Guinea, where she examined the degree to which the temperamental differences between men and women were innate versus culturally determined. She found different patterns of gender behavior in the cultures she analyzed compared to gender expectations in the United States at the time: For example, for the Tchambuli, now Chambri, men were emotionally dependent on the dominant women.

During World War II, she worked as an anthropologist for the U.S. government, studying food habits. At this time, she wrote her first book on American culture, *And Keep Your Powder Dry* (1943), which examined the cultural characteristics and attitudes of Americans, to help the country cope with wartime challenges.

Goodell noted that Mead understood the organizational routines and demands of news media and was an extremely quotable source for reporters, as she had a gift for phrase making and tended to avoid the qualifiers and disclaimers that frequently diluted the impact of scientists' public comments.

In 1973, Mead was elected to the National Academy of Sciences. She received 28 honorary degrees and 40 distinguished awards for science and citizenship, including the Viking Medal in general anthropology. She was posthumously awarded the Presidential Medal of Freedom.

The Margaret Mead Papers and South Pacific Ethnographic Archives is held at the U.S. Library of Congress, Washington, D.C. Containing more than 500,000 items, it features collections of Mead's manuscripts, letters, field notes, diaries, drawings, photographs, and broadcast recordings.

Mead wrote an autobiography, *Blackberry Winter: My Earlier Years* (1972), which covered her life from birth to the beginning of World War II. She was married three times: to Luther Cressman, Reo Fortune, and Gregory Bateson, with whom she had one daughter, Mary Catherine.

Margaret Mead died of cancer on November 15, 1978, in New York City.

Declan Fahy

See also Visible Scientist

Further Readings

Freeman, D. (1983). *Margaret Mead and Samoa: The making and unmaking of an anthropological myth.* Cambridge, MA: Harvard University Press.

Freeman, D. (1998). *The fateful hoaxing of Margaret Mead: A historical analysis of her Samoan research.* New York: Basic Books.

Goodell, R. (1975). *The visible scientists.* Boston: Little, Brown.

Mead, M. (1928). *Coming of age in Samoa: A psychological study of primitive youth for Western civilisation.* New York: William Morrow.

Mead, M. (1930). *Growing up in New Guinea: A comparative study of primitive education.* New York: William Morrow.

Mead, M. (1930). *The social organization of Manua.* Honolulu, HI: Bernice P. Bishop Museum.

Mead, M. (1935). *Sex and temperament in three primitive societies.* New York: William Morrow.

Mead, M. (1943). *And keep your powder dry: An anthropologist looks at America.* New York: William Morrow.

Mead, M. (1972). *Blackberry winter: My earlier years.* New York: William Morrow.

MEDIA CONVERGENCE

In a technological sense, *media convergence* is all about integration and interoperability, the coming together of computing networks, information and communication technologies, and digital forms of information that are inherently adaptable, delivered via "intelligent" platforms, applications, and devices. The processes that facilitate media convergence are shaped by, while also shaping, social practices and cultural values; the ways that we produce and consume digital media to communicate science (as well as politics, sports, and so on) are changing. Where once people had opportunities to collate and filter scientific information via various "traditional" communication channels, now digital technologies are also playing an important role.

From an end user's perspective—both those consuming and those contributing—media convergence involves digital technologies that encode and decode multiple streams of (in this case) science content. This can involve sending linked and aggregated text, galleries of still images, moving pictures, digital simulations, sounds, music, or any combination thereof, to one or more devices and platforms of the end user's choosing, such as a mobile phone or personal digital assistant (PDA). And these media can be customized and consumed "automatically" via feeds that match the user's profile as specified on the device(s) of their choice; change your profile and you rearrange the content to be downloaded or reorder the aggregated content that you have received.

This entry maps some of the current landscape for media convergence with a particular focus on what it means for communicating the sciences. It has been written with two notes of caution that are worth bearing in mind. First, the choice of examples illustrates the realized potential of some digital media for the sciences, but also the continuing potential. These selections have necessarily been small in number, and they are described here via a non-converged medium, a printed or electronic book. Second, what follows is an attempt to map what is a rapidly developing landscape, technologically, socially, economically, politically, legally, and culturally. No entry that discusses media convergence could ever claim to be future proof, but the hope is that this will provide a useful introduction for those approaching these issues for the first time.

In the spirit of the information age, it is up to the reader to use their scholarly skills to seek out further examples of media convergence in action, perhaps applying what follows to their scholarly background (be that arts, humanities, social science, or the natural sciences) or area of practical application (as a practicing scientist, media professional, student of science communication, or interested citizen).

Representing the Sciences in Popular Media

How might a newspaper or magazine feature a scientific story? How might a scientific issue be broadcast on television or radio? These used to be questions that had, relatively speaking at least, simple answers. Science in newspapers, for example, involved a printed copy that someone had delivered or bought from a newsstand. These printed copies had pretty standardized formats with news, comments, leading articles, features, letters, cartoons, obituaries, and so on. And science news had to compete with politics, economics, and sports for column inches in these printed media; so far, pretty straightforward.

With the introduction of digital technologies and media convergence much, but not all, of this has changed. Scientific issues still feature in printed newspapers, and although they still have to compete for column inches, they also now compete for time and space in multiplatform newsrooms in the converged, 24/7, rolling news media landscape. Many online editions of newspapers now routinely produce text and photos, as they always have, but with additional content in the form of audio, photo galleries, moving images, computer simulations and graphics, online quizzes and glossaries, links to other selected and recommended Web sites, and so on. Where someone once read a newspaper and turned the pages, they can now "select and click," and they can also watch, listen, subscribe to digests, and even contribute—for example, by commenting on an article—as well as have selected content routinely downloaded directly to the device of their choosing. It is hardly surprising, then, that science communication researchers are talking not of consumers but of *users* of science in media. Similarly, conceptions of what it means to be a media professional are being rethought to consider the additional skills that may be required to produce multiple forms of digital science content.

Similarly there are now greater opportunities to listen to a wide range of genres on "digital radio" (more accurately called multiplatform audio)—for example, through networked desktop computers, digital television, digital radio, and as podcasts to subscribe to or download to a device of the user's choice. And at least some of these streams will be multiple, with the option of additional online content; it is now possible to listen to, "read," and "watch" radio at the same time. You may even choose to produce your own podcast about a scientific subject, following in the well-trodden footsteps of many amateur radio enthusiasts, and contribute in real-time to radio via blogs, text messaging, and phone-ins.

Meanwhile, digital television has introduced additional digital-only channels that are "broadcast" to television sets and via the Web, while "watch again" facilities allow viewers to move beyond the limitations of channel schedules. As James Bennett notes, perhaps the most interesting development with digital television is the ability to call up additional on-demand content. Although currently limited in scope, such developments have the potential to change how we watch science on television.

What Media Convergence Means for the Sciences

The phrase *media for the sciences* has always been plural—since ancient times scientific information has been spoken, drawn, and written. The sciences would not exist without media. As Scott Montgomery has noted, it is no coincidence that when scientific information became more available via translations, printed and circulated without the need for scribes, what we now call modern science began to flourish. (Of course, other factors were also important in the development of modern science.) More recently, the introduction of digital technologies has seen a proliferation in the number of media for science. So what has changed?

In some respects, convergence involves media forms that are not that different from their non-converged equivalents: Devices that host them often provide fairly standard computing facilities, such as the ability to search for (and within) digitally stored content on a given device and/or network. Convergence means that the same digital content can now be stored, retrieved, filtered, shared, and aggregated via multiple devices and applications. It can also be rendered in multiple forms; for example, the same text can be printed, rendered as a series of linked Web pages, or "screen-read" as spoken word. And all this takes place at the click of a mouse. Where previously someone may have needed multiple devices to communicate science, now they may be able to survive with one, or at least far fewer than before, and they can even be "on the move" while using a wireless-enabled device or static by using a fairly standard networked desktop computer.

These developments require technological solutions that make the same content available in multiple forms, although much of the technology remains "black boxed" to the end user. However, users do need to adapt the ways they communicate science, requiring some level of information literacy (and the ability to re-skill) and a desire to purchase the devices that facilitate media convergence. Indeed, the careful promotion and cultural fetishization of certain devices are two of the reasons why media convergence has become popular, ensuring a continuing market for upgrades to the latest model.

This economic reality is reinforced through social practices and developing cultural norms. For example, it is almost without countenance in the information age to be out of electronic contact for any length of time; to be without sufficient numbers of online "friends" and to know their location and what they are doing; to be unable to know one's precise location and how to get to your next one; to be out of the loop in terms of the latest developments in the important news (global, national, playground, or otherwise); or to lack the ability to digitally photograph and distribute that image at a moment's notice. And all this can be done via the same networked device.

Converging Media, Changing Practices

It follows that the ways in which many media professionals, scientists, other stakeholders, and citizens produce, consume, share, interact with, and create portrayals of the sciences via digital media are also evolving. For example, media that facilitate convergence are changing the ways that at least some scientists conduct and communicate their science with their peers and how this scientific information is distributed and shared within the public sphere. Such developments require networks that can be "public," such as the Internet, or "private," including intranets, SMS (Short Message Service used for text messaging), file transfer sites, and other password-protected Web sites.

As a result, scientists can now collect, analyze, and output data using the same device, or via a series of devices that are coordinated by a team of scientists working in different locations, or while working remotely "in the field." Alternatively, they can work at a distance from the point of data collection, accessing, sharing, and analyzing data collected from remotely located sensors, telescopes, and so on.

Meanwhile, Stefano Cozzini has discussed the importance of grid technology for the sciences, which facilitates distributed networked computing. In essence, this involves the linking of secure computing infrastructure, experimental facilities, and data storage among two or more institutions to address complex scientific challenges. Cozzini notes that developments such as these are improving the chances of solving complex problems in high-energy physics, astronomy, meteorology, and computational biology.

Similarly, media and publishing industries are adapting to, as well as promoting, consumption via new social practices that extend market reach beyond traditional mass audiences bounded by national borders. These new markets include consumers that can be geographically distributed, downloading or streaming (and potentially making contributions to) representations of science from a number of countries. Crucial for the converged business model, however, is the fact that at least some of these consumers are also willing to consume (and pay for) a lot of converged information about a particular area of scientific investigation. Although they may be smaller in their absolute numbers, these consumers are targeted via promotional strategies that facilitate marketing synergies via branded nests of products: buy the science documentary once it has been aired on television and receive additional content, receive automatic updates to the device and platform of your choice, and so on; alternatively, consumers may receive some of the content for free as a "loss leader" but pay for additional products.

Media convergence, in this instance, has the potential to deliver customized packages of scientific knowledge to those with and without formal qualifications in the sciences, and potentially all from the comfort of an armchair or even a makeshift laboratory in the garage. Over time, this may further extend ideas about who counts as a "scientific expert" to include those without formal qualifications in a scientific subject.

Producing and Consuming Science via Digital Media

The changes in how science is produced for, and consumed via, digital media have been profound for *early adopters,* a term that includes many science publishers, some scientific institutions and scientists, almost all media industry companies and corporations and the professionals working for them, and also other citizen consumers. These changes will continue to be felt as *late adopter* citizens are forced to embrace the digital switchover in broadcast (television and radio) media. But, as this encyclopedia illustrates, print media, for the foreseeable future at least, will still be consumed by physically turning the pages.

As Matthew Chalmers notes, some scientists (and media professionals and citizens, for that matter) will be more willing to embrace these changes than others, and people should not overlook the challenges that shifts toward digital technologies can bring. Concepts such as the *digital divide* between those who are information rich or information poor illustrate that lack of access to information, scientific or otherwise, can reinforce preexisting structural inequalities as easily as it can create new ones. Information literacy skills, so necessary for navigating what Christine Borgman has described as the data deluge, also come more easily to some than others. It is within this context that some understanding of media convergence is of fundamental importance to those wishing to study science communication in the information age.

Conclusion

The introduction of digital technologies and their ability to facilitate convergence means that we have more media and greater choice in how science communication is produced and consumed. This results in several challenges for science communication scholars. How do we make sense of the increased number of channels that filter and collate scientific information? Can we deliver suitable theories that take account of the ever-shifting processes of media convergence for science where neologisms and evolving social practices abound? Can we easily delineate media industries, where a taxonomy based on the media form used to make sense? Should we increasingly rely on distinctions between commercial and public service media or between elite and popular brands or titles? Meanwhile science communication researchers continue to search for reliable and valid ways of collecting data from what are often transitory and ephemeral forms. It is clear that science communication has changed because of media convergence. The challenge for science communication scholars—and practitioners—is to continue to develop the skills to stay ahead of the curve.

Richard Holliman

See also Internet, History of; Online Media and the Sciences

Further Readings

Bennett, J. (2009). From flow to user flows: Understanding "good science" programming in the UK digital television landscape. In R. Holliman, E. Whitelegg, E. Scanlon, S. Smidt, & J. Thomas (Eds.), *Investigating science communication in the information age: Implications for public engagement and popular media* (pp. 183–204). Oxford, UK: Oxford University Press.

Borgman, C. (2007). *Scholarship in the digital age: Information, infrastructure and the Internet.* Cambridge: MIT Press.

Castells, M. (2001). *The Internet galaxy: Reflections on the Internet, business, and society.* Oxford, UK: Oxford University Press.

Chalmers, M. (2009). Communicating physics in the information age. In R. Holliman, J. Thomas, S. Smidt, E. Scanlon, & E. Whitelegg (Eds.), *Practising science communication in the information age: Theorising professional practices* (pp. 67–80). Oxford, UK: Oxford University Press.

Cozzini, S. (2008). Grid computing and e-science: A view from inside. *Journal of Science Communication, 7*(2), 1–4.

Eysenbach, G. (2008). Medicine 2.0: Social networking, collaboration, participation, apomediation, and openness. *Journal of Medical Internet Research, 10*(3), e22.

Montgomery, S. (2009). Science and the online world: Realities and issues for discussion. In R. Holliman, J. Thomas, S. Smidt, E. Scanlon, & E. Whitelegg (Eds.), *Practising science communication in the information age: Theorising professional practices* (pp. 83–97). Oxford, UK: Oxford University Press.

MEDICAL JOURNALISM

Medical journalism refers both to the process and the product of gathering information on medical topics and presenting it via the mass media or specialized media. This entry describes the scope of medical journalism, identifies needed skills, notes some issues that can arise, and briefly discusses the education of medical journalists.

Scope of Medical Journalism

Medical journalism can encompass a wide variety of topics, media, and genres. Among major topics of medical journalism are medical research findings, disease outbreaks and other public health concerns, healthful living, and health policy. Traditionally, medical journalism has consisted primarily of newspaper health reporting. Today, however, medical journalism appears in a wide range of media, including not only newspapers but also consumer magazines, specialized magazines for health professionals, radio, television, and Web sites. It also appears in news sections of medical journals. *Genres* of medical journalism include news stories, various types of feature stories (such as overview stories, narratives, and profiles), columns, and investigative stories.

Skills

The skills entailed in medical journalism include the ability to identify story ideas, gather information, evaluate information, and craft the piece.

Good medical journalism begins with a good story idea. Newly announced research findings that can aid in preventing or treating major diseases tend to be newsworthy, as well as current disease outbreaks, recently discovered threats to public health, newly exposed problems in medical care, newly disclosed diseases of public figures, and current or potential developments in health policy. Topics for medical feature stories can include diseases of current concern, achievements by noteworthy medical researchers and health professionals, and issues in health care.

Gathering information well is essential to high-quality medical journalism. In the popular media, most reports on medical research are based on newly published articles in medical journals. Medical journals are also information sources for other medical stories. In addition, information for medical stories comes from government agencies, such as the U.S. National Institutes of Health,

Centers for Disease Control and Prevention, and Food and Drug Administration. Other information sources include organizations such as the American Cancer Society, the American Heart Association, medical and other health professional schools, hospitals and other health care institutions, and pharmaceutical companies and other corporations relating to health care.

Much of the information from such sources is now available on the World Wide Web. However, good medical journalism also entails interviewing—for example, to obtain the most recent information, gain additional perspective, and add human interest. People who are interviewed often include researchers, health care providers, and patients as well as health care administrators, medical ethicists, and (with permission) family members and friends of patients.

Evaluating information that has been gathered is important in deciding whether—and if so, how—to include the information in a medical story. In this evaluation, basic understanding of research design and statistics can help greatly. Among questions to consider when evaluating medical information are the following: Is the source credible? Was the study large enough and otherwise well designed? Is there more than one possible explanation for the findings? Are the findings from different studies consistent?

In medical journalism, crafting the piece entails following various principles of science writing. Aspects especially applicable to medical journalism include explaining concepts clearly, incorporating human interest, presenting numbers and sizes effectively, and noting sources of further information. Because the information in medical stories can influence decisions affecting health, fact-checking is especially important.

Issues

Specialized ethical and other issues can arise in medical journalism. Examples of *ethical issues* include what story topics would best serve the public's health, how to respect privacy when writing about patients, and how to choose visuals that communicate accurately and do not sensationalize. Sometimes issues of fairness arise, for example, when friends or family members of some patients seek media attention in the hope of obtaining resources.

Issues of sensitivity in language choice also arise. For example, wording that negates individuality ("the mentally ill") or defines people by their disease ("a diabetic") should generally be avoided; a guideline is to "put 'people' first" (as in "people with mental illnesses" or "a person with diabetes"). Similarly, melodramatic wording (such as "cancer victim" rather than "person with cancer") should be avoided. For accuracy as well as sensitivity, aids such as wheelchairs should be presented as enabling rather than limiting ("uses a wheelchair," not "is confined to a wheelchair").

Some specialized aspects of usage and style arise in medical journalism. One example is to minimize use of the word *breakthrough* because advances in medicine generally reflect long research. Other examples include remembering not to capitalize disease names except for parts that are proper nouns (rheumatoid arthritis versus Parkinson's disease), using mainly generic rather than brand names for drugs, and capitalizing brand names but not generic names. Good medical journalism also entails proper use of terms commonly confused with each other (for example, *incidence* and *prevalence*, *life expectancy* and *life span*, and *psychiatrist* and *psychologist*).

Education and Organizations

Traditionally, most medical journalists have come from general journalism backgrounds. However, some medical journalists have been educated as physicians or other health professionals. Increasingly, medical journalism is being done by individuals with undergraduate or graduate education specifically in medical journalism or science journalism. Organizations serving medical journalists include the Association of Health Care Journalists.

Barbara Gastel

See also American Medical Writers Association; Career Paths, Medical Writing/Medical Journalism; Government Public Information; Interviewing Scientists

Further Readings

Albert, T. (1995). *Medical journalism: The writer's guide to getting published*. New York: Radcliffe Medical Press.

Cohn, V., & Cope, L. (2001). *News and numbers: A guide to reporting statistical claims and controversies in health and other fields* (2nd ed.). Ames: Iowa State University Press.

Gastel, B. (2005). *Health writer's handbook* (2nd ed.). Ames, IA: Blackwell.

Levi, R. (2001). *Medical journalism: Exposing fact, fiction, fraud*. Ames: Iowa State University Press.

MENDEL, GREGOR (1822–1884)

Gregor Mendel was an Augustinian monk and botanist who is considered the founder of genetics for having formulated a series of laws regulating the transmission of features through different generations of plants. In a series of experiments with peas during the 1850s and 1860s, he proved that characteristics such as size and color were combined independently in hybrid plants from different parents. He also demonstrated that there was a hierarchy in transmission of certain contrasting characteristics—for example, a crossing between a tall and a short pea plant always yielded tall—and that a given characteristic could be transmitted to further generations despite not being visibly shown in an offspring pea—two tall plants could yield a short one due to their ancestors. In the early 20th century, Mendel's laws were reinterpreted after a long period of oblivion and incorporated into the core of genetics, the discipline studying how genes convey features that are inherited in different species.

Mendel was born in a small town of the Austrian Silesia, currently part of the Czech Republic but in the mid-19th century belonging to the Austrian Empire. During his childhood, he combined animal and plant care at a family farm with formal education. His religious career started at age 21, when his family, unable to fund his studies, sent him to the Abbey of Saint Thomas in Brünn—now the city of Brno. Due to his intellectual potential, Mendel was allowed to attend the University of Vienna, where he studied physics, mathematics, and natural sciences.

The results of Mendel's degree were not fully satisfactory, due to his frail physical and psychological health. Three years after returning to Brünn (1856), he started his experiments with peas in an allotment belonging to the abbey and devoted to hybridization of agricultural variants. Mendel crossed different types of pea plants and observed the similarities and differences of their descendants. By repeating this operation various thousands of times, he obtained a large record of generations that allowed him to quantify the transmission of characteristics.

Mendel applied combinatorial mathematics to determine how often certain features—green or yellow color, round or wrinkled seeds—were transmitted over others to the offspring after the crossing of different plants. He concluded, from the frequencies of transmission, that there were dominant and recessive characteristics. The former were always preferentially transmitted, but recessive characteristics could be transmitted to further generations by the offspring despite remaining invisible during their lifetime. If, for instance, green color was a dominant characteristic and yellow was recessive, the offspring of a green and yellow plant would always be green, but could have yellow descendents.

The results of Mendel's experiments were published at the *Proceedings of the Natural History Society of Brünn* in 1866, after he presented them at the meetings of this society. However, the local nature of this publication, together with the state of the life sciences at that time, led Mendel's conclusions to go largely unnoticed. Only 7 years before, in 1859, Charles Darwin had published *The Origin of Species* and triggered an increasing debate on the mechanisms of evolution of different organisms, among them animals and plants. Despite Mendel being aware of this debate, he barely mentioned it in his paper, and this resulted in his laws not being connected with one of the main topics of late-19th-century life sciences. The growing opposition of religious institutions to Darwinism and evolution further obstructed this connection.

Darwin himself postulated a theory of inheritance in 1868 that was different from Mendel's, known as pangenesis. According to this theory, the cells inside the body produced a series of particles called gemmules, which traveled to the reproductive organs and were involved in the transmission of characteristics from parent to offspring. Also in 1868, Mendel became Abbot of Saint Thomas and gradually abandoned his investigations due to his increasing official duties.

Mendel's results remained outside the mainstream life sciences community until the first decade of the 20th century. At that time, a number of researchers within the emerging field of genetics adopted them in what has been termed the rediscovery of Mendel's laws. Microscope observations in the late 19th century had identified the chromosomes as a series of particles located in the cell nucleus and involved in the division of cells during the development of the embryo and later adult life. In 1907, Danish botanist Wilhelm Johannsen raised for the first time the concept of the gene as the putative unit located in the chromosomes and involved in inheritance. Since then, an increasing number of researchers— among them William Bateson, T. H. Morgan, and R. A. Fisher—adopted the gene as the physical entity directing hereditary transmission from parents to offspring according to Mendel's laws.

This rediscovery led Mendel to be seen as the founder of genetics, even though he conducted his experiments 50 years before the concept of the gene was formulated. Between the 1910s and 1930s, Mendel's laws were extended to animals and humans, and they fostered movements such as eugenics, which sought initiatives to improve hereditary outcomes within communities and families. Most defenders of eugenics held a deterministic view, according to which genes unconditionally shaped the hereditary fate of a group. Their proposals spanned from progressive sociomedical projects (socialist geneticists seeking to avoid diseases among the working classes) to reactionary and totalitarian policies, such as sterilization of the handicapped in the United States and of minority racial and ethnic populations in Nazi Germany.

Between the 1930s and 1940s, a union between Mendel's laws and evolutionary theory was achieved in the so-called modern synthesis. According to this view, recombination between dominant and recessive characteristics was the source of variation during genetic transmission from parent to offspring. The Darwinian mechanism of natural selection then led the better-adapted descendants to survive from one generation to another within a given environment. For instance, in Soviet Siberia, only those genetically better adapted to cold temperatures would resist the weather and be able to transmit their features to further generations.

The gene remained an uncertain entity within the chromosome until the late 1940s and early 1950s, when it was discovered that deoxyribonucleic acid (DNA), whose structure was first described by James D. Watson, Francis Crick, and others, was its constituent substance. This has been considered the transition point from classical to molecular genetics and the beginning of a detailed explanation of the physics and chemistry behind Mendel's laws.

Miguel García-Sancho

See also Darwin, Charles; Eugenics; Gene; Watson, James D.

Further Readings

Allen, G. E. (2002). The ideology of elimination: American and German eugenics, 1900–1945. In F. R. Nicosia & J. Huener (Eds.), *Medicine and medical ethics in Nazi Germany*. New York: Berghahn Books.

Corcos, A. F., & Monaghan, F. V. (Eds.). (1993). *Gregor Mendel's experiments on plant hybrids: A guided study*. New Brunswick, NJ: Rutgers University Press.

Duchesneau, F. (2007). The delayed linkage of heredity with the cell theory. In S. Müller-Wille & H. J. Rheinberger (Eds.), *Heredity produced: At the crossroads of biology, politics, and culture, 1500–1870* (pp. 293–314). Cambridge: MIT Press.

Falk, R., & Sarkar, S. (1991). The real objective of Mendel's paper: A response to Monaghan and Corcos. *Biology and Philosophy, 6*(4), 447–451.

Harwood, J. (2004). Linkage before Mendelism? Plant breeding research in Central Europe, c. 1880–1910. In H. J. Rheinberger & J. P. Gaudillière (Eds.), *Classical genetic research and its legacy: The mapping cultures of twentieth century genetics* (pp. 9–20). New York: Routledge.

Monaghan, F. V., & Corcos, A. F. (1990). The real objective of Mendel's paper. *Biology and Philosophy, 5*(3), 267–292.

MERTON, ROBERT K. (1910–2003)

American sociologist Robert K. Merton may be best known in communication studies, as well as sociology, for having urged researchers to concentrate on "middle range" problems: Instead of trying to develop broad, abstract, "grand theories" that attempt to explain numerous social phenomena but are difficult or impossible to test, Merton argued social scientists would be better off working on smaller, more manageable problems where empirical data can be gathered.

The familiar idea of "agenda setting" that was developed later on by mass communication scholars might be considered a middle range theory; for example, the notion that the media's issue agenda influences the popular issue agenda is an example of a theory focused on a narrow range of phenomena that has been clearly demonstrated by empirical research. By working on middle range problems, Merton suggested, we could gradually build up to creating more overarching theories about society. Merton has also been credited with inventing the focus group, a staple research method within media studies to this day. But perhaps most importantly, from the point of view of science communication specialists, Merton made a much more specific contribution as one of the first sociologists to analyze the social organization of science.

As a functionalist sociologist, Merton tended to see society as a collection of interrelated social institutions and professions that generally work (or function) together to meet society's various needs. Functionalism concentrates on analyzing these institutions and how they fit into the broader structure of society, rather than (more narrowly) the specific dynamics of how individuals interact or (more broadly) explanations that try to address society as a whole, such as questions of the distribution of power. It makes sense, therefore, that a functionalist should be the one to advocate for middle range empirical research. Functionalism's distinction between "manifest" and "latent" functions—meaning those that are stated and obvious versus those that are hidden, less obvious, and often unintended, generally requiring thoughtful analysis to uncover—has also been carried over into media content analysis, which generally recognizes that only some of the meanings of messages are on the surface, while others lie hidden beneath and require active interpretation and analysis to reveal.

Importantly, Merton was concerned with society's "dysfunctions" as well as its functions. Because of its assumption that the different parts of society function smoothly together, functionalism has been criticized for accepting, even implicitly supporting, the status quo social system, rather than addressing its problems. However, the idea of "dysfunctions" explicitly recognizes that not all elements of the social structure necessarily contribute to harmony, opening the door for the analysis of both social conflict and social change.

One particularly important set of institutions that Merton analyzed was the institutions of science. He may be best remembered, in this regard, for his description of the ethical principles or values that he identified as broadly shared among members of the scientific community, which he called the "ethos" of science. His interest in this aspect of the social organization of science was consistent with his more general interest in processes of socialization—that is, his concern with how people learn to become members of particular social groups and to adopt the norms and values of those groups in the process. Merton is often considered the founder of the sociology of science.

The notion of *scientific ethos,* as developed by Merton, consists of four principles: universalism (the evaluation of truth by means of universal criteria), communalism (the common ownership of scientific knowledge), disinterestedness (scientific activities being undertaken without concern for immediate self-interest), and organized skepticism (reliance on procedures for subjecting work to evaluation by the scientific community). However, as publicity surrounding cases of scientific fraud has increased, some scholars have questioned whether these four principles still underpin the present-day scientific enterprise, which has become increasingly privatized and commercialized.

Merton (born Meyer R. Schkolnick, into a working-class Jewish family of Eastern European descent) grew up in modest circumstances in South Philadelphia and began his career in sociology as a student of George Simpson at Temple University. He later attended Harvard, where he studied with a number of well-known sociologists, including Talcott Parsons; received his doctorate in sociology; and taught for a number of years before moving on to faculty positions at Tulane and Columbia. At Columbia, he was associate director of the Bureau of Applied Social Research from 1942 to 1971. He has been described as a "lifelong friend" of another Columbia sociologist and the bureau's founder, Paul Lazarsfeld, whose influence on media studies can also still be felt today.

Merton married Suzanne Carhart in 1934; they separated in 1968, and, in 1993, Merton married sociologist Harriet Zimmerman. Merton was an extremely well-known figure in American sociology and won numerous major awards, including membership in the U.S. National Academies of Science, receipt of a Guggenheim Fellowship and a National Medal of Science, and being named a MacArthur Fellow.

Among Merton's best-known works are *Social Theory and Social Structure* (1968), *The Sociology of Science* (1979), and *On the Shoulders of Giants: A Shandean Postscript* (1993). The latter departs from the usual academic mold to build on a provocative quote from Isaac Newton, in the process illuminating both Merton's own career and the sociology of knowledge.

Susanna Hornig Priest

See also Agenda Setting and Science; Scientific Ethos; Scientific Journal, History of; Scientific Publishing, Overview; Scientific Societies

Further Readings

Baran, S., & Davis, D. (2008). *Mass communication theory: Foundations, ferment, and future* (5th ed.). Boston: Wadsworth.

Kauffman, M. (2003, February 24). Robert K. Merton, versatile sociologist and father of the focus group, dies at 92. *The New York Times*, p. B7. Retrieved December 1, 2009, from www.nytimes.com/2003/02/24/nyregion/robert-k-merton-versatile-sociologist-and-father-of-the-focus-group-dies-at-92.html

Merton, R. K. (1968). *Social theory and social structure.* New York: Free Press.

Merton, R. K. (1979). *The sociology of science: Theoretical and empirical investigations.* Chicago: University of Chicago Press.

Merton, R. K. (1993). *On the shoulders of giants: A Shandean postscript.* Chicago: University of Chicago Press.

Sztompka, P. (2007). Trust in science: Robert K. Merton's inspirations. *Journal of Classical Sociology,* 7(2), 211–220.

METAPHORS IN SCIENCE COMMUNICATION

Metaphors have played a foundational role in the communication of science; in fact, they have indispensable functions in the theorizing and practice of science. They can be defined, depending on the perspectives of various theorists, as depicting, interpreting, or experiencing one entity, concept, or phenomenon (source X) in terms of another (target Y) via the mapping of relationships between the source (domain X) and target (domain Y). Classic examples of metaphors are "Life is a journey" and "DNA is a code."

Metaphors are essential for teaching and learning novel, complex, or abstract notions. In science, metaphors are described as serving in three capacities: explanatory, constitutive, and communicative. When employed in scientific communication, metaphors are posited to be of two types that serve two distinct functions, explanatory and constitutive. One fundamental type of metaphor is regarded as *pedagogical* or *exegetical*. These metaphors are considered to enhance insight and understanding and foster memorableness of science-related material. As such, pedagogical metaphors are posited to best serve the description and explanation process when communicating about science.

In essence, the elegance of the teaching and explanation nature of pedagogical metaphors is that of framing new concepts or constructs in relation to known subject matter of message receivers. However, there are concerns and a variety of opinions regarding the function and use of pedagogical metaphors. For instance, if the metaphor used to explicate over-assesses the knowledge of the receivers at hand, the communicator increases the risk of receivers misunderstanding the metaphor. As such, estimating the amount and nature of receivers' content-related knowledge is recommended before using a particular pedagogical metaphor. Experts in science communication often recommend using multiple metaphors to enhance the accuracy of an explanation.

Another type of scientific metaphor, which corresponds to the second function of metaphor in science, is said to be *theory constructive*. Considered to be an essential factor in the linguistic composition of scientific theory, theory-constructive metaphors are suggested to reflect scientific constructs and related nomenclature that in all probability are difficult to articulate using literal terminology. Theory-constructive metaphors are said to function by encouraging receivers to contemplate the similarities or mappings between the two domains, as well as to visualize new domain relationships.

Perspectives vary regarding whether pedagogical metaphors and theory-constitutive metaphors exist as exclusive linguistic forms, considering their respective functions. It may be that some metaphors may serve either role, depending on the case and context of application or use.

Finally, as author Tim Giles has noted, metaphors serve an essential communicative function in scientific discourse. Metaphors function as a dominant rhetorical strategy in science communication; the elegance of metaphor use in communicating about science is that they can be effectively chosen and directed to a spectrum of science information receivers. They are essential to scientists communicating with scientists. Metaphors are the vernacular—linguistic heuristics—used by scientists to explicate to others with the same background of specialized knowledge, as well as to construct bridges from one scientific area of inquiry to another.

The use of metaphors in the sharing of science with the public is as critical as the role they serve in the practice of science and the interaction among scientists. They are used by scientists to describe complex concepts with the lay or "general" public in the understanding and "misunderstanding" of science. The heuristic nature of metaphor allows scientists to explicate science to lay audiences by virtue of the very nature of metaphor—the mapping or transfer between metaphoric domains that they make possible. Pragmatically, as well, the communicative effect of metaphor has been recognized in attracting public interest in various areas of science, in garnering public and government financial support, in public deliberations of science, and in consideration of government guidelines for the practice of science. A popular metaphor for explicating science can also be an effective persuasive metaphor for public support and policy issues. The inherent effect of metaphors on framing information helps journalists make science newsworthy, trendy, and fashionable and produces an increased probability of being accepted (or, in some cases, rejected). The metaphor has and will continue to be an elemental and indispensable force in the discovery, theorizing, and communication of science.

Bryan B. Whaley

See also Discourse Analysis and Science; Rhetoric of Science

Further Readings

Brown, T. L. (2003). *Making truth: Metaphor in science.* Urbana: University of Illinois Press.

Cheng, D., Claessens, M., Gascoigne, T., Metcalfe, J., Schiele, B., & Shi, S. (Eds.). (2008). *Communicating science in social contexts: New models, new practices.* New York: Springer.

Giles, T. D. (2001). The missing metaphor. *Journal of Technical Writing and Communication, 31*(4), 373–390.

Giles, T. D. (2008). *Motives for metaphor in scientific and technical communication.* Amityville, NY: Baywood.

Gross, A. G. (1990). *The rhetoric of science.* Cambridge, MA: Harvard University Press.

Hellsten, I., & Nerlich, B. (2008). Genetics and genomics: The politics and ethics of metaphorical framing. In M. Bucchi & B. Trench (Eds.), *Handbook of public communication of science and technology* (pp. 93–110). New York: Routledge.

Knudsen, S. (2003). Scientific metaphors going public. *Journal of Pragmatics, 35,* 1247–1263.

Knudsen, S. (2005). Communicating novel and conventional scientific metaphors: A study of the development of the metaphor of genetic code. *Public Understanding of Science, 14,* 373–392.

Lopez, J. J. (2007). Notes on metaphors, notes as metaphors: The genome as musical spectacle. *Science Communication, 29*(1), 7–34.

McReynolds, P. (1990). Motives and metaphors: A study in scientific creativity. In D. E. Leary (Ed.), *Metaphors in the history of psychology* (pp. 133–172). Cambridge, UK: Cambridge University Press.

Van Besien, F. (1989). Metaphors in scientific language. *Communication & Cognition, 22*(1), 5–22.

MEXICO, SCIENCE COMMUNICATION IN

The public communication of science has a long tradition in Mexico. As far back as the colonial period in the 17th century, the Mexican scientist and historian Carlos de Sigüenza y Góngora published a pamphlet in which he set forth scientific arguments to demonstrate that comets were a natural phenomenon, with nothing supernatural about them. The first scientific journals in New Spain, the *Diario Literario de México* and the *Mercurio Volante,* came out in the 18th century.

The public communication of science has been primarily linked to Mexico's universities and research institutes. Some projects, however, have been undertaken through the private initiatives of scientists, communicators, and investigators working either individually or in groups. This tradition has found its main outlet in print publications, especially books and periodicals. Over the last few decades, science journalism has had a sporadic presence in supplements attached to print and digital media. Interactive science and technology museums have been built in different parts of the country, and innovative channels of communication are being explored in informal settings, such as science cafés and itinerant workshops and exhibits. And in the last 10 years, graduate programs have been set up to provide professional preparation in the public communication of science.

The establishment in 1980 of the University Center for the Communication of Science, known today as the Dirección General de Divulgación de la Ciencia (DGDC), or General Directorate for the Dissemination of Science, at the National Autonomous University of Mexico (UNAM), was an important milestone in the institutionalization of scientific dissemination in this country.

Then, in 1986, the Mexican Association for the Dissemination of Science and Technology (SOMEDICYT in its initials in Spanish) was set up to integrate the various projects and initiatives developed by both institutions and individuals and aimed at fostering the public communication of science in Mexico.

Main Trends in the Public Communication of Science in Mexico

Mexican universities that conduct scientific research have projects for communicating science to the public. Their aims and scope vary widely depending on each institution's resources. Since its establishment, the General Directorate for the Dissemination of Science has developed projects for scientific communication both in print media (it publishes a number of book collections, as well as the magazine ¿Cómo ves?) and in radio and television broadcasts. It has also developed science and technology museums in the nation's capital. It helps to publicize scientific and technological discoveries from around the world, as well as the

findings of national researchers, especially those working at the UNAM's research institutes.

Other universities and research centers around the country, such as the National Polytechnic Institute, the University of Guadalajara, and the University of Baja California, have communication projects aimed primarily at disseminating the research done by their own scientists.

One of the problems that has held back this work in Mexico is the lack of multidimensional projects that combine the promotion of scientific vocations with the playful dimension of the public communication of science, together with references to relevant public issues in which scientific knowledge has a decisive role to play in generating comprehensive solutions in dialogue with stakeholder communities. Examples of these issues are environmental and health challenges, water management, and the use of alternative energy sources.

Main Scientific Topics Communicated in Mexico

Topics related to scientific disciplines (drawn from basic research), such as those in physics, astronomy, biology, chemistry, and mathematics, are among the main subjects of concern to science communicators in Mexico. Other important topics are those related to regional or global issues (drawn from applied research): biotechnology, pollution, global warming, environmental problems, and, more generally, health and technology.

Institutions and Associations

The Mexican Society for the Dissemination of Science and Technology, or SOMEDICYT, has 120 full members. Every year it organizes the National Congress for the Dissemination of Science and Technology, which brings together most of the country's communicators of science.

The Mexican Association of Museums and Centers of Science and Technology (AMMCCYT, for its initials in Spanish), the Mexican Academy of Sciences, and the National Council for Science and Technology (CONACYT) are also important agencies. The Asociación Mexicana de Planetarios (AMPAC), the Mexican Association of Planetariums, represents 38 planetariums from around the country, 11 of them in Mexico City. It was incorporated as a nonprofit organization on September 23, 1980, at the Luis Enrique Erro Planetarium of the National Polytechnic Institute.

The Foro Consultivo de Ciencia y Tecnología, or the Advisory Committee for Science and Technology, provides expert advice for the Mexican President's Office. State councils for science and technology are also important. Most of the national scientific associations, as well as public and private universities, devote resources to disseminating their specialties.

Media for the Public Communication of Science

Collections of Books by Mexican Authors

Mexican authors have published an extensive list of books devoted to the public communication of science. Deserving special mention are the collection *La Ciencia para Todos,* published by the Fondo de Cultura Económica, aimed at a younger audience and published by ADN Editores; the *Croma* collection by Editorial Paidós; and the *¿Cómo ves?* collection put out by the UNAM.

Periodicals

Among magazines in Mexico that seek to communicate scientific topics to a general audience, *¿Cómo ves?* is the most respected; in fact, it is taken as the national benchmark for this type of publication. Targeting a younger audience, it has been published for 10 years without interruption under the auspices of the DGDC of the UNAM and with the collaboration of Mexican scientists and communicators.

Other Mexican publications that disseminate scientific information include the magazines *Ciencia* of the Mexican Academy of Sciences; *Ciencia y Desarrollo* of the National Council for Science and Technology; *Ciencias,* published by the Faculty of Science of the UNAM; and *Conversus* of the National Polytechnic Institute. There are also a number of magazines published by state universities that dedicate all or part of their pages to the dissemination of scientific topics, such as *La Ciencia y el Hombre* of the University of Veracruz and *Elementos,* published by the Autonomous University of Puebla. Some educational institutions and research centers have electronic magazines that

include information on science. In addition, Spanish versions of international magazines such as *National Geographic, Muy Interesante,* and *Quo* also circulate in the country, often with sections developed in Mexico.

Mexican communicators can also be found in cyberspace, using different formats in addition to the periodical publications mentioned previously: blogs published by scientists and communicators of science, scientific news agency sites, and other Web pages devoted explicitly to the public communication of science. Some examples include sites titled "Imágenes en la Ciencia" by Sergio de Régules, "La Ciencia por Gusto" by Martín Bonfil, and "El Cierzo" by Carlos Enrique Orozco.

Newspapers

Most newspapers published in Mexico set aside some space for scientific information, either in their printed or in their electronic version, but not many do it regularly. Even fewer have a section or supplement devoted exclusively to science. A review of 294 newspapers published in the country found that only 69 had a specific space set aside for information about science and technology, and only 4 devoted a supplement to these topics. Much of the information published came from international agencies.

Among national newspapers that regularly cover scientific issues and that have specialized scientific journalists, four stand out: *La Jornada, El Universal, Reforma,* and *Milenio.*

Radio and Television

Public radio—university stations, primarily—has traditionally devoted much more time to the public communication of science than commercial radio, but public radio has low levels of listeners. In recent years, some radio consortia have included more news and reports on science in their programming, and there are a few programs devoted exclusively to scientific topics, such as Enrique Ganem's *El Explicador* ("The Explainer"), broadcast by MVS Radio. One formula that some of these consortia use is to partner with universities to produce sections or news programs on science; such segments can be heard on Televisa Radio, through the station XEW, or on Radio Imagen.

Nevertheless, the coverage of science on the radio is still meager compared to the time dedicated to sports, politics, the economy, or entertainment.

The same holds for television. Nationally produced programming that looks at science, either in program or documentary format, usually comes out of public universities or cultural channels funded by the federal government or state governments. TV UNAM, Channel 11 (run by the National Polytechnic Institute) and Channel 22—with José Gordon's outstanding program *La Oveja Eléctrica. Ciencia Subversiva* ("The Electric Sheep: Subversive Science")—have specific time slots set aside for the public communication of science. Programs about science broadcast by commercial channels tend to be foreign productions, and the most extensive coverage can be found on cable television, such as the Discovery Channel and the National Geographic Channel. The quality of this programming notwithstanding, unfortunately it almost completely disregards the science done in this country, which only commands significant air time when there are newsworthy incidents to report, such as the H1N1 flu outbreak.

Science and Technology Museums

Mexico currently has 24 museums and centers of dissemination that focus on science and technology, as reported by the AMMCCYT. They are distributed around the country in 17 different states; 6 of them are located in Mexico City. The primary objective of these centers is to educate children and young adults by enriching their scientific culture through interaction with permanent and temporary exhibits, as well as to develop entertaining workshops and other activities that sensitize participants to their regional and national context. In recent years, these centers have come to be seen as teaching resources and often have a specific mandate to support formal education. They have also undertaken research into the professional formation of communicators of science.

Scientific Cafés

The *café scientifique* is a project with roots in France, but now there are Mexican versions in a number of states around the country. One project in the state of Jalisco, organized by the Cultural Promotion Office and the Master's Degree Program in the Communication of Science and Culture at ITESO University, deserves special mention, as it has been running successfully for 5 years. Scientists from all over the country have participated in informal talks, where the audience is encouraged to take an active part in the conversation.

Professionalization and Research

Professional development for communicators of science has taken place primarily in graduate education programs. The pioneer in this field has been the Master's Degree Program in the Communication of Science and Culture at ITESO University in Jalisco, which started up in 1998. It is grounded in a sociocultural approach that seeks to equip students with elements that will allow them to contextualize and understand the relationships between practices such as the production of scientific knowledge, its impact on different areas of social life, technological development and the specific ways in which it is incorporated into social life, and the meaning that social actors give to these relationships in everyday practice. Subsequently, a specialization in the communication of science was set up within the graduate program in philosophy at the UNAM. Both programs include research on the public communication of science and undertake projects that contribute to the construction of knowledge in this academic field. The UNAM also offers a diploma course in the dissemination of science that has been attracting students for over a decade.

Susana Herrera Lima and Estrella Burgos

See also International Science Journalism Associations; Latin America, Science Communication in; Science Café; Science Centers and Science Museums

Further Readings

Consej Nacional de Ciencia y Tecnología. (n.d.). *Ciencia y desarrollo* [Science and development]. Available at www.conacyt.gob.mx (in Spanish)

Dirección General de Divulgación de la Ciencia. (1998–2007). *Colección divulgación para divulgadores* [Collection of materials for popularizers]. Mexico City, Mexico: Universidad Nacional Autónoma de México.

Dirección General de Divulgación de la Ciencia. (n.d.). *¿Cómo ves?* [You see?]. Mexico City,

Mexico: Universidad Nacional Autónoma de México.

Fondo de Cultura Económica and Consej Nacional de Ciencia y Tecnología. (n.d.). *La ciencia para todos* [Science for all]. Mexico City, Mexico: Author.

Instituto Tecnológico y de Estudios Superiores de Occidente. (n.d.). *Nautilus*. Available online at www.nautilus.iteso.mx (in Spanish)

Universidad Nacional Autónoma de México. (n.d.). *Cienciorama*. Available online at www .cienciorama.unam.mx (in Spanish)

MUIR, JOHN (1838–1914)

John Muir is considered to be one of the founding figures of the American conservation movement, which evolved into what we now know as environmentalism. Muir was born in Scotland but was raised in Wisconsin in a home governed by a very strict Christian father. Muir attended university in Wisconsin, where he took some classes that spurred his interest in nature. Instead of graduating, Muir undertook a walk to the American South. After this walk, he moved to California.

Muir eventually settled in the area of Yosemite. His experiences there inspired and confirmed his tendency to supplement traditional Christian religion with a spiritual view of nature. Viewing Yosemite, he saw nature as a temple. He undertook various jobs in the area, all the while nurturing his interest in the geological origins of the spectacular formations that surrounded him. At the same time, he became concerned about the despoliation being caused by livestock and tourists. Muir's view was that such mercenary pursuits were a blight on one of God's holiest creations.

Muir became an avid mountaineer. During his expeditions, he began to speculate that Yosemite's features were the result of glacial action, which was not in accord with the dominant theories of his day. However, his speculations did start to receive some notice from the scientific community. Muir is best known for his writings describing and defending the preservation of natural environments and for helping to form the Sierra Club.

Muir was well educated and was influenced by the transcendentalist literary movement, which sought understanding through intuition, often seeing in nature the inscription of God's intent. But Muir's literary efforts were formed just as much by his own hands—based on his own experience with nature. He traveled not only in the mountains of California but also in Alaska. He began supplementing his income by writing articles about his trips; these were published in Eastern newspapers or literary monthlies. These articles began to draw some attention, and he gained some minor recognition from them. The American print media audience of the time was interested in stories of the New West, and Muir's florid yet fluent writing style suited the popular taste.

His most important activity was to draw attention to the cause of setting aside Yosemite as a national park. Robert Underwood Johnson, publisher of *The Century Magazine*, persuaded Muir to write two articles proposing Yosemite as a national park, modeled on the example of Yellowstone. These articles appeared in the magazine in the fall of 1890. Political opposition from economic interests eventually disappeared, and the bill to create the park was passed. Later, Muir would attempt to preserve the nearby Hetch Hetchy Valley, which was desired as a water source for San Francisco. Although Muir had hosted President Theodore Roosevelt on a camping trip in Yosemite, he was unable to persuade later governments, and the valley was eventually taken. Muir died not long after this fight was lost.

Muir's other notable achievement, the founding of the Sierra Club, used the Appalachian Mountain Club, an association of moutaineering enthusiasts, as a model. Muir was elected the Sierra Club's first president. The organization has grown to become one of the preeminent environmental protection groups in the United States.

Muir was also associated with the debate over preservation versus conservation. He wanted to preserve natural spaces, to keep them in their natural state. Others preferred conservation, which sought to protect environments with an eye toward their continued use by humans. Conservation tended to predominate, as conservation advocates such as Gifford Pinchot were appointed by the government to oversee the government's forests and other holdings. But preservation did not lose out completely, as more national parks were added to the list of preserved areas throughout the 1900s.

From the standpoint of the communication of science and technology, Muir embodied an interesting model. He had some scientific training but no professional credentials as a scientist. Nevertheless, his theories about the glacial origins of Yosemite turned out to be on the right track. Muir was one of a few "amateur" scientists to exert significant influence on government policy. In some ways, he bears resemblance to Rachel Carson, whose seminal *Silent Spring* spawned the modern environmental movement. Carson did have an advanced degree as a biologist, but she shared with Muir an intense love of being in nature and an excellent ability to communicate through the written word. Muir's campaign for Yosemite was arguably the first to achieve environmental goals through the mass media. Carson's campaign followed a similar trajectory: publication in influential literary monthlies (in this case, *The New Yorker*), followed by influential books. In Carson's case, the issue was eventually taken up in the electronic mass media as well, which did not exist in Muir's day. But they both shared an ability to communicate environmental facts through the medium of storytelling and had created an audience for their works through previous descriptive works about nature.

Muir Woods is part of the Golden Gate National Recreation Area in California. Said Muir of the redwoods in the area, "This is the best tree-lovers monument" in any forest in the world.

James Shanahan

See also Carson, Rachel; Environmental Journalism

Further Readings

Fox, S. (1985). *The American conservation movement: John Muir and his legacy.* Madison: University of Wisconsin Press.

Muir, J. (1890). Features of the proposed Yosemite National Park. *The Century Magazine, 40*(5), 656–667.

Muir, J. (1901). *Our national parks.* Boston: Houghton Mifflin.

Muir, J. (1909). *Stickeen: The story of a dog.* Boston: Houghton Mifflin.

NANOTECHNOLOGY

Seen by some as a transformative, almost revolutionary, set of technologies, nanotechnology represents a substantial investment of research dollars on the part of the U.S. government and many other governments around the world. While it has not received as much public attention as some might predict, nanotechnology has been the subject of an increasing number of news reports in recent years as its products begin to appear in the marketplace and knowledge of both its risks and its benefits grows. Part of the strategy for rolling out nanotechnology products in the United States, the United Kingdom, and elsewhere has involved a new emphasis on public communication and public engagement.

Nanotechnology can, however, be particularly difficult for nonspecialists to grasp. In short, the more that scientists and engineers can control matter at the atomic and molecular scale, the more power they have to shape our material world, whether in medicine, electronics, materials science, environmental science, or other areas.

While scientists and engineers have known a great deal about atoms and molecules for more than a century, a family of instruments called scanning probe microscopy, developed over the past 30 years, has greatly improved the ability to see the three-dimensional topography of atomic-scale surfaces, including molecules, proteins, and viruses. The scientific images produced by these instruments (especially the scanning tunneling microscope and the atomic force microscope) then make it possible to do extremely sophisticated before-and-after experiments, to see the results, and thus to learn to control matter at that scale.

Nanotechnology is the name for those activities. *Nano* is a scientific prefix meaning "one billionth." A nanometer is one billionth of a meter (or 10^{-9} m in scientific notation), and from this scale we get the word *nanotechnology*, a collective term for several dozen related techniques that observe, manipulate, and manufacture matter that is measured at the scale of the nanometer. The diameter of a hydrogen atom, for example, is one tenth of a nanometer, and the water molecule (H_2O) is approximately one third of a nanometer across. The DNA molecule is about 2 nanometers across, and the smallest viruses are roughly 15 nanometers. There is a well-accepted three-part definition of nanotechnology (also shortened to nanotech): It deals with matter that is 100 nanometers or less in at least one dimension; it takes advantage of forces like catalysis, magnetism, or conductivity, the effects of which are different at the nanoscale than at larger scales; and it generates material applications, which is a way of saying that it is *not* merely an exercise in scientific curiosity. While there are some limits to what nanotech can do because of certain intractable behaviors of atoms and molecules, this family of technologies nevertheless has great potential to affect almost everything material.

Nanotechnology and Science Communication

Nanotechnology entails some daunting challenges for science communication, especially for the task

485

of explaining nanotech to individuals who have little scientific background. At the same time, anyone can be a stakeholder in nanotech in the sense that it will affect each of us, regardless of whether we have strong scientific backgrounds. Things measured by billionths of a meter can be difficult to imagine, doubly difficult to explain, and downright impossible to depict visually in a way that is truly faithful to the original nanosized object. Three features of nanotech are especially important for the challenge of communicating this technology to those who have a stake in its effects on our lives.

First, nanotechnology is not confined to a single scientific discipline. On the contrary, it is a scale of scientific investigation defined by size, the nanometer scale. Among the scientific disciplines engaged in nanotech research are atomic physics, quantum physics, synthetic chemistry, catalytic chemistry, microbiology, molecular biology, chemical engineering, materials science, and more.

Second, nanotech is a generalized technology platform, not a single technology like cell phones, and not a single process like the polymerase chain reaction, but rather a broad collection of techniques, procedures, and instruments for controlling matter at the nanoscale. Earlier examples of generalized technology platforms are the assembly line and commercially available electricity.

Third, nanotechnology is an emerging technology, meaning that it is changing, it is incomplete, and its consequences for the material and social conditions in which we live are not entirely clear. The science is well established, but the applications are mostly in the future. As a consequence, many of the political and ethical discussions about the place of nanotechnology in our lives are highly speculative.

These three features—that nanotech is defined by scale rather than discipline, that it is a generalized technology, and that it is an emerging technology—combine to make nanotech a classic polysemic (or multivalent) signifier: The same thing can mean very different things to different people. The science may be universal, but the expectations for its results can be quite personal. These expectations are often framed as hyperbole. To some technophilic visionaries, nanotech will deliver a set of magical tools that will free us from common human problems like disease and aging and thus enable us to become superhumans, but to some

traditionalists and humanists, nanotech will lead to the end of humanity as we know it, beginning with the end of personal privacy. Some expect nanotech to produce miracles of environmental remediation, while others believe it will bring nothing but environmental catastrophe. It is expected by some that nanotech will bring an end to hunger and poverty, but it is also expected by others that nanotech will increase the gap between the rich and the poor.

Nanomedicine is an especially salient locus of nanorelated hyperbole. It comes to us packaged in amazing promises and expectations: smaller, faster, more accurate diagnostics; targeted chemotherapy with few or no side effects; platforms for reconstructing damaged tissue; extension of the human life span; the end of cancer, supposedly; and, some say, the end of death. A small number of diagnostic and therapeutic products are very close to clinical reality, but much of what nanomedicine promises is still far in the future. This condition entails a series of problems. How can one tell what is realistic and what is fantasy? If someone is ill, when can that person expect nanomedicine to produce a cure? What forces or influences will nurture some forms of nanomedicine and neglect other forms?

Regardless of which aspects turn out to be realistic and which are not, nanomedicine arouses powerful feelings of hope. Those who are healthy now, but who know not to take good health for granted, have reason to hope that nanomedicine will profoundly affect their lives for the better within a decade or two. Those who are ill, especially those whose conditions are beyond the therapeutic powers of the current state of medicine, may be strongly motivated to believe that nanomedicine will soon deliver them from their illness. As noble as it is to produce better therapeutics, it is regrettable to the same degree to raise false hopes when describing the ways nanomedicine will touch our lives.

These expressions of hyperbole, whether in nanomedicine or elsewhere, cause one to wonder whether they are grounded in the scientific and technical realities of nanotech. Or, do they express hopes and fears unrelated to nanotech reality but gratuitously superimposed on nanotechnology? Another question is the changing relation between the technology and the hyperbole. Is the antinano hype discredited when beneficial applications come into our lives? Is there potential for a nanophobic backlash—do poli-cymakers and nonexperts feel deceived by extravagant promises that turn out to be unrealistic? Social scientists have been tracking these questions of hope and trust. Furthermore, changes in relations between the technology and the hyperbole do not necessarily constitute a victory of one form of hype over another. They can also take the form of centrist positions displacing either form of hype.

This reminds us that polysemic signifiers can also have a diachronic dimension: The relation between the signifier and the signified can change over time, either because the signifiers are changing in contrast with stable signifieds, or vice versa, or perhaps because both are changing at the same time. Thus, one might expect understandings of nanotech to change one way or another.

These relations are also contestable: People can argue about what a signifier means. And finally, signifier-signified relations can be political. In weighing these competing speculations and predictions about nanotech, one sees an ideological landscape of explicit and implicit assumptions, with much competition to establish definitions, iconic images, and authoritative meanings, not to mention priorities for government funding.

Visual Representation of Nanotechnology

A second interesting problem of communication concerns visual images. When exciting developments in nanotech are communicated to the public, the news is often accompanied by a striking visual image of atoms or molecules. The media of popular science make the nanoscale comprehensible by showing what its pieces look like to the human eye—if the human eye could see things that small. But none of these objects are truly visible the same way that an object in a photograph is visible. The process of making pictures with scanning probe microscopy is totally different from that of either photography or electron microscopy. This raises the issue of the relation between an object and an image of the object. What is a faithful reproduction? How do technical processes affect the image?

The process for making pictures with a scanning tunneling microscope is as follows: an ultrafine metal probe, ideally one atom wide at the end, is brought to within less than a nanometer from an atomic surface. An electric current runs from surface to tip, causing electrons to move from surface to tip in a process called "tunneling." When there is a depression on the surface (for example, a gap between atoms), the tip moves into the depression to maintain the steady electrical current. When there is a topographical elevation (for example, a molecule or a raised surface), the tip rises up to ride over the elevation. There are some exceptions in which the tunneling signal is affected by phenomena other than topography, but scanning probe microscopy is the best method for collecting three-dimensional data about the topography of an atomic surface.

This means that these instruments "know" the surface in terms of numerical data that record topographical variation, not visual impressions. Next, software converts the data into a simple two-dimensional image. These are often shades of gray, but they can be depicted in any color that ranges from light to dark. Objects imaged this way are smaller than the wavelength of visible light, so they literally reflect no color, and they have no shadows to make them look three-dimensional. Color, shading, and other three-dimensional effects are created after the fact.

The difference between the beginning and the end of the process is so great that it is virtually impossible for a picture of an atom or a molecule to be faithful to the object the way we think a photograph is. If someone asks, "Is that what an atom really looks like?" then the honest answer is, "No, but this is the best approximation we can create." Few people seriously argue that atoms and molecules are fictitious, but there is no picture or model of an atom that is equivalent to a photograph of an object at the human scale. Some people caution that the process of making pictures with scanning probe microscopy can lead to excessive manipulation of variables like color, and that this is tantamount to misrepresentation. But there is simply no such thing as a simple and direct photograph of an atom. Unavoidably, there are only mediated visual interpretations of atoms.

Why Communicate About Nanotechnology?

The third set of issues revolves around the question of *why* institutions communicate information about nanotechnology to the lay public. No one favors scientific illiteracy per se, but there are several different reasons for communicating knowledge of nanotechnology, and different reasons lead to different consequences.

Since the late 1970s, there has been a concern, both in the United States and the United Kingdom, that public support for scientific research, and especially for government funding of research, might not be as stable and friendly as some would hope. One consequence of this concern was a series of projects in the United Kingdom known as "public understanding of science," that is, a program for communicating science to the lay public to enhance public support for scientific research. This came to be seen as a misguided project for several reasons. First, it was patronizing and condescending to have one-way communications: The scientists talk, the nonscientists passively listen, and the problem is supposedly solved. Second, it was unrealistic. People are seldom enthusiastic about being on the receiving end of a condescending one-way process of communication. Third, there is good reason to conclude that public support for scientific research is largely independent of public understanding of science.

A related research program in the United States has been concerned with "civic scientific literacy," based on a series of large-scale surveys used to measure scientific knowledge and understanding across four decades. The results are consistently grim. Very few adult Americans seem to possess much knowledge of science, measured in this way. A complicated topic like nanotechnology is going to face extraordinary challenges in that situation. But in the United States too, strong public support for scientific research coexists with weak levels of civic scientific literacy.

In the United Kingdom, more recently there emerged a program known as upstream public engagement, which is based on the idea that nonexperts who might be affected by a given form of science or technology ought to have a voice in the early stages of research, before each policy decision becomes a fait accompli. This program was developed partly by a group of researchers at Lancaster University and is sometimes called the Lancaster Discourse.

The United States had a somewhat different experience with the question of how the lay public would have voices in science policy decisions.

Numerous stakeholders and advocacy groups demanded and successfully achieved active roles. Perhaps the most notable case was that of gay activists becoming involved in AIDS/HIV-related epidemiology and clinical trials. Other cases are that of nonscientists serving on review panels for the National Institutes of Health; environmentalist groups influencing environmental policy; and the Cambridge, Massachusetts, advisory board involvement in safe procedures for recombinant DNA research.

Processes like these combine two trends. In *stakeholder democracy,* the general population may be uninterested and inert about a particular policy question, but those who see themselves as being affected by a given policy will nevertheless take an active interest. In *participatory democracy,* nonexperts also take active roles designed to influence policy. Both stakeholder democracy and participatory democracy can apply to science policy, as well as to many other policy questions. Furthermore, these two trends are corroborated by observations that show that nonexperts can acquire, understand, and deploy technical information when they have to.

Promoting Upstream Engagement

While encouraging public engagement is part of official American policy for nanotechnology, the U.S. experience to date is the sum of numerous independent events and experiments, known collectively as *democratizing science.* These approaches are promoted as critical and activist alternatives to programs that feed scientific knowledge to the lay public only for the purpose of gaining uncritical support for scientific research. Nanotechnology is not necessarily more suitable to upstream engagement or democratizing science than other scientific topics, but it gained attention among nonexperts at the same time that these discourses matured. And so, by historical coincidence, nanotechnology has became a platform for experimenting with mechanisms and processes by which nonexperts can have more active and constructive roles in the creation of science policy.

Some of these mechanisms are meant to measure or model public opinion about nanotechnology, using survey research and focus groups, for example. Others are intended to generate policy guidelines as nonexperts delve more deeply into nanotech. In the United States, Patrick Hamlett has conducted a series of consensus conferences on nanotech, based loosely on models developed in Denmark and elsewhere. Hamlett's project has experimented with conventional face-to-face conferences, computer-mediated ("keyboard-to-keyboard") conferences, syntheses of the two styles, and synchronized consensus conferences taking place at multiple sites to increase the representativeness of this process by increasing the number and variety of participants who are included.

Another approach has been to assemble large audiences and then divide them into small groups to discuss nanotechnology. This is seen in the Nano Forums project of the Nanoscale Informal Science Education Network, and in the Nano Future Forums that were executed in Boston, Massachusetts; Columbia, South Carolina; Berkeley, California; and St. Louis, Missouri, in 2007 and 2008.

The South Carolina Citizens' School of Nanotechnology offers a different model in which a limited number of participants engage in face-to-face dialogue with scientific experts over a sustained period of time, with the result that the participants gain both knowledge and the confidence to participate in science policy discussions. In addition, the scientific experts learn about the layperson's values and concerns, which they might not ordinarily be aware of.

The Role of Critical Scholarship

Not only does nanotechnology find itself subject to social scientists experimenting with various versions of upstream public engagement and democratizing science, it also comes to the attention of scholars in the humanities and social sciences at a time when many of them have gained considerable expertise through studying issues of biotechnology, including genetically modified organisms, the Human Genome Project, and technology-assisted fertilization. Nanotech cannot be reduced to biotech, and approaches for studying nanotech are not limited to those for studying biotech. Still, it is beneficial that this newer family of technologies has been greeted by a research community that knows more about how to ask critical questions about the societal issues that come with an emerging technology than have previous generations of scholars.

Some researchers in the humanities and social sciences are primarily interested in the point that nanotechnology has the unique power to shape our material world in many ways, and to change our social, cultural, political, and economic landscape, and their work is specifically focused on the topic of nanotechnology. Others see nanotech as a case study of either an emerging technology or a generalized technology platform (or both), which is to say that nanotech ought to be one example within a bigger model of how science and technology interact with society, culture, politics, or economy. Both approaches have much to offer.

Both approaches need to be grounded in good understandings of the science that makes nanotechnology possible. This point may seem obvious, but in fact, the interdisciplinary field of Science and Technology Studies (STS) has sometimes been accused of delivering vapid commentaries on science and technology that are uninformed by knowledge of the relevant science or technology. Sometimes this criticism has been unfair, but not always. Those in the humanities and social sciences who would enhance our understandings of nanotechnology have the undeniable advantage that their disciplines can explore a phenomenon in terms of its history, its social dynamics, its cultural meanings, its political dynamics, and its economic consequences, and thus greatly enrich the ways we come to terms with an interesting phenomenon. So be it. However, these perspectives are most valuable when they take into account the science that underlies the technology.

Chris Toumey

See also Deliberative Democracy; Nanotechnology, Regulation of; Public Understanding of Science; Upstream Engagement; Visual Images in Science Communication

Further Readings

Binnig, G., & Rohrer, H. (1985, August). The scanning tunneling microscope. *Scientific American, 253*, 50–56.

Macnaghten, P., Kearnes, M., & Wynne, B. (2005). Nanotechnology, governance, and public deliberation. *Science Communication, 27*(2), 268–291.

Nanotech: The science of the small gets down to business. (2001). *Scientific American, 285*(3) [Special issue].

Robinson, C. (2004). Images in nanoscience/technology. In D. Baird, A. Nordmann, & J. Schummer (Eds.), *Discovering the nanoscale* (pp. 165–169). Amsterdam: IOS Press.

Royal Society and Royal Academy of Engineering. (2004). *Nanoscience and nanotechnologies: Opportunities and uncertainties.* London: The Royal Society.

Toumey, C. (2006). National discourses on democratizing nanotechnology. *Quaderni, 61,* 81–101.

NANOTECHNOLOGY, REGULATION OF

Nanotechnology takes place at the scale of 1 to 100 nanometers, about the size of only several atoms or 1 biological molecule, such as a protein. Matter at this scale takes on novel properties, and humans have recently been able to use nanotechnology for products and applications in many sectors of society. Nanotechnology might have large benefits to society, but it also presents risks and social, cultural, and ethical challenges. In this entry, issues regarding the oversight and regulation of nanotechnology are explored. Accurate, clear, and informative communication about nanotechnology and its oversight is important for providing stakeholders and the public with the knowledge to make informed decisions. Nanotechnology has not been a big news item up until now and therefore is not very much in the public eye, but because of both its potential benefits and its likely risks, it is quite likely to receive more communication attention and discussion in coming years. The regulatory decisions we make today will have important ramifications in the future.

Applications and Benefits

Nanotechnology encompasses a diverse set of applications and tools linked together primarily by scale. At the scale of nanotechnology (1 billionth of a meter), matter takes on novel properties, such as greater reactivity, electrical conductivity, and abilities to penetrate. Although nanoparticles exist in nature, recent tools and scientific understanding have allowed humans to manipulate matter at the nanoscale and create novel products.

Nanotechnology is being applied to health and medicine, food and agriculture, chemical and product manufacturing, and environmental science and remediation. In medicine, dendrimers (nanoscale, complex organic molecules) are being studied to specifically target and destroy cancer cells without the side effects of chemotherapy. Nanomaterials are being piloted for use in solar panels to lower the cost of solar energy. In agriculture, sensors based on nanotechnology are being developed for detecting environmental conditions and responding only when needed for the timed release of fertilizer, water, or pesticides. Iron oxide nanoparticles are being used to remove arsenic, a toxic contaminant, from drinking water. Carbon nanotubes (thin-walled tubes made of carbon atoms) are much stronger than steel and are used in consumer goods like tennis rackets, building materials, and computers. Products of nanotechnology are progressing from passive structures like chemical nanomaterials to more active structures that can respond, change, and move through human and natural systems.

Japan, the United States, and the European Union are leaders in nanotechnology research and development, although several other countries have emerging programs. The United States first funded nanotechnology in a coordinated fashion at the federal level in 2000. The U.S. National Nanotechnology Initiative (NNI) has grown from U.S.$400 million to over U.S.$1.3 billion from 2000 to 2008. Over half of this funding goes to the U.S. Department of Defense, and a significant proportion goes to the National Science Foundation, the Department of Energy, and the National Institutes of Health. Smaller amounts are allocated to several other agencies. Most public agencies have some responsibility for nanotechnology on account of its diverse products and applications.

Concerns and Risks

Scientists point out that human exposure to nanoparticles has significantly increased over the last century due to anthropogenic sources, and they are finding important safety issues associated with nanotechnology products. As such, there have been debates about how much funding should go to the study of risks of nanotechnology. Some scholars and practitioners argue that the funding for the study of environmental health and safety (EHS) issues associated with nanotechnology has been too low. In 2006, funding for risk-related research was estimated to be about 1% of total NNI budget, according to Andrew Maynard of the Woodrow Wilson Project on Emerging Nanotechnologies. The lack of significant levels of funding for environmental health and safety issues has created a situation in which over 500 nanotechnology products are on the market while very little is known about human and ecosystem exposure levels, health effects, or environmental fate and transport.

There have been some laboratory studies suggesting that nanoparticles are more toxic at lower concentrations than their larger counterparts due to their higher surface area-to-mass ratio and greater reactivity. Nanoparticles are also likely to penetrate more readily through human tissues and in ecosystems given their smaller size. Most toxicity studies have been on buckyballs (made out of 60 carbon atoms and shaped like a soccer ball), carbon nanotubes, silver, or titanium dioxide. Buckyballs have been shown to be harmful to fish and aquatic microorganisms. Titanium dioxide nanoparticles, used in commercial sunscreens, and silver particles, used as antimicrobials, impair cell function in cell-culture experiments. Inhaled nanoparticles more readily migrate into lung tissues after inhalation and from the lungs to the bloodstream. Carbon nanotubes can cause inflammation and toxicological changes in the lung and skin damage.

There is general consensus among toxicology experts that nanomaterials have unique characteristics and pose special safety issues that warrant attention. In 2008, government organizations in Japan, the European Union, and the United States proposed increasing resources for environmental health and safety studies of nanotechnology applications.

Nanotechnology also presents social, cultural, economic, and ethical issues, some of which are tied to risk and safety, and others that are not. Ethical principles of fairness and justice are related to oversight through the distribution of risks and benefits among human communities and ecosystems. Another broader oversight issue is whether consumers and patients should have rights to know and choose products generated from nanotechnology, an idea that is related to informed consent or the ethical principle of autonomy.

Current Regulatory Approaches

Regulation, a component of oversight, is typically limited to considerations of the risks, costs, and benefits in making decisions about the commercial approval of technological products. Regulation of nanotechnology currently relies on traditional mechanisms that have been developed for related products and applications. Current debate about nanotechnology regulation is focused on whether special consideration should be given to nanotechnology products and, if so, whether new laws or regulations are needed to do so. As of 2008, there is currently not a specific law or mechanism for the oversight of nanotechnology products in the United States. The European Union is determining whether nanomaterials will be treated separately under its new regulation on Registration, Evaluation, Authorisation and Restriction of Chemicals (REACH). Whatever its regulatory future, nanotechnology provides an interesting parallel to other emerging technologies in terms of the uncertainty that surrounds discussions of the best way to manage it.

In the United States, most chemical and consumer nanotechnology products do not require premarket testing or safety data. For example, the U.S. Environmental Protection Agency (EPA) does not necessarily regulate manufactured nanomaterials under the Toxic Substances Control Act (TSCA) if they have molecular formulas of chemicals already on the market. The U.S. Food and Drug Administration (FDA) only investigates nanotechnology-based cosmetics if safety questions emerge after the products are on the marketplace, and there is no premarket approval process for cosmetics.

However, both the EPA and FDA have been active in policies and programs surrounding nanotechnology regulation. In 2007, the EPA decided to administer a voluntary stewardship program for nanomaterials, in which data generated by industry is collected by the agency but there are no formal requirements for regulatory approval. In the same year, the FDA published a policy document stating that it will treat nanoscale drugs, devices, food products, and biologics as substantially equivalent to their larger-scale counterparts. The FDA indicated that it will not take a special look at nanomaterials in products under the agency's jurisdiction and that current laws and regulations are sufficient to cover both nano- and larger-sized products. Also, the FDA did not support mandatory labeling of nanotechnology products, and manufacturers are not required to tell the agency if they are using nanotechnology.

The EPA did decide on a mandatory premarket testing approach for regulation of silver nanoparticles under its pesticide statute. Silver nanoparticles are being used in washing machines, refrigerators, socks, and food-packaging materials to kill microorganisms and keep products fresh longer. Initially, these products were entering the marketplace with no premarket testing. However, several environmental and other interest groups brought attention to the potential release of silver ions into the environment from these products and petitioned the EPA to regulate them. In 2007, the agency decided to regulate nanosilver under the U.S. Federal Insecticide, Fungicide, and Rodenticide Act (FIFRA). This statute requires premarket tests to be submitted to the agency and products using nanosilver to be registered. However, to trigger regulation, the manufacturer must claim that its product is designed to kill pests. As a result, some companies that produce nanosilver materials are removing pest-killing claims from their products to avoid formal regulation.

Nonfederal oversight programs for nanomaterials have recently emerged. At the local level, the city of Berkeley, California, passed an ordinance that requires companies that manufacture or use nanoparticles to submit written toxicology disclosures and describe how the facility will handle disposal of nanomaterials. Cambridge, Massachusetts, is also considering such an ordinance and has established an advisory group to make recommendations to its Department of Health. Voluntary collaborative efforts for risk management of nanomaterials have also been initiated. The nonprofit group Environmental Defense has partnered with DuPont to develop a risk analysis framework for nanomaterials. On the international level, the Organisation for Economic Co-operation and Development is helping to form partnerships among nations to generate and share data about the safety of nanomaterials, and the International Standards Organization is working toward safety standards for nanomaterials.

Proposals for Regulation and Oversight

Some stakeholders are skeptical of the promise of nanotechnology, citing negative past experiences with other emerging technologies, such as biotechnology. Several interest groups have objected to the current voluntary approaches to overseeing nanotechnology. The International Center for Technology Assessment, in partnership with several other nonprofit organizations, developed proposed principles for regulating nanomaterials, including public transparency and mandatory premarket testing done by independent experts. The center has also filed a legal petition against the FDA for its lack of premarket safety testing of cosmetics and sunscreens incorporating nanoparticles.

Some scholars have suggested new laws specifically designed for formal regulation of nanotechnology. An argument for a new law for nanoproducts was promoted by Clarence Davies in 2007, who pointed out the limitations of TSCA, the Occupational Safety and Health Act (OSHA), and the federal Food, Drug and Cosmetics Act (FDCA) to adequately address the risks from nanomaterials. Other scholars and organizations have argued that current environmental and health statutes are sufficient but might need to be altered in interpretation or application. The American Bar Association concluded that TSCA, FIFRA, Clean Air Act, Clean Water Act, Resource Conservation and Recovery Act, and Comprehensive Environmental Response, Compensation, and Liability Act provide the EPA with sufficient legal authority to regulate nanochemicals and deal with the risks and benefits of using nanotechnology.

In a 2008 article, Gary Marchant, Douglas Sylvester, and Kenneth Abbott suggested a reflexive, incremental, and cooperative approach to risk management, a component of oversight, that is based on "soft law," including product stewardship, professional ethics of researchers, stakeholder participation, and transparency to address both the definitional uncertainty of what nanotechnology is and also the uncertainty in human health and environmental risks. This approach is proposed as a way to address public affect (or feelings) and trust about nanotechnology, as well as collect more information on the nature, magnitude, and perception of risks.

Currently, manufacturers hold most of the information about nanotechnology products and their safety, largely because of confidential business information. They also are the ones who are primarily responsible for ensuring safety of nanotechnology products through voluntary programs. According to the International Risk Governance Council's "Role of Industry" report in 2006, industry groups believe that without clear data and standards for nanotechnology products, the current state of knowledge is insufficient to set new mandatory federal regulations. However, there is a body of literature suggesting that citizens are less confident when technology oversight is placed in the hands of those who have potential conflicts of interest. Some studies have shown little trust in government or industry to effectively manage the possible risks associated with nanotechnology. The majority of participants in nanotechnology perception studies think that voluntary standards are insufficient and prefer mandatory regulation, access to more information, and increased safety testing for nanotechnology products.

To explore and increase societal dialogue about these and other oversight policy issues, several scholars have called for upstream public engagement as a mechanism for integrating the public's views about nanotechnology into decision making early in the process. Some public-engagement exercises have been conducted for nanotechnology, although there is not yet a formal and systematic way to get the public's input on nanotechnology regulation and oversight. This gap makes accurate and informed scientific communication about nanotechnology through traditional venues like the media even more important.

Jennifer Kuzma

See also Environmental Protection Agency, U.S.; Food and Drug Administration, U.S.; Nanotechnology; Risks and Benefits; Technology Assessment

Further Readings

American Bar Association. (2006). Section of environment, energy, and resources, *Nanotechnology Briefing Papers*. Retrieved June 30, 2008, from www.abanet.org/environ/nanotech/

Davies, C. J. (2007). *EPA and nanotechnology: Oversight for the 21st century* (PEN 9). Washington, DC: Project on Emerging Nanotechnologies.

International Risk Governance Council. (2006). *Survey on nanotechnology governance, volume B. The role of industry*. Retrieved June 30, 2008, from www.irgc.org/IMG/pdf/Survey_on_Nanotechnology_Governance_-_Part_B_The_Role_of_Industry-2.pdf

Kuzma, J. (2006). Nanotechnology oversight: Just do it. *Environmental Law Reporter, 36*, 10913–10923.

Macoubrie, J. (2006). Nanotechnology: Public concerns, reasoning, and trust in government. *Public Understanding of Science, 15*, 221–241.

Marchant, G. E., Sylvester, D. J., & Abbott, K. W. (2008). Risk management principles for nanotechnology. *Nanoethics, 2*, 43–60.

Paradise, J., Wolf, S., Ramachandran, G., Kokkoli, E., Hall, R., & Kuzma, J. (2008). Developing oversight frameworks for nanobiotechnology. *Minnesota Journal of Law, Science, and Technology, 9*(1), 399–416.

Priest, S. H. (2001). Misplaced faith: Communication variables as predictors of encouragement for biotechnology development. *Science Communication, 23*(2), 97–100.

Roco, M. C., & Bainbridge, W. S. (2005). Societal implications of nanoscience and nanotechnology: Maximizing human benefit. *Journal of Nanoparticle Research, 7*, 1–13.

Wilsdon, J., & Willis, R. (2004). *See-through science: Why public engagement needs to move upstream*. London: Demos. Retrieved June 30, 2008, from www.demos.co.uk/files/Seethroughsciencefinal.pdf

NARRATIVE IN SCIENCE COMMUNICATION

Narrative, or the telling of stories, plays an important role in how science is done and more especially in how it is communicated to the public. However, the role of narrative is controversial, as most scientists would probably eschew narrative descriptions of their own work (preferring straightforward retelling of the facts and procedures of any given scientific investigation), while the public seems to demand science in narrative packages, and the media seem more than willing to provide these stories.

A narrative is basically a story, typically with a beginning, middle, and end. Characters play an important role in narratives; especially important are protagonists and antagonists, and a variety of characters are often deployed in supporting roles to support the realism of the plot and to provide variety. Stories often fall into genres (the two most basic being comedy and tragedy). Most stories develop a narrative arc, with the protagonists facing some challenge, overcoming various hurdles along the way, and finally meeting that challenge in a denouement (ending). Further, most stories often conclude with a lesson or moral; the reader is supposed to get a final message from the narrative.

It is beyond the scope of this entry to review various theories of narrative; such theories are really the province of literary and dramatic criticism. Nevertheless, narrative has figured prominently in some communication work, and there are important applications to problems of science communication.

Do Scientists Use Narrative?

Typically one thinks of the scientist as adhering to a strict procedure, governed by the rules of the scientific method. In crafting a study and eventually reporting it, the scientist should review the literature on the topic, determine the questions to be investigated, conduct the study according to well-understood rules, and report the results in a straightforward way. The introduction of narrative elements into such a product would be seen as out of place in the standard scientific report, whose main goal is to advance the theory and report the results in such a way that other investigators could replicate them. While scientific investigations could and often do make for interesting narratives, the actual product of science, most often seen in the peer-reviewed journal article, is normally rigorously screened to remove any narrative elements that would be seen as inappropriate. Thus, in such reports, the narrative, such as it is, is fairly straightforward: Previous investigators found certain results, they raise unanswered questions, the investigator answers them, and science moves on.

However, scientists are of course human and thus not immune from the almost universal human interest in narrative. In 1985, the *Journal of Communication* presented a special issue on *Homo narrans* (humans as a storytelling species). In it Walter Fisher argued that narratives are the principal means by which humans reason. He put forth the idea that people use "good reasons" to evaluate problems, and that these good reasons are derived from stories that have good "narrative probability" and "narrative fidelity." That is, if a person hears a story that rings true with their lived experience and their social and cultural knowledge, people are likely to adopt its claims as valid.

Fisher and others think that this is a fairly naturalistic way for humans to process information. Indeed, psychologists and other social scientists are giving renewed attention to narrative as the preferred and natural way that we perceive, store, and use information. But the development of the scientific method tended to push narrative onto the back burner. Francis Bacon (1561–1626) was perhaps the most influential figure in the early development of the scientific method; he felt that scientists should start from observation, proceeding through inductive reasoning to facts and laws. While his method has been greatly revised since then—there are still disputes about proper scientific method—*narrative* reasoning was not in the forefront. Summing up, scientists have tended toward a "rational" and "technical" discourse in presenting their findings.

Meanwhile, the public and the media—especially with the development of modern mass media—have continued to rely on narrative. News is presented as "stories," and people are much more likely to look for stories that resonate with their experiences than to mine scientific data to reach conclusions that they might consider valid.

This yields a persistent dilemma of science communication: Scientists speak in rational and technical terms, while journalists and audiences still rely on narratives. This creates many occasions for problems of communication, as well as dissatisfaction among scientists, the media, and even the public as to how science is communicated.

Is There a "Metanarrative" of Science?

The history of science cannot help but be a narrative, and scientists are of course instructed in the history of their particular discipline. One of the conventional wisdoms that seeped into the history—or *his "story"*—of science was that progress is made in a cumulative fashion: Individual scientists contribute small building blocks that are placed on the achievements of others. But the actual notion of history—and therefore narrative—was somewhat hidden. That is, scientists did not think that history itself had any force; scientists were merely following the most reasonable path suggested by the most promising results in their field.

However, Thomas Kuhn, in *The Structure of Scientific Revolutions* (1970), showed that history, narrative, society, and culture did and do play an important role in how scientific discoveries are made. He argued that science advanced through revolutionary "paradigm" shifts. Kuhn saw a paradigm as a worldview that would guide scientists in choosing their research questions, methods, and how they would report results. Importantly, the worldview was not restricted to what was empirically observable but was also influenced by the philosophy, sociology, and culture of the time. Thus, for instance, theories and observations of heavenly bodies by the Greek astronomers were guided by contemporary philosophy, history, and culture as much as by mere empiricism. While their theories were very successful for a number of purposes, it was not until the time of Copernicus that scientists could begin to reject some of the assumptions of classical astronomy, eventually resulting in the Copernican revolution and movement toward a new paradigm of how the solar system should be viewed. But even the new paradigm had to contend with its own demons, such as objections from the Catholic Church.

In sum, in Kuhn's view, science progresses not through incremental innovation (which he sees as mere "puzzle-solving") but through dramatic breakthroughs that are able to challenge and change the story of science and relate science to a cultural metanarrative in a new way. Thus, science is both restricted and guided by master cultural narratives, but science can also change the course of these narratives.

Science Communication, Risk Communication, and Other Modern Dilemmas of Science and Narrative

In the 20th century and beyond, science and technology have assumed increasingly important roles in social, economic, and political development. Thus, a "master narrative" of the importance of science and technology can readily be found within our educational system, the media system, and other arenas of discourse. At the same time, competing narratives have not gone away. In the United States, the rise of Evangelical Christianity challenges the authority of science on questions such as the creation of the universe, abortion/right to life, and evolutionary theories. Around the world,

resurgent religious fundamentalisms still carry much weight. In short, not everyone has accepted the narrative of science as inevitably and inexorably answering all the important questions.

However, even within the public sphere that does accept the central importance of the role of science, there are still problems that often revolve around how science is communicated. This brings us back to the question of narrative. Because the main vehicle through which people receive information about science is through the media, and because media almost always package scientific news into stories, it has become evident that "science-speak" (rational/technical discourse) and "media-speak" (narrative/story) are not always commensurate with each other.

"Science communication" is often seen as the "translation" of scientific information for lay audiences. For a long time, it was assumed that a "deficit model" explained what needed to be done: Citizens lacked the "correct" information, and scientists could simply provide them with what was lacking. However, the sociology of science and work in science communication has revealed that simple lack of data is often not the problem. First, it has become clear that scientists themselves are still influenced by society, institutions, and culture in the ways they produce science. Scientific knowledge is at least partly "socially constructed." Moreover, citizens are capable of understanding scientific information, though scientists may need to present this information in ways other than straightforward reports of findings. That is, people still rely on narratives, and thus an effective approach to science communication needs to take into account how narratives work.

An example can be found in how the issue of climate change is communicated. At the time of the writing of this entry, nearly every climate scientist agrees that climate change is happening and that it is anthropogenic. However, there are still significant portions of the public that downplay climate change or even those who think it is a hoax. What explains this? Anthony Downs suggested in the early 1970s that issues go through "attention cycles" in which the public becomes alarmed about an issue with potentially dangerous consequences but then loses interest in the issue as the cost of solving the problem is realized. Downs was referring specifically to the issue of ecology in this work. Others, testing his theory, have since found that narrative factors also play a role. Because science is so often communicated through the media, which relies on narratives, science itself is not enough to sustain a story over time. Beyond results, political and economic controversy can eventually take over for the reporting of "raw" data and conclusions. Also, if the predicted consequences do not materialize soon, that which the media had sensationally predicted may come to be seen as a foolish whipping up of hysteria. Finally, vested interests that may wish to downplay scientific findings can also influence the media reporting of the issue.

Public relations effects and industry-sponsored science can also be brought forth to question the validity of scientific claims. Thus, while climate change has been on the public and media agenda since the late 1980s, attention has waxed and waned over the years, as various forces have contributed to a confusing picture and ultimately a lack of public pressure for concrete action on the issue. In sum, even if scientists wanted to ignore the role that narratives play in how the public understands and acts on scientific issues, they could and should not. Scientists, under this view, need to pay more attention to how issues will be framed by journalists and received by the public. If they do not, their research, even when solid and valid, may go unnoticed by the public, or policymakers may be able to frame the issues in ways that meet political or economic needs.

Another issue involving narrative is the area of "risk communication." This is the communication of information about hazards from scientists and policymakers to publics. The science community would prefer to rely on a technical/rational form of discourse, in which hazards and risks are communicated precisely—mathematically—to relevant audiences. However, publics do not necessarily understand risk in the same way as scientists. Often the public will see something as more risky if it is out of their control or if there is more "dread" associated with the risk. Oftentimes, in the various forums in which scientists present risk information to publics, there is a fundamental disconnection between the ways the two parties perceive the interchange. While scientists may feel that they have done their job if they give an accurate statistical account of the chances of an individual being harmed, citizens may feel that they are being duped,

especially if they see the process and procedure as being unbalanced, biased, or unfair. That is, while scientists may think that their "expert" stance is what is needed, citizens may well discount scientists' presentations as attempts to get them to acquiesce to a policy that has already been decided. Scientists often see such reactions as illogical or uninformed, but there is often no way around the fact that people will use a narrative logic (as described by Fisher) in reaching their conclusions. Additionally, because the media often present science in narrative packages, it is often the case that publics have received more than just the scientific findings. The media will also have focused on controversy among scientists (even if only a few disagree with the consensus view), as well as on the political and economic aspects of the controversy.

While "pure" scientific discourse would probably eschew what we normally think of as narrative, it is evident that narrative is inscribed within all aspects of the science communication process, from production of science to its reporting and reception by audiences. While communication researchers are seeking ways to improve the commensurability of communication between scientists and the public, this search is ongoing.

James Shanahan

See also Deficit Model; Discourse Analysis and Science; Kuhn, Thomas; Rhetoric of Science; Risk Communication, Overview

Further Readings

Downs, A. (1972). Up and down with ecology—the "issue-attention" cycle. *Public Interest, 28,* 38–51.

Fisher, W. (1985). The narrative paradigm: In the beginning. *Journal of Communication, 35*(4), 74.

Kuhn, T. (1970). *The structure of scientific revolutions.* Chicago: University of Chicago Press.

Miller, S. (2001). Public understanding of science at the crossroads. *Public Understanding of Science, 10*(1), 115–120.

NATIONAL ACADEMIES, U.S.

The National Academies are a conglomerate of four nonprofit honorary societies of distinguished scholars engaged in scientific and engineering research and dedicated to the advancement of science and technology and to their use for the general welfare. The first of those institutions was the National Academy of Sciences, established by President Abraham Lincoln in 1863. To keep pace with the growing role that science and technology would play in public life, the National Academies later also incorporated the National Research Council (established in 1916), the National Academy of Engineering (1964), and the Institute of Medicine (1970). The name National Academies now refers to these four institutions collectively. Because of the organization's stature, reports and other publications of the National Academies and its National Research Council, which address a broad range of topics in science policy and science education, are influential; their conclusions and findings appear regularly in the news.

The National Academy of Sciences (NAS) was chartered to look into and report on any subject whenever called on to do so by any branch of government. It has about 2,100 members and 380 foreign associates, including nearly 200 Nobel Prize winners. The academy is governed by a council consisting of 12 members (councilors) and 5 officers, who are elected from among the academy's membership.

The National Academy of Engineering (NAE) provides engineering leadership by focusing on projects that address the relationships among engineering, technology, and the quality of life. The NAE also conducts independent studies to examine important topics in engineering and technology. The NAE has more than 2,000 members and foreign associates, senior professionals in business, academia, and government, who are among the world's most accomplished engineers.

The Institute of Medicine (IOM) has as its main mission to serve as adviser to the nation on strategies to improve health, and it does so by providing scientific advice on matters of biomedical science, medicine, and general health. It has nearly 1,700 members, of which about 80 are foreign associates.

The National Research Council (NRC) functions under the auspices of the three other National Academies mentioned previously and can be considered the operating arm of those academies. The mission of the NRC is to improve government

decision making and public policy, increase public education and understanding, and promote the acquisition and dissemination of knowledge in matters involving science, engineering, technology, and health by providing advice to elected officials, policymakers, and the public in general. The NRC is administered jointly by the NAS, NAE, and the IOM through the NRC Governing Board. The NRC also administers a number of fellowships.

Each of the academies is a nonprofit organization composed of members elected by their peers. Being a member of any of these academies is one of the highest honors bestowed on an individual in a scientific, engineering, or medical profession; election represents recognition of an outstanding sustained record of accomplishments in one's field.

Each of the National Academies organizes its work through committees of individuals who volunteer their time and effort in projects aimed at addressing critical national issues by giving expert advice to the federal government and the public. Historically, the results of the committees' deliberations have guided policy decisions in many different areas of science, technology, and education. Both Congress and the executive branch have used their advice, both in establishing legislation and in issuing executive orders. Yet all of the academies work outside the formal framework of government to ensure the provision of both scientifically and technically informed analysis and independent direction.

None of the four institutions that compose the National Academies receives direct federal appropriations for its work. Individual projects may be funded by federal agencies, foundations, other governmental and private sources, or the institution's own endowment. The work is made possible by the participation of the nearly 6,000 of the world's top scientists, engineers, and other professionals who are members of the National Academies.

The academies' committee reports must go through a rigorous peer-review process at the academy level as well as at the NRC level. Each report must be based on solid evidence, supplemented in many cases by expert opinion. The committees that prepare these reports are made up of those experts appropriate to the topics to be discussed. Membership on these committees is determined as the result of a complex process: soliciting and receiving nominations for candidates from a wide number of sources, presenting a proposed slate and alternatives to the academy leadership group, receiving approval from the academy president, and then formally requesting appointment from the NRC chairperson. The selection process is designed to make sure that there are no particular biases or potential conflicts of interest involving the composition of the committees.

The committee meetings convened may take place either in public or in private. During the information-gathering phase of the committee work, members may hear from those who are not committee members or employees, officials, or agents of the academy in question. These meetings are generally open to the public, while the deliberations (involving discussion of the specific findings or recommendations to be included in a report) usually take place in private. This is aimed at avoiding bias in the deliberations that might otherwise result from public pressure and also allows committee members to change their positions freely during the course of the deliberations.

The entire process is usually aimed at achieving a consensus among members of the committee. Where the published data are insufficient to support a conclusion, the committee may use its collective knowledge alongside available data to argue for its conclusions. Once an NAS report draft is finished, it is reviewed according to the policies of the academy in question and also by the NRC Report Review Committee (RRC). Reviews are provided to the study staff by the review office and are blinded. The study staff must respond to each review, either by making appropriate changes or providing a rationale for not doing so, prior to the document's becoming finalized.

Aldemaro Romero

See also Issues in Science and Technology; Royal Society

Further Readings

The National Academies: Advisors to the Nation on Science, Engineering, and Medicine: www .nationalacademies.org

National Aeronautics and Space Administration, U.S.

The National Aeronautics and Space Administration (NASA) is an independent agency within the government of the United States, having a mission to pioneer future space exploration, scientific discovery, and aeronautics research. It is led by an administrator who is appointed by the president and confirmed by the U.S. Senate, and within Congress the agency reports to the Senate Committee on Commerce, Science and Transportation and to the House Committee on Science and Technology. NASA's accomplishments are often in the news; the agency distributes extensive information about its activities to the media and other audiences via its Web site, including press kits and fact sheets; it operates its own cable television channel, NASA TV, in some markets; and it broadcasts NASA news on the full range of new media technologies, from podcasts to Twitter.

Following World War II, the U.S. Department of Defense (DoD) began a serious push into the fields of rocketry and upper stratosphere science. Aircraft research was performed both by DoD and by the National Advisory Committee for Aeronautics (NACA). Largely due to Soviet space successes such as the *Sputnik* satellite, President Dwight D. Eisenhower called for a renewed focus on space science. The first successful space missions, launches of suborbital satellites of the Jupiter series, were by the DoD. Suborbital satellite *Jupiter* C RS-40, which was launched on August 8, 1957, provided the first nose cone ever to be recovered following entry into space. On January 31, 1958, suborbital satellite *Jupiter* C RS-29 was launched containing the *Explorer I* payload; the first scientific experiment in space, it measured radiation. The architect of the *Explorer I* payload was Professor James Van Allen of the University of Iowa, and the Van Allen Radiation Belt was named in his honor.

President Eisenhower, in calling for orbital satellite research, mandated that this effort be undertaken by a civilian, rather than a military, organization. On October 1, 1958, following the passage of the National Aeronautics and Space Act, NASA absorbed NACA with its 8,000 employees,

$100 million budget, and 3 major research facilities and added space exploration to its aeronautics research portfolio. The NASA research enterprise has grown from 3 to 10 research facilities and to an annual budget over $17 billion.

While continuing a focus on aeronautics, NASA has had a rich history in space exploration, including human spaceflight, missions to the moon and planets, the use of satellites for Earth observation by remote sensing, and gravitational science. To facilitate this distributed research portfolio, NASA has four "mission directorates" (in aeronautics research, science, space operations, and exploration systems) that manage a number of research laboratory facilities scattered throughout the United States.

President John F. Kennedy, based on a suggestion made by Vice President Lyndon B. Johnson, announced the intention for the United States to land a man on the moon and to reclaim from the Soviets superiority in space research. Project Mercury was the first high-profile human spaceflight program and was designed to learn if humans could withstand the space environment. This program utilized three different rocket systems. *Little Joe* and *Redstone* rockets provided initial testing, including suborbital flights with chimpanzees. Manned flights utilized the *Atlas* rocket booster. On May 5, 1961, Alan B. Shepard Jr. became the first American in space on a 15-minute suborbital flight, and John H. Glenn Jr. was the first American to orbit Earth on February 20, 1962.

Project Gemini followed Project Mercury, with 10 flights in 1965 and 1966. This program, powered by *Titan II* rockets, perfected the operating procedures involved in orbital spaceflight, including rendezvous/docking, extravehicular spacewalk operations, and reentry/recovery. On June 3, 1965, Edward H. White Jr. became the first American to perform a spacewalk.

Based on the successes of Projects Mercury and Gemini, Project Apollo provided the push that resulted in humans walking on the moon. Powered by the *Saturn V* rocket, these spaceflights represented the first and, to date, the last times that humans left low Earth orbit to venture more deeply into space. It was not without cost. A January 1967 fire in an *Apollo* capsule on the ground cost the lives of Roger B. Chaffee, Virgil "Gus" Grissom, and Edward H. White Jr. *Apollo XIII*

was not able to complete its mission to land on the moon. However, on July 20, 1969, Neil Armstrong became the first human to walk on the moon, and on December 13, 1972, Eugene A. Cernan was the last human to leave a human lunar footprint. The Apollo-Soyuz Test Project successfully tested rendezvous and docking procedures between U.S. and Soviet spacecraft.

From the 1980s on, NASA has concentrated on its space shuttle program to bring both humans and materials such as satellites into low Earth orbit. The space shuttle, officially called the Space Transportation System (STS), is delivered into space by a complex propulsion system using solid rocket boosters, shuttle rockets, and an external tank. The shuttle glides back to Earth for an airplanelike runway landing. There is room in the shuttle mid-deck for experimental packages, and modules such as Spacelab can be housed in the cargo bay, adding experimental flexibility. Dedicated research missions have been extraordinarily successful, exploring the effects of the space environment on material science, physical science, neurobiology, immunology, developmental biology, and plant physiology. This research has been international in scope. For example, STS-87 (May 1997) had a mid-deck locker experiment that was collaborative, using a multi-investigator team from the United States and Ukraine, and had astronauts from the United States, Ukraine, and Japan. The space shuttle program was not without human cost, however, with the losses of *Challenger* (STS-51L, January 28, 1986) and *Columbia* (STS-107, February 1, 2003). In all, 14 astronauts lost their lives.

In 1984, Congress authorized the construction of a new space station, built in a modular fashion with the shuttle as the vehicle to deliver the station into orbit. This is an international partnership with Russia, Japan, the European Union, and others. Both the shuttle and Russian spacecraft, and more recently the European Space Agency's spacecraft, resupply the station at regular intervals.

The focus of this entry has largely been human space exploration; however, NASA's successes include many other elements as well. Technology spinoffs from space exploration have been credited with breakthroughs in computing and communication. Construction and launch of the Hubble Space Telescope has provided a new window into the vastness of space, while the Landsat satellite series has provided new insights through remote sensing of the ecology of the Earth, and meteorological satellites have become important tools for weather forecasting. NASA has not forgotten that "Aeronautics" is the first "A" in NASA, with technology and data on propulsion systems, aerodynamics, and composite research impacting both military and civilian aircraft. After 50 years of service, NASA retains its original purposes of pioneering space exploration, engaging in scientific discovery, and conducting aeronautics research.

James A. Guikema

See also Colonizing Other Worlds; European Space Agency; Hubble Space Telescope; Space Program, Overview; Space Shuttle

Further Readings

U.S. National Aeronautics and Space Administration: www.nasa.gov

NATIONAL ASSOCIATION OF SCIENCE WRITERS

Founded in 1934, the National Association of Science Writers (NASW) is the largest organization devoted to the professional interests of science writers. As stated on the association's Web site, NASW was incorporated in 1955 with a charter to "foster the dissemination of accurate information" about science through the media to the public. In other words, NASW fights for the free flow of science news. What began as a group of colleagues meeting informally to discuss the field has grown into a 2,600-member organization that holds annual workshops, publishes a quarterly magazine, hosts an active Web site, funds travel and reporting fellowships, and conducts activities designed to advance the field and craft of science writing. Though it has grown, NASW still fosters a collegial atmosphere for members, creating networking opportunities, both virtual and physical, that bring together science writers from all over the United States and multiple foreign countries.

NASW is fueled by volunteer power. Four officers and an 11-member executive board, elected for 2-year terms, lead NASW. Officers are required to be working members of the press. Over the years, NASW officers have included employees of most of the major newspapers, wire services, magazines, and broadcast outlets in the United States. Board membership is open to any NASW member in good standing. Committees change over time to reflect the needs and interests of members and to keep up with a changing field; volunteer liaisons form a bridge between NASW and other journalistic organizations.

Membership in this professional society is achieved through an application process in which the applicant demonstrates evidence of published work. Regular memberships are for working journalists, authors, editors, producers, public information officers, science-writing educators, and people who write and produce films, museum exhibits, and other material intended to inform the public about science and technology. Student memberships were established to foster interest in the field and do not require the same stringent application process as regular memberships. Student memberships exist for those currently enrolled in a journalism or science program or who are serving as a reporter or editor at a school newspaper.

NASW's code of ethics stipulates that NASW or its members, when invoking their NASW membership, must act in accordance with the organization's aims, in keeping with the highest standards of journalism. NASW does not take political positions, endorse candidates, support specific legislation, or allow the use of its name in connection with any political events. NASW may, however, take a position on issues related to journalism, freedom of information, and other public policy debates that relate to the members' ability to act in keeping with the highest standards of journalism.

Resources for members focus on professional development. An annual meeting that is held in a different region of the country each year offers skills and topical workshops as well as copious social opportunities. Other regional workshops are held as topics and interest arise. NASW sponsors travel fellowships for the annual meeting as well as other meetings relevant for members. The quarterly magazine, *ScienceWriters*, in publication since 1952, highlights developments, issues, and controversies relevant to the field with reports by members and outside experts. Members also have access to a jobs board, a grievance system that helps freelancers get paid for their work, and professional e-mail and Web hosting services. Other member services are periodically added to reflect the changing needs of members.

NASW runs a series of programs especially for student members to encourage entry into the field. Programs include one-on-one mentoring sessions at national meetings and an annual internship fair that draws a large number of potential employers and students alike.

NASW recognizes outstanding contributions to the field by sponsoring the annual Science in Society awards, established in 1972. The awards, which include a cash prize, recognize writing and multimedia packages or shows that specifically address the impact of science on society. The awards are funded solely by NASW without support from any professional or commercial interest.

In seeking to foster science writing across the globe, NASW is itself an active member of the World Federation of Science Journalists and participates in its worldwide gatherings with other members of the profession. As part of its international activities, NASW has recently partnered with the Arab Science Journalists Association to foster development of new science writing groups and increase cross-cultural learning.

Tinsley Davis

See also American Medical Writers Association; Career Paths, Medical Writing/Medical Journalism; Career Paths, Science/Environmental Journalism; Council for the Advancement of Science Writing

Further Readings

National Association of Science Writers: www.nasw.org

NATIONAL DEVELOPMENT, SCIENCE AND TECHNOLOGY IN

Today, large-scale science and technology (S&T) and the information, knowledge, and news that these generate are concentrated in the so-called developed world. Major international collaborations in science and technology today that will extend into the first few decades of the 21st century include such projects as the Large Hadron Collider of the European Organization for Nuclear Research (or Conseil Européen pour la Recherche Nucléaire, known as CERN) in Geneva, Switzerland; the International Thermonuclear Experimental Reactor (ITER) in Cadarache, France; and the International Space Station. Each of these collaborations costs billions of dollars, employs thousands of scientists and engineers with advanced degrees, and requires meticulous planning, coordination, and project management. They are led and participated in mostly by advanced countries.

Contrast these collaborations with the S&T activities in many developing countries, where most activities are at a more rudimentary level: improving science education, identifying indigenous resources that can substitute for expensive imported materials, and innovating at an appropriate technological level. Inventors still generally work alone in their shops creating useful devices that make use of indigenous materials to respond to the needs of the community. Yet stories of "inventions" that violate the laws of physics and propose fantastic solutions to important problems occasionally appear in the media, reflecting the low level of science understanding by both media practitioners and the public in many developing countries.

Because S&T is so important for national economic development, the widening gap in this area between developed and developing countries will continue to exacerbate the wealth gap between nations. This is rooted in history and in the differences between the S&T policies and strategies carried out by countries on each side of the economic divide. The present distribution of S&T activities has not always been the situation, however, and has complex historical roots.

A Brief History

Up until the late Middle Ages (beginning in the 14th century), Western Europeans lagged behind the Middle East, South Asia, and China both scientifically and technologically. The West's ascendancy began during the Renaissance and Scientific Revolution era and was completed during the

Industrial Revolution. That the West drew heavily from the East's technology is shown in the West's adoption of gunpowder, magnetic compass, horse harness, and printing press from China and the windmill and waterwheel from the Middle East. In mathematics, the origin of the number system adopted by the West and the whole world is clear from its name, the Hindu-Arabic system. In science, the Copernican revolution that defined the Earth as the center of the solar system also relied on works from the Middle East. Yet it was the once-backward Western Europeans who developed modern science. The risk-taking of the merchant capitalists there created an environment conducive to new ideas on nature, society, and man's role in the order of things. The result was technology that made possible the economic and political domination by Europeans that has lasted from the Renaissance era up until the present.

If societal factors affect the development of science, the converse is equally true. Science affects the development of society, and this became clear during the Industrial Revolution of the mid-19th to early 20th centuries. In particular, unlike the technologies developed in earlier eras, those based on the physics of electromagnetism (including the telegraph and early wireless communication) require an understanding of the works of Michael Faraday and James Clerk Maxwell. Aside from spawning new industries (including communication and entertainment) and facilitating the flow of capital and information, the new technologies also led to better science because of greater precision in measurements. As a result, from the mid-19th century onward, we see evidence of the symbiotic linkage between S&T development and the significant, long-term effects of S&T on society.

The Industrial Revolution led to the rapid economic growth of European countries such as England, France, Germany, and the Netherlands, as well as the two newly industrializing countries of the late 19th century, the United States and Japan. This rapid growth fueled the political rivalry among these countries, which spilled over into a competition for control of other countries. Countries in Africa, the Americas, and Asia, including those that earlier had educated the West on science, mathematics, and technology (including India, China, and the Middle East), became colonies, protectorates, or "spheres of influence"

of the more advanced countries. The need for markets and sources of raw materials for their new industries meant that the colonizers slowed down, if not stopped, a colony's incipient industrialization, as Ian Inkster has argued happened to India in his 1991 book *Science and Technology in History*. The developing world showed little growth in the applied sciences and engineering because of little demand. At best, a country dominated in this way practices a form of science that is strongly dependent on the science done in the colonizing country, serving in part to convey the colonizer's cultural "superiority."

In contrast to the case of India, in the Philippines, the country's second colonial master, the United States, early on established public institutions for higher learning, health, agriculture, and science, yet discovered very little interest in the sciences and the technical areas on the part of Filipinos. This can be explained by the fact that the country's first colonial master for more than 300 years, Spain, was not itself a party to the Scientific and Industrial Revolutions that swept Europe in the 18th and 19th centuries. At the beginning of the 20th century, the Americans themselves were in no position to transfer some areas of science to the Filipinos because they themselves were just learning these fields from the Germans, French, and English.

The first half of the 20th century saw two world wars, conflicts between advanced countries that were fought also on the soils of developing countries, especially World War II. This era is significant for a number of reasons. Although both wars made use of weapons based on the technology of the times, it was during World War II that scientific analysis was first used in military operations. Then, through the Manhattan Project, the United States showed that directed military research based on a frontier area of science (in this case nuclear fission) and involving hundreds of scientists and military personnel can realize ambitious goals in a short period of time. At the end of World War II, the power of the atom was unleashed. Ironically, nuclear weapons have since helped keep world peace through the threat of mutual destruction. Finally, the wars led indirectly to the independence of the former colonies.

The neocolonial period was also the era of the cold war, when the world was divided into two camps—the Soviets and Eastern Bloc on one side, and the United States and its Western allies on the other. During this period, the weapons and space race resulted in a more potent nuclear arsenal (using the hydrogen bomb), the development of better delivery systems (missiles), the use of satellites for communications, and the landing on the moon. The economic and military competition also accelerated the developments of later technologies, such as microelectronics, advances in material science, and recombinant DNA technology, which in turn spawned new industries. Universities in developed countries increased enrollment, secured more funding for basic and applied research, and developed new linkages with industry. "Proxy wars" between the cold war adversaries began in some developing countries (such as Vietnam and Afghanistan) that had begun asserting their independence.

Beginning with the late 1980s, the Soviet Union and the Eastern Bloc began to unravel, eventually leading to the thawing of relations between the former ideological rivals. The intense competition in space and nuclear technologies at the height of the cold war shifted to cooperation. For example, the forerunner of the present International Space Station project was the Shuttle-Mir Program that emerged between 1986 and 1996. Many former colonies, later classified as third world countries and now more commonly referred to as developing countries, have not achieved substantial progress. By the late 20th century, only a very few had attained a standard of living that compares to and can compete with the advanced technology industrial societies of the West. India and China, the two most populous nations in the world, only integrated their economies into the world market in the 1990s. However, these two countries have already made considerable economic progress. China is now the world's factory and India is the world's foremost provider of information technology services.

Global Initiatives for S&T Development in Developing Countries

The historical account of the previous section shows that S&T is a common heritage of both developed and developing nations; thus, developing countries should have the opportunity to participate in S&T activities even though most do not have the resources to participate in big-ticket programs such as the three listed in the introduction. Furthermore, as the European experience during the Renaissance period shows, it is possible for the next major development in S&T to come not from Harvard or Cambridge but from an institution in a developing country. Policymakers and leaders of advanced countries understand this, which may be part of the reason why their aid to developing countries includes S&T development.

In today's global economy, helping developing countries improve science and engineering education will also redound to the benefit of the advanced country. Practices such as business process outsourcing and locating manufacturing in developing countries lower business costs, which improves the profits of multinational corporations. Multinational corporations can also lower the cost of research and development (R&D) by locating in developing countries with strong programs in science and engineering. Examples are Intel and Microsoft, which have established R&D units in India and China.

Helping developing countries improve their S&T also benefits advanced countries directly. Even before the world economy became highly integrated, the advanced countries, in particular the United States, drew much of their supply of graduate students in the sciences and engineering from universities in developing countries. Many of these students stayed on in the United States to become faculty members in universities or work in industry. And these people could not have qualified in American universities as graduate students if the education they received from their home countries was not up to the standard of American academic institutions. In a number of developing countries, aid provided by foundations such as Rockefeller and Ford, as well as the U.S.-based Fulbright-Hays program, have helped universities with upgrading their faculties and the acquisition of laboratories and books, thus helping to improve at least undergraduate education.

A number of other programs assist at higher levels of professional training. For example, the Alexander von Humboldt Stiftung allows doctoral academics in developing countries to spend a year or two in German universities and research laboratories as Humboldt Fellows. A variety of both short- and long-term programs are offered by the Abdus Salam International Center for Theoretical Physics in Trieste, Italy. The brainchild of Nobel

Laureate Abdus Salam, the center is a joint program of the Italian government, the International Atomic Energy Agency, and the United Nations Educational, Scientific and Cultural Organization, with funding from many other sources. The Association of Southeast Asian Nations (ASEAN) and the European Union (EU) help academic departments in ASEAN member nations by partnering their faculty in sciences, mathematics, and engineering with EU counterparts to jointly develop course materials. A broader EU program in Asia, the Asia Link Program, has provided support for 175 institutions. And yet another EU program provides thousands of Erasmus Mundus scholarships for citizens of developing countries to study in Europe. The World Bank's Millennium Science Initiative provides loans to developing countries for improving science and technology at the highest level, hoping to alleviate the problem of "brain drain" in developing countries.

Another, perhaps even more important, problem is the increasing information and digital divide, which puts children in developing countries at a clear disadvantage compared to children in developed countries. This been addressed by the One Laptop Per Child program, a brainchild of Nicholas Negroponte of the Massachusetts Institute of Technology (MIT) Media Lab that was supported by a consortium of information technology and semiconductor companies. The goal is to produce cheap laptop computers (valued at around U.S.$100) that can be provided to children in developing countries.

S&T Programs of Successful Developing Countries

How did some formerly colonized countries, like South Korea and Taiwan, achieve spectacular economic growth and move up to the ranks of scientifically advanced countries, while others stagnated economically and remained laggards in S&T? What role did S&T development play in these countries' economic success? Or is it the other way around, that their economic success enabled them to develop their own S&T? While some of these countries mention S&T in their national constitutions, there is little evidence that this has a consistent impact. What, then, explains the observed differences? Obviously, history and the environment play important roles. However, there are a number of developing countries that have had a similar past and exist in the same general geographical location, yet having divergent development pathways.

Development theorists today generally agree that a country's national innovation system is the main determining factor in explaining a country's success or failure. Roughly speaking, the *innovation system* can be defined as the institutions and arrangements that contribute to a country's accumulation of wealth and generation of knowledge. Key institutions will include the government, the educational system, and the private sector. Important arrangements include socioeconomic policies, the laws of the land, and the relationships defined between academe, industry, and government institutions. Leaders can also play key roles. For example, in the case of South Korea, a key leader in the development of S&T was Park Chung Hee, who presided over the country's industrialization from the early 1960s to 1979.

In the 1950s and 1960s, some newly independent developing countries adopted the policy of import substitution to protect their fledgling industries. Tariffs and quotas on imports were used to encourage the use of local products. This is where South Korea and Taiwan differed from many countries in Latin America and Asia. Very early on, the two countries realized that their limited domestic market would not be able to sustain their industries; thus they looked to exports to sustain industrial growth. Unlike the situation in countries with an inward orientation where industries can become complacent, resulting in stunted growth, an export perspective forces local industries to improve productivity, lowering production cost, and raising product quality because of the demanding foreign market. This is one major difference between both South Korea and Taiwan and the rest of the developing world.

Both South Korea and Taiwan also effectively practiced industrial policy in which the government defined direction for the private sector by providing direct support and incentives only for specific industries—or, in other words, by "picking winners." This is contrary to the philosophy of laissez-faire economics—the view that the government's only role is to provide a conducive macroeconomic environment and it should be the private sector that establishes which industries will move ahead, given the demands of the market. Because South Korea and Taiwan implemented this successful industrial policy, like their former colonizer Japan, they were able to give advanced countries a run for their money in the semiconductor and electronics industry, shipbuilding, car manufacturing (South Korea), and car parts manufacturing (Taiwan). However, the secret of long-term success here may be to know when to let go. Both South Korea and Taiwan have since modified these policies.

Aside from adopting an export-oriented strategy and practicing an effective industrial policy, these two countries implemented what the World Bank called "getting the basics right." They both invested heavily in infrastructure—power plants, telecommunications, and roads. They invested in education in all levels at rates much higher than most countries in the region. And they focused their educational systems to produce technical people—technicians, scientists, and engineers with advanced education. By the 1980s, these two countries had much higher numbers of R&D personnel per 100,000 population than most countries in the world, although still lagging behind the most advanced countries. These investments made the two countries attractive to multinationals. Also, the two countries had high rates of savings and deliberately lowered the cost of money, which made capital affordable to their industries.

The most important strategy used by these two countries, belatedly recognized by other developing countries, is technology acquisition. Before the global trend to claim and safeguard intellectual property rights (IPR), developing countries had been practicing reverse engineering of technologies from advanced countries. Other methods used have included joint ventures and licensing agreements with multinationals and even outright purchases of technology. One very effective strategy is through the original equipment manufacturing system, whereby a multinational firm transfers the manufacturing know-how to a firm in a developing country for as long as the local firm is able to produce the product more cheaply. The constraint is that the product is then sold under the multinational's brand name. This strategy was used extensively by both South Korea and Taiwan. They were in a position to do so because they invested

heavily in technical education. The two countries also established government research and training institutions when their own universities were slow to develop needed applied fields.

Later, many of these countries' firms moved up to an original design manufacturing system where the local firm has the freedom to make its own designs based on the overall requirements of the multinational. The last stage of the learning process is original brand name manufacturing, where the local firm can now market a product using its own brand name because the entire manufacturing process is its own.

One major difference between the two countries is that South Korea's economic growth is centered on the development of big business conglomerates, which follows the Japanese development model. Taiwan's strategy is focused on the growth of the small and medium enterprises, which more closely follows the German growth model. But regardless of which sector of the industry they focused their growth on, the two successful countries essentially followed the same strategies of (a) export orientation very early in their independence, (b) effective industrial policy, (c) "getting the basics right," and (d) technology acquisition. The two countries invested in S&T at the same time they were carrying out programs for industrial growth. The investment in S&T paid off when their industries reached the stage of technological sophistication, which required advanced knowledge in the sciences and engineering.

Free Trade, IPR, and Developing Countries

The rest of the developing countries today are faced with both a threat and an opportunity as they strive to improve their economies. The threat comes from free trade and strict IPR protections. Strict IPR will make technologies expensive and difficult to reverse engineer. The free flow of goods and services will make it harder for industries in developing countries to compete with those from the advanced countries. Barriers such as quotas and tariffs can no longer be used to protect local industries. On the other hand, since these defense mechanisms were not used sensibly in the past by many developing countries, resulting in stunted growth for their industries, maybe the reality of open competition will force them to become efficient. Nevertheless, many existing firms will probably not be able to survive.

Strict IPR protections should also make the developing countries learn the sciences and take R&D seriously. This is the opportunity. Advanced countries are quite open with the sciences, with respect to knowledge that is not proprietary. There are many opportunities that developing countries can take advantage of to enhance higher education, as mentioned previously. The Internet also makes it easy to get materials on any topic and to access online journals, databases, and archives of papers. A scientist in a developing country these days is no longer isolated from the rest of his or her professional community. A scholar shielded from the maelstrom of fashionable ideas and who has less in life but does have access to information may just have the best of both worlds—the hungry tradition of the old Renaissance scholars and access to the knowledge that feeds the imagination. Behold, the next major development in the sciences may just come from the developing world.

Jose A. Magpantay

See also Cold War Rhetoric; Science Communication and Indigenous North America

Further Readings

Hobday, M. (1997). *Innovation in East Asia: The challenge to Japan.* Northampton, MA: Edward Elgar.

Inkster, I. (1991). *Science and technology in history: An approach to industrial development.* New Brunswick, NJ: Rutgers University Press.

Sapolsky, H. (1977). Science, technology, and military policy. In I. Spiegel-Rosing & D. de Solla Price (Eds.), *Science, technology and society: A cross-disciplinary perspective* (pp. 443–471). Beverly Hills, CA: Sage.

Teresi, D. (2003). *Lost discoveries: The ancient roots of modern science—from the Babylonians to the Maya.* New York: Simon & Schuster.

Wagner, C. S., Brahmakulam, I., Jackson, B., Wong, A., & Yoda, T. (2001). *Science and technology collaboration: Building capacity in developing countries?* (RAND Science and Technology Report MR-1357.0-WB). Santa Monica, CA: RAND.

NATIONAL INSTITUTES OF HEALTH, U.S.

The U.S. National Institutes of Health (NIH), located in Bethesda, Maryland, is the primary federal agency responsible for conducting and supporting health-related research. The work of NIH scientists has helped prevent disease, improved health outcomes, and saved lives in the United States and across the globe. In 2008, it had a budget of $29 billion and employed 18,000 workers, 6,000 of them scientists. The extensive public information, outreach, and education efforts that are an integral part of NIH activities make sure that news about NIH research is widely publicized.

Improving health care is, indeed, NIH's history. In the 1880s, according to historical records compiled by NIH, Congress had mandated the screening of immigrants arriving in ships from Europe to ports in the United States for cholera and yellow fever. Congress was concerned about epidemics of these diseases spreading from infected immigrants to affect the entire country. Cholera is contracted though drinking contaminated water or eating contaminated food, according to the federal Centers for Disease Control and Prevention. Symptoms include vomiting, dehydration, muscular cramps, and collapse. Yellow fever is transmitted when infected mosquitoes bite humans. Initial symptoms include fever, chills, nausea, and fatigue, followed by more serious effects. Cramped and unsanitary passenger ships were likely breeding grounds for these diseases.

Dr. Joseph J. Kinyoun, a student of famed microbiologist Louis Pasteur and NIH's first director, isolated the cholera virus in a one-room laboratory on Staten Island in 1887 and helped keep it from spreading into New York City. Immigrants arriving at Ellis Island with these diseases were quarantined. Kinyoun's research laid the groundwork for what NIH does today.

On May 26, 1930, President Herbert Hoover signed legislation officially establishing the NIH in downtown Washington, D.C. Soon after, in 1935, Congress approved a 45-acre site in Bethesda for an expanded facility.

As one of 13 agencies within the U.S. Department of Health and Human Services, NIH is composed of 27 centers and institutes that carry out the medical research mission of NIH. For example, these include the National Cancer Institute, the National Eye Institute, and the National Heart, Blood and Lung Institute. Each institute is dedicated to conducting scientific research on a particular disease or a part of the human body, how to reduce people's chances of acquiring disease, or particular health-related societal problems such as drug abuse.

In addition to the work of scientists at NIH headquarters in Bethesda, the agency has awarded nearly 50,000 competitive grants to more than 325,000 researchers at over 3,000 universities and medical schools who are seeking cures for cancer, diabetes, and other health ailments. More than 100 scientists who have worked on NIH projects have received Nobel Prizes. Their medical discoveries are put to use by health care providers, patients, and caregivers. For example, in 1977, it was a group of NIH researchers and collaborators who recommended that women begin getting regular breast exams as an early warning against breast cancer, according to an NIH press release. Twenty years later, new research showed that mammography screenings should be conducted on a regular basis for women in certain age groups.

In fact, NIH-sponsored research has been deemed responsible for the following medical improvements: (a) a decrease in heart and stroke death rates, from 51% in 1975 to 40% in 2000; (b) a 70% decline in the number of AIDS-related deaths between 1995 and 2001; (c) an increase in life expectancy from 47 years in 1900 to nearly 77 years by 2000; and, (d) thanks to vaccines produced by NIH, a reduction in major infectious diseases like whooping cough, rubella, and pneumococcal pneumonia, which used to kill millions.

NIH tackles other health-related issues, too. In June 2009, for example, NIH released a study concluding that school-based prevention programs in elementary school can reduce problem behaviors in students. The study found that fifth graders were almost 50% less likely to engage in substance abuse or violent or sexual behavior if they participated in a comprehensive interactive school prevention program for 1 to 4 years, versus students who did not participate in the program. The study was supported by the National Institute on Drug Abuse, one of the NIH institutes.

Other NIH research grants allow researchers in underdeveloped countries to collaborate with those in developing countries to build research and training centers to prevent and control chronic diseases, such as heart and lung disease and diabetes. As of 2009, the National Heart, Blood and Lung Institute planned to award 10 contracts worth $34 million in the Collaborating Centers of Excellence, or CCOE, network. A CCOE consists of a research institution in a low- or middle-income developing country, which is paired with at least one partner academic institution in a developed country in a collaborative effort to address chronic diseases on a global scale. Bangladesh, China, Guatemala, and India are among the countries where these CCOEs will be established. Heart and lung disease, cancer, and type 2 diabetes account for more than 50% of deaths worldwide, according to the World Health Organization, a United Nations agency that monitors health and shapes health research on a global scale.

Kim Smith

See also Cancer Prevention and Risk Communication; Centers for Disease Control and Prevention, U.S.; Health Communication, Overview; Health Literacy; Public Health Service, U.S.

Further Readings

Centers for Disease Control and Prevention. (n.d.). *What is cholera?* Available at www.cdc.gov/nczved/dfbmd/disease_listing/cholera_gi.html#What is cholera

Centers for Disease Control and Prevention. (n.d.). *What is yellow fever?* Available at www.cdc.gov/ncidod/dvbid/yellowfever/YF_FactSheet.html

Hamowy, R. (2007). *Government and public health in America.* Cheltenham, UK: Edward Elgar.

Leuchtenburg, W. (2009). *Herbert Hoover: The 31st president, 1929–1933.* New York: Henry Holt.

A Short History of the National Institutes of Health: http://history.nih.gov/exhibits/history/index.html

NATIONAL SCIENCE FOUNDATION, U.S.

The National Science Foundation (NSF) was created by the U.S. Congress in 1950 as an independent federal agency with a general mandate to promote the progress of science, particularly in the areas of national health, prosperity, welfare, and national defense. Later on, this federal agency concentrated on areas of basic research in science and engineering, leaving other areas such as health and national defense to different agencies. Today, NSF is the only U.S. federal agency with a mandate to support all nonmedical fields of research. NSF is the most important source of basic science funding in the world, with a budget that by the year 2008 surpassed $6 billion. In the United States especially, a good portion of the scientific progress with which science communicators are most concerned is generated from this investment; in addition, NSF is an important source of background statistics on all areas of science and education, including statistics on science literacy and public understanding of science.

Although the budget for NSF comes from the U.S. Congress, the agency has usually been able to stay away from political turmoil and severe budgetary constraints. In fact, NSF usually garners bipartisan support in Congress, which sometimes funds it with even more money than it requests. Thus, this federal agency has seen its budget increase steadily over the years. That support has increased significantly after events such as the launch of the Soviet satellite *Sputnik* in 1957 and the technological boom of the 1980s. Most recipients of the money NSF grants are America's colleges and universities. Although the NSF budget is less than 5% of the federal budget for research and development, it provides about 20% of the federal money that U.S. academic institutions of higher education receive.

NSF has its headquarters in Arlington, Virginia, and has a staff of about 1,700 employees who are overseen by a director, who works together with a 24-member National Science Board. Both the director and the board members serve for 6-year terms and are appointed by the president of the United States and confirmed by the U.S. Senate. The board meets six times a year to establish the general policies of the foundation.

In addition to funding research in the traditional academic research areas, NSF dollars support less traditional areas considered high-risk, either those pursuing less conventional directions or those representing novel collaborations among people from different disciplines. Sometimes NSF

also supports international ventures. Some NSF funding goes to educational projects in the sciences and social sciences, ranging from public outreach efforts to formal education at all levels—from primary school to postsecondary education.

As part of its mandate, NSF identifies areas of science that need federal funding and establishes programs to address those needs. To that end, NSF constantly gathers information about research activities in the United States and other countries. Among the data they gather and analyze is information about the levels of public understanding of science in the United States and the world, education from the elementary to the postdoctoral level, demographics of colleges and universities both nationally and internationally, research and development in the United States in general, the impact and needs of industry in scientific areas, science-related facilities, and information technologies. Reports by NSF are made public in print as well as in electronic documents through its Web site.

Funding to applicants is generally decided through a complex and highly competitive process that is executed by the directors of the different programs. The process is as follows: (a) NSF announces funding opportunities that include guidelines and deadlines; (b) after the proposals are received, the program director selects a number of external reviewers from U.S. colleges and universities, who submit their recommendations back to the program director; (c) the program director makes a number of recommendations that are submitted to the division director for review; (d) the division director makes a final decision; (e) this decision is reviewed by the Division of Grants and Agreements, which looks into the business, financial, and policy implications of the grant or cooperative agreement; and (f) after the program director negotiates details with the grantees, the final decision is announced.

The merits of the proposal are judged based on a series of criteria that vary from program to program but generally include elements such as the scientific rigor of the proposal, its societal impact, the level of innovation it represents, the background of the investigators involved, and evidence of good planning and budgeting. Based on the availability of funds, the best projects are recommended for funding. Some types of projects can be renewed after the initial funding period.

NSF has given increasing priority to collaborative projects among two or more institutions, particularly if one of those institutions has a sizable representation of ethnic group members from groups historically underrepresented in the sciences. Depending on the specific discipline, gender is also taken into consideration. For example, mathematics and engineering have traditionally had a low representation of women. The same can be said of people with disabilities.

Another area that has received increasing attention by NSF relates to projects that are interdisciplinary in nature, bringing in different perspectives and backgrounds aimed at solving specific problems.

Projects that are aimed at improving public understanding of science among people of all ages, children through adults, as well as more formal education projects, are supported by NSF through a diversity of programs and initiatives. Other awards go to science and engineering infrastructure.

NSF also administers a number of other programs, such as the President's National Medal of Science, the Presidential Awards for Excellence in Mathematics and Science Teaching, the Presidential Early Career Awards for Scientists and Engineers, and the Presidential Awards for Excellence in Science, Mathematics, and Engineering Mentoring.

Aldemaro Romero

See also Big Science; National Academies, U.S.; Science Indicators, History of the NSB Project on

Further Readings

National Science Board, U.S. (2008). *Science and engineering indicators*. Available at www.nsf .gov/statistics/seind08/

National Science Foundation, U.S. (2008). *About the National Science Foundation*. Available at www.nsf .gov/about/

NATURE

Nature is the flagship journal of the Nature Publishing Group (NPG) and is one of the most prestigious scientific journals worldwide. It was founded in 1869 and works editorially independently from its publisher. Like its American counterpart *Science*, the international weekly journal *Nature* publishes important scientific findings from almost every scientific field and is therefore called multidisciplinary. Its original mission statement was revised in 2000 and defines the publication as primarily concerned with "prompt publication" of important results in any scientific field, as well as reports and discussion of news and issues in the world of science.

Nature is ranked among the top 10 of 6,426 listed journals ranked in the *Journal Citation Reports 2007,* provided by Thomson Reuters. *Nature* is not only famous for its papers on basic research, particularly in the life sciences, but also for its news stories on scientific developments and research policy.

The *Nature* Family

Nature's headquarters are in London. The journal's publisher, NPG, is a division of Macmillan, in turn affiliated with the German publishing group Georg von Holtzbrinck. Compared to its main competitor, the society-based journal *Science, Nature*'s print circulation is much lower, yet the trend toward electronic publishing arguably makes circulation figures less significant. In addition, a large number of reputable *Nature* sister journals are published, devoted to special research areas. Currently, the *Nature* family consists of 15 *Nature Research* journals, such as *Nature Genetics,* which was the first and was launched in 1992, *Nature Reviews* journals, *Nature Clinical Practice* journals, and *Nature Protocols,* an online resource for information on scientific protocols. All *Nature* sister journals operate independently. Recently, NPG expanded with new online products in Asia, like *Nature China* and *Nature India*. As bibliometric analyses have shown, *Nature* has a wider international scope than *Science*. In 2007, NPG launched a free preprint server called *Nature Precedings,* which allows an informal exchange among researchers on new preliminary findings.

Role in Science Communication

Nature is considered one of the most relevant journals to science communication for the following reasons: (a) its high impact factor (a measure of citation frequencies and an indicator of scientific relevance), (b) its high circulation, (c) its multidisciplinary orientation, and (d) its professional press service. As announced on its Web site, *Nature* ensures" receive its authors maximum exposure for their work" in the world's mass media, both print and broadcast. Because of its high visibility in the research community and beyond, a publication in *Nature* is very beneficial to scientists for career purposes. Similar to the trend for other high-impact journals, the submissions to *Nature* have slightly increased in the last decade. By its own account, *Nature* received 10,332 submissions in 2007, of which 7.82% were actually published.

Editorial Process

Nature's editors are looking for interesting papers that will have an impact beyond a specific field. Unlike the journal *Science*, *Nature* has no external editorial board. A team of science-trained editors makes all decisions. As submissions are triaged, only a small fraction of submitted manuscripts are sent out for review, while the others are promptly rejected. The decisions about which papers will eventually be accepted are based on the criteria of scientific quality, novelty, and the potential interest of a broad readership. Papers are usually sent to two or three referees. On the basis of the reviews, the final decision on publication is made by the manuscript editor, who is advised by staff members.

The Peer-Review System

A formal peer-review system at *Nature* was initially installed during the editorship of John Maddox in 1967. In a previous era, under the editorship of Jack Brimble, papers were only randomly distributed to scientists for reviewing purposes. As expressed in many editorials, Maddox is known to have given *Nature* a "voice." Due to his experiences as a scientist as well as a newspaper science correspondent, he introduced this twofold perspective on the evaluation of manuscripts.

Just like other scholarly journals, *Nature* has had to deal with published papers that turned out to be fraudulent. Well-known examples are the paper series by the physicist Jan Hendrik Schön and the collaborations of Friedhelm Herrmann and Marion Brach from the biomedical field. In the aftermath of the highly publicized case of fraud in the field of cloning and stem cell research by Hwang Woo Suk and colleagues involving papers published in *Science*, *Nature* began to introduce stricter guidelines on data submission to prevent future transgressions, even though the Hwang events did not directly affect it. One example is the development of a special guideline for papers that deal with cloning. Since 2006, any cloning experiments must be replicated by an independent team before publication.

In June 2006, *Nature* conducted an open peer-review trial to make the peer-review system more transparent and more interactive. The low participation rate of authors and the quality of the public comments on the papers under consideration could not justify further engagement in this direction, however, or so the editors concluded from this experience.

Nature as a Source for Science Journalism

Nature, just like *Science*, is widely seen as a news agency for science journalism. The journal is also divided into a scientific paper section in the back and a news section in the front, which aims to increase the level of general understanding of different fields of science.

Nature, like other high-profile journals, offers a press release service for registered journalists, alerting them to individual papers that will be published in the upcoming issue. The press releases are under strict embargo, and journalists have to accept the embargo or are removed from the mailing list. Violations against the embargo are generally quite rare. One of the exceptions was the famous "Dolly" cloning paper published in 1997, which attracted a lot of attention before its formal publication. While from the journal's point of view, providing the advance information enables journalists to have time enough to investigate their stories thoroughly, the embargo system also has its critics. Vincent Kiernan, for example, argues that the embargo controls the information flow from science to the public improperly and serves primarily to maximize the publicity the journal receives.

Nature and Web 2.0

The Nature Publishing Group has been a pioneer in the application of Web 2.0 technologies, and its

Web services are rapidly expanding. It started with a Web-based daily news program, *Nature News*, followed by *Nature Network* as a social platform, and nowadays provides podcasts and video streams, which since November 2008 are also available on the YouTube Web site. Quite unusual for a scientific journal, *Nature* launched a virtual presence in *Second Life* in November 2006, later developed under the name *Eluician Islands*. A professional online editor organizes seminar series and conferences in this virtual world. *Nature*'s Web site is being transformed into a multimedia platform that attracts scientists (as the primary readership) as well as nonscientists.

Nature's Web site was nominated as the Best Science Web site in the annual Webby awards in 2008. In 2007, both *Nature* and *Science* were awarded the Prince of Asturias Award for Communication and Humanities. Because of its impact on science and the media alike, *Nature*, as well as its competitor *Science*, holds an exceptional position in the world of scientific journals.

Martina Franzen

See also Embargo System; Peer Review; Science; Science in Virtual Worlds

Further Readings

Abbott, A. (2006). Wissenschaft bei einer internationalen Fachzeitschrift I [Science in an international journal I]: Between peer review and a science journalism generator. In H. Wormer (Ed.), *Die Wissensmacher. Profile und Arbeitsfelder von Wissenschaftsredaktionen in Deutschland* [The knowledge makers: Profiles and fields of science editorial departments in Germany] (pp. 299–313). Wiesbaden, Germany: VS Verlag für Sozialwissenschaften.

Ackerson, L. G., & Chapman, K. (2003). Identifying the role of multidisciplinary journals in scientific research. *College & Research Libraries, 64*, 468–478.

Franzen, M. (2009). Torwächter der Wissenschaft oder Einfallstor für die Massenmedien? Zur Rolle von *Science* und *Nature* an der Schnittstelle von Wissenschaft und Öffentlichkeit [Gatekeeper of science or gateway for the mass media? The role of *Science* and *Nature* at the interface of science and the public]. In S. Stöckel, W. Lisner, & G. Rüve (Eds.), *Das Medium Wissenschaftszeitschrift seit dem 19. Jahrhundert. Verwissenschaftlichung der Gesellschaft—Vergesellschaftung von Wissenschaft* [The medium of the scientific journal since the 19th century: Scientific transformation of society—Socialization of science] (pp. 229–252). Stuttgart, Germany: Franz Steiner Verlag.

Garfield, E. (1981). *Nature*: 112 years of continuous publication of high impact research and science journalism. *Current Comments, 40*, 5–12.

Kaneiwa, K., Adachi, J., Aoiki, M., Masuda, T., Midorikawa, A., Tanimura, A., et al. (1988). A comparison between the journals *Nature* and *Science*. *Scientometrics, 13*(3–4), 125–133.

Kiernan, V. (1997). Ingelfinger, embargoes, and other controls on the dissemination of science news. *Science Communication, 18*(4), 297–319.

Maddox, J. (1995). Valediction from an old hand. *Nature, 378*, 521–523.

Nature: www.nature.com

Peer review and fraud. (2006). *Nature* [Editorial], *444*, 971–972.

Standards for papers on cloning. (2006). *Nature* [Editorial], *439*, 243.

NELKIN, DOROTHY (1933–2003)

A sociologist and prolific author, Dorothy Nelkin chronicled the tense relationships among science, technology, and society. With a natural curiosity and the research skills of a social scientist, she explored complex controversies such as creationism, animal rights legislation, and genetic testing. Her research also led to a greater understanding of how the media and scientists shape the public's perception of science and technology. She was the author, coauthor, or editor of 26 books and numerous journal articles. Her writing, known for its journalistic attention to detail and accessible style, found an audience in both the academic and public spheres. Scholars in science studies, bioethics, and the politics of science and technology benefited from her research, and many scientific advisory boards sought her expertise.

Nelkin was born July 30, 1933, in Boston, Massachusetts, and grew up in nearby Brookline. She was the daughter of Henry L. Wolfers, who founded and operated the Henry L. Wolfers lighting company in Boston, and Helen (Fine) Wolfers, a homemaker. Nelkin, the first in her family to attend college, received a bachelor's degree in philosophy in 1954 from Cornell University. There she met her husband, Mark Nelkin, a physicist and university professor. They were married August 31, 1952, and had two daughters, Lisa and Laurie. A homemaker for more than a decade, Nelkin began to pursue her research interests again in 1963, and by 1970, she had published her first book, *On the Season: Aspects of the Migrant Labor System*. Three more books followed the next year.

Nelkin's academic career was unusual in a number of ways. Although she never received formal credentials higher than a bachelor's degree, Nelkin rose to prestigious academic positions at both Cornell and New York University. At Cornell, from 1963 to 1972, she worked as a research associate, and from 1972 to 1989 she advanced through the ranks to become a professor of sociology. Colleagues there credit her with helping to develop the university's Department of Science and Technology Studies. At New York University, where she began teaching in 1990, she was a professor of sociology and an affiliated professor of law. At the time of her death, she held that school's highest rank of university professor. Another unique aspect of Nelkin's career was that her scholarship crossed typical academic boundaries. She was educated in the social sciences and humanities but at ease in the world of science. She unabashedly tackled scientific topics, whether AIDS or biotechnology, with the same intellectual zeal she brought to social issues. She had entered the academic world of the 1960s with considerable deficits: being female, having stayed home to raise children, and lacking a graduate degree or background in many of the areas she researched. Yet succeed she did.

As she gained a reputation as an international scholar, she increasingly became involved with work on editorial boards of journals in sociology, law, science studies, and public health and on the boards of scientific organizations. In particular, she was a member of the founding editorial board of the journal *Public Understanding of Science*, a founding member of the Society for the Social Studies of Science, a fellow of the American Association for the Advancement of Science, and a member of the National Academy of Sciences' Institute of Medicine. She received Guggenheim and Russell Sage Fellowships, respectively, in 1983 and 1984. She was an adviser to the federal government's Human Genome Project and a supporter of the National Center for Science Education. In 1981, she testified for the plaintiffs in the highly charged *McLean v. Arkansas Public Board of Education* case involving the teaching of creationism in the public schools.

When asked during that court case to explain her work, Nelkin said that controversies intrigued her. She explained that they let her study how people use science to articulate their arguments and to legitimize their claims. She also said her work often began with a sense of sympathy for people worried that scientific research threatened their values.

Much of Nelkin's work reflects this sensitivity to a public that is increasingly disenchanted with decisions requiring scientific or technological assessments in which they have little opportunity to participate. In her early research, she studied the rights of migrant workers and the location of nuclear power plants in the United States and Europe, along with many other issues. Her book *Science Textbook Controversies: The Politics of Equal Time* (1977) questioned why the movement to teach creationism in the schools should re-emerge during a time when science enjoyed such widespread credibility.

With *Selling Science: How the Press Covers Science and Technology* (1987), Nelkin turned her attention to the packaging of science news. In this influential science communication history, Nelkin wrote that journalists and scientists share the blame for poor science reporting in which imagery trumps content. She found that metaphors of war and competition dominated many science stories, a fact that caused her to question if such dramatic accounts add to the public's perceiving scientists with awe and reverence, not healthy skepticism. She noted that journalists announce many scientific discoveries with excessive optimism but dismiss others initially considered negative as laboratory monsters. As always, Nelkin was interested in the social context in which individuals operate, and in this book she analyzed the internal culture of the fields of journalism and science. She explained that both professions share a reverence for objectivity. However, journalists' work is hampered by competition, deadline pressures, and assumptions about audience interest. Scientists, many of whom enjoy considerable commercial support, seek positive press to garner more research dollars. Thus, their well-oiled public relations apparatus and their tendency to suppress information about risks contribute to the public's lack of understanding of science. Although others had studied science journalism before her, Nelkin provided the big picture, one that illustrated how individual institutional needs shape what the public learns about science.

Later in Nelkin's career, her focus shifted to biotechnology topics. In *Dangerous Diagnostics: The Social Power of Biological Information* (1989), Nelkin and coauthor Lawrence Tancredi warned of the potential for employers and health care insurers to abuse information gained from genetic tests. Other books sounded alarms about the medical market for human tissue by medical researchers and the societal trend to view human behavior as solely determined by genes.

Nelkin reported complex science issues in a way that reviewers have described as engaging, thoughtful, and captivating. Her unceasing curiosity and daunting work ethic inspired students and scholars alike. Nelkin, a lifelong observer of the interactions between science and the public, provoked much-needed debate on timely topics.

Ellen J. Gerl

See also Newspaper Science Pages; Public Understanding of Science; Scientist–Journalist Relations

Further Readings

Lindee, M. S. (2004). Obituary: Dorothy Nelkin (30 July 1933–28 May 2003). *New Genetics and Society, 23*(2), 131–135.

Nagourney, E. (2003, June 2). Dorothy Nelkin, 69, expert on science and society, dies. *The New York Times*, p. A16.

Nelkin, D. (1995). *Selling science: How the press covers science and technology* (Expanded ed.). New York: W. H. Freeman. (Original work published 1987)

Raymond, J. G. (2001, April 11). The body business. *The Washington Post*, C9.

NEWSPAPER SCIENCE PAGES

Newspapers, especially daily newspapers, organize their content into separate sections. Common sections include local news, business, sports, and lifestyle. Some sections appear daily, while others may appear on a weekly or biweekly basis. Organizing newspapers into sections serves several purposes, including facilitating reader navigation of the material. People interested primarily in business coverage or sports news can turn directly to those pages. Newspapers are able to sell advertising into these separate sections to help advertisers reach a specialized and engaged audience. For example, home and garden sections are common weekly segments, and newspapers can sell ad space in that section to companies that wish to market products—from lumber to lawn services—to an interested, involved audience. Organizing content into sections also allows newspapers to highlight content and promote particular coverage areas. Science, health, and technology sections are among the weekly sections often featured in daily newspapers. However, the number of those sections is on the decline as newspapers struggle with declining advertising and declining profits.

In 1978, the *New York Times* launched a separate section for science news called *Science Times*. Other newspapers followed. In 1986, a survey by the Scientists' Institute for Public Information found that 66 other daily papers had weekly science sections and another 80 had science pages. But after reaching its height in the mid-1990s, the number of papers with science sections has fallen. The falloff has not been limited to smaller papers; the top 20 circulation papers like the *Dallas Morning News* and the *Boston Globe* have dissolved their science sections. The decline in science news sections has been traced to a decrease in retail computer ads in the late 1990s and to a general decline in media revenue—and subsequent cutbacks and staff layoffs—since the early 2000s.

A multiyear study of the *Science Times* section found that the size of the section grew in the 1980s and early 1990s, reaching a peak average size of 9 pages in 1995, but that the average size had decreased to 7 pages by 2000. However, the amount of science content increased despite a decrease in the number of total pages. The loss in total page size was a result of a sharp decrease in advertising, going from an average of 6 pages to an average of 2 pages. Computer retailers accounted for 95% of the advertising in the *Science Times* between the mid-1980s and the mid-1990s. By

2000, a little over half of the ads in *Science Times* were computer related, and health-related ads had climbed to 46.5%.

Effect on Science Coverage

Early critics of separate science sections and pages argued the sections would lead to the "ghettoization" of science news, concentrating science coverage in the weekly section and stripping science news from the remainder of the newspaper. The argument was that this ghettoization of science news would actually reduce a general reader's exposure to science news, since a reader could choose to skip the special section altogether. However, a study of papers with science sections found that papers that instituted science sections show improved coverage of science issues throughout the newspaper, nearly doubling the amount of science coverage in some cases. As might be expected, newspapers with science sections publish more science news than newspapers without separate sections. Yet the presence of a science section affected more than the bottom-line number of stories. The newspapers with science sections were found to increase the number of stories and the length of those stories in other, non-science sections of the paper as well as increase the number of illustrations included with science stories throughout the newspaper.

The other effect that science pages have had on overall newspaper coverage of science is in the depth and breadth of coverage. Newspapers, especially in the United States, tend to print more medicine and health news with less emphasis on other science, engineering, and technology topics, with limited coverage of basic research. One criticism of science coverage in general has been the overemphasis on consumer-oriented health news and the de-emphasis of important scientific developments outside of medical news. In newspapers with science pages, medicine and health stories still account for the largest segment of stories, especially in the general news sections, but they provide more coverage of the less common science topics such as technology and basic research.

Future

Declining numbers of science sections do not bode well for the future of science journalism at U.S. newspapers or for the coverage of science in general. While the introduction of science sections expanded science coverage and improved the depth, breadth, and presentation of science news in daily newspapers, the deletion of a science section is likely to lead to a corresponding decline in the amount and quality of coverage. Science news coverage does not currently reflect the variety and extent of scientific inquiry in the United States, and the move toward fewer science sections certainly will not help remedy this problem. Cutting science sections often goes hand-in-hand with the layoff of veteran science reporters. Increasing numbers of science journalists work as freelancers or for online publications. Ironically, the migration of science news to the Internet has raised fears that science news will be further ghettoized, with people who are interested in science news turning to specialty Web sites but general news readers being exposed to fewer and fewer science stories.

Long term, the decrease in the news hole devoted to science news and the cutting of experienced science reporters will affect not only how national science stories are covered but also, more immediately, the coverage of local science news. The wire services and the remaining daily science sections will still cover major scientific stories, but other stories—once produced by regional reporters—covering "local" research efforts and specific community-based scientific concerns will not come to fruition, leaving several significant holes in the coverage of science.

S. Camille Broadway

See also Audiences for Science; Beat Reporting; Career Paths, Science/Environmental Journalism; Popular Science, Overview; Scientists Institute for Public Information

Further Readings

Bader, R. (1990). How science news sections influence newspaper science coverage: A case study. *Journalism Quarterly, 67*(1), 88–96.

Clark, F., & Illman, D. L. (2006). A longitudinal study of the *New York Times* Science Times section. *Science Communication, 27*(4), 496–513.

Cornell, J. (2009, July). The rise and fall—and possible rise again—of science journalism. In B. Gallavotti

(Chair), *Communicating energy.* Symposium conducted at the meeting of the First International School of Scientific Journalism and Communication, Erice, Italy. Available at www.internationalsciencewriters.org/sicily.htm

Dawson, J. (2002, Fall). The devolution of a science page. *Nieman Reports,* 16–17.

Pinholster, G., & O'Malley, C. (2006). EurekaAlert! Survey confirms challenges for science communicators in the post-print era [Comment]. *Journal of Science Communication, 5*(3), 1–12.

NIMBY ("Not In My Back Yard")

NIMBY ("Not In My Back Yard") is an acronym describing opposition to something newly proposed for the neighborhood of the opponent. Synonyms include NIMBYism and the NIMBY syndrome. The opponents themselves are often referred to as NIMBYs, less often as NIMBYists. Understanding NIMBY dynamics can be important to communicators who want to understand public reactions to controversial planning decisions involving technology and environment.

Print use of NIMBY dates back only to 1980, when the term appeared in the *Christian Science Monitor.* By then it was already in widespread use at angry public meetings. The phrase NIMBY is intrinsically pejorative, keeping company with adjectives like *irrational* and *selfish.* Only proponents of a development refer to its opponents as NIMBYs. This entry, however, will use the term without the pejorative subtext.

Good for the World, Bad for the Neighborhood

The purest, most literal example of the NIMBY attitude is opposition to something that virtually everyone (including the opponents) agrees ought to be built somewhere, but virtually everyone would prefer not to live near. Examples include airports, jazz clubs, superhighways, slaughterhouses, prisons, and wind farms. These are all developments that offer significant benefits to the overall community at the expense of their nearest neighbors. They bring with them noise, odor, pollution, traffic, crime, or other undesirable side effects. Opposing them is certainly not irrational, though it is demonstrably selfish (that is, rationally self-interested).

Rutgers University Planning Professor Frank J. Popper coined the term LULU (Locally Unwanted Land Use) to refer to developments of this sort. His 1981 article "Siting LULUs," published in the journal *Planning,* had a major influence on planning professionals. Unlike NIMBY, LULU isn't pejorative; the term captures the reality that some projects are genuinely good for the world but bad for the neighborhood. That's probably why it did not catch on the way NIMBY did. In the contentious environment of siting controversies, there wasn't much demand for a neutral term.

Developments that are good for the world but bad for the neighborhood tend to get built in the end. The big question is how and where such developments are sited. The following are among the options:

1. *Oppression.* In the normal course of events, LULUs end up in neighborhoods too weak to oppose them successfully. That usually means poor neighborhoods and often means minority neighborhoods. The environmental justice movement is thus inextricably tied to the NIMBY concept. In 1987, the United Church of Christ's Commission for Racial Justice published a landmark study entitled "Toxic Wastes and Race in the United States," concluding that race—even more than income—determined what communities ended up with hazardous waste sites. Few would argue that the leaky and poorly regulated "hazwaste" facilities of the past were "good for the world," but they were surely bad for the neighborhood—and they tended to wind up in predictable neighborhoods.

2. *Market mechanisms.* A variety of market mechanisms have been devised as possible replacements for oppression. A "reverse Dutch auction," for example, requires the siting authority to "buy" the site from whichever community offers the lowest "selling price." Market siting is voluntary by definition; communities that do not bid are assured

of not getting the development. Like oppression, market mechanisms usually end up putting LULUs in neighborhoods with desperate needs, simply because their price is likely to be lower than the price of affluent neighborhoods. But at least they are paid their price.

3. *Greenfields development.* Because rich neighborhoods have the power and poor neighborhoods have the moral high ground, siting authorities sometimes try to put LULUs in nobody's neighborhood. That does not usually work very well either. For one thing, greenfields are increasingly hard to find, especially if the development in question needs to be near population centers and infrastructure. And ruining pristine territory is hardly the ideal solution. Nor is it guaranteed to succeed; in many places the constituency for protecting untouched land is nearly as powerful as the constituency for protecting affluent neighborhoods.

4. *LULU trade-offs.* People who have thought hard about siting often wind up proposing some sort of scheme to balance which neighborhoods get which LULUs. If you accept the airport, you get a pass on the power plant and the prison. Some have described elaborate point systems, grounded in empirical data on how undesirable people say various LULUs actually are. Neighborhoods that exceed the point quota are out of the running for new LULUs (perhaps even if they want one—thus preventing poor neighborhoods from selling their quality of life the same way we prevent poor people from selling their organs). Neighborhoods below the quota are vulnerable.

It is not that hard to come up with a combo that makes sense: LULU trade-offs to determine which neighborhoods are fair game; a market mechanism to choose among the neighborhoods that are below the point quota; a special dispensation to keep pristine land pristine. But nobody has come up with a way to turn such ideas into public policy. The dominant LULU siting strategy today is still oppression: coercing the weak.

Oppression isn't working as well these days as it once worked; the weak are less weak than they used to be. One result, for better or worse (or both), is that many LULUs languish without a site for decades. This may offer reason to hope that a better way—better for the world *and* for the neighborhood—will eventually replace oppression as the siting strategy of choice.

Bad for Everybody

Often, opponents of a controversial development have objections that go beyond the concept of Not In My Back Yard. Opposition to nuclear power plants and hazardous waste incinerators, for example, is grounded in the view that these technologies are fundamentally flawed, that they should be abandoned altogether. Some have tried to popularize the acronym NIABY (Not In Anybody's Back Yard) to emphasize that these are not simply NIMBYs.

There is nothing disreputable about the straightforward NIMBY position. Neighborhoods are entitled to try to protect themselves from becoming unwilling National Sacrifice Areas for the benefit of others. But stopping developments that one considers bad for the world as well as the neighborhood is a different and higher priority. Calling NIABYs NIMBYs is not just insulting, it is inaccurate as well.

Often the two impulses are merged. National and international organizations that are opposed to putting X anywhere help organize neighbors who are opposed to putting it here. The locals learn the global principles; some come to believe them fervently, while others parrot them for tactical reasons.

Both NIMBY and NIABY, by the way, are politically diverse phenomena. Opponents of casinos and abortion clinics express the same mix of local dismay and global disapproval as opponents of power plants and incinerators. In fact, most of the environment-focused literature on NIMBY and related phenomena dates back to the 1990s or earlier; the literature from the 2000s is primarily about the difficulty of siting low-income apartment developments, psychiatric halfway houses, and the like.

Like LULU, NIABY has not caught on because it is not pejorative. But there's a pejorative exaggeration of NIABY that has gained currency among developers: BANANA (Build Absolutely Nothing Anywhere Near Anybody).

Between NIMBY ("I approve of X in principle but I don't want it here") and NIABY ("I disapprove of X anywhere") is a range of motives without unique acronyms. Some of the important ones:

- *I disapprove of something else that will be facilitated by X.* Opponents of nuclear power, for example, have wisely opposed Nevada's radioactive waste repository. If there is no place to put the waste, it will be harder to site new plants and maybe even to keep existing ones open. This position is likely to masquerade as, and merge with, NIABY. Opponents of a "radwaste" repository do not have to say whether they oppose it for its own sake, as a stand-in for nuclear power, or both.

- *I disapprove of the particulars of this version of X.* A good one might be okay, but opponents object to cutting corners, building a sloppy one. NIMBYs and NIABYs alike point out defects in the particulars of the proposal at hand. They often fail to stop it but succeed in remedying some of its defects, thus making it a whole lot better and safer. That may have been their goal in the first place, or it may be a fallback position, or they may see it simply as defeat.

- *I disapprove of how many X's you're building and how hurriedly you're building them.* We may need some X's eventually, but we haven't exhausted Y and Z yet, and they should come first. Throughout the 1980s and 1990s, opponents of landfills advanced a variety of NIMBY and NIABY arguments. But their strongest argument, in hindsight, was the value of source reduction and recycling as ways of reducing waste and thus landfill demand. By stopping landfill after landfill, they bought time for better solutions (not to mention better landfills).

- *I disapprove of where you chose to put your X.* We simply should not put a nuclear plant in an earthquake zone or a hog farm near a residential neighborhood. NIMBYs invariably make this claim: It is not that it is my neighborhood; it is just the wrong neighborhood. And coercive siting, as opposed to market siting, justifies the claim. When a siting authority spends years evolving elaborate criteria for finding the very best location to put an X, and finally chooses my backyard, it gives me both ammunition and motivation to claim that the criteria were wrongly chosen, or that they were wrongly weighted, or that they were wrongly applied . . . and someplace else is actually the best location.

- *I disapprove of your process.* Someone is accused of telling when they should be asking.

The last bullet point—process—needs elaborating. Imagine a homeowner pulling into their driveway after a long day's work and noticing that there are strangers picnicking in their backyard. "Get out of my backyard!" they demand. "Why?" the strangers inquire. "We've done a site analysis. Your backyard is a prime location for our picnic. And we've done a risk assessment. Our picnic is unlikely to do any significant permanent damage to your backyard." They did not ask permission; they did not invite the homeowner to the picnic; they will not even tell them exactly what they are eating. Odds are the homeowner is pretty steamed.

Of course, in this example, it is literally *your* backyard that is in question. Owners have a legal right to forbid trespassing on their own property. The principle is slightly different when it is not necessarily a backyard owned by an invaded individual that is in question; it might be the developer's property but someone else's neighborhood and community. But the feeling of being invaded by outsiders is much the same.

This is the key legitimacy battleground that underlies many NIMBY controversies. Should newly acquired land in a community be seen as *the owner's* land or as *the residents'* community? How should we reconcile individuals' right to do what they want with their land against a community's right, collectively, to control the future of the community? There is a long tradition of balancing the two: Zoning laws, for example, apportion rights in both directions. And the process is intentionally and appropriately political. When people fight a political fight to stop something they do not want in their neighborhood, they are acting in the best democratic tradition—whether it is a hazardous waste dump or an abortion clinic that they are opposing. But the community is not always supposed to win either; democracies do sometimes exercise coercion. Still, the best response to process objections is voluntary siting.

Rights, Substance, and Outrage

In any siting controversy, three conflicting rights are at stake: the right of developers to do what they want with their land; the right of neighborhoods to control what developers do in their neighborhood; and the right of the larger community (city, state, country) to constrain the neighborhoods' control or, in other words, to coerce the neighborhoods for the greater good.

This conflict takes place in the context of substantive disagreement over whether the development in question is wise or unwise—whether it is good or bad for the neighborhood and whether it is good or bad for the larger community. And it takes place in the context of outrage. Quite apart from the rights of the parties and the wisdom of the development, coercive siting arouses more outrage than voluntary siting. Similarly, unfair siting arouses more outrage than fair siting. A market mechanism is both more voluntary and more fair than oppression—but even a coercive process can at least be made fairer by compensating the victims of the coercion for the burdens they are being forced to bear. A variety of other outrage factors (control, trust, dread, responsiveness, and so on) also influence the likelihood and strength of the NIMBY response.

In most cases, in fact, neighborhood opposition to LULUs—that is, NIMBY—is fueled chiefly by outrage. When outrage is high, neighborhood opponents are driven to assert their rights. They bolster their assertion of rights by claiming that the development in question is substantively unwise, that it is bad for the neighborhood and/or bad for the world. These substantive claims may be correct or mistaken—or they may be grounded more in opinions and values than in science, and so "correct" and "mistaken" may be the wrong categories. But however strong or weak the substantive arguments local opponents deploy, their urge to fight usually results more from outrage than from substance.

Those who seek to stop a development they consider substantively unwise should therefore try to manage local outrage upward, thus triggering a more vigorous NIMBY response. Those who seek to consummate a development they consider substantively sound should try to manage local outrage downward, thus muting the NIMBY response. A smart opponent underlines how arrogant, unaccountable, and sleazy the developer is; a smart developer works to be humble, accountable, and honest.

When it comes to NIMBY, rights are usually divided. Substance is usually debatable. Outrage is usually what determines the outcome.

Peter M. Sandman

See also Community "Right to Know"; Environmental Impact Statements; Environmental Justice

Further Readings

Lesbirel, S. H., & Shaw, D. (Eds.). (2005). *Managing conflict in facility siting*. Cheltenham, UK: Edward Elgar.

Popper, F. J. (1981). Siting LULUs. *Planning, 47*(4), 12–15.

Popper, F. J. (1992). The great LULU trading game. *Planning, 58*(5), 15–17.

Sandman, P. M. (1986). Getting to maybe: Some communications aspects of siting hazardous waste facilities. *Seton Hall Legislative Journal, 9*, 437–465. Available at www.psandman.com/articles/seton .htm

Sandman, P. M. (1992, July). Siting controversial facilities: Some principles, paradoxes, and heresies. *Consensus, 2.* Available at www.psandman.com/ articles/siting.htm

Nuclear Power

After scientists at the end of the 19th century began exploring the composition of matter, it didn't take them long to realize the enormous energy contained within atoms—as summed up in Albert Einstein's equation $E = mc^2$ (energy equals mass times the speed of light squared). Early on, scientists speculated that the release of such energy could result in the most powerful explosions ever created. They also predicted that, if controlled, the released energy could be used to power vehicles or make electricity. In 1904, for example, British chemist Frederick Soddy declared that a ship could make a round-trip voyage from England to Australia fueled by the energy in a pint of uranium. As nuclear energy production continues to be controversial and to appear regularly in the news media, this entry is designed to provide some of the context and background needed to understand the current status of this endeavor.

The first significant use of nuclear energy came in the form of the atomic bombs the United States tested in July 1945 and dropped on the Japanese cities of Hiroshima and Nagasaki the following month as World War II came to an end. Those latter two bombs, one created by splitting the atoms of uranium and the other those of plutonium, killed an estimated 210,000 people immediately and in the short term. While the uranium was produced by a process called *enrichment,* which will be discussed in further sections, the plutonium was created as a *by-product* of the operation of uranium-fueled nuclear reactors and was then separated from other residual products and manufactured into bombs. After World War II, nuclear reactors were used for many years only for plutonium bomb production as the nuclear arms race developed between the United States and the Soviet Union and then their allies.

Scientists soon figured out how the uranium-fueled reactors could produce electricity as well as bomb material, so they created dual-use reactors. The Soviets introduced a small dual-use reactor in 1954, and the British put their first dual-use reactor online in 1956 to produce plutonium and generate electricity for public use. The next year at Shippingport, Pennsylvania, the United States began operating the world's first nuclear power plant dedicated to electricity production. This reactor was a larger version of a reactor design employed by the Westinghouse Electric Corporation to build nuclear-powered submarines, the first of which—the *Nautilus*—was launched by the U.S. Navy in 1955.

Civilian Nuclear Plants

During the 50 years between civilian nuclear power's advent in 1957 until the end of 2007, some 558 nuclear power plants were constructed around the world. And during that period, 119 of those reactors were permanently shut down, including Shippingport after 25 years of operation, with most turned into nuclear waste, according to International Atomic Energy Agency (IAEA) figures. Some plants—notably the Chernobyl reactor unit 4 in Ukraine that suffered a gas explosion in 1986—were closed after accidents, and others had operational problems, but most simply became obsolete. The projected life span of a nuclear plant can vary country by country. In the United States, for example, the federal Nuclear Regulatory Commission (NRC) licenses plants for 40 years and has extended the licenses another 20 years for many plants.

In 2008, 30 countries operated 439 nuclear power plants with a production capacity of some 372,000 megawatts, equivalent to about 16% of the world's electricity consumption. With 104 nuclear reactors, the United States is the world's largest nuclear operator, but meets just 20% of its high electricity demand with nuclear power. France, with 59 reactors, comes in second in total production, but those plants supply 78% of the country's electricity. Japan has the third largest number of reactors with 55 in operation. Throughout the world, in 2008, another 35 nuclear plants were under construction, including 7 in Russia, which operates 31 reactors; 6 in India, which already has 17 nuclear plants; and 6 in China, with 11 nuclear reactors operating, according to the IAEA. (In addition, 56 countries operate 284 small research reactors, military reactors are run by some of the world's 9 nuclear weapons states, and more than 200 reactors propel submarines and ships.)

It is unclear whether the 2008 nuclear reactor construction activity signifies a reversal in the fortunes of nuclear power. Many countries, with the notable exception of France, went into a holding pattern regarding this source of electricity after the partial meltdown of the Three Mile Island reactor in Pennsylvania in 1979 and the Chernobyl disaster of 1986. Indeed, some countries, including Italy and Germany, renounced nuclear power, with Germany vowing to shut down its reactors (17 in 2008 producing 28% of the country's electricity) by 2021. In most countries, negative public attitudes, coupled with weak economic performance, left the nuclear industry limping along. But that started changing in about 2005, when the reality of global warming entered the picture.

Global Warming and the New Nuclear Debate

A few scientists began warning in the 1980s that human activities, particularly the burning of fossil fuels such as oil in motor vehicles and coal in power plants, were pumping carbon dioxide and other greenhouse gases into the atmosphere and trapping so much heat that the earth was warming at a dangerous rate. Public awareness of the issue grew gradually and was then jolted in 2004 when several prominent environmentalists long opposed to nuclear power declared that the global warming threat was so dire that nuclear power was needed to address it. Among them was James Lovelock, the British environmentalist who had propounded the hypothesis that Earth is a self-regulating organism, which he dubbed *Gaia*. Global warming is "the greatest danger" civilization has ever faced, he wrote in an editorial for *The Independent* newspaper in May 2004. He argued that although renewable energy could contribute a little to the solution, nuclear energy is "the only immediately available source" that would not result in further warming.

The nuclear industry and other advocates of this technology were thrilled by the endorsement from Lovelock and some other environmentalists, although most environmental organizations remained opposed to nuclear power. The advocates stepped up their discussion of a nuclear "renaissance," as can be roughly indicated by the number of times the term occurs in a computer search of the LexisNexis database of major world publications. While the term appeared in article headlines just 8 times in 2005, it appeared 17 times in 2006 and 24 times in 2007. The nuclear proponents considered their stance bolstered by increasing evidence that human behavior was the major factor in the warming climate picture. In 2007, thousands of scientists from around the globe issued the strongest predictions yet about global warming in four reports produced by the Intergovernmental Panel on Climate Change.

Proponents of nuclear power argue (correctly) that, unlike burning fossil fuels such as coal, nuclear power generation does not create greenhouse gases. And they said that worldwide demand for electricity, projected by the International Energy Agency to grow 30% to 50% by 2030, required large nuclear power plants to meet global demand. Opponents countered that nuclear power should not be considered part of the solution to global warming for several reasons, including the arguments that an expansion of nuclear power would increase the risk of nuclear weapons proliferation, that nuclear waste problems had not been resolved, that dangers exist from accidents or terrorist attacks, and that the money and public subsidies provided to the nuclear industry could be better spent on renewable technologies.

The Nuclear Fuel Cycle: Where Power and Weapons Converge

In trying to sort out the facts from the rhetoric in the debate over nuclear power, it is important to have a basic understanding of uranium and the nuclear fuel cycle—the steps involved in taking uranium from the ground, using it to produce electricity or weapons, and dealing with the waste material.

Uranium is a dense, silver-gray metal that is the heaviest of the 92 naturally occurring elements found on Earth. Thus, a uranium atom has an atomic number of 92, which reflects the number of protons in its nucleus as well as the number of electrons surrounding the nucleus. An element's atomic weight equals the protons plus the number of neutrons in the nucleus. Natural uranium found in the Earth's crust is comprised principally of two atoms designated by their atomic weight—uranium 238, which makes up about 99.3%, and uranium 235, which makes up about 0.7 of 1%. Uranium 235 is the uranium atom of interest for nuclear power production because it is fissile, meaning that it can split (or fission) and sustain a chain reaction. In a nuclear reactor, the energy released during the fissioning of uranium 235 atoms is used to heat water and create steam, which through turbines is turned into electricity. As explained in the following paragraphs, uranium 235 is one of two elements used for nuclear weapons.

Mining is the first step in the nuclear fuel cycle. While natural uranium exists in many countries around the world, in 2007, Canada was the largest producer; and Australia, followed by Kazakhstan, held the largest deposits, according to the Australian-based Uranium Information Centre (UIC). The amount of uranium in the surrounding rock also varies, with some rich deposits containing percentages in the teens, but other ore containing as little as 0.1% uranium. The ore is shipped to a mill where it is processed to extract the uranium, creating uranium oxide (commonly known as yellowcake), usually containing more than 80% uranium. The yellowcake is shipped to a conversion plant that turns it into a gas called uranium hexafluoride, a form of the element needed for enrichment.

Uranium enrichment is the stage where nuclear power and nuclear weapons developments first converge. That's because both require higher concentrations of the uranium 235 atoms for the chain reactions that in one case create power and in the other create nuclear explosions. The uranium hexafluoride gas resulting from the conversion process is suitable for separation into uranium 238 and uranium 235 atoms. The most modern way to accomplish the separation is with highly sophisticated cylindrical centrifuges whose rapid whirring propels the slightly heavier uranium 238 atoms to the outside walls while leaving the lighter uranium 235 atoms in the center to be collected. The uranium atoms are sent through banks of hundreds of centrifuges for months-long time periods until the desired concentration of uranium 235 of 4% to 5% for nuclear power plant fuel or about 90% for nuclear bombs is achieved. Experts say the bulk of the enrichment task is completed in getting the uranium 235 to the 4% level, which makes any uranium enrichment plant a concern with regard to its bomb-making potential. A prime example is the dispute over Iran's enrichment facility, which the country's leaders say is solely for civilian purposes but the United States and other countries say could be used for bomb making.

Low-enriched uranium hexafluoride gas designated for power plants is converted back into a solid uranium oxide form and then sent to a fuel fabrication facility. There it is pressed into ceramic pellets, baked at high temperatures, and then encased in metal tubes known as "fuel rods." The thin, finger-sized fuel rods, which can be about 12 feet tall, are placed into fuel assemblies that, depending on the reactor, can hold from a few dozen to a few hundred rods. The reactor at a nuclear power plant initiates a controlled chain reaction, and when the uranium 235 atoms split, their energy turns water into steam that drives an electricity-generating turbine.

The chain reaction in the reactor is the second place where nuclear power and nuclear weapons can converge, as indeed they do in dual-use reactors. The Chernobyl plant, for example, was just such a dual-use reactor. Such duality occurs because during the chain reaction, some of the uranium 238 is turned into plutonium 239, an element with atomic number 94 that, like uranium 235, is fissile and thus usable for nuclear bombs. Physicists employ a rule of thumb calculating that the fissioning of 1 megawatt in a uranium reactor produces 1 gram of plutonium per day. Using current figures, then, the 439 reactors operating in the world produce about 372 kilograms of plutonium a day, more than 15 kilograms each hour. But the plutonium created in the fuel rods is mixed with uranium 238 and some unfissioned uranium 235, as well as other elements created during the fission process.

Fuel rods are used in reactors for various amounts of time. In reactors aimed at producing plutonium for weapons, the fuel rods are usually left in only a few months to minimize the creation of too much undesirable fission product material; in strictly civilian power reactors, the rods can be left in for up to 2 years. The used fuel, known as spent fuel, is then removed. If the plutonium in the spent fuel is to be used in bombs or reused as reactor fuel, it must first be separated from the other material in a reprocessing plant. Such plants are operated by countries possessing nuclear weapons, the most recent of which is North Korea, which operated a secret reprocessing facility to create a handful of nuclear weapons.

Under initiatives designed to impede nuclear weapons proliferation, Presidents Gerald Ford and Jimmy Carter successfully pushed for a 1979 ban on reprocessing U.S. civilian spent fuel. Today that ban is being challenged by some pronuclear advocates. They point out that several other countries, including France, the United Kingdom, Russia, and Japan, possess reprocessing capabilities enabling them to separate out plutonium and reuse it as mixed oxide fuel for reactors. The plutonium normally replaces the uranium 235 in such fuel. But civilian spent fuel in the United States is considered high-level waste and is designated for permanent disposal. To date, however, disagreements have prevented the Yucca Mountain waste site in Nevada from opening. Countries that do reprocess spent reactor fuel still end up with high-level waste needing disposal. No country has, as yet, opened a permanent disposal site for high-level waste.

Pros and Cons of Nuclear Power

Many advocates of nuclear power acknowledge problems with the technology but argue that the threat of global warming is so great that nuclear power must be embraced, at least for the time being. Stewart Brand, the founder of the progressive *Whole Earth Catalog* in 1968, made that point in a May 2005 article for *Technology*

Review. "Nuclear certainly has problems," he wrote, ranging from accidents to the storage of waste, the cost of construction, and the potential for weapons use. But he considers the problems solvable, including proliferation. To stop weapons from proliferating, he suggested that the international community set up a reactor fuel supplier that would take back spent fuel for processing, which he described as an idea that could "go from 'Impractical!' to 'Necessary!'" in short order, as a result of world events. World events, the reality of nuclear "haves" and "have-nots," and countries' perceptions of their own interests have so far hindered that approach and similar ones offered by others. Iran, for instance, flatly rejected proposals that it leave uranium enrichment to other supplier countries, even its putative ally Russia.

Nuclear power opponents typically point to Chernobyl in warning that a growth in the number of nuclear reactors around the world could lead to serious accidents, caused by either problematic technology or operator error. Proponents note that no Chernobyl-type reactors are being built today, that no sizable accidents have occurred since 1986, and that modern reactors, such as those using the pebble-bed design, are considered inherently safe from reactor core meltdowns. Pebble-bed reactors, whose cores consist of several hundred thousand tennis-ball-sized "pebbles" made of 4% uranium, are one of several Generation IV nuclear reactors under development. Skeptics, such as former NRC commission member Peter A. Bradford, say that the nuclear industry continually claims that fail-safe reactors are right around the corner.

Similarly, nuclear proponents and opponents square off on the issues of nuclear waste and the threat of terrorism. Physicist Brice Smith summed up the state of the overall debate in an interview in the November/December 2007 issue of the *Bulletin of the Atomic Scientists,* arguing that the risks of nuclear power "are rivaled only by climate change" in their complexity and in the challenges of addressing them, adding that the risk of nuclear technology also involves its expense.

And nuclear reactors are expensive. A typical 1,000-megawatt reactor in the United States, which generates enough electricity to supply 4 million to 10 million American homes (depending on the part of the country, use of appliances like air conditioners, and the actual operating time of the reactor), costs between $2.5 and $4 billion to build, according to many experts. But cost overruns can occur anywhere, such as in the case of a French-built reactor under construction in Finland estimated to cost $2.3 billion in 2002, a figure that has doubled (even without figuring in the declining value of the U.S. dollar in Europe).

Another factor to consider is the number of nuclear reactors needed to make a significant impact in reducing global warming. To address that question, it is necessary to distinguish between electricity generation and other energy consumption that produces greenhouse gases. For example, an April 2008 report from the U.S. Environmental Protection Agency concludes that U.S. electricity generating plants, primarily coal-fired plants, account for 41% of the country's carbon dioxide emissions. But vehicle use accounts for 33% of the carbon dioxide emissions, with over 60% of those emissions attributed to gasoline consumption by personal vehicles.

Former NRC commission member Bradford argued in an October 2006 talk that even tripling worldwide nuclear power production with new plants constructed at a 15% annual growth rate over the next 50 years would be unable to provide more than 10% to 15% of the necessary displacement of greenhouse gases. He said that when retirements of old nuclear power plants are put into the equation, the current annual growth rate of nuclear reactors is only about 5%. Moreover, Bradford argued that a large increase in nuclear power plants would have to be accompanied by the construction of an additional 15 uranium enrichment plants, the equivalent of 14 Yucca Mountain waste repositories, and possibly reprocessing plants. He cited estimates by the Natural Resources Defense Council that such a ramping up of the nuclear power industry would cost between $2 and $3 trillion. He maintained that such a sum could go a long way toward supporting the development of much less risky renewable sources of energy.

Len Ackland

See also Chernobyl; Climate Change, Communicating; Nuclear Waste; Nuclear Weapons; Three Mile Island

Further Readings

Brand, S. (2005). Environmental heresies. *Technology Review, 108*(5), 60–64.

Deutch, J., Moniz, E. J., Ansolabehere, S., Driscoll, M., Gray, P. E., Holdren, J. P., et al. (2003). *The future of nuclear power: An interdisciplinary MIT study.* Cambridge, MA: Report for Massachusetts Institute of Technology. Retrieved January 1, 2009, from http://web.mit.edu/nuclearpower/pdf/nuclearpower-full.pdf

Garwin, R. L., & Charpak, G. (2001). *Megawatts and megatons: A turning point in the nuclear age?* New York: Knopf.

Lovelock, J. (2004, May 24). Nuclear power is the only green solution. *The Independent.*

Makhijani, A. (2007). *Carbon-free and nuclear free: A roadmap for U.S. energy policy.* Takoma Park, MD: IEER Press.

Rezek, J. (2007). Interview: Brice Smith. *Bulletin of the Atomic Scientists, 63*(6), 22–27.

Weart, S. R. (1988). *Nuclear fear: A history of images.* Cambridge, MA: Harvard University Press.

Nuclear Waste

More than 20 years after the U.S. Congress in 1987 designated Yucca Mountain in western Nevada as the sole geological repository for used, or spent, American nuclear reactor fuel and high-level nuclear waste, the repository still hasn't opened. Ongoing media coverage of nuclear waste issues generally, and the Yucca Mountain proposal specifically, builds on a long history of controversy and a host of complex technical arguments. While billions of dollars have been spent in constructing the underground site at Yucca Mountain, Nevadans have charged that it would endanger the state's health and safety along with imperiling people in states through which the waste would be shipped by rail or highway. And in late 2007, Senate majority leader Harry Reid of Nevada succeeded in having the Department of Energy's (DOE) Yucca Mountain budget cut by $108 million, leading to layoffs among the site's 2,400 workers.

In the meantime, more than 54,000 metric tons of spent nuclear fuel has been generated by U.S. nuclear reactors, according to the federal U.S. Nuclear Regulatory Commission (NRC). And more than 90 million gallons of high-level waste from the country's nuclear weapons program also await disposal. All of this waste contains highly radioactive elements, such as plutonium, cesium, and neptunium. With no permanent destination available, the waste is being temporarily stored at the country's 104 operating nuclear reactors, at designated off-site facilities, and at DOE nuclear weapons sites. While government and nuclear industry officials say the temporary storage poses no problems, nuclear power opponents argue that the lack of permanent waste disposal is a major reason that this source of electricity should be abandoned. Moreover, with the capacity of Yucca Mountain legislatively set at 70,000 metric tons, the site is likely to be filled shortly after its opening, now projected at 2018—although opponents say it will never open.

The lack of a high-level nuclear waste repository in the United States, which operates the largest number of nuclear power plants in the world, is mirrored by the other 29 nations operating a total of 335 reactors. Even France, which generates 78% of its electricity with 59 reactors, is still studying the environmental consequences of disposing of high-level waste in underground clay deposits at its Bure laboratory in northwestern France. While French legislation called for a permanent disposal site to be opened in 2006, that year the decision was delayed another 10 years. And Finland, constructing what is considered by some to be the most sophisticated underground repository, won't open the facility until 2020, at the earliest. The waste from the cores of nuclear reactors is just one of the radioactive by-products from the various ways humans use energy from the nuclei of atoms.

Categories of Nuclear Waste

Nations put nuclear wastes into categories to establish appropriate waste-management rules while at the same time protecting human health. The United States, for example, makes certain distinctions based on whether the waste originated from the manufacture of nuclear weapons or from commercial activities, including nuclear power. In France, the categories are based on the type of radiation and an element's radioactive half-life, the time period in which half of an unstable (radioactive) material emits particles (decays) and turns into a more stable material. For example, plutonium 239—used to make nuclear bombs—has a half-life of about 24,000 years.

Nuclear enterprises of all sorts begin with the mining of uranium from the earth's crust and then milling it to extract the uranium from the ore. The two major applications of uranium are for nuclear weapons and nuclear waste, and the production stages and by-products are described as the nuclear "fuel cycle." The nuclear stages will vary, of course, for other applications of nuclear technology, such as in medicine, but radioactive waste of some kind results from most stages.

This entry will use the U.S. categories to illustrate the different types of nuclear waste and how they are handled. The waste in each category, as well as the total amount of waste and its radioactivity, are difficult to calculate because of the different measures used and the range of activities performed, such as mining or reprocessing the fuel from nuclear reactors. Essentially, however, the majority of the radioactivity in nuclear waste resides in the spent fuel and the reprocessing waste from weapons production. The majority of the volume comes from mine and mill tailings and low-level waste.

Uranium Mining and Milling Waste

Uranium and the elements created as it undergoes half-life decay can create health and environmental hazards. In the western United States, in particular, the leftover ore from uranium mining can be found in many areas. The U.S. Environmental Protection Agency (EPA) estimated in a 2006 report that the waste from surface uranium mining ranges from 1 to 8 billion metric tons, while that from underground mining ranges from 5 to 100 million metric tons. The broad estimates for the hazards presented by mine tailings underscore how little attention has been paid until recently. Recent media articles about the health consequences of uranium mine tailings on Navajo land, followed by congressional hearings in 2007, have focused some attention on this issue. Yet by early 2008, little cleanup of mine tailings had been done.

Uranium mill tailings resulting from the processes that create "yellowcake," containing at least 80% uranium, have higher concentrations of radium and also pose risks from the radioactive radon gas created when it decays. The hazard from tailings has been recognized for some time and falls under the Uranium Mill Tailings Radiation Control Act of 1978. The tailings are estimated to exceed 260 million tons. An exceptionally large pile—16 million tons located on 130 acres on one bank of the Colorado River near Moab, Utah—is being relocated as part of the federal government's tailings cleanup. Modern uranium mines are often in situ facilities, which greatly reduce the amount of tailings waste because they drill wells into rock formations and use liquids to dissolve the uranium into groundwater that is pumped to the surface. Tailings piles at the sites hold waste from this process.

Low-Level Radioactive Waste

NRC classifies low-level waste that doesn't result from uranium milling into a complex system of four categories (A to C and greater than C), with class A considered the least radioactive. Low-level wastes can include contaminated gloves and clothing used by nuclear workers, carcasses of laboratory animals containing radioactive material, and some decommissioned equipment from nuclear weapons production facilities. Individual states are responsible for low-level waste under the 1980 Low-Level Radioactive Waste Policy Act, and most states formed compacts to develop regional facilities. In 2007, three facilities existed: one in Barnwell, South Carolina; one in Hanford, Washington; and the most active, EnergySolutions (formerly Envirocare) in Clive, Utah. The total low-level waste being stored at these sites exceeds 475 million cubic feet. Of 4 million cubic feet and 530,000 curies of low-level radioactive waste disposed of in 2005, 3.9 million cubic feet went to EnergySolutions, according to NRC figures.

By summer 2008, EnergySolutions, which lies 85 miles west of Salt Lake City and runs a square-mile disposal site for radioactive and toxic waste, will be the only low-level waste site still accepting deliveries, according to an April 2008 article by Judy Fahys in the *Salt Lake Tribune*. Early in 2008, the privately owned company, which imports some waste from overseas, stirred controversy with its plans to import 20,000 tons of waste from dismantled Italian nuclear reactors.

Transuranic Waste From Nuclear Weapons Production

Transuranic (or TRU) waste is waste containing elements such as plutonium and neptunium with atomic numbers (the number of protons in the nucleus) greater than uranium's 92. This waste was created during the production of U.S. nuclear weapons. Around 250,000 cubic meters of this waste is estimated to have been created. The government's permanent disposal site near Carlsbad, New Mexico, is called the Waste Isolation Pilot Plant (WIPP). It opened in March 1999 and accepts shipments from other nuclear weapons sites. The bulk of the waste was produced at the now-demolished Rocky Flats bomb plant near Denver, Colorado, which processed plutonium and made it into nuclear bombs used primarily to detonate thermonuclear weapons. By April 2008, WIPP had stored some 58,000 cubic meters of transuranic waste more than 1,000 feet underground in salt formations. Over time, the natural movement of salt will encase the waste.

High-Level Waste From Weapons Production

Producing radioactive materials, including plutonium, for U.S. nuclear weapons resulted in 53 million gallons of radioactive waste stored in 177 huge refinery-like tanks at the Hanford site in southeastern Washington State and 37 million gallons in 49 tanks at the Savannah River plant in South Carolina. The government's main military nuclear reactors operated at those two sites. DOE estimated in 2006 that cleanup at Savannah River would be completed in 2025 for $32.1 billion and at Hanford in 2035 for $60 billion. The Hanford cleanup is widely regarded as the most challenging in the weapons complex.

High-Level Waste From Civilian Reactors

Ceramic uranium pellets contained in thin metal tubes called fuel rods and arranged by the hundreds in assemblies—like bowling pins in frames—make nuclear reactors work. As the uranium 235 atoms making up 4% to 5% of the fuel rods split (fission), energy released in the process heats water to steam for turbines that generate electricity. But the chain reactions also transform the uranium 238 in the fuel rods into plutonium and other fission products so that the rods are not practical to use after a period of 1 to 2 years and must be removed from the reactor. This used, or spent, fuel contains an estimated 95% uranium 238, 1% plutonium, 1% unfissioned uranium 235, and 3% highly radioactive fission products. The spent fuel is typically put into a storage pool at the nuclear power plant so the radiation levels can dissipate. After a period of months or years, the fuel is removed.

In some countries, such as France, the fuel rods are reprocessed to separate out the plutonium and uranium for further use. But in the United States, where civilian reprocessing is currently not allowed, the used fuel is treated as high-level waste. NRC has designated the pools as one of two acceptable methods of storage. The other method is to store the fuel in dry storage casks. The storage sites are licensed by the NRC and can either be on the reactor site or off-site.

The agency currently licenses independent storage installations in 30 states. One of those sites, on Goshute Indian tribal land in western Utah, has been extremely contentious. Private Fuel Storage (a consortium of eight utilities) plans to store 40,000 metric tons of spent fuel in 4,000 casks on Goshute land. After the NRC approved the license in early 2006, the Interior Department objected. The state of Utah also opposed the storage facility, which has been the subject of lawsuits. Opponents of the site express the concern that the temporary storage there could become permanent due to the fight over Yucca Mountain mentioned at the beginning of this entry.

Future Nuclear Waste

Concern about nuclear waste and nuclear weapons proliferation are seen as two of the biggest challenges facing the nuclear power industry's growth plans. But the nuclear waste problem will grow even if no more nuclear power plants are built. That's because the 439 reactors now operated by 30 countries will continue producing spent fuel as well as low-level nuclear waste for as long as they operate. It will need to go somewhere. Then when the plants are shut down and demolished, they will become waste. If the so-called nuclear renaissance does take place, the waste issue will be even greater.

Len Ackland

See also Chernobyl; Nuclear Power; Nuclear Weapons; Three Mile Island

Further Readings

Ackland, L. (2002). *Making a real killing: Rocky Flats and the nuclear west* (2nd ed.). Albuquerque: University of New Mexico Press.

Long, M. E. (2002). Half life: The lethal legacy of America's nuclear waste. *National Geographic, 202*(1), 2–33.

Smith, B. (2006). *Insurmountable risks: The dangers of using nuclear power to combat global climate change.* Takoma Park, MD: IEER Press.

U.S. Nuclear Regulatory Commission: www.nrc.gov

Nuclear Weapons

The material power of nuclear weapons is universally recognized, but their communicative power is equally extraordinary. The strategist Carl von Clausewitz argued that war is fundamentally a social activity, a form of persuasion guided by rules of grammar more than by strict logic. He also took pains to distinguish between the abstract concept of "absolute" or "ideal" war and the inevitable particularity of "real" war. Both of those insights apply to nuclear weapons viewed as devices of communication; that is, both *products* and *instruments* of communication.

Nuclear weapons could not have arisen without two kinds of organized communication: the organized inquiry of Big Science and the organized production of 20th-century industry. Those two institutions emerged at a historical moment that led to their application, at an unprecedented scale, to the invention of the most destructive weapons ever created. The threat of a Nazi nuclear weapon that motivated this invention had disappeared by the time it came to fruition, but it was nonetheless used on Japan. Some historians argue that the primary reason for that use was communicative: to make a statement to the Soviet Union about U.S.

military power. Other commentators, such as the physicist Robert Oppenheimer, have noted that the use of such "technically sweet" inventions seems inevitable once they become possible.

Irrespective of these controversial claims, the subsequent history of the cold war is largely one of intentional and accidental communication though the medium of nuclear weapons. The U.S.–Soviet arms race operated through a grammar of threats, responses, and counterresponses and through a vocabulary of weapons systems, force deployments, and strategic postures. The highly rationalized models of defense strategists, which guided this dangerous conversation, may represent the closest approximation yet to Clausewitz's ideal war. Meanwhile, the horrific scenarios and moral objections offered by critics and protesters sought to capture the implications of a real nuclear war. The "nuclear criticism" movement that emerged in the 1980s was founded on the principle that nuclear extinction is the ultimate symbol, a "transcendental signifier" that organized all other aspects of society and culture. Accordingly, the literary critic Alan Nadel argues that the cold war principle of "containment" extended beyond the U.S. policy directed at the Soviet Union to a parallel containment of social norms, roles, values, and practices in the name of national security.

Many scholars of the cold war argue that it persisted for four decades without another use of nuclear weapons because the conversation was relatively simple, with two principal actors who shared an understanding of its grammar and vocabulary. Throughout that period, the number of players in the "nuclear club" stayed small, with their roles subordinated to those of the two superpowers. Nuclear communication played out within that framework around topics including arms control, nuclear testing, civil defense measures, and missile defense systems. Across those areas, communication scholars have examined practical and theoretical questions from a range of perspectives, including presidential rhetoric, negotiation and conflict management, public discourse, and the rhetoric of science and technology.

The grammar, vocabulary, and scope of the nuclear conversation changed with the end of the cold war. New nations have now joined the nuclear club, while others threaten to do so, seeking to communicate their status as modern players on the world stage. New concerns have emerged about nonstate actors' access to nuclear technologies, as nuclear commerce becomes globalized and nuclear knowledge disseminates. Meanwhile, the material and communicative legacies of the superpowers' commitment to nuclear weapons have become more evident, from environmental and public health damages to compromises of democracy made under the umbrella of nuclear secrecy.

Four interrelated themes interact and appear consistently in nuclear discourse. *Mystery,* an almost religious sense of awe, surrounds the forces of nature on which these weapons are based and the scientists who harness those forces. The material and symbolic *potency* of nuclear weapons is unparalleled. *Secrecy* pervades their development and deployment and much of nuclear policy making. *Entelechy,* or presumed inevitability, seems to have guided their invention and proliferation and threatens to guarantee their eventual use again in the future. More than six decades after their invention, nuclear weapons still set a standard of fear that drives international relations, national security policies, and military budgets across the world. Fears of global terrorism and the proliferation of weapons of mass destruction almost invariably culminate in visions of nuclear mushroom clouds. From the cold war "doomsday machine" of Stanley Kubrick's fictional Dr. Strangelove to the "smoking gun" feared to be immanent in Saddam Hussein's Iraq, the messages communicated by nuclear weapons are as powerful as the weapons themselves.

William J. Kinsella

See also Manhattan Project; Oppenheimer, J. Robert; Physicians for Social Responsibility; Teller, Edward; Union of Concerned Scientists

Further Readings

Chernus, I. (1986). *Dr. Strangegod: On the symbolic meaning of nuclear weapons.* Columbia: University of South Carolina Press.

Kinsella, W. J. (2005). One hundred years of nuclear discourse: Four master themes and their implications for environmental communication. In S. L. Senecah (Ed.), *Environmental communication yearbook* (Vol. 2, pp. 49–72). Mahwah, NJ: Erlbaum.

Nadel, A. (1995). *Containment culture: American narratives, postmodernism, and the atomic age.* Durham, NC: Duke University Press.

Ruthven, K. (1993). *Nuclear criticism.* Carlton, Australia: Melbourne University Press.

Taylor, B. C. (1998). Nuclear weapons and communication studies: A review essay. *Western Journal of Communication, 62*(3), 300–315.

Taylor, B. C., Kinsella, W. J., Depoe, S. P., & Metzler, M. S. (Eds.). (2007). *Nuclear legacies: Communication, controversy, and the U.S. nuclear weapons complex.* Lanham, MD: Lexington.

Weart, S. (1989). *Nuclear fear: A history of images.* Cambridge, MA: Harvard University Press.

NUTRIGENOMICS

The 1953 discovery of the DNA double helix marked a new beginning in understanding the genetic basis of inheritance and, more recently, the Human Genome Project exponentially advanced our knowledge about genetic factors that shape a broad group of diseases. These advances facilitated the advent of genetic testing, which is currently available for over 1,200 medical conditions. The plethora of information that became available has many health-related implications and regularly receives extensive media attention, but news stories often appear with little background to help the reader understand the significance of the various concepts.

In addition to identifying a large number of genes relevant for human disease, sequencing of the human genome revealed an interesting fact: It became apparent that any two unrelated individuals are 99.9% identical at the DNA level. The remaining 0.1% represents sites of variation, also known as single nucleotide polymorphisms (SNPs). Approximately 3.1 million SNPs were identified throughout the human genome, and some estimates predict that their actual number is approximately 10 million. These sites are particularly important, as they are thought to explain why individuals respond differently to the same nutrients and environmental chemicals or why, in different individuals, very different adverse effects to the same medication are observed.

As genetic factors are linked to increasing numbers of disease predispositions and inherited traits, it is essential to remember that most conditions are not simply determined by our chromosomes but shaped by complex interactions between genetic and environmental influences. The environment comprises a very diverse group of factors, including nutrients, smoking, alcohol, medications, microorganisms, radiation, chemicals, and social influences, all of which affect the way we develop and impact our susceptibility to disease. In other words, our genes are not our destiny. Of the many environmental influences to which humans are invariably exposed throughout their lives, food intake is thought to exert the most influential impact on diseases.

The importance of nutritional intake for human health has been recognized throughout history and in many different societies. With recent analyses estimating that 33% of the world's adult population was overweight or obese in 2005, and that by 2030 this number could exceed 57%, the nutritional sciences are expected to increasingly emerge as a public health focus. At the convergence between nutritional science and genomics, two new fields, nutrigenetics and nutrigenomics, are being shaped; while the two terms are often used interchangeably, *nutrigenetics* investigates how discrete genetic variations such as SNPs affect individual responses to specific dietary compounds, while *nutrigenomics* focuses on understanding how food components modulate changes in the gene expression profile of an individual.

Nutrients and the Human Genome

Nutrients interact with the human genome in a bidirectional fashion. Food constituents not only provide energy but shape gene expression by complex mechanisms, and, at the same time, our individual genetic makeup influences our nutritional choices. By examining interindividual differences in the response to dietary compounds, nutrigenomics promises to explain how nutrients shape the gene–environment interactions in complex disorders such as obesity, type 2 diabetes mellitus, cardiovascular disease, and cancer, and opens the way toward the era of personalized nutrition. While many previous studies investigated the relationship between single genes and specific nutrients, nutrigenomics opens the possibility of exploring interactions that simultaneously involve several nutrients and multiple genes, under a variety of

conditions, a scenario that more accurately reflects events occurring in live organisms.

For certain metabolic conditions, genetic testing can help suggest dietary interventions that, if implemented early, are lifesaving. Phenylketonuria is perhaps one of the most frequently mentioned gene–nutrient interactions. In this metabolic condition that affects 1 in 10,000 newborn infants, deficiency of the enzyme phenylalanine hydroxylase leads to elevated blood levels of the amino acid phenylalanine, which is toxic to the nervous system and causes severe brain damage and delayed physical development. No cure is currently available, but restricting phenylalanine from the diet soon after birth can prevent these complications.

A more complex scenario is familial hypercholesterolemia, an inherited metabolic condition that affects over half a million people in the United States and over 10 million individuals worldwide. In this condition, mutations in the gene encoding the low-density lipoprotein (LDL) receptor cause a reduced uptake of LDL cholesterol ("bad cholesterol") from the plasma, and the resulting increased circulatory LDL levels predispose these individuals to cardiovascular disease and stroke. Over 700 mutations in the LDL receptor gene have been described, and even individuals harboring the same mutation sometimes exhibit different clinical manifestations. A study that examined individuals from several generations of affected Utah families carrying mutations in this gene revealed that four men born before 1880 lived between 62 and 81 years, while their great-grandsons died of coronary disease at an average age of 45. This points toward the importance of environmental factors, such as diet and lifestyle, in addition to the mere presence of a mutation, in shaping the disease.

A relevant example illustrating how genetic information can guide dietary choices comes from studies of methylenetetrahydrofolate (MTHFR), the enzyme responsible for generating the major form of circulating folic acid (vitamin B_9). A single base pair substitution in MTHFR changes cytosine (C) to thymine (T), replacing the amino acid alanine with valine in the resulting protein, and this change has been linked to increased risk for neural tube defects, neuropsychiatric conditions, and cardiac malformations. MTHFR polymorphisms have also been implicated in colon cancer. Individuals harboring this mutation in a homozygous form (when both copies of the mutated gene are present in their chromosome), called the TT genotype, have a 30% to 40% lower risk for colorectal cancer when these individuals consume adequate amounts of folic acid but face increased risk when dietary folic acid intake is insufficient. Genetic testing can reveal the presence of this polymorphism and thus inform understanding of individual dietary folic acid requirements, allowing for appropriate dietary intervention.

Another interesting example is provided by fish oil, long appreciated for its cardioprotective benefits. Most recently, considerable interindividual variations in LDL cholesterol, ranging from a 40% decrease to a 113% increase, were observed in a group of subjects in response to dietary fish oil. Several genes were implicated, the apolipoprotein E (ApoE) gene being one of them. The ApoE protein is a central player in lipid metabolism, and two SNPs are involved in creating three major variants or isoforms, E2, E3, and E4, of which E4 confers higher risk for Alzheimer's disease and cardiovascular conditions. This gene recently found itself in the middle of a controversy when the same isoform was shown to predict the severity of brain damage subsequent to head trauma, opening controversial discussions about the possibility of predicting future damage in individuals who practice sports with high risks for head injury.

Ethical and Legal Implications

As the previous example demonstrates, mutations implicated in one medical condition may, at the same time, be informative about predispositions to additional conditions or risks. With increasing amounts of genomic data becoming available, it is crucial to focus on how to interpret the findings in the most accurate and meaningful manner. Recent surveys predict that by 2010, 33% of U.S. consumers might collect and use nutrigenomic information, suggesting that this topic is poised to become an increasingly important health communication issue. Unveiling gene–diet links provides opportunities for increased awareness and active surveillance as well as allows interventions such as nutritional changes, more frequent screenings, or differing reproductive choices.

At present, insufficient information is available to explain how particular mutations are linked to

disease predisposition, and this leads to a discrepancy between the expanding volume of information and our ability to understand its significance. There are instances when the same polymorphism is associated with up to seven different conditions. For example, in the case of MTHFR, described previously, the same polymorphism has been linked to venous thrombosis, schizophrenia, depression, gastric cancer, stroke, and coronary artery disease and can represent a risk factor or a protective one, depending on the particular condition. Moreover, a particular polymorphism may be just one of many variations connected to the same condition. For example, 52 genes that belong to several pathways are in some way linked to type 2 diabetes mellitus, and 14 of these have been confirmed by at least four studies, with more associations expected as additional research is conducted. At the same time, genes that appear to be associated with a specific condition in one population are not necessarily relevant in other populations, and extreme caution is necessary when interpreting the data; for example, genetic factors linked to rheumatoid arthritis have been reported to differ between Caucasian and Korean individuals examined to date.

Our limited ability to understand genomic information becomes particularly important when considering the direct-to-consumer availability of genetic tests relevant to nutrigenomics. Approximately 30 companies are estimated to have commercialized health-related direct-to-consumer genetic tests, which provide the results directly to consumers and, in many instances, do not involve health professionals and/or counseling in this process. One study reported that of 56 genes that 7 companies used for SNP testing, 24 were not reviewed in the literature. The published SNP–disease associations were statistically significant for only 38% of the remaining 32 genes and, even in those, only to a moderate extent. Another study examined 24 companies offering direct-to-consumer genetic tests and reported that, compared to diagnostic tests (for example, to unveil a Tay-Sachs disease carrier state) or predictive tests (for example, to examine the risk for conditions such as breast cancer or Huntington's disease), the commercialization of nutrigenetic tests reduced the likelihood of requiring physician involvement and provision of pre- or posttest counseling.

In 2006, the U.S. Government Accountability Office (GAO) purchased direct-to-consumer genetic tests from four Web sites and submitted DNA samples from several individuals for analysis, creating fictitious profiles based on different lifestyle and personal characteristics. The investigation reported that the tests were misleading and made claims that are medically unproven and ambiguous, such as informing consumers that they "may" be at increased risk for heart disease. In addition, most recommendations were not based on personalized genetic profiles, but represented general health advice, and two of the Web sites recommended, based on the test results, expensive personalized supplements that GAO reported to be similar to antioxidants and vitamins sold at much lower prices in stores. One Web site recommended an expensive supplement that can "repair damaged DNA," even though no product with such an effect is currently known, based on medical and scientific findings. These examples underscore the need for strong and active regulatory oversight.

It is essential to appreciate that most genetic tests are not true diagnostic tools but have a predictive value and are simply informative about disease susceptibility over an individual's lifetime. In this context, public education is fundamental and needs to emphasize that for most medical conditions, the final outcome will be shaped by a complex interplay between genes, their context within the organism, and environmental influences, an interaction that Richard Lewontin describes in his book so appropriately entitled *The Triple Helix* (2002).

Richard A. Stein

See also Gene; Human Genome Project; Toxicogenomics

Further Readings

Bergmann, M. M., Gorman, U., & Mathers, J. C. (2008). Bioethical considerations for human nutrigenomics. *Annual Review of Nutrition, 28,* 447–467.

Genuis, S. J. (2008). Our genes are not our destiny: Incorporating molecular medicine into clinical practice. *Journal of Evaluation in Clinical Practice, 14*(1), 94–102.

Geransar, R., & Einsiedel, E. (2008). Evaluating online direct-to-consumer marketing of genetic tests: Informed choices or buyers beware? *Genetic Testing, 12*(1), 13–23.

Godard, B., & Ozdemir, V. (2008). Nutrigenomics and personalized diet: From molecules to intervention and nutri-ethics. *OMICS, 12*(4), 227–229.

Government Accountability Office. (2006). *Nutrigenetic testing: Tests purchased from four Web sites mislead consumers.* Accessed September 4, 2009, from www.gao.gov/products/GAO-06–977T

Janssens, A. C., Gwinn, M., Bradley, L. A., Oostra, B. A., van Duijn, C. M., & Khoury, M. J. (2008). A critical appraisal of the scientific basis of commercial genomic profiles used to assess health risks and personalize health interventions. *American Journal of Human Genetics, 82*(3), 593–599.

Jongbloet, P. H., Verbeek, A. L., den Heijer, M., & Roeleveld, N. (2008). Methylenetetrahydrofolate reductase (MTHFR) gene polymorphisms resulting in suboptimal oocyte maturation: A discussion of folate status, neural tube defects, schizophrenia, and vasculopathy. *Journal of Experimental and Clinical Assisted Reproduction, 5*(5), 5–12.

Kaput, J., Noble, J., Hatipoglu, B., Kohrs, K., Dawson, K., & Bartholomew, A. (2007). Application of nutrigenomic concepts to type 2 diabetes mellitus. *Nutrition, Metabolism and Cardiovascular Diseases, 17*(2), 89–103.

Kelly, T., Yang, W., Chen, C. S., Reynolds, K., & He, J. (2008). Global burden of obesity in 2005 and projections to 2030. *International Journal of Obesity, 32*(9), 1431–1437.

Lau, F. C., Bagchi, M., Sen, C., Roy, S., & Bagchi, D. (2008). Nutrigenomic analysis of diet-gene interactions on functional supplements for weight management. *Current Genomics, 9*(4), 239–251.

Lee, H. S., Korman, B. D., Le, J. M., Kastner, D. L., Remmers, E. F., Gregersen, P. K., et al. (2009). Genetic risk factors for rheumatoid arthritis differ in Caucasian and Korean populations. *Arthritis & Rheumatism, 60*(2), 364–371.

Lewontin, R. (2002). *The triple helix: Gene, organism and environment.* Cambridge, MA: Harvard University Press.

Lovegrove, J. A., & Gitau, R. (2008). Nutrigenetics and CVD: What does the future hold? *Proceedings of the Nutrition Society, 67,* 206–213.

Ordovas, J. M., & Corella, D. (2004). Nutritional genomics. *Annual Review of Genomics and Human Genetics, 5,* 71–118.

Ries, N. M., & Castle, D. (2008). Nutrigenomics and ethics interface: Direct-to-consumer services and commercial aspects. *OMICS, 12*(4), 245–250.

Savulescu, J. (2005). Compulsory genetic testing for APOE Epsilon 4 and boxing. *Genetic Technology and Sport, 1*(4), 136–146.

Williams, R. R., Hasstedt, S. J., Wilson, D. E., Ash, K. O., Yanowitz, F. F., Reiber, G. E., et al. (1986). Evidence that men with familial hypercholesterolemia can avoid early coronary death: An analysis of 77 gene carriers in four Utah pedigrees. *Journal of the American Medical Association, 255*(2), 219–224.

NUTRITION AND MEDIA

The media play a significant role in bringing nutrition information to the American public. This entry describes how the media influence food-related behaviors and how health professionals can use media to communicate nutrition issues to the public.

The media influence how Americans think and feel about food in relation to politics, culture, and health. Media help to form and to communicate cultural norms and images around nutrition, provide avenues for nutrition education, and create channels for food advertising and product promotion. Nutrition information has been communicated via a variety of media, including print, radio, television, and the Internet.

Media Effects on Health

The mass media exert both positive and negative effects on individuals and populations. The media may provide information on nutrition related to health conditions, such as those available on health Web sites or newspaper and magazine health columns, and this information can have positive benefits for those who receive and understand the information. Media may also convey negative health messages, such as promotions for sugary cereals and drinks, especially those targeted to children.

Food Advertisements and Commercial Marketing

Americans see tens of thousands of food advertisements every year. The majority of these advertisements promote unhealthy foods and beverages. In 1997, food companies reportedly spent $11 billion dollars on advertising alone. The large amount of food advertising and commercial marketing in the media influences eating and shopping behaviors in children and adults.

Evidence exists that commercial food marketing can decrease elementary school children's ability to differentiate healthful products from nonhealthful ones. Commercial food marketing also impacts children's food preferences; a number of studies have shown that food advertising influences children's food selection, either in school or at the grocery store.

Children's food preferences, molded by advertising, influence the purchasing and eating habits of their family. Research has shown that the amount of time a child spends watching television is a predictor of how often they request a food at the grocery store.

Food content in television shows and movies can also have an impact on adult and child eating behavior. High calorie–low nutrient food choices are much more likely to be advertised on television and in the movies, encouraging consumers to eat a diet that contributes to diabetes and obesity. One study found that foods high in fat and sugar are disproportionately shown over fruits and vegetables in high-grossing films.

Media and Body Image

The media greatly influence American norms around physical attractiveness. Obese or overweight television characters tend to be portrayed as unpopular and unsuccessful, while thin characters are portrayed as having positive characteristics. There are fewer overweight and obese characters on television than exist in real life, and nearly a third of women on television are underweight. Although researchers have not found a direct association between television viewing and eating disorders, studies have shown that increased exposure to media is associated with higher levels of body dissatisfaction.

Media to Promote Nutrition Information

Using the media to raise public awareness, widely disseminate nutrition education messages, and advocate for changes in public policy have proven to be useful strategies.

Social Marketing

Using techniques such as market research, product positioning, pricing, physical distribution, and promotion, social marketing programs seek to influence nutrition behavior to improve individual health.

Several social marketing campaigns have focused on promoting healthy eating. For example, the national Project LEAN campaign promoted low-fat eating through public service announcements (PSAs) and various other communication channels. Findings from the campaign indicated that PSAs in combination with other public relations and communication strategies generated media attention and awareness of the importance of low-fat eating. The "California Children's 5 a Day—Power Play!" is a social marketing campaign aimed at increasing fruit and vegetable consumption among children and their families. The campaign promoted fruits and vegetables through media in schools and neighborhoods and was able to increase the number of children believing they should consume more fruits and vegetables as well as achieve a slight increase in reported fruit and vegetable consumption.

While social marketing campaigns have shown some effect in promoting healthy eating and activity in children who have not yet formed habits, success of social marketing interventions with adults has been limited.

Media Advocacy

The focus of a media advocacy campaign is to set the agenda and shape the public debate to include policy solutions in news coverage of nutrition issues. Media advocacy targets policymakers, advocates, and community members who can become active in the political process of making change. Media advocacy has been used to advocate for policy change in schools and neighborhoods to increase access to healthy foods and reduce access to high calorie–low nutrient foods. Media advocacy differs from other types of health communication because it seeks to change the social, physical, or policy environment surrounding individuals, rather than seeking to change individual behavior.

Because most nutrition issues are complicated and deeply imbedded in social organization and behavior routines, they require long-term and evolving communications strategies. Promoting good nutrition requires motivations for individuals to adopt healthy eating behavior; social marketing campaigns may help inform them about the most effective ways to do that. But to be successful, people will have to find affordable access to healthy food, conditions that will require policy change in many communities. Media advocacy is likely to be a very useful tool to help nutrition advocates make the case to policymakers for those policies.

Regulating Food Marketing in the Media

Policy strategies to address the role of media in promoting particular foods are under consideration in Congress and state legislatures across the country. For example, Senator Tom Harkin of Iowa introduced legislation in May 2005 that would, among other provisions, restore the authority of the Federal Trade Commission to regulate the advertising and marketing of food and beverage products to children. Increasing the understanding of the impact of both the new and old media on children may provide further avenues for intervening to protect and promote child health and wellness.

Lisa Craypo, Sally Lawrence, and Sarah Samuels

See also Center for Science in the Public Interest; Communication Campaigns in Health and Environment; Health Communication and the Internet; Health Communication, Overview

Further Readings

Alcalay, R., & Bell, R. (2000). *Promoting nutrition and physical activity through social marketing: Current practices and recommendations.* Sacramento: University of California, Davis, Center for Advanced Studies in Nutrition and Social Marketing.

Center for Science in the Public Interest. (2003). *Pestering parents: How food companies market obesity to children.* Retrieved July 12, 2009, from www.cspinet.org/pesteringparents

Dorfman, L. (2008). Using media advocacy to influence policy. In R. J. Bensley & J. Brookins-Fisher (Eds.), *Community health education methods: A practical guide* (3rd ed., pp. 383–410). Sudbury, MA: Jones & Bartlett.

Hastings, G., Stead, M., McDermott, L., Forsyth, A., Macintosh, A. M., Rayner, M., et al. (2003). *Review of research on the effects of food promotion to children* (Prepared for the Food Standards Agency). Glasgow, Scotland: University of Strathclyde, Center for Social Marketing.

NYE, BILL (1955–)

Bill Nye once dropped into Mount St. Helens's crater to explain how volcanoes work. He has parasailed over a lake to illustrate air pressure. He has stripped to shorts in a meat locker to make the point that freezing temperatures do not cause colds, but germs do. A scientist-turned-comic and producer of educational media, Nye shows the public how science affects their everyday lives. Nye is best known for his Emmy Award–winning television series *Bill Nye the Science Guy*. The show entertained and educated millions of young viewers in the 1990s with madcap antics, MTV-style pacing, and the silly, bowtie-wearing Nye as host. The program showed kids that science was "way cool." It also set new standards for educational programming aimed at children. Nye continues to popularize science. He writes children's science books, creates games and media products for all ages, and appears on television specials. Disney's Epcot Center even features a "Bill Nye the Science Guy" exhibit.

Nye was born November 27, 1955, to Ned Nye and Jacqueline Jenkins-Nye and raised in Washington, D.C. The young Nye was fascinated with how things work. He took apart his bicycle. He tinkered with a rubber band–powered airplane to make it turn left. Growing up during a time when the U.S. space program often made front-page news, he loved learning about airplanes and flight. He attended the private Sidwell Friends School where, as he told Peter Carlin in *People* magazine, he was a member of the science club and "a big-time nerd." He went on to earn a bachelor's degree in mechanical engineering from Cornell University in 1977. While at Cornell, he took an astronomy class from Carl Sagan. He lists the famous astronomer among his heroes, along with comedian Steve Martin and his mom, whom

the Navy's cryptography division recruited in 1942 for her math and science skills. After graduation, Nye worked as an engineer for the Boeing Corporation and Sundstrand Data Control near Seattle. At Boeing, he invented a hydraulic resonance suppressor tube used on 747 airplanes.

In Seattle, his flair for comedy became evident. He started moonlighting as a stand-up comic and, in 1986, landed a regular gig as a writer and performer for the local KING-TV comedy show, *Almost Live!* The same year, he debuted the character of the Science Guy on KJR Radio. He created a television pilot of a Science Guy episode for the local PBS station in 1992 and the next year signed a major deal with the Walt Disney Company's syndication arm, Buena Vista Television. The *Puget Sound Business Journal* reported that the agreement took "the quirky science booster" into just about every U.S.television market. In some cities, children could watch the *Science Guy* 7 days a week on public and commercial television stations.

From 1993 to 1998, Nye was the writer and on-air "talent" of *Bill Nye the Science Guy*, coproduced by Disney and Seattle public television station KCTS. The National Science Foundation (NSF) and the Corporation for Public Broadcasting contributed funding. Kids loved the zany mix of science and fun and so did the broadcasting industry. The television show reached more than 4 million viewers in the United States and Canada. The *New York Times* wrote that the February 1997 industry ratings earned the series the status of most popular syndicated educational show among children ages 6 to 11. During its 5-year run, the show won 28 Emmy Awards. In 1999, the Annenberg Public Policy Center recognized *Bill Nye the Science Guy* as an excellent educational and informational program. Research also showed that the program featured a high percentage of women and minorities among its guests, helping to counter the stereotype of scientists as white men.

Other television educational programs for school-aged children, such as *Mr. Wizard's World, Beakman's World, and Newton's Apple,* covered science topics. But *Bill Nye the Science Guy* was different, "a hipper, hyper Mr. Wizard of the 1990's," the *New York Times* wrote. Flashy graphics and silly stunts kept the 26-minute episodes moving at a frantic clip. Nye disco danced, bungee jumped, and skydived to illustrate points. He demonstrated do-it-yourself experiments that sent kids running to kitchen cupboards for baking soda and vinegar, or other ingredients, so they could try them too.

Perhaps most important, Nye had a knack for making complex topics understandable. Each show was sharply focused. Every experiment or crazy caper reinforced the day's theme, which helped viewers retain one or two key points. The series covered three main categories: planetary science, physical science, and life science. The 100 episodes, correlated to National Science Education Standards (NSES), ranged from the first program on flight to the last one on motion.

Nye's "Science Guy" brand extends from television to books, videos, DVDs, and games. He is the author or coauthor of five children's books. His first, *Bill Nye the Science Guy's Big Blast of Science,* came out in 1993. With NSF support, a *Bill Nye the Science Guy* classroom series of the program was released on video in 1997. "The Way Cool Game of Science: Populations and Ecosystems," produced in 2007, is an example of one of his interactive games.

He has been the host of a variety of television series and specials targeted to adult viewers as well, such as the PBS series *The Eyes of Nye* and *The 100 Greatest Discoveries* on Discovery's Science Channel. In 2008, Discovery launched the series *Stuff Happens* on its Planet Green Channel with Nye as host. Here viewers see Nye, in his familiar lab coat, showing how daily decisions such as eating bacon for breakfast have an impact on the environment and the world.

Television persona aside, Nye enjoys hands-on science himself. The engineer, who as a boy tried to invent a bicycle-powered vacuum cleaner, holds two patents on educational items and is working on other inventions, including an improved toe shoe for ballerinas. He has taught as a visiting professor at Cornell University, and he holds honorary doctorates from Rensselaer Polytechnic Institute and Goucher College.

Using humor, simple experiments, and everyday examples, Nye communicates to nonscientists how science works and why it is important. He shares an infectious passion for all things scientific. As the *Bill Nye the Science Guy* program often reminds viewers: "Science Rules."

Ellen J. Gerl

See also Children's Television and Science; Television Science

Further Readings

Carlin, P. (1996). Force of nature: Emmy-winning Bill Nye mixes science and silliness to make quality TV for kids. *People, 46*(17), 69.

Goldberg, C. (1997, April 9). Pondering fire, infinity and a head of lettuce (Cool!). *New York Times,* C1.

Harrison, L. (1993). "Science guy" goes national with syndicated kids' series. *Puget Sound Business Journal, 14*(19, Sec. 1), 16.

Trumbull, M. (1995). "Science guy" mixes facts and fun. *Christian Science Monitor, 87*(47), 12.